MW00564654

LEARNING LEGISLATION AND REGULATION

AN INTRODUCTION TO LAWMAKING PROCESSES IN THE MODERN AMERICAN LEGAL SYSTEM

...

Steven F. Huefner

*C. William O'Neill Professor in Law and Judicial Administration,
The Ohio State University Moritz College of Law*

Anuj C. Desai

*Volkman-Bascom Professor of Law,
University of Wisconsin Law School*

LEARNING SERIES

© 2024 LEG, Inc. d/b/a West Academic
    860 Blue Gentian Road, Suite 350
    Eagan, MN 55121
    1-877-888-1330

West, West Academic Publishing, and West Academic are trademarks of West Publishing Corporation, used under license.

Published in the United States of America

ISBN: 978-1-64020-625-0

DEDICATION

To my parents, whose public service in and out of government began
teaching me from an early age the value of democratic government and the importance of legislative accountability, administrative process, and personal
and public integrity.

SFH

To RCD and KSD for making the long voyage more than six decades ago . . .
and for staying; to NDC for putting up with me . . . and with this book; to the
dedicated public servants at OMB OGC and throughout the federal government; to teachers too numerous to name; and to the future lawyers who are just
getting started but who will grapple with the complex but fascinating problems
of the legal process over the course of their legal careers.

ACD

PREFACE

This book provides an introduction to the critically important subjects of how both legislatures and public agencies function and how the legal texts that these government institutions produce are interpreted. The title of the book "Legislation and Regulation" comes from the names of these legal texts: legislatures create legislation, and agencies create regulation. In discussing these subjects, the book also addresses the subject of how courts function and, in particular, how courts resolve ambiguities in the texts that legislatures and agencies produce. The book thus offers an important perspective on the operation of all three branches of government. As you will see, lawyers play a crucial role in all the lawmaking processes that this book addresses, legislative, regulatory, and judicial.

The content is designed to actively engage you with a combination of explanatory discussion, examples of primary source materials, and **"Do-It-Yourself"** (DIY) learning exercises. The DIY exercises, which are identified with this "tools" icon, provide opportunities for you to put yourself in the place of the judge, or the attorney, or the law professor—in short, for you to engage more directly in the activities of lawyering. By taking a few minutes to develop and write down your own response to these exercises (which frequently concern how to read, understand, and apply legal texts, before discovering what other interpreters may have said about the same issue), you will develop a deeper understanding of the material than you might acquire through reading alone. You will get the most out of this book by spending a few minutes with each of these exercises to develop your own response before continuing.

The book is organized into eight parts and approximately three dozen chapters, many of which could serve as the background reading for a single day of class discussion. Each chapter begins with a list of some "Key Concepts," followed by a "Chapter Summary." A set of "Notes & Questions" often follows many of the principal cases or concludes a section. At many other points throughout the text, "sidebar" boxes add additional content.

Sidebars that reinforce critical ideas and content are identified with this exclamation-point icon, meaning **"take special note."**

Sidebars that provide background information are identified with this **"FYI"** icon.

And sidebars that raise additional questions are identified with this **"food for thought"** question-mark icon.

Excerpts of court opinions, longer quotes from books and articles, and extended constitutional or statutory provisions are distinguished from the primary text by appearing on a light grey background, while the DIY exercises, Key Concepts, Chapter Summaries, and sidebars appear on a light blue background. For readability, our excerpts omit many citations from the original judicial opinions. We also have omitted most footnotes from the judicial opinion excerpts. When we have omitted substantive language from court opinions, or from book or article excerpts, we have designated our omissions with three asterisks (* * *), to distinguish our omissions from omissions found in the original sources, which remain designated using traditional ellipses (. . .).

ACKNOWLEDGEMENTS

We are grateful for the excellent contributions of many research assistants at both The Moritz College of Law and the University of Wisconsin Law School, including Miles Carlson, Keith Darsee, Christopher Deucher, Sarah Grupp, Matthew Hawk, Jimmy Hinton, Timothy Lanzendorfer, Kevin McCarthy, Reem Mohamed, Zach Renier, Sarah Rhodes, Greyson Teague, Will White, and Kelly Wu.

We are especially grateful to our colleague and friend Dean Daniel Tokaji for his support and collaboration over the years on both our teaching and our scholarly activities, and for his generous permission to let us borrow extensively from his excellent ELECTION LAW IN A NUTSHELL in Part II of the book. We also gratefully acknowledge Hillel Levin for permission to include in Chapter 2 his essay "The Food Stays in the Kitchen," which originally appeared in *The Green Bag* in 2009.

SUMMARY OF CONTENTS

DETAILED TABLE OF CONTENTS

TABLE OF CASES

Principal cases are in bold.

TABLE OF STATUTES

TABLE OF REGULATIONS

TABLE OF WORKS CITED

Aleinikoff, T. Alexander, Updating Statutory Interpretation, 87 Mich. L. Rev. 20 (1988), 673

American Bar Association Task Force on Federal Lobbying Laws, Lobbying Law in the Spotlight: Challenges and Proposed Improvements, 63 Admin. L. Rev. 419 (2011), 231

American College Dictionary (1970), 1002

American Heritage Dictionary (3d ed. 1992), 537

American Heritage Dictionary (4th ed. 2000), 470

Anderson, William R., Chevron in the States: An Assessment and A Proposal, 58 Admin. L. Rev. 1017 (2006), 989

Barrett, A., Substantive Canons and Faithful Agency, 90 B.U. L. Rev. 109 (2010), 975

Bell, Derrick A., Jr., The Referendum: Democracy's Barrier to Racial Equality, 54 Wash. L. Rev. 1 (1978), 299

Benson, Jocelyn, A Shared Existence: The Current Compatibility of the Equal Protection Clause and Section 5 of the Voting Rights Act, 88 Neb. L. Rev. 124 (2009), 133

Bix, Brian H., Jurisprudence: Theory and Context (8th ed. 2019), 363

Black's Law Dictionary (3d ed. 1933), 915

Black's Law Dictionary (6th ed. 1990), 446, 736, 908

Black's Law Dictionary (7th ed. 1999), 470

Black's Law Dictionary (10th ed. 2014), 488

Blackstone, W., Commentaries (1766), 1000

Blackstone, William, Commentaries (Cooley ed., 1879), 338

Bork, Neutral Principles and Some First Amendment Problems, 47 Ind. L.J. 1 (1971), 205

Boyd, T. & S. Markman, The 1982 Amendments to the Voting Rights Act: A Legislative History, 40 Wash. & Lee L. Rev. 1347 (1983), 370

Breyer, Judicial Review of Questions of Law and Policy, 38 Admin. L.Rev. 363 (1986), 927

Breyer, S., Making Our Democracy Work: A Judge's View (2010), 976

Breyer, Stephen, The Legislative Veto After Chadha, 72 Geo. L.J. 785 (1984), 753

Brudney, James J.: Canon Shortfalls and the Virtues of Political Branch Interpretive Assets, 98 Cal. L. Rev. 1199 (2010), 561

Brudney, James J. & Corey Ditslear, Canons of Construction and the Elusive Quest for Neutral Reasoning, 58 Vand. L. Rev. 1 (2005), 458, 561

Burke, Edmund, Speech to the Electors of Bristol (1774), 65

Friendly, Henry J., Mr. Justice Frankfurter and the Reading of Statutes, in Benchmarks (1967), 455, 512, 618

Fuller, Lon L., The Case of the Speluncean Explorers, Harv. L. Rev. 616 (1949), 321

Galanter, Marc, Why the "Haves" Come out Ahead: Speculations on the Limits of Legal Change, 9 Law & Society Rev. 95 (1974), 240

Gellhorn, Ernest, Ronald M. Levin & Jeffrey Lubbers, Administrative Law & Process in A Nutshell (6th ed. 2016), 786

Gluck, Abbe R. & Lisa Schultz Bressman, Statutory Interpretation from the Inside: An Empirical Study of Congressional Drafting, Delegation and the Canons, 65 Stan. L. Rev. 901 (2013), 443, 494

Gluck, Abbe R., The States as Laboratories of Statutory Interpretation: Methodological Consensus and the New Modified Textualism, 119 Yale L.J. 1750 (2010), 435

Gray, John Chipman, The Nature and Sources of the Law 119 (1909), 365

Greco, Gary J., Survey, Standards or Safeguards: A Survey of the Delegation Doctrine in the States, 8 Admin. L. J. Am. U. 567 (1994), 752

Greenawalt, Kent, Statutory Interpretation: 20 Questions (1999), 377

Griffith, E., The Rise and Development of the Gerrymander (1907), 152

Grofman, Bernard, Lisa Handley, & Richard G. Niemi, Minority Representation And The Quest For Voting Equality (1992), 103

Hand, L., How Far Is a Judge Free in Rendering a Decision?, in The Spirit of Liberty 103 (I. Dilliard ed. 1952), 577

Hart and Sacks' The Legal Process: Basic Problems in the Making and Application of Law (William N. Eskridge Jr. & Philip P. Frickey eds., 1994), 77

Hart and Sacks' The Legal Process: Basic Problems in the Making and Application of Law (William N. Eskridge Jr. & Philip P. Frickey eds., 2006), 344, 437, 444

Hart, H.L.A., The Concept of Law (1961), 363

Harvard Law School, The Antonin Scalia Lecture Series: A Dialogue with Justice Elena Kagan on the Reading of Statutes (Nov. 25, 2015), 983

Heinzerling, Lisa, The Major Answers Doctrine, 16 NYU J. L. & Lib. 506 (2023), 985

HHS, A. Burke, A. Misra, & S. Sheingold, Premium Affordability, Competition, and Choice in the Health Insurance Marketplace (2014), 45

Holmes, Oliver Wendell, The Path of the Law, 10 Harv. L. Rev. 457 (1897), 365

Holmes, Oliver Wendell, The Theory of Legal Interpretation, 12 Harv. L. Rev. 417 (1899), 618

Holtzoff, A., Report on Proposed Federal Tort Claims Bill (1931), 470

Htun, Mala, Is Gender Like Ethnicity? The Political Representation of Identity Groups, 2 Perspectives on Politics 439 (2004), 74

Hunter, The First Gerrymander? 9 Early Am. Studies 792 (2011), 152

Iuliano, Jason & Keith E. Whittington, The Nondelegation Doctrine: Alive and Well, 93 Notre Dame L. Rev. 619 (2017), 751

Jaffe, L., Judicial Control of Administrative Action (1965), 959

Katzmann, Robert A., Judging Statutes (2014), 453

Kennedy, John F., Profiles in Courage (1956), 69

Klarman, M., The Framers' Coup: The Making of the United States Constitution 340–342 (2016), 153

Koch, Jr., Charles H. & Richard Murphy, 3 Administrative Law and Practice § 7.32 (3d ed.), 767

Krishnakumar, Anita S., Dueling Canons, 65 Duke L. J. 909 (2016), 559

Lawson, Gary, Outcome, Procedures, and Process: Agency Duties of Explanation for Legal Conclusions, 48 Rutgers L. Rev. 313 (1996), 813

Levin, Ronald M., The Anatomy of Chevron: Step Two Reconsidered, 72 Chi.-Kent L. Rev. 1253 (1997), 935

Lieber, Francis, Legal and Political Hermeneutics, Or, Principles of Interpretation and Construction in Law and Politics: With Remarks on Precedents and Authorities (1839), 335

Linde, Hans A., When Initiative Lawmaking Is Not "Republican Government": The Campaign Against Homosexuality, 72 Or. L. Rev. 19 (1993), 299

Lippmann, Walter, Public Opinion (1922), 836

Llewellyn, Karl, Remarks on the Theory of Appellate Decision and the Rules or Canons About How Statutes Are to be Construed, 3 Vand. L. Rev. 395 (1950), 550

Magleby, David B., Direct Legislation in the American States, in Referendums Around the World (1994), 298

Manning, John F., Textualism and the Equity of the Statute, 101 Colum. L. Rev. 1 (2001), 347

Manning, John F., The Absurdity Doctrine, 116 Harv. L. Rev. 2387 (2003), 395

Manz, William H., Guide to State Legislation, Legislative History, and Administrative Materials (7th ed. 2008), 605

Mashaw, Jerry L., Norms, Practices, and the Paradox of Deference: A Preliminary Inquiry into Agency Statutory Interpretation, 57 Admin. L. Rev. 501 (2005), 843

Mashaw, Jerry L., Recovering American Administrative Law: Federalist Foundations, 1787–1801, 115 Yale L.J. 1256 (2006, 706

Melville, H., Moby Dick (U. Chicago 1952), 503

Merrill, Thomas W., Capture Theory and the Courts: 1967–1983, 72 Chi.-Kent L. Rev. 1039 (1997), 840, 976

Metzger, Gillian E., The Constitutional Duty to Supervise, 124 Yale L.J. 1836 (2015), 758

Miller, Geoffrey P., Pragmatics and the Maxims of Interpretation, 1990 Wisc. L. Rev. 1179 (1990), 458

Sinclair, Barbara, Unorthodox Lawmaking: New Legislative Processes in the U.S. Congress (1997), 244

Sinclair, Michael, "Only a Sith Thinks Like That": Llewelyn's "Dueling Canons" Eight to Twelve, 51 N.Y. L. Sch. L. Rev. 1003 (2006–07), 558

Smith, Bradley A., Unfree Speech: The Folly of Campaign Finance Reform (2001), 177

Squire, Peverill & Gary Moncrief, State Legislatures Today: Politics Under the Domes (2d ed. 2015), 244

Stack, Kevin M., Purposivism in the Executive Branch: How Agencies Interpret Statutes, 109 Nw. U. L. Rev. 871 (2015), 843

Stephanopoulos, Nicholas, Our Electoral Exceptionalism, 80 U. Chi. L. Rev. 769 (2013), 74

Stephenson, Matthew C. & Adrian Vermeule, Chevron Has Only One Step, 95 Va. L. Rev. 597 (2009), 946

Stigler, George J., The Theory of Economic Regulation, 2 Bell J. Econ. & Mgmt. Sci 3 (1971), 839

Strauss, Peter L., "Deference" is Too Confusing—Let's Call Them "Chevron Space" and "Skidmore Weight," 112 Colum. L. Rev. 1143 (2012), 947

Strauss, Peter L., When the Judge Is Not the Primary Official with Responsibility to Read: Agency Interpretation and the Problem of Legislative History, 66 Chi.-Kent L. Rev. 321 (1990), 843

Sunstein, Cass R., Beyond Marbury: The Executive's Power to Say What the Law Is, 115 Yale L.J. 2580 (2006), 948

Sunstein, Cass R., Nondelegation Canons, 67 U. Chi. L. Rev. 315 (2000), 904

Sutherland, J., Statutory Construction 5201 (3d F. Horack ed. 1943), 570

Sutherland, Statutes and Statutory Construction (6th ed. 2000), 475

Sutherland, Statutes and Statutory Construction (7th ed. 2014), 457, 475

The Barnhart Dictionary of Etymology 146 (1988), 503

The Case of the Speluncean Explorers: Contemporary Proceedings, 61 Geo. Wash. U. L. Rev. 1754 (1993), 78

The Documentary History of the Ratification of the Constitution: Massachusetts (J. Kaminski & G. Saladino eds. 2000), 153

The Federalist No. 10 (B. Wright ed. 1961), 201

The Federalist No. 11 (C. Rossiter ed. 1961), 976

The Federalist No. 37 (J. & A. McLean eds. 1788), 165

The Federalist No. 47 (J. Madison), 976

The Federalist No. 48 (J. Cooke ed. 1961), 540

The Federalist No. 59 (C. Rossiter ed. 1961), 154

The Oxford Dictionary of English Etymology (C. Onions ed. 1966), 503

The Random House Dictionary of the English Language Unabridged 319 (2d ed. 1987), 503

LEARNING LEGISLATION AND REGULATION

AN INTRODUCTION TO LAWMAKING PROCESSES IN THE MODERN AMERICAN LEGAL SYSTEM

Part I—An Introduction to the Study of Legislation and Regulation

Even before law school, most law students recognize that both the federal government and the state governments of the United States are composed of three distinct branches: judicial, legislative, and executive. Much less well understood is that these three branches interact constantly in adopting, revising, and clarifying the law. This book will give you a more sophisticated understanding of the nature and complexities of these interactions among the organs of American government.

On the conventional account of separation of powers, courts expound the common law, while legislatures enact statutory law. Yet this account vastly oversimplifies how American law is made today. Legislatures charge executive branch agencies with enforcing statutory requirements, and in doing so they also demand that agencies develop implementing regulations. These agency regulations inevitably refine, clarify, and sometimes expand what the legislature has done. Courts, meanwhile, are routinely called upon to decide how to interpret ambiguities in the law, ambiguities that can arise easily in the text of either a legislative enactment or an agency regulation.

These realities of modern lawmaking give rise to important but contested questions of how courts should perform their interpreting role, and how agencies should perform their implementing role, without usurping legislative authority. This book is about these questions. It will provide you with a grounding in the functioning of legislatures and agencies today, as well as an in-depth exposure to the theories and doctrines of judicial statutory interpretation. Your study of these topics will also deepen your understanding of the relationship among the three branches of government. We begin in this Part with a chapter on the various sources of lawmaking authority, followed by two chapters introducing the problem of textual interpretation.

Part I—An Introduction to the Study of
Legislation and Regulation

1

Sources and Hierarchy of Lawmaking Authority

Key Concepts

- Lawmaking authority
- Constitutional government
- Ballot initiative
- Enumerated congressional powers
- Implied congressional powers
- Plenary state powers
- Dual sovereignty
- Supremacy Clause
- Supreme Court review of congressional action
- Delegation of lawmaking authority

Chapter Summary

This chapter begins by discussing the U.S. Constitution and the authority it grants to the three branches of federal government, before turning to a consideration of the place of state constitutions and local governments in our democratic processes. The chapter then examines the key structural features of Congress and state legislatures, as well as the constitutional limitations placed on these legislative institutions. A brief introduction to the concept of delegation of lawmaking authority from legislatures to agencies concludes this chapter.

Today, a thorough grounding in legislative and regulatory processes—how legislatures and agencies function—is essential to understand the sources and authority of American law, which in turn is crucial to being a practicing lawyer. While the court-centric common-law tradition to which American law traces its roots continues to profoundly shape the U.S. legal system, state and federal legislatures have

> **FYI** "Common law" refers to law developed over time and enunciated exclusively by the judicial branch—the courts.

long displaced courts as the primary creators of law. In turn, as American society and government have grown more complex, legislatures have increasingly shared their lawmaking authority with administrative agencies, whose regulations now comprise another substantial layer of American law. Accordingly, this chapter briefly identifies the sources and hierarchy of legislative and regulatory lawmaking authority. Later chapters will then provide more detail about the function and operation of contemporary legislatures and administrative agencies.

A. Constitutional Democracy: Lawmaking Authority Derives from the People

In the United States, the foundational legal document of both the state and federal levels of government is a written constitution that defines the scope of governmental powers and duties. But the constitutions themselves derive their ultimate authority from the citizenry. Either through their designated representatives, or through processes of direct democracy, citizens have the authority to ratify, amend, or replace these foundational documents. Each of these state and federal constitutions in turn then establishes a legislative body as the primary lawmaking institution of their respective system of government; many state constitutions also establish mechanisms of direct democracy, typically called the "initiative" process, which allow the citizens themselves to initiate and enact state statutes in supplement of their state legislature.

> An "Initiative" is a measure initiated directly by the people themselves, which becomes law if supported by the requisite vote of the people at a general election. **FYI**

1. The United States Constitution

The United States Constitution stands as a model of the democratic principle, explicitly articulated a decade earlier in the Declaration of Independence, that governments must derive their just powers "from the consent of the governed." DECLARATION OF INDEPENDENCE. The U.S. Constitution's framework for a set of government powers and institutions for the new federal republic—including the commitment to a government of separated legislative, executive, and judicial powers—resulted not only from the collective wisdom of the group of drafters drawn from twelve of the thirteen original states, but also from a ratification process through which the citizens of each of the thirteen states accepted the document and imbued it with authority. As new states have been added to the Union, each in turn has recognized the Constitution's place as the country's foundational legal document.

> The 1776 adoption of The Declaration **FYI** of Independence by representatives of the original American colonies set the stage for the American Revolutionary War, and for the subsequent drafting (in 1787) and adoption (in 1789) of the Constitution of the United States.

> **FYI** As you may be aware, in the 18th century the term "citizens" covered a far more limited group of people than it does today.

As further confirmation that the people of the nation remain the ultimate sovereign over the federal government, the Constitution itself establishes a process for its own amendment that depends on popular approval. This process provides that amendments to the Constitution will take effect only upon the assent of state conventions or state legislatures representing three-fourths of the several states. *See* U.S. CONST. art. V. The amendment process is deliberately difficult, reflecting a judgment that the national constitution should not undergo frequent change, and instead should express the country's foundational principles with a relatively high degree of permanence and stability.

To date, some twenty-seven amendments have been added to the U.S. Constitution, and only one amendment has ever been repealed. Some of these amendments have altered the way the federal government operates, as for instance by limiting the President to two elected terms, U.S. CONST. amend. XXII; granting presidential

> Some observers today argue that the **FYI** U.S. Constitution is too hard to amend, making it more difficult for the national government to evolve with society.

electors to the District of Columbia, U.S. CONST. amend. XXIII; or specifying when members of Congress can receive pay increases, U.S. CONST. amend. XXVII. But many of these twenty-seven amendments, including the first ten amendments, constituting the Bill of Rights, as well as the Fourteenth Amendment's guarantees of due process and equal protection of law, and the Twenty-Fourth Amendment's prohibition of poll taxes, impose constraints on the reach of government power over the lives of U.S. citizens.

From the outset, it is important to recognize that even without these amendments, the U.S. Government is a government of limited powers, having only those powers and authorities that the people, through the Constitution, have given it. This stands in direct contrast to state governments, which are understood to possess plenary power to control and regulate all aspects of society, unless some provision of either the pertinent state constitution or the U.S. Constitution disables the state government from exercising power in some specified arena. These limits on the legislative powers of the federal and state governments will be discussed further in section B below.

Nevertheless, the U.S. Constitution gives the federal legislature—the Congress of the United States—broad authority to legislate in many areas. For instance, among other powers, the Constitution expressly permits Congress to:

- impose taxes and spend the proceeds thereof;

- establish a national military;

- develop a body of law to protect copyrights and patents;

- regulate commerce among the states;

- admit additional states into the Union; and

- enforce the Fourteenth Amendment's guarantees of due process and equal protection of law for all citizens.

Whenever Congress legislates, it must rely, at least implicitly, on some grant of authority found in the Constitution.

2. State Constitutions

As a second foundational legal document, functioning in tandem with the U.S. Constitution, all fifty states have a written state constitution that structures the operation of their state government. Like their federal counterpart, these state constitutions establish a legislative, executive, and judicial branch of government and have been adopted through some process that required the assent of that state's citizens. Each state constitution, except for Delaware's, can be amended by an action of the people. (Delaware's constitution can only be amended by the state legislature.)

A state-by-state description of the differences between federal and state procedures for adopting a constitutional amendment would be impractical to detail here, given the variety of state processes. It is helpful, however, to outline some typical structural features, as well as to highlight a few noteworthy outliers.

As a general matter, every state except Delaware provides for some method of constitutional amendment by legislative initiative. These legislatively referred amendments must first be proposed and passed by a state's legislature, and then be presented to the voting public for approval on a general election ballot. In four states—Connecticut, Hawaii, New Jersey, and Pennsylvania—legislative approval requires either super-majority approval of one legislative session, or simple-majority approvals of two consecutive legislative sessions, prior to a proposed amendment going to the ballot for popular ratification in a general election. Eleven other states require majority legislative approval to occur in two consecutive legislative sessions. The Delaware Constitution's amendment process, spelled out in Article XVI, is unique in that it requires two consecutive super-majority legislative session approvals to effectuate a constitutional amendment, but no popular ratification is required.

Another mechanism by which state constitutions are altered is through the ballot initiative process. Eighteen state constitutions provide some mechanism whereby the voters directly, without the participation of the legislature, may propose and adopt an amendment to their state constitution. Ballot initiative requirements among these states vary widely in their particulars. Indeed, in some states (e.g., Illinois, Massachusetts, Mississippi, and Oklahoma) the amendment process is rendered practically illusory by onerous procedural obstacles. Nevada, uniquely, requires amendments to be ratified at two general elections before taking effect.

Yet another method of state constitutional amendment is by commission referral. For instance, the Florida Taxation and Budget Reform Commission, established by Article XI of the Florida Constitution, convenes every twenty years to propose amendments for statewide ballot ratification. Eight such amendments were referred to the general electorate in 2008 (the most recent meeting of the Commission). New Mexico adopted a constitutional amendment in 1996 that created a process whereby proposed amendments are referred to the state legislature by a commission.

Finally, rather than merely providing means for amending their founding documents, forty-four states have adopted methods to replace their constitution entirely via constitutional convention. A number of states automatically place before their voters every ten, sixteen, or twenty years a general election ballot question about whether to call a constitutional convention. Other states permit only the legislature to initiate a constitutional convention, without requiring direct input from the voters. Still other states provide for the legislature to propose a constitutional convention by submitting the question to the voters through a ballot measure. Requirements vary by state concerning, for example, what percentage of the voting public must approve the measure, as well as what proportion of the legislature must vote in favor, or for how many consecutive legislative sessions, before the proposal to call a convention is placed on a ballot.

Most state constitutions have been amended much more frequently than the U.S. Constitution; indeed, many have even been completely replaced, sometimes more than once, by an entirely new foundational document. The frequency with which state constitutions are amended reflects both the comparative ease of the amendment process in most states, and the fact that many state constitutions serve as the locus for a much greater range of substantive law provisions than does the U.S. Constitution. For instance, it is not uncommon for state constitutions to have provisions about public schools, natural resources, labor and unions, and rights to judicial remedies. As a result, state constitutions tend to be substantially longer than the U.S. Constitution.

Collectively, the fifty state constitutions and the U.S. Constitution give rise to a complex system, in which Congress is supreme in its power to legislate for certain enumerated federal purposes (as provided by the Supremacy Clause, U.S. CONST. art. VI, cl. 2), while states regulate many other areas. As a result, unless constrained by federal law or the U.S. Constitution, substantial variation often exists in how state governments choose to handle specific issues within their purview, such as the status of marijuana under state law, how to fund public education, how to conduct elections, or whether, and if so how, to punish criminal activity, including whether to impose the death penalty for certain crimes. Indeed, this variation is the key ingredient that allows states to experiment with novel solutions to the challenges of governance, serving as the "laboratories" of democracy, as Justice Brandeis famously put it. *See New State Ice Co. v. Liebmann*, 285 U.S. 262, 311 (1932). Although these state policies are generally established primarily by state legislatures, in certain states they may also result from the popular initiative processes of direct democracy (described in Chapter 13).

FYI The Supremacy Clause of the U.S. Constitution provides that federal law is "the supreme Law of the Land," notwithstanding what a state constitution or state legislature might want the law to be. As a result, federal law supersedes any conflicting state laws.

3. Local Governments

A brief word is also in order about the source of local government power in the United States. Although local legislative and regulatory bodies also are responsible for the creation of important portions of American law, in contrast to the federal and state governments they do not derive their authority directly from the people. Instead, throughout the United States, local governments (as well as various special improvement districts, utility districts, and the like) are legal creations of the state in which they exist.

As required by state law, municipalities may need to adopt a charter in order to incorporate or otherwise be recognized, but this is not an act of independent authority. Rather, it is an act dependent on the state, which chooses to bestow a portion of the state's authority upon a locality provided the locality has complied with state-imposed requirements. Counties, meanwhile, are typically established by the state legislature and given the ability to control specified matters of governance through county commissions or councils.

Many states grant "home rule" authority to cities and towns, giving these municipalities additional freedom from state legislative control of certain local affairs. But the precise manner in which municipalities exercise governmental power—the role of the city council, town manager, mayor, and other officials or entities—is either established in the state constitution or subject to the control of the state legislature, even if the legislature allows localities to make certain choices between various forms of governance.

B. From Constitutions to Legislatures: Legislative Structures and Limitations

As described in section A above, the state and federal constitutions are the supreme law within their respective spheres at the state or federal level. Other sources of law—statutes, regulations, judicial orders, executive orders, local ordinances—all derive their ultimate authority from these constitutions. These constitutions, in turn, impose important structural features and substantive limits upon the subordinate powers of federal and state lawmaking.

1. Constitutional Structures of Congress

In establishing Congress as the source of federal lawmaking authority, the very first provision of the U.S. Constitution provides, "All legislative Powers herein granted shall be vested in a Congress of the United States, which shall consist of a Senate

> **FYI** Article I of the U.S. Constitution establishes the structure of the legislative branch—Congress. Article II establishes the structure of the executive branch—the Presidency. Article III establishes the structure of the judicial branch—the federal courts.

and a House of Representatives." U.S. CONST. art. I, sec. 1. The remainder of Article I of the U.S. Constitution then goes on to specify a number of fundamental requirements that shape the structure of Congress and its two chambers.

One essential characteristic of Congress established by the Constitution is the representational nature of the two chambers. As a result of the Great Compromise, by constitutional design the U.S. Senate has always consisted of two Senators from each state, regardless of a state's population, thus giving residents of small states disproportionate influence. From twenty-six members at its founding, the Senate has grown to one hundred members today, each serving for six years at a time. Meanwhile, although the U.S. Constitution initially gave state legislatures the authority to appoint their state's two U.S. Senators, since the adoption of the Seventeenth Amendment in 1913, the people of each state have directly elected their Senators.

> The "Great Compromise" refers to a bargain struck at the Constitutional Convention between delegates of larger states and delegates of smaller states, whereby every state would have equal representation in the U.S. Senate, while representation in the U.S. House would be proportional to each state's population. **FYI**

Senators are elected "at large," meaning each Senator is understood to represent the state's entire population. Some additional considerations about the representational roles of elected legislators generally, both federal and state, including the scope of the one-person, one-vote requirements, are discussed in Chapters 4 and 5.

> **FYI** Before the Seventeenth Amendment, state legislatures chose their state's U.S. Senators, rather than letting the state's residents elect them directly.

Meanwhile, the U.S. House of Representatives is composed of Representatives apportioned among the states according to each state's population, with each state guaranteed at least one Representative, and all Representatives elected for two-year terms. Although the Constitution initially provided for a House consisting of 65 members, *see* U.S. CONST. art. I, sec. 2, cl. 3, since 1913 the total number of Representatives has been set by Congress at 435. *See* THE APPORTIONMENT ACT OF 1911, PUBLIC LAW 62–5. Today, every state with more than one Representative must subdivide the state into geographical districts of equal population, with each district electing its own member of the House of Representatives. *See Wesberry v. Sanders*, 376 U.S. 1 (1964). But dividing states into congressional districts is not a constitutional requirement, and in the early years, many states elected their Representatives at-large, rather than by district. After 1967, Congress entirely prohibited at-large representation for states entitled to more than one Representative. The apportionment and districting processes are also discussed in more detail in Chapter 5.

Another bedrock constitutional requirement is that before any measure can become a law, both the Senate and the House must be in complete agreement upon its text. U.S. CONST. art. I, sec. 7, cl. 2. This "bicameralism" requirement usually requires that the two respective chambers negotiate and compromise, a process that sometimes can give rise to interpretive problems later, when statutes are being construed and implemented. Occasionally, however, the bicameral bargaining process can provide understanding and insight about the meaning of ambiguities in the resulting text. These topics are also discussed in greater detail later.

Article I of the Constitution also provides that before any measure can become a law, either the President also must approve its text, or else if the President does not approve it, both Houses of Congress must each agree to the measure by a two-thirds supermajority to "override" a President's disapproval ("veto") of the measure. U.S. CONST. art. I, sec. 7, cl. 2. This requirement of Presidential "presentment" derives its name from the provision in Article I of the U.S. Constitution requiring that bills "be presented" to the President to trigger the President's responsibility to either approve or disapprove the measure. *Id.* Give-and-take occurring between Congress and the President in the shadow of this presentment requirement also can sometimes be instructive in understanding statutory meaning.

The U.S. Constitution leaves to Congress most decisions about its internal legislative operations, including whether and how to use committees, what role to ascribe to political parties, how and when to limit legislative debate, and whether to keep a full transcript of proceedings. The effect on the legislative process of these and other internal operating procedures, rules, and norms is also discussed later.

DIY
Legislative Powers Under Article I of the U.S. Constitution

 Take a few minutes right now to read Article I of the U.S. Constitution, which you can find here: https://constitutioncenter.org/interactive-constitution/articles/article-i. As you read, pay extra attention to the highlighted portions, which are provisions that have been amended (as explained when the highlighted portions are selected). **Also, begin thinking about how you might alter any provision of Article I, if you had the power.** Then continue reading below.

2. Constitutional Structures of State Legislatures

Except for Nebraska, all fifty states follow the federal model of establishing a bicameral legislature. Nebraska departs from this model by establishing a unicameral legislature, consisting of only one chamber. (The District of Columbia, along with the territories of Guam and the Virgin Islands, also have unicameral legislative assemblies). But unlike the federal model, in which members of the U.S. Senate from different states represent constituencies of very different population sizes, the one-person, one-vote requirement of *Reynolds v. Sims*, 377 U.S. 533 (1964), requires that all state legislators be elected from districts of approximately equal population (unless they are elected from multi-member rather than single-member districts, an option that ten state legislatures presently use for at least one of their two legislative chambers).

As specified in individual state constitutions, the number of members of each state's legislative bodies varies substantially from state to state, as does the relative size of the larger and smaller chambers of each bicameral legislature. At 49 members, the unicameral Nebraska Legislature is the smallest state legislature, although Alaska's 60-member bicameral legislature is composed of the yet-smaller 40-member House of Representatives and 20-member Senate. Meanwhile, the largest state legislature, with 424 members, is New Hampshire. The average size of the 49 bicameral state legislatures is 150 members.

Of more importance, however, is the ratio of representation, or in other words, the number of citizens that each legislator represents. This varies from just over 3000 residents per representative in the New Hampshire House of Representatives to over 465,000 residents per representative in California's lower house. The size of this ratio may affect the legislative process, to the extent that legislators who represent a smaller number of constituents may naturally be more responsive to those individual constituents.

Also following the federal model, each state constitution provides that legislation cannot become law without either the approval of the state's Governor, or if that approval is not given, the subsequent approval of a legislative supermajority, the size of which is specified in the state constitution. But in a departure from the federal model, many states allow their governor to disapprove individual parts or "items" of a legislative measure, rather than limiting the executive veto to the entirety of a measure. This "line-item veto" or item veto authority can have a substantial impact on the legislative dynamic between the executive and legislative branches, even in states that limit these partial vetoes to only the dollar amounts of individual items in legislative appropriations (funding) measures.

> The "line-item veto" authority given to governors in many states allows the governor to disapprove ("veto") particular parts of a legislative enactment. In contrast, under the U.S. Constitution, the President's veto authority allows the President only to disapprove a congressional enactment in its entirety.

In most bicameral state legislatures, the members of one chamber, typically called the lower chamber, serve two-year terms, while the members of the other chamber, typically called the upper chamber, serve either two-year or four-year terms. State legislatures, like Congress, establish many of their own internal operating procedures, rules, and norms. However, many state constitutions also establish additional procedural requirements having no analog in the U.S. Constitution. These include, for example, requirements concerning the number of "readings" that a measure must receive (or times that a legislature must make the measure its formal business) before it can become law; requirements concerning the contents of a measure's official title; and single-subject requirements, intended to prevent combining two or more unrelated measures into one bill in an effort to increase the measure's overall legislative support.

DIY
Legislative Powers Under Article II of the Ohio Constitution

 Take a few minutes right now to look at Article II of the Ohio Constitution. You can find it here: https://codes.ohio.gov/ohio-constitution/article-2. It is much longer than Article I of the U.S. Constitution, and it is not necessary for you to read every section carefully at this point. Instead you should read it to get a sense of its structure and coverage. **As you review it, begin thinking about how you might alter any provision of Article II, if you had the power.** Also think about any differences you notice between this article of a state constitution and Article I of the U.S. constitution, which you read previously. Then continue reading below.

3.   Constitutional Limits on Congressional Legislation

As mentioned above, for Congress to enact any particular measure, the federal Constitution must grant Congress authority to legislate that particular measure. To enforce this general principle, the U.S. Supreme Court has the ultimate responsibility, once a case raising the issue is properly before it, to determine whether Congress has overreached its constitutional powers in any specific legislative enactment, and if so to invalidate the congressional action as unconstitutional. *See Marbury v. Madison*, 5 U.S. 137 (1803). Over the years, numerous Supreme Court decisions have helped to clarify the limits of Congress's legislative powers, both those enumerated and those implied.

> **!** *Marbury v. Madison* established the principle of judicial review, which allows courts to invalidate legislative actions that the courts deem to violate the Constitution.

Among the various powers of Congress specifically enumerated in Article I, Section 8 of the Constitution, the authority to regulate interstate commerce and the power to tax have both been frequent subjects of Supreme Court decisions regarding the scope of congressional power. For instance, in *National Federation of Independent Business (NFIB) v. Sebelius*, 567 U.S. 519 (2012), the Court held (by a 5–4 majority) that the individual mandate of the Patient Protection and Affordable Care

Act of 2010—the requirement that every individual have health care insurance coverage—could not be justified as an exercise of Congress's power to regulate interstate commerce, despite the substantial impact of health care expenditures on the national economy. But in the same decision the Court also held (by a different 5–4 majority) that the individual mandate was justified as an exercise of Congress's power to tax because the mandate relied on imposing a fine (or tax) on those who did not comply.

Many other cases have required the Court to determine the scope of Congress's implied power under the Constitution's "Necessary and Proper" clause, U.S. CONST. art. I, sec. 8, cl. 18. This clause, also called the "Elastic Clause," grants Congress the authority "to make all Laws which shall be necessary and proper" for executing any of the other powers expressly given to Congress. In 1819, in the foundational case of *McCulloch v. Maryland*, 17 U.S. 316 (1819), the Court gave a generally broad ambit to this clause, unanimously holding that Congress had the implied power to establish a national bank in order to effectuate its enumerated powers "to lay and collect taxes; to borrow money; to regulate commerce; to declare and conduct a war; and to raise and support armies and navies." In 2012, however, the Court in *NFIB v. Sebelius* rejected the Necessary and Proper Clause as a justification for the individual mandate of the Affordable Care Act.

Congress's legislative authority is further limited by the Constitution's explicit protections of individual rights, especially the protections contained in the Bill of Rights, which operate to disable congressional power where Congress might otherwise be empowered to act. For instance, the Fifth Amendment prevents the government from taking private property for public use without just compensation, and more generally from depriving anyone of life, liberty, or property without due process of law; and the Eighth Amendment prohibits the imposition of cruel and unusual punishments or excessive bail. The language of the First Amendment contains the clearest textual limitation of Congress's legislative power, expressly providing that "Congress shall make no law respecting an establishment of religion, or prohibiting the free exercise thereof; or abridging the freedom of speech, or of the press; or the right of the people peaceably to assemble, and to petition the Government for a redress of grievances."

> Although not the only constitutional constraint on Congress's power, the First Amendment is well known as a direct limit on what Congress can do.

Here too, courts regularly play an essential role in enforcing limits on congressional power, reviewing specific legislative enactments to determine whether they impermissibly encroach upon protected liberties, and striking down those that do. Thus, congressional power is limited by the language of the Constitution, as interpreted by an independent judiciary with the power of judicial review over congressional action to enforce these constitutional limits.

Another limitation on congressional power comes through the independence of the executive branch, most saliently the President's power to veto congressional enactments. Although a presidential veto typically is simply an expression of a policy disagreement, a veto (or even the threat of a veto) also can serve as an additional check on legislative overreach.

4. Constitutional Limits on State Legislation

Although it was not always the case, state legislatures operate today under many limits that are similar to the limits under which Congress operates. At the same time, state legislatures also confront several types of limitations not applicable to Congress.

Until early in the twentieth century, the federal Bill of Rights was generally understood to limit only the federal government. Beginning in 1925, however, the Supreme Court in a series of cases began to hold that many of the rights in the Bill of Rights applied to the states: the Court interpreted the Fourteenth Amendment's Due Process Clause to "incorporate" those rights. As a result, states today must also ensure, for instance, that no state action violates the individual rights to freedom of speech, press, assembly, or religion protected by the First Amendment; deprives an individual of property without just compensation in violation of the Fifth Amendment; or imposes cruel or unusual punishment contrary to the Eighth Amendment.

> **!** The Fourteenth Amendment's Due Process Clause states, "No State shall. . .deprive any person of life, liberty, or property, without due process of law. . . ."

In addition, even before the process of selective incorporation made most of the federal Bill of Rights applicable to the states, almost all states had in their constitutions their own versions of a bill of rights, which similarly protected citizens from government actions that might otherwise limit their individual freedoms. Moreover, in many states these provisions comprise the first article of the state constitution, taking a position of prominence in the constitutional firmament. These state bills of rights are often even more protective of individual liberties than is their federal counterpart. For instance, several states include a guarantee that citizens have a right to a judicial remedy for a legal wrong done to them.

Apart from the expansive scope of many state constitutions' bills of rights, the plenary nature of state legislative authority also provides reason to build additional limits on state legislative authority into many specific provisions of state constitutions, lest the state legislature have too much free rein to establish any policy it wishes. One feature that is almost universal, and which stands in contrast to federal congressional authority, is the requirement that state legislatures keep the state budget in balance. Another common feature is a constitutional mandate that the state legislature fund a system of public schools. And almost all states have at least one constitutional provision addressing the issue of natural resource management or the environment, ranging from general policy statements regarding environmental protection to specific prohibitions on types of fishing nets.

A limit that state legislatures often must confront that has no analog at the congressional level is the principle of federal supremacy. That is, if Congress has legislated in an area within its jurisdiction, a state legislature is precluded from adopting an overtly contravening rule. Federal supremacy further means, because of what is labeled the "preemption doctrine," that state legislatures sometimes may not even pass a complementary measure if congressional action in that area indicates that Congress intended to exclusively "occupy the field." *See, e.g., Fid. Fed. Sav. & Loan Ass'n v. de la Cuesta*, 458 U.S. 141 (1982).

Finally, the fact that most state governors wield some version of an item veto authority serves as a greater limit on state legislatures than does the federal system's all-or-nothing presidential veto authority.

C. From Legislatures to Agencies: Delegation of Lawmaking Authority

So far, we have considered how the power to make laws reposes first in the people, and then is given by them, through state and federal constitutions, to the people's representatives, constituted as legislatures. Legislatures then may use this power as they see fit, subject to various procedural and substantive limits, including those described briefly above. In turn, one choice that legislatures routinely make is to delegate elements of this lawmaking authority to executive branch departments and independent government agencies.

In the federal government, there are two categories of agencies, "executive agencies" and "independent agencies." As a formal matter, federal agencies fall into one category or the other (although as we will see there are some reasons to think of the executive agency/independent agency distinction as more of a continuum). We discuss this in more detail in Chapter 28.

FYI At the risk of stating the obvious, note the etymological connection between "execution" of law and the "executive" branch of government.

To better facilitate the implementation and execution of law, it has long been an accepted feature of American government for legislatures to create departments within the executive branch to administer government policies over specified subject matters. Indeed, in 1789, several of the First Congress's earliest and most important actions were to establish the Departments of State, War, and Treasury. But today, the duties given to government departments and agencies routinely include more than the mere execution of law, and also comprehend the development of substantive regulations and the adjudication of disputes. Indeed, although the text of Article I, Section 1 of the U.S. Constitution might be read to grant Congress exclusive federal legislative authority, Congress routinely allocates to federal departments and agencies the authority to promulgate regulations that clarify, extend, or otherwise fine-tune statutory law in areas overseen by the relevant department or agency.

Recall that the first clause of Article I of the U.S. Constitution states that "*[a]ll* legislative Power herein granted shall be vested in a Congress of the United States." U.S. Const. art. I, sec. 1 (emphasis added).

At the federal level, a long doctrinal history has developed concerning the extent of permissible delegations of lawmaking authority from Congress to executive branch departments and independent agencies. Variably labeled either the "delegation doctrine" or the "nondelegation doctrine," this doctrine holds that Congress cannot delegate its legislative powers to actors outside the legislative branch unless Congress establishes an "intelligible principle" to guide the delegate's exercise of the delegated authority. See *J.W. Hampton, Jr. & Co. v. United States*, 276 U.S. 394, 409 (1928). In practice, this doctrine has been largely toothless and has not seriously limited Congress's power of delegation. Recently, however, several Justices on the Supreme Court have expressed interest in strengthening it. We will discuss this further in Chapter 29.

State practice is consistent: state legislatures are allowed to share lawmaking authority with state agencies and departments for the purpose of filling in the gaps in more broadly stated statutory schemes. For instance, although the Wisconsin Supreme Court observed in the 1945 case of *Clintonville Transfer Line v. Public Service Commission*, 21 N.W.2d 5, 11 (Wis. 1945), that "the power to declare whether or not there shall be a law, to determine the general policy to be achieved by the law, and to fix the limits within which the law shall operate is vested by our constitution in the legislature and may not be delegated," the court also explained that nonetheless "when the legislature has laid down the fundamentals of the law, it may delegate to administrative agencies such legislative powers as may be necessary to carry into effect the general legislative purpose." All states permit their state legislature to give agencies the authority to promulgate rules provided they are doing so in furtherance of a specific purpose or policy that the legislature has established.

In large part because Congress can delegate its lawmaking powers, Congress has repeatedly created specialized agencies with regulatory authority beyond the existing fifteen cabinet-level executive branch departments and their subsidiary offices. The now-defunct Interstate Commerce Commission, created in 1887 as part of the Interstate Commerce Act, is usually considered the federal government's first independent regulatory agency, but similar agencies proliferated in the twentieth century. Today, other prominent independent federal agencies include the Federal Communications Commission (FCC), the Federal Energy Regulatory Commission (FERC), the Federal Reserve (the Fed), the Federal Trade Commission (FTC), the National Labor Relations Board (NLRB), and the Securities and Exchange Commission (SEC), to name only a few. These agencies, along with the cabinet departments and other executive agencies, are an essential contributor to the contemporary body of federal law.

Typically, when federal agencies and departments promulgate regulations, they do so by engaging in a statutorily prescribed "notice and comment" rule-making process. This process, described in more detail in Part VII, provides the public—including lobbyists and interest group representatives—with an opportunity for input, and thus an opportunity to shape the resulting policies. Many state agency rulemaking processes are analogous, although state agencies also may often have the power to use different processes to promulgate regulations.

An essential component of a legislature's ability—and willingness—to delegate some portion of its lawmaking authority to agencies is its ability to maintain a measure of oversight of the way that the delegated authority is used. Thus, as agencies have come to play a larger role in promulgating law and implementing policy, the processes of legislative oversight of agency behavior have also become increasingly important. These tools of legislative oversight are also discussed in greater detail in Part VII.

DIY
Improving the Constitutional Structures for Legislating

 Based on your reading of Article I of the U.S. Constitution and Article II of the Ohio Constitution, as well as the other readings above, identify and briefly describe (in writing or to another person) one change you would make to either the U.S. Constitution or to the Ohio Constitution to improve how laws are made.

* * *

We will explore the operations of legislatures and administrative agencies in greater detail later. First, however, the next two chapters will introduce the problem of textual interpretation. Why is textual interpretation important and what does it have to do with legislatures and administrative agencies? In short, textual interpretation is a fundamental aspect of law practice. Legislatures adopt statutes, and administrative agencies adopt regulations. Statutes and regulations are the principal forms of law in the American legal system, and just like judicial precedents, they are legal texts that must be interpreted. Thus, for most lawyers much of the time, legal practice consists of reading those texts, interpreting them, and applying those interpretations to factual scenarios in the world. Moreover, as we will see, courts usually have the final word on the meaning of legal texts in our system of government. So, understanding not only how to interpret those texts in the abstract but also how courts will interpret those texts—what techniques courts use and what considerations courts factor into their interpretations—is critical to being a good lawyer. The next two chapters will begin to give you a taste of this important aspect of lawyering.

Test Your Understanding

 To assess your understanding of the material in this chapter, click here to take a quiz.

2

The Interpretive Problem, All Around Us

Key Concepts

- Textual interpretation
- Ambiguity in language
- Tools of interpretation
- Customary usage
- Authorial intent
- Precedent
- Plain language
- Context

Chapter Summary

This chapter consists of a few thought experiments to introduce you to statutory, or more generally textual, interpretation. The first problem, reprinting an essay applying the command "The Food Stays in the Kitchen," concerns a household "ordinance" barring food from leaving a home kitchen. The essay will introduce you to a variety of approaches to understanding this command and will encourage you to evaluate the scope of the ordinance on your own. The chapter also introduces another famous interpretative problem involving the command "no vehicles in the park," inviting you to think about how you would go about interpreting this text.

Chapter 1 introduced the constitutional framework for the governmental institutions that produce the statutes and regulations at the heart of our system of laws. Before digging more deeply into the operation of these institutions, it is worth a short detour to introduce the kinds of interpretive issues generated by the statutes and regulations that these institutions produce. In later chapters we will then return in much greater depth to how to approach these interpretive problems.

Of course, interpretive problems are not unique to the written law of legislative statutes or administrative regulations. Consider the following essay, only somewhat tongue-in-cheek, which presents a familiar non-legal kind of interpretive problem dressed in the garb of a legal dispute.

The Food Stays in the Kitchen: Everything I Needed to Know About Statutory Interpretation I Learned by the Time I Was Nine
© 2009 Hillel Y. Levin
(originally appeared in THE GREEN BAG in 2009)

On March 23, 1986, the following proclamation, henceforth known as Ordinance 7.3, was made by the Supreme Lawmaker, Mother:

> I am tired of finding popcorn kernels, pretzel crumbs, and pieces of cereal all over the family room. From now on, no food may be eaten outside the kitchen.

Thereupon, litigation arose.

FATHER, C.J., issued the following ruling on March 30, 1986:

Defendant Anne, age 14, was seen carrying a glass of water into the family room. She was charged with violating Ordinance 7.3 ("the Rule"). We hold that drinking water outside of the kitchen does not violate the Rule. The Rule prohibits "food" from being eaten outside of the kitchen. This prohibition does not extend to water, which is a beverage rather than food. Our interpretation is confirmed by Webster's Dictionary, which defines food to mean, in relevant part, a "material consisting essentially of protein, carbohydrate, and fat used in the body of an organism to sustain growth, repair, and vital processes and to furnish energy" and "nutriment in solid form." Plainly, water, which contains no protein, carbohydrate, or fat, and which is not in solid form, is not a food.

Customary usage further substantiates our distinction between "food" and water. Ordinance 6.2, authored by the very same Supreme Lawmaker, declares: "[a]fter you get home from school, have some food and something to drink, and then do your homework." This demonstrates that the Supreme Lawmaker speaks of food and drink separately and is fully capable of identifying one or both as appropriate. After all, if "food," as used in the Family Code, included beverages, then the word "drink" in Ordinance 6.2 would be redundant and mere surplusage. Thus, had the Supreme Lawmaker wished to prohibit beverages from being taken out of the kitchen, she could easily have done so by declaring that "no food or drink is permitted outside the kitchen."

Our understanding of the word "food" to exclude water is further buttressed by the evident purpose of the Rule. The Supreme Lawmaker enacted the Rule as a response to the mess produced by solid foods. Water, even when spilled, does not produce a similar kind of mess.

Some may argue that the cup from which the Defendant was drinking water may, if left in the family room, itself be a mess. But we are not persuaded. The language of the Rule speaks to the Supreme Lawmaker's concern with small particles of food rather than to a more generalized concern with the containers in which food is held. A cup or other container bears a greater resemblance to other bric-a-brac, such as toys and backpacks, to which the Rule does not speak, than it does to the food spoken of in the Rule. Although we need not divine the Supreme Lawmaker's reasons for such a distinction, there are at least two plausible explanations. First, it could be that small particles of food left around the house are more problematic than the stray cup or bowl because they find their way into hard-to-reach places and may lead to rodent infestation. Second, it is possible that the Supreme Lawmaker was unconcerned with containers being left in the family room because citizens of this jurisdiction have been meticulous about removing such containers.

BABYSITTER SUE, J., issued the following ruling on April 12, 1986:

Defendant Beatrice, age 12, is charged with violating Ordinance 7.3 by drinking a beverage, to wit: orange juice, in the family room.

The Defendant relies on our ruling of March 30, 1986, which "h[e]ld that drinking water outside of the kitchen does not violate the [Ordinance]," and urges us to conclude that all beverages are permitted in the family room under Ordinance 7.3. While we believe this is a difficult case, we agree. As we have previously explained, the term "food" does not extend to beverages.

Our hesitation stems not from the literal meaning of the Ordinance, which strongly supports the Defendant's claim, but rather from an understanding of its purpose. As we have previously stated, and as evidenced by the language of the Ordinance itself, the Ordinance was enacted as a result of the Supreme Lawmaker's concern with mess. Unlike the case with water, if the Defendant were to spill orange juice on the couch or rug in the family room, the mess would be problematic—perhaps even more so than the mess produced by crumbs of food. It is thus difficult to infer why the Supreme Lawmaker would choose to prohibit solid foods outside of the kitchen but to permit orange juice.

Nevertheless, we are bound [by] the plain language of the Ordinance and by precedent. We are confident that if the Supreme Lawmaker disagrees with the outcome in this case, she can change or clarify the law accordingly.

GRANDMA, SENIOR J., issued the following ruling on May 3, 1986:

Defendant Charlie, age 10, is charged with violating Ordinance 7.3 by eating popcorn in the family room. The Defendant contends, and we agree, that the Ordinance does not apply in this case.

Ordinance 7.3 was enacted to prevent messes outside of the kitchen. This purpose is demonstrated by the language of the Ordinance itself, which refers to food being left "all over the family room" as the immediate cause of its adoption.

Such messes are produced only when one transfers food from a container to his or her mouth outside of the kitchen. During that process—what the Ordinance refers to as "eat[ing]"—crumbs and other food particles often fall out of the eater's hand and onto the floor or sofa.

As the record shows, the Defendant placed all of the popcorn into his mouth prior to leaving the kitchen. He merely masticated and swallowed while in the family room. At no time was there any danger that a mess would be produced.

We are certain that there was no intent to prohibit merely the chewing or swallowing of food outside of the kitchen. After all, the Supreme Lawmaker has expressly permitted the chewing of gum in the family room. It would be senseless and absurd to treat gum differently from popcorn that has been ingested prior to leaving the kitchen.

If textual support is necessary to support this obvious and commonsensical interpretation, abundant support is available. First, the Ordinance prohibits food from being "eaten" outside of the kitchen. The term "eat" is defined to mean "to take in through the mouth as food: ingest, chew, and swallow in turn." The Defendant, having only chewed and swallowed, did not "eat." Further, the Ordinance prohibits the "eat[ing]" rather than the "bringing" of food outside of the kitchen; and indeed, food is often brought out of the kitchen and through the family room, as when school lunches are delivered to the front door for carpool pickup. There is no reason to treat food enclosed in a brown bag any differently from food enclosed within the Defendant's mouth.

Finally, if any doubt remains as to the meaning of this Ordinance as it pertains to the chewing and swallowing of food, we cannot punish the Defendant for acting reasonably and in good faith reliance upon the text of the Ordinance and our past pronouncements as to its meaning and intent.

UNCLE RICK, J., issued the following ruling on May 20, 1986:

Defendant Charlie, age 10, is charged with violating Ordinance 7.3 ("the Rule") by bringing a double thick mint chocolate chip milkshake into the family room.

Were I writing on a clean slate, I would surely conclude that the Defendant has violated the Rule. A double thick milkshake is "food" because it contains protein, carbohydrate, and/or fat. Further, the purpose of the Rule—to prevent messes—would be undermined by permitting a double thick milkshake to be brought into the family room. Indeed, it makes little sense to treat a milkshake differently from a pretzel or a scoop of ice cream.

However, I am not writing on a clean slate. Our precedents have now established that all beverages are permitted outside of the kitchen under the Rule. The Defendant relied on those precedents in good faith. Further, the Supreme Lawmaker has had ample opportunity to clarify or change the law to prohibit any or all beverages from being brought out of the kitchen, and she has elected not to exercise that authority. I can only conclude that she is satisfied with the status quo.

GRANDMA, SENIOR J., issued the following ruling on July 2, 1986:

Defendant Anne, age 14, is charged with violating Ordinance 7.3 by eating apple slices in the family room.

As we have repeatedly held, the Ordinance pertains only to messy foods. Moreover, the Ordinance explicitly refers to "popcorn kernels, pretzel crumbs, and pieces of cereal." Sliced apples, not being messy (and certainly being no worse than orange juice and milkshakes, which have been permitted by our prior decisions), and being wholly dissimilar from the crumbly foods listed in the Ordinance, do not come within the meaning of the Ordinance.

We also find it significant that the consumption of healthy foods such as sliced apples is a behavior that this jurisdiction supports and encourages. It would be odd to read the Ordinance in a way that would discourage such healthy behaviors by limiting them to the kitchen.

AUNT SARAH, J., issued the following ruling on August 12, 1986:

Defendant Beatrice, age 13, is charged with violating Ordinance 7.3 by eating pretzels, popcorn, cereal, and birthday cake in the family room. Under ordinary circumstances, the Defendant would clearly be subject to the Ordinance. However, the circumstances giving rise to the Defendant's action in this case are far from ordinary.

The Defendant celebrated her thirteenth birthday on August 10, 1986. For the celebration, she invited four of her closest friends to sleep over. During the evening, and as part of the festivities, the celebrants watched a movie in the family room. Chief Justice Father provided those present with drinks and snacks, including the aforesaid pretzels, popcorn, and cereal, for consumption during the movie-watching. Father admonished the Defendant to clean up after the movie, and there is no evidence in the record suggesting that the Defendant failed to do so.

We frankly concede that the Defendant's action were violative of the plain meaning of the Ordinance. However, given the special and unique nature of the occasion, the fact that Father, a representative of the Supreme Lawmaker—as well as of this Court—implicitly approved of the Defendant's actions, and the apparent efforts of the Defendant in upholding the spirit of the Ordinance by cleaning up after her friends, we believe that the best course of action is to release the Defendant.

In light of the growing confusion in the interpretation of this ambiguous Ordinance, we urge the Supreme Lawmaker to exercise her authority to clarify and/or change the law if and as she deems it appropriate.

FATHER, C.J., issued the following ruling on September 17, 1986:

Defendant Derek, age 9, was charged with violating Ordinance 7.3 ("the Rule") by eating pretzels, potato chips, popcorn, a bagel with cream cheese, cottage cheese, and a chocolate bar in the family room.

The Defendant argues that our precedents have clearly established a pattern permitting food to be eaten in the family room so long as the eater cleans up any mess. He further maintains that it would be unjust for this Court to punish him after having permitted past actions such as drinking water, orange juice, and a milkshake, as well as swallowing popcorn, eating apple slices, and eating pretzels, popcorn, and cereal on a special occasion. The Defendant avers that there is no rational distinction between his sister's eating foods in the family room during a movie on a special occasion and his eating foods in the family room during a weekly television show. We agree. The citizens of this jurisdiction look to the rulings of this Court, as well as to general practice, to understand their rights and obligations as citizens. In the many months since the Rule was originally announced, the cumulative rulings of this Court on the subject would signify to any citizen that, whatever the technical language of the Rule, the real Rule is that they must clean up after eating any food outside of the kitchen. To draw and enforce any other line now would be arbitrary and, as such, unjust.

On November 4, 1986, the following proclamation, henceforth known as The New Ordinance 7.3, was made by the Supreme Lawmaker, Mother:

> Over the past few months, I have found empty cups, orange juice stains, milkshake spills, slimy spots of unknown origin, all manner of crumbs, melted chocolate, and icing from cake in the family room. I thought I was clear the first time! And you've all had a chance to show me that you could use your common sense and clean up after yourselves. So now let me be clearer: No food, gum, or drink of any kind, on any occasion or in any form, is permitted in the family room. Ever. Seriously. I mean it.

NOTES & QUESTIONS

1. At what point did the various interpreters construing the command that "the food stay in the kitchen" make an interpretive mistake? From the very first case? Only later? From the very first case, but only in light of what came later?

2. How much does the explanatory statement included in the first sentence of New Ordinance 7.3 shed light on the purpose of this revised ordinance? Does the new ordinance shed any light on the purpose of the original command? The first sentence of the new ordinance is broader than the first sentence of the original command, which referred to "pop-

corn kernels, pretzel crumbs, and pieces of cereal." But is it not fair to view the new ordinance's expression of broader concerns as also capturing what motivated the original command?

3. The interpretive problems presented in "The Food Stays in the Kitchen" vividly illustrate the reality that textual commands often do not anticipate the range of circumstances they will be asked to address, and that the resulting interpretive process can be influenced by such factors as precedent, perspective, and principle. In later chapters we will explore these factors in greater depth in the context of the interpretation of legal rules.

Interpretive ambiguities also can arise even without text or words. Consider a pictorial command like the one on the following page. It involves signage along a trail in a public park at a point where the trail divides into two parallel paths. The pictorial command, consisting of one depiction of a bicycle and a second depiction of a person walking, each depiction with an arrow pointing (in opposite directions from each other) to one of the two paths, appears simple enough: bicycles to the left path, pedestrians to the right path.

Before going on to the page after this picture, think for a moment about whether you can imagine possible ambiguities in these pictorial commands . . . .

Now consider the dilemma facing a pair of "pedestrian bikers" (pedestrians walking beside their bikes) when confronted with the signage above at the fork in the path.

DIY
Walking with Your Bicycle: Interpreting a Pictorial Command

How should these pedestrian bikers decide which of the two paths to take as they continue to walk with their bikes? Is the answer easy? If so, what makes it easy? If it is not, why not? Are the relevant factors inherent in the nature of the picture or the command "bicycles to the left, pedestrians to the right"? Or do they depend on *your* understanding of why the sign is there, or on facts about the world not present in the pictures themselves? Take two minutes to write down your thoughts.

Finally, we consider a prototypical problem of textual statutory interpretation. H.L.A. Hart, one of the most important jurisprudential thinkers of the 20th century, posed this famous hypothetical in 1958:

> A legal rule forbids you to take a vehicle into the public park. Plainly this forbids an automobile, but what about bicycles, roller skates, toy

automobiles? What about airplanes? Are these, as we say, to be called "vehicles" for the purpose of the rule or not?

In addition to the interpretive difficulties that Hart himself identified in this brief hypothetical, we can imagine countless other difficulties associated with the same municipal ordinance, which might simply read "No vehicles in the park." For instance, should the text of this five-word prohibition be understood to exclude from the park:

a) A baby stroller?

b) A scooter?

c) A sled on a snowy day?

d) A police cruiser?

e) An ambulance?

f) A tank on a war memorial pedestal?

g) A horse and buggy?

h) A horse?

i) A canoe?

j) A sanitation truck?

What other problem conveyances can you identify?

DIY
"No Vehicles in the Park"

 With H.L.A. Hart's "no vehicles in the park" hypothetical in mind, consider the following six questions and write a brief response to each:

1. What do you think a "no vehicles in the park" ordinance is meant to prohibit?

2. Why do you think this?

3. Given your response to question 1, what type of conveyance or other item, whether already on the list or not, would pose the greatest interpretive difficulty (that is, would be the hardest problem to resolve) under your understanding of the ordinance?

4. What could persuade you that the ordinance prohibits something other than what you described in your response to question 1?

5. What interpretive tools or sources of authority or guidance ought to be most relevant in construing the ordinance?

6. Who should be responsible for construing the ordinance?

In legal practice, interpretive problems can arise for a host of reasons, including ones beyond those identified in "The Food Stays in the Kitchen." (So, despite Professor Levin's tongue-in-cheek claim with his article's subtitle, you did not learn everything you need to know about statutory interpretation by the time you were nine!) Because the future is difficult to predict, law will almost inevitably be unable to anticipate every possible future problem. Lawmaking—whether by legislatures, agencies, or courts—occurs in a particular context and is usually designed to address identified, pre-existing problems in the world that need fixing. But the world changes. Those changes can be social, cultural, technological, or some combination. As we will see as the book progresses, many of the most difficult interpretive problems arise because of some kind of societal change, generating a mismatch between the words the lawmakers wrote at one point in time and a problem arising in a different context. This is one reason good lawyers in any area of practice are attuned to both the words of legal texts and the underlying aspects of the world that those texts were written to address. It is also why good lawyers understand who the legal decisionmakers—whether judges, legislators, or agency officials—are, and the institutional context in which they make their decisions and interpretations, considerations that Parts II and III will address.

Test Your Understanding

 To assess your understanding of the material in this chapter, click here to take a quiz.

3

The Interpretive Problem: A Full-Blown Judicial Response

Key Concepts

- Agency responsibilities
- Agency interpretation
- *Chevron* Doctrine

Chapter Summary

This chapter considers the Supreme Court's response to an interpretive issue in the text of the Affordable Care Act, addressed in the 2015 case of *King v. Burwell*. While the facts of the case are fascinating, pay close attention to the process that the Court uses in reaching its decision. The chapter first examines the reasoning of the majority, authored by Chief Justice John Roberts. It then includes key portions of Justice Scalia's dissent. As you read both opinions, pay close attention to the statutory interpretation tools that each opinion deploys, including the two opinions' treatment of Congress and the legislative process. Meanwhile, reflect on what you think the role of the judiciary should be in a case like *King v. Burwell*.

We complete this introductory Part of the book with a real and relatively recent interpretive problem arising from a federal statute, the Patient Protection and Affordable Care Act (ACA, colloquially known as Obamacare), which Congress enacted in 2010 to respond to the issue of rising health care costs and the large numbers of Americans without health insurance. The problem comes to us in the 2015 case of *King v. Burwell*, one of several major U.S. Supreme Court decisions growing out of the ACA. As you will see, each of the three branches of government is involved in the dispute: Congress passed the statute; then, federal agencies interpreted the law in the course of implementing it; and then the federal courts (eventually, the

Supreme Court) interpreted the law in the course of a lawsuit brought by several individuals who objected to the agency interpretation.

The case raises important questions both of statutory interpretation and of agency implementation of congressional enactments. Although the case is somewhat complex, the interpretive issue that it raises—the meaning of the statutory phrase "established by the state"—seems quite straightforward. In fact, however, the issue is far from straightforward: in contrast to the interpretive questions we raised in Chapter 2, this one arises in the context of a complex statute regulating one of the most significant aspects of the American economy, the multi-trillion dollar health-care industry.

In thinking about the agency roles here, you also may find it helpful to reread the last section (Part C) of Chapter 1. The excerpts of the case that follow include portions of the majority and dissenting opinions.

DIY
Interpreting a Complex Statute: *King v. Burwell*

As you read the excerpts of *King v. Burwell* that follow, see if you can find answers to these questions:

1. Who is David King and why is he involved?

2. Who is Sylvia Burwell and why is she involved?

3. What federal agencies are involved, and why?

4. How did the text of the Affordable Care Act come to have within it the interpretive ambiguity at issue in the case? Do the origins of that ambiguity help explain the disagreement between the majority and the dissent?

5. What do you think is the appropriate resolution of this interpretive issue?

David King v. Sylvia Burwell, Sec'y of Health and Human Services
576 U.S. 473 (2015)

CHIEF JUSTICE ROBERTS delivered the opinion of the Court.

The Patient Protection and Affordable Care Act adopts a series of interlocking reforms designed to expand coverage in the individual health insurance market. First, the Act bars insurers from taking a person's health into account when deciding whether to sell health insurance or how much to charge. Second, the Act generally requires each person to maintain insurance coverage or make a payment to the Internal Revenue Service. And third, the Act gives tax credits to certain people to make insurance more affordable.

In addition to those reforms, the Act requires the creation of an "Exchange" in each State—basically, a marketplace that allows people to compare and purchase insurance plans. The Act gives each State the opportunity to establish its own Exchange, but provides that the Federal Government will establish the Exchange if the State does not.

This case is about whether the Act's interlocking reforms apply equally in each State no matter who establishes the State's Exchange. Specifically, the question presented is whether the Act's tax credits are available in States that have a Federal Exchange.

I

A

The Patient Protection and Affordable Care Act, 124 Stat. 119, grew out of a long history of failed health insurance reform. In the 1990s, several States began experimenting with ways to expand people's access to coverage. One common approach was to impose a pair of insurance market regulations—a "guaranteed issue" requirement, which barred insurers from denying coverage to any person because of his health, and a "community rating" requirement, which barred insurers from charging a person higher premiums for the same reason. Together, those requirements were designed to ensure that anyone who wanted to buy health insurance could do so.

The guaranteed issue and community rating requirements achieved that goal, but they had an unintended consequence: They encouraged people to wait until they got sick to buy insurance. Why buy insurance coverage when you are healthy, if you can buy the same coverage for the same price when you become ill? This consequence—known as "adverse selection"—led to a second: Insurers were forced to increase premiums to account for the fact that, more and more, it was the sick rather than the healthy who were buying insurance. And that consequence fed back into the first: As the cost of insurance rose, even more people waited until they became ill to buy it.

This led to an economic "death spiral." As premiums rose higher and higher, and the number of people buying insurance sank lower and lower, insurers began to leave the market entirely. As a result, the number of people without insurance increased dramatically.

This cycle happened repeatedly during the 1990s.

* * *

In 1996, Massachusetts adopted the guaranteed issue and community rating requirements and experienced similar results. But in 2006, Massachusetts added two more reforms: The Commonwealth required individuals to buy insurance or pay a penalty, and it gave tax credits to certain individuals to ensure that they could afford the insurance they were required to buy. The combination of these three reforms—insurance market regulations, a coverage mandate, and tax credits—reduced the uninsured rate in Massachusetts to 2.6 percent, by far the lowest in the Nation.

B

The Affordable Care Act adopts a version of the three key reforms that made the Massachusetts system successful. First, the Act adopts the guaranteed issue and community rating requirements. The Act provides that "each health insurance issuer that offers health insurance coverage in the individual . . . market in a State must accept every . . . individual in the State that applies for such coverage." 42 U.S.C. § 300gg–1(a). The Act also bars insurers from charging higher premiums on the basis of a person's health. § 300gg.

FYI The Internal Revenue Service (or IRS) is the agency within the Department of the Treasury tasked with administering the internal federal tax laws. ("Internal" is as opposed to taxes like tariffs and customs duties, which are imposed on transnational transactions.)

Second, the Act generally requires individuals to maintain health insurance coverage or make a payment to the IRS. 26 U.S.C. § 5000A. Congress recognized that, without an incentive, "many individuals would wait to purchase health insurance until they needed care." 42 U.S.C. § 18091(2)(I). So Congress adopted a coverage requirement to "minimize this adverse selection and broaden the health insurance risk pool to include healthy individuals, which will lower health insurance premiums." *Ibid.* In Congress's view, that coverage requirement was "essential to creating effective health insurance markets." *Ibid.* Congress also provided an exemption from the coverage requirement for anyone who has to spend more than eight percent of his income on health insurance. 26 U.S.C. §§ 5000A(e)(1)(A), (e)(1)(B)(ii).

Third, the Act seeks to make insurance more affordable by giving refundable tax credits to individuals with household incomes between 100 percent and 400 percent of the federal poverty line. § 36B. Individuals who meet the Act's requirements may purchase insurance with the tax credits, which are provided in advance directly to the individual's insurer. 42 U.S.C. §§ 18081, 18082.

These three reforms are closely intertwined. As noted, Congress found that the guaranteed issue and community rating requirements would not work without the coverage requirement. § 18091(2)(I). And the coverage requirement would not work without the tax credits. The reason is that, without the tax credits, the cost of buying insurance would exceed eight percent of income for a large number of individuals, which would exempt them from the coverage requirement. Given the relationship between these three reforms, the Act provided that they should take effect on the same day—January 1, 2014.

> This is the Court's description of the broader statutory scheme. If on your first reading you don't understand who is getting the tax credits and why, be sure to re-read this Section I.B.

C

In addition to those three reforms, the Act requires the creation of an "Exchange" in each State where people can shop for insurance, usually online. 42 U.S.C. § 18031(b)(1). An Exchange may be created in one of two ways. First, the Act provides that "[e]ach State shall . . . establish an American Health Benefit Exchange . . . for the State." *Ibid.* Second, if a State nonetheless chooses not to establish its own Exchange, the Act provides that the Secretary of Health and Human Services "shall . . . establish and operate such Exchange within the State." § 18041(c)(1).

The issue in this case is whether the Act's tax credits are available in States that have a Federal Exchange rather than a State Exchange. The Act initially provides that tax credits "shall be allowed" for any "applicable taxpayer." 26 U.S.C. § 36B(a). The Act then provides that the amount of the tax credit depends in part on whether the taxpayer has enrolled in an insurance plan through "an Exchange established by the State under section 1311 of the Patient Protection and Affordable Care Act [hereinafter 42 U.S.C. § 18031]." 26 U.S.C. §§ 36B(b)–(c) (emphasis added).

The IRS addressed the availability of tax credits by promulgating a rule that made them available on both State and Federal Exchanges. 77 Fed.Reg. 30378 (2012). As relevant here, the IRS Rule provides that a taxpayer is eligible for a tax credit if he enrolled in an insurance plan through "an Exchange," 26 CFR § 1.36B–2 (2013), which is defined as "an Exchange serving the individual market . . . regardless of whether the Exchange is established and operated by a State . . . or by HHS," 45 CFR § 155.20 (2014). At this point, 16 States and the District of Columbia have established their own Exchanges; the other 34 States have elected to have HHS do so.

D

Petitioners are four individuals who live in Virginia, which has a Federal Exchange. They do not wish to purchase health insurance. In their view, Virginia's Exchange does not qualify as "an Exchange established by the State under [42 U.S.C. § 18031]," so they should not receive any tax credits. That would make the cost of buying insurance more than eight percent of their income, which would exempt them from the Act's coverage requirement. 26 U.S.C. § 5000A(e)(1).

Under the IRS Rule, however, Virginia's Exchange *would* qualify as "an Exchange established by the State under [42 U.S.C. § 18031]," so petitioners would receive tax credits. That would make the cost of buying insurance *less* than eight percent of petitioners' income, which would subject them to the Act's coverage requirement. The IRS Rule therefore requires petitioners to either buy health insurance they do not want, or make a payment to the IRS.

Petitioners challenged the IRS Rule in Federal District Court. The District Court dismissed the suit, holding that the Act unambiguously made tax credits available to individuals enrolled through a Federal Exchange. *King v. Sebelius*, 997 F.Supp.2d 415 (E.D.Va.2014). The Court of Appeals for the Fourth Circuit affirmed. 759 F.3d 358 (2014). The Fourth Circuit viewed the Act as "ambiguous and subject to at least two different interpretations."

Id., at 372. The court therefore deferred to the IRS's interpretation under *Chevron U.S.A. Inc. v. Natural Resources Defense Council, Inc.*, 467 U.S. 837, 104 S.Ct. 2778, 81 L.Ed.2d 694 (1984). 759 F.3d, at 376.

The same day that the Fourth Circuit issued its decision, the Court of Appeals for the District of Columbia Circuit vacated the IRS Rule in a different case, holding that the Act "unambiguously restricts" the tax credits to State Exchanges. *Halbig v. Burwell*, 758 F.3d 390, 394 (2014). We granted certiorari in the present case.

II

The Affordable Care Act addresses tax credits in what is now Section 36B of the Internal Revenue Code. * * *

The parties dispute whether Section 36B authorizes tax credits for individuals who enroll in an insurance plan through a Federal Exchange. Petitioners argue that a Federal Exchange is not "an Exchange established by the State under [42 U.S.C. § 18031]," and that the IRS Rule therefore contradicts Section 36B. The Government responds that the IRS Rule is lawful because the phrase "an Exchange established by the State under [42 U.S.C. § 18031]" should be read to include Federal Exchanges.

When analyzing an agency's interpretation of a statute, we often apply the two-step framework announced in *Chevron*, 467 U.S. 837. Under that framework, we ask whether the statute is ambiguous and, if so, whether the agency's interpretation is reasonable. *Id.*, at 842–843. This approach "is premised on the theory that a statute's ambiguity constitutes an implicit delegation from Congress to the agency to fill in the statutory gaps." *FDA v. Brown & Williamson Tobacco Corp.*, 529 U.S. 120 (2000). "In extraordinary cases, however, there may be reason to hesitate before concluding that Congress has intended such an implicit delegation." *Ibid.*

> This discussion is about the *"Chevron* doctrine," named after a 1984 case involving the energy company Chevron as one of the parties. We turn to this doctrine in Part VIII of the book. For now, it is enough to know that sometimes an agency, not a court, gets the first crack at interpreting a statute in the course of implementing it and that, when it does, the agency's interpretation can sometimes affect how a court addresses the interpretive question.

This is one of those cases. The tax credits are among the Act's key reforms, involving billions of dollars in spending each year and affecting the price of health insurance for millions of people.

Whether those credits are available on Federal Exchanges is thus a question of deep "economic and political significance" that is central to this statutory scheme; had Congress wished to assign that question to an agency, it surely would have done so expressly. *Utility Air Regulatory Group v. EPA*, 573 U.S. 302, 324 (2014) (quoting *Brown & Williamson*, 529 U.S., at 160). It is especially unlikely that Congress would have delegated this decision to the *IRS*, which has no expertise in crafting health insurance policy of this sort. This is not a case for the IRS.

It is instead our task to determine the correct reading of Section 36B. If the statutory language is plain, we must enforce it according to its terms. But oftentimes the "meaning—or ambiguity—of certain words or phrases may only become evident when placed in context." *Brown & Williamson*, 529 U.S., at 132. So when deciding whether the language is plain, we must read the words "in their context and with a view to their place in the overall statutory scheme." *Id.*, at 133 (internal quotation marks omitted). Our duty, after all, is "to construe statutes, not isolated provisions." *Graham County Soil and Water Conservation Dist. v. United States ex rel. Wilson*, 559 U.S. 280, 290 (2010) (internal quotation marks omitted).

A

We begin with the text of Section 36B. As relevant here, Section 36B allows an individual to receive tax credits only if the individual enrolls in an insurance plan through "an Exchange established by the State under [42 U.S.C. § 18031]." In other words, three things must be true: First, the individual must enroll in an insurance plan through "an Exchange." Second, that Exchange must be "established by the State." And third, that Exchange must be established "under [42 U.S.C. § 18031]." We address each requirement in turn.

First, all parties agree that a Federal Exchange qualifies as "an Exchange" for purposes of Section 36B. Section 18031 provides that "[e]ach State shall . . . establish an American Health Benefit Exchange . . . for the State." § 18031(b)(1). Although phrased as a requirement, the Act gives the States "flexibility" by allowing them to "elect" whether they want to establish an Exchange. § 18041(b). If the State chooses not to do so, Section 18041 provides that the Secretary "shall . . . establish and operate such *Exchange* within the State." § 18041(c)(1) (emphasis added).

By using the phrase "such Exchange," Section 18041 instructs the Secretary to establish and operate the same Exchange that the State was directed to establish under Section 18031. See BLACK'S LAW DICTIONARY 1661 (10th ed. 2014) (defining "such" as "That or those; having just been mentioned"). In other words, State Exchanges and Federal Exchanges are equivalent—they must meet the same requirements, perform the same functions, and serve the same purposes. Although State and Federal Exchanges are established by different sovereigns, Sections 18031 and 18041 do not suggest that they differ in any meaningful way. A Federal Exchange therefore counts as "an Exchange" under Section 36B.

Second, we must determine whether a Federal Exchange is "established by the State" for purposes of Section 36B. At the outset, it might seem that a Federal Exchange cannot fulfill this requirement. After all, the Act defines "State" to mean "each of the 50 States and the District of Columbia"—a definition that does not include the Federal Government. 42 U.S.C. § 18024(d). But when read in context, "with a view to [its] place in the overall statutory scheme," the meaning of the phrase "established by the State" is not so clear. *Brown & Williamson*, 529 U.S., at 133 (internal quotation marks omitted).

After telling each State to establish an Exchange, Section 18031 provides that all Exchanges "shall make available qualified health plans to qualified individuals." 42 U.S.C. § 18031(d)(2)(A). Section 18032 then defines the term "qualified individual" in part as an individual who "resides in the State that established the Exchange." § 18032(f)(1)(A). And that's a problem: If we give the phrase "the State that established the Exchange" its most natural meaning, there would be no "qualified individuals" on Federal Exchanges. But the Act clearly contemplates that there will be qualified individuals on every Exchange. As we just mentioned, the Act requires all Exchanges to "make available qualified health plans to qualified individuals"—something an Exchange could not do if there were no such individuals. § 18031(d)(2)(A). And the Act tells the Exchange, in deciding which health plans to offer, to consider "the interests of qualified individuals . . . in the State or States in which such Exchange operates"—again, something the Exchange could not do if qualified individuals did not exist. § 18031(e)(1)(B). This problem arises repeatedly throughout the Act. See, *e.g.,* § 18031(b)(2) (allowing a State to create "one Exchange . . . for providing . . . services to both qualified individuals and qualified small employers," rather than creating separate Exchanges for those two groups).

These provisions suggest that the Act may not always use the phrase "established by the State" in its most natural sense. Thus, the meaning of that phrase may not be as clear as it appears when read out of context.

Third, we must determine whether a Federal Exchange is established "under [42 U.S.C. § 18031]." This too might seem a requirement that a Federal Exchange cannot fulfill, because it is Section 18041 that tells the Secretary when to "establish and operate such Exchange." But here again, the way different provisions in the statute interact suggests otherwise.

The Act defines the term "Exchange" to mean "an American Health Benefit Exchange established under section 18031." § 300gg–91(d)(21). If we import that definition into Section 18041, the Act tells the Secretary to "establish and operate such 'American Health Benefit Exchange established under section 18031.' " That suggests that Section 18041 authorizes the Secretary to establish an Exchange under Section 18031, not (or not only) under Section 18041. Otherwise, the Federal Exchange, by definition, would not be an "Exchange" at all. See *Halbig*, 758 F.3d, at 399–400 (acknowledging that the Secretary establishes Federal Exchanges under Section 18031).

This interpretation of "under [42 U.S.C. § 18031]" fits best with the statutory context. All of the requirements that an Exchange must meet are in Section 18031, so it is sensible to regard all Exchanges as established under that provision. In addition, every time the Act uses the word "Exchange," the definitional provision requires that we substitute the phrase "Exchange established under section 18031." If Federal Exchanges were not established under Section 18031, therefore, literally none of the Act's requirements would apply to them. Finally, the Act repeatedly uses the phrase "established under [42 U.S.C. § 18031]" in situations where it would make no sense to distinguish between State and Federal Exchanges. See, *e.g.*, 26 U.S.C. § 125(f)(3)(A) (2012 ed., Supp. I) ("The term 'qualified benefit' shall not include any qualified health plan . . . offered through an Exchange established under [42 U.S.C. § 18031]"); 26 U.S.C. § 6055(b)(1)(B)(iii)(I) (2012 ed.) (requiring insurers to report whether each insurance plan they provided "is a qualified health plan offered through an Exchange established under [42 U.S.C. § 18031]"). A Federal Exchange may therefore be considered one established "under [42 U.S.C. § 18031]."

The upshot of all this is that the phrase "an Exchange established by the State under [42 U.S.C. § 18031]" is properly viewed as ambiguous. The phrase may be limited in its reach to State Exchanges. But it is also possible that the phrase refers to *all* Exchanges—both State and Federal—at least for purposes of the tax credits. If a State chooses not to follow the directive in Section 18031 that it establish an Exchange, the Act tells the Secretary to establish "such Exchange." § 18041. And by using the words "such Exchange," the Act indicates that State and Federal Exchanges should be the same. But State and Federal Exchanges would differ in a fundamental way if tax credits were available only on State Exchanges—one type of Exchange would help make insurance more affordable by providing billions of dollars to the States' citizens; the other type of Exchange would not.

The conclusion that Section 36B is ambiguous is further supported by several provisions that assume tax credits will be available on both State and Federal Exchanges. For example, the Act requires all Exchanges to create outreach programs that must "distribute fair and impartial information concerning . . . the availability of premium tax credits under section 36B." § 18031(i)(3)(B). The Act also requires all Exchanges to "establish and make available by electronic means a calculator to determine the actual cost of coverage after the application of any premium tax credit under section 36B." § 18031(d)(4)(G). And the Act requires all Exchanges to report to the Treasury Secretary information about each health plan they sell, including the "aggregate amount of any advance payment of such credit," "[a]ny information . . . necessary to determine eligibility for, and the amount of, such credit," and any "[i]nformation necessary to determine whether a taxpayer has received excess advance payments." 26 U.S.C. § 36B(f)(3). If tax credits were not available on Federal Exchanges, these provisions would make little sense.

Petitioners and the dissent respond that the words "established by the State" would be unnecessary if Congress meant to extend tax credits to both State and Federal Exchanges. Brief for Petitioners 20; *post*, at 2497–2498. But "our preference for avoiding surplusage constructions is not absolute." *Lamie v. United States Trustee*, 540 U.S. 526, 536 (2004); see also *Marx v. General Revenue Corp.*, 568 U.S. 371, 385 (2013) ("The canon against surplusage is not an absolute rule"). And specifically with respect to this Act, rigorous application of the canon does not seem a particularly useful guide to a fair construction of the statute.

The Affordable Care Act contains more than a few examples of inartful drafting. (To cite just one, the Act creates three separate Section 1563s. See 124 Stat. 270, 911, 912.) Several features of the Act's passage contributed to that unfortunate reality. Congress wrote key parts of the Act behind closed doors, rather than through "the traditional legislative process." Cannan, *A Legislative History of the Affordable Care Act: How Legislative Procedure Shapes Legislative History*, 105 L. LIB. J. 131, 163 (2013). And Congress passed much of the Act using a complicated budgetary procedure known as "reconciliation," which limited opportunities for debate and amendment, and bypassed the Senate's normal 60-vote filibuster requirement. *Id.*, at 159–167. As a result, the Act does not reflect the type of care and deliberation that one might expect of such significant legislation. *Cf.* Frankfurter, *Some Reflections on the Reading of Statutes*, 47 COLUM. L. REV. 527, 545 (1947) (describing a cartoon "in which a senator tells his colleagues 'I admit this new bill is too complicated to understand. We'll just have to pass it to find out what it means.' ").

> **?** Does this tell you something about the legislative process that occurred here? Notice that the Court is contrasting the process for the ACA with the process used for other statutes, "the traditional legislative process." Why do you think the Court views aspects of the legislative process as important here? Is this part of the Court's justification for reading the words "established by the State" in this rather unconventional way? Note too that the ACA is 906 pages long!

Anyway, we "must do our best, bearing in mind the fundamental canon of statutory construction that the words of a statute must be read in their context and with a view to their place in the overall statutory scheme." *Utility Air Regulatory Group*, 573 U.S., at 320 (internal quotation marks omitted). After reading Section 36B along with other related provisions in the Act, we cannot conclude that the phrase "an Exchange established by the State under [Section 18031]" is unambiguous.

B

Given that the text is ambiguous, we must turn to the broader structure of the Act to determine the meaning of Section 36B. "A provision that may seem ambiguous in isolation is often clarified by the remainder of the statutory scheme . . . because only one of the permissible meanings produces a substantive effect that is compatible with the rest of the law." *United Sav. Assn. of Tex. v. Timbers of Inwood Forest Associates, Ltd.*, 484 U.S. 365, 371 (1988). Here, the statutory scheme compels us to reject petitioners' interpretation because it would destabilize the individual insurance market in any State with a Federal Exchange, and likely create the very "death spirals" that Congress designed the Act to avoid. See *New York State Dept. of Social*

Servs. v. Dublino, 413 U.S. 405, 419–420 (1973) ("We cannot interpret federal statutes to negate their own stated purposes.").

As discussed above, Congress based the Affordable Care Act on three major reforms: first, the guaranteed issue and community rating requirements; second, a requirement that individuals maintain health insurance coverage or make a payment to the IRS; and third, the tax credits for individuals with household incomes between 100 percent and 400 percent of the federal poverty line. In a State that establishes its own Exchange, these three reforms work together to expand insurance coverage. The guaranteed issue and community rating requirements ensure that anyone can buy insurance; the coverage requirement creates an incentive for people to do so before they get sick; and the tax credits—it is hoped—make insurance more affordable. Together, those reforms "minimize . . . adverse selection and broaden the health insurance risk pool to include healthy individuals, which will lower health insurance premiums." 42 U.S.C. § 18091(2)(I).

Under petitioners' reading, however, the Act would operate quite differently in a State with a Federal Exchange. As they see it, one of the Act's three major reforms—the tax credits—would not apply. And a second major reform—the coverage requirement—would not apply in a meaningful way. As explained earlier, the coverage requirement applies only when the cost of buying health insurance (minus the amount of the tax credits) is less than eight percent of an individual's income. 26 U.S.C. §§ 5000A(e)(1)(A), (e)(1)(B)(ii). So without the tax credits, the coverage requirement would apply to fewer individuals. And it would be a lot fewer. In 2014, approximately 87 percent of people who bought insurance on a Federal Exchange did so with tax credits, and virtually all of those people would become exempt. HHS, A. Burke, A. Misra, & S. Sheingold, *Premium Affordability, Competition, and Choice in the Health Insurance Marketplace* 5 (2014); Brief for Bipartisan Economic Scholars as *Amici Curiae* 19–20. If petitioners are right, therefore, only one of the Act's three major reforms would apply in States with a Federal Exchange.

The combination of no tax credits and an ineffective coverage requirement could well push a State's individual insurance market into a death spiral. * * *

It is implausible that Congress meant the Act to operate in this manner. See *National Federation of Independent Business v. Sebelius*, 567 U.S. 519, 702 (2012) (SCALIA, KENNEDY, THOMAS, AND ALITO, JJ., dissenting) ("Without the federal subsidies . . . the exchanges would not operate as Congress intended and may not operate at all."). Congress made the guaranteed issue and community rating requirements applicable in every State in the Nation. But those requirements only work when combined with the coverage requirement and the tax credits. So it stands to reason that Congress meant for those provisions to apply in every State as well.

Petitioners respond that Congress was not worried about the effects of withholding tax credits from States with Federal Exchanges because "Congress evidently believed it was offering states a deal they would not refuse." Brief for Petitioners 36. Congress may have been wrong about the States' willingness to establish their own Exchanges, petitioners continue, but that does not allow this Court to rewrite the Act to fix that problem. That is particularly true, petitioners conclude, because the States likely *would* have created their own Exchanges in the absence of the IRS Rule, which eliminated any incentive that the States had to do so. *Id.*, at 36–38.

Section 18041 refutes the argument that Congress believed it was offering the States a deal they would not refuse. That section provides that, if a State elects not to establish an Exchange, the Secretary "shall . . . establish and operate such Exchange within the State." 42 U.S.C. § 18041(c)(1)(A). The whole point of that provision is to create a federal fallback in case a State chooses not to establish its own Exchange. Contrary to petitioners' argument, Congress did not believe it was offering States a deal they would not refuse—it expressly addressed what would happen if a State did refuse the deal.

C

Finally, the structure of Section 36B itself suggests that tax credits are not limited to State Exchanges. Section 36B(a) initially provides that tax credits "shall be allowed" for any "applicable taxpayer." Section 36B(c)(1) then defines an "applicable taxpayer" as someone who (among other things) has a household income between 100 percent and 400 percent of the federal poverty line. Together, these two provisions appear to make anyone in the specified income range eligible to receive a tax credit.

According to petitioners, however, those provisions are an empty promise in States with a Federal Exchange. In their view, an applicable taxpayer in such a State would be *eligible* for a tax credit—but the *amount* of that tax credit would always be zero. * * *

D

Petitioners' arguments about the plain meaning of Section 36B are strong. But while the meaning of the phrase "an Exchange established by the State under [42 U.S.C. § 18031]" may seem plain "when viewed in isolation," such a reading turns out to be "untenable in light of [the statute] as a whole." *Department of Revenue of Ore. v. ACF Industries, Inc.*, 510 U.S. 332, 343 (1994). In this instance, the context and structure of the Act compel us to depart from what would otherwise be the most natural reading of the pertinent statutory phrase.

Reliance on context and structure in statutory interpretation is a "subtle business, calling for great wariness lest what professes to be mere rendering becomes creation and attempted interpretation of legislation becomes legislation itself." *Palmer v. Massachusetts*, 308 U.S. 79, 83 (1939). For the reasons we have given, however, such reliance is appropriate in this case, and leads us to conclude that Section 36B allows tax credits for insurance purchased on any Exchange created under the Act. Those credits are necessary for the Federal Exchanges to function like their State Exchange counterparts, and to avoid the type of calamitous result that Congress plainly meant to avoid.

* * *

In a democracy, the power to make the law rests with those chosen by the people. Our role is more confined—"to say what the law is." *Marbury v. Madison*, 1 Cranch 137, 177 (1803). That is easier in some cases than in others. But in every case we must respect the role of the Legislature, and take care not to undo what it has done. A fair reading of legislation demands a fair understanding of the legislative plan.

Congress passed the Affordable Care Act to improve health insurance markets, not to destroy them. If at all possible, we must interpret the Act in a way that is consistent with the former, and avoids the latter. Section 36B can fairly be read consistent with what we see as Congress's plan, and that is the reading we adopt.

The judgment of the United States Court of Appeals for the Fourth Circuit is *Affirmed*.

FYI Throughout his years on the Supreme Court, Justice Scalia was known for his occasionally biting critiques of his colleagues' work, often expressed in colorful language.

JUSTICE SCALIA, with whom JUSTICE THOMAS and JUSTICE ALITO join, dissenting.

The Court holds that when the Patient Protection and Affordable Care Act says "Exchange established by the State" it means "Exchange established by the State or the Federal Government." That is of course quite absurd, and the Court's 21 pages of explanation make it no less so.

I

* * *

This case requires us to decide whether someone who buys insurance on an Exchange established by the Secretary [of Health and Human Services] gets tax credits. You would think the answer would be obvious—so obvious there would hardly be a need for the Supreme Court to hear a case about it. In order to receive any money under § 36B, an individual must enroll in

Would Justice Scalia similarly have said that an ordinance reading "No vehicles in the park" obviously prohibits a maintenance vehicle? Why (not)?

an insurance plan through an "Exchange established by the State." The Secretary of Health and Human Services is not a State. So an Exchange established by the Secretary is not an Exchange established by the State— which means people who buy health insurance through such an Exchange get no money under § 36B.

Words no longer have meaning if an Exchange that is not established by a State is "established by the State." It is hard to come up with a clearer way to limit tax credits to state Exchanges than to use the words "established by the State." And it is hard to come up with a reason to include the words "by the State" other than the purpose of limiting credits to state Exchanges. "[T]he plain, obvious, and rational meaning of a statute is always to be preferred to any curious, narrow, hidden sense that nothing but the exigency of a hard case and the ingenuity and study of an acute and powerful intellect would discover." *Lynch v. Alworth-Stephens Co.*, 267 U.S. 364, 370

(1925) (internal quotation marks omitted). Under all the usual rules of interpretation, in short, the Government should lose this case. But normal rules of interpretation seem always to yield to the overriding principle of the present Court: The Affordable Care Act must be saved.

> The quip that ends this paragraph is a reference to a 2012 case, *NFIB v. Sebelius*, which challenged the constitutionality of the ACA. In that case, the Court upheld the ACA as constitutional, with Justice Scalia dissenting. Justice Scalia explains this point further in the concluding paragraphs of this opinion.

II

The Court interprets § 36B to award tax credits on both federal and state Exchanges. It accepts that the "most natural sense" of the phrase "Exchange established by the State" is an Exchange established by a State. *Ante*, at ____. (Understatement, thy name is an opinion on the Affordable Care Act!) Yet the opinion continues, with no semblance of shame, that "it is also possible that the phrase refers to *all* Exchanges—both State and Federal." *Ante*, at ____. (Impossible possibility, thy name is an opinion on the Affordable Care Act!) The Court claims that "the context and structure of the Act compel [it] to depart from what would otherwise be the most natural reading of the pertinent statutory phrase." *Ante*, at ____.

I wholeheartedly agree with the Court that sound interpretation requires paying attention to the whole law, not homing in on isolated words or even isolated sections. Context always matters. Let us not forget, however, *why* context matters: It is a tool for understanding the terms of the law, not an excuse for rewriting them.

Any effort to understand rather than to rewrite a law must accept and apply the presumption that lawmakers use words in "their natural and ordinary signification." *Pensacola Telegraph Co. v. Western Union Telegraph Co.*, 96 U.S. 1, 12 (1878). Ordinary connotation does not always prevail, but the more unnatural the proposed interpretation of a law, the more compelling the contextual evidence must be to show that it is correct. Today's interpretation is not merely unnatural; it is unheard of. Who would ever have dreamt that "Exchange established by the State" means "Exchange established by the State or *the Federal Government*"? Little short of an express statutory definition could justify adopting this singular reading. Yet the only pertinent definition here provides that "State" means "each of the 50 States and the District of Columbia." 42 U.S.C. § 18024(d). Because the Secretary is neither one of the 50 States nor the District of Columbia, that definition positively contradicts the eccentric theory that an Exchange established by the Secretary has been established by the State.

Far from offering the overwhelming evidence of meaning needed to justify the Court's interpretation, other contextual clues undermine it at every turn. To begin with, other parts of the Act sharply distinguish between the establishment of an Exchange by a State and the establishment of an Exchange by the Federal Government. The States' authority to set up Exchanges comes from one provision, § 18031(b); the Secretary's authority comes from an entirely different provision, § 18041(c). Funding for States to establish Exchanges comes from one part of the law, § 18031(a); funding for the Secretary to establish Exchanges comes from an entirely different part of the law, § 18121. States generally run state-created Exchanges; the Secretary generally runs federally created Exchanges. § 18041(b)–(c). And the Secretary's authority to set up an Exchange in a State depends upon the State's "*[f]ailure* to establish [an] Exchange." § 18041(c) (emphasis added). Provisions such as these destroy any pretense that a federal Exchange is in some sense also established by a State.

Reading the rest of the Act also confirms that, as relevant here, there are *only* two ways to set up an Exchange in a State: establishment by a State and establishment by the Secretary. §§ 18031(b), 18041(c). So saying that an Exchange established by the Federal Government is "established by the State" goes beyond giving words bizarre meanings; it leaves the limiting phrase "by the State" with no operative effect at all. That is a stark violation of the elementary principle that requires an interpreter "to give effect, if possible, to every clause and word of a statute." *Montclair v. Ramsdell*, 107 U.S. 147, 152 (1883). In weighing this argument, it is well to remember the difference between giving a term a meaning that duplicates another part of the law, and giving a term no meaning at all. Lawmakers sometimes repeat themselves—whether out of a desire to add emphasis, a sense of belt-and-suspenders caution, or a lawyerly penchant for doublets (aid and abet, cease and desist, null and void). Lawmakers do not, however, tend to use terms that "have no operation at all." *Marbury v. Madison*, 1 Cranch 137, 174 (1803). So while the rule against treating a term as a redundancy is far from categorical, the rule against treating it as a nullity is as close to absolute as interpretive principles get. The Court's reading does not merely give "by the State" a duplicative effect; it causes the phrase to have no effect whatever.

Making matters worse, the reader of the whole Act will come across a number of provisions beyond § 36B that refer to the establishment of Exchanges by States. Adopting the Court's interpretation means nullifying the term "by the State" not just once, but again and again throughout the Act. * * *

Congress did not, by the way, repeat "Exchange established by the State under [§ 18031]" by rote throughout the Act. Quite the contrary, clause after clause of the law uses a more general term such as "Exchange" or "Exchange established under [§ 18031]." See, *e.g.*, 42 U.S.C. §§ 18031(k), 18033; 26 U.S.C. § 6055. It is common sense that any speaker who says "Exchange" some of the time, but "Exchange established by the State" the rest of the time, probably means something by the contrast.

Equating establishment "by the State" with establishment by the Federal Government makes nonsense of other parts of the Act. The Act requires States to ensure (on pain of losing Medicaid funding) that any "Exchange established by the State" uses a "secure electronic interface" to determine an individual's eligibility for various benefits (including tax credits). 42 U.S.C. § 1396w–3(b)(1)(D). How could a State control the type of electronic interface used by a federal Exchange? The Act allows a State to control contracting decisions made by "an Exchange established by the State." § 18031(f)(3). Why would a State get to control the contracting decisions of a federal Exchange? The Act also provides "Assistance to States to establish American Health Benefit Exchanges" and directs the Secretary to renew this funding "if the State . . . is making progress . . . toward . . . establishing an Exchange." § 18031(a). Does a State that refuses to set up an Exchange still receive this funding, on the premise that Exchanges established by the Federal Government are really established by States? It is presumably in order to avoid these questions that the Court concludes that federal Exchanges count as state Exchanges only "for purposes of the tax credits." *Ante*, at ___. (Contrivance, thy name is an opinion on the Affordable Care Act!)

It is probably piling on to add that the Congress that wrote the Affordable Care Act knew how to equate two different types of Exchanges when it wanted to do so. The Act includes a clause providing that "[a] *territory* that . . . establishes . . . an Exchange . . . shall be treated as a State" for certain purposes. § 18043(a) (emphasis added). Tellingly, it does not include a comparable clause providing that the *Secretary* shall be treated as a State for purposes of § 36B when *she* establishes an Exchange.

Faced with overwhelming confirmation that "Exchange established by the State" means what it looks like it means, the Court comes up with argument after feeble argument to support its contrary interpretation. None of its tries comes close to establishing the implausible conclusion that Congress used "by the State" to mean "by the State or not by the State."

* * *

Least convincing of all, however, is the Court's attempt to uncover support for its interpretation in "the structure of Section 36B itself." *Ante*, at ___. The Court finds it strange that Congress limited the tax credit to state Exchanges in the formula for calculating the amount of the credit, rather than in the provision defining the range of taxpayers *eligible* for the credit. Had the Court bothered to look at the rest of the Tax Code, it would have seen that the structure it finds strange is in fact quite common. Consider, for example, the many provisions that initially make taxpayers of all incomes eligible for a tax credit, only to provide later that the amount of the credit is zero if the taxpayer's income exceeds a specified threshold. See, *e.g.*, 26 U.S.C. § 24 (child tax credit); § 32 (earned-income tax credit); § 36 (first-time-homebuyer tax credit). Or consider, for an even closer parallel, a neighboring provision that initially makes taxpayers of all States eligible for a credit, only to provide later that the amount of the credit may be zero if the taxpayer's State does not satisfy certain requirements. See § 35 (health-insurance-costs tax credit). One begins to get the sense that the Court's insistence on reading things in context applies to "established by the State," but to nothing else.

For what it is worth, lawmakers usually draft tax-credit provisions the way they do—*i.e.*, the way they drafted § 36B—because the mechanics of the credit require it. Many Americans move to new States in the middle of the year. Mentioning state Exchanges in the definition of "coverage month"— rather than (as the Court proposes) in the provisions concerning taxpayers' eligibility for the credit—accounts for taxpayers who live in a State with a state Exchange for a part of the year, but a State with a federal Exchange for the rest of the year. In addition, § 36B awards a credit with respect to insurance plans "which cover the taxpayer, *the taxpayer's spouse, or any dependent* . . . of the taxpayer and which were enrolled in through an Exchange established by the State." § 36B(b)(2)(A) (emphasis added). If Congress had mentioned state Exchanges in the provisions discussing taxpayers' eligibility for the credit, a taxpayer who buys insurance from a federal Exchange would get no money, even if he has a spouse or dependent who buys insurance from a state Exchange—say a child attending college in a different State. It thus makes perfect sense for "Exchange established by the State" to appear where it does, rather than where the Court suggests. Even if that were not so, of course, its location would not make it any less clear.

The Court has not come close to presenting the compelling contextual case necessary to justify departing from the ordinary meaning of the terms of the law. Quite the contrary, context only underscores the outlandishness of the Court's interpretation. Reading the Act as a whole leaves no doubt about the matter: "Exchange established by the State" means what it looks like it means.

III

For its next defense of the indefensible, the Court turns to the Affordable Care Act's design and purposes. As relevant here, the Act makes three major reforms. The guaranteed-issue and community-rating requirements prohibit insurers from considering a customer's health when deciding whether to sell insurance and how much to charge, 42 U.S.C. §§ 300gg, 300gg–1; its famous individual mandate requires everyone to maintain insurance coverage or to pay what the Act calls a "penalty," 26 U.S.C. § 5000A(b)(1), and what we have nonetheless called a tax, see *National Federation of Independent Business v. Sebelius*, 567 U.S. 519, 570 (2012); and its tax credits help make insurance more affordable. The Court reasons that Congress intended these three reforms to "work together to expand insurance coverage"; and because the first two apply in every State, so must the third. *Ante*, at ___.

This reasoning suffers from no shortage of flaws. To begin with, "even the most formidable argument concerning the statute's purposes could not overcome the clarity [of] the statute's text." *Kloeckner v. Solis*, 568 U.S. 41, 56, n. 4 (2012). Statutory design and purpose matter only to the extent they help clarify an otherwise ambiguous provision. Could anyone maintain with a straight face that § 36B is unclear? To mention just the highlights, the Court's interpretation clashes with a statutory definition, renders words inoperative in at least seven separate provisions of the Act, overlooks the contrast between provisions that say "Exchange" and those that say "Exchange established by the State," gives the same phrase one meaning for purposes of tax credits but an entirely different meaning for other purposes, and (let us not forget) contradicts the ordinary meaning of the words Congress used. On the other side of the ledger, the Court has come up with nothing more than a general provision that turns out to be controlled by a specific one, a handful of clauses that are consistent with either understanding of establishment by the State, and a resemblance between the tax-credit provision and the rest of the Tax Code. If that is all it takes to make something ambiguous, everything is ambiguous.

Having gone wrong in consulting statutory purpose at all, the Court goes wrong again in analyzing it. The purposes of a law must be "collected chiefly from its words," not "from extrinsic circumstances." *Sturges v. Crowninshield*, 4 Wheat. 122, 202 (1819) (MARSHALL, C.J.). Only by concentrating on the law's terms can a judge hope to uncover the scheme *of the statute*, rather than some other scheme that the judge thinks desirable. Like it or not, the express terms of the Affordable Care Act make only two of the three reforms mentioned by the Court applicable in States that do not establish Exchanges. It is perfectly possible for them to operate independently of tax credits. The guaranteed-issue and community-rating requirements continue to ensure that insurance companies treat all customers the same no matter their health, and the individual mandate continues to encourage people to maintain coverage, lest they be "taxed."

The Court protests that without the tax credits, the number of people covered by the individual mandate shrinks, and without a broadly applicable individual mandate the guaranteed-issue and community-rating requirements "would destabilize the individual insurance market." *Ante*, at ___. If true, these projections would show only that the statutory scheme contains a flaw; they would not show that the statute means the opposite of what it says. Moreover, it is a flaw that appeared as well in other parts of the Act. A different title established a long-term-care insurance program with guaranteed-issue and community-rating requirements, but without an individual mandate or subsidies. §§ 8001–8002, 124 Stat. 828–847 (2010). This program never came into effect "only because Congress, in response to actuarial analyses predicting that the [program] would be fiscally unsustainable, repealed the provision in 2013." *Halbig*, 758 F.3d, at 410. How could the Court say that Congress would never dream of combining guaranteed-issue and community-rating requirements with a narrow individual mandate, when it combined those requirements with no individual mandate in the context of long-term-care insurance?

Similarly, the Department of Health and Human Services originally interpreted the Act to impose guaranteed-issue and community-rating requirements in the Federal Territories, even though the Act plainly does not make the individual mandate applicable there. *Ibid.*; see 26 U.S.C. § 5000A(f)(4); 42 U.S.C. § 201(f). "This combination, predictably, [threw] individual insurance markets in the territories into turmoil." *Halbig, supra*, at 410. Responding to complaints from the Territories, the Department at first insisted that it had "no statutory authority" to address the problem and suggested that the

Territories "seek legislative relief from Congress" instead. Letter from G. Cohen, Director of the Center for Consumer Information and Insurance Oversight, to S. Igisomar, Secretary of Commerce of the Commonwealth of Northern Mariana Islands (July 12, 2013). The Department changed its mind a year later, after what it described as "a careful review of [the] situation and the relevant statutory language." Letter from M. Tavenner, Administrator of the Centers for Medicare and Medicaid Services, to G. Francis, Insurance Commissioner of the Virgin Islands (July 16, 2014). How could the Court pronounce it "implausible" for Congress to have tolerated instability in insurance markets in States with federal Exchanges, *ante*, at ___, when even the Government maintained until recently that Congress did exactly that in American Samoa, Guam, the Northern Mariana Islands, Puerto Rico, and the Virgin Islands?

Compounding its errors, the Court forgets that it is no more appropriate to consider one of a statute's purposes in isolation than it is to consider one of its words that way. No law pursues just one purpose at all costs, and no statutory scheme encompasses just one element. Most relevant here, the Affordable Care Act displays a congressional preference for state participation in the establishment of Exchanges: Each State gets the first opportunity to set up its Exchange, 42 U.S.C. § 18031(b); States that take up the opportunity receive federal funding for "activities . . . related to establishing" an Exchange, § 18031(a)(3); and the Secretary may establish an Exchange in a State only as a fallback, § 18041(c). But setting up and running an Exchange involve significant burdens—meeting strict deadlines, § 18041(b), implementing requirements related to the offering of insurance plans, § 18031(d)(4), setting up outreach programs, § 18031(i), and ensuring that the Exchange is self-sustaining by 2015, § 18031(d)(5)(A). A State would have much less reason to take on these burdens if its citizens could receive tax credits no matter who establishes its Exchange. (Now that the Internal Revenue Service has interpreted § 36B to authorize tax credits everywhere, by the way, 34 States have failed to set up their own Exchanges. *Ante*, at ___.) So even if making credits available on all Exchanges advances the goal of improving healthcare markets, it frustrates the goal of encouraging state involvement in the implementation of the Act. *This* is what justifies going out of our way to read "established by the State" to mean "established by the State or not established by the State"?

Worst of all for the repute of today's decision, the Court's reasoning is largely self-defeating. The Court predicts that making tax credits unavailable in States that do not set up their own Exchanges would cause disastrous economic consequences there. If that is so, however, wouldn't one expect States to react by setting up their own Exchanges? And wouldn't that outcome satisfy two of the Act's goals rather than just one: enabling the Act's reforms to work and promoting state involvement in the Act's implementation? The Court protests that the very existence of a federal fallback shows that Congress expected that some States might fail to set up their own Exchanges. *Ante*, at ___. So it does. It does not show, however, that Congress expected the number of recalcitrant States to be particularly large. The more accurate the Court's dire economic predictions, the smaller that number is likely to be. That reality destroys the Court's pretense that applying the law as written would imperil "the viability of the entire Affordable Care Act." *Ante*, at ___. All in all, the Court's arguments about the law's purpose and design are no more convincing than its arguments about context.

IV

Perhaps sensing the dismal failure of its efforts to show that "established by the State" means "established by the State or the Federal Government," the Court tries to palm off the pertinent statutory phrase as "inartful drafting." *Ante*, at ___. This Court, however, has no free-floating power "to rescue Congress from its drafting errors." *Lamie v. United States Trustee*, 540 U.S. 526, 542 (2004) (internal quotation marks omitted). Only when it is patently obvious to a reasonable reader that a drafting mistake has occurred may a court correct the mistake. The occurrence of a misprint may be apparent from the face of the law, as it is where the Affordable Care Act "creates three separate Section 1563s." *Ante*, at ___. But the Court does not pretend that there is any such indication of a drafting error on the face of § 36B. The occurrence of a misprint may also be apparent because a provision decrees an absurd result—a consequence "so monstrous, that all mankind would, without hesitation, unite in rejecting the application." *Sturges*, 4 Wheat., at 203. But § 36B does not come remotely close to satisfying that demanding standard. It is entirely plausible that tax credits were restricted to state Exchanges deliberately—for example, in order to encourage States to establish their own Exchanges. We therefore have no authority to dismiss the terms of the law as a drafting fumble.

Let us not forget that the term "Exchange established by the State" appears twice in § 36B and five more times in other parts of the Act that mention tax credits. What are the odds, do you think, that the same slip of the pen occurred in seven separate places? No provision of the Act—none at all—contradicts the limitation of tax credits to state Exchanges. And as I have already explained, uses of the term "Exchange established by the State" beyond the context of tax credits look anything but accidental. Supra, at 2487. If there was a mistake here, context suggests it was a substantive mistake in designing this part of the law, not a technical mistake in transcribing it.

> Recall the Court majority's discussion of the ACA's "inartful drafting." Does Justice Scalia's view of the legislative process seem different? Or, is he implicitly making a claim not about the legislative process, but instead about the judicial process (i.e., the role of judges in determining whether a statute contains "inartful drafting")? Read on. See if the next Part of Justice Scalia's opinion, Part V, has more to say on this topic.

V

The Court's decision reflects the philosophy that judges should endure whatever interpretive distortions it takes in order to correct a supposed flaw in the statutory machinery. That philosophy ignores the American people's decision to give *Congress* "[a]ll legislative Powers" enumerated in the Constitution. Art. I, § 1. They made Congress, not this Court, responsible for both making laws and mending them. This Court holds only the judicial power—the power to pronounce the law as Congress has enacted it. We lack the prerogative to repair laws that do not work out in practice, just as the people lack the ability to throw us out of office if they dislike the solutions we concoct. We must always remember, therefore, that "[o]ur task is to apply the text, not to improve upon it." *Pavelic & LeFlore v. Marvel Entertainment Group, Div. of Cadence Industries Corp.*, 493 U.S. 120, 126 (1989).

Trying to make its judge-empowering approach seem respectful of congressional authority, the Court asserts that its decision merely ensures that the Affordable Care Act operates the way Congress "meant [it] to operate." *Ante,* at ___. First of all, what makes the Court so sure that Congress "meant" tax credits to be available everywhere? Our only evidence of what Congress meant comes from the terms of the law, and those terms show beyond all question that tax credits are available only on state Exchanges. More importantly, the Court forgets that ours is a government of laws and not of men. That means we are governed by the terms of our laws, not by the unenacted will of our lawmakers. "If Congress enacted into law something different from what it intended, then it should amend the statute to conform to its intent." *Lamie, supra*, at 542. In the meantime, this Court "has no roving license . . . to disregard clear language simply on the view that . . . Congress 'must have intended' something broader." *Bay Mills*, 572 U.S., at 794.

Even less defensible, if possible, is the Court's claim that its interpretive approach is justified because this Act "does not reflect the type of care and deliberation that one might expect of such significant legislation." *Ante*, at ___. It is not our place to judge the quality of the care and deliberation that went into this or any other law. A law enacted by voice vote with no deliberation whatever is fully as binding upon us as one enacted after years of study, months of committee hearings, and weeks of debate. Much less is it our place to make everything come out right when Congress does not do its job properly. It is up to Congress to design its laws with care, and it is up to the people to hold them to account if they fail to carry out that responsibility.

Rather than rewriting the law under the pretense of interpreting it, the Court should have left it to Congress to decide what to do about the Act's limitation of tax credits to state Exchanges. If Congress values above everything else the Act's applicability across the country, it could make tax credits available in every Exchange. If it prizes state involvement in the Act's implementation, it could continue to limit tax credits to state Exchanges while taking other steps to mitigate the economic consequences predicted by the Court. If Congress wants to accommodate both goals, it could make tax credits available everywhere while offering new incentives for States to set up their own Exchanges. And if Congress thinks that the present design of the Act works well enough, it could do nothing. Congress could also do something else altogether, entirely abandoning the structure of the Affordable Care Act. The Court's insistence on making a choice that should be made by Congress both aggrandizes judicial power and encourages congressional lassitude.

* * *

Today's opinion changes the usual rules of statutory interpretation for the sake of the Affordable Care Act. That, alas, is not a novelty. In *National Federation of Independent Business v. Sebelius*, 567 U.S. 519, this Court revised major components of the statute in order to save them from unconstitutionality. The Act that Congress passed provides that every individual "shall" maintain insurance or else pay a "penalty." 26 U.S.C. § 5000A. This Court, however, saw that the Commerce Clause does not authorize a federal mandate to buy health insurance. So it rewrote the mandate-cum-penalty as a tax. 567 U.S., at 547–75 (principal opinion). The Act that Congress passed also requires every State to accept an expansion of its Medicaid program, or else risk losing *all* Medicaid funding. 42 U.S.C. § 1396c. This Court, however, saw that the Spending Clause does not authorize this coercive condition. So it rewrote the law to withhold only the incremental funds associated with the Medicaid expansion. 567 U.S., at 575–88 (principal opinion). Having transformed two major parts of the law, the Court today has turned its attention to a third. The Act that Congress passed makes tax credits available only on an "Exchange established by the State." This Court, however, concludes that this limitation would prevent the rest of the Act from working as well as hoped. So it rewrites the law to make tax credits available everywhere. We should start calling this law SCOTUScare.

> SCOTUS is a colloquial abbreviation **FYI** for the "Supreme Court of the United States."

> **FYI** The Social Security Act of 1935 established a system of Federal old-age benefits, among other things. That system is now so embedded in law that politicians often view touching it as the "third-rail" of politics. Meanwhile, the 1947 Taft-Hartley Act is a statute addressing management-labor relations. It was fiercely opposed by labor unions, and President Truman vetoed it, but Congress overrode Truman's veto. It is today a cornerstone of labor relations.

Perhaps the Patient Protection and Affordable Care Act will attain the enduring status of the Social Security Act or the Taft-Hartley Act; perhaps not. But this Court's two decisions on the Act will surely be remembered through the years. The somersaults of statutory interpretation they have performed ("penalty" means tax, "further [Medicaid] payments to the State" means only incremental Medicaid payments to the State, "established by the State" means not established by the State) will be cited by litigants endlessly, to the confusion of honest jurisprudence. And the cases will publish forever the discouraging truth that the Supreme Court of the United States favors some laws over others, and is prepared to do whatever it takes to uphold and assist its favorites.

I dissent.

DIY
Interpreting a Complex Statute: *King v. Burwell* (reprise)

 After you have read the excerpts of *King v. Burwell* and responded to the questions that preceded the case, spend a few more minutes pondering what role each of the three branches of government should play in a dispute like this. Make a few notes about this question and be ready to share your thoughts. You might think about Justice Scalia's assertion that the Supreme Court "holds only the judicial power—the power to pronounce the law as Congress has enacted it." What exactly does this mean?

Test Your Understanding

To assess your understanding of the material in this chapter, click here to take a quiz.

Part II—The Shaping of Legislative Representation and Influence

In Part I, we commenced our study of Legislation and Regulation with an overview of the constitutional frameworks of legislatures and regulatory bodies, followed by an introduction to the problem of how courts—and thus, lawyers—interpret the work product of these governmental institutions. We will return to regulatory bodies and to the interpretive problem in later Parts of the book. But understanding legislation—one of the central types of law you as a lawyer will confront in helping your clients—requires an understanding of the legislative actors and institutions that create legislation.

Accordingly, in the next two Parts (Part II and Part III), we turn to the structure, composition, and operation of the legislature itself. Because the United States is a representative democracy, we elect representatives to serve as legislators—or, as they are also called, "lawmakers," the makers of the form of law known as statutes or legislation. In Part III, we will study the process of lawmaking, or in other words how legislatures, made up of these legislators, produce legislation. First, however, in this Part II we look at the composition of the legislature itself.

As you no doubt know, individuals become legislators through the political process of regularly held elections. In this Part, we tackle some of the law that regulates that political process, including key elements of the representational structures, and the sources of influence that shape the operation of legislative institutions in the United States. This will help you better understand how the people who do that lawmaking—the legislators—get their positions. We discuss the role(s) of elected representatives, how these representatives are matched with their constituents, and the efforts to constrain the influence of wealth and money on political campaigns and on democratic deliberation.

4

Legislative Representation

Key Concepts

- Representative democracy
- Representatives as agents
- Representatives as trustees
- Classical pluralism
- Classical republicanism

Chapter Summary

We commonly think of the United States as a democracy. The term "democracy," from its Ancient Greek origins, means "government by the people." Thus, at some level, this means that the "law" derives from (or at least has some connection with) "the people." As we have already seen in Part I and will see in more detail later, legal institutions—rather than some unmediated action of "the people"—produce law, and lawyers play a crucial role in that production. In this chapter, we look at the connection between "the people" and their legislators, considering different theories of democratic representation. In the chapters that follow, we will consider how these legislators are organized into a legislature, the legal institution that theoretically most directly represents "the people" in the broader governmental system.

In some places at some times, "pure" democracy, in which every citizen participates in every decision about public policy, has existed. But our modern world is sufficiently large and complex that we have chosen to delegate most public decision-making to designated "representatives," who make decisions on

A "representative democracy," in which citizens choose representatives who will make government decisions, stands in contrast with a "direct democracy," in which citizens themselves make decisions about government policy. **FYI** behalf of their constituents. This more complex democratic system is often called a republican form of government. It turns out, however, that no single agreed-upon theory exists about the role of the representative in a republican government. The following two short readings will give you a flavor of these theories.

From DANIEL P. TOKAJI, ELECTION LAW IN A NUTSHELL (2d ed. 2017):

FYI As students of history (and fans of "Hamilton" the musical) know, THE FEDERALIST PAPERS (of which *Federalist #10* is one entry) are a series of essays authored in 1787 and 1788 by Alexander Hamilton, John Jay, and James Madison, to build public support for the ratification of the U.S. Constitution.

Federalist #10 (1787), written by James Madison as part of the effort to encourage the original thirteen states to ratify the newly drafted U.S. Constitution, is perhaps the most famous articulation of the rationale for the republican form of government. Madison argued that republican government at the national level would control the undesirable effects of "faction," which he defined as a group of citizens "united and actuated by some common impulse of passion, or of interest, adverse to the rights of other citizens, or to the permanent and aggregate interests of the community." Madison believed that factions are inevitable in a society committed to the preservation of liberty, but that they would have negative effects on governance unless their effects were cabined. He argued that a republican form of government, in which citizens delegate power to a relatively small number of representatives, would guard against the negative effects of faction. Those elected to the national legislature would have the wisdom and capacity to rise above parochial considerations and promote the "public good."

? In what ways do "factions," as Madison called them, operate in the United States today? As Madison postulated, how well does our republican form of government help to cabin their negative effects?

One of the major questions of democratic theory underlying the republican system of government is how elected officials should conceive of their responsibilities. Should they serve as the direct agents of those who elected them, giving the people who elected them what the people want? Or should legislators exercise their own independent judgment, supporting policies that promote what the legislators conceive of as the public good? This is the question underlying the so-called "Burkean debate," named for the great British statesman and Member of Parliament Edmund Burke and his classic *Speech to the Electors of Bristol* (1774). The speech was given after his election to the House of Commons, and in response to another Member of Parliament who had given a speech supporting the practice of constituents giving "instructions" to their representatives regarding how to vote.

From Edmund Burke, *Speech to the Electors of Bristol* (1774):

Certainly, gentlemen, it ought to be the happiness and glory of a representative to live in the strictest union, the closest correspondence, and the most unreserved communication with his constituents. Their wishes ought to have great weight with him; their opinion, high respect; their business, unremitted attention. It is his duty to sacrifice his repose, his pleasures, his satisfactions, to theirs; and above all, ever, and in all cases, to prefer their interest to his own. But his unbiased opinion, his mature judgment, his enlightened conscience, he ought not to sacrifice to you, to any man, or to any set of men living. These he does not derive from your pleasure; no, nor from the law and the constitution. They are a trust from Providence, for the abuse of which he is deeply answerable. Your representative owes you, not his industry only, but his judgment; and he betrays, instead of serving you, if he sacrifices it to your opinion.

My worthy colleague says, his will ought to be subservient to yours. If that be all, the thing is innocent. If government were a matter of will upon any side, yours, without question, ought to be superior. But government and legislation are matters of reason and judgment, and not of inclination; and what sort of reason is that, in which the determination precedes the discussion; in which one set of men deliberate, and another decide; and where those who form the conclusion are perhaps three hundred miles distant from those who hear the arguments?

> What does Burke mean here? How are "reason" and "judgment" distinct from "inclination"? If so, when might they clash? As we go through the rest of the course, think about the role that "reason" and "judgment" play in the lawmaking processes, not only in the legislature, but also in agencies and courts.

To deliver an opinion, is the right of all men; that of constituents is a weighty and respectable opinion, which a representative ought always to rejoice to hear; and which he ought always most seriously to consider. But *authoritative* instructions; *mandates* issued, which the member is bound blindly and implicitly to obey, to vote, and to argue for, though contrary to the clearest conviction of his judgment and conscience—these are things utterly unknown to the laws of this land, and which arise from a fundamental mistake of the whole order and tenor of our constitution.

> **?** In what sense is Burke using the word "congress"? Does it matter that the "parliament" (i.e., the legislature) in the United States is actually called "the Congress"?

Parliament is not a *congress* of ambassadors from different and hostile interests; which interests each must maintain, as an agent and advocate, against other agents and advocates; but parliament is a *deliberative* assembly of *one* nation, with *one* interest, that of the whole; where, not local purposes, not local prejudices, ought to guide, but the general good, resulting from the general reason of the whole. You choose a member indeed; but when you have chosen him, he is not member of Bristol, but he is a member of *parliament*. If the local constituent should have an interest, or should form an hasty opinion, evidently opposite to the real good of the rest of the community, the member for that place ought to be as far, as any other, from any endeavour to give it effect. I beg pardon for saying so much on this subject. I have been unwillingly drawn into it; but I shall ever use a respectful frankness of communication with you. Your faithful friend, your devoted servant, I shall be to the end of my life: a flatterer you do not wish for.

DIY
The Role of a Representative

Do you agree with Burke's view that the obligation of an elected representative is to follow his or her own judgment about what is in the interests of the country as a whole? Is this conception of the legislator's role realistic? Does the fact that most legislators in the United States (indeed, in most developed democracies in the world) are members of a political party affect this way of thinking about the role of a "representative" in the modern American legal system? See if you can formulate not just one alternative, but two or three alternative conceptions of the role of a legislator, and record them in your notes. Then continue reading below.

A. Conceptions of the Role of the Legislator

Edmund Burke is deservedly famous for his *Speech to the Electors of Bristol*. But are his view of representatives as trustees and the contrasting view of representatives as agents mutually exclusive? Might they somehow be harmonized? Or might representatives conceive of their roles in yet other ways, or be chosen for yet other purposes?

1. Legislators as Agents

The view that elected representatives should function as the agents of their constituents—a view obviously of some currency in eighteenth century Britain when Burke, who went on to lose his next election, challenged it—also holds great favor in America today. Also sometimes called the "delegate" view, it is the conception that the role of a representative is to carry her constituents' wishes with her to the Capitol building or Statehouse, and once there to act in her constituents' stead by voting in the manner that the constituents themselves would vote were they present. In its most extreme form, this is a view that the function of a legislature is to aggregate the preferences of the public it serves by having legislators deliver the proxies of their constituents.

In terms of a pure democratic ideal of every citizen having an equal say in government and in the setting of public policy, this agency view of representative democracy has some inherent appeal. It also can be a deeply attractive notion to constituents choosing between political candidates at the ballot box. Indeed, as American voters are aware, candidates frequently campaign for votes on the basis that other politicians do not sufficiently respect the voters' political preferences, and that the candidate, if elected, will better honor the voters' wishes. As a result, a great deal of political polling and opinion research occurs to help candidates and legislators match their campaign commitments and voting records with constituent views, so that they can promote themselves as better "agents."

Of course, this is an oversimplification. It assumes that a majority of the constituents of a given legislator all share the same wishes, when in fact constituents typically hold a range of views, even on one issue. Political scientists therefore sometimes speak in terms of a constituency's "median" or "pivotal" voter. Although this too remains an oversimplification, in today's connected world it is becoming easier and easier for representatives to be aware not only of which voters will be the determinative ones (whether in the general election or in the increasingly critical primary elections), but also of the views or wishes of those voters.

A legislator who conceives of her legislative role in agency terms need not always vote in lockstep with what she understands to be the views of her constituents, however. At times, the legislator might be privy to more and better information about an issue because the legislator participates in information-gathering and negotiation processes as a legislator. In such circumstances, the agent legislator might depart from her constituency if she in good faith believes that the views of her constituency (or, perhaps more precisely, of the "pivotal" voter in her constituency) would align with her legislative actions were her constituents in her shoes; that is, if the constituents were informed by the same information-gathering and negotiation processes in which the representative has participated on behalf of her constituents. On some more nuanced agency conceptions, therefore, the task of an agent legislator is not necessarily to do what she is told, but to honor what she assumes *would be* the fully informed preferences of her constituents, who are her principals. This description of the agent's task may seem to blur the role of an agent with the role of a trustee (discussed next), but the key distinction remains that agents are acting to effectuate what they understand to be their principals' fully informed preferences, while trustees are acting in what they themselves believe is in the best interests of their beneficiaries.

2. Legislators as Trustees

On the trusteeship model of representation, the legislator's role is not to determine how her principals would have behaved, even in light of the information-gathering and negotiation processes in which the legislator participates. Rather, it is to use the legislative process as a collective act of public deliberation about the common good, and then to draw upon the legislator's own wisdom and experience, combined with that of the legislator's colleagues, to make an independent decision about what either is in the constituents' best interests, or best serves the public at large. These two formulations of a trustee's duties are not necessarily the same thing—indeed, one open question is whether the trustee's foremost responsibility should be to the trustee's constituents, or instead to the greater public. But in either case, on a trusteeship model, the constituents are the beneficiaries of the legislator's work, not the principals who direct that work.

> **?** Should legislators be trusted to act as trustees and depart from the wishes of their constituency? Under what circumstances? What can voters do to ensure their elected officials continue to act in the public interest rather than in their own selfish interests?

Following Burke, this conception has a rich tradition in American politics as well. For instance, James Madison, writing in *Federalist #10*, argued that a chief advantage of representative democracy over pure democracy was that a representative democracy would:

> refine and enlarge the public views by passing them through the medium of a chosen body of citizens, whose wisdom may best discern the true interest of their country and whose patriotism and love of justice will be least likely to sacrifice it to temporary or partial considerations. Under such a regulation it may well happen that the public voice, pronounced by the representatives of the people, will be more consonant to the public good than if pronounced by the people themselves, convened for the purpose.

More recently, John F. Kennedy, while serving as a U.S. Senator, similarly observed,

> It is difficult to accept [the] narrow view of the role of United States Senator—a view that assumes the people of Massachusetts sent me to Washington to serve merely as a seismograph to record shifts in popular opinion . . . . The voters selected us, in short, because they had confidence in our judgment and our ability to exercise that judgment from a position where we could determine what were their own best interests, as a part of the nation's interest. This may mean that we must on occasion lead, inform, correct and sometimes even ignore constituent opinion, if we are to exercise fully that judgment for which we were elected.

JOHN F. KENNEDY, PROFILES IN COURAGE 16 (1956).

Indeed, politicians who are too much like a seismograph—too responsive to public opinion, in exactly the way a legislator-as-agent might justifiably behave in response to the evolving views of their constituent principals—often are pilloried as opportunistic "flip-floppers" who lack their own judgment or convictions. Yet in today's politics, it understandably would be politically difficult (impossible?!) for candidates to seek representative office primarily by touting their personal wisdom, or by flaunting their confidence that they understand the public interest better than do their constituents. Rather, it is next to impossible for politicians to ignore the repeated complaints that legislators (and thus legislatures) are out of touch with the wishes of the greater public, or to resist the popular appeals for legislators to be more responsive to the demands of their constituents. A fundamental tension therefore exists between these two primary ways of conceptualizing the role of a legislator.

3. Hybrid Conceptions of the Legislator's Role

The trustee-versus-agent dichotomy is a valuable tool for reflection about how we would like our legislative institutions to function, and about how we therefore might shape other electoral and structural features of these institutions to foster that function, as discussed further in Chapters 5 through 10 below. But both as a normative and a descriptive matter, this dichotomy presents a false choice about the role of elected representatives. Instead, several hybrid characterizations are also possible, and, in fact, most legislators behave in some fashion as both agent and trustee.

> **FYI** You will often hear your professors, legal textbook authors, and other legal scholars use the terms "normative" and "descriptive." If you haven't gathered already, the term "descriptive" refers to any statement about the world as it **is in fact**; and the term "normative" refers to any statement about the world as **it should be**.

One idealized hybrid view imagines that, if the representatives are well-chosen and the society is well-informed, then the action that a legislator would take as an agent will align with the choice that the legislator would make as a trustee. Of course, were that the case, either conception of the role of an elected representative would be adequate to the task, and the explanatory value of the two distinctive conceptions would largely evaporate. In particular, there would be little reason to argue for the trustee role, which implicitly depends on the assumption that elected representatives will be more capable than the public-at-large at identifying the common good, an assumption that is inconsistent with the premise of the idealized view. But the real world clearly is not one in which representatives' judgments consistently align with constituent preferences.

Another possible hybrid model invites distinguishing among specific legislative issues, categorizing some as more appropriate for the agency model, and others as more appropriate for the trustee model. This is a view that fits with the notion that a few high-profile legislative issues will have sufficient public salience that legislators should respect and follow the resulting public opinion, while many other issues will not generate either any meaningful public discussion or any reliable measure of informed public opinion, and so should be left for legislators to address using their own best judgment, perhaps influenced by the judgment and advice of experts. This view also accords with the substantial delegation of lawmaking authority to agencies, where greater specialization and expert knowledge can be brought to bear on issues of public policy, as discussed further in Part VII.

Indeed, on some versions of this view, the public should welcome being relieved of the responsibility to have an informed opinion about each of the myriad issues that a modern legislature typically addresses. The range and complexity of issues coming before legislatures and agencies today argue for the view that, at least for many of these issues, the task of the legislator is not to determine what the fully informed pivotal constituent would want, but rather to determine what in the legislator's own judgment is best, or when to delegate the development of specific rules and standards to agencies that have greater expertise.

One potential framework for distinguishing among types of legislative issues is to consider the distribution of their costs and benefits. In a landmark study of the regulatory process, political scientist James Q. Wilson suggested the following two-by-two categorization, in which the distribution of the costs of legislative action is represented on the horizontal axis, and the distribution of the benefits of legislative action is represented on the vertical axis:

> The chart below is derived from the work of American political scientist James Q. Wilson, and his 1980 book "The Politics of Regulation."

Chart 1—Categories of Legislative Activity

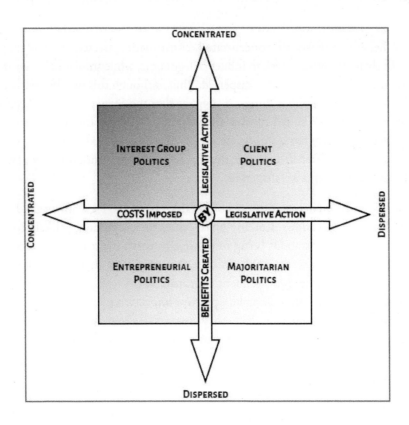

For instance, in this typology, the upper left quadrant of "Interest Group Politics" involves policy issues where the costs and the benefits are each concentrated upon some small segments of society. An example of Interest Group Politics might be

> As you might imagine, these are stylized examples and the real world is generally a mix of these four matrices. So, even in this example, it could be the case that one type of weapons system is better for national defense. If so, there would also be dispersed costs or benefits of the choice. But, as we lay the example out here, that concern does not play a role.

when two competing defense contractors are lobbying Congress to enact different statutory requirements for the latest weapons system. Each of the individual defense contractors would be an example of a "concentrated" interest. So, in this example, both the costs and the benefits of one choice or the other would go to a concentrated interest. Meanwhile, "Client Politics" could be in play when an industry group lobbies for a specific tax benefit. Since all tax benefits ultimately reduce the tax revenues in the public fisc, revenues that can be used for the general welfare, the public at large will have to bear the cost of that benefit. In contrast, many environmental protection measures, which may target specific polluters to benefit the broad public, are examples of "Entrepreneurial Politics." Finally, other environmental laws, which increase costs to consumers broadly in order to foster public health, offer examples of "Majoritarian Politics."

When benefits or costs are concentrated, constituents affected thereby may be more likely to mobilize to seek to influence legislators, while similar behavior is less likely when benefits or costs are dispersed. Thus, although this two-by-two matrix undoubtedly oversimplifies things, it suggests that the agency model of legislator behavior may be well suited to what the matrix identifies as Interest Group Politics (where legislative costs and benefits are both concentrated), while the trustee model may be a better fit for what the matrix calls Majoritarian Politics (where both costs and benefits are dispersed).

A third hybrid view recognizes the complexity not of the legislative agenda, but of legislators' motivations. On any given issue, each legislator is likely to have some mix of concerns about being responsive to constituent interests and some desire to wisely promote the public interest. It bears noting that almost all elected representatives, despite their frequent caricature as primarily self-interested and ambitious, genuinely aspire to make a positive impact on matters of public policy and governance. Yet understandably they also worry about their own re-election, even if only out of their desire to continue to pursue their roles as public servants.

They therefore work to protect their electoral prospects both by listening to the concerns of their constituents and by building a base of donors who will contribute campaign funds.

On this view, it can be a complicated calculation for a legislator to balance her genuine belief in the importance of serving as her constituents' agent or delegate, on the one hand, with her equally genuine belief in the importance of serving as her constituents' trustee, on the other hand. This third hybrid view accepts that for each legislative issue or action, a thoughtful legislator may make this calculation anew, even if subconsciously. The legislator not only will be attuned to her constituents' views, to the strength of those views, and to how well informed those views are, but also will remain focused on understanding and promoting the overall well-being of society.

A final, now vestigial, hybrid model might be identified with the structure of Congress prior to adoption of the Seventeenth Amendment in 1913. Before that amendment provided for the direct election of U.S. Senators, one might argue that Senators and Representatives were intended to have different kinds of electoral responsibilities. On this view, popularly elected Representatives would function more like agents of their constituents, while Senators appointed by their state legislatures would fulfill the role of trustees for the citizens of their states. The bicameral Congress thus would bring to bear both types of representation in establishing federal policy. Popular election of U.S. Senators has eliminated this hybrid model.

In connection with this 'hybrid" model, it is **FYI** worth noting that U.S. Senators are elected for 6-year terms (with roughly one third of the Senators elected every two years), while U.S. Representatives are elected for 2-year terms. So, theoretically, Senators have more leeway to think longer term than do Representatives. This might then give them more latitude to pursue the trustee role.

4. Legislators as a Collective Microcosm, a Portrait-in-Miniature

Other conceptions of representation depend neither on the trustee model nor the agent model. In particular, a descriptive model, championed in the founding generation most famously by John Adams, and still favored by some today, takes as its reference point the view that the representative body should be a descriptively accurate sampling of the public at large, a "portrait, in miniature." 4 THE WORKS OF JOHN ADAMS 205 (1850). Its claim is that legislative outcomes will be improved by populating the legislature with individuals whose demographic characteristics, taken collectively, closely match the characteristics of the society at large.

One difficulty, of course, is deciding just what characteristics are relevant to assessing a legislature's descriptive accuracy. Today, characteristics such as race, gender, income, age, sexual orientation, occupation, and religion would all be likely candidates. In some descriptive models, political party or ideology will be especially relevant. Yet John Adams' list surely would have been different, and there is no settled list of relevant characteristics (nor, if there were, of how to create an appropriate cross-section when any given legislator could represent multiple characteristics).

Nonetheless, the notion of creating a descriptively accurate representative institution has intrinsic appeal. A sense of its potential value underlies contemporary frustrations with partisan gerrymandering (discussed more in section F below), as well as concerns about the underrepresentation in legislatures of minority groups and women. It also lies behind other countries' practices of reserving certain numbers of legislative seats for representatives of specified groups (see Mala Htun, *Is Gender Like Ethnicity? The Political Representation of Identity Groups*, 2 PERSPECTIVES ON POLITICS 439 (2004)), or of using systems of proportional representation rather than winner-take-all elections (see Nicholas Stephanopoulos, *Our Electoral Exceptionalism*, 80 U. CHI. L. REV. 769 (2013)).

Moreover, even contemplating a descriptive model of the role of the legislator invites additional attention and insight into what it is that we expect our representatives to do when they "represent" us. It also invites us to think more carefully about how the structures of our election processes affect who become our representatives, and why our representative institutions have substantially less diversity along many dimensions than our overall population.

B. Conceptions of the Role of the Legislature

 The term "liberal" here is distinct from the common use of the term today to refer to views on the left side of the political spectrum.
Similarly, the term "republican" here is distinct from the use of the term "Republican" (with a capital "R") when referring to the Republican Party.

In the previous subsection, we looked at conceptions of the role of elected representatives, the legisla**tors**. In this subsection, we turn to the two main conceptions of the institutional role of the legisla**ture**, the institution where legislators perform these roles. One main conception of the legislature derives from classical liberal theory and is somewhat akin to what is also often called pluralist theory. The other main conception derives from republican political theory. In addition, since the later twentieth century, several critical theories also have invited attention to perceived shortcomings in the role and operation of representative institutions.

1.   Classical Liberal or Pluralist Conceptions

Classical liberalism, often associated with 17th-century English philosopher John Locke, is built upon ideas of natural rights to promote the ideals of individualism and liberty, particularly by protecting economic freedom and civil liberties, within certain limits. As applied to legislative politics, liberalism conceives of representative government as a system in which diverse, legitimate viewpoints are allowed to clash and compete for official recognition, within a framework that ensures the protection of minority rights against the threat of majority tyranny. The process is expected to result in legislative proposals that can garner more support, and in which factional or interest group bargaining is encouraged as a means of promoting equilibrium through compromise.

Classical liberalism favors the protection of individual liberties.

This liberal conception of the role of a legislature aligns more closely (though not coextensively) with the agency model of representatives than with the trustee model of representatives. Legislators-as-agents bring to the legislature their constituents' views about their individual interests (e.g., economic, political, etc.), and each legislator then must bargain and compromise with others in seeking the best outcomes for their respective groups of constituents. In this clash of interests, legislators-as-agents also are free to support and adopt the ideas of other legislators, provided they conclude that their constituents would likewise be persuaded to do the same.

Because liberalism seeks to protect and promote individualism, it expects that a range of diverse interests will be represented and contested in the legislative arena. This view often is also labeled "pluralist," because it welcomes and responds to a multiplicity of positions. The legislative arena thereby functions as the forum for evaluating, refining, and choosing among these multiple positions.

At its heart, the pluralist conception incorporates aspects of Madisonian thinking in its recognition, as a descriptive matter, that society will have many narrow interests or factions. But, as a normative matter, Madison saw factions as tending toward mischief, most famously in *Federalist #10*, and he defended representative government as a mechanism for controlling what would otherwise be the detrimental impacts of these factions. In contrast, many pluralists see factions or interest groups more favorably, as the most obvious way for citizens in a diverse society to participate in lawmaking and to share political power. Pluralists therefore welcome many competing diverse interests into the legislative arena on the view that this is more likely to lead to socially desirable outcomes. *See, e.g.*, ROBERT A. DAHL, PLURALIST DEMOCRACY IN THE UNITED STATES: CONFLICT & CONSENT (1968).

But classical liberalism is not just pluralistic in the sense of having government represent the cacophony of society's interests. An important strand of classic liberalism emphasizes the importance of individual rights, including political, civil, and economic rights. So, a classically liberal conception of the role of the legislature can also embrace the trustee model of legislators. For a trustee legislator, one important question can be how best to advance the liberal virtues of civil liberties and economic freedom. If legislators themselves have more wisdom or experience in these matters than their constituents, it would be in the constituents' best interests for the legislators, as trustees, to pursue these liberal ends even when their constituents desire otherwise. Constituent preferences may be inflamed by bias against certain minority rights, for instance, or may otherwise reflect some popular but misguided movement that in the long run will undermine liberal virtues. (Similar concerns may partially explain the Framers' decision to make the U.S. Constitution difficult to amend. It likely does explain the Framers' decision to make it so difficult to pass laws in the federal system, a topic we address in Chapter 11.) In these circumstances, rejecting the legislator-as-agent role and ignoring constituent views can be defended as advancing a liberal conception of the legislature.

2. Classical Republican Conceptions

> **!** Classical republicanism favors the promotion of the public good. The 18th-century Swiss political philosopher Jean-Jacques Rousseau spoke of there being a "general will," a common interest shared by all citizens.

Classical republican theory (again, "republican" with a small r, not to be confused with today's Republican Party) focuses on the improved social benefits achievable through democratic institutions, and thus may offer a more idealized or optimistic conception of representative government than does liberal theory. Tracing its ideas to ancient Greece, republican theory strives to promote a vision of the common good and to foster a commitment to civic virtue. It expects that legislators not only will eschew their own personal interests, but also will deliberate together about a common interest greater than can be achieved for or by their individual constituencies alone. Thus, deliberation itself is a civic act that can lead to the creation of better public policies.

This republican conception is also fundamentally Madisonian, but in a very different way than the liberal conception's focus on the abundance of diverse interest groups. Rather, in arguing for the supremacy of a republican form of government, Madison claimed that it would produce representatives with "enlightened views and virtuous sentiments" who could be "guardians of the public weal." FEDERALIST #59. As one twentieth-century scholar summarized this Madisonian view, a representative was to be "an independent man of republican virtue, tied to his constituents by duty, gratitude, and ambition and serving them with the affection of friends and the impartiality of judges." Robert J. Morgan, *Madison's Theory of Representation in the Tenth Federalist*, 36 J. POLITICS 852, 853 (1974).

The republican conception of the role of the legislature thus aligns more closely (though also not coextensively) with the representative-as-trustee conception of the role of the legislator. On the republican view, the legislature is a forum for acts of public deliberation. This deliberation occurs not primarily as a contest of ideas competing for acceptance or acclaim, but as a creative process in which solutions are forged in a cooperative effort to maximize the public interest or common weal. In undertaking that enterprise, legislators are expected to model civic virtue through self-sacrifice and avoidance of self-interest.

However, for Madison, the size and the scale of the new nation were critical to what he saw as Congress's ability to realize this vision of legislative deliberation. Indeed, he was often skeptical about the ability of state legislatures to replicate this vision. Nevertheless, his vision generally caught on, and today state legislatures are also routinely (if inaccurately) conceived of in republican terms.

In part, the continuing strength of the republican conception of legislatures reflects the influence of the "Legal Process" school of thought, developed in the mid-twentieth century largely by Harvard Law Professors Henry Hart & Albert Sacks. *See* HART AND SACKS' THE LEGAL PROCESS: BASIC PROBLEMS IN THE MAKING AND APPLICATION OF LAW (William N. Eskridge Jr. & Philip P. Frickey eds., 1994). Writing at a time when the administrative state was just blossoming

> **FYI**
> Hart & Sacks' famous "Legal Process" materials were developed to be (and were used as) a law school textbook. But the materials were not published until 1994, after both Hart and Sacks had passed away. For decades, generations of law students used unpublished mimeographed copies of a 1958 "tentative edition."

into its modern complexity, Hart and Sacks argued that the function of elected representatives is to take part in a legislative process that is open, informed, and deliberative, in order to be able to enact rules or principles for the good of society. This focus on both the public good and the value of the deliberative process continues to echo in many descriptions of the legislature's role, as well as to shape various interpretive theories, as discussed in Part IV.

3. Critical Theories

In contrast to the preceding accounts of the legislature, some observers have eschewed efforts to defend any normative conception of the legislative process, and instead have offered descriptive accounts that are deeply cynical or pessimistic. On these accounts, the institutions of representative democracy function to secure a privileged position and status for some subset of society, merely offering lip service to ideals of full democratic participation and class mobility for all citizens, while actually doing little to deliver on those ideals.

Some versions of these critical accounts of the legislative process took root in the thinking of a number of eminent legal scholars in the early twentieth century, a group known loosely as the "Legal Realists." Building on the work of late-nineteenth-century thinkers such as Oliver Wendell Holmes, these Legal Realists rejected what they saw as legal formalism's overly formalistic or scientific attribution to the legal system of logic, order, and idealized free-market relations, and instead characterized law as consisting essentially of the raw exercise of judicial and political power. For the Legal Realists, both the economic marketplace and the political arena operated as a melee of individuals, groups, and institutions struggling to create value for themselves through whatever levers of power they could bring to bear.

Critical perspectives intensified with the emergence of the Critical Legal Studies (CLS) movement in the late 1970s. Drawing primary strength from individuals recently involved in the civil rights and anti-war struggles, the CLS movement characterized the quest for political and legal dominance as slanted in favor of the particular social stratum of those already in power. CLS thinkers viewed the law not as a democratic creation applied in particular cases via impartial legal reasoning, but as the embodiment of a preexisting hegemony of privileged social elites, structured and deployed to preserve that social preeminence.

Different subsets of this view, such as Critical Race Studies and Critical Gender Studies, have focused on specific aspects of the perceived power imbalance. One aspiration of CLS scholarship is to bring to light previously unnoticed or ignored power dynamics to prompt scrutiny and correction in the open forum of public discourse, scrutiny that in theory could provoke counter-hegemonic ways of understanding and interpreting the meanings of legal text such as the statutes and regulations discussed in more detail below in Parts V through VIII. *See, e.g., The*

Case of the Speluncean Explorers: Contemporary Proceedings, 61 GEO. WASH. U. L. REV. 1754 (1993).

* * *

As these competing visions suggest, representative democracy is complex. Furthermore, the complexity of the interactions between the many competing interests can make the practice of politics quite different from its theory.

NOTES & QUESTIONS

1. What do you think the role of an elected representative in the U.S. today *ought* to be? Is this the same role that elected representatives have played historically? Is this role in fact the role that you currently anticipate your elected representatives will perform? If not, why not?

2. How might one's perspective on the role of a legislator, or on the role of the legislature, affect the interpretive enterprise? That is, do differing perspectives affect the way in which statutes (the legislative work product) are construed?

3. How might one's perspective on the role of a legislator affect one's view about the ideal or most appropriate way to separate the represented population into districts, or otherwise to assign representatives to constituencies?

Test Your Understanding

To assess your understanding of the material in this chapter, click here to take a quiz.

5

Political Districts and the "One Person, One Vote" Principle

Key Concepts

- One Person, One Vote
- Malapportionment
- "Political Questions"
- Decennial census
- Redistricting authorities
- Redistricting criteria

Chapter Summary

In 1964, the U.S. Supreme Court declared that, with the exception of the U.S. Senate, legislative bodies composed of geographic districts with different population sizes deprived individual voters of equal voting power. The result was a constitutional requirement that legislative districts contain roughly equal populations, though just how to measure the population can be complicated. Now, after each decennial census, some redistricting body must redraw legislative districts to equalize the population in light of demographic changes during the previous decade. Many considerations in addition to equal population can influence the drawing of legislative districts.

Individual legislators can only perform their representative role as part of a collective assembly. But additional questions remain regarding how to assemble this collective body. In the United States, state legislatures and the U.S. House of Representatives consist of representatives each elected by voters of a specific geographic district, with each district electing one representative. Meanwhile, because the U.S. Senate consists of two Senators per state, each state is essentially a multi-member district. Many local councils also use multi-member districts. A critical question in structuring legislative institutions is how to draw these geographic districts. For many years, states were left free to answer this question without many legal constraints. That began to change in the mid-20th century.

A. One Person, One Vote

The relationship between "the people" and the lawmakers—their elected representatives in the legislature—is itself shaped by law. In the United States, that law is both state and federal, and both constitutional and statutory. The individuals who directly participate in the creation of legislation—the lawmakers—are thus shaped by that law, because that law structures how they become legislators (and in turn who can—or at least, who is likely to—become a legislator). So, in this and the following two chapters, we introduce you to some of that law, or what is sometimes called the law of the political process. You can think of this law—these rules—as the framework for how legislators get elected, and thus as one aspect of the framework for how the legal system responds to the needs of "the people" in our democratic republic.

The first aspect of this legal framework that we address is the "one person, one vote" principle. You will read excerpts from an excellent primer on election law that lays out some of the basics about this idea, as well as excerpts from the seminal 1964 Supreme Court case that established the principle as a constitutional mandate.

From Daniel P. Tokaji, Election Law in a Nutshell (2d ed. 2017):

The U.S. Constitution does not expressly confer a general right to vote, but instead leaves the regulation of elections to the states and Congress. Qualifications for voting in congressional elections are tied to qualifications for voting in state legislative elections under Article I, Section 2 of the original Constitution and the Seventeenth Amendment. The Elections Clause, in Article I, Section 4 of the Constitution, gives states the authority to regulate the "Times, Places, and Manner" of holding congressional elections, while authorizing Congress to "make or alter such Regulations." Under the original structure of the Constitution, then, the setting of qualifications and the

FYI The Seventeenth Amendment, adopted in 1913, established the popular election of U.S. Senators. Prior to that time, Senators were formally chosen by state legislatures under Article I, Section 3 of the original Constitution.

regulation of elections was left to the states, with Congress authorized to make or alter rules for the conduct of congressional elections.

Since the late Nineteenth Century, the Supreme Court has declared the right to vote "fundamental" because it is "preservative of all rights." The Court first characterized voting as a fundamental right in *Yick Wo v. Hopkins,* 118 U.S. 356 (1886). While that case did not involve voting, the Court has repeated its statement that voting is a fundamental right many times. The idea is that the vote—and by extension, representation in government—is essential to ensure that all our other interests are protected.

The primary source of the fundamental right to vote is the Fourteenth Amendment. Other provisions of the Constitution provide additional protection for the vote:

- *The Fifteenth Amendment* (1870) prohibits the denial or abridgement of the vote based on race, color, or previous condition of servitude.

- *The Nineteenth Amendment* (1920) prohibits denial or abridgement of the vote on account of sex.

- *The Twenty-Fourth Amendment* (1964) prohibits the denial or abridgement of the vote in federal elections based on the failure to pay a poll tax or other tax.

- *The Twenty-Sixth Amendment* (1971) prohibits the denial or abridgement of the vote on account of age to citizens 18 and over.

Note that these constitutional amendments prohibit the exclusion of people from voting on certain grounds, but do not confer an affirmative right to vote on all citizens.

Despite the specific clauses regarding voting and the longstanding characterization of the right to vote as fundamental, the Court has not always treated voting as a fundamental right. Ironically, at the same time that the Supreme Court declared the right to vote "funda-

Also note the number of constitutional amendments that in some way protect voting rights. Note too when each of these amendments was adopted. As you might imagine, the Fifteenth, Nineteenth, Twenty-Fourth, and Twenty-Sixth Amendments were each adopted to respond to specific concerns about denials or abridgements of the right to vote at the time.

mental" in *Yick Wo*, white Democrats in the South were employing practices designed to ensure the mass disenfranchisement of African Americans. * * *

[The Supreme Court mostly avoided entering the fray with respect to the disenfranchisement of African Americans until the 1960s. An important exception was the White Primary Cases, decided between the 1920s and the 1950s. Back then, the South was solidly Democratic. In Texas and some other states, African Americans were excluded from voting in primary elections, used to select a political party's nominee. White Democrats unsuccessfully argued that there was no state action and, therefore, that all-white primaries did not violate the Fourteenth Amendment or Fifteenth Amendment. The last of the White Primary Cases was *Terry v. Adams,* 345 U.S. 461 (1953), striking down a straw vote from which blacks were excluded but functioned as the de facto Democratic Primary.

[Another voting rights issue that developed during this period of time arose from the states' failure to redraw congressional and state legislative districts. This problem came to the fore in the mid-Twentieth Century, because many states had failed to redraw their legislative districts, despite the mass migration of people from rural to urban and suburban areas.]

FYI The U.S. Senate, which gives each state two senators regardless of a state's population, is an example of a malapportioned legislative body.

Malapportionment exists when districts with different populations have the same representation. Until the 1960s, for example, one district might have ten times the population of a neighboring district, even though both had one representative in the legislature. People in larger districts—which tended to be in urban and suburban areas—were effectively underrepresented. By contrast, people in rural districts were overrepresented, sometimes enjoying a majority of representatives in the legislature even though they were a minority of the overall population.

For a long time, malapportionment was considered to be a nonjusticiable "political question," one that was left to the political branches of government and thus deemed beyond the power of federal courts to decide. But in *Baker v. Carr*, 369 U.S. 186 (1962), the Court reversed course to hold malapportionment claims justiciable. In the succeeding years, it issued a series of decisions—collectively known as the "one person, one vote" line of cases—requiring that each legislative district's representation correspond to its population. * * *

[In] *Wesberry v. Sanders*, 376 U.S. 1 (1964), [the Supreme Court] ruled that the malapportionment of congressional districts within a state violated Article I, Section 2 of the Constitution. *Wesberry* arose from Georgia, in which the most populous congressional district (consisting of Fulton County) was two to three times as large as some other districts. Justice Black wrote the majority opinion, which held that Article I, Section 2's requirement that U.S. House Representatives be chosen "by the People of the several States" meant that each person's vote be worth as much as that of others. Although the text of the Constitution does not mandate equally populated House districts, the Court rested its opinion on originalist grounds, concluding that the intent of the Framers was that "in allocating Congressman the number assigned to each State

The "political question" doctrine is one of several legal doctrines in federal courts known as "avoidance doctrines." These doctrines are designed to keep the courts from having to resolve certain kinds of disputes. The "political question" doctrine gives the courts the opportunity to abstain from deciding an issue if the courts believe it is better resolved by another branch (or both of the other branches) of government. In *Baker v. Carr*, before deciding that malapportionment claims were justiciable, the Supreme Court laid out principles for deciding when an issue would be treated as a nonjusticiable "political question." As you might imagine, there are heated debates about what constitutes a "political question" (which you will likely learn about in your Constitutional Law course), but it is important to realize that the phrase is a legal term-of-art.

should be determined solely by the number of the State's inhabitants." The Court thus held that the one person, one vote rule applies to congressional districts. * * *

Notice that while *Wesberry* involved congressional districts, *Reynolds* involved state legislative districts.

Four months after *Wesberry*, the Court decided *Reynolds v. Sims*, 377 U.S. 533 (1964), probably the most important of the one person, one vote cases. * * * The case arose from Alabama, which had population disparities [across districts] of up to 16 to 1 in the state house and 41 to 1 in the state senate.

Reynolds v. Sims
377 U.S. 533 (1964)

MR. CHIEF JUSTICE WARREN delivered the opinion of the Court.

Involved in these cases are an appeal and two cross-appeals from a decision of the Federal District Court for the Middle District of Alabama holding invalid, under the Equal Protection Clause of the Federal Constitution, the existing and two legislatively proposed plans for the apportionment of seats in the two houses of the Alabama Legislature, and ordering into effect a temporary reapportionment plan comprised of parts of the proposed but judicially disapproved measures. * * *

Undeniably the Constitution of the United States protects the right of all qualified citizens to vote, in state as well as in federal elections. A consistent line of decisions by this Court in cases involving attempts to deny or restrict the right of suffrage has made this indelibly clear. * * *

In *Wesberry v. Sanders*, 376 U.S. 1, decided earlier this Term, we held that attacks on the constitutionality of congressional districting plans enacted by state legislatures do not present nonjusticiable questions and should not be dismissed generally for "want of equity." We determined that the constitutional test for the validity of congressional districting schemes was one of substantial equality of population among the various districts established by a state legislature for the election of members of the Federal House of Representatives. * * *

[O]ur decision in *Wesberry* was of course grounded on that language of the Constitution which prescribes that members of the Federal House of Representatives are to be chosen "by the People," while attacks on state legislative apportionment schemes, such as that involved in the instant cases, are principally based on the Equal Protection Clause of the Fourteenth Amendment. Nevertheless, *Wesberry* clearly established that the fundamental principle of representative government in this country is one of equal representation for equal numbers of people, without regard to race, sex, economic status, or place of residence within a State. Our problem, then, is to ascertain, in the instant cases, whether there are any constitutionally cognizable principles which would justify departures from the basic standard of equality among voters in the apportionment of seats in state legislatures. * * *

A predominant consideration in determining whether a State's legislative apportionment scheme constitutes an invidious discrimination violative of rights asserted under the Equal Protection Clause is that the rights allegedly impaired are individual and personal in nature. As stated by the Court in *United States v. Bathgate*, 246 U.S. 220, 227, "[t]he right to vote is personal . . . ." While the result of a court decision in a state legislative apportionment controversy may be to require the restructuring of the geographical distribution of seats in a state legislature, the judicial focus must be concentrated upon ascertaining whether there has been any discrimination against certain of the State's citizens which constitutes an impermissible impairment of their constitutionally protected right to vote. * * * Undoubtedly, the right of suffrage is a fundamental matter in a free and democratic society. Especially since the right to exercise the franchise in a free and unimpaired manner is preservative of other basic civil and political rights, any alleged infringement of the right of citizens to vote must be carefully and meticulously scrutinized. Almost a century ago, in *Yick Wo v. Hopkins*, 118 U.S. 356, the Court referred to "the political franchise of voting" as "a fundamental political right, because preservative of all rights." 118 U.S., at 370.

Legislators represent people, not trees or acres. Legislators are elected by voters, not farms or cities or economic interests. As long as ours is a representative form of government, and our legislatures are those instruments of government elected directly by and directly representative of the people, the right to elect legislators in a free and unimpaired fashion is a bedrock of our political system. It could hardly be gainsaid that a constitutional claim had been asserted by an allegation that certain otherwise qualified voters had been entirely prohibited from voting for members of their state legislature. And, if a State should provide that the votes of citizens in one part of the State should be given two times, or five times, or 10 times the weight of votes of citizens in another part of the State, it could hardly be contended that the right to vote of those residing in the disfavored areas had not been effectively diluted. It would appear extraordinary to suggest that a State could be constitutionally permitted to enact a law providing that certain of the State's voters could vote two, five, or 10 times for their legislative representatives, while voters living elsewhere could vote only once. And it is inconceivable that a state law to the effect that, in counting votes for legislators, the votes of citizens in one part of the State would be multiplied by two, five, or 10, while the votes of persons in another area would be counted only at face value, could be constitutionally sustainable. Of course, the effect of state legislative districting schemes which give the same number of representatives to unequal numbers of constituents is identical. Overweighting and overvaluation of the votes of those living here has the certain effect of dilution and undervaluation of the votes of those living there. The resulting discrimination against those individual voters living in disfavored areas is easily demonstrable mathematically. Their right to vote is simply not the same right to vote as that of those living in a favored part of the State. Two, five, or 10 of them must vote before the effect of their voting is equivalent to that of their favored neighbor. Weighting the votes of citizens differently, by any method or means, merely because of where they happen to reside, hardly seems justifiable. * * * As we stated in *Wesberry v. Sanders*:

? As a historical matter, does this quote from *Wesberry* seem correct? In addition to the malapportionment of the U.S. Senate and (to a lesser extent) the U.S. House of Representatives embedded into the Constitution, the original Constitution also contained the infamous "Three-Fifths Clause," which counted slaves as three-fifths of a person for purposes of apportionment of congressional seats, but which did not permit slaves to vote. The effect of this provision was a malapportionment giving voters in slave states greater federal congressional representation.

"We do not believe that the Framers of the Constitution intended to permit the same vote-diluting discrimination to be accomplished through the device of districts containing widely varied numbers of inhabitants. To say that a vote is worth more in one district than in another would . . . run counter to our fundamental ideas of democratic government . . . ."

State legislatures are, historically, the fountainhead of representative government in this country. A number of them have their roots in colonial times, and substantially antedate the creation of our Nation and our Federal Government. In fact, the first formal stirrings of American political independence are to be found, in large part, in the views and actions of several of the colonial legislative bodies. With the birth of our National Government, and the adoption and ratification of the Federal Constitution, state legislatures retained a most important place in our Nation's governmental structure. But representative government is in essence self-government through the medium of elected representatives of the people, and each and every citizen has an inalienable right to full and effective participation in the political processes of his State's legislative bodies. Most citizens can achieve this participation only as qualified voters through the election of legislators to represent them. Full and effective participation by all citizens in state government requires, therefore, that each citizen have an equally effective voice in the election of members of his state legislature. Modern and viable state government needs, and the Constitution demands, no less.

Logically, in a society ostensibly grounded on representative government, it would seem reasonable that a majority of the people of a State could elect a majority of that State's legislators. To conclude differently, and to sanction minority control of state legislative bodies, would appear to deny majority rights in a way that far surpasses any possible denial of minority rights that might otherwise be thought to result. Since legislatures are responsible for enacting laws by which all citizens are to be governed, they should be bodies which are collectively responsive to the popular will. And the concept of equal protection has been traditionally viewed as requiring the uniform treatment of persons standing in the same relation to the governmental action questioned or challenged. With respect to the allocation of legislative representation, all voters, as citizens of a State, stand in the same relation regardless of where they live. Any suggested criteria for the differentiation of citizens are insufficient to justify any discrimination, as to the weight of their votes, unless relevant to the permissible purposes of legislative apportionment. Since the achieving of fair and effective representation for all citizens is concededly the basic aim of legislative apportionment, we conclude that the Equal Protection Clause guarantees the opportunity for equal participation by all voters in the election of state legislators. Diluting the weight of votes because of place of residence impairs basic constitutional rights under the Fourteenth Amendment just as much as invidious discriminations based upon factors such as race, *Brown v. Board of Education*, 347 U.S. 483, or economic status, *Griffin v. Illinois*, 351 U.S. 12, *Douglas v. California*, 372 U.S. 353. Our constitutional system amply provides for the protection of minorities by means other than giving them majority control of state legislatures. And the democratic ideals of equality and majority rule, which have served this Nation so well in the past, are hardly of any less significance for the present and the future. * * *

To the extent that a citizen's right to vote is debased, he is that much less a citizen. The fact that an individual lives here or there is not a legitimate reason for overweighting or diluting the efficacy of his vote. The complexions of societies and civilizations change, often with amazing rapidity. A nation once primarily rural in character becomes predominantly urban.

Representation schemes once fair and equitable become archaic and out-dated. But the basic principle of representative government remains, and must remain, unchanged—the weight of a citizen's vote cannot be made to depend on where he lives. Population is, of necessity, the starting point for consideration and the controlling criterion for judgment in legislative apportionment controversies. A citizen, a qualified voter, is no more nor no less so because he lives in the city or on the farm. This is the clear and strong command of our Constitution's Equal Protection Clause. This is an essential part of the concept of a government of laws and not men. This is at the heart of Lincoln's vision of "government of the people, by the people, [and] for the people." The Equal Protection Clause demands no less than substantially equal state legislative representation for all citizens, of all places as well as of all races. * * *

We hold that, as a basic constitutional standard, the Equal Protection Clause requires that the seats in both houses of a bicameral state legislature must be apportioned on a population basis. Simply stated, an individual's right to vote for state legislators is unconstitutionally impaired when its weight is in a substantial fashion diluted when compared with votes of citizens living in other parts of the State. Since, under neither the existing apportionment provisions nor either of the proposed plans was either of the houses of the Alabama Legislature apportioned on a population basis, the District Court correctly held that all three of these schemes were constitutionally invalid. * * *

Since neither of the houses of the Alabama Legislature, under any of the three plans considered by the District Court, was apportioned on a population basis, we would be justified in proceeding no further. However, one of the proposed plans * * * at least superficially resembles the scheme of legislative representation followed in the Federal Congress. Under this plan, each of Alabama's 67 counties is allotted one senator, and no counties are given more than one Senate seat. Arguably, this is analogous to the allocation of two Senate seats, in the Federal Congress, to each of the 50 States, regardless of population. Seats in the Alabama House, under the proposed constitutional amendment, are distributed by giving each of the 67 counties at least one, with the remaining 39 seats being allotted among the more populous counties on a population basis. This scheme, at least at first glance, appears to resemble that prescribed for the Federal House of Representatives, where the 435 seats are distributed among the States on a population basis, although each State, regardless of its population, is given at least one Congressman. * * *

We agree with the District Court, and find the federal analogy inapposite and irrelevant to state legislative districting schemes. Attempted reliance on the federal analogy appears often to be little more than an after-the-fact rationalization offered in defense of maladjusted state apportionment arrangements. The original constitutions of 36 of our States provided that representation in both houses of the state legislatures would be based completely, or predominantly, on population. And the Founding Fathers clearly had no intention of establishing a pattern or model for the apportionment of seats in state legislatures when the system of representation in the Federal Congress was adopted. * * *

The system of representation in the two Houses of the Federal Congress is one ingrained in our Constitution, as part of the law of the land. It is one conceived out of compromise and concession indispensable to the establishment of our federal republic. Arising from unique historical circumstances, it is based on the consideration that in establishing our type of federalism a group of formerly independent States bound themselves together under one national government. * * * The developing history and growth of our republic cannot cloud the fact that, at the time of the inception of the system of representation in the Federal Congress, a compromise between the larger and smaller States on this matter averted a deadlock in the Constitutional Convention which had threatened to abort the birth of our Nation. * * *

For Georgia's malapportioned districts to be constitutional, does it need to be the case that "the Founding Fathers . . . had [an] intention of establishing a pattern or model for the apportionment of seats in state legislatures"? Isn't Georgia just saying that a structure of apportionment that parallels that of the federal Congress can't be deemed a violation of the federal Constitution? Read on and see what the Court has to say about the relationship between federal malapportionment written into the Constitution itself and the constitutionality of malapportionment at the state level.

Political subdivisions of States—counties, cities, or whatever—never were and never have been considered as sovereign entities. Rather, they have been traditionally regarded as subordinate governmental instrumentalities created by the State to assist in the carrying out of state governmental functions. As stated by the Court in *Hunter v. City of Pittsburgh*, 207 U.S. 161, 178, these governmental units are "created as convenient agencies for exercising such of the governmental powers of the State as may be entrusted to them," and the "number, nature and duration of the powers conferred upon [them]

... and the territory over which they shall be exercised rests in the absolute discretion of the State." The relationship of the States to the Federal Government could hardly be less analogous.

Thus, we conclude that the plan contained in the 67-Senator Amendment for apportioning seats in the Alabama Legislature cannot be sustained by recourse to the so-called federal analogy. Nor can any other inequitable state legislative apportionment scheme be justified on such an asserted basis. This does not necessarily mean that such a plan is irrational or involves something other than a "republican form of government." We conclude simply that such a plan is impermissible for the States under the Equal Protection Clause, since perforce resulting, in virtually every case, in submergence of the equal-population principle in at least one house of a state legislature.

* * *

[W]e affirm the judgment below and remand the cases for further proceedings consistent with the views stated in this opinion.

It is so ordered.

> **FYI** The phrase "republican form of government" is a reference to another clause in the federal Constitution, the so-called "Guarantee Clause," Article IV, Section 4, which states that "[t]he United States shall guarantee to every State in this Union a Republican Form of Government . . . ." Again, the reference to "Republican" here evokes the classical republican ideas of virtue and the common good that we discussed in Section A and not necessarily the modern-day "Republican" Party.

NOTES & QUESTIONS

1. Does the *Reynolds* opinion embody a particular theory of representation? How would you describe that theory? Under what representational theory would the one person, one vote principle matter the *least*?

2. Is the Court's distinction between the U.S. Constitution's scheme for electing U.S. Senators and the state's system for allocating representation in the state legislature persuasive?

3. The consequence of *Wesberry and Reynolds* was a monumental restructuring of legislative bodies, to equalize the population disparities that

had developed in the preceding decades and place urban and suburban areas on comparable footing. Though not grounded in the need to redress race discrimination, the one person, one vote doctrine did provide some improvements here, as malapportionment had generally worked to the disadvantage of African Americans, many of whom had moved from farms to cities during the Great Migration of the early and mid-20th century. "One person, one vote" also became a rallying cry of the voting rights movement, fueling the push toward enactment of the Voting Rights Act of 1965, discussed below.

4.   Another consequence of the one person, one vote cases is that congressional and state legislative districts must be redrawn every ten years, immediately after each U.S. Census. Usually, the state legislature redraws the districts lines. Does that create a conflict of interest? We look at the redistricting process in the next section, Section B.

5.   The Court would later extend the one person, one vote principle to local elections (*e.g.*, city councils and school boards elected from districts). But some of the complications in applying the one person, one vote rule remained in dispute for decades—and have yet to be fully resolved.

The "one person, one vote" principle has given rise to a host of subsidiary legal issues. Two of these, discussed next, are (1) how much "equality" is required, and (2) what individuals to include in the population count.

From DANIEL P. TOKAJI, ELECTION LAW IN A NUTSHELL (2d ed. 2017):

1.   The Degree of Equality Required

The first round of one person, one vote cases established that districts must be of at least approximately equal population, but they did not establish the degree of equality that must obtain. Put another way, they did not settle the question of how much departure from precise numerical equality is constitutionally permitted. In cases that followed, the answer turned out to be different for challenges to *congressional* malapportionment than for challenges to *state legislative* malapportionment, with greater deviation being allowed under the latter than the former.

Recall that Article I, Section 2 is the textual source for the equal population rule for congressional districts under *Wesberry*, while the Equal Protection Clause is the textual source of the equal population rule for state legislative districts under *Reynolds*. For congressional districts, the Court has required that districts "as nearly as practicable" be of precisely equal population. Applying this standard, the Court in *Kirkpatrick v. Preisler,* 394 U.S. 526 (1969), struck down a Missouri congressional redistricting plan in which the most populous district was 3.13% above the ideal and the least populous district 2.84% below it. And in *Karcher v. Daggett,* 462 U.S. 725 (1983), the Court struck down a New Jersey congressional plan in which the difference in population between the largest and smallest district was less than one percent (0.6984% to be exact). * * *

The Court clarified the standard for congressional districts in *Tennant v. Jefferson County Commission,* 567 U.S. 758 (2012). That case involved a "minor" deviation (0.79%) between the largest and smallest districts. Such a deviation, *Tennant* held, need only be justified by a "legitimate" state objective. The Court found there to be legitimate state interests in preserving local boundaries, avoiding contests between incumbents, and minimizing shifts between old and new districts.

> **!** With respect to congressional districts, the *Tennant* decision permits deviations in district population of under 1% when justified by a legitimate reason.

The Court has been more tolerant of population deviations in state and local redistricting plans, as opposed to congressional redistricting plans. * * * In *Gaffney v. Cummings,* 412 U.S. 735 (1973), the Court upheld a Connecticut state house plan with a total maximum deviation of 7.83%. The state justified the deviations in the plan as an attempt to ensure a plan that would roughly approximate the political strengths of the two major parties. Justice White's opinion for the Court accepted this justification.

After *Gaffney,* it was generally presumed that state and local plans with a total maximum deviation over 10% required justification, while those with a deviation under 10% did not. * * *

> With respect to state legislative districts, decisions such as *Harris* and *Gaffney* have permitted larger deviations, of up to 10%, unless a deviation can be shown to reflect illegitimate factors. **!**

In *Harris v. Arizona Independent Redistricting Commission,* 578 U.S. 253 (2016), the Supreme Court refined the constitutional standard applicable to minor departures from population equality. Arizona has an independent redistricting commission, which drew a state legislative plan with an

8.8% total maximum deviation. Although this fell squarely within the 10% threshold, plaintiffs argued that the plan violated the one person, one vote rule because it systematically overpopulated Republican districts while underpopulating Democratic districts. The Commission defended this asymmetrical deviation on the ground that it was necessary to comply with the Voting Rights [Act].

> As a policy matter, does it make sense to allow greater deviation in state and local districts? Is the justification connected with the two different constitutional provisions at issue? Or, is something else going on?

Harris rejected the constitutional challenge to Arizona's districts, with Justice Breyer writing for the unanimous Court. He explained that minor deviations from population equality—under 10% total maximum deviation—do not ordinarily require justification. To challenge a plan within this threshold, plaintiffs must show that it is "more probable than not" that the deviation "reflects the predominance of illegitimate reapportionment factors rather than the 'legitimate considerations.'" Legitimate considerations include traditional redistricting criteria like compactness, contiguity, and the preservation of political subdivisions. The Court assumed without deciding that partisanship would be an illegitimate consideration, but upheld Arizona's districts based on the commission's good-faith effort to comply with the Voting Rights Act. * * * *Harris* also held that compliance with the Voting Rights Act's preclearance requirement was an acceptable justification for the commission's minor deviation from population equality, even though preclearance was effectively suspended by the Court's subsequent decision in *Shelby County [v. Holder*, 570 U.S. 529 (2013)].

2. Measurement of Equal Population

Reynolds speaks of both equal population and equal voters. But not everyone who lives in a district is a voter. Many people are not eligible to vote, among them children, noncitizens, people with criminal convictions (in some places), and people who are incarcerated (almost everywhere). Moreover, many people who are eligible to vote do not in fact vote.

In determining whether districts are equally populated, it can make a big difference whether to count the total population, the voting-age population, the citizen-voting-age population, the voting-eligible population, registered voters, or actual voters. That is because some places will have many more noncitizens, children, and other nonvoters than others. Which measure is most appropriate is likely to depend on whether one thinks the rule is designed to protect all people within the jurisdiction (regardless of whether they can vote), only those who vote, or perhaps some but not all of those who reside in the jurisdiction but do not vote.

The usual practice is for those drawing legislative maps to consider *total population* in determining whether districts are equally populated. That does not necessarily mean that the use of total population is constitutionally required. In *Burns v. Richardson,* 384 U.S. 73 (1966), the Court upheld Hawaii's use of registered voters to draw state legislative districts. *Burns* emphasized the particular circumstances of Hawaii that justified its decision to depart from total population—in particular, the large number of non-resident military personnel and tourists included in the U.S. Census.

In *Evenwel v. Abbott,* 136 S. Ct. 1120 (2016), the Supreme Court rejected a constitutional challenge to the use of total population to draw state legislative districts. Like all the other states, Texas used total population to draw its state legislative districts after the 2010 census, but the number of eligible voters within each district varied substantially. Plaintiffs argued that the state was required to equalize *eligible voters* among districts. The Court unanimously rejected this argument, with Justice Ginsburg writing for the majority. She relied heavily on the history of the original Constitution and the Fourteenth Amendment, which use total population as the basis for apportioning U.S. representatives among the states. This history, the majority concluded, undermined the argument that state legislative districts must be drawn to equalize eligible voters rather than total population. The Court expressly left open the question whether states *must* use total population to draw state legislative districts or, alternatively, may choose to use eligible voters or some other metric. * * *

> *!* Notice that in *Evenwel,* the Court specifically relies on the idea that it is constitutionally permissible for the states to structure their approach to districting on the way federal districting was done based on the original constitutional scheme. In contrast, recall that this is precisely the argument the Court rejects in *Reynolds v. Sims*.

DIY
Whom to Include in District Population Counts?

 In the round of redistricting following the 2010 federal census, all of the states used the total population of each district as the measure of equality, a practice upheld in *Evenwel*. But a state might seek to use a different measure. Do you think that it would violate the one person, one vote rule if a state chose to equalize the *voting-eligible population* (i.e., citizens of voting age who are not disqualified from voting) within each district, rather than the *total population*? Why or why not? Does one's theory of representation shape the response to this question? Who would be advantaged and disadvantaged if only eligible voters were considered in drawing districts?

B. The Redistricting Process

Drawing political or representational districts *geographically* is a long-standing though by no means constitutionally compelled practice. (For instance, districts could be structured by age bands, which would give new meaning to the idea of "the youth vote.") Before the arrival of the one person, one vote requirement, districts could be drawn geographically largely on the basis of existing political boundaries and natural geographic characteristics. But drawing geographic districts of equal population usually necessitates departing from existing municipal lines or topographic features.

Each state makes its own choice about who will draw its congressional districts and its state legislative districts. A few states have established independent redistricting commissions to do this work, but in most states today a partisan body or the state legislature itself has the responsibility for drawing districts. Occasionally, courts are called upon to draw legislative districts when the regular redistricting process has failed for some reason, although federal courts are expected to defer to state court proceedings as much as possible. *See Growe v. Emison*, 507 U.S. 25 (1993).

When those responsible for drawing district lines perform their work, a number of considerations can come into play. In some jurisdictions, some of these considerations are spelled out in statute or the state constitution. For instance, the Florida Constitution has a provision that prohibits drawing districts with "the intent to favor or disfavor a political party or an incumbent." Where there are no constitutional or statutory constraints, the line-drawers can make their own decisions about what considerations to favor. Currently, federal law (2 U.S.C. § 2c) also requires that all congressional districts be single-member districts, and the federal Voting Rights Act, discussed below, also affects the line-drawing process.

In 2023, the Supreme Court decided a case that had threatened to deprive state courts of the ability to enforce state constitutional constraints on the drawing of congressional districts. The case, *Moore v. Harper*, 600 U.S. 1, 143 S. Ct. 2065 (2023), presented the Court with what was called the "Independent State Legislature Theory." In its most extreme form, this theory claimed that because Article I of the U.S. Constitution provides that the "Manner of holding [congressional] Elections" is to be "prescribed in each State by the Legislature thereof," a state legislature had unreviewable authority to set the terms of these elections. However, the Court rejected this theory, explaining that state legislatures were creatures of their state constitutions and thus bound by the terms of those constitutions, as construed and applied by the state high court, provided that state court was acting within the "ordinary bounds of judicial review." 600 U.S. at ___, 143 S. Ct. at 2089. In what circumstances a state court might be seen to have exceeded the "ordinary bounds of judicial review" must await another day, but at least for now the teaching of *Moore v. Harper* is that state courts may continue to play their traditional role of construing their state constitutions with respect to how congressional districts are drawn. *Moore v. Harper*, 600 U.S. at ___, 143 S. Ct. at 2081.

Whether specified in a state constitution, required by a state redistricting statute, or simply of interest to a redistricting body, various considerations can play a role in how districts are drawn. Here is a typical list of possible districting considerations:

From Daniel P. Tokaji, Election Law in a Nutshell (2d ed. 2017):

- *Compactness.* This criterion focuses on the shape of the district. A district shaped in a circle is compact, while an irregularly shaped district with multiple tentacles or appendages is not.

- *Contiguity.* A district is contiguous if one can travel from one point in the district to any other, without entering another district. The main complication that arises is whether a district is contiguous if two parts are separated by water, as is necessary in the case of an island. Districts connecting across water are generally considered contiguous, so long as district lines do not cross. Another question is whether "Figure 8" districts, which connect at a point, are contiguous. If contiguity is required by state law, the answer will depend on how that law is written and interpreted.

- *Communities of Interest.* This term is generally understood to mean a group of people that shares some common interest, such as those defined by politics, culture, or religion. As with other redistricting criteria, there is no uniform definition of a community of interest, but some jurisdictions require it to be considered.

- *Political Boundaries.* Some states require that lines be drawn so as to avoid breaking up local governmental entities like counties, municipalities, wards, and precincts, and requiring that whole governmental units be joined together when possible or practicable.

- *Geographic Boundaries.* Another criterion is to avoid crossing important geographic markers, like mountain ranges or rivers. This may be justified by the interest in making it relatively easy for candidates and others to travel through the district. It may also be related to the preservation of communities of interest.

- *Census Tracts.* These are geographic groupings defined by the U.S. Census Bureau, generally consisting of 1,200 to 8,000 people with an optimum size of 4,000. Keeping census tracts together may be justified by the interest in administrative convenience. It may also help keep communities of interest together.

- *Nesting.* This means putting two or more districts of the lower chamber of the state legislature wholly within each district of the upper chamber. For example, each senate district might contain three whole house districts. In addition to making the map look "cleaner" it may promote administrative convenience by reducing the number of ballot formats that must be created. It may also avoid voters' confusion about who represents them.

- *Partisanship.* Districts may be drawn so as to favor one party over another or, on the other hand, to avoid favoritism for any party by drawing plans that roughly correspond to the political makeup of the jurisdiction as a whole. A plan strongly favoring one major party over the other is a partisan gerrymander. Alternatively, partisan fairness—that is, a rough correspondence between each party's popular support and its share of seats—may be a criterion for drawing district lines.

- *Incumbency.* As with partisanship, plans may be drawn either to maximize the advantage of incumbents, or to avoid any favoritism for incumbents. The two major parties will sometimes agree (some would say collude) to draw a map that maximizes the number of safe seats that both parties control. Such a plan effectively insulates incumbent legislators from competition, arguably making them less accountable to voters.

- *Competitiveness.* This is the flip side of plans that are drawn to favor a political party or incumbents generally. A plan may be drawn to promote competitive districts, ones that contain roughly the same number of voters from both major parties. This gives both parties a chance to win the district. The asserted benefits of competitive districts include sensitivity to changes in the electorate's political views and an incentive for candidates to appeal to the median voter. In the aggregate, this may encourage moderation and diminish partisan polarization.

- *Minority Protection.* Redistricting plans may be drawn to enhance the representation of a minority group defined by race, ethnicity, language, religion, or some other characteristic. The most important example of a law that requires minority representation to be taken into account is the Voting Rights Act of 1965 (VRA), as amended, which protects racial minorities' opportunity to elect their candidates of choice. * * *

NOTES & QUESTIONS

1. What criteria should states follow when drawing congressional and state legislative district lines? Should states adopt a requirement like Florida's?

2. Is it best to entrust redistricting to state legislatures? Or to some other body? If to some other body, how should that body be designed to ensure that lines are drawn fairly?

3. As a last resort, should courts be able to draw districts to satisfy specified districting standards?

Test Your Understanding

To assess your understanding of the material in this chapter, click here to take a quiz.

6

Racial Considerations in Districting

Key Concepts

- The Voting Rights Act
- Discriminatory intent vs. discriminatory impact
- *Thornburg v. Gingles*
- *Allen v. Milligan*
- Equal Protection
- Racial gerrymandering
- *Shaw v. Reno*

Chapter Summary

Shortly after the Civil War, the Fifteenth Amendment to the Constitution guaranteed equal voting rights regardless of a citizen's race or color. Yet this guarantee was largely hollow, until Congress passed the Voting Rights Act of 1965. The Voting Rights Act has dramatically transformed American elections, significantly improving the voting rights of racial minorities, including in how representational districts are constructed. Meanwhile, the contours of the VRA continue to evolve in response to a series of Supreme Court decisions, and the Court also has developed a distinct but related line of jurisprudence under the Constitution's Equal Protection Clause that greatly limits the government's ability to take race into account in the drawing of legislative districts.

The "one person, one vote" principle discussed in the previous chapter is a *constitutional* doctrine. In this chapter, we first introduce a companion *statutory* measure, enacted over a half-century ago, that has been critical to the fuller realization of the right to vote for racial minority voters throughout the United States. We then introduce a countervailing constitutional doctrine developed under the Equal Protection Clause that limits the degree to which race can be considered in drawing legislative districts.

A.   The Voting Rights Act*

A central concern of voting rights law is to ensure fair representation for political minorities, including racial and ethnic minorities. In the U.S., the struggle for racial justice is inextricably intertwined with the right to vote. During the period when Jim Crow segregation reigned throughout the states of the former Confederacy, Black Americans were systematically denied the right to vote, making it far more difficult to secure equality in other walks of life such as education, employment, housing, and public accommodations. Despite the country's adoption of the Fifteenth Amendment to the Constitution in 1870, the exclusion of Black Americans from voting persisted throughout the latter part of the Nineteenth and most of the Twentieth Century.

> **FYI** "Jim Crow" laws were state laws that enforced racial segregation in a host of ways from the post-Reconstruction era of the 1870s through the Civil Rights era of the 1960s.

The pivotal event was not a decision from the Supreme Court enforcing the Fifteenth Amendment, but the enactment during the Civil Rights Era of the Voting Rights Act of 1965 (VRA). This statute ended the system of mass disenfranchisement that had long excluded southern Blacks from voting. The VRA had three key sections:

> You'll recall from Chapter 5 that the Fifteenth Amendment states that "[t]he right of citizens of the United States to vote shall not be denied or abridged . . . on account of race, color, or previous condition of servitude."

Section 2, which until its 1982 amendment basically just reiterated the Fifteenth Amendment's prohibition against racial discrimination in voting;

Section 4, which prohibited the use of literacy tests and other voter exclusion methods in "covered states," where Black voter disenfranchisement had been most severe. Covered states were defined as those in which less than half the voting age population had voted in 1964 and that had used some form of test to exclude some of its citizens from voting;

Section 5, which required any of the jurisdictions identified by the section 4 coverage formula to receive federal approval ("pre-clearance") of any new voting rules.

---

*   The material in this section is drawn from DANIEL P. TOKAJI, ELECTION LAW IN A NUTSHELL (2d ed. 2017).

Sections 4 and 5 were initially intended to be temporary, but Congress renewed them for additional terms of years in 1970, 1975, 1982, and 2006. In 1970, Congress also extended the prohibition on literacy tests nationwide, rather than just to the covered states. Then, in *Shelby County v. Holder*, 570 U.S. 529 (2013), the Supreme Court found section 4's coverage formula to be unconstitutional, thus also eviscerating the pre-clearance requirement of section 5, at least until Congress could develop a revised (and constitutional) coverage formula. But Congress has made no attempt to do so. However, the VRA has clearly had a significant impact in protecting minority voting rights.

The first generation of VRA enforcement activity focused on putting an end to the literacy tests, poll taxes, and other practices that had been used to deny the vote to members of racial minority groups (practices termed "vote denial"), especially in the seven southern states initially covered under the coverage formula of section 4 of the Act. In the Act's early years, the VRA had an immediate

> You'll recall from Chapter 5 that the Twenty-Fourth Amendment to the Constitution, adopted in 1964, one year before the Voting Rights Act, prohibits the denial or abridgment of the right to vote by reason of failure to pay a poll tax or other tax.

impact on voter participation, as Black voter registration rates in these seven states increased from under 30% to over 50% in just its first two years. *See* BERNARD GROFMAN, LISA HANDLEY, & RICHARD G. NIEMI, MINORITY REPRESENTATION AND THE QUEST FOR VOTING EQUALITY (1992).

But over time, advocates of minority voting rights recognized that access to the ballot box was not sufficient to achieve equality in the political process. Thus,

> Notice that the concept of "vote dilution" is in effect the idea underlying the "one person, one vote" principle we discussed in Chapter 5. The claim of the urban voters in *Reynolds v. Sims* was that under the Alabama districting plan they challenged their votes were effectively worth less, as a mathematical matter, than the votes of rural voters—in essence, a claim that their votes were "diluted" relative to rural voters.

the second generation of VRA enforcement focused on practices—most notably *at-large elections* and *redistricting schemes*—that diluted the voting strength of racial, ethnic, and language minorities as a group, making it difficult for these groups to elect any of their own members as representatives (practices termed "vote dilution"). However, in *City of Mobile v. Bolden*, 446 U.S. 55 (1980), the Court held that a deliberate intent to discriminate against a protected group, and not just a discriminatory impact, was required to establish unconstitutional vote dilution under the Fifteenth Amendment, as well as a violation of section 2 of the VRA, as originally enacted. In response, in 1982 Congress amended section 2 to protect against electoral practices whose effect was vote dilution.

As amended in 1982, section 2 of the Voting Rights Act states:

 What do you think are legitimate voting qualifications or prerequisites?

(a)   No voting qualification or prerequisite to voting or standard, practice, or procedure shall be imposed or applied by any State or political subdivision in a manner which results in a denial or abridgement of the right of any citizen of the United States to vote on account of race or color . . . , as provided in subsection (b).

(b)   A violation of subsection (a) is established if, based on the totality of circumstances, it is shown that the political processes leading to nomination or election in the State or political subdivision are not equally open to participation by members of a class of citizens protected by subsection (a) in that its members have less opportunity than other members of the electorate to participate in the political process and to elect representatives of their choice. The extent to which members of a protected class have been elected to office in the State or political subdivision is one circumstance which may be considered: *Provided*, That nothing in this section establishes a right to have members of a protected class elected in numbers equal to their proportion in the population.

52 U.S.C. § 10301.

The amendment's key change to the statute was the addition of the "results" standard, in place of the former language that had been construed to prohibit only intentional race discrimination. This amendment was not an easy lift for Congress. Some Senators objected that the "results" standard would give rise to a quota system, but Senator Robert Dole shepherded a compromise that was eventually incorporated in subsection (b) above.

Subsection (b) did not provide additional guidance about how to employ its "totality of the circumstances" standard to identify a violation, but the Report of the Senate Judiciary Committee listed a host of "typical" factors for consideration:

1. the extent of any history of official discrimination in the state or political subdivision that touched the right of members of the minority group to register, to vote, or otherwise to participate in the democratic process;

2. the extent to which voting in the elections of the state or political subdivision is racially polarized;

3. the extent to which the state or political subdivision has used unusually large election districts, majority vote requirements, anti-single shot provisions, or other voting practices or procedures that may enhance the opportunity for discrimination against the minority group;

> Single-shot voting, also known as "bullet voting," is a voting tactic, usually in multiple-winner elections, for when a voter is entitled to vote for several candidates but instead chooses to vote for only one. **FYI**

4. if there is a candidate slating process, whether the members of the minority group have been denied access to that process;

5. the extent to which members of the minority group in the state or political subdivision bear the effects of discrimination in such areas as education, employment and health, which hinder their ability to participate effectively in the political process;

6. whether political campaigns have been characterized by overt or subtle racial appeals;

7. the extent to which members of the minority group have been elected to public office in the jurisdiction.

8. whether there is a significant lack of responsiveness on the part of elected officials to the particularized needs of the members of the minority group; and

9. whether the policy underlying the state or political subdivision's use of such voting qualification, prerequisite to voting, or standard, practice or procedure is tenuous.

Because the new language of Section 2 was not crystal clear, it was left to the Supreme Court to provide a standard for vote dilution claims under the amended version of Section 2. The Court did so in *Thornburg v. Gingles*, 478 U.S. 30 (1986), articulating three preconditions for vote dilution claims under Section 2 that remain in effect today.

Gingles involved a challenge to a state legislative districting plan in North Carolina, a state with a long and ugly history of race discrimination in voting. During and for several decades after Reconstruction, a number of Black men had been elected to the North Carolina legislature, and three to Congress. But in 1900, the state adopted a state constitutional amendment that effectively disenfranchised the Black voting population. Thereafter, although some Black voters in North Carolina were occasionally able to exercise their right to vote, none were elected to Congress or the state legislature. As late as the early 1980s, the North Carolina legislature still had only four Black Americans among its 170 members—just 2.3% of the seats—despite the fact that this minority group constituted around 22% of the state's population.

The plaintiffs in *Gingles* alleged that the state's districts diluted Black voting strength, preventing them from electing their candidates of choice. Most of the challenged districts were "multi-member" districts, meaning that more than one representative was elected from the same geographic area. These larger districts allegedly made it more difficult for African Americans to elect their preferred candidates. Accordingly, the *Gingles* plaintiffs wanted them broken up into smaller districts, so that Black voters would have a better chance of electing Black candidates from at least some of these districts. The case therefore raised the question of whether Section 2, although it explicitly did not mandate a right to proportional representation, might sometimes demand the creation of electoral districts populated by a majority of voters of a single racial minority group.

The district court concluded that several of the districts violated Section 2 of the VRA, and the Supreme Court agreed as to all but one of these districts. Justice Brennan's opinion for the Court held that in the redistricting context, plaintiffs seeking to establish a violation of Section 2 must show three things: "First, the minority group must be able to demonstrate that it is sufficiently large and geographically compact to constitute a majority in a single-member district. . . . Second, the minority group must be able to show that it is politically cohesive. . . . Third, the minority must be able to demonstrate that the white majority votes sufficiently as a bloc to enable it—in the absence of special circumstances, such as the minority candidate running unoppo-

> **!** This is the three-part so-called *Gingles* test for vote-dilution claims under Section 2 of the Voting Rights Act. Note that the plaintiff must establish *all three* of these circumstances.

sed. . .usually to defeat the minority's preferred candidate." Justice O'Connor wrote a concurring opinion cautioning against misreading the majority opinion as giving rise to a right to proportional representation.

The *Gingles* decision immediately drew criticism from some quarters that in fact it did amount to a proportionality test. After Justice Clarence Thomas became a member of the Court, he made clear his opposition to the *Gingles* approach. Criticism of the *Gingles* decision persisted, until in 2023 the Supreme Court decided *Allen v. Milligan*, a case that had threatened to undo the *Gingles* test and to gut Section 2's impact on redistricting processes. But to the surprise of many, the Court reaffirmed the *Gingles* test in its *Milligan* decision, excerpted below.

> We present additional excerpts of **FYI** *Allen v. Milligan* in Chapter 16 below as part of the discussion of the concept of "statutory *stare decisis*," which appears in this excerpt as well.

Allen v. Milligan
599 U.S. 1 (2023)

CHIEF JUSTICE ROBERTS **delivered the opinion of the Court, except as to Part III-B-1.**

* * *

I-B

For the first 115 years following Reconstruction, the State of Alabama elected no black Representatives to Congress. In 1992, several plaintiffs sued the State, alleging that it had been impermissibly diluting the votes of black Alabamians in violation of § 2 [of the Voting Rights Act]. The lawsuit produced a majority-black district in Alabama for the first time in decades. And that fall, Birmingham lawyer Earl Hillard became the first black Representative from Alabama since 1877.

Alabama's congressional map has "remained remarkably similar" after [that lawsuit]. The map contains seven congressional districts, each with a single representative. * * *

In 2020, the decennial census revealed that Alabama's population had grown by 5.1%. A group of plaintiffs led by Alabama legislator Bobby Singleton sued the State, arguing that the existing congressional map was malapportioned and racially gerrymandered in violation of the Equal Protection Clause. While litigation was proceeding, the Alabama Legislature's Committee on Reapportionment began creating a new districting map.

* * *

II

The District Court found that plaintiffs demonstrated a reasonable likelihood of success on their claim that [the new map] violates § 2. We affirm that determination.

A

For the past forty years, we have evaluated claims brought under § 2 using the three-part framework developed in our decision *Thornburg v. Gingles*, 478 U.S. 30 (1986). * * *

Gingles began by describing what § 2 guards against. "The essence of a § 2 claim," the Court explained, "is that a certain electoral law, practice, or structure interacts with social and historical conditions to cause an inequality in the opportunities enjoyed by black and white voters." *Id.*, at 47. That occurs where an "electoral structure operates to minimize or cancel out" minority voters' "ability to elect their preferred candidates." *Id.*, at 48. Such a risk is greatest "where minority and majority voters consistently prefer different candidates" and where minority voters are submerged in a majority voting population that "regularly defeat[s]" their choices. *Ibid.*

To succeed in proving a § 2 violation under *Gingles*, plaintiffs must satisfy three "preconditions." * * *

Each *Gingles* precondition serves a different purpose. The first, focused on geographical compactness and numerosity, is "needed to establish that the minority has the potential to elect a representative of its own choice in some single-member district." *Growe v. Emison*, 507 U.S. 25, 40 (1993). The second, concerning the political cohesiveness of the minority group, shows that a representative of its choice would in fact be elected. See *ibid*. The third precondition, focused on racially polarized voting, "establish[es] that the challenged districting thwarts a distinctive minority vote" at least plausibly on account of race. *Ibid*. And finally, the totality of circumstances inquiry recognizes that application of the *Gingles* factors is "peculiarly dependent upon the facts of each case." 478 U.S., at 79. Before courts can find a violation of § 2, therefore, they must conduct "an intensely local appraisal" of the electoral mechanism at issue, as well as a "searching practical evaluation of the 'past and present reality.' " *Ibid.*

Gingles has governed our Voting Rights Act jurisprudence since it was decided 37 years ago. Congress has never disturbed our understanding of § 2 as *Gingles* construed it. And we have applied *Gingles* in one § 2 case after another, to different kinds of electoral systems and to different jurisdictions in States all over the country. * * *

B

As noted, the District Court concluded that plaintiffs' § 2 claim was likely to succeed under *Gingles*. [*Singleton v. Merrill*,] 582 F. Supp. 3d [924], at 1026 [(ND Ala. 2022) (per curiam)]. Based on our review of the record, we agree.

With respect to the first *Gingles* precondition, the District Court correctly found that black voters could constitute a majority in a second district that was "reasonably configured." The plaintiffs adduced eleven illustrative maps—that is, example districting maps that Alabama could enact—each of which contained two majority-black districts that comported with traditional districting criteria. * * *

As to the second and third *Gingles* preconditions, the District Court determined that there was "no serious dispute that Black voters are politically cohesive, nor that the challenged districts' white majority votes sufficiently as a bloc to usually defeat Black voters' preferred candidate." 582 F. Supp. 3d, at 1016 (internal quotation marks omitted). The Court noted that, "on average, Black voters supported their candidates of choice with 92.3% of the vote" while "white voters supported Black-preferred candidates with 15.4% of the vote." *Id.*, at 1017 (internal quotation marks omitted). Plaintiffs' experts described the evidence of racially polarized voting in Alabama as "intens[e]," "very strong," and "very clear." *Ibid.* Even Alabama's expert conceded "that the candidates preferred by white voters in the areas that he looked at regularly defeat the candidates preferred by Black voters." *Id.*, at 1018.

Finally, the District Court concluded that plaintiffs had carried their burden at the totality of circumstances stage. The Court observed that elections in Alabama were racially polarized; that "Black Alabamians enjoy virtually zero success in statewide elections"; that political campaigns in Alabama had been "characterized by overt or subtle racial appeals"; and that "Alabama's extensive history of repugnant racial and voting-related discrimination is undeniable and well documented." *Id.*, at 1018–1024.

We see no reason to disturb the District Court's careful factual findings, which are subject to clear error review and have gone unchallenged by Alabama in any event. Nor is there a basis to upset the District Court's legal conclusions. The Court faithfully applied our precedents and correctly determined that, under existing law, HB1 violated § 2.

III

The heart of these cases is not about the law as it exists. It is about Alabama's attempt to remake our § 2 jurisprudence anew.

The centerpiece of the State's effort is what it calls the "race-neutral benchmark." The theory behind it is this: Using modern computer technology, mapmakers can now generate millions of possible districting maps for a given State. The maps can be designed to comply with traditional districting criteria but to not consider race. The mapmaker can determine how many majority-minority districts exist in each map, and can then calculate the median or average number of majority-minority districts in the entire multimillion-map set. That number is called the race-neutral benchmark.

Before reading further, what defect can you identify in this argument Alabama is making about Section 2?

The State contends that this benchmark should serve as the point of comparison in § 2 cases. The benchmark, the State says, was derived from maps that were "race-blind"—maps that cannot have "deni[ed] or abridge[d]" anyone's right to vote "on account of race" because they never took race into "account" in the first place. 52 U.S.C. § 10301(a). Courts in § 2 cases should therefore compare the number of majority-minority districts in the State's plan to the benchmark. If those numbers are similar—if the State's map "resembles" the benchmark in this way—then, Alabama argues, the State's map also cannot have "deni[ed] or abridge[d]" anyone's right to vote "on account of race." *Ibid.*

Alabama contends that its approach should be adopted for two reasons. First, the State argues that a race-neutral benchmark best matches the text of the Voting Rights Act. Section 2 requires that the political processes be "equally open." § 10301(b). What that means, the State asserts, is that the

State's map cannot impose "obstacles or burdens that block or seriously hinder voting on account of race." Brief for Alabama 43. These obstacles do not exist, in the State's view, where its map resembles a map that never took race into "account." *Ibid.* Second, Alabama argues that the *Gingles* framework ends up requiring racial proportionality in districting. According to the State, *Gingles* demands that where "another majority-black district could be drawn, it must be drawn." Brief for Alabama 71 (emphasis deleted). And that sort of proportionality, Alabama continues, is inconsistent with the compromise that Congress struck, with the text of § 2, and with the Constitution's prohibition on racial discrimination in voting.

To apply the race-neutral benchmark in practice, Alabama would require § 2 plaintiffs to make at least three showings. First, the illustrative plan that plaintiffs adduce for the first *Gingles* precondition cannot have been "based" on race. Brief for Alabama 56. Second, plaintiffs must show at the totality of circumstances stage that the State's enacted plan diverges from the average plan that would be drawn without taking race into account. And finally, plaintiffs must ultimately prove that any deviation between the State's plan and a race-neutral plan is explainable "only" by race—not, for example, by "the State's naturally occurring geography and demography." *Id.*, at 46.

As we explain below, we find Alabama's new approach to § 2 compelling neither in theory nor in practice. We accordingly decline to recast our § 2 case law as Alabama requests.

A-1

Section 2 prohibits States from imposing any "standard, practice, or procedure . . . in a manner which results in a denial or abridgement of the right of any citizen . . . to vote on account of race or color." 52 U.S.C. § 10301(a). What that means, § 2 goes on to explain, is that the political processes in the State must be "equally open," such that minority voters do not "have less opportunity than other members of the electorate to participate in the political process and to elect representatives of their choice." § 10301(b).

We have understood the language of § 2 against the background of the hard-fought compromise that Congress struck. To that end, we have reiterated that § 2 turns on the presence of discriminatory effects, not discriminatory intent. And we have explained that "[i]t is patently clear that Congress has used the words 'on account of race or color' in the Act to mean 'with respect to' race or color, and not to connote any required purpose of racial discrimination." *Gingles*, 478 U.S., at 71, n. 34 (plurality opinion) (some

alterations omitted). Individuals thus lack an equal opportunity to participate in the political process when a State's electoral structure operates in a
manner that "minimize[s] or cancel[s] out the[ir] voting strength." *Id.*, at
47. That occurs where an individual is disabled from "enter[ing] into the
political process in a reliable and meaningful manner" "in the light of past
and present reality, political and otherwise." *White [v. Regester]*, 412 U.S.
[755], at 767, 770 [(1973)]. A district is not equally open, in other words,
when minority voters face—unlike their majority peers—bloc voting along
racial lines, arising against the backdrop of substantial racial discrimination within the State, that renders a minority vote unequal to a vote by a
nonminority voter.

The State's reading of § 2, by contrast, runs headlong into our precedent.
Alabama asserts that a State's map does not "abridge[ ]" a person's right to
vote "on account of race" if the map resembles a sufficient number of race-
neutral alternatives. See Brief for Alabama 54–56. But our cases have consistently focused, for purposes of litigation, on the specific illustrative maps
that a plaintiff adduces. Deviation from that map shows it is possible that
the State's map has a disparate effect on account of race. The remainder of
the *Gingles* test helps determine whether that possibility is reality by looking
to polarized voting preferences and the frequency of racially discriminatory
actions taken by the State, past and present.

A State's liability under § 2, moreover, must be determined "based on the
totality of circumstances." 52 U.S.C. § 10301(b). Yet Alabama suggests there
is only one "circumstance[ ]" that matters—how the State's map stacks up
relative to the benchmark. That single-minded view of § 2 cannot be squared
with the VRA's demand that courts employ a more refined approach. And
we decline to adopt an interpretation of § 2 that would "revise and reformulate the *Gingles* threshold inquiry that has been the baseline of our § 2
jurisprudence" for nearly forty years. *Bartlett [v. Strickland]*, 556 U.S. [1], at
16 [(2009)] (plurality opinion); see also *Wisconsin Legislature [v. Wisconsin
Elections Comm'n]*, 595 U.S. [___], at ___ (slip op., at 7) [(2022)] (faulting
lower court for "improperly reduc[ing] *Gingles'* totality-of-circumstances
analysis to a single factor"); *[Johnson v.] De Grandy*, 512 U.S. [997], at 1018
[(1994)] ("An inflexible rule would run counter to the textual command
of § 2, that the presence or absence of a violation be assessed 'based on the
totality of circumstances.' ").

2

Alabama also argues that the race-neutral benchmark is required because our existing § 2 jurisprudence inevitably demands racial proportionality in districting, contrary to the last sentence of § 2(b). But properly applied, the *Gingles* framework itself imposes meaningful constraints on proportionality, as our decisions have frequently demonstrated.

In *Shaw v. Reno*, for example, we considered the permissibility of a second majority-minority district in North Carolina, which at the time had 12 seats in the U.S. House of Representatives and a 20% black voting age population. 509 U.S. 630, 633–634 (1993). The second majority-minority district North Carolina drew was "160 miles long and, for much of its length, no wider than the [interstate] corridor." *Id.*, at 635. The district wound "in snakelike fashion through tobacco country, financial centers, and manufacturing areas until it gobble[d] in enough enclaves of black neighborhoods." *Id.*, at 635–636. Indeed, the district was drawn so imaginatively that one state legislator remarked: "[I]f you drove down the interstate with both car doors open, you'd kill most of the people in the district." *Id.*, at 636.

Though North Carolina believed the additional district was required by § 2, we rejected that conclusion, finding instead that those challenging the map stated a claim of impermissible racial gerrymandering under the Equal Protection Clause. *Id.*, at 655, 658. In so holding, we relied on the fact that the proposed district was not reasonably compact. *Id.*, at 647. North Carolina had "concentrated a dispersed minority population in a single district by disregarding traditional districting principles such as compactness, contiguity, and respect for political subdivisions." *Ibid.* (emphasis added). And "[a] reapportionment plan that includes in one district individuals who belong to the same race, but who are otherwise separated by geographical and political boundaries," we said, raised serious constitutional concerns. *Ibid.* (emphasis added).

The same theme emerged in our 1995 decision *Miller v. Johnson*, where we upheld a district court's finding that one of Georgia's ten congressional districts was the product of an impermissible racial gerrymander. 515 U.S. 900, 906, 910–11 (1995). * * *

The point of all this is a simple one. Forcing proportional representation is unlawful and inconsistent with this Court's approach to implementing § 2. The numbers bear the point out well. At the congressional level, the fraction of districts in which black-preferred candidates are likely to win "is currently below the Black share of the eligible voter population in every state but three." Brief for Professors Jowei Chen *et al.* as Amici Curiae 3 (Chen Brief). Only one State in the country, meanwhile, "has attained a proportional share" of districts in which Hispanic-preferred candidates are likely to prevail. *Id.*, at 3–4. That is because as residential segregation decreases—as it has "sharply" done since the 1970s—satisfying traditional districting criteria such as the compactness requirement "becomes more difficult." T. Crum, *Reconstructing Racially Polarized Voting*, 70 DUKE L. J. 261, 279, and n. 105 (2020).

* * *

Reapportionment, we have repeatedly observed, "is primarily the duty and responsibility of the State[s]," not the federal courts. *Id.*, at ___ (slip op., at 21). Properly applied, the *Gingles* factors help ensure that remains the case. As respondents themselves emphasize, § 2 "never require[s] adoption of districts that violate traditional redistricting principles." Brief for Respondents in No. 21-1087, p. 3. Its exacting requirements, instead, limit judicial intervention to "those instances of intensive racial politics" where the "excessive role [of race] in the electoral process . . . den[ies] minority voters equal opportunity to participate." Senate Report 33–34.

B

Although we are content to reject Alabama's invitation to change existing law on the ground that the State misunderstands § 2 and our decisions implementing it, we also address how the race-neutral benchmark would operate in practice. Alabama's approach fares poorly on that score, which further counsels against our adopting it.

1

The first change to existing law that Alabama would require is prohibiting the illustrative maps that plaintiffs submit to satisfy the first *Gingles* precondition from being "based" on race. Brief for Alabama 56. Although Alabama is not entirely clear whether, under its view, plaintiffs' illustrative plans must not take race into account at all or whether they must just not "prioritize" race, *ibid.*, we see no reason to impose such a new rule.

When it comes to considering race in the context of districting, we have made clear that there is a difference "between being aware of racial considerations and being motivated by them." *Miller*, 515 U.S., at 916. The former is permissible; the latter is usually not. That is because "[r]edistricting legislatures will . . . almost always be aware of racial demographics," *Miller*, 515 U.S., at 916, but such "race consciousness does not lead inevitably to impermissible race discrimination," *Shaw*, 509 U.S., at 646. Section 2 itself "demands consideration of race." *Abbott [v. Perez]*, 581 U.S. [___], at ___ (slip op., at 4) [(2018)]. The question whether additional majority-minority districts can be drawn, after all, involves a "quintessentially race-conscious calculus." *De Grandy*, 512 U.S., at 1020.

At the same time, however, race may not be "the predominant factor in drawing district lines unless [there is] a compelling reason." *Cooper [v. Harris]*, 581 U.S. [285], at 291 [(2017)]. Race predominates in the drawing of district lines, our cases explain, when "race-neutral considerations [come] into play only after the race-based decision had been made." *Bethune-Hill v. Virginia State Bd. of Elections*, 580 U.S. 178, 189 (2017) (internal quotation marks omitted). That may occur where "race for its own sake is the overriding reason for choosing one map over others." *Id.*, at 190.

While the line between racial predominance and racial consciousness can be difficult to discern, *see Miller*, 515 U.S., at 916, it was not breached here. The [ ] plaintiffs relied on illustrative maps produced by expert Bill Cooper. See 2 App. 591–592. Cooper testified that while it was necessary for him to consider race, he also took several other factors into account, such as compactness, contiguity, and population equality. *Ibid*. Cooper testified that he gave all these factors "equal weighting." *Id.*, at 594. And when asked squarely whether race predominated in his development of the illustrative plans, Cooper responded: "No. It was a consideration. This is a Section 2 lawsuit, after all. But it did not predominate or dominate." *Id.*, at 595.

The District Court agreed. It found "Cooper's testimony highly credible" and commended Cooper for "work[ing] hard to give 'equal weight[ ]' to all traditional redistricting criteria." 582 F. Supp. 3d, at 1005–1006; see also *id.*, at 978–979. The court also explained that Alabama's evidence of racial predominance in Cooper's maps was exceedingly thin. * * *

The dissent contends that race nevertheless predominated in both Cooper's and Duchin's maps because they were designed to hit " 'express racial target[s]' "—namely, two "50%-plus majority-black districts." *Post*, at 15 (opinion of THOMAS, J.) (quoting *Bethune-Hill*, 580 U.S., at 192). This argument fails in multiple ways. First, the dissent's reliance on *Bethune-Hill* is mistaken. In that case, this Court was unwilling to conclude that a State's maps were produced in a racially predominant manner. Instead, we remanded for the lower court to conduct the predominance analysis itself, explaining that "the use of an express racial target" was just one factor among others that the court would have to consider as part of "[a] holistic analysis." *Id.*, at 192. Justice Thomas dissented in relevant part, contending that because "the legislature sought to achieve a [black voting-age population] of at least 55%," race necessarily predominated in its decisionmaking. *Id.*, at 198 (opinion concurring in part and dissenting in part). But the Court did not join in that view, and Justice Thomas again dissents along the same lines today.

The second flaw in the dissent's proposed approach is its inescapable consequence: *Gingles* must be overruled. According to the dissent, racial predominance plagues every single illustrative map ever adduced at the first step of *Gingles*. For all those maps were created with an express target in mind—they were created to show, as our cases require, that an additional majority-minority district could be drawn. That is the whole point of the enterprise. The upshot of the approach the dissent urges is not to change how *Gingles* is applied, but to reject its framework outright.

The contention that mapmakers must be entirely "blind" to race has no footing in our § 2 case law. The line that we have long drawn is between consciousness and predominance. Plaintiffs adduced at least one illustrative map that comported with our precedents. They were required to do no more to satisfy the first step of *Gingles*.

* * *

C

Alabama finally asserts that the Court should outright stop applying § 2 in cases like these because the text of § 2 does not apply to single-member redistricting and because § 2 is unconstitutional as the District Court applied it here. We disagree on both counts.

Alabama first argues that § 2 does not apply to single-member redistricting. Echoing Justice Thomas's concurrence in *Holder v. Hall*, Alabama reads § 2's reference to "standard, practice, or procedure" to mean only the "methods for conducting a part of the voting process that might . . . be used to interfere with a citizen's ability to cast his vote." 512 U.S. [874], at 917–918 [(1994)] (opinion concurring in judgment). Examples of covered activities would include "registration requirements, . . . the locations of polling places, the times polls are open, the use of paper ballots as opposed to voting machines, and other similar aspects of the voting process." *Id.,* at 922. But not "a single-member districting system or the selection of one set of districting lines over another." *Id.,* at 923.

This understanding of § 2 cannot be reconciled with our precedent. As recounted above, we have applied § 2 to States' districting maps in an unbroken line of decisions stretching four decades. * * * Alabama's approach would require "abandoning" this precedent, "overruling the interpretation of § 2" as set out in nearly a dozen of our cases. *Holder,* 512 U.S., at 944 (opinion of THOMAS, J.).

We decline to take that step. Congress is undoubtedly aware of our construing § 2 to apply to districting challenges. It can change that if it likes. But until and unless it does, statutory *stare decisis* counsels our staying the course.

The statutory text in any event supports the conclusion that § 2 applies to single-member districts. Alabama's own proffered definition of a "procedure is the manner or method of proceeding in a process or course of action." Brief for Alabama 51 (internal quotation marks omitted). But the manner of proceeding in the act of voting entails determining in which districts voters will vote. The fact that the term "procedure" is preceded by the phrase "qualification or prerequisite to voting," 52 U.S.C. § 10301(a), does not change its meaning. It is hard to imagine many more fundamental "prerequisites" to voting than determining where to cast your ballot or who you are eligible to vote for. Perhaps for that reason, even Alabama does not bear the courage of its conviction on this point. It refuses to argue that § 2 is inapplicable to multimember districting, though its textual arguments apply with equal force in that context.

The dissent, by contrast, goes where even Alabama does not dare, arguing that § 2 is wholly inapplicable to districting because it "focuses on ballot access and counting" only. *Post,* at 2 (opinion of THOMAS, J.). But the statutory text upon which the dissent relies supports the exact opposite conclusion. The relevant section provides that "[t]he terms 'vote' or 'voting' shall include all action necessary to make a vote effective." *Ibid.* (quoting 52 U.S.C. § 10310(c)(1); emphasis added). Those actions "includ[e], but [are] not limited to, . . . action[s] required by law prerequisite to voting, casting a ballot, and having such ballot counted properly and included in the appropriate totals of votes cast." § 10310(c)(1). It would be anomalous to read the broad language of the statute—"all action necessary," "including but not limited to"—to have the crabbed reach that Justice Thomas posits. And we have already discussed why determining where to cast a ballot constitutes a "prerequisite" to voting, as the statute requires.

The dissent also contends that "applying § 2 to districting rests on systematic neglect of . . . the ballot-access focus of the 1960s' voting-rights struggles." *Post*, at 3 (opinion of THOMAS, J.). But history did not stop in 1960. As we have explained, Congress adopted the amended § 2 in response to the 1980 decision *City of Mobile*, a case about districting. And—as the dissent itself acknowledges—"Congress drew § 2(b)'s current operative language" from the 1973 decision *White v. Regester, post*, at 4, n. 3 (opinion of THOMAS, J.), a case that was also about districting (in fact, a case that invalidated two multimember districts in Texas and ordered them redrawn into single-member districts, 412 U.S., at 765). This was not lost on anyone when § 2 was amended. Indeed, it was the precise reason that the contentious debates over proportionality raged—debates that would have made little sense if § 2 covered only poll taxes and the like, as the dissent contends.

We also reject Alabama's argument that § 2 as applied to redistricting is unconstitutional under the Fifteenth Amendment. According to Alabama, that Amendment permits Congress to legislate against only purposeful discrimination by States. See Brief for Alabama 73. But we held over 40 years ago "that, even if § 1 of the [Fifteenth] Amendment prohibits only purposeful discrimination, the prior decisions of this Court foreclose any argument that Congress may not, pursuant to § 2 [of the Fifteenth Amendment] outlaw voting practices that are discriminatory in effect." *City of Rome v. United States*, 446 U.S. 156, 173 (1980). The VRA's "ban on electoral changes that are discriminatory in effect," we emphasized, "is an appropriate method of promoting the purposes of the Fifteenth Amendment." *Id.*, at 177. As *City of Rome* recognized, we had reached the very same conclusion in *South Carolina v. Katzenbach*, a decision issued right after the VRA was first enacted.

Alabama further argues that, even if the Fifteenth Amendment authorizes the effects test of § 2, that Amendment does not authorize race-based redistricting as a remedy for § 2 violations. But for the last four decades, this Court and the lower federal courts have repeatedly applied the effects test of § 2 as interpreted in *Gingles* and, under certain circumstances, have authorized race-based redistricting as a remedy for state districting maps that violate § 2. In light of that precedent, including *City of Rome*, we are not persuaded by Alabama's arguments that § 2 as interpreted in *Gingles* exceeds the remedial authority of Congress.

The concern that § 2 may impermissibly elevate race in the allocation of political power within the States is, of course, not new. *See, e.g., Shaw,* 509 U.S., at 657 ("Racial gerrymandering, even for remedial purposes, may balkanize us into competing racial factions; it threatens to carry us further from the goal of a political system in which race no longer matters."). Our opinion today does not diminish or disregard these concerns. It simply holds that a faithful application of our precedents and a fair reading of the record before us do not bear them out here.

* * *

JUSTICE KAVANAUGH, concurring in all but Part III-B-1.

I agree with the Court that Alabama's redistricting plan violates § 2 of the Voting Rights Act as interpreted in *Thornburg v. Gingles,* 478 U.S. 30 (1986). I write separately to emphasize four points.

First, the upshot of Alabama's argument is that the Court should overrule *Gingles.* But the *stare decisis* standard for this Court to overrule a statutory precedent, as distinct from a constitutional precedent, is comparatively strict. Unlike with constitutional precedents, Congress and the President may enact new legislation to alter statutory precedents such as *Gingles.* In the past 37 years, however, Congress and the President have not disturbed *Gingles,* even as they have made other changes to the Voting Rights Act. Although statutory *stare decisis* is not absolute, "the Court has ordinarily left the updating or correction of erroneous statutory precedents to the legislative process." *Ramos v. Louisiana,* 590 U.S. ___, ___ (2020) (KAVANAUGH, J., concurring in part) (slip op., at 4). * * *

Second, Alabama contends that *Gingles* inevitably requires a proportional number of majority-minority districts, which in turn contravenes the proportionality disclaimer in § 2(b) of the Voting Rights Act. 52 U.S.C. § 10301(b). But Alabama's premise is wrong. As the Court's precedents make clear, *Gingles* does not mandate a proportional number of majority-minority districts. *Gingles* requires the creation of a majority-minority district only when, among other things, (i) a State's redistricting map cracks or packs a large and "geographically compact" minority population and (ii) a plaintiff's proposed alternative map and proposed majority-minority district are "reasonably configured"—namely, by respecting compactness principles and other traditional districting criteria such as county, city, and town lines. * * *

If *Gingles* demanded a proportional number of majority-minority districts, States would be forced to group together geographically dispersed minority voters into unusually shaped districts, without concern for traditional districting criteria such as county, city, and town lines. But *Gingles* and this Court's later decisions have flatly rejected that approach. * * *

Third, Alabama argues that courts should rely on race-blind computer simulations of redistricting maps to assess whether a State's plan abridges the right to vote on account of race. It is true that computer simulations might help detect the presence or absence of intentional discrimination. For example, if all of the computer simulations generated only one majority-minority district, it might be difficult to say that a State had intentionally discriminated on the basis of race by failing to draw a second majority-minority district.

But as this Court has long recognized—and as all Members of this Court today agree—the text of § 2 establishes an effects test, not an intent test. And the effects test, as applied by *Gingles* to redistricting, requires in certain circumstances that courts account for the race of voters so as to prevent the cracking or packing—whether intentional or not—of large and geographically compact minority populations. * * *

Fourth, Alabama asserts that § 2, as construed by *Gingles* to require race-based redistricting in certain circumstances, exceeds Congress's remedial or preventive authority under the Fourteenth and Fifteenth Amendments. As the Court explains, the constitutional argument presented by Alabama is not persuasive in light of the Court's precedents. Justice Thomas notes, however, that even if Congress in 1982 could constitutionally authorize race-based redistricting under § 2 for some period of time, the authority to conduct race-based redistricting cannot extend indefinitely into the future. But Alabama did not raise that temporal argument in this Court, and I therefore would not consider it at this time.

For those reasons, I vote to affirm, and I concur in all but Part III-B-1 of the Court's opinion.

JUSTICE THOMAS, with whom JUSTICE GORSUCH joins, with whom JUSTICE BARRETT joins as to Parts II and III, and with whom JUSTICE ALITO joins as to Parts II-A and II-B, dissenting.

These cases "are yet another installment in the 'disastrous misadventure' of this Court's voting rights jurisprudence." *Alabama Legislative Black Caucus* v. *Alabama*, 575 U.S. 254, 294 (2015) (THOMAS, J., dissenting) (quoting *Holder* v. *Hall*, 512 U.S. 874, 893 (1994) (THOMAS, J., concurring in judgment)). What distinguishes them is the uncommon clarity with which they lay bare the gulf between our "color-blind" Constitution, *Plessy* v. *Ferguson*, 163 U.S. 537, 559 (1896) (HARLAN, J., dissenting), and "the consciously segregated districting system currently being constructed in the name of the Voting Rights Act." *Holder*, 512 U.S., at 907 (opinion of THOMAS, J.). The question presented is whether § 2 of the Act, as amended, requires the State of Alabama to intentionally redraw its longstanding congressional districts so that black voters can control a number of seats roughly proportional to the black share of the State's population. Section 2 demands no such thing, and, if it did, the Constitution would not permit it.

I

At the outset, I would resolve these cases in a way that would not require the Federal Judiciary to decide the correct racial apportionment of Alabama's congressional seats. Under the statutory text, a § 2 challenge must target a "voting qualification or prerequisite to voting or standard, practice, or procedure." 52 U.S.C. § 10301(a). I have long been convinced that those words reach only "enactments that regulate citizens' access to the ballot or the processes for counting a ballot"; they "do not include a State's . . . choice of one districting scheme over another." *Holder*, 512 U.S., at 945 (opinion of THOMAS, J.). "Thus, § 2 cannot provide a basis for invalidating any district." *Abbott v. Perez*, 585 U.S. ___, ___ (2018) (THOMAS, J., concurring) (slip op., at 1). * * *

"Vote" and "voting" are defined terms under the Act, and the Act's definition plainly focuses on ballot access and counting:

"The terms 'vote' or 'voting' shall include all action necessary to make a vote effective in any primary, special, or general election, including, but not limited to, registration, listing pursuant to this chapter, or other action required by law prerequisite to voting, casting a ballot, and having such ballot counted properly and included in the appropriate totals of votes cast with respect to candidates for public or party office and propositions for which votes are received in an election." § 10310(c)(1).

* * *

II

Even if § 2 applies here, however, Alabama should prevail. The District Court found that Alabama's congressional districting map "dilutes" black residents' votes because, while it is *possible* to draw two majority-black districts, Alabama's map only has one. But the critical question in all vote-dilution cases is: "Diluted relative to what benchmark?" *Gonzalez* v. *Aurora*, 535 F.3d 594, 598 (CA7 2008) (Easterbrook, C. J.). Neither the District Court nor the majority has any defensible answer. The text of § 2 and the logic of vote-dilution claims require a meaningfully race-neutral benchmark, and no race-neutral benchmark can justify the District Court's finding of vote dilution in these cases. The only benchmark that can justify it—and the one that the District Court demonstrably applied—is the decidedly nonneutral benchmark of proportional allocation of political power based on race. * * *

D

* * * The majority gives the impression that, in applying [the *Gingles*] framework, the District Court merely followed a set of well-settled, determinate legal principles. But it is widely acknowledged that "*Gingles* and its progeny have engendered considerable disagreement and uncertainty regarding the nature and contours of a vote dilution claim," with commentators "noting the lack of any 'authoritative resolution of the basic questions one would need to answer to make sense of [§ 2's] results test.' " *Merrill* v. *Milligan*, 595 U.S. ___, ___–___ (2022) (Roberts, C.J., dissenting from grant of applications for stays) (slip op., at 1–2) (quoting C. Elmendorf, *Making Sense of Section 2: Of Biased Votes, Unconstitutional Elections, and Common Law Statutes*, 160 U. Pa. L. Rev. 377, 389 (2012)). * * *

The source of this confusion is fundamental: Quite simply, we have never succeeded in translating the *Gingles* framework into an objective and workable method of identifying the undiluted benchmark. The second and third preconditions are all but irrelevant to the task. They essentially collapse into one question: Is voting racially polarized such that minority-preferred candidates consistently lose to majority-preferred ones? See *Gingles*, 478 U.S., at 51. Even if the answer is yes, that tells a court nothing about "how hard it 'should' be for minority voters to elect their preferred candidates under an acceptable system." *Id.*, at 88 (O'Connor, J., concurring in judgment). Perhaps an acceptable system is one in which the minority simply cannot elect its preferred candidates; it is, after all, a minority. Rejecting that outcome as "dilutive" requires a value judgment relative to a benchmark that polarization alone cannot provide. * * *

III

As noted earlier, the Court has long recognized the need to avoid interpretations of § 2 that " 'would unnecessarily infuse race into virtually every redistricting, raising serious constitutional questions.' " *Bartlett*, 556 U.S., at 21 (plurality opinion) (quoting *LULAC [League of United Latin American Citizens v. Perry]*, 548 U.S. [399], at 446 [(2006)] (opinion of KENNEDY, J.)). Today, however, by approving the plaintiffs' racially gerrymandered maps as reasonably configured, refusing to ground § 2 vote-dilution claims in a race-neutral benchmark, and affirming a vote-dilution finding that can only be justified by a benchmark of proportional control, the majority holds, in substance, that race belongs in virtually every redistricting. It thus drives headlong into the very constitutional problems that the Court has long sought to avoid. The result of this collision is unmistakable: If the District Court's application of § 2 was correct as a statutory matter, § 2 is unconstitutional as applied here.

Because the Constitution "restricts consideration of race and the [Voting Rights Act] demands consideration of race," *Abbott*, 585 U.S., at ___ (slip op., at 4), strict scrutiny is implicated wherever, as here, § 2 is applied to require a State to adopt or reject any districting plan on the basis of race. See *Bartlett*, 556 U.S., at 21–22 (plurality opinion). At this point, it is necessary to confront directly one of the more confused notions inhabiting our redistricting jurisprudence. In several cases, we have "assumed" that compliance with § 2 of the Voting Rights Act could be a compelling state interest, before proceeding to *reject* race-predominant plans or districts as insufficiently tailored to that asserted interest. See, *e.g.*, *Wisconsin Legislature*, 595 U.S., at ___ (slip op., at 3); *Cooper* v. *Harris*, 581 U.S. 285, 292 (2017); *Shaw II [Shaw v. Hunt]*, 517 U.S. [899], at 915 [(1996)]; *Miller*, 515 U.S., at 921. But we have never applied this assumption to *uphold* a districting plan that would otherwise violate the Constitution, and the slightest reflection on first principles should make clear why it would be problematic to do so. The Constitution is supreme over statutes, not vice versa. *Marbury* v. *Madison*, 1 Cranch 137, 178 (1803). Therefore, if complying with a federal statute would require a State to engage in unconstitutional racial discrimination, the proper conclusion is not that the statute excuses the State's discrimination, but that the statute is invalid.

If Congress has any power at all to require States to sort voters into congressional districts based on race, that power must flow from its authority to "enforce" the Fourteenth and Fifteenth Amendments "by appropriate legislation." Amdt. 14, § 5; Amdt. 15, § 2. Since Congress in 1982 replaced intent with effects as the criterion of liability, however, "a violation of § 2 is no longer *a fortiori* a violation of" either Amendment. *[Reno v.] Bossier Parish School Bd.*, 520 U.S. [471], at 482 [(1997)]. Thus, § 2 can be justified only under Congress' power to "enact reasonably prophylactic legislation to deter constitutional harm." *Allen* v. *Cooper*, 589 U.S. ___, ___ (2020) (slip op., at 11) (alteration and internal quotation marks omitted). Because Congress' prophylactic- enforcement authority is "remedial, rather than substantive," "[t]here must be a congruence and proportionality between the injury to be prevented or remedied and the means adopted to that end." *Id.*, at 520. Congress' chosen means, moreover, must " 'consist with the letter and spirit of the constitution.' " *Shelby County* v. *Holder*, 570 U.S. 529, 555 (2013) (quoting *McCulloch* v. *Maryland*, 4 Wheat. 316, 421 (1819)); accord, *Miller*, 515 U.S., at 927.

Here, as with everything else in our vote-dilution jurisprudence, the task of sound analysis is encumbered by the lack of clear principles defining § 2 liability in districting. It is awkward to examine the "congruence" and "proportionality" of a statutory rule whose very meaning exists in a perpetual state of uncertainty. The majority makes clear, however, that the primary factual predicate of a vote-dilution claim is "bloc voting along racial lines" that results in majority-preferred candidates defeating minority-preferred ones. *Ante*, at 17; accord, *Gingles*, 478 U.S., at 48 ("The theoretical basis for [vote-dilution claims] is that where minority and majority voters consistently prefer different candidates, the majority, by virtue of its numerical superiority, will regularly defeat the choices of minority voters"). And, as I have shown, the remedial logic with which the District Court's construction of § 2 addresses that "wrong" rests on a proportional-control benchmark limited only by feasibility. Thus, the relevant statutory rule may be approximately stated as follows: If voting is racially polarized in a jurisdiction, and if there exists any more or less reasonably configured districting plan that would enable the minority group to constitute a majority in a number of districts roughly proportional to its share of the population, then the jurisdiction must ensure that its districting plan includes that number of majority-minority districts "or something quite close." 582 F. Supp. 3d, at 1033. Thus construed and applied, § 2 is not congruent and proportional to any provisions of the Reconstruction Amendments.

To determine the congruence and proportionality of a measure, we must begin by "identify[ing] with some precision the scope of the constitutional right at issue." *Board of Trustees of Univ. of Ala.* v. *Garrett*, 531 U.S. 356, 365 (2001). The Reconstruction Amendments "forbi[d], so far as civil and political rights are concerned, discrimination . . . against any citizen because of his race," ensuring that "[a]ll citizens are equal before the law." *Gibson* v. *Mississippi*, 162 U.S. 565, 591 (1896) (HARLAN, J.). They dictate "that the Government must treat citizens as individuals, not as simply components of a racial, religious, sexual or national class." *Miller*, 515 U.S., at 911 (internal quotation marks omitted). These principles are why the Constitution presumptively forbids race-predominant districting, "even for remedial purposes." *Shaw I*, 509 U.S., at 657.

These same principles foreclose a construction of the Amendments that would entitle members of racial minorities, *qua* racial minorities, to have their preferred candidates win elections. Nor do the Amendments limit the rights of members of a racial majority to support *their* preferred candidates—regardless of whether minorities prefer different candidates and of whether "the majority, by virtue of its numerical superiority," regularly prevails. *Gingles*, 478 U.S., at 48. Nor, finally, do the Amendments establish a norm of proportional control of elected offices on the basis of race. See *Parents Involved [in Community Schools v. Seattle School Dist. No. 1]*, 551 U.S. [701], at 730–731 [(2007)] (plurality opinion); *Shaw I*, 509 U.S., at 657. And these notions are not merely *foreign to* the Amendments. Rather, they are *radically inconsistent* with the Amendments' command that government treat citizens as individuals and their "goal of a political system in which race no longer matters." *Ibid.*

* * *

In short, as construed by the District Court, § 2 does not remedy or deter unconstitutional discrimination in districting in any way, shape, or form. On the contrary, it *requires* it, hijacking the districting process to pursue a goal that has no legitimate claim under our constitutional system: the proportional allocation of political power on the basis of race. Such a statute "cannot be considered remedial, preventive legislation," and the race-based redistricting it would command cannot be upheld under the Constitution. *City of Boerne [v. Flores]*, 521 U.S. [507], at 532 [(1997)].

[Justice Alito's dissenting opinion has been omitted.]

NOTES & QUESTIONS

1. What does the *Gingles* test require a plaintiff to prove in order to establish a violation of Section 2? Why did the Court adopt this test? Is this an appropriate interpretation of the statute?

2. How is the approach suggested by Justice Thomas's dissenting opinion different? Note that both the majority and dissenting opinions are trying to square Section 2's focus on results (rather than intent) with its statement that proportional representation is not required. Is Justice Thomas right that the *Gingles* test in fact amounts to a requirement of proportional representation based on race? What is the majority's response to that accusation?

3. The 1982 amendments to the VRA, as construed in *Gingles*, had an enormous impact on the composition of legislative bodies. The number of African Americans and Latinos serving in Congress and state legislative bodies increased dramatically. The *Gingles* standard was ultimately applied in cases challenging at-large elections and single-member redistricting plans, as well as multi-member districts. Do these results vindicate the approach taken in *Gingles*?

4. Do you agree with Justice Thomas that Section 2 should not apply to the redistricting of single-member districts? Is his view of Section 2 consistent with the language of the statute? What exactly is meant by the individual terms in the phrase "standard, practice, or procedure" in subsection (a)? Can a districting system such as a multi-member district be thought of as a voting "standard, practice, or procedure"? Note too that subsection (b) says that a violation is established if "it is shown that the *political processes* leading to nomination or election . . . are not equally open" (emphasis added)? Can a type of districting system be viewed as part of the "political processes"?

Even if you disagree with Justice Thomas on the question of how to interpret the Voting Rights Act, think about the principles he is articulating. They will return in the next section on racial gerrymandering.

B.   Racial Gerrymandering*

As just described, the Voting Rights Act (VRA) does sometimes require the consideration of race in redistricting. However, the Supreme Court has also interpreted the U.S. Constitution to constrain when and how much race can be a consideration in the redistricting process. The principal case is *Shaw v. Reno*, 509 U.S. 630 (1993), which held that districts drawn primarily on the basis of race violate the Equal Protection Clause of the Fourteenth Amendment. The Court concluded that "[r]acial gerrymandering, even for a remedial purpose, may balkanize us into competing racial factions," something the Court majority viewed as antithetical to a race-neutral political process that it believed should be the end goal of remedial legislation. *Id.* at 657. In every subsequent redistricting cycle, the *Shaw* decision has created conflict with the VRA over the role that race should play in the redistricting process.

> The term "gerrymander" refers **FYI** to the practice of drawing electoral districts or other boundaries so as to advantage one group while disadvantaging another. It often has negative connotations and usually (but not always) implies an intentional attempt to avoid drawing boundaries that would more accurately reflect the democratic will. The term originated in the early nineteenth century when then-Massachusetts Governor (and later Vice-President of the United States) Elbridge **Gerry** signed into law a bill that created a partisan district that was said to resemble a sala**mander**.

1.   Background

With the end of Reconstruction and the emergence of Jim Crow discrimination in the late 1800s, Black voters quickly became scarce in the South. Through the Great Migration (the internal migration of Black Americans from the South to Northern and Western states), Black voters were occasionally able to establish political footholds in various Northern and Western cities. In New York, for example, local Black politicians in the Harlem section of Manhattan successfully lobbied for a majority Black congressional district in the early 1940s. This district in turn elected Adam Clayton Powell, a Black preacher with the nickname "Mr. Civil Rights" thanks to his national advocacy for civil rights. But it took the Voting Rights Act of 1965 to begin to restore Black voting rights nationwide.

The VRA led to a dramatic increase in minority politicians being elected to state and federal office. In 1964, for example, Mississippi had single-digit Black voter registration, but by the end of the decade it not only had approximately 66% Black

---

*   The material in this section is drawn from DANIEL P. TOKAJI, ELECTION LAW IN A NUTSHELL (2d ed. 2017), and Daniel Tokaji, *Restricting Race-Conscious Redistricting*, *Regulatory Review* (July 31, 2017), https://www.theregreview.org/2017/07/31/tokaji-restricting-race-conscious-redistricting/.

voter registration, but also had a few Black members of the state legislature for the first time since the late 1800s. The VRA also had ameliorative effects on the redistricting process, including in non-Southern states like Ohio, which saw the creation of majority-minority districts in the late 1960s. This early wave of new minority politicians led to the creation of groups like the Congressional Black Caucus and Congressional Hispanic Caucus.

Activists, politicians, and Civil Rights groups suffered a setback in the 1980 redistricting cycle in the form of the Court's decision in *City of Mobile*, but the ensuing 1982 VRA amendment gave them new life in the 1990 cycle. Their efforts were bolstered by career lawyers in the Department of Justice who wanted to enforce the VRA to its fullest effect. The administration of President George H.W. Bush also actively pushed for the creation of new majority-minority districts for more self-interested political reasons: If reliably Democratic Black voters in the South could be concentrated in a few districts, that would allow Republicans a better chance at capturing the remaining districts in the region. This was especially true in North Carolina, the state at the heart of the case that follows.

2. *Shaw v. Reno (Shaw I)*

Plaintiffs in *Shaw v. Reno,* 509 U.S. 630 (1993) (*Shaw I*) challenged two majority-Black congressional districts in North Carolina, a state that had not elected a single African American to Congress between 1900 and 1990, even though the state's population was approximately 20% Black. Both districts had a rather odd shape under the 1991 redistricting plan. One of the congressional districts (CD 1) was described as looking like a "bug splattered on a windshield," the other (CD 12) as "snake-like," winding along a major highway, I-85, from one part of the state to another "until it gobble[d] in enough enclaves of black neighborhoods" to create a Black majority.

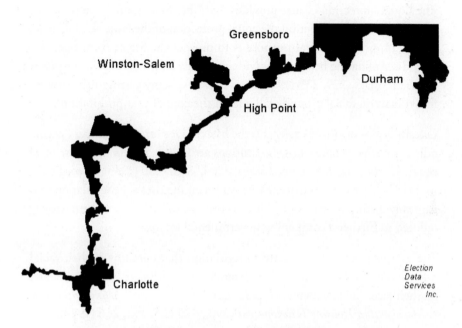

North Carolina's 12th Congressional District (1992)

In truth, the unusual shape of these districts was the consequence of two factors: first, North Carolina's attempt, as a condition of VRA preclearance, to satisfy the Department of Justice's demand for two Black-majority districts in the state; and second, the desire of the state legislature's Democratic majority to protect the seats of *white* Democrats in Congress.

The *Shaw* plaintiffs, who were white, challenged these two districts on the ground that they violated the Equal Protection Clause by excessively relying on race. Justice O'Connor's opinion for the majority in *Shaw I* allowed these claims to proceed, reversing the lower court's order dismissing them. This was, the Court recognized, a new kind of equal protection claim, analytically distinct from ones recognized before:

Recall again that neither the Voting Rights Act nor the relevant provisions of the Constitution (the Fourteenth and Fifteenth Amendments) make any specific reference to "minorities" or "Blacks." Thought of through the lens of representation, what exactly are the white plaintiffs claiming? Is the claim that being in a district that is very likely to elect a Black representative discriminates against them as whites?

The Equal Protection Clause provides that "[n]o State shall . . . deny to any person within its jurisdiction the equal protection of the laws." U.S. Const., Amdt. 14, § 1. Its central purpose is to prevent the States from purposefully discriminating between individuals on the basis of race. *Washington v. Davis,* 426 U.S. 229, 239 (1976). Laws that explicitly distinguish between individuals on racial grounds fall within the core of that prohibition. * * *

Classifications of citizens solely on the basis of race "are by their very nature odious to a free people whose institutions are founded upon the doctrine of equality." *Hirabayashi v. United States,* 320 U.S. 81, 100 (1943). Accordingly, we have held that the Fourteenth Amendment requires state legislation that expressly distinguishes among citizens because of their race to be narrowly tailored to further a compelling governmental interest.

These principles apply not only to legislation that contains explicit racial distinctions, but also to those "rare" statutes that, although race neutral, are, on their face, "unexplainable on grounds other than race." *Arlington Heights v. Metropolitan Housing Development Corp.,* 429 U.S. 252, 266 (1977). * * *

[W]e believe that reapportionment is one area in which appearances do matter. A reapportionment plan that includes in one district individuals who belong to the same race, but who are otherwise widely separated by geographical and political boundaries, and who may have little in common with one another but the color of their skin, bears an uncomfortable resemblance to political apartheid. It reinforces the perception that members of the same racial group—regardless of their age, education, economic status, or the community in which they live—think alike, share the same political interests, and will prefer the same candidates at the polls. We have rejected such perceptions elsewhere as impermissible racial stereotypes. By perpetuating such notions, a racial gerrymander may exacerbate the very patterns of racial bloc voting that majority-minority districting is sometimes said to counteract.

? Note that, in this passage, the Court is directly tying its reasoning to the nature of representation. What exactly is the point here? Is the claim that a Black representative elected from a racially gerrymandered district will be less responsive to the concerns of non-Black constituents? Can this idea be squared with the rationale underlying *Gingles'* interpretation of the Voting Rights Act, that, when voting is in fact racially polarized, a failure to give racial minorities representatives of their choice amounts to a dilution of the minorities' vote?

> The message that such districting sends to elected representatives is equally pernicious. When a district obviously is created solely to effectuate the perceived common interests of one racial group, elected officials are more likely to believe that their primary obligation is to represent only the members of that group, rather than their constituency as a whole. * * *
>
> For these reasons, we conclude that a plaintiff challenging a reapportionment statute under the Equal Protection Clause may state a claim by alleging that the legislation, though race-neutral on its face, rationally cannot be understood as anything other than an effort to separate voters into different districts on the basis of race, and that the separation lacks sufficient justification.

Shaw I, 509 U.S. at 642, 647–49. Justices White, Blackmun, Stevens, and Souter dissented.

3. Post-*Shaw I* Cases

Shaw I held that the use of race in drawing districts sometimes triggers judicial review according to the Court's standard of "strict scrutiny." But *Shaw I* left open two significant questions about when race may and may not be considered in drawing district lines. The first question is when strict scrutiny applies. The second was what could justify the use of race in those cases in which strict scrutiny applied.

The Court provided guidance on these questions in subsequent cases arising from the post-1990 redistricting cycle. On the first question, the Court clarified in *Miller v. Johnson,* 515 U.S. 900 (1995), that strict scrutiny applies when race is the *predominant factor* in drawing district lines. *Miller* arose from Georgia's post-1990 congressional redistricting. The district challenged in *Miller* was not as oddly shaped as the ones in *Shaw,* but the Court nevertheless held that it was subject to strict scrutiny. Again, the vote was 5–4. The Court later applied this standard in *Shaw v. Hunt,* 517 U.S. 899 (1996) (*Shaw II*), to hold that North Carolina's 12th congressional district was subject to strict scrutiny and to strike down that district by another 5–4 vote.

> **FYI**
>
> "Strict scrutiny" is a term used in constitutional litigation when someone is challenging the constitutionality of government action (including legislation). It is the most demanding degree of judicial review of government action, requiring that the government show both that it has a "compelling interest" for its action and that the action is "narrowly tailored" or "the least restrictive" alternative for furthering its compelling interest, i.e., that it cannot further this government interest with some alternative that would encroach less on a protected right.

On the second question, the Court clarified what must be shown to satisfy strict scrutiny in two cases decided in 1996. In *Bush v. Vera*, 517 U.S. 952 (1996), the Court struck down three Texas congressional districts by another 5–4 vote, without a majority opinion. Justice O'Connor's lead opinion (joined by only two other justices) assumed that compliance with the VRA could be a compelling interest, but concluded that the districts were not narrowly tailored to serve this interest. In addition, Justice O'Connor took the unusual step of writing a separate concurring opinion, speaking only for herself. That opinion took the position that compliance with Section 2 of the VRA *is* a compelling interest. Combined with the four dissenting justices, that made a majority for the proposition that compliance with the VRA can be a compelling interest. But Chief Justice Rehnquist's opinion for the majority in *Shaw II* clarified that merely avoiding VRA litigation is *not* a sufficient justification. The state must have a "strong basis in evidence" for believing it is violating the VRA, not just reason to believe it will be sued.

The final and perhaps most important case in the *Shaw* line is *Easley v. Cromartie*, 532 U.S. 234 (2001). That case also concerned North Carolina's 12th congressional district, as redrawn in 1997, after the decision in *Shaw II*. The district court had initially granted summary judgment for plaintiffs, concluding that the new 12th district—which now had less than a majority (47%) of African Americans—violated the *Shaw* doctrine. The Court unanimously remanded and ordered the district court to hold a trial on the reasons for drawing the districts. After a trial, the district court again held the new district unconstitutional. And again, the Supreme Court reversed. This time, Justice O'Connor—who wrote *Shaw I* and was part of the majority in all the subsequent cases noted above—switched sides, joining Justice Breyer's majority opinion in *Easley* (along with Justices Stevens, Souter, and Ginsburg).

? How difficult do you think it is for plaintiffs to show that race, rather than politics, is the predominant reason for a districting decision?

The *Easley* majority concluded that *politics*, not race, was the predominant factor in drawing the challenged district. While race was a consideration, the Court rejected the district court's conclusion that race was predominant. That conclusion was based upon the district's shape, its splitting of political subdivisions, and its high percentage of African Americans. The *Easley* majority found this evidence insufficient to prove that race was the predominant factor, given other evidence showing that political considerations played a role in the district's boundaries.

Whether because of *Easley* or because of the Justice Department's less vigorous enforcement of the VRA, *Shaw* litigation dramatically declined in the post-2000 redistricting cycle. None of these claims were successful at the statewide level. *See* Jocelyn Benson, *A Shared Existence: The Current Compatibility of the Equal Protection Clause and Section 5 of the Voting Rights Act,* 88 NEB. L. REV. 124 (2009).

4.   Issues from the 2010 and 2020 Redistricting Cycles

A tension remains between the VRA—which sometimes requires race to be considered in drawing district lines—and the *Shaw* doctrine, which limits consideration of race in drawing district lines. Taken together, the VRA and *Shaw* cases impose a "Goldilocks" obligation on those responsible for drawing district lines, requiring them to engage in some—but not too much—consideration of race. After the 2010 redistricting cycle, the Supreme Court reinvigorated the *Shaw* racial gerrymandering doctrine, applying it in several cases involving Republican-drawn plans that packed Democratic-leaning racial minorities together into fewer districts.

Bethune-Hill v. Virginia State Board of Elections, 580 U.S. 178 (2017), is notable because it was the first time that the Court, applying strict scrutiny under the *Shaw* doctrine, had upheld a district drawn predominantly on the basis of race. Though race was the predominant factor, the Court concluded that its use was narrowly tailored to meet the state's asserted interest of complying with the Voting Rights Act, which the Court assumed without deciding was a compelling interest. The Court vacated and remanded the lower court's decision that eleven other districts were not drawn primarily on the basis of race.

Cooper v. Harris, 581 U.S. 285 (2017), involved a constitutional challenge to North Carolina's 1st and 12th congressional districts—the same districts that were at issue in the original racial gerrymandering decision, *Shaw v. Reno*. Again, the central claim was that Republicans had packed Black residents into these two districts without a sufficient justification under the Voting Rights Act. In the 5–3 decision excerpted below, the Court held that both districts violated the *Shaw* doctrine.

Cooper v. Harris
581 U.S. 285 (2017)

JUSTICE KAGAN **delivered the opinion of the Court.**

The Constitution entrusts States with the job of designing congressional districts. But it also imposes an important constraint: A State may not use race as the predominant factor in drawing district lines unless it has a compelling reason. In this case, a three-judge District Court ruled that North

Carolina officials violated that bar when they created two districts whose voting-age populations were majority black. Applying a deferential standard of review to the factual findings underlying that decision, we affirm.

I

A

The Equal Protection Clause of the Fourteenth Amendment limits racial gerrymanders in legislative districting plans. It prevents a State, in the absence of "sufficient justification," from "separating its citizens into different voting districts on the basis of race." *Bethune-Hill v. Virginia State Bd. of Elections*, 580 U.S. ___, ___, 137 S.Ct. 788, 797, 197 L.Ed.2d 85 (2017) (internal quotation marks and alteration omitted). When a voter sues state officials for drawing such race-based lines, our decisions call for a two-step analysis.

First, the plaintiff must prove that "race was the predominant factor motivating the legislature's decision to place a significant number of voters within or without a particular district." *Miller v. Johnson*, 515 U.S. 900, 916 (1995). * * * The plaintiff may make the required showing through "direct evidence" of legislative intent, "circumstantial evidence of a district's shape and demographics," or a mix of both. *Ibid.*

Second, if racial considerations predominated over others, the design of the district must withstand strict scrutiny. The burden thus shifts to the State to prove that its race-based sorting of voters serves a "compelling interest" and is "narrowly tailored" to that end. *Ibid.* This Court has long assumed that one compelling interest is complying with operative provisions of the Voting Rights Act of 1965 (VRA or Act), 79 Stat. 437, as amended, 52 U.S.C. § 10301 *et seq.* * * *

When a State invokes the VRA to justify race-based districting, it must show (to meet the "narrow tailoring" requirement) that it had "a strong basis in evidence" for concluding that the statute required its action. *Alabama Legislative Black Caucus v. Alabama*, 575 U.S. ___, ___, 135 S.Ct. 1257, 1274, 191 L.Ed.2d 314 (2015). Or said otherwise, the State must establish that it had "good reasons" to think that it would transgress the Act if it did not draw race-based district lines. *Ibid.* That "strong basis" (or "good reasons") standard gives States "breathing room" to adopt reasonable compliance measures that may prove, in perfect hindsight, not to have been needed. *Bethune-Hill*, 580 U.S. at ___, 137 S.Ct. at 802.

B

This case concerns North Carolina's most recent redrawing of two congressional districts, both of which have long included substantial populations of black voters. In its current incarnation, District 1 is anchored in the northeastern part of the State, with appendages stretching both south and west (the latter into Durham). District 12 begins in the south-central part of the State (where it takes in a large part of Charlotte) and then travels northeast, zig-zagging much of the way to the State's northern border. * * *

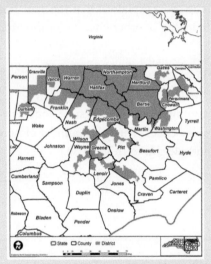

Congressional District 1 (Enacted 2011)   Congressional District 12 (Enacted 2011)

The [2011] map (among other things) significantly altered both District 1 and District 12. The 2010 census had revealed District 1 to be substantially underpopulated: To comply with the Constitution's one-person-one-vote principle, the State needed to place almost 100,000 new people within the district's boundaries. [The mapmakers] chose to take most of those people from heavily black areas of Durham, requiring a finger-like extension of the district's western line. With that addition, District 1's [Black voting-age population or BVAP] rose from 48.6% to 52.7%. District 12, for its part, had no need for significant total-population changes: It was overpopulated by fewer than 3,000 people out of over 730,000. Still, [the mapmakers] decided to reconfigure the district, further narrowing its already snakelike body while adding areas at either end—most relevantly here, in Guilford County. Those changes appreciably shifted the racial composition of District 12: As the district gained some 35,000 African-Americans of voting age and lost some 50,000 whites of that age, its BVAP increased from 43.8% to 50.7%.

Registered voters in the two districts (David Harris and Christine Bowser) * * * brought this suit against North Carolina officials (collectively, "the State" or "North Carolina"), complaining of impermissible racial gerrymanders. After a bench trial, a three-judge District Court held both districts unconstitutional. All the judges agreed that racial considerations predominated in the design of District 1. And in then applying strict scrutiny, all rejected the State's argument that it had a "strong basis" for thinking that the VRA compelled such a race-based drawing of District 1's lines. As for District 12, a majority of the panel held that "race predominated" over all other factors, including partisanship. And the court explained that the State had failed to put forward any reason, compelling or otherwise, for its attention to race in designing that district. * * *

II

[Part II of the opinion rejected the argument that a prior state-court lawsuit should have claim or issue preclusive effect. This is a reminder of how important civil procedure is, but is not relevant to this course.]

DIY
Predicting the Outcome of a Racial Gerrymandering Case

Before reading how the Court handled the merits of this case, take a minute to make a prediction about the disposition. Then continue reading the rest of the Court's opinion.

III

With that out of the way, we turn to the merits of this case, beginning (appropriately enough) with District 1. As noted above, the court below found that race furnished the predominant rationale for that district's redesign. And it held that the State's interest in complying with the VRA could not justify that consideration of race. We uphold both conclusions.

A

Uncontested evidence in the record shows that the State's mapmakers, in considering District 1, purposefully established a racial target: African-Americans should make up no less than a majority of the voting-age population. [The Court summarized the evidence.]

Faced with this body of evidence—showing an announced racial target that subordinated other districting criteria and produced boundaries amplifying divisions between blacks and whites—the District Court did not clearly err in finding that race predominated in drawing District 1. Indeed, as all three judges recognized, the court could hardly have concluded anything but.

B

The more substantial question is whether District 1 can survive the strict scrutiny applied to racial gerrymanders. As noted earlier, we have long assumed that complying with the VRA is a compelling interest. And we have held that race-based districting is narrowly tailored to that objective if a State had "good reasons" for thinking that the Act demanded such steps. * * *

This Court identified, in *Thornburg v. Gingles*, three threshold conditions for proving vote dilution under § 2 of the VRA. First, a "minority group" must be "sufficiently large and geographically compact to constitute a majority" in some reasonably configured legislative district. Second, the minority group must be "politically cohesive." And third, a district's white majority must "vote [ ] sufficiently as a bloc" to usually "defeat the minority's preferred candidate." Those three showings, we have explained, are needed to establish that "the minority [group] has the potential to elect a representative of its own choice" in a possible district, but that racially polarized voting prevents it from doing so in the district as actually drawn because it is "submerg[ed] in a larger white voting population." *Growe v. Emison*, 507 U.S. 25, 40 (1993). If a State has good reason to think that all the *"Gingles* preconditions" are met, then so too it has good reason to believe that § 2 requires drawing a majority-minority district. See *Bush v. Vera*, 517 U.S. 952, 978 (1996) (plurality opinion). But if not, then not.

Here, electoral history provided no evidence that a § 2 plaintiff could demonstrate the third *Gingles* prerequisite—effective white bloc-voting. For most of the twenty years prior to the new plan's adoption, African-Americans had made up less than a majority of District 1's voters; the district's BVAP usually hovered between 46% and 48%. Yet throughout those two decades, as the District Court noted, District 1 was "an extraordinarily safe district for African-American preferred candidates." In the closest election during that period, African-Americans' candidate of choice received 59% of the total vote; in other years, the share of the vote garnered by those candidates rose to as much as 70%. Those victories (indeed, landslides) occurred because the district's white population did not "vote [ ] sufficiently as a bloc" to thwart black voters' preference, *Gingles*, 478 U.S., at 51; rather, a meaningful number of white voters joined a politically cohesive black community to elect that group's favored candidate. In the lingo of voting law, District 1 functioned, election year in and election year out, as a "crossover" district, in which members of the majority help a "large enough" minority to elect its candidate of choice. *Bartlett v. Strickland*, 556 U.S. 1, 13 (2009) (plurality opinion).* * *

To have a strong basis in evidence to conclude that § 2 demands such race-based steps, the State must carefully evaluate whether a plaintiff could establish the *Gingles* preconditions—including effective white bloc-voting—in a new district created without those measures. We see nothing in the legislative record that fits that description. * * *

In sum: Although States enjoy leeway to take race-based actions reasonably judged necessary under a proper interpretation of the VRA, that latitude cannot rescue District 1. We by no means "insist that a state legislature, when redistricting, determine *precisely* what percent minority population [§ 2 of the VRA] demands." But neither will we approve a racial gerrymander whose necessity is supported by no evidence and whose *raison d'être* is a legal mistake. Accordingly, we uphold the District Court's conclusion that North Carolina's use of race as the predominant factor in designing District 1 does not withstand strict scrutiny.

IV

We now look west to District 12, making its fifth(!) appearance before this Court. This time, the district's legality turns, and turns solely, on which of two possible reasons predominantly explains its most recent reconfiguration. * * *

[W]e review a district court's finding as to racial predominance only for clear error, except when the court made a legal mistake. Under that standard of review, we affirm the court's finding so long as it is "plausible"; we reverse only when "left with the definite and firm conviction that a mistake has been committed." *Anderson [v. City of Besemmer City]*, 470 U.S. [564], at 573, 574 [(1985)]. * * *

In light of those principles, we uphold the District Court's finding of racial predominance respecting District 12. The evidence offered at trial, including live witness testimony subject to credibility determinations, adequately supports the conclusion that race, not politics, accounted for the district's reconfiguration. And no error of law infected that judgment: Contrary to North Carolina's view, the District Court had no call to dismiss this challenge just because the plaintiffs did not proffer an alternative design for District 12 as circumstantial evidence of the legislature's intent.

A

Begin with some facts and figures, showing how the redistricting of District 12 affected its racial composition. As explained above, District 12 (unlike District 1) was approximately the right size as it was: North Carolina did not—indeed, could not—much change its total population. But by further slimming the district and adding a couple of knobs to its snakelike body (including in Guilford County), the General Assembly incorporated tens of thousands of new voters and pushed out tens of thousands of old ones. And those changes followed racial lines: To be specific, the new District 12 had 35,000 more African-Americans of voting age and 50,000 fewer whites of that age. (The difference was made up of voters from other racial categories.) Those voter exchanges produced a sizable jump in the district's BVAP, from 43.8% to 50.7%. The Assembly thus turned District 12 (as it did District 1) into a majority-minority district. * * *

[The Court summarized the evidence showing that mapmakers attempted to keep the BVAP above 50%, purportedly to comply with the VRA.]

Perhaps the most dramatic testimony in the trial came when Congressman Mel Watt (who had represented District 12 for some 20 years) recounted a conversation he had with Rucho [one of the mapmakers] in 2011 about the district's future make-up. According to Watt, Rucho said that "his leadership had told him that he had to ramp the minority percentage in [District 12] up to over 50 percent to comply with the Voting Rights Law." * * * The District Court credited Watt's testimony about the conversation, citing his courtroom demeanor and "consistent recollection" under "probing cross-examination." In the court's view, Watt's account was of a piece with all the other evidence—including the redistricters' on-the-nose attainment of a 50% BVAP—indicating that the General Assembly, in the name of

VRA compliance, deliberately redrew District 12 as a majority-minority district. * * *

The District Court's assessment that all this evidence proved racial predominance clears the bar of clear error review. The court emphasized that the districting plan's own architects had repeatedly described the influx of African-Americans into District 12 as a § 5 compliance measure, not a side-effect of political gerrymandering. * * * No doubt other interpretations of that evidence were permissible. Maybe we would have evaluated the testimony differently had we presided over the trial; or then again, maybe we would not have. Either way—and it is only this which matters—we are far from having a "definite and firm conviction" that the District Court made a mistake in concluding from the record before it that racial considerations predominated in District 12's design.

B

The State mounts a final, legal rather than factual, attack on the District Court's finding of racial predominance. When race and politics are competing explanations of a district's lines, argues North Carolina, the party challenging the district must introduce a particular kind of circumstantial evidence: "an alternative [map] that achieves the legislature's political objectives while improving racial balance." * * *

We have no doubt that an alternative districting plan, of the kind North Carolina describes, can serve as key evidence in a race-versus-politics dispute. One, often highly persuasive way to disprove a State's contention that politics drove a district's lines is to show that the legislature had the capacity to accomplish all its partisan goals without moving so many members of a minority group into the district. * * *

But they are hardly the *only* means. Suppose that the plaintiff in a dispute like this one introduced scores of leaked emails from state officials instructing their mapmaker to pack as many black voters as possible into a district, or telling him to make sure its BVAP hit 75%. Based on such evidence, a court could find that racial rather than political factors predominated in a district's design, with or without an alternative map. And so too in cases lacking that kind of smoking gun, as long as the evidence offered satisfies the plaintiff's burden of proof. * * *

A plaintiff's task, in other words, is simply to persuade the trial court—without any special evidentiary prerequisite—that race (not politics) was the "predominant consideration in deciding to place a significant number of voters within or without a particular district." *Alabama*, 575 U.S., at ___, 135 S.Ct., at 1265 (internal quotation marks omitted). * * * An alternative map is merely an evidentiary tool to show that such a substantive violation has occurred; neither its presence nor its absence can itself resolve a racial gerrymandering claim. * * *

* * * This case turned not on the possibility of creating more optimally constructed districts, but on direct evidence of the General Assembly's intent in creating the actual District 12, including many hours of trial testimony subject to credibility determinations. That evidence, the District Court plausibly found, itself satisfied the plaintiffs' burden of debunking North Carolina's "it was really politics" defense; there was no need for an alternative map to do the same job. * * *

V

Applying a clear error standard, we uphold the District Court's conclusions that racial considerations predominated in designing both District 1 and District 12. For District 12, that is all we must do, because North Carolina has made no attempt to justify race-based districting there. For District 1, we further uphold the District Court's decision that § 2 of the VRA gave North Carolina no good reason to reshuffle voters because of their race. We accordingly affirm the judgment of the District Court.

It is so ordered.

[JUSTICE THOMAS joined the majority opinion but wrote a brief concurring opinion, agreeing that race was the predominant factor in creating both districts and asserting that compliance with Section 2 of the VRA cannot justify the use of race in drawing districts, a position consistent with his *Allen v. Milligan* dissent excerpted in Section A above.

JUSTICE ALITO wrote a dissenting opinion, which CHIEF JUSTICE ROBERTS and JUSTICE KENNEDY joined. The dissenters disagreed only with the majority's conclusion on District 12, not District 1. They thought that plaintiffs had failed to show that race was the predominant factor in drawing District 12, given the plaintiffs' failure to come forward with an alternative map that did not have the same racial effects.

JUSTICE GORSUCH took no part in the decision of the case]

NOTES & QUESTIONS

1. In what circumstances does the consideration of race in drawing legislative district lines require strict scrutiny under the Equal Protection Clause? What interests may justify the consideration of race in drawing a district?

2. Note that the districts challenged in *Cooper v. Harris* were oddly shaped, like those challenged in *Shaw*. Should the shape of the district matter in determining whether there has been an unconstitutional racial gerrymander? Go back and look at some of the traditional criteria for districting discussed in Chapter 5, Section B above (pp. 98–100).

3. Should the Equal Protection Clause be understood to require mapmakers to be completely "race-blind" in drawing district lines? Why or why not?

4. Why do you think the North Carolina legislature decided to draw Districts 1 and 12 in the way they did? Was race—in particular, compliance with the VRA—the only reason, or were there other considerations? Does it matter that Blacks in North Carolina overwhelmingly support Democratic candidates over Republican candidates irrespective of race? Bear in mind that the legislature was controlled by the Republican Party at the time.

5. Finally, as already discussed above in section A, in 2023 the Supreme Court heard *Allen v. Milligan*, a case that threatened to eviscerate the *Gingles* test for applying the Voting Rights Act to redistricting processes. Yet in the end, a 5–4 majority in *Milligan* reaffirmed the *Gingles* test as a settled matter of statutory *stare decisis*. Thus, the tension between the VRA and the *Shaw* doctrine persists.

What does all this racial gerrymandering jurisprudence mean, and how can you keep it straight? To the extent it is helpful, we include below a table summarizing the key cases, followed by a schematic flowchart for thinking about the viability of a claim.

Chronological Summary of Key Racial Gerrymandering Cases

Case	Factual Context	Holding	Effect
Shaw v. Reno (1993) **Shaw I**	NC Districts 1 & 12—white plaintiffs challenged districts as violation of Equal Protection Clause for excessively relying on race	- cannot rely on race unless State can prove **'sufficient justification'** **(strict scrutiny rule)**	Creation of standard for determining when racial gerrymandering violates the Equal Protection Clause
Miller v Johnson (1995)	GA's post-1990 congressional districting	- strict scrutiny applies when race is the **predominant factor** in drawing districts	Clarification of when the EPC standard of strict scrutiny applies
Bush v. Vera (1996)	TX's post-1990 congressional redistricting	- compliance with VRA could be a **compelling interest** (and so pass strict scrutiny)	Identification of how a state might satisfy strict scrutiny
Shaw v. Hunt (1996) **Shaw II**	NC's 12th district	- because race was a predominant factor, strict scrutiny applies - just avoiding VRA litigation is *not* sufficient justification - must show **'strong basis in evidence'** for believing that VRA would otherwise be violated	Clarification of when and how the strict scrutiny standard applies
Easley v. Cromartie (2001)	NC's 12th District	- because politics, not race, was the predominant factor (race was a factor but not predominant), no violation of EPC	Decline in VRA litigation

Case	Factual Context	Holding	Effect
Bethune-Hill v. VA State Board of Elections (2017)	Challenge to 12 VA districts	- race was a predominant factor in one district - one district passed strict scrutiny: **'narrowly tailored to comply with VRA'**	
Cooper v. Harris (2017)	NC Districts 1 & 12	- race was a predominant factor - NC did not pass strict scrutiny - NC claimed VRA interest for District 1 but failed the *Gingles* test as whites were not voting as a racial bloc (crossover votes)	Use of the *Gingles* test to determine whether "majority minority district" was actually required to comply with the VRA
Allen v. Milligan (2023)	AL's number of majority-minority districts	- Alabama's post-2020 redistricting violated VRA by not creating adequate majority-minority districts	*Gingles* test reaffirmed by current Supreme Court

**Flowchart of an EPC Claim alleging a state has drawn legislative
districts unconstitutionally on the basis of race**

Is race a 'predominant factor' (*Miller*)?

If no (race may be a factor, but not predominant, *Easley*), then no claim.

If yes, can the reliance on race pass strict scrutiny?

Does the government allege a "compelling interest' to use race (*Shaw I*)?

If no, then plaintiffs prevail.

If yes, is the government's alleged compelling interest compliance with the VRA
(*Bush*)?

If yes, can government demonstrate district was 'narrowly tailored' (which
requires that there be a 'strong basis in evidence' for believing a VRA violation is
likely (*Shaw II*))?

To prove 'strong basis in evidence,' would the previous district lines
likely pass the *Gingles* Test? (*Cooper*)

If the previous district lines likely fail the *Gingles* Test, redistricting unjustified
for a VRA Claim, and state loses.

If the previous district lines likely pass the *Gingles* Test, redistricting may be
justified to comply with VRA.

Test Your Understanding

To assess your understanding of the material in this chapter, <u>click here</u> to take a quiz.

7

Partisan Gerrymandering

Key Concepts

- Partisan gerrymandering
- Justiciability
- Political questions
- Equal Protection
- Representational fairness

Chapter Summary

Politicians have long engaged in self-interested calculations when drawing legislative districts, including the gerrymandering of district lines to gain partisan advantage. For decades, federal courts wrestled with whether they had the ability to identify and prohibit certain forms of partisan gerrymandering. A number of standards were proposed over the years, but none gained majority support on the Supreme Court. In the 2019 case of *Rucho v. Common Cause*, the Court majority held that claims of partisan gerrymandering presented nonjusticiable political questions.

One of the oldest features of American politics in many states is that the state legislature draws state legislative and Congressional districts after each decennial census. Although an increasing number of states have created independent redistricting commissions for this task, typically the state legislature passes a map through a bill or a joint resolution, and then the governor signs off on the map. Since the early days of the Republic, however, politicians have used their line-drawing authority to

FYI

A "partisan" gerrymander should be distinguished from other forms of gerrymanders, such as a racial gerrymander (which deliberately uses race to draw political districts), or an incumbent protection gerrymander (which draws district lines to protect the re-election prospects of one or more incumbent office holders).

draw districts that favor themselves and their allies, usually their co-partisans. This process is usually called *partisan gerrymandering*, and often maligned—truthfully—as a process that lets representatives choose their voters, rather than vice-versa.

Today, these gerrymanders occur when politicians, using detailed voting data from recent elections, identify where Democratic and Republican voters live and then either "pack" their opponents' supporters into one district or "crack" them among multiple districts. The first process sacrifices a few districts to the disfavored party in order to ensure that the favored party can dominate the other districts. The second process splits a cluster of voters affiliated with the disfavored party into multiple districts so that the favored party can dilute the power of this cluster of voters to prevent the election of politicians from the disfavored party. Either way, the goal of this process is to limit the power that voters from one political party wield in the political process. These gerrymandered districts otherwise comply with the requirements of equal population and other constitutional and statutory demands.

On many occasions, advocates have tried to argue that the Constitution's Equal Protection Clause forbids partisan gerrymandering, at least when done to excess. Versions of this argument reached the Supreme Court in cases like *Davis v. Bandemer*, 478 U.S. 109 (1986), and *Vieth v. Jubelirer*, 541 U.S. 267 (2004). Neither case, however, produced a majority opinion, and lower courts had no standard to apply, so partisan gerrymandering continued. In 2019, the Supreme Court issued a definitive decision in *Rucho v. Common Cause*, excerpted below. Its essential holding is that partisan gerrymandering presents a nonjusticiable political question beyond the purview of the federal courts. The excerpt below provides the Court's explanation of this, as well as a summary of earlier Supreme Court cases challenging partisan gerrymandering.

Rucho v. Common Cause
588 U.S. ___, 139 S.Ct. 2484 (2019)

CHIEF JUSTICE ROBERTS **delivered the opinion of the Court.**

Voters and other plaintiffs in North Carolina and Maryland challenged their States' congressional districting maps as unconstitutional partisan gerrymanders. The North Carolina plaintiffs complained that the State's districting plan discriminated against Democrats; the Maryland plaintiffs complained that their State's plan discriminated against Republicans. The plaintiffs alleged that the gerrymandering violated the First Amendment, the Equal Protection Clause of the Fourteenth Amendment, the Elections

Clause, and Article I, § 2, of the Constitution. The District Courts in both cases ruled in favor of the plaintiffs, and the defendants appealed directly to this Court.

These cases require us to consider once again whether claims of excessive partisanship in districting are "justiciable"—that is, properly suited for resolution by the federal courts. This Court has not previously struck down a districting plan as an unconstitutional partisan gerrymander, and has struggled without success over the past several decades to discern judicially manageable standards for deciding such claims. The districting plans at issue here are highly partisan, by any measure. The question is whether the courts below appropriately exercised judicial power when they found them unconstitutional as well.

I-A

The first case involves a challenge to the congressional redistricting plan enacted by the Republican-controlled North Carolina General Assembly in 2016. The Republican legislators leading the redistricting effort instructed their mapmaker to use political data to draw a map that would produce a congressional delegation of ten Republicans and three Democrats. [*Rucho v. Common Cause*,] 318 F. Supp. 3d 777, 807–808 (MDNC 2018). As one of the two Republicans chairing the redistricting committee stated, "I think electing Republicans is better than electing Democrats. So I drew this map to help foster what I think is better for the country." *Id.*, at 809. He further explained that the map was drawn with the aim of electing ten Republicans and three Democrats because he did "not believe it [would be] possible to draw a map with 11 Republicans and 2 Democrats." *Id.*, at 808. One Democratic state senator objected that entrenching the 10–3 advantage for Republicans was not "fair, reasonable, [or] balanced" because, as recently as 2012, "Democratic congressional candidates had received more votes on a statewide basis than Republican candidates." *Ibid.* The General Assembly was not swayed by that objection and approved the 2016 Plan by a party-line vote. *Id.*, at 809.

In November 2016, North Carolina conducted congressional elections using the 2016 Plan, and Republican candidates won 10 of the 13 congressional districts. *Id.*, at 810. In the 2018 elections, Republican candidates won nine congressional districts, while Democratic candidates won three. The Republican candidate narrowly prevailed in the remaining district, but the State Board of Elections called a new election after allegations of fraud.

* * *

The plaintiffs challenged the 2016 Plan on multiple constitutional grounds. First, they alleged that the Plan violated the Equal Protection Clause of the Fourteenth Amendment by intentionally diluting the electoral strength of Democratic voters. Second, they claimed that the Plan violated their First Amendment rights by retaliating against supporters of Democratic candidates on the basis of their political beliefs. Third, they asserted that the Plan usurped the right of "the People" to elect their preferred candidates for Congress, in violation of the requirement in Article I, § 2, of the Constitution that Members of the House of Representatives be chosen "by the People of the several States." Finally, they alleged that the Plan violated the Elections Clause by exceeding the State's delegated authority to prescribe the "Times, Places and Manner of holding Elections" for Members of Congress.

After a four-day trial, the three-judge District Court unanimously concluded that the 2016 Plan violated the Equal Protection Clause and Article I of the Constitution.

* * *

I-B

The second case before us is *Lamone v. Benisek*, No. 18–726. In 2011, the Maryland Legislature—dominated by Democrats—undertook to redraw the lines of that State's eight congressional districts. The Governor at the time, Democrat Martin O'Malley, led the process. He appointed a redistricting committee to help redraw the map, and asked Congressman Steny Hoyer, who has described himself as a "serial gerrymanderer," to advise the committee. 348 F. Supp. 3d 493, 502 (Md. 2018). The Governor later testified that his aim was to "use the redistricting process to change the overall composition of Maryland's congressional delegation to 7 Democrats and 1 Republican by flipping" one district. *Ibid*. "[A] decision was made to go for the Sixth," *ibid*., which had been held by a Republican for nearly two decades. To achieve the required equal population among districts, only about 10,000 residents needed to be removed from that district. *Id*., at 498. The 2011 Plan accomplished that by moving roughly 360,000 voters out of the Sixth District and moving 350,000 new voters in. Overall, the Plan reduced the number of registered Republicans in the Sixth District by about 66,000 and increased the number of registered Democrats by about 24,000. *Id*., at 499–501. The map was adopted by a party-line vote. *Id*., at 506. It was used in the 2012 election and succeeded in flipping the Sixth District. A Democrat has held the seat ever since.

In November 2013, three Maryland voters filed this lawsuit. They alleged that the 2011 Plan violated the First Amendment, the Elections Clause, and Article I, § 2, of the Constitution. After considerable procedural skirmishing and litigation over preliminary relief, the District Court entered summary judgment for the plaintiffs. 348 F. Supp. 3d 493. It concluded that the plaintiffs' claims were justiciable, and that the Plan violated the First Amendment by diminishing their "ability to elect their candidate of choice" because of their party affiliation and voting history, and by burdening their associational rights. *Id.*, at 498. On the latter point, the court relied upon findings that Republicans in the Sixth District "were burdened in fundraising, attracting volunteers, campaigning, and generating interest in voting in an atmosphere of general confusion and apathy." *Id.*, at 524.

* * *

II-A

Article III of the Constitution limits federal courts to deciding "Cases" and "Controversies." We have understood that limitation to mean that federal courts can address only questions "historically viewed as capable of resolution through the judicial process." *Flast v. Cohen*, 392 U.S. 83, 95 (1968). In these cases we are asked to decide an important question of constitutional law. "But before we do so, we must find that the question is presented in a 'case' or 'controversy' that is, in James Madison's words, 'of a Judiciary Nature.' " *DaimlerChrysler Corp. v. Cuno*, 547 U.S. 332, 342 (2006) (quoting 2 RECORDS OF THE FEDERAL CONVENTION OF 1787, p. 430 (M. Farrand ed. 1966)).

* * *

Last Term in *Gill v. Whitford*, we reviewed our partisan gerrymandering cases and concluded that those cases "leave unresolved whether such claims may be brought." 585 U.S. ___, at ___ (slip op., at 13) [(2018)]. This Court's authority to act, as we said in *Gill*, is "grounded in and limited by the necessity of resolving, according to legal principles, a plaintiff's particular claim of legal right." *Ibid*. The question here is whether there is an "appropriate role for the Federal Judiciary" in

FYI

You may recall that we first encountered the "political question" doctrine in Chapter 5 above (pp. 84–85) as one of several "avoidance" doctrines that federal courts use when deciding whether even to decide a legal issue. The Court here is asking a variation of the same question it did in those one person, one vote cases: should the federal courts be the place to resolve the ultimate question of whether, and in what circumstances, partisan gerrymandering is unconstitutional?

remedying the problem of partisan gerrymandering—whether such claims are claims of *legal* right, resolvable according to *legal* principles, or political questions that must find their resolution elsewhere. *Id.*, at ___ (slip op., at 8).

II-B

Partisan gerrymandering is nothing new. Nor is frustration with it. The practice was known in the Colonies prior to Independence, and the Framers were familiar with it at the time of the drafting and ratification of the Constitution. See *Vieth* [*v. Jubelirer,*] 541 U.S. [267], at 274 [(2004)] (plurality opinion). During the very first congressional elections, George Washington and his Federalist allies accused Patrick Henry of trying to gerrymander Virginia's districts against their candidates—in particular James Madison, who ultimately prevailed over fellow future President James Monroe. Hunter, *The First Gerrymander?* 9 EARLY AM. STUDIES 792–794, 811 (2011). See 5 *Writings of Thomas Jefferson* 71 (P. Ford ed. 1895) (Letter to W. Short (Feb. 9, 1789)) ("Henry has so modelled the districts for representatives as to tack Orange [county] to counties where he himself has great influence that Madison may not be elected into the lower federal house").

In 1812, Governor of Massachusetts and future Vice President Elbridge Gerry notoriously approved congressional districts that the legislature had drawn to aid the Democratic-Republican Party. The moniker "gerrymander" was born when an outraged Federalist newspaper observed that one of the misshapen districts resembled a salamander. See *Vieth*, 541 U.S., at 274 (plurality opinion); E. GRIFFITH, THE RISE AND DEVELOPMENT OF THE GERRYMANDER 17–19 (1907). "By 1840, the gerrymander was a recognized force in party politics and was generally attempted in all legislation enacted for the formation of election districts. It was generally conceded that each party would attempt to gain power which was not proportionate to its numerical strength." *Id.*, at 123.

The Framers addressed the election of Representatives to Congress in the Elections Clause. Art. I, § 4, cl. 1. That provision assigns to state legislatures the power to prescribe the "Times, Places and Manner of holding Elections" for Members of Congress, while giving Congress the power to "make or alter" any such regulations. Whether to give that supervisory authority to the National Government was debated at the Constitutional Convention. When those opposed to such congressional oversight moved to strike the relevant language, Madison came to its defense:

> [T]he State Legislatures will sometimes fail or refuse to consult the common interest at the expense of their local coveniency or prejudices. . . .

> Whenever the State Legislatures had a favorite measure to carry, they
> would take care so to mould their regulations as to favor the candidates
> they wished to succeed.

2 RECORDS OF THE FEDERAL CONVENTION OF 1787, at 240–241.

During the subsequent fight for ratification, the provision remained a subject
of debate. Antifederalists predicted that Congress's power under the Elections Clause would allow Congress to make itself "omnipotent," setting the
"time" of elections as never or the "place" in difficult to reach corners of the
State. Federalists responded that, among other justifications, the revisionary
power was necessary to counter state legislatures set on undermining fair
representation, including through malapportionment. M. KLARMAN, THE
FRAMERS' COUP: THE MAKING OF THE UNITED STATES CONSTITUTION
340–342 (2016). The Federalists were, for example, concerned that newly
developing population centers would be deprived of their proper electoral
weight, as some cities had been in Great Britain. See 6 THE DOCUMENTARY
HISTORY OF THE RATIFICATION OF THE CONSTITUTION: MASSACHUSETTS
1278–1279 (J. Kaminski & G. Saladino eds. 2000).

Congress has regularly exercised its Elections Clause power, including to
address partisan gerrymandering. The Apportionment Act of 1842, which
required single-member districts for the first time, specified that those
districts be "composed of contiguous territory," Act of June 25, 1842, ch.
47, 5 Stat. 491, in "an attempt to forbid the practice of the gerrymander,"
Griffith, *supra*, at 12. Later statutes added requirements of compactness and
equality of population. Act of Jan. 16, 1901, ch. 93, § 3, 31 Stat. 733; Act
of Feb. 2, 1872, ch. 11, § 2, 17 Stat. 28. (Only the single member district
requirement remains in place today. 2 U.S.C. § 2c.) See *Vieth*, 541 U.S.,
at 276 (plurality opinion). Congress also used its Elections Clause power
in 1870, enacting the first comprehensive federal statute dealing with elections as a way to enforce the Fifteenth Amendment. Force Act of 1870,
ch. 114, 16 Stat. 140. Starting in the 1950s, Congress enacted a series of
laws to protect the right to vote through measures such as the suspension
of literacy tests and the prohibition of English-only elections. See, *e.g.*, 52
U.S.C. § 10101 *et seq.*

Appellants suggest that, through the Elections Clause, the Framers set aside
electoral issues such as the one before us as questions that only Congress can
resolve. See *Baker*, 369 U.S., at 217. We do not agree. In two areas—one-
person, one-vote and racial gerrymandering—our cases have held that there

is a role for the courts with respect to at least some issues that could arise from a State's drawing of congressional districts. See *Wesberry* v. *Sanders*, 376 U.S. 1 (1964); *Shaw v. Reno*, 509 U.S. 630 (1993) (*Shaw I*).

But the history is not irrelevant. The Framers were aware of electoral districting problems and considered what to do about them. They settled on a characteristic approach, assigning the issue to the state legislatures, expressly checked and balanced by the Federal Congress. As Alexander Hamilton explained, "it will . . . not be denied that a discretionary power over elections ought to exist somewhere. It will, I presume, be as readily conceded that there were only three ways in which this power could have been reasonably modified and disposed: that it must either have been lodged wholly in the national legislature, or wholly in the State legislatures, or primarily in the latter, and ultimately in the former." THE FEDERALIST No. 59, p. 362 (C. Rossiter ed. 1961). At no point was there a suggestion that the federal courts had a role to play. Nor was there any indication that the Framers had ever heard of courts doing such a thing.

II-C

Courts have nevertheless been called upon to resolve a variety of questions surrounding districting. Early on, doubts were raised about the competence of the federal courts to resolve those questions. See *Wood v. Broom*, 287 U.S. 1 (1932); *Colegrove v. Green*, 328 U.S. 549 (1946).

[The Court then summarized the history of its one-person, one vote jurisprudence and its racial gerrymandering jurisprudence.]

Partisan gerrymandering claims have proved far more difficult to adjudicate. The basic reason is that, while it is illegal for a jurisdiction to depart from the one-person, one-vote rule, or to engage in racial discrimination in districting, "a jurisdiction may engage in constitutional political gerrymandering." *Hunt v. Cromartie*, 526 U.S. 541, 551 (1999). * * *

To hold that legislators cannot take partisan interests into account when drawing district lines would essentially countermand the Framers' decision to entrust districting to political entities. The "central problem" is not determining whether a jurisdiction has engaged in partisan gerrymandering. It is "determining when political gerrymandering has gone too far." *Vieth*, 541 U.S., at 296 (plurality opinion). See *League of United Latin American Citizens v. Perry*, 548 U.S. 399, 420 (2006) (*LULAC*) (opinion of KEN-

NEDY, J.) (difficulty is "providing a standard for deciding how much partisan dominance is too much").

We first considered a partisan gerrymandering claim in *Gaffney v. Cummings* in 1973. There we rejected an equal protection challenge to Connecticut's redistricting plan, which "aimed at a rough scheme of proportional representation of the two major political parties" by "wiggl[ing] and joggl[ing] boundary lines" to create the appropriate number of safe seats for each party. 412 U.S. [735], at 738, 752, n. 18 [(1973)] (internal quotation marks omitted). In upholding the State's plan, we reasoned that districting "inevitably has and is intended to have substantial political consequences." *Id.*, at 753.

Thirteen years later, in *Davis v. Bandemer*, we addressed a claim that Indiana Republicans had cracked and packed Democrats in violation of the Equal Protection Clause. 478 U.S. 109, 116–117 (1986) (plurality opinion). A majority of the Court agreed that the case was justiciable, but the Court splintered over the proper standard to apply. Four Justices would have required proof of "intentional discrimination against an identifiable political group and an actual discriminatory effect on that group." *Id.*, at 127. Two Justices would have focused on "whether the boundaries of the voting districts have been distorted deliberately and arbitrarily to achieve illegitimate ends." *Id.*, at 165 (POWELL, J., concurring in part and dissenting in part). Three Justices, meanwhile, would have held that the Equal Protection Clause simply "does not supply judicially manageable standards for resolving purely political gerrymandering claims." *Id.*, at 147 (O'CONNOR, J., concurring in judgment). At the end of the day, there was "no 'Court' for a standard that properly should be applied in determining whether a challenged redistricting plan is an unconstitutional partisan political gerrymander." *Id.*, at 185, n. 25 (opinion of POWELL, J.). In any event, the Court held that the plaintiffs had failed to show that the plan violated the Constitution.

Eighteen years later, in *Vieth*, the plaintiffs complained that Pennsylvania's legislature "ignored all traditional redistricting criteria, including the preservation of local government boundaries," in order to benefit Republican congressional candidates. 541 U.S., at 272–273 (plurality opinion) (brackets omitted). Justice Scalia wrote for a four-Justice plurality. He would have held that the plaintiffs' claims were nonjusticiable because there was no "judicially discernible and manageable standard" for deciding them. *Id.*, at 306. Justice Kennedy, concurring in the judgment, noted "the lack of comprehensive and neutral principles for drawing electoral boundaries [and] the absence of rules to limit and confine judicial intervention." *Id.*, at

306–307. He nonetheless left open the possibility that "in another case a standard might emerge." *Id.*, at 312. Four Justices dissented.

In *LULAC*, the plaintiffs challenged a mid-decade redistricting map approved by the Texas Legislature. Once again a majority of the Court could not find a justiciable standard for resolving the plaintiffs' partisan gerrymandering claims. See 548 U.S., at 414 (noting that the "disagreement over what substantive standard to apply" that was evident in *Bandemer* "persists").

As we summed up last Term in *Gill*, our "considerable efforts in *Gaffney*, *Bandemer*, *Vieth*, and *LULAC* leave unresolved whether . . . claims [of legal right] may be brought in cases involving allegations of partisan gerrymandering." 585 U.S., at ___ (slip op., at 13). Two "threshold questions" remained: standing, which we addressed in *Gill*, and "whether [such] claims are justiciable." *Ibid.*

III-A

In considering whether partisan gerrymandering claims are justiciable, we are mindful of Justice Kennedy's counsel in *Vieth*: Any standard for resolving such claims must be grounded in a "limited and precise rationale" and be "clear, manageable, and politically neutral." 541 U.S., at 306–308 (opinion concurring in judgment). An important reason for those careful constraints is that, as a Justice with extensive experience in state and local politics put it, "[t]he opportunity to control the drawing of electoral boundaries through the legislative process of apportionment is a critical and traditional part of politics in the United States." *Bandemer*, 478 U.S., at 145 (opinion of O'CONNOR, J.). See *Gaffney*, 412 U.S., at 749 (observing that districting implicates "fundamental 'choices about the nature of representation' " (quoting *Burns v. Richardson*, 384 U.S. 73, 92 (1966))). An expansive standard requiring "the correction of all election district lines drawn for partisan reasons would commit federal and state courts to unprecedented intervention in the American political process," *Vieth*, 541 U.S., at 306 (opinion of KENNEDY, J.).

> **?** Having the power to control the drawing of district lines may well be a "critical" and "traditional" part of a legislature's (and hence, incumbent legislators') power, but should it be? What does does partisan gerrymandering's role in districting tell us about the nature of representation and the makeup of the legislature, that is, who our lawmakers are?

As noted, the question is one of degree: How to "provid[e] a standard for deciding how much partisan dominance is too much." *LULAC*, 548 U.S., at 420 (opinion of KENNEDY, J.). And it is vital in such circumstances that the Court act only in accord with especially clear standards: "With uncertain limits, intervening courts—even when proceeding with best intentions—would risk assuming political, not legal, responsibility for a process that often produces ill will and distrust." *Vieth*, 541 U.S., at 307 (opinion of KENNEDY, J.). If federal courts are to "inject [themselves] into the most heated partisan issues" by adjudicating partisan gerrymandering claims, *Bandemer*, 478 U.S., at 145 (opinion of O'CONNOR, J.), they must be armed with a standard that can reliably differentiate unconstitutional from "constitutional political gerrymandering." *Cromartie*, 526 U.S., at 551.

III-B

Partisan gerrymandering claims rest on an instinct that groups with a certain level of political support should enjoy a commensurate level of political power and influence. Explicitly or implicitly, a districting map is alleged to be unconstitutional because it makes it too difficult for one party to translate statewide support into seats in the legislature. But such a claim is based on a "norm that does not exist" in

> Note that one can argue that this is the same instinct driving the Voting Rights Act's attempt to increase racial minority representation in elected bodies, "an instinct that [racial] groups with a certain level of support should enjoy a commensurate level of political power and influence."

our electoral system—"statewide elections for representatives along party lines." *Bandemer*, 478 U.S., at 159 (opinion of O'CONNOR, J.).

Partisan gerrymandering claims invariably sound in a desire for proportional representation. As Justice O'Connor put it, such claims are based on "a conviction that the greater the departure from proportionality, the more suspect an apportionment plan becomes." *Ibid.* "Our cases, however, clearly foreclose any claim that the Constitution requires proportional representation or that legislatures in reapportioning must draw district lines to come as near as possible to allocating seats to the contending parties in proportion to what their anticipated statewide vote will be." *Id.*, at 130 (plurality opinion). See *Mobile v. Bolden*, 446 U.S. 55, 75–76 (1980) (plurality opinion) ("The Equal Protection Clause of the Fourteenth Amendment does not require proportional representation as an imperative of political organization.").

The Founders certainly did not think proportional representation was required. For more than 50 years after ratification of the Constitution, many States elected their congressional representatives through at-large or "general ticket" elections. * * * When Congress required single-member districts in the Apportionment Act of 1842, it was not out of a general sense of fairness, but instead a (mis)calculation by the Whigs that such a change would improve their electoral prospects.

Unable to claim that the Constitution requires proportional representation outright, plaintiffs inevitably ask the courts to make their own political judgment about how much representation particular political parties *deserve*—based on the votes of their supporters—and to rearrange the challenged districts to achieve that end. But federal courts are not equipped to apportion political power as a matter of fairness, nor is there any basis for concluding that they were authorized to do so. As Justice Scalia put it for the plurality in *Vieth*:

> 'Fairness' does not seem to us a judicially manageable standard. . . . Some criterion more solid and more demonstrably met than that seems to us necessary to enable the state legislatures to discern the limits of their districting discretion, to meaningfully constrain the discretion of the courts, and to win public acceptance for the courts' intrusion into a process that is the very foundation of democratic decisionmaking.

541 U.S., at 291.

> ❗ Note that in this and the two paragraphs to follow the Court identifies three possible kinds of fairness: 1) competitiveness, 2) proportionality, and 3) adherence to "traditional" districting criteria. (Can you think of others?)

The initial difficulty in settling on a "clear, manageable and politically neutral" test for fairness is that it is not even clear what fairness looks like in this context. There is a large measure of "unfairness" in any winner-take-all system. Fairness may mean a greater number of competitive districts. Such a claim seeks to undo packing and cracking so that supporters of the disadvantaged party have a better shot at electing their preferred candidates. But making as many districts as possible more competitive could be a recipe for disaster for the disadvantaged party. As Justice White has pointed out, "[i]f all or most of the districts are competitive . . . even a narrow statewide preference for either party would produce an overwhelming majority for the winning party in the state leg-islature." *Bandemer*, 478 U.S., at 130 (plurality opinion).

On the other hand, perhaps the ultimate objective of a "fairer" share of seats in the congressional delegation is most readily achieved by yielding to the gravitational pull of proportionality and engaging in cracking and packing, to ensure each party its "appropriate" share of "safe" seats. Such an approach, however, comes at the expense of competitive districts and of individuals in districts allocated to the opposing party.

Or perhaps fairness should be measured by adherence to "traditional" dis-tricting criteria, such as maintaining political subdivisions, keeping com-munities of interest together, and protecting incumbents. But protecting incumbents, for example, enshrines a particular partisan distribution. And the "natural political geography" of a State—such as the fact that urban electoral districts are often dominated by one political party—can itself lead to inherently packed districts. As Justice Kennedy has explained, tra-ditional criteria such as compactness and contiguity "cannot promise polit-ical neutrality when used as the basis for relief. Instead, it seems, a decision under these standards would unavoidably have significant political effect, whether intended or not." *Vieth*, 541 U.S., at 308–309 (opinion concurring in judgment).

Deciding among just these different visions of fairness (you can imagine many others) poses basic questions that are political, not legal. There are no legal standards discernible in the Constitution for making such judg-ments, let alone limited and precise standards that are clear, manageable,

> How does this statement compare with the Court's *Gingles* test for district-ing challenges under Section 2 of the Voting Rights Act? Are the *Gingles* factors "clear, manageable, and politically neutral"?

and politically neutral. Any judicial decision on what is "fair" in this con-text would be an "unmoored determination" of the sort characteristic of a political question beyond the competence of the federal courts. *Zivotof-sky v. Clinton*, 566 U.S. 189, 196 (2012).

And it is only after determining how to define fairness that you can even begin to answer the determinative question: "How much is too much?" At what point does permissible partisanship become unconstitutional? If compliance with traditional districting criteria is the fairness touchstone, for example, how much deviation from those criteria is constitutionally acceptable and how should mapdrawers prioritize competing criteria? Should a court "reverse gerrymander" other parts of a State to counteract "natural" gerrymandering caused, for example, by the urban concentration of one party? If a districting plan protected half of the incumbents but redistricted the rest into head to head races, would that be constitutional? A court would have to rank the relative importance of those traditional criteria and weigh how much deviation from each to allow.

If a court instead focused on the respective number of seats in the legislature, it would have to decide the ideal number of seats for each party and determine at what point deviation from that balance went too far. If a 5–3 allocation corresponds most closely to statewide vote totals, is a 6–2 allocation permissible, given that legislatures have the authority to engage in a certain degree of partisan gerrymandering? Which seats should be packed and which cracked? Or if the goal is as many competitive districts as possible, how close does the split need to be for the district to be considered competitive? Presumably not all districts could qualify, so how to choose? Even assuming the court knew which version of fairness to be looking for, there are no discernible and manageable standards for deciding whether there has been a violation. The questions are "unguided and ill suited to the development of judicial standards," *Vieth*, 541 U.S., at 296 (plurality opinion), and "results from one gerrymandering case to the next would likely be disparate and inconsistent," *id.*, at 308 (opinion of KENNEDY, J.).

Appellees contend that if we can adjudicate one-person, one-vote claims, we can also assess partisan gerrymandering claims. But the one-person, one-vote rule is relatively easy to administer as a matter of math. The same cannot be said of partisan gerrymandering claims, because the Constitution supplies no objective measure for assessing whether a districting map treats a political party fairly. It hardly follows from the principle that each person must have an equal say in the election of representatives that a person is entitled to have his political party achieve representation in some way commensurate to its share of statewide support.

More fundamentally, "vote dilution" in the one-person, one-vote cases refers to the idea that each vote must carry equal weight. In other words, each representative must be accountable to (approximately) the same number of constituents. That requirement does not extend to political parties. It does not mean that each party must be influential in proportion to its number of supporters. As we stated unanimously in *Gill*, "this Court is not responsible for vindicating generalized partisan preferences. The Court's constitutionally prescribed role is to vindicate the individual rights of the people appearing before it." 585 U.S., at ___ (slip op., at 21).

Nor do our racial gerrymandering cases provide an appropriate standard for assessing partisan gerrymandering. "[N]othing in our case law compels the conclusion that racial and political gerrymanders are subject to precisely the same constitutional scrutiny. In fact, our country's long and persistent history of racial discrimination in voting—as well as our Fourteenth Amendment jurisprudence, which always has reserved the strictest scrutiny for discrimination on the basis of race—would seem to compel the opposite conclusion." *Shaw I*, 509 U.S., at 650 (citation omitted). Unlike partisan gerrymandering claims, a racial gerrymandering claim does not ask for a fair share of political power and influence, with all the justiciability conundrums that entails. It asks instead for the elimination of a racial classification. A partisan gerrymandering claim cannot ask for the elimination of partisanship.

> Does this seem right to you? Go back and look at *Allen v. Milligan* in Chapter 6. Doesn't a claim under Section 2 of the Voting Rights Act effectively "ask for a fair share of political power and influence"?

IV

[In Part IV the Court rejected a number of "tests" for evaluating partisan gerrymandering claims, concluding that "none meets the need for a limited and precise standard that is judicially discernible and manageable. And none provides a solid grounding for judges to take the extraordinary step of reallocating power and influence between political parties."]

V

Excessive partisanship in districting leads to results that reasonably seem unjust. But the fact that such gerrymandering is "incompatible with democratic principles," *Arizona State Legislature*, 576 U.S., at 591, does not mean that the solution lies with the federal judiciary. We conclude that partisan gerrymandering claims present political questions beyond the reach of the federal courts. * * *

Today the dissent essentially embraces the argument that the Court unanimously rejected in *Gill*: "this Court can address the problem of partisan gerrymandering because it *must*." 585 U.S., at ___ (slip op., at 12). That is not the test of our authority under the Constitution; that document instead "confines the federal courts to a properly judicial role." *Town of Chester v. Laroe Estates, Inc.*, 581 U.S. 433, 438 (2017).

What the appellees and dissent seek is an unprecedented expansion of judicial power. We have never struck down a partisan gerrymander as unconstitutional—despite various requests over the past 45 years. The expansion of judicial authority would not be into just any area of controversy, but into one of the most intensely partisan aspects of American political life. That intervention would be unlimited in scope and duration—it would recur over and over again around the country with each new round of districting, for state as well as federal representatives. Consideration of the impact of today's ruling on democratic principles cannot ignore the effect of the unelected and politically unaccountable branch of the Federal Government assuming such an extraordinary and unprecedented role. See *post*, at 32–33.

Our conclusion does not condone excessive partisan gerrymandering. Nor does our conclusion condemn complaints about districting to echo into a void. The States, for example, are actively addressing the issue on a number of fronts. In 2015, the Supreme Court of Florida struck down that State's congressional districting plan as a violation of the Fair Districts Amendment to the Florida Constitution. *League of Women Voters of Florida v. Detzner*, 172 So. 3d 363 (2015). The dissent wonders why we can't do the same. See *post*, at 31. The answer is that there is no "Fair Districts Amendment" to the Federal Constitution. Provisions in state statutes and state constitutions can provide standards and guidance for state courts to apply. (We do not understand how the dissent can maintain that a provision saying that no districting plan "shall be drawn with the intent to favor or disfavor a political party" provides little guidance on the question. See *post*, at 31, n. 6.) Indeed, numerous other States are restricting partisan considerations in districting through legislation. One way they are doing so is by placing power to draw electoral districts in the hands of independent commissions. For example, in November 2018, voters in Colorado and Michigan approved constitutional amendments creating multimember commissions that will be responsible in whole or in part for creating and approving district maps for congressional and state legislative districts. See Colo. Const., Art. V, §§ 44, 46; Mich. Const., Art. IV, § 6. Missouri is trying a different tack. Voters there overwhelmingly approved the creation of a new position—state demographer—to draw state legislative district lines. Mo. Const., Art. III, § 3.

Other States have mandated at least some of the traditional districting criteria for their mapmakers. Some have outright prohibited partisan favoritism in redistricting. See Fla. Const., Art. III, § 20(a) ("No apportionment plan or individual district shall be drawn with the intent to favor or disfavor a political party or an incumbent."); Mo. Const., Art. III, § 3 ("Districts shall be designed in a manner that achieves both partisan fairness and, secondarily, competitiveness. 'Partisan fairness' means that parties shall be able to translate their popular support into legislative representation with approximately equal efficiency."); Iowa Code § 42.4(5) (2016) ("No district shall be drawn for the purpose of favoring a political party, incumbent legislator or member of Congress, or other person or group."); Del. Code Ann., Tit. xxix, § 804 (2017) (providing that in determining district boundaries for the state legislature, no district shall "be created so as to unduly favor any person or political party").

As noted, the Framers gave Congress the power to do something about partisan gerrymandering in the Elections Clause. The first bill introduced in the 116th Congress would require States to create 15-member independent commissions to draw congressional districts and would establish certain redistricting criteria, including protection for communities of interest, and ban partisan gerrymandering. H. R. 1, 116th Cong., 1st Sess., §§ 2401, 2411 (2019).

[The Court then summarized other congressional proposals to limit partisan gerrymandering.]

We express no view on any of these pending proposals. We simply note that the avenue for reform established by the Framers, and used by Congress in the past, remains open.

* * *

No one can accuse this Court of having a crabbed view of the reach of its competence. But we have no commission to allocate political power and influence in the absence of a constitutional directive or legal standards to guide us in the exercise of such authority. "It is emphatically the province and duty of the judicial department to say what the law is." *Marbury v. Madison*, 1 Cranch, at 177. In this rare circumstance, that means our duty is to say "this is not law."

The judgments of the United States District Court for the Middle District of North Carolina and the United States District Court for the District of Maryland are vacated, and the cases are remanded with instructions to dismiss for lack of jurisdiction.

It is so ordered.

Justice Kagan, with whom Justice Ginsburg, Justice Breyer, and Justice Sotomayor join, dissenting.

For the first time ever, this Court refuses to remedy a constitutional violation because it thinks the task beyond judicial capabilities.

And not just any constitutional violation. The partisan gerrymanders in these cases deprived citizens of the most fundamental of their constitutional rights: the rights to participate equally in the political process, to join with others to advance political beliefs, and to choose their political representatives. In so doing, the partisan gerrymanders here debased and dishonored our democracy, turning upside-down the core American idea that all governmental power derives from the people. These gerrymanders enabled politicians to entrench themselves in office as against voters' preferences. They promoted partisanship above respect for the popular will. They encouraged a politics of polarization and dysfunction. If left unchecked, gerrymanders like the ones here may irreparably damage our system of government.

And checking them is *not* beyond the courts. The majority's abdication comes just when courts across the country, including those below, have coalesced around manageable judicial standards to resolve partisan gerrymandering claims. Those standards satisfy the majority's own benchmarks. They do not require—indeed, they do not permit—courts to rely on their own ideas of electoral fairness, whether proportional representation or any other. And they limit courts to correcting only egregious gerrymanders, so judges do not become omnipresent players in the political process. But yes, the standards used here do allow—as well they should—judicial intervention in the worst-of-the-worst cases of democratic subversion, causing blatant constitutional harms. In other words, they allow courts to undo partisan gerrymanders of the kind we face today from North Carolina and Maryland. In giving such gerrymanders a pass from judicial review, the majority goes tragically wrong.

I

Maybe the majority errs in these cases because it pays so little attention to the constitutional harms at their core. After dutifully reciting each case's facts, the majority leaves them forever behind, instead immersing itself in everything that could conceivably go amiss if courts became involved. So it is necessary to fill in the gaps. To recount exactly what politicians in North Carolina and Maryland did to entrench their parties in political office, whatever the electorate might think. And to elaborate on the constitutional injury those politicians wreaked, to our democratic system and to individuals' rights. All that will help in considering whether courts confronting partisan gerrymandering claims are really so hamstrung—so unable to carry out their constitutional duties—as the majority thinks.

A

The plaintiffs here challenge two congressional districting plans—one adopted by Republicans in North Carolina and the other by Democrats in Maryland—as unconstitutional partisan gerrymanders. As I relate what happened in those two States, ask yourself: Is this how American democracy is supposed to work?

[Justice Kagan's opinion then recounted in greater detail than had the majority opinion the sordid partisan machinations that produced the districting maps at issue in both North Carolina and Maryland.]

B

Now back to the question I asked before: Is that how American democracy is supposed to work? I have yet to meet the person who thinks so.

"Governments," the Declaration of Independence states, "deriv[e] their just Powers from the Consent of the Governed." The Constitution begins: "We the People of the United States." The Gettysburg Address (almost) ends: "[G]overnment of the people, by the people, for the people." If there is a single idea that made our Nation (and that our Nation commended to the world), it is this one: The people are sovereign. The "power," James Madison wrote, "is in the people over the Government, and not in the Government over the people." 4 *Annals of Cong.* 934 (1794).

Free and fair and periodic elections are the key to that vision. The people get to choose their representatives. And then they get to decide, at regular intervals, whether to keep them. Madison again: "[R]epublican liberty" demands "not only, that all power should be derived from the people; but that those entrusted with it should be kept in dependence on the people." 2 THE FEDERALIST NO. 37, p. 4 (J. &

> Notice Justice Kagan's explicit evocation of the idea of representation and relationship between "the people" and their elected representatives. Although the majority does not include a paragraph like this, do you think the majority would agree? [Read on. Justice Kagan certainly thinks so!] If so, why are the two sides disagreeing about the outcome?

A. McLean eds. 1788). Members of the House of Representatives, in particular, are supposed to "recollect[ ] [that] dependence" every day. *Id.*, No. 57, at 155. To retain an "intimate sympathy with the people," they must be "compelled to anticipate the moment" when their "exercise of [power] is to be reviewed." *Id.*, Nos. 52, 57, at 124, 155. Election day—next year, and two years later, and two years after that—is what links the people to their representatives, and gives the people their sovereign power. That day is the foundation of democratic governance.

And partisan gerrymandering can make it meaningless. At its most extreme—as in North Carolina and Maryland—the practice amounts to "rigging elections." *Vieth v. Jubelirer*, 541 U.S. 267, 317 (2004) (Kennedy, J., concurring in judgment) (internal quotation marks omitted). By drawing districts to maximize the power of some voters and minimize the power of others, a party in office at the right time can entrench itself there for a decade or more, no matter what the voters would prefer. Just ask the people of North Carolina and Maryland. The "core principle of republican government," this Court has recognized, is "that the voters should choose their representatives, not the other way around." *Arizona State Legislature v. Arizona Independent Redistricting Comm'n*, 576 U.S. 787, 824 (2015) (internal quotation marks omitted). Partisan gerrymandering turns it the other way around. By that mechanism, politicians can cherry-pick voters to ensure their reelection. And the power becomes, as Madison put it, "in the Government over the people." 4 *Annals of Cong.* 934.

The majority disputes none of this. I think it important to underscore that fact: The majority disputes none of what I have said (or will say) about how gerrymanders undermine democracy. Indeed, the majority concedes (really, how could it not?) that gerrymandering is "incompatible with democratic principles." *Ante*, at 30 (quoting *Arizona State Legislature*, 576 U.S., at 791. And therefore what? That recognition would seem to demand a response. The majority offers two ideas that might qualify as such. One is that the political process can deal with the problem—a proposition so dubious on its face that I feel secure in delaying my answer for some time. See *ante*, at 31–33; *infra*, at 29–31. The other is that political gerrymanders have always been with us. See *ante*, at 8, 24. To its credit, the majority does not frame that point as an originalist constitutional argument. After all (as the majority rightly notes), racial and residential gerrymanders were also once with us, but the Court has done something about that fact. See *ante*, at 10. The majority's idea instead seems to be that if we have lived with partisan gerrymanders so long, we will survive.

That complacency has no cause. Yes, partisan gerrymandering goes back to the Republic's earliest days. (As does vociferous opposition to it.) But big data and modern technology—of just the kind that the mapmakers in North Carolina and Maryland used—make today's gerrymandering altogether different from the crude linedrawing of the past. Old-time efforts, based on little more than guesses, sometimes led to so-called dummymanders—gerrymanders that went spectacularly wrong. Not likely in today's world. Mapmakers now have access to more granular data about party preference and voting behavior than ever before. * * * Just as important, advancements in computing technology have enabled mapmakers to put that information to use with unprecedented efficiency and precision. While bygone mapmakers may have drafted three or four alternative districting plans, today's mapmakers can generate thousands of possibilities at the touch of a key—and then choose the one giving their party maximum advantage (usually while still meeting traditional districting requirements). The effect is to make gerrymanders far more effective and durable than before, insulating politicians against all but the most titanic shifts in the political tides. These are not your grandfather's—let alone the Framers'—gerrymanders.

* * * And gerrymanders will only get worse * * * with developments like machine learning. And someplace along this road, "we the people" become sovereign no longer.

C

Partisan gerrymandering of the kind before us not only subverts democracy (as if that weren't bad enough). It violates individuals' constitutional rights as well. That statement is not the lonesome cry of a dissenting Justice. This Court has recognized extreme partisan gerrymandering as such a violation for many years.

Partisan gerrymandering operates through vote dilution—the devaluation of one citizen's vote as compared to others. A mapmaker draws district lines to "pack" and "crack" voters likely to support the disfavored party. See generally *Gill v. Whitford*, 585 U.S.

Recall again that this idea of "vote dilution" is the basis of claims under Section 2 of the Voting Rights Act—and ultimately, claims under the "one person, one vote" principle too! [Read on. Justice Kagan explains more!]

___, ___–___ (2018) (slip op., at 14–16). He packs supermajorities of those voters into a relatively few districts, in numbers far greater than needed for their preferred candidates to prevail. Then he cracks the rest across many more districts, spreading them so thin that their candidates will not be able to win. Whether the person is packed or cracked, his vote carries less weight—has less consequence—than it would under a neutrally drawn (non-partisan) map. See *id.*, at ___ (KAGAN, J., concurring) (slip op., at 4). In short, the mapmaker has made some votes count for less, because they are likely to go for the other party.

That practice implicates the Fourteenth Amendment's Equal Protection Clause. The Fourteenth Amendment, we long ago recognized, "guarantees the opportunity for equal participation by all voters in the election" of legislators. *Reynolds v. Sims*, 377 U.S. 533, 566 (1964). And that opportunity "can be denied by a debasement or dilution of the weight of a citizen's vote just as effectively as by wholly prohibiting the free exercise of the franchise." *Id.*, at 555. Based on that principle, this Court in its one-person-one-vote decisions prohibited creating districts with significantly different populations. A State could not, we explained, thus "dilut[e] the weight of votes because of place of residence." *Id.*, at 566. The constitutional injury in a partisan gerrymandering case is much the same, except that the dilution is based on party affiliation. In such a case, too, the districters have set out to reduce the weight of certain citizens' votes, and thereby deprive them of their capacity to "full[y] and effective[ly] participat[e] in the political process[ ]." *Id.*, at 565. As Justice Kennedy (in a controlling opinion) once hypothesized: If districters declared that they were drawing a map "so as most to burden [the votes of] Party X's" supporters, it would violate the Equal Protection Clause. *Vieth*, 541 U.S., at 312. * * *

And partisan gerrymandering implicates the First Amendment too. That Amendment gives its greatest protection to political beliefs, speech, and association. Yet partisan gerrymanders subject certain voters to "disfavored treatment"—again, counting their votes for less—precisely because of "their voting history [and] their expression of political views." *Vieth*, 541 U.S., at 314 (opinion of KENNEDY, J.). And added to that strictly personal harm is an associational one. Representative democracy is "unimaginable without the ability of citizens to band together in [support of] candidates who espouse their political views." *California Democratic Party v. Jones*, 530 U.S. 567, 574 (2000). By diluting the votes of certain citizens, the State frustrates their efforts to translate those affiliations into political effectiveness. See *Gill*,

585 U.S., at ___ (KAGAN, J., concurring) (slip op., at 9) ("Members of the disfavored party[,] deprived of their natural political strength[,] may face difficulties fundraising, registering voters, [and] eventually accomplishing their policy objectives"). In both those ways, partisan gerrymanders of the kind we confront here undermine the protections of "democracy embodied in the First Amendment." *Elrod* v. *Burns*, 427 U.S. 347, 357 (1976) (internal quotation marks omitted).

Though different Justices have described the constitutional harm in diverse ways, nearly all have agreed on this much: Extreme partisan gerrymandering (as happened in North Carolina and Maryland) violates the Constitution. [quoting statements from the opinions in *Vieth* and *Bandemer*.] Once again, the majority never disagrees; it appears to accept the "principle that each person must have an equal say in the election of representatives." *Ante*, at 20. And indeed, without this settled and shared understanding that cases like these inflict constitutional injury, the question of whether there are judicially manageable standards for resolving them would never come up.

II

So the only way to understand the majority's opinion is as follows: In the face of grievous harm to democratic governance and flagrant infringements on individuals' rights—in the face of escalating partisan manipulation whose compatibility with this Nation's values and law no one defends—the majority declines to provide any remedy. For the first time in this Nation's history, the majority declares that it can do nothing about an acknowledged constitutional violation because it has searched high and low and cannot find a workable legal standard to apply.

The majority gives two reasons for thinking that the adjudication of partisan gerrymandering claims is beyond judicial capabilities. First and foremost, the majority says, it cannot find a neutral baseline—one not based on contestable notions of political fairness—from which to measure injury. See *ante*, at 15–19. According to the majority, "[p]artisan gerrymandering claims invariably sound in a desire for proportional representation." *Ante*, at 16. But the Constitution does not mandate proportional representation. So, the majority contends, resolving those claims "inevitably" would require courts to decide what is "fair" in the context of districting. *Ante*, at 17. They would have "to make their own political judgment about how much representation particular political parties deserve" and "to rearrange the challenged districts to achieve that end." *Ibid.* (emphasis in original). And second, the majority argues that even after establishing a baseline, a court would have no way to answer "the determinative question: 'How much is too much?'" *Ante*, at 19. No "discernible and manageable" standard is available, the majority claims—and so courts could willy-nilly become embroiled in fixing every districting plan. *Ante*, at 20; see *ante*, at 15–16.

I'll give the majority this one—and important—thing: It identifies some dangers everyone should want to avoid. Judges should not be apportioning political power based on their own vision of electoral fairness, whether proportional representation or any other. And judges should not be striking down maps left, right, and center, on the view that every smidgen of politics is a smidgen too much. Respect for state legislative processes—and restraint in the exercise of judicial authority—counsels intervention in only egregious cases.

But in throwing up its hands, the majority misses something under its nose: What it says can't be done *has* been done. Over the past several years, federal courts across the country—including, but not exclusively, in the decisions below—have largely converged on a standard for adjudicating partisan gerrymandering claims (striking down both Democratic and Republican districting plans in the process). And that standard does what the majority says is impossible. The standard does not use any judge-made conception of electoral fairness—either proportional representation or any other; instead, it takes as its baseline a State's *own* criteria of fairness, apart from partisan gain. And by requiring plaintiffs to make difficult showings relating to both purpose and effects, the standard invalidates the most extreme, but only the most extreme, partisan gerrymanders.

[JUSTICE KAGAN's opinion then discussed how lower courts had developed and applied what she saw as a judicially manageable framework for identifying unconstitutional partisan gerrymanders.]

The majority, in the end, fails to understand both the plaintiffs' claims and the decisions below. Everything in today's opinion assumes that these cases grew out of a "desire for proportional representation" or, more generally phrased, a "fair share of political power." *Ante*, at 16, 21. And everything in it assumes that the courts below had to (and did) decide what that fair share would be. But that is not so. The plaintiffs objected to one specific practice—the extreme manipulation of district lines for partisan gain. Elimination of that practice could have led to proportional representation. Or it could have led to nothing close. What was left after the practice's removal could have been fair, or could have been unfair, by any number of measures. That was not the crux of this suit. The plaintiffs asked only that the courts bar politicians from entrenching themselves in power by diluting the votes of their rivals' supporters. And the courts, using neutral and manageable—and eminently legal—standards, provided that (and only that) relief. This Court should have cheered, not overturned, that restoration of the people's power to vote.

III

This Court has long understood that it has a special responsibility to remedy violations of constitutional rights resulting from politicians' districting decisions. Over 50 years ago, we committed to providing judicial review in that sphere, recognizing as we established the one-person-one-vote rule that "our oath and our office require no less." *Reynolds*, 377 U.S., at 566. Of course, our oath and our office require us to vindicate all constitutional rights. But the need for judicial review is at its most urgent in cases like these. "For here, politicians' incentives conflict with voters' interests, leaving citizens without any political remedy for their constitutional harms." *Gill*, 585 U.S., at ___ (KAGAN, J., concurring) (slip op., at 14). Those harms arise because politicians want to stay in office. No one can look to them for effective relief.

* * *

And gerrymandering is, as so many Justices have emphasized before, antidemocratic in the most profound sense. In our government, "all political power flows from the people." *Arizona State Legislature*, 576 U.S., at ___ (slip op., at 35). And that means, as Alexander Hamilton once said, "that the people should choose whom they please to govern them." 2 DEBATES ON THE CONSTITUTION 257 (J. Elliot ed. 1891). But in Maryland and North Carolina they cannot do so. In Maryland, election in and election out, there are 7 Democrats and 1 Republican in the congressional delegation. In North Carolina, however the political winds blow, there are 10 Republicans and 3 Democrats. Is it conceivable that someday voters will be able to break out of that prefabricated box? Sure. But everything possible has been done to make that hard. To create a world in which power does not flow from the people because they do not choose their governors.

Of all times to abandon the Court's duty to declare the law, this was not the one. The practices challenged in these cases imperil our system of government. Part of the Court's role in that system is to defend its foundations.

None is more important than free and fair elections. With respect but deep sadness, I dissent.

NOTES & QUESTIONS

1. Why should the Equal Protection Clause allow the adjudication of claims of racial gerrymandering, but not allow claims of partisan gerrymandering?

2. What, if anything, is wrong with partisan gerrymandering? How should legislative districts be drawn?

3. Were the *Rucho* plaintiffs asking for a kind of *proportionality* in political districts?

4. What is the best remedy today for excessive partisan gerrymandering?

5. How does partisan gerrymandering affect the makeup of the legislature (and in turn who participates directly in the lawmaking process)? In *Rucho* and its companion case from Maryland, *Lamone v. Benisek*, one political party entrenched itself at the expense of the other, but notice that in North Carolina, it was the Republicans, and in Maryland, the Democrats. Does that mean that in the aggregate, partisan gerrymanders might cancel each other out in Congress? If they did cancel each other out, so that the number of Democrats and Republicans matched their percentage of voters in the population of the country as a whole, would that take care of the problem?

6. How important is a representative's political party to her "representativeness"? Is it more or less important than the representative's race? If you live in a district in which the representative is always from a different party from you, do you feel more "represented" by a Congressperson from your party who comes from a different district?

Test Your Understanding

To assess your understanding of the material in this chapter, click here to take a quiz.

8

Regulating Campaign Spending

Key Concepts

- Campaign expenditure
- Campaign contribution
- Public financing
- Campaign finance disclosure
- *Quid pro quo* corruption
- Bipartisan Campaign Reform Act
- Issue ads
- Electioneering communications

Chapter Summary

This chapter first describes several different modes of regulating the financing of electoral campaigns and then reviews the Supreme Court's 1976 landmark decision in *Buckley* v. *Valeo*, a case that established the basic framework for judicial review of campaign finance laws. Following the discussion of *Buckley*, the chapter introduces the Bipartisan Campaign Reform Act of 2002 (BCRA) and the judicial responses to that law.

The laws surrounding the financing of election campaigns for legislative and other public offices are complicated. Federal campaign finance laws govern the financing of campaigns for Congress and the President. A federal agency, the Federal Election Commission (FEC), is responsible for administering and enforcing this law. In addition, each state has its own laws governing the financing of state legislative, executive, and judicial branch elections in that state. All federal and state laws governing campaign finance must also comply with the U.S. Constitution, including the First Amendment, which protects freedom of speech and association. The First

Amendment has long been understood to provide some degree of constitutional protection for campaign contributions and expenditures, and therefore to limit government regulation of the flow of money into electoral campaigns, as discussed below. This chapter will focus primarily on *federal* campaign finance laws and the federal constitutional constraints on campaign finance regulation.

A. Background*

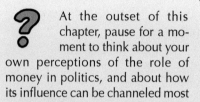 At the outset of this chapter, pause for a moment to think about your own perceptions of the role of money in politics, and about how its influence can be channeled most productively.

Election campaigns cost money, and lots of it. Much of that money is spent on advertising and other communications designed to influence votes for particular candidates or ballot measures. Election-related communications are protected by the First Amendment, as are the contributions and expenditures that fund them. Yet there are serious concerns about the influence that campaign money may have, both on election results and on the decisions that public officials make once elected. For over a century, Congress and other legislative bodies have tried to limit the influence of campaign money on elections and politics.

As an initial matter, it is helpful to have a basic understanding of both the various *modes of regulating campaign finance* and the *underlying values* animating both the desire to regulate campaign finance and the view that doing so is problematic. An understanding of these modes of regulation and these competing values will help inform discussion of the court decisions discussed in the remainder of this chapter.

Consider four basic modes of regulating the financing of electoral campaigns:

- *Expenditure restrictions* regulate the direct spending of money to influence election campaigns. This mode of regulation includes laws imposing a specific dollar limit on the amount that may be spent in support of or against candidates, as well as outright bans on certain entities (such as corporations or unions) spending money to influence elections. As we shall see, the U.S. Supreme Court has looked with skepticism on expenditure limits.

---

*   The material in this chapter is drawn from Daniel P. Tokaji, Election Law in a Nutshell (2d ed. 2017).

- *Contribution restrictions* regulate the giving of money to another person or entity to support an election campaign. The most prominent example is the limit on how much each person may give to an individual candidate. There are also limits on how much may be given to party organizations.

- *Public financing* is the provision of public funds to candidates or parties, to reduce their reliance on private donors. Rather than imposing a ceiling on expenditures or contributions, public financing attempts to raise the floor. Candidates typically obtain public financing by making a threshold showing of viability—for example, by raising a certain number of small-dollar contributions.

- *Disclosure* requires that information be made available to the public about contributions or expenditures. Candidates, political parties, and other entities may be required to disclose their donors, the amounts they receive, and how much they spend on campaign-related activities. Another form of disclosure is to require a disclaimer in advertisements, indicating the person or entity responsible.

As a general matter, expenditure limits are considered the most intrusive form of regulation and disclosure requirements the least. Contribution limits and public financing fall somewhere in between. The constitutional standards applied to these different forms of regulation are discussed in greater detail below.

Important values are at stake on both sides of the debate over campaign finance regulation. These values come into play in political discourse over whether and how much to regulate, as well as judicial consideration of the laws that have been adopted.

The most prominent argument made in support of campaign finance regulation is the prevention of *corruption and the appearance of corruption*. This is the only argument that the Supreme Court has accepted as a justification for contribution limits. As you will see, the Court has defined corruption narrowly, as limited to the exchange of campaign contributions for political favors. This is known as *quid pro quo* corruption or, more commonly, bribery. In general, bribery is an offer or agreement to exchange something of value for the performance of an "official act."

Another important value asserted in support of regulation is the *promotion of equality* or a "level playing field." *See* Edward B. Foley, *Equal-Dollars-Per-Voter: A Constitutional Principle of Campaign Finance*, 94 COLUM. L. REV. 1204 (1994). The concern is that people and entities with large amounts of wealth will have disproportionate influence on either election results or policymaking. This is closely related to the "anti-distortion" rationale, the concern that democratic politics will be distorted if wealthy entities—especially large corporations—have a stronger voice than ordinary people and are thus able to drown out ordinary voices. This argument often dovetails with the claim that uncontrolled campaign influence by the wealthy has a disproportionately negative impact on racial minorities, thus denying them equal participation in the political process.

> **?** Take another look at the categories of legislative activity we introduced near the beginning of Chapter 4, structured around the 2 x 2 matrix based on the work of political scientist James Q. Wilson (pp. 71–72). Does the concern about the influence of wealth play out differently in different categories, based on how concentrated or how diffuse the costs or benefits of a measure might be?

Other values cited in support of campaign finance regulation include the *promotion of competitive elections, protecting candidates' time*, and *informing the electorate*. Some forms of campaign finance regulation may promote competition by making it easier for candidates without personal wealth or wealthy friends to run for office. Regulation may also help prevent entrenchment by allowing challengers to compete more successfully against incumbents. Another asserted rationale for regulation is to ensure that candidates—including current officeholders—are not forced to spend too much of their time raising money. The reality of contemporary politics is that candidates for office must raise considerable sums to fund their campaigns. For those who are current officeholders, this necessarily limits the time they can spend performing their official duties. Finally, disclosure rules are justified as a way to inform the electorate. Disclosure may help voters make better decisions by letting them know candidates' sources of financial support. It may also help inform citizens of the interest groups seeking to influence public officials, thus allowing those officials to be held accountable.

On the other side of the debate, regulatory skeptics cite First Amendment values in support of their arguments. They argue that contribution and expenditure limits are a *threat to liberty and autonomy* because they limit the ability of individuals to express their political views. Political speech enjoys an especially high level of protection under our First Amendment. *See* BRADLEY A. SMITH, UNFREE SPEECH: THE FOLLY OF CAMPAIGN FINANCE REFORM (2001).

In addition, campaign finance regulation may be seen as an *infringement on political association*. One of the ways that individuals organize politically is by pooling their resources for campaign-related activities. This may be done by donating to a candidate's campaign, political party, or other group seeking to influence an election. Rights of political association also enjoy strong constitutional protection. Opponents of regulation believe that some campaign finance regulations interfere with protected associational activity.

Regulatory skeptics also deny that campaign finance regulation meaningfully advances the values its supporters tout. Instead, regulation's unintended consequences may compromise those values. Limits on campaign finance regulation are enacted by legislative bodies, which have a strong incentive to protect their own interests and those of their parties. Far from promoting competition, skeptics argue, some regulations have *anti-competitive effects*—tending to advance the interests of the party in power or of incumbents generally. Challengers may find it more difficult to wage a viable campaign with regulations than without them.

Skeptics also argue that some campaign finance regulations *increase the time candidates spend fundraising*. In particular, contribution limits force candidates to spend considerable time raising small-dollar contributions from a large number of donors, rather than obtaining big donations from just a few people, which would take less time.

Finally, skeptics argue that some forms of regulation cause a *weakening of political parties* and *degradation of political discourse*. An unintended consequence of our current regime is that more money tends to flow to outside groups. As we shall see, candidates and parties may be subject to contribution limits, but groups engaged solely in independent expenditures may not. This tends to push more money to outside groups, weakening parties. It may also result in a less civil political discourse, since outside groups are not accountable to the people in the same way that candidates are, and therefore may be more willing to run negative ads. Even if those ads are effective, they may have a negative effect on political discourse.

DIY
The Regulation of Campaign Finance: What Do You Think?

 Before turning to the judicial doctrines surrounding campaign finance, take a minute to consider the pros and cons concerning campaign finance regulation described above. Which of these points resonate(s) most with you?

B. The Constitutional Framework: *Buckley v. Valeo*

The Supreme Court established the basic framework for judicial review of campaign finance laws in *Buckley v. Valeo,* 424 U.S. 1 (1976). Although this framework has been refined over the years, it remains basically in place with respect to the four modes of regulation discussed above, all of which were present in the case: expenditure limits, contribution limits, public financing, and disclosure requirements.

> "FECA" is the acronym for the Federal Election Campaign Act, the 1974 amended version of which was at issue in the *Buckley* case.

At issue in *Buckley* were the 1974 amendments to the Federal Election Campaign Act of 1971 (FECA), codified at 52 U.S.C. § 30101 *et seq*. These amendments established a comprehensive scheme of campaign finance regulation for federal elections, including both congressional and presidential elections. *Buckley* upheld some provisions of this scheme while striking down others under the First Amendment. The court's unsigned *per curiam* opinion consumed 138 pages, with another 83 pages of concurring and dissenting opinions. As explained below, the *Buckley* court struck down FECA's expenditure limits, upheld its contribution limits, upheld presidential public financing, and upheld its disclosure requirements (with some limitations) against facial constitutional challenges.

In this chapter, we will focus on what *Buckley* said about campaign contribution and expenditure limits. The 1974 FECA amendments imposed a $1000 limit on individual *contributions* to federal election campaigns. It also imposed various restrictions on *expenditures* by federal candidates, political parties, and others. The court in *Buckley* drew a sharp line between expenditure limits and contribution limits, holding that the former enjoy a greater degree of constitutional protection than the latter.

Buckley v. Valeo
424 U.S. 1 (1976)

PER CURIAM

These appeals present constitutional challenges to the key provisions of the Federal Election Campaign Act of 1971 (Act) * * * as amended in 1974. * * *

I. Contribution and Expenditure Limitations

The intricate statutory scheme adopted by Congress to regulate federal election campaigns includes restrictions on political contributions and expenditures that apply broadly to all phases of and all participants in the election process. The major contribution and expenditure limitations in the Act prohibit individuals from contributing more than $25,000 in a single year or more than $1,000 to any single candidate for an election campaign and from spending more than $1,000 a year "relative to a clearly identified candidate." Other provisions restrict a candidate's use of personal and family resources in his campaign and limit the overall amount that can be spent by a candidate in campaigning for federal office.

The constitutional power of Congress to regulate federal elections is well established and is not questioned by any of the parties in this case. Thus, the critical constitutional questions presented here go not to the basic power of Congress to legislate in this area, but to whether the specific legislation that Congress has enacted interferes with First Amendment freedoms. * * *

A. General Principles

The Act's contribution and expenditure limitations operate in an area of the most fundamental First Amendment activities. Discussion of public issues and debate on the qualifications of candidates are integral to the operation of the system of government established by our Constitution. The First Amendment affords the broadest protection to such political expression in order "to assure (the) unfettered interchange of ideas for the bringing about of political and social changes

> Notice that the Court begins its analysis with principles about freedom of discussion, freedom of association, and (what we discussed in Chapter 4) the nature of representation in a republic. These principles are all relatively uncontroversial. As you read on, think about the relationship between these principles and the campaign finance regulations being challenged in the case.

desired by the people." *Roth v. United States*, 354 U.S. 476, 484 (1957). * * *
In a republic where the people are sovereign, the ability of the citizenry to
make informed choices among candidates for office is essential, for the
identities of those who are elected will inevitably shape the course that we
follow as a nation. * * *

The First Amendment protects political association as well as political
expression. The constitutional right of association * * * stemmed from the
court's recognition that "(e)ffective advocacy of both public and private
points of view, particularly controversial ones, is undeniably enhanced by
group association." Subsequent decisions have made clear that the First and
Fourteenth Amendments guarantee " 'freedom to associate with others for
the common advancement of political beliefs and ideas,'" a freedom that
encompasses " '(t)he right to associate with the political party of one's
choice.' " *Kusper v. Pontikes*, 414 U.S. 51, 56 (1973). * * *

> **!** Notice this core disagreement right at the beginning. Although you do not need to understand all of First Amendment law, the parties' disagreement here is key to First Amendment jurisprudence: "speech" is protected by the First Amendment, but "conduct" generally is not. Is spending money in favor of a preferred candidate "speech" or "conduct"? Read on, and see what the Court has to say about this.

It is with these principles in mind that we consider the primary contentions of the parties with respect to the Act's limitations upon the giving and spending of money in political campaigns. Those conflicting contentions could not more sharply define the basic issues before us. Appellees contend that what the Act regulates is conduct, and that its effect on speech and association is incidental at most. Appellants respond that contributions and expenditures are at the very core of political speech, and that the Act's limitations thus constitute restraints on First Amendment liberty that are both gross and direct. * * *

A restriction on the amount of money a person or group can spend on political communication during a campaign necessarily reduces the quantity of expression by restricting the number of issues discussed, the depth of their exploration, and the size of the audience reached. This is because virtually every means of communicating ideas in today's mass society requires the expenditure of money. The distribution of the humblest handbill or leaflet entails printing, paper, and circulation costs. Speeches and rallies generally necessitate hiring a hall and publicizing the event. The electorate's increasing dependence on television, radio, and other mass media for news and information has made these expensive modes of communication indispensable instruments of effective political speech.

The expenditure limitations contained in the Act represent substantial rather than merely theoretical restraints on the quantity and diversity of political speech. The $1,000 ceiling on spending "relative to a clearly identified candidate" would appear to exclude all citizens and groups except candidates, political parties, and the institutional press from any significant use of the most effective modes of communication. Although the Act's limitations on expenditures by campaign organizations and political parties provide substantially greater room for discussion and debate, they would have required restrictions in the scope of a number of past congressional and presidential campaigns and would operate to constrain campaigning by candidates who raise sums in excess of the spending ceiling.

By contrast with a limitation upon expenditures for political expression, a limitation upon the amount that any one person or group may contribute to a candidate or political committee entails only a marginal restriction upon the contributor's ability to engage in free communication. A contribution serves as a general expression of support for the candidate and his views, but does not communicate the underlying basis for the support. The quantity of communication by the contributor does not increase perceptibly with the size of his contribution, since the expression rests solely on the undifferentiated, symbolic act of contributing. At most, the size of the contribution provides a very rough index of the intensity of the contributor's support for the candidate. A limitation on the amount of money a person may give to a candidate or campaign organization thus involves little direct restraint on his political communication, for it permits the symbolic expression of support evidenced by a contribution but does not in any way infringe the contributor's freedom to discuss candidates and issues. While contributions may result in political expression if spent by a candidate or an association to present views to the

> What does the Court mean here? Assuming, as the Court does, that a contribution to a campaign is a "communication," i.e., expressive activity protected by the First Amendment, is the Court saying that the message sent by, say, a $1 contribution is effectively the same message sent by, say, a $1 million contribution? Is the basic idea that a campaign contribution, no matter the amount, is just a "symbolic act"?

voters, the transformation of contributions into political debate involves speech by someone other than the contributor.

Does this seem right to you? Recall from Section A above that one of the arguments against contribution limits is that it is more efficient for a candidate to raise money from a small number of wealthy donors' large contributions than from a large number of small donations.

Given the important role of contributions in financing political campaigns, contribution restrictions could have a severe impact on political dialogue if the limitations prevented candidates and political committees from amassing the resources necessary for effective advocacy. There is no indication, however, that the contribution limitations imposed by the Act would have any dramatic adverse effect on the funding of campaigns and political associations. * * *

The Act's contribution and expenditure limitations also impinge on protected associational freedoms. Making a contribution, like joining a political party, serves to affiliate a person with a candidate. In addition, it enables likeminded persons to pool their resources in furtherance of common political goals. The Act's contribution ceilings thus limit one important means of

An "independent expenditure" refers to money spent directly by individuals and organizations other than the candidate, as opposed to a "contribution," which is money given by individuals and/or organizations to the candidate for the candidate to choose how to spend.

associating with a candidate or committee, but leave the contributor free to become a member of any political association and to assist personally in the association's efforts on behalf of candidates. And the Act's contribution limitations permit associations and candidates to aggregate large sums of money to promote effective advocacy. By contrast, the Act's $1,000 limitation on independent expenditures "relative to a clearly identified candidate" precludes most associations from effectively amplifying the voice of their adherents, the original basis for the recognition of First Amendment protection of the freedom of association. * * *

In sum, although the Act's contribution and expenditure limitations both implicate fundamental First Amendment interests, its expenditure ceilings impose significantly more severe restrictions on protected freedoms of political expression and association than do its limitations on financial contributions.

B. Contribution Limitations

1. The $1,000 Limitation on Contributions by Individuals and Groups to Candidates and Authorized Campaign Committees

Section 608(b) provides, with certain limited exceptions, that "no person shall make contributions to any candidate with respect to any election for federal office which, in the aggregate, exceed $1,000." The statute defines "person" broadly to include "an individual, partnership, committee, association, corporation, or any other organization or group of persons." * * *

[T]he primary First Amendment problem raised by the Act's contribution limitations is their restriction of one aspect of the contributor's freedom of political association. The court's decisions involving associational freedoms establish that the right of association is a "basic constitutional freedom," *Kusper v. Pontikes*, 414 U.S., at 57, that is "closely allied to freedom of speech and a right which, like free speech, lies at the foundation of a free society." *Shelton v. Tucker*, 364 U.S. 479, 486 (1960). * * * Yet, it is clear that "(n)either the right to associate nor the right to participate in political activities is absolute." *CSC v. Letter Carriers*, 413 U.S. 548, 567 (1973). Even a " 'significant interference' with protected rights of political association" may be sustained if the state demonstrates a sufficiently important interest and employs means closely drawn to avoid unnecessary abridgment of associational freedoms. *Cousins v. Wigoda*, supra, 419 U.S., at 488.

Recall in Chapter 6, when discussing the constitutional challenges to racial gerrymandering (p. 131), we encountered the idea of "strict scrutiny," which requires the government to show that it has a "compelling" interest and that its action is the "least restrictive" alternative for furthering that interest. Here, we are encountering a less stringent form of judicial review: the government's interest must only be "important" and the government action need only be "closely drawn." We look at this more closely in Note 4 below.

What do you think about this premise? Are large contributions given with the goal of securing a political *quid pro quo*? Always? Sometimes? Rarely? Never?

* * * According to the parties and amici, the primary interest served by the limitations and, indeed, by the Act as a whole, is the prevention of corruption and the appearance of corruption spawned by the real or imagined coercive influence of large financial contributions on candidates' positions

and on their actions if elected to office. [The Court also mentioned two other interests.]

? Among the examples Congress relied on were a $2 million donation to the Nixon campaign by the dairy industry to get a meeting with White House officials on price supports and numerous individuals who donated large sums in order to get Ambassadorships. Do these seem like "pernicious practices"? Or just the way politics works?

It is unnecessary to look beyond the Act's primary purpose to limit the actuality and appearance of corruption resulting from large individual financial contributions in order to find a constitutionally sufficient justification for the $1,000 contribution limitation. * * * To the extent that large contributions are given to secure a political *quid pro quo* from current and potential office holders, the integrity of our system of representative democracy is undermined. Although the scope of such pernicious practices can never be reliably ascertained, the deeply disturbing examples surfacing after the 1972 election demonstrate that the problem is not an illusory one.

Of almost equal concern as the danger of actual quid pro quo arrangements is the impact of the appearance of corruption stemming from public awareness of the opportunities for abuse inherent in a regime of large individual financial contributions. * * * Congress could legitimately conclude that the avoidance of the appearance of improper influence "is also critical . . . if confidence in the system of representative government is not to be eroded to a disastrous extent." * * *

The Act's $1,000 contribution limitation focuses precisely on the problem of large campaign contributions—the narrow aspect of political association where the actuality and potential for corruption have been identified— while leaving persons free to engage

Notice that preventing the appearance of corruption is a distinct rationale from preventing actual corruption.

in independent political expression, to associate actively through volunteering their services, and to assist to a limited but nonetheless substantial extent in supporting candidates and committees with financial resources. Significantly, the Act's contribution limitations in themselves do not undermine to any material degree the potential for robust and effective discussion of candidates and campaign issues by individual citizens, associations, the institutional press, candidates, and political parties.

We find that, under the rigorous standard of review established by our prior decisions, the weighty interests served by restricting the size of financial contributions to political candidates are sufficient to justify the limited effect upon First Amendment freedoms caused by the $1,000 contribution ceiling. * * *

[The Court went on to uphold other contribution limits in the Act.]

C. Expenditure Limitations

The Act's expenditure ceilings impose direct and substantial restraints on the quantity of political speech. The most drastic of the limitations restricts individuals and groups, including political parties that fail to place a candidate on the ballot, to an expenditure of $1,000 "relative to a clearly identified candidate during a calendar year." Other expenditure ceilings limit spending by candidates, their campaigns, and political parties in connection with election campaigns. It is clear that a primary effect of these expenditure limitations is to restrict the quantity of campaign speech by individuals, groups, and candidates. The restrictions, while neutral as to the ideas expressed, limit political expression "at the core of our electoral process and of the First Amendment freedoms." *Williams v. Rhodes*, 393 U.S. 23, 32 (1968). * * *

Section 608(e)(1) provides that "(n)o person may make any expenditure . . . relative to a clearly identified candidate during a calendar year which, when added to all other expenditures made by such person during the year advocating the election or defeat of such candidate, exceeds $1,000." The plain effect * * * is to prohibit all individuals,

> Notice this real-world point. Do you find it convincing? If the cost of a quarter-page ad in a newspaper is more than $1,000 at the time, does this law effectively prohibit individuals from taking out ads supporting or opposing specific candidates?

who are neither candidates nor owners of institutional press facilities, and all groups, except political parties and campaign organizations, from voicing their views "relative to a clearly identified candidate" through means that entail aggregate expenditures of more than $1,000 during a calendar year. The provision, for example, would make it a federal criminal offense for a person or association to place a single one-quarter page advertisement "relative to a clearly identified candidate" in a major metropolitan newspaper.

[To avoid vagueness, the Court understood this provision "as limited to communications that include explicit words of advocacy of election or defeat of a candidate."]

We turn then to the basic First Amendment question whether § 608(e)(1), even as thus narrowly and explicitly construed, impermissibly burdens the constitutional right of free expression. * * *

[T]he independent advocacy restricted by the provision does not presently appear to pose dangers of real or apparent corruption comparable to those identified with large campaign contributions. The parties defending § 608(e)(1) contend that it is necessary to prevent would-be contributors from avoiding the contribution limitations by the simple expedient of paying directly for media advertisements or for other portions of the candidate's campaign activities. They argue that expenditures controlled by or coordinated with the candidate and his campaign might well have virtually the same value to the candidate as a contribution and would pose similar dangers of abuse. Yet such controlled or coordinated expenditures are treated as contributions rather than expenditures under the Act. Section 608(b)'s contribution ceilings rather than § 608(e)(1)'s independent expenditure limitation prevent attempts to circumvent the Act

> Notice again the distinction between a "contribution" to a candidate and an "independent expenditure." The concept of a "contribution" includes any expenditures if the expenditure is "controlled" by or even "coordinated with" the candidate's campaign, even if someone else makes the actual expenditure.

through prearranged or coordinated expenditures amounting to disguised contributions. By contrast, § 608(e)(1) limits expenditures for express advocacy of candidates made totally independently of the candidate and his campaign. Unlike contributions, such independent expenditures may well provide little assistance to the candidate's campaign and indeed may prove counterproductive. The absence of prearrangement and coordination of an expenditure with the candidate or his agent not only undermines the value of the expenditure to the candidate, but also alleviates the danger that expenditures will be given as a quid pro quo for improper commitments from the candidate. Rather than preventing circumvention of the contribution limitations, § 608(e)(1) severely restricts all independent advocacy despite its substantially diminished potential for abuse.

While the independent expenditure ceiling thus fails to serve any substantial governmental interest in stemming the reality or appearance of corruption in the electoral process, it heavily burdens core First Amendment expression. * * * Advocacy of the election or defeat of candidates for federal office is no less entitled to protection under the First Amendment than the discussion of political policy generally or advocacy of the passage or defeat of legislation.

> In the next paragraph, notice the reference to an interest distinct from preventing corruption or the appearance of corruption. This is the interest in countering the inequality inherent in the fact that, if engaging in speech costs money, people with more money have a greater ability to speak—or, at least, a greater ability to get their views heard.

It is argued, however, that the ancillary governmental interest in equalizing the relative ability of individuals and groups to influence the outcome of elections serves to justify the limitation on express advocacy of the election or defeat of candidates imposed by § 608(e)(1)'s expenditure ceiling. But the concept that government may restrict the speech of some elements of our society in order to enhance the relative voice of others is wholly foreign to the First Amendment, which was designed "to secure 'the widest possible dissemination of information from diverse and antagonistic sources,'" and " 'to assure unfettered interchange of ideas for the bringing about of political and social changes desired by the people.'" *New York Times Co. v. Sullivan*, supra, 376 U.S., at 266, 269, quoting *Associated Press v. United States*, 326 U.S. 1, 20 (1945), and *Roth v. United States*, 354 U.S., at 484. The First Amendment's protection against governmental abridgment of free expression cannot properly be made to depend on a person's financial

> The second sentence of this paragraph is one of the most famous lines in the history of the First Amendment. Can you see why? But, if the government can't "restrict" some speech to further the interest in creating an equal playing field in political campaigns, what can it do? Recall from Chapter 5 that we have a one-person, one-vote principle as to the actual mechanisms for voting (i.e., each person Is supposed to have the same influence when counting votes to determine who becomes a representative). How does the fact that we do not have an equivalent "one person, one speech" principle (i.e., each person does not have the same influence on the broader ecosystem of ideas about and arguments in favor of or against candidates when determining who becomes a representative) matter in determining who becomes a representative?

ability to engage in public discussion. *Cf. Eastern R. Conf. v. Noerr Motors*, 365 U.S. 127, 139 (1961). * * *

For the reasons stated, we conclude that § 608(e)(1)'s independent expenditure limitation is unconstitutional under the First Amendment.

[For similar reasons, the Court proceeded to strike down the limitation on candidate expenditures from personal or family resources, and the limitations on overall campaign expenditures by candidates. Neither were adequately tailored to address the interest in preventing the reality or appearance of corruption, and the interest in equalizing resources was deemed inadequate under the First Amendment.]

In sum, the provisions of the Act that impose a $1,000 limitation on contributions to a single candidate, a $5,000 limitation on contributions by a political committee to a single candidate, and a $25,000 limitation on total contributions by an individual during any calendar year, are constitutionally valid. These limitations, along with the disclosure provisions, constitute the Act's primary weapons against the reality or appearance of improper influence stemming from the dependence of candidates on large campaign contributions. The contribution ceilings thus serve the basic governmental interest in safeguarding the integrity of the electoral process without directly impinging upon the rights of individual citizens and candidates to engage in political debate and discussion. By contrast, the First Amendment requires the invalidation of the Act's independent expenditure ceiling, its limitation on a candidate's expenditures from his own personal funds, and its ceilings on overall campaign expenditures. These provisions place substantial and direct restrictions on the ability of candidates, citizens, and associations to engage in protected political expression, restrictions that the First Amendment cannot tolerate.

[Part II addressed and upheld the disclosure requirements of the 1974 FECA amendments. Part III upheld the public financing scheme that the statute adopted for presidential elections. Part IV invalidated the structure created for the FEC. The statute was later amended to fix this problem.]

[The concurring and dissenting opinions are omitted.]

NOTES & QUESTIONS

1. Why did the *Buckley* court conclude that contributions and expenditures were distinguishable from each other as a matter of First Amendment law? Is this distinction persuasive?

2. What interest did the *Buckley* court accept as a permissible rationale for campaign contribution limits. Is the opinion's reasoning on this point persuasive?

3. Why did the court conclude that the government had failed to justify the FECA restrictions on campaign expenditures?

4. If the government can't "restrict" some speech to further the interest in creating an equal playing field in political campaigns, what can it do? Recall from Chapter 5 that the one person, one vote principle means that each person is supposed to have the same influence when counting votes to determine who becomes a representative. How does the fact that we do not have an equivalent "one person, one speech" principle, in which each person might have roughly equivalent influence on the broader ecosystem of political ideas and arguments, matter in determining who becomes a representative?

5. *Buckley* was decided before the Supreme Court created the current tiers of scrutiny in constitutional-law jurisprudence and so was not very precise about the level of scrutiny applicable to contribution and expenditure limits under the First Amendment. Subsequent cases have clarified the constitutional standard. Expenditure restrictions are subject to *strict scrutiny*, which means they must be narrowly tailored to serve a compelling interest. Contribution restrictions, meanwhile, must only be "closely drawn" to further a "sufficiently important interest," under *Nixon v. Shrink Missouri Government PAC,* 528 U.S. 377 (2000). This is a form of heightened scrutiny, but perhaps still less stringent than strict scrutiny. *Shrink Missouri* upheld contribution limits applicable to candidates for state office, which ranged from $275 for candidates for state representative to $1,075 for candidates for statewide office. On the other hand, in *Randall v. Sorrell,* 548 U.S. 230 (2006), a splintered Court struck down Vermont's very low contribution limits: $200 for state representative candidates, $300 for state senate candidates, and $400 for candidates for statewide office.

6. Although *Buckley* prohibited restrictions on *individual* expenditures, the court subsequently upheld restrictions on *corporate* expenditures in *Austin v. Michigan Chamber of Commerce,* 494 U.S. 652 (1990). *Austin* involved a Michigan law prohibiting corporations from using their funds to support or oppose candidates for state office. The court upheld Michigan's ban on corporate expenditures on a 6–3 vote. Justice Marshall's opinion for the Court applied strict scrutiny under the First Amendment, but found that the law was narrowly tailored to serve a compelling interest: "Michigan's regulation aims at a different type of corruption in the political arena: the corrosive and distorting effects of immense aggregations of wealth that are accumulated with the help of the corporate form and that have little or no correlation to the public's support for the corporation's political ideas." *Id.* at 660. This is sometimes referred to as the "antidistortion" rationale for campaign finance regulation.

7. How different is the "antidistortion" rationale from the interest in countering the effect that wealth inequality has on elections, the "equal the playing field" rationale that *Buckley* rejected? Or, put another way, was *Austin* consistent with *Buckley*? As we shall see, two decades later in *Citizens United v. FEC* the Supreme Court overruled *Austin.*

C. The Bipartisan Campaign Reform Act (BCRA)

The Bipartisan Campaign Reform Act of 2002 (BCRA, also known as McCain-Feingold) further amended FECA. BCRA was mainly designed to close two loopholes in federal campaign finance law that had emerged in the decades following *Buckley,* loopholes commonly referred to as "soft money" and "issue ads."

1. Soft Money Versus Hard Money

> **!** "Soft money" refers to unregulated political contributions, in other words donations intended to further a political purpose but made in a manner that does not implicate contribution limits.

Before BCRA, contributors who had reached FECA's $1,000 "hard money" limit often gave money to political party committees. These donations, which were not subject to limits, came to be known as "soft money." Candidates for office and their campaigns would sometimes encourage donors who had "maxed out" on the hard money limit to make soft money contributions instead. In theory, these funds were supposed to be used for activities influencing state elections. But the FEC ruled that parties could fund mixed-purpose activities—designed to influence federal elections as well as state and local elections—with soft money. As a result, the amount of soft money raised by the political parties increased significantly.

In response to these developments, Title I of BCRA banned soft money while raising the limits on hard money. It prohibited national political party committees from soliciting, receiving, or spending these previously unregulated monies. BCRA also enacted restrictions on state and local parties, to prevent soft money from finding new channels. Finally, BCRA prohibited federal candidates and officeholders from receiving, spending, or soliciting soft money.

BCRA also raised the hard money limit on individual contributions to candidates from $1000 to $2000, now indexed for inflation. In the 2023–24 election cycle, the inflation-adjusted limit is $3300. That means that an individual could give up to $3300 to each candidate's primary campaign and an additional $3300 to her general election campaign, for an effective total of $6600 per candidate in each election cycle.

2. Issue Ads and Electioneering Communications

The other major loophole that BCRA sought to close was issue ads. Federal law had long prohibited corporations and unions from making campaign contributions and expenditures from their general accounts or treasuries, instead requiring them to form a separate segregated fund (or PAC). However, under *Buckley*'s interpretation of FECA, the expenditure

> A "PAC," or Political Action Committee, is an entity organized to accumulate political contributions from multiple donors for the purpose of spending those funds to influence elections.

ban was limited to *express advocacy*—that is, to ads using so-called magic words like "vote for" or "vote against." This construction of FECA made it very easy for corporations and unions to get around the ban, by running ads purporting to address policy issues that were really campaign ads. Proponents of campaign finance reform often referred to these as "sham issue ads."

In response, BCRA created a broader category of regulated campaign expenditures that included "electioneering communications," defined as broadcast, cable, and satellite communications referring to a specific candidate for federal office aired within 30 days of a primary election or 60 days of a general election.

3.   *McConnell v. FEC*

In *McConnell v. Federal Election Commission*, 540 U.S. 93 (2003), the Court upheld BCRA's restrictions on both soft money and electioneering communications.

> As we also saw in *Buckley v. Valeo*, the Supreme Court has viewed preventing both corruption and the appearance of corruption as important government interests justifying some forms of campaign finance regulation. It is worth thinking about the harms caused by the appearance of corruption.

The relevant portion of the majority opinion was jointly authored by Justices Stevens and O'Connor. They treated the soft money ban as a contribution limit, requiring only that it be closely drawn to a sufficiently important interest, as *Buckley* and *Shrink Missouri* prescribe. The Court upheld the soft money ban based on the government's interest in curbing corruption and the appearance of corruption. Key to this ruling was the majority's broad conception of the anti-corruption interest. This interest was not limited to *quid pro quo* corruption, but also included the unequal access—and possible influence—that big soft-money donors enjoyed.

McConnell also upheld BCRA's ban on corporate- and union-funded electioneering communications against a First Amendment challenge. The court relied on its prior decision in *Austin*, extending that decision to union-funded expenditures as well as those from the treasuries of for-profit corporations. That aspect of *McConnell*, however, was subsequently overruled in *Citizens United*, the subject of the next chapter.

Test Your Understanding

To assess your understanding of the material in this chapter, click here to take a quiz.

9

The *Citizens United* Decision

Key Concepts

- Independent expenditures
- General treasury funds vs. segregated political funds
- "Antidistortion" rationale
- Super PACs
- Disclosure of campaign contributions and expenditures
- Chilling effect
- Heightened scrutiny

Chapter Summary

In 2010, the Supreme Court decided a major case that has significantly reshaped campaign finance jurisprudence and dramatically transformed the ways that money influences political campaigns. In *Citizens United v. Federal Election Commission*, the Court held that corporations, both non-profit and for-profit, have the same First Amendment right as private individuals to spend as much of their corporate funds as they wish on political speech. The ruling extends to unions and other organizations as well. Although limits on the amount that can be contributed directly to candidates remain constitutional, the ability of organizations to spend unlimited amounts on independent political activities has transformed political campaigns, including giving rise to Super PACs. Meanwhile, measures that require public disclosure of campaign contributions and expenditures remain constitutional for now.

In Chapter 8, we saw that in its 1990 *Austin* decision the Supreme Court had concluded that campaign expenditure restrictions targeting corporations could pass muster under the First Amendment in light of what the Court called "the corrosive and distorting effects of immense aggregations of wealth that are accumulated with the help of the corporate form and that have little or no correlation to the public's support for the corporation's political ideas." Although the Court made exceptions for "ideological" corporations or organizations whose *raison d'etre* might be precisely to take part in political advocacy, it continued to affirm long-standing prohibitions on for-profit corporations and unions using their general treasury funds for most political activities. Instead, these entities had to create separate political accounts, funded by the voluntary contributions of their members and employees (rather than funded by a corporation's profits or a union's required member dues), to engage in political activities.

Two decades after *Austin*, and seven years after *McConnell v. FEC* had similarly upheld BCRA's ban on corporate funding of electioneering communications, a new Court took up the issue of corporate rights to engage in political activity. In *Citizens United v. Federal Election Commission*, 558 U.S. 310 (2010), the Court reached a very different result with respect to the ability of corporations and unions to spend their general treasury funds, although from the opening paragraphs of its decision the Court reaffirmed the appropriateness of disclosure requirements in the political speech context.

A. Corporate and Union Campaign Expenditures

FYI Senator Hillary Clinton lost the Democratic nomination to then-Senator Barack Obama, who then defeated Senator John McCain (R-AZ), one of the principal authors of BCRA, in the general election.

On a 5–4 vote, the Supreme Court in *Citizens United* struck down BCRA's prohibition on corporate electioneering communications, overruling the portions of *McConnell* mentioned above. The Citizens United organization, a nonprofit corporation, had produced a film called *Hillary: The Movie*. The film portrayed then-Senator Hillary Clinton (D-NY) in an unfavorable light, and the group desired to run ads promoting the movie in 2008, when Clinton was a Democratic candidate for President. Fearing that the ads might violate BCRA's prohibition on corporate electioneering, Citizens United brought a First Amendment challenge to the constitutionality of the prohibition.

As you read the excerpts of the *Citizens United* decision below, be thinking about the purposes of the First Amendment and how to promote the "unfettered interchange of ideas" concerning political and social change, *Buckley*, 424 U.S. at 14 (quoting *Roth v. United States*, 354 U.S. 476, 484 (1957)).

Citizens United v. Federal Election Commission
558 U.S. 310 (2010)

JUSTICE KENNEDY delivered the opinion of the Court.

Federal law prohibits corporations and unions from using their general treasury funds to make independent expenditures for speech defined as an "electioneering communication" or for speech expressly advocating the election or defeat of a candidate. 2 U.S.C. § 441b. Limits on electioneering communications were upheld in *McConnell v. Federal Election Comm'n*, 540 U.S. 93, 203–209 (2003). The holding of *McConnell* rested to a large extent on an earlier case, *Austin v. Michigan Chamber of Commerce*, 494 U.S. 652 (1990). *Austin* had held that political speech may be banned based on the speaker's corporate identity.

In this case we are asked to reconsider *Austin* and, in effect, *McConnell*. It has been noted that "*Austin* was a significant departure from ancient First Amendment principles," *Federal Election Comm'n v. Wisconsin Right to Life, Inc.,* 551 U.S. 449, 490 (2007) *(WRTL)* (SCALIA, J., concurring in part and concurring in judgment). We agree with that conclusion and hold that *stare decisis* does not compel the continued acceptance of *Austin.* The government may regulate corporate political speech through disclaimer and disclosure requirements, but it may not suppress that speech altogether. We turn to the case now before us.

I

A

Citizens United is a nonprofit corporation. It brought this action in the United States District Court for the District of Columbia. A three-judge Court later convened to hear the cause. The resulting judgment gives rise to this appeal. * * *

In January 2008, Citizens United released a film entitled *Hillary: The Movie.* We refer to the film as *Hillary.* It is a 90-minute documentary about then-senator Hillary Clinton, who was a candidate in the Democratic Party's 2008 presidential primary elections. *Hillary* mentions Senator Clinton by name and depicts interviews with political commentators and other persons, most of them quite critical of Senator Clinton. *Hillary* was released in theaters and on DVD, but Citizens United wanted to increase distribution by making it available through video-on-demand. * * *

To implement the proposal, Citizens United was prepared to pay for the video-on-demand; and to promote the film, it produced two 10-second ads and one 30-second ad for *Hillary.* Each ad includes a short (and, in our view, pejorative) statement about Senator Clinton, followed by the name of the movie and the movie's website address. Citizens United desired to promote the video-on-demand offering by running advertisements on broadcast and cable television.

B

Before the Bipartisan Campaign Reform Act of 2002 (BCRA), federal law prohibited—and still does prohibit—corporations and unions from using general treasury funds to make direct contributions to candidates or independent expenditures that expressly advocate the election or defeat of a candidate, through any form of media, in connection with certain qualified federal elections. BCRA § 203 amended § 441b to prohibit any "electioneering communication" as well. An electioneering communication is defined as "any broadcast, cable, or satellite communication" that "refers to a clearly identified candidate for federal office" and is made within 30 days of a primary or 60 days of a general election. § 434(f)(3)(a). * * * Corporations and unions are barred from using their general treasury funds for express advocacy or electioneering communications. They may establish, however, a "separate segregated fund" (known as a political action committee, or PAC) for these purposes. 2 U.S.C. § 441b(b)(2). The moneys received by the segregated fund are limited to donations from stockholders and employees of the corporation or, in the case of unions, members of the union.

C

Citizens United wanted to make *Hillary* available through video-on-demand within 30 days of the 2008 primary elections. It feared, however, that both the film and the ads would be covered by § 441b's ban on corporate-funded independent expenditures, thus subjecting the corporation to civil and criminal penalties under § 437g. In December 2007, Citizens United sought declaratory and injunctive relief against the FEC. It argued that (1) § 441b is unconstitutional as applied to *Hillary;* and (2) BCRA's disclaimer and disclosure requirements, BCRA §§ 201 and 311, are unconstitutional as applied to *Hillary* and to the three ads for the movie.

The District Court * * * granted the FEC's motion for summary judgment, the Court held that § 441b was facially constitutional under *McConnell,* and that § 441b was constitutional as applied to *Hillary* because it was "susceptible of no other interpretation than to inform the electorate that Senator Clinton is unfit for office, that the United States would be a dangerous place in a President Hillary Clinton world, and that viewers should vote against her." 530 F.Supp.2d, at 279. * * *

II

[In part II, the Court rejected several arguments that *Hillary* did not come within the scope of BCRA § 441b, and that the Court therefore need not reach the question of whether § 441b was unconstitutional.]

III

The First Amendment provides that "Congress shall make no law . . . abridging the freedom of speech." Laws enacted to control or suppress speech may operate at different points in the speech process. * * *

The law before us is an outright ban, backed by criminal sanctions. Section 441b makes it a felony for all corporations—including nonprofit advocacy corporations—either to expressly advocate the election or defeat of candidates or to broadcast electioneering communications within 30 days of a primary election and 60 days of a general election. Thus, the following acts would all be felonies under § 441b: the Sierra Club runs an ad, within the crucial phase of 60 days before the general election, that exhorts the public to disapprove of a Congressman who favors logging in national forests; the National Rifle Association publishes a book urging the public to vote for the challenger because the incumbent U.S. Senator supports a handgun ban; and the American Civil Liberties Union creates a web site telling the public to vote for a presidential candidate in light of that candidate's defense of free speech. These prohibitions are classic examples of censorship. * * *

> Notice this point. When you think of the term "corporations," does the Sierra Club or NRA come to mind? Or is the term more likely to evoke ExxonMobil or Walmart? Like the Sierra Club, NRA, and ACLU, Citizens United is a nonprofit. Does this matter? Should it? What if the law only applied to for-profit corporations?

Section 441b's prohibition on corporate independent expenditures is thus a ban on speech. As a "restriction on the amount of money a person or group can spend on political communication during a campaign," that statute "necessarily reduces the quantity of expression by restricting the number of issues discussed, the depth of their exploration, and the size of the audience reached." *Buckley v. Valeo*, 424 U.S. 1, 19 (1976) *(per curiam)*. Were the Court to uphold these restrictions, the government could repress speech by silencing certain voices at any of the various points in the speech process. If § 441b applied to individuals, no one would believe that it is merely a time, place, or manner restriction on speech. Its purpose and effect are to silence entities whose voices the government deems to be suspect.

 As noted above, the law only applies to corporations and unions, and so it treats corporations (and unions) differently from individuals. What does the Court mean here when it says that the law's "purpose and effect are to silence entities whose voices the Government deems to be suspect"?

Speech is an essential mechanism of democracy, for it is the means to hold officials accountable to the people. The right of citizens to inquire, to hear, to speak, and to use information to reach consensus is a precondition to enlightened self-government and a necessary means to protect it. * * *

For these reasons, political speech must prevail against laws that would suppress it, whether by design or inadvertence. Laws that burden political speech are "subject to strict scrutiny," which requires the government to prove that the restriction "furthers a compelling interest and is narrowly tailored to achieve that interest." *WRTL*, 551 U.S., at 464 (opinion of ROBERTS, C.J.). * * *

Premised on mistrust of governmental power, the First Amendment stands against attempts to disfavor certain subjects or viewpoints. As instruments to censor, these categories are interrelated: speech restrictions based on the identity of the speaker are all too often simply a means to control content.

Is it accurate to call this a law "based on the identity of the speaker"?

Quite apart from the purpose or effect of regulating content, moreover, the government may commit a constitutional wrong when by law it identifies certain preferred speakers. By taking the right to speak from some and giving it to others, the government deprives the disadvantaged person or class of the right to use speech to strive to establish worth, standing, and respect for the speaker's voice. The government may not by these means deprive the public of the right and privilege to determine for itself what speech and speakers are worthy of consideration. The First Amendment protects speech and speaker, and the ideas that flow from each. * * *

We find no basis for the proposition that, in the context of political speech, the government may impose restrictions on certain disfavored speakers. Both history and logic lead us to this conclusion.

A

The Court has recognized that First Amendment protection extends to corporations. * * *

At least since the latter part of the 19th century, the laws of some states and of the United States imposed a ban on corporate direct contributions to candidates. See B. SMITH, UNFREE SPEECH: THE FOLLY OF CAMPAIGN FINANCE REFORM 23 (2001). Yet not until 1947 did Congress first prohibit independent expenditures by corporations and labor unions in § 304 of the Labor Management Relations Act of 1947, 61 Stat. 159 (codified at 2 U.S.C. § 251 (1946 ed., supp. I)). * * *

> Recall that the text of the First Amendment is as follows: "Congress shall make no law. . .abridging the freedom of speech. . . ." It does not say, for example, "The people have the right to freedom of speech" or "No person shall have his freedom of speech abridged." Does that textual formulation matter? Should it?

For almost three decades thereafter, the Court did not reach the question whether restrictions on corporate and union expenditures are constitutional. * * *

Buckley did not consider § 610's separate ban on corporate and union independent expenditures. * * *

* * * *Austin* "uph[eld] a direct restriction on the independent expenditure of funds for political speech for the first time in [this Court's] history." 494 U.S., at 695 (KENNEDY, J., dissenting). There, the Michigan Chamber of Commerce sought to use general treasury funds to run a newspaper ad supporting a specific candidate. Michigan law, however, prohibited corporate independent expenditures that supported or opposed any candidate for state office. A violation of the law was punishable as a felony. The Court sustained the speech prohibition.

To bypass *Buckley* * * *, the *Austin* Court identified a new governmental interest in limiting political speech: an antidistortion interest. *Austin* found a compelling governmental interest in preventing "the corrosive and distorting effects of immense aggregations of wealth that are accumulated with the help of the corporate form and that have little or no correlation to the public's support for the corporation's political ideas." 494 U.S., at 660. * * *

? What do you think about this "anti-distortion" rationale? It is obviously distinct from the anti-corruption rationale the Court viewed as acceptable in upholding contribution limits in *Buckley v. Valeo*. But, how does it compare with "the concept that government may restrict the speech of some elements of our society in order to enhance the relative voice of others," an idea that the *Buckley* Court called "wholly foreign to the First Amendment" (p. 187)? Is it the same? If so, did the *Buckley* Court effectively already reject this anti-distortion rationale? What might be different about the issue in *Austin*?

B

The Court is thus confronted with conflicting lines of precedent: a pre-*Austin* line that forbids restrictions on political speech based on the speaker's corporate identity and a post-*Austin* line that permits them. No case before *Austin* had held that Congress could prohibit independent expenditures for political speech based on the speaker's corporate identity. * * *

If the First Amendment has any force, it prohibits Congress from fining or jailing citizens, or associations of citizens, for simply engaging in political speech. If the antidistortion rationale were to be accepted, however, it would permit government to ban political speech simply because the speaker is an association that has taken on the corporate form. * * *

Political speech is "indispensable to decisionmaking in a democracy, and this is no less true because the speech comes from a corporation rather than an individual." [*First Nat'l Bank of Boston v.*] *Bellotti*, 435 U.S. 765, at 777 (footnote omitted). * * * This protection for speech is inconsistent with *Austin*'s antidistortion rationale. * * *

It is irrelevant for purposes of the First Amendment that corporate funds may "have little or no correlation to the public's support for the corporation's political ideas." [*Austin,* 494 U.S.], at 660 (majority opinion). All speakers, including individuals and the media, use money amassed from the economic marketplace to fund their speech. The First Amendment protects the resulting speech, even if it was enabled by economic transactions with persons or entities who disagree with the speaker's ideas. * * *

The censorship we now confront is vast in its reach. The government has "muffle[d] the voices that best represent the most significant segments of the economy." *McConnell, supra,* at 257–258 (opinion of SCALIA, J.). And "the electorate [has been] deprived of information, knowledge and opinion vital to its function." [*United States v.*] *CIO*, 335 U.S. [106], at 144 [(1948)] (RUTLEDGE, J., concurring in result). By suppressing the speech of manifold corporations, both for-profit and nonprofit, the government prevents their voices and viewpoints from reaching the public and advising voters on which persons or entities are hostile to their interests. Factions will necessarily form in our republic, but the remedy of "destroying the liberty" of some factions is "worse than the disease." THE FEDERALIST No. 10, p. 130 (B. Wright ed. 1961) (J. Madison). Factions should be checked by permitting them all to speak, see *ibid.,* and by entrusting the people to judge what is true and what is false.

The purpose and effect of this law is to prevent corporations, including small and nonprofit corporations, from presenting both facts and opinions to the public. This makes *Austin's* antidistortion rationale all the more an aberration. * * *

When government seeks to use its full power, including the criminal law, to command where a person may get his or her information or what distrusted source he or she may not hear, it uses censorship to control thought. This is unlawful. The First Amendment confirms the freedom to think for ourselves. * * *

[T]he government falls back on the argument that corporate political speech can be banned in order to prevent corruption or its appearance. In *Buckley,* the Court found this interest "sufficiently important" to allow limits on contributions but did not extend that reasoning to expenditure limits. 424 U.S., at 25. When *Buckley* examined an expenditure ban, it found "that the governmental interest in preventing corruption and the appearance of corruption [was] inadequate to justify [the ban] on independent expenditures." *Id.,* at 45. * * *

When *Buckley* identified a sufficiently important governmental interest in preventing corruption or the appearance of corruption, that interest was limited to *quid pro quo* corruption. The fact that speakers may have influence over or access to elected officials does not mean that these officials are corrupt. * * *

The appearance of influence or access, furthermore, will not cause the electorate to lose faith in our democracy. By definition, an independent expenditure is political speech presented to the electorate that is not coordinated with a candidate. The fact that a corporation, or any other speaker, is willing to spend money to try to persuade voters presupposes that the people have the ultimate influence over elected officials. This is inconsistent with any suggestion that the electorate will refuse " 'to take part in democratic governance' " because of additional political speech made by a corporation or any other speaker. *McConnell, supra,* at 144 (quoting *Nixon v. Shrink Missouri Government PAC,* 528 U.S. 377, 390 (2000)). * * *

> What is the assumption the Court is making here about the relationship between political speech (including by corporations) and representative government? In contrast, what assumption did the drafters and defenders of the BCRA make about that relationship based on the anti-distortion rationale?

The remedies enacted by law * * * must comply with the First Amendment; and, it is our law and our tradition that more speech, not less, is the governing rule. An outright ban on corporate political speech during the critical preelection period is not a permissible remedy. Here Congress has created categorical bans on speech that are asymmetrical to preventing *quid pro quo* corruption.

[The Court proceeded to reject the government's attempt to justify BCRA's ban on corporate electioneering based on its asserted interests in protecting shareholders and preventing foreign influence. It also held that *stare decisis* was not an adequate reason for adhering to its holdings in *Austin* and *McConnell.*]

D

Austin is overruled, so it provides no basis for allowing the government to limit corporate independent expenditures. As the government appears to concede, overruling *Austin* "effectively invalidate[s] not only BCRA Section 203, but also 2 U.S.C. 441b's prohibition on the use of corporate treasury funds for express advocacy." Section 441b's restrictions on corporate independent expenditures are therefore invalid and cannot be applied to *Hillary.*

> Recall again that BCRA Section 203 expanded the prohibition on corporations and unions using their general treasury funds to cover any "electioneering communication."

Given our conclusion we are further required to overrule the part of *McConnell* that upheld BCRA § 203's extension of § 441b's restrictions on corporate independent expenditures. The *McConnell* Court relied on the antidistortion interest recognized in *Austin* to uphold a greater restriction on speech than the restriction upheld in *Austin,* see 540 U.S., at 205, and we have found this interest unconvincing and insufficient. This part of *McConnell* is now overruled.

[Part IV upheld BCRA's disclosure requirements. That portion of the opinion is excerpted and discussed in Section B of this chapter below.]

V

When word concerning the plot of the movie *Mr. Smith Goes to Washington* reached the circles of government, some officials sought, by persuasion, to discourage its distribution. Under *Austin,* though, officials could have done more than discourage its distribution—they could have banned the film. After all, it, like *Hillary,* was speech funded by a corporation that was critical of members of Congress. *Mr. Smith Goes to Washington* may be fiction and caricature; but fiction and caricature can be a powerful force. * * *

Some members of the public might consider *Hillary* to be insightful and instructive; some might find it to be neither high art nor a fair discussion on how to set the nation's course; still others simply might suspend judgment on these points but decide to think more about issues and candidates. Those choices and assessments, however, are not for the government to make. "the First Amendment underwrites the freedom to experiment and to create in the realm of thought and speech. Citizens must be free to use new forms, and new forums, for the expression of ideas. The civic discourse belongs to the people, and the government may not prescribe the means used to conduct it." *McConnell, supra,* at 341 (opinion of KENNEDY, J.).

The judgment of the District Court is reversed with respect to the constitutionality of 2 U.S.C. § 441b's restrictions on corporate independent expenditures. * * * The case is remanded for further proceedings consistent with this opinion.

It is so ordered.

[CHIEF JUSTICE ROBERTS and JUSTICE SCALIA wrote concurring opinions, which are omitted. JUSTICE STEVENS wrote a very long dissent, only a brief portion of which is excerpted here.]

Justice Stevens, with whom Justice Ginsburg, Justice Breyer, and Justice Sotomayor join, concurring in part and dissenting in part.

The real issue in this case concerns how, not if, the appellant may finance its electioneering. Citizens United is a wealthy nonprofit corporation that runs a political action committee (PAC) with millions of dollars in assets. Under the Bipartisan Campaign Reform Act of 2002 (BCRA), it could have used those assets to televise and promote *Hillary: The Movie* wherever and whenever it wanted to. It also could have spent unrestricted sums to broadcast *Hillary* at any time other than the 30 days before the last primary election. Neither Citizens United's nor any other corporation's speech has been "banned." All that the parties dispute is whether Citizens United had a right to use the funds in its general treasury to pay for broadcasts during the 30-day period. The notion that the First Amendment dictates an affirmative answer to that question is, in my judgment, profoundly misguided. Even more misguided is the notion that the Court must rewrite the law relating to campaign expenditures by *for-profit* corporations and unions to decide this case.

> **!** Notice how different this framing of the case is from the majority's framing.

The basic premise underlying the Court's ruling is its iteration, and constant reiteration, of the proposition that the First Amendment bars regulatory distinctions based on a speaker's identity, including its "identity" as a corporation. While that glittering generality has rhetorical appeal, it is not a correct statement of the law. Nor does it tell us when a corporation may engage in electioneering that some of its shareholders oppose. It does not even resolve the specific question whether Citizens United may be required to finance some of its messages with the money in its PAC. The conceit that corporations must be treated identically to natural persons in the political sphere is not only inaccurate but also inadequate to justify the court's disposition of this case.

> **?** Is this argument about "the distinction between corporate and human speakers" the same as the anti-distortion rationale? If not, what more does it add?

In the context of election to public office, the distinction between corporate and human speakers is significant. Although they make enormous contributions to our society, corporations are not actually members of it. They cannot vote or run for office. Because they may be managed and controlled by nonresidents, their interests may conflict in fundamental respects with the interests of eligible voters. The financial resources, legal structure, and instrumental orientation of corporations raise legitimate concerns about their role in the electoral process. Our lawmakers have a compelling constitutional basis, if not also a democratic duty, to take measures designed to guard against the potentially deleterious effects of corporate spending in local and national races. * * *

Let us start from the beginning. The Court invokes "ancient First Amendment principles" and original understandings to defend today's ruling, yet it makes only a perfunctory attempt to ground its analysis in the principles or understandings of those who drafted and ratified the amendment. Perhaps this is because there is not a scintilla of evidence to support the notion that anyone believed it would preclude regulatory distinctions based on the corporate form. To the extent that the Framers' views are discernible and relevant to the disposition of this case, they would appear to cut strongly against the majority's position.

This is not only because the Framers and their contemporaries conceived of speech more narrowly than we now think of it, see Bork, *Neutral Principles and Some First Amendment Problems*, 47 IND. L.J. 1, 22 (1971), but also because they held very different views about the nature of the First Amendment right and the role of corporations in society. Those few corporations that existed at the founding were authorized by grant of a special legislative charter. * * *

The individualized charter mode of incorporation reflected the "cloud of disfavor under which corporations labored" in the early years of this nation. 1 W. FLETCHER, CYCLOPEDIA OF THE LAW OF CORPORATIONS § 2, p. 8 (rev. ed. 2006). * * * Thomas Jefferson famously fretted that corporations would subvert the republic. * * *

The Framers thus took it as a given that corporations could be comprehensively regulated in the service of the public welfare. Unlike our colleagues, they had little trouble distinguishing corporations from human beings, and when they constitutionalized the right to free speech in the First Amendment, it was the free speech of individual americans that they had in mind. While individuals might join together to exercise their speech rights, business corporations, at least, were plainly not seen as facilitating such associational or expressive ends. * * *

A century of more recent history puts to rest any notion that today's ruling is faithful to our First Amendment tradition. At the federal level, the express distinction between corporate and individual political spending on elections stretches back to 1907, when Congress passed the Tillman Act, banning all corporate contributions to candidates. The Senate Report on the legislation observed that "[t]he evils of the use of [corporate] money in connection with political elections are so generally recognized that the committee deems it unnecessary to make any argument in favor of the general purpose of this measure. It is in the interest of good government and calculated to promote purity in the selection of public officials." S.Rep. No. 3056, 59th Cong., 1st Sess., 2 (1906). * * *

By the time Congress passed FECA in 1971, the bar on corporate contributions and expenditures had become such an accepted part of federal campaign finance regulation that when a large number of plaintiffs, including several nonprofit corporations, challenged virtually every aspect of the act in *Buckley,* 424 U.S. 1, no one even bothered to argue that the bar as such was unconstitutional. * * *

In the 20 years since *Austin,* we have reaffirmed its holding and rationale a number of times, * * * most importantly in *McConnell,* 540 U.S. 93, where we upheld the provision challenged here, § 203 of BCRA. * * *

> **?** Notice the array of different government interests Justice Stevens is referring to? Does the law further each of these interests? If so, how?

In sum, over the course of the past century Congress has demonstrated a recurrent need to regulate corporate participation in candidate elections to " '[p]reserv[e] the integrity of the electoral process, preven[t] corruption, . . . sustai[n] the active, alert responsibility of the individual citizen,' " protect the expressive interests of shareholders, and " '[p]reserv[e] . . . the individual citizen's confidence in government.' " * * * Time and again, we have recognized these realities in approving measures that Congress and the states have taken. None of the cases the majority cites is to the contrary. * * *

Undergirding the majority's approach to the merits is the claim that the only "sufficiently important governmental interest in preventing corruption or the appearance of corruption" is one that is "limited to *quid pro quo* corruption." This is the same "crabbed view of corruption" that was espoused by Justice Kennedy in *McConnell* and squarely rejected by the Court in that case. 540 U.S., at 152. While it is true that we have not always spoken about corruption in a clear or consistent voice, the approach taken by the majority cannot be right, in my judgment. It disregards our constitutional history and the fundamental demands of a democratic society.

On numerous occasions we have recognized Congress' legitimate interest in preventing the money that is spent on elections from exerting an " 'undue influence on an officeholder's judgment'" and from creating " 'the appearance of such influence,'" beyond the sphere of *quid pro quo* relationships. * * * Corruption can take many forms. Bribery may be the paradigm case. But the difference between selling a vote and selling access is a matter of degree, not kind. And selling access is not qualitatively different from giving special preference to those who spent money on one's behalf. Corruption operates along a spectrum, and the majority's apparent belief that *quid pro quo* arrangements can be neatly demarcated from other improper influences does not accord with the theory or reality of politics. It certainly does not accord with the record Congress developed in passing BCRA, a record that stands as a remarkable testament to the energy and ingenuity with which corporations, unions, lobbyists, and politicians may go about scratching each other's backs—and which amply supported Congress' determination to target a limited set of especially destructive practices. * * *

> **?** What do you think of this argument? What kind of influence on the political process should be viewed as appropriate advocacy in favor of one's interests? And what sort of advocacy should be deemed "corrupt," akin to, or at least comparable with, bribery or quid-pro-quo arrangements? In Chapter 10, we look at lobbying. Keep these ideas in mind when we get there.

> **?** If "corruption" and "undue influence" are interchangeable, then perhaps the important question is whether certain influence is "undue." What do you think? Is Citizens United using its general treasury funds to distribute and advertise *Hillary: The Movie* giving Citizens United (or its donors) "undue" influence on political discourse or, in turn, on the legislative process?

Unlike the majority's myopic focus on *quid pro quo* scenarios and the free-floating "First Amendment principles" on which it rests so much weight, this broader understanding of corruption has deep roots in the nation's history. "During debates on the earliest [campaign finance] reform acts, the terms 'corruption' and 'undue influence' were used nearly interchangeably." Pasquale, *Reclaiming Egalitarianism in the Political Theory of Campaign Finance Reform,*

2008 U. ILL. L. REV. 599, 601. * * * And whereas we have no evidence to support the notion that the Framers would have wanted corporations to have the same rights as natural persons in the electoral context, we have ample evidence to suggest that they would have been appalled by the evidence of corruption that Congress unearthed in developing BCRA and that the Court today discounts to irrelevance. * * * When they brought our constitutional order into being, the Framers had their minds trained on a threat to republican self-government that this Court has lost sight of. * * *

In a democratic society, the longstanding consensus on the need to limit corporate campaign spending should outweigh the wooden application of judge-made rules. * * * At bottom, the Court's opinion is thus a rejection of the common sense of the American people, who have recognized a need to prevent corporations from undermining self-government since the founding, and who have fought against the distinctive corrupting potential of corporate electioneering since the days of Theodore Roosevelt. It is a strange time to repudiate that common sense. While American democracy is imperfect, few outside the majority of this Court would have thought its flaws included a dearth of corporate money in politics.

I would affirm the judgment of the District Court.

NOTES & QUESTIONS

1. Was the *Citizens United* majority correct to conclude that campaign expenditures by for-profit corporations should receive protection under the First Amendment? Why or why not?

2. Why did the Court conclude that BCRA's ban on corporate electioneering was not narrowly tailored to prevent either the reality or the appearance of corruption? Why did it reject *Austin's* "antidistortion" rationale? Are its arguments persuasive? Consider Justice Stevens's dissent.

3. After *Buckley* and *Citizens United*, no limits are permitted on independent expenditures by wealthy individuals or corporations. How do you think this changes the incentives that members of Congress face?

4. After the decision in *Citizens United*, a new kind of organization began to proliferate. The technical term is "independent-expenditure only committees," but they are commonly called "Super PACs." These entities only make independent expenditures, and do not make contributions to candidates. Super PACs may receive unlimited contributions. The proliferation of Super PACs followed quickly after the D.C. Circuit's decision in *Speechnow.org v. Federal Election Commission*, 599 F.3d 686 (D.C. Cir. 2010) (en banc). The D.C. Circuit concluded that it violates the First Amendment to limit contributions to an organization that only makes independent expenditures. The court relied on the holding in *Citizens United* that there is no valid constitutional interest in limiting independent expenditures, unanimously concluding that limiting contributions to independent-expenditure only committees likewise serves no cognizable government interest.

5. In addition to Super PACs and other political action committees, a number of groups organized under Section 501(c) of the Internal Revenue Code now routinely engage in independent spending to influence election results. Under current law, contributions to these entities only need to be disclosed if they are made "for the purpose of" election-related activity. These groups are, however, required to disclose their expenditures for express advocacy and electioneering communications.

6. What effects do you think the proliferation of independent spending by outside groups (that is, groups other than candidates and parties) is likely to have on the legislative process? Consider this perspective, drawn from a study of outside spending in congressional elections:

    > Perhaps most important is the impact of independent spending on governance. We did not find evidence of *quid pro quo* corruption, in the form of exchange of money for political favors, which the Supreme Court holds to be the only rationale for restricting the flow of campaign funding. Without additional evidence, then, reformers will have a hard time making a case for new contribution limits under existing First Amendment precedent. What we did find was evidence of other effects of outside spending. The primary effects include threats of making or withholding outside spending—usually implicit, but occasionally explicit—as well as changes to the legislative agenda. Some of our interviewees also believe that outside spending has more subtle, secondary effects on the legislative process, by consuming members' time,

fraying relationships, contributing to polarization, and spurring greater public distrust of Congress.

Daniel P. Tokaji & Renata E.B. Strause, The New Soft Money: Outside Spending in Congressional Elections (2014).

B. Disclosure Requirements*

Federal and state laws also require the disclosure of certain campaign-related expenditures and contributions. Disclosure requirements have generally been viewed with less suspicion than limits on expenditures and contributions. That is because requiring disclosure of campaign-related money does not necessarily impede it from being given or spent. On the other hand, compelled disclosure may have a chilling effect on would-be donors and spenders. People may fear negative consequences if the government or someone else (such as an employer) finds out they have financially supported a candidate, party, or other group that is regarded with disfavor.

> **FYI** The Supreme Court first held that the First Amendment prohibits mandatory disclosure in a 1958 case, *NAACP v. Alabama*. Think about the parties to that litigation. The Court held that the State of Alabama could not compel the NAACP to disclose its membership list. Why do you think the State of Alabama would have wanted the NAACP's membership list in the 1950s? What do you think of the context of the NAACP's claim that its "right of association" would be infringed if it were forced to turn over its membership list? How does it compare with, say, a Super PAC's claim that it should have a right not to disclose its donors?

The Supreme Court accords heightened scrutiny to disclosure requirements, in recognition of their potential chilling effects and impact on privacy. The Court has subjected mandatory disclosure rules to "exacting scrutiny" under the First Amendment, a standard that requires a substantial relation between the disclosure requirement and a sufficiently important government interest. Although this may sound stringent, it is less so than the strict scrutiny standard applied to expenditure limits. As a practical matter, it is also less stringent than the scrutiny accorded to contribution limits. That is

---

*   The material in this section is drawn from Daniel P. Tokaji, Election Law in a Nutshell (2d ed. 2017).

largely because the Court has been relatively generous in the government interests that it recognizes as justifications for disclosure.

Starting with *Buckley*, the Court has recognized three interests that may justify disclosure requirements: (1) *informing the electorate* of where campaign money comes from and how it is spent, (2) *deterring corruption and avoiding the appearance of corruption*, by exposing large contributors who may be seeking special treatment, and (3) *gathering information needed to detect violations of contribution limits*. Based on these interests, *Buckley* upheld FECA's disclosure requirements,

Campaign finance disclosures can serve three related interests:
(1) informing the public
(2) deterring corruption
(3) detecting violations

including the requirement that political committees register and report and that those making contributions over $100 be disclosed. To save expenditure disclosure from a vagueness challenge, the Court narrowed FECA's scope. It interpreted "political committees" to include only those under the control of a candidate or having the major purpose of influencing elections.

Relying on *Buckley*, the Supreme Court upheld BCRA's expansion of FECA's disclosure requirements in both *McConnell* and *Citizens United*. Under BCRA, anyone spending more than $10,000 on electioneering communications must file a disclosure statement identifying the person making the expenditure, the amount spent, the election to which it was directed, and the names of certain contributors. BCRA § 201. BCRA also required that electioneering communications include a disclaimer, indicating that "_____ is responsible for the content of this advertising." BCRA § 311. Eight of the nine justices joined Part IV of the *Citizens United* majority opinion, upholding BCRA's disclosure and disclaimer requirements:

> Disclaimer and disclosure requirements may burden the ability to speak, but they "impose no ceiling on campaign-related activities," *Buckley*, 424 U.S., at 64, and "do not prevent anyone from speaking," *McConnell*, supra, at 201, (internal quotation marks and brackets omitted). The Court has subjected these requirements to "exacting scrutiny," which requires a "substantial relation" between the disclosure requirement and a "sufficiently important" governmental interest.
>
> In *Buckley*, the Court explained that disclosure could be justified based on a governmental interest in "provid[ing] the electorate with information" about the sources of election-related spending. 424 U.S., at 66. The *McConnell* Court applied this interest in rejecting facial challenges to BCRA

§§ 201 and 311. 540 U.S., at 196. There was evidence in the record that independent groups were running election-related advertisements " 'while hiding behind dubious and misleading names.'" *id.*, at 197 (quoting *McConnell I*, 251 F.Supp.2d, at 237). The Court therefore upheld BCRA §§ 201 and 311 on the ground that they would help citizens " 'make informed choices in the political marketplace.' " 540 U.S., at 197 (quoting *McConnell I, supra*, at 237) * * *

[W]e find the statute valid as applied to the ads for the movie and to the movie itself. * * *

> **!** This is the requirement that the communication state "___ is responsible for the content of this advertisement."

Citizens United argues that the disclaimer requirements in § 311 are unconstitutional as applied to its ads. It contends that the governmental interest in providing information to the electorate does not justify requiring disclaimers for any commercial advertisements, including the ones at issue here. We disagree. * * * At the very least, the disclaimers avoid confusion by making clear that the ads are not funded by a candidate or political party. * * *

Citizens United also disputes that an informational interest justifies the application of § 201 to its ads, which only attempt to persuade viewers to see the film. Even if it disclosed the funding sources for the ads, Citizens United says, the information would not help viewers make informed choices in the

> This is the rule that any person who spends more than $10,000 on electioneering communication in a calendar year must file a disclosure statement with the FEC. **!**

political marketplace. This is similar to the argument rejected above with respect to disclaimers. Even if the ads only pertain to a commercial transaction, the public has an interest in knowing who is speaking about a candidate shortly before an election. Because the informational interest alone is sufficient to justify application of § 201 to these ads, it is not necessary to consider the government's other asserted interests.

Last, Citizens United argues that disclosure requirements can chill donations to an organization by exposing donors to retaliation. * * * Citizens United, however, has offered no evidence that its members may face similar threats or reprisals. To the contrary, Citizens United has been disclosing its donors for years and has identified no instance of harassment or retaliation. * * *

With the advent of the Internet, prompt disclosure of expenditures can provide shareholders and citizens with the information needed to hold corporations and elected officials accountable for their positions and supporters. * * * The First Amendment protects political speech; and disclosure permits citizens and shareholders to react to the speech of corporate entities in a proper way. This transparency enables the electorate to make informed decisions and give proper weight to different speakers and messages.

Only Justice Thomas dissented from *Citizens United*'s upholding of BCRA's disclosure and disclaimer requirements:

I dissent from Part IV of the Court's opinion * * * because the court's constitutional analysis does not go far enough. The disclosure, disclaimer, and reporting requirements in BCRA §§ 201 and 311 are also unconstitutional.

Congress may not abridge the "right to anonymous speech" based on the " 'simple interest in providing voters with additional relevant information.' " in continuing to hold otherwise, the Court misapprehends the import of "recent events" that some amici describe "in which donors to certain causes were blacklisted, threatened, or otherwise targeted for retaliation."

* * * Amici's examples relate principally to Proposition 8, a state ballot proposition that California voters narrowly passed in the 2008 general election. Proposition 8 amended California's constitution to provide that "[o]nly marriage between a man and a woman is valid or recognized in California." Cal. Const., Art. I, § 7.5. Any donor who gave more than $100 to any committee supporting or opposing Proposition 8 was required to disclose his full name, street address, occupation, employer's name (or business name, if self-employed), and the total amount of his contributions. See Cal. Govt. Code Ann. § 84211(f) (West 2005). The California Secretary of State was then required to post this information on the Internet.

Some opponents of Proposition 8 compiled this information and created web sites with maps showing the locations of homes or businesses of Proposition 8 supporters. Many supporters (or their customers) suffered property damage, or threats of physical violence or death, as a result. They cited these incidents in a complaint they filed after the 2008 election, seeking to invalidate California's mandatory disclosure laws. Supporters recounted being told: "consider yourself lucky. If I had a gun I would have gunned you down along with each and every other supporter," or, "we have plans for you and your friends." Proposition 8 opponents also allegedly harassed the measure's supporters by defacing or damaging their property. Two religious organizations supporting Proposition 8 reportedly received through the mail envelopes containing a white powdery substance. * * *

> **?** What do you think of Justice Thomas's references to retaliation in the Prop 8 example here? Recall that the Supreme Court first prohibited mandatory disclosure of membership lists in the 1958 case of *NAACP v. Alabama*. Are the concerns of the supporters of Prop 8 that Justice Thomas references similar to the kind of concerns NAACP members would have had in Alabama in the 1950s?

The success of such intimidation tactics has apparently spawned a cottage industry that uses forcibly disclosed donor information to pre-empt citizens' exercise of their First Amendment rights. Before the 2008 presidential election, a "newly formed nonprofit group . . . plann[ed] to confront donors to conservative groups, hoping to create a chilling effect that will dry up contributions." Luo, *Group Plans Campaign Against G.O.P. Donors*, N.Y. TIMES, Aug. 8, 2008, p. A15. Its leader, "who described his effort as 'going for the jugular,'" detailed the group's plan to send a "warning letter . . . alerting donors who might be considering giving to right-wing groups to a variety of potential dangers, including legal trouble, public exposure and watchdog groups digging through their lives." *Ibid.* * * *

My point is not to express any view on the merits of the political controversies I describe. Rather, it is to demonstrate—using real-world, recent examples—the fallacy in the court's conclusion that "[d]isclaimer and disclosure requirements * * * impose no ceiling on campaign-related activities, and do not prevent anyone from speaking." Of course they do. Disclaimer and disclosure requirements enable private citizens and elected officials to implement political strategies specifically calculated to curtail campaign-related activity and prevent the lawful, peaceful exercise of First Amendment rights. * * *

Now more than ever, §§ 201 and 311 will chill protected speech because—as California voters can attest—"the advent of the Internet" enables "prompt disclosure of expenditures," which "provide[s]" political opponents "with the information needed" to intimidate and retaliate against their foes. Thus, "disclosure permits citizens . . . to react to the speech of [their political opponents] in a proper"—or undeniably improper—"way" long before a plaintiff could prevail on an as-applied challenge.

I cannot endorse a view of the First Amendment that subjects citizens of this nation to death threats, ruined careers, damaged or defaced property, or pre-emptive and threatening warning letters as the price for engaging in "core political speech, the 'primary object of First Amendment protection.' " *McConnell*, 540 U.S., at 264 (THOMAS, J., concurring in part, concurring in judgment in part, and dissenting in part). Accordingly, I respectfully dissent from the Court's judgment upholding BCRA §§ 201 and 311.

NOTES & QUESTIONS

1. What interests did the *Citizens United* majority find persuasive in upholding BCRA's disclosure and disclaimer requirements?

2. Do you find Justice Thomas's counterarguments persuasive? Is he right to suggest that mandatory disclosure could deter some citizens from making political contributions or expenditures? Should the First Amendment protect speakers from the social ramifications of their political speech activities?

3. What effect is mandatory disclosure of campaign contributions and expenditures likely to have on the legislative process? Are disclosure requirements a satisfactory substitute for limits on campaign contributions and expenditures? Why or why not?

What do you make of all these various forms of campaign finance regulation, and the complicated jurisprudential landscape that surrounds them? In the table below, we offer a simplified summary of the jurisprudence we have covered in this and the previous chapter.

Constitutional Scrutiny of Campaign Regulations

Regulation:	*Expenditure Limits*	*Contribution Limits*	*Disclosure Requirements*
Standard of Judicial Scrutiny	*Strict Scrutiny:* Limits must be "narrowly tailored" to serve a "compelling" interest	*Exacting Scrutiny:* Limits must be "closely drawn" to further a "sufficiently important" interest	*Exacting Scrutiny:* "substantial relation" between the requirement and a "sufficiently important" interest
Reason for the Standard	Expenditure limits necessarily reduce amount of protected speech; little risk of corruption	Even limited contributions still permit expressive activity; preventing corruption is important	Informing the electorate, preventing corruption, and enabling enforcement of other limits are important

Test Your Understanding

To assess your understanding of the material in this chapter, click here to take a quiz.

10

Lobbying

Key Concepts

- Right to petition the government
- Direct lobbying
- Indirect lobbying
- Grass roots lobbying
- Lobbying Disclosure Act of 1995
- Honest Leadership and Open Government Act of 2007

Chapter Summary

This chapter turns its attention to the practice of lobbying, an activity used to influence and inform our government representatives. After a brief discussion of the Federal Regulation of Lobbying Act (FRLA) of 1946, the chapter shifts to the current federal lobbying regulation regime, as structured principally by the Federal Lobbying Disclosure Act (FLDA) of 1995 and the Honest Leadership and Open Government Act (HLOGA) of 2007.

A. Background

Money has the potential to influence not only how our elected representatives are chosen, but also how they behave once in office. As early as seventeenth-century England, members of the public would frequent the hallways and lobbies of Parliament outside the chamber of the House of Commons in an effort to gain an audience with their representatives. Thus apparently was born the verb "to lobby," meaning to seek to persuade or influence government officials in the performance of their public duties. Of course, lobbying can occur not only in legislative ante-rooms, but also wherever and whenever interested parties can obtain access to government officials—restaurants, country clubs, home districts, conferences, by telephone or letter, and so on. (Indeed, today the actual chambers and antechambers of legislative bodies typically are private spaces, to which the public is not admitted, other than the observation galleries).

In the United States, the right to petition government for the "redress of grievances" is one of the cherished rights protected by the First Amendment. This right recognizes that public input is critical to the legislative process. Interest groups from across the spectrum are perhaps the most important forces influencing U.S. politics today. But in popular parlance, the term "lobbying" often is used not to describe a process of healthy public petitioning and input concerning governmental policy, but to convey concerns about privileged access available only to moneyed interests and perceived as antithetical to norms of democratic equality.

 Why do you think lobbying is so widely looked on with disdain?

As you read this chapter, think of the different branches of government and the ways in which advocates try to further their clients' interests in those different venues. In many of your courses (and later in this one too!), you focus on courts and their decision-making processes. Keep in mind that lawyers litigating in court are also "seek[ing] to persuade or influence government officials in the performance of their public duties." It is just that the "government officials" are judges, and the ways in which advocates may "persuade or influence" those officials are far more regulated. (For example, you may have already encountered the Federal Rules of Civil Procedure in your Civil Procedure course. Those rules and a host of "ethical" precepts embedded in the Rules of Professional Responsibility constrain how lawyers can "persuade or influence" judges.) As you go through this course, think about the following: How is "lobbying" before a legislature different from litigating in court? How is it different from lobbying before an agency? As you pursue your studies to become a lawyer, keep in mind that government officials in every branch of government make decisions about law that affect the public. Advocates for their clients' interests participate in shaping those decisions, but because the way in which the government officials make their decisions differ, so too does the way in which advocates "lobby" on behalf of their clients' interests.

During the twentieth century, concerns about corruption and distortion repeatedly led to legislative efforts to regulate the lobbying process at both the federal and state levels. In this chapter, we will focus on *federal* lobbying regulation. Efforts at regulation have intensified as the lobbying industry has expanded and become more sophisticated, and as many of the interest groups active in lobbying activities also have become central players in election campaigns. Today, the Lobbying Disclosure Act of 1995 is the main law regulating federal lobbying activity. As its title suggests, this law focuses on required *disclosure* of lobbying activities, rather than direct restraints on lobbying activities or expenditures. But there is strong resistance even to these efforts, grounded in First Amendment concerns as well as in questions about the efficacy of lobbying regulation.

B. Direct and Indirect Lobbying

The term lobbying usually is used to describe efforts by an organized group to influence government officials, particularly legislators and agency officials. At the outset, it is worth distinguishing between two methods for seeking to persuade or influence legislators and other officials: "direct" lobbying and "indirect" lobbying.

Direct lobbying refers to efforts to communicate a group's position or interests by having a group representative, or "lobbyist," meet, speak with, or write to government officials and their key staff members. This direct communication between an interest group and governmental actors may occur either at public hearings or in private meetings or correspondence. A close relationship exists between direct lobbying and campaign financing. Lobbyists (or their clients) often spend or give money to influence election campaigns. Incumbent legislators are in this sense dependent upon people and groups with an interest in influencing the legislative process.

Indirect lobbying refers to interest group efforts to cultivate broad public support for a group's position, and then to turn that support into grassroots pressure on legislators or agencies. Sometimes, what may superficially appear to be spontaneous popular support for (or opposition to) a particular legislative or agency measure may in fact reflect an organized campaign by an interest group to spur participation of citizens-at-large (or at least of the interest group's own members, in the case of large membership-based organizations like the Sierra Club or the National Rifle Association). Groups cultivate popular support through mass mailings, mass emailings, and media campaigns, which often incorporate explicit requests for the public to contact government officials, especially their legislators.

> Recall from the last chapter that the Sierra Club and the NRA were two of the examples the majority used in *Citizens United v. FEC* in concluding that corporations should have a First Amendment right to make unfettered independent expenditures related to campaigns (see p. 197).

C. An Early Regulatory Effort: The Federal Regulation of Lobbying Act

Until the New Deal dramatically expanded the reach of the federal government, interest groups tended to focus more on what was happening in state legislatures, where matters of economic policy typically were shaped. Exceptions of course existed, for instance involving Gilded Age matters of tariffs or railroad rates, when lobbyists turned their attention to Congress. In the public mind, lobbying practices were often connected with corruption and scandal, so that by the early twentieth century state lobbying had become one target of Progressive Era reforms.

Some members of Congress took up the reform mantle in the 1930s, largely in response to concerns about lobbyists' influence on tariff legislation. Proposed reforms were intended primarily to bring public accountability and disclosure to lobbying activities, not to limit the activities themselves. The reform effort languished for a decade, however, until Congress enacted the Federal Regulation of Lobbying Act of 1946 (FRLA), 60 Stat. 839.

The FRLA was directed primarily at disclosure of federal lobbying activities and was limited to lobbying before Congress (and thus did not apply to lobbying of Executive Branch officials). The Act provided that violations were punishable with fines and imprisonment. But the Act was not a model of legislative clarity in establishing what those violations were. Enacted as but one minor part of a broader Legislative Reorganization Act, 60 Stat. 812 (1946) (a measure that had drawn much more attention to its other provisions) and pieced together from various measures that had been considered over the previous ten years, the FRLA gave rise to several crucial interpretative issues.

The U.S. Supreme Court resolved several of these issues in *United States v. Harriss,* 347 U.S. 612 (1954). To avoid problems of both constitutional vagueness and potential infringement upon the First Amendment, Chief Justice Warren's opinion for the Court essentially rewrote the FRLA. In particular, the Court held that the disclosure requirements applied only to those who had raised outside money to lobby and did not apply to groups spending their own funds. *Id.* at 619. The Court also held that all sections of the Act applied only to "lobbying in its commonly accepted sense," by which the Court meant *direct* communications with members of Congress. *Id.* at 620. As thus interpreted in *Harriss*, the FLRA did not cover indirect lobbying, nor did it cover communication with legislative staffers other than members.

The Court adopted these narrowing constructions of the statute to avoid constitutional problems—specifically, conflict with the First Amendment. As so narrowed, the Court concluded that the statute was constitutional:

> Thus construed, [the challenged provisions of the FLRA] do not violate the freedoms guaranteed by the First Amendment—freedom to speak, publish, and petition the Government.
>
> Present-day legislative complexities are such that individual members of Congress cannot be expected to explore the myriad pressures to which they are regularly subjected. Yet full realization of the American ideal of government by elected representatives depends to no small extent on their ability to properly evaluate such pressures. Otherwise, the voice of the people may all too easily be drowned out by the voice of special interest groups seeking favored treatment while masquerading as proponents of the public weal. This is the evil which the Lobbying Act was designed to help prevent.

When the Court talks about the voice of the people being "drowned out" by the voice of special interest groups, what kind of an interest is the Court giving credence too? Think back to the last two chapters and the campaign-finance cases. Is this a rationale based on "anti-corruption"? Or, is it the "anti-distortion" rationale?

What types of situations is the Court thinking of here? Recall again political scientist James Q. Wilson's paradigm for thinking about concentrated versus diffuse costs and benefits. (Chapter 4, p. 71) Where does the type of problem the Court is alluding to fit in Wilson's 2 x 2 matrix?

> Toward that end, Congress has not sought to prohibit these pressures. It has merely provided for a modicum of information from those who for hire attempt to influence legislation or who collect or spend funds for that purpose. It wants only to know who is being hired, who is putting up the money, and how much. * * *
>
> Under these circumstances, we believe that Congress, at least within the bounds of the Act as we have construed it, is not constitutionally forbidden to require the disclosure of lobbying activities. To do so would be to deny Congress in large measure the power of self-protection. And here Congress has used that power in a manner restricted to its appropriate end. We conclude that [the challenged provisions of the FRLA] do not offend the First Amendment.

Id. at 625–26. Yet the Court's narrowing construction of the FRLA rendered it toothless in the eyes of most observers, and the U.S. Department of Justice rarely sought to enforce the FRLA (although some groups and individuals continued to register with Congress under the Act). Forty years would pass before Congress undertook another serious effort to establish a meaningful disclosure regime for federal lobbying.

D. The Current Regime: The Federal Lobbying Disclosure Act of 1995

During the second half of the twentieth century, lobbying as an industry exploded, at both the state and federal levels. By one analysis, by the beginning of the 21st century some 12,000 registered lobbyists were spending over $1.5 billion a year in reported federal lobbying expenditures, compared to an estimated $10.3 million in 1950 (itself an aberrationally large year). By 2020, that figure had more than doubled to over $3.5 billion. *See* OpenSecrets.org, *Lobbying Data Summary*, at https://www.opensecrets.org/federal-lobbying.

A variety of factors have contributed to this development. In part, lobbying activity has increased because of the growth in the scope and complexity of government regulation and activity itself, which provides more and more businesses and other groups with greater and greater motivation to influence government policy. In addition, lobbying, like campaign financing, tends to become more expensive each cycle, as participants must defend against the competing activities of other participants, who all seek to outperform the previous round. Lobbying activities also have grown in tandem with the increased participation of interest groups in political campaigns. Meanwhile, the practice of earmarking, or specifying a particular recipient of a portion of a federal appropriation, which had its heyday at the end of the twentieth century and in the first decade of the twenty-first century, provided additional incentives for businesses and industries to hire lobbyists to compete for government benefits.

But perhaps as important as any of these factors is that corporate America has simply become increasingly convinced of, and eager to capitalize on, the potential value of a large and well-managed lobbying operation. For many large corporations, this involves a team of both in-house lobbyists and hired government relations firms, whose activities often involve collectively monitoring hundreds of different proposed legislative and administrative actions, first identifying and then working to control the most important opportunities and risks. For many corporate clients, lobbyists' most valuable contributions can be defensive efforts to prevent the enactment of an undesirable piece of legislation, capitalizing on the many obstacles or "vetogates" that exist in the legislative process.

We discuss the legislative process in general, including "vetogates," in Part III of this book, Chapter 11.

The importance of lobbying to most American corporations is evidenced by the fact that they spend substantially more resources on lobbying than on efforts to influence elections. By some accounts, in recent years corporations have favored spending on congressional lobbying over elections by five (or more) to one, even after *Citizens United. See, e.g.*, ROBERT J. SHAPIRO & DOUGLAS DAWSON, CORPORATE POLITICAL SPENDING: WHY THE NEW CRITICS ARE WRONG 11 (2012). Lobbying by nonprofit organizations, although it accounts for only a small percentage of total federal lobbying, has also been increasing rapidly in recent decades.

By the late 20th century, the growth of the number of professional lobbyists, and of the amount of money flowing into the legislative and regulatory processes as a result, had given rise to increasing calls for Congress to regulate the lobbying industry further. Meanwhile, many states enacted laws to regulate the lobbying process, through disclosure requirements and sometimes through direct restraints on lobbying. For instance, some states prohibit lobbyists from contributing to legislative campaign funds while the state legislature is in session, or even from contributing to campaigns at all. Other states have "revolving door" measures that prohibit former state legislators from conducting any lobbying activities within one or two years of when their legislative terms ended. In at least one case, however, a lower federal court has found it unconstitutional to preclude former state legislators from engaging in *uncompensated* lobbying. *See Brinkman v. Budish*, 692 F. Supp. 2d 855, 863 (S.D. Ohio 2010).

By the early 1990s, increasing public concern over the impact of professional lobbyists prompted Congress to begin working on a new law to regulate federal lobbying, focused on promoting greater transparency concerning the influence of lobbying on policy. These efforts eventually replaced the Federal Regulation of Lobbying Act of 1946 with the Federal Lobbying Disclosure Act of 1995 (FLDA), 109 Stat. 691. The FLDA then was amended in 2007 by provisions of the Honest Leadership and Open Government Act ("HLOGA"), 121 Stat. 735, passed partly in response to a major lobbying scandal. In addition to strengthening certain provisions of the FLDA, the HLOGA imposed or strengthened constraints intended to control the "revolving door" of politics, primarily by prohibiting former members of Congress, as well as former congressional staffers, from taking positions as paid lobbyists for one or two years after leaving their government posts.

Today the FLDA is the primary mechanism for regulating congressional and federal agency lobbying. The FLDA is substantially more detailed than the 1946 Act, with elaborate definitions that specify its scope with precision, but which often require careful analysis to apply.

Here are the key provisions of the FLDA, as amended by the HLOGA:

2 U.S.C. §§ 1601–1604

§ 1601. Findings.

The Congress finds that—

> **!** The actual text of much of these sections is included here partly to give you experience reading a somewhat complicated statute and seeing how its components fit together.

(1) responsible representative Government requires public awareness of the efforts of paid lobbyists to influence the public decisionmaking process in both the legislative and executive branches of the Federal Government;

(2) existing lobbying disclosure statutes have been ineffective because of unclear statutory language, weak administrative and enforcement provisions, and an absence of clear guidance as to who is required to register and what they are required to disclose; and

(3) the effective public disclosure of the identity and extent of the efforts of paid lobbyists to influence Federal officials in the conduct of Government actions will increase public confidence in the integrity of Government.

> **?** How do these rationales for lobbying disclosure compare with the rationales for regulating campaign finance that we discussed in Chapter 8?

§ 1602. Definitions.

As used in this chapter:

* * *

(2) *Client.* The term "client" means any person or entity that employs or retains another person for financial or other compensation to conduct lobbying activities on behalf of that person or entity. A person or entity whose employees act as lobbyists on its own behalf is both a client and an employer of such employees. In the case of a coalition or association that employs or

retains other persons to conduct lobbying activities, the client is the coalition or association and not its individual members. * * *

(3) *Covered executive branch official.* The term "covered executive branch official" means—

> (A) the President;

> (B) the Vice President;

> (C) any officer or employee, or any other individual functioning in the capacity of such an officer or employee, in the Executive Office of the President; * * *

(4) *Covered legislative branch official.* The term "covered legislative branch official" means—

> (A) a Member of Congress;

> (B) an elected officer of either House of Congress;

> (C) any employee of, or any other individual functioning in the capacity of an employee of—

>> (i) a Member of Congress; * * *

(7) *Lobbying activities.* The term "lobbying activities" means lobbying contacts and efforts in support of such contacts, including preparation and planning activities, research and other background work that is intended, at the time it is performed, for use in contacts, and coordination with the lobbying activities of others. * * *

(8) *Lobbying contact*

> (A) Definition. The term "lobbying contact" means any oral or written communication (including an electronic communication) to a covered executive branch official or a covered legislative branch official that is made on behalf of a client with regard to—

>> (i) the formulation, modification, or adoption of Federal legislation (including legislative proposals);

>> (ii) the formulation, modification, or adoption of a Federal rule, regulation, Executive order, or any other program, policy, or position of the United States Government;

(iii) the administration or execution of a Federal program or policy (including the negotiation, award, or administration of a Federal contract, grant, loan, permit, or license); or

(iv) the nomination or confirmation of a person for a position subject to confirmation by the Senate.

(B) Exceptions. The term "lobbying contact" does not include a communication that is—

(i) made by a public official acting in the public official's official capacity;

(ii) made by a representative of a media organization if the purpose of the communication is gathering and disseminating news and information to the public;

(iii) made in a speech, article, publication or other material that is distributed and made available to the public, or through radio, television, cable television, or other medium of mass communication; * * *

(v) a request for a meeting, a request for the status of an action, or any other similar administrative request, if the request does not include an attempt to influence a covered executive branch official or a covered legislative branch official; * * *

(vii) testimony given before a committee, subcommittee, or task force of the Congress, or submitted for inclusion in the public record of a hearing conducted by such committee, subcommittee, or task force;

(viii) information provided in writing in response to an oral or written request by a covered executive branch official or a covered legislative branch official for specific information;

(ix) required by subpoena, civil investigative demand, or otherwise compelled by statute, regulation, or other action of the Congress or an agency, including any communication compelled by a Federal contract, grant, loan, permit, or license;

(x) made in response to a notice in the Federal Register, Commerce Business Daily, or other similar publication soliciting communications from the public and directed to the agency official specifically designated in the notice to receive such communications. * * *

(10) *Lobbyist.* The term "lobbyist" means any individual who is employed or retained by a client for financial or other compensation for services that include more than one lobbying contact, other than an individual whose lobbying activities constitute less than 20 percent of the time engaged in the services provided by such individual to that client over a 3-month period. * * *

§ 1603. Registration of lobbyists

(a) Registration

(1) General rule. No later than 45 days after a lobbyist first makes a lobbying contact or is employed or retained to make a lobbying contact, whichever is earlier, or on the first business day after such 45th day if the 45th day is not a business day, such lobbyist (or, as provided under paragraph (2), the organization employing such lobbyist), shall register with the Secretary of the Senate and the Clerk of the House of Representatives.

> Later in the course, we will discuss the decision-making **!** processes in administrative agencies. In one very important process—what is called "Notice & Comment Rulemaking"—everyone in the public is invited, pursuant to a "notice in the Federal Register," to provide input about an agency's proposed Rule (an administrative agency equivalent of a statute). This is a crucial venue for advocacy within the Executive Branch, and one where lots of lawyers participate on behalf of their clients. Notice that this form of advocacy is not treated as "lobbying" under the FLDA definitions.

(2) Employer filing. Any organization that has 1 or more employees who are lobbyists shall file a single registration under this section on behalf of such employees for each client on whose behalf the employees act as lobbyists.

(3) Exemption

(A) General rule. Notwithstanding paragraphs (1) and (2), a person or entity whose—

(i) total income for matters related to lobbying activities on behalf of a particular client (in the case of a lobbying firm) does not exceed and is not expected to exceed $2,500; or

(ii) total expenses in connection with lobbying activities (in the case of an organization whose employees engage in lobbying activities on its own behalf) do not exceed or are not expected to exceed $10,000 (as estimated under section 1604 of this title) in the quarterly period described in section 1604(a) of this title during which the registration would be made is not required to register under this subsection with respect to such client.

(B) Adjustment. The dollar amounts in subparagraph (A) shall be adjusted [for inflation]. * * *

(b) Contents of registration. Each registration under this section shall contain—

(1) the name, address, business telephone number, and principal place of business of the registrant, and a general description of its business or activities;

(2) the name, address, and principal place of business of the registrant's client, and a general description of its business or activities (if different from paragraph (1));

(3) the name, address, and principal place of business of any organization, other than the client, that—

(A) contributes more than $5,000 to the registrant or the client in the quarterly period to fund the lobbying activities of the registrant; and

(B) actively participates in the planning, supervision, or control of such lobbying activities;

* * *

§ 1604. Reports by registered lobbyists

(a) Quarterly report. No later than 20 days after the end of the quarterly period beginning on the first day of January, April, July, and October of each year in which a registrant is registered under section 1603 of this title, or on the first business day after such 20th day if the 20th day is not a business day, each registrant shall file a report with the Secretary of the Senate and the Clerk of the House of Representatives on its lobbying activities during such quarterly period. A separate report shall be filed for each client of the registrant.

(b) Contents of report. Each quarterly report filed under subsection (a) shall contain—

(1) the name of the registrant, the name of the client, and any changes or updates to the information provided in the initial registration, including information under section 1603(b)(3) of this title;

(2) for each general issue area in which the registrant engaged in lobbying activities on behalf of the client during the quarterly period—

(A) a list of the specific issues upon which a lobbyist employed by the registrant engaged in lobbying activities, including, to the maximum extent practicable, a list of bill numbers and references to specific executive branch actions;

(B) a statement of the Houses of Congress and the Federal agencies contacted by lobbyists employed by the registrant on behalf of the client;

(C) a list of the employees of the registrant who acted as lobbyists on behalf of the client; and

(D) a description of the interest, if any, of any foreign entity identified under section 1603(b)(4) of this title in the specific issues listed under subparagraph (A);

(3) in the case of a lobbying firm, a good faith estimate of the total amount of all income from the client (including any payments to the registrant by any other person for lobbying activities on behalf

of the client) during the quarterly period, other than income for matters that are unrelated to lobbying activities;

(4) in the case of a registrant engaged in lobbying activities on its own behalf, a good faith estimate of the total expenses that the registrant and its employees incurred in connection with lobbying activities during the quarterly period. * * *

NOTES & QUESTIONS

1. How does the FLDA define a "lobbyist"? What is a "client"? How much of a person's time working for a client must be spent on "lobbying activities" for the person to be considered a lobbyist? What purposes does this definition serve? Is it a reasonable standard?

2. Under what circumstances is a lobbyist (or their employer) required to register?

3. How often must reports be filed by registered lobbyists? What must those reports include?

4. As a result of the FLDA, substantially more information about federal lobbying is now publicly available. Not only has the number of registered lobbyists increased (from about 6,000 under the old FRLA just before passage of the FLDA, to double that number today), but each of these registrants must disclose details about their lobbying activities.

5. The reports required by the FLDA are made publicly available over the Internet by the Clerks of the U.S. Senate and the House of Representatives. Lobbyists also must file semiannual reports of their campaign contributions. Violations of the Act are subject to both civil and criminal penalties. Annual reports by the Government Accountability Office suggest both that there is a high degree of compliance with the Act, and that the Department of Justice has increased its enforcement activity in recent years.

Passage of the FLDA did not bring about an end to perceived lobbying abuses. Indeed, according to some analyses, the added requirements of the HLOGA may be driving an increase in the amount of "shadow" lobbying, in which former government officials find ways to sell their expertise without having to register as lobbyists. Furthermore, in the eyes of many reformers the available information remains incomplete. Perceived deficiencies, among others, include the Act's lack of any requirements to identify the extent to which lobbyists engage in grassroots (indirect) lobbying; the fact that lobbyists are not required to disclose the individuals, offices, or committees that they contact; and the exception from the Act's coverage for individuals who spend less than 20% of their work hours lobbying. *See* American Bar Association Task Force on Federal Lobbying Laws, *Lobbying Law in the Spotlight: Challenges and Proposed Improvements*, 63 ADMIN. L. REV. 419 (2011).

On the other hand, some believe the FLDA impermissibly burdens their First Amendment rights. In the following case, the National Association of Manufacturers challenged the requirement that a registrant disclose information about any organization that contributed more than $5,000 to support its lobbying activities. The United States Court of Appeals for the District of Columbia Circuit ("D.C. Circuit") rejected this challenge in an opinion written by Judge Garland (who was later nominated to serve on the Supreme Court, but was never confirmed, and who later became the U.S. Attorney General in the Biden administration).

National Association of Manufacturers v. Taylor
582 F.3d 1 (D.C. Cir. 2009)

Before GINSBURG, HENDERSON, and GARLAND, CIRCUIT JUDGES.

GARLAND, CIRCUIT JUDGE.

More than fifty years ago, the Supreme Court held that the public disclosure of "who is being hired, who is putting up the money, and how much" they are spending to influence legislation is "a vital national interest." *United States v. Harriss,* 347 U.S. 612, 625–26 (1954). Today, we consider a constitutional challenge to Congress' latest effort to ensure greater transparency, the Honest Leadership and Open Government Act of 2007. Because nothing has transpired in the last half century to suggest that the national interest in public disclosure of lobbying information is any less vital than it was when the Supreme Court first considered the issue, we reject that challenge.

I

A

Congress first enacted comprehensive lobbying regulation in 1946 with passage of the Federal Regulation of Lobbying Act (FRLA), Pub.L. No. 79–601, tit. III, 60 Stat. 839 (1946). The Act required paid lobbyists, defined as persons whose services were engaged for the purpose of influencing legislation, to register with the Secretary of the Senate and the Clerk of the House of Representatives. *Id.* § 308(a), 60 Stat. at 841. * * * The FRLA remained on the books as the primary font of federal lobbying regulation for fifty years.

In 1995, concerned that the FRLA had "failed to ensure the public disclosure of meaningful information about individuals who attempt to influence the conduct of officials of the Federal government," H.R. REP. No. 104–339, pt. 1, at 5 (1995), the 104th Congress scrapped the Act and started from scratch. By unanimous vote of both Houses, Congress passed the Lobbying Disclosure Act of 1995 (LDA), Pub.L. No. 104–65, 109 Stat. 691 (codified as amended at 2 U.S.C. §§ 1601 *et seq.*). * * *

* * * Congress enacted a new statutory scheme containing broader disclosure obligations, a more expansive definition of lobbying, and a more robust enforcement scheme. The LDA requires lobbyists (or their employers) to register with the Secretary of the Senate and Clerk of the House within 45 days of making or being retained to make lobbying contacts. 2 U.S.C. § 1603(a)(1), (2). Each registration must contain identifying information regarding the registrant (*i.e.*, the lobbyist or employer of lobbyists) and each of its clients. *Id.* § 1603(b)(1), (2). It must also contain a statement of "the general issue areas in which the registrant expects to engage in lobbying activities on behalf of the client" and specific issues that have already been or are likely to be addressed in its lobbying activities. *Id.* § 1603(b)(5). Each registrant must then submit periodic reports updating those disclosures and stating the income received from its clients as well as the expenses the registrant incurred in connection with lobbying activities conducted on its own behalf. *Id.* § 1604(b).

Particularly relevant here, the LDA provides that, "[i]n the case of a coalition or association that employs or retains other persons to conduct lobbying activities, the client is the coalition or association and not its individual members." *Id.* § 1602(2). For the first time, however, Congress took steps to partially pierce the veil of coalitions and associations that lobby Congress on behalf of their members. LDA § 4 required registrants—including coalitions and associations—to disclose not only their clients, but also:

> (3) the name, address, and principal place of business of any
> organization, other than the client, that—

(A) contributes more than $10,000 toward the lobbying activities of the registrant in a semiannual period. . .; and

(B) in whole or in major part plans, supervises, or controls such lobbying activities.

2 U.S.C. § 1603(b)(3) (1995). According to the House Judiciary Committee Report that recommended passage of the LDA, this provision was "intended to preclude evasion of the disclosure requirements of the Act through the creation of ad hoc lobbying coalitions behind which real parties in interest can hide." H.R. REP. No. 104–339, U.S. Code Cong. & Admin. News 1996, 644, pt. 1, at 18.

In 2007, after twelve years of experience with the LDA, and spurred by a series of lobbying-related scandals, *see* H.R. REP. No. 110–161, pt. 1, at 9 (2007), Congress again enacted lobbying reform. According to the House Judiciary Committee Report, Congress' purpose was to close "loopholes in current law." *Id.* This time, it did not repeal its earlier handiwork. Instead, Congress amended the LDA while keeping much of it intact, including its statement of legislative findings and most of its definitions. The result was the Honest Leadership and Open Government Act of 2007 (HLOGA), Pub.L. No. 110–81, 121 Stat. 735.

Section 207 of HLOGA is the provision at issue on this appeal. It amends * * * 2 U.S.C. § 1603(b)(3), by altering both the monetary and level-of-participation thresholds necessary to trigger disclosure of organizations other than clients. The participation threshold is our focus here. Instead of only requiring the disclosure of an organization that "in whole or in major part" plans, supervises, or controls the lobbying activities of the registrant, HLOGA requires the disclosure of any organization that "actively participates" in the planning, supervision, or control of such lobbying activities.

Amended § 1603(b) now requires that each registration contain (and that each quarterly report update):

(3) the name, address, and principal place of business of any organization, other than the client, that—

(A) contributes more than $5,000 to the registrant or the client in the quarterly period to fund the lobbying activities of the registrant; and

(B) *actively participates* in the planning, supervision, or control of such lobbying activities[.]

2 U.S.C. § 1603(b)(3) (emphasis added). HLOGA also increased the civil penalties for anyone who "knowingly" fails to make the disclosures required by this and other sections, and added criminal penalties for "knowingly and corruptly" failing to do so. * * *

B

The plaintiff in this case, the National Association of Manufacturers (NAM), is "the nation's largest industrial trade association, representing small and large manufacturers in every industrial sector and in all 50 states." Although some of NAM's more than 11,000 corporate members choose to disclose their affiliation with the association, NAM's policy is to keep its membership list confidential. NAM employs approximately 35 people who make lobbying contacts with the federal government, and it therefore must make disclosures under the LDA. * * *

According to NAM, hundreds of its corporate members make contributions that exceed the monetary threshold of amended § 1603(b)(3)(A). * * * The amended version of § 1603(b)(3), * * * requires disclosure of any member who "actively participates" in planning, supervision, or control of lobbying activities, and this will require disclosure of many NAM members. * * *

The district court concluded that amended § 1603(b)(3) does not violate the First Amendment because the section is narrowly tailored to serve compelling governmental interests, and it further found that the section was not unconstitutionally vague. Accordingly, it denied NAM's motion and dismissed the complaint. *Id.* at 68. NAM now appeals. * * *

? How does the compelled disclosure of NAM's membership compare with the compelled disclosure we discussed in the last chapter on campaign finance (Chapter 9, Section B)? Does it seem similar to the compelled disclosure the Supreme Court upheld in Part IV of the *Citizens United* decision (pp. 211–213)? What about Justice Thomas's dissent from that portion of the opinion and his point about supporters of California Prop 8? How about the concerns about disclosure of membership lists raised in the 1958 *NAACP v. Alabama* case we discussed in that same portion of Chapter 9?

II

Amended § 1603(b)(3) does not prohibit lobbyists from saying anything. It requires only disclosure. Nonetheless, NAM explains that "the disclosures mandated by [amended § 1603(b)(3)] will discourage and deter speech, petitioning, and expressive association." We agree with NAM that these are substantial First Amendment interests and that requiring disclosure can burden them. As the Supreme Court has noted, "compelled disclosure, in itself, can seriously infringe on privacy of association and belief guaranteed by the First Amendment." *Buckley v. Valeo*, 424 U.S. 1, 64 (1976). * * *

But we also note that the Court, recognizing the lesser burdens that disclosure generally imposes on First Amendment interests, has upheld numerous statutes requiring disclosures by those endeavoring to influence the political system. For example, in *United States v. Harris* the Court upheld lobbying disclosure requirements of the FRLA on the ground that the statute served a "vital national interest" in a "manner restricted to its appropriate end." 347 U.S. at 626. In so doing, the Court emphasized that Congress had "not sought to prohibit [lobbying] pressures," but had "merely provided for a modicum of information." Similarly, in *Buckley v. Valeo,* the Court rejected a First Amendment challenge to campaign finance disclosure requirements of the Federal Election Campaign Act (FECA), holding that a disclosure requirement was a "reasonable and minimally restrictive method of furthering First Amendment values by opening the basic processes of our federal election system to public view." 424 U.S. at 82. * * * The courts of appeals have been similarly deferential to disclosure statutes.

The question we face at the outset is the level of scrutiny we should apply to NAM's First Amendment challenge. The parties vigorously debate whether the Supreme Court applies "strict," or some lesser-but-still-heightened form of scrutiny to disclosure statutes. On the one hand, the government notes that in *Buckley,* the Court used the term "exacting" rather than "strict" to describe the scrutiny it applied to the disclosure requirements of FECA. On the other hand, NAM notes that the Supreme Court has, on occasion, used the terms "exacting" and "strict" interchangeably to describe the same First Amendment test. * * *

[T]he debate over the appropriate test to apply is irrelevant because it makes no difference to our disposition. As we said in *Blount v. SEC,* "if [a statute] can withstand strict scrutiny there is no need to decide the issue" of which test to apply. 61 F.3d 938, 943 (D.C.Cir.1995). To satisfy strict scrutiny, the government must establish three elements: (1) "the interests the government proffers in support" of the statute must be "properly characterized as 'compelling' "; (2) the statute must "effectively advance[ ] those interests"; and (3) the statute must be "narrowly tailored to advance the compelling interests asserted." *Id.* at 944. * * * We conclude, in agreement with the district court, that the statute satisfies the requirements of strict scrutiny.

> Notice that First Amendment jurisprudence has **!** changed over time. This second element was not part of the doctrinal articulation of the "means-ends" test in 1976 when the Court decided *Buckley v. Valeo* (Chapter 8, Section B). It is also not included in the formulation of the strict-scrutiny test in race-based challenges under the Fourteenth Amendment such as the racial gerrymandering cases we looked at in Chapter 6 (see, e.g., *Cooper v. Harris*).

A

We begin our examination of the first element of strict scrutiny—the requirement that the governmental interest supporting the statute be "compelling"—by asking just what that interest is in this case. * * *

Here, the statutory language is quite clear. In enacting the LDA, Congress found that "responsible representative Government requires public awareness of the efforts of paid lobbyists to influence the public decisionmaking process in both the legislative and executive branches of the Federal Government." 2 U.S.C. § 1601(1). "[P]ublic confidence in the integrity of Government" will be increased, Congress declared, by "effective public disclosure of the identity and extent of the efforts of paid lobbyists to influence Federal officials in the conduct of Government actions." *Id.* § 1601(3). In short, and not surprisingly, the purpose of the lobbying disclosure statute is to provide greater public information about who is lobbying Congress and what they are lobbying about. * * *

Having identified the governmental interest at issue, we next ask whether it is sufficient to justify compelled disclosure. In making such a determination, we do not write on a blank slate. Not long after Congress first waded into the lobbying reform arena with the FRLA, the Supreme Court examined the law's validity under the First Amendment. In *Harriss,* a decision that NAM does not currently seek to overturn, the Court upheld the Act. The Court premised that result on the same informational interest upon which the defendants in this case rely. * * * This goal of providing Congress with information with which to evaluate the pressures that lobbyists bring to bear upon it, the Court concluded, is "a vital national interest."

Two decades later, in *Buckley,* the Court held that information about efforts to influence the political system is not only important to government officials (or candidates for office), but is also important for the public at large. In reviewing a statute requiring disclosure of campaign contributions and expenditures, the Court declared "that there are governmental interests sufficiently important to outweigh the possibility of infringement" of First Amendment rights, "particularly when the 'free functioning of our national institutions' is involved." 424 U.S. at 66. "The governmental interests sought to be vindicated by the disclosure" of such contributions and expenditures, the Court said, "are of this magnitude." *Id.* * * *

There is nothing to suggest that the public interest in this type of information is diminished once the candidate has attained office and is exposed to the pressures of lobbying. Indeed, just as disclosure serves the important "informational interest" of "help[ing] voters to define more of the candidates' constituencies," *id.* at 81, it likewise helps the public to understand the constituencies behind legislative or regulatory proposals. Transparency in government, no less than transparency in choosing our government, remains a vital national interest in a democracy. * * *

In sum, we conclude that Congress' interest in increasing "public awareness of the efforts of paid lobbyists to influence the public decisionmaking process," 2 U.S.C. § 1601(1), is sufficiently compelling to withstand strict scrutiny.

B

We next consider whether amended § 1603(b)(3) "effectively advances" the interest the government proffers in support of it. *Blount,* 61 F.3d at 944. On its face, it certainly appears to. By requiring registrants to disclose the "name, address, and principal place of business" of any organization that contributes the monetary threshold and actively participates in the planning, supervision, or control of the registrant's lobbying activities, the section provides the very information—"who is being hired, who is putting up the money, and how much"—that *Harriss* found to be "a vital national interest." 347 U.S. at 625–26. As *Buckley* held with respect to the disclosure of independent expenditures supporting political candidates, amended § 1603(b)(3) serves the "informational interest" of "increas[ing] the fund of information concerning those who support" legislation. 424 U.S. at 81. And like the FECA provision upheld in *Buckley,* the amended section "goes beyond the general disclosure requirements" of the LDA "to shed the light of publicity" on lobbying activities that "would not otherwise be reported" because they do not come under the pre-amendment thresholds. *Id.* * * *

[A]s we have said, "neither a perfect nor even the best available fit between means and ends is required" to satisfy this prong of the strict scrutiny test. *Blount*, 61 F.3d at 946. It is sufficient that amended § 1603(b)(3) effectively advances the LDA's general purpose of increasing "public awareness of the efforts of paid lobbyists to influence the public decisionmaking process," as well as the amended section's specific purpose of requiring disclosure of organizations that "actively participate[ ] in the planning, supervision, or control" of a registrant's lobbying activities.

C

Finally, we consider whether amended § 1603(b)(3) is narrowly tailored. Under the strict scrutiny test, "narrowly tailored" means that "less restrictive alternatives" to the statute would not "accomplish the government's goals equally or almost equally effectively." *Blount*, 61 F.3d at 944. * * *

By choosing a regime based upon disclosure, Congress already opted for a regime considerably less restrictive than one based upon the direct regulation of lobbying. In *Buckley*, the Court said that "disclosure requirements certainly in most applications appear to be the least restrictive means of curbing the evil[ ]" of ignorance regarding the source and expenditure of campaign funds. 424 U.S. at 68. Indeed, *Buckley* described a disclosure regime as a "reasonable and minimally restrictive method of *furthering* First Amendment values." *Id.* at 81 (emphasis added). We have no doubt, then, that amended § 1603(b)(3) readily passes the "narrow tailoring" element of the strict scrutiny test.

D

For the reasons discussed above, we conclude that amended § 1603(b)(3) meets the demands of strict scrutiny. A fortiori, the section also satisfies the test the Court specifically applied to disclosure requirements in [cases including *McConnell* and *Buckley*], whatever it is called. As we have noted, to survive scrutiny under that test, there must be "a 'relevant correlation' or 'substantial relation' between the governmental interest and the information required to be disclosed," and * * * the strength of the governmental interest must reflect the seriousness of the actual burden on First Amendment rights. * * *

[In Part II.E, the court rejected NAM's argument that its members faced a sufficient risk of retaliation that it should be excused from disclosure. Part III rejected its argument that the statute was unconstitutionally vague.]

IV

For more than sixty years, Congress has sought to expose the lobbying of government officials to public scrutiny. Acronyms and intricacies aside, the progression from the FRLA to the LDA to the HLOGA marks the legislature's attempt to shine increasing light on the efforts of paid lobbyists to influence the public decisionmaking process. We find nothing unconstitutional in the way Congress has gone about that task. Accordingly, the decision of the district court, rejecting the appellant's challenge to the constitutionality of section 207 of the Honest Leadership and Open Government Act of 2007, is

Affirmed.

NOTES & QUESTIONS

1. What are the purposes of the Federal Lobbying Disclosure Act, as amended? Do you think the statute is likely to achieve those purposes? Why or why not?

2. What constitutional standard does the D.C. Circuit apply to the amended FLDA's requirements requiring the disclosure of lobbying activities? What standard do you think should apply?

3. What interest does the D.C. Circuit find sufficient to justify the Act's lobbying disclosure requirements? Note that *NAM* was decided before *Citizens United*. Would the *NAM* case have been resolved differently after *Citizens United*?

4. What amendments to the FLDA would you recommend?

5. Aside from disclosure, can you imagine any other regulations on lobbying activities that would effectively address the goals that Congress was seeking to accomplish? If Congress attempted to impose direct restraints on lobbying activities—for example, prohibiting corporations from spending over a certain dollar amount on lobbying in support of

or against a particular bill—what constitutional standard would apply? Are such restraints likely to be deemed constitutional?

DIY
Combatting Corruption in the Lawmaking Process

 Before concluding this Part of the book, spend a few minutes thinking about whether our legislatures, courts, administrative agencies, other institutions, and we as citizens are doing enough to prevent corruption and the appearance of corruption in our politics. In addition to corruption and the appearance of corruption, how about the potential for "distortion" in the legislative and executive branches that spending of large sums of money in campaigns and lobbying by those with greater financial resources can cause? Think also about how the legislative, executive, and judicial branches compare on this score. As you may have learned in Civil Procedure or one of your other courses, litigation costs a lot of money too. Those with greater means may well prevail in the legislative and executive branches, but they also generally prevail in court. *See* Marc Galanter, *Why the "Haves" Come out Ahead: Speculations on the Limits of Legal Change*, 9 LAW & SOCIETY REV. 95 (1974). You are taking this course to become a lawyer. Is there a special role for lawyers in combatting these problems?

Test Your Understanding

To assess your understanding of the material in this chapter, click here to take a quiz.

Part III—The Processes of Statutory Creation

In Part II, we looked at some important aspects of representation in a republic. In a representative democracy like the United States, the underlying ideal is that "the people" are responsible for their own governance—and are thus involved in the making of "law." Of course, as we have previously noted, "the people" don't ordinarily make the law directly. Rather, they elect legislators, and these legislators (to whom we often refer, quite literally, as "lawmakers") make the law. Meanwhile, the reference to "law" in the previous sentence is to a very specific form of law called "legislation," or "statutory law." As you have seen in other classes, judges in the Anglo-American system of law also make a kind of law, one known as the "common law." In fact, as a practical matter, judges also make "constitutional law," as you probably gathered from some of the cases you read in Part II (such as the cases addressing racial gerrymandering—e.g., *Shaw v. Reno; Cooper v. Harris*—and campaign finance—*Buckley v. Valeo; Citizens United v. FEC*), although with constitutional law, judges must do so by interpreting constitutional language that in the first place was adopted by the people.

In this Part, we turn our attention more specifically to the category of law we call "legislation" and explore the processes that representatives use to create or enact this statutory law. We note, however, that today these processes unfortunately are affected by a prolonged period of increasing political dysfunction. As a result of that dysfunction, many of the norms and customs of American law that have tended to shape and constrain the legislative and regulatory arenas are now under profound stress, to the point that some of our descriptive accounts of the lawmaking processes may seem outdated or quaint. Nevertheless, we retain these accounts for two purposes: first, because many of the interpretive problems that lawyers will continue to confront in the short-term will have arisen from statutes and regulations enacted in times past, when many of these norms and customs held sway; and second, because in the longer term it is worth aspiring for the return to a healthier political process that might again function something along these descriptive lines.

With that caveat, this Part first provides an overview of the prototypical lawmaking process in a bicameral legislature, and then it looks a little more closely at the critical role that legislatures play in the allocation of government funds. The Part concludes on what we might call a "comparative" note, considering the processes of direct democracy, which offer a different way to enact legislation. Many states permit their citizens to enact some laws directly, without going through their state legislatures. This process is of course somewhat different from the legislative process, but it produces statutory law nonetheless. (At times the processes of direct democracy also can enact state constitutional amendments as well.)

Understanding how statutes come into being has both inherent value and instrumental value. As a lawyer, no matter what area of practice you choose, you will inevitably have to read and interpret legislation. This task of "statutory interpretation" can take place in many different contexts: a client wants to know, "Can I do such-and-such?"; a client wants to sue someone who allegedly violated the law; a client wants to draft a will or conclude a contract with some other party; a client needs to get a permit or license from a government agency to do something; a client wants to get a government agency to regulate in a certain way. When we turn to the statutory interpretation enterprise in Part IV, we will see that no matter the context, *interpreting legislation requires some understanding of the process by which that legislation was created.*

So, as you work through this Part, think about both how the legislative process connects with representation and the people (as we explored in Part II), and how you think the process should affect the interpretation of legislation (as we will explore beginning in Part IV).

11

How a Bill Becomes a Law

Key Concepts

- From policy idea to enacted statute
- Constitutional requirements
- Internal rules
- Vetogates
- Bicameralism
- Presentment
- Legislative privilege

Chapter Summary

At both the state and federal levels, laws usually begin as ideas in the heads of legislators, government agency personnel, lobbyists, issue organization leaders, or constituents. After introduction by a legislator, a proposed law becomes a bill and is usually assigned to a legislative committee for hearings. A small portion of those bills are then "voted out of committee" (in other words, favorably recommended by the committee) for potential consideration by the entire legislative chamber. If placed on the chamber's calendar of business, the full legislative body then debates, amends, and votes on the measure. If a majority votes yes, the bill then goes to the other legislative chamber to repeat the same process (except in Nebraska, which has a unicameral legislature). If both chambers pass the same measure, it then goes to the President or Governor for approval or disapproval.

Yet many roadblocks, or "vetogates," prevent most bills from becoming laws. The committee stage is where most bills die, although the process involves many other stages. But despite the complex process, the only explicit elements that the United States Constitution requires are bicameralism (both chambers agreeing to the same language), majoritarianism (majority vote needed), and presentment (Presidential approval), with the additional limit that measures appropriating funds must start in the House of Representatives.

As one additional constitutional dimension, the Speech or Debate Clause of the United States Constitution creates a legal privilege for members of Congress and their staff. This legislative privilege is designed to facilitate legislative deliberation by preventing the Executive or Judicial branches from questioning or interfering with official legislative work. Most state legislators have an analogous privilege.

"Laws, like sausages, cease to inspire respect in proportion as we know how they are made."

—John Godfrey Saxe, 1869

Some version of the above aphorism, often wrongly attributed to nineteenth century German Chancellor Otto von Bismarck, is frequently invoked to disparage how legislatures function, and sometimes even to discourage paying attention to them. Yet many aspects of the legislative process are worthy of respect, notwithstanding the presence of ample elements of distortion and dysfunction. Furthermore, all aspects of the process are deserving of close study, especially by lawyers, whose professional lives revolve so heavily around the work and work product of legislatures.

This chapter offers a synopsis of the legislative process, from bill introduction through presentment to the President or Governor. In addition to providing an abbreviated summary of the classic process through which an idea for legislation becomes a law, the synopsis stresses the most critical steps, which have the potential to offer the greatest insight into matters of statutory interpretation. It also acknowledges that in recent years many major pieces of federal legislation have not followed the classic process. *See* WALTER J. OLESZEK, ET AL., CONGRESSIONAL PROCEDURES AND THE POLICY PROCESS (10th ed. 2016); PEVERILL SQUIRE & GARY MONCRIEF, STATE LEGISLATURES TODAY: POLITICS UNDER THE DOMES (2d ed. 2015); BARBARA SINCLAIR, UNORTHODOX LAWMAKING: NEW LEGISLATIVE PROCESSES IN THE U.S. CONGRESS (1997).

A. How a Bill Becomes a Law: From Introduction to Enactment

The process by which a legislative idea becomes an enacted statute usually (though not always) plays out over at least several months, and often years. But once a specific bill is formally introduced, it must be completed within the constitutionally defined term of the legislature (two years for each Congress, as well as for many state legislatures) or the proposal will die and must be reintroduced from scratch in the next legislative cycle. Outlined below are the key elements of this process (with the caveat that the rampant dysfunctionality of politics at the federal level today has prompted increasing departures from this traditional process). For convenience and clarity, this synopsis focuses primarily on congressional procedures, although most of its principles also apply to state legislatures.

One overarching point about the legislative process is that executive agencies are heavily involved in many of the steps in this process, contributing their expertise to individual legislative proposals in several different ways. Of course, one form of agency or executive branch participation in the lawmaking process is when an agency (or the President or Governor) promotes its own legislative agenda, finding a legislator to sponsor a bill on behalf of the agency (or President or Governor). In addition to this frequent form of agency participation in the legislative process, agencies also often play an instrumental role by helping to refine a bill as it works its way through various stages of the process. Agencies may make these contributions publicly, as when agency personnel testify at legislative hearings or submit other kinds of evidence to legislative committees. Perhaps more influentially, agencies

This role that executive agencies play is an important and understudied aspect of the legislative process. It is, however, a well-documented fact: even though the branch of government that is empowered to pass laws is the legislature, it is often the executive branch that actually drafts the language in those laws. What are the implications of this fact, if any, for subsequent interpretation? Does it matter that the very agency officials whom the law empowers may well have been the ones who drafted the law in the first place?

also may participate in the legislative process behind the scenes, providing what at the federal level is often called "technical drafting assistance." This is a relatively understudied aspect of the lawmaking process, which sometimes can take the form of truly "technical" advice, but often instead involves the agency's sharing of its substantive views about the desirability of particular measures. *See* Christopher J. Walker, *Legislating in the Shadows,* 165 U. PENN. L. REV. 1377 (2017).

For many legislative proposals, any of several steps in the process can prove to be difficult obstacles, or "vetogates," which may prevent the proposal from ever becoming law. Understanding these obstacles and how proponents strive to avoid or overcome them can be valuable for purposes of resolving interpretive issues in statutory text, which we will consider in Parts V and VI of the book. Likewise, an awareness of the substantial amount of agency participation in the legislative process also can be relevant to understanding the agency's subsequent involvement in the interpretive enterprise, as we explore in Parts VII and VIII.

1. External Rules, Internal Rules, and Norms

As a threshold matter, it is helpful to have some familiarity with the body of rules and norms that governs the activities of a legislature. Each legislative chamber sets most of its own procedural rules, subject to several general procedural requirements imposed upon the lawmaking process from outside the legislature.

At the federal level, the U.S. Constitution creates a Congress with two chambers, the Senate and the House of Representatives, and then imposes on these two bodies some—albeit, only a few—constraints on their lawmaking processes. In addition to the bicameralism requirement of Article I, Section 7, which provides that both houses must agree before a measure can become law, these few external requirements include the following: that a majority of members must be present to constitute a quorum sufficient to conduct any official business; that neither house may adjourn for more than three days without the consent of the other house; and that each house "shall keep a Journal of its Proceedings." U.S. CONST. art. I, sec. 5, cl. 3. Beyond that, the Constitution provides that "[e]ach House may determine the Rules of its Proceedings," *id.* art. I, sec. 5, cl. 2, as well as that each House "shall chuse" [sic] its officers, other than the President of the Senate, who is to be the Vice-President of the United States, *id.* art. I, secs. 2 & 3.

At least implicit in the structure of Congress and state legislatures is that the concurrence of a simple majority of the members present is both necessary and sufficient, not only in choosing the officers of a legislative body, but also in agreeing to any other pending motion or matter of business, unless some supermajority is otherwise specified for particular matters. In the U.S. Constitution, this default decision rule is suggested, for instance, by explicit exceptions requiring "the Concurrence of two thirds of the Members present" for the Senate to convict on charges of impeachment, *id.* art. I, sec. 3, cl. 6, and also requiring the same supermajority for the Senate to ratify a treaty, *id.* art. II, sec. 2, cl. 2.

The "Journal" that Article I requires Congress to keep is not the relatively familiar Congressional Record. The Congressional Record instead is a transcript of the proceedings on the floor of both the U.S. House and Senate, which Congress since 1873 has independently opted, but is not required, to keep. (It was preceded by the Annals of Congress, the Register of Debates, and the Congressional Globe, a series of less comprehensive records). Meanwhile, the Journal of each house is a short but official summary of the business conducted in that chamber, including records of the votes on pending legislation. But it is not a record of all the words spoken.

State constitutions occasionally impose additional requirements on the functioning of state legislatures. For instance, some state constitutions require that a measure address only one subject, or that a bill's title accurately describe what the measure will do. Other state constitutions require that state legislation operate uniformly throughout the state, thus precluding legislation that expressly targets a specific business or locality. In addition to these requirements that address the substance of a bill's text, many state constitutions impose requirements concerning purely procedural matters, such as requiring three "readings" of a bill (on different days, ostensibly to promote greater collective deliberation, though actual reading of the full text is usually waived) before a vote; specifying mandatory time periods between a bill's introduction and a vote; and imposing moratoriums on any substantial alterations of the purpose of a bill between introduction and enactment. But sometimes these constitutionally imposed procedural requirements are construed as not judicially enforceable (or not ordinarily enforceable), and instead subject only to internal enforcement by the legislature itself.

The internal rules, which typically are adopted (or re-adopted) as the first official act undertaken at the opening of each Congress or legislature, then specify a host of additional requirements to govern the legislative process. These requirements include specifying the order of business, setting the schedule of the legislative session, assigning the power to appoint committees, and imposing specific rules regarding attendance and voting requirements for all members, among many others. Most legislatures today opt to do much of their work in committees, and the internal rules of each chamber also define the scope and operations of the chamber's committees. Great variation exists across the states in the level of specificity of their procedures.

Robert's Rules of Order is probably the best-known set of these legislative rules, but it is not the set of rules used in most state legislatures nor in Congress. Instead, Mason's Manual of Legislative Procedure, as modified to fit each state, is the dominant rulebook in most state legislatures (used in 70 of the 99 state legislative chambers). Meanwhile, the U.S. Senate publishes its own set of rules as the Senate Manual, and the corresponding publication in the U.S. House of Representatives is entitled "Constitution, Jefferson's Manual, and Rules of the House of Representatives."

Not only are the requirements of these rules wholly within the control of the legislature, but the enforcement of these rules is also a matter entirely internal to the legislature. In other words, violations of these rules do not give rise to enforceable obligations elsewhere. Instead, enforcement generally occurs by a member of the legislature raising a point of order or an objection. For instance, a U.S. Senator could object to the consideration of a measure because it includes a substantive, non-clerical amendment proposed by a committee on a matter outside that committee's jurisdiction, in violation of Senate Rule XV, § 5. But if no one in the Senate raises this objection and the measure eventually is enacted into law, the procedural defect that occurred during the Senate consideration of the measure cannot be used to challenge or invalidate the law. Expressed in more general terms, courts will not look beyond Congress's own attestation that a measure was duly enacted. *See Field v. Clark,* 143 U.S. 649 (1892). Most states have their own versions of this "enrolled bill" doctrine. *See, e.g., Consumer Party of Pa. v. Commonwealth,* 507 A.2d 323, 331–33 (Pa. 1986).

In the first instance, responsibility for ruling on a point of order usually rests with the legislative body's parliamentarian, an unelected staff member appointed by the legislative leadership whose job is to interpret and apply the internal rules. However, the parliamentarian's decisions and interpretations are always subject to being overruled by the will of the body, expressed through a majority vote.

In addition to being governed by the many formal rules, both internal and constitutional, most legislative chambers also are deeply influenced by a set of norms that have developed over time. These include whether and how to appoint a parliamentarian, and what other officers and staff assistants to appoint or hire. They also include various seniority norms, under which Members who have been serving in the legislature the longest are given favored positions or leadership roles, or are looked to for guidance; the creation and use of a variety of "caucuses" or subsets of Members, organized not only around political parties (the House Republican Conference, for instance) but also around ideology or subject area (the Blue Dog Coalition or the Congressional Bike Caucus, for instance), or racial or ethnic groups (the Legislative Black Caucus, for instance); and the manner in which the majority and minority parties organize themselves, establish their legislative agendas, and control their members.

Legislative norms also can include understandings concerning how committees will operate (for instance, when to issue published committee reports, or how to select witnesses to appear at hearings); the ways in which legislators communicate with each other (for instance, through "Dear Colleague" letters); and expectations surrounding the identification and addition of co-sponsors for legislative measures. Expectations concerning how lobbyists share information with legislators may also be part of the institutional culture, or norms, of a legislature, and may be constrained by lobbying regulations and ethics rules.

2. Bill Introduction and Committee Referral

Only duly recognized members of a legislature have the privilege of introducing a legislative proposal to their respective legislative chamber. When a new proposal is introduced, it becomes a "bill" and is given a bill number, usually chronologically in numerical order starting at "1" with the first measure in each term of the legislature. Each chamber assigns its own bill numbers, in Congress using a prefix of "S." or "H.R." to distinguish Senate bills from House bills.

Individual members can be motivated to introduce a bill for many different reasons. Often legislators will be motivated to introduce a new law or law reform proposal by their own personal experience, by a constituent confronting an issue, or based on staff advice. Legislative leaders may introduce a measure on behalf of an entire party caucus, endorsing it as part of the party's broader legislative agenda. Legislators also will often work closely with lobbyists in introducing measures that are supported (and often even drafted) by particular interest groups. And it is obviously important for a President or a Governor to have allies in the legislature who can introduce measures at the chief executive's request. State budget bills routinely begin with a courtesy introduction of the Governor's own budget proposal.

After a bill is formally introduced in a particular house of the legislature, internal rules generally provide for a number of steps before it can be voted on, and indeed often even before it can become the topic of debate for the full chamber. Typically, the next step is for the parliamentarian of the chamber to refer the bill to a particular legislative committee. Legislative committees are usually constituted around subject areas, again entirely as a matter of internal process or custom. In Congress, some of these committees' subject areas include Aging; Agriculture; Appropriations; Armed Services; Energy and Commerce; Foreign Affairs; Health, Education, Labor, and Pensions; Homeland Security; Judiciary; Small Business; and Veterans' Affairs. Bills are then also classified by subject, in order to match them with the most appropriate committee. In Congress, for example, when a measure covers subjects within the ambit of more than one committee, the "weight of the bill" test may be used to determine the appropriate committee assignment according to the bill's "predominant subject." Alternatively, a bill implicating multiple subjects may receive referrals to multiple committees. Committees in turn

> Committees play a crucial role in the legislative process. Think about the pros and cons of their influence as you read on.

often have authority to organize subcommittees, with each subcommittee having some further substantive specialization.

Reliance on legislative committees is not a constitutional requirement, but instead is the legislature's deliberate delegation of its legislative workload to a trusted subsidiary body. Occasionally—and perhaps more frequently during periods of intense partisanship and legislative dysfunction—legislative leaders may keep a measure before the entire body (as happened, for instance, in the U.S. House's consideration of the Senate version of the Patient Protection and Affordable Care Act of 2010), rather than letting the measure be referred to a committee. But the expertise cultivated in various subject-matter committees and subcommittees continues to enhance the efficiency and sophistication with which bills are considered.

3. Committee Consideration

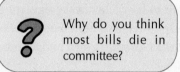

Why do you think most bills die in committee?

The committee stage is critical to the traditional legislative process. In part this is because most bills "die" in committee, as can be seen by comparing the number of measures referred to committees in any given legislature to the number of measures reported out of committees. Not only is the committee phase crucial because most legislative proposals fail to survive the committee "gatekeeping" process, but also because, even for those that do survive, it is where the vast majority of substantive changes—amendments—are considered.

By internal rules, committees are led by a chair, typically appointed by the majority leader of the legislative chamber. The leader of the chamber also appoints the remaining members of each committee, drawing members of the minority party from the recommendations of the minority leadership, and in rough proportion to the parties' overall numbers in the full chamber. Thus, political control over a legislative chamber brings with it control of all committees. In many legislatures, the position of committee chair typically goes to the committee member of the majority party with the most seniority, although this usually is a mere institutional norm. Because of the gatekeeping role of committees and subcommittees, these chairs exercise enormous power. The committee members of the minority party also will have a minority leader on the committee, often called the "ranking member," who also is typically the most senior of the minority party's committee members.

Committees and subcommittees perform two primary and related functions in connection with the bills referred to them. First, they conduct hearings on the bill; and second, they "mark-up," or debate and amend, the bill. When committees delegate consideration of a bill to a subcommittee, the subcommittee eventually must return the bill to the parent committee, rather than to the full chamber. As a result, hearings and mark-ups may occur at both the subcommittee and committee levels.

Hearings are an opportunity for committees (and subcommittees) to seek advice and input about the bill from a variety of knowledgeable experts and affected individuals, including lobbyists. Although most witnesses appear voluntarily, congressional committees, as well as some state legislative committees, have explicit authority, as necessary, to issue subpoenas to compel witnesses to appear and testify. These witnesses may testify in support of or in opposition to a bill, or they may simply provide information for the committee members to consider in deciding whether to support, amend, or oppose the bill.

Most committee hearings are public events, attended by representatives of interested parties, perhaps a few media organizations, and some members of the general public. On occasion, a hearing for a high-profile bill will draw a large public crowd and many media representatives, but many committee hearings are subdued affairs. Representatives of concerned interest groups are a consistent presence at almost all hearings. As public events, hearings can also provide opportunities for legislators to "grandstand" to some degree, as they declare their own views, justify their positions, or seek to undermine opposing views.

A committee's (or subcommittee's) mark-up sessions are also typically public events. During mark-up, committees use their subject matter expertise, as informed by the information gathered through the hearings process, to recommend changes to the bill as it was originally introduced. Changes are suggested through proposed amendments, which must then be approved by a majority vote of the committee. Often, however, a committee will informally agree to a whole host of changes to a bill, and then formally adopt all these changes at once by agreeing to an "amendment in the nature of a substitute," which replaces the original bill with a wholly new measure.

After the conclusion of all the hearings and mark-up sessions, legislative committees have a third primary responsibility, discussed in the next subsection: to report back to the full body about the committee's work on a specific piece of legislation. When a subcommittee has finished its work, it returns the measure to the parent committee, perhaps with a draft committee report for the committee to decide whether to adopt and send on to the full chamber. Occasionally (and with increasing frequency), several congressional committees will collaborate in preparing a piece of "omnibus" legislation that combines the work of these multiple committees into one bill with multiple "titles" or parts (each of which may have formerly been a separate bill) for full chamber consideration as a whole.

4. Committee Reports

When a committee is done considering a particular measure, it may report the measure to the full chamber. In Congress, the action of reporting a measure is almost always accompanied by a published document: the committee's formal report. This document typically contains the full text of the bill, as amended by the committee; summarizes the bill; and presents the committee's views on the measure. The report also will often present accompanying views of dissenting members of the committee. As we will explore in subsequent portions of the book, committee reports are often used as an aid in interpreting ambiguous provisions.

Many state legislative committees do not have a rule (or custom or practice) of preparing a published report to accompany bills sent back to the full legislature. Instead, the committee "report" consists of the procedural step of informing the leadership that the committee has completed its hearings and mark-up and is ready to reintroduce the measure, as amended by the committee, to the full chamber. Usually this step comes with the committee's endorsement of the measure, although occasionally a committee will report a measure "without recommendation."

Committee reports play a crucial role in the life of a bill. In Congress, committee reports are required, by internal rule, to be available to all members "at least 48-hours before" the time when the Senate plans to take up or debate the measure, and three calendar days prior to consideration in the House. *See* Senate Rule XXVIII, 10(a)(1); House Rule XIII, 4(a)(1). These requirements serve not only to provide members with advance notice of the upcoming agenda, but also to give them time to consider the merits of the bill, in light of the committee's careful evaluation and amendment. Furthermore, for some legislative proposals, committee reports can be a more accessible and efficient means for legislators to understand how a proposed law would operate than reading the full text of the proposed measure. Finally, legislators often will rely on members of their staff to digest these committee reports, especially in areas of less interest or familiarity to the legislator, and then to brief the legislator on the merits of the bill. In the life of a busy legislator, this staff role can be an especially critical one.

5. Getting a Measure to the Floor

Committees perform a significant "gatekeeping" function in winnowing down the number of measures that receive full consideration by a legislative chamber, but committee approval is no guarantee that a measure will reach the floor to receive the formal attention of the full chamber. Before a measure can become the pending business of a legislative chamber, it must be placed on the "calendar" (or one of several calendars) of that chamber. The leaders of the majority party in each chamber control the calendar and thus have substantial influence in setting the agenda of measures that the full chamber will take up.

For instance, in recent Congresses, the Speaker of the U.S. House of Representatives has followed an internal norm ("the Hastert Rule") of not bringing a measure to the floor unless it appears that a majority of the Members of the controlling party supports the measure. The House Rules Committee also can often prevent a measure from reaching the floor simply by refusing to adopt a "rule" to govern how floor debate concerning the measure will occur. Though procedural devices, such as a "discharge petition," exist to circumvent some of this foot-dragging, use of these devices is unusual under congressional norms.

In the U.S. Senate, meanwhile, bringing a measure to the floor for consideration typically requires adoption of a "motion to proceed." Under the Senate's internal rules, both this motion and the underlying legislative proposal are subject to a potential "filibuster," in which opponents of a measure take advantage of the Senate's norm of permitting unlimited debate to keep the motion to proceed pending indefinitely. Under current Senate rules, ending a filibuster (and even a threatened filibuster) takes the agreement of a three-fifths supermajority, or sixty Senators in today's 100-member Senate.

> We also discuss the "filibuster" in the next subsection, "6. Floor Debate and Voting."

6. Floor Debate and Voting

The most visible stage of the legislative process is the "floor debate," or in other words the formal consideration that a measure receives in a particular legislative chamber by the full membership of that chamber. But in the typical congressional case, not much of interest actually occurs here. Instead, floor debate often takes place with very few members present in an almost empty chamber and is mostly a dramatic show that precedes the official vote on a bill. Those substantive developments that do occur at this relatively late stage, primarily in terms of amendments, are usually highly scripted or noncontroversial. Floor debate in state legislatures can be somewhat more influential and often occurs in front of a full chamber, as a result of both its importance and strict attendance rules.

In both Congress and state legislatures, legislative leaders will not allow a measure they support to become the official business of the legislative chamber until they are confident that the measure has sufficient votes to pass. Conversely, if it is a high-profile measure to which they are opposed, they may work to hurry it to a floor vote if they are confident it will fail, in order to demonstrate that the measure lacked sufficient support. As a result, the "debate" that occurs at this stage often is primarily an opportunity for both proponents and opponents publicly to make their best case, justifying their position to both their constituents and the broader public, but not primarily to persuade their colleagues to support their position. In Congress, it also is an opportunity for members to have these statements of position published as part of the Congressional Record, a practice with the potential to influence subsequent interpretation of an enacted law, as we will see later.

In the U.S. House of Representatives, floor debate is usually structured by a rule (promulgated by the House Rules Committee) crafted specifically for each measure that specifies how much total time will be spent debating the measure, how that time will be divided (including how many minutes any one member may speak about the measure), and how many amendments may be offered. The House Rules Committee is incredibly powerful and important because of its authority to set the terms of debate on any measure.

In the U.S. Senate, internal rules establish a default floor process that permits unlimited debate, although by internal rule this default may be altered by a three-fifths supermajority vote (sixty votes) to limit or close debate. The Senate's practice of generally permitting unlimited debate on occasion gives rise to a filibuster, a strategic effort to kill a measure by debating it incessantly until its proponents are forced to withdraw it, unless the measure can draw the support of a three-fifths supermajority to end the filibuster. In recent decades, it is the mere threat of a filibuster that achieves this end, rather than the actual deployment of an unending oral debate. The mechanism for overcoming a Senate filibuster is a "cloture motion," or a motion to close debate. Under the Senate's current cloture rule, three-fifths of the Senate must vote in favor of a cloture motion for it to pass. In an earlier era, the cloture rule required a larger two-thirds supermajority to pass.

> **!** A Senate filibuster is a means of preventing a vote on a measure until a three-fifths supermajority of the Senate agrees to end debate on the measure. The practice, which is entirely a matter of the Senate's internal rules, is under increasing criticism, even as its defenders assert that it promotes bipartisanship.

Once a measure has become the official business of a legislative body, debate concerning proposed amendments to the measure (sometimes with a little more in the way of member attendance) often consumes as much time as debate over the merits of the underlying proposal itself. Usually, the outcome of these amendment attempts is a foregone conclusion, with some doomed to fail, and others anticipated to succeed. In either case their discussion can bring into relief what the bill would do with or without the amendment, again providing arguments of potential relevance to the interpretive problems we will address in later chapters. Individual legislatures have internal rules governing whether or when amendments must be "germane" to the measure they are amending.

Floor amendments can be both strategically important and politically important. As a strategic matter, amendments may be essential to garnering sufficient support to ensure passage of the underlying measure. Amendments also may be offered in an attempt to weaken the underlying measure, or occasionally even with the hope that adoption of the amendment will amount to a "poison pill" that dooms the underlying measure, perhaps by fracturing whatever coalition had been prepared to support it, or by complicating its implementation. As a political matter, amendments also sometimes may be offered to enable legislators to go on record with a more detailed or nuanced demonstration of their position than would be possible by a simple vote up or down on the underlying measure. Meanwhile, as we will see later, even amendments that were proposed but not adopted can subsequently serve as interpretive tools when questions arise about the meaning of a provision.

At some point, consideration of amendments ceases and debate on the underlying bill (as amended) begins. Here, committee leaders and sponsors of the measure usually take a lead role in promoting the measure. Because of their familiarity with the bill, their representations about its meaning and impact may be given great weight by colleagues who are unfamiliar with the bill. Opponents also have an opportunity to characterize the problems and weaknesses of the measure; their arguments are occasionally viewed as potentially more exaggerated, hyperbolic, or untrustworthy than are supporters' arguments.

Once the time for debate on the bill has expired, or if a motion to proceed to the vote (often termed a motion "to call the question" or "to order the previous question") succeeds, members then vote on the measure. The results of this vote, often termed the vote on "final passage," are recorded in the Journal of the chamber, the official record of its actions.

7.   The Second Body—Bicameralism in Action

A measure that has succeeded in one house then must complete the same process all over again in the other house (except in unicameral Nebraska). Sometimes members of each body will introduce identical or similar measures in both houses at approximately the same time, and let each house proceed to consider the measures in due course. Eventually, one measure will be allowed to function as the primary measure, if only because it is the first one to have passed the chamber where it originated. This first chamber then formally notifies the other of its action and transmits its bill to the other chamber for consideration. At that point, the second house will put the measure through essentially the same process, beginning with referral to the appropriate committee; then committee hearings, mark-up, and reporting to the floor; followed by floor debate, amendment, and voting.

The second house has the full right to refuse to consider the measure at any stage, including holding it up in committee; to consider it and vote against it; or to amend it and pass it as amended. But unless the second house passes the measure exactly as it was received from the first house, the bicameralism requirement has not been met. At that point, if changes have been made, the measure may be sent back to the originating chamber, where more work is required.

8.   Conference Committees

As just indicated, what often emerges from the second body is no longer the same measure that went in. In the typical case, either the two houses of the legislature then must work together to iron out the differences between the two versions that have each passed only one house, or one of the houses must acquiesce to the version that the other has passed. The two houses are equal in this regard, with neither having a superior position, either by dint of having passed the first version of the measure, or because of any difference between the so-called "upper" and "lower" houses of the legislature.

Differences are usually ironed out by appointing a "conference committee," consisting of members of both chambers appointed by their leaders specifically for the one-time purpose of resolving differences between the two versions of a particular bill. For instance, the conference committee formed for a prison bill will be different from the conference committee for a hydraulic fracturing bill. Conference committee members are chosen based on their position as leaders in their respective chamber, or their substantive expertise concerning the specific measure at issue (often, though not necessarily, including members who have already helped handle the measure in a standing committee, before it passed their chamber).

The role of the conference committee is to get supporters of the two versions to come to an agreement on one common measure. To that end, internal rules in Congress specifically prohibit a conference committee from taking up new matters or revisiting elements already common to both chambers' versions of the measure. But enforcement of this limitation is also entirely an internal matter, and conference committees may take up matters outside their jurisdiction if they are prepared to take the risk that some member of either chamber may raise an objection when the conference committee version is subsequently presented.

> The phrase "standing committee" refers to a regular and continuing committee in one of the legislative chambers. This contrasts with an *"ad hoc* committee." A conference committee is one type of *ad hoc* committee.

Assuming a conference committee is able to develop a compromise measure that it anticipates will be acceptable to both chambers, the conference committee then prepares its own committee report to explain its work and support its recommendations. This report, including the full text of the proposed compromise measure, is then submitted to and voted on by both houses. If both houses agree to it, the bicameralism requirement of Article I at last is satisfied. If either chamber fails to agree to the conference report, it is back to the drawing board.

It also is possible for a conference committee to entirely fail to produce a conference agreement, or to conclude that one of the two measures with which it began should simply be reconsidered by the second house.

Once a measure has passed both houses, it is "enrolled." This means that an official version is prepared and certified by the chamber in which it originated, then signed by the presiding officers of each chamber (in Congress, the Speaker of the House and the President Pro Tempore of the Senate). The enrolled bill then is presented to the President or Governor for approval or disapproval (veto).

9.   Presentment to the President or Governor

Again, as part of the checks and balances built into a system of separated governmental powers, once a legislative measure has satisfied the bicameralism requirement, it cannot become law without its presentment to the head of the executive branch for approval or veto. If the measure is vetoed, it can only become law if the legislature, after an opportunity to consider the chief executive's explanation for disapproving it, then passes it again, notwithstanding the veto, by a specified supermajority vote.

The presentment requirement provides the President or Governor more than just an opportunity to veto a measure. It also can serve as a moment for another necessary actor in the lawmaking process—and the only individual actor personally necessary—to reflect upon and articulate an understanding of the intended purpose and effect of the measure, and to consider whether the text of the measure is adequate to effectuate that purpose. While on occasion this opportunity also may devolve into mere "grandstanding," it also can serve as a reference point, both for understanding how the lawmaking process works generally as well as for understanding the specific measure approved or vetoed.

> **FYI** In 1990, President George H.W. Bush vetoed amendments to the Civil Rights Act of 1964 (what would have been the Civil Rights Act of 1990). In his veto message, the President specifically mentioned his concerns that the bill's retroactivity provisions, which would have applied the bill's changes to cases then pending in court, would have been unfair to defendants in those pending cases. The following year, when Congress passed the Civil Rights Act of 1991, the law did not include the same retroactivity language, and President Bush signed the bill into law. In a 1994 case, *Landgraf v. USI Film Products*, 511 U.S. 244 (1994), the Supreme Court treated the absence of that language in the statute as important because of the President's earlier veto message.

As explored in Chapter 26, the practice of deriving interpretive guidance from statements that a chief executive makes upon signing a measure into law is not without some controversy. Also controversial are attempts at this stage by the chief executive to amend the enactment implicitly, for instance by purporting to condition approval of the measure on a claim that the measure can only be read in a particular way and would not have received the executive's approval were it to be read otherwise. Meanwhile, veto messages can be especially instructive when they shape a subsequent legislative measure intended to respond to or accommodate the executive's stated objections.

In the federal system, once the President signs a measure, it is immediately effective, unless the measure by its own terms provides for a subsequent effective date. The Office of the Federal Register then publishes a hardcopy of each new law as a "slip law," which can also be accessed electronically through the website of the Government Printing Office. The new law also will be included in the United States Statutes at Large, a published volume of "session laws," comprising all the measures enacted into law during that same session of Congress.

If the President instead disapproves (vetoes) a measure, the measure is returned, along with the President's veto message, to the house of Congress that originated the measure. There, Congress can begin considering whether to enact the measure into law notwithstanding the President's veto. Both houses must approve the measure by a two-thirds supermajority to enact the measure into law over the President's objections. If both houses obtain the required supermajority, the Office of the Federal Register then publishes the "slip law" version of the law.

In about half the states, measures signed by the Governor ordinarily are not immediately effective (unless they are passed as "emergency" measures, which require the vote of a supermajority of the state legislature). Instead, these measures must wait a specified period (usually ninety days) in order to provide the state's voters their own opportunity to disapprove the measure using the popular referendum process (discussed further in Chapter 13 concerning Direct Democracy). In most cases, however, no referendum occurs and the measure becomes effective after the specified time elapses.

And with that, the legislative process is complete!

> "Session laws," which are a chronological compilation of a legislature's output, need to be distinguished from "codified laws," or the "code," which is a collection of statutory law organized by topic or subject matter (for example, collecting all the laws about motor vehicles in one title of a state code). As a formal matter, usually only the "session laws" are the official law, because they are what the legislature has passed and the chief executive has signed. But as a practical matter, nearly every lawyer (and judge!) reads and interprets the "code" because the codified version's topical organization makes it easier to use. The code, for example, will incorporate statutory amendments affecting one section of law all in one single place, making it more accessible.

FYI

DIY
The Hurdles to Making Law

As the preceding summary of the legislative process suggests, proposed legislation must overcome many hurdles to become law. Take a minute to think about whether the legislative process makes enacting new law too difficult, too easy, or is just right, and write down in your notes why you think what you think.

B. Fostering Robust Deliberation: Legislative Privilege

This chapter's description of the legislative process now turns briefly to an over-view of the "legislative privilege," an underappreciated topic of great importance to a legislature's ability to engage in robust, thoughtful deliberation in the public interest at all stages of the process. The legislative privilege is a long-standing pro-tection of the independence of the legislative branch that shields legislators from harassment or intimidation by the other branches of government concerning the legislators' performance of their legislative work. However, this is a protection that occasionally complicates the enforcement of bribery laws and other external efforts to mon-itor and constrain legislative deliberations.

> **!** Recall that the campaign finance laws we discussed in Chapters 8 and 9 and the lobbying laws we discussed in Chapter 10 were premised in part on an anti-corruption rationale. Probably obviously, bribery laws have much the same rationale.

The Framers of the U.S. Constitution en-shrined in Article I the principle that legis-lators should be responsible for how they perform their legislative work only at the voting booth or within their legislative body. They did so by adopting in the Constitution's "Speech or Debate Clause" a form of the Eng-lish parliamentary privilege. This clause assures Members of Congress that "for any Speech or Debate in either House, they shall not be questioned in any other Place." U.S. CONST. art. I, § 6, cl. 1. Almost all states' constitutions contain an analogous pro-tection for their state legislators, and the remaining states recognize an analogous legislative privilege at common law.

At the federal level, the central elements of this legislative privilege (which oc-casionally also goes by the name of "legislative immunity") are well settled. It precludes both (1) imposing legal liability on legislators for how they legislate (a prototypical "immunity"), as well as (2) compelling them to explain their legisla-tive activities (a prototypical "privilege"). It applies only to activities that are "an integral part of the deliberative and communicative processes by which Members participate" in considering matters within the constitutional jurisdiction of their chamber, *Gravel v. United States,* 408 U.S. 606, 625 (1972), and does not extend to the full range of a Member's official activities and duties (such as constituent services, guest appearances, and administrative responsibilities, among other func-tions outside the scope of the Speech or Debate Clause). But where the privilege applies, it is an absolute rather than a qualified privilege, meaning that it is not subject to a balancing of interests. It applies both to Members of Congress as well as to their staff, at least on those occasions when staff are assisting the Member with essential legislative activities.

The Supreme Court has described the fundamental purpose of the legislative privilege as "to prevent intimidation of legislators by the Executive and accountability before a possibly hostile judiciary." *Gravel*, 408 U.S. at 617. But it also has been understood as necessary to protect legislators against the burdens of defending themselves in civil or criminal matters, as well as against the burdens of responding to discovery requests in third-party lawsuits. In this last regard, the Speech or Debate Clause's protection against being "questioned" in any place other than Congress also has regularly been applied to a Member's legislative documents, as well as to personal testimony. The legislative privilege thus provides Members of Congress with both an evidentiary and a testimonial privilege, as well as immunity from suit.

In providing Members of Congress liability immunity for the performance of their legislative duties, the Speech or Debate Clause does not preclude the prosecution of a Member for violation of the federal bribery statute. It does, however, make these prosecutions more difficult. Consider the following case excerpt.

United States v. Helstoski
442 U.S. 477 (1979)

MR. CHIEF JUSTICE BURGER delivered the opinion of the Court.

We granted certiorari in this case to resolve important questions concerning the restrictions the Speech or Debate Clause places on the admissibility of evidence at a trial on charges that a former Member of the House had, while a Member, accepted money in return for promising to introduce and introducing private bills.

I

Respondent Helstoski is a former Member of the United States House of Representatives from New Jersey. In 1974, while Helstoski was a Member of the House, the Department of Justice began investigating

A "private bill" **FYI** is a proposal for a law that would apply only to a particular individual, group of individuals, or corporate entity. This contrast with a "public bill," which applies to everyone in a jurisdiction. Private bills are relatively rare these days. For instance, in August 2022, one recent private bill (which did in fact become a "private *law*") authorized the President to award the Medal of Honor to Gunnery Sergeant John L. Canley for acts of valor during the Vietnam war. See Prvt. L. No. 115-1 (Jan. 29, 2018).

reported political corruption, including allegations that aliens had paid money for the introduction of private bills which would suspend the application of the immigration laws so as to allow them to remain in this country.

* * * [Before the grand jury,] Helstoski testified as to his practices in introducing private immigration bills, and he produced his files on numerous private bills. Included in the files were correspondence with a former legislative aide and with individuals for whom bills were introduced. He also provided copies of 169 bills introduced on behalf of various aliens. * * *

II

In June 1976, a grand jury returned a multiple-count indictment charging Helstoski and others with various criminal acts [including official bribery, in violation of 18 U.S.C. § 201]. Helstoski moved to dismiss the indictment, contending that the grand jury process had been abused and that the indictment violated the Speech or Debate Clause.

[The District Court denied the motion, but also ruled that the Government would not be allowed to offer evidence of Helstoski's actual performance of any legislative acts. The government appealed that evidentiary ruling, and the Third Circuit affirmed it.]

III

The Court's holdings in *United States v. Johnson*, 383 U.S. 169 (1966), and *United States v. Brewster*, [408 U.S. 501 (1972)], leave no doubt that evidence of a legislative act of a Member may not be introduced by the Government in a prosecution under [18 U.S.C. § 201]. In *Johnson* there had been extensive questioning of both Johnson, a former Congressman, and others about a speech which Johnson had delivered in the House of Representatives and the motive for the speech. The Court's conclusion was unequivocal:

"We see no escape from the conclusion that such an intensive judicial inquiry, made in the course of a prosecution by the Executive Branch under a general conspiracy statute, violates the express language of the Constitution and the policies which underlie it." 383 U.S., at 177.

In *Brewster*, we explained the holding of *Johnson* in this way:

"*Johnson* thus stands as a unanimous holding that a Member of Congress may be prosecuted under a criminal statute provided that the Government's case does not rely on legislative acts or the motivation for legislative acts. A legislative act has consistently been defined as an act generally done in

Congress in relation to the business before it. In sum, the Speech or Debate Clause prohibits inquiry only into those things generally said or done in the House or the Senate in the performance of official duties and into the motivation for those acts." 408 U.S., at 512.

The Government, however, argues that exclusion of references to past legislative acts will make prosecutions more difficult because such references are essential to show the motive for taking money. In addition, the Government argues that the exclusion of references to past acts is not logically consistent. In its view, if jurors are told of promises to perform legislative acts they will infer that the acts were performed, thereby calling the acts themselves into question.

We do not accept the Government's arguments; without doubt the exclusion of such evidence will make prosecutions more difficult. Indeed, the Speech or Debate Clause was designed to preclude prosecution of Members for legislative acts. The Clause protects "against inquiry into acts that occur in the regular course of the legislative process and into the motivation for those acts." *Id.*, at 525. It "precludes any showing of how [a legislator] acted, voted, or decided." *Id.*, at 527. Promises by a Member to perform an act in the future are not legislative acts. *Brewster* makes clear that the "compact" may be shown without impinging on the legislative function. *Id.*, at 526.

> What is the distinction the Court is drawing here? Does it make sense? Why should evidence of a legislator's promise to vote a certain way be admissible, but the legislator's actual vote not be?

We therefore agree with the Court of Appeals that references to past legislative acts of a Member cannot be admitted without undermining the values protected by the Clause. We implied as much in *Brewster* when we explained: "To make a prima facie case under [the] indictment, the Government need not show any act of [Brewster] subsequent to the corrupt promise for payment, for it is taking the bribe, not performance of the illicit compact, that is a criminal act." *Ibid.* (Emphasis altered.) A similar inference is appropriate from *Johnson* where we held that the Clause was violated by questions about motive addressed to others than Johnson himself. That holding would have been unnecessary if the Clause did not afford protection beyond legislative acts themselves.

MR. JUSTICE STEVENS misconstrues our holdings on the Speech or Debate Clause in urging: "The admissibility line should be based on the purpose of the offer rather than the specificity of the reference." *Post*, at 496. The Speech or Debate Clause does not refer to the prosecutor's purpose in offering evidence. The Clause does not simply state, "No proof of a legislative act shall be offered"; the prohibition of the Clause is far broader. It provides that Members "shall not be questioned in any other Place." Indeed, as MR. JUSTICE STEVENS recognizes, the admission of evidence of legislative acts "may reveal [to the jury] some information about the performance of legislative acts and the legislator's motivation in conducting official duties." *Post*, at 496. Revealing information as to a legislative act—speaking or debating—to a jury would subject a Member to being "questioned" in a place other than the House or Senate, thereby violating the explicit prohibition of the Speech or Debate Clause.

As to what restrictions the Clause places on the admission of evidence, our concern is not with the "specificity" of the reference. Instead, our concern is whether there is mention of a legislative act. To effectuate the intent of the Clause, the Court has construed it to protect other "legislative acts" such as utterances in committee hearings and reports. E. g., *Doe v. McMillan*, 412 U.S. 306 (1973). But it is clear from the language of the Clause that protection extends only to an act that has already been performed. A promise to deliver a speech, to vote, or to solicit other votes at some future date is not "speech or debate." Likewise, a promise to introduce a bill is not a legislative act. Thus, in light of the strictures of *Johnson* and *Brewster*, the District Court order prohibiting the introduction of evidence "of the performance of a past legislative act" was redundant.

[The Court then rejected the government's argument that Representative Helstoski had waived the protections of the Speech or Debate Clause.]

The Speech or Debate Clause was designed neither to assure fair trials nor to avoid coercion. Rather, its purpose was to preserve the constitutional structure of separate, coequal, and independent branches of government. The English and American history of the privilege suggests that any lesser standard would risk intrusion by the Executive and the Judiciary into the sphere of protected legislative activities. The importance of the principle was recognized as early as 1808 in *Coffin v. Coffin*, 4 Mass. 1, 27, where the court said that the purpose of the principle was to secure to every member "exemption from prosecution, for every thing said or done by him, as a representative, in the exercise of the functions of that office." (Emphasis added.)

This Court has reiterated the central importance of the Clause for preventing intrusion by Executive and Judiciary into the legislative sphere.

> [I]t is apparent from the history of the clause that the privilege was not born primarily of a desire to avoid private suits . . . but rather to prevent intimidation by the executive and accountability before a possibly hostile judiciary. . . .
>
> There is little doubt that the instigation of criminal charges against critical or disfavored legislators by the executive in a judicial forum was the chief fear prompting the long struggle for parliamentary privilege in England and, in the context of the American system of separation of powers, is the predominate thrust of the Speech or Debate Clause.

United States v. Johnson, 383 U.S., at 180–181, 182.

We reaffirmed that principle in *Gravel v. United States*, 408 U.S. 606, 618 (1972), when we noted that the "fundamental purpose" of the Clause was to free "the legislator from executive and judicial oversight that realistically threatens to control his conduct as a legislator."

* * *

The Government also argues that there has been a sort of institutional waiver by Congress in enacting § 201. According to the Government, § 201 represents a collective decision to enlist the aid of the Executive Branch and the courts in the exercise of Congress' powers under Art. I, 5, to discipline its Members. This Court has twice declined to decide whether a Congressman could, consistent with the Clause, be prosecuted for a legislative act as such, provided the prosecution were "founded upon a narrowly drawn statute passed by Congress in the exercise of its legislative power to regulate the conduct of its members." *Johnson*, supra, at 185; *United States v. Brewster*, 408 U.S., at 529 n. 18. We see no occasion to resolve that important question. We hold only that § 201 does not amount to a congressional waiver of the protection of the Clause for individual Members.

We recognize that an argument can be made from precedent and history that Congress, as a body, should not be free to strip individual Members of the protection guaranteed by the Clause from being "questioned" by the Executive in the courts. The controversy over the Alien and Sedition Acts reminds us how one political party in control of both the Legislative and the Executive Branches sought to use the courts to destroy political opponents.

FYI The Alien and Seditions Acts were controversial laws passed in 1798 by the Federalist Party in Congress. The Sedition Act in particular was used (and was intended to be used) by the Administration of John Adams (a Federalist) to, among other things, suppress criticism of Adams and the Federalists by their opponents, those supporting the Democratic-Republican Party, the other major party in the U.S. at the time. Many prominent Democratic-Republicans were prosecuted under the law.

The Supreme Judicial Court of Massachusetts noted in *Coffin* that "the privilege secured . . . is not so much the privilege of the house as an organized body, as of each individual member composing it, who is entitled to this privilege, even against the declared will of the house." 4 Mass., at 27 (emphasis added). In a similar vein in *Brewster* we stated:

"The immunities of the Speech or Debate Clause were not written into the Constitution simply for the personal or private benefit of Members of Congress, but to protect the integrity of the legislative process by insuring the independence of individual legislators." 408 U.S., at 507 (emphasis added).

See also *id.*, at 524. We perceive no reason to undertake, in this case, consideration of the Clause in terms of separating the Members' rights from the rights of the body.

Assuming, arguendo, that the Congress could constitutionally waive the protection of the Clause for individual Members, such waiver could be shown only by an explicit and unequivocal expression. There is no evidence of such a waiver in the language or the legislative history of § 201 or any of its predecessors.

We conclude that there was neither individual nor institutional waiver and that the evidentiary barriers erected by the Speech or Debate Clause must stand. Accordingly, the judgment of the Court of Appeals is

Affirmed.

[JUSTICE STEVENS, joined by JUSTICE STEWART, dissented in part, and JUSTICE BRENNAN dissented.]

NOTES & QUESTIONS

1. In today's politics, where do legislative proposals typically originate, and what are the typical influences that affect potential legislation? Is anything wrong with this picture?

2. What are the most difficult "hurdles" that a piece of legislation must surmount?

3. At which stage(s) of the legislative process, and why, might you be most likely to find salient information for understanding the legislature's intended meaning of a statute?

4. Do you think the fact that statutes are difficult to pass should affect how statutes should be interpreted? Some scholars and judges argue that one reason statutes are difficult to pass is as a protection for minority interests and that almost all statutes are thus compromises between different factions. These scholars and judges argue that courts should therefore limit their interpretive inquiry to the final text of the statute and should generally ignore legislative history and other evidence that might help one understand a statute's purpose. We will look at this more closely beginning in Part IV.

5. Is the filibuster, as practiced today in the U.S. Senate, a desirable feature of the federal legislative process?

6. Is the legislative privilege of the Speech or Debate Clause a good thing? How far should it go?

7. The broad contours of the legislative privilege, and its purpose of ensuring that legislators can conduct their legislative debates and deliberations without fear of liability or harassment, are relatively well-settled. Nevertheless, many subsidiary issues occasionally arise at both the state and federal levels, including questions at the margins about whether something is protected legislative activity, as well as questions about what kinds of executive branch investigatory activities unconstitutionally infringe upon the independence of the legislative branch. Meanwhile, state courts are under no obligation to construe their analogous state provisions in lockstep with the federal jurisprudence, and indeed they have not, occasionally declining to extend the legislative privilege to staff, or refusing to apply it to protect testimony or documents. On the other hand, at least one state court has construed its legislative

privilege more broadly also to protect legislators for their statements to the press about legislative activities, *see Abercrombie v. McClung,* 525 P.2d 594 (Haw. 1974), a coverage that the U.S. Supreme Court has not made available to members of Congress, *see Hutchinson v. Proxmire,* 443 U.S. 111 (1979).

Test Your Understanding

To assess your understanding of the material in this chapter, click here to take a quiz.

12

Budgets and Appropriations of Funds

Key Concepts

- Federal funding process
- Budget resolution
- Origination Clause
- Authorizing measures
- Annual appropriations
- Discretionary spending
- Mandatory (direct) spending
- Reconciliation
- Line Item Veto

Chapter Summary

One aspect of the legislative branch that is woefully under-appreciated by most Americans is the budget process by which legislatures provide funds for government activities. Yet far more than just providing funding, the budget process is really where the legislature establishes the government's priorities.

The federal budget process starts with *authorizing* measures that give agencies and departments the authority to spend money. Once passed, these measures can have effect for decades. However, they do not actually provide any funding. Instead, Congress must also annually pass a set of a*ppropriations* bills, which actually allocate federal dollars to respective units of the federal government for them to spend. Meanwhile, on an annual basis Congress also strives to pass a *budget resolution*, an internal statement of principle about how money will be spent. Congressional *reconciliation* then is a process used to match actual appropriations to the spending limits agreed upon in the budget resolution.

When the executive branch does not spend all of the money allocated by the legislative branch, it has some authority to *impound* the funds. Otherwise, if the President does not want to spend the money allocated, the President may submit to Congress a request for *rescission*.

Near the end of the 20th Century, Congress attempted to give the President a Line Item Veto authority, the power to cancel individual appropriations within a larger bill. However, the Supreme Court found this mechanism unconstitutional.

A. Budget and Appropriations Measures

Perhaps a legislature's most fundamental responsibility is to decide how to spend public money, or in other words to decide for what purposes to appropriate government funds. Most state legislatures exercise this "power of the purse" through the enactment of a state budget bill, which controls the uses to which public revenue will be directed. Although Congress also may adopt a federal budget resolution, Congress formally controls and directs the uses of federal funds not with the budget resolution but through a set of appropriations acts, which in turn are constrained by a separate set of spending authorization acts. The congressional budget resolution, meanwhile, is in reality only a nonbinding statement of principle and priorities, not a necessary component of the federal spending process. Indeed, in recent years political difficulties have sometimes entirely prevented Congress from adopting the annual budget resolution. Federal budget, authorization, and appropriation measures are discussed further below.

Several factors influence how legislatures perform the critical function of appropriating government funds. First, before government can spend money, it must be able to raise or borrow it. At the federal level, the Constitution provides that all bills for raising revenue must originate in the House of Representatives. U.S. CONST. art. I, sec. 7, cl. 1. The Founders included this "Origination Clause" in order to ensure that the branch of the federal legislature closest to the people controlled the government's purse strings. The Origination Clause (or Revenue Clause) has been construed to pertain only to general tax measures, and not to preclude the Senate from originating bills having an incidental effect of raising revenue.

The federal government also may (and does) borrow money to fund its expenses. By statute, Congress has established a limit on the cumulative amount of debt the federal government may accumulate. But the limit does not operate as much of a constraint, as Congress routinely raises the debt limit in order to prevent the federal government from defaulting on its obligations. Other budgetary rules seek to control the size of the annual deficit in the federal government's fiscal year operating budget, or to require that any new federal spending be tied to a source of funds. These constraints can substantially limit congressional activity in a wide variety of areas.

> The government borrows money by **FYI** issuing federal government bonds, commonly referred to as "Treasuries." Those who purchase Treasuries are in essence lending the federal government money. Treasuries can be one of three types— "Treasury Bonds," "Treasury Notes," or "Treasury Bills" (or "T-Bills"), depending on how long the loan is for and how the interest is paid.

> **FYI** The "budget deficit" is the amount by which government spending exceeds tax receipts and other government income in a given year. The opposite of a deficit is a budget surplus, which occurs when the government takes in more in revenue than it spends. With the exception of a short period between 1998 and 2001, the federal government has run a deficit every year since 1970. So, except for the 1998–2001 period, the government's cumulative amount of debt has continued to climb. This is why Congress has needed to repeatedly raise the debt limit, or "debt ceiling" as it is sometimes called.

In order for a federal government department or agency to spend money, Congress first must authorize the expenditure, usually through enactment of an *authorization* measure. But authorization alone is not sufficient, as the department or agency also must have the funds at its disposal. The separate *appropriations* acts are the vehicles through which Congress actually makes funds available for specific purposes. It is not uncommon for a particular federal program to have statutory authority to spend more money than Congress has made available to it through an appropriation.

One additional critical element of how Congress decides to spend federal funds is the "Reconciliation" process. Reconciliation has proven critical because it can provide a means of circumventing a Senate filibuster, allowing legislation to pass with a simple majority rather than a super-majority vote. Developed entirely as a matter of the internal rules by which Congress has chosen to structure its deliberations, the Reconciliation process was intended to help Congress align ("reconcile") spending and revenue-raising measures with the annual congressional budget resolution. The budget resolution typically includes an instruction to certain committees to achieve certain budget effects through development of a Reconciliation bill. The Reconciliation bill is limited in the content it can contain but receives expedited consideration under a privileged status that limits the terms of debate and precludes the possibility of a Senate filibuster. The parliamentary details governing exactly what can be in the Reconciliation bill and how the Reconciliation process can be used are complex, but it has increasingly become the means of accomplishing significant non-budgetary goals, for instance enacting parts of the Patient Protection and Affordable Care Act in 2010.

Some state constitutions, like the U.S. Constitution, also provide that revenue measures must originate in the lower chamber of the legislature. But far more important than this constraint is that 49 states (all except Vermont) have some sort of balanced budget requirement that precludes deficit spending, at least with respect to the state's operating budget. (Many of these states are permitted to incur debt for purposes of capital projects, such as constructing roads or buildings, financed by specific bonding legislation.) Some states, like Congress, appropriate operating funds on an annual basis, while other states use a biennial budget cycle. Appropriating only those funds that will be available during the budget cycle, without any possibility of deficit spending, is a complex task, and may require states to make mid-year budget corrections or adjustments when actual revenues fall short of estimates.

At the federal level, the following excerpts from the Congressional Research Service Report R46468, *"A Brief Overview of the Congressional Budget Process"* (2023), provide additional description of the series of steps involved in the congressional budget and appropriations processes:

A Brief Overview of the Congressional Budget Process

The Budget Cycle

Since FY1977, the federal fiscal year has run from October 1 through September 30, and much of the focus of the budget process for Congress concerns the upcoming fiscal year (referred to as the budget year). The Budget and Accounting Act of 1921 established a requirement that the President submit a budget request for the next fiscal year at the beginning of each calendar year. Likewise, the Congressional Budget Act of 1974 (CBA) provides for the consideration of a concurrent resolution on the budget (i.e., a budget resolution) to allow Congress to make decisions about fiscal policy and budget priorities on an annual basis. In addition, since appropriations legislation typically provides budget authority to be obligated over the course of a single fiscal year, Congress must enact new appropriations legislation each year prior to the start of the fiscal year.

On the other hand, while much of the congressional agenda and workload in any given session is focused on annual budgetary actions, most federal spending (in the form of direct, or mandatory, spending), as well as most revenue, occurs as a consequence of permanent law or laws with sunset dates beyond the next fiscal year. While changes to laws concerning direct spending or revenue are not tied directly to the annual budget cycle, such legislation may be a necessary part of budgetary actions in any given year.

FYI "FY1997" means "Fiscal Year 1997," and a fiscal year is essentially the "budget year," which is distinct from the calendar year. In recent decades, almost every year Congress has been pressed to complete the legislative process necessary to fund the government for the coming fiscal year by the time the fiscal year begins, on October 1. This difficulty typically results in the enactment of just a temporary funding measure, called a "continuing resolution," until Congress can complete its regular appropriations measures.

The President's Budget

The Constitution does not assign a formal role in the federal budget process to the President. This was changed by the Budget and Accounting Act of 1921, which established the requirement for a consolidated budget proposal to be developed by the President, with the assistance of the Office of Management and Budget (OMB), and submitted to Congress. Although it also does not have the force of law, the President's budget submission reflects his policy priorities and offers a set of recommendations regarding federal programs, projects, and activities funded through appropriations acts, as well as any proposed changes to revenue and direct spending laws. As currently provided under 31 U.S.C. § 1105, the President is to submit the request "on or after the first Monday in January but not later than the first Monday in February of each year." In support of the President's appropriations requests, executive branch agencies prepare additional materials, frequently referred to as congressional budget justifications. These materials provide more detail than is contained in the President's budget documents and are used in support of agency testimony during Appropriations subcommittee hearings on the President's budget.

The Budget Resolution and Reconciliation

Until the 1970s, congressional consideration of the multiple budgetary measures considered every year lacked any formal coordination. Instead,

Congress considered these various budgetary measures separately, sometimes informally comparing them to proposals in the President's budget. The CBA changed that. It provides for the adoption of a concurrent resolution on the budget, allowing Congress to make decisions about overall fiscal policy and priorities, as well as coordinate and establish guidelines for the consideration of various budget related measures. This budget resolution sets aggregate budget policies and functional priorities for the upcoming budget year as well as at least four additional fiscal years. In recent practice, budget resolutions have often covered a 10-year period.

Because a concurrent resolution is not presented to the President and cannot become law, it has no statutory effect, and no money can be raised or spent pursuant to it. The main purpose of the budget resolution is to establish a framework within which Congress can consider separate revenue, spending, and other budget-related legislation. Revenue and spending amounts set in the budget resolution establish the basis for the enforcement of congressional budget policies through points of order during House and Senate floor consideration. Most budget points of order in the Senate require a three-fifths supermajority to be waived. The budget resolution may also be used to initiate the reconciliation process (described below) for conforming existing revenue and direct spending laws to congressional budget policies.

> **FYI** A "point of order" is a mechanism in parliamentary procedure whereby a legislator can call attention to a potential rules violation during a legislative session, and seek an immediate ruling whether a procedural defect has occurred.

In the absence of a budget resolution, Congress may use alternative means to establish enforceable budget levels. When Congress has been late in reaching final agreement on a budget resolution, or has not reached agreement at all, the House and Senate, often acting separately, have established alternate legislative procedures to deal with enforcement issues on an ad hoc basis. These alternatives are typically referred to as "deeming resolutions," because they are deemed to serve in place of an agreement between the two chambers on an annual budget resolution for the purposes of establishing enforceable budget levels for the upcoming fiscal year (or multiple fiscal years).

The budget resolution represents an agreement between the House and Senate concerning the overall size of the federal budget and the general composition of the budget in terms of functional categories. The amounts in functional categories are translated into allocations to each House or Senate committee with jurisdiction over spending in a process called "cross-walking" under Section 302(a) of the CBA. Legislation considered by the House and Senate must be consistent with these allocations, as well as with the aggregate levels of spending and revenues. Both the allocations and aggregates are enforceable through points of order that may be made during House or Senate floor consideration of such legislation. These allocations are supplemented by nonbinding assumptions concerning the substance of possible budgetary legislation that are included in the report from the Budget Committee that accompanies each chamber's respective budget resolution.

"Functional categories" are broad areas, such as "International Affairs," "Agriculture," and "Health." The federal budget has approximately twenty functional categories.

In some years, the budget resolution includes reconciliation instructions. Reconciliation instructions identify the committees that must recommend changes in laws affecting revenues or direct spending programs within their jurisdiction in order to implement the priorities agreed to in the budget resolution. Although the level of budgetary changes in a committee's instructions are enforceable, the choice of policy changes necessary to achieve it remains the prerogative of the committee. In some instances, reconciliation instructions have included particular policy options or assumptions regarding how an instructed committee might be expected to achieve its reconciliation target, but such language has not been considered binding or enforceable. Reconciliation instructions may further direct the committee to report the legislation for consideration in its respective chamber or to submit the legislation to the Budget Committee to be included in an omnibus reconciliation measure. If it will be included in an omnibus measure, Section 310(b)(2) of the CBA requires that the Budget Committee report such a measure "without any substantive revision."

Once it is reported, a reconciliation bill may then be considered, and possibly amended, by the full House or Senate. In the House, reconciliation bills are typically considered under the terms of a special rule setting any limits on debate or amending. In the Senate, reconciliation legislation is eligible to be considered under expedited procedures. The CBA (primarily in Sections 305, 310, and 313) provides for limits on the contents and consideration of a reconciliation bill. The limits on the contents of the measure and any amendments are enforced by points of order and would require a three-fifths supermajority to be waived in the Senate. In addition, debate on a reconciliation bill is limited to 20 hours. Because the 20-hour limit is on debate rather than consideration, after debate time has expired, Senators may continue to offer amendments and make other motions or appeals but without further debate (often referred to as a "vote-a-rama"). The time limit on floor debate has meant that, in practice, reconciliation bills can be passed by the Senate by a simple majority without the need for a supermajority of three-fifths of the Senate to first invoke cloture.

FYI Recall from Chapter 11 that cloture is the Senate's process for overcoming a filibuster to close debate on a particular measure.

Direct Spending Legislation

Congressional budgetary procedures distinguish between two types of spending: discretionary spending (which is controlled through the annual appropriations process) and direct spending (also referred to as mandatory spending, for which the level of funding is controlled outside of the annual appropriations process). Discretionary and direct spending are both included in the President's budget and the congressional budget resolution, and they both provide statutory authority for agencies to enter into obligations for payments from the Treasury. The two forms of spending, however, are distinct in most other respects in terms of both formulation and consideration.

In the federal budget lexicon, "discretionary spending" **FYI** refers to the amounts Congress decides to spend in an annual appropriation for a specific purpose, such as for Amtrak or the military. Meanwhile, "direct spending" refers to commitments of federal funds already made through previously established programs, such as Social Security, but which still must be paid out in the current fiscal year. Direct spending is also often called "entitlement" spending.

Direct spending characteristically provides budget authority in the form of a requirement to make payments to individual recipients according to a formula that establishes eligibility criteria and a program of benefits. The resulting overall level of outlays for a direct spending program represents an aggregation of obligations for these individual benefits. In general, direct spending programs are established in permanent law that continues in effect until such time as it is revised or terminated. In some cases, however, such as the Child Health Insurance Program (CHIP) and Temporary Assistance for Needy Families (TANF), the program may require periodic reauthorization. For some programs (termed "appropriated entitlements"), appropriations legislation may provide the means of financing, but, in practice, the requirements for funding such programs are determined through their authorizing legislation so that the Appropriations Committees have little or no discretion over the amounts provided.

Jurisdiction over direct spending programs (including those funded in annual appropriations acts) is exercised in the House and Senate through legislative committees (such as the Senate Committee on Health, Education, Labor and Pensions or the House Agriculture Committee) based on their jurisdiction over legislation concerning the structure of direct spending programs including formulas regarding eligibility criteria and benefit payments.

While direct spending legislation may be included in reconciliation legislation, it may also be considered under the regular procedures of the House and Senate. The scheduling for consideration of legislation making such changes is determined by congressional leadership through their agenda-setting authority rather than keyed to the beginning of the fiscal year.

The Authorization/Appropriations Process

Discretionary spending is provided through a characteristically annual process in which Congress enacts regular appropriations measures. As an exercise of their constitutional authority to determine their rules of proceeding, both chambers have adopted rules that broadly distinguish between legislation that addresses questions of policy on the one hand and, on the other, legislation that addresses questions of funding and that also provide for their separate consideration. In common usage, the terms used to describe these types of measures are authorizations and appropriations, respectively.

An authorization may generally be described as a statutory provision that defines the authority of the government to act. It can establish or continue a federal agency, program, policy, project, or activity. Further, it may establish policies and restrictions and deal with organizational and administrative matters. It may also, explicitly or implicitly, authorize subsequent congressional action to provide appropriations. By itself, however, an authorization of discretionary spending does not provide funding for government activities.

> In other words, an authorization is like **FYI** giving permission for an activity but without the funding for it, and an appropriation is providing the funding for it.

An appropriation may generally be described as a statutory provision that provides budget authority, thus permitting a federal agency to incur obligations and make payments from the Treasury for specified purposes, usually during a specified period of time.

Congress regularly considers three main types of appropriations measures: regular annual appropriations to provide budget authority to fund programs and agency activities for the next fiscal year, supplemental appropriations to provide additional budget authority during the current fiscal year if the regular appropriation is insufficient or to finance activities not provided for in the regular appropriation, and continuing appropriations (often referred to as continuing resolutions or CRs) to provide interim (or sometimes full-year) funding to agencies for activities or programs not yet covered by a regular appropriation. By custom, appropriations bills originate in the House but may be amended by the Senate, as with other legislation.

The House and Senate Appropriations Committees are organized into subcommittees, each of which is responsible for developing one of the regular annual appropriations bills. Appropriations bills are constrained in terms of both their purpose and the amount of funding they provide. Appropriations are broadly constrained in terms of purpose because the rules of both the House (Rule XXI) and the Senate (Rule XVI) generally limit appropriations to programs and purposes previously authorized by law.

Constraints in terms of the amount of funding exist on several levels. For individual items or programs, funding may be limited to the level recommended in authorizing legislation. The overall level of discretionary spending provided in all appropriations acts is limited by the allocation of discretionary spending in the budget resolution to the Appropriations Committees under Section 302(a) of the CBA. Section 302(b) of the CBA further requires the House and Senate Appropriations Committees to subdivide the overall amount of discretionary spending among their subcommittees. Section 302(b) further requires these suballocations to be made "as soon as practicable after a concurrent resolution on the budget is agreed to." Because each subcommittee is responsible for developing a single general appropriations bill, the process of making suballocations effectively determines a spending limit for each of the regular annual appropriations bills. Legislation (or amendments) that would cause the suballocations made under Section 302(b) to be exceeded is subject to a point of order during floor consideration. The Appropriations Committees can (and do) issue revised subdivisions over the course of appropriations actions to reflect changes in spending priorities effected during floor consideration or in conference committee actions.

Revenue and Public Debt Legislation

The budget resolution provides a guideline for the overall level of revenues but not for their composition. Legislation controlling revenues is reported by the committees of jurisdiction (the House Ways and Means Committee and the Senate Finance Committee). The revenue level agreed to in the budget resolution acts as a minimum, limiting consideration of revenue legislation that would decrease revenue below that level. In addition, Article I, Section 7, of the Constitution requires that all revenue measures originate in the House of Representatives, although the Senate may amend them, as with other legislation. Revenue legislation may be considered at any time, although revenue provisions are often included in reconciliation legislation.

When the receipts collected by the federal government are not sufficient to cover outlays, it is necessary for the Treasury to finance the shortfall through the sale of various types of debt instruments to the public and federal agencies. Federal borrowing is subject to a statutory limit on public debt (referred to as the debt limit or debt ceiling). The budget resolution includes an appropriate level for the public debt that reflects the budgetary policies agreed to in the resolution. However, any change to the authorized limit on the public debt must be implemented through a statutory enactment. In recent years, Congress has chosen to suspend the debt limit for a set amount of time instead of raising the debt limit by a fixed dollar amount. When a suspension ends, the debt limit is reestablished at a dollar level that accommodates the level of federal debt issued during the suspension period.

Budget Enforcement and Sequestration

The CBA includes several provisions designed to encourage congressional compliance with the budget resolution. The House and Senate have also adopted other limits as part of their standing rules, as procedural provisions in budget resolutions, or as parts of some other measures to establish other budgetary rules, limits, and requirements. In particular, the overall spending ceiling, revenue floor, and committee allocations of spending determined in a budget resolution are all enforceable by points of order in both the House and the Senate during floor consideration. In addition, Appropriations Committees are required to make subdivisions of their committee allocation, and these too are enforceable. Legislation breaching other budgetary limits or causing increases in the deficit would also generally be subject to points of order.

Points of order enforce prohibitions against certain types of legislation or other congressional actions being taken in the legislative process. Points of order are not self-enforcing, however. A point of order must be raised by a Member on the floor of the chamber before the presiding officer can rule on its application and, thus, for its enforcement.

In the Senate, most points of order related to budget enforcement may be waived by a vote of three-fifths of all Senators (60 if there is no more than one vacancy). As with other provisions of Senate rules, budget enforcement points of order may also be waived by unanimous consent. In the House, points of order, including those for budget enforcement, may be waived by the adoption of special rules, although other means (such as unanimous consent or suspension of the rules) may also be used.

Since 1985, budgetary decision-making has often been subject to various budget control statutes designed to restrict congressional budgetary actions or enforce particular budgetary outcomes in order to reduce the budget deficit, limit spending, or prevent deficit increases. The mechanisms included in these acts have sought to supplement and modify the existing budget process and also added statutory budget controls, in some cases seeking to require future deficit reduction legislation or limit future congressional budgetary actions and in some cases seeking to preserve deficit reduction achieved in accompanying legislation. These control statutes have used sequestration as a means for their enforcement. Sequestration involves a presidential order that permanently cancels non-exempt budgetary resources for the purpose of achieving a required amount of outlay savings. Once an executive determination triggers sequestration, spending reductions are made automatically.

Between FY2012 and FY2021, the Budget Control Act of 2011 (BCA) reestablished statutory limits on discretionary spending, divided into separately enforceable defense and nondefense limits, for FY2012–FY2021. Several measures were subsequently enacted that modified the spending limits or enforcement procedures included in the BCA.

Currently, sequestration is used as an enforcement mechanism associated with the Statutory Pay-As-You-Go (PAYGO) Act of 2010. In the case of the Statutory PAYGO Act, OMB is required to record the budgetary effects of revenue and direct spending provisions enacted into law, including both costs and savings, on two PAYGO scorecards covering five- and 10-year periods. The budgetary effect of PAYGO measures is determined by statements inserted into the Congressional Record by the chairmen of the House and Senate Budget Committees and referenced in the text of the measures. If this procedure is not followed, the budgetary effect of the measure is determined by OMB. If OMB reports the net impact of changes to direct spending and revenue laws over the course of an annual session of Congress is projected to increase the deficit over either of these time periods, the President is required to issue a sequester order to eliminate it.

B. Item Vetoes

When spending legislation is presented to state governors for approval or veto, most of them have the authority not only to veto the entire measure, but also to veto individual items of spending authority contained in the measure. The federal lawmaking process, however, does not grant the U.S. President an item veto authority. But U.S. Presidents have long wished for and sought it. To that end, in 1996 Congress enacted the Line Item Veto Act, structured as an amendment to the 1974 Congressional Budget and Impoundment Control Act. The 1974 Impoundment Control Act authorized the President to "impound" (rather than spend) appropriated funds in certain circumstances, in two ways: either through temporary deferrals, or through submitting a request that Congress rescind (cancel) the appropriation. The Line Item Veto Act enhanced the rescission process.

The next case considers the Line Item Veto Act's constitutionality. As you read it, think not just about your own view of the constitutionality of the Act, but also about what the case teaches more generally about the federal lawmaking process.

Clinton v. City of New York
524 U.S. 417 (1998)

JUSTICE STEVENS delivered the opinion of the Court.

[Shortly after the Line Item Veto Act became effective on January 1, 1997,] the President exercised his authority [under the Act] to cancel one provision in the Balanced Budget Act of 1997, Pub. L. 105–33, 111 Stat. 251, 515, and two provisions in the Taxpayer Relief Act of 1997, Pub. L. 105–34, 111 Stat. 788, 895–896, 990–993. Appellees, claiming that they had been injured by two of those cancellations, filed these cases in the District Court. [That court held the statute unconstitutional, and we expedited our review.]

IV

The Line Item Veto Act gives the President the power to "cancel in whole" three types of provisions that have been signed into law: "(1) any dollar amount of discretionary budget authority; (2) any item of new direct spending; or (3) any limited tax benefit." 2 U.S.C. § 691(a) (1994 ed., Supp. II). * * *

The Act requires the President to adhere to precise procedures whenever he exercises his cancellation authority. In identifying items for cancellation he must consider the legislative history, the purposes, and other relevant information about the items. See 2 U.S.C. § 691(b) (1994 ed., Supp. II). He must determine, with respect to each cancellation, that it will "(i) reduce the Federal budget deficit; (ii) not impair any essential Government functions; and (iii) not harm the national interest." § 691(a)(3)(A). Moreover, he must transmit a special message to Congress notifying it of each cancellation within five calendar days (excluding Sundays) after the enactment of the canceled provision. See § 691(a)(3)(B). It is undisputed that the President meticulously followed these procedures in these cases.

A cancellation takes effect upon receipt by Congress of the special message from the President. See § 691b(a). If, however, a "disapproval bill" pertaining to a special message is enacted into law, the cancellations set forth in that message become "null and void." *Ibid.* The Act sets forth a detailed expedited procedure for the consideration of a "disapproval bill," see § 691d, but no such bill was passed for either of the cancellations involved in these cases. A majority vote of both Houses is sufficient to enact a disapproval bill. The Act does not grant the President the authority to cancel a disapproval bill, see § 691(c), but he does, of course, retain his constitutional authority to veto such a bill.

The effect of a cancellation is plainly stated in § 691e, which defines the principal terms used in the Act. With respect to both an item of new direct spending and a limited tax benefit, the cancellation prevents the item "from having legal force or effect." §§ 691e(4)(B)–(C). Thus, under the plain text of the statute, the two actions of the President that are challenged in these cases prevented one section of the Balanced Budget Act of 1997 and one section of the Taxpayer Relief Act of 1997 "from having legal force or effect." The remaining provisions of those statutes, with the exception of the second canceled item in the latter, continue to have the same force and effect as they had when signed into law. [opinion continues after the exercise]

DIY
Should the President Have a Line-Item Veto?

Pause for a moment and consider your own views about whether the Constitution should be read to allow Congress to grant the President this authority to cancel an item of spending. Once you have decided how you would construe the Constitution, continue reading the Court's opinion.

In both legal and practical effect, the President has amended two Acts of Congress by repealing a portion of each. "[R]epeal of statutes, no less than enactment, must conform with Art. I." *INS v. Chadha*, 462 U.S. 919, 954 (1983). There is no provision in the Constitution that authorizes the President to enact, to amend, or to repeal statutes. Both Article I and Article II assign responsibilities to the President that directly relate to the lawmaking process, but neither addresses the issue presented by these cases. The President "shall from time to time give to the Congress Information on the State of the Union, and recommend to their Consideration such Measures as he shall judge necessary and expedient. . . ." Art. II, § 3. Thus, he may initiate and influence legislative proposals. Moreover, after a bill has passed both Houses of Congress, but "before it become[s] a Law," it must be presented to the President. If he approves it, "he shall sign it, but if not he shall return it, with his Objections to that House in which it shall have originated, who shall enter the Objections at large on their Journal, and proceed to reconsider it." Art. I, § 7, cl. 2. His "return" of a bill, which is usually described as a "veto," is subject to being overridden by a two-thirds vote in each House.

> This is the majority's key point: the President "cancelling" the spending is the equivalent, "[i]n both legal and practical effect," to his "amending" the statute by "repealing" the relevant spending provision. As you read through the rest of the majority opinion, notice how much depends on this point. When you get to the dissent, notice what the dissent says about this.

There are important differences between the President's "return" of a bill pursuant to Article I, § 7, and the exercise of the President's cancellation authority pursuant to the Line Item Veto Act. The constitutional return takes place before the bill becomes law; the statutory cancellation occurs after the bill becomes law. The constitutional return is of the entire bill; the statutory cancellation is of only a part. Although the Constitution expressly authorizes the President to play a role in the process of enacting statutes, it is silent on the subject of unilateral Presidential action that either repeals or amends parts of duly enacted statutes.

There are powerful reasons for construing constitutional silence on this profoundly important issue as equivalent to an express prohibition. The procedures governing the enactment of statutes set forth in the text of Article I were the product of the great debates and compromises that produced the Constitution itself. Familiar historical materials provide abundant support for the conclusion that the power to enact statutes may only "be exercised in accord with a single, finely wrought and exhaustively considered, procedure." *Chadha*, 462 U.S., at 951. Our first President understood the text of the Presentment Clause as requiring that he either "approve all the parts of a Bill, or reject it in toto." What has emerged in these cases from the President's exercise of his statutory cancellation powers, however, are truncated versions of two bills that passed both Houses of Congress. They are not the product of the "finely wrought" procedure that the Framers designed.

At oral argument, the Government suggested that the cancellations at issue in these cases do not effect a "repeal" of the canceled items because under the special "lockbox" provisions of the Act, a canceled item "retain[s] real, legal budgetary effect" insofar as it prevents Congress and the President from spending the savings that result from the cancellation. Tr. of Oral Arg. 10. The text of the Act expressly provides, however, that a cancellation prevents a direct spending or tax benefit provision "from having legal force or effect." 2 U.S.C. §§ 691e(4)(B)–(C). That a canceled item may have "real, legal budgetary effect" as a result of the lockbox procedure does not change the fact that by canceling the items at issue in these cases, the President made them entirely inoperative as to appellees. Section 968 of the Taxpayer Relief Act no longer provides a tax benefit, and § 4722(c) of the Balanced Budget Act of 1997 no longer relieves New York of its contingent liability. Such significant changes do not lose their character simply because the canceled provisions may have some continuing financial effect on the Government. The cancellation of one section of a statute may be the functional equivalent of a partial repeal even if a portion of the section is not canceled.

V

The Government advances two related arguments to support its position that despite the unambiguous provisions of the Act, cancellations do not amend or repeal properly enacted statutes in violation of the Presentment Clause. First, relying primarily on *Field v. Clark*, 143 U.S. 649 (1892), the Government contends that the cancellations were merely exercises of discretionary authority granted to the President by the Balanced Budget Act and the Taxpayer Relief Act read in light of the previously enacted Line Item Veto Act. Second, the Government submits that the substance

> What constitutional significance should attach to the fact that when Congress authorizes the President to decide not to spend an appropriation, and the President then decides not to spend that appropriation, the result is that this appropriation is "entirely inoperative" as to the potential beneficiaries of the appropriation?

of the authority to cancel tax and spending items "is, in practical effect, no more and no less than the power to 'decline to spend' specified sums of money, or to 'decline to implement' specified tax measures." Brief for Appellants 40. Neither argument is persuasive.

* * *

VI

Although they are implicit in what we have already written, the profound importance of these cases makes it appropriate to emphasize three points.

First, we express no opinion about the wisdom of the procedures authorized by the Line Item Veto Act. Many members of both major political parties who have served in the Legislative and the Executive Branches have long advocated the enactment of such procedures for the purpose of "ensur[ing] greater fiscal accountability in Washington." H.R. Conf. Rep. 104–491, p. 15 (1996). The text of the Act was itself the product of much debate and deliberation in both Houses of Congress and that precise text was signed into law by the President. We do not lightly conclude that their action was unauthorized by the Constitution. We have, however, twice had full argument and briefing on the question and have concluded that our duty is clear.

Second, although appellees challenge the validity of the Act on alternative grounds, the only issue we address concerns the "finely wrought" procedure commanded by the Constitution. *Chadha*, 462 U.S., at 951. We have been favored with extensive debate about the scope of Congress' power to delegate lawmaking authority, or its functional equivalent, to the President. The excellent briefs filed by the parties and their amici curiae have provided us with valuable historical information that illuminates the delegation issue but does not really bear on the narrow issue that is dispositive of these cases. Thus, because we conclude that the Act's cancellation provisions violate Article I, § 7, of the Constitution, we find it unnecessary to consider the District Court's alternative holding that the Act "impermissibly disrupts the balance of powers among the three branches of government." 985 F.Supp., at 179.

Third, our decision rests on the narrow ground that the procedures authorized by the Line Item Veto Act are not authorized by the Constitution. The Balanced Budget Act of 1997 is a 500-page document that became "Public Law 105–33" after three procedural steps were taken: (1) a bill containing its exact text was approved by a majority of the Members of the House of Representatives; (2) the Senate approved precisely the same text; and (3) that text was signed into law by the President. The Constitution explicitly requires that each of those three steps be taken before a bill may "become a law." Art. I, § 7. If one paragraph of that text had been omitted at any one of those three stages, Public Law 105–33 would not have been validly enacted. If the Line Item Veto Act were valid, it would authorize the President to create a different law—one whose text was not voted on by either House of Congress or presented to the President for signature. Something that might be known as "Public Law 105–33 as modified by the President" may or may not be desirable, but it is surely not a document that may "become a law" pursuant to the procedures designed by the Framers of Article I, § 7, of the Constitution.

If there is to be a new procedure in which the President will play a different role in determining the final text of what may "become a law," such change must come not by legislation but through the amendment procedures set forth in Article V of the Constitution. * * *

The judgment of the District Court is affirmed.

It is so ordered.

JUSTICE BREYER, with whom JUSTICE O'CONNOR and JUSTICE SCALIA join as to Part III, dissenting.

* * *

II

I approach the constitutional question before us with three general considerations in mind. First, the Act represents a legislative effort to provide the President with the power to give effect to some, but not to all, of the expenditure and revenue-diminishing provisions contained in a single massive appropriations bill. And this objective is constitutionally proper.

When our Nation was founded * * *, a Congress, wishing to give a President the power to select among appropriations, could simply have embodied each appropriation in a separate bill, each bill subject to a separate Presidential veto.

Today, however, our population is about 250 million * * *, the annual federal budget is $1.5 trillion * * *, and a typical budget appropriations bill may have a dozen titles, hundreds of sections, and spread across more than 500 pages of the Statutes at Large. * * * Congress cannot divide such a bill into thousands, or tens of thousands, of separate appropriations bills, each one of which the President would have to sign, or to veto, separately. Thus, the question is whether the Constitution permits Congress to choose a particular novel means to achieve this same, constitutionally legitimate, end.

Second, the case in part requires us to focus upon the Constitution's generally phrased structural provisions, provisions that delegate all "legislative" power to Congress and vest all "executive" power in the President. See Part IV, infra. The Court, when applying these provisions, has interpreted them generously in terms of the institutional arrangements that they permit.

Indeed, Chief Justice Marshall, in a well-known passage, explained,

> To have prescribed the means by which government should, in all future time, execute its powers, would have been to change, entirely, the character of the instrument, and give it the properties of a legal code. It would have been an unwise attempt to provide, by immutable rules, for exigencies which, if foreseen at all, must have been seen dimly, and which can be best provided for as they occur.

McCulloch v. Maryland, 4 Wheat. 316 (1819).

This passage, like the cases I have just mentioned, calls attention to the genius of the Framers' pragmatic vision, which this Court has long recognized in cases that find constitutional room for necessary institutional innovation.

Third, we need not here referee a dispute among the other two branches. And, as the majority points out:

" 'When this Court is asked to invalidate a statutory provision that has been approved by both Houses of the Congress and signed by the President, particularly an Act of Congress that confronts a deeply vexing national problem, it should only do so for the most compelling constitutional reasons.' " Ante, at 2107, n. 42 (quoting *Bowsher v. Synar,* 478 U.S. 714, 736 (1986) (STEVENS J., concurring in judgment)). * * *

These three background circumstances mean that, when one measures the literal words of the Act against the Constitution's literal commands, the fact that the Act may closely resemble a different, literally unconstitutional, arrangement is beside the point. To drive exactly 65 miles per hour on an interstate highway closely resembles an act that violates the speed limit. But it does not violate that limit, for small differences matter when the question is one of literal violation of law. No more does this Act literally violate the Constitution's words. See Part III, infra.

The background circumstances also mean that we are to interpret nonliteral separation-of-powers principles in light of the need for "workable government." *Youngstown Sheet and Tube Co.*, supra, at 635 (JACKSON, J., concurring). If we apply those principles in light of that objective, as this Court has applied them in the past, the Act is constitutional. See Part IV, infra.

III

The Court believes that the Act violates the literal text of the Constitution. A simple syllogism captures its basic reasoning:

Major Premise: The Constitution sets forth an exclusive method for enacting, repealing, or amending laws. See ante, at 2103–2104.

Minor Premise: The Act authorizes the President to "repea[l] or amen[d]" laws in a different way, namely by announcing a cancellation of a portion of a previously enacted law. See ante, at 2102–2103.

Conclusion: The Act is inconsistent with the Constitution. See ante, at 2108.

I find this syllogism unconvincing, however, because its Minor Premise is faulty. When the President "canceled" the two appropriation measures now before us, he did not repeal any law nor did he amend any law. He simply followed the law, leaving the statutes, as they are literally written, intact.

To understand why one cannot say, literally speaking, that the President has repealed or amended any law, imagine how the provisions of law before us might have been, but were not, written. Imagine that the canceled New York health care tax provision at issue here, Pub.L. 105–33, § 4722(c), 111 Stat. 515 (quoted in full ante, at 2095, n. 2), had instead said the following:

> You can see here that the dissent is quite explicit about where it disagrees with the majority. Read on and see why. But, as you do, ask yourself why the two sides are disagreeing about this.

"Section One. Taxes. . .that were collected by the State of New York from a health care provider before June 1, 1997, and for which a waiver of the provisions [requiring payment] have been sought. . .are deemed to be permissible health care related taxes. . .*provided however that the President may prevent the just-mentioned provision from having legal force or effect if he determines x, y, and z*." (Assume x, y and z to be the same determinations required by the Line Item Veto Act).

Whatever a person might say, or think, about the constitutionality of this imaginary law, there is one thing the English language would prevent one from saying. One could not say that a President who "prevent[s]" the deeming language from "having legal force or effect," see 2 U.S.C. § 691e(4)(B) (1994 ed., Supp. II), has either repealed or amended this particular hypothetical statute. Rather, the President has followed that law to the letter. He has exercised the power it explicitly delegates to him. He has executed the law, not repealed it.

It could make no significant difference to this linguistic point were the italicized proviso to appear, not as part of what I have called Section One, but, instead, at the bottom of the statute page, say, referenced by an asterisk, with a statement that it applies to every spending provision in the Act next to which a similar asterisk appears. And that being so, it could make no difference if that proviso appeared, instead, in a different, earlier enacted law, along with legal language that makes it applicable to every future spending provision picked out according to a specified formula. See, e.g., Balanced Budget and Emergency Deficit Control Act of 1985 (Gramm-Rudman-Hollings

Act), Pub.L. 99–177, 99 Stat. 1063, 2 U.S.C. § 901 et seq. (enforcing strict spending and deficit-neutrality limits on future appropriations statutes); see also 1 U.S.C. § 1 (in "any Act of Congress" singular words include plural, and vice versa) (emphasis added). * * *

NOTES & QUESTIONS

1. At the federal level, what is the difference between a budget resolution, an authorizing statute, and an appropriations statute? What is the purpose of the "reconciliation" process?

2. When and how often does Congress enact typical appropriations statutes?

3. How might the budgetary and appropriations history of a law later affect a question of statutory interpretation?

4. What differences can you identify between state and federal budget and spending processes?

5. In *Clinton v. City of New York* the majority and the dissent appear to disagree about whether "cancelling" an item of spending is functionally the same as repealing the item. But is the disagreement really about whether the Line Item Veto Act authorizes the President to "repeal" or "amend" laws? Why can't they agree on whether the Act does or does not actually give the President the power to "repeal" or "amend" laws? Isn't that just a factual question about what the law does? Why do the two sides see what the "Line Item Veto Act" is doing so differently? Does one side just not understand how the Act really works? Or, is something else going on in why the two sides are disagreeing?

6. Was the Supreme Court right to have held the Line Item Veto Act unconstitutional? Why or why not? How could Congress have altered the Line Item Veto Act to improve the chances that a majority of the Court would find it constitutional?

Test Your Understanding

To assess your understanding of the material in this chapter, click here to take a quiz.

13

Direct Democracy

Key Concepts

- Initiative
- Referendum
- Recall
- The gun behind the door
- Constraints on direct democracy
- Tyranny of the majority

Chapter Summary

Direct Democracy in contemporary America arose out of the Populist and Progressive movements, seeking to return more lawmaking power to the people, although it exists only at the state level. The *initiative* allows the public to enact a new law, the *referendum* allows the public to reject a piece of new legislation enacted by the legislature, and the *recall* allows the public to remove an elected official from office before the term of office expires.

Occasionally, Direct Democracy's threat of a public vote can operate like a "gun behind the door," spurring the legislature to act on an issue that it might otherwise have preferred to ignore.

Because Direct Democracy does increase the risk of the "tyranny of the majority," some constraints are often placed on the processes of Direct Democracy. These constraints generally either restrict its substantive scope or set procedural requirements.

Up to this point, we have focused on representative democracy: the election of candidates to Congress, state legislatures, and other public offices, where these representatives then make policy for the larger society. This chapter detours briefly to direct democracy, which allows the people to vote directly on proposed laws, as well as on the retention of public officials. We summarize the history and principal mechanisms of direct democracy—the initiative, referendum, and recall—as well as its pros and cons.

A. Background

Direct democracy has a venerable history, stretching from the plebiscites of Ancient Greece and Rome, to New England town meetings, to state and local ballot initiatives of today. James Madison famously contrasted a "pure democracy," in which citizens govern directly, with a "republic," in which the people delegate power to representatives who govern. In *Federalist #10*, he argued that pure democracy was more vulnerable to the mischief caused by faction, which he argued would inevitably lead to "turbulence and contention." The Constitution instead established a republican form of democracy at the federal level, in which the people act not directly but through their chosen representatives.

FYI Even the election of the President is formally done through a system of "electors" in the "electoral college." *See* U.S. Const. art. II, sec. 1; U.S. Const. amend XII. So, not only the drafting of laws, but also the choosing of the nation's chief executive is mediated through "representatives."

Although no mechanisms of direct democracy exist at the federal level, most states have some form of direct democracy that supplements representative democracy. Every state but Delaware requires a public vote to amend the state constitution. Starting in the late Nineteenth Century, Populists and then Progressives urged the expansion of direct democracy. The Populist movement was a late 19th century political movement, strongest in the Midwest and South, that pushed for agrarian reforms. The Progressive movement of the late 19th and early 20th century is usually associated with reformers who sought to use government to respond to the impact of capitalism and industrialization on workers, the urban poor, and others. To both Populists and Progressives, direct democracy was viewed as a way to return power to the people and check the influence of wealthy spe-

FYI By 1892, the Populist, or People's, Party formed, and its presidential candidate James Weaver garnered more than a million votes (out of about 12 million votes cast), winning 4 Western states and 22 electoral votes. Though the Populist Party itself effectively collapses after the 1896 presidential election, some of its ideas continued to have influence.

cial interests, such as railroads (the mega-corporations of the day), interests that were thought to have undue influence in legislatures.

The three main instruments of direct democracy are (1) initiatives, (2) referenda, and (3) recalls. The *initiative* is the mechanism of direct democracy that usually receives the most attention. Initiatives allow voters to enact changes to state law directly, rather than going through the state legislature. The process begins with a petition drive, setting forth the precise law to be enacted. If an initiative petition receives the requisite number of sig-

> Progressive reformers played **FYI** important roles in the adoption of the first post-Reconstruction Amendments to the U.S. Constitution: the Sixteenth (1913, authorizing a federal income tax), Seventeenth (1913, providing for popular election of Senators), Eighteenth (1919, prohibiting the sale of alcohol), and Nineteenth (1920, prohibiting sex discrimination in voting).

natures, as set forth in state law, then the measure will appear on the ballot and become law if voters approve it. States may allow initiatives to be used for the enactment of statutes, constitutional amendments, or both.

> **?** As you think about this process in comparison with the process in the legislature we looked at in Chapter 11, keep in mind your future role as a lawyer. This process also creates law that will inevitably need interpretation; how might this different creation process affect how the law is interpreted?

The *referendum*, by contrast, allows voters to reject a statute that has already been enacted by the legislature (somewhat like a gubernatorial veto). As with initiatives, referenda qualify for the ballot through the collection of petition signatures. Usually, the collection of sufficient signatures prevents the challenged statute from going into effect, until the referendum question can be put to the voters at the next election. If voters then disapprove of the statute enacted by the state legislature, it will never take effect.

Today, most states' laws provide for initiatives, referenda, or both. The terms "ballot measures" and "ballot propositions" are generally used, and will be used here, to include both initiatives and referenda. Ballot propositions were widely used in the early decades of the Twentieth Century. Their use declined significantly from the 1940s through 1960s, but increased again in the ensuing decades. *See* RICHARD J. ELLIS, DEMOCRATIC DELUSIONS: THE INITIATIVE PROCESS IN AMERICA (2002). Historically, most initiative activity has been concentrated in a handful of states. M. DANE WATERS, INITIATIVE AND REFERENDUM ALMANAC (2003).

A third form of direct democracy is the *recall*, which allows citizens to remove an elected official before the expiration of the term of office. Like the initiative and referendum, a proposed recall is placed on the ballot by collecting sufficient petition signatures.

Ballot measures are sometimes referred to as a "gun behind the door," suggesting that the threat of their use alone may influence how legislatures behave. Nevertheless, in some states ballot measures are in fact used quite frequently. In California, for example, more initiatives were approved in the last two decades of the Twentieth Century than in the preceding 68 years, dating back to the establishment of the initiative process in the state. Nationwide, between 1990 and 2000, 458 initiatives appeared on the ballot.

Direct democracy has generated a vigorous public and scholarly debate about its benefits, with sharply differing perspectives on its pros and cons. The arguments commonly made in favor of direct democracy include the following:

- It enables the people to hold elected officials and governments generally *accountable*.

- It provides a *safety valve* against government being dominated by special interests, especially those with considerable resources to devote to legislative lobbying.

- It promotes *democratic self-government* by giving the people a direct voice in the lawmaking process and spurring public debate over important issues.

- It allows *less powerful groups* to propose ideas to the public.

- It may help increase *voter turnout*.

The arguments commonly made against direct democracy include the following:

- It undermines *representative* democracy and the virtues of representation.

- It creates *voter confusion* due to the large number and complexity of ballot measures, which many voters lack the interest, energy, or competency to understand or assess.

- It leads to *unsound legislation*, given the absence of a review process (comparable to legislative committees) by which to fix drafting problems.

- It actually *exacerbates the disproportionate influence of wealthy interests*, because of the high cost of qualifying a ballot measure and running a direct democracy campaign.

- It *distorts the lawmaking agenda*, especially when it comes to funding, and leads to undesirable "ballot-box budgeting."

- It enables the *tyranny of the majority*, endangering the rights of unpopular individuals and groups who constitute a numerical minority of voters.

See Thomas E. Cronin, Direct Democracy: The Politics of Initiative, Referendum, and Recall (1989).

Despite varying opinions on the desirability of direct democracy, there is little question that the process for qualifying initiatives, referendums, and recalls today is quite different from what was envisioned by their original Populist and Progressive advocates. Today, getting something on the ballot is an expensive endeavor, in which professional consultants and paid signature gatherers play an important role. In a large state, it costs many millions of dollars to get a ballot proposition or recall on the ballot. Campaigns for ballot measures are also expensive. Although the literature on the effect of money on direct democracy is mixed, some evidence suggests that large expenditures can be effective when used to oppose a ballot measure, but are less effective when used in support.

NOTES AND QUESTIONS

1. Are some kinds of issues better suited for direct democracy than others? Which ones?

2. What would direct democracy at the federal level look like? Would it be a good idea?

3. Think in comparative terms about the pros and cons of direct democracy. How does it differ from the legislative process? Is it better? Worse? Just different? Is it good to have two different—and alternative—processes of adopting legislation, either because of the gun-behind-the-door argument or just to give proponents of legislative change different avenues to pursue their goals?

B. Constraints on Direct Democracy

State laws impose both substantive and procedural constraints on direct democracy. One of the most prominent content limitations is the single-subject rule. States also have detailed procedural rules governing how initiatives and referenda qualify to be on the ballot.

1. State Laws Regulating the Content of Initiatives

Most initiative and referendum states have some form of a "single subject" rule. As the name suggests, this rule requires that a ballot measure address only one subject. Some states also have single-subject rules that apply to laws enacted by legislative bodies. Most states purport to use the same version of their single-subject rule for ballot measures as for legislative enactments, although some courts apply the rule more strictly to ballot measures.

Two main justifications support the application of the single-subject rule to initiatives. One is that it prevents *voter confusion* that might arise from an initiative encompassing multiple subjects. The other is that it prevents *logrolling*, the practice of packaging multiple items together in a single initiative, one or more of which would lack majority support if proposed on its own. Florida, Colorado, and Washington are among the states to have applied a strict version of the single subject requirement to initiatives. In addition, some states have "separate vote" requirements, which perform a similar function by requiring separate votes on items that are not sufficiently related. Oregon and Montana are notable for their application of a strong version of the separate vote requirement.

Single-subject requirements have engendered a great deal of litigation, largely because it can be difficult to agree on the precise "subject" addressed by almost any ballot measure. The more broadly an initiative's subject matter is characterized, the more likely it will be found to satisfy the single subject rule. Conversely, the more narrowly an initiative's subject is described, the more likely it will be found in violation of this rule.

For instance, Ohio is among the states that has a single-subject rule for state initiatives. The Ohio Constitution first provides that

> [t]he legislative power of the state shall be vested in a general assembly consisting of a senate and house of representatives but the people reserve to themselves the power to propose to the general assembly laws and amendments to the constitution, and to adopt or reject the same at the polls on a referendum vote as hereinafter provided.

Ohio Const., Art. I, § 1. An Ohio statute further provides that

> [o]nly one proposal of law or constitutional amendment to be proposed
> by initiative petition shall be contained in an initiative petition to en-
> able the voters to vote on that proposal separately.

Ohio Rev. Code § 3519.01. In the first instance, it is up to the Ohio Ballot Board
to determine whether an initiative petition involves more than one subject, and if
so, to break it into multiple initiatives. Ohio Rev. Code § 3505.062.

DIY
What Is a "Single Subject"?

1.   Would a single constitutional initiative that set campaign contribution limits and reformed the redistricting
process for drawing Ohio legislative districts be consistent
with the single-subject requirement?

2.   What about a single initiative that reforms the process
for redistricting both congressional and state legislative districts?

States have various other restrictions on the content of ballot measures, including
limits on initiatives that

- *Levy taxes or make appropriations.* The rationale is that, without
  such a restriction, a large percentage of the state's budget would be
  controlled by past initiatives—as is the case in California. *See* Philip L. Dubois & Floyd Feeney, Lawmaking by Initiative (1998);

- *Resolve administrative questions,* as opposed to legislative questions.
  See Foster v. Clark, 790 P.2d 1 (Or. 1990) (rejecting an initiative
  to change a street name because it was an administrative issue);

- *Reverse decisions made by the legislature,* although such changes may
  be permitted by referendum;

- *Declare an opinion* on a public policy question, without legislating
  on the subject. *See AFL-CIO v. Eu,* 686 P.2d 609 (Cal. 1984).

2. State Procedural Requirements

States vary dramatically in the frequency with which the mechanisms of direct democracy are used. This variation is attributable in no small part to variations in states' procedural requirements for getting on the ballot. Here are some typical requirements:

- *Number of Signatures.* All direct-democracy states require that petitioners gather a prescribed number of signatures to qualify a measure for the ballot. The requisite number is often set as a proportion of votes cast for governor in the most recent gubernatorial election. Those signing must be registered voters, except in North Dakota, which does not have voter registration.

- *Geographic Distribution.* Some states require that petitioners show support throughout the state, not just in larger counties, by requiring that signatures be obtained from a prescribed number of counties.

- *Time Period for Collection.* States vary in their limitations on the time period in which petitions may be circulated for signatures, ranging from 50 days to 360 days.

- *Title and Summary.* Because initiatives and referenda can be lengthy, all states require a brief summary of the proposal and most require an even shorter title, usually written by a state official.

- *Voting Requirements.* Some states require a majority of those *voting on the measure* to enact it, while others require a majority of all people *voting in that election* (including those who abstain from the measure). Some states require a supermajority.

See David B. Magleby, *Direct Legislation in the American States*, in REFERENDUMS AROUND THE WORLD (1994).

NOTES & QUESTIONS

1. What purpose is served by restrictions on the *content* of ballot initiatives? Which content restrictions do you favor? Are there others you would suggest beyond those in subsection 1 above?

2.   What purpose do the procedural requirements serve? Is it better to have more relaxed requirements for qualification of ballot measures, or more stringent ones?

3.   Judicial Review

Litigation surrounding direct democracy is common. A frequent subject of litigation is compliance with procedural requirements. For example, a ballot measure's proponents may challenge a state official's decision that an initiative petition has not obtained the requisite number of valid signatures, or opponents may challenge the decision that it has. Proponents or opponents of ballot measures may also challenge the title and summary written by a state official, such as the Attorney General or Secretary of State. Lawsuits also often arise over a ballot measure's consistency with substantive requirements of state law, such as the single subject rule.

Some scholars have argued that direct democracy is especially likely to lead to the tyranny of the majority, because ballot initiatives lack the checks on majoritarianism—and therefore the protection for minorities—that exist with representative democracy. *See, e.g.*, Derrick A. Bell, Jr., *The Referendum: Democracy's Barrier to Racial Equality*, 54 WASH. L. REV. 1 (1978). While this critique of direct democracy has partly focused on racial minorities, it has also included other groups constituting a numerical minority, such as gay, lesbian, bisexual, and transgender people, who are arguably less able to protect their interests through direct democracy than through representative democracy. *See* Hans A. Linde, *When Initiative Lawmaking Is Not "Republican Government": The Campaign Against Homosexuality*, 72 OR. L. REV. 19 (1993). For this reason, some have argued that initiatives affecting minorities should receive more searching judicial review, or "hard looks." *See* Julian N. Eule, *Judicial Review of Direct Democracy*, 99 YALE L.J. 1503 (1990).

> Recall again how difficult it is to pass legislation through a legislative process with bicameralism and presentment and the various "vetogates" we described in Chapter 11.

Several cases have challenged ballot initiatives under the Equal Protection Clause of the Fourteenth Amendment to the U.S. Constitution, on the ground that they unduly infringe on the political rights of a numerical minority. In *Hunter v. Erickson,* 393 U.S. 385 (1969), the Supreme Court struck down an initiative amending the City Charter of Akron, Ohio, in reaction to a fair housing ordinance that the Akron City Council had adopted. The initiative required that any ordinances regulating race discrimination in housing be approved by a majority of voters before they could become law. *Hunter* found this initiative to be an explicit racial classification, because it treated racial housing matters differently from other housing matters, placing "special burdens on racial minorities within the governmental process."

On the other hand, in *Schuette v. Coalition to Defend Affirmative Action,* 572 U.S. 291 (2014), the Court rejected a challenge to a Michigan initiative prohibiting race-based preferences in university admissions. There was no majority opinion. Justice Kennedy's opinion (joined by Chief Justice Roberts and Justice Alito) concluded that, in contrast to *Hunter* and another important case, *Washington v. Seattle School District No. 1.,* 458 U.S. 457 (1982), the Michigan initiative did not have the "serious risk, if not specific purpose, of causing injuries on account of race." Instead, "Michigan voters exercised their privilege to enact laws as a basic exercise of their democratic power, bypassing public officials they deemed not responsive to their concerns about a policy of granting race-based preferences." Justice Breyer concurred in the judgment, arguing that *Hunter* and *Seattle* involved efforts to limit racial minorities' ability to participate in the political process by taking decision-making authority from one level of the political process, where the minorities had prevailed, to another level, where they were less likely to. In contrast, the Michigan initiative "took decision-making authority away from … *unelected actors* [university faculty and administrators] and placed it in the hands of voters." Also concurring in the judgment, Justice Scalia (joined by Justice Thomas) would have overruled *Hunter* and *Seattle.* Justice Sotomayor (joined by Justice Ginsburg) dissented, concluding that "a majority of the Michigan electorate changed the basic rules of the political process in that State in a manner that uniquely disadvantaged racial minorities." She emphasized that the only aspect of university admissions policy that was taken out of the hands of the university governance system was the question of race-conscious admissions.

Initiatives disadvantaging gays and lesbians have also been challenged under the Equal Protection Clause. In *Romer v. Evans,* 517 U.S. 620 (1996), the Court struck down a Colorado initiative prohibiting localities from adopting or enforcing anti-discrimination protections for gays and lesbians. Justice Kennedy's majority opinion focused on two aspects of the initiative. First, the Court noted the initiative's imposition of a "broad and undifferentiated disability on a single named group." According to the Court, making it more difficult for gays and lesbians to seek aid from the government than other groups was "a denial of equal protection of the laws in the most literal sense." Second, *Romer* concluded that the Colorado initiative could only be understood as the product of discriminatory animus, given the discontinuity between its breadth and the reasons offered for it. Because Colorado's initiative lacked a rational relationship to legitimate government interests, it violated the Equal Protection Clause.

Direct democracy was also an important part of the backdrop in the debate over same-sex marriage. In *Obergefell v. Hodges,* 576 U.S. 644 (2015), the Supreme Court held that the right to marry is fundamental under the Fourteenth Amendment, and that same-sex couples may not be denied that right. Justice Kennedy wrote for the five-justice majority. Although the same-sex marriage bans before the Court in *Obergefell* were partly the product of direct democracy, the Court's opinion did not rest on this ground. Each of the four dissenting justices (Chief Justice Roberts, Justice Scalia, Justice Thomas, and Justice Alito), however, complained that the Court was substituting its own policy preferences for those arrived at through democratic processes.

C. Case Study: Ohio Redistricting Reform

One of the central ideas behind direct democracy is that it will allow citizens to make laws that serve the public interest in circumstances where elected officials are unlikely to do so on their own. Political reform is one area in which direct democracy—particularly the citizen initiative—is especially important. Incumbent legislators might generally be expected to be averse to changing the rules through which they themselves were elected.

Ohio has seen more than its share of controversy over the manner in which its congressional and state legislative district lines are drawn. Under the Ohio Constitution, the state's congressional districts have long been drawn by the state legislature enacting a districting law. Meanwhile, its 99 state house districts and 33 state senate districts were, until recently, drawn by a five-member commission with bipartisan representation. As a practical matter, however, one major party or the other always controlled that commission: whichever party won at least two of three positions elected on a statewide basis (Governor, Secretary of State, and Auditor) would control the redistricting process.

The consequence was that districting plans reflected the preferences of the dominant party at the time of redistricting. When Democrats controlled the process in the 1970s and 1980s, they used their advantage to draw pro-Democratic plans. When Republicans controlled the process in the 1990s, 2000s, and 2010s, they used their power to the same effect. As the technological means for drawing district lines improved, the dominant party's ability to entrench itself in power correspondingly increased.

Over the years, attempts to reform Ohio's congressional and state legislative re-districting process have occurred. Because this process is prescribed by the Ohio Constitution, a state constitutional amendment was required to change the pro-cess. That in turn would require either a citizens' initiative be put on the ballot by obtaining signatures of ten percent of electors, or a legislative initiative be put on the ballot through a joint resolution approved by both chambers of the state legislature.

In 2005, a coalition of groups came together under the name "Reform Ohio Now" to propose a package of state constitutional amendments, one of which would have reformed the redistricting process. This proposed initiative took a formulaic, math-ematical approach that emphasized drawing *competitive* districts. It was opposed by the Republican Party, which at the time controlled the state legislature and a majority of the state's congressional delegation. Although the initiative qualified for the ballot, the initiative failed by a 70–30% margin. The next year, a legislative attempt at reforming the redistricting process—this one supported by many of the state's Republican leaders—failed, when Ohio Democrats refused to support it.

Citizen groups took another stab at reforming Ohio's redistricting process in 2012, through a coalition called "Voters First Ohio." They proposed an initiative constitutional amendment that would have vested control over the congressional and state legislative redistricting process in a nonpartisan commission, which was required to prioritize four criteria in drawing district lines: (1) compactness; (2) community preservation, (3) competitiveness, and (4) partisan representational fairness. Again, the initiative qualified for the ballot, and again the Ohio Repub-lican Party opposed it. The measure was defeated 63–37%

A breakthrough appeared to have occurred in 2015. Republicans and Democrats in the state legislature came to agreement on a referendum—the Ohio Bipartisan Redistricting Commission Amendment—that would amend the state constitution to change the process for drawing state legislative districts. The amendment created a seven-person Ohio Redistricting Commission, to replace the five-person board formerly responsible for drawing state legislative districts. In addition to three statewide elected officials (the Governor, Secretary of State, and Auditor), the com-mission includes the legislative leaders of the two largest parties in both the state house of representatives and the state senate. In effect, this means that there will be at least two members of each major political party on the commission. The most important requirement of this amendment is to require at least two votes from the minority party to approve a state legislative redistricting plan, if that plan is to remain in effect for ten years. It also imposes geographical constraints on districts and prohibits plans that unduly favor either political party. With no organized opposition, the referendum was approved 71%–29% in the November 2015 election.

However, when this new process took effect following the 2020 Census, it quickly devolved into a partisan affair, which made no serious effort to garner support from the minority party. The result was a map adopted unilaterally by Republican leaders that set state legislative district boundaries for only the next four years, rather than the next decade. Meanwhile, the four-year map was immediately challenged in court by minority Democrats and others as not complying with the requirements of the 2015 referendum. The Ohio Supreme Court, in a series of decisions, repeatedly struck down the legislative map as unduly favoring the Republican Party, but the court was unable to prod the commission to develop a constitutional map in time for the 2022 election, so the state used the map that the court had held to be unconstitutional. The litigation evaporated prior to the 2024 election, after the composition of the state Supreme Court changed.

While the 2015 amendment reformed the process for drawing state legislative districts, control over *congressional* redistricting remained with the state's legislature—at least for the moment. In early 2018, with Republicans firmly in control of the Ohio legislature, Republicans and Democrats in the legislature again came together, reaching agreement on another referendum to amend the state constitution. This new amendment, which the voters approved in May 2018, also reformed the process for congressional redistricting in Ohio after the 2020 census. Unfortunately, it too devolved into a partisan process in the last quarter of 2021, and the Ohio Supreme Court was unable to enforce its rulings that the congressional map violated the amended constitutional process.

This 2018 amendment added the provision below (amended Article XIX) to the Ohio Constitution. As you read it, see if you can identify several ways in which it seeks to reduce the amount of partisan favoritism that affects the congressional map drawing process in Ohio.

OHIO CONSTITUTION

ARTICLE XIX

Section 1. (A) Except as otherwise provided in this section, the general assembly shall be responsible for the redistricting of this state for congress based on the prescribed number of congressional districts apportioned to the state pursuant to Section 2 of Article I of the Constitution of the United States.

Not later than the last day of September of a year ending in the numeral one, the general assembly shall pass a congressional district plan in the form of a bill by the affirmative vote of three-fifths of the members of each house of the general assembly, including the affirmative vote of at least one-half of the members of each of the two largest political parties represented in that house. A congressional district plan that is passed under this division and becomes law shall remain effective until the next year ending in the numeral one, except as provided in Section 3 of this article.

(B) If a congressional district plan is not passed not later than the last day of September of a year ending in the numeral one and filed with the secretary of state in accordance with Section 16 of Article II of this constitution, then the Ohio redistricting commission described in Article XI of this constitution shall adopt a congressional district plan not later than the last day of October of that year by the affirmative vote of four members of the commission, including at least two members of the commission who represent each of the two largest political parties represented in the general assembly. The plan shall take effect upon filing with the secretary of state and shall remain effective until the next year ending in the numeral one, except as provided in Section 3 of this article.

(C)(1) If the Ohio redistricting commission does not adopt a plan not later than the last day of October of a year ending in the numeral one, then the general assembly shall pass a congressional district plan in the form of a bill not later than the last day of November of that year.

(2) If the general assembly passes a congressional district plan under division (C)(1) of this section by the affirmative vote of three-fifths of the members of each house of the general assembly, including the affirmative vote of at least one-third of the members of each of the two largest political parties represented in that house, and the plan becomes law, the plan shall remain effective until the next year ending in the numeral one, except as provided in Section 3 of this article.

(3) If the general assembly passes a congressional district plan under division (C)(1) of this section by a simple majority of the members of each house of the general assembly, and not by the vote described in division (C)(2) of this section, all of the following shall apply:

(a) The general assembly shall not pass a plan that unduly favors or disfavors a political party or its incumbents.

(b) The general assembly shall not unduly split governmental units, giving preference to keeping whole, in the order named, counties, then townships and municipal corporations.

(c) Division (B)(2) of Section 2 of this article shall not apply to the plan. The general assembly shall attempt to draw districts that are compact.

(d) The general assembly shall include in the plan an explanation of the plan's compliance with divisions (C)(3)(a) to (c) of this section.

(e) If the plan becomes law, the plan shall remain effective until two general elections for the United States house of representatives have occurred under the plan, except as provided in Section 3 of this article.

(D) Not later than the last day of September of the year after the year in which a plan expires under division (C)(3)(e) of this section, the general assembly shall pass a congressional district plan in the form of a bill by the affirmative vote of three-fifths of the members of each house of the general assembly, including the affirmative vote of at least one-half of the members of each of the two largest political parties represented in that house. A congressional district plan that is passed under this division and becomes law shall remain effective until the next year ending in the numeral one, except as provided in Section 3 of this article.

A congressional district plan passed under this division shall be drawn using the federal decennial census data or other data on which the previous redistricting was based.

(E) If a congressional district plan is not passed not later than the last day of September of the year after the year in which a plan expires under division (C)(3)(e) of this section and filed with the secretary of state in accordance with Section 16 of Article II of this constitution, then the Ohio redistricting commission described in Article XI of this constitution shall be reconstituted and reconvene and shall adopt a congressional district plan not later than the last day of October of that year by the affirmative vote of four members of the commission, including at least two members of the commission who represent each of the two largest political parties represented in the general assembly. A congressional district plan adopted under this division shall take effect upon filing with the secretary of state and shall remain effective until the next year ending in the numeral one, except as provided in Section 3 of this article.

A congressional district plan adopted under this division shall be drawn using the federal decennial census data or other data on which the previous redistricting was based.

(F)(1) If the Ohio redistricting commission does not adopt a congressional district plan not later than the last day of October of the year after the year in which a plan expires under division (C)(3)(e) of this section, then the general assembly shall pass a congressional district plan in the form of a bill not later than the last day of November of that year.

A congressional district plan adopted under this division shall be drawn using the federal decennial census data or other data on which the previous redistricting was based.

(2) If the general assembly passes a congressional district plan under division (F)(1) of this section by the affirmative vote of three-fifths of the members of each house, including the affirmative vote of at least one-third of the members of each of the two largest political parties represented in that house, and the plan becomes law, it shall remain effective until the next year ending in the numeral one, except as provided in Section 3 of this article.

(3) If the general assembly passes a congressional district plan under division (F)(1) of this section by a simple majority vote of the members of each house of the general assembly, and not by the vote described in division (F)(2) of this section, all of the following shall apply:

(a) The general assembly shall not pass a plan that unduly favors or disfavors a political party or its incumbents.

(b) The general assembly shall not unduly split governmental units, giving preference to keeping whole, in the order named, counties, then townships and municipal corporations.

(c) Division (B)(2) of Section 2 of this article shall not apply to the plan. The general assembly shall attempt to draw districts that are compact.

(d) The general assembly shall include in the plan an explanation of the plan's compliance with divisions (F)(3)(a) to (c) of this section.

(e) If the plan becomes law, the plan shall remain effective until the next year ending in the numeral one, except as provided in Section 3 of this article.

(G) Before the general assembly passes a congressional district plan under any division of this section, a joint committee of the general assembly shall hold at least two public committee hearings concerning a proposed plan. Before the Ohio redistricting commission adopts a congressional district plan under any division of this section, the commission shall hold at least two public hearings concerning a proposed plan.

(H) The general assembly and the Ohio redistricting commission shall facilitate and allow for the submission of proposed congressional district plans by members of the public. The general assembly shall provide by law the manner in which members of the public may do so.

(I) For purposes of filing a congressional district plan with the governor or the secretary of state under this article, a congressional district plan shall include both a legal description of the boundaries of the congressional districts and all electronic data necessary to create a congressional district map for the purpose of holding congressional elections.

(J) When a congressional district plan ceases to be effective under this article, the district boundaries described in that plan shall continue in operation for the purpose of holding elections until a new congressional district plan takes effect in accordance with this article. If a vacancy occurs in a district that was created under the previous district plan, the election to fill the vacancy for the remainder of the unexpired term shall be held using the previous district plan.

Section 2. (A)(1) Each congressional district shall be entitled to a single representative in the United States house of representatives in each congress.

(2) The whole population of the state, as determined by the federal decennial census or, if the federal decennial census is unavailable, another basis as directed by the general assembly, shall be divided by the number of congressional districts apportioned to the state pursuant to Section 2 of Article I of the Constitution of the United States, and the quotient shall be the congressional ratio of representation for the next ten years.

(3) Notwithstanding the fact that boundaries of counties, municipal corporations, and townships within a district may be changed, district boundaries shall be created by using the data from the most recent federal decennial census or from the basis directed by the general assembly, as applicable.

(B) A congressional district plan shall comply with all of the following requirements:

(1) The plan shall comply with all applicable provisions of the constitutions of Ohio and the United States and of federal law, including federal laws protecting racial minority voting rights.

(2) Every congressional district shall be compact.

(3) Every congressional district shall be composed of contiguous territory, and the boundary of each district shall be a single nonintersecting continuous line.

(4) Except as otherwise required by federal law, in a county that contains a population that exceeds the congressional ratio of representation, the authority drawing the districts shall take the first of the following actions that applies to that county:

(a) If a municipal corporation or township located in that county contains a population that exceeds the congressional ratio of representation, the authority shall attempt to include a significant portion of that municipal corporation or township in a single district and may include in that district other municipal corporations or townships that are located in that county and whose residents have similar interests as the residents of the municipal corporation or township that contains a population that exceeds the congressional ratio of representation. In determining whether the population of a municipal corporation or township exceeds the congressional ratio of representation for the purpose of this division, if the territory of that municipal corporation or township completely surrounds the territory of another municipal corporation or township, the territory of the surrounded municipal corporation or township shall be considered part of the territory of the surrounding municipal corporation or township.

(b) If one municipal corporation or township in that county contains a population of not less than one hundred thousand and not more than the congressional ratio of representation, that municipal corporation or township shall not be split. If that county contains two or more such municipal corporations or townships, only the most populous of those municipal corporations or townships shall not be split.

(5) Of the eighty-eight counties in this state, sixty-five counties shall be contained entirely within a district, eighteen counties may be split not more than once, and five counties may be split not more than twice. The authority drawing the districts may determine which counties may be split.

(6) If a congressional district includes only part of the territory of a particular county, the part of that congressional district that lies in that particular county shall be contiguous within the boundaries of the county.

(7) No two congressional districts shall share portions of the territory of more than one county, except for a county whose population exceeds four hundred thousand.

(8) The authority drawing the districts shall attempt to include at least one whole county in each congressional district. This division does not apply to a congressional district that is contained entirely within one county or that cannot be drawn in that manner while complying with federal law.

(C)(1) Except as otherwise provided in division (C)(2) of this section, for purposes of this article, a county, municipal corporation, or township is considered to be split if, based on the census data used for the purpose of redistricting, any contiguous portion of its territory is not contained entirely within one district.

(2) If a municipal corporation or township has territory in more than one county, the contiguous portion of that municipal corporation or township that lies in each county shall be considered to be a separate municipal corporation or township for purposes of this section.

Section 3. (A) The supreme court of Ohio shall have exclusive, original jurisdiction in all cases arising under this article.

(B)(1) In the event that any section of this constitution relating to congressional redistricting, any congressional district plan, or any congressional district or group of congressional districts is challenged and is determined to be invalid by an unappealed final order of a court of competent jurisdiction then, notwithstanding any other provisions of this constitution, the general assembly shall pass a congressional district plan in accordance with the provisions of this constitution that are then valid, to be used until the next time for redistricting under this article in accordance with the provisions of this constitution that are then valid.

The general assembly shall pass that plan not later than the thirtieth day after the last day on which an appeal of the court order could have been filed or, if the order is not appealable, the thirtieth day after the day on which the order is issued.

A congressional district plan passed under this division shall remedy any legal defects in the previous plan identified by the court but shall include no changes to the previous plan other than those made in order to remedy those defects.

(2) If a new congressional district plan is not passed in accordance with division (B)(1) of this section and filed with the secretary of state in accordance with Section 16 of Article II of this constitution, the Ohio redistricting commission shall be reconstituted and reconvene and shall adopt a congressional district plan in accordance with the provisions of this constitution that are then valid, to be used until the next time for redistricting under this article in accordance with the provisions of this constitution that are then valid.

The commission shall adopt that plan not later than the thirtieth day after the deadline described in division (B)(1) of this section.

A congressional district plan adopted under this division shall remedy any legal defects in the previous plan identified by the court but shall include no other changes to the previous plan other than those made in order to remedy those defects.

NOTES & QUESTIONS

1. In what ways does this constitutional amendment attempt to reduce the extent of partisan gerrymandering in drawing Ohio's congressional districts?

2. Would you have voted for this proposal if you were in the Democratic minority in the Ohio legislature in 2018? If you were in the Republican majority?

3. This proposal was approved unanimously in the Ohio Senate and by an overwhelming majority in the Ohio House of Representatives, with only a handful of members in each party voting against it. Why do you think this measure had such strong bipartisan support?

4. Section 2(B)(4) refers to "a county that contains a population that exceeds the congressional ratio of representation." What does that mean? Does it mean anything to you? Without knowing much about Ohio demographics, do you have a sense of which county or counties might

satisfy this criterion? In other words, do you have a sense, as a practical matter, of how and when this language applies?

Now, think about the drafters of this initiative language. Would they have known exactly to which county (or counties) this refers? How about the voters who voted on it? But if this language had been part of a bill brought before the legislature, would the legislators have known what it meant, as a practical matter? (Three Ohio counties, encompassing the state's three largest cities, satisfy this criterion.)

5. Article I, Section 4 of the U.S. Constitution states:

    > The Times, Places and Manner of holding Elections for Senators and Representatives, shall be prescribed in each State by the Legislature thereof; but the Congress may at any time by Law make or alter such Regulations, except as to the Places of chusing Senators.

    Does Ohio's 2018 amendment comply with this requirement, given that it was adopted by voters, and not, as the U.S. Constitution's language puts it, "by the legislature thereof"? At least under current doctrine, it appears that the answer is yes: *Arizona State Legislature v. Arizona Indep. Redistricting Commission*, 576 U.S. 787 (2015). Meanwhile, a variation on the claim that Article I, Section 4 gives state legislatures *alone* the exclusive authority over federal election processes, a claim called the "independent state legislature theory," was largely rejected by the Supreme Court in *Moore v. Harper*, 600 U.S. 1 (2023).

6. What do you see as the pros and cons of representative democracy, as compared to direct democracy?

Test Your Understanding

To assess your understanding of the material in this chapter, click here to take a quiz.

Part IV—Foundations of Statutory Interpretation

Parts II and III provided a grounding in some of the key structural features that shape how legislatures are organized and how they operate. In the rest of the book we turn our attention to the output that these legislative institutions generate, in the form of the many statutes across the full range of American law.

As noted in Part I, statutes frequently contain provisions whose meaning is unclear or contested. Later Parts will take up in some depth a variety of tools and doctrines that courts often deploy to resolve disputes about the meaning of enacted text, that is, to *interpret* a statute. First, however, in this Part we expose you to the principal theoretical frameworks that courts and scholars frequently offer or invoke for confronting issues of statutory meaning, especially Textualism and Purposivism. Recognizing some of the key tensions in these frameworks then will facilitate a closer study of the interpretive techniques covered in later Parts of the book.

In the United States, at both the state and federal levels, courts have the final word on what statutes mean and how they apply. Much interpretation, however, is done by other participants in the legal system, including lawyers advising their clients, not just by courts. Indeed, *most* interpretation is done outside of the courts. But because our system of government gives courts the ultimate legal authority to interpret statutes, your job as a future lawyer will often entail asking, and then trying to determine, how a court will interpret. Thus, all lawyers need to understand how courts think about statutory interpretation and the techniques, tools, and modes of argumentation courts use when interpreting statutes. This Part, along with Parts V and VI, will introduce you to this fascinating and indispensable subject, statutory interpretation.

14

The Interpretive Problem

Chapter Summary

Statutes can be ambiguous for many reasons. While most statutory language is clear in most circumstances, sources of confusion also frequently exist. When interpreters of statutory text encounter challenges such as incomplete definitions, potential drafting errors, seemingly absurd results, changed circumstances, unanticipated consequences, or conflicting provisions, they rely on—implicitly or explicitly—some theory of statutory interpretation to decide how to apply the words of a statute to a real-world situation.

So far, our focus has been on how legislatures are structured and how they function in the American legal system, including the processes through which these institutions create law. We now turn to the output of these lawmaking processes, or statutes. In particular, we address the reality that the words that emerge from these processes require interpretation. Often, it is unclear whether the words apply to a factual situation in the world. In such circumstances, we refer to the statute as being "ambiguous," even though those same words may well be crystal clear when applied to a whole host of other factual situations. The primary focus of this portion of the book is on how these ambiguities in the law are resolved, and by whom. We begin with an overview of why legal interpretation is necessary and the challenge this poses.

A. The Basic Problem of Meaning and Interpretation

Though as a historical matter the law has not always been reduced to writing, all modern legal systems depend on written, accessible statements of the law. In the common law tradition, that is one reason why for centuries judicial decisions have been "reported" in published volumes or Reports, to which lawyers, and citizens generally, can refer for guidance and advice. In turn, part of being a lawyer then involves recognizing when the implications of the reported or recorded law are not clear, in which case the lawyer's role includes marshaling arguments for how to understand, construe, extend, and refine the words of the reported law when these statements of the law are being applied to a new or unaddressed circumstance.

But interpretive ambiguities are not confined to matters of judge-made or common law. Similar challenges also routinely arise in determining the meaning of the statutes that legislatures enact, as well as of regulations promulgated by agencies. Indeed, as you likely have already seen in other courses, and as the many examples we will consider throughout the rest of this book reflect, statutes and regulations are replete with interpretive ambiguities.

The reasons ambiguities arise in law generally fall into two categories: (1) because the legal institutions that enact law using English as their tool are, as a practical matter, not always able to delineate fully the line between the real-world circumstances they wish a law to cover and those they do not; and (2) because human language itself, including English, cannot always capture the world precisely.

Consider the first category. Ambiguities result in part because lawmakers simply cannot craft language that covers all existing circumstances. Ambiguities also can arise when circumstances change or unanticipated developments happen; when a legislature deliberately uses vague or broad terms; or when a drafting error or sloppiness occurs in the lawmaking process. Legislatures are simply not structured to be nimble enough to resolve all these ambiguities themselves (agencies, by contrast, as we will consider in later chapters, are often better able to do so than are legislatures). As we saw in Chapter 11, enacting a statute is a difficult task, particularly with the numerous vetogates in the legislative process. Moreover, even if legislatures could somehow constantly refine statutory language, legislatures are generally only permitted to make law prospectively. So, legislatures will often not be able to clarify an ambiguity until after a factual scenario arises that raises the ambiguity. It therefore frequently falls to the courts to construe these provisions.

Of course, the problem of linguistic interpretation is not unique to law. This points to the second category of reasons for ambiguity noted above. Human language is inherently incomplete, imperfect, and imprecise. We have already seen several examples of this earlier. Indeed, ordinary interpersonal communication routinely depends on the listener making a host of assumptions, informed by context and usage, about the implication of the speaker's words. As Wittgenstein and other philosophers of language have argued, a speaker's words do not have intrinsic meaning, but instead are only linguistic signifiers that connect with a variety of social conventions to convey content. These shared assumptions on which all communication depends also mean that in ordinary conversation, a directive like "no vehicles in the park" can often be successfully reinterpreted when an unanticipated application arises, without the need for a new directive.

> Contrast a human language like English with a computer language such as HTML or Javascript. What is it about traditional computer languages that allow them to avoid ambiguity?

> **FYI** Ludwig Wittgenstein was an especially important 20th century philosopher who taught at Cambridge University.

Because of these interpretive assumptions or conventions, a statement's literal meaning often gives way to another understanding, shared by both parties to the communication. This is obviously true for idiomatic expressions, such as "bite your tongue," "hit the hay," or "not in a million years," but it is also true for a range of ordinary statements. For example, "please take a picture" means one thing when standing at the edge of the Grand Canyon and means something very different when helping an artist pack up framed photographs after a photography exhibit. Similarly, the imperative "we need to do this right away" could imply any of a variety of possible timelines, depending entirely on circumstance, though it also might be ambiguous. An understanding of context likewise may dramatically shape the answer one gives to the question, "Where are you from?" Thus, language scholars sometimes distinguish between semantic (or literal) meaning and pragmatic (or contextual) meaning. In the end, no matter how clear we may attempt to make our words, ordinary human communication requires, as Francis Lieber famously put it in the nine-

> Francis Lieber was a nineteenth **FYI** century German-American legal and political philosopher.

teenth century, that we "trust at last to common sense and good faith." Even then, ambiguities will still arise.

Is the same approach relevant to the interpretation of law? Or does legal interpretation require its own set of tools? Interpreters of legal texts are not of one mind about how to solve interpretive problems in the law. Instead, they have injected different jurisprudential views of language and meaning (and different views of the judicial role) into the task of resolving textual ambiguity. Stripped to its barest bones, the interpretive problem can often be framed as whether to find (if that is possible) and follow the purpose behind a piece of legal text, or whether to find (if that is possible) and follow the objective meaning of the words of the text. The following two examples of interpretive problems in legal text will help set the stage for our exploration of this fundamental difficulty.

DIY
How Do Textual Ambiguities Arise?

 What follows are two quite different problems of statutory interpretation, one a contemporary real-world problem, and the other a famous law review hypothetical. As you read, compare the 2015 Ohio Court of Appeals decision in *West Jefferson v. Cammelleri* immediately below with the excerpt that follows it from the famous 1949 law review article *The Case of the Speluncean Explorers*. Think about the differences in the source(s) of the textual difficulty in each, as well as how the judicial bodies involved went about developing a resolution.

Village of West Jefferson v. Cammelleri
2015 Ohio 2463 (Ohio Ct. App. 2015)

ROBERT ALLEN HENDRICKSEN, J.

{¶ 1} Defendant-appellant, Andrea Cammelleri, appeals from a decision of the Madison County Municipal Court finding her guilty of violating a parking time limit ordinance. * * *

{¶ 2} At approximately 5:30 p.m. on February 13, 2014, Cammelleri had just woken up after working third shift when she looked out her window and noticed her pickup truck was no longer parked on the street in front of her house. Thinking her pickup truck had been stolen, Cammelleri called 911. The dispatcher inquired as to the make and model of Cammelleri's vehicle and told Cammelleri that her pickup truck had not been stolen, but had been impounded. A police officer later went to Cammelleri's house and gave her the parking citation.

{¶ 3} Cammelleri was cited for violating West Jefferson Codified Ordinances 351.16(a), which states:

> It shall be unlawful for any person . . . to park . . . upon any street . . . in the Village, any motor vehicle camper, trailer, farm implement and/or non-motorized vehicle for a continued period of twenty-four hours. . . .

{¶ 4} Cammelleri contested the citation, and on March 18, 2014, the matter proceeded to a bench trial. At trial, Cammelleri stipulated that her 1993 Ford pickup truck was parked on the street outside of her house located in West Jefferson in excess of 24 hours. The only issue was whether the ordinance actually applied to Cammelleri's pickup truck. Cammelleri argued the ordinance did not apply because the language prohibits a motor vehicle camper from being parked on the street for an extended period of time. The village contended the ordinance did apply because a comma was inadvertently omitted between the phrase "motor vehicle" and the word "camper."

{¶ 5} The trial court held that when reading the ordinance in context, it unambiguously applied to motor vehicles and "anybody reading [the ordinance] would understand that it is just missing a comma." The trial court then found Cammelleri guilty of violating West Jefferson Codified Ordinances 351.16(a) and ordered her to pay court costs.

{¶ 6} Cammelleri now appeals and asserts three assignments of error for review.

* * *

{¶ 13} [In her first assignment of error,] Cammelleri argues her pickup truck does not constitute a motor vehicle camper as identified by the ordinance. By using the phrase "motor vehicle camper," Cammelleri asserts the ordinance specifically identified and prohibited a camper that is propelled by an engine from parking on the street in excess of 24 hours. In contrast, the village argues it is clear a comma is missing between the phrase "motor vehicle" and the word "camper," and thus, the ordinance applies to Cammelleri's pickup truck as a motor vehicle. We agree with Cammelleri.

{¶ 14} Interpretation of a statute or ordinance is a matter of law, and thus, the proper standard of review is de novo. *State v. Straley*, 139 Ohio St.3d 339, 2014–Ohio–2139, ¶ 9. The paramount concern is determining legislative intent in enacting the statute. * * * To discern this intent by looking at the language used in the statute itself, we must read words and phrases in context and construe them in accordance with rules of grammar and common usage. * * * "[I]f such intent is clearly expressed therein, the statute may not be restricted, constricted, qualified, narrowed, enlarged or abridged." *State ex rel. McGraw v. Gorman*, 17 Ohio St.3d 147, 149 (1985). In other words, if the meaning is unambiguous and definite, then the statute is to be applied as written and needs no further interpretation. * * *

{¶ 15} In this instance, the intent of the ordinance is plain from the grammar and language used in West Jefferson Codified Ordinances 351.16(a). According to ordinary grammar rules, items in a series are normally separated by commas. *Chicago Manual of Style* 312 (16th ed.2010). The items included in the series of motor vehicle camper, trailer, and farm implement are separated by commas. In order to interpret the ordinance in the way the village suggests, prohibiting parking either a motor vehicle *or* a camper upon a street in the village for over 24 hours, a comma must be inserted between the phrase "motor vehicle" and the word "camper." However, no such comma exists. According to the rules of grammar, "motor vehicle camper" is one item. * * *

> **?** Would the rules of grammar alone be enough to convince you of this interpretation? Why or why not? What else does the court go on to use to reinforce this reading?

{¶ 16} Furthermore, the structure of the sentence is consistent with the meaning of "motor vehicle camper." According to West Jefferson Codified Ordinances 301.20, subject to exceptions, "motor vehicle" is defined as "every vehicle propelled or drawn by power other than muscular power." The ordinary definition of "camper," among others, is "any of various motor vehicles or trailers equipped for camping out." WEBSTER'S NEW WORLD COLLEGE DICTIONARY 211 (4th Ed.1999). When considering the plain meaning of the terms taken together, a motor vehicle camper is a vehicle propelled or drawn by power other than muscular power equipped for camping. In line with this definition, a motor vehicle camper could be a type of motor home equipped for camping that is self-propelled by an engine, a type of trailer equipped for camping that is drawn by a truck or other motor vehicle, or a truck or other motor vehicle equipped for camping by placement of an attachment onto the vehicle itself.

{¶ 17} Finally, reading "motor vehicle camper" as one item does not produce an absurd result. The definition of "motor vehicle camper" is consistent with the Ohio Revised Code's definition of "recreational vehicle." R.C. 4501.01(Q) defines "recreational vehicle," subject to certain requirements, as "a vehicular portable structure" that "is designed for the sole purpose of recreational travel." R.C. 4501.01(Q) also lists specific types of recreational vehicles, including travel trailer, motor home, truck camper, fifth wheel trailer, and park trailer. Cammelleri testified when she typed "motor vehicle camper" into an internet search engine, the results produced were of recreational vehicles.

{¶ 18} By utilizing rules of grammar and employing the common meaning of terms, "motor vehicle camper" has a clear definition that does not produce an absurd result. If the village desires a different reading, it should amend the ordinance and insert a comma between the phrase "motor vehicle" and the word "camper." As written, however, legislative intent is clear from looking at the language used in the ordinance itself.

> What does this assertion that "legislative intent is clear" mean? Do you agree with it?

* * *

{¶ 21} Judgment reversed, Cammelleri's conviction is vacated, and Cammelleri is hereby discharged.

The Case of the Speluncean Explorers
Lon L. Fuller
62 Harv. L. Rev. 616 (1949)

IN THE SUPREME COURT OF NEWGARTH, 4300

The defendants, having been indicted for the crime of murder, were convicted and sentenced to be hanged by the Court of General Instances of the County of Stowfield. They bring a petition of error before this Court. The facts sufficiently appear in the opinion of the Chief Justice.

TRUEPENNY, C. J. The four defendants are members of the Speluncean Society, an organization of amateurs interested in the exploration of caves. Early in May of 4299 they, in the company of Roger Whetmore, then also a member of the Society, penetrated into the interior of a limestone cavern of the type found in the Central Plateau of this Commonwealth. While they were in a position remote from the entrance to the cave, a landslide occurred. Heavy boulders fell in such a manner as to block completely the only known opening to the cave. When the men discovered their predicament they settled themselves near the obstructed entrance to wait [rescue]. * * *

The task of rescue proved one of overwhelming difficulty. It was necessary to supplement the forces of the original party by repeated increments of men and machines, which had to be conveyed at great expense to the remote and isolated region in which the cave was located. A huge temporary camp of workmen, engineers, geologists, and other experts was established. The work of removing the obstruction was several times frustrated by fresh landslides. In one of these, ten of the workmen engaged in clearing the entrance were killed. The treasury of the Speluncean Society was soon exhausted in the rescue effort, and the sum of eight hundred thousand frelars, raised partly by popular subscription and partly by legislative grant, was expended before the imprisoned men were rescued. Success was finally achieved on the thirty-second day after the men entered the cave.

FYI Though Lon Fuller set this hypothetical well into the future, he wrote it long before even cell phones!

* * * On the twentieth day of their imprisonment * * * communication [through a wireless machine was] established with the unfortunate men within the mountain. They asked to be informed how long a time would be required to release them. The engineers in charge of the project answered that at least ten days would be required even if no new landslides occurred. The explorers then asked if any physicians were present, and were placed in communication with a committee of medical experts. The imprisoned men described their condition and the rations they had taken with them, and asked for a medical opinion whether they would be likely to live without food for ten days longer. The chairman of the committee of physicians told them that there was little possibility of this. The wireless machine within the cave then remained silent for eight hours. When communication was re-established the men asked to speak again with the physicians. The chairman of the physicians' committee was placed before the apparatus, and

Whetmore, speaking on behalf of himself and the defendants, asked whether they would be able to survive for ten days longer if they consumed the flesh of one of their number. The physicians' chairman reluctantly answered this question in the affirmative. Whetmore asked whether it would be advisable for them to cast lots to determine which of them should be eaten. None of the physicians present was willing to answer. * * * When the imprisoned men were finally released it was learned that on the twenty-third day after their entrance into the cave Whetmore had been killed and eaten by his companions.

From the testimony of the defendants, which was accepted by the jury, it appears that it was Whetmore who first proposed that they might find the nutriment without which survival was impossible in the flesh of one of their own number. It was also Whetmore who first proposed the use of some method of casting lots, calling the attention of the defendants to a pair of dice he happened to have with him. The defendants were at first reluctant to adopt so desperate a procedure, but after the conversations by wireless related above, they finally agreed on the plan proposed by Whetmore. After much discussion of the mathematical problems involved, agreement was finally reached on a method of determining the issue by the use of the dice.

Before the dice were cast, however, Whetmore declared that he withdrew from the arrangement, as he had decided on reflection to wait for another week before embracing an expedient so frightful and odious. The others charged him with a breach of faith and proceeded to cast the dice. When it came Whetmore's turn, the dice were cast for him by one of the defendants, and he was asked to declare any objections he might have to the fairness of the throw. He stated that he had no such objections. The throw went against him, and he was then put to death and eaten by his companions.

After the rescue of the defendants, and after they had completed a stay in a hospital where they underwent a course of treatment for malnutrition and shock, they were indicted for the murder of Roger Whetmore. [After the trial,] in a lengthy special verdict the jury found the facts as I have related them above, and found further that if on these facts the defendants were guilty of the crime charged against them, then they found the defendants guilty. On the basis of this verdict, the trial judge ruled that the defendants were guilty of murdering Roger Whetmore. The judge then sentenced them to be hanged, the law of our Commonwealth permitting him no discretion with respect to the penalty to be imposed. After the release of the jury, its members joined in a communication to the Chief Executive asking that the sentence be commuted to an imprisonment of six months. The trial judge addressed a similar communication to the Chief Executive. As yet no action with respect to these pleas has been taken, as the Chief Executive is apparently awaiting our disposition of this petition of error.

> **?** How would you characterize this interpretive approach? That is, what sorts of jurisprudential views about the role of the courts does it appear to reflect? And what does the next paragraph's call for executive clemency say about this approach?

It seems to me that in dealing with this extraordinary case the jury and the trial judge followed a course that was not only fair and wise, but the only course that was open to them under the law. The language of our statute is well known: "Whoever shall willfully take the life of another shall be punished by death." N.C.S.A. (N.S.) § 12–A. This statute permits of no exception applicable to this case, however our sympathies may incline us to make allowance for the tragic situation in which these men found themselves.

In a case like this the principle of executive clemency seems admirably suited to mitigate the rigors of the law, and I propose to my colleagues that we follow the example of the jury and the trial judge by joining in the communications they have addressed to the Chief Executive. There is every reason to believe that these requests for clemency will be heeded. * * * If this is done, then justice will be accomplished without impairing either the letter or spirit of our statutes and without offering any encouragement for the disregard of law.

FOSTER, J. I am shocked that the Chief Justice, in an effort to escape the embarrassments of this tragic case, should have adopted, and should have proposed to his colleagues, an expedient at once so sordid and so obvious. I believe something more is on trial in this case than the fate of these unfortunate explorers; that is the law of our Commonwealth. If this Court declares that under our law these men have committed a crime, then our law is itself convicted in the tribunal of common sense, no matter what happens to the individuals involved in this petition of error. For us to assert that the law we uphold and expound compels us to a conclusion we are ashamed of, and from which we can only escape by appealing to a dispensation resting within the personal whim of the Executive, seems to me to amount to an admission that the law of this Commonwealth no longer pretends to incorporate justice.

For myself, I do not believe that our law compels the monstrous conclusion that these men are murderers. I believe, on the contrary, that it declares them to be innocent of any crime. I rest this conclusion on two independent grounds, either of which is of itself sufficient to justify the acquittal of these defendants.

The first of these grounds rests on a premise that may arouse opposition until it has been examined candidly. I take the view that the enacted or positive law of this Commonwealth, including all of its statutes and precedents, is inapplicable to this case, and that the case is governed instead by what ancient writers in Europe and America called "the law of nature."

* * *

Had the tragic events of this case taken place a mile beyond the territorial limits of our Commonwealth, no one would pretend that our law was applicable to them. We recognize that jurisdiction rests on a territorial basis. The grounds of this principle are by no means obvious and are seldom examined. I take it that this principle is supported by an assumption that it is feasible to impose a single legal order upon a group of men only if they live together within the confines of a given area of the earth's surface. The premise that men shall coexist in a group underlies, then, the territorial principle, as it does all of law. Now I contend that a case may be removed morally from the force of a legal order, as well as geographically. If we look to the purposes of law and government, and to the premises underlying our positive law, these men when they made their fateful decision were as remote from our legal order as if they had been a thousand miles beyond our boundaries. Even in a physical sense, their underground prison was separated from our courts and writ-servers by a solid curtain of rock that could be removed only after the most extraordinary expenditures of time and effort.

I conclude, therefore, that at the time Roger Whetmore's life was ended by these defendants, they were, to use the quaint language of nineteenth-century writers, not in a "state of civil society" but in a "state of nature." This has the consequence that the law applicable to them is not the enacted and established law of this Commonwealth, but the law derived from those principles that were appropriate to their condition. I have no hesitancy in saying that under those principles they were guiltless of any crime.

What these men did was done in pursuance of an agreement accepted by all of them and first proposed by Whetmore himself. Since it was apparent that their extraordinary predicament made inapplicable the usual principles that regulate men's relations with one another, it was necessary for them to draw, as it were, a new charter of government appropriate to the situation in which they found themselves.

* * *

This concludes the exposition of the first ground of my decision. My second ground proceeds by rejecting hypothetically all the premises on which I have so far proceeded. I concede for purposes of argument that I am wrong in saying that the situation of these men removed them from the effect of our positive law, and I assume that the Consolidated Statutes have the power to penetrate five hundred feet of rock and to impose themselves upon these starving men huddled in their underground prison.

Now it is, of course, perfectly clear that these men did an act that violates the literal wording of the statute which declares that he who "shall willfully take the life of another" is a murderer. But one of the most ancient bits of legal wisdom is the saying that a man may break the letter of the law without breaking the law itself. Every proposition of positive law, whether contained in a statute or a judicial precedent, is to be interpreted reasonably, in the light of its evident purpose. This is a truth so elementary that it is hardly necessary to expatiate on it. Illustrations of its application are numberless and are to be found in every branch of the law. In *Commonwealth v. Staymore* the defendant was convicted under a statute making it a crime to leave one's car parked in certain areas for a period longer than two hours. The defendant had attempted to remove his car, but was prevented from doing so because the streets were obstructed by a political demonstration in which he took no part and which he had no reason to anticipate. His conviction was set aside by this Court, although his case fell squarely within the wording of the statute. Again, in *Fehler v. Neegas* there was before this Court for construction a statute in which the word "not" had plainly been transposed from its intended position in the final and most crucial section of the act. This transposition was contained in all the successive drafts of the act, where it was apparently overlooked by the draftsmen and sponsors of the legislation. No one was able to prove how the error came about, yet it was apparent that, taking account of the contents of the statute as a whole, an error had been made, since a literal reading of the final clause rendered it inconsistent with everything that had gone before and with the object of the enactment as stated in its preamble. This Court refused to accept a literal interpretation of the statute, and in effect rectified its language by reading the word "not" into the place where it was evidently intended to go.

The statute before us for interpretation has never been applied literally. Centuries ago it was established that a killing in self-defense is excused. There is nothing in the wording of the statute that suggests this exception. Various attempts have been made to reconcile the legal treatment of self-defense with the words of the statute, but in my opinion these are all merely ingenious sophistries. The truth is that the exception in favor of self-defense cannot be reconciled with the *words* of the statute, but only with its *purpose*.

The true reconciliation of the excuse of self-defense with the statute making it a crime to kill another is to be found in the following line of reasoning. One of the principal objects underlying any criminal legislation is that of deterring men from crime. Now it is apparent that if it were declared to be the law that a killing in self-defense is murder such a rule could not operate in a deterrent manner. A man whose life is threatened will repel his aggressor, whatever the law may say. Looking therefore to the broad purposes of criminal legislation, we may safely declare that this statute was not intended to apply to cases of self-defense.

When the rationale of the excuse of self-defense is thus explained, it becomes apparent that precisely the same reasoning is applicable to the case at bar. If in the future any group of men ever find themselves in the tragic predicament of these defendants, we may be sure that their decision whether to live or die will not be controlled by the contents of our criminal code. Accordingly, if we read this statute intelligently it is apparent that it does not apply to this case. The withdrawal of this situation from the effect of the statute is justified by precisely the same considerations that were applied by our predecessors in office centuries ago to the case of self-defense.

There are those who raise the cry of judicial usurpation whenever a court, after analyzing the purpose of a statute, gives to its words a meaning that is not at once apparent to the casual reader who has not studied the statute closely or examined the objectives it seeks to attain. Let me say emphatically that I accept without reservation the proposition that this Court is bound by the statutes of our Commonwealth and that it exercises its powers in subservience to the duly expressed will of the Chamber of Representatives. The line of reasoning I have applied above raises no question of fidelity to enacted law, though it may possibly raise a question of the distinction between intelligent and unintelligent fidelity.

> How would you characterize this interpretive approach, and its contrast with the approach of Chief Justice Truepenny?

No superior wants a servant who lacks the capacity to read between the lines. The stupidest housemaid knows that when she is told "to peel the soup and skim the potatoes" her mistress does not mean what she says. She also knows that when her master tells her to "drop everything and come running" he has overlooked the possibility that she is at the moment in the act of rescuing the baby from the rain barrel. Surely we have a right to expect the same modicum of intelligence from the judiciary. The correction of obvious legislative errors or oversights is not to supplant the legislative will, but to make that will effective.

I therefore conclude that on any aspect under which this case may be viewed these defendants are innocent of the crime of murdering Roger Whetmore, and that the conviction should be set aside.

KEEN, J. I should like to begin by setting to one side two questions which are not before this Court.

The first of these is whether executive clemency should be extended to these defendants if the conviction is affirmed. Under our system of government, that is a question for the Chief Executive, not for us. I therefore disapprove of that passage in the opinion of the Chief Justice in which he in effect gives instructions to the Chief Executive as to what he should do in this case and suggests that some impropriety will attach if these instructions are not heeded. This is a confusion of governmental functions—a confusion of which the judiciary should be the last to be guilty. I wish to state that if I were the Chief Executive I would go farther in the direction of clemency than the pleas addressed to him propose. I would pardon these men altogether, since I believe that they have already suffered enough to pay for any offense they may have committed. I want it to be understood that this remark is made in my capacity as a private citizen who by the accident of his office happens to have acquired an intimate acquaintance with the facts of this case. In the discharge of my duties as judge, it is neither my function to address directions to the Chief Executive, nor to take into account what he may or may not do, in reaching my own decision, which must be controlled entirely by the law of this Commonwealth.

The second question that I wish to put to one side is that of deciding whether what these men did was "right" or "wrong," "wicked" or "good." That is also a question that is irrelevant to the discharge of my office as a judge sworn to apply, not my conceptions of morality, but the law of the land. In putting this question to one side I think I can also safely dismiss without comment the first and more poetic portion of my brother Foster's opinion.

The element of fantasy contained in the arguments developed there has been sufficiently revealed in my brother Tatting's somewhat solemn attempt to take those arguments seriously.

The sole question before us for decision is whether these defendants did, within the meaning of N. C. S. A. (N. S.) § 12–A, willfully take the life of Roger Whetmore. The exact language of the statute is as follows: "Whoever shall willfully take the life of another shall be punished by death." Now I should suppose that any candid observer, content to extract from these words their natural meaning, would concede at once that these defendants did "willfully take the life" of Roger Whetmore.

Whence arise all the difficulties of the case, then, and the necessity for so many pages of discussion about what ought to be so obvious? The difficulties, in whatever tortured form they may present themselves, all trace back to a single source, and that is a failure to distinguish the legal from the moral aspects of this case. To put it bluntly, my brothers do not like the fact that the written law requires the conviction of these defendants. Neither do I, but unlike my brothers I respect the obligations of an office that requires me to put my personal predilections out of my mind when I come to interpret and apply the law of this Commonwealth.

Now, of course, my brother Foster does not admit that he is actuated by a personal dislike of the written law. Instead he develops a familiar line of argument according to which the court may disregard the express language of a statute when something not contained in the statute itself, called its "purpose," can be employed to justify the result the court considers proper. Because this is an old issue between myself and my colleague, I should like, before discussing his particular application of the argument to the facts of this case, to say something about the historical background of this issue and its implications for law and government generally.

There was a time in this Commonwealth when judges did in fact legislate very freely, and all of us know that during that period some of our statutes were rather thoroughly made over by the judiciary. That was a time when the accepted principles of political science did not designate with any certainty the rank and function of the various arms of the state. We all know the tragic issue of that uncertainty in the brief civil war that arose out of the conflict between the judiciary, on the one hand, and the executive and the legislature, on the other. There is no need to recount here the factors that contributed to that unseemly struggle for power, though they included the unrepresentative character of the Chamber, resulting from a division of the country into election districts that no longer accorded with the actual distribution of the population, and the forceful personality and wide popular following of the then Chief Justice. It is enough to observe that those days are behind us, and that in place of the uncertainty that then reigned we now have a clear-cut principle, which is the supremacy of the legislative branch of our government. From that principle flows the obligation of the judiciary to enforce faithfully the written law, and to interpret that law in accordance with its plain meaning without reference to our personal desires or our individual conceptions of justice. I am not concerned with the question whether the principle that forbids the judicial revision of statutes is right or wrong, desirable or undesirable; I observe merely that this principle has become a tacit premise underlying the whole of the legal and governmental order I am sworn to administer.

Yet though the principle of the supremacy of the legislature has been accepted in theory for centuries, such is the tenacity of professional tradition and the force of fixed habits of thought that many of the judiciary have still not accommodated themselves to the restricted role which the new order imposes on them. My brother Foster is one of that group; his way of dealing with statutes is exactly that of a judge living in the 3900's.

We are all familiar with the process by which the judicial reform of disfavored legislative enactments is accomplished. Anyone who has followed the written opinions of Mr. Justice Foster will have had an opportunity to see it at work in every branch of the law. I am personally so familiar with the process that in the event of my brother's incapacity I am sure I could write a satisfactory opinion for him without any prompting whatever, beyond being informed whether he liked the effect of the terms of the statute as applied to the case before him.

The process of judicial reform requires three steps. The first of these is to divine some single "purpose" which the statute serves. This is done although not one statute in a hundred has any such single purpose, and although the objectives of nearly every statute are differently interpreted by the different classes of its sponsors. The second step is to discover that a mythical being called "the legislator," in the pursuit of this imagined "purpose," overlooked something or left some gap or imperfection in his work. Then comes the final and most refreshing part of the task, which is, of course, to fill in the blank thus created. *Quod erat faciendum.*

My brother Foster's penchant for finding holes in statutes reminds one of the story told by an ancient author about the man who ate a pair of shoes. Asked how he liked them, he replied that the part he liked best was the holes. That is the way my brother feels about statutes; the more holes they have in them the better he likes them. In short, he doesn't like statutes.

One could not wish for a better case to illustrate the specious nature of this gap-filling process than the one before us. My brother thinks he knows exactly what was sought when men made murder a crime, and that was something he calls "deterrence." My brother Tatting has already shown how much is passed over in that interpretation. But I think the trouble goes deeper. I doubt very much whether our statute making murder a crime really has a "purpose" in any ordinary sense of the term. Primarily, such a statute reflects a deeply-felt human conviction that murder is wrong and that something should be done to the man who commits it. * * *

If we do not know the purpose of § 12–A, how can we possibly say there is a "gap" in it? How can we know what its draftsmen thought about the question of killing men in order to eat them? My brother Tatting has revealed an understandable, though perhaps slightly exaggerated revulsion to cannibalism. How do we know that his remote ancestors did not feel the same revulsion to an even higher degree? Anthropologists say that the dread felt for a forbidden act may be increased by the fact that the conditions of a tribe's life create special temptations toward it, as incest is most severely condemned among those whose village relations make it most likely to occur. Certainly the period following the Great Spiral was one that had implicit in it temptations to anthropophagy. Perhaps it was for that very reason that our ancestors expressed their prohibition in so broad and unqualified a form. All of this is conjecture, of course, but it remains abundantly clear that neither I nor my brother Foster knows what the "purpose" of § 12–A is.

Considerations similar to those I have just outlined are also applicable to the exception in favor of self-defense, which plays so large a role in the reasoning of my brothers Foster and Tatting. It is of course true that in *Commonwealth v. Parry* an obiter dictum justified this exception on the assumption that the purpose of criminal legislation is to deter. It may well also be true that generations of law students have been taught that the true explanation of the exception lies in the fact that a man who acts in self-defense does not act "willfully," and that the same students have passed their bar examinations by repeating what their professors told them. These last observations I could dismiss, of course, as irrelevant for the simple reason that professors and bar examiners have not as yet any commission to make our laws for us. But again the real trouble lies deeper. As in dealing with the statute, so in dealing with the exception, the question is not the conjectural *purpose* of the rule, but its *scope*. Now the scope of the exception in favor of self-defense as it has been applied by this Court is plain: it applies to cases of resisting an aggressive threat to the party's own life. It is therefore too clear for argument that this case does not fall within the scope of the exception, since it is plain that Whetmore made no threat against the lives of these defendants.

* * *

How would you characterize this interpretive approach, and how would you contrast it with the approaches of Justices Foster and Truepenny?

Now I know that the line of reasoning I have developed in this opinion will not be acceptable to those who look only to the immediate effects of a decision and ignore the long-run implications of an assumption by the judiciary of a power of dispensation. A hard decision is never a popular decision. Judges have been celebrated in literature for their sly prowess in devising some quibble by which a litigant could be deprived of his rights where the public thought it was wrong for him to assert those rights. But I believe that judicial dispensation does more harm in the long run than hard decisions. Hard cases may even have a certain moral value by bringing home to the people their own responsibilities toward the law that is ultimately their creation, and by reminding them that there is no principle of personal grace that can relieve the mistakes of their representatives.

Indeed, I will go farther and say that not only are the principles I have been expounding those which are soundest for our present conditions, but that we would have inherited a better legal system from our forefathers if those principles had been observed from the beginning. For example, with respect to the excuse of self-defense, if our courts had stood steadfast on the language of the statute the result would undoubtedly have been a legislative revision of it. Such a revision would have drawn on the assistance of natural philosophers and psychologists, and the resulting regulation of the matter would have had an understandable and rational basis, instead of the hodgepodge of verbalisms and metaphysical distinctions that have emerged from the judicial and professorial treatment.

These concluding remarks are, of course, beyond any duties that I have to discharge with relation to this case, but I include them here because I feel deeply that my colleagues are insufficiently aware of the dangers implicit in the conceptions of the judicial office advocated by my brother Foster.

I conclude that the conviction should be affirmed.

[The opinions of Justices Tatting and Handy have been omitted.]

NOTES & QUESTIONS

1. In a brief "postscript" to his essay, Lon Fuller included this reflection:

   > The case was constructed for the sole purpose of bringing into a common focus certain divergent philosophies of law and government. These philosophies presented men with live questions of choice in the days of Plato and Aristotle. Perhaps they will continue to do so when our era has had its say about them. If there is any element of prediction in the case, it does not go beyond a suggestion that the questions involved are among the permanent problems of the human race.

2. Judge Foster and Judge Keen clash over whether the statute must be construed in light of its purpose, or instead must be applied faithfully according to its terms. How does each approach find justification in a sense of loyalty and service to the legislative institution that enacted the statute? These two approaches share some similarities with the "Purposivist" and "Textualist" approaches we will consider further in Chapters 17–19, the two approaches that dominate interpretive theory today. What does each approach imply about the role of judges in the broader lawmaking process?

3. In 1999, on the 50th anniversary of Professor Fuller's article, the *Harvard Law Review* invited a number of prominent judges and scholars to write their own opinions in the Case of the Speluncean Explorers. Judge Frank Easterbrook, a well-known Textualist judge on the United States Court of Appeals for the Seventh Circuit, would have reversed the de-

fendants' convictions. He began his opinion by noting that, "Were the language of the statute the end of matters, the right judgment would be straightforward, as [Justice Keen concludes]." The problem, though, as he then pointed out, was that then, "when the hangman had finished implementing the judgment, he too would be doomed, for the executioner takes life willfully." Easterbrook went on to draw on the longstanding background principle that "criminal statutes have been understood to operate only when the acts were unjustified," and he then concluded that the defendants' acts were in fact justified. Where does this "background principle" come from, and what does it mean?

4. Another famous interpretive problem is this one posed by nineteenth century political philosopher Francis Lieber in 1839:

> Suppose a housekeeper says to a domestic: "fetch some soupmeat," accompanying the act with giving some money to the latter; he will be unable to execute the order without interpretation, however easy and, consequently, rapid the performance of the process may be. Common sense and good faith tell the domestic, that the housekeeper's meaning was this: 1. He should go immediately, or as soon as his other occupations are finished; or, if he be directed to do so in the evening, that he should go the next day at the usual hour; 2. that the money handed him by the housekeeper is intended to pay for the meat thus ordered, and not as a present to him; 3. that he should buy such meat and of such parts of the animal, as, to his knowledge, has commonly been used in the house he stays at, for making soups; 4. that he buy the best meat he can obtain, for a fair price; 5. that he go to that butcher who usually provides the family, with whom the domestic resides, with meat, or to some convenient stall, and not to any unnecessarily distant place; 6. that he return the rest of the money; 7. that he bring home the meat in good faith, neither adding anything disagreeable nor injurious; 8. that he fetch the meat for the use of the family and not for himself.

> Suppose, on the other hand, the housekeeper, afraid of being misunderstood, had mentioned these eight specifications, she would not have obtained her object, if it were to exclude all possibility of misunderstanding. For, the vari-

ous specifications would have required new ones. Where would be the end? We are constrained then, always, to leave a considerable part of our meaning to be found out by interpretation. . . .

FRANCIS LIEBER, LEGAL AND POLITICAL HERMENEUTICS, OR, PRINCIPLES OF INTERPRETATION AND CONSTRUCTION IN LAW AND POLITICS: WITH REMARKS ON PRECEDENTS AND AUTHORITIES 28–30 (1839).

Can you see how many dimensions of the direction to "fetch some soupmeat" could give rise to ambiguities in its execution? How does the domestic servant minimize the risk of not complying with the directive properly? As you probably gathered, the analogy to law has the housekeeper in the role of the legislature and the domestic in the role of the court. In what ways is a judge like the domestic in this example? In what ways not? Put another way, once we see from Lieber's example that ambiguity is inevitable, does it matter that the interpreter is a judge and not (as in Lieber's example) the domestic? In particular, note that the domestic must actually carry out the housekeeper's instructions (must actually "fetch [the] soup meat"), whereas judges interpret statutes that someone else (the litigants before them) must ultimately implement. Judges generally never have to actually "fetch [the] soup meat," so to speak. We will return to this conundrum in Parts VII and VIII.

B. Categories of Common Interpretive Problems in the Law

At this point it should not come as a surprise that statutes and regulations contain a trove of interpretive challenges. These challenges can be grouped into various occasionally overlapping categories, organized by the cause or source of the interpretive difficulty. One possible categorization includes ambiguities that (1) result from incomplete or vague terms; (2) result from drafting errors, including "scrivener's" errors; (3) lead to absurd results; (4) result from new or changed circumstances; (5) produce unanticipated consequences; and (6) arise from conflicting provisions. These categories nicely capture the kinds of problems that legal interpreters see again and again.

1. Incomplete or Vague Terms

The largest category of interpretive problems in statutes and regulations arises when the meaning of some textual word or phrase, such as "any other immoral purpose," or "established by the state" is incompletely specified or understood. The interpreter is left to assign a meaning to this term for purposes of the statute or regulation in which it is used, relying on any number of possible interpretive tools, such as those discussed below in Chapters 20–27. Notwithstanding these tools, however, some of those interpretive problems may be quite difficult to resolve.

Many other instances of this kind of interpretive problem involve a statute or regulation that includes a definition of a key term, yet still leaves questions about how to apply that term in some specific case. For instance, the Endangered Species Act makes it unlawful to "take" any endangered species of fish or wildlife and further defines "take" to mean "to harass, harm, pursue, hunt, shoot, wound, kill, trap, capture, or collect, or to attempt to engage in any such conduct." Notice the word "harm" in the list of verbs in this definition. Is it appropriate to understand "harm" to encompass "significant habitat modification or degradation where it actually kills or injures wildlife"? The Secretary of the Interior thought so. In an important case concerning the adverse impact of timber logging on the northern spotted owl and red-cockaded woodpecker (which you will read in the book's final chapter), the Supreme Court considered that interpretation. *See Babbitt v. Sweet Home Chapter of Communities for a Greater Oregon*, 515 U.S. 687 (1995). It is not hard to see how Congress's effort to be thorough in defining the statutory term "take" nonetheless left room for debate about what "harm" meant— and thus what "take" meant—much as Francis Lieber had cautioned about the difficulties of trying to respond in advance to all the interpretive issues that might arise in connection with the instruction to "fetch some soupmeat."

2. Drafting Errors, Including "Scrivener's Errors"

A different kind of interpretive challenge arises when the legislative text might be thought to contain a drafting error. For instance, in the *Cammelleri* case above, the municipal ordinance provided: "It shall be unlawful for any person . . . to park . . . upon any street . . . in the Village, any *motor vehicle camper*, trailer, farm implement and/or non-motorized vehicle for a continued period of twenty-four hours." *See West Jefferson v. Cammelleri*, 2015-Ohio-2463 (Ohio App. 2015) (emphasis added). Notice the absence of a comma within the three-word phrase italicized above. The reviewing court construed this ordinance literally—as not containing a comma between "motor vehicle" and "camper"—throwing out a citation against the owner of a pick-up truck, a simple "motor vehicle," because it was not a "motor vehicle camper." But might the Village council perhaps have intended for this ordinance to have prohibited "any motor vehicle, camper, trailer," etc., from parking for over twenty-four hours, and merely omitted a comma from the published ordinance? If so, has this careless omission of a comma, potentially even by a scribe or secretary (a scrivener), given rise to a needless interpretive problem?

> You might wonder who exactly the **FYI** "scrivener" might be. As discussed in Part III, the legislative drafting process has many players from staffers and lobbyists to members of Congress themselves.

Of course, one critical step in dealing with this kind of interpretive problem is deciding that in fact the problematic text is, simply, an error. What evidence of error might be relevant? In arguing for a fairly narrow ambit for correcting drafting errors in construing statutes, Justice Scalia once argued that it should be "clear to the reader" that a scrivener's error has occurred, in which case it will also be "clear to the reader . . . what *the text* means." *See* Antonin Scalia & John F. Manning, *A Dialogue on Statutory and Constitutional Interpretation*, 80 Geo. Wash. L. Rev. 1610, 1613 (2012). But will drafting errors, even scrivener's errors, in fact always be so clear? Keep this issue in mind as you continue to explore various interpretive problems.

3. Absurdity

Occasionally interpreters will decline to follow the literal language of a law because following the language would be "absurd." Absurdity can be based on either just the text itself (as with syntactical or grammatical errors) or the consequences. The former is a variation of the "drafting error" idea discussed above. So, consider a statute that requires a document to be submitted to a government agency "prior to December 31." Does that really mean it must be submitted on or before December 30th? Or is that absurd and the statute really means that the document must be submitted on or before December 31 ("prior to [the end of the year]")? In *United States v. Locke*, 471 U.S. 94 (1985), the Supreme Court held that it was the former. Or, consider a statute that requires the filing of an appeal "not less than 7 days after" the trial court issues a particular order? Wait, stop! Before going on, read that language again. What exactly does it mean? Does it really mean you could file your appeal after, say, twenty years (which is "not less than 7 days")? Or does it actually mean "not *more* than 7 days after" the order? When faced with exactly this text, experienced judges disagreed on whether its literal interpretation was "absurd." *Compare Pritchett v. Office Depot, Inc.*, 420 F.3d 1090, 1093 n.2 (10th Cir. 2005) *with Amalgamated Transit Union Local 1309 v. Laidlaw Transit Services, Inc.*, 448 F.3d 1092, 109 (9th Cir. 2006) (Bybee, J., dissenting from the denial of rehearing en banc); *see also Spivey v. Vertrue, Inc.*, 528 F.3d 98 (7th Cir. 2008). After four years, Congress amended the language, replacing it with "not more than 10 days."

> **FYI** William Blackstone (1723–1780) is best known for his four-volume "Commentaries on the Laws of England," the first comprehensive treatise of its kind. He also was an Oxford professor, a member of Parliament, and a jurist. Many contemporary jurists and scholars view Blackstone's "Commentaries" as important evidence of the law of the United States at the time of the Founding.

Although some judges believe "absurdity" should be limited to textual absurdity, many others view absurdity through the lens of consequences. The idea that a statute should not be applied to produce absurd or unjust results was a settled rule at least by the time of the famed eighteenth century British legal commentator William Blackstone. *See* 1 WILLIAM BLACKSTONE, COMMENTARIES 60 (Cooley ed., 1879).

For instance, Blackstone (citing Pufendorf before him) related that the ancient Bolognian law "that whoever

> **FYI** Samuel von Pufendorf was a 17th-century German jurist and political philosopher.

drew blood in the streets should be punished with utmost severity" was deemed inapplicable to a surgeon providing emergency care by drawing the blood of the victim of a seizure (an accepted medical procedure of the day). In essence, this construction amounted to the simple triumph of common sense over literal text. Is this because the phrase "drew blood" was inapt or not adequately specified? Or did the provision imply some limiting connotation? Similarly, in *United States v. Kirby*, 74 U.S. 482 (1868), the Supreme Court invoked common sense in construing a federal criminal statute that prohibited the willful obstruction of "the passage of the mail, or of any driver or carrier" of the mail. The Court refused to apply the statute to a sheriff executing an arrest warrant upon a mail carrier who had been charged with murder. The Court wrote that a statute's "[g]eneral terms should be so limited in their application as to not lead to injustice, oppression, or an absurd consequence." *Id.* at 486.

Whether a particular result is absurd is often the source of disagreement. One interpreter's absurd or unjust application can be another interpreter's proper construction of a legal text, as for instance in the Supreme Court's disagreement in *Tennessee Valley Authority v. Hill,* 437 U.S. 153 (1978), about whether the Endangered Species Act required the cessation of construction of a federally funded hydroelectric dam in order to protect a threatened fish species (we will briefly share the resolution of this case in in subsection 6 at pp. 340–341 below). One implication of this matter of perspective is that problems of statutory interpretation simply do not generate obvious answers, nor is there even a settled methodology for resolving them, though courts have developed a variety of interpretive tools.

> Are these merely examples of what Judge Easterbrook called the "background principle" that criminal statutes should apply only where the conduct was "unjustified" (see Note 3 on pp. 333–334)? Or is something more going on here??

4. New or Changed Circumstances

A different interpretive problem can arise when the text of a law must be applied to a circumstance that the enacting lawmakers likely did not foresee because of social, technological, or other legal changes. Consider a late 20th century example arising out of changing social norms and the advent of gay parenting. The New York adoption statute had long provided that upon the making of an adoption order, all parental rights and responsibilities of the natural (biological) parent(s) would cease. Meanwhile, by 1995, changes in New York legal doctrine permitted unmarried individuals and gay couples to adopt. The case of *In the Matter of Jacob,* 660 N.E.2d 397 (N.Y. 1995), which we will read in Chapter 27, then confronted the circumstance in which the gay partner of the biological mother of a child wished to become an adoptive parent. No legal barrier prevented this, except that the adoption statute, if applied according to its terms, would then require the natural mother (the partner of the adoptive mother) to lose all her parental rights. The state high court, in a divided opinion, rejected this "Catch-22" and construed the problematic provision not to apply. One could also call this the avoidance of an "absurd result," albeit one occasioned by changed circumstances.

We will see other examples in subsequent chapters of interpretive issues in light of changed circumstances, in which the courts addressing the statutory issue divided on whether the changed circumstances provided information or context relevant to the question of how to apply or construe the textual provision. This division is emblematic of the reality that many interpretive problems do not have universally accepted answers. Furthermore, as is often true, the divide also tracks a divide between "Purposivist" interpretation and "Textualist" interpretation, which we will consider in more detail in Chapters 17–19.

5.   Unanticipated Consequences

In a similar vein, a statutory interpreter sometimes will need to apply a statute to a situation that, although not necessarily new or the result of changes in circumstance, nevertheless simply may not have been anticipated. This category also often overlaps with the "absurdity" category. In Chapter 17, in the 2020 Supreme Court case *Bostock v. Clayton County,* 590 U.S. 644 (2020), we will see an application of the Civil Rights Act of 1964 that arguably fits this category.

6.   Conflicting Provisions

Occasionally, a statute will contain conflicting directives, or will conflict with another related statute. For instance, consider two of the state statutory provisions at issue in the Florida contest over the outcome of the 2000 presidential election. After the Democratic Party requested a manual recount of the presidential race in several key Florida counties, a question arose about the deadline for completing these recounts. One provision of Florida law, enacted in 1951, provided that county election returns (results) not received by the Secretary of State by 5 p.m. on the seventh day after the election "shall be ignored." But another provision, enacted in 1989, provided that if a county's returns were not received by 5 p.m. on the seventh day after the election, the returns "may be ignored," and that county board members then were subject to fines for each day thereafter that their county's returns were late. These two provisions conflicted about whether the Secretary of State had discretion to accept returns after the deadline. For multiple reasons, the Florida Supreme Court concluded that the more recent statute governed and that the Secretary of State therefore had the discretion to accept late returns. The court also concluded that in the circumstances of the 2000 election the Secretary of State had abused that discretion, acting unreasonably and unlawfully in not accepting late-arriving recount totals from two counties. *See Palm Beach County Canvassing Board v. Harris,* 772 So.2d 1220 (Fla. 2000), *vacated sub nom. Bush v. Palm Beach Canvassing Board,* 531 U.S. 70 (2000).

As another example, consider again the provision of the Endangered Species Act at issue in *Tennessee Valley Authority v. Hill,* which required all federal agencies to "insure that actions [of such agency] do not jeopardize the continued existence of [an] endangered species." Yet in 1975 and 1976, even after Congress became aware that a species of small fish called a snail darter had been listed as endangered and was threatened by completion of a federally funded dam, congressional budget and appropriations committees continued to approve the use of federal funds to complete the dam, directing in one committee report that the dam "be completed as promptly as possible." In 1976, Congress enacted a spending measure appropriating all the remaining funding necessary for the purpose of completing the dam. In the face of this conflict between the ESA and a more recent congressional appropriation (itself also fully law), the Court chose to enforce the ESA. But the dissent argued the Congress that had enacted the ESA in 1973 not only had shown no awareness that the act might preclude the completion of the dam in question, but also that the subsequent Congress's continuing appropriation of funds for the dam showed that Congress intended the ESA not to interfere with the dam.

NOTES & QUESTIONS

1. Interpretive problems can certainly be categorized in ways other than those described above. These categories are typical, however, and are intended to invite reflection concerning the difficulties of crafting written text to avoid interpretive issues. Occasionally, lawmakers may justifiably be faulted for sloppiness, but it is unrealistic to expect them to avoid all potential errors or ambiguities, and in any event, interpretive problems frequently result from other causes. Recognizing that interpretive issues are inevitable is an important foundation for considering how to approach them.

2. Reconsider the interpretive problems in *Cammelleri* and *The Speluncean Explorers:* Into which categories would you place each of those problems?

3. How would you have resolved *Cammelleri*? *The Speluncean Explorers?*

4. Might identifying the category (or cause) of an interpretive problem affect the way in which an interpreter makes an interpretive choice? How?

 ## Test Your Understanding

To assess your understanding of the material in this chapter, click here to take a quiz.

15

Statutory Text and Statutory Purpose: Some Historical Background

Key Concepts

- Legislative intent
- Canons of construction
- *Heydon's Case* & the Mischief Rule
- Plain meaning of the letter of the law
- *Holy Trinity* & the Spirit of the Law

Chapter Summary

Early theories of statutory interpretation offer insight into its role today. One of the earliest cases in the field is *Heydon's Case*, where a British court resolved the statutory meaning by identifying the "mischief" that the statute was intended to remedy. While this case is not often cited today as legal doctrine, its underlying approach lives on as foundational to some modern interpretive theories.

As time progressed, courts became increasingly focused on the textual output of the legislature's lawmaking processes. By the late 19th century, American jurists routinely prioritized the "plain meaning" of the words in statutes. A departure from that approach is what made *Holy Trinity Church v. United States* stand out in 1892: The United States Supreme Court decided that honoring the legislature can sometimes mean ignoring the literal meaning of the written text and looking instead to the "spirit of the law." Today, courts still frequently cite *Holy Trinity* to justify looking beyond the text, although the Supreme Court has not cited the case in a majority opinion since the 1980s.

As the preceding chapter has suggested, issues of statutory interpretation have long abounded in the law. Over the years, courts, practitioners, and scholars have employed a variety of techniques and approaches to resolve these interpretive problems. These approaches have ebbed and flowed across a landscape marked with changing views about the respective roles of courts and legislatures in articulating what law is, as we will explore in Chapter 16. But especially during the twentieth century, as statutes grew in importance at both the federal and state levels, several distinct interpretive theories flourished, generating increasingly widespread attention and commentary in recent decades.

This chapter provides a very brief historical overview of the interpretive theories that courts in earlier eras used to address problems of statutory interpretation. Building on that history, the chapters that follow will expose you to several famous and interesting cases that highlight the difference between the two approaches to statutory interpretation that are most relevant today, namely Purposivism and (New) Textualism. Across time other interpretive theories have sometimes been ascendant, but we will focus on Purposivism and Textualism (with an additional summary of both Intentionalism and Plain Meaning Interpretation at the end of this Part, and a brief discussion at the end of Part VI of what could be considered an offshoot of Purposivism, namely, Pragmatic or Dynamic Interpretation).

At the outset, it bears noting that the meaning of most statutes and regulations, as applied to most circumstances, is usually clear. For instance, when a state statute provides that public schools shall provide their pupils with 180 days of annual instruction, public school districts generally understand what this obligation requires as they go about setting their academic calendar. Or when federal law provides that a voter who appears at a polling place without a required form of identification must at least be allowed to cast a provisional ballot, the fundamental obligation that this law imposes on election workers and election systems is clear. Yet even for the clearest of legal texts, circumstances may arise for which the meaning of the words is no longer obvious. It is primarily to the difficult cases that the theories and tools of interpretation discussed in this book are directed.

It also bears noting that, with respect to the small minority of occasions when the meaning of statutory text is contested, no single theory of interpretation is universally accepted. As Harvard Law Professors Henry Hart and Albert Sacks, two prominent scholars of statutory interpretation more than half a century ago, famously said: "Do not expect anybody's theory of statutory interpretation . . . to be an accurate statement of what courts actually do with statutes. The hard truth of the matter is that American courts have no intelligible, generally accepted, and consistently applied theory of statutory interpretation." Hart and Sacks' The Legal Process: Basic Problems in the Making and Application of Law 1169 (William N. Eskridge Jr. & Philip P. Frickey eds., 2006). That mid-twentieth century warning continues to be apt today. Since that time, arguments about the major interpretive theories have often been spirited, but the basic point remains: courts continue to rely on various interpretive theories without much uniformity. Courts are also eclectic in how these theories affect their actual interpretive process. Nonetheless, understanding these theories is important for every lawyer: predicting how a court will interpret a statute will often turn on knowing what interpretive technique or tool the court is likely use, and the choice of technique or tool will often depend on the court's underlying theoretical framework (sometimes without explicit recognition of any theoretical framework).

A. Early Approaches to Problems of Statutory Interpretation

From before the Founding, the most frequently invoked method for resolving ambiguities in statutory text was typically expressed in terms of finding and following the **"legislative intent"** behind the language in question. The same standard remains in widespread though not universal use today. In practice, however, this simple touchstone permitted the courts, as the primary interpreters, to use a variety of methods to decide what the legislature that had enacted the provision had intended. These methods included reading the full text of the statute, to consider how it held together as a whole; examining the immediate circumstances surrounding the measure's enactment, to identify evidence of the legislature's motive; considering the broader context of the times, in an effort to understand the problem or "mischief" at which the statute was directed; and applying any of numerous "canons of construction" (such as *"exceptions to a measure should be narrowly construed,"* or *"qualifying words should apply only to the last antecedent"*), which were understood to specify norms that would advance the will or intent of the enacting legislature. Although these "canons of construction" were (and are) often fictions, you can think of them as probabilistic assessments of what the statutory language likely meant when the interpreting court does not have any better evidence.

Centuries earlier, in the initial years of the British parliamentary system, judges (who themselves were often also members of Parliament) conducted the interpretive task quite differently, functioning essentially as collaborators or partners with legislators. Parliament was not an independent branch of government and the idea of legislative supremacy had not yet taken root. In this era, statutes were hardly more constraining of judges than was the common law. Indeed, courts could deploy their equitable powers to correct what they often saw as defects in the work-product of Parliament. For a rich treatment of the history of both British and American courts in interpreting statutes, see WILLIAM D. POPKIN, STATUTES IN COURT 7-151 (1999).

Among the most famous of the early expositions of the judiciary's role in the interpretive enterprise is *Heydon's Case*, 76 Eng. Rep. 637 (1584). It identified four considerations relevant to the judicial construction of the meaning of an ambiguous statutory provision:

(1) the pre-existing common law;

(2) "the mischief and defect for which the common law did not provide";

(3) the remedy chosen by the legislature;

(4) "the true reason of the remedy."

This last consideration suggests an effort to understand the legislature's actual or "true" motive for its remedial requirement, though it also could invite attention to how the remedy might be expected specifically to address the defect. After listing these considerations, *Heydon's Case* then described the court's role as follows: to construe the statute in order to "suppress the mischief, and advance the remedy . . . according to the true intent of the makers of the Act, *pro bono publico*."

The concluding phrase *pro bono publico*, or "for the public good," adds an interesting gloss to the interpretive enterprise, suggesting that interpretive problems should be resolved in a manner that promotes the public interest. On the one hand, this statement might be rather unremarkable. To the extent that the legislative process itself is often similarly described as a process by which elected representatives pursue the public interest, this coda to *Heydon's Case* might be just a final way of saying "honor the intent of the legislators *because* they have been acting for the public good." But the command *pro bono publico* could also be understood as saying that the interpreters themselves, in their own judgment, should ensure that the constructions they assign to ambiguous provisions are in the public interest. On this reading, *Heydon's Case* seems explicitly to give the interpreter some discretionary choice. The question of how to cabin this discretionary power, or potential willfulness, of the statutory interpreter looms large today over all theories—and the practice—of statutory interpretation. As explored further below, this concern has particular resonance in the contemporary debate between *Purposivists* and *Textualists*.

At the time of *Heydon's Case*, however, a different form of discretionary influence—a court's equitable powers—also sometimes played a role in the resolution of interpretive problems. When confronting an ambiguous statutory provision, courts up through the late eighteenth century might have used their equitable powers to do something quite distinct from advancing the intent of the legislature. Instead, they might have used the statutory ambiguity as an opportunity to achieve what they viewed as the fair, just, or *equitable* application of the statute. Indeed, in this earlier era, courts could rely on their own training, judgment, and authority to identify the "spirit" or "soul" of an enactment, in order to construe the textual meaning so as to advance their vision of the law. (For a history of the development of equitable interpretation, see Popkin, *supra*, at 11–19; *see also* John F. Manning, *Textualism and the Equity of the Statute,* 101 Colum. L. Rev. 1 (2001).) In the courts, both common law cases and statutory cases therefore could be vehicles for judicial exposition and development of the law.

> **FYI**
>
> A court's "equitable powers" are its powers to impose a decision that it believes is the fair or just outcome. "Equity" is a body of jurisprudence distinct from the common law. Traditionally, courts of equity were also distinct from common-law courts. Today, federal courts and most state courts have power to administer both "legal" and "equitable" rights and remedies.

Yet by the time of the Founding, the supremacy of legislative enactments over the common law had already been clearly established, at least as a matter of theory. As a result, when these two sources of law have conflicting clear meanings, the statutory expression prevails. However, when the meaning of a statute is unclear, courts often have construed the statute in light of their reading of the surrounding law, to avoid or minimize any conflict. Thus, courts might refer to the common law in resolving a matter of statutory interpretation not only for its potential as a tool for understanding what defect the legislature was seeking to remedy, per *Heydon's Case*, but also to further the ideal of making only the most incremental changes in the overall body of the law, except when the enacting legislature has clearly intended a more dramatic change. Put another way, the legislature is often presumed to understand the existing common law and to intend its continuation, unless a legislative enactment clearly shows otherwise. (This is an example of another of the many "canons" of interpretation, which later chapters will discuss in their own right.)

By the latter nineteenth century, the idea of courts deploying equitable powers had waned and observers of the problems of statutory interpretation were urging courts to show greater deference to the legislature. A number of treatises and legal commentaries of this Formalist era argued that statutory interpretation was reducible to a science, which when properly applied to a legal text would yield but one definitive meaning. Still, where the meaning was not clear, courts frequently adhered to the interpretive canon that statutes in derogation of the common law were to be strictly or narrowly construed.

With the ascendance of the idea of legislative supremacy, one widely accepted interpretive theory was that the judiciary should fulfill its duty to effectuate the legislature's intent by following the ordinary or "plain" meaning of a statute's words. Indeed, in the view of some, a court was to do so even if the court thought this reading of the words was "injudicious." *River Wear Commissioners v. Adamson*, [1877] App. Cas. 743 (H.L.). Some dimensions of **Plain Meaning Interpretation** undergird the contemporary interpretive theory known as New Textualism discussed further in Chapters 17–19 below. But as a historical matter, one well-known and relatively strict statement of this plain meaning approach came from Lord Atkinson of the British House of Lords, who said that where the language of a statute is plain, it must be enforced even if it is unjust, unwise, or produces "absurd or mischievous results." *Vacher & Sons Ltd. v. London Society of Compositors*, [1913] A.C. 107 (Eng.). This staunch adherence to the literal meaning of the legislature's chosen text was defended as the most appropriate way to respect and honor the legislature's superior lawmaking authority.

This extreme defense of enforcing the plain language of a statute regardless of outcome was something of a pushback against a competing approach that invited interpreting courts to disregard the letter of the law in favor of its spirit if following the letter would produce what the court thought was an absurd or obviously unintended result. The most famous example of the deployment of this rule is the *Holy Trinity* case, considered next.

B. *Holy Trinity Church v. United States*

DIY
The *Holy Trinity* Problem

First read the fact summary below, and then the accompanying statutory text at issue, as reproduced from the 1885 volume of the U.S. Statutes at Large. Then, *before you read the case excerpt*, complete the brief exercise that follows the statutory text.

Fact Summary:

In the latter nineteenth century, Holy Trinity Church was an organization incorporated as a religious society under the laws of the state of New York. Until September 1887, a pastor named Walpole Warren was an alien residing in England. In that month Holy Trinity Church contracted with Warren for him to come to New York City and enter into service as rector and pastor of the church; and, in pursuance of such contract, Warren did come to the U.S. and enter upon such service. The United States claims that these actions violated section 1 of the 1885 statute titled *"An act to prohibit the importation and migration of foreigners and aliens under contract or agreement to perform labor in the United States, its Territories, and the District of Columbia,"* reproduced below. Accordingly, the United States has now commenced an action to recover the penalty described in section 3 of the act.

Statutory Text:

332   FORTY-EIGHTH CONGRESS. Sess. II. Ch. 161–164. 1885.

February 26, 1885.   **CHAP. 164.**—An act to prohibit the importation and migration of foreigners and aliens under contract or agreement to perform labor in the United States, its Territories, and the District of Columbia.

Prepayment for transportation of, or assisting foreign emigrants under contract for labor or service made previous to emigration, unlawful.

Be it enacted by the Senate and House of Representatives of the United States of America in Congress assembled, That from and after the passage of this act it shall be unlawful for any person, company, partnership, or corporation, in any manner whatsoever, to prepay the transportation, or in any way assist or encourage the importation or migration of any alien or aliens, any foreigner or foreigners, into the United States, its Territories, or the District of Columbia, under contract or agreement, parol or special, express or implied, made previous to the importation or migration of such alien or aliens, foreigner or foreigners, to perform labor or service of any kind in the United States, its Territories, or the District of Columbia.

Such contracts void.

SEC. 2. That all contracts or agreements, express or implied, parol or special, which may hereafter be made by and between any personl company, partnership, or corporation, and any foreigner or foreigners, alien or aliens, to perform labor or service or having reference to the performance of labor or service by any person in the United States, its Territories, or the District of Columbia previous to the migration or

FORTY-EIGHTH CONGRESS. Sess. II. Ch. 164, 165. 1885.   333

importation of the person or persons whose labor or service is contracted for into the United States, shall be utterly void and of no effect.

SEC. 3. That for every violation of any of the provisions of section one of this act the person, partnership, company, or corporation violating the same, by knowingly assisting, encouraging or soliciting the migration or importation of any alien or aliens, foreigner or foreigners, into the United States, its Territories, or the District of Columbia, to perform labor or service of any kind under contract or agreement, express or implied, parol or special, with such alien or aliens, foreigner or foreigners, previous to becoming residents or citizens of the United States, shall forfeit and pay for every such offence the sum of one thousand dollars, which may be sued for and recovered by the United States or by any person who shall first bring his action therefor including any such alien or foreigner who may be a party to any such contract or agreement, as debts of like amount are now recovered in the circuit courts of the United States; the proceeds to be paid into the Treasury of the United States; and separate suits may be brought for each alien or foreigner being a party to such contract or agreement aforesaid. And it shall be the duty of the district attorney of the proper district to prosecute every such suit at the expense of the United States.

Penalty for violation of first section, fine; how recovered.

SEC. 4. That the master of any vessel who shall knowingly bring within the United States on any such vessel, and land, or permit to be landed, from any foreign port or place, any alien laborer, mechanic, or artisan who, previous to embarkation on such vessel, had entered into contract or agreement, parol or special, express or implied, to perform labor or service in the United States, shall be deemed guilty of a misdemeanor, and on conviction thereof, shall be punished by a fine of not more than five hundred dollars for each and every such alien laborer, mechanic or artisan so brought as aforesaid, and may also be imprisoned for a term not exceeding six months.

Master of vessel, knowingly bringing such emigrant laborer, guilty of misdemeanor, punishable by fine or imprisonment.

SEC. 5. That nothing in this act shall be so construed as to prevent any citizen or subject of any foreign country temporarily residing in the United States, either in private or official capacity, from engaging, under contract or otherwise, persons not residents or citizens of the United States to act as private secretaries, servants, or domestics for such foreigner temporarily residing in the United States as aforesaid; nor shall this act be so construed as to prevent any person, or persons, partnership, or corporation from engaging, under contract or agreement, skilled workman in foreign countries to perform labor in the United States in or upon any new industry not at present established in the United States: *Provided,* That skilled labor for that purpose cannot be otherwise obtained; nor shall the provisions of this act apply to professional actors, artists, lecturers, or singers, nor to persons employed strictly as personal or domestic servants: *Provided,* That nothing in this act shall be construed as prohibiting any individual from assisting any member of his family or any relative or personal friend, to migrate from any foreign country to the United States, for the purpose of settlement here.

Foreigners temporarily residing in the United States may engage other foreigners as private secretaries, servants, etc. Skilled workman in foreign countries may be engaged to perform labor in any new industry not established in the United States. Proviso. Artists, lecturers, servants, etc., excepted. Proviso, as to assisting relatives and friends.

SEC. 6. That all laws or parts of laws conflicting herewith be, and the same are hereby, repealed.

Laws conflicting herewith, repealed.

Approved, February 26, 1885.

DIY (continued)

Before you read the Supreme Court's decision in the case, spend ten minutes developing the best argument you can make that the church's contract with Walpole Warren does not violate section 1 of the act. Then spend another five minutes to decide how you would resolve the question of whether the church has violated the statute, and to write down a brief explanation of why you have reached that decision. (Note that sections 4 and 5 of the act also may affect your thinking about how you would argue or decide the issue.) *Only after you have written out your thoughts, go on to read the decision excerpt below.*

Holy Trinity Church v. United States
143 U.S. 457 (1892)

MR. JUSTICE BREWER delivered the opinion of the court.

[After describing the facts, Justice Brewer explained that the circuit court had held that the contract violated the statute], and the single question presented for our determination is whether it erred in that conclusion.

The first section describes the act forbidden, and is in these words:

> Be it enacted by the Senate and House of Representatives of the United States of America, in Congress assembled, that from and after the passage of this act it shall be unlawful for any person, company, partnership, or corporation, in any manner whatsoever, to prepay the transportation, or in any way assist or encourage the importation or migration, of any alien or aliens, any foreigner or foreigners, into the United States, its Territories, or the District of Columbia, under contract or agreement, parol or special, express or implied, made previous to the importation or migration of such alien or aliens, foreigner or foreigners, to perform labor or service of any kind in the United States, its Territories, or the District of Columbia.

It must be conceded that the act of the corporation is within the letter of this section, for the relation of rector to his church is one of service, and implies labor on the one side with compensation on the other. Not only are the general words "labor" and "service" both used, but also, as it were to guard against any narrow interpretation and emphasize a breadth of meaning, to them is added "of any kind," and, further, as noticed by the circuit judge in his opinion, the fifth section, which makes specific exceptions, among them professional actors, artists, lecturers, singers, and domestic servants, strengthens the idea that every other kind of labor and service was intended to be reached by the first section. While there is great force to this reasoning, we cannot think Congress intended to denounce with penalties a transaction like that in the present case. It is a familiar rule that a thing may be within the letter of the statute and yet not within the statute, because not within its spirit nor within the intention of its makers. This has been often asserted, and the Reports are full of cases illustrating its application. This is not the substitution of the will of the judge for that of the legislator; for frequently words of general meaning are used in a statute, words broad enough to include an act in question, and yet a consideration of the whole legislation, or of the circumstances surrounding its enactment, or of the absurd results which follow from giving such broad meaning to the words, makes it unreasonable to believe that the legislator intended to include the particular act. As said in *Stradling v. Morgan*, Plow. 205:

> This "familiar rule" is the most famous line of the *Holy Trinity* opinion.

> From which cases it appears that the sages of the law heretofore have construed statutes quite contrary to the letter in some appearance, and those statutes which comprehend all things in the letter they have expounded to extend to but some things, and those which generally prohibit all people from doing such an act they have interpreted to permit some people to do it, and those which include every person in the letter they have adjudged to reach to some persons only, which expositions have always been founded upon the intent of the legislature, which they have collected sometimes by considering the cause and necessity of making the act, sometimes by comparing one part of the act with another, and sometimes by foreign circumstances.

* * * In *U.S. v. Kirby*, 7 Wall. 482, 486, the defendants were indicted for the violation of an act of Congress providing

> that if any person shall knowingly and willfully obstruct or retard the passage of the mail, or of any driver or carrier, or of any horse or carriage carrying the same, he shall, upon conviction, for every such offense, pay a fine not exceeding one hundred dollars.

The specific charge was that the defendants knowingly and willfully retarded the passage of one Farris, a carrier of the mail, while engaged in the performance of his duty, and also in like manner retarded the steam-boat Gen. Buell, at that time engaged in carrying the mail. To this indictment the defendants pleaded specially that Farris had been indicted for murder by a court of competent authority in Kentucky; that a bench-warrant had been issued and placed in the hands of the defendant Kirby, the sheriff of the county, commanding him to arrest Farris, and bring him before the court to answer to the indictment; and that, in obedience to this warrant, he and the other defendants, as his posse, entered upon the steamboat Gen. Buell and arrested Farris, and used only such force as was necessary to accomplish that arrest. The question as to the sufficiency of this plea was certified to this Court, and it was held that the arrest of Farris upon the warrant from the state court was not an obstruction of the mail, or the retarding of the passage of a carrier of the mail, within the meaning of the act. In its opinion the Court says:

> All laws should receive a sensible construction. General terms should be so limited in their application as not to lead to injustice, oppression, or an absurd consequence. It will always, therefore, be presumed that the legislature intended exceptions to its language which would avoid results of this character. The reason of the law in such cases should prevail over its letter. The common sense of man approves the judgment mentioned by Pufendorf, that the Bolognian law which enacted "that whoever drew blood in the streets should be punished with the utmost severity," did not extend to the surgeon who opened the vein of a person that fell down in the street in a fit. The same common sense accepts the ruling, cited by Plowden, that the statute of 1 Edw. II., which enacts that a prisoner who breaks prison shall be guilty of felony, does not extend to a prisoner who breaks out when the prison is on fire, "for he is not to be hanged because he would not stay to be burnt." And we think that a like common sense will sanction the ruling we make, that the act of Congress which punishes the obstruction or retarding of the passage of the mail, or of its carrier, does not apply to a case of temporary detention of the mail caused by the arrest of the carrier upon an indictment for murder. * * *

If there is a potential conflict, when should the "reason of the law" prevail over the law's letter?

Among other things which may be considered in determining the intent of the legislature is the title of the act. We do not mean that it may be used to add to or take from the body of the statute, (*Hadden v. Collector*, 5 Wall.

107,) but it may help to interpret its meaning. In the case of *U.S. v. Fisher*, 2 Cranch, 358, 386, CHIEF JUSTICE MARSHALL said:

> On the influence which the title ought to have in construing the enacting clauses, much has been said, and yet it is not easy to discern the point of difference between the opposing counsel in this respect. Neither party contends that the title of an act can control plain words in the body of the statute; and neither denies that, taken with other parts, it may assist in removing ambiguities. Where the intent is plain, nothing is left to construction. Where the mind labors to discover the design of the legislature, it seizes everything from which aid can be derived; and in such case the title claims a degree of notice, and will have its due share of consideration. * * *

It will be seen that words as general as those used in the first section of this act were by that decision limited, and the intent of Congress with respect to the act was gathered partially, at least, from its title. Now, the title of this act is, "An act to prohibit the importation and migration of foreigners and aliens under contract or agreement to perform labor in the United States, its territories, and the District of Columbia." Obviously the thought expressed in this reaches only to the work of the manual laborer, as distinguished from that of the professional man. No one reading such a title would suppose that Congress had in its mind any purpose of staying the coming into this country of ministers of the gospel, or, indeed, of any class whose toil is that of the brain. The common understanding of the terms "labor" and "laborers" does not include preaching and preachers, and it is to be assumed that words and phrases are used in their ordinary meaning. So whatever of light is thrown upon the statute by the language of the title indicates an exclusion from its penal provisions of all contracts for the employment of ministers, rectors, and pastors.

? How might statutory interpreters identify the "common understanding"?

Again, another guide to the meaning of a statute is found in the evil which it is designed to remedy; and for this the court properly looks at contemporaneous events, the situation as it existed, and as it was pressed upon the attention of the legislative body. * * * The situation which called for this statute was briefly but fully stated by MR. JUSTICE BROWN when, as district judge, he decided the case of *U.S. v. Craig*, 28 Fed. Rep. 795, 798:

The motives and history of the act are matters of common knowledge. It had become the practice for large capitalists in this country to contract with their agents abroad for the shipment of great numbers of an ignorant and servile class of foreign laborers, under contracts by which the employer agreed, upon the one hand, to prepay their passage, while, upon the other hand, the laborers agreed to work after their arrival for a certain time at a low rate of wages. The effect of this was to break down the labor market, and to reduce other laborers engaged in like occupations to the level of the assisted immigrant. The evil finally became so flagrant that an appeal was made to congress for relief by the passage of the act in question, the design of which was to raise the standard of foreign immigrants, and to discountenance the migration of those who had not sufficient means in their own hands, or those of their friends, to pay their passage.

It appears, also, from the petitions, and in the testimony presented before the committees of Congress, that it was this cheap, unskilled labor which was making the trouble, and the influx of which Congress sought to prevent. It was never suggested that we had in this country a surplus of brain toilers, and, least of all, that the market for the services of Christian ministers was depressed by foreign competition. Those were matters to which the attention of Congress, or of the people, was not directed. So far, then, as the evil which was sought to be remedied interprets the statute, it also guides to an exclusion of this contract from the penalties of the act.

A singular circumstance, throwing light upon the intent of Congress, is found in this extract from the report of the Senate committee on education and labor, recommending the passage of the bill:

> The general facts and considerations which induce the committee to recommend the passage of this bill are set forth in the report of the committee of the house. The committee report the bill back without amendment, although there are certain features thereof which might well be changed or modified, in the hope that the bill may not fail of passage during the present session. Especially would the committee have otherwise recommended amendments,

> Whether interpreters should use committee reports (a type of "legislative history") is at the heart of the debate we will explore later between Textualists and Purposivists. **FYI**

substituting for the expression, "labor and service," whenever it occurs in the body of the bill, the words "manual labor" or "manual service," as sufficiently broad to accomplish the purposes of the bill, and that such amendments would remove objections which a sharp and perhaps unfriendly criticism may urge to the proposed legislation. The committee, however, believing that the bill in its present form will be construed as including only those whose labor or service is manual in character, and being very desirous that the bill become a law before the adjournment, have reported the bill without change.

Page 6059, Congressional Record, 48th Cong.

And, referring back to the report of the committee of the house, there appears this language:

It seeks to restrain and prohibit the immigration or importation of laborers who would have never seen our shores but for the inducements and allurements of men whose only object is to obtain labor at the lowest possible rate, regardless of the social and material well-being of our own citizens, and regardless of the evil consequences which result to American laborers from such immigration. This class of immigrants care nothing about our institutions, and in many instances never even heard of them. They are men whose passage is paid by the importers. They come here under contract to labor for a certain number of years. They are ignorant of our social condition, and, that they may remain so, they are isolated and prevented from coming into contact with Americans. They are generally from the lowest social stratum, and live upon the coarsest food, and in hovels of a character before unknown to American workmen. They, as a rule, do not become citizens, and are certainly not a desirable acquisition to the body politic. The inevitable tendency of their presence among us is to degrade American labor, and to reduce it to the level of the imported pauper labor.

Page 5359, Congressional Record, 48th Cong.

We find, therefore, that the title of the act, the evil which was intended to be remedied, the circumstances surrounding the appeal to Congress, the reports of the committee of each house, all concur in affirming that the intent of congress was simply to stay the influx of this cheap, unskilled labor.

But, beyond all these matters, no purpose of action against religion can be imputed to any legislation, state or national, because this is a religious people. This is historically true. From the discovery of this continent to the present hour, there is a single voice making this affirmation. The commission to Christopher Columbus, prior to his sail westward, is from 'Ferdinand and Isabella, by the grace of God, king and queen of Castile,' etc., and recites that 'it is hoped that by God's assistance some of the continents and islands in the ocean will be discovered,' etc. The first colonial grant, that made to Sir Walter Raleigh in 1584, was from 'Elizabeth, by the grace of God, of England, France and Ireland, queene, defender of the faith,' etc.; and the grant authorizing him to enact statutes of the government of the proposed colony provided that 'they be not against the true Christian faith nowe professed in the Church of England.' The first charter of Virginia, granted by King James I. in 1606, after reciting the application of certain parties for a charter, commenced the grant in these words: 'We, greatly commending, and graciously accepting of, their Desires for the Furtherance of so noble a Work, which may, by the Providence of Almighty God, hereafter tend to the Glory of his Divine Majesty, in propagating of Christian Religion to such People, as yet live in Darkness and miserable Ignorance of the true Knowledge and Worship of God, and may in time bring the Infidels and Savages, living in those parts, to human Civility, and to a settled and quiet Government; DO, by these our Letters-Patents, graciously accept of, and agree to, their humble and well-intended Desires.'

[omitting seven extended paragraphs about religious influences on American law.]

If we pass beyond these matters to a view of American life, as expressed by its laws, its business, its customs, and its society, we find everywhere a clear recognition of the same truth. Among other matters note the following: The form of oath universally prevailing, concluding with an appeal to the Almighty; the custom of opening sessions of all deliberative bodies and most conventions with prayer; the prefatory words of all wills, "In the name of God, amen;" the laws respecting the observance of the Sabbath, with the general cessation of all secular business, and the closing of courts, legislatures, and other similar public assemblies on that day; the churches and church organizations which abound in every city, town, and hamlet; the multitude of charitable organizations existing everywhere under Christian auspices; the gigantic missionary associations, with general support, and aiming to establish Christian missions in every quarter of the globe. These, and many other matters which might be noticed, add a volume of unofficial declarations to the mass of organic utterances that this is a Christian nation. In the face of all these, shall it be believed that a Congress of the United States intended to make it a misdemeanor for a church of this country to contract for the services of a Christian minister residing in another nation?

Suppose, in the Congress that passed this act, some member had offered a bill which in terms declared that, if any Roman Catholic church in this country should contract with Cardinal Manning to come to this country, and enter into its service as pastor and priest, or any Episcopal church should enter into a like contract with Canon Farrar, or any Baptist church should make similar arrangements with Rev. Mr. Spurgeon, or any Jewish synagogue with some eminent rabbi, such contract should be adjudged unlawful and void, and the church making it be subject to prosecution and punishment. Can it be believed that it would have received a minute of approving thought or a single vote? Yet it is contended that such was, in effect, the meaning of this statute. The construction invoked cannot be accepted as correct. It is a case where there was presented a definite evil, in view of which the legislature used general terms with the purpose of reaching all phases of that evil; and thereafter, unexpectedly, it is developed that the general language thus employed is broad enough to reach cases and acts which the whole history and life of the country affirm could not have been intentionally legislated against. It is the duty of the courts, under those circumstances, to say that, however broad the language of the statute may be, the act, although within the letter, is not within the intention of the legislature, and therefore cannot be within the statute.

> **?** What does Justice Brewer's use of the word "duty" in this concluding sentence suggest about what he views the judicial role to be?

The judgment will be reversed, and the case remanded for further proceedings in accordance with this opinion.

NOTES & QUESTIONS

1. The *Holy Trinity* case remains among the most widely cited cases in the field of statutory interpretation, in part because of how clearly it juxtaposes the choice between enforcing a statute according to its "letter" (its literal terms) and enforcing it according to its "spirit" (its purpose). The

Court explicitly states, "It must be conceded that the act of the corporation is within the letter of this section." But is that necessarily right? Is there an argument that the church's paying of Reverend Walpole's travel from England did *not* violate the literal statutory language? Hint: Think about possible narrow meanings of the words "labor" and "service."

2. What do you make of how the section 4 misdemeanor for vessel masters defines the scope to which that section applies?

3. What, if anything, do the exclusions in section 5 of the act say about the issue in this case?

4. How would you characterize the way in which Justice Brewer approaches the interpretive problem? Does it suggest a particular interpretive philosophy (in other words, a philosophy about how the Court should go about assigning meaning to the words of a legislative act)?

5. How does Justice Brewer's opinion make use of extrinsic evidence (evidence beyond the text of the statute) of the enacting Congress's intended meaning?

6. What does the Court conclude is the purpose of the act? Do you agree?

7. Did the Court need to exclude from the act's scope the contract at issue in *Holy Trinity* in order for the act to achieve the congressional purpose that the Court concluded was the foundation for the act?

8. What role does Justice Brewer's assertion that "this is a Christian nation" and the rest of that portion of his opinion play in his analysis?

9. What are some objections to Justice Brewer's approach? Imagine what a dissenting opinion might say.

10. By the time the Court decided the *Holy Trinity* case, Congress had amended the act to exclude from its coverage (in future cases) the importing of ministers. Should this amendment have figured in the Court's resolution of the case involving Walpole Warren? If so, how?

Test Your Understanding

To assess your understanding of the material in this chapter, click here to take a quiz.

16

The Several Lawmaking Institutions and Their Relationship

Key Concepts

- Evolution of the judicial role
- Legal Formalism
- Legal Realism
- Judicial willfulness
- Legal Process Theory
- The Age of the Statute
- Statutory *stare decisis*
- Modern characterizations of legal interpreters
- Dutiful executor
- Faithful agent
- Cooperative partner

Chapter Summary

Before the founding of the United States, English and colonial courts approached statutes with freedom to apply statutory texts as they saw fit. In the early decades of the American republic, many viewed courts as normatively superior to the legislature and its "crude" political lawmaking. Later, Legal Realists like Oliver Wendell Holmes challenged the exalted role of courts, while also arguing for a less disdainful view of statutes.

By the middle of the 20th Century, the rise of the administrative state contributed to the advent of the Legal Process Theory. This theory saw legislatures and agencies as rational bodies making rational laws using a rational process. The job of the courts was to honor and effectuate the results of these rational processes.

Yet today, a key question remains: How exalted should legislatures be, and how much freedom should courts have when interpreting the law? Three alternative characterizations of the proper judicial role in "saying what the law is" bring this issue into focus: should courts function as the dutiful executor, the faithful agent, or the cooperative partner of the legislature?

A. What Is Law? Distinctive Roles of Courts, Legislatures, and Agencies

As the examples in the two previous chapters help to demonstrate, legal text can be rife with interpretative problems much like those that affect other forms of communication. But problems of legal interpretation also present a special case. In a fundamental sense, the words of the law are themselves *the law*, and the ideal of the "rule of law" is predicated in turn on the existence—and settled meaning—of these words. It is these words that give rise to enforceable rights and obligations, shared among all citizens. As Justice Scalia observed thirty-five years ago in a famous law review article, ordinary citizens ought to be able to read the words of the law and to rely on their understanding of the words' ordinary meaning. *See* Antonin Scalia, *The Rule of Law as a Law of Rules*, 56 U. CHI. L. REV. 1175 (1989). Accordingly, even as we concede that the meaning of the written law will sometimes be ambiguous, we aspire for the law to be specified with sufficient clarity that it will consistently convey the same meaning to a variety of listeners or audiences.

? Do you think present-day laws are understandable to ordinary citizens? Some more so than others perhaps? Just as importantly, is Justice Scalia right? Should *all* laws be written so that ordinary citizens can read and understand them? How often do ordinary citizens read the actual words of law and adjust their behavior accordingly? How do ordinary citizens know what the law is? As you continue through this book, keep this question in mind: who exactly is the audience for *the language* of any given statute?

Indeed, in an earlier era, most statutory interpreters presumed that legal text had an inherent or intrinsic meaning, which courts and other readers could and should find primarily through textual analysis. Today, however, legal interpreters generally recognize that meaning is to some degree contingent and contextual, dependent on at least some unstated assumptions shared between author and audience. Thus, Lieber's notion (see pp. 318, 334 above) of "common sense and good faith," an essential component of ordinary communication, also could play a valuable role in how judges should interpret ambiguities in legal text.

Yet when what is at issue is the meaning of an authoritative statement of public law, with its power to determine rights, privileges, duties, and obligations, some may view common sense and good faith as improper or at least insufficient bases for an interpretive methodology. How then should ambiguities in legal text be resolved? Who should resolve them? What are the appropriate ways of identifying, and then drawing from, the shared assumptions upon which legal communication also depends? What should be the role of context? How much clarity of meaning can there be without an understanding of context? How should the context of a statute or regulation be identified, understood, and assessed? How much attention should be placed on determining the written law's underlying purpose? What sources can reliably establish this purpose?

These and other questions of interpretive methodology were implicit in the example problems we have considered in the previous two chapters, and we will continue to explore them throughout the remainder of this book. But first, as additional foundation for that exploration, this chapter will reflect briefly on what "law" itself is and where it comes from, including both the role of courts as well as the place of statutes and regulations in American law. Some theory of law and how it is created, even if it is entirely implicit, inevitably undergirds one's theory of textual interpretation (as does some theory of language, even if also implicit). Although the general question "what is law?" is far too broad for this text to even begin to address well, a few thoughts will provide some relevant background. For a more expansive but accessible treatment of what "law" is, see BRIAN H. BIX, JURISPRUDENCE: THEORY AND CONTEXT (8th ed. 2019); for a famous and in-depth exploration, see H.L.A. HART, THE CONCEPT OF LAW (1961).

1. Early Jurisprudential Theories: Legal Formalism and Legal Realism

Many jurisprudential theories focus heavily or entirely on the role of courts, sometimes even describing "law" simply as "what courts do." Moreover, that is the framework around which the case method of much of American legal education has been built. Yet any sophisticated understanding of law today also requires an understanding of how legislatures and agencies behave, as well as of the relationships among courts, legislatures, and agencies.

Chief Justice Marshall famously said in *Marbury v. Madison,* 5 U.S. 137, 177 (1803), that it was emphatically the duty of the courts "to say what the law is." This pronouncement was not a truism solely about the judiciary's role in promulgating common law, but a claim about its authority to have the last word regarding the meaning of all legal text, including statutory and regulatory text. Frequently, many other types of people besides judges also take on the role of legal interpreters, including agency officials, lawyers, politicians, and citizens. But all must take cognizance that as a general matter courts have the authority to be the final interpreters of the work of legislatures and agencies. Therefore anyone hoping to understand the meaning of legal texts should be attentive to how judges may ultimately assign a definitive interpretation to ambiguous language.

> **?** What do you think the process of "finding" or discovering the law might have consisted of?

On the **Legal Formalist** account of law that dominated American jurisprudence at the beginning of the twentieth century, the role of courts was to "find" the law through the application of neutral principles. On this conception, the common law already existed, waiting to be discovered. Legislatures, meanwhile, were viewed as institutions that could "make" law as a matter of pure political will (with state legislatures sometimes even viewed as examples of "mob rule"). Typically, this account exalted courts as normatively superior because in their hands law was a deductive science involving the logical application of accepted rules and doctrines to the problems of social living and circumstance, while statutory lawmaking in the hands of a legislature was simply crass power politics. Statutes might be formally and hierarchically superior to common law, but in practice they might often be functionally inferior, diminished by social attitudes and a pejorative perception that legislative outputs reflected only the non-rational exercise of raw political power.

Formalists viewed courts as deductive not only in the ways in which they fostered the development of the common law, but also in the ways in which they interpreted and applied—arguably even refined—the crude statutory law. Under a Formalist account, the role of the court as the interpreter of legal text was to find the intrinsic meaning of that text. Hierarchical relationships among written constitutions, legislative statutes, and agency regulations helped courts to identify and prioritize the application of these rules and principles.

Over the years, many critics challenged the Formalist view of how courts operate. These critics typically did so, however, without challenging the exalted position of the courts as the central institution in the American legal system. For instance, Justice Oliver Wendell Holmes once declared, in a speech that is often seen as the opening salvo of the **Legal Realism** movement of the first half of the twentieth century, that rather than being a deductive process, law was nothing more than a prediction of what the courts will do. *See* Oliver Wendell Holmes, *The Path of the Law,* 10 HARV. L. REV. 457 (1897). On Holmes' still court-centric view, the task of the lawyer was to understand, and exploit, the range of reasons or motivations that might sway the courts, but not to expect that this was a matter of simple deduction. Statutes were important primarily because of how they might figure in predictions of how courts would act. As Holmes' contemporary John Chipman Gray famously said: "legislative acts, statutes, are to be dealt with as sources of Law, and not as part of the Law itself." JOHN CHIPMAN GRAY, THE NATURE AND SOURCES OF THE LAW 119 (1909). On this view of the law, statutes remained functionally inferior to what judges did, even though what judges did was no longer merely deductive.

But while Holmes rejected the fiction that judges simply "found" the law deductively, he recognized that judges are not completely unconstrained or willful. Rather, judges develop a legal result by attending to an accepted set of precepts and precedents, and by honoring the work of the legislatures, at least to some degree. Thus, even on his view of law as prediction, law was a prediction about how courts will use legal rules, principles, and philosophies in resolving the matters that come before them. Courts do not function without guidelines and constraints.

Nevertheless, Holmes' view was still a somewhat skeptical one, espousing the notion that courts, like legislatures, in fact also "make" rather than "find" the law. Specifically with respect to matters of statutory interpretation, the Legal Realists who followed Holmes similarly argued that courts were making rather than finding the law because a court often could have articulated several equally defensible arguments to support contrasting interpretive results, allowing the court to choose, rather than deduce, a particular outcome. This Realist view explicitly acknowledged the idea of judicial power and discretion. Ever since, the prospect of judicial willfulness has raised important questions of objectivity and subjectivity in law and judicial interpretation.

> The idea of "judicial willfulness" suggests that the judicial branch is imposing its own will, rather than simply applying law enunciated by other lawgivers.

2. Legal Process Theory: A 20th-Century Reply

By the mid-twentieth century, other legal thinkers were pushing back against Holmes' and the Legal Realists' more skeptical views of law. So too was the rapid expansion of the administrative state, with its reliance on bureaucratic expertise.

As part of what would become known as the **Legal Process** school, these thinkers argued that rather than being primarily a prediction of how courts will use their authority, law was a complex arrangement of obligations that depended, for their acceptance and validity, on being the output of legal institutions (courts, legislatures, and agencies) governed by a set of rational processes. These processes were public, accessible, deliberative, reasonable, and stable. They brought a form of coherence to the legal system, a system that depended on the institutional competence of distinctive bodies such as courts, legislatures, and agencies, each operating in their own spheres yet each dependent on the sound and often-collaborative operation of the other institutions.

In pushing back against the Legal Realists, these Legal Process thinkers certainly did not reassert the notion that the role of courts was to "find" the law. But they did argue, much more than Holmes, that the processes by which courts "make" law were regularized and carefully constrained. Judicial law creation, they asserted, involved a "reasoned elaboration" of each issue before the court, premised on neutral principles generally applicable to any case and typically justified in written opinions. Legal Process thinkers also defended legislatures as worthy institutions in which the citizens' representatives pursued reasonable purposes through reasonable means in a process that permitted public observation and accountability. On this account, statutory law not only was still formally superior to common law, but also was now embraced as functionally superior as well. Each resulting statute was entitled to full respect not merely as a reference source for law but as part of the law itself.

Meanwhile, at both the federal and state levels, the twentieth century witnessed an explosion of lawmaking activity by legislatures and agencies, ushering in what has sometimes been called "The Age of the Statute." As a result, law today is a complex hybrid of legislative statutes, agency regulations, and common law, all subject to overarching constitutional rules and principles. Each of these various sources of law is enforced primarily by courts and agencies, who thereby also are inevitably responsible for interpreting the law (once the fiction is abandoned that their role is merely to find the law), but with a recognition of the legislature's superior authority to make the law.

3.   Lingering Concerns About Willfulness in Interpretation: Who Is to Say "What the Law Is"?

In the hybrid state of law just described, the problem of potential judicial willfulness is, if anything, more acute than in Justice Holmes' day. Meanwhile, the related issue (which we will take up in Part VII) of how much lawmaking authority agencies may properly exercise also remains a significant one. Thus, an essential concern is how to prevent or discourage excessive willfulness on the part of both courts and agencies, whose law "elaboration" role is significant but understood to be subservient to that of legislatures.

The Legal Process defense of the reasoned operations and individual competencies of courts, legislatures, and agencies can assist in thinking about the nature of each of these lawmaking institution's responsibilities to "say what the law is." The question of the proper relationship between legislatures and courts lurks in the shadows almost every time a court faces an interpretive problem, but in some circumstances the issue comes directly to the surface, and the relationship becomes the very focus of the interpretive problem itself. One instance of this involves *stare decisis* in statutory interpretation, to which we turn in the next section.

B. Statutory *Stare Decisis*

You likely have already encountered the concept of *stare decisis* in some of your other courses. *Stare decisis*, which is Latin for "to stand by things decided," is the policy of a court to stand by its own precedents. The idea is that once a court has laid down a principle of law, the court adheres to that principle and applies it to all future cases where the facts are substantially the same. When applying the common law, courts will usually adhere to *stare decisis*, although they will on occasion overrule their precedent. As you know, though, the common law is judge-made law, and so a court that overrules one of its past

> *Stare decisis* can be either "horizontal" **FYI** or "vertical." "Horizontal *stare decisis*" refers to *stare decisis* by the same court that decided the previous case, whereas "vertical *stare decisis*" refers to the fact that lower courts in the judicial hierarchy are bound to follow the law as declared by higher courts. Our discussion here focuses solely on horizontal *stare decisis*.

precedents is simply modifying law that the court itself originally created. So, to the extent that we can think of the court as a continuing institution over time (even when its membership changes), we can think of the overruling of a past common-law precedent as the court itself just changing its mind within its own lawmaking sphere.

But what about a *statutory* precedent? How should the principle of *stare decisis* operate to constrain a court once the court has construed the meaning of a statute (or regulation)? When a court interprets a statute, it determines the meaning of language adopted by a legislature. Once the court has done so, can that same court change its mind and overrule its past precedent interpreting a statute? On the one hand, if the kinds of considerations that would lead the court to reject *stare decisis* in the context of a common-law decision also apply to a statutory decision (considerations such as the quality of the past decision's reasoning, its consistency with related decisions, legal developments since the past decision, and the extent of the legal system's and society's reliance on the decision), then why shouldn't the court feel free to revisit its prior statutory decisions? On the other hand, in the context of statutory interpretation (as opposed to the common law), it is the legislature, not the court, that serves as the principal lawmaking institution. So, perhaps a court should be more reluctant to overrule a precedent interpreting a statute than one declaring the common law.

The question of whether the principle of *stare decisis* in the context of statutory interpretation should be sacrosanct (or, at least, stronger than in the context of the common law) raises fundamental questions about the relationship between legislatures and courts as lawmaking institutions. As a principle of judicial restraint, *stare decisis* is often understood to have even stronger force with respect to judicial precedents that have resolved questions of statutory meaning. The underlying rationale for this strong form of statutory *stare decisis*, predicated heavily on Legal Process ideas, is that once a court has clarified a textual ambiguity in the legislature's handiwork, the legislature, not the judiciary, is in the vastly superior institutional position to revise this meaning at some subsequent time, if it wishes. But if the legislature does not do so, courts should not lightly second-guess that legislative inaction, even when the courts might no longer be persuaded by the reasoning of their original precedent.

An especially famous and somewhat thorny examination of this question involves a series of three U.S. Supreme Court decisions about the application of the federal antitrust statute to Major League Baseball, culminating in the 1972 case *Flood v. Kuhn*, which you will encounter in Chapter 27. But you have already seen a more recent example, namely, the 2023 decision in *Allen v. Milligan*, discussed above in Chapter 6.

When the Supreme Court stayed the district court decisions at issue in *Allen v. Milligan*, many observers predicted the Court was preparing to overrule its own prior interpretations of section 2 of the Voting Rights Act of 1965. To the surprise of these observers, the Court instead reaffirmed those prior interpretations, notwithstanding arguments that subsequent developments had left those precedents weakened. Below we present key excerpts from *Allen v. Milligan* concerning the principle of statutory *stare decisis*, including part of Justice Alito's dissent, in which he argued for a reinterpretation of those precedents. As you read, be thinking about whether and in what circumstances "statutory *stare decisis*" should have heightened import.

Allen v. Milligan
599 U.S. 1 (2023)

CHIEF JUSTICE ROBERTS delivered the opinion of the Court, except as to Part III-B-1.

In January 2022, a three-judge District Court sitting in Alabama preliminarily enjoined the State from using the districting plan it had recently adopted for the 2022 congressional elections, finding that the plan likely violated Section 2 of the Voting Rights Act, 52 U.S.C. § 10301. This Court stayed the District Court's order pending further review. 595 U.S. ___ (2022). After conducting that review, we now affirm.

I-A

Shortly after the Civil War, Congress passed and the States ratified the Fifteenth Amendment, providing that "[t]he right of citizens of the United States to vote shall not be denied or abridged . . . on account of race, color, or previous condition of servitude." U.S. Const., Amdt. 15, § 1. In the century that followed, however, the Amendment proved little more than a parchment promise. Jim Crow laws like literacy tests, poll taxes, and "good-morals" requirements abounded, *South Carolina v. Katzenbach*, 383 U.S. 301, 312–313 (1966), "render[ing] the right to vote illusory for blacks," *Northwest Austin Municipal Util. Dist. No. One v. Holder*, 557 U.S. 193, 220–221 (2009) (THOMAS, J., concurring in judgment in part and dissenting in part). Congress stood up to little of it; "[t]he first century of congressional enforcement of the [Fifteenth] Amendment . . . can only be regarded as a failure." *Id.*, at 197 (majority opinion).

That changed in 1965. Spurred by the Civil Rights movement, Congress enacted and President Johnson signed into law the Voting Rights Act. 79 Stat. 437, as amended, 52 U.S.C. § 10301 et seq. The Act "create[d] stringent new remedies for voting discrimination," attempting to forever "banish the blight of racial discrimination in voting." *Katzenbach*, 383 U.S., at 308. By 1981, in only sixteen years' time, many considered the VRA "the most successful civil rights statute in the history of the Nation." S. Rep. No. 97–417, p. 111 (1982) (Senate Report).

These cases concern Section 2 of that Act. In its original form, "§ 2 closely tracked the language of the [Fifteenth] Amendment" and, as a result, had little independent force. *Brnovich v. Democratic National Committee*, 594 U.S. ___, ___ (2021) (slip op., at 3). Our leading case on § 2 at the time was *City of Mobile v. Bolden*, which involved a claim by black voters that the City's at-large election system effectively excluded them from participating in the election of city commissioners. 446 U.S. 55 (1980). The commission had three seats, black voters comprised one-third of the City's population, but no black-preferred candidate had ever won election.

The Court ruled against the plaintiffs. The Fifteenth Amendment—and thus § 2—prohibits States from acting with a "racially discriminatory motivation" or an "invidious purpose" to discriminate. *Id.*, at 61–65 (plurality opinion). But it does not prohibit laws that are discriminatory only in effect. *Ibid.* The *Mobile* plaintiffs could "register and vote without hindrance"—"their freedom to vote ha[d] not been denied or abridged by anyone." *Id.*, at 65. The fact that they happened to lose frequently was beside the point. Nothing the City had done "purposeful[ly] exclu[ded]" them "from participati[ng] in the election process." *Id.*, at 64.

Almost immediately after it was decided, *Mobile* "produced an avalanche of criticism, both in the media and within the civil rights community." T. Boyd & S. Markman, *The 1982 Amendments to the Voting Rights Act: A Legislative History*, 40 WASH. & LEE L. REV. 1347, 1355 (1983) (Boyd & Markman). * * * By focusing on discriminatory intent and ignoring disparate effect, critics argued, the Court had abrogated "the standard used by the courts to determine whether [racial] discrimination existed. . .: Whether such discrimination existed." *It's Results That Count*, Philadelphia Inquirer, Mar. 3, 1982, p. 8-A.

But *Mobile* had its defenders, too. In their view, abandoning the intent test in favor of an effects test would inevitably require a focus on proportionality—wherever a minority group won fewer seats in the legislature than its share of the population, the charge could be made that the State law had a discriminatory effect. That, after all, was the type of claim brought in *Mobile*. But mandating racial proportionality in elections was regarded by many as intolerable. * * *

This sharp debate arrived at Congress's doorstep in 1981. The question whether to broaden § 2 or keep it as is, said [Senator Orrin] Hatch—by then Chairman of the Senate Subcommittee before which § 2 would be debated—"involve[d] one of the most substantial constitutional issues ever to come before this body." 2 Hearings before the Subcommittee on the Constitution of the Senate Committee on the Judiciary, 97th Cong., 2d Sess., pt. 1, p. 1 (1982). * * *

The impasse was not resolved until late April 1982, when Senator Bob Dole proposed a compromise. Boyd & Markman 1414. Section 2 would include the effects test that many desired but also a robust disclaimer against proportionality. * * *

> For the language of VRA amended section 2, see the discussion in Chapter 6 at p. 104.

The Dole compromise won bipartisan support and, on June 18, the Senate passed the 1982 amendments by an overwhelming margin, 85–8. Eleven days later, President Reagan signed the Act into law. * * *

B

> **FYI** The portion of *Allen v. Milligan* you read in Chapter 6 includes an extended excerpt of this section.

[Here the Court described the history of Alabama's congressional maps, including the adoption of a new congressional map under the name HB1 in 2021, and summarized the decisions below.]

* * *

II-A

For the past forty years, we have evaluated claims brought under § 2 using the three-part framework developed in our decision *Thornburg v. Gingles*, 478 U.S. 30 (1986). *Gingles* concerned a challenge to North Carolina's multimember districting scheme, which allegedly diluted the vote of its black citizens. *Id.*, at 34–36. The case presented the first opportunity since the 1982 amendments to address how the new § 2 would operate.

Gingles began by describing what § 2 guards against. "The essence of a § 2 claim," the Court explained, "is that a certain electoral law, practice, or structure interacts with social and historical conditions to cause an inequality in the opportunities enjoyed by black and white voters." *Id.*, at 47. That occurs where an "electoral structure operates to minimize or cancel out" minority voters' "ability to elect their preferred candidates." *Id.*, at 48. Such a risk is greatest "where minority and majority voters consistently prefer different candidates" and where minority voters are submerged in a majority voting population that "regularly defeat[s]" their choices. *Ibid.*

[The Court then summarized the three *Gingles* preconditions for proving a violation of section 2.]

> **FYI** The specifics of the *Gingles* test are covered in Chapter 6.

Gingles has governed our Voting Rights Act jurisprudence since it was decided 37 years ago. Congress has never disturbed our understanding of § 2 as *Gingles* construed it. And we have applied *Gingles* in one § 2 case after another, to different kinds of electoral systems and to different jurisdictions in States all over the country. * * *

B

As noted, the District Court concluded that plaintiffs' § 2 claim was likely to succeed under *Gingles*. 582 F. Supp. 3d, at 1026. Based on our review of the record, we agree. * * *

We see no reason to disturb the District Court's careful factual findings, which are subject to clear error review and have gone unchallenged by Alabama in any event. Nor is there a basis to upset the District Court's legal conclusions. The Court faithfully applied our precedents and correctly determined that, under existing law, HB1 violated § 2.

> **!** The point of the certiorari petition, and the Court's stay of the district court decision pending its review, was to consider whether to overrule the existing law.

III

The heart of these cases is not about the law as it exists. It is about Alabama's attempt to remake our § 2 jurisprudence anew. * * *

As we explain below, we find Alabama's new approach to § 2 compelling neither in theory nor in practice. We accordingly decline to recast our § 2 case law as Alabama requests.

A-1

Section 2 prohibits States from imposing any "standard, practice, or procedure . . . in a manner which results in a denial or abridgement of the right of any citizen . . . to vote on account of race or color." 52 U.S.C. § 10301(a). What that means, § 2 goes on to explain, is that the political processes in the State must be "equally open," such that minority voters do not "have less opportunity than other members of the electorate to participate in the political process and to elect representatives of their choice." § 10301(b).

We have understood the language of § 2 against the background of the hard-fought compromise that Congress struck. To that end, we have reiterated that § 2 turns on the presence of discriminatory effects, not discriminatory intent. And we have explained that "[i]t is patently clear that Congress has used the words 'on account of race or color' in the Act to mean 'with respect to' race or color, and not to connote any required purpose of racial discrimination." *Gingles*, 478 U.S., at 71, n. 34 (plurality opinion) (some alterations omitted). Individuals thus lack an equal opportunity to participate in the political process when a State's electoral structure operates in a manner that "minimize[s] or cancel[s] out the[ir] voting strength." *Id.*, at 47. * * *

The State's reading of § 2, by contrast, runs headlong into our precedent. Alabama asserts that a State's map does not "abridge[ ]" a person's right to vote "on account of race" if the map resembles a sufficient number of race-neutral alternatives. See Brief for Alabama 54–56. But our cases have consistently focused, for purposes of litigation, on the specific illustrative maps that a plaintiff adduces. Deviation from that map shows it is possible that the State's map has a disparate effect on account of race. The remainder of the *Gingles* test helps determine whether that possibility is reality by looking to polarized voting preferences and the frequency of racially discriminatory actions taken by the State, past and present.

A State's liability under § 2, moreover, must be determined "based on the totality of circumstances." 52 U.S.C. § 10301(b). Yet Alabama suggests there is only one "circumstance[ ]" that matters—how the State's map stacks up relative to the benchmark. That single-minded view of § 2 cannot be squared with the VRA's demand that courts employ a more refined approach. And we decline to adopt an interpretation of § 2 that would "revise and reformulate the *Gingles* threshold inquiry that has been the baseline of our § 2 jurisprudence" for nearly forty years.

* * *

C

Alabama finally asserts that the Court should outright stop applying § 2 in cases like these because the text of § 2 does not apply to single-member redistricting and because § 2 is unconstitutional as the District Court applied it here. We disagree on both counts. * * *

This understanding of § 2 cannot be reconciled with our precedent. As recounted above, we have applied § 2 to States' districting maps in an unbroken line of decisions stretching four decades. In doing so, we have unanimously held that § 2 and *Gingles* "[c]ertainly . . . apply" to claims challenging single-member districts. *Growe [v. Emison]*, 507 U.S. [25,] 40 [(1993)]. And we have even invalidated portions of a State's single-district map under § 2. See *LULAC [v. Perry]*, 548 U.S. [399,] 427–29 [(2006)]. Alabama's approach would require "abandoning" this precedent, "overruling the interpretation of § 2" as set out in nearly a dozen of our cases. *Holder [v. Hall]*, 512 U.S. [874,] 944 [(1994)] (opinion of THOMAS, J.).

We decline to take that step. Congress is undoubtedly aware of our construing § 2 to apply to districting challenges. It can change that if it likes. But until and unless it does, statutory *stare decisis* counsels our staying the course.

[Here the Court included this footnote: Justice Alito argues that "[t]he *Gingles* framework should be [re]interpreted" in light of changing methods in statutory interpretation. Post, at 10 (dissenting opinion). But as we have explained, *Gingles* effectuates the delicate legislative bargain that § 2 embodies. And statutory *stare decisis* counsels strongly in favor of not "undo[ing] . . . the compromise that was reached between the House and Senate when § 2 was amended in 1982." *Brnovich*, 594 U.S., at ___ (slip op., at 22).]

* * *

The judgments of the District Court * * * are affirmed.

JUSTICE KAVANAUGH, concurring in all but Part III-B-1.

I agree with the Court that Alabama's redistricting plan violates § 2 of the Voting Rights Act as interpreted in *Thornburg v. Gingles,* 478 U.S. 30 (1986). I write separately to emphasize four points.

First, the upshot of Alabama's argument is that the Court should overrule *Gingles.* But the *stare decisis* standard for this Court to overrule a statutory precedent, as distinct from a constitutional precedent, is comparatively strict. Unlike with constitutional precedents, Congress and the President may enact new legislation to alter statutory precedents such as *Gingles.* In the past 37 years, however, Congress and the President have not disturbed *Gingles,* even as they have made other changes to the Voting Rights Act. Although statutory *stare decisis* is not absolute, "the Court has ordinarily left the updating or correction of erroneous statutory precedents to the legislative process." *Ramos v. Louisiana*, 590 U.S. ___, ___ (2020) (KAVANAUGH, J., concurring in part) (slip op., at 4)

* * *

JUSTICE ALITO, with whom JUSTICE GORSUCH joins, dissenting.

Based on a flawed understanding of the framework adopted in *Thornburg v. Gingles*, 478 U.S. 30 (1986), the Court now holds that the congressional districting map adopted by the Alabama Legislature violates § 2 of the Voting Rights Act. Like the Court, I am happy to apply *Gingles* in these cases. But I would interpret that precedent in a way that heeds what § 2 actually says, and I would take constitutional requirements into account. When the *Gingles* framework is viewed in this way, it is apparent that the decisions below must be vacated.

* * *

III

The Court spends much of its opinion attacking what it takes to be the argument that Alabama has advanced in this litigation. I will not debate whether the Court's characterization of that argument is entirely correct, but as applied to the analysis I have just set out, the Court's criticisms miss the mark.

A

The major theme of this part of the Court's opinion is that Alabama's argument, in effect, is that "*Gingles* must be overruled." Ante, at 25. But as I wrote at the beginning of this opinion, I would decide these cases under the *Gingles* framework. We should recognize, however, that the *Gingles* framework is not the same thing as a statutory provision, and it is a mistake to regard it as such. In applying that framework today, we should keep in mind subsequent developments in our case law.

One important development has been a sharpening of the methodology used in interpreting statutes. *Gingles* was decided at a time when the Court's statutory interpretation decisions sometimes paid less attention to the actual text of the statute than to its legislative history, and *Gingles* falls into that category. The Court quoted § 2 but then moved briskly to the Senate Report. See 478 U.S., at 36–37, 43, and n. 7. Today, our statutory interpretation decisions focus squarely on the statutory text. And as we held in

> **FYI** "Legislative history" is a term of art that describes a set of documentary records produced as part of the legislative process for a particular measure, usually including committee reports and testimony, as well as statements legislators make about the measure.

Brnovich, "[t]he key requirement" set out in the text of § 2 is that a State's electoral process must be " 'equally open' " to members of all racial groups. [594 U.S. ____], at ____ (slip op., at 15). The *Gingles* framework should be interpreted in a way that gives effect to this standard.

* * *

[Justice Thomas's dissenting opinion has been omitted here.]

NOTES AND QUESTIONS

1. Section I-A of the Court's *Allen* opinion is a short history of the Voting Rights Act, including the 1982 amendment of section 2. Why does the Court include this much historical detail? How important is this statutory history to the Court's view of the principle of statutory *stare decisis*?

2. Justice Kavanaugh's concurrence notes that in the 37 years since the *Gingles* decision, "Congress and the President have made other changes to the Voting Rights Act." What is the significance of this observation? Would it matter if Congress had not revisited any part of the Voting Rights Act since 1982?

3. What does Justice Alito mean when he asserts that since *Gingles*, there "has been a sharpening of the methodology used in interpreting statutes"? Assuming for the moment that his assertion is correct, should that even matter to the principle of statutory *stare decisis*?

C. Characterizing the Role of the Legal Interpreter

In *Allen v. Milligan*, we saw that the principle of statutory *stare decisis* reflects a judicial reluctance to intrude upon the legislature's perceived prerogatives because of the legislature's superior institutional competence to establish public policy. A sense of the legislature's institutional abilities may affect not only the notion of *stare decisis*, but also a sort of inverse question of to what extent courts should look to statutes (or regulations) to derive policy guidance to help refine the common law. A Legal Process approach suggests that, at least on occasion, courts might profitably take note of legislatively established policies as a basis for updating or filling-in gaps in the common law doctrines that are primarily the courts' responsibility. Thus, ideas from the Legal Process School have affected the Supreme Court's understanding of its relationship to Congress in multiple ways.

But perhaps more important than its influence on ideas about either *stare decisis* or incorporating legislative policy into common law, the Legal Process school can offer a set of principles to constrain the amount of willfulness with which courts and agencies might approach issues of statutory and regulatory interpretation generally. As a threshold matter, consider again the question of whether an interpreter *finds* the meaning of an ambiguous text, or *creates* the meaning. Interpretive issues can be placed along a continuum between the easiest cases, where an interpreter might truly only need to find or "discover" the meaning of the term of a legal text, a task with relatively little room for willfulness, and the hardest cases, where to reach a decision, it might be necessary for the interpreter willfully to "create" that meaning. Yet for many interpretive problems, the reality is that "it is extremely difficult to say in practice and in conceptualization just where discovery gives way to creation." Kent Greenawalt, Statutory Interpretation: 20 Questions 17–18 (1999); *see* Reed Dickerson, The Interpretation and Application of Statutes 22–23 (1975).

For instance, consider a provision of the now-archaic White Slave Traffic Act that once criminalized the transportation of any woman in interstate commerce "for the purpose of prostitution or debauchery, or for any other immoral purpose." How should an interpreter determine the meaning of the phrase "any other immoral purpose," as used in this provision? *See Caminetti v. United States,* 242 U.S. 470 (1917). Does that task involve *finding* the meaning implicit in the words chosen by the enacting Congress? Or does it involve *creating* the meaning, either on behalf of the enacting Congress or as an independent act, through subsequent application of various tools of legal interpretation?

Of central importance to thinking about this question is to ask what the interpreter's responsibility is to the legislature or agency, as the author of the text. Consciously or subconsciously, interpreters may conceive of their role in at least three distinct ways: as dutiful executors, as faithful agents, or as cooperative partners. Whichever role the interpreter assumes in turn will affect the amount of freedom that the interpreter feels in seeking to further the work of that author. These distinct conceptions of the interpreters' roles deserve brief elaboration as points of reference for the discussion in ensuing chapters of various interpretive theories or methodologies.

On the conception of the interpreter as a **"Dutiful Executor,"** the interpreter's role is to hew as closely as possible to the instructions given by the author, just as the executor of a will must seek to effectuate the precise written directions made by a deceased testator. This view provides the interpreter little latitude, and to the extent that ambiguities arise in administering the author's wishes, the executor may be bound by (and perhaps therefore take comfort in) established default rules. In subsequent chapters we will explore some interpretive theories and doctrines that rely heavily on a variety of such default rules, even though in the statutory interpretation context they may not be binding in the way that they are in the interpretation of wills.

A less constraining model is to view the interpreter as a **"Faithful Agent"** of the enacting legislature or promulgating agency. In this conception, the role of the interpreter, as the agent, is to honor the principal's desires above all, including by exercising some discretion to adjust, as appropriate, the means of fulfilling these desires. Accordingly, a faithful agent model depends on the agent having a means of knowing or ascertaining the principal's desires. The chapters that follow will continue to explore some theories and doctrines of statutory interpretation that address the question of how to determine the enacting legislature's underlying desire or will, whether characterized as legislative intent or legislative purpose. But identifying this desire often may be a difficult enterprise, and as a practical matter some interpretation must occur even when the agent does not or cannot know the principal's wishes.

An even less constraining model is to view the interpreter as a **"Cooperative Partner"** of the legislature, working to effectuate the broader public good by building upon the policies embodied in the legislature's work and striving to make the overall body of the law as coherent and public-regarding as possible. This model is not unconstrained, as the aspiration of making the law "coherent" incorporates the notion that the interpreter cannot just ignore the statutory law; rather, statutory text must still provide a foundation and a tether for any such cooperative lawmaking. Later we will also consider some theoretical and doctrinal perspectives relevant to statutory interpretation on something like a "Cooperative Partner" model.

The Cooperative Partner model of interpretation is in some respects closest to how government agencies (rather than courts) work to effectuate legislative policies in the statutes that they administer, within general limits set by the legislature. But as we will discuss later, all three of these models of the interpreter's role may have some validity in thinking about the many circumstances in which agencies construe and enforce statutory text, as well as the various ways in which courts construe and enforce agency regulations in addition to statutes.

NOTES & QUESTIONS

1. Which of the three preceding conceptions of the interpreter's role best squares with your sense of how courts should function when applying statutory provisions? Of how agencies should function?

2. How much does your perception of how *legislatures* function affect your response to question 1? What other factors influence your view? Does it matter that legislatures adopt statutes before the precise interpretive questions arise? Relatedly, does it matter that courts ordinarily have a concrete dispute with specific facts before them when they interpret statutory language? Or that agencies must implement the statutes they interpret, not just interpret statutory language for other parties who appear before them, as courts do?

3. Which conception of the interpreter's role would be the best approach for Francis Lieber's domestic servant to follow in resolving ambiguities that arise in responding to the direction to "fetch some soupmeat"? *See supra* Chapter 14, pp. 334–335. Is your response to this question different from your response to question 1? If so, why?

4. We have considered the hybrid quality of law, in terms of its collective origins in the legislative, executive, and judicial branches, and we have seen the critical interpretive and law-elaborating role that courts and agencies can play. We will turn now to the current theories, doctrines, and tools of statutory interpretation that are of greatest potential relevance in addressing the kinds of interpretive problems that we have begun to study.

Test Your Understanding

To assess your understanding of the material in this chapter, <u>click here</u> to take a quiz.

17

Emphasizing Text in Interpretation

Key Concepts

- Ordinary public meaning
- Literal meaning
- Extratextual sources of meaning
- Textualism
- Purposivism
- Legislative history

Chapter Summary

This chapter centers around two interpretive problems whose resolutions provide rich demonstrations of a Textualist emphasis in interpretation. Along the way these two illustrations also offer explicit contrasts with other modes of resolving the interpretive issues. One problem, confronted in the 2020 Supreme Court decision in *Bostok v. Clayton County*, is whether a federal law passed in 1964 prohibiting employment discrimination "because of . . . sex" should be interpreted to prohibit employment discrimination on the basis of sexual orientation or transgender status. A divided Court said "yes," but justices on both sides of the decision claimed that they were more faithfully applying the statutory text.

The other problem involves a federal drug statute whose mandatory minimum prison sentences were triggered by the weight of the drug that the defendant distributed. The *en banc* Seventh Circuit divided over how to apply this statute to doses of LSD distributed in blotter paper that significantly increased the weight. In *United States v. Marshall*, the majority held that the text of the statute required that the blotter paper be included in the weight, while the dissent took a more pragmatic approach to interpretation, arguing that including the blotter paper in the weight was completely irrational and could not have been what the legislature would have wanted.

Having invited you in the previous chapter to think about the respective roles of legislatures and courts in determining what the law is (and the complexity of that task), in the next two chapters we will read excerpts of several instructive cases that will expose you to current debates about how to interpret statutes. We begin with two cases that emphasize Textualist thinking yet raise important questions about whether Textualism actually furthers the values its adherents claim for it—objectivity, fair notice, and judicial constraint—or is consistent with another important value, legislative intent. The first involves a question of the meaning of Title VII of the Civil Rights Act of 1964, another of the country's most important pieces of civil rights legislation (along with the Voting Rights Act of 1965, which you have already encountered several times above). The second case involves a counterintuitive application of a mandatory minimum prison sentence that Congress enacted as part of the federal Sentencing Guidelines, an important criminal justice reform effort begun in the 1980s.

A. The Meaning of Title VII's Prohibition on Sex Discrimination in Employment

DIY
The Sexual Orientation Discrimination Question

 In 1964, in a culmination of a multi-year effort, Congress enacted the Civil Rights Act of 1964, the country's most sweeping civil rights law ever. The measure contained several separate divisions or "titles," which prohibited discrimination in voting, in places of public accommodation, in state and local government programs, in schools, by recipients of federal funds, and in employment. Title VII is the title concerning employment.

Section 703 in Title VII of the Civil Rights Act prohibits larger private employers from hiring, firing, or otherwise discriminating in the terms and conditions of any individual's employment "because of such individual's race, color, religion, sex, or national origin." In 2020, the Supreme Court considered three consolidated Title VII cases raising the question whether it was a violation of section 703 for an employer to fire an employee on the basis of the employee's transgender or homosexual status. Before reading the Court's treatment of this issue, take five minutes to think about the following related questions:

1. How would you make the strongest argument that the employer has not violated section 703?

2. How would you make the strongest argument that the employer has violated section 703?

3. Which argument do you find easier to craft?

4. Which argument do you find more persuasive?

Once you have settled on your tentative views on these questions, go on to the case excerpted below.

Bostock v. Clayton County
<u>590 U.S. 644 (2020)</u>

JUSTICE GORSUCH delivered the opinion of the Court.

Sometimes small gestures can have unexpected consequences. Major initiatives practically guarantee them. In our time, few pieces of federal legislation rank in significance with the Civil Rights Act of 1964. There, in Title VII, Congress outlawed discrimination in the workplace on the basis of race, color, religion, sex, or national origin. Today, we must decide whether an employer can fire someone simply for being homosexual or transgender. The answer is clear. An employer who fires an individual for being homosexual or transgender fires that person for traits or actions it would not have questioned in members of a different sex. Sex plays a necessary and undisguisable role in the decision, exactly what Title VII forbids.

> What does the observation in Justice Gorsuch's opening sentence suggest about the lawmaking process? The statutory interpretation process?

Those who adopted the Civil Rights Act might not have anticipated their work would lead to this particular result. Likely, they weren't thinking about many of the Act's consequences that have become apparent over the years, including its prohibition against discrimination on the basis of motherhood

> Do you have a sense of what Justice Gorsuch means by "extratextual considerations" at this point? Keep this question in mind.

or its ban on the sexual harassment of male employees. But the limits of the drafters' imagination supply no reason to ignore the law's demands. When the express terms of a statute give us one answer and extratextual considerations suggest another, it's no contest. Only the written word is the law, and all persons are entitled to its benefit.

I

Few facts are needed to appreciate the legal question we face. Each of the three cases before us started the same way: An employer fired a long-time employee shortly after the employee revealed that he or she is homosexual or transgender—and allegedly for no reason other than the employee's homosexuality or transgender status. [The Court went on to describe each case, and the circuit split that arose in the Courts of Appeals.]

II

This Court normally interprets a statute in accord with the ordinary public meaning of its terms at the time of its enactment. After all, **only the words on the page constitute the law** adopted by Congress and approved by the President. If judges could add to, remodel, update, or detract from

> This statement (bold emphasis added) is a prototypical assertion of the "Textualist" position that laws must be interpreted based on the enacted text.

old statutory terms inspired only by extratextual sources and our own imaginations, we would risk amending statutes outside the legislative process reserved for the people's representatives. And we would deny the people the right to continue relying on the original meaning of the law they have counted on to settle their rights and obligations.

> What significance does this constraint (of looking at the time of the statute's adoption) have?

With this in mind, our task is clear. We must determine the ordinary public meaning of Title VII's command that it is "unlawful. . .for an employer to fail or refuse to hire or to discharge any individual, or otherwise to discriminate against any individual with respect to his compensation, terms, conditions, or privileges of employment, because of such individual's race, color, religion, sex, or national origin." § 2000e–2(a)(1). To do so, we orient ourselves to the time of the statute's adoption, here 1964, and begin by examining the key statutory terms in turn before assessing their impact on the cases at hand and then confirming our work against this Court's precedents.

A

The only statutorily protected characteristic at issue in today's cases is "sex"—and that is also the primary term in Title VII whose meaning the parties dispute. Appealing to roughly contemporaneous dictionaries, the employers say that, as used here, the term "sex" in 1964 referred to "status as either male or female [as] determined by reproduc-

> Take note of how the next four paragraphs engage solely in an exploration of the words of the statute and their resulting meaning.

tive biology." The employees counter by submitting that, even in 1964, the term bore a broader scope, capturing more than anatomy and reaching at least some norms concerning gender identity and sexual orientation. But because nothing in our approach to these cases turns on the outcome of the parties' debate, and because the employees concede the point for argument's sake, we proceed on the assumption that "sex" signified what the employers suggest, referring only to biological distinctions between male and female.

Still, that's just a starting point. The question isn't just what "sex" meant, but what Title VII says about it. Most notably, the statute prohibits employers from taking certain actions "because of" sex. And, as this Court has previously explained, "the ordinary meaning of 'because of' is 'by reason of' or 'on account of.'" In the language of law, this means that Title VII's "because of" test incorporates the " 'simple' " and "traditional" standard of but-for causation. * * *

As sweeping as even the but-for causation standard can be, Title VII does not concern itself with everything that happens "because of" sex. The statute imposes liability on employers only when they "fail or refuse to hire," "discharge," "or otherwise. . .discriminate against" someone because of a statutorily protected characteristic like sex. *Ibid.* The employers acknowledge that they discharged the plaintiffs in today's cases, but assert that the statute's list of verbs is qualified by the last item on it: "otherwise. . .discriminate against." By virtue of the word otherwise, the employers suggest, Title VII concerns itself not with every discharge, only with those discharges that involve discrimination.

Accepting this point, too, for argument's sake, the question becomes: What did "discriminate" mean in 1964? As it turns out, it meant then roughly what it means today: "To make a difference in treatment or favor (of one as compared with others)." WEBSTER'S NEW INTERNATIONAL DICTIONARY 745 (2d ed. 1954). To "discriminate against" a person, then, would seem to mean treating that individual worse than others who are similarly situated. * * *

B

? Now that you have seen the phrase "ordinary public meaning" used repeatedly, what do you think it means?

From the ordinary public meaning of the statute's language at the time of the law's adoption, a straightforward rule emerges: An employer violates Title VII when it intentionally fires an individual employee based in part on sex. It doesn't matter if other factors besides the plaintiff's sex con-tributed to the decision. And it doesn't matter if the employer treated women as a group the same when compared to men as a group. If the employer intentionally relies in part on an individual employee's sex when deciding to discharge the employee—put differently, if changing the employee's sex would have yielded a different choice by the employer—a statutory violation has occurred. Title VII's message is "simple but momentous": An individual employee's sex is "not relevant to the selection, evaluation, or compensa-tion of employees." *Price Waterhouse v. Hopkins*, 490 U. S. 228, 239 (1989) (plurality opinion).

The statute's message for our cases is equally simple and momentous: An individual's homosexuality or transgender status is not relevant to employ-ment decisions. That's because it is impossible to discriminate against a person for being homosexual or transgender without discriminating against that individual based on sex. Consider, for example, an employer with two employees, both of whom are attracted to men. The two individuals are, to the employer's mind, materially identical in all respects, except that one is a man and the other a woman. If the employer fires the male employee for no reason other than the fact he is attracted to men, the employer discrimi-nates against him for traits or actions it tolerates in his female colleague. Put differently, the employer intentionally singles out an employee to fire based in part on the employee's sex, and the affected employee's sex is a but-for cause of his discharge. Or take an employer who fires a transgender person who was identified as a male at birth but who now identifies as a female. If the employer retains an otherwise identical employee who was identified as female at birth, the employer intentionally penalizes a person identified as male at birth for traits or actions that it tolerates in an employee identified as female at birth. Again, the individual employee's sex plays an unmistakable and impermissible role in the discharge decision. * * *

An employer musters no better a defense by responding that it is equally happy to fire male and female employees who are homosexual or transgender. Title VII liability is not limited to employers who, through the sum of all of their employment actions, treat the class of men differently than the class of women. Instead, the law makes each instance of discriminating against an individual employee because of that individual's sex an independent violation of Title VII. So just as an employer who fires both Hannah and Bob for failing to fulfill traditional sex stereotypes doubles rather than eliminates Title VII liability, an employer who fires both Hannah and Bob for being gay or transgender does the same.

At bottom, these cases involve no more than the straightforward application of legal terms with plain and settled meanings. For an employer to discriminate against employees for being homosexual or transgender, the employer must intentionally discriminate against individual men and women in part because of sex. That has always been prohibited by Title VII's plain terms—and that "should be the end of the analysis." 883 F. 3d, at 135 (CABRANES, J., concurring in judgment). * * *

III

What do the employers have to say in reply? * * * [T]he employers submit that even intentional discrimination against employees based on their homosexuality or transgender status supplies no basis for liability under Title VII.

The employers' argument proceeds in two stages. Seeking footing in the statutory text, they begin by advancing a number of reasons why discrimination on the basis of homosexuality or transgender status doesn't involve discrimination because of sex. But each of these arguments turns out only to repackage errors we've already seen and this Court's precedents have already rejected. In the end, the employers are left to retreat beyond the statute's text, where they fault us for ignoring the legislature's purposes in

> This summary of the defendants' argument focuses on what the enacting Congress might have intended section 703 to mean, a "purposivist" interpretive approach that the Court's opinion rejects.

enacting Title VII or certain expectations about its operation. They warn, too, about consequences that might follow a ruling for the employees. But none of these contentions about what the employers think the law was meant to do, or should do, allow us to ignore the law as it is.

A

Maybe most intuitively, the employers assert that discrimination on the basis of homosexuality and transgender status aren't referred to as sex discrimination in ordinary conversation. If asked by a friend (rather than a judge) why they were fired, even today's plaintiffs would likely respond that it was because they were gay or transgender, not because of sex. According to the employers, that conversational answer, not the statute's strict terms, should guide our thinking and suffice to defeat any suggestion that the employees now before us were fired because of sex. *Cf.* post, at 3 (ALITO, J., dissenting); post, at 8–13 (KAVANAUGH, J., dissenting).

But this submission rests on a mistaken understanding of what kind of cause the law is looking for in a Title VII case. In conversation, a speaker is likely to focus on what seems most relevant or informative to the listener. So an employee who has just been fired is likely to identify the primary or most direct cause rather than list literally every but-for cause. To do otherwise would be tiring at best. But these conversational conventions do not control Title VII's legal analysis, which asks simply whether sex was a but-for cause. * * *

Trying another angle, the defendants before us suggest that an employer who discriminates based on homosexuality or transgender status doesn't intentionally discriminate based on sex, as a disparate treatment claim requires. *See* post, at 9–12 (ALITO, J., dissenting); post, at 12–13 (KAVANAUGH, J., dissenting). But, as we've seen, an employer who discriminates against homosexual or transgender employees necessarily and intentionally applies sex-based rules. An employer that announces it will not employ anyone who is homosexual, for example, intends to penalize male employees for being attracted to men and female employees for being attracted to women.

What, then, do the employers mean when they insist intentional discrimination based on homosexuality or transgender status isn't intentional discrimination based on sex? Maybe the employers mean they don't intend to harm one sex or the other as a class. But as should be clear by now, the statute focuses on discrimination against individuals, not groups. Alternatively, the employers may mean that they don't perceive themselves as motivated by a desire to discriminate based on sex. But nothing in Title VII turns on the employer's labels or any further intentions (or motivations) for its conduct beyond sex discrimination. * * *

Next, the employers turn to Title VII's list of protected characteristics—race, color, religion, sex, and national origin. Because homosexuality and transgender status can't be found on that list and because they are conceptually distinct from sex, the employers reason, they are implicitly excluded from Title VII's reach. Put another way, if Congress had wanted to address these matters in Title VII, it would have referenced them specifically. *Cf.* post, at 7–8 (Alito, J., dissenting); post, at 13–15 (Kavanaugh, J., dissenting).

But that much does not follow. We agree that homosexuality and transgender status are distinct concepts from sex. But, as we've seen, discrimination based on homosexuality or transgender status necessarily entails discrimination based on sex; the first cannot happen without the second. Nor is there any such thing as a "canon of donut holes," in which Congress's failure to speak directly to a specific case that falls within a more general statutory rule creates a tacit exception. Instead, when Congress chooses not to include any exceptions to a broad rule, courts apply the broad rule. And that is exactly how this Court has always approached Title VII. * * *

The employers try the same point another way. Since 1964, they observe, Congress has considered several proposals to add sexual orientation to Title VII's list of protected characteristics, but no such amendment has become law. Meanwhile, Congress has enacted other statutes addressing other topics that do discuss sexual orientation. This postenactment legislative history, they urge, should tell us something. *Cf.* post, at 2, 42–43 (Alito, J., dissenting); post, at 4, 15–16 (Kavanaugh, J., dissenting).

But what? There's no authoritative evidence explaining why later Congresses adopted other laws referencing sexual orientation but didn't amend this one. Maybe some in the later legislatures understood the impact Title VII's broad language already promised for cases like ours and didn't think a revision needed. Maybe others knew about its impact but hoped no one else would notice. Maybe still others, occupied by other concerns, didn't consider the issue at all. All we can know for certain is that speculation about why a later Congress declined to adopt new legislation offers a "particularly dangerous" basis on which to rest an interpretation of an existing law a different and earlier Congress did adopt. *Pension Benefit Guaranty Corporation v. LTV Corp.*, 496 U. S. 633, 650 (1990); *see also United States v. Wells*, 519 U. S.

482, 496 (1997); *Sullivan v. Finkelstein*, 496 U. S. 617, 632 (1990) (SCALIA, J., concurring) ("Arguments based on subsequent legislative history. . .should not be taken seriously, not even in a footnote"). * * *

B

Ultimately, the employers are forced to abandon the statutory text and precedent altogether and appeal to assumptions and policy. Most pointedly, they contend that few in 1964 would have expected Title VII to apply to discrimination against homosexual and transgender persons. And whatever the text and our precedent indicate, they say, shouldn't this fact cause us to pause before recognizing liability?

It might be tempting to reject this argument out of hand. This Court has explained many times over many years that, when the meaning of the statute's terms is plain, our job is at an end. The people are entitled to rely on the law as written, without fearing that courts might disregard its plain terms based on some extratextual consideration. Of course, some Members of this Court have consulted legislative history when interpreting ambiguous statutory language. *Cf.* post, at 40 (ALITO, J., dissenting). But that has no bearing here. "Legislative history, for those who take it into account, is meant to clear up ambiguity, not create it." *Milner v. Department of Navy*, 562 U. S. 562, 574 (2011). * * *

> ❗ Here, the Court contemplates the use of "legislative history," an "extratextual" tool for understanding legislative text. But in this case the Court rejects any reason to rely on legislative history.

Still, while legislative history can never defeat unambiguous statutory text, historical sources can be useful for a different purpose: Because the law's ordinary meaning at the time of enactment usually governs, we must be sensitive to the possibility a statutory term that means one thing today or in one context might have meant something else at the time of its adoption or might mean something different in another context. And we must be attuned to the possibility that a statutory phrase ordinarily bears a different meaning than the terms do when viewed individually or literally. To ferret out such shifts in linguistic usage or subtle distinctions between literal and ordinary meaning, this Court has sometimes consulted the understandings of the law's drafters as some (not always conclusive) evidence. * * *

The employers, however, advocate nothing like that here. They do not seek to use historical sources to illustrate that the meaning of any of Title VII's language has changed since 1964 or that the statute's terms, whether viewed individually or as a whole, ordinarily carried some message we have missed. To the contrary, as we have seen, the employers agree with our understanding of all the statutory language—"discriminate against any individual. . .because of such individual's. . .sex." Nor do the competing dissents offer an alternative account about what these terms mean either when viewed individually or in the aggregate. Rather than suggesting that the statutory language bears some other meaning, the employers and dissents merely suggest that, because few in 1964 expected today's result, we should not dare to admit that it follows ineluctably from the statutory text. When a new application emerges that is both unexpected and important, they would seemingly have us merely point out the question, refer the subject back to Congress, and decline to enforce the plain terms of the law in the meantime.

That is exactly the sort of reasoning this Court has long rejected. * * *

The employer's position also proves too much. If we applied Title VII's plain text only to applications some (yet-to-be-determined) group expected in 1964, we'd have more than a little law to overturn. Start with *Oncale* [*v. Sundowner Offshore Services, Inc.*, 523 U.S. 75 (1998)]. How many people in 1964 could have expected that the law would turn out to protect male employees? Let alone to protect them from harassment by other male employees? As we acknowledged at the time, "male-on-male sexual harassment in the workplace was assuredly not the principal evil Congress was concerned with when it enacted Title VII." 523 U. S., at 79. Yet the Court did not hesitate to recognize that Title VII's plain terms forbade it. Under the employer's logic, it would seem this was a mistake.

That's just the beginning of the law we would have to unravel. As one Equal Employment Opportunity Commission (EEOC) Commissioner observed shortly after the law's passage, the words of " 'the sex provision of Title VII [are] difficult to. . .control.' " Franklin, *Inventing the "Traditional Concept" of Sex Discrimination*, 125 HARV. L. REV. 1307, 1338 (2012) (quoting *Federal Mediation Service To Play Role in Implementing Title VII*, [1965–1968 Transfer Binder] CCH Employment Practices ¶ 8046, p. 6074). The "difficult[y]" may owe something to the initial proponent of the sex discrimination rule in Title VII, Representative Howard Smith. On some accounts, the congressman may have wanted (or at least was indifferent to the possibility of) broad language with wide-ranging effect. Not necessarily because he was interested in rooting out sex discrimination in all its forms, but because he may have hoped to scuttle the whole Civil Rights Act and thought that adding language covering sex discrimination would serve as a poison pill. *See* C. WHALEN & B. WHALEN, THE LONGEST DEBATE: A LEGISLATIVE HISTORY OF THE 1964 CIVIL RIGHTS ACT 115–118 (1985). Certainly nothing in the meager legislative history of this provision suggests it was meant to be read narrowly.

Whatever his reasons, thanks to the broad language Representative Smith introduced, many, maybe most, applications of Title VII's sex provision were "unanticipated" at the time of the law's adoption. * * *

Over time, though, the breadth of the statutory language proved too difficult to deny. By the end of the 1960s, the EEOC reversed its stance on sex-segregated job advertising. *See* Franklin, 125 HARV. L. REV., at 1345. In 1971, this Court held that treating women with children differently from men with children violated Title VII. *Phillips* [*v. Martin Marietta Corp.,* 400 U. S. 542, 544 (1971)]. And by the late 1970s, courts began to recognize that sexual harassment can sometimes amount to sex discrimination. *See, e.g., Barnes v. Castle,* 561 F. 2d 983, 990 (CADC 1977). While to the modern eye each of these examples may seem "plainly [to] constitut[e] discrimination because of biological sex," post, at 38 (ALITO, J., dissenting), all were hotly contested for years following Title VII's enactment. And as with the discrimination we consider today, many federal judges long accepted interpretations of Title VII that excluded these situations. * * * Would the employers have us undo every one of these unexpected applications too? * * *

With that, the employers are left to abandon their concern for expected applications and fall back to the last line of defense for all failing statutory interpretation arguments: naked policy appeals. If we were to apply the statute's plain language, they complain, any number of undesirable policy consequences would follow. *Cf.* post, at 44–54 (ALITO, J., dissenting). Gone here is any pretense of statutory interpretation; all that's left is a suggestion we should proceed without the law's guidance to do as we think best. But that's an invitation no court should ever take up. The place to make new legislation, or address unwanted consequences of old legislation, lies in Congress. * * *

> **?** In whose eyes might the consequences of old legislation be "unwanted"? Should it matter if the enacting Congress, not the current Congress, would see the consequences as unwanted?

Ours is a society of written laws. Judges are not free to overlook plain statutory commands on the strength of nothing more than suppositions about intentions or guesswork about expectations. In Title VII, Congress adopted broad language making it illegal for an employer to rely on an employee's sex when deciding to fire that employee. We do not hesitate to recognize today a necessary consequence of that legislative choice: An employer who fires an individual merely for being gay or transgender defies the law.

* * *

JUSTICE ALITO, with whom JUSTICE THOMAS joins, dissenting.

There is only one word for what the Court has done today: legislation. The document that the Court releases is in the form of a judicial opinion interpreting a statute, but that is deceptive.

Title VII of the Civil Rights Act of 1964 prohibits employment discrimination on any of five specified grounds: "race, color, religion, sex, [and] national origin." 42 U. S. C. § 2000e–2(a)(1). Neither "sexual orientation" nor "gender identity" appears on that list. For the past 45 years, bills have been introduced in Congress to add "sexual orientation" to the list, and in recent years, bills have included "gender identity" as well. But to date, none has passed both Houses.

Last year, the House of Representatives passed a bill that would amend Title VII by defining sex discrimination to include both "sexual orientation" and "gender identity," H. R. 5, 116th Cong., 1st Sess. (2019), but the bill has stalled in the Senate. An alternative bill, H. R. 5331, 116th Cong., 1st Sess. (2019), would add similar prohibitions but contains provisions to protect religious liberty. This bill remains before a House Subcommittee.

Because no such amendment of Title VII has been enacted in accordance with the requirements in the Constitution (passage in both Houses and presentment to the President, Art. I, § 7, cl. 2), Title VII's prohibition of discrimination because of "sex" still means what it has always meant. But the Court is not deterred by these constitutional niceties. Usurping the constitutional authority of the other branches, the Court has essentially taken H. R. 5's provision on employment discrimination and issued it under the guise of statutory interpretation. A more brazen abuse of our authority to interpret statutes is hard to recall.

The Court tries to convince readers that it is merely enforcing the terms of the statute, but that is preposterous. Even as understood today, the concept of discrimination because of "sex" is different from discrimination because of "sexual orientation" or "gender identity." And in any event, our duty is to interpret statutory terms to "mean what they conveyed to reasonable people *at the time they were written*." A. SCALIA & B. GARNER, READING LAW: THE INTERPRETATION OF LEGAL TEXTS 16 (2012) (emphasis added). If every single living American had been surveyed in 1964, it would have been hard to find any who thought that discrimination because of sex meant discrimination because of sexual orientation—not to mention gender identity, a concept that was essentially unknown at the time.

The Court attempts to pass off its decision as the inevitable product of the textualist school of statutory interpretation championed by our late colleague Justice Scalia, but no one should be fooled. The Court's opinion is like a pirate ship. It sails under a textualist flag, but what it actually represents is a theory of statutory interpretation that Justice Scalia excoriated—the theory that courts should "update" old statutes so that they better reflect the current values of society. See A. SCALIA, A MATTER OF INTERPRETATION 22 (1997). If the Court finds it appropriate to adopt this theory, it should own up to what it is doing.

> **FYI** Here is another interpretive theory, which sometimes goes by the name of "dynamic" interpretation. We explore this "updating" approach a little more in Chapter 27 of Part VI.

Many will applaud today's decision because they agree on policy grounds with the Court's updating of Title VII. But the question in these cases is not whether discrimination because of sexual orientation or gender identity *should be* outlawed. The question is *whether Congress did that in 1964*.

It indisputably did not.

* * *

I respectfully dissent.

JUSTICE KAVANAUGH, dissenting.

* * *

For the sake of argument, I will assume that firing someone because of their sexual orientation may, as a very literal matter, entail making a distinction based on sex. But to prevail in this case with their literalist approach, the plaintiffs must also establish one of two other points. The plaintiffs must establish that courts, when interpreting a statute, adhere to literal meaning rather than ordinary meaning. Or alternatively, the plaintiffs must establish that the ordinary meaning of "discriminate because of sex"—not just the literal meaning—encompasses sexual orientation discrimination. The plaintiffs fall short on both counts.

First, courts must follow ordinary meaning, not literal meaning. And courts must adhere to the ordinary meaning of phrases, not just the meaning of the words in a phrase.

There is no serious debate about the foundational interpretive principle that courts adhere to ordinary meaning, not literal meaning, when interpreting statutes. As Justice Scalia explained, "the good textualist is not a literalist." A. SCALIA, A MATTER OF INTERPRETATION 24 (1997). Or as Professor Eskridge stated: The "prime directive in statutory interpretation is to apply the meaning that a reasonable reader would derive from the text of the law," so that "for hard cases as well as easy ones, the ordinary meaning (or the 'everyday meaning' or the 'commonsense' reading) of the relevant statutory text is the anchor for statutory interpretation." W. ESKRIDGE, INTERPRETING LAW 33, 34–35 (2016) (footnote omitted). Or as Professor Manning put it, proper statutory interpretation asks "how a reasonable person, conversant with the relevant social and linguistic conventions, would read the text in context. This approach recognizes that the literal or dictionary definitions of words will often fail to account for settled nuances or background conventions that qualify the literal meaning of language and, in particular, of legal language." Manning, *The Absurdity Doctrine*, 116 HARV. L. REV. 2387, 2392–2393 (2003). Or as Professor Nelson wrote: No "mainstream judge is interested solely in the literal definitions of a statute's words." Nelson, *What Is Textualism?*, 91 VA. L. REV. 347, 376 (2005). The ordinary meaning that counts is the ordinary public meaning at the time of enactment—although in this case, that temporal principle matters little because the ordinary meaning of "discriminate because of sex" was the same in 1964 as it is now.

Judges adhere to ordinary meaning for two main reasons: rule of law and democratic accountability. A society governed by the rule of law must have laws that are known and understandable to the citizenry. And judicial adherence to ordinary meaning facilitates the democratic accountability of America's elected representatives for the laws they enact. Citizens and legislators must be able to ascertain the law by reading the words of the statute. Both the rule of law and democratic accountability badly suffer when a court adopts a hidden or obscure interpretation of the law, and not its ordinary meaning.

Consider a simple example of how ordinary meaning differs from literal meaning. A statutory ban on "vehicles in the park" would literally encompass a baby stroller. But no good judge would interpret the statute that way because the word "vehicle," in its ordinary meaning, does not encompass baby strollers.

The ordinary meaning principle is longstanding and well settled. Time and again, this Court has rejected literalism in favor of ordinary meaning. * * *

Those cases exemplify a deeply rooted principle: When there is a divide between the literal meaning and the ordinary meaning, courts must follow the ordinary meaning.

Next is a critical point of emphasis in this case. The difference between literal and ordinary meaning becomes especially important when—as in this case—judges consider phrases in statutes. (Recall that the shorthand version of the phrase at issue here is "discriminate because of sex.") Courts must heed the ordinary meaning of the phrase as a whole, not just the meaning of the words in the phrase. That is because a phrase may have a more precise or confined meaning than the literal meaning of the individual words in the phrase. Examples abound. An "American flag" could literally encompass a flag made in America, but in common parlance it denotes the Stars and Stripes. A "three-pointer" could literally include a field goal in football, but in common parlance, it is a shot from behind the arc in basketball. A "cold war" could literally mean any wintertime war, but in common parlance it signifies a conflict short of open warfare. A "washing machine" could literally refer to any machine used for washing any item, but in everyday speech it means a machine for washing clothes.

* * *

If the usual evidence indicates that a statutory phrase bears an ordinary meaning different from the literal strung-together definitions of the individual words in the phrase, we may not ignore or gloss over that discrepancy. "Legislation cannot sensibly be interpreted by stringing together dictionary synonyms of each word and proclaiming that, if the right example of the meaning of each is selected, the 'plain meaning' of the statute leads to a particular result. No theory of interpretation, including textualism itself, is premised on such an approach." 883 F.3d 100, 144, n. 7 (CA2 2018) (LYNCH, J., dissenting).

* * *

Second, in light of the bedrock principle that we must adhere to the ordinary meaning of a phrase, the question in this case boils down to the ordinary meaning of the phrase "discriminate because of sex." Does the ordinary meaning of that phrase encompass discrimination because of sexual orientation? The answer is plainly no.

On occasion, it can be difficult for judges to assess ordinary meaning. Not here. Both common parlance and common legal usage treat sex discrimination and sexual orientation discrimination as two distinct categories of discrimination—back in 1964 and still today.

As to common parlance, few in 1964 (or today) would describe a firing because of sexual orientation as a firing because of sex. As commonly understood, sexual orientation discrimination is distinct from, and not a form of, sex discrimination. The majority opinion acknowledges the common understanding, noting that the plaintiffs here probably did not tell their friends that they were fired because of their sex. Ante, at 16. That observation is clearly correct. In common parlance, Bostock and Zarda were fired because they were gay, not because they were men.

Contrary to the majority opinion's approach today, this Court has repeatedly emphasized that common parlance matters in assessing the ordinary meaning of a statute, because courts heed how "most people" "would have understood" the text of a statute when enacted. * * *

Consider the employer who has four employees but must fire two of them for financial reasons. Suppose the four employees are a straight man, a straight woman, a gay man, and a lesbian. The employer with animosity against women (animosity based on sex) will fire the two women. The employer with animosity against gays (animosity based on sexual orientation) will fire the gay man and the lesbian. Those are two distinct harms caused by two distinct biases that have two different outcomes. To treat one as a form of the other—as the majority opinion does—misapprehends common language, human psychology, and real life.

It also rewrites history. Seneca Falls was not Stonewall. The women's rights movement was not (and is not) the gay rights move

> **FYI**
>
> Seneca Falls is a reference to an 1848 convention in the town of Seneca Falls, New York, dedicated to women's rights. Stonewall is a reference to the 1969 protests and ensuing gay rights activism precipitated by New York City police raiding the Stonewall Inn, a gay club in Greenwich Village.

> ❓ Should these considerations of history and sociology matter to the interpretive process?

ment, although many people obviously support or participate in both. So to think that sexual orientation discrimination is just a form of sex discrimination is not just a mistake of language and psychology, but also a mistake of history and sociology.

Importantly, an overwhelming body of federal law reflects and reinforces the ordinary meaning and demonstrates that sexual orientation discrimination is distinct from, and not a form of, sex discrimination. Since enacting Title VII in 1964, Congress has never treated sexual orientation discrimination the same as, or as a form of, sex discrimination. Instead, Congress has consistently treated sex discrimination and sexual orientation discrimination as legally distinct categories of discrimination.

Many federal statutes prohibit sex discrimination, and many federal statutes also prohibit sexual orientation discrimination. But those sexual orientation statutes expressly prohibit sexual orientation discrimination in addition to expressly prohibiting sex discrimination. Every single one. To this day, Congress has never defined sex discrimination to encompass sexual orientation discrimination. Instead, when Congress wants to prohibit sexual orientation discrimination in addition to sex discrimination, Congress explicitly refers to sexual orientation discrimination.

* * *

Instead of a hard-earned victory won through the democratic process, today's victory is brought about by judicial dictate—judges latching on to a novel form of living literalism to rewrite ordinary meaning and remake American law. Under the Constitution and laws of the United States, this Court is the wrong body to change American law in that way. The Court's ruling "comes at a great cost to representative self-government." *Hively [v. Ivy Tech. Community College]*, 853 F. 3d [339,] 360 [(7th Cir. 2017)] (SYKES, J., dissenting). And the implications of this Court's usurpation of the legislative process will likely reverberate in unpredictable ways for years to come.

* * *

NOTES & QUESTIONS

1. Both Justice Gorsuch's majority opinion and the two dissenting opinions assert that they are bound by the text of section 703, yet they reach opposite conclusions about what it means in the context of this case. Why?

2. Justice Alito's dissent says that the majority decision "sails under a textualist flag" but (in a portion not excerpted above) "cannot be defended on textualist grounds." Why do you think he says that?

3. How relevant to what you view to be the correct resolution of this case is the question of whether the members of Congress who voted for Title VII would have intended or expected section 703 to cover the discrimination at issue here? Is "intended to cover" the same question as "expected to cover"? How relevant to your view of the correct resolution of this case is the question of what members of the *public* in 1964 would have thought? How about members of the public in 2020 (when the case was decided)?

4. Justice Kavanaugh argues in the final paragraph of our excerpt that the Court majority has usurped the legislative role, and Justice Alito asserts in his first paragraph that what the majority has done amounts to "legislation," and later that it is a "brazen" abuse of the judicial branch's responsibility to interpret statutes. Are they correct? Note that Justice Gorsuch explicitly and repeatedly declares just the opposite.

5. How significant to the analysis are the other congressional statutes, besides Title VII, that explicitly protect against sexual orientation discrimination in other contexts? What about Congress's failed attempts to amend Title VII to add "sexual orientation" to its employment discrimination prohibitions?

6. The Court's opinion makes several references to the phrase "ordinary public meaning." What do you think this phrase means? What role should "ordinary public meaning" have in interpreting statutes?

7. Justice Kavanaugh's dissent claims that the Court in fact has *not* relied on an "ordinary meaning" analysis. How do you explain this disagreement?

8.   Is either side conclusively correct about the semantic meaning of the phrase "because of such individual's . . . sex"? The majority uses what is in effect a comparative approach to the meaning of the statute. The majority says that firing a male employee who is attracted to a man, when the employer would not fire a female employee who is attracted to a man, is "because of . . . sex" because the employer is treating the male employee different from the female employee. But consider this: can't the employer just say it is firing the male employee because of the sex of *the person the employee is attracted to*, not because of the sex of the employee? And if so, the employer did not fire the employee because of, in the words of the statute, "such individual's [the employee's] . . . sex." Rather, it fired the employee because of *someone else's* sex! Is there any necessarily correct way to resolve this linguistically? For an argument that there isn't, see Anuj C. Desai, *Text is Not Enough*, 93 U. Colo. L. Rev. 1 (2022).

B. A Problem in Applying the Federal Sentencing Guidelines

DIY
Mandatory Minimum Sentences for Distributing LSD

In 1984, in an effort to standardize prison sentences for federal crimes, Congress established the federal Sentencing Commission to promulgate Sentencing Guidelines. As part of this effort, Congress later set mandatory minimum sentences for certain offenses. In particular, the sentencing scheme imposed upon drug dealers a mandatory minimum prison sentence based on the quantity of illegal drugs they had been convicted of distributing, typically depending on the weight of the illegal drugs. With respect to LSD, the Guidelines provided for a five-year minimum for distributing one gram of a "mixture or substance containing a detectable amount" of LSD, and a ten-year minimum for distributing ten grams. But LSD is typically purchased not by weight, but by the dose, with doses frequently contained on sheets of blotter paper or in sugar cubes. In determining whether a defendant is subject to a 5-year or 10-year mandatory minimum sentence, should the weight of the sugar cubes, blotter paper, or other carrier medium (for instance, orange juice) be included in determining the weight? This question repeatedly vexed the federal courts more than three decades ago. Take two minutes to collect your thoughts on this question and write down your response.

The Seventh Circuit, sitting *en banc*, issued a particularly interesting and divided decision on this issue, in which Judge Frank Easterbrook sought to resolve the interpretive problem from a Textualist perspective, while his colleague Richard Posner rejected that approach. Both judges are known as part of the "Chicago School" of jurisprudence that often relies on economic analysis and reasoning to help resolve cases. As you read each of their opinions, think about their contrasting approaches to the interpretive problem.

United States v. Marshall
908 F.2d 1312 (7th Cir. 1990)

EASTERBROOK, CIRCUIT JUDGE.

Two cases consolidated for decision in banc present [a question] concerning the application and constitutionality of the statute and sentencing guidelines that govern sales of lysergic acid diethylamide (LSD). Stanley J. Marshall was convicted after a bench trial and sentenced to 20 years' imprisonment for conspiring to distribute, and distributing, more than ten grams of LSD, enough for 11,751 doses. * * * Patrick Brumm, Richard L. Chapman, and John M. Schoenecker were convicted by a jury of selling ten sheets (1,000 doses) of paper containing LSD. Because the total weight of the paper and LSD was 5.7 grams, a five-year mandatory minimum applied. The district court sentenced Brumm to 60 months (the minimum), Schoenecker to 63 months, and Chapman to 96 months' imprisonment. All four defendants confine their arguments on appeal to questions concerning their sentences.

[The question we must resolve is whether] 21 U.S.C. § 841(b)(1)(A)(v) and (B)(v), which set mandatory minimum terms of imprisonment—five years for selling more than one gram of a "mixture or substance containing a detectable amount" of LSD, ten years for more than ten grams—exclude the weight of a carrier medium. * * *

According to the Sentencing Commission, the LSD in an average dose weighs 0.05 milligrams. Twenty thousand pure doses are a gram. But 0.05

mg is almost invisible, so LSD is distributed to retail customers in a carrier. Pure LSD is dissolved in a solvent such as alcohol and sprayed on paper or gelatin; alternatively the paper may be dipped in the solution. After the solvent evaporates, the paper or gel is cut into one-dose squares and sold by the square. Users swallow the squares or may drop them into a beverage, releasing the drug. Although the gelatin and paper are light, they weigh much more than the drug. Marshall's 11,751 doses weighed 113.32 grams; the LSD accounted for only 670.72 mg of this, not enough to activate the five-year mandatory minimum sentence, let alone the ten-year minimum. The ten sheets of blotter paper carrying the 1,000 doses Chapman and confederates sold weighed 5.7 grams; the LSD in the paper did not approach the one-gram threshold for a mandatory minimum sentence. This disparity between the weight of the pure LSD and the weight of LSD-plus-carrier underlies the defendants' arguments. * * *

If the carrier counts in the weight of the "mixture or substance containing a detectable amount" of LSD, some odd things may happen. Weight in the hands of distributors may exceed that of manufacturers and wholesalers. Big fish then could receive paltry sentences or small fish draconian ones. Someone who sold 19,999 doses of pure LSD (at 0.05 mg per dose) would escape the five-year mandatory minimum of § 841(b)(1)(B)(v) and be covered by § 841(b)(1)(C), which lacks a minimum term and has a maximum of "only" 20 years. Someone who sold a single hit of LSD dissolved in a tumbler of orange juice could be exposed to a ten-year mandatory minimum. Retailers could fall in or out of the mandatory terms depending not on the number of doses but on the medium: sugar cubes weigh more than paper, which weighs more than gelatin. One way to eliminate the possibility of such consequences is to say that the carrier is not a "mixture or substance containing a detectable amount" of the drug. Defendants ask us to do this.

Defendants' submission starts from the premise that the interaction of the statutory phrase "mixture or substance" with the distribution of LSD by the dose in a carrier creates a unique probability of surprise results. The premise may be unwarranted. The paper used to distribute LSD is light stuff, not the kind used to absorb ink. Chapman's 1,000 doses weighed about 0.16 ounces. More than 6,000 doses, even in blotter paper, weigh less than an ounce. Because the LSD in one dose weighs about 0.05 milligrams, the combination of LSD-plus-paper is about 110 times the weight of the LSD. The impregnated paper could be described as "0.9% LSD." Gelatin carrying LSD could be described as "2.5% LSD", if the weight for gelatin given in *United States v. McGeehan*, 824 F.2d 677, 680 (8th Cir.1987), is accurate.

This is by no means an unusual dilution rate for illegal drugs. Heroin sold on the street is 2% to 3% opiate and the rest filler. * * * Sometimes the mixture is even more dilute, approaching the dilution rate for LSD in blotter paper. * * * Heroin and crack cocaine, like LSD, are sold on the streets by the dose, although they are sold by weight higher in the distributional chain. All of the "designer drugs" and many of the opiates are sold by the dose, often conveniently packaged in pills. The Sentencing Commission lists MDA, PCP, psilocin, psilocybin, methaqualone, phenmetrazine, and amphetamines (regular and meth-) along with LSD as drugs sold by the dose in very dilute form. * * *

It is not possible to construe the words of § 841 to make the penalty turn on the net weight of the drug rather than the gross weight of carrier and drug. The statute speaks of "mixture or substance containing a detectable amount" of a drug. "Detectable amount" is the opposite of "pure"; the point of the statute is that the "mixture" is not to be converted to an equivalent amount of pure drug.

> This is a quintessential Textualist observation.

The structure of the statute reinforces this conclusion. The 10-year minimum applies to any person who possesses, with intent to distribute, "100 grams or more of phencyclidine (PCP) or 1 kilogram or more of a mixture or substance containing a detectable amount of phencyclidine (PCP)", § 841(b)(1)(A)(iv). Congress distinguished the pure drug from a "mixture or substance containing a detectable amount of" it. All drugs other than PCP are governed exclusively by the "mixture or substance" language. Even brute force cannot turn that language into a reference to pure LSD. Congress used the same "mixture or substance" language to describe heroin, cocaine, amphetamines, and many other drugs that are sold after being cut—sometimes as much as LSD. There is no sound basis on which to treat the words "substance or mixture containing a detectable amount of", repeated verbatim for every drug mentioned in § 841 except PCP, as different things for LSD and cocaine although the language is identical, while treating the "mixture or substance" language as meaning the same as the reference to pure PCP in 21 U.S.C. § 841(b)(1)(A)(iv) and (B)(iv).

Although the "mixture or substance" language shows that the statute cannot be limited to pure LSD, it does not necessarily follow that blotter paper is a "mixture or substance containing" LSD. That phrase cannot include all "carriers". One gram of crystalline LSD in a heavy glass bottle is still

> **?** Is Judge Easter-
> brook suggesting
> that he might have
> been willing to consider legis-
> lative history, if it had anything
> to say on the question?

only one gram of "statutory LSD". So is a gram of LSD being "carried" in a Boeing 747. How much mingling of the drug with something else is essential to form a "mixture or substance"? The legislative history is silent, but ordinary usage is indicative.

"Substance" may well refer to a chemical compound, or perhaps to a drug in a solvent. LSD does not react chemically with sugar, blotter paper, or gelatin, and none of these is a solvent. "Mixture" is more inclusive. Cocaine often is mixed with mannitol, quinine, or lactose. These white powders do not react, but it is common ground that a cocaine-mannitol mixture is a statutory "mixture."

LSD and blotter paper are not commingled in the same way as cocaine and lactose. What is the nature of their association? The possibility most favorable to defendants is that LSD sits on blotter paper as oil floats on water. Immiscible substances may fall outside the statutory definition of "mixture". The possibility does not assist defendants—not on this record, anyway. LSD is applied to paper in a solvent; after the solvent evaporates, a tiny quantity of LSD remains. Because the fibers absorb the alcohol, the LSD solidifies inside the paper rather than on it. You cannot pick a grain of LSD off the surface of the paper. Ordinary parlance calls the paper containing tiny crystals of LSD a mixture.

United States v. Rose, 881 F.2d 386 (7th Cir.1989), like every other appellate decision that has addressed the question, concludes that the carrier medium for LSD, like the "cut" for heroin and cocaine, is a "mixture or substance containing a detectable amount" of the drug. Although a chemist might be able to offer evidence bearing on the question whether LSD and blotter paper "mix" any more fully than do oil and water, the record contains no such evidence. Without knowing more of the chemistry than this record reveals, we adhere to the unanimous conclusion of the other courts of appeals that blotter paper treated with LSD is a "mixture or substance containing a detectable quantity of" LSD. * * *

POSNER, CIRCUIT JUDGE, joined by BAUER, CHIEF JUDGE, and CUMMINGS, WOOD JR., and CUDAHY, CIRCUIT JUDGES, dissenting.

* * * Based as it is on weight, the system [at issue] works well for drugs that are sold by weight; and ordinarily the weight quoted to the buyer is the

weight of the dilute form, although of course price will vary with purity. The dilute form is the product, and it is as natural to punish its purveyors according to the weight of the product as it is to punish moonshiners by the weight or volume of the moonshine they sell rather than by the weight of the alcohol contained in it. So, for example, under Florida law it is a felony to possess one or more gallons of moonshine, and a misdemeanor to possess less than one gallon, regardless of the alcoholic content. Fla.Stat. §§ 561.01, 562.451.

LSD, however, is sold to the consumer by the dose; it is not cut, diluted, or mixed with something else. Moreover, it is incredibly light. An average dose of LSD weighs .05 milligrams, which is less than two millionths of an ounce. To ingest something that small requires swallowing something much larger. Pure LSD in granular form is first diluted by being dissolved, usually in alcohol, and then a quantity of the solution containing one dose of LSD is sprayed or eyedropped on a sugar cube, or on a cube of gelatin, or, as in the cases before us, on an inch-square section of "blotter" paper. * * * After the solution is applied to the carrier medium, the alcohol or other solvent evaporates, leaving an invisible (and undiluted) spot of pure LSD on the cube or blotter paper. The consumer drops the cube or the piece of paper into a glass of water, or orange juice, or some other beverage, causing the LSD to dissolve in the beverage, which is then drunk. * * * But a quart of orange juice containing one dose of LSD is not more, in any relevant sense, than a pint of juice containing the same one dose, and it would be loony to punish the purveyor of the quart more heavily than the purveyor of the pint. It would be like basing the punishment for

> Be sure to think about the potential sentencing difference that would arise from a dose of LSD in a quart of orange juice rather than in a glass of orange juice.

selling cocaine on the combined weight of the cocaine and of the vehicle (plane, boat, automobile, or whatever) used to transport it or the syringe used to inject it or the pipe used to smoke it. The blotter paper, sugar cubes, etc. are the vehicles for conveying LSD to the consumer.

The weight of the carrier is vastly greater than that of the LSD, as well as irrelevant to its potency. There is no comparable disparity between the pure and the mixed form (if that is how we should regard LSD on blotter paper or other carrier medium) with respect to the other drugs in section 841, with the illuminating exception of PCP. There Congress specified alternative weights, for the drug itself and for the substance or mixture containing the drug. For example, the five-year minimum sentence for a seller of PCP requires the sale of either ten grams of the drug itself or one hundred grams of a substance or mixture containing the drug. 21 U.S.C. § 841(b)(1)(B)(iv).

Ten sheets of blotter paper, containing a thousand doses of LSD, weigh almost six grams. The LSD itself weighs less than a hundredth as much. If the thousand doses are on gelatin cubes instead of sheets of blotter paper, the total weight is less, but it is still more than two grams * * *, which is forty times the weight of the LSD. In both cases, if the carrier plus the LSD constitutes the relevant "substance or mixture" (the crucial "if" in this case), the dealer is subject to the minimum mandatory sentence of five years. One of the defendants before us (Marshall) sold almost 12,000 doses of LSD on blotter paper. This subjected him to the ten-year minimum, and the Guidelines then took over and pushed him up to twenty years. Since it takes 20,000 doses of LSD to equal a gram, Marshall would not have been subject to even the five-year mandatory minimum had he sold the LSD in its pure form. And a dealer who sold fifteen times the number of doses as Marshall—180,000—would not be subject to the ten-year mandatory minimum sentence if he sold the drug in its pure form, because 180,000 doses is only nine grams.

At the other extreme, if Marshall were not a dealer at all but dropped a square of blotter paper containing a single dose of LSD into a glass of orange juice and sold it to a friend at cost (perhaps 35 cents), he would be subject to the ten-year minimum. The juice with LSD dissolved in it would be the statutory mixture or substance containing a detectable amount of the illegal drug and it would weigh more than ten grams (one ounce is about 35 grams, and the orange juice in a glass of orange juice weighs several ounces). So a person who sold one dose of LSD might be subject to the ten-year mandatory minimum sentence while a dealer who sold 199,999 doses in pure form would be subject only to the five-year minimum. Defendant Dean sold 198 doses, crowded onto one sheet of blotter paper: this subjected him to the five-year mandatory minimum, too, since the ensemble weighed slightly more than a gram. * * *

All this seems crazy but we must consider whether Congress might have had a reason for wanting to key the severity of punishment for selling LSD to the weight of the carrier rather than to the number of doses or to some reasonable proxy for dosage (as weight is, for many drugs). The only one suggested is that it might be costly to determine the weight of the LSD in the blotter paper, sugar cube, etc., because it is so light! That merely underscores the irrationality of basing the punishment for selling this drug on weight rather than on dosage. But in fact the weight is reported in every case I have seen, so apparently it can be determined readily enough; it has to be determined in any event, to permit a purity adjustment under the Guidelines. If the weight of the LSD is difficult to determine, the difficulty is easily overcome by basing punishment on the number of doses, which makes much more sense in any event. To base punishment on the weight of the carrier medium makes about as much sense as basing punishment on the weight of the defendant. * * *

This is a quilt the pattern whereof no one has been able to discern. The legislative history is silent, and since even the Justice Department cannot explain the why of the punishment scheme that it is defending, the most plausible inference is that Congress

> What should an interpreting court do when faced with a "crazy quilt" statute?

simply did not realize how LSD is sold. The inference is reinforced by the statutory treatment of PCP. * * *

That irrationality is magnified when we compare the sentences for people who sell other drugs prohibited by 21 U.S.C. § 841. Marshall, remember, sold fewer than 12,000 doses and was sentenced to twenty years. Twelve thousand doses sounds like a lot, but to receive a comparable sentence for selling heroin Marshall would have had to sell ten kilograms, which would yield between one and two million doses. * * * To receive a comparable sentence for selling cocaine he would have had to sell fifty kilograms, which would yield anywhere from 325,000 to five million doses. * * * While the corresponding weight is lower for crack—half a kilogram—this still translates into 50,000 doses. * * *

Well, what if anything can we judges do about this mess? The answer lies in the shadow of a jurisprudential disagreement that is not less important

> Here Judge Posner is cueing his own brief explication in the paragraphs that follow of the benefits of what he calls "pragmatic" interpretation, as contrasted with Textualism, or what he calls "positivist" interpretation.

by virtue of being unavowed by most judges. It is the disagreement between the severely positivistic view that the content of law is exhausted in clear, explicit, and definite enactments by or under express delegation from legislatures, and the natural lawyer's or legal pragmatist's view that the practice of interpretation and the general terms of the Constitution (such as

> **!** Note that here Judge Posner is staking out a judicial role that involves more than just seeking to effectuate what the enacting Congress intended.

"equal protection of the laws") authorize judges to enrich positive law with the moral values and practical concerns of civilized society. Judges who in other respects have seemed quite similar, such as Holmes and Cardozo, have taken opposite sides of this issue. Neither approach is entirely satisfactory. The first buys political neutrality and a type of objectivity at the price of substantive injustice, while the second buys justice in the individual case at the price of considerable uncertainty and, not infrequently, judicial willfulness. It is no wonder that our legal system oscillates between the approaches. The positivist view, applied unflinchingly to this case, commands the affirmance of prison sentences that are exceptionally harsh by the standards of the modern Western world, dictated by an accidental, unintended scheme of punishment nevertheless implied by the words (taken one by one) of the relevant enactments. The natural law or pragmatist view leads to a freer interpretation, one influenced by norms of equal treatment; and let us explore the interpretive possibilities here. One is to interpret "mixture or substance containing a detectable amount of [LSD]" to exclude the carrier medium – the blotter paper, sugar or gelatin cubes, and orange juice or other beverage. That is the course we rejected in *United States v. Rose* * * *, as have the other circuits. I wrote *Rose*, but I am no longer confident that its literal interpretation of the statute, under which the blotter paper, cubes, etc. are "substances" that "contain" LSD, is inevitable. The blotter paper, etc. are better viewed, I now think, as carriers, like the package in which a kilo of cocaine comes wrapped or the bottle in which a fifth of liquor is sold.

Interpreted to exclude the carrier, the punishment schedule for LSD would make perfectly good sense; it would not warp the statutory design. The comparison with heroin and cocaine is again illuminating. The statute imposes the five-year mandatory minimum sentence on anyone who sells a substance or mixture containing a hundred grams of heroin, equal to 10,000 to 20,000 doses. One gram of pure LSD, which also would trigger the five-year minimum, yields 20,000 doses. The comparable figures for cocaine are 3250 to 50,000 doses, placing LSD in about the middle. So Congress may have wanted to base punishment for the sale of LSD on the weight of the pure drug after all, using one and ten grams of the pure drug to trigger the five-year and ten-year minima (and corresponding maxima—twenty years and forty years). This interpretation leaves "substance or mixture containing" without a referent, so far as LSD is concerned. But we must remember that Congress used the identical term in each subsection that specifies the quantity of a drug that subjects the seller to the designated minimum and maximum punishments. In thus automatically including the same term in each subsection, Congress did not necessarily affirm that, for each and every drug covered by the statute, a substance or mixture containing the drug must be found.

The flexible interpretation that I am proposing is decisively strengthened by the constitutional objection to basing punishment of LSD offenders on the weight of the carrier medium rather than on the weight of the LSD. Courts often do interpretive handsprings to avoid having even to decide a constitutional question. * * * In doing so they expand, very questionably in my view, the effective scope of the Constitution, creating a constitutional penumbra in which statutes wither, shrink, are deformed. A better case for flexible interpretation is presented when the alternative is to nullify Congress's action: when in other words there is not merely a constitutional question about, but a constitutional barrier to, the statute when interpreted literally. * * * This is such a case.

* * * The literal interpretation adopted by the majority is not inevitable. All interpretation is contextual. The words of the statute—interpreted against a background that includes a constitutional norm of equal

> What does Judge Posner mean by this?

treatment, a (closely related) constitutional commitment to rationality, an evident failure by both Congress and the Sentencing Commission to consider how LSD is actually produced, distributed, and sold, and an equally evident failure by the same two bodies to consider the interaction between heavy mandatory minimum sentences and the Sentencing Guidelines—will bear an interpretation that distinguishes between the carrier vehicle of the illegal drug and the substance or mixture containing a detectable amount of the drug. The punishment of the crack dealer is not determined by the weight of the glass tube in which he sells the crack; we should not lightly attribute to Congress a purpose of punishing the dealer in LSD according to the weight of the LSD carrier. We should not make Congress's handiwork an embarrassment to the members of Congress and to us.

[The dissenting opinion of JUDGE CUMMINGS is omitted.]

NOTES & QUESTIONS

1. What clues to the interpretive philosophies of these two prominent Seventh Circuit judges can you identify in their opinions?

2. Beyond labeling their philosophies, what else can you say about the underlying reasons that seem to animate these contrasting interpretations?

3. Judge Easterbrook agrees that the phrase "mixture or substance" is not self-defining. How does he decide what the phrase does and does not include?

4. What anomalies does the majority's interpretation potentially create?

5. Do any of these anomalies raise the specter of an absurd result?

6. In *Chapman v. United States*, 500 U.S. 453 (1991), a divided Supreme Court affirmed the Seventh Circuit's decision in *Marshall*.

7. At this point in our consideration of the problems of statutory interpretation, what do you think the role of the courts should be with respect to a problem like the issue in *Marshall*?

Test Your Understanding

To assess your understanding of the material in this chapter, click here to take a quiz.

18

An Eye to Purpose in Interpretation

Key Concepts

- Legislative intent
- Legislative purpose
- Legislative history
- Affirmative action
- Multiple or conflicting legislative purposes

Chapter Summary

This chapter focuses on ways in which sources of under- standing outside the text of a statute might clarify the stat- ute's meaning, if those sources help illuminate the enacting legislature's intended purpose. As one way of reflecting on the potential value of knowing something about the pur- pose of a statute, we consider a famous problem involving the classification of fruits and vegetables in a 19th century tariff statute, with respect to which very little actually was known about its purpose. A second case addresses another interpretive issue involving Title VII of the Civil Rights Act of 1964, namely, whether the Act's prohibition of racial discrimination in employment prohibited a private employer from engaging in voluntary "affirma- tive action" efforts to rectify historical imbalances in the racial composition of its workforce. A divided Supreme Court concluded that although the text of the Act could be read to prohibit the affirmative action plan, such a reading would be antithetical to the underlying purpose of Title VII. But dissenters argued that there was more than one way of describing the purpose of Title VII.

The previous chapter presented two problems rich with Textualist approaches to interpretation. This chapter will consider two interpretive problems through a more Purposivist approach. Searching for the "spirit" of the law as a means for resolving interpretive problems, as the Supreme Court did in the *Holy Trinity* case, is certainly one (though not the only) way of being guided by legislative purpose.

But is the result of doing so greater *judicial* willfulness? Or is it instead the better effectuation of the *legislative* will? This is a critical question to consider.

Before we proceed, note that interpretive theorists sometimes distinguish between legislative intent, or how the enacting legislature intended the words of its statutory text to apply, and legislative purpose, an often broader conception of the animating motive behind the legislation. For present purposes, we will lump Purposivism and Intentionalism together. Later, in Chapter 19, we will then offer a few thoughts about their differences.

A. The Potential Significance of Knowing Legislative Intent or Purpose

Textualists argue that only the enacted text is law and therefore that any evidence about the enacting legislature's intent should come through the legislature's chosen text. But might circumstances arise in which extra-textual evidence of legislative intent would also be helpful in resolving an interpretive problem? Once again, we begin with an exercise from a real statute.

DIY
Is the Tomato a Fruit or a Vegetable?

 A produce company imported tomatoes from the West Indies in the spring of 1886. The federal customs officer at the Port of New York assessed and collected import duties on the tomatoes under a provision of the Tariff Act of March 3, 1883, a sweeping tariff measure that imposed varying duties on hundreds of import goods. One of these provisions imposed a ten percent duty on "vegetables in their natural state, or in salt or brine, not specially enumerated or provided for in this act." The produce company paid this tariff duty on its tomatoes under protest, claiming that the tomatoes instead should have been classified under the "Free List" section of the same act, a provision that exempted from import duties a host of items, including "fruits, green, ripe, or dried, not specially enumerated or provided for in this act." Tomatoes were not specifically enumerated or provided for in any provision of the act. The company then filed a court action seeking to recover the ten percent duties it had paid on the tomatoes.

How should the court resolve this issue? Are tomatoes "fruits" or "vegetables"? Does it seem like there is an easy answer to this question? If so, then we encourage you to think about any counterarguments to your intuition, whatever it might be. Assume that the text of the Tariff Act itself offers no other help. Take five minutes to ponder these questions and to write down your thoughts.

Once you have thought about these questions, ask yourself one more thing: Assuming for a moment that you want to determine legislative intent, what other information might be helpful? (We will revisit this interpretive problem at the end of this chapter.)

Only after you have pondered this problem on your own, consider the following possible responses to the final question above. Perhaps the most obvious possibility is to want to conduct a bit of historical research about the origins of the tariff statute. One very specific question might be "Did the Congress that enacted this tariff intend for the measure to treat tomatoes as a type of fruit, or instead as a type of vegetable?" A Purposivist interpreter might choose to explore and examine a variety of sources of information to resolve this question. For instance, other provisions of the statute, without directly answering the question, might nonetheless shed light on whether Congress intended terms like "fruits" and "vegetables" to have a technical, scientific definition, or instead an ordinary produce market definition. Or legislators involved in the passage of the measure, during the course of its enactment, might have said something in a committee report or a legislative debate specifically about tomatoes, or about the meaning of the terms "fruit" and "vegetable." Or perhaps during consideration of the measure participants in the legislative process other than Members of Congress might have behaved in ways that provided information potentially relevant to the question, for instance if trade groups active in the issue had assumed in testimony before a congressional committee that tomatoes were fruits. The term "legislative history" is typically used to identify these extra-textual sources of information.

A broader question, not specifically focused on tomatoes but still potentially helpful in classifying them, might be "Why did Congress impose high tariffs on vegetables, but entirely exempt fruits?" If the answer to this question was that the tariffs were intended to protect certain domestic agricultural producers, that answer might shed light on how to classify tomatoes for purposes of the tariff statute. But if Congress instead was in fact attempting to distinguish between different geographic regions from which various agricultural products originated, that factor could differently influence how a Purposivist would construe the statute for purposes of classifying tomatoes.

Yet even if the interpreter can find evidence in the legislative history that sheds light on the enacting legislature's intended meaning, that does not answer the normative question of whether it is appropriate for the interpreter to go about interpreting in this way. Textualists argue that it is never (or rarely) appropriate to rely on legislative evidence outside the enacted text to determine the textual meaning. They object to searching for legislative intent evidence in legislative history materials outside the statute in part because this evidence can often be manipulated and may not be reliable or truly reflect the will of the legislature as a body. Instead, Textualists may look to places within the text, such as a statement of purpose section, or a statutory preface, to glean more information about the legislative intent.

Another argument against seeking to find the purpose behind a statute is that the enacting legislature may not have had one single purpose. The following case provides a possible example of this difficulty, which arose in an early interpretation of Title VII of the Civil Rights Act.

B. Affirmative Action Under Title VII of The Civil Rights Act of 1964

As you know from the previous chapter, the several different titles of the Civil Rights Act of 1964 prohibit discrimination in voting, in places of public accommodation, in state and local government programs, in schools, by recipients of federal funds, and in employment. Title VII is the title concerning employment. It contains the following provisions, among many others:

Section 703:

(a) Employer practices

It shall be an unlawful employment practice for an employer—

(1) to fail or refuse to hire or to discharge any individual, or otherwise to discriminate against any individual with respect to his compensation, terms, conditions, or privileges of employment, because of such individual's race, color, religion, sex, or national origin; or

(2) to limit, segregate, or classify his employees or applicants for employment in any way which would deprive or tend to deprive any individual of employ-

ment opportunities or otherwise adversely affect his status as an employee, because of such individual's race, color, religion, sex, or national origin.

. . .

(d) Training programs

It shall be an unlawful employment practice for any employer, labor organization, or joint labor-management committee controlling apprenticeship or other training or retraining, including on-the-job training programs to discriminate against any individual because of his race, color, religion, sex, or national origin in admission to, or employment in, any program established to provide apprenticeship or other training.

. . .

(j) Preferential treatment on account of existing number or percentage imbalance

Nothing contained in this subchapter shall be interpreted to require any employer, employment agency, labor organization, or joint labor-management committee subject to this subchapter to grant preferential treatment to any individual or to any group because of the race, color, religion, sex, or national origin of such individual or group on account of an imbalance which may exist with respect to the total number or percentage of persons of any race, color, religion, sex, or national origin employed by any employer, referred or classified for employment by any employment agency or labor organization, admitted to membership or classified by any labor organization, or admitted to, or employed in, any apprenticeship or other training program, in comparison with the total number or percentage of persons of such race, color, religion, sex, or national origin in any community, State, section, or other area, or in the available work force in any community, State, section, or other area.

DIY
Does Affirmative Action in Employment Violate Title VII?

Kaiser Aluminum & Chemical Corporation (Kaiser) operated a plant in Gramercy, Louisiana. The plant had various categories of employees, including "craftworkers." Until 1974, Kaiser had hired as craftworkers only persons with prior craft experience, something available to very few

Black Americans at the time. Not surprisingly, the result was that only 5 out of 273 (1.83%) of the craftworkers at the Gramercy plant were Black, despite a surrounding population that was approximately 40% Black. This disparity left Kaiser worried that it could be vulnerable to an unlawful discrimination lawsuit under section 703(a) of Title VII (above), as the Supreme Court had recently construed that section in the case of *Griggs v. Duke Power*, 401 U.S. 424 (1971).

In 1974, Kaiser and United Steelworkers of America (USWA) reached a collective bargaining agreement in which Kaiser agreed to establish a training program to train some of its unskilled production workers for craftworker positions. Trainees were to be selected by seniority, except that 50% of the trainee positions were to be reserved for Kaiser's Black employees until their proportion in the craftworker ranks matched their proportion in the local labor force.

During the first year of the training program, seven Black and six white production workers were selected as trainees at Kaiser. Several white production workers with greater seniority than all the Black trainees were denied trainee positions. One of these white Kaiser employees filed a lawsuit against Kaiser and USWA alleging that the training program discriminated against him in violation of section 703 (a) and (d).

Before reading how the Supreme Court resolved the case, decide whether you think the Kaiser-USWA plan is permissible *under the statute*. Take at least ten minutes to think about how an effort to understand and further the purpose of Title VII might affect the analysis of *whether the terms of section 703 prohibit a **voluntary**, **temporary** affirmative action program adopted by a **private** employer*. (In the preceding sentence's italicized statement of the issue, each of the highlighted words could have significance.) Make some written notes about these questions:

1.   Prior to Title VII, what ability would a private employer have had to adopt a preferential training program?

2.   What do you think the purpose of Title VII is, as it relates to the lawfulness of a training program like Kaiser's?

3.   Does the text of Title VII help demonstrate this purpose? Look first at 703(d) and at 703(a). After you have read them, take a look at 703(j). The white Kaiser employees are ultimately asking the court to interpret 703(d), but does 703(j) tell you anything else about the purpose of Title VII?

4.   What does the word "discriminate," as used in Title VII in 1964, mean? Does it mean the same thing today? In 1974?

Only once you have put your ten minutes to good use, go on and read the following case excerpt.

United Steelworkers of America v. Weber
443 U.S. 193 (1979)

Mr. Justice Brennan delivered the opinion of the Court.

Challenged here is the legality of an affirmative action plan—[the Kaiser-USWA training program,] collectively bargained by an employer and a union—that reserves for black employees 50% of the openings in an in-plant craft-training program until the percentage of black craftworkers in the plant is commensurate with the percentage of blacks in the local labor force. The question for decision is whether Congress, in Title VII of the Civil Rights Act of 1964, 78 Stat. 253, as amended, 42 U.S.C. 2000e et seq., left employers and unions in the private sector free to take such race-conscious steps to eliminate manifest racial imbalances in traditionally segregated job categories. [The Circuit Court held that Title VII prohibited the Kaiser-USWA plan.] We hold that Title VII does not prohibit such race-conscious affirmative action plans.

* * *

II

We emphasize at the outset the narrowness of our inquiry. Since the Kaiser-USWA plan does not involve state action, this case does not present an alleged violation of the Equal Protection Clause of the Fourteenth Amendment. Further, since the Kaiser-USWA plan was adopted voluntarily, we are not concerned with what Title VII requires or with what a court might order to remedy a past proved violation of the Act. The only question before us is the narrow statutory issue of whether Title VII forbids private employers and unions from voluntarily agreeing upon bona fide affirmative action plans that accord racial preferences in the manner and for the purpose provided in the Kaiser-USWA plan. That question was expressly left open in *McDonald v. Santa Fe Trail Transp. Co.*, 427 U.S. 273, 281 n. 8 (1976), which held, in a case not involving affirmative action, that Title VII protects whites as well as blacks from certain forms of racial discrimination.

Respondent argues that Congress intended in Title VII to prohibit all race-conscious affirmative action plans. Respondent's argument rests upon a literal interpretation of 703 (a) and (d) of the Act. Those sections make it unlawful to "discriminate. . .because of. . .race" in hiring and in the selection of apprentices for training programs. Since, the argument runs, *McDonald v. Santa Fe Trail Transp. Co., supra*, settled that Title VII forbids discrimination against whites as well as blacks, and since the Kaiser-USWA affirmative action plan operates to discriminate against white employees solely because they are white, it follows that the Kaiser-USWA plan violates Title VII.

FYI Note that by the time the Court was hearing the *Weber* case, it had already held in *McDonald* that Title VII prohibited discrimination not only against Black employees but also against white employees. That gave the *Weber* plaintiffs a basis to think they could invalidate the affirmative action plan.

Respondent's argument is not without force. But it overlooks the significance of the fact that the Kaiser-USWA plan is an affirmative action plan voluntarily adopted by private parties to eliminate traditional patterns of racial segregation. In this context respondent's reliance upon a literal construction of 703 (a) and (d) and upon *McDonald* is misplaced. See *McDonald v. Santa Fe Trail Transp. Co.*, supra, at 281 n. 8. It is a "familiar rule, that a thing may be within the letter of the statute and yet not within the statute, because not within its spirit, nor within the intention of its makers." *Holy Trinity Church v. United States*, 143 U.S. 457, 459 (1892). The prohibition against racial discrimination in 703 (a) and (d) of Title VII must therefore be read against the background of the legislative history of Title VII and the historical context from which the Act arose. Examination

The first sentence of this paragraph is acknowledging the strength of the "literal" interpretation it had described in the previous paragraph. (Does this remind you of anything in the Court's *Holy Trinity* decision?)

But the Court is preparing to dismiss the literal interpretation on the basis of both legislative history and context.

of those sources makes clear that an interpretation of the sections that forbade all race-conscious affirmative action would "bring about an end completely at variance with the purpose of the statute" and must be reject-ed. *United States v. Public Utilities Comm'n*, 345 U.S. 295, 315 (1953). * * *

Congress' primary concern in enacting the prohibition against racial discrimination in Title VII of the Civil Rights Act of 1964 was with "the plight of the Negro in our economy." 110 Cong. Rec. 6548 (1964) (remarks of Sen. Humphrey). Before 1964, blacks were largely relegated to "unskilled and semi-skilled jobs." *Ibid.* (remarks of Sen. Humphrey); *id.*, at 7204 (remarks of Sen.

> This paragraph be-gins an extended discussion of a number of pieces of the "legis-lative history" of Title VII. Take note of how many different pieces the Court compiles.

Clark); *id.*, at 7379–7380 (remarks of Sen. Kennedy). Because of automation the number of such jobs was rapidly decreasing. See *id.*, at 6548 (remarks of Sen. Humphrey); *id.*, at 7204 (remarks of Sen. Clark). As a consequence, "the relative position of the Negro worker [was] steadily worsening. In 1947 the nonwhite unemployment rate was only 64 percent higher than the white rate; in 1962 it was 124 percent higher." *Id.*, at 6547 (remarks of Sen. Humphrey). See also *id.*, at 7204 (remarks of Sen. Clark). Congress considered this a serious social problem. As Senator Clark told the Senate:

> The rate of Negro unemployment has gone up consistently as compared with white unemployment for the past 15 years. This is a social malaise and a social situation which we should not toler-ate. That is one of the principal reasons why the bill should pass.

Id., at 7220.

Congress feared that the goals of the Civil Rights Act – the integration of blacks into the mainstream of American society – could not be achieved unless this trend were reversed. And Congress recognized that that would not be possible unless blacks were able to secure jobs "which have a future." *Id.*, at 7204 (remarks of Sen. Clark). See also *id.*, at 7379–7380 (remarks of Sen. Kennedy). As Senator Humphrey explained to the Senate:

> What good does it do a Negro to be able to eat in a fine restaurant if he cannot afford to pay the bill? What good does it do him to be accepted in a hotel that is too expensive for his modest income? How can a Negro child be motivated to take full advantage of integrated educational facilities if he has no hope of getting a job where he can use that education?

Id., at 6547.

> Without a job, one cannot afford public convenience and accommodations. Income from employment may be necessary to further a man's education, or that of his children. If his children have no hope of getting a good job, what will motivate them to take advantage of educational opportunities?

Id., at 6552.

These remarks echoed President Kennedy's original message to Congress upon the introduction of the Civil Rights Act in 1963. "There is little value in a Negro's obtaining the right to be admitted to hotels and restaurants if he has no cash in his pocket and no job." 109 Cong. Rec. 11159.

Accordingly, it was clear to Congress that "[t]he crux of the problem [was] to open employment opportunities for Negroes in occupations which have been traditionally closed to them," 110 Cong. Rec. 6548 (1964) (remarks of Sen. Humphrey), and it was to this problem that Title VII's prohibition against racial discrimination in employment was primarily addressed.

It plainly appears from the House Report accompanying the Civil Rights Act that Congress did not intend wholly to prohibit private and voluntary affirmative action efforts as one method of solving this problem. The Report provides:

> No bill can or should lay claim to eliminating all of the causes and consequences of racial and other types of discrimination against minorities. There is reason to believe, however, that national leadership provided by the enactment of Federal legislation dealing with the most troublesome problems *will create an atmosphere conducive to voluntary or local resolution of other forms of discrimination.*

H. R. Rep. No. 914, 88th Cong., 1st Sess., pt. 1, p. 18 (1963). (Emphasis supplied.)

Given this legislative history, we cannot agree with respondent that Congress intended to prohibit the private sector from taking effective steps to accomplish the goal that Congress designed Title VII to achieve. The very statutory words intended as a spur or catalyst to cause "employers and unions to self-examine and to self-evaluate their employment practices and to endeavor to eliminate, so far as possible, the last vestiges of an unfortunate and ignominious page in this country's history," *Albemarle Paper Co. v. Moody*, 422 U.S. 405, 418 (1975), cannot be interpreted as an absolute prohibition against all private, voluntary, race-conscious affirmative action efforts to hasten the elimination of such vestiges. It would be ironic indeed if a law triggered by a Nation's concern over centuries of racial injustice and intended to improve the lot of those who had "been excluded from the American dream for so long," 110 Cong. Rec. 6552 (1964) (remarks of Sen. Humphrey), constituted the first legislative prohibition of all voluntary, private, race-conscious efforts to abolish traditional patterns of racial segregation and hierarchy.

Our conclusion is further reinforced by examination of the language and legislative history of 703(j) of Title VII. Opponents of Title VII raised two related arguments against the bill. First, they argued that the Act would be interpreted to require employers with racially imbalanced work forces to grant preferential treatment to racial minorities in order to integrate. Second, they argued that employers with racially imbalanced work forces would grant preferential treatment to racial minorities, even if not required to do so by the Act. See 110 Cong. Rec. 8618–8619 (1964) (remarks of Sen. Sparkman). Had Congress meant to prohibit all race-conscious affirmative action, as respondent urges, it easily could have answered both objections by providing that Title VII would not require or permit racially preferential integration efforts. But Congress did not choose such a course. Rather, Congress added 703(j) which addresses only the first objection. The section provides that nothing contained in Title VII "shall be interpreted to require any employer. . .to grant preferential treatment. . .to any group because of the race. . .of such. . .group on account of" a de facto racial imbalance in the employer's work force. The section does not state that "nothing in Title VII shall be interpreted to permit" voluntary affirmative efforts to correct racial imbalances. The natural inference is that Congress chose not to forbid all voluntary race-conscious affirmative action.

The reasons for this choice are evident from the legislative record. Title VII could not have been enacted into law without substantial support from legislators in both Houses who traditionally resisted federal regulation of private business. Those legislators demanded as a price for their support that "management prerogatives, and union freedoms. . .be left undisturbed to the greatest extent possible." H. R. Rep. No. 914, 88th Cong., 1st Sess., pt. 2, p. 29 (1963). Section 703(j) was proposed by Senator Dirksen to allay any fears that the Act might be interpreted in such a way as to upset this compromise. The section was designed to prevent 703 of Title VII from being interpreted in such a way as to lead to undue "Federal Government interference with private businesses because of some Federal employee's ideas about racial balance or racial imbalance." 110 Cong. Rec. 14314 (1964) (remarks of Sen. Miller). See also *id.*, at 9881 (remarks of Sen. Allott); *id.*, at 10520 (remarks of Sen. Carlson) *id.*, at 11471 (remarks of Sen. Javits); *id.*, at 12817 (remarks of Sen. Dirksen). Clearly, a prohibition against all voluntary, race-conscious, affirmative action efforts would disserve these ends. Such a prohibition would augment the powers of the Federal Government and diminish traditional management prerogatives while at the same time impeding attainment of the ultimate statutory goals. In view of this legislative history and in view of Congress' desire to avoid undue federal regulation of private businesses, use of the word "require" rather than the phrase "require or permit" in 703 (j) fortifies the conclusion that Congress did not intend to limit traditional business freedom to such a degree as to prohibit all voluntary, race-conscious affirmative action.

We therefore hold that Title VII's prohibition in 703 (a) and (d) against racial discrimination does not condemn all private, voluntary, race-conscious affirmative action plans.

III

We need not today define in detail the line of demarcation between permissible and impermissible affirmative action plans. It suffices to hold that the challenged Kaiser-USWA affirmative action plan falls on the permissible side of the line. The purposes of the plan mirror those of the statute. Both were designed to break down old patterns of racial segregation and hierarchy. Both were structured to "open employment opportunities for Negroes in occupations which have been traditionally closed to them." 110 Cong. Rec. 6548 (1964) (remarks of Sen. Humphrey).

At the same time, the plan does not unnecessarily trammel the interests of the white employees. The plan does not require the discharge of white workers and their replacement with new black hirees. Nor does the plan create an absolute bar to the advancement of white employees; half of those trained in the program will be white. Moreover, the plan is a temporary measure; it is not intended to maintain racial balance, but simply to eliminate a manifest racial imbalance. Preferential selection of craft trainees at the Gramercy plant will end as soon as the percentage of black skilled craftworkers in the Gramercy plant approximates the percentage of blacks in the local labor force.

We conclude, therefore, that the adoption of the Kaiser-USWA plan for the Gramercy plant falls within the area of discretion left by Title VII to the private sector voluntarily to adopt affirmative action plans designed to eliminate conspicuous racial imbalance in traditionally segregated job categories. Accordingly, the judgment of the Court of Appeals for the Fifth Circuit is

Reversed.

[The concurring opinion of Justice Blackmun, and the dissenting opinions of Chief Justice Burger and Justice Rehnquist, are omitted here.]

> Excerpts of Justice Blackmun's con- **FYI** currence in this case are included in Chapter 27 (pp. 668–673) below, as an example of "pragmatic" interpretation. Justice Rehnquist's dissent is described in Note 4 immediately below.

NOTES & QUESTIONS

1. What does Justice Brennan's opinion identify as the congressional purpose of Title VII?

2. How does the language of section 703 support this purpose? How does it detract from it?

3. What parts of the "legislative history"—in other words the statements from committee reports and individual legislators' floor speeches—are most helpful to Justice Brennan's analysis?

4. Justice Rehnquist (who was an Associate Justice at the time of *Weber*) wrote a long and impassioned dissent, joined by Chief Justice Burger, taking a different view of the purpose of the statute. He argued both that the language of section 703(a) and 703(d) on its face prohibited the training program at issue, because the program differentiated between employees on the basis of their race, and that the purpose of Title VII also prohibited the training program, because the statute's purpose was *to eliminate race-based distinctions in employment opportunities*. In support of his purpose argument, he included his own extensive presentation of statements from committee reports and floor speeches. Furthermore, he found in many of these legislative history materials what he regarded as specific intent evidence that the enacting Congress fully intended to prohibit all race-based distinctions in employment. What do you make of these conflicting claims about the purpose of Title VII?

5.   Now consider how your own DIY reasoning compares. Does your view fall closer to the majority opinion, or to the dissent just described above?

The possibility that a Purposivist inquiry may identify multiple purposes—indeed, as in *Weber*, purposes that potentially conflict in some circumstances—is one reason that its critics see it as potentially vulnerable to judicial willfulness. For instance, do the two quite distinct purposes of Title VII seen in the contrasting *Weber* opinions of Justice Brennan and Justice Rehnquist simply reflect these jurists' own preferences, rather than congressional purpose?

In the next chapter, we will explore further some of the nuances of the principal interpretive theories. First, however, we return to an earlier question.

C. The Tomato Problem (Resolved?)

As a coda to this chapter, consider the Supreme Court's resolution of The Tomato Problem, introduced at the beginning of this chapter. Before reading the Court's opinion below, review the notes you previously made about the problem, including whatever thoughts you had about the possible interpretive assistance that legislative history materials might provide. In actual fact, the Court did not have any legislative history materials from which it could identify a legislative purpose or intent. Does that make it easier to resolve the interpretive issue, or harder?

FYI The issue again was whether tomatoes were "vegetables" or "fruit" within the meaning of a law imposing tariffs (*i.e.*, taxes) on imported produce.

Nix v. Hedden
149 U.S. 304 (1893)

This was an action brought February 4, 1887, against the collector of the port of New York to recover back duties paid under protest on tomatoes imported by the plaintiff from the West Indies in the spring of 1886, which the collector assessed under "Schedule G.—Provisions" of the Tariff Act of March 3, 1883, c. 121, imposing a duty on "vegetables in their natural state, or in salt or brine, not specially enumerated or provided for in this act, ten percentum *ad valorem*," and which the plaintiffs contended came within the clause in the free list of the same act, "Fruits, green, ripe, or dried, not specially enumerated or provided for in this act." 22 Stat. 504, 519.

At the trial, the plaintiff's counsel, after reading in evidence definitions of the words "fruit" and "vegetables" from Webster's Dictionary, Worcester's Dictionary, and the Imperial Dictionary, called two witnesses, who had been for thirty years in the business of selling fruit and vegetables, and asked them, after hearing these definitions, to say whether these words had "any special meaning in trade or commerce, different from those read."

One of the witnesses answered as follows:

"Well, it does not classify all things there, but they are correct as far as they go. It does not take all kinds of fruit or vegetables; it takes a portion of them. I think the words 'fruit' and 'vegetable' have the same meaning in trade today that they had on March 1, 1883. I understand that the term 'fruit' is applied in trade only to such plants or parts of plants as contain the seeds. There are more vegetables than those in the enumeration given in Webster's Dictionary under the term 'vegetable,' as 'cabbage, cauliflower, turnips, potatoes, peas, beans, and the like,' probably covered by the words 'and the like.'"

The other witness testified:

"I don't think the term 'fruit' or the term 'vegetables' had, in March, 1883, and prior thereto, any special meaning in trade and commerce in this country different from that which I have read here from the dictionaries."

The plaintiff's counsel then read in evidence from the same dictionaries the definitions of the word "tomato."

The defendant's counsel then read in evidence from Webster's Dictionary the definitions of the words "pea," "eggplant," "cucumber," "squash," and "pepper."

The plaintiff then read in evidence from Webster's and Worcester's dictionaries the definitions of "potato," "turnip," "parsnip," "cauliflower," "cabbage," "carrot," and "bean."

No other evidence was offered by either party. The court, upon the defendant's motion, directed a verdict for him, which was returned, and judgment rendered thereon. 39 F. 109. The plaintiffs duly excepted to the instruction, and sued out this writ of error.

Mr. Justice Gray, after stating the facts in the foregoing language, delivered the opinion of the Court.

The single question in this case is whether tomatoes, considered as provisions, are to be classed as "vegetables" or as "fruit" within the meaning of the Tariff Act of 1883.

The only witnesses called at the trial testified that neither "vegetables" nor "fruit" had any special meaning in trade or commerce different from that given in the dictionaries, and that they had the same meaning in trade today that they had in March, 1883.

The passages cited from the dictionaries define the word "fruit" as the seed of plants, or that part of plants which contains the seed, and especially the juicy, pulpy products of certain plants covering and containing the seed. These definitions have no tendency to show that tomatoes are "fruit," as distinguished from "vegetables" in common speech or within the meaning of the Tariff Act.

There being no evidence that the words "fruit" and "vegetables" have acquired any special meaning in trade or commerce, they must receive their ordinary meaning. Of that meaning the court is bound to take judicial notice, as it does in regard to all words in our own tongue, and upon such a question dictionaries are admitted not as evidence, but only as aids to the memory and understanding of the court.

> **FYI** The phrase "judicial notice" refers to the process by which a court recognizes the truth of certain relevant facts without any evidence. Here, the court is treating the ordinary meaning of "all words in our own tongue" (*i.e.*, English!) as something that the court itself gets to decide.

Botanically speaking, tomatoes are the fruit of a vine, just as are cucumbers, squashes, beans, and peas. But in the common language of the people, whether sellers or consumers of provisions, all these are vegetables which are grown in kitchen gardens, and which, whether eaten cooked or raw, are, like potatoes, carrots, parsnips, turnips, beets, cauliflower, cabbage, celery, and lettuce, usually served at dinner in, with, or after the soup, fish, or meats which constitute the principal part of the repast, and not, like fruits generally, as dessert.

* * *

Judgment affirmed.

NOTES & QUESTIONS

1. How important to the Court's decision in *Nix* were the following factors:

    Ordinary meaning?

    Technical meaning?

    Contemporary dictionaries?

    Specific legislative intent?

    Broader legislative purpose?

2. How much room do you see for "judicial willfulness" in deciding whether imported tomatoes are fruits or vegetables? How would you want to cabin or constrain whatever potential willfulness you see?

3. Would legislative history materials that spoke to the interpretive question provide a constraint?

Test Your Understanding

To assess your understanding of the material in this chapter, click here to take a quiz.

19

An Overview of the Primary Interpretive Theories

Key Concepts

- Intentionalism
- Specific intent
- Imagined intent
- Purposivism
- "Legal Process" school
- Professors Hart & Sacks
- Plain Meaning
- Moderate Plain Meaning
- Soft Plain Meaning
- Ordinary versus literal meaning
- Technical meaning
- Strict construction
- New Textualism
- Text and context
- Legislative supremacy

Chapter Summary

The theories of Intentionalism and Purposivism both seek to resolve interpretive problems by understanding what the enacting legislature was trying to do. Intentionalism asks what the enacting legislature would have intended the text to mean in a given situation. When confronting ambiguous text, an Intentionalist looks first to find evidence of specific intent, or a "smoking gun," somewhere in the legislative record concerning the exact issue at hand. Absent success finding this, an Intentionalist may *imagine*

what the enacting legislature would have said had they been asked. To an Intentionalist, a textual difficulty is answered based on how the enacting legislature would have wanted it to be solved.

Purposivists undertake a similar analysis when resolving a textual difficulty, but they direct their focus on a bigger picture. Unlike Intentionalists, Purposivists are not as tied to the details of what the enacting legislators said or might have said about the meaning of the particular text at issue. Instead, they seek to identify what is the greater underlying purpose of the statute and the problem that the legislature was trying to solve. A Purposivist will then construe the ambiguous text to advance this purpose. Purposivists thus are much more likely to adopt a statutory construction that the enacting legislature did not specifically consider, so long as this construction advances the legislature's purpose for the law, as understood by the interpreter.

Plain Meaning Interpretation is a theory of statutory interpretation that dates back centuries. While somewhat superseded or at least overshadowed today by New Textualism, it represents the proposition that an interpreter should give legal effect to the plain meaning of words in statutes. In concept, Plain Meaning Interpretation is straightforward: the legislature intended what it said.

New Textualism is a modern, influential, and contested theory of statutory interpretation. A reaction to Purposivism, New Textualism not only looks to the text itself as the best tool for interpretation, but also generally rejects using legislative history as an interpretive aid. Since legislative history itself is not voted on by legislators, a New Textualist argues, it is not part of the law to be interpreted. New Textualism's influence has reshaped the landscape of statutory interpretation. Today, most interpreters of any philosophy will focus first on the text of the statute before using any other tool.

Previous chapters have introduced several well-known interpretive problems and explored some of the difficulties that the interpretive theories of Textualism and Purposivism have had in resolving these problems. In Parts V and VI that follow, we present a number of tools or doctrines to help resolve interpretive disputes. Learning these tools will help you both to be a successful attorney and to develop your own views about the best interpretive approach. But first, we conclude this Part of the book with brief summaries of four distinct categories of interpretive theory: Intentionalism, Purposivism, Plain Meaning Interpretation, and Textualism.

As you will see throughout Parts V and VI (and may have already gathered), no interpreter or judge represents an archetype of any of these theories (though some will claim to!). These theories do, however, underlie when and how judges use various interpretive tools and doctrines, and different judges definitely have tendencies about these theories that make them draw on some interpretive tools or doctrines more than others. As we will see, the various interpretive tools and doctrines often lead to conflicting results. That is why understanding these theories will help you better understand why a judge might favor one tool or doctrine over another in a given case. It will also help you identify the underlying assumptions in a particular argument about interpretation, which will in turn help you think concretely about potential counter-arguments, something good lawyers need to do all the time.

A. Intentionalism

Intentionalism and Purposivism are similar methods for construing ambiguous statutory language by seeking to understand and effectuate the will of the enacting legislature. In both, the interpreter's role could be described as being a *faithful agent* of the enacting legislature, seeking to complete the legislature's work. The principal difference between these two theories is the level of generality at which the legislative will is assessed. Intentionalism is attentive to the enacting legislature's specific intent about the language at issue—or, at times, about the specific facts to which that language is to be applied—while Purposivism focuses on the legislature's more general intent or purpose animating the statute. These two theories also have somewhat different philosophical groundings.

Intentionalism asks, "What did the enacting legislature believe (or intend) that the text of its statute would mean as applied to this interpretive problem?" The text of the measure itself is generally the most reliable evidence for ascertaining intent, whenever it sheds light on the question. But when the text does not supply an understanding of the intent, Intentionalist interpretation presumes (often counterfactually) that the enacting legislature

> Intentionalism presumes the enacting legislature had a view about how the statutory provision should apply to the specific interpretive problem that the interpreter seeks to resolve.

nevertheless knew how it would have wanted its statute to apply to the interpretative problem, and simply failed to use sufficiently clear language to that effect in the statutory text. Intentionalism then seeks to ascertain that intent through other evidence. It thus partakes of something of an "originalist" quality, inasmuch as its touchstone is identifying what the original authors of a measure meant, in order then to seek to implement that meaning faithfully.

Intentionalist interpretation can be used most successfully when the interpreter is able to identify a figurative "smoking gun" of some sort, which provides evidence that the enacting legislature both contemplated applying its statute to the issue at hand and said something specific about how to apply it to that issue. In practice, however, it is often difficult to find a reliable smoking gun.

For instance, if we return to the *Cammelleri* case you read in Chapter 14, imagine that the minutes of the Village Council meeting at which the ordinance that prohibited the parking of a "motor vehicle camper" for over 24 hours contained clear or repeated evidence of the Council's understanding that the parking prohibition would apply to cars, as well as to trucks, campers, and a range of other vehicles. Such intent evidence might persuade a court to read the phrase "motor vehicle camper" as if it were two terms separated by a comma, and that the omission of the comma after "vehicle" is a pure scrivener's error (in contrast to the reading of the appellate court that actually heard this issue, *see* pp. 318–321, which instead insisted on construing the provision precisely as written). On the other hand, the court might find evidence that the Council's only concern was in fact campers, evidence that would indicate that the Council really meant there not to be a comma. But Council meeting minutes may not exist. Or if they do exist, they may not contain any indication of what the Council intended.

? What problems might arise in asking the enacting legislators what they intended? See if you can identify several.

In theory, if not too much time has passed, one way of filling this evidentiary gap regarding the legislative intent behind a measure would be to interrogate the Council members or legislators themselves, after the interpretive issue has arisen, asking them what they had intended their words to mean in this specific case. But doing so would raise significant reliability problems. First, at least in many contexts there would be a risk that the legislators would not in fact even have had, or at least would not recall, a specific intent concerning the interpretive problem. Moreover, in the absence of an actual historical intent, some legislators nonetheless might claim (counterfactually though not necessarily deceitfully or maliciously) to know what the intent was. Other legislators, meanwhile, might disagree. (Indeed, as discussed further below, the idea of an institution having its own singular intent might be problematic.) Furthermore, such after-the-fact disagreement could arise even in circumstances in which the legislature may have had an actual historical intent. Finally, in any of these scenarios, ulterior motives might cause a legislator to claim falsely that the legislature did have a particular intent at the time of enactment, even though that claimed intent in fact bears no relationship to what the legislature had actually intended. Thus, the idea of obtaining first-person testimony *after* the interpretive problem arises is fraught with difficulty. Perhaps, on balance, a court could take the evidence and exercise its discretion as to whether to believe the evidence based on an assessment of its reliability. After all, judges assess the reliability of evidence in all sorts of other situations. Nonetheless, in the American approach to statutory interpretation, even judges with Intentionalist tendencies will generally not admit such evidence. Besides the reliability issues, one other reason courts tend not to allow such evidence is concerns about separation of powers, a sense that the legislators had their say at the time they adopted the law and should not be interfering in the interpretive process.

Instead, the Intentionalist therefore typically resorts to evidence produced at the time of enactment, principally documents produced during the legislative process, or what is known as "legislative history," which we will discuss in greater detail in future chapters. Legislative history materials can include published committee reports and records of legislative debates, to name the kinds of records usually seen as providing the most reliable evidence of specific legislative intent. Judges will generally view these extrinsic materials as having greater reliability the more they establish that they reflect a widespread or consensus view of the enacting legislature.

Textualists and other critics of Intentionalism argue that the legislature as an institution may not have had *any* intent other than what it expressed in its enactment. Indeed, these critics point to the difficulty of identifying the intent of an institutional or corporate entity because an institution itself lacks a will or motive. Instead, it is composed of many individuals, each with their own wills and motives, which may have combined to cause the institution to adopt a particular position or course of conduct but will not always combine to produce a single collective intent. Professor Max Radin remains famous today for articulating this concern almost a century ago. *See* Max Radin, *Statutory Interpretation*, 43 HARV. L. REV. 863, 870–71 (1930). Furthermore, each of these individuals may have their own way of expressing their view of the collective intent of the entity and be unable to speak definitively for the collective. Just as no single legislator, acting alone, can bestow legal force on the enacted text, one might say that no single legislator's statement of an underlying intent should govern the interpretation of a piece of legislative text. Textualism therefore argues for an interpretive methodology independent of any attempt to find the legislative intent, except as it may have been collectively expressed by the institution in the words of the statute itself.

Intentionalism nonetheless has many defenders, who observe that in other contexts the law routinely assumes that institutions and groups, though not strictly willful actors themselves, can be presumed to have an intent that motivates their actions. In interpreting private contracts, for instance, it is common to seek to understand the intent or purpose behind a provision to which a corporation or organization has agreed. The crucial interpretive question is what evidence will suffice to establish the intent of the institution. Similarly for legislatures, the question is whether certain forms of extra-textual evidence, alone or in combination with text and context, suffice to establish an underlying legislative intent. Later chapters will discuss in more detail some of the principal sources of extrinsic evidence typically used to ascertain legislative intent, as well as ways to assess the reliability of these sources.

In the absence of contemporaneous evidence of the enacting legislature's intent, and as an alternative to interrogating legislators after the fact about their intent, one instead could simply *imagine* asking the legislators what they had intended their words to mean, as Judge Learned Hand (in the twentieth century), and British commentator Edmund Plowden long before him (in the sixteenth century), had encouraged. *See* WILLIAM D. POPKIN, STATUTES IN COURT 12 (1999). Some Intentionalist theories of statutory interpretation thus distinguish between "Specific" Intent and "Imagined" or "Reconstructed" Intent. *See* Roscoe Pound, *Spurious Interpretation*, 7 COLUM. L. REV. 379 (1907). Imagined intent, however, obviously lacks any "smoking gun" evidence about what the enacting legislature meant and instead is a speculative reconstruction about what the legislature would have said about the interpretive problem, had it specifically contemplated and addressed it.

> **!** "Imagined Intent" or "Reconstructed Intent" appears on the scene when the enacting legislature provided no direct evidence of its specific intent, but the interpreter nonetheless feels able to channel what the enacting legislature would have intended with respect to the specific interpretive problem, had it been asked.

For instance, in 1976 the question arose whether employment discrimination based on pregnancy amounted to a violation of Title VII of the Civil Rights Act of 1964, the text of which prohibited discrimination on the basis of "race, color, religion, sex, or national origin." *See General Electric Co. v. Gilbert*, 429 U.S. 125 (1976). An Intentionalist approach might imagine putting this specific question to the enacting Congress. In other words, would Congress in 1964 have said that discrimination on the basis of pregnancy was discrimination on the basis of sex, as prohibited by Title VII? Notice the use of the conditional in the framing of the question: what *would* the 1964 Congress have thought? This is what makes this approach "*imagined*" reconstruction of intent. It is not hard to imagine the enacting Congress giving a negative response to this question in 1964. But the Intentionalist interpreter may never be entirely sure of the answer to this or any other effort to imagine or reconstruct the intent.

In today's debates about theories of statutory interpretation, Intentionalism is often overshadowed by Purposivism. Nevertheless, Intentionalism still has plenty of adherents, especially in the state systems. For instance, New York has long followed a set of statutory interpretation guidelines that specifically invite its courts to be Intentionalist interpreters. These guidelines provide that "[t]he primary consideration of the courts" is to "give effect to the intention of the Legislature," first "from a literal reading of the act itself," and then "if the meaning is still not clear. . .from such facts [as may] legitimately reveal it." *See* N.Y. STAT. LAW § 92 (McKinney 2016). Minnesota has a statute providing that "[t]he object of all interpretation. . .is to ascertain and effectuate the intention of the legislature," and to do so using a range of sources "[w]hen the words of a law are not explicit." MINN. STAT. 645.16 (2016). Many other state legislatures have codified a requirement that courts construe their statutes so as to be consistent with the "manifest intent of the legislature," although the phrase "manifest intent" in these provisions is sometimes a limiting phrase understood to describe only the intent that is evident from either the measure itself or the rest of the body of law, rather than through the analysis of legislative history. For more detailed discussion of Intentionalism in all fifty states, see Jacob Scott, *Codified Canons and the Common Law of Interpretation*, 98 GEO. L.J. 341 (2010); Abbe R. Gluck, *The States as Laboratories of Statutory Interpretation: Methodological Consensus and the New Modified Textualism*, 119 YALE L.J. 1750 (2010).

B. Purposivism

Purposivism, like Intentionalism, also looks beyond the literal meaning of the words of a law in its effort to understand the underlying legislative will. As distinguished from Intentionalism, however, Purposivism asks not, "What did the enacting legislature expect that the statute's words would mean as applied to this specific interpretive problem?," but instead, "What purpose did the enacting legislature expect that the statute would serve, and how might the statute's text fairly be construed to serve that purpose in this instance?" Focusing on this question may not lead as directly to an answer as might Intentionalism in those cases in which the interpreter can find evidence of specific intent, but in cases in which there is little or no evidence of the legislature's specific intent, Purposivism may be a preferable way of furthering the legislative will.

> Purposivism seeks to construct an ambiguous provision in a way that will further what the interpreter concludes is the underlying purpose behind the statute, whether or not the enacting legislature had a specific intent regarding the particular interpretive problem.

Indeed, to some observers, the effort to identify the general "purpose" may be a more objective enterprise than trying to identify specific "intent" because purpose might often be more evident from just the text alone, taken as a whole, without reference to extrinsic sources of meaning. However, the interpretive theory that today is called "Purposivism" wholeheartedly embraces the use of extrinsic sources as well, not just the text, and therefore must be distinguished from a narrower use of text alone to identify the general purpose. Because of its reliance on legislative history materials, Purposivism draws all the same critiques that Intentionalism does, including a concern about the difficulty of imputing a motive or purpose to an institution except through the institution's official actions (namely, the enactment of the statute), and a concern about the reliability of legislative history materials. Moreover, many critics worry that once extra-textual sources are part of the interpretive enterprise, the effort to identify a measure's general purpose may well be *less* objective than an effort to identify the legislature's specific intent, precisely because a variety of "purposes" may be found at different levels of abstraction, rather than being limited like Intentionalism by the particular interpretive problem that has arisen.

One of the more famous judicial statements of a Purposivist approach is from the Supreme Court's 1940 opinion in *United States v. American Trucking Associations*, 310 U.S. 534, 543 (1940):

> There is, of course, no more persuasive evidence of the purpose of a statute than the words by which the legislature undertook to give expression to its wishes. Often these words are sufficient, in and of themselves, to determine the purpose of the legislation. In such cases, we have followed their plain meaning. When that meaning has led to absurd or futile results, however, this Court has looked beyond the words to the purpose of the act. Frequently, however, even when the plain meaning did not produce absurd results but merely an unreasonable one "plainly at variance with the policy of the legislation as a whole," this Court has followed that purpose, rather than the literal words. **When aid to construction of the meaning of words, as used in the statute, is available, there certainly can be no "rule of law" which forbids its use, however clear the words may appear on "superficial examination"** (emphasis added).

As the *American Trucking* opinion suggests, American courts in the mid-twentieth century were departing from a strict plain meaning approach to statutory interpretation. In part, this likely reflected the growing influence of ideas that would

shortly lead to the mid-century emergence of the "Legal Process" school of jurisprudence, noted above. Indeed, Purposivism is often equated with Legal Process
interpretation, and while Purposivism had previously flourished on its own, today
it certainly owes much of its contemporary theoretical basis to the Legal Process
school.

Harvard law professors Henry Hart and Albert Sacks are credited with playing
leading roles in the development of Legal Process theory, including developing
their own rubric of the "Rudiments of Statutory Interpretation." This was a detailed and nuanced set of guidelines for courts to follow when interpreting a statute. Central to the Hart & Sacks Purposivist rubric were the following points,
worth comparing to those in *Heydon's Case* in Chapter 15 above:

- courts should "[r]espect the position of the legislature as the chief
  policy-determining agency of society";

- courts should "[b]e mindful. . .that every statute is a part of the
  law" and should be part of "striving for even-handed justice";

- with these premises, courts should "[d]ecide what purpose ought
  to be attributed to the statute";

- courts should then interpret the statute "so as to carry out the
  purpose as best [they] can";

- except if doing so would require giving the words of a statute "a
  meaning they will not bear," or would violate a policy that certain
  types of laws (such as those establishing the boundaries of criminal
  conduct) must be clear on their face.

See HART AND SACKS' THE LEGAL PROCESS: BASIC PROBLEMS IN THE MAKING AND
APPLICATION OF LAW 1374 (William N. Eskridge Jr. & Philip P. Frickey eds.,
2006).

As part of seeking to understand the legislature's purpose in enacting a measure, Hart &
Sacks, in a pithy statement of a core tenet of
the Legal Process school, called on the interpreter to "assume, unless the contrary unmistakably appears, that the legislature was made
up of ***reasonable persons pursuing reasonable purposes reasonably***" (emphasis added).
Id. at 1378. Meanwhile, the interpreter was

Hart & Sacks were
important jurispru-
dential figures in
the mid-20th century, playing
a key role in the development
of Legal Process theory. *See
also* Chapter 16, Section A.2.

then likewise called upon to continue this same enterprise as a faithful agent of the legislature, reasonably furthering the legislature's reasonable purposes.

Hart & Sacks explicitly acknowledged that a statute might have multiple purposes. In such a case, their interpretive guidance for identifying the most relevant purpose was for the court to imagine being in the position of the enacting legislature, with a *modus operandi* of "pursuing reasonable purposes reasonably," rather than of being influenced by "short-run currents of political expedience." HART & SACKS, *supra*, at 1378. How akin is this guidance to the *Heydon's Case* instruction to construe ambiguities *"pro bono publico"*? Is this guidance enough to help a judicial interpreter decide neutrally between competing purposes in a typical case? If not, is that a problem with Purposivism? Or is it inevitable when interpreting statutory texts that cannot—and so do not—resolve every possible interpretive issue that arises?

On a related note, Purposivist interpretation also may be less constrained by the idea that textual meaning must not change over time. In particular, a Purposivist might well argue that while the original purpose of a measure does not change, the meaning that an interpreter gives to a vague or broadly worded statutory phrase might well evolve in light of current conditions, in order to advance that original purpose. Arguably, this is one way of understanding Justice Brennan's majority opinion in *Weber*, which discounted specific intent evidence that some members of the enacting Congress thought Title VII would prohibit all race-based distinctions in employment.

A key question for Purposivism is what sources to consult in the effort to understand the enacting legislature's purpose. As with Intentionalism, the context of the enactment, including legislative documents that appear to reflect the views of the legislators involved, will often play a central role. These "legislative history" materials (whose interpretive use again will be the focus of future chapters) can include official committee reports; committee hearing transcripts, testimony, and exhibits; records of legislative debates; and even correspondence between legislators and constituents, interest groups, or other legislators. Beyond legislative history materials, Purposivists may also explore the broader context of an enactment, with an eye to identifying the "mischief" to which the measure was directed or even perhaps to finding some broader values implicitly embodied in the measure.

At the state level, state courts construing state legislation do not engage in Purposivist interpretation nearly as much as do their federal counterparts construing congressional legislation. As noted above at the end of section A of this chapter, however, many states direct their courts to construe ambiguous statutes to further

"legislative intent" or "legislative purpose." Yet, it is only in a small number of these states that this instruction explicitly permits courts to use any available legislative history materials when determining the pur-
pose. This divergence between state courts and federal courts partly reflects the fact that state legislatures historically have not produced as much in the way of the kinds of legislative history materials that Congress has long pre-pared, and upon which Purposivist interpreta-tion typically depends. But the historical lack of state legislative history materials is slowly

> State legislatures have been much slower than Con-gress in creating detailed ar-chival records of their delib-erative processes.

changing, as more and more state legislatures have begun to prepare transcripts of committee meetings and floor debates, or to produce searchable video archives of their proceedings.

C. Plain Meaning Interpretation

In contrast to both Intentionalism and Purposivism, many interpreters in many eras have argued for the fundamental primacy of the text itself. As Oliver Wendell Holmes expressed it, "We do not inquire what the legislature meant; we ask only what the statute means." For generations of lawyers, this approach was typically described as interpretation according to the "plain meaning" of the text. Be mind-ful, however, that as a jurist Justice Holmes on occasion relied on legislative his-tory to decide "what the statute means," even to give it a meaning at odds with its apparent plain meaning. *See, e.g., Boston Sand & Gravel Co. v. United States,* 278 U.S. 41 (1928).

As noted in Chapter 15, Plain Meaning Interpretation has long been a rejoinder to an interpretive approach that places primacy not on the text but on legislative intent determined through whatever means possible. As Justice Frankfurter once cautioned, interpreters should be careful not "to give point to the quip that only when legislative history is doubtful do you go the statute." Felix Frankfurter, *Some Reflections on the Reading of Statutes,* 47 COLUM. L. REV. 527, 543. Plain Meaning interpretation is particularly critical of any intent-based approach that encourages creative usage—or even distortion—of the text in order to promote the perceived intent. *E.g., Christian Disposal, Inc. v. Village of Eolia,* 895 S.W.2d 632, 634 (Mo. Ct. App. 1995) (claiming "courts have not hesitated to hold that legislative intent will prevail over common meaning"). Meanwhile, some interpreters view a plain meaning approach as a narrow type of intentionalist theory, in which the text itself is the only (or by far the most reliable) evidence of the underlying legislative intent. *See American Trucking,* 310 U.S. at 543.

At its core, the Plain Meaning approach—often characterized as interpretation according to what is called the **Plain Meaning Rule**—reflects that sometimes an interpretive issue arises not because the meaning of a key statutory term is textually ambiguous, but because applying what appears to be a clear legal provision to a particular circumstance seems counterintuitive or otherwise contrary to what the lawmaker likely intended. Examples might include whether an ordinance prohibiting all vehicles in a public park applies to a construction vehicle bringing in playground equipment, or whether a prohibition against importing a foreign laborer precludes importing a religious pastor. But it is precisely to these circumstances that the Plain Meaning Rule is most obviously directed.

> **!** Sometimes the plain meaning of a statute becomes muddy because its application to a specific circumstance seems out of place. The question then becomes how strongly to insist on following the plain meaning.

However, the Rule also pertains to circumstances in which the literal text alone simply is not plain, providing that in a case of genuine ambiguity, the interpreter should work outward from the key text to related statutory provisions, then to the act as a whole, and eventually to a host of "intrinsic" or textual interpretive aids (of the kind described in Part V below), in order to find the meaning that then would be characterized as "plain."

The Plain Meaning Rule provides that even when the result seems contrary to what the interpreter believes the lawmaker intended, the interpreter should apply the law according to its plain meaning. As the Supreme Court wrote over one hundred years ago, "if [the meaning of a law] is plain,. . .the sole function of the courts is to enforce it according to its terms." *Caminetti v. United States,* 242 U.S. 470, 485 (1917). Plain meaning interpretation views the interpreter as more of a dutiful executor than a faithful agent or cooperative partner of the legislature. Updating this idea almost a century later, Justice Thomas in 2003 called this a "seemingly obvious rule": "Unless Congress explicitly states otherwise, 'we construe a statutory term in accordance with its ordinary or natural meaning.' " *Barnhart v. Peabody Coal Co.,* 537 U.S. 149, 184 (2003) (THOMAS, J., dissenting) (*quoting FDIC v. Meyer,* 510 U.S. 471, 476 (1994)).

Yet judges, even those on the Supreme Court, do not agree about precisely how far to follow the Plain Meaning Rule. A strict version of the rule, such as the version that Lord Atkinson articulated in 1913 (see Chapter 15, page 348), would insist on adhering to the text even when it produces a ridiculous outcome. But a competing rule against interpreting a law to produce absurd results might justify a more **"moderate" plain meaning** approach, in which the interpreter is willing to look for guidance outside the text when reliance on the text alone would lead to an absurd result or an interpretive stalemate. However, there is no obvious standard for determining when a plain meaning interpretation is "absurd," as arguably might be the case in not allowing a

> Strict plain mean-
> ing, which would **FYI**
> follow the literal
> terms at all costs, has few ad-
> herents.

vehicle into the park to deliver playground equipment, but might less arguably be the case in refusing to allow the importation of a foreign pastor.

Legal interpreters also may differ in their willingness to apply the Plain Meaning Rule in the face of evidence that doing so would violate the intent or purpose behind the measure. The result is that the Plain Meaning Rule can be formulated and deployed in varying degrees. For instance, a weak version of the rule is that "absent clear evidence of a contrary legislative intention, a statute should be interpreted according to its plain language." *United States v. Apfelbaum*, 445 U.S. 115, 121 (1980). This version, in striking contrast to the formulations in *Caminetti* and *Meyer* described above, explicitly invites the interpreter to look for evidence sufficient to depart from the plain meaning. This formulation typifies the approach of the majority opinion in *United States v. Weber*, 443 U.S. 193 (1979), discussed in the preceding chapter, which conceded that a literal application of the antidiscrimination provisions of Title VII of the Civil Rights Act might well invalidate a private employer's voluntary affirmative action plan. The Court's opinion rejected this literal reading of the statute on the basis that it would thwart what the Court, after considering a variety of extrinsic sources of legislative history, concluded was Congress's underlying purpose: "the integration of [B]lacks into the mainstream of American society," without disrupting private employers' traditional prerogatives any more than necessary.

Meanwhile, a **"soft" plain meaning** approach, while seeking to ground its interpretation solidly in the plain meaning of the text, is also open to using a range of additional interpretive tools, including extrinsic evidence found in an act's legislative history, to confirm or fine tune its understanding of just what the plain meaning is. For instance, in *Tennessee Valley Authority v. Hill*, 437 U.S. 153 (1978), the Supreme Court relied on several arguments from legislative history materials to reinforce its conclusion that the plain meaning of the Endangered Species Act, specifically its provision that all federal agencies must ensure that their actions "not jeopardize the continued existence" of an endangered species, was that the federally owned Tennessee Valley Authority could not complete the nearly finished—and fully funded—Tellico Dam, as draconian as this result might be.

In its typical formulation, the Plain Meaning Rule invites attention to what is often called the **"ordinary or natural meaning"** of the text at issue. For instance, in the *Bostock* case above we saw Justices Gorsuch and Kavanaugh disagree about the ordinary public meaning of "because of . . . sex." In the famous case of *McBoyle v. United States,* 283 U.S. 25 (1931), the Court confronted the question of whether an airplane was a vehicle for purposes of the National Motor Vehicle Theft Act, which criminalized the interstate transportation of a stolen vehicle. Writing for the Court, Justice Holmes explained that the statute's definition of a vehicle, namely "an automobile, automobile truck, automobile wagon, motor cycle, or any other self-propelled vehicle not designed for running on rails," called to mind the "everyday" or "popular" meaning of the term as "a thing moving on land," and should not be construed to include something that flies, even though an airplane literally fit within the category of "any other self-propelled vehicle not designed for running on rails." Here, the Court's conception of the ordinary or natural meaning limited the category of "vehicle" to its prototypical, rather than its broader literal, meaning. Implicitly, the Court was thus limiting the term according to how it thought the text would most naturally strike a typical reader.

But this focus gives rise to another issue about the application of the Rule, namely, how to determine what meaning is the "plain" meaning. The ordinary meaning is often distinguishable from the **literal meaning** of the text. If construed literally, the National Motor Vehicle Theft Act would have applied to a stolen airplane, but the Court in *McBoyle* thought a literal meaning was at odds with the plain or ordinary meaning. Nevertheless, one strict version of the plain meaning rule does call for the words of a statute to be construed literally. So a literal or **"strict" construction** approach to interpretation should not be confused with the prototypical or ordinary meaning approach.

The meaning of a term may also depend on context and audience. Indeed, depending on audience, determining the plain meaning sometimes may require understanding a term's technical or scientific or legal meaning. For instance, to the general public, the ordinary meaning of a term in the statute of wills may be different from the meaning of that same term to an estate lawyer. If the language in the statute of wills is directed primarily to estate lawyers and probate courts, then perhaps it is this audience's reading of the term that should establish its plain meaning. Or a public health statute replete with scientific and medical terms concerning disease tracking and prevention may invite interpretation according to the "plain" *technical* meaning of its terms, as understood by the medical and public health communities. Thus, the plain meaning rule occasionally can be applied with respect to the meaning that a particular intended audience would most naturally ascribe to the text, even if this is not the ordinary meaning for the average citizen. Importantly, sometimes the "technical" meaning of a phrase or term can be a specialized *legal* meaning, not just technical in a scientific sense.

> Arguably, in *Nix v. Hedden* the Court chose not to construe the tariff statute's terms "fruits" and "vegetables" as though the target audience was botanists, rather than tradespeople or ordinary consumers.

One increasingly frequent aid in applying the plain meaning rule is to turn to **dictionaries** as a source for understanding the text. Of course, an enacting legislature can always include its own definitions of critical statutory terms for purposes of a given measure, and many statutes have a separate section devoted to definitions. But absent these internal definitions (and sometimes even in spite of them, or in order to understand undefined terms contained within a statutory definition), courts, agencies, and other interpreters may choose to consult dictionaries, on the theory that dictionaries can help identify the ordinary or natural meaning of a term. Moreover, dictionary definitions can be used not only to develop an understanding of the ordinary meaning of a term, but also to identify technical, scientific, or legal definitions of a term, in contexts in which those specialized uses may be the more appropriate "plain" meanings.

> What risks might overreliance on dictionaries entail?

In fact, however, some recent empirical research suggests that legislative drafters rarely draft with dictionary definitions in mind. *See* Abbe R. Gluck & Lisa Schultz Bressman, *Statutory Interpretation from the Inside: An Empirical Study of Congressional Drafting, Delegation and the Canons*, 65 STAN. L. REV. 901 (2013). Should this matter to one's theory of interpretation, or should interpretation nonetheless presume that drafters ought to be familiar with dictionary definitions? Some interpreters have long worried that relying on dictionary definitions in interpreting ambiguous legal text can be misleading. Judge Learned Hand once cautioned against "mak[ing] a fortress out of the dictionary," and urged the interpreter instead to remain focused on understanding the statute's actual purpose. *See Cabell v. Markham,* 148 F.2d 737 (2d Cir. 1945). On the other hand, as Hart and Sacks observed, "reputable dictionaries" may provide more reliable and "impersonal" sources of understanding than the idiosyncratic meanings that a particular judge may assign to ambiguous text based on the judge's own personal experience. *See*

Hart and Sacks' The Legal Process: Basic Problems in the Making and Application of Law 1190 (William N. Eskridge Jr. & Philip P. Frickey eds., 2006).

D. New Textualism

Today's New Textualism is clearly an outgrowth of Plain Meaning interpretation. It can trace its roots to the final two decades of the 20th century, when a group of jurists and theorists, led by U.S. Supreme Court Justice Antonin Scalia and other jurists such as U.S. Court of Appeals Judge Frank Easterbrook, developed and forcefully advocated for a version of Plain Meaning interpretation that relies almost exclusively on the enacted text, and eschews the use of any legislative history materials. This movement, sometimes called simply Textualism but also appropriately known as New Textualism to distinguish it from earlier Plain Meaning or "textualist" approaches to interpretation, continues to have a profound influence on interpretive methodology today. It has dramatically reinvigorated the Plain Meaning doctrine, which in the eyes of many jurists and observers had become largely moribund at the federal level by the time of New Textualism's arrival in the 1980s. New Textualism also has reshaped the way most other interpreters structure their analyses, leading all theories of interpretation to focus substantial attention on the text itself, and only thereafter to evaluate whatever extrinsic sources also may have interpretive value in light of the implications of the text.

> **?** Before reading further, you might think about how many of the New Textualists' arguments against using legislative history as a tool of statutory interpretation you can anticipate at this point.

Recall that Plain Meaning Interpretation, in its earlier formulations, was driven fundamentally by the rise of a positive view of legislative supremacy in the nineteenth century. Although New Textualism builds upon this same foundation, its proponents also raise concerns about the dangers of judicial willfulness in matters of interpretation. New Textualists accordingly seek to limit the courts' interpretive discretion as much as possible and argue that an important way of doing so is to insist on adhering almost exclusively to the text and to reject the use of legislative history materials. New Textualism thus generally opposes both a "soft" version of Plain Meaning Interpretation (which as described above is willing to supplement the text with legislative history materials in a wide range of cases), as well as a "moderate" version (which as also previously described is willing to look beyond the text for clues to meaning in legislative history materials when the text alone would lead to an absurd result or an interpretive impasse).

New Textualism's insistence that it is generally improper to resort to legislative history does not mean that it embraces the extreme version of the Plain Meaning Rule that Lord Atkinson championed a century ago, in which the interpreter must adhere to the text even when it produces absurd results. Rather, New Textualism insists only that the tools for resolving interpretive problems not include looking to legislative history. When the text alone does not avoid the problems of an absurd result or an interpretive impasse, New Textualism typically resolves the

> Can you think of a circumstance in which a New Textualist might decide that consulting legislative history *is* appropriate?

problem by construing the text in light of the larger body of the law or by relying on other "canons" of interpretation, as described further in Chapters 20–23. These canons are widely known interpretive guidelines or maxims that, like dictionaries, can help to choose between interpretive possibilities. Nor does New Textualism amount to a form of "strict constructionism" that calls for a hyperliteral reading of the text. Rather, it depends on identifying ordinary, "fair," and sensible readings of the text, through use of canons of construction and other interpretive tools as necessary. Most contemporary Textualists reject being equated with Strict Constructionists.

E. A Problem from the Text of a Firearms Statute

As a final DIY exercise in Part IV, consider how a Textualist might approach the following well-known problem involving a federal criminal statute.

DIY
The "Uses ... a Firearm" Conundrum

A federal firearms statute, 18 U.S.C. § 924(c), provides the following sentencing enhancement:

924(c)(1)(A): Except to the extent that a greater minimum sentence is otherwise provided by this subsection or by any other provision of law, any person who, during and in relation to any crime of violence or drug trafficking crime (including a crime of violence or drug trafficking crime that provides for an enhanced punishment if committed by the use of a deadly or dangerous weapon or device) for which the person may be prosecuted in a court of the United States, uses or carries a firearm, or who, in furtherance of any such crime, possesses a firearm, shall, in addition to the punishment provided for such crime of violence or drug trafficking crime—

(i)   be sentenced to a term of imprisonment of not less than 5 years. . .

Under this provision, does bartering a gun for illegal narcotics amount to "us[ing]" a firearm during and in relation to a drug trafficking crime? What other information would you like to have in analyzing this question? Reflect for a few minutes on how you believe this statute should be applied to a defendant who, for instance, traded a gun for cocaine.

After you have reached your own conclusion, Compare Justice O'Connor's and Justice Scalia's responses to the issue in the following case:

Smith v. United States
508 U.S. 223 (1993)

JUSTICE O'CONNOR delivered the opinion of the Court.

We decide today whether the exchange of a gun for narcotics constitutes "use" of a firearm "during and in relation to. . .[a] drug trafficking crime" within the meaning of 18 U.S.C. 924(c)(1). We hold that it does.

* * *

When a word is not defined by statute, we normally construe it in accord with its ordinary or natural meaning. * * * Surely petitioner's treatment of his MAC-10 [gun] can be described as "use" within the everyday meaning of that term. Petitioner "used" his MAC-10 in an attempt to obtain drugs by offering to trade it for cocaine. Webster's defines "to use" as "[t]o convert to one's service" or "to employ." WEBSTER'S NEW INTERNATIONAL DICTIONARY 2806 (2d ed. 1939). Black's Law Dictionary contains a similar definition: "[t]o make use of; to convert to one's service; to employ; to avail oneself of; to utilize; to carry out a purpose or action by means of." BLACK'S LAW DICTIONARY 1541 (6th ed. 1990). Indeed, over 100 years ago we gave the word "use" the same gloss, indicating that it means " 'to employ' " or " 'to derive service from.'" *Astor v. Merritt*, 111 U.S. 202, 213 (1884). Petitioner's handling of the MAC-10 in this case falls squarely within those definitions. By attempting to trade his MAC-10 for the drugs, he "used" or "employed" it as an item of barter to obtain cocaine; he "derived service" from it because it was going to bring him the very drugs he sought.

In petitioner's view, 924(c)(1) should require proof not only that the defendant used the firearm, but also that he used it as a weapon. But the words "as a weapon" appear nowhere in the statute. Rather, 924(c)(1)'s language sweeps broadly, punishing any "us[e]" of a firearm, so long as the use is "during and in relation to" a drug trafficking offense. * * * Had Congress intended the narrow construction petitioner urges, it could have so indicated. It did not, and we decline to introduce that additional requirement on our own.

Language, of course, cannot be interpreted apart from context. The meaning of a word that appears ambiguous if viewed in isolation may become clear when the word is analyzed in light of the terms that surround it. Recognizing this, petitioner and the dissent argue that the word "uses" has a somewhat reduced scope in 924(c)(1) because it appears alongside the word "firearm." Specifically, they contend that the average person on the street would not think immediately of a guns-for-drugs trade as an example of "us[ing] a firearm." Rather, that phrase normally evokes an image of the most familiar use to which a firearm is put—use as a weapon. Petitioner and the dissent therefore argue that the statute excludes uses where the weapon is not fired or otherwise employed for its destructive capacity. See post, at 242–244. Indeed, relying on that argument—and without citation to authority—the dissent announces its own, restrictive definition of "use." "To use an instrumentality," the dissent argues, "ordinarily means to use it for its intended purpose." Post, at 242.

There is a significant flaw to this argument. It is one thing to say that the ordinary meaning of "uses a firearm" includes using a firearm as a weapon, since that is the intended purpose of a firearm and the example of "use" that most immediately comes to mind. But it is quite another to conclude that, as a result, the phrase also excludes any other use. Certainly that conclusion does not follow from the phrase "uses. . .a firearm" itself. As the dictionary definitions and experience make clear, one can use a firearm in a number of ways. That one example of "use" is the first to come to mind when the phrase "uses. . .a firearm" is uttered does not preclude us from recognizing that there are other "uses" that qualify as well. In this case, it is both reasonable and normal to say that petitioner "used" his MAC-10 in

448 • Learning Legislation and Regulation •

his drug trafficking offense by trading it for cocaine; the dissent does not contend otherwise. Post, at 2.

The dissent's example of how one might "use" a cane, post, at 2, suffers from a similar flaw. To be sure, "use" as an adornment in a hallway is not the first "use" of a cane that comes to mind. But certainly it does not follow that the only "use" to which a cane might be put is assisting one's grandfather in walking. Quite the opposite: the most infamous use of a cane in American history had nothing to do with walking at all, see J. McPherson, Battle Cry of Freedom 150 (1988) (describing the caning of Senator Sumner in the United States Senate in 1856); and the use of a cane as an instrument of punishment was once so common that "to cane" has become a verb meaning "[t]o beat with a cane." WEBSTER'S NEW INTERNATIONAL DICTIONARY, *supra*, at 390. In any event, the only question in this case is whether the phrase "uses . . . a firearm" in 924(c)(1) is most reasonably read as excluding the use of a firearm in a gun-for-drugs trade. The fact that the phrase clearly includes using a firearm to shoot someone, as the dissent contends, does not answer it.

* * *

In any event, the "intended purpose" of a firearm is not that it be used in any offensive manner whatever, but rather that it be used in a particular fashion - by firing it. The dissent's contention therefore cannot be that the defendant must use the firearm "as a weapon," but rather that he must fire it or threaten to fire it, "as a gun." Under the dissent's approach, then, even the criminal who pistol-whips his victim has not used a firearm within the meaning of 924(c)(1), for firearms are intended to be fired or brandished, not used as bludgeons. It appears that the dissent similarly would limit the scope of the "othe[r] use[s]" covered by USSG 2B3.1(b)(2)(B). The universal view of the courts of appeals, however, is directly to the contrary. No court of appeals ever has held that using a gun to pistol-whip a victim is anything but the "use" of a firearm; nor has any court ever held that trading a firearm for drugs falls short of being the "use" thereof. * * *

JUSTICE SCALIA, with whom JUSTICE STEVENS and JUSTICE SOUTER join, dissenting.

Section 924(c)(1) mandates a sentence enhancement for any defendant who "during and in relation to any crime of violence or drug trafficking crime. . .uses. . .a firearm." 18 U.S.C. 924(c)(1). The Court begins its analysis by focusing upon the word "use" in this passage, and explaining that the dictionary definitions of that word are very broad. See ante, at 228–229. It is, however, a "fundamental principle of statutory construction (and, indeed, of language itself) that the meaning of a word cannot be determined in isolation, but must be drawn from the context in which it is used." *Deal v. United States*, ante, at 132. That is particularly true of a word as elastic as "use," whose meanings range all the way from "to partake of" (as in "he uses tobacco") to "to be wont or accustomed" (as in "he used to smoke tobacco"). See WEBSTER'S NEW INTERNATIONAL DICTIONARY 2806 (2d ed. 1939).

In the search for statutory meaning, we give nontechnical words and phrases their ordinary meaning. To use an instrumentality ordinarily means to use it for its intended purpose. When someone asks, "Do you use a cane?," he is not inquiring whether you have your grandfather's silver-handled walking stick on display in the hall; he wants to know whether you walk with a cane. Similarly, to speak of "using a firearm" is to speak of using it for its distinctive purpose, *i.e.,* as a weapon. To be sure, "one can use a firearm in a number of ways," ante, at 7, including as an article of exchange, just as one can "use" a cane as a hall decoration - but that is not the ordinary meaning of "using" the one or the other. The Court does not appear to grasp the distinction between how a word can be used and how it ordinarily is used. It would, indeed, be "both reasonable and normal to say that petitioner 'used' his MAC-10 in his drug trafficking offense by trading it for cocaine." *Ibid*. It would also be reasonable and normal to say that he "used" it to scratch his head. When one wishes to describe the action of employing the instrument of a firearm for such unusual purposes, "use" is assuredly a verb one could select. But that says nothing about whether the ordinary meaning of the phrase "uses a firearm" embraces such extraordinary employments. It is unquestionably not reasonable and normal, I think, to say simply "do not use firearms" when one means to prohibit selling or scratching with them.

The normal usage is reflected, for example, in the United States Sentencing Guidelines, which provide for enhanced sentences when firearms are "discharged," "brandished, displayed, or possessed," or "otherwise used." See, e.g., United States Sentencing Commission, Guidelines Manual 2B3.1(b)(2) (Nov. 1992). As to the latter term, the Guidelines say: " 'Otherwise used' with reference to a dangerous weapon (including a firearm) means that the conduct did not amount to the discharge of a firearm, but was more than brandishing, displaying, or possessing a firearm or other dangerous weapon." USSG 1B1.1, comment, n. 1(g) (definitions). "Otherwise used" in this provision obviously means "otherwise used as a weapon."

Given our rule that ordinary meaning governs, and given the ordinary meaning of "uses a firearm," it seems to me inconsequential that "the words 'as a weapon' appear nowhere in the statute," ante, at 6; they are reasonably implicit. Petitioner is not, I think, seeking to introduce an "additional requirement" into the text, *ibid.*, but is simply construing the text according to its normal import. * * *

Another consideration leads to the same conclusion: 924(c)(1) provides increased penalties not only for one who "uses" a firearm during and in relation to any crime of violence or drug trafficking crime, but also for one who "carries" a firearm in those circumstances. The interpretation I would give the language produces an eminently reasonable dichotomy between "using a firearm" (as a weapon) and "carrying a firearm" (which, in the context "uses or carries a firearm," means carrying it in such manner as to be ready for use as a weapon). The Court's interpretation, by contrast, produces a strange dichotomy between "using a firearm for any purpose whatever, including barter," and "carrying a firearm." * * *

For the foregoing reasons, I respectfully dissent

NOTES & QUESTIONS

1. Notice the majority's reliance upon dictionaries while the dissent focuses on the "normal usage" of the words. Is one of these approaches more convincing to you? What happens if the "normal usage" of a word is quite different from its technical or its dictionary meaning?"

2. Justice Stevens and Justice Scalia were often on opposite sides of statutory interpretation questions, and they each had very different interpretive philosophies. But in *Smith*, they agreed on the proper interpretation, even joining the same opinion. What if anything does that tell you?

F.   New Textualism's Impact Today

Before concluding this chapter (and this Part), several points about New Textualism (often today just labelled Textualism) as an interpretive theory merit brief mention. One is that although New Textualism appears to be radically different from Purposivism, it too grounds itself on a sense that the interpreter's role is to serve as a faithful agent of the enacting legislature. But Textualism has a different view of what it means to serve as such an agent: because Textualism questions the coherence of the notion of subjective legislative intent, a Textualist approach focuses on the meaning of the words to the objective reader, rather than any other evidence of actual legislative intent. The only "intent" that matters is what Textualists refer to as an "objectified" intent, one that can be gleaned from the words of the statute, not one that depends on evidence from the legislative process that might shed further light on the words' meaning.

> Here, the adjective "subjective" refers to the purpose from the perspective of the *drafter* of language, whereas "objective" refers to the purpose from the perspective of a *reader* of the language.

As we will see, all judges, including those who call themselves Textualists, use a whole host of techniques when interpreting statutes, including some techniques that are independent of text and legislative intent. But a Textualist approach to interpretation would generally avoid the search for a statute's intent or purpose outside of the words of the statute—or, more precisely, an intent or purpose distinct from one that a reader of the statute would find in the words themselves. Textualism is premised on the idea that limiting the inquiry to the words of the statute will better constrain courts and thus more faithfully further legislative supremacy, thereby preserving the legislature's role as the principal policymaking body in society.

Independently important for Textualism is the fact that the text is legitimate. To a Textualist, allowing illegitimate sources to alter the meaning contained in legal text would undermine the idea of legislative supremacy.

Of almost equal concern to New Textualists is their view that extrinsic sources of interpretive guidance are not reliable. The Textualists' repeated refrain, discussed in greater detail in Part VI, is that evidence of legislative purpose or intent found in committee reports, floor statements, and other legislative history materials cannot be trusted to express the view of a majority of legislators, but rather may reflect the results of strategic manipulation. In other words, because the full legislative body does not approve legislative history materials by a majority vote the way the legislature must approve the enacted text, individual legislators or even their staff members may be able to incorporate in speeches or legislative reports statements of intent that in fact do not reflect a broadly held view. Indeed, they may do so primarily or even exclusively for the purpose of seeding the historical record with statements that can be used in court when interpretive issues arise, rather than for the purpose of persuading or influencing their legislative colleagues during the enactment process. In contrast, enacted text is fully reliable.

Critics of New Textualism offer two fundamental critiques. One is that its formalist insistence on honoring only whatever legislative intent is apparent in the enacted text disserves and disrespects the legislative branch in any case in which the text alone lacks a sufficiently clear or plain meaning. In those cases, Purposivists and others insist that extrinsic sources of meaning at least deserve to be consulted, albeit with an awareness of their potential pitfalls. Only by thoughtfully considering in each specific case whether these materials provide reliable evidence of legislative purpose or intent can the interpreter truly function as a faithful agent of the enacting legislature; Textualist interpretation often leads to results that diverge from actual legislative intent. New Textualists respond that it is not the role of the interpreter to seek to accomplish what the legislature may have intended but simply failed to effectuate; the legislature, through new lawmaking, is free to correct any judicial or agency interpretation it finds unjust or with which it disagrees. Critics reply that the notion that legislatures can readily correct interpretations with which they disagree ignores the difficulties inherent in the legislative process and slights the complexities of the relationships between the various institutions of government.

Another criticism of Textualism is that it is vulnerable to the influence of the interpreter's personal preferences in those cases in which the statutory text lacks a sufficiently plain meaning. This argument claims that while a good-faith examination of legislative history materials operates to constrain an interpreter's freedom, Textualist interpretation leaves the interpreter with *greater* freedom to roam the many interpretive canons, various dictionaries, and whatever arguably related textual provisions the interpreter can find elsewhere in statutory law to justify whatever particular interpretive choice may happen to align with the interpreter's own preferences, consciously or subconsciously. New Textualists counter that when an interpretive issue does not have a clear answer, Textualism's reliance on interpretive doctrines developed independently of any specific issue reduces the risks of importing judicial preferences into the interpretive enterprise, as compared to Purposivist interpretation, which often may provide the interpreter a host of competing legislative history evidence from which to choose.

Yet a third and related critique is that New Textualism is not ideologically neutral, because the typical result of interpreting language textually is to interpret it narrowly, and thereby to constrain the reach of government action or impact.

Thus, despite both its trenchant identification of several hazards of Purposivist interpretation, and its proffer of a conceptually simple alternative, Textualism is still only one competing approach to interpretation (though the current U.S. Supreme Court has tilted that way in just the past few years). It has, however, significantly altered the way in which interpretive problems are analyzed and argued. Much more than in the heyday of unconstrained Purposivism, today almost all litigants, jurists, and agency officials focus substantial attention on the enacted text before turning to extrinsic tools. Justice Kagan's 2015 widely repeated comment "We are all textualists now" reflects this increased focus on text, rather than suggesting that all jurists today have adopted the New Textualist position of wholly shunning legislative history. *See* Kevin Tobia, *We're Not All Textualists Now*, 78 NYU Ann. Surv. Am. L. 243 (2023). Indeed, debates about interpretive theory continue to rage, both within the academy as well as among judicial interpreters and the practicing bar.

An excellent treatise of New Textualism is Antonin Scalia & Bryan Garner, Reading Law: The Interpretation of Legal Texts (2012). For some Purposivist responses, see William N. Eskridge Jr., Interpreting Law: A Primer on How to Read Statutes and the Constitution (2016); Robert A. Katzmann, Judging Statutes (2014).

Test Your Understanding

To assess your understanding of the material in this chapter, click here to take a quiz.

Part V—Canons of Construction in Statutory Interpretation

For all interpreters, the process of statutory and regulatory interpretation begins with a close reading of the words of the measure. As Justice Felix Frankfurter, while a professor at Harvard Law School, famously urged his students, the three critical interpretive steps are: "(1) Read the statute; (2) read the statute; (3) read the statute." *See* Henry J. Friendly, *Mr. Justice Frankfurter and the Reading of Statutes*, in Benchmarks 202 (1967); *cf.* Felix Frankfurter, *Some Reflections on the Reading of Statutes*, 1947 Colum. L. Rev. 527. When faced with difficult questions, interpreters may deploy a wide range of interpretive tools to refine their understanding of the meaning of the words of the statute, but the words themselves are crucial for all judges in the modern American system, no matter how they characterize their interpretive approach.

The interpretive tools and techniques judges use are often divided into two categories: "intrinsic" and "extrinsic." "Intrinsic" tools are those that are said to derive solely from the statutory text itself, whereas "extrinsic" tools are those that depend on evidence from outside the text. For analytic purposes, this Part and the next one will take this framework as given, with this Part addressing "intrinsic" tools and Part VI addressing "extrinsic" tools. This framework is important to help you structure your thinking about the statutory interpretation problem, and some courts (particularly, state courts) even use that terminology. But the line between "intrinsic" and "extrinsic" is not as simple as it might seem at first blush. For example, judges often turn to dictionaries to determine the meaning of words in statutes, but this is viewed as an "intrinsic" technique even though the dictionary is not part of the statutory text. Similarly, judges rely on values in the legal system, values that instantiate themselves in what are known as "substantive canons." Yet, many also view these substantive canons as "intrinsic" tools of interpretation. On the other hand, evidence about the meaning of the words in statutes often comes from the meaning of the same words used elsewhere ***within the law***, whether in the common law or other related statutes. Yet when a judge draws on the common law or other related statutes, this is sometimes viewed as an "extrinsic" technique. So, it is important not to make too much of the distinction between intrinsic and extrinsic tools. The key thing you must understand is the techniques themselves and when they come into play.

We turn now to the intrinsic tools referred to as "canons of construction." These "canons" fall into two categories: (1) textual and (2) substantive. Textual canons are those about **language**—how language is generally used—whereas substantive canons derive from some kind of **normative value** or **policy** found outside the statute, usually elsewhere in the legal system (for example, in the Constitution). While at the federal level most of these interpretive canons or maxims exist only as rules of thumb, many states have now codified a number of these canons as interpretive instructions. *See* Jacob Scott, *Codified Canons and the Common Law of Interpretation*, 98 GEO. L. J. 341 (2010).

We begin our exploration of these canons of construction with a chapter discussing three categories of "textual canons" of interpretation: (1) semantic canons; (2) grammar canons; and (3) the "Whole Act Rule" and its corollaries and variants. The next two chapters will then consider several examples of "substantive canons." The final chapter of this Part offers some reflections on the use of these intrinsic tools. Part VI then will explore extrinsic tools of interpretation.

20

Textual Canons: Maxims of Word Meanings

A. Background

Interpretation of legal text, including statutes, generally begins with a reading of the words attuned to their plain meaning. In other words, interpreters look at a legal text such as a statute as though it were any other communication in (American) English, and they use the same techniques to understand the language of the statute as they would use to understand any other written communication in the English language. Indeed, the Plain Meaning approach to legal interpretation, which we described in Chapter 19 as one approach to interpretive theory, is also frequently characterized as a rule or canon of interpretation and included among the list of intrinsic tools of interpretation. For instance, see 2A SUTHERLAND, STATUTES AND STATUTORY CONSTRUCTION §§ 46:1 & 47:27 (7th ed. 2014); REED DICKERSON, THE INTERPRETATION AND APPLICATION OF STATUTES 190 (1975).

As noted in Chapter 19, however, the plain meaning of a text may not always be the accepted interpretive touchstone, particularly when the result seems at odds with a sensible construction. In addition, the reality is that plenty of statutory provisions lack a plain meaning as applied to some contexts, at least without additional attention to the linguistic structure and the relationship of the words at issue to each other and to other parts of the statute. Over the years, a number of canons of construction have developed concerning these linguistic relationships to help refine one's understanding of what might otherwise be ambiguous legal text. These quite sensible, even intuitive, interpretive presumptions include linguistic maxims, grammar rules, and principles concerning how to read an ambiguous provision in light of the larger body of legal text to which it relates. Many of these canons of construction share similarities with interpretive principles that have been used for millennia. *See* Geoffrey P. Miller, *Pragmatics and the Maxims of Interpretation*, 1990 WISC. L. REV. 1179, 1183-89. Given that they are attempts to capture the meaning of linguistic communication, this should not be surprising: people have been communicating through language for millennia! Most importantly for your purposes, these canons are a staple of modern American jurisprudence. *See, e.g.,* James J. Brudney & Corey Ditslear, *Canons of Construction and the Elusive Quest for Neutral Reasoning*, 58 VAND. L. REV. 1 (2005).

Before we delve into these intrinsic interpretive tools more specifically, consider the following problem.

DIY
Fishing for Red Grouper

The *Miss Katie* is a commercial fishing vessel operating out of Florida in the Gulf of Mexico with a crew of three. An officer of the Florida Fish and Wildlife Conservation Commission, deputized as a federal agent by the National Marine Fisheries Service, boarded the *Miss Katie* in the middle of the Gulf of Mexico to ensure that it was complying with federal regulations. It wasn't. One federal conservation regulation requires immediate release of red grouper under 20 inches long, and imposes civil penalties and potential license suspension for violations. The officer found six dozen undersized red grouper, measuring between 18.75 inches and 20 inches. The officer measured and recorded the length of each undersized fish, segregated them from the rest of the *Miss Katie*'s cargo, ordered the captain of the *Miss Katie* to leave them thus segregated and return to port, and issued the captain a citation.

> **FYI** A red grouper is a commercially important species of fish found in the western Atlantic Ocean and the Gulf of Mexico.

In port four days later, the officer remeasured the segregated red grouper, and found that the measurements did not match those he had recorded previously. A crew member confessed that the captain had directed him to throw overboard some of the grouper that the officer had previously measured and segregated, and that he and the captain had replaced the discarded grouper with additional but previously undetected undersized fish from the rest of the catch.

Eventually, the captain was indicted for two federal crimes: destroying property to prevent a federal seizure, in violation of 18 U.S.C. § 2232(a), and destroying, concealing, and covering up undersized fish to impede a federal investigation, in violation of 18 U.S.C. § 1519. Our focus is on whether § 1519, reproduced here, is applicable to this conduct:

> Section 1519. Destruction, alteration, or falsification of records in Federal investigations and bankruptcy.

> Whoever knowingly alters, destroys, mutilates, conceals, covers up, falsifies, or makes a false entry in any record, document, or tangible object with the intent to impede, obstruct, or influence the investigation or proper administration of any matter within the jurisdiction of any department or agency of the United States or any case filed under title 11, or in relation to or contemplation of any such matter or case, shall be fined under this title, imprisoned not more than 20 years, or both.

Title 11 of the U.S. Code is the title of the code dedicated to bankruptcy. **FYI**

Assume you are the defense attorney for the captain of the *Miss Katie*. Spend five minutes thinking about how you could argue that § 1519 does not apply to your client's conduct, and also about what additional research you might undertake to look for ways to strengthen your argument or respond to counterarguments. Write your thoughts in your notes and save them for later.

Now let's consider the most common textual canons, in three categories: semantic canons, grammar canons, and the Whole Act Rule.

B. Semantic Canons: Maxims of Word Meaning and Association

Key Concepts

- Semantic canons
- *Noscitur a sociis* ("known by its associates")
- *Ejusdem generis* ("of the same general class")
- *Expressio unius est exclusio alterius* ("the expression of one implies the exclusion of others")

Summary

Semantic canons are maxims of word meaning and association employed by judges to find meaning in ambiguous statutes. Although jurists continue to debate how much interpretive weight to give them, these canons are widely used.

When encountering a list of terms, *noscitur a sociis* tells an interpreter to give meaning to an ambiguous word or term in relation to the other terms around it, its "associates." Similarly, when there is a catch-all term at the end of a list of terms (for example "any other person"), *ejusdem generis* tells the interpreter to give meaning to the catch-all term in relation to the words or terms that preceded it. Together, both canons represent the common-sense proposition that the unambiguous terms in a list can provide evidence of the legislature's intent concerning an ambiguous term.

Expressio unius est exclusio alterius is an example of reasoning by negative inference. It tells interpreters that when the legislature clearly could have included a term in a list, but did not, the omission is understood to be intentional: in essence, the interpreter can infer meaning from silence. Much like *noscitur or ejusdem*, the interpreter takes clues of intent from the unambiguous terms in a list. Unlike those other canons, however, the interpreter finds meaning in the absence of a term, often concluding that the statute was not intended to apply to the problem confronting the interpreter.

The primary semantic canons are three maxims of word meaning and association, each often still known by its Latin name: (a) *noscitur a sociis*, (b) *ejusdem generis*, and (c) *expressio unius est exclusio alterius*. (In the United Kingdom, more than in the United States, many additional semantic canons remain in use today, often also still known by their Latin names.) Although legislatures rarely draft with the names of these semantic canons in mind, they often are consciously or subconsciously aware of the underlying intuitive logic of these canons. This can lead legislators to try to be exhaustive, only to find later that they still omitted something unanticipated.

1.   *Noscitur a sociis*—"[a word is] known by its associates." This maxim invites the interpreter to assign meaning to an ambiguous word or phrase in light of the company it keeps, namely the surrounding terms, especially if the word is part of a list.

For instance, the Endangered Species Act makes it unlawful for anyone to "take" any endangered species. In *Babbitt v. Sweet Home Chapter of Communities for a Greater Oregon,* 515 U.S. 687 (1995), an opinion that you will read in full glory later in the final chapter, at issue was the meaning of the term "harm," as used in the statute's definition of the term "take." The definition provision stated that "take" meant: "to harass, *harm*, pursue, hunt, shoot, wound, kill, trap, capture, or collect, or to attempt to engage in any such conduct" (emphasis added). The Secretary of the Interior had promulgated a regulation further specifying that "harm . . . means an act which actually kills or injures wildlife," including "significant habitat modification or degradation. . . ." The Court divided, with three dissenters invoking the *noscitur* canon to argue that "harm" should be understood, like the other words in the definition of "take," to require affirmative conduct "directed immediately and intentionally against a particular animal," and not to include acts that only affected protected wildlife "indirectly and by accident." 515 U.S. at 718, 720. But the majority upheld the Secretary's much broader application of the term as a reasonable interpretation (under the principles of judicial review of agency interpretations that we will consider in Part VIII).

2.   *Ejusdem generis*—"of the same class or kind." The point of this canon is that a broad or generic catch-all term, particularly at the end of a list of specific terms, should be understood as a catch-all only for the same kinds of things that have been more specifically identified by the associated terms. In a sense, this maxim is a variant of the *noscitur* canon, which suggests that the meaning of an ambiguous word can be determined by the surrounding words.

For instance, a Utah state statute required a plaintiff to file a bond in connection with any civil action against "any sheriff, constable, peace officer, state road officer, or *any other person charged with the duty of enforcement of the criminal laws* of this state. . . ." In *Heathman v. Giles,* 374 P.2d 839 (Utah 1962), the state Supreme

Court decided that this statute did not apply to an action against a prosecutor or deputy prosecutors, but was limited to a class of "badge-carrying officers . . . in the front line of law enforcement . . . charged with . . . seeking out persons suspected of crime; and of making arrests. . . ." The court further explained that prosecutors, "although 'charged with the duty of enforcement of the criminal laws,' are officers of such a significantly different character" as to fall outside the meaning of the statute's catch-all phrase. *Id.* at 840.

Now consider the following two contrasting opinions from this more recent Supreme Court case.

Ali v. Federal Bureau of Prisons
552 U.S. 214 (2008)

Justice Thomas delivered the opinion of the Court.

* * * In December 2003, petitioner [who was serving a prison sentence on a federal criminal conviction was] transferred to the United States Penitentiary Big Sandy (USP Big Sandy) in Inez, Kentucky. * * * [H]is bags arrived some days later. Upon inspecting his property, he noticed that several items were missing. The staff at USP Big Sandy's Receiving and Discharge Unit told him that he had been given everything that was sent, and that if things were missing he could file a claim. Many of the purportedly missing items were of religious and nostalgic significance, including two copies of the Qur'an, a prayer rug, and religious magazines. Petitioner estimated that the items were worth $177.

Petitioner filed an administrative tort claim. In denying relief, the agency noted that, by his signature on the receipt form, petitioner had certified the accuracy of the inventory listed thereon and had thereby relinquished any future claims relating to missing or damaged property. Petitioner then filed a complaint alleging, *inter alia*, violations of the Federal Tort Claims Act (FTCA), 28 U. S. C. §§ 1346, 2671 *et seq*. The BOP [Bureau of Prisons] maintained that petitioner's claim was barred by the exception in § 2680(c) for property claims against law enforcement officers. The District Court agreed and dismissed petitioner's FTCA claim for lack of subject-matter jurisdiction.

* * * We granted certiorari to resolve the disagreement among the Courts of Appeals as to the scope of § 2680(c).

II

In the FTCA, Congress waived the United States' sovereign immunity for claims arising out of torts committed by federal employees. See 28 U. S. C. § 1346(b)(1). As relevant here, the FTCA authorizes "claims against the United States, for money damages . . . for injury or loss of property . . . caused by the negligent or wrongful act or omission of any employee of the Government while acting within the scope of his office or employment." *Ibid.* The FTCA exempts from this waiver certain categories of claims. See §§ 2680(a)–(n). Relevant here is the exception in subsection (c), which provides that § 1346(b) shall not apply to "[a]ny claim arising in respect of the assessment or collection of any tax or customs duty, or the detention of any goods, merchandise, or other property by any officer of customs or excise or any other law enforcement officer." § 2680(c).

This case turns on whether the BOP officers who allegedly lost petitioner's property qualify as "other law enforcement officer[s]" within the meaning of § 2680(c). Petitioner argues that they do not because "any other law enforcement officer" includes only law enforcement officers acting in a customs or excise capacity. Noting that Congress referenced customs and excise activities in both the language at issue and the preceding clause in § 2680(c), petitioner argues that the entire subsection is focused on preserving the United States' sovereign immunity only as to officers enforcing those laws.

Petitioner's argument is inconsistent with the statute's language. The phrase "*any* other law enforcement officer" suggests a broad meaning. *Ibid.* (emphasis added). We have previously noted that "[r]ead naturally, the word 'any' has an expansive meaning, that is, 'one or some indiscriminately of whatever kind.'" *United States v. Gonzales*, 520 U. S. 1, 5 (1997) (quoting WEBSTER'S THIRD NEW INTERNATIONAL DICTIONARY 97 (1976)). * * *

We think [this reasoning] applies equally to the expansive language Congress employed in 28 U. S. C. § 2680(c). Congress' use of "any" to modify "other law enforcement officer" is most naturally read to mean law enforcement officers of whatever kind. The word "any" is repeated four times in the relevant portion of § 2680(c), and two of those instances appear in the particular phrase at issue: "*any* officer of customs or excise or *any* other law enforcement officer." (Emphasis added.) Congress inserted the word "any" immediately before "other law enforcement officer," leaving no doubt that it modifies that phrase. To be sure, the text's references to "tax or customs duty" and "officer[s] of customs or excise" indicate that Congress intended to preserve immunity for claims arising from an officer's enforcement of tax and customs laws. The text also indicates, however, that Congress intended to preserve immunity for claims arising from the detention of property, and there is no indication that Congress intended immunity for those claims to turn on the type of law being enforced.

Petitioner would require Congress to clarify its intent to cover all law enforcement officers by adding phrases such as "performing any official law enforcement function," or "without limitation." But Congress could not have chosen a more all-encompassing phrase than "any other law enforcement officer" to express that intent. We have no reason to demand that Congress write less economically and more repetitiously. * * *

Against this textual and structural evidence that "any other law enforcement officer" does in fact mean any other law enforcement officer, petitioner invokes numerous canons of statutory construction. He relies primarily on *ejusdem generis*, or the principle that "when a general term follows a specific one, the general term should be understood as a reference to subjects akin to the one with specific enumeration." *Norfolk & Western R. Co. v. Train Dispatchers*, 499 U. S. 117, 129 (1991). In petitioner's view, "any officer of customs or excise or any other law enforcement officer" should be read as a three-item list, and the final, catchall phrase "any other law enforcement officer" should be limited to officers of the same nature as the preceding specific phrases.

Petitioner likens his case to two recent cases in which we found the canon useful. In *Washington State Dept. of Social and Health Servs. v. Guardianship Estate of Keffeler*, 537 U. S. 371, 375 (2003), we considered the clause "execution, levy, attachment, garnishment, or other legal process" in 42 U. S. C. § 407(a). Applying *ejusdem generis*, we concluded that "other legal process" was limited to legal processes of the same nature as the specific items listed. 537 U. S., at 384–385. The department's scheme for serving as a representative payee of the benefits due to children under its care, while a "legal process," did not share the common attribute of the listed items, viz., "utilization of some judicial or quasi-judicial mechanism . . . by which control over property passes from one person to another in order to discharge" a debt. 537 U. S., at 385. Similarly, in *Dolan v. Postal Service*, 546 U. S. 481 (2006), the Court considered whether an exception to the FTCA's waiver of sovereign immunity for claims arising out of the " 'loss, miscarriage, or negligent transmission of letters or postal matter' " barred a claim that mail negligently left on the petitioner's porch caused her to slip and fall. *Id.*, at 485 (quoting 28 U. S. C. § 2680(b)). Noting that "loss" and "miscarriage" both addressed "failings in the postal obligation to deliver mail in a timely manner to the right address," 546 U. S., at 487, the Court concluded that "negligent transmission" must be similarly limited, *id.*, at 486–489, and rejected the Government's argument that the exception applied to "all torts committed in the course of mail delivery," *id.*, at 490.

* * * The structure of the phrase "any officer of customs or excise or any other law enforcement officer" does not lend itself to application of the canon. The phrase is disjunctive, with one specific and one general category, not—like the clauses at issue in *Keffeler* and *Dolan*—a list of specific items separated by commas and followed by a general or collective term. The absence of a list of specific items undercuts the inference embodied in *ejusdem generis* that Congress remained focused on the common attribute when it used the catchall phrase. Cf. *United States v. Aguilar*, 515 U. S. 593, 615 (1995) (Scalia, J., concurring in part and dissenting in part) (rejecting the canon's applicability to an omnibus clause that was "one of . . . several distinct and independent prohibitions" rather than "a general or collective term following a list of specific items to which a particular statutory command is applicable"). * * *

Petitioner's appeals to other interpretive principles are also unconvincing. Petitioner contends that his reading is supported by the canon *noscitur a sociis*, according to which "a word is known by the company it keeps." *S. D. Warren Co. v. Maine Bd. of Environmental Protection*, 547 U. S. 370, 378 (2006). But the cases petitioner cites in support of applying *noscitur a sociis* involved statutes with stronger contextual cues. See *Gutierrez v. Ada*, 528 U. S. 250, 254–258 (2000) (applying the canon to narrow the relevant phrase, "any election," where it was closely surrounded by six specific references to gubernatorial elections); *Jarecki, supra,* at 306–309 (applying the canon to narrow the term "discoveries" to discoveries of mineral resources where it was contained in a list of three words, all of which applied to the oil, gas, and mining industries and could not conceivably all apply to any other industry). Here, although customs and excise are mentioned twice in § 2680(c), nothing in the overall statutory context suggests that customs and excise officers were the exclusive focus of the provision. The emphasis in subsection (c) on customs and excise is not inconsistent with the conclusion that "any other law enforcement officer" sweeps as broadly as its language suggests.

Similarly, the rule against superfluities lends petitioner sparse support. The construction we adopt today does not necessarily render "any officer of customs or excise" superfluous; Congress may have simply intended to remove any doubt that officers of customs or excise were included in "law enforcement officers." See *Fort Stewart Schools v. FLRA*, 495 U. S. 641, 646 (1990) (noting that "technically unnecessary" examples may have been "inserted out of an abundance of caution"). Moreover, petitioner's construction threatens to render "any other law enforcement officer" superfluous because it is not clear when, if ever, "other law enforcement officer[s]" act in a customs or excise capacity. In any event,

FYI This is also often called the "rule against surplusage," and is discussed in its own right in section C below.

we do not woodenly apply limiting principles every time Congress includes a specific example along with a general phrase.

In the end, we are unpersuaded by petitioner's attempt to create ambiguity where the statute's text and structure suggest none. Had Congress intended to limit § 2680(c)'s reach as petitioner contends, it easily could have written "any other law enforcement officer *acting in a customs or excise capacity.*" Instead, it used the unmodified, all-

What do you make of this characterization? If there is ambiguity, where does the ambiguity come from?

encompassing phrase "any other law enforcement officer." Nothing in the statutory context requires a narrowing construction—indeed, as we have explained, the statute is most consistent and coherent when "any other law enforcement officer" is read to mean what it literally says. See *Norfolk & Western R. Co.*, 499 U. S., at 129 (noting that interpretive canons must yield "when the whole context dictates a different conclusion"). It bears emphasis, moreover, that § 2680(c), far from maintaining sovereign immunity for the entire universe of claims against law enforcement officers, does so only for claims "arising in respect of" the "detention" of property. We are not at liberty to rewrite the statute to reflect a meaning we deem more desirable. Instead, we must give effect to the text Congress enacted: Section 2680(c) forecloses lawsuits against the United States for the unlawful detention of property by "any," not just "some," law enforcement officers.

JUSTICE KENNEDY, with whom JUSTICE STEVENS, JUSTICE SOUTER, and JUSTICE BREYER join, dissenting.

Statutory interpretation, from beginning to end, requires respect for the text. The respect is not enhanced, however, by decisions that foreclose consideration of the text within the whole context of the statute as a guide to determining a legislature's intent. To prevent textual analysis from becoming so rarefied that it departs from how a legislator most likely understood the words when he or she voted for the law, courts use certain interpretative rules to consider text within the statutory design. These canons do not demand wooden reliance and are not by themselves dispositive, but they do function as helpful guides in construing ambiguous statutory provisions. Two of these accepted rules are *ejusdem generis* and *noscitur a sociis,* which together instruct that words in a series should be interpreted in relation to one another.

Today the Court holds, if my understanding of its opinion is correct, that there is only one possible way to read the statute. Placing implicit reliance upon a comma at the beginning of a clause, the Court says that the two maxims noted, and indeed other helpful and recognized principles of statutory analysis, are not useful as interpretative aids in this case because the clause cannot be understood by what went before. In my respectful submission the Court's approach is incorrect as a general rule and as applied to the statute now before us. Both the analytic framework and the specific interpretation the Court now employs become binding on the federal courts, which will confront other cases in which a series of words operate in a clause similar to the one we consider today. So this case is troubling not only for the result * * * but also for the analysis it employs. * * *

The Federal Tort Claims Act (FTCA) allows those who allege injury from governmental actions over a vast sphere to seek damages for tortious conduct. The enacting Congress enumerated 13 exceptions to the Act's broad waiver of sovereign immunity, all of which shield the Government from suit in specific instances. These exceptions must be given careful consideration in order to prevent interference with the governmental operations described. As noted in *Kosak v. United States,* 465 U. S. 848, 853, n. 9 (1984), however, "unduly generous interpretations of the exceptions run the risk of defeating the central purpose of the statute."

* * * Both on first reading and upon further, close consideration, the plain words of the statute indicate that the [§ 2680(c)] exception is concerned only with customs and taxes. The provision begins with a clause dealing exclusively with customs and tax duties. And the provision as a whole contains four express references to customs and tax, making revenue duties and customs and excise officers its most salient features.

This is not to suggest that the Court's reading is wholly impermissible or without some grammatical support. After all, detention of goods is not stated until the outset of the second clause and at the end of the same clause the words "any other law enforcement officer" appear; so it can be argued that the first and second clauses of the provision are so separate that all detentions by all law enforcement officers in whatever capacity they might act are covered. Still, this ought not be the preferred reading; for between the beginning of the second clause and its closing reference to "any other law enforcement officer" appears another reference to "officer[s] of customs or excise," this time in the context of property detention. This is quite sufficient, in my view, to continue the limited scope of the exception. At the very least, the Court errs by adopting a rule which simply bars all consideration of the canons of *ejusdem generis* and *noscitur a sociis*. And when those canons are consulted, together with other common principles of interpretation, the case for limiting the exception to customs and tax more than overcomes the position maintained by the Government and adopted by the Court.

The *ejusdem generis* canon provides that, where a seemingly broad clause constitutes a residual phrase, it must be controlled by, and defined with reference to, the "enumerated categories . . . which are recited just before it," so that the clause encompasses only objects similar in nature. *Circuit City Stores, Inc. v. Adams*, 532 U. S. 105, 115 (2001). The words "any other law enforcement officer" immediately follow the statute's reference to "officer[s] of customs or excise," as well as the first clause's reference to the assessment of tax and customs duties.

The Court counters that § 2680(c) "is disjunctive, with one specific and one general category," rendering *ejusdem generis* inapplicable. *Ante*, at 10. The canon's applicability, however, is not limited to those statutes that include a laundry list of items. See, *e.g., Norfolk & Western R. Co. v. Train Dispatchers*, 499 U. S. 117, 129 (1991) ("[W]hen a general term follows a specific one, the general term should be understood as a reference to subjects akin to the one with specific enumeration"). In addition, *ejusdem generis* is often invoked in conjunction with the interpretative canon *noscitur a sociis,* which provides that words are to be " 'known by their companions.' " *Washington State Dept. of Social and Health Servs. v. Guardianship Estate of Keffeler*, 537 U. S. 371, 384 (2003) (quoting *Gutierrez, supra,* at 255). The general rule is that the "meaning of a word, and, consequently, the intention of the legislature," should be "ascertained by reference to the context, and by considering whether the word in question and the surrounding words are, in fact, *ejusdem generis*, and referable to the same subject-matter." *Neal v. Clark*, 95 U. S. 704, 709 (1878) (internal quotation marks omitted)).

A proper reading of § 2680(c) thus attributes to the last phrase ("any other law enforcement officer") the discrete characteristic shared by the preceding phrases ("officer[s] of customs or excise" and "assessment or collection of any tax or customs duty"). See also *Norton v. Southern Utah Wilderness Alliance*, 542 U. S. 55, 62–63 (2004) (applying *ejusdem generis* to conclude that " 'failure to act' " means "failure to take an *agency action*" (emphasis in original)); *Washington State Dept. of Social and Health Servs., supra,* at 384–385 (holding that the phrase "other legal process" in 42 U.S.C. § 407(a) refers only to the utilization of a judicial or quasi-judicial mechanism, the common attribute shared by the phrase and the statutory enumeration preceding it). Had Congress intended otherwise, in all likelihood it would have drafted the section to apply to "any law enforcement officer, including officers of customs and excise," rather than tacking "any other law enforcement officer" on the end of the enumerated categories as it did here.

The common attribute of officers of customs and excise and other law enforcement officers is the performance of functions most often assigned to revenue officers, including, *inter alia,* the enforcement of the United States' revenue laws and the conduct of border searches. Although officers of customs and officers of excise are in most instances the only full-time staff charged with this duty, officers of other federal agencies and general law enforcement officers often will be called upon to act in the traditional capacity of a revenue officer. * * *

The Court reaches its contrary conclusion by concentrating on the word "any" before the phrase "other law enforcement officer." 28 U. S. C. § 2680(c). It takes this single last phrase to extend the statute so that it covers all detentions of property by any law enforcement officer in whatever capacity he or she acts. There are fundamental problems with this approach, in addition to the ones already mentioned.

First, the Court's analysis cannot be squared with the longstanding recognition that a single word must not be read in isolation but instead defined by reference to its statutory context. This is true even of facially broad modifiers. The word "any" can mean "different things depending upon the setting," *Nixon v. Missouri Municipal League*, 541 U. S. 125, 132 (2004), and must be limited in its application "to those objects to which the legislature intended to apply them," *United States v. Palmer*, 3 Wheat. 610, 631 (1818). * * *

Further, § 2680(c) provides that there will be immunity only where there has been a "detention" of goods, merchandise, or property. "[D]etention" is defined by legal and nonlegal dictionaries alike as a "compulsory," "forced," or "punitive" containment. BLACK's LAW DICTIONARY 459 (7th ed. 1999) (compulsory); AMERICAN HERITAGE DICTIONARY 494 (4th ed. 2000) (forced or punitive). The issue whether petitioner's property was "detained" within the meaning of the statute was not raised in this case; and so the Court leaves for another day the exception's applicability to these facts. See *ante,* at 4, n. 2. It is important, however, to bear in mind that, in the context of detention of goods by customs and tax agents, it will be the rare case when property is voluntarily turned over, rather than forcibly appropriated; indeed, customs and tax agents are in the regular business of seizing and forfeiting property, as are law enforcement agents acting in the capacity of revenue enforcement. * * *

In other contexts, however, the word "detention" may or may not accurately describe the nature of the Government action. A prisoner's voluntary decision to deliver property for transfer to another facility, for example, bears a greater similarity to a "bailment"—the delivery of personal property after being held by the prison in trust, see AMERICAN HERITAGE DICTIONARY, *supra,* at 134—than to a "detention."

* * * Second, the Court's construction of the phrase "any other law enforcement officer" runs contrary to " 'our duty "to give effect, if possible, to every clause and word of a statute." ' " *Duncan v. Walker,* 533 U. S. 167, 174 (2001) (quoting *United States v. Menasche,* 348 U. S. 528, 538–539 (1955)). The Court's reading renders "officer[s] of customs or excise" mere surplusage, as there would have been no need for Congress to have specified that officers of customs and officers of excise were immune if they indeed were subsumed within the allegedly all-encompassing "any" officer clause.

Third, though the final reference to "any other law enforcement officer" does result in some ambiguity, the legislative history, by virtue of its exclusive reference to customs and excise, confirms that Congress did not shift its attention from the context of revenue enforcement when it used these words at the end of the statute. See, *e.g.,* S. Rep. No. 1400, 79th Cong., 2d Sess., 33 (1946) (in discussing 28 U. S. C. § 2680(c) referring only to "the detention of goods by customs officers"); A. Holtzoff, *Report on Proposed Federal Tort Claims Bill* 16 (1931) (noting that the property-detention exception was added to the legislation to "include immunity from liability in respect of loss in connection with the detention of goods or merchandise by any officer of customs or excise").

Indeed, the Court's construction reads the exception to defeat the central purpose of the statute, an interpretative danger the Court has warned against in explicit terms. See *Kosak*, 465 U. S., at 854, n. 9 (the Court must identify only " 'those circumstances which are within the words and reason of the exception'—no less and no more" (quoting *Dalehite v. United States*, 346 U. S. 15, 31 (1953)). It is difficult to conceive that the FTCA, which was enacted by Congress to make the tort liability of the United States "the same as that of a private person under like circumstance[s]," S. Rep. No. 1400, at 32, would allow any officer under any circumstance to detain property without being accountable under the Act to those injured by his or her tortious conduct. If Congress wanted to say that all law enforcement officers may detain property without liability in tort, including when they perform general law enforcement tasks, it would have done so in more express terms; one would expect at least a reference to law enforcement officers outside the customs or excise context either in the text of the statute or in the legislative history. In the absence of that reference, the Court ought not presume that the liberties of the person who owns the property would be so lightly dismissed and disregarded. * * *

If Congress had intended to give sweeping immunity to all federal law enforcement officials from liability for the detention of property, it would not have dropped this phrase onto the end of the statutory clause so as to appear there as something of an afterthought. The seizure of property by an officer raises serious concerns for the liberty of our people and the Act should not be read to permit appropriation of property without a remedy in tort by language so obscure and indirect.

NOTES & QUESTIONS

1. What canons of construction can you find being used in each opinion?

2. Another example of the use of the *ejusdem generis* canon involves the Federal Arbitration Act of 1926, which excluded from its coverage "contracts of employment of seamen, railroad employees, or any other class of workers engaged in foreign or interstate commerce." Although standing alone, the phrase "any other class of workers engaged in foreign or interstate commerce" is quite broad, potentially excluding all employment contracts from the arbitration act's coverage, the *ejusdem* canon would suggest that, as used in this act, the phrase should be limited to

workers like seamen or railroad employees. The Supreme Court adopted this narrow reading in *Circuit City Stores, Inc. v. Adams*, 532 U.S. 105 (2001), thus excluding from the Federal Arbitration Act's coverage only contracts of transportation workers, and not of the retail sales employee who also wanted to be excluded from the act's coverage.

3.   What explains the different result in *Circuit City*, a case cited in *Ali*?

4.   The *Ali* case demonstrates that while interpreters of many stripes may agree about the potential value of textual canons in the abstract, they often disagree about when and how to apply them. In particular, notice the way the majority's use of the Plain Meaning Rule directly conflicts with the dissent's use of *noscitur a sociis* and *ejusdem generis*. Isn't this conflict inevitable here? If so, does this inevitable conflict help you understand something about the role of semantic canons in statutory interpretation?

3.   ***Expressio unius est exclusio alterius***—"the expression of one thing implies the exclusion of other things (not expressed)." This maxim is typically deployed when a statute contains a list of items or terms, identifying with some specificity when or to what the statute should apply, and the omission from that list of some other possible item or term suggests that the statute does not apply to it.

For example, the Resource Conservation and Recovery Act permits private suits against anyone "who has contributed [to the] handling, storage, treatment, transportation, or disposal of any solid waste [that] may present an imminent and substantial endangerment to health or the environment." The act in turn defines "disposal" as "the *discharge, deposit, injection, dumping, spilling, leaking, or placing* of any solid waste . . . into or on any land or water so that such solid waste . . . may enter the environment or be emitted into the air or discharged into any waters . . ." (emphasis added). Relying on the *expressio unius* canon, the Ninth Circuit concluded that two railroad companies had not violated the act's prohibition against disposal of solid waste by emitting diesel particulates directly into the air, because "emitting" into the air was not included among the defined ways that prohibited solid waste disposal could occur. Even though the definition did make reference to the possible subsequent emission into the air of a solid waste after its disposal "into or on any land or water," the definition first required that disposal itself involve one of seven specified types of conduct, which did not include emitting solid waste into the air. *See Center for Community Action v. BNSF Ry. Co.*, 764 F.3d 1019 (9th Cir. 2014).

In an earlier case, the Supreme Court considered the Warsaw Convention in light of the *expressio* canon. The Convention has several provisions that limit the liability of commercial airlines for loss of baggage or cargo but waive the liability limits if the carrier has not provided the customer with adequate notice of these limits. The Convention also has another provision that limits the airlines' liability for passenger injury or death but does not include any waiver of the limit in the absence of adequate notice to the passenger. In *Chan v. Korean Air Lines,* 490 U.S. 122 (1989), the Court invoked the *expressio* canon to conclude that airlines that had not provided passengers with notice of the liability limits for injury or death were still entitled to the protections of these limits because the Convention had expressly provided in other contexts that lack of notice would mean the waiver of the liability limits, but said nothing about waiving the liability limits for lack of notice in this context.

As one more example, in the *Holy Trinity* case, the *expressio* canon could have undermined the Court's conclusion. The statute at issue, which prohibited contracts to import foreigners to perform "labor or service of any kind," contained a set of exceptions that expressly excluded from its coverage "professional actors, lecturers, or singers, [or] personal or domestic servants." Under the *expressio unius* canon, because pastors and ministers were not included in this list of very specific types of labor or service, that could have implied that pastors and ministers were not intended to be among the exceptions (and therefore *were* meant to be covered by the act). Of course, that the Court did not use this canon to reach the result opposite of what it actually held confirms that the canons are merely a source of interpretive guidance, not binding interpretive methods.

On many occasions statutory language merely identifies examples of the type of items to which a statute applies, rather than exhausting all possible items. The phrase "including but not limited to," when it precedes a list of covered items, is the most obvious example. But sometimes the word "including" alone is used to introduce the list, and other comparable phrases such as "for instance" or "for example" may be used to identify representative items within a set without intending to exclude other items not specified. Consider *United States v. Phillip Morris U.S.A. Inc.,* 566 F.3d 1095, 1110–16 (D.C. Cir. 2009), in which the District of Columbia Circuit construed language in the federal RICO statute (the Racketeer Influenced and Corrupt Organizations Act) providing that " 'enterprise' includes any individual, partnership, corporation, association, or other legal entity, and any union or group of individuals associated in fact although not a legal entity." The court rejected the argument that the list of included entities was exclusive. Instead, the court viewed the mere fact that the statute used the term "includes" as sufficient to make the list non-exclusive.

Thus, interpreters must be cautious in their deployment of these semantic canons. As indicated by the number of occasions when the Supreme Court itself has divided on the appropriateness of using one or more of these canons, there is no accepted criterion for determining when a particular canon fits a textual problem. Instead, even the choice to use a canon is contextual. As Justice Souter wrote in 2003 specifically about the *expressio* canon, "[the canon] does not apply to every statutory listing or grouping; it has force only when the items expressed are members of an 'associated group or series,' justifying the inference that items not mentioned were excluded by deliberate choice, not inadvertence." *Barnhardt v. Peabody Coal Co.*, 537 U.S. 149, 168 (2003). With respect to canons more generally, Justice Scalia has observed (jointly with his co-author Bryan Garner) that canons should not be used thoughtlessly, but must be deployed in light of context: "The skill of sound construction lies in assessing the clarity and weight of each clue and deciding where the balance lies." SCALIA & GARNER, *supra*, at 59.

C. Grammar Canons

Key Concepts

- Grammar canons
- Punctuation canon
- The last antecedent
- May vs. shall
- And vs. or
- Plural vs. singular
- Gendered pronouns

Summary

Grammar canons employ basic rules of sentence structure to ascertain legal meanings. By employing them, the interpreter assumes that legislators, whether deliberately or subconsciously, intended that the statute be understood by following the common rules of grammar. While this is a seemingly unremarkable assumption, it is not always clear if drafters actually follow these rules.

> For instance, the punctuation canon tells an interpreter to give legal effect to the placing of periods, commas, colons, and semi-colons. Another canon, dubbed the last antecedent canon, limits the legal effect of modifying clauses following a list of terms, only giving the modifier its effect with respect to the last term in the list. The may vs. shall canon says that when the legislature uses mandatory words like "shall," the interpreter should give them mandatory meaning, and when it uses words like "may," the interpreter should treat them as discretionary. Similarly, when the legislature uses "and," the clause should be given conjunctive effect, while use of "or" tells of a disjunctive effect. The canons involving plural vs. singular and gendered pronouns both have diminished importance today as interpretive tools, but can still be employed.

Grammar canons are another class of interpretive textual canon. These are rules of English grammar that arguably have special force in legal writing, precisely in order to reduce ambiguity. Some of these rules themselves have evolved over time, and they also are not necessarily universally embraced in the same form. Even where they are widely followed or accepted, they are only rebuttable presumptions, not hard-and-fast requirements.

1.   The Punctuation Canon. For generations, the rule in English law was that the punctuation of a statute could not be used to resolve (or create!) ambiguity. This was because in an earlier era, marks of punctuation typically were added to the written law after the fact by clerks or recorders, rather than being added by Parliament itself during the process of enactment.

In contrast, as Sutherland's famous statutory interpretation treatise explains, "The better rule is that punctuation is part of an act and courts may consider punctuation to interpret an act but not to create doubt or to distort or defeat legislative intent." 2A Sutherland Statutes and Statutory Construction § 47.15 (7th ed. 2014). (Until the 2014 release of the 7th edition, the Sutherland treatise had provided that in the United States statutes are typically "read as punctuated unless there is some reason to do otherwise." 2A Sutherland Statutes and Statutory Construction § 47.15 (6th ed. 2000).) Commas can

> Jabez Gridley Sutherland was a **FYI** nineteenth century lawyer, judge, and politician who represented Michigan in the U.S. House of Representatives from 1871 to 1873. He later served as a law professor and in 1891 penned an influential treatise on statutory interpretation, which the publishers continue to update and publish under his name today.

often be especially significant in determining meaning, helping to establish how words and phrases relate to each other, as for instance in distinguishing the phrase "motor vehicle trailer" from the phrase "motor vehicle, trailer." Semicolons likewise can be especially helpful. Yet where punctuation seems problematic, the punctuation rule can easily give way to judicial adjustment of punctuation under the theory of a scrivener's error.

2.   The Last Antecedent. A second grammatical canon, which for its proper application may often depend in turn upon the proper use of serial commas, is the rule of the last antecedent. This rule provides that words of limitation, qualification, or clarification that follow and relate back to a set of terms or clauses should be understood to modify only the most immediately preceding antecedent to which they can sensibly apply, unless punctuation, context, or "other indicia of meaning," *Barnhart v. Thomas,* 540 U.S. 20, 26 (2003), clearly suggest otherwise. Determining when to apply this canon is not always easy, however.

For instance, 18 U.S.C. § 2252(b)(2) prescribes a more severe criminal sentence for a defendant convicted on federal child pornography charges if the defendant already has a previous state law conviction "relating to aggravated sexual abuse, sexual abuse, or abusive sexual conduct *involving a minor or ward*" (emphasis added). Should the qualifying language "involving a minor or ward" be understood to limit only the final type of state law crime listed, that of "abusive sexual conduct"? Or should it apply to all three of the possible kinds of state law crimes listed? How would the interpretive dilemma have differed if a comma followed the phrase "abusive sexual conduct"? Without that comma, the rule of the last antecedent would support applying the limiting phrase to only the final category of state law crime. In a 6–2 opinion, the Supreme Court followed this approach in *Lockhart v. United States,* 577 U.S. 347 (2016). But the dissenters thought this a patent misuse of the last antecedent rule (as well as contrary to clear legislative history about congressional intent) and invoked a contrary maxim that " '[w]hen there is a straightforward, parallel construction that involves all nouns or verbs in a series,' a modifier at the end of the list 'normally applies to the entire series' " (quoting SCALIA & GARNER, *supra,* at 147).

3.   May Versus Shall. A more straightforward maxim is that mandatory words ordinarily should be given a mandatory meaning, while hortatory or precatory words should not. Yet on occasion, "may" has been construed to carry a mandatory meaning. *See In re Cartmell's Estate,* 138 A.2d 588 (Vt. 1958). Meanwhile, sometimes the extent to which "shall" is mandatory may also be at issue. *See Barnhart v. Peabody Coal Co.,* 537 U.S. 149 (2003).

The usually significant difference between "may" and "shall" also figured importantly in one of the central legal issues surrounding the 2000 presidential election in Florida. Florida law had two seemingly conflicting provisions, one of which told the Secretary of State that county election totals arriving after the statutory canvassing deadline "shall be ignored," and another providing that late-arriving canvass totals "may be ignored," with specified fines for each day that a county's returns were late. The Florida Supreme Court concluded that the permissive provision controlled the result because (1) it was more recently enacted; (2) it was more specific; and (3) it better made sense of the overall statutory scheme. See *Palm Beach County Canvassing Board v. Harris*, 772 So.2d 1220 (Fla.), *vacated sub nom Bush v. Palm Beach Canvassing Board*, 531 U.S. 70 (2000).

4.   And Versus Or. As a matter of English grammar, "and" is conjunctive and "or" is disjunctive. Unfortunately, these terms can be used ambiguously. As a result, one formulation of a relevant canon is that "terms connected by a disjunctive [should] be given separate meanings, unless the context dictates otherwise." *Reiter v. Sonotone Corp.*, 442 U.S. 330, 339 (1979). But "or" can be read to mean "and" when to do otherwise would frustrate legislative intent. See *De Sylva v. Ballantine*, 351 U.S. 570 (1956).

5.   Plural Versus Singular Nouns; Gendered Pronouns. In theory, a drafter's choice to use a plural noun or pronoun might be cause for distinguishing its meaning from a singular construction, and the use of a gendered pronoun to exclude the opposite gender. For instance, in *People v. Rodriguez*, 290 P.3d 1143 (2012), the Supreme Court of California construed a state criminal statute that targeted the activities of street gangs. Elements of the offense included that the alleged perpetrator (1) participates in a street gang, and (2) "willfully promotes, furthers, or assists in any felonious criminal conduct by members of that gang." The court concluded that the statute's plural term "members" precluded convicting a gang-member who acted alone; multiple gang "members" had to participate.

Unless the specific context shows otherwise, however, the plural is generally understood to include the singular, and vice-versa; gendered pronouns similarly are usually construed to be all-embracing. Indeed, as a matter of federal law, the Dictionary Act has codified these rules of construction in section 1 of Title 1 of the United States Code: "In determining the meaning of any Act of Congress, unless the context indicates otherwise—words importing the singular include and apply to several persons, parties, or things; words importing the plural include the singular; words importing the masculine gender include the feminine as well. . . ." 1 U.S.C. § 1. Most states have analogous interpretive directions in their codes (and similar directions are found in the United Kingdom under the Interpretation Act of 1889). Meanwhile, 1 U.S.C. § 1 further provides that in federal statutes, "the words 'person' and 'whoever' include corporations, companies, associations, firms, partnerships, societies, and joint stock companies, as well as individuals."

D. The Whole Act Rule and Its Corollaries

Key Concepts

- Reading statutory text in context
- Whole Act Rule
- The Rule Against Surplusage
- The Rule of Consistent Usage
- Titles and headings
- Preambles, legislative findings, and statements of purpose
- Provisos and exceptions
- The Whole Code Rule

Summary

The overarching idea of the Whole Act Rule as an interpretive canon is that ambiguity in a certain term or clause of a statute can often best be resolved not in isolation, but in the context of the larger body of the rest of the text enacted alongside it. The interpreter assumes the legislature has rationally adopted a cohesive law whose functions and terminology are in harmony. As we saw in Part III, however, methods of modern lawmaking do not always in fact give rise to cohesive and harmonious laws.

Within the broad ambit of the Whole Act Rule are corollaries that function as canons themselves. The Rule Against Surplusage assumes that legislators do not add unnecessary or redundant words to statutes, and that every word was intended to have meaning and thus impact its operation. The Rule of Consistent Usage says that when a term is used more than once, its meaning should be consistent everywhere. Titles and Headings in a statute can give an interpreter some clue as to how the text within that section operates, as can Preambles and Statements of Purpose. Provisos and exceptions that limit the operation of a statute are assumed to have a narrow legal effect. Finally, the Whole Code Rule extends these same ideas to continuities in the greater body of law beyond the statute in question.

A final text-based canon is the Whole Act Rule. This canon is one of many interpretive tools that address how to understand text *in context*. The Whole Act Rule encourages the interpreter to be attentive not only to the way that the specific term in question interacts with the immediately surrounding words, but also how it fits with the entire statute of which it is a part. In its simplest form, this rule applies to situations in which the same term is used in multiple places within a statute. The Rule would assign a single consistent meaning to the term throughout the entire act to resolve an interpretive ambiguity that otherwise would remain if there were just a single isolated usage of the term. Even when the term in question is not used elsewhere in the act, occasionally the interpretive difficulty can be resolved by considering how the various interpretive possibilities will affect the functioning of other parts of the act.

Implicit in the Whole Act Rule are the assumptions that a statute should function as a coherent whole and that it is drafted as a coherent whole, whether or not this is an accurate description of the actual drafting process. The many corollaries of the Whole Act Rule discussed below also are based on this idea of coherence. In practice, however, legislatures often cobble together several distinct parts, purposes, or ideas into one act, without always having time or opportunity (or even desire) to ensure consistency or integration among the many constituent pieces (a practice that has become a recurring hallmark of today's era of increasingly "unorthodox" lawmaking). Thus, the assumption of internal coherence is to a certain degree based on a legal fiction, or at best is a probabilistic assessment of the likely meaning of statutory text, rather than being a statute-specific claim about legislative intent. Nevertheless, the rest of an act is the most immediate source of context for understanding the meaning of a provision at issue, and it is eminently sensible to construe individual components of an act to enhance the act's overall coherence.

> The Whole Act Rule strives to resolve a textual ambiguity **!** by construing the text in the way that will best align with the entirety of the statute.

Indeed, Justice Scalia liked to argue that courts should use textual canons like the Whole Act Rule if only to encourage legislatures to write their statutes more carefully and with greater coherence. See SCALIA & GARNER, at 51.

> **FYI** Recall that in Chapter 11 we recognized that in recent decades Congress has increasingly departed from its traditional process of letting a standing committee have primary responsibility for determining the content of a specific bill.

We will see many examples of this Rule in cases we will read in the materials ahead; what follows immediately below is a summary of the Rule's main corollaries:

1.   **The Rule Against Surplusage.** This rule, which again is only a rule of thumb and not a hard and fast requirement, suggests that each unique word or phrase in a statute ought to be construed to add meaning, and not just to repeat a meaning adequately covered by other terms. Consider the applicability of this corollary to our previous discussion of *ejusdem generis* in *Ali v. Federal Bureau of Prisons,* 552 U.S. 214 (2008) (which turned on the question of whether Bureau of Prisons employees were "other law enforcement officers" for purposes of an exception to government liability in the Federal Tort Claims Act).

Of course, the problem with this rule is that legislators not only have no obligation to follow this rule in drafting their enactments, but also frequently depart from it. In drafting legislative measures, overkill is typical and legislators routinely include redundancies and surplusage to be sure that all bases are covered.

2.   **The Presumption of Consistent Usage and Meaningful Variation.** The point of this corollary of the Whole Act Rule is that a term repeated in multiple places within a statute ought to be presumed to have a consistent meaning throughout. In contrast, a different term used where the same term might have fit should therefore be understood to reflect the drafters' deliberate choice to convey a different meaning.

3.   **Titles and Headings.** The Whole Act Rule also invites legal interpreters to look at titles and section headings, common parts of most legislative enactments and regulations today, for clues about meaning. For instance, you may recall that as far back as the 1892 *Holy Trinity* case (in Chapter 15), the Supreme Court turned to the statute's title as an aid "in determining the intent of the legislature." 143 U.S. 457, 462 (1892). Another example is *Almendarez-Torres v. United States,* 523 U.S. 224 (1998), where the Supreme Court relied upon a section heading's title of "criminal penalties" to help determine that the section did not define a separate crime but only specified punishments. The general rule here is that while headings and titles may be considered, they should not trump the text itself. *See Intel Corp. v. Advanced Micro Devices, Inc.,* 542 U.S. 241 (2004). Furthermore, in a number of enactments dating back over a hundred years, Congress has instructed interpreters not to consider certain titles and headings, although courts routinely do so anyway.

4.   **Preambles, Legislative Findings, and Statements of Purpose.** Similarly, in modern legislatures, it has become increasingly common to include some background for an act in the statute itself, at least in major pieces of legislation. While historically "preambles" and "whereas" clauses were seen as preceding the enacted text, it has become routine for similar statements of background and purpose to be incorporated as components of the duly enacted law itself, even if taken alone these provisions typically do not create or impose new legal obligations. Either explicitly

or implicitly, these components may explain something about the enacting legislature's intent or in other ways provide the context for the measure. And because they are fully "law," interpreters may see these sources of context and legislative intent as more reliable than extrinsic pieces of legislative history.

For instance, in *Sutton v. United Airlines*, 527 U.S. 471 (1999), the Supreme Court relied on the preamble to the Americans with Disabilities Act ("ADA") to conclude that myopia was not a protected disability under the ADA. The act's preamble had specified that some 43 million Americans were affected with a disability and therefore would be the beneficiaries of the act. The number of Americans Congress identified in the preamble as disabled was significant because had Congress considered myopia to be a disability for which the ADA offered protections, it would have needed to specify a much larger number in the preamble.

5.   Provisos and Exceptions. Another Whole Act Rule corollary is that provisos and exceptions in an act ought to be narrowly construed. The idea behind this corollary is to keep the exception from swallowing the rule by construing ambiguous exceptions to do less rather than more. Consider the applicability of this corollary as well to the exception to the Federal Tort Claims Act at issue in *Ali v. Federal Bureau of Prisons*, 552 U.S. 214 (2008).

6.   The Whole Code Rule. The Whole Act Rule also partakes of a variant known as the "Whole Code Rule." This corollary seeks to assign meaning to an ambiguous term by construing it not only to accord with the rest of the particular enactment of which it is a part, but also with the rest of the statutory law in the jurisdiction. Chapter 23 concludes with excerpts of the case *West Virginia University Hospitals Inc. v. Casey*, 499 U.S. 83 (1991), which demonstrates this corollary in full flower. But even more so than the Whole Act Rule, the assumption of internal coherence that underlies the Whole Code Rule—that all sorts of different laws necessarily cohere or are in harmony with each other—is almost certainly factually false. Thus, the Whole Code Rule too usually depends on a probabilistic assessment of likely meaning and on the broader value of promoting coherence in the law, not on the legislature's actual intent as to a specific piece of legislation.

DIY
Fishing for Red Grouper (reprise)

Recall the issue of undersized red grouper on the *Miss Katie* at the beginning of this chapter. The fish appear in the following case, in which our captain is now John Yates. The three opinions in the case deploy a host of interpretive tools. See how many interpretive tools you can find, while paying particular attention to ways that the Whole Act Rule is (or is not) put to use.

Yates v. United States
574 U.S. 528 (2015)

JUSTICE GINSBURG announced the judgment of the Court and delivered an opinion, in which THE CHIEF JUSTICE, JUSTICE BREYER, and JUSTICE SOTOMAYOR join.

* * * Section 1519 was enacted as part of the Sarbanes-Oxley Act of 2002, 116 Stat. 745, legislation designed to protect investors and restore trust in financial markets following the collapse of Enron Corporation. A fish is no doubt an object that is tangible; fish can be seen, caught, and handled, and a catch, as this case illustrates, is vulnerable to destruction. But it would cut § 1519 loose from its financial-fraud mooring to hold that it encompasses any and all objects, whatever their size or significance, destroyed with obstructive intent. Mindful that in Sarbanes-Oxley, Congress trained its attention on corporate and accounting deception and cover-ups, we conclude that a matching construction of § 1519 is in order: A tangible object captured by § 1519, we hold, must be one used to record or preserve information.

* * * The ordinary meaning of an "object" that is "tangible," as stated in dictionary definitions, is "a discrete . . . thing," WEBSTER'S THIRD NEW INTERNATIONAL DICTIONARY 1555 (2002), that "possess[es] physical form," BLACK'S LAW DICTIONARY 1683 (10th ed. 2014). From this premise, the Government concludes that "tangible object," as that term appears in § 1519, covers the waterfront, including fish from the sea.

Whether a statutory term is unambiguous, however, does not turn solely on dictionary definitions of its component words. Rather, "[t]he plainness or ambiguity of statutory language is determined [not only] by reference to the language itself, [but as well by] the specific context in which that language is used, and the broader context of the statute as a whole." *Robinson v. Shell Oil Co.*, 519 U. S. 337, 341 (1997). See also *Deal v. United States*, 508 U. S. 129, 132 (1993) (it is a "fundamental principle of statutory construction (and, indeed, of language itself) that the meaning of a word cannot be determined in isolation, but must be drawn from the context in which it is used"). Ordinarily, a word's usage accords with its dictionary definition. In law as in life, however, the same words, placed in different contexts, sometimes mean different things.

We have several times affirmed that identical language may convey varying content when used in different statutes, sometimes even in different provisions of the same statute. * * * As the Court observed in *Atlantic Cleaners & Dyers*, 286 U. S., at 433:

> Most words have different shades of meaning and consequently may be variously construed. . . . Where the subject matter to which the words refer is not the same in the several places where [the words] are used, or the conditions are different, or the scope of the legislative power exercised in one case is broader than that exercised in another, the meaning well may vary to meet the purposes of the law, to be arrived at by a consideration of the language in which those purposes are expressed, and of the circumstances under which the language was employed.

> **FYI** Note that this approach would seem to depart from a prototypical use of the Whole Act Rule, in which the same word used in multiple places would receive the same meaning. Think about what the Court describes as reasons for this departure from the Whole Act Rule.

* * *

Familiar interpretive guides aid our construction of the words "tangible object" as they appear in § 1519. We note first § 1519's caption: "Destruction, alteration, or falsification of records in Federal investigations and bankruptcy." That heading conveys no suggestion that the section prohibits spoliation of any and all physical evidence, however remote from records. Neither does the title of the section of the Sarbanes-Oxley Act in which § 1519 was placed, § 802: "Criminal penalties for altering documents." 116 Stat. 800. Furthermore, § 1520, the only other provision passed as part of § 802, is titled "Destruction of corporate audit records" and addresses only that specific subset of records and documents. While these headings are not commanding, they supply cues that Congress did not intend "tangible object" in § 1519 to sweep within its reach physical objects of every kind, including things no one would describe as records, documents, or devices closely associated with them. See *Almendarez-Torres v. United States*, 523 U. S. 224, 234 (1998) ("[T]he title of a statute and the heading of a section are tools available for the resolution of a doubt about the meaning of a statute." (internal quotation marks omitted)). If Congress indeed meant to make § 1519 an all-encompassing ban on the spoliation of evidence, as the dissent believes Congress did, one would have expected a clearer indication of that intent.

Section 1519's position within Chapter 73 of Title 18 further signals that § 1519 was not intended to serve as a cross-the-board ban on the destruction of physical evidence of every kind. Congress placed § 1519 (and its companion provision § 1520) at the end of the chapter, following immediately after the pre-existing § 1516, § 1517, and § 1518, each of them prohibiting obstructive acts in specific contexts. See § 1516 (audits of recipients of federal funds); § 1517 (federal examinations of financial institutions); § 1518 (criminal investigations of federal health care offenses). See also S. Rep. No. 107–146, at 7 (observing that § 1517 and § 1518 "apply to obstruction in certain limited types of cases, such as bankruptcy fraud, examinations of financial institutions, and healthcare fraud").

But Congress did not direct codification of the Sarbanes-Oxley Act's other additions to Chapter 73 adjacent to these specialized provisions. Instead, Congress directed placement of those additions within or alongside retained provisions that address obstructive acts relating broadly to official proceedings and criminal trials: Section 806, "Civil Action to protect against retaliation in fraud cases," was codified as § 1514A and inserted between the pre-existing § 1514, which addresses civil actions to restrain harassment of victims and witnesses in criminal cases, and § 1515, which defines terms used in § 1512 and § 1513. Section 1102, "Tampering with a record or otherwise impeding an official proceeding," was codified as § 1512(c) and inserted within the pre-existing § 1512, which addresses tampering with a victim, witness, or informant to impede any official proceeding. Section 1107, "Retaliation against informants," was codified as § 1513(e) and inserted within the pre-existing § 1513, which addresses retaliation against a victim, witness, or informant in any official proceeding. Congress thus ranked § 1519, not among the broad proscriptions, but together with specialized provisions expressly aimed at corporate fraud and financial audits. This placement accords with the view that Congress' conception of § 1519's coverage was considerably more limited than the Government's.

The contemporaneous passage of § 1512(c)(1), which was contained in a section of the Sarbanes-Oxley Act discrete from the section embracing § 1519 and § 1520, is also instructive. Section 1512(c)(1) provides:

> (c) Whoever corruptly—
>
> (1) alters, destroys, mutilates, or conceals a record, document, or other object, or attempts to do so, with the intent to impair the object's integrity or availability for use in an official proceeding. . .
>
> shall be fined under this title or imprisoned not more than 20 years, or both.

The legislative history reveals that § 1512(c)(1) was drafted and proposed after § 1519. See 148 Cong. Rec. 12518, 13088–13089 (2002). The Government argues, and Yates does not dispute, that § 1512(c)(1)'s reference to "other object" includes any and every physical object. But if § 1519's reference to "tangible object" already included all physical objects, as the Government and the dissent contend, then Congress had no reason to enact § 1512(c)(1): Virtually any act that would violate § 1512(c)(1) no doubt would violate § 1519 as well, for § 1519 applies to "the investigation or proper administration of any matter within the jurisdiction of any department or agency of the United States . . . or in relation to or contemplation of any such matter," not just to "an official proceeding."

The Government acknowledges that, under its reading, § 1519 and § 1512(c)(1) "significantly overlap." Brief for United States 49. Nowhere does the Government explain what independent function § 1512(c)(1) would serve if the Government is right about the sweeping scope of § 1519. We resist a reading of § 1519 that would render superfluous an entire provision passed in proximity as part of the same Act. See *Marx v. General Revenue Corp.*, 568 U. S. ___, ___ (2013) (slip op., at 14) ("[T]he canon against surplusage is strongest when an interpretation would render superfluous another part of the same statutory scheme.").

The words immediately surrounding "tangible object" in § 1519—"falsifies, or makes a false entry in any record [or] document"—also cabin the contextual meaning of that term. As explained in *Gustafson v. Alloyd Co.*, 513 U. S. 561,

575 (1995), we rely on the principle of *noscitur a sociis*—a word is known by the company it keeps—to "avoid ascribing to one word a meaning so broad that it is inconsistent with its accompanying words, thus giving unintended breadth to the Acts of Congress." (internal quotation marks omitted). * * *

The *noscitur a sociis* canon operates in a similar manner here. "Tangible object" is the last in a list of terms that begins "any record [or] document." The term is therefore appropriately read to refer, not to any tangible object, but specifically to the subset of tangible objects involving records and documents, *i.e.,* objects used to record or preserve information.

This moderate interpretation of "tangible object" accords with the list of actions § 1519 proscribes. The section applies to anyone who "alters, destroys, mutilates, conceals, covers up, *falsifies*, or *makes a false entry in* any record, document, or tangible object" with the requisite obstructive intent. (Emphasis added.) The last two verbs, "falsif[y]" and "mak[e] a false entry in," typically take as grammatical objects records, documents, or things used to record or preserve information, such as logbooks or hard drives. It would be unnatural, for example, to describe a killer's act of wiping his fingerprints from a gun as "falsifying" the murder weapon. But it would not be strange to refer to "falsifying" data stored on a hard drive as simply "falsifying" a hard drive. Furthermore, Congress did not include on § 1512(c)(1)'s list of prohibited actions "falsifies" or "makes a false entry in." See § 1512(c)(1) (making it unlawful to "alte[r], destro[y], mutilat[e], or concea[l] a record, document, or other object" with the requisite obstructive intent). That contemporaneous omission also suggests that Congress intended "tangible object" in § 1519 to have a narrower scope than "other object" in § 1512(c)(1).

A canon related to *noscitur a sociis*, *ejusdem generis*, counsels: "Where general words follow specific words in a statutory enumeration, the general words are [usually] construed to embrace only objects similar in nature to those objects enumerated by the preceding specific words." *Washington State Dept. of Social and Health Servs. v. Guardianship Estate of Keffeler*, 537 U. S. 371, 384 (2003) (internal quotation marks omitted). * * * Had Congress intended "tangible object" in § 1519 to be interpreted so generically as to capture physical objects as dissimilar as documents and fish, Congress would have had no reason to refer specifically to "record" or "document." The Government's unbounded reading of "tangible object" would render those words misleading surplusage.

Having used traditional tools of statutory interpretation to examine markers of congressional intent within the Sarbanes-Oxley Act and § 1519 itself, we are persuaded that an aggressive interpretation of "tangible object" must be rejected. It is highly improbable that Congress would have buried a general spoliation statute covering objects of any and every kind in a provision targeting fraud in financial record-keeping.

* * * [Here the Court invoked the Rule of Lenity, discussed in Chapter 21.]

For the reasons stated, we resist reading § 1519 expansively to create a coverall spoliation of evidence statute, advisable as such a measure might be. Leaving that important decision to Congress, we hold that a "tangible object" within § 1519's compass is one used to record or preserve information. The judgment of the U. S. Court of Appeals for the Eleventh Circuit is therefore reversed, and the case is remanded for further proceedings.

Justice Alito, concurring in the judgment.

This case can and should be resolved on narrow grounds. And though the question is close, traditional tools of statutory construction confirm that John Yates has the better of the argument. Three features of 18 U. S. C. § 1519 stand out to me: the statute's list of nouns, its list of verbs, and its title. Although perhaps none of these features by itself would tip the case in favor of Yates, the three combined do so.

Start with the nouns. Section 1519 refers to "any record, document, or tangible object." The *noscitur a sociis* canon instructs that when a statute contains a list, each word in that list presumptively has a "similar" meaning. See, *e.g.*, *Gustafson v. Alloyd Co.*, 513 U. S. 561, 576 (1995). A related canon, *ejusdem generis* teaches that general words following a list of specific words should usually be read in light of those specific words to mean something "similar." See, *e.g.*, *Christopher v. SmithKline Beecham Corp.*, 567 U. S. ___, ___ (2012) (slip op., at 18). Applying these canons to § 1519's list of nouns, the term "tangible object" should refer to something similar to records or documents. A fish does not spring to mind—nor does an antelope, a colonial farmhouse, a hydrofoil, or an oil derrick. All are "objects" that are "tangible." But who wouldn't raise an eyebrow if a neighbor, when asked to identify something similar to a "record" or "document," said "crocodile"?

This reading, of course, has its shortcomings. For instance, this is an imperfect *ejusdem generis* case because "record" and "document" are themselves quite general. And there is a risk that "tangible object" may be made superfluous—what is similar to a "record" or "document" but yet is not one? An e-mail, however, could be such a thing. See *United States Sentencing*

Commission, Guidelines Manual § 2J1.2 and comment. (Nov. 2003) (reading "records, documents, or tangible objects" to "includ[e]" what is found on "magnetic, optical, digital, other electronic, or other storage mediums or devices"). An e-mail, after all, might not be a "document" if, as was "traditionally" so, a document was a "piece of paper with information on it," not "information stored on a computer, electronic storage device, or any other medium." BLACK'S LAW DICTIONARY 587–588 (10th ed. 2014). E-mails might also not be "records" if records are limited to "minutes" or other formal writings "designed to memorialize [past] events." *Id.,* at 1465. A hard drive, however, is tangible and can contain files that are precisely akin to even these narrow definitions. Both "record" and "document" can be read more expansively, but adding "tangible object" to § 1519 would ensure beyond question that electronic files are included. To be sure, "tangible object" presumably can capture more than just e-mails; Congress enacts "catchall[s]" for "known unknowns." *Republic of Iraq v. Beaty*, 556 U. S. 848, 860 (2009). But where *noscitur a sociis* and *ejusdem generis* apply, "known unknowns" should be similar to known knowns, *i.e.,* here, records and documents. This is especially true because reading "tangible object" too broadly could render "record" and "document" superfluous.

Next, consider § 1519's list of verbs: "alters, destroys, mutilates, conceals, covers up, falsifies, or makes a false entry in." Although many of those verbs could apply to nouns as far-flung as salamanders, satellites, or sand dunes, the last phrase in the list—"makes a false entry in"—makes no sense outside of filekeeping. How does one make a false entry in a fish? "Alters" and especially "falsifies" are also closely associated with filekeeping. Not one of the verbs, moreover, *cannot* be applied to filekeeping—certainly not in the way that "makes a false entry in" is always inconsistent with the aquatic.

Again, the Government is not without a response. One can imagine Congress trying to write a law so broadly that not every verb lines up with every noun. But failure to "line up" may suggest that something has gone awry in one's interpretation of a text. Where, as here, each of a statute's verbs applies to a certain category of nouns, there is some reason to think that Congress had that category in mind. Categories, of course, are often underinclusive or overinclusive—§ 1519, for instance, applies to a bomb-threatening letter but not a bomb. But this does not mean that categories are not useful or that Congress does not enact them. Here, focusing on the verbs, the category of nouns appears to be filekeeping. This observation is not dispositive, but neither is it nothing. The Government also contends that § 1519's verbs cut both ways because it is unnatural to apply "falsifies" to tangible objects, and that is certainly true. One does not falsify the outside casing of a hard drive, but one could falsify or alter data physically recorded on that hard drive.

Finally, my analysis is influenced by § 1519's title: "Destruction, alteration, or falsification of *records* in Federal investigations and bankruptcy." (Emphasis added.) This too points toward filekeeping, not fish. Titles can be useful devices to resolve " 'doubt about the meaning of a statute.' " *Porter v. Nussle*, 534 U. S. 516–528 (2002) (quoting *Almendarez-Torres v. United States*, 523 U. S. 224, 234 (1998)). The title is especially valuable here because it reinforces what the text's nouns and verbs independently suggest—that no matter how other statutes might be read, this particular one does not cover every noun in the universe with tangible form.

Titles, of course, are also not dispositive. Here, if the list of nouns did not already suggest that "tangible object" should mean something similar to records or documents, especially when read in conjunction with § 1519's peculiar list of verbs with their focus on filekeeping, then the title would not be enough on its own. In conjunction with those other two textual features, however, the Government's argument, though colorable, becomes too implausible to accept.

JUSTICE KAGAN, with whom JUSTICE SCALIA, JUSTICE KENNEDY, and JUSTICE THOMAS join, dissenting.

* * * This case raises the question whether the term "tangible object" means the same thing in § 1519 as it means in everyday language—any object capable of being touched. The answer should be easy: Yes. The term "tangible object" is broad, but clear. Throughout the U. S. Code and many States' laws, it invariably covers physical objects of all kinds. And in § 1519, context confirms what bare text says: All the words surrounding "tangible object" show that Congress meant the term to have a wide range. That fits with Congress's evident purpose in enacting § 1519: to punish those who alter or destroy physical evidence—*any* physical evidence—with the intent of thwarting federal law enforcement.

The plurality instead interprets "tangible object" to cover "only objects one can use to record or preserve information." The concurring opinion similarly, if more vaguely, contends that "tangible object" should refer to "something similar to records or documents"—and shouldn't include colonial farmhouses, crocodiles, or fish. In my view, conventional tools of statutory construction all lead to a more conventional result: A "tangible object" is an object that's tangible. I would apply the statute that Congress enacted and affirm the judgment below.

I

Is this fair? Doesn't the plurality also start with the text, and then turn to the heading as the "first" interpretive guide only after articulating why the text might be ambiguous?

While the plurality starts its analysis with § 1519's heading ("We note first § 1519's caption"), I would begin with § 1519's text. When Congress has not supplied a definition, we generally give a statutory term its ordinary meaning. As the plurality must acknowledge, the ordinary meaning of "tangible object" is "a discrete thing that possesses physical form." A fish is, of course, a discrete thing that possesses physical form. See generally DR. SEUSS, ONE FISH TWO FISH RED FISH BLUE FISH (1960). So the ordinary meaning of the term "tangible object" in § 1519, as no one here disputes, covers fish (including too-small red grouper).

That interpretation accords with endless uses of the term in statute and rule books as construed by courts. Dozens of federal laws and rules of procedure (and hundreds of state enactments) include the term "tangible object" or its first cousin "tangible thing"—some in association with documents, others not. * * * No surprise, then, that—until today—courts have uniformly applied the term "tangible object" in § 1519 in the same way.

That is not necessarily the end of the matter; I agree with the plurality (really, who does not?) that context matters in interpreting statutes. We do not "construe the meaning of statutory terms in a vacuum." *Tyler v. Cain*, 533 U. S. 656,662 (2001). Rather, we interpret particular words "in their context and with a view to their place in the overall statutory scheme." *Davis v. Michigan Dept. of Treasury*, 489 U. S. 803, 809 (1989). And sometimes that means, as the plurality says, that the dictionary definition of a disputed term cannot control. But this is not such an occasion, for here the text and its context point the same way. Stepping back from the words "tangible object" provides only further evidence that Congress said what it meant and meant what it said.

A reference, of course, to another famous Dr. Seuss work, *Horton Hatches an Egg*: "I meant what I said and I said what I meant. An elephant's faithful one-hundred percent!"

Begin with the way the surrounding words in § 1519 reinforce the breadth of the term at issue. Section 1519 refers to "any" tangible object, thus indicating (in line with *that* word's plain meaning) a tangible object "of whatever kind." WEBSTER'S THIRD NEW INTERNATIONAL DICTIONARY 97 (2002). This Court has time and again recognized that "any" has "an expansive meaning," bringing within a statute's reach *all* types of the item (here, "tangible object") to which the law refers. * * * *Ali v. Federal Bureau of Prisons*, 552 U. S. 214–220 (2008). And the adjacent laundry list of verbs in § 1519 ("alters, destroys, mutilates, conceals, covers up, falsifies, or makes a false entry") further shows that Congress wrote a statute with a wide scope. Those words are supposed to ensure—just as "tangible object" is meant to—that § 1519 covers the whole world of evidence-tampering, in all its prodigious variety. * * *

The words "record, document, or tangible object" in § 1519 also track language in 18 U. S. C. § 1512, the federal witness-tampering law covering (as even the plurality accepts) physical evidence in all its forms. Section 1512, both in its original version (preceding § 1519) and today, repeatedly uses the phrase "record, document, or other object"—most notably, in a provision prohibiting the use of force or threat to induce another person to withhold any of those materials from an official proceeding. § 4(a) of the Victim and Witness Protection Act of 1982, 96 Stat.1249, as amended, 18 U. S. C. § 1512(b)(2). * * *

And legislative history, for those who care about it, puts extra icing on a cake already frosted. Section 1519, as the plurality notes, was enacted after the Enron Corporation's collapse, as part of the Sarbanes-Oxley Act of 2002, 116 Stat.745. But the provision began its life in a separate bill, and the drafters emphasized that Enron was "only a case study exposing the shortcomings in our current laws" relating to both "corporate and criminal" fraud. S. Rep. No. 107–146, pp. 2, 11 (2002). The primary "loophole[ ]" Congress identified, see *id.*, at 14, arose from limits in the part of § 1512 just described: That provision, as uniformly construed, prohibited a person from inducing another to destroy "record[s], document[s], or other object[s]"—of every type—but not from doing so himself. § 1512(b)(2); see *supra*, at 5. Congress (as even the plurality agrees) enacted § 1519 to close that yawning gap. But § 1519 could fully achieve that goal only if it covered all the records, documents, and objects § 1512 did, as well as all the means of tampering with them. And so § 1519 was written to do exactly that—"to apply broadly to any acts to destroy or fabricate physical evidence," as long as performed with the requisite intent. S. Rep. No. 107–146, at 14. "When a person destroys evidence," the drafters explained, "overly technical legal distinctions should neither hinder nor prevent prosecution." *Id.*, at 7. Ah well: Congress, meet today's Court, which here invents just such a distinction with just such an effect. See *United States v. Philadelphia Nat. Bank*, 374 U. S. 321,343 (1963) ("[C]reat[ing] a large loophole in a statute designed to close a loophole" is "illogical and disrespectful of . . . congressional purpose").

As Congress recognized in using a broad term, giving immunity to those who destroy non-documentary evidence has no sensible basis in penal policy. A person who hides a murder victim's body is no less culpable than one who burns the victim's diary. A fisherman, like John Yates, who dumps undersized fish to avoid a fine is no less blameworthy than one who shreds his vessel's catch log for the same reason. Congress thus treated both offenders in the same way. It understood, in enacting § 1519, that destroying evidence is destroying evidence, whether or not that evidence takes documentary form.

II

A

The plurality searches far and wide for anything—*anything*—to support its interpretation of § 1519. But its fishing expedition comes up empty.

The plurality's analysis starts with § 1519's title: "Destruction, alteration, or falsification of records in Federal investigations and bankruptcy." That's already a sign something is amiss. I know of no other case in which we have *begun* our interpretation of a statute with the title, or relied on a title to override the law's clear terms. Instead, we have followed "the wise rule that the title of a statute and the heading of a section cannot limit the plain meaning of the text." *Trainmen v. Baltimore & Ohio R. Co.*, 331 U. S. 519–529 (1947).

The reason for that "wise rule" is easy to see: A title is, almost necessarily, an abridgment. Attempting to mention every term in a statute "would often be ungainly as well as useless"; accordingly, "matters in the text . . . are frequently unreflected in the headings." *Id.*, at 528. * * *

The plurality next tries to divine meaning from § 1519's "position within Chapter 73 of Title 18." But that move is yet odder than the last. As far as I can tell, this Court has never once suggested that the section number assigned to a law bears upon its meaning. Cf. [A. SCALIA & B. GARNER,

READING LAW: THE INTERPRETATION OF LEGAL TEXTS (2012)], *supra*, at xi–xvi (listing more than 50 interpretive principles and canons without mentioning the plurality's new number-in-the-Code theory). And even on its own terms, the plurality's argument is hard to fathom. The plurality claims that if § 1519 applied to objects generally, Congress would not have placed it "after the pre-existing § 1516, § 1517, and § 1518" because those are "specialized provisions." But search me if I can find a better place for a broad ban on evidence-tampering. The plurality seems to agree that the law properly goes in Chapter 73—the criminal code's chapter on "obstruction of justice." But the provision does not logically fit into any of that chapter's pre-existing sections. And with the first 18 numbers of the chapter already taken (starting with § 1501 and continuing through § 1518), the law naturally took the 19th place. That is standard operating procedure. Prior to the Sarbanes-Oxley Act of 2002, all of Chapter 73 was ordered chronologically: Section 1518 was later enacted than § 1517, which was later enacted than § 1516, which was . . . well, you get the idea. And after Sarbanes-Oxley, Congress has continued in the same vein. Section 1519 is thus right where you would expect it (as is the contemporaneously passed § 1520)—between § 1518 (added in 1996) and § 1521 (added in 2008).

The plurality's third argument, relying on the surplusage canon, at least invokes a known tool of statutory construction—but it too comes to nothing. Says the plurality: If read naturally, § 1519 "would render superfluous" § 1512(c)(1), which Congress passed "as part of the same act." But that is not so: Although the two provisions significantly overlap, each applies to conduct the other does not. The key difference between the two is that § 1519 protects the integrity of "matter[s] within the jurisdiction of any [federal] department or agency" whereas § 1512(c)(1) safeguards "official proceeding[s]" as defined in § 1515(a)(1)(A). Section 1519's language often applies more broadly than § 1512(c)(1)'s, as the plurality notes. For example, an FBI investigation counts as a matter within a federal department's jurisdiction, but falls outside the statutory definition of "official proceeding" as construed by courts. See, *e.g.*, *United States v. Gabriel*, 125 F. 3d 89, 105, n. 13 (CA2 1997). But conversely, § 1512(c)(1) sometimes reaches more widely than § 1519. For example, because an "official proceeding" includes any "proceeding before a judge or court of the United States," § 1512(c)(1) prohibits tampering with evidence in federal litigation between private parties. See § 1515(a)(1)(A). By contrast, § 1519 wouldn't ordinarily operate in that context because a federal court isn't a "department or agency." See *Hubbard v. United States*, 514 U. S. 695, 715 (1995). So the surplusage canon doesn't come into play. Overlap—even significant overlap—abounds in the criminal law. This Court has never thought that of such ordinary stuff surplusage is made.

And the legislative history to which the plurality appeals only cuts against it because those materials show that lawmakers knew that § 1519 and § 1512(c)(1) share much common ground. Minority Leader Lott introduced the amendment that included § 1512(c)(1) (along with other criminal and corporate fraud provisions) late in the legislative process, explaining that he did so at the specific request of the President. See 148 Cong. Rec. 12509, 12512 (2002) (remarks of Sen. Lott). Not only Lott but several other Senators noted the overlap between the President's package and provisions already in the bill, most notably § 1519. See *id.*, at 12512 (remarks of Sen. Lott); *id.*, at 12513 (remarks of Sen. Biden); *id.*, at 12517 (remarks of Sens. Hatch and Gramm). The presence of both § 1519 and § 1512(c)(1) in the final Act may have reflected belt-and-suspenders caution: If § 1519 contained some flaw, § 1512(c)(1) would serve as a backstop. Or the addition of § 1512(c)(1) may have derived solely from legislators' wish "to satisfy audiences other than courts"—that is, the President and his Justice Department. Gluck & Bressman, *Statutory Interpretation from the Inside*, 65 STAN. L. REV. 901, 935 (2013) (emphasis deleted). Whichever the case, Congress's consciousness of overlap between the two provisions removes any conceivable reason to cast aside § 1519's ordinary meaning in service of preventing some statutory repetition.

Indeed, the inclusion of § 1512(c)(1) in Sarbanes-Oxley creates a far worse problem for the plurality's construction of § 1519 than for mine. Section 1512(c)(1) criminalizes the destruction of any "record, document, or other object"; § 1519 of any "record, document, or tangible object." On the plurality's view, one "object" is really an object, whereas the other is only an object that preserves or stores information. But "[t]he normal rule of statutory construction assumes that identical words used in different parts of the same act," passed at the same time, "are intended to have the same meaning." *Sorenson v. Secretary of Treasury*, 475 U. S. 851, 860 (1986) (internal quotation marks omitted). And that is especially true when the different provisions pertain to the same subject. See *supra*, at 5–6. The plurality doesn't—really, can't—explain why it instead interprets the same words used in two provisions of the same Act addressing the same basic problem to mean fundamentally different things.

Getting nowhere with surplusage, the plurality switches canons, hoping that *noscitur a sociis* and *ejusdem generis* will save it. The first of those related canons advises that words grouped in a list be given similar meanings. The second counsels that a general term following specific words embraces only things of a similar kind. According to the plurality, those Latin maxims change the English meaning of "tangible object" to only things, like records and documents, "used to record or preserve information." But understood as this Court always has, the canons have no such transformative effect on the workaday language Congress chose.

As an initial matter, this Court uses *noscitur a sociis* and *ejusdem generis* to resolve ambiguity, not create it. Those principles are "useful rule[s] of construction where words are of obscure or doubtful meaning." *Russell Motor Car Co. v. United States*, 261 U. S. 514, 520 (1923). But when words have a clear definition, and all other contextual clues support that meaning, the canons cannot properly defeat Congress's decision to draft broad legislation. See, *e.g.*, *Ali*, 552 U. S., at 227 (rejecting the invocation of these canons as an "attempt to create ambiguity where the statute's text and structure suggest none").

Anyway, assigning "tangible object" its ordinary meaning comports with *noscitur a sociis* and *ejusdem generis* when applied, as they should be, with attention to § 1519's subject and purpose. Those canons require identifying a common trait that links all the words in a statutory phrase. In responding to that demand, the plurality characterizes records and documents as things that preserve information—and so they are. But just as much, they are things that provide information, and thus potentially serve as evidence relevant to matters under review. And in a statute pertaining to obstruction of federal investigations, that evidentiary function comes to the fore. The destruction of records and documents prevents law enforcement agents from gathering facts relevant to official inquiries. And so too does the destruction of tangible objects—of whatever kind. Whether the item is a fisherman's ledger or an undersized fish, throwing it overboard has the identical effect on the administration of justice. For purposes of § 1519, records, documents, and (all) tangible objects are therefore alike.

Indeed, even the plurality can't fully credit its *noscitur/ejusdem* argument. The same reasoning would apply to *every* law placing the word "object" (or "thing") after "record" and "document." But as noted earlier, such statutes are common: The phrase appears (among other places) in many state laws based on the Model Penal Code, as well as in multiple provisions of § 1512. See *supra*, at 4–5. The plurality accepts that in those laws "object" means object; its argument about superfluity positively *depends* on giving § 1512(c)(1) that broader reading. What, then, is the difference here? The plurality proposes that some of those statutes describe less serious offenses than § 1519. How and why that distinction affects application of the *noscitur a sociis* and *ejusdem generis* canons is left obscure: Count it as one more of the plurality's never-before-propounded, not-readily-explained interpretive theories. But in any event, that rationale cannot support the plurality's

> **?** What do you make of this critique? How might the plurality respond?

willingness to give "object" its natural meaning in § 1512, which (like § 1519) sets out felonies with penalties of up to 20 years. See §§ 1512(a)(3)(C), (b), (c). The canons, in the plurality's interpretive world, apparently switch on and off whenever convenient.

And the plurality's invocation of § 1519's verbs does nothing to buttress its canon-based argument. The plurality observes that § 1519 prohibits "falsif[ying]" or "mak[ing] a false entry in" a tangible object, and no one can do those things to, say, a murder weapon (or a fish). But of course someone can alter, destroy, mutilate, conceal, or cover up such a tangible object, and § 1519 prohibits those actions too. The Court has never before suggested that all the verbs in a statute need to match up with all the nouns. And for good reason. It is exactly when Congress sets out to draft a statute broadly—to include every imaginable variation on a theme—that such mismatches will arise. To respond by narrowing the law, as the plurality does, is thus to flout both what Congress wrote and what Congress wanted.

* * *

III

If none of the traditional tools of statutory interpretation can produce today's result, then what accounts for it? The plurality offers a clue when it emphasizes the disproportionate penalties § 1519 imposes if the law is read broadly. Section 1519, the plurality objects, would then "expose[ ] individuals to 20-year prison sentences for tampering with *any* physical object that *might* have evidentiary value in *any* federal investigation into *any* offense." That brings to the surface the real issue: overcriminalization and excessive punishment in the U. S. Code.

Now as to this statute, I think the plurality somewhat—though only somewhat—exaggerates the matter. The plurality omits from its description of § 1519 the requirement that a person act "knowingly" and with "the intent to impede, obstruct, or influence" federal law enforcement. And in highlighting § 1519's maximum penalty, the plurality glosses over the absence of any prescribed minimum. (Let's not forget that Yates's sentence was not 20 years, but 30 days.) Congress presumably enacts laws with high maximums and no minimums when it thinks the prohibited conduct may run the gamut from major to minor. That is assuredly true of acts obstructing justice. . . . Still and all, I tend to think, for the reasons the plurality gives, that § 1519 is a bad law—too broad and undifferentiated, with too-high maximum penalties, which give prosecutors too much leverage and sentencers too much discretion. And I'd go further: In those ways, § 1519 is unfortunately not an outlier, but an emblem of a deeper pathology in the federal criminal code.

But whatever the wisdom or folly of § 1519, this Court does not get to rewrite the law. "Resolution of the pros and cons of whether a statute should sweep broadly or narrowly is for Congress." *Rodgers*, 466 U. S., at 484. If judges disagree with Congress's choice, we are perfectly entitled to say so—in lectures, in law review articles, and even in dicta. But we are not entitled to replace the statute Congress enacted with an alternative of our own design.

I respectfully dissent.

NOTES & QUESTIONS

1. How many canons and other tools of interpretation can you find in each of the *Yates* opinions?

2. Which tools (or doctrines) are most persuasive to you? Why?

3. Has the Court majority overly complicated a straightforward provision? Why or why not?

4. At this point, what do you think about the role the judiciary should play in addressing an interpretive issue like the one in *Yates*?

5. For a fishy corollary, consider a 2022 California appellate court decision holding that the state Fish and Game Commission could classify "bumblebees" as "fish," within the meaning of the California Endangered Species Act (CESA) (a precursor of the federal Endangered

Species Act). The CESA definition of "fish" was "a wild fish, mollusk, crustacean, invertebrate, amphibian, or part, spawn, or ovum of any of these animals," which the court viewed as converting the ordinary meaning of "fish" into a legal term of art for purposes of the CESA, and thus permitting bumblebees to be covered as "invertebrates." The court was careful to note that it was not saying that bumblebees are fish for all purposes! *See Almond Alliance v. Fish and Game Comm'n*, 294 Cal. Rptr.3d 603 (Cal. Ct. App.), *review denied*, 79 Cal.App.5th 337 (Cal. Sup. Ct. 2022).

6.   For a marvelous exposition of the various ways in which the word "any" in statutory text has repeatedly and for centuries affected the interpretive enterprise (including in *Ali v. Federal Bureau of Prisons* and *Yates v. United States*), and the proposal of a new "any" canon of interpretation, *see* James J. Brudney & Ethan J. Lieb, "Any," 49 BYU L. Rev. 465 (2023).

Test Your Understanding

To assess your understanding of the material in this chapter, click here to take a quiz.

21

Substantive (Policy) Canons: Lenity and Constitutional Avoidance

Key Concepts

- Substantive canons
- The Rule of Lenity
- The Constitutional Avoidance Canon
- Tie-breaker
- Rebuttable presumption
- Clear-statement rule

Chapter Summary

Substantive canons are principles of interpretation based not on the way in which language is used but structured instead to further some policy objective. For this reason, they play a distinctly different role from the textual canons we studied in the last chapter. Some substantive canons are long-standing and respected tools for settling ambiguity, while others have fallen out of favor. In part because they are grounded in societal policy preferences, substantive canons are apt to evolve and change over time, sometimes abruptly. In this chapter, we explore two examples, but there are many, many more, including specialized substantive canons within particular fields of law.

The first example is the Rule of Lenity, a longstanding principle of criminal law which states that ambiguity in a criminal statute should be construed in favor of the accused. In the past, this was a broad presumption existing in the background of most criminal proceedings. Today, it operates primarily as a last resort tie-breaker to settle textual ambiguity. In other words, its use and influence has waned.

The second example, the Constitutional Avoidance Canon, has also seen evolution in recent years. In its most widely accepted and least controversial form, it states that, when possible, judges should avoid an interpretation of a statute that would render the statute unconstitutional. But a variation of this canon states that interpreters should avoid not just an unconstitutional interpretation of a statute but even an interpretation that would raise "serious doubt" about its constitutionality. The rationale is to steer jurists away from even needing to consider a constitutional question if a fair alternative textual interpretation does not implicate the Constitution. Because rulings interpreting the Constitution have profound ripple effects throughout the law, the canon attempts to limit how often the Supreme Court issues decisions about constitutional law.

In contrast to the textual canons discussed in the previous chapter, which at least on their face appear to be policy neutral (and are often defended as such, although as Chapter 23 will suggest there may be reason to be cautious about this claim), a

> **FYI** By "policy neutral," we mean without favoring any particular kinds of legislative policies or ideologies.

number of interpretive canons explicitly embody some substantive preference about the law. This chapter and the next introduce a half-dozen of the best known of these substantive policy canons. A key question with respect to how to use each of these canons is whether its substantive preference should operate merely as a "tie-breaker," when no better basis exists for choosing between several possible interpretations; as a mild and rebuttable presumption to be followed unless the interpreter finds evidence of contrary legislative intent; or as a heavy presumption unless the legislature has made a *clear statement* of its contrary intent.

A. The Rule of Lenity

One ancient canon, with roots in medieval England, is that a law imposing a penalty should be narrowly construed. Known as the Rule of Lenity (which you may already have encountered in a Criminal Law course), this canon is most applicable to criminal statutes and invites courts to interpret statutory ambiguities in favor of the defendant. For instance, Justice Holmes' opinion in *McBoyle v. United States*, 283 U.S. 25 (1931), invoked the Rule of Lenity in declining to include an airplane within the National Motor Vehicle Theft Act's definition of vehicle. He explained that penal statutes should give the public fair notice of exactly what conduct will be penalized, something that an ambiguous provision simply does not

> **?** Even before considering any of the following examples of substantive canons, think about whether you are predisposed to want these canons to operate strictly as tie-breakers, or instead as presumptions of some sort. Then see if your view changes as you consider some specific examples.

do. The dissenting justices in *Smith v. United States*, 508 U.S. 223 (1993), which we saw in Chapter 19, also drew on the Rule of Lenity to support their conclusion that the phrase "uses a gun" in 18 U.S.C. § 924(c)(1) should be interpreted narrowly to require that the gun be used *as a weapon*.

Next we will read another case involving 18 U.S.C. § 924(c)(1), the same provision at issue in *Smith* in Chapter 19. As you read each of the two contrasting opinions, watch for the different ways in which they relate the Rule of Lenity to the other interpretive tools they deploy. But first, take a few minutes to reflect on this DIY exercise about the issue in the case.

DIY
The "Carries a Firearm" Conundrum

 As we have seen, 18 U.S.C. § 924(c)(1) is a sentencing provision that imposes a mandatory five-year sentence on a person who "uses or carries a firearm" during and in relation to a drug trafficking crime. We have previously considered how broadly to construe the word "uses"; now consider how broadly to construe the word "carries." Reflect for a few minutes on what sorts of fact patterns might constitute an unlawful carrying: Having a firearm in a locked suitcase while smuggling drugs? Transporting a firearm in the trunk of a vehicle while traveling to a drug rendezvous? Can you think of more ambiguous applications? Where would you draw the line on what amounts to "carrying" a firearm within the meaning of this statute? After you have a tentative view on this interpretive issue, go on and read the case excerpt below (remembering to watch for potential deployments of the Rule of Lenity).

Muscarello v. United States
524 U.S. 125 (1998)

JUSTICE BREYER delivered the opinion of the Court.

A provision in the firearms chapter of the federal criminal code imposes a 5-year mandatory prison term upon a person who "uses or carries a firearm" "during and in relation to" a "drug trafficking crime." 18 U.S.C. § 924(c)(1). The question before us is whether the phrase "carries a firearm" is limited to the carrying of firearms on the person. We hold that it is not so limited. * * *

I

? This is the same statute at issue in *Smith v. United States* (1993), considered in Chapter 19, where the interpretive issue was whether one who trades a firearm for drugs thereby "uses" the firearm within the meaning of this statute. In *Muscarello*, the Court now must determine what the phrase "carries a firearm" in this statute means.

The question arises in two [consolidated cases]. The defendant in the first case, Frank J. Muscarello, unlawfully sold marijuana, which he carried in his truck to the place of sale. Police officers found a handgun locked in the truck's glove compartment. During plea proceedings, Muscarello admitted that he had "carried" the gun "for protection in relation" to the drug offense, though he later claimed to the contrary, and added that, in any event, his "carr[ying]" of the gun in the glove compartment did not fall within the scope of the statutory word "carries."

The defendants in the second case, Donald Cleveland and Enrique Gray-Santana, placed several guns in a bag, put the bag in the trunk of a car, and then traveled by car to a proposed drug-sale point, where they intended to steal drugs from the sellers. Federal agents at the scene stopped them, searched the cars, found the guns and drugs, and arrested them.

In both cases the Courts of Appeals found that the defendants had "carrie[d]" the guns during and in relation to a drug trafficking offense. We granted certiorari to determine whether the fact that the guns were found in the locked glove compartment, or the trunk, of a car, precludes application of § 924(c)(1). We conclude that it does not.

II

A

We begin with the statute's language. The parties vigorously contest the ordinary English meaning of the phrase "carries a firearm." Because they essentially agree that Congress intended the phrase to convey its ordinary, and not some special legal, meaning, and because they argue the linguistic point at length, we too have looked into the matter in more than usual depth. Although the word "carry" has many different meanings, only two are relevant here. When one uses the word in the first, or primary, meaning, one can, as a matter of ordinary English, "carry firearms" in a wagon, car, truck, or other vehicle that one accompanies. When one uses the word in a different, rather special, way, to mean, for example, "bearing" or (in slang) "packing" (as in "packing a gun"), the matter is less clear. * * *

Consider first the word's primary meaning. The Oxford English Dictionary gives as its first definition "convey, originally by cart or wagon, hence in any vehicle, by ship, on horseback, etc." 2 OXFORD ENGLISH DICTIONARY 919 (2d ed. 1989); see also WEBSTER'S THIRD NEW INTERNATIONAL DICTIONARY 343 (1986) (first definition: "move while supporting (as in a vehicle or in one's hands or arms)"); THE RANDOM HOUSE DICTIONARY OF THE ENGLISH LANGUAGE UNABRIDGED 319 (2d ed. 1987) (first definition: "to take or support from one place to another; convey; transport").

The origin of the word "carries" explains why the first, or basic, meaning of the word "carry" includes conveyance in a vehicle. See THE BARNHART DICTIONARY OF ETYMOLOGY 146 (1988) (tracing the word from Latin "carum," which means "car" or "cart"); 2 OXFORD ENGLISH DICTIONARY, supra, at 919 (tracing the word from Old French "carier" and the late Latin "carricare," which meant to "convey in a car"); THE OXFORD DICTIONARY OF ENGLISH ETYMOLOGY 148 (C. Onions ed. 1966) (same); THE BARNHART DICTIONARY OF ETYMOLOGY, supra, at 143 (explaining that the term "car" has been used to refer to the automobile since 1896).

The greatest of writers have used the word with this meaning. See, e.g., the KING JAMES BIBLE, 2 Kings 9:28 ("[H]is servants carried him in a chariot to Jerusalem"); id., Isaiah 30:6 ("[T]hey will carry their riches upon the shoulders of young asses"). Robinson Crusoe says, "[w]ith my boat, I carry'd away every Thing." D. DEFOE, ROBINSON CRUSOE 174 (J. Crowley ed. 1972). And the owners of Queequeg's ship, Melville writes, "had lent him a [wheelbarrow], in which to carry his heavy chest to his boardinghouse." H. MELVILLE, MOBY DICK 43 (U. Chicago 1952). This Court, too, has spoken of the "carrying" of drugs in a car or in its "trunk." *California v. Acevedo*, 500 U.S. 565, 572–573 (1991); *Florida v. Jimeno*, 500 U.S. 248, 249 (1991).

These examples do not speak directly about carrying guns. But there is nothing linguistically special about the fact that weapons, rather than drugs, are being carried. Robinson Crusoe might have carried a gun in his boat; Queequeg might have borrowed a wheelbarrow in which to carry, not a chest, but a harpoon. And, to make certain that there is no special ordinary

English restriction (unmentioned in dictionaries) upon the use of "carry" in respect to guns, we have surveyed modern press usage, albeit crudely, by searching computerized newspaper databases-both the New York Times database in Lexis/Nexis, and the "US News" database in Westlaw. We looked for sentences in which the words "carry," "vehicle," and "weapon" (or variations thereof) all appear. We found thousands of such sentences, and random sampling suggests that many, perhaps more than one third, are sentences used to convey the meaning at issue here, i.e., the carrying of guns in a car. * * *

> **?** What significance, if any, should attach to the portion of sentences that convey this meaning of "carry"?

Now consider a different, somewhat special meaning of the word "carry"—a meaning upon which the linguistic arguments of petitioners and the dissent must rest. The Oxford English Dictionary's twenty-sixth definition of "carry" is "bear, wear, hold up, or sustain, as one moves about; habitually to bear about with one." 2 OXFORD ENGLISH DICTIONARY, supra, at 921. Webster's defines "carry" as "to move while supporting," not just in a vehicle, but also "in one's hands or arms." WEBSTER'S THIRD NEW INTERNATIONAL DICTIONARY, supra, at 343. And Black's Law Dictionary defines the entire phrase "carry arms or weapons" as "To wear, bear or carry them upon the person or in the clothing or in a pocket, for the purpose of use, or for the purpose of being armed and ready for offensive or defensive action in case of a conflict with another person." BLACK'S LAW DICTIONARY 214.

These special definitions, however, do not purport to limit the "carrying of arms" to the circumstances they describe. No one doubts that one who bears arms on his person "carries a weapon." But to say that is not to deny that one may also "carry a weapon" tied to the saddle of a horse or placed in a bag in a car. Nor is there any linguistic reason to think that Congress intended to limit the word "carries" in the statute to any of these special definitions. To the contrary, all these special definitions embody a form of an important, but secondary, meaning of "carry," a meaning that suggests support rather than movement or transportation, as when, for example, a column "carries" the weight of an arch. * * *

We recognize, as the dissent emphasizes, that the word "carry" has other meanings as well. But those other meanings are not relevant here. And the fact that speakers often do not add to the phrase "carry a gun" the words "in a car" is of no greater relevance here than the fact that millions of Americans did not see Muscarello carry a gun in his car. The relevant linguistic facts are that the word "carry" in its ordinary sense includes carrying in a car and that the word, used in its ordinary sense, keeps the same meaning whether one carries a gun, a suitcase, or a banana. * * *

B

We now explore more deeply the purely legal question of whether Congress intended to use the word "carry" in its ordinary sense, or whether it intended to limit the scope of the phrase to instances in which a gun is carried "on the person." We conclude that neither the statute's basic purpose nor its legislative history support circumscribing the scope of the word "carry" by applying an "on the person" limitation.

This Court has described the statute's basic purpose broadly, as an effort to combat the "dangerous combination" of "drugs and guns." *Smith v. United States*, 508 U.S. 223, 240 (1993). And the provision's chief legislative sponsor has said that the provision seeks "to persuade the man who is tempted to commit a Federal felony to leave his gun at home." 114 Cong. Rec. 22231 (1968) (Rep. Poff); see *Busic v. United States*, 446 U.S. 398, 405 (1980) (describing Poff's comments as "crucial material" in interpreting the purpose of § 924(c)). * * *

From the perspective of any such purpose (persuading a criminal "to leave his gun at home") what sense would it make for this statute to penalize one who walks with a gun in a bag to the site of a drug sale, but to ignore a similar individual who, like defendant Gray-Santana, travels to a similar site with a similar gun in a similar bag, but instead of walking, drives there with the gun in his car? How persuasive is a punishment that is without effect until a drug dealer who has brought his gun to a sale (indeed has it available for use) actually takes it from the trunk (or unlocks the glove compartment) of his car? It is difficult to say that, considered as a class, those who prepare, say, to sell drugs by placing guns in their cars are less dangerous, or less deserving of punishment, than those who carry handguns on their person.

We have found no significant indication elsewhere in the legislative history of any more narrowly focused relevant purpose. * * *

C

We are not convinced by petitioners' remaining arguments to the contrary. First, they say that our definition of "carry" makes it the equivalent of "transport." Yet, Congress elsewhere in related statutes used the word "transport" deliberately to signify a different, and broader, statutory coverage. The immediately preceding statutory subsection, for example, imposes a different set of penalties on one who, with an intent to commit a crime, "ships, transports, or receives a firearm" in interstate commerce. 18 U.S.C. § 924(b). Moreover, § 926A specifically "entitle[s]" a person "not otherwise prohibited . . . from transporting, shipping, or receiving a firearm" to "transport a firearm . . . from any place where he may lawfully possess and carry" it to "any other place" where he may do so. Why, petitioners ask, would Congress have used the word "transport," or used both "carry" and "transport" in the same provision, if it had intended to obliterate the distinction between the two?

The short answer is that our definition does not equate "carry" and "transport." "Carry" implies personal agency and some degree of possession, whereas "transport" does not have such a limited connotation and, in addition, implies the movement of goods in bulk over great distances. * * *

The dissent refers to § 926A and to another statute where Congress used the word "transport" rather than "carry" to describe the movement of firearms. 18 U. S. C. § 925(a)(2)(B). According to the dissent, had Congress intended "carry" to have the meaning we give it, Congress would not have needed to use a different word in these provisions. But as we have discussed above, we believe the word "transport" is broader than the word "carry."

And, if Congress intended "carry" to have the limited definition the dissent contends, it would have been quite unnecessary to add the proviso in § 926A requiring a person, to be exempt from penalties, to store her firearm in a locked container not immediately accessible. See § 926A (quoted in full at post, 8-9) (exempting from criminal penalties one who transports a firearm from a place where "he may lawfully possess and carry such firearm" but not exempting the "transportation" of a firearm if it is "readily accessible or is directly accessible from the passenger compartment of transporting vehicle"). The statute simply could have said that such a person may not "carry" a firearm. But, of course, Congress did not say this because that is not what "carry" means.

As we interpret the statutory scheme, it makes sense. Congress has imposed a variable penalty with no mandatory minimum sentence upon a person who "transports" (or "ships" or "receives") a firearm knowing it will be used to commit any "offense punishable by imprisonment for [more than] one year," § 924(b), and it has imposed a 5-year mandatory minimum sentence upon one who "carries" a firearm "during and in relation to" a "drug trafficking crime," § 924(c). The first subsection imposes a less strict sentencing regime upon one who, say, ships firearms by mail for use in a crime elsewhere; the latter subsection imposes a mandatory sentence upon one who, say, brings a weapon with him (on his person or in his car) to the site of a drug sale.

Second, petitioners point out that, in *Bailey v. United States*, 516 U.S. 137 (1995), we considered the related phrase "uses . . . a firearm" found in the same statutory provision now before us. See 18 U.S.C. § 924(c)(1) ("uses or carries a firearm"). We construed the term "use" narrowly, limiting its application to the "active employment" of a firearm. *Bailey*, 516 U.S., at 144. Petitioners argue that it would be anomalous to construe broadly the word "carries," its statutory next-door neighbor.

In *Bailey*, however, we limited "use" of a firearm to "active employment" in part because we assumed "that Congress . . . intended each term to have a particular, nonsuperfluous meaning." Id., at 146. A broader interpretation of "use," we said, would have swallowed up the term "carry." Ibid. But "carry" as we interpret that word does not swallow up the term "use." "Use" retains the same independent meaning we found for it in *Bailey*, where we provided examples involving the displaying or the bartering of a gun. Ibid. "Carry" also retains an independent meaning, for, under *Bailey*, carrying a gun in a car does not necessarily involve the gun's "active employment." More importantly, having construed "use" narrowly in *Bailey*, we cannot also construe "carry" narrowly without undercutting the statute's basic objective. For the narrow interpretation would remove the act of carrying a gun in a car entirely from the statute's reach, leaving a gap in coverage that we do not believe Congress intended.

Third, petitioners say that our reading of the statute would extend its coverage to passengers on buses, trains, or ships, who have placed a firearm, say, in checked luggage. To extend this statute so far, they argue, is unfair, going well beyond what Congress likely would have thought possible. They add that some lower courts, thinking approximately the same, have limited the scope of "carries" to instances where a gun in a car is immediately accessible, thereby most likely excluding from coverage a gun carried in a car's trunk or locked glove compartment. See, e.g., *Foster*, 133 F. 3d, at 708 (concluding that person "carries" a firearm in a car only if the firearm is immediately accessible); *Giraldo*, 80 F. 3d, at 676 (same).

In our view, this argument does not take adequate account of other limiting words in the statute-words that make the statute applicable only where a defendant "carries" a gun *both* "during *and* in relation to" a drug crime.

§ 924(c)(1) (emphasis added). Congress added these words in part to prevent prosecution where guns "played" no part in the crime. See S. Rep. No. 98–225, at 314, n. 10. * * *

Fourth, petitioners argue that we should construe the word "carry" to mean "immediately accessible." And, as we have said, they point out that several Circuit Courts of Appeals have limited the statute's scope in this way. * * * That interpretation, however, is difficult to square with the statute's language, for one "carries" a gun in the glove compartment whether or not that glove compartment is locked. Nothing in the statute's history suggests that Congress intended that limitation. And, for reasons pointed out above, we believe that the words "during" and "in relation to" will limit the statute's application to the harms that Congress foresaw.

Finally, petitioners and the dissent invoke the "rule of lenity." The simple existence of some statutory ambiguity, however, is not sufficient to warrant application of that rule, for most statutes are ambiguous to some degree. Cf. *Smith*, 508 U.S., at 239 ("The mere possibility of articulating a narrower construction . . . does not by itself make the rule of lenity applicable"). " 'The rule of lenity applies only if, "after seizing everything from which aid can be derived,". . . we can make "no more than a guess as to what Congress intended." ' " *United States v. Wells*, 519 U.S. 482, 499 (1997) [quoting other cases]. To invoke the rule, we must conclude that there is a " 'grievous ambiguity or uncertainty' in the statute." *Staples v. United States*, 511 U.S. 600, 619, n. 17 (1994) (quoting *Chapman v. United States*, 500 U.S. 453, 463 (1991)). Certainly, our decision today is based on much more than a "guess as to what Congress intended," and there is no "grievous ambiguity" here. The problem of statutory interpretation in this case is indeed no different from that in many of the criminal cases that confront us. Yet, this Court has never held that the rule of lenity automatically permits a defendant to win. * * *

 What kind of use of the Rule of Lenity is this? Do you think the Court should have been willing to use a stronger version of the Rule here?

Justice Ginsburg with whom The Chief Justice, Justice Scalia, and Justice Souter join, dissenting.

* * * Without doubt, "carries" is a word of many meanings, definable to mean or include carting about in a vehicle. But that encompassing definition is not a ubiquitously necessary one. Nor, in my judgment, is it a proper con-

struction of "carries" as the term appears in § 924(c)(1). In line with *Bailey* and the principle of lenity the Court has long followed, I would confine "carries a firearm," for § 924(c)(1) purposes, to the undoubted meaning of that expression in the relevant context. I would read the words to indicate not merely keeping arms on one's premises or in one's vehicle, but bearing them in such manner as to be ready for use as a weapon.

* * * I note first what is at stake for petitioners. The question before the Court "is not whether possession of a gun [on the drug offender's premises or in his car, during and in relation to commission of the offense,] means a longer sentence for a convicted drug dealer. It most certainly does. * * * Rather, the question concerns which sentencing statute governs the precise length of the extra term of punishment," § 924(c)(1)'s "blunt 'mandatory minimum' " five-year sentence, or the more finely tuned "sentencing guideline statutes, under which extra punishment for drug-related gun possession varies with the seriousness of the drug crime." *United States v. McFadden*, 13 F. 3d 463, 466 (CA1 1994) (Breyer, C. J., dissenting).

Accordingly, there would be no "gap," no relevant conduct "ignore[d]," were the Court to reject the Government's broad reading of § 924(c)(1). * * *

In Muscarello's case, for example, * * * the less rigid (tailored to "the seriousness of the drug crime," *McFadden*, 13 F. 3d, at 466) Guidelines regime would have added four months to Muscarello's prison time, in contrast to the five-year minimum addition the Court's reading of § 924(c)(1) mandates. In sum, drug traffickers will receive significantly longer sentences if they are caught travelling in vehicles in which they have placed firearms. The question that divides the Court concerns the proper reference for enhancement in the cases at hand, the Guidelines or § 924(c)(1).

* * * I do not think dictionaries, surveys of press reports, or the Bible tell us, dispositively, what "carries" means embedded in § 924(c)(1). * * *

At issue here is not "carries" at large but "carries a firearm." The Court's computer search of newspapers is revealing in this light. Carrying guns in a car showed up as the meaning "perhaps more than one third" of the time. One is left to wonder what meaning showed up some two thirds of the time. Surely a most familiar meaning is, as the Constitution's Second Amendment ("keep and *bear* Arms") (emphasis added) and Black's Law Dictionary, at 214, indicate: "wear, bear, or carry . . . upon the person or in the clothing or in a pocket, for the purpose . . . of being armed and ready for offensive or defensive action in a case of conflict with another person."

On lessons from literature, a scan of Bartlett's and other quotation collections shows how highly selective the Court's choices are. If "[t]he greatest of writers" have used "carry" to mean convey or transport in a vehicle, so have they used the hydra-headed word to mean, inter alia, carry in one's hand, arms, head, heart, or soul, sans vehicle. * * * [T]he Court's lexicological sources demonstrate vividly that "carry" is a word commonly used to convey various messages. Such references, given their variety, are not reliable indicators of what Congress meant, in § 924(c)(1), by "carries a firearm."

* * * Noting the paradoxical statement, " 'I use a gun to protect my house, but I've never had to use it,' " the Court in *Bailey*, 516 U.S., at 143, emphasized the importance of context-the statutory context. Just as "uses" was read to mean not simply "possession," but "active employment," so "carries," correspondingly, is properly read to signal the most dangerous cases-the gun at hand, ready for use as a weapon.

It is reasonable to comprehend Congress as having provided mandatory minimums for the most life-jeopardizing gun-connection cases (guns in or at the defendant's hand when committing an offense), leaving other, less imminently threatening, situations for the more flexible guidelines regime.

* * * For indicators from Congress itself, it is appropriate to consider word usage in other provisions of Title 18's chapter on "Firearms." * * * The Court, however, does not derive from the statutory complex at issue its thesis that " '[c]arry' implies personal agency and some degree of possession, whereas 'transport' does not have such a limited connotation and, in addition, implies the movement of goods in bulk over great distances." Looking to provisions Congress enacted, one finds that the Legislature did not acknowledge or routinely adhere to the distinction the Court advances today; instead, Congress sometimes employed "transports" when, according to the Court, "carries" was the right word to use.

Section 925(a)(2)(B), for example, provides that no criminal sanction shall attend "the transportation of [a] firearm or ammunition carried out to enable a person, who lawfully received such firearm or ammunition from the Secretary of the Army, to engage in military training or in competitions." The full text of § 926A, rather than the truncated version the Court presents, see ante, at 9, is also telling:

> Notwithstanding any other provision of any law or any rule or regulation of a State or any political subdivision thereof, any person who is not otherwise prohibited by this chapter from transport-

ing, shipping, or receiving a firearm shall be entitled to transport a firearm for any lawful purpose from any place where he may lawfully possess and carry such firearm to any other place where he may lawfully possess and carry such firearm if, during such transportation the firearm is unloaded, and neither the firearm nor any ammunition being transported is readily accessible or is directly accessible from the passenger compartment of such transporting vehicle: Provided, That in the case of a vehicle without a compartment separate from the driver's compartment the firearm or ammunition shall be contained in a locked container other than the glove compartment or console.

In describing when and how a person may travel in a vehicle that contains his firearm without violating the law, §§ 925(a)(2)(B) and 926A use "transport," not "carry," to "impl[y] personal agency and some degree of possession." See ante, at 9.

Reading "carries" in § 924(c)(1) to mean "on or about [one's] person" is fully compatible with these and other "Firearms" statutes. * * *

II

Section 924(c)(1), as the foregoing discussion details, is not decisively clear one way or another. The sharp division in the Court on the proper reading of the measure confirms, "[a]t the very least, . . . that the issue is subject to some doubt. Under these circumstances, we adhere to the familiar rule that, 'where there is ambiguity in a criminal statute, doubts are resolved in favor of the defendant.' " *Adamo Wrecking Co. v. United States*, 434 U.S. 275, 284–285 (1978) (citation omitted); see *United States v. Granderson*, 511 U.S. 39, 54 (1994) ("[W]here text, structure, and history fail to establish that the Government's position is unambiguously correct, we apply the rule of lenity and resolve the ambiguity in [the defendant's] favor."). "Carry" bears many meanings, as the Court and the "Firearms" statutes demonstrate. The narrower "on or about [one's] person" interpretation is hardly implausible nor at odds with an accepted meaning of "carries a firearm."

Overlooking that there will be an enhanced sentence for the gun-possessing drug dealer in any event, the Court asks rhetorically: "How persuasive is a punishment that is without effect until a drug dealer who has brought his gun to a sale (indeed has it available for use) actually takes it from the trunk (or unlocks the glove compartment) of his car?" Correspondingly, the Court defines "carries a firearm" to cover "a person who knowingly possesses and conveys firearms [anyplace] in a vehicle . . . which the person accompanies." Congress, however, hardly lacks competence to select the words "possesses" or "conveys" when that is what the Legislature means.

Notably in view of the Legislature's capacity to speak plainly, and of over-riding concern, the Court's inquiry pays scant attention to a core reason for the rule of lenity: "[B]ecause of the seriousness of criminal penalties, and because criminal punishment usually represents the moral condemnation of the community, legislatures and not courts should define criminal activity. This policy embodies 'the instinctive distaste against men languishing in prison unless the lawmaker has clearly said they should.' " *United States v. Bass*, 404 U.S. 336, 348 (1971) (quoting H. Friendly, *Mr. Justice Frankfurter and the Reading of Statutes*, in *Benchmarks* 196, 209 (1967)). * * *

NOTES & QUESTIONS

1. The majority begins its analysis by noting that the Oxford English Dictionary lists "convey by vehicle" as its "first definition" and so refers to that as the "word's primary meaning." Does "convey by vehicle" seem like the *primary* meaning of "carry" to you? Why might the Oxford English Dictionary list this as its first definition? Is it perhaps a British, rather than American, usage? In fact, it turns out that Oxford places its definitions in *chronological* order, so the first definition is merely the oldest known use of the word, not the most widespread contemporary use of it. Doesn't this undermine the majority's conclusion? What does the majority's (pretty fundamental) mistake in using a dictionary tell us about the appropriateness of using dictionaries to resolve questions of statutory meaning?

2. As the dissenters in *Muscarello* make apparent, the Rule of Lenity is not consistently favored or followed. Indeed, it has been falling out of favor in recent decades. For instance, it was not followed in *Moskal v. United States*, 498 U.S. 103 (1990), to avoid treating vehicle titles with erroneous odometer readings as "falsely made" securities. At one time, more than two-thirds of the states had codified some version of the Rule of Lenity, but most of those states eventually repealed their version of this

rule, often in favor of a non-substantive canon that instructs courts to construe penal statutes "according to their terms to promote justice."

3. Although the Rule of Lenity is typically applicable to criminal statutes, it can occasionally figure in civil contexts as well, when what is at issue is some form of civil penalty. Moreover, many statutes, for instance including the federal RICO statute, 18 U.S.C. §§ 1962–1964, are effectively civil-criminal hybrids, imposing both civil and criminal liability under the same substantive standard. Should the Rule apply to a statute like RICO?

4. An interesting and important point of disagreement concerning the Rule's application is whether to use it as a heavy presumption, favoring the defendant whenever there is ambiguity in a penal measure, or just as a tiebreaker, when all other sources of clarifying textual ambiguity leave the issue unresolved. Do you see why Justice Breyer's majority opinion consigns the rule to tiebreaker status?

5. How would you have resolved the meaning of "carries a firearm" for purposes of this statute?

B. The Constitutional Avoidance Canon

Another substantive canon is that statutory provisions should be construed to avoid giving rise to a serious constitutional question. In other words, if two (or more) interpretations of a measure are possible, but one interpretation might place the constitutionality of the underlying measure genuinely at issue, the interpreter should choose another interpretation that would not raise a constitutional issue: "[I]f a serious doubt of constitutionality is raised, it is a cardinal principle that this Court will first ascertain whether a construction of the statute is fairly possible by which the question may be avoided." *Ashwander v. Tennessee Valley Authority*, 297 U.S. 288, 348 (1936) (Brandeis, J., concurring). At one time, the Constitutional Avoidance Canon took a narrower form, providing that only when an interpretation would actually make a measure unconstitutional should it be avoided if any other interpretation was fairly possible. But today, the canon is used to avoid even needing to resolve a serious question about a law's constitutionality.

Consider the following well-known example. The constitutional question involved the First Amendment's Free Exercise Clause, which limits government involvement in religion. The Clause provides that "*Congress shall make no law* respecting an establishment of religion or *prohibiting the free exercise thereof.*" The constitutional

> **FYI** In this usage, "lay teachers" means teachers without formal religious training hired to teach secular rather than religious subject matter.

question in the case is whether the National Labor Relations Act's requirement that an employer recognize and bargain with an employee union would violate the First Amendment when the employees are lay teachers at Catholic high schools. Note that the specific text of the act in question, the National Labor Relations Act of 1935, does not show up until the dissenting opinion!

National Labor Relations Board v. Catholic Bishop
440 U.S. 490 (1979)

MR. CHIEF JUSTICE BURGER delivered the opinion of the Court.

This case arises out of the National Labor Relations Board's exercise of jurisdiction over lay faculty members at two groups of Catholic high schools. We granted certiorari to consider two questions: (a) Whether teachers in schools operated by a church to teach both religious and secular subjects are within the jurisdiction granted by the National Labor Relations Act; and (b) if the Act authorizes such jurisdiction, does its exercise violate the guarantees of the Religion Clauses of the First Amendment?

I

[The Court described the religious purposes of the two groups of schools, along with their goal of providing traditional secular education, their state recognitions and certifications, and their accreditations by regional educational organizations. In 1974 and 1975, union organizations filed petitions with the National Labor Relations Board to represent the lay teachers at the schools.] The schools challenged the assertion of jurisdiction on two grounds: (a) that the schools do not fall within the Board's discretionary jurisdictional criteria; and (b) that the Religion Clauses of the First Amendment preclude the Board's jurisdiction. The Board rejected the jurisdictional arguments on the basis * * * that its policy was to decline jurisdiction over religiously sponsored organizations "only when they are completely religious, not just religiously associated." Because neither group of schools was found to fall within the Board's "completely religious" category, the Board asserted jurisdiction and ordered elections.

[After union elections occurred, the schools refused to recognize or bargain with the prevailing union organizations.] The Board concluded that the schools had violated the Act and ordered that they cease their unfair labor practices and that they bargain collectively with the unions. * * * The schools challenged the Board's orders in petitions to the Court of Appeals for the Seventh Circuit. That court denied enforcement of the Board's orders. * * *

III

The [National Labor Relations] Board's assertion of jurisdiction over private schools is * * * a relatively recent development. * * * The Board now asserts jurisdiction over all private, nonprofit, educational institutions with gross annual revenues that meet its jurisdictional requirements whether they are secular or religious. * * *

That broad assertion of jurisdiction has not gone unchallenged. But the Board has rejected the contention that the Religion Clauses of the First Amendment bar the extension of its jurisdiction to church-operated schools. Where the Board has declined to exercise jurisdiction, it has done so only on the grounds of the employer's minimal impact on commerce. * * *

When it ordered an election for the lay professional employees at five parochial high schools in Baltimore in 1975, the Board reiterated its belief that exercise of its jurisdiction is not contrary to the First Amendment:

> [T]he Board's policy in the past has been to decline jurisdiction over similar institutions only when they are completely religious, not just religiously associated, and the Archdiocese concedes that instruction is not limited to religious subjects. That the Archdiocese seeks to provide an education based on Christian principles does not lead to a contrary conclusion. Most religiously associated institutions seek to operate in conformity with their religious tenets.

Roman Catholic Archdiocese of Baltimore, 216 N. L. R. B., at 250.

The Board also rejected the First Amendment claims in *Cardinal Timothy Manning, Roman Catholic Archbishop of the Archdiocese of Los Angeles*, 223 N. L. R. B. 1218, 1218 (1976): "Regulation of labor relations does not violate the First Amendment when it involves a *minimal intrusion* on religious conduct and is necessary to obtain [the Act's] objective." (Emphasis added.)

The Board thus recognizes that its assertion of jurisdiction over teachers in religious schools constitutes some degree of intrusion into the administration of the affairs of church-operated schools. Implicit in the Board's distinction between schools that are "completely religious" and those "religiously associated" is also an acknowledgment of some degree of entanglement. * * *

IV

That there are constitutional limitations on the Board's actions has been repeatedly recognized by this Court even while acknowledging the broad scope of the grant of jurisdiction. The First Amendment, of course, is a limitation on the power of Congress. Thus, if we were to conclude that the Act granted the challenged jurisdiction over these teachers we would be required to decide whether that was constitutionally permissible under the Religion Clauses of the First Amendment.

Although the respondents press their claims under the Religion Clauses, the question we consider first is whether Congress intended the Board to have jurisdiction over teachers in church-operated schools. In a number of cases the Court has heeded the essence of Mr. Chief Justice Marshall's admonition in *Murray v. The Charming Betsy*, 2 Cranch 64, 118 (1804), by holding that an Act of Congress ought not be construed to violate the Constitution if any other possible construction remains available. Moreover, the Court has followed this policy in the interpretation of the Act now before us and related statutes.

In *Machinists v. Street*, 367 U.S. 740 (1961), for example, the Court considered claims that serious First Amendment questions would arise if the Railway Labor Act were construed to allow compulsory union dues to be used to support political candidates or causes not approved by some members. The Court looked to the language of the Act and the legislative history and concluded that they did not permit union dues to be used for such political purposes, thus avoiding "serious doubt of [the Act's] constitutionality."

> **FYI** The constitutional issue the Court avoided in *Machinists* was whether compulsory union dues used for the union's political activities infringed upon the First Amendment's protection of freedom of association.

Similarly in *McCulloch v. Sociedad Nacional de Marineros de Honduras*, 372 U.S. 10 (1963), a case involving the Board's assertion of jurisdiction over foreign seamen, the Court declined to read the National Labor Relations Act so as to give rise to a serious question of separation of powers which in turn would have implicated sensitive issues of the authority of the Executive over relations with foreign nations. The international implications of the case led the Court to describe it as involving "public questions particularly high in the scale of our national interest." Id., at 17. Because of those questions the Court held that before sanctioning the Board's exercise of jurisdiction " 'there must be present the affirmative intention of the Congress clearly expressed.' "

The values enshrined in the First Amendment plainly rank high "in the scale of our national values." In keeping with the Court's prudential policy it is incumbent on us to determine whether the Board's exercise of its jurisdiction here would give rise to serious constitutional questions. If so, we must first identify "the affirmative intention of the Congress clearly expressed" before concluding that the Act grants jurisdiction.

V

In recent decisions involving aid to parochial schools we have recognized the critical and unique role of the teacher in fulfilling the mission of a church-operated school. What was said of the schools in *Lemon v. Kurtzman*, 403 U.S. 602, 617 (1971), is true of the schools in this case: "Religious authority necessarily pervades the school system." The key role played by teachers in such a school system has been the predicate for our conclusions that governmental aid channeled through teachers creates an impermissible risk of excessive governmental entanglement in the affairs of the church-operated schools. * * *

The Board argues that it can avoid excessive entanglement since it will resolve only factual issues such as whether an anti-union animus motivated an employer's action. But at this stage of our consideration we are not compelled to determine whether the entanglement is excessive as we would were we considering the constitutional issue. Rather, we make a narrow inquiry whether the exercise of the Board's jurisdiction presents a significant risk that the First Amendment will be infringed.

Moreover, it is already clear that the Board's actions will go beyond resolving factual issues. The Court of Appeals' opinion refers to charges of unfair labor practices filed against religious schools. The court observed that in those cases the schools had responded that their challenged actions were mandated by their religious creeds. The resolution of such charges by the Board, in many instances, will necessarily involve inquiry into the good faith of the position asserted by the clergy-administrators and its relationship to the school's religious mission. It is not only the conclusions that may be reached by the Board which may impinge on rights guaranteed by the Religion Clauses, but also the very process of inquiry leading to findings and conclusions.

The Board's exercise of jurisdiction will have at least one other impact on church-operated schools. The Board will be called upon to decide what are "terms and conditions of employment" and therefore mandatory subjects of bargaining. See 29 U.S.C. 158(d). Although the Board has not interpreted that phrase as it relates to educational institutions, similar state provisions provide insight into the effect of mandatory bargaining. * * * Inevitably the Board's inquiry will implicate sensitive issues that open the door to conflicts between clergy-administrators and the Board, or conflicts with negotiators for unions. * * *

The church-teacher relationship in a church-operated school differs from the employment relationship in a public or other nonreligious school. We see no escape from conflicts flowing from the Board's exercise of jurisdiction over teachers in church-operated schools and the consequent serious First Amendment questions that would follow. We therefore turn to an examination of the National Labor Relations Act to decide whether it must be read to confer jurisdiction that would in turn require a decision on the constitutional claims raised by respondents.

VI

There is no clear expression of an affirmative intention of Congress that teachers in church-operated schools should be covered by the Act. Admittedly, Congress defined the Board's jurisdiction in very broad terms; we must therefore examine the legislative history of the Act to determine whether Congress contemplated that the grant of jurisdiction would include teachers in such schools.

In enacting the National Labor Relations Act in 1935, Congress sought to protect the right of American workers to bargain collectively. The concern that was repeated throughout the debates was the need to assure workers the right to organize to counterbalance the collective activities of employers which had been authorized by the National Industrial Recovery Act. But congressional attention focused on employment in private industry and on industrial recovery. * * *

Our examination of the statute and its legislative history indicates that Congress simply gave no consideration to church-operated schools. It is not without significance, however, that the Senate Committee on Education and Labor chose a college professor's dispute with the college as an example of employer-employee relations not covered by the Act. S. Rep. No. 573, 74th Cong., 1st Sess., 7 (1935), 2 Legislative History, supra, at 2307.

Congress' next major consideration of the jurisdiction of the Board came during the passage of the Labor Management Relations Act of 1947—the Taft-Hartley Act. In that Act Congress amended the definition of "employer" in § 2 of the original Act to exclude nonprofit hospitals. 61 Stat. 137, 29 U.S.C. 152(2) (1970 ed.). There was some discussion of the scope of the Board's jurisdiction but the consensus was that nonprofit institutions in general did not fall within the Board's jurisdiction because they did not affect commerce. * * *

The most recent significant amendment to the Act was passed in 1974, removing the exemption of nonprofit hospitals. Pub. L. 93–360, 88 Stat. 395. The Board relies upon that amendment as showing that Congress approved the Board's exercise of jurisdiction over church-operated schools. A close examination of that legislative history, however, reveals nothing to indicate an affirmative intention that such schools be within the Board's jurisdiction. Since the Board did not assert jurisdiction over teachers in a church-operated school until after the 1974 amendment, nothing in the history of the amendment can be read as reflecting Congress' tacit approval of the Board's action.

During the debate there were expressions of concern about the effect of the bill on employees of religious hospitals whose religious beliefs would not permit them to join a union. * * * [The result] was an amendment which reflects congressional sensitivity to First Amendment guarantees:

> Any employee of a health care institution who is a member of and adheres to established and traditional tenets or teachings of a bona fide religion, body, or sect which has historically held conscientious objections to joining or financially supporting labor organizations shall not be required to join or financially support any labor organization as a condition of employment; except that such employee may be required, in lieu of periodic dues and initiation fees, to pay sums equal to such dues and initiation fees to a nonreligious charitable fund exempt from taxation under

> section 501(c)(3) of title 26, chosen by such employee from a list
> of at least three such funds, designated in a contract between
> such institution and a labor organization, or if the contract fails
> to designate such funds, then to any such fund chosen by the
> employee.

29 U.S.C. 169.

The absence of an "affirmative intention of the Congress clearly expressed" fortifies our conclusion that Congress did not contemplate that the Board would require church-operated schools to grant recognition to unions as bargaining agents for their teachers.

The Board relies heavily upon *Associated Press v. NLRB*, 301 U.S. 103 (1937). There the Court held that the First Amendment was no bar to the application of the Act to the Associated Press, an organization engaged in collecting information and news throughout the world and distributing it to its members. Perceiving nothing to suggest that application of the Act would infringe First Amendment guarantees of press freedoms, the Court sustained Board jurisdiction. Id., at 131–132. Here, on the contrary, the record affords abundant evidence that the Board's exercise of jurisdiction over teachers in church-operated schools would implicate the guarantees of the Religion Clauses.

Accordingly, in the absence of a clear expression of Congress' intent to bring teachers in church-operated schools within the jurisdiction of the Board, we decline to construe the Act in a manner that could in turn call upon the Court to resolve difficult and sensitive questions arising out of the guarantees of the First Amendment Religion Clauses.

MR. JUSTICE BRENNAN, with whom MR. JUSTICE WHITE, MR. JUSTICE MARSHALL, and MR. JUSTICE BLACKMUN join, dissenting.

The Court today holds that coverage of the National Labor Relations Act does not extend to lay teachers employed by church-operated schools. That construction is plainly wrong in light of the Act's language, its legislative history, and this Court's precedents. It is justified solely on the basis of a canon of statutory construction seemingly invented by the Court for the purpose of deciding this case. I dissent.

I

The general principle of construing statutes to avoid unnecessary constitutional decisions is a well-settled and salutary one. The governing canon, however, is not that expressed by the Court today. The Court requires that there be a "clear expression of an affirmative intention of Congress" before it will bring within the coverage of a broadly worded regulatory statute certain persons whose coverage might raise constitutional questions. But those familiar with the legislative process know that explicit expressions of congressional intent in such broadly inclusive statutes are not commonplace. Thus, by strictly or loosely applying its requirement, the Court can virtually remake congressional enactments. This flouts Mr. Chief Justice Taft's admonition "that amendment may not be substituted for construction, and that a court may not exercise legislative functions to save [a] law from conflict with constitutional limitation." *Yu Cong Eng v. Trinidad*, 271 U.S. 500, 518 (1926). * * *

The settled canon for construing statutes wherein constitutional questions may lurk was stated in *Machinists v. Street*, 367 U.S. 740 (1961), cited by the Court: " 'When the validity of an act of the Congress is drawn in question, and even if a serious doubt of constitutionality is raised, it is a cardinal principle that this Court will first ascertain whether a construction of the statute is *fairly possible* by which the question may be avoided.' *Crowell v. Benson*, 285 U.S. 22, 62." *Id.*, at 749–750 (emphasis added).

This limitation to constructions that are "fairly possible," and "reasonable," *see Yu Cong Eng*, acts as a brake against wholesale judicial dismemberment of congressional enactments. It confines the judiciary to its proper role in construing statutes, which is to interpret them so as to give effect to congressional intention. The Court's new "affirmative expression" rule releases that brake.

II

The interpretation of the National Labor Relations Act announced by the Court today is not "fairly possible." The Act's wording, its legislative history, and the Court's own precedents leave "the intention of the Congress . . . revealed too distinctly to permit us to ignore it because of mere misgivings as to power." *Moore Ice Cream Co. v. Rose*, supra, at 379. Section 2 (2) of the Act, 29 U.S.C. 152 (2), defines "employer" as

> . . . any person acting as an agent of an employer, directly or
> indirectly, *but shall not include* the United States or any wholly
> owned Government corporation, or any Federal Reserve Bank,
> or any State or political subdivision thereof, or any person subject
> to the Railway Labor Act, as amended from time to time, or any
> labor organization (other than when acting as an employer), or
> anyone acting in the capacity of officer or agent of such labor
> organization.

(Emphasis added.)

Thus, the Act covers all employers not within the eight express exceptions.
The Court today substitutes amendment for construction to insert one more
exception—for church-operated schools. This is a particularly transparent
violation of the judicial role: The legislative history reveals that Congress
itself considered and rejected a very similar amendment.

The pertinent legislative history of the NLRA begins with the Wagner Act of
1935, 49 Stat. 449. Section 2(2) of that Act, identical in all relevant respects
to the current section, excluded from its coverage neither church-operated
schools nor any other private nonprofit organization. Accordingly, in applying
that Act, the National Labor Relations Board did not recognize an exception
for nonprofit employers, even when religiously associated. An argument for
an implied nonprofit exemption was rejected because the design of the Act
was as clear then as it is now: "[N]either charitable institutions nor their
employees are exempted from operation of the Act by its terms, although
certain other employers and employees are exempted." *Central Dispensary
& Emergency Hospital*, 44 N. L. R. B. 533, 540 (1942). * * * Both the lower
courts and this Court concurred in the Board's construction. * * *

The Hartley bill, which passed the House of Representatives [440 U.S. 490,
513] in 1947, would have provided the exception the Court today writes into
the statute: "The term 'employer'. . . shall not include . . . any corporation,
community chest, fund, or foundation organized and operated exclusively
for *religious*, charitable, scientific, literary, or *educational* purposes, . . . no
part of the net earnings of which inures to the benefit of any private shareholder or individual. . . ." (Emphasis added.) H. R. 3020, 80th Cong., 1st
Sess., 2(2) (Apr. 18, 1947), reprinted in National Labor Relations Board,
Legislative History of the Labor Management Relations Act, 1947, pp.
160–161 (hereinafter, 1947 Leg. Hist.).

But the proposed exception was not enacted. The bill reported by the Senate Committee on Labor and Public Welfare did not contain the Hartley exception. Instead, the Senate proposed an exception limited to nonprofit hospitals, and passed the bill in that form. The Senate version was accepted by the House in conference, thus limiting the exception for nonprofit employers to nonprofit hospitals. Ch. 120, 61 Stat. 136.

Even that limited exemption was ultimately repealed in 1974. Pub. L. 93–360, 88 Stat. 395. In doing so, Congress confirmed the view of the Act expressed here: that it was intended to cover all employers—including nonprofit employers—unless expressly excluded, and that the 1947 amendment excluded only nonprofit hospitals. * * * Moreover, it is significant that in considering the 1974 amendments, the Senate expressly rejected an amendment proposed by Senator Ervin that was analogous to the one the Court today creates—an amendment to exempt nonprofit hospitals operated by religious groups. 120 Cong. Rec. 12950, 12968 (1974), 1974 Leg. Hist. 119, 141. Senator Cranston, floor manager of the Senate Committee bill and primary opponent of the proposed religious exception, explained:

"[S]uch an exception for religiously affiliated hospitals would seriously erode *the existing national policy which holds religiously affiliated institutions generally such as* proprietary nursing homes, residential communities, and *educational facilities to the same standards as their nonsectarian counterparts*." 120 Cong. Rec. 12957 (1974), 1974 Leg. Hist. 137 (emphasis added). * * *

In construing the Board's jurisdiction to exclude church-operated schools, therefore, the Court today is faithful to neither the statute's language nor its history. Moreover, it is also untrue to its own precedents. "This Court has consistently declared that in passing the National Labor Relations Act, Congress intended to and did vest in the Board the fullest *jurisdictional* breadth constitutionally permissible under the Commerce Clause [citing cases]." *NLRB v. Reliance Fuel Oil Corp.*, 371 U.S. 224, 226 (1963) (emphasis in original). As long as an employer is within the reach of Congress' power under the Commerce Clause—and no one doubts that respondents are—the Court has held him to be covered by the Act regardless of the nature of his activity. Indeed, *Associated Press v. NLRB*, 301 U.S. 103 (1937), construed the Act to cover editorial employees of a nonprofit news-gathering organization despite a claim—precisely parallel to that made here—that their inclusion rendered the Act in violation of the First Amendment. Today's opinion is simply unable to explain the grounds that distinguish that case from this one.

Thus, the available authority indicates that Congress intended to include—not exclude—lay teachers of church-operated schools. The Court does not counter this with evidence that Congress did intend an exception it never stated. Instead, despite the legislative history to the contrary, it construes the Act as excluding lay teachers only because Congress did not state explicitly that they were covered. In Mr. Justice Cardozo's words, this presses "avoidance of a difficulty . . . to the point of disingenuous evasion." *Moore Ice Cream Co. v. Rose*, 289 U.S., at 379. 11

> **?** What is your view of the implications of what the Court calls "the available authority" on the question of what was Congress's intent?

III

Under my view that the NLRA includes within its coverage lay teachers employed by church-operated schools, the constitutional questions presented would have to be reached. I do not now do so only because the Court does not. I repeat for emphasis, however, that while the resolution of the constitutional question is not without difficulty, it is irresponsible to avoid it by a cavalier exercise in statutory interpretation which succeeds only in defying congressional intent. * * *

NOTES & QUESTIONS

1. Is the statutory text at issue in the *Catholic Bishop* case issue ambiguous? If not, why not? If so, what is the ambiguity and what is its cause?

2. What is the difference between the *Machinists v. Street* version of the Constitutional Avoidance Canon, discussed in the *Catholic Bishop* case, and the version that the majority follows in *Catholic Bishop*? Which do you find most appropriate?

3. The Constitutional Avoidance Canon often comes in for some criticism. One criticism is that it permits the judiciary to issue stealth advisory opinions about the constitutionality of various measures. At the same time, because its use typically means a court has not opined on the underlying constitutionality, the canon deprives the legislature of the opportunity to learn the true limits of its constitutional power. A third

criticism is that at least in some instances, the effect of a court's reliance on the canon will be to expand the degree to which a constitutional provision constrains the legislature's authority beyond what the provision would require if squarely interpreted, thus limiting a statutory measure's scope to less than the full scope of the legislature's constitutional power.

Test Your Understanding

To assess your understanding of the material in this chapter, click here to take a quiz.

22

Substantive (Policy) Canons: Federalism and Common Law Canons

---

Key Concepts

- New Federalism canons
- Presumption against preemption of state law
- Clear statement canons
- Derogation canon
- Remedial canon

Chapter Summary

The New Federalism Canons are relatively new canons used in federal courts. They rose to prominence as an effort to promote greater federal deference to the sovereign authority of the states. For example, absent a clear statement of intent from Congress, a court should not construe a federal statute to interfere with areas of traditional state regulation (e.g., professional licensure). Another related canon is a Presumption Against Preemption of State Law, which says that federal law should not be construed to preempt state law without clear evidence that Congress intended that the law do so.

Two additional substantive canons, the Derogation Canon and the Remedial Canon, run directly counter to each other. The Derogation Canon says statutes that depart from the common law should be construed narrowly, so as to alter the common law as little as possible. On the other hand, the Remedial Canon argues that "remedial" statutes should be construed broadly to increase their remedial effect. Since there is no universal way to say what is a "remedial" statute, the Remedial Canon is not widely accepted, though its underlying premise often makes an appearance.

A. "New Federalism" Canons—Discouraging Intrusions on State Sovereignty

An entire group of substantive canons operates to protect specific constitutional values even when the interpretive issue is not likely to raise any concern about possible unconstitutionality. Among the most widely employed of such canons are those that protect state government sovereignty from federal encroachment unless Congress has clearly stated in the statute that Congress intended to infringe on state authority. These are often collectively called the "New Federalism" canons, reflecting their relatively recent creation or reinvigoration during the 1980s and 1990s, when the U.S. Supreme Court repeatedly articulated various ways of narrowly construing the reach of federal statutes to promote America's system of dual sovereignty.

The New Federalism canons include a canon against abrogating a state's immunity under the Eleventh Amendment to the Constitution absent a clear textual statement, *see Atascadero State Hospital v. Scanlon,* 473 U.S. 234 (1985), and a canon requiring that Congress clearly state in the statute any conditions it imposes on federal funding of state programs, *see Pennhurst State School & Hospital v. Halderman,* 451 U.S. 1 (1981).

> **!** "Clear statement" rules require the legislature to have in some fashion squarely revealed an intent that a statute be construed in a particular way, or the interpreter will not construe it in that way. You will recall that the majority in *NLRB v. Catholic Bishop* took a "clear statement" approach to the Constitutional Avoidance canon you read in the last chapter.

But perhaps the best known of the New Federalism canons is the canon against construing a federal statute to interfere with traditional state government prerogatives absent the statute's clear statement to this effect. This version of a New Federalism canon traces to *Gregory v. Ashcroft,* 501 U.S. 452 (1991). At issue was whether the Age Discrimination in Employment Act (ADEA) protected state court judges in Missouri against a mandatory retirement provision of the Missouri Constitution. By its terms, the ADEA prohibits covered employers from imposing a mandatory retirement age on covered employees. State governments are covered employers under the ADEA, but the ADEA excluded "appointees on the policymaking level" from the category of "covered employees." The interpretive issue before the U.S. Supreme Court was whether Missouri's state court judges were "appointees on the policymaking level."

A range of interpretive tools could have been brought to bear on this question. But the Court instead relied on a historical and political account of the nature of America's system of dual sovereignty to explain that construing the ADEA to limit how a state structures its government operations would intrude on "the most fundamental sort" of decision "at the heart of representative government" through which "a State defines itself as a sovereign." The Court decided that because this area of sovereignty was "traditionally regulated by the States," it should be protected from federal interference unless it was clear that Congress intended to "upset the usual constitutional balance of federal and state powers." In applying this New Federalism canon, the Court wrote: "We will not read the ADEA to cover state judges unless Congress has made it clear that judges are *included.* . . . [I]t must be plain to anyone reading the Act that it covers judges." Unable to find that degree of clarity, the Court concluded that the ADEA did not apply to Missouri's judges to protect them from the state's mandatory retirement age. Id. at 460–67.

A more recent application of this canon follows. Consider first this DIY exercise, then read the Supreme Court's disposition of the issue.

DIY
A Jilted Spouse Seeks Revenge

 A federal statute, the Chemical Weapons Convention Implementation Act, makes it a crime to "use, or threaten to use, any chemical weapon," among other things. The statute defines "chemical weapon" as "[a] toxic chemical and its precursors," but contains an exception for using these kinds of chemicals for "any peaceful purpose related to an industrial, agricultural, research, medical, or pharmaceutical activity." § 229F(1)(A). The statute defines "toxic chemical" as "any chemical which through its chemical action on life processes can cause death, temporary incapacitation or permanent harm to humans or animals."

Carol Anne Bond took a toxic chemical from her workplace, and ordered another toxic chemical from Amazon.com, which she then spread on her best friend's doorknob, mailbox, and car door, after learning that her best friend had an affair with Bond's husband. The friend suffered minor injuries. Federal prosecutors charged Bond with several federal crimes, including violating the Chemical Weapons Convention Implementation Act.

Has Bond violated the Act? What other information would you like to know to help decide this question? How might the New Federalism canon against construing a federal statute to interfere with traditional state government prerogatives be brought to bear on the question? Should the canon be a factor in the analysis? Why or why not? Spend at least a few minutes thinking about these questions and writing down your thoughts in your notes. Then go on to read the case excerpt below.

Bond v. United States
572 U.S. 844 (2014)

CHIEF JUSTICE ROBERTS delivered the opinion of the Court.

The horrors of chemical warfare were vividly captured by John Singer Sargent in his 1919 painting *Gassed*. The nearly life-sized work depicts two lines of soldiers, blinded by mustard gas, clinging single file to orderlies guiding them to an improvised aid station. There they would receive little treatment and no relief; many suffered for weeks only to have the gas claim their lives. The soldiers were shown staggering through piles of comrades too seriously burned to even join the procession.

The painting reflects the devastation that Sargent witnessed in the aftermath of the Second Battle of Arras during World War I. That battle and others like it led to an overwhelming consensus in the international community that toxic chemicals should never again be used as weapons against human beings. Today that objective is reflected in the international Convention on Chemical Weapons, which has been ratified or acceded to by 190 countries. The United States, pursuant to the Federal Government's constitutionally enumerated power to make treaties, ratified the treaty in 1997. * * *

I

A

[The Court's opinion then described in more detail the development of the Convention on the Prohibition of the Development, Production, Stockpiling, and Use of Chemical Weapons and on Their Destruction, S. Treaty Doc. No. 103–21, 1974 U. N. T. S. 317, traceable to World War I, and its aspirations to achieve "general and complete disarmament under strict and effective international control, including the prohibition and elimination of all types of weapons of mass destruction." The Court then explained that although ratified by the Senate, the treaty is not self- executing in that "the Convention creates obligations only for State Parties and 'does not by itself give rise to domestically enforceable federal law' absent 'implementing legislation passed by Congress.' *Medellín v. Texas*, 552 U.S. 491, n. 2 (2008)."]

Congress gave the Convention domestic effect in 1998 when it passed the Chemical Weapons Convention Implementation Act. See 112 Stat. 2681–856. The Act closely tracks the text of the treaty: It forbids any person knowingly "to develop, produce, otherwise acquire, transfer directly or indirectly, receive, stockpile, retain, own, possess, or use, or threaten to use, any chemical weapon." 18 U.S.C. § 229(a)(1). It defines "chemical weapon" in relevant part as "[a] toxic chemical and its precursors, except where intended for a purpose not prohibited under this chapter as long as the type and quantity is consistent with such a purpose." § 229F(1)(A). "Toxic chemical," in turn, is defined in general as "any chemical which through its chemical action on life processes can cause death, temporary incapacitation or permanent harm to humans or animals. The term includes all such chemicals, regardless of their origin or of their method of production, and regardless of whether they are produced in facilities, in munitions or elsewhere." § 229F(8)(A). Finally, "purposes not prohibited by this chapter" is defined as "[a]ny peaceful purpose related to an industrial, agricultural, research, medical, or pharmaceutical activity or other activity," and other specific purposes. § 229F(7). A person who violates section 229 may be subject to severe punishment: imprisonment "for any term of years," or if a victim's death results, the death penalty or imprisonment "for life." § 229A(a).

B

Petitioner Carol Anne Bond is a microbiologist from Lansdale, Pennsylvania. In 2006, Bond's closest friend, Myrlinda Haynes, announced that she was pregnant. When Bond discovered that her husband was the child's father, she sought revenge against Haynes. Bond stole a quantity of 10-chloro-10H-phenoxarsine (an arsenic-based compound) from her employer, a chemical manufacturer. She also ordered a vial of potassium dichromate (a chemical commonly used in printing photographs or cleaning laboratory equipment) on Amazon.com. Both chemicals are toxic to humans and, in high enough doses, potentially lethal. It is undisputed, however, that Bond did not intend to kill Haynes. She instead hoped that Haynes would touch the chemicals and develop an uncomfortable rash.

* * * Bond went to Haynes's home on at least 24 occasions and spread the chemicals on her car door, mailbox, and door knob. These attempted assaults were almost entirely unsuccessful. The chemicals that Bond used are easy to see, and Haynes was able to avoid them all but once. On that occasion, Haynes suffered a minor chemical burn on her thumb, which she treated by rinsing with water. Haynes repeatedly called the local police to report the suspicious substances, but they took no action. When Haynes found powder on her mailbox, she called the police again, who told her to call the post office. Haynes did so, and postal inspectors placed surveillance cameras around her home. The cameras caught Bond opening Haynes's mailbox, stealing an envelope, and stuffing potassium dichromate inside the muffler of Haynes's car.

Federal prosecutors naturally charged Bond with two counts of mail theft, in violation of 18 U.S.C. § 1708. More surprising, they also charged her with two counts of possessing and using a chemical weapon, in violation of section 229(a). Bond moved to dismiss the chemical weapon counts on the ground that section 229 exceeded Congress's enumerated powers and invaded powers reserved to the States by the Tenth Amendment. The District Court denied Bond's motion. She then entered a conditional guilty plea that reserved her right to appeal. The District Court sentenced Bond to six years in federal prison plus five years of supervised release, and ordered her to pay a $2,000 fine and $9,902.79 in restitution.

Bond appealed, raising a Tenth Amendment challenge to her conviction. * * * She also argued that section 229 does not reach her conduct because the statute's exception for the use of chemicals for "peaceful purposes" should be understood in contradistinction to the "warlike" activities that the Convention was primarily designed to prohibit. Bond argued that her conduct, though reprehensible, was not at all "warlike." The Court of Appeals rejected this argument. The court acknowledged that the Government's reading of section 229 would render the statute "striking" in its "breadth" and turn every "kitchen cupboard and cleaning cabinet in America into a potential chemical weapons cache." But the court nevertheless held that Bond's use of " 'highly toxic chemicals with the intent of harming Haynes' can hardly be characterized as 'peaceful' under that word's commonly understood meaning."

The Third Circuit also rejected Bond's constitutional challenge to her conviction, holding that section 229 was "necessary and proper to carry the Convention into effect." The Court of Appeals relied on this Court's opinion in *Missouri v. Holland*, 252 U.S. 416 (1920), which stated that "[i]f the treaty is valid there can be no dispute about the validity of the statute" that implements it "as a necessary and proper means to execute the powers of the Government." * * *

II

In our federal system, the National Government possesses only limited powers; the States and the people retain the remainder. The States have broad authority to enact legislation for the public good—what we have often called a "police power." *United States v. Lopez*, 514 U.S. 549, 567 (1995). The Federal Government, by contrast, has no such authority and "can exercise only the powers granted to it," *McCulloch v. Maryland*, 4 Wheat. 316, 405 (1819), including the power to make "all Laws which shall be necessary and proper for carrying into Execution" the enumerated powers, U.S. Const., Art. I, § 8, cl. 18. For nearly two centuries it has been "clear" that, lacking a police power, "Congress cannot punish felonies generally." *Cohens v. Virginia*, 6 Wheat. 264, 428 (1821). A criminal act committed wholly within a State "cannot be made an offence against the United States, unless it have some relation to the execution of a power of Congress, or to some matter within the jurisdiction of the United States." *United States v. Fox*, 95 U.S. 670, 672 (1878).

The Government frequently defends federal criminal legislation on the ground that the legislation is authorized pursuant to Congress's power to regulate interstate commerce. In this case, however, the Court of Appeals held that the Government had explicitly disavowed that argument before the District Court. As a result, in this Court the parties have devoted significant effort to arguing whether section 229, as applied to Bond's offense, is a necessary and proper means of executing the National Government's power to make treaties. U.S. Const., Art. II, § 2, cl. 2. Bond argues that the lower court's reading of *Missouri v. Holland* would remove all limits on federal authority, so long as the Federal Government ratifies a treaty first. She insists that to effectively afford the Government a police power whenever it implements a treaty would be contrary to the Framers' careful decision to divide power between the States and the National Government as a means of preserving liberty. To the extent that *Holland* authorizes such usurpation of traditional state authority, Bond says, it must be either limited or overruled.

The Government replies that this Court has never held that a statute implementing a valid treaty exceeds Congress's enumerated powers. To do so here, the Government says, would contravene another deliberate choice of the

Framers: to avoid placing subject matter limitations on the National Government's power to make treaties. And it might also undermine confidence in the United States as an international treaty partner.

Notwithstanding this debate, it is "a well-established principle governing the prudent exercise of this Court's jurisdiction that normally the Court will not decide a constitutional question if there is some other ground upon which to dispose of the case." *Escambia County v. McMillan*, 466 U.S. 48, 51 (1984) (per curiam); see also *Ashwander v. TVA*, 297 U.S. 288, 347 (1936) (Brandeis, J., concurring). Bond argues that section 229 does not cover her conduct. So we consider that argument first.

III

Section 229 exists to implement the Convention, so we begin with that international agreement. As explained, the Convention's drafters intended for it to be a comprehensive ban on chemical weapons. But even with its broadly worded definitions, we have doubts that a treaty about chemical weapons has anything to do with Bond's conduct. The Convention, a product of years of worldwide study, analysis, and multinational negotiation, arose in response to war crimes and acts of terrorism. There is no reason to think the sovereign nations that ratified the Convention were interested in anything like Bond's common law assault.

Even if the treaty does reach that far, nothing prevents Congress from implementing the Convention in the same manner it legislates with respect to innumerable other matters—observing the Constitution's division of responsibility between sovereigns and leaving the prosecution of purely local crimes to the States. The Convention, after all, is agnostic between enforcement at the state versus federal level: It provides that "[e]ach State Party shall, *in accordance with its constitutional processes*, adopt the necessary measures to implement its obligations under this Convention." Art. VII(1), 1974 U. N. T. S. 331 (emphasis added). * * *

Fortunately, we have no need to interpret the scope of the Convention in this case. Bond was prosecuted under section 229, and the statute—unlike the Convention—must be read consistent with principles of federalism inherent in our constitutional structure.

A

In the Government's view, the conclusion that Bond "knowingly" "use[d]" a "chemical weapon" in violation of section 229(a) is simple: The chemicals that Bond placed on Haynes's home and car are "toxic chemical[s]" as defined by the statute, and Bond's attempt to assault Haynes was not a "peaceful purpose." §§ 229F(1), (8), (7). The problem with this interpretation is that it would "dramatically intrude[ ] upon traditional state criminal jurisdiction," and we avoid reading statutes to have such reach in the absence of a clear indication that they do. *United States v. Bass*, 404 U.S. 336, 350 (1971).

Part of a fair reading of statutory text is recognizing that "Congress legislates against the backdrop" of certain unexpressed presumptions. *EEOC v. Arabian American Oil Co.*, 499 U.S. 244, 248 (1991). As Justice Frankfurter put it in his famous essay on statutory interpretation, correctly reading a statute "demands awareness of certain presuppositions." *Some Reflections on the Reading of Statutes*, 47 COLUM. L. REV. 527, 537 (1947). For example, we presume that a criminal statute derived from the common law carries with it the requirement of a culpable mental state—even if no such limitation appears in the text—unless it is clear that the Legislature intended to impose strict liability. *United States v. United States Gypsum Co.*, 438 U.S. 422, 437 (1978). To take another example, we presume, absent a clear statement from Congress, that federal statutes do not apply outside the United States. *Morrison v. National Australia Bank Ltd.*, 561 U.S. 247, 255 (2010). So even though section 229, read on its face, would cover a chemical weapons crime if committed by a U.S. citizen in Australia, we would not apply the statute to such conduct absent a plain statement from Congress. The notion that some things "go without saying" applies to legislation just as it does to everyday life.

Among the background principles of construction that our cases have recognized are those grounded in the relationship between the Federal Government and the States under our Constitution. It has long been settled, for example, that we presume federal statutes do not abrogate state sovereign immunity, *Atascadero State Hospital v. Scanlon*, 473 U.S. 234, 243 (1985), impose obligations on the States pursuant to section 5 of the Fourteenth Amendment, *Pennhurst State School and Hospital v. Halderman*, 451 U.S. 1 –17 (1981), or preempt state law, *Rice v. Santa Fe Elevator Corp.*, 331 U.S. 218, 230 (1947).

Closely related to these is the well-established principle that " 'it is incumbent upon the federal courts to be certain of Congress' intent before finding that federal law overrides' " the "usual constitutional balance of federal and state powers." *Gregory v. Ashcroft*, 501 U.S. 452, 460 (1991) (quoting *Atascadero*, supra, at 243). To quote Frankfurter again, if the Federal Government would " 'radically readjust[ ] the balance of state and national authority, those charged with the duty of legislating [must be] reasonably explicit' " about it. *BFP v. Resolution Trust Corporation*, 511 U.S. 531, 544 (1994) (quoting *Some Reflections*, supra, at 539–540; second alteration in original). Or as explained by Justice Marshall, when legislation "affect[s] the federal balance, the requirement of clear statement assures that the legislature has in fact faced, and intended to bring into issue, the critical matters involved in the judicial decision." *Bass*, supra, at 349.

We have applied this background principle when construing federal statutes that touched on several areas of traditional state responsibility. See *Gregory*, supra, at 460 (qualifications for state officers); *BFP*, supra, at 544 (titles to real estate); *Solid Waste Agency of Northern Cook Cty. v. Army Corps of Engineers*, 531 U.S. 159, 174 (2001) (land and water use). Perhaps the clearest example of traditional state authority is the punishment of local criminal activity. *United States v. Morrison*, 529 U.S. 598, 618 (2000). Thus, "we will not be quick to assume that Congress has meant to effect a significant change in the sensitive relation between federal and state criminal jurisdiction." *Bass*, 404 U.S., at 349.

In *Bass*, we interpreted a statute that prohibited any convicted felon from " 'receiv[ing], possess[ing], or transport[ing] in commerce or affecting commerce . . . any firearm.' " *Id.*, at 337. The Government argued that the statute barred felons from possessing all firearms and that it was not necessary to demonstrate a connection to interstate commerce. We rejected that reading, which would "render[ ] traditionally local criminal conduct a matter for federal enforcement and would also involve a substantial extension of federal police resources." *Id.*, at 350. We instead read the statute more narrowly to require proof of a connection to interstate commerce in every case, thereby "preserv[ing] as an element of all the offenses a requirement suited to federal criminal jurisdiction alone." *Id.*, at 351.

Similarly, in *Jones v. United States*, 529 U.S. 848, 850 (2000), we confronted the question whether the federal arson statute, which prohibited burning " 'any . . . property used in interstate or foreign commerce or in any activity affecting interstate or foreign commerce,' " reached an owner-occupied private residence. Once again we rejected the Government's "expansive interpretation," under which "hardly a building in the land would fall outside the federal statute's domain." *Id.*, at 857. We instead held that the statute was "most sensibly read" more narrowly to reach only buildings used in "active employment for commercial purposes." *Id.*, at 855. We noted that "arson is a paradigmatic common-law state crime," *id.*, at 858, and that the Government's proposed broad reading would " 'significantly change[ ] the federal-state balance,' " *ibid.* (quoting *Bass*, 404 U.S., at 349), "mak[ing] virtually every arson in the country a federal offense," 529 U.S., at 859.

These precedents make clear that it is appropriate to refer to basic principles of federalism embodied in the Constitution to resolve ambiguity in a federal statute. In this case, the ambiguity derives from the improbably broad reach of the key statutory definition given the term—"chemical weapon"—being defined; the deeply serious consequences of adopting such a boundless reading; and the lack of any apparent need to do so in light of the context from which the statute arose—a treaty about chemical warfare and terrorism. We conclude that, in this curious case, we can insist on a clear indication that Congress meant to reach purely local crimes, before interpreting the statute's expansive language in a way that intrudes on the police power of the States. See *Bass*, supra, at 349.

B

We do not find any such clear indication in section 229. "Chemical weapon" is the key term that defines the statute's reach, and it is defined extremely broadly. But that general definition does not constitute a clear statement that Congress meant the statute to reach local criminal conduct.

In fact, a fair reading of section 229 suggests that it does not have as expansive a scope as might at first appear. To begin, as a matter of natural meaning, an educated user of English would not describe Bond's crime as involving a "chemical weapon." Saying that a person "used a chemical weapon" conveys a very different idea than saying the person "used a chemical in a way that caused some harm." The natural meaning of "chemical weapon" takes account of both the particular chemicals that the defendant used and the circumstances in which she used them.

When used in the manner here, the chemicals in this case are not of the sort that an ordinary person would associate with instruments of chemical warfare. The substances that Bond used bear little resemblance to the deadly toxins that are [the particular target of the Convention]. More to the point, the use of something as a "weapon" typically connotes "[a]n instrument of offensive or defensive combat," WEBSTER'S THIRD NEW INTERNATIONAL DICTIONARY 2589 (2002), or "[a]n instrument of attack or defense in combat, as a gun, missile, or sword," AMERICAN HERITAGE DICTIONARY 2022 (3d ed. 1992). But no speaker in natural parlance would describe Bond's feud-driven act of spreading irritating chemicals on Haynes's door knob and mailbox as "combat." Nor do the other circumstances of Bond's offense—an act of revenge born of romantic jealousy, meant to cause discomfort, that produced nothing more than a minor thumb burn—suggest that a chemical weapon was deployed in Norristown, Pennsylvania. Potassium dichromate and 10-chloro-10H-phenoxarsine might be chemical weapons if used, say, to poison a city's water supply. But Bond's crime is worlds apart from such hypotheticals, and covering it would give the statute a reach exceeding the ordinary meaning of the words Congress wrote.

In settling on a fair reading of a statute, it is not unusual to consider the ordinary meaning of a defined term, particularly when there is dissonance between that ordinary meaning and the reach of the definition. * * * The ordinary meaning of "chemical weapon" plays a similar limiting role here.

The Government would have us brush aside the ordinary meaning and adopt a reading of section 229 that would sweep in everything from the detergent under the kitchen sink to the stain remover in the laundry room. Yet no one would ordinarily describe those substances as "chemical weapons." The Government responds that because Bond used "specialized, highly toxic" (though legal) chemicals, "this case presents no occasion to address whether Congress intended [section 229] to apply to common household substances." That the statute would apply so broadly, however, is the inescapable conclusion of the Government's position: Any parent would be guilty of a serious federal offense—possession of a chemical weapon—when, exasperated by the children's repeated failure to clean the goldfish tank, he considers poisoning the fish with a few drops of vinegar. We are reluctant to ignore the ordinary meaning of "chemical weapon" when doing so would transform a statute passed to implement the international Convention on Chemical Weapons into one that also makes it a federal offense to poison goldfish. That would not be a "realistic assessment[ ] of congressional intent." Post, at 6 (SCALIA, J., concurring in judgment).

In light of all of this, it is fully appropriate to apply the background assumption that Congress normally preserves "the constitutional balance between the National Government and the States." That assumption is grounded in the very structure of the Constitution. * * * [M]aintaining that constitutional balance is not merely an end unto itself. Rather, "[b]y denying any one government complete jurisdiction over all the concerns of public life, federalism protects the liberty of the individual from arbitrary power."

The Government's reading of section 229 would " 'alter sensitive federal-state relationships,' " convert an astonishing amount of "traditionally local criminal conduct" into "a matter for federal enforcement," and "involve a substantial extension of federal police resources." *Bass*, 404 U.S., at 349–350. It would transform the statute from one whose core concerns are acts of war, assassination, and terrorism into a massive federal anti-poisoning regime that reaches the simplest of assaults. As the Government reads section 229, "hardly" a poisoning "in the land would fall outside the federal statute's domain." *Jones*, 529 U.S., at 857. Of course Bond's conduct is serious and unacceptable—and against the laws of Pennsylvania. But the background principle that Congress does not normally intrude upon the police power of the States is critically important. In light of that principle, we are reluctant to conclude that Congress meant to punish Bond's crime with a federal prosecution for a chemical weapons attack.

> How significant is this concern about altering federal-state relationships?

In fact, with the exception of this unusual case, the Federal Government itself has not looked to section 229 to reach purely local crimes. The Government has identified only a handful of prosecutions that have been brought under this section. Most of those involved either terrorist plots or the possession of extremely dangerous substances with the potential to cause severe harm to many people. * * * The Federal Government undoubtedly has a substantial interest in enforcing criminal laws against assassination, terrorism, and acts with the potential to cause mass suffering. Those crimes have not traditionally been left predominantly to the States, and nothing we have said here will disrupt the Government's authority to prosecute such offenses.

It is also clear that the laws of the Commonwealth of Pennsylvania (and every other State) are sufficient to prosecute Bond. Pennsylvania has several statutes that would likely cover her assault. * * *

The Government objects that Pennsylvania authorities charged Bond with only a minor offense based on her "harassing telephone calls and letters," and declined to prosecute her for assault. But we have traditionally viewed the exercise of state officials' prosecutorial discretion as a valuable feature of our constitutional system. And nothing in the Convention shows a clear intent to abrogate that feature. Prosecutorial discretion involves carefully weighing the benefits of a prosecution against the evidence needed to convict, the resources of the public fisc, and the public policy of the State. Here, in its zeal to prosecute Bond, the Federal Government has "displaced" the "public policy of the Commonwealth of Pennsylvania, enacted in its capacity as sovereign," that Bond does not belong in prison for a chemical weapons offense. * * *

As we have explained, "Congress has traditionally been reluctant to define as a federal crime conduct readily denounced as criminal by the States." *Bass*, 404 U.S., at 349. There is no clear indication of a contrary approach here. Section 229 implements the Convention, but Bond's crime could hardly be more unlike the uses of mustard gas on the Western Front or nerve agents in the Iran-Iraq war that form the core concerns of that treaty. There are no life-sized paintings of Bond's rival washing her thumb. And there are no apparent interests of the United States Congress or the community of nations in seeing Bond end up in federal prison, rather than dealt with (like virtually all other criminals in Pennsylvania) by the State. * * *

This case is unusual, and our analysis is appropriately limited. Our disagreement with our colleagues reduces to whether section 229 is "utterly clear." Post, at 5 (SCALIA, J., concurring in judgment). We think it is not, given that the definition of "chemical weapon" in a particular case can reach beyond any normal notion of such a weapon, that the context from which the statute arose demonstrates a much more limited prohibition was intended, and that the most sweeping reading of the statute would fundamentally upset the Constitution's balance between national and local power. This exceptional convergence of factors gives us serious reason to doubt the Government's expansive reading of section 229, and calls for us to interpret the statute more narrowly.

In sum, the global need to prevent chemical warfare does not require the Federal Government to reach into the kitchen cupboard, or to treat a local assault with a chemical irritant as the deployment of a chemical weapon. There is no reason to suppose that Congress—in implementing the Convention on Chemical Weapons—thought otherwise. * * *

JUSTICE SCALIA, with whom JUSTICE THOMAS joins, and with whom JUSTICE ALITO joins as to Part I, concurring in the judgment.

Somewhere in Norristown, Pennsylvania, a husband's paramour suffered a minor thumb burn at the hands of a betrayed wife. The United States Congress—"everywhere extending the sphere of its activity, and drawing all power into its impetuous vortex," THE FEDERALIST No. 48—has made a federal case out of it. What are we to do?

It is the responsibility of "the legislature, not the Court, . . . to define a crime, and ordain its punishment." *United States v. Wiltberger*, 5 Wheat. 76, 95 (1820) (Marshall, C. J., for the Court). And it is "emphatically the province and duty of the judicial department to say what the law [including the Constitution] is." *Marbury v. Madison*, 1 Cranch 137, 177 (1803) (same). Today, the Court shirks its job and performs Congress's. As sweeping and unsettling as the Chemical Weapons Convention Implementation Act of 1998 may be, it is clear beyond doubt that it covers what Bond did; and we have no authority to amend it. So we are forced to decide—there is no way around it—whether the Act's application to what Bond did was constitutional. * * *

I. The Statutory Question

A. Unavoidable Meaning of the Text

The meaning of the Act is plain. No person may knowingly "develop, produce, otherwise acquire, transfer directly or indirectly, receive, stockpile, retain, own, possess, or use, or threaten to use, any chemical weapon." 18 U.S.C. § 229(a)(1). A "chemical weapon" is "[a] toxic chemical and its precursors, except where intended for a purpose not prohibited under this chapter as long as the type and quantity is consistent with such a purpose." § 229F(1)(A). A "toxic chemical" is "any chemical which through its chemical action on life processes can cause death, temporary incapacitation or permanent harm to humans or animals. The term includes all such chemicals, regardless of their origin or of their method of production, and regardless of whether they are produced in facilities, in munitions or elsewhere." § 229F(8)(A). A "purpose not prohibited" is "[a]ny peaceful purpose related to an industrial, agricultural, research, medical, or pharmaceutical activity or other activity." § 229F(7)(A).

Applying those provisions to this case is hardly complicated. Bond possessed and used "chemical[s] which through [their] chemical action on life processes can cause death, temporary incapacitation or permanent harm." Thus, she possessed "toxic chemicals." And, because they were not possessed or used only for a "purpose not prohibited," § 229F(1)(A), they were "chemical weapons." Ergo, Bond violated the Act. End of statutory analysis, I would have thought.

> **?** Is this an accurate characterization of the majority opinion? Why or why not?

The Court does not think the interpretive exercise so simple. But that is only because its result-driven antitextualism befogs what is evident.

B. The Court's Interpretation

The Court's account of the clear-statement rule reads like a really good lawyer's brief for the wrong side, relying on cases that are so close to being on point that someone eager to reach the favored outcome might swallow them. The relevance to this case of *United States v. Bass*, 404 U.S. 336 (1971), and *Jones v. United States*, 529 U.S. 848 (2000), is, in truth, entirely made up. In *Bass*, we had to decide whether a statute forbidding " 'receiv[ing], possess[ing], or transport[ing] in commerce or affecting commerce . . . any firearm' " prohibited possessing a gun that lacked any connection to interstate commerce. 404 U.S., at 337–339. Though the Court relied in part on a federalism-inspired interpretive presumption, it did so only after it had found, in Part I of the opinion, applying traditional interpretive tools, that the text in question was ambiguous, *id.*, at 339–347. Adopting in Part II the narrower of the two possible readings, we said that *"unless Congress conveys its purpose clearly*, it will not be deemed to have significantly changed the federal-state balance." *Id.*, at 349 (emphasis added). Had Congress "convey[ed] its purpose clearly" by enacting a clear and even sweeping statute, the presumption would not have applied.

Jones is also irrelevant. To determine whether an owner-occupied private residence counted as a " 'property used in interstate or foreign commerce or in any activity affecting interstate or foreign commerce' " under the federal arson statute, 529 U.S., at 850–851, our opinion examined not the federal-jurisdiction-expanding consequences of answering yes but rather the ordinary meaning of the words—and answered no, *id.*, at 855–857. Then, in a separate part of the opinion, we observed that our reading was consistent with the principle that we should adopt a construction that avoids "grave and doubtful constitutional questions," *id.*, at 857, and, quoting *Bass*, the principle that Congress must convey its purpose clearly before its laws will be " 'deemed to have significantly changed the federal-state balance,' " 529 U.S., at 858. To say that the best reading of the text conformed to those principles is not to say that those principles can render clear text ambiguous.

The latter is what the Court says today. Inverting *Bass* and *Jones*, it starts with the federalism-related consequences of the statute's meaning and reasons backwards, holding that, if the statute has what the Court considers a disruptive effect on the "federal-state balance" of criminal jurisdiction that effect causes the text, even if clear on its face, to be ambiguous. Just ponder what the Court says: "[The Act's] ambiguity *derives* from the improbably broad reach of the key statutory definition, . . . the deeply serious consequences of adopting such a boundless reading; and the lack of any apparent need to do so. . . ." *Ibid.* (emphasis added). Imagine what future courts can do with that judge-empowering principle: Whatever has improbably broad, deeply serious, and apparently unnecessary consequences * * * *is ambiguous*!

 Is this an accurate characterization? Why or why not?

The same skillful use of oh-so-close-to-relevant cases characterizes the Court's *pro forma* attempt to find ambiguity in the text itself, specifically, in the term "[c]hemical weapon." The ordinary meaning of weapon, the Court says, is an instrument of combat, and "no speaker in natural parlance would describe Bond's feud-driven act of spreading irritating chemicals on Haynes's door knob and mailbox as 'combat.' " Undoubtedly so, but undoubtedly beside the point, since the Act supplies its own definition of "chemical weapon," which unquestionably does bring Bond's action within the statutory prohibition. The Court retorts that "it is not unusual to consider the ordinary meaning of a defined term, particularly when there is dissonance between that ordinary meaning and the reach of the definition." So close to true! What is "not unusual" is using the ordinary meaning of the term being defined for the purpose of resolving an ambiguity in the definition. When, for example, "draft," a word of many meanings, is one of the words used in a definition of "breeze," we know it has nothing to do with military conscription or beer. * * *

In this case, by contrast, the ordinary meaning of the term being defined is irrelevant, because the statute's own definition—however expansive—is utterly clear: any "chemical which through its chemical action on life processes can cause death, temporary incapacitation or permanent harm to humans or animals," § 229F(8)(A), unless the chemical is possessed or used for a "peaceful purpose," § 229F(1)(A), (7)(A). The statute parses itself. There is no opinion of ours, and none written by any court or put forward by any commentator since Aristotle, which says, or even suggests, that "dissonance" between ordinary meaning and the unambiguous words of a definition is to be resolved in favor of ordinary meaning. If that were the case, there would hardly be any use in providing a definition. No, the true rule is entirely clear: "When a statute includes an explicit definition, we must follow that definition, *even if it varies from that term's ordinary meaning.*" *Stenberg v. Carhart*, 530 U.S. 914, 942 (2000) (emphasis added). Once again, contemplate the judge-empowering consequences of the new interpretive rule the Court today announces: When there is "dissonance" between the statutory definition and the ordinary meaning of the defined word, the latter may prevail.

But even text clear on its face, the Court suggests, must be read against the backdrop of established interpretive presumptions. Thus, we presume "that a criminal statute derived from the common law carries with it the requirement of a culpable mental state—even if no such limitation appears in the text." And we presume that "federal statutes do not apply outside the United States." Both of those are, indeed, established interpretive presumptions that are (1) based upon realistic assessments of congressional intent, and (2) well known to Congress—thus furthering rather than subverting genuine legislative intent. To apply these presumptions, then, is not to rewrite clear text; it is to interpret words fairly, in light of their statutory context. But there is nothing either (1) realistic or (2) well known about the presumption the Court shoves down the throat of a resisting statute today. Who in the world would have thought that a definition is inoperative if it contradicts ordinary meaning? When this statute was enacted, there was not yet a "*Bond* presumption" to that effect—though presumably Congress will have to take account of the *Bond* presumption in the future, perhaps by adding at the end of all its definitions that depart from ordinary connotation "and we really mean it."

* * *

II. The Constitutional Question

Since the Act is clear, the real question this case presents is whether the Act is constitutional as applied to petitioner. [Justice Scalia then went on to answer this question "no."]

* * * We have here [in the Court's disposition] a supposedly "narrow" opinion which, in order to be "narrow," sets forth interpretive principles never before imagined that will bedevil our jurisprudence (and proliferate litigation) for years to come. The immediate product of these interpretive novelties is a statute that should be the envy of every lawmaker bent on trapping the unwary with vague and uncertain criminal prohibitions. All this to * * * enable[ ] the fundamental constitutional principle of limited federal powers to be set aside by the President and Senate's exercise of the treaty power. We should not have shirked our duty and distorted the law to preserve that [misunderstanding of the treaty power]; we should have welcomed and eagerly grasped the opportunity—nay, the obligation—to consider and repudiate it.

[The concurring opinions of JUSTICE THOMAS and JUSTICE ALITO are omitted.]

NOTES & QUESTIONS

1. Is the statutory text at issue in *Bond* ambiguous? If not, why not? If so, what is the ambiguity and what is its cause?

2. Are there similarities between the statutory text in *Bond* and the text of the National Labor Relations Act in the *NLRB v. Catholic Bishop* case you read in the previous chapter? Can you see any similarities between the approach the majority used in the two cases? Is the Court actually interpreting the text of the statute in either case?

3. Could the Court have used the Rule of Lenity here? If not, why not?

4. What should be the judicial role in this case? As you think about that question, keep in mind the role that substantive canons play in statutory interpretation: they involve policy choices, not linguistic decoding. They might be policy choices that the legislature implicitly made— that's the point Chief Justice Roberts makes when he says, for example, that "some things 'go without saying'" and "we are reluctant to conclude that Congress meant to punish Bond's crime with a federal prosecution for a chemical weapons attack"—but when a case using a substantive canon does arise, it is the Court that is deciding to further that policy.

5. We know what Justice Scalia's interpretive theory in this case was, but what interpretive theory do you think best describes Chief Justice Roberts' approach?

6. What advice would you now give Congress when drafting legislation to implement a treaty?

B. Presumption Against Preemption of State Law

Under Article VI, clause 2 of the U.S. Constitution, the "Supremacy Clause," federal law is legally superior to conflicting provisions of all state constitutions and laws. Thus, federal laws preempt (in other words take precedence over) any conflicting state laws.

Another federalism-based canon, but a more long-standing and less restrictive one, is the presumption that a federal statute does not preempt state law. As articulated in 1947 in *Rice v. Santa Fe Elevator Corporation*, 331 U.S. 218, 230 (1947), "the historic police powers of the States were not to be superseded by [a congressional statute in a field of law that the States have traditionally occupied] unless that was the clear and manifest purpose of Congress." Unlike the New Federalism canons, which in their typical formulation can only be overcome by a clear statement in the text of the statute itself, the presumption against federal preemption can be overcome by evidence outside the statute of congressional purpose or intent to preempt state law, including evidence of an actual conflict between federal and state law, *see, e.g., Geier v. American Honda Motor Co., Inc.*, 529 U.S. 861 (2000), or evidence that Congress intended its enactment to "occupy the field," *see, e.g., Fid. Fed. Sav. & Loan Ass'n v. de la Cuesta*, 458 U.S. 141 (1982).

C. Narrowly Construe Statutes in Derogation of the Common Law

An even more long-standing canon, reflecting the functional supremacy of the common law in an earlier era, as discussed previously, is the Derogation Canon: Statutes in derogation of the common law are to be narrowly construed. In other words, the legislature's output should be interpreted so as to change the underlying common law as little as possible. For instance, in *Norfolk Southern Railway Co. v. Sorrell*, 549 U.S. 158 (2007), a negligence action brought under the Federal Employers' Liability Act (FELA), the Supreme Court held that common-law principles of causation survived FELA's enactment because the text of the act did not expressly reject those common-law principles. Notwithstanding *Sorrell*, the Derogation Canon has become disfavored. So many modern statutes are now built upon pre-existing statutory law (rather than just the common law) that the Derogation Canon plays a minimal role these days. The fact that Congress adopted FELA in 1908 and created a cause of action that incorporated other common-law elements was relevant in the *Sorrell* Court's decision to draw on the Derogation Canon.

D. Broadly Construe "Remedial Measures"

A final substantive canon, which sometimes runs counter to the Derogation Canon, is the Remedial Canon: a remedial statute should be construed broadly to effectuate its public-regarding purposes. For its proper application, this canon obviously depends on classifying a particular statute as "remedial," a task fraught with subjectivity. This canon also does not by its own terms identify what amounts to a broad construction. But in determining what makes for a remedial statute, it may be worth recalling our consideration in Chapter 4 of the "economic" analysis potentially at work in the consideration of the differences between statutes that result from narrow interest group bargaining in a legislature, on the one hand, and statutes that reflect a more thorough republican deliberation about what will best promote the public interest, an analysis that resembles a relatively simplistically form of Public Choice Theory.

> Recall the two-by-two categorization of the costs and benefits of legislative activity, attributed to political scientist James Q. Wilson, as in Chart 1 on p. 71.

Because of its indeterminacy and potential over-inclusivity, today the Remedial Canon is widely derided. But its underlying principle has occasionally featured in important cases. For instance, in *Griggs v. Duke Power Co.,* 401 U.S. 424 (1971), the Supreme Court concluded that an employer had violated Title VII of the Civil Rights Act by relying on an ability test that operated to disadvantage minority workers, even though there was no evidence that the employer had intended to discriminate. The statutory text at issue included a provision that made it unlawful for an employer to "adversely affect" an individual's employment opportunities "because of such individual's race," which on a broad reading could prohibit actions with a disparate impact even without discriminatory intent. But a separate provision nonetheless allowed an employer to use a "professionally developed ability test" as long as the test was "not designed, intended or used to discriminate because of race." A narrow reading of this provision would suggest that an employer must have had a discriminatory purpose or intent in order to violate the act.

Focusing on what it saw as the underlying remedial purpose of Title VII to "remove barriers that have operated in the past to favor [white employees]," the Court construed the act broadly to also cover employment practices "neutral on their face, and even neutral in terms of intent, . . . if they operate to 'freeze' the status quo of prior discriminatory practices." *Id.* at 430. This was a significant departure from the plain meaning of the statute, in service of what the Court saw as its underlying remedial purpose.

Test Your Understanding

To assess your understanding of the material in this chapter, click here to take a quiz.

23

Some Reflections on the Value and Proper Use of Canons

Key Concepts

- Karl Llewellyn's "Thrust and Parry"
- Interpretive directions in statutes
- The neutrality of canons

Chapter Summary

The appropriate use of canons is hotly debated, and their ostensible neutrality has been questioned. As renowned 20th century legal scholar Karl Llewellyn pointed out, for every canon employed, a counter canon can be asserted. As a result, some argue that the interpreter's role is essentially to choose which canon to employ, cherry-picking canons to reach a preferred policy outcome, rather than finding the meaning inherent in the text.

Canons are not without their defenders, however, and they have seen a resurgence in recent years. Defenders argue that by employing canons, the interpreter can fix the textual meaning without relying on more subjective tools like legislative history, which can become an exercise of cherry-picking in itself.

Canons have an obvious appeal because of both their simplicity and their seeming independence from any particular interpretive issue. But as we have seen in some of the preceding examples. they are not always as clear or helpful as they may first appear. Three main concerns have arisen about the use of canons: (1) they require a fair amount of judgment concerning when to deploy a given one; (2) if structured as binding requirements, they may encroach upon the judicial function; and (3) they may not be as neutral as they claim or appear to be, at least in their application.

A. When to Deploy What Canon? Karl Llewellyn's "Thrust and Parry"

FYI Karl Llewellyn was a law professor at Columbia University and the University of Chicago in the mid-twentieth century. He was a primary drafter of the Uniform Commercial Code, and many generations of law students also knew him for his primer on law "The Bramble Bush."

As suggested, for instance, by the tension noted in the previous chapter between the Remedial Canon and the Derogation Canon, an interpreter often faces a choice between two or more competing canons. Renowned Legal Realist Karl Llewellyn illustrated this point straightforwardly in an appendix to a brief 1950 law review article, describing what has become known as Llewellyn's "Thrust and Parry" of dueling canons. The appendix, which juxtaposes more than two dozen pairs of competing canons, follows below; for the full article, see Karl Llewellyn, *Remarks on the Theory of Appellate Decision and the Rules or Canons About How Statutes Are to be Construed*, 3 VAND. L. REV. 395, 401–06 (1950).

To some Legal Realists like Llewellyn, the point of this juxtaposition of competing canons was to show that because judges and other interpreters might simply pick whichever canon served their preconceived notion of how to interpret the text, canons therefore might not actually provide a neutral basis for interpretation. But many Legal Process thinkers have countered that canons can still be matched to circumstance, and that at least in many instances, the choice between two competing canons may come down to a question of fit, with some amount of objective rationality supporting the choice of which canon best responds to a given interpretive problem. Furthermore, it is often the case that several canons can be brought to bear collectively on an interpretive problem, mutually reinforcing each other. Nonetheless, Llewellyn's argument introduces a strong note of caution about the use of interpretive canons.

DIY
Dueling Canons

Before reading Llewellyn's appendix below, take a few minutes to think about the canons that you have already met. Which are most compelling to you, and why? Think back to the Derogation Canon and the Remedial Canon. Do they conflict? If so, in what sense? Is the conflict inherent in the canons as they are abstractly articulated as rules? Or would any conflict only occur in the application of the rules to particular interpretive problems? In addition to the Remedial Canon and the Derogation Canon, can you identify any other pairs of potentially conflicting or competing canons? And do you think a judge's judicial philosophy is more legitimate if the judge uses particular canons consistently, rather than using "opposite" canons in various cases? Or should a judge be free to pick the "best" canon on a case-by-case basis?

Llewellyn's "Thrust and Parry" (1950)

1950] *REMARKS ON THEORY OF APPELLATE DECISION*   401

* * *

III

When it comes to presenting a proposed construction in court, there is an accepted conventional vocabulary. As in argument over points of case-law, the accepted convention still, unhappily requires discussion as if only one single correct meaning could exist. Hence there are two opposing canons on almost every point. An arranged selection is appended. Every lawyer must be familiar with them all: they are still needed tools of argument. At least as early as Fortescue the general picture was clear, on this, to any eye which would see.

Plainly, to make any canon take hold in a particular instance, the construction contended for must be sold, essentially, by means other than the use of the canon: The good sense of the situation and a *simple* construction of the available language to achieve that sense, *by tenable means, out of the statutory language.*

CANONS OF CONSTRUCTION

Statutory interpretation still speaks a diplomatic tongue. Here is some of the technical framework for maneuver.

THRUST	BUT	PARRY
1. A statute cannot go beyond its text.[3]		1. To effect its purpose a statute may be implemented beyond its text.[4]
2. Statutes in derogation of the common law will not be extended by construction.[5]		2. Such acts will be liberally construed if their nature is remedial.[6]
3. Statutes are to be read in the light of the common law and a statute affirming a common law rule is to be construed in accordance with the common law.[7]		3. The common law gives way to a statute which is in consistent with it and when a statute is designed as a revision of a whole body of law applicable to a given subject it supersedes the common law.[8]

3. First National Bank v. DeBerriz, 87 W. Va. 477, 105 S.E. 900 (1921); SUTHERLAND, STATUTORY CONSTRUCTION § 388 (2d ed. 1904); 59 C.J., *Statutes*, § 575 (1932).

4. Dooley v. Penn. R.R., 250 Fed. 142 (D. Minn. 1918); 59 C.J., *Statutes* § 575 (1932).

5. Devers v. City of Scranton, 308 Pa. 13, 161 Atl. 540 (1932); BLACK, CONSTRUCTION AND INTERPRETATION OF LAWS § 113 (2d ed. 1911); SUTHERLAND, STATUTORY CONSTRUCTION § 573 (2d ed. 1904); 25 R.C.L., *Statutes* § 281 (1919).

6. Becker v. Brown, 65 Neb. 264, 91 N.W. 178 (1902); BLACK, CONSTRUCTION AND INTERPRETATION OF LAWS § 113 (2d ed. 1911); SUTHERLAND, STATUTORY CONSTRUCTION §§ 573-75 (2d ed. 1904); 59 C.J., *Statutes* § 657 (1932).

7. Bandfield v. Bandfield, 117 Mich. 80, 75 N.W. 287 (1898); 25 R.C.L., *Statutes* § 280 (1919).

8. Hamilton v. Rathbone, 175 U.S. 414, 20 Sup. Ct. 155, 44 L. Ed. 219 (1899); State v. Lewis, 142 N.C. 626, 55 S.E. 600 (1906); 25 R.C.L., *Statutes* §§ 280, 289 (1919).

VANDERBILT LAW REVIEW [VOL. 3

4. Where a foreign statute which has received construction has been adopted, previous construction is adopted too.[9]

4. It may be rejected where there is conflict with the obvious meaning of the statute or where the foreign decisions are unsatisfactory in reasoning or where the foreign interpretation is not in harmony with the spirit or policy of the laws of the adopting state.[10]

5. Where various states have already adopted the statute, the parent state is followed.[11]

5. Where interpretations of other states are inharmonious, there is no such restraint.[12]

6. Statutes *in pari materia* must be construed together.[13]

6. A statute is not *in pari materia* if its scope and aim are distinct or where a legislative design to depart from the general purpose or policy of previous enactments may be apparent.[14]

7. A statute imposing a new penalty or forfeiture, or a new liability or disability, or creating a new right of action will not be construed as having a retroactive effect.[15]

7. Remedial statutes are to be liberally construed and if a retroactive interpretation will promote the ends of justice, they should receive such construction.[16]

8. Where design has been distinctly stated no place is left for construction.[17]

8. Courts have the power to inquire into real—as distinct from ostensible—purpose.[18]

---

9. Freese v. Tripp, 70 Ill. 496 (1873); Black, Construction and Interpretation of Laws § 176 (2d ed. 1911); 59 C.J., *Statutes*, §§ 614, 627 (1932); 25 R.C.L., *Statutes* § 294 (1919).

10. Bowers v. Smith, 111 Mo. 45, 20 S.W. 101 (1892); Black, Construction and Interpretation of Laws § 176 (2d ed. 1911); Sutherland, Statutory Construction § 404 (2d ed. 1904); 59 C.J., *Statutes* § 628 (1932).

11. Burnside v. Wand, 170 Mo. 531, 71 S.W. 337 (1902).

12. State v. Campbell, 73 Kan. 688, 85 Pac. 784 (1906).

13. Milner v. Gibson, 249 Ky. 594, 61 S.W.2d 273 (1933); Black, Construction and Interpretation of Laws § 104 (2d ed. 1911); Sutherland, Statutory Construction §§ 443-48 (2d ed. 1904); 25 R.C.L., *Statutes* § 285 (1919).

14. Wheelock v. Myers, 64 Kan. 47, 67 Pac. 632 (1902); Black, Construction and Interpretation of Laws § 104 (2d ed. 1911); Sutherland, Statutory Construction § 449 (2d ed. 1904); 59 C.J., *Statutes* § 620 (1932).

15. Keeley v. Great Northern Ry., 139 Wis. 448, 121 N.W. 167 (1909); Black, Construction and Interpretation of Laws § 119 (2d ed. 1911).

16. Falls v. Key, 278 S.W. 893 (Tex. Civ. App. 1925); Black, Construction and Interpretation of Laws § 120 (2d ed. 1911).

17. Federoff v. Birks Bros., 75 Cal. App. 345, 242 Pac. 885 (1925); Sutherland, Statutory Construction § 358 (2d ed. 1904); 59 C.J., *Statutes* § 570 (1932).

18. Coulter v. Pool, 187 Cal. 181, 201 Pac. 120 (1921); 59 C.J., *Statutes* § 570 (1932).

9. Definitions and rules of construction contained in an interpretation clause are part of the law and binding.[19]

9. Definitions and rules of construction in a statute will not be extended beyond their necessary import nor allowed to defeat intention otherwise manifested.[20]

10. A statutory provision requiring liberal construction does not mean disregard of unequivocal requirements of the statute.[21]

10. Where a rule of construction is provided within the statute itself the rule should be applied.[22]

11. Titles do not control meaning; preambles do not expand scope; section headings do not change language.[23]

11. The title may be consulted as a guide when there is doubt or obscurity in the body; preambles may be consulted to determine rationale, and thus the true construction of terms; section headings may be looked upon as part of the statute itself.[24]

12. If language is plain and unambiguous it must be given effect.[25]

12. Not when literal interpretation would lead to absurd or mischievous consequences or thwart manifest purpose.[26]

13. Words and phrases which have received judicial construction before enactment are to be understood according to that construction.[27]

13. Not if the statute clearly requires them to have a different meaning.[28]

---

19. Smith v. State, 28 Ind. 321 (1867); BLACK, CONSTRUCTION AND INTERPRETATION OF LAWS § 89 (2d ed. 1911); 59 C.J., *Statutes* § 567 (1932).

20. *In re* Bissell, 245 App. Div. 395, 282 N.Y. Supp. 983 (4th Dep't 1935); BLACK, CONSTRUCTION AND INTERPRETATION OF LAWS § 89 (2d ed. 1911); 59 C.J., *Statutes* § 566 (1932).

21. Los Angeles County v. Payne, 82 Cal. App. 210, 255 Pac. 281 (1927); SUTHERLAND, STATUTORY CONSTRUCTION § 360 (2d ed. 1904); 59 C.J., *Statutes* § 567 (1932).

22. State *ex rel.* Triay v. Burr, 79 Fla. 290, 84 So. 61 (1920); SUTHERLAND, STATUTORY CONSTRUCTION § 360 (2d ed. 1904); 59 C.J., *Statutes* § 567 (1932).

23. Westbrook v. McDonald, 184 Ark. 740, 44 S.W. 2d 331 (1931); Huntworth v. Tanner, 87 Wash. 670, 152 Pac. 523 (1915); BLACK, CONSTRUCTION AND INTERPRETATION OF LAWS §§ 83-85 (2d ed. 1911); SUTHERLAND, STATUTORY CONSTRUCTION §§ 339-42 (2d ed. 1904); 59 C.J., *Statutes* § 599 (1932); 25 R.C.L., *Statutes* §§ 266-267 (1919).

24. Brown v. Robinson, 275 Mass. 55, 175 N.E. 269 (1931); Gulley v. Jackson, 165 Miss. 103, 145 So. 905 (1933); BLACK, CONSTRUCTION AND INTERPRETATION OF LAWS §§ 83-85 (2d ed. 1911); SUTHERLAND, STATUTORY CONSTRUCTION §§ 339-42 (2d ed. 1904); 59 C.J., *Statutes* §§ 598-99 (1932); 25 R.C.L., *Statutes* §§ 266, 267 (1919).

25. Newhall v. Sanger, 92 U.S. 761, 23 L. Ed. 769 (1875); BLACK, CONSTRUCTION AND INTERPRETATION OF LAWS § 51 (2d ed. 1911); 59 C.J., *Statutes* § 569 (1932); 25 R.C.L., *Statutes* §§ 213, 225 (1919).

26. Clark v. Murray, 141 Kan. 533, 41 P.2d 1042 (1935); SUTHERLAND, STATUTORY CONSTRUCTION § 363 (2d ed. 1904); 59 C.J., *Statutes* § 573 (1932); 25 R.C.L., *Statutes* §§ 214, 257 (1919).

27. Scholze v. Sholze, 2 Tenn. App. 80 (M.S. 1925); BLACK, CONSTRUCTION AND INTERPRETATION OF LAWS § 65 (2d ed. 1911); SUTHERLAND, STATUTORY CONSTRUCTION § 363 (2d ed. 1904).

28. Dixon v. Robbins, 246 N.Y. 169, 158 N.E. 63 (1927); BLACK, CONSTRUCTION AND INTERPRETATION OF LAWS § 65 (2d ed. 1911); SUTHERLAND, STATUTORY CONSTRUCTION § 363 (2d ed. 1904).

14. After enactment, judicial decision upon interpretation of particular terms and phrases controls.[29]

14. Practical construction by executive officers is strong evidence of true meaning.[30]

15. Words are to be taken in their ordinary meaning unless they are technical terms or words of art.[31]

15. Popular words may bear a technical meaning and technical words may have a popular signification and they should be so construed as to agree with evident intention or to make the statute operative.[32]

16. Every word and clause must be given effect.[33]

16. If inadvertantly inserted or if repugnant to the rest of the statute, they may be rejected as surplusage.[34]

17. The same language used repeatedly in the same connection is presumed to bear the same meaning throughout the statute.[35]

17. This presumption will be disregarded where it is necessary to assign different meanings to make the statute consistent.[36]

18. Words are to be interpreted according to the proper grammatical effect of their arrangement within the statute.[37]

18. Rules of grammar will be disregarded where strict adherence would defeat purpose.[38]

19. Exceptions not made cannot be read.[39]

19. The letter is only the "bark." Whatever is within the reason of the law is within the law itself.[40]

---

29. Eau Claire National Bank v. Benson, 106 Wis. 624, 82 N.W. 604 (1900); BLACK, CONSTRUCTION AND INTERPRETATION OF LAWS § 93 (2d ed. 1911).
30. State *ex rel.* Bashford v. Frear, 138 Wis. 536, 120 N.W. 216 (1909); BLACK, CONSTRUCTION AND INTERPRETATION OF LAWS § 94 (2d ed. 1911); 25 R.C.L., *Statutes* § 274 (1919).
31. Hawley Coal Co. v. Bruce, 252 Ky. 455, 67 S.W.2d 703 (1934); BLACK, CONSTRUCTION AND INTERPRETATION OF LAWS § 63 (2d ed. 1911); SUTHERLAND, STATUTORY CONSTRUCTION, §§ 390, 393 (2d ed. 1904); 59 C.J., *Statutes*, §§ 577, 578 (1932).
32. Robinson v. Varnell, 16 Tex. 382 (1856); BLACK, CONSTRUCTION AND INTERPRETATION OF LAWS § 63 (2d ed. 1911); SUTHERLAND, STATUTORY CONSTRUCTION § 395 (2d ed. 1904); 59 C.J., *Statutes* §§ 577, 578 (1932).
33. *In re* Terry's Estate, 218 N.Y. 218, 112 N.E. 931 (1916); BLACK, CONSTRUCTION AND INTERPRETATION OF LAWS § 60 (2d ed. 1911); SUTHERLAND, STATUTORY CONSTRUCTION § 380 (2d ed. 1904).
34. United States v. York, 131 Fed. 323 (C.C.S.D.N.Y. 1904); BLACK, CONSTRUCTION AND INTERPRETATION OF LAWS § 60 (2d ed. 1911); SUTHERLAND, STATUTORY CONSTRUCTION §§ 384 (2d ed. 1904).
35. Spring Canyon Coal Co. v. Industrial Comm'n, 74 Utah 103, 277 Pac. 206 (1929); BLACK, CONSTRUCTION AND INTERPRETATION OF LAWS § 53 (2d ed. 1911).
36. State v. Knowles, 90 Md. 646, 45 Atl. 877 (1900); BLACK, CONSTRUCTION AND INTERPRETATION OF LAWS § 53 (2d ed. 1911).
37. Harris v. Commonwealth, 142 Va. 620, 128 S.E. 578 (1925); BLACK, CONSTRUCTION AND INTERPRETATION OF LAWS § 55 (2d ed. 1911); SUTHERLAND, STATUTORY CONSTRUCTION § 408 (2d ed. 1904).
38. Fisher v. Connard, 100 Pa. 63 (1882); BLACK, CONSTRUCTION AND INTERPRETATION OF LAWS § 55 (2d ed. 1911); SUTHERLAND, STATUTORY CONSTRUCTION § 409 (2d ed. 1904).
39. Lima v. Cemetery Ass'n, 42 Ohio St. 128 (1884); 25 R.C.L., *Statutes* § 230 (1919).
40. Flynn v. Prudential Ins. Co., 207 N.Y. 315, 100 N.E. 794 (1913); 59 C.J., *Statutes* § 573 (1932).

1950] *REMARKS ON THEORY OF APPELLATE DECISION*   405

20. Expression of one thing excludes another.[41]	20. The language may fairly comprehend many different cases where some only are expressly mentioned by way of example.[42]
21. General terms are to receive a general construction.[43]	21. They may be limited by specific terms with which they are associated or by the scope and purpose of the statute.[44]
22. It is a general rule of construction that where general words follow an enumeration they are to be held as applying only to persons and things of the same general kind or class specifically mentioned (*ejusdem generis*).[45]	22. General words must operate on something. Further, *ejusdem generis* is only an aid in getting the meaning and does not warrant confining the operations of a statute within narrower limits than were intended.[46]
23. Qualifying or limiting words or clauses are to be referred to the next preceding antecedent.[47]	23. Not when evident sense and meaning require a different construction.[48]
24. Punctuation will govern when a statute is open to two constructions.[49]	24. Punctuation marks will not control the plain and evident meaning of language.[50]

---

41. Detroit v. Redford Twp., 253 Mich. 453, 235 N.W. 217 (1931); BLACK, CONSTRUCTION AND INTERPRETATION OF LAWS § 72 (2d ed. 1911); SUTHERLAND, STATUTORY CONSTRUCTION §§ 491-94 (2d ed. 1904).

42. Springer v. Philippine Islands, 277 U.S. 189, 48 Sup. Ct. 480, 72 L. Ed. 845 (1928); BLACK, CONSTRUCTION AND INTERPRETATION OF LAWS § 72 (2d ed. 1911); SUTHERLAND, STATUTORY CONSTRUCTION § 495 (2d ed. 1904).

43. De Witt v. San Francisco, 2 Cal. 289 (1852); BLACK, CONSTRUCTION AND INTERPRETATION OF LAWS § 68 (2d ed. 1911); 59 C.J., *Statutes* § 580 (1932).

44. People *ex rel.* Krause v. Harrison, 191 Ill. 257, 61 N.E. 99 (1901); BLACK, CONSTRUCTION AND INTERPRETATION OF LAWS § 69 (1911); SUTHERLAND, STATUTORY CONSTRUCTION § 347 (2d ed. 1904).

45. Hull Hospital v. Wheeler, 216 Iowa 1394, 250 N.W. 637 (1933); BLACK, CONSTRUCTION AND INTERPRETATION OF LAWS § 71 (2d ed. 1911); SUTHERLAND, STATUTORY CONSTRUCTION §§ 422-34 (2d ed. 1904); 59 C.J., *Statutes* § 581 (1932); 25 R.C.L., *Statutes* § 240 (1919).

46. Texas v. United States, 292 U.S. 522, 54 Sup. Ct. 819, 78 L. Ed. 1402 (1934); Grosjean v. American Paint Works, 160 So. 449 (La. App. 1935); BLACK, CONSTRUCTION AND INTERPRETATION OF LAWS § 71 (2d ed. 1911); SUTHERLAND, STATUTORY CONSTRUCTION, §§ 437-41 (2d ed. 1904); 59 C.J., *Statutes* § 581 (1932); 25 R.C.L., *Statutes* § 240 (1919).

47. Dunn v. Bryan, 77 Utah 604, 299 Pac. 253 (1931); BLACK, CONSTRUCTION AND INTERPRETATION OF LAWS § 73 (2d ed. 1911); SUTHERLAND, STATUTORY CONSTRUCTION §§ 420, 421 (2d ed. 1904); 59 C.J., *Statutes* § 583 (1932).

48. Myer v. Ada County, 50 Idaho 39, 293 Pac. 322 (1930); BLACK, CONSTRUCTION AND INTERPRETATION OF LAWS § 73 (2d ed. 1911); SUTHERLAND, STATUTORY CONSTRUCTION §§ 420, 421 (2d ed. 1904); 59 C.J., *Statutes* § 583 (1932).

49. United States v. Marshall Field & Co., 18 C.C.P.A. 228 (1930); BLACK, CONSTRUCTION AND INTERPRETATION OF LAWS § 88 (2d ed. 1911); SUTHERLAND, STATUTORY CONSTRUCTION § 361 (2d ed. 1904); 59 C.J., *Statutes* § 590 (1932).

50. State v. Baird, 36 Ariz. 531, 288 Pac. 1 (1930); BLACK, CONSTRUCTION AND INTERPRETATION OF LAWS § 87 (2d ed. 1911); SUTHERLAND, STATUTORY CONSTRUCTION § 361 (2d ed. 1904); 59 C.J., *Statutes* § 590 (1932).

VANDERBILT LAW REVIEW [VOL. 3

25. It must be assumed that language has been chosen with due regard to grammatical propriety and is not interchangeable on mere conjecture.[51]

25. "And" and "or" may be read interchangeably whenever the change is necessary to give the statute sense and effect.[52]

26. There is a distinction between words of permission and mandatory words.[53]

26. Words imparting permission may be read as mandatory and words imparting command may be read as permissive when such construction is made necessary by evident intention or by the rights of the public.[54]

27. A proviso qualifies the provision immediately preceding.[55]

27. It may clearly be intended to have a wider scope.[56]

28. When the enacting clause is general, a proviso is construed strictly.[57]

28. Not when it is necessary to extend the proviso to persons or cases which come within its equity.[58]

51. Hines v. Mills, 187 Ark. 465, 60 S.W.2d 181 (1933); BLACK, CONSTRUCTION AND INTERPRETATION OF LAWS § 75 (2d ed. 1911).

52. Fulghum v. Bleakley, 177 S.C. 286, 181 S.E. 30 (1935); SUTHERLAND, STATUTORY CONSTRUCTION § 397 (2d ed. 1904); 25 R.C.L., *Statutes* § 226 (1919).

53. Koch & Dryfus v. Bridges, 45 Miss. 247 (1871); BLACK, CONSTRUCTION AND INTERPRETATION OF LAWS § 150 (2d ed. 1911).

54. Jennings v. Suggs, 180 Ga. 141, 178 S.E. 282 (1935); Ewing v. Union Central Bank, 254 Ky. 623, 72 S.W.2d 4 (1934); BLACK, CONSTRUCTION AND INTERPRETATION OF LAWS § 151 (2d ed. 1911); 59 C.J., *Statutes* § 631 (1932).

55. State *ex rel.* Higgs v. Summers, 118 Neb. 189, 223 N.W. 957 (1929); BLACK, CONSTRUCTION AND INTERPRETATION OF LAWS § 130 (2d ed. 1911); SUTHERLAND, STATUTORY CONSTRUCTION § 352 (2d ed. 1904); 59 C.J., *Statutes* § 640 (1932).

56. Reuter v. San Mateo County, 220 Cal. 314, 30 P.2d 417 (1934); BLACK, CONSTRUCTION AND INTERPRETATION OF LAWS § 130 (2d ed. 1911).

57. Montgomery v. Martin, 294 Pa. 25, 143 Atl. 505 (1928); BLACK, CONSTRUCTION AND INTERPRETATION OF LAWS § 131 (2d ed. 1911); SUTHERLAND, STATUTORY CONSTRUCTION § 322 (2d ed. 1904).

58. Forscht v. Green, 53 Pa. 138 (1866); BLACK, CONSTRUCTION AND INTERPRETATION OF LAWS § 131 (2d ed. 1911).

NOTES & QUESTIONS

1. What do you make of Llewellyn's juxtaposition of dueling canons? Do you think that an interpreter will be able to identify the better choice between two dueling canons in many, or at least some, instances?

2. As you can see, some of Llewellyn's "parries" don't really conflict with the "thrusts." Instead, they *modify* the thrusts. Consider thrust-parry combination number 12: The thrust is, "If language is plain and unambiguous, it must be given effect," while the parry is "Not when literal interpretation would lead to absurd or mischievous consequences or thwart manifest purpose." As we noted in Chapter 14, there is debate these days about the appropriateness of the "parry," the absurdity doctrine or the use of "manifest purpose" to override a statute's text. But even assuming its appropriateness, is there really a "conflict" between the thrust and the parry? Don't the thrust and parry together simply reflect the fact that, yes, judges follow the plain meaning unless it leads to an absurd result? It is of course true that there will be debate about whether a result is "absurd" enough, but is there really any conflict here? *See* Michael Sinclair, *"Only a Sith Thinks Like That": Llewelyn's "Dueling Canons" Eight to Twelve*, 51 N.Y. L. Sch. L. Rev. 1003, 1008–18 (2006–07). Is Llewellyn's point simply to illustrate that judges have discretion, that we should not think of canons as algorithms that will automatically yield a single definitive correct answer to an interpretive question? If so, notice what that means for you as a lawyer: to understand statutory interpretation, you need to understand not only the canons themselves, but also how judges decide when to use which ones. As Llewelyn himself puts it, "to make any canon take hold in a particular instance, the construction contended for must be sold, essentially, by means other than the use of the canon . . . ."

3. Llewellyn's appendix ought to make apparent that the universe of interpretive canons is broader than the subset of canons we have explicitly considered in this book. Although we will not touch on all of Llewellyn's canons, there are still more to come. We turn to some of them (for instance, numbers 4 and 6) in the next chapter.

4. Just as important as Llewellyn's "thrust and parry" is the fact that completely unrelated canons can sometimes point in opposite directions. Thought of through the Llewelyn's fencing metaphor, the problem is

that two different "thrusts" can lead to two different interpretive results. The two canons may not be inherently contradictory, but in the context of a specific interpretive question, one canon favors one interpretation, while the other canon favors another. Look again at the *Yates* case, for example, and see if you can identify the various "thrusts" that conflict with each other in applying the statutory term "tangible object" to fish.

5. For a more contemporary look at examples of two (or more) competing interpretive canons at work in opposing interpretive arguments, see Anita S. Krishnakumar, *Dueling Canons*, 65 DUKE L. J. 909 (2016).

B. Interpretive Directions in Statutes

As noted earlier, an interpreter who might otherwise struggle to choose between competing maxims may sometimes find that context can help identify the most appropriate canon(s). Another way that interpreters might be guided in their choice of which canon(s) to apply is when statutes themselves specify the enacting legislature's interpretive expectations. Perhaps the most common such direction is when a statute says something like "[t]he provisions of this title shall be liberally construed to effectuate its remedial purposes," as Congress provided in enacting the Racketeer Influenced and Corrupt Organizations Act of 1970. *See* Pub. L. No. 91–452, § 904(a), 84 Stat. 941, 947 (1970).

Alternatively, separately codified rules of interpretation may offer guidance or direction. For instance, as a matter of federal law, Congress has provided some minimal guidance in what is known as the Dictionary Act, including that the singular usage includes the plural and that "words importing the masculine gender include the feminine as well." *See* 1 U.S.C. § 1. Many more examples of codified interpretive directions exist as a matter of state law, including states that have codified the Plain Meaning Rule, states that have codified the presumption of consistent usage, and even states that have codified a presumption that the legislature intends its statutes to be "reasonable," to name only a few of various state interpretive directions. Some states also have codified that legislative history (to be discussed in detail in coming chapters) may be used to construe an ambiguous statute.

An important issue related to the enactment into law of interpretive directions or canons is whether these legislative instructions to courts encroach upon the judicial function. That is, do they amount to the legislature telling the judiciary how to do the judiciary's job? Obviously, courts have the last word, and so may with impunity ignore these directions if they feel that the directions constrain the courts' ability to determine the appropriate interpretive methodology. At the same time, these directions do amount to law and plainly establish the legislature's intent concerning some interpretive difficulties. It is hard to imagine these kinds of directions not having at least some impact at the margin on how a court will think about—and articulate its resolution of—a problem of statutory construction.

C. Canons as "Neutral" Tools—or Not

FYI Although the policies embedded in substantive canons are independent of any particular interpretive problem, many of them apply only to a specific area of law and may consistently favor a certain type of party, like the Rule of Lenity, which favors criminal defendants every time. Or the canon to construe income tax deductions strictly, *see INDOPOCO, Inc. v. Comm'n of Internal Revenue*, 503 U.S. 79, 84 (1992), which always favors the government. Another example is the principle that veterans' benefits statutes be construed liberally for their beneficiaries, *see King v. St. Vincent's Hosp.*, 502 U.S. 215, 220 n.9 (1991), which always favors veterans.

One reason courts seem to like interpretive canons is that they are seen as either neutral, in the case of the textual canons, or as expressing widely accepted policy preferences divorced from a particular interpretive problem, in the case of the substantive canons. In theory they thereby may give the interpreter some protection against being accused of interpretation based on personal preference or ideology (about which briefly more below). Meanwhile, canons have experienced something of a resurgence in the past quarter century because of the impact of the New Textualist school of interpretation, which often requires additional sources of interpretative direction other than the extrinsic tools.

But with the resurgence of canons of interpretation also has come increased attention to whether the textual canons in fact are neutral, or just how appropriate the substantive canons' policy preferences are. Justice Scalia often expressed skepticism about the value of the substantive policy canons, precisely because their embodiment of a substantive position made them the equivalent of "dice-loading rules." His dissent in the *Bond* case that you read in the previous chapter is an example of that skepticism. In this respect, he contrasted substantive canons with textual canons, which he viewed as neutral. Later, however, he appeared to become more open to the value of at least a few of the substantive canons, including the Constitutional Avoidance Canon and the Rule of Lenity. *See* SCALIA & GARNER, *supra*, at 249, 299–301.

Others, meanwhile, have challenged the assertion that any of the canons can be deployed neutrally. For instance, one study found that in the latter half of the twentieth century, liberal Supreme Court Justices were more likely to use canons to justify liberal outcomes, and conservative Supreme Court Justices were more likely to use canons to justify conservative outcomes. The same study also found that in close cases, conservative Justices used canons to reach conservative results, while liberal justices argued that legislative history favored reaching liberal results. The researchers concluded that canons are often used for ideological ends, even if subconsciously. *See* James J. Brudney & Corey Ditslear, *Canons of Construction and the Elusive Quest for Neutral Reasoning*, 58 VAND. L. REV. 1 (2005); *see also* James J. Brudney: *Canon Shortfalls and the Virtues of Political Branch Interpretive Assets*, 98 CAL. L. REV. 1199 (2010).

> Do you agree that interpretive canons are often used for ideological ends? How would you design a study to test this claim? Is there a meaningful difference between using canons to serve an ideological end, and using canons for their own sake but thereby producing an ideological bias?

D. *West Virginia University Hospitals v. Casey*: A Transition Case

In the next chapter we will turn our attention to extrinsic interpretive aids. In preparation, here is a transition case, *West Virginia University Hospitals v. Casey*.

DIY
Searching for Interpretive Tools in *Casey*

As you read the *Casey* case below, make a list of how many interpretive tools you can find in use.

West Virginia University Hospitals v. Casey
499 U.S. 83 (1991)

Justice Scalia delivered the opinion of the Court.

> **FYI** The concept of "fee shifting" involves imposing at least some portions of the financial expenses associated with prevailing in a court action on the losing party, requiring the losing party in certain cases to reimburse the prevailing party for its court costs and attorneys' fees.

This case presents the question whether fees for services rendered by experts in civil rights litigation may be shifted to the losing party pursuant to 42 U.S.C. § 1988 [which provides in relevant part: "In any action or proceeding to enforce a provision of sections 1981, 1982, 1983, 1985, and 1986 of this title, title IX of Public Law 92–318, or title VI of the Civil Rights Act of 1964, the court, in its discretion, may allow the prevailing party, other than the United States, a reasonable attorney's fee as part of the costs."]

I

Petitioner West Virginia University Hospitals, Inc. (WVUH), operates a hospital in Morgantown, W. Va., near the Pennsylvania border. The hospital is often used by Medicaid recipients living in southwestern Pennsylvania. In January 1986, Pennsylvania's Department of Public Welfare notified WVUH of new Medicaid reimbursement schedules for services provided to Pennsylvania residents by the Morgantown hospital. In administrative proceedings, WVUH unsuccessfully objected to the new reimbursement rates on both federal statutory and federal constitutional grounds. After exhausting administrative remedies, WVUH filed suit in Federal District Court under 42 U.S.C. § 1983. Named as defendants (respondents here) were Pennsylvania Governor Robert Casey and various other Pennsylvania officials.

Counsel for WVUH employed Coopers & Lybrand, a national accounting firm, and three doctors specializing in hospital finance to assist in the preparation of the lawsuit and to testify at trial. WVUH prevailed at trial in May 1988. The District Court subsequently awarded fees pursuant to 42 U.S.C. § 1988, including over $100,000 in fees attributable to expert services. The District Court found these services to have been "essential" to presentation of the case—a finding not disputed by respondents.

Respondents appealed both the judgment on the merits and the fee award. The Court of Appeals for the Third Circuit affirmed as to the former, but reversed as to the expert fees, disallowing them except to the extent that they fell within the $30-per-day fees for witnesses prescribed by 28 U.S.C. § 1821. WVUH petitioned this Court for review of that disallowance; we granted certiorari.

II

28 U.S.C. § 1920 provides:

> A judge or clerk of any court of the United States may tax as costs the following:
>
> (1) Fees of the clerk and marshal;
>
> (2) Fees of the court reporter for all or any part of the stenographic transcript necessarily obtained for use in the case;
>
> (3) Fees and disbursements for printing and witnesses;
>
> (4) Fees for exemplification and copies of papers necessarily obtained for use in the case;
>
> (5) Docket fees under section 1923 of this title;
>
> (6) Compensation of court appointed experts, compensation of interpreters, and salaries, fees, expenses, and costs of special interpretation services under section 1828 of this title.

28 U.S.C. § 1821(b) limits the witness fees authorized by § 1920(3) as follows: "A witness shall be paid an attendance fee of $30 per day for each day's attendance. A witness shall also be paid the attendance fee for the time necessarily occupied in going to and returning from the place of attendance. . . ." In *Crawford Fitting Co. v. J. T. Gibbons, Inc.,* 482 U.S. 437 (1987), we held that these provisions define the full extent of a federal court's power to shift litigation costs absent express statutory authority to go further. "[W]hen," we said, "a prevailing party seeks reimbursement for fees paid to its own expert witnesses, a federal court is bound by the limits of § 1821(b), absent contract or explicit statutory authority to the contrary." *Id.,* at 439. * * *

As to the testimonial services of the hospital's experts, therefore, *Crawford Fitting* plainly requires, as prerequisite to reimbursement, the identification of "explicit statutory authority." WVUH argues, however, that some of the expert fees it incurred in this case were unrelated to expert testimony, and that, as to those fees, the § 1821(b) limits, which apply only to witnesses in attendance at trial, are of no consequence. We agree with that, but there remains applicable the limitation of § 1920. *Crawford Fitting* said that we would not lightly find an implied repeal of §§ 1821 or of 1920, which it held to be an express limitation upon the types of costs which, absent other authority, may be shifted by federal courts. 482 U.S., at 441. None of the categories of expenses listed in § 1920 can reasonably be read to include fees for services rendered by an expert employed by a party in a nontestimonial advisory capacity. The question before us, then, is—with regard to both testimonial and nontestimonial expert fees—whether the term "attorney's fee" in § 1988 provides the "explicit statutory authority" required by *Crawford Fitting*.

III

The record of statutory usage demonstrates convincingly that attorney's fees and expert fees are regarded as separate elements of litigation cost. While some fee-shifting provisions, like § 1988, refer only to "attorney's fees," see, *e. g.*, Civil Rights Act of 1964, 42 U.S.C. § 2000e–5(k), many others explicitly shift expert witness fees *as well as* attorney's fees. In 1976, just over a week prior to the enactment of § 1988, Congress passed those provisions of the Toxic Substances Control Act, 15 U.S.C. §§ 2618(d), 2619(c)(2), which provide that a prevailing party may recover "the costs of suit and reasonable fees for attorneys *and expert witnesses*." (Emphasis added.) Also in 1976, Congress amended the Consumer Product Safety Act, 15 U.S.C. §§ 2060(c), 2072(a), 2073, which as originally enacted in 1972 shifted to the losing party "cost[s] of suit, including a reasonable attorney's fee," see 86 Stat. 1226. In the 1976 amendment, Congress altered the fee shifting provisions to their present form by adding a phrase shifting expert witness fees *in addition to* attorney's fees. See Pub. L. 94–284, 10, 90 Stat. §§ 506, 507. Two other significant acts passed in 1976 contain similar phrasing: The Resource Conservation and Recovery Act of 1976, 42 U.S.C. § 6972(e) ("costs of litigation (including reasonable attorney and expert witness fees)"), and the Natural Gas Pipeline Safety Act Amendments of 1976, 49 U.S.C. App. § 1686(e) ("costs of suit, including reasonable attorney's fees and reasonable expert witnesses fees").

Congress enacted similarly phrased fee-shifting provisions in numerous statutes both before 1976, see, *e.g.*, Endangered Species Act of 1973, 16 U.S.C. § 1540(g)(4) ("costs of litigation (including reasonable attorney and expert witness fees)"), and afterwards, see, *e.g.,* Public Utility Regulatory Policies Act of 1978, 16 U.S.C. § 2632(a)(1) ("reasonable attorneys' fees, expert witness fees, and other reasonable costs incurred in preparation and advocacy of [the litigant's] position"). These statutes encompass diverse categories of legislation, including tax, administrative procedure, environmental protection, consumer protection, admiralty and navigation, utilities regulation, and, significantly, civil rights: The Equal Access to Justice Act (EAJA), the counterpart to § 1988 for violation of federal rights by federal employees, states that " 'fees and other expenses' [as shifted by § 2412(d)(1)(A)] includes the reasonable expenses of expert witnesses . . . reasonable attorney fees." 28 U.S.C. § 2412(d)(2)(A). At least 34 statutes in 10 different titles of the U.S. Code explicitly shift attorney's fees *and* expert witness fees.

The laws that refer to fees for nontestimonial expert services are less common, but they establish a similar usage both before and after 1976: Such fees are referred to *in addition to* attorney's fees when a shift is intended. A provision of the 1964 Criminal Justice Act, 18 U.S.C. § 3006A(e), directs the court to reimburse appointed counsel for expert fees necessary to the defense of indigent criminal defendants—even though the immediately preceding provision, § 3006A(d), already directs that appointed defense counsel be paid a designated hourly rate plus "expenses reasonably incurred." WVUH's position must be that expert fees billed to a client through an attorney are "attorney's fees" because they are to be treated as part of the expenses of the attorney; but if this were normal usage, they would have been reimbursable under the Criminal Justice Act as "expenses reasonably incurred"—and subsection § 3006A(e) would add nothing to the recoverable amount. The very heading of that subsection, "Services *other than* counsel" (emphasis added), acknowledges a distinction between services provided by the attorney himself and those provided to the attorney (or the client) by a nonlegal expert.

To the same effect is the 1980 EAJA, which provides: " 'fees and other expenses' [as shifted by § 2412(d)(1)(A)] includes the reasonable expenses of expert witnesses, *the reasonable cost of any study, analysis, engineering report, test, or project* which is found by the court to be necessary for the preparation of the party's case, and reasonable attorney fees." 28 U.S.C. § 2412(d)(2)(A) (emphasis added). If the reasonable cost of a "study" or "analysis"—which is but another way of describing nontestimonial expert services—is by common usage already included in the "attorney fees," again a significant and highly detailed part of the statute becomes redundant. The Administrative Procedure Act, 5 U.S.C. § 504(b)(1)(A) (added 1980), and the Tax Equity and Fiscal Responsibility Act of 1982, 26 U.S.C. § 7430(c)(1), contain similar language. Also reflecting the same usage are two railroad regulation statutes, the Regional Rail Reorganization Act of 1976, 45 U.S.C. §§ 726(f)(9), 741(i) ("costs and expenses (including reasonable fees of accountants, experts, and attorneys) actually incurred"), and the Railroad Revitalization and Regulatory Reform Act of 1976, 45 U.S.C. § 854(g) ("costs and expenses (including fees of accountants, experts, and attorneys) actually and reasonably incurred").[5]

We think this statutory usage shows beyond question that attorney's fees and expert fees are distinct items of expense. If, as WVUH argues, the one includes the other, dozens of statutes referring to the two separately become an inexplicable exercise in redundancy.

IV

WVUH argues that at least in pre-1976 *judicial* usage the phrase "attorney's fees" included the fees of experts. To support this proposition, it relies upon two historical assertions: first, that pre-1976 courts, when exercising traditional equitable discretion in shifting attorney's fees, taxed as an element of such fees the expenses related to expert services; and second, that pre-1976 courts shifting attorney's fees pursuant to statutes identical in phrasing to 1988 allowed the recovery of expert fees. We disagree with these assertions. The judicial background against which Congress enacted 1988 mirrored the statutory background: expert fees were regarded not as a subset of attorney's fees, but as a distinct category of litigation expense.

Certainly it is true that prior to 1976 some federal courts shifted expert fees to losing parties pursuant to various equitable doctrines—sometimes in conjunction with attorney's fees. But they did not shift them *as an element of* attorney's fees. * * * We have found no support for the proposition that, at common law, courts shifted expert fees *as an element of* attorney's fees.

Of arguably greater significance than the courts' treatment of attorney's fees *versus* expert fees at common law is their treatment of those expenses under statutes containing fee shifting provisions similar to § 1988. The

---

5 WVUH cites a House Conference Committee report from a statute passed in 1986, stating "The conferees intend that the term 'attorneys' fees as part of the costs' include reasonable expenses and fees of expert witnesses and the reasonable costs of any test or evaluation which is found to be necessary for the preparation of the . . . case." H. R. Conf. Rep. No. 687, 99th Cong., 2d sess. 5, *reprinted in* 1986 U. S. Code Cong. & Admin. News 1798, 1808 (discussing the Handicapped Children's Protection Act of 1986, 20 U.S.C. § 1415(e)(4)(B)). In our view this undercuts rather than supports WVUH's position: The specification would have been quite unnecessary if the ordinary meaning of the term included those elements. The statement is an apparent effort to *depart* from ordinary meaning and to define a term of art.

hospital contends that in some cases courts shifted expert fees as well as the statutorily authorized attorney's fees—and thus must have thought that the latter included the former. We find, however, that the practice, at least in the overwhelming majority of cases, was otherwise.

Prior to 1976, the leading fee-shifting statute was the Clayton Act. As of 1976 four Circuits (six Circuits, if one includes summary affirmances of district court judgments) had held that this provision did not permit a shift of expert witness fees. No court had held otherwise. Also instructive is pre-1976 practice under the federal patent laws, which provided, 35 U.S.C. § 285 that "[t]he court in exceptional cases may award reasonable attorney fees to the prevailing party." Again, every court to consider the matter as of 1976 thought that this provision conveyed no authority to shift expert fees.

In sum, we conclude that at the time this provision was enacted neither statutory nor judicial usage regarded the phrase "attorney's fees" as embracing fees for experts' services.

V

WVUH suggests that a distinctive meaning of "attorney's fees" should be adopted with respect to § 1988 because this statute was meant to overrule our decision in *Alyeska Pipeline Service Co. v. Wilderness Society,* 421 U.S. 240 (1975). As mentioned above, prior to 1975 many courts awarded expert fees and attorney's fees in certain circumstances pursuant to their equitable discretion. In *Alyeska,* we held that this discretion did not extend beyond a few exceptional circumstances long recognized by common law. Specifically, we rejected the so-called "private attorney general" doctrine recently created by some lower federal courts, which allowed equitable fee shifting to plaintiffs in certain types of civil rights litigation. 421 U. S., at 269. WVUH argues that 1988 was intended to restore the pre-*Alyeska* regime—and that, since expert fees were shifted then, they should be shifted now.

Both chronology and the remarks of sponsors of the bill that became § 1988 suggest that at least some members of Congress viewed it as a response to *Alyeska*. See, *e.g.,* S. Rep. No. 1011, 94th Cong., 2d Sess. 4, 6, *repr. in* 1976 U. S. CODE CONG. & ADMIN. NEWS 5911, 5913. It is a considerable step, however, from this proposition to the conclusion the hospital would have us draw, namely, that § 1988 should be read as a reversal of *Alyeska* in all respects.

By its plain language and as unanimously construed in the courts, § 1988 is both broader and narrower than the pre-*Alyeska* regime. Before *Alyeska,* civil rights plaintiffs could recover fees pursuant to the private attorney general doctrine only if private enforcement was necessary to defend important rights benefiting large numbers of people, and cost barriers might otherwise preclude private suits. Section 1988 contains no similar limitation—so that in the present suit there is no question as to the propriety of shifting WVUH's *attorney's* fees, even though it is highly doubtful they could have been awarded under pre-*Alyeska* equitable theories. In other respects, however, § 1988 is not as broad as the former regime. It is limited, for example, to violations of specified civil rights statutes—which means that it would not have reversed the outcome of *Alyeska* itself, which involved not a civil rights statute but the National Environmental Policy Act of 1969, 42 U.S.C. §§ 4321 *et seq*. Since it is clear that, in many respects, § 1988 was not meant to return us precisely to the pre-*Alyeska* regime, the objective of achieving such a return is no reason to depart from the normal import of the text.

WVUH further argues that the congressional purpose in enacting § 1988 must prevail over the ordinary meaning of the statutory terms. It quotes, for example, the House Committee Report to the effect that "the judicial remedy [must be] full and complete," H. R. Rep. No. 1558, 94th Cong. 2d sess. 1 (1976), and the Senate Committee Report to the effect that "[c]itizens must have the opportunity to recover what it costs them to vindicate [civil] rights in court," S. Rep. No. 1011, 94th Cong. 2d Sess. 2, repr. in 1976 U. S. Code Cong. & Admin. News 5908, 5910. As we have observed before, however, the purpose of a statute includes not only what it sets out to change, but also what it resolves to leave alone. The best evidence of that purpose is the statutory text adopted by both Houses of Congress and submitted to the President. Where that contains a phrase that is unambiguous—that has a clearly accepted meaning in both legislative and judicial practice—we do not permit it to be expanded or contracted by the statements of individual legislators or committees during the course of the enactment process. See *United States v. Ron Pair Enterprises, Inc.,* 489 U.S. 235, 241 (1989) ("[W]here, as here, the statute's language is plain, 'the sole function of the court is to enforce it according to its terms.' "), quoting *Caminetti v. United States,* 242 U.S. 470, 485 (1917). Congress could easily have shifted "attorney's fees and expert witness fees," or "reasonable litigation expenses," as it did in contemporaneous statutes; it chose instead to enact more restrictive language, and we are bound by that restriction.

WVUH asserts that we have previously been guided by the "broad remedial purposes" of § 1988, rather than its text, in a context resolving an "analogous issue": In *Missouri v. Jenkins,* 491 U.S. 274, 285 (1989), we concluded that § 1988 permitted separately billed paralegal and law-clerk time to be charged to the losing party. The trouble with this argument is that *Jenkins* did *not* involve an "analogous issue," insofar as the relevant considerations are concerned. The issue there was not, as WVUH contends, whether we would permit our perception of the "policy" of the statute to overcome its "plain language." It was not remotely plain in *Jenkins* that the phrase "attorney's fee" did not include charges for law-clerk and paralegal services. Such services, like the services of "secretaries, messengers, librarians, janitors, and others whose labor contributes to the work product," 491 U. S., at 285, had traditionally been included in calculation of the lawyers' hourly rates. Only recently had there arisen "the 'increasingly widespread custom of separately billing for [such] services,' " *id.*, at 286 (quoting from *Ramos v. Lamm,* 713 F. 2d 546, 558 (CA10 1983). By contrast, there has never been, to our knowledge, a practice of including the cost of expert services within attorneys' hourly rates. There was also no record in *Jenkins* —as there is a lengthy record here—of statutory usage that recognizes a distinction between the charges at issue and attorney's fees. We do not know of a single statute that shifts clerk or paralegal fees separately; and even those, such as the EAJA, which comprehensively define the assessable "litigation costs" make no separate mention of clerks or paralegals. In other words, *Jenkins* involved a respect in which the term "attorney's fees" (giving the losing argument the benefit of the doubt) was genuinely ambiguous; and we resolved that ambiguity not by invoking some policy that supersedes the text of the statute, but by concluding that charges of this sort had traditionally been included in attorney's fees, and that separate billing should make no difference. The term's application to expert fees is not ambiguous; and if it were the means of analysis employed in *Jenkins* would lead to the conclusion that since such fees have not traditionally been included within the attorney's hourly rate they are not attorney's fees.

WVUH's last contention is that, even if Congress plainly did not include expert fees in the fee-shifting provisions of § 1988, it would have done so had it thought about it. Most of the pre-§ 1988 statutes that explicitly shifted expert fees dealt with environmental litigation, where the necessity of expert advice was readily apparent; and when Congress later enacted the EAJA, the federal counterpart of § 1988, it explicitly included expert fees. Thus, the argument runs, the 94th Congress simply forgot; it is our duty to ask how they would have decided had they actually considered the question. See *Friedrich v. City of Chicago,* 888 F. 2d 511, 514 (CA7 1989) (awarding expert fees under § 1988 because a court should "complete . . .

the statute by reading it to bring about the end that the legislators would have specified had they thought about it more clearly").

This argument profoundly mistakes our role. Where a statutory term presented to us for the first time is ambiguous, we construe it to contain that permissible meaning which fits most logically and comfortably into the body of both previously and subsequently enacted law. See 2 J. SUTHERLAND, STATUTORY CONSTRUCTION 5201 (3d F. Horack ed. 1943). We do so not because that precise accommodative meaning is what the lawmakers must have had in mind (how could an earlier Congress know what a later Congress would enact?) but because it is our role to make sense rather than nonsense out of the *corpus juris*. But where, as here, the meaning of the term prevents such accommodation, it is not our function to eliminate clearly expressed inconsistency of policy, and to treat alike subjects that different Congresses have chosen to treat differently. The facile attribution of congressional "forgetfulness" cannot justify such a usurpation. Where what is at issue is not a contradictory disposition within the same enactment, but merely a difference between the more parsimonious policy of an earlier enactment and the more generous policy of a later one, there is no more basis for saying that the earlier Congress forgot than for saying that the earlier Congress felt differently. In such circumstances, the attribution of forgetfulness rests in reality upon the judge's assessment that the later statute contains the *better* disposition. But that is not for judges to prescribe. We thus reject this last argument for the same reason that Justice Brandeis, writing for the Court, once rejected a similar (though less explicit) argument by the United States:

> [The statute's] language is plain and unambiguous. What the Government asks is not a construction of a statute, but, in effect, an enlargement of it by the court, so that what was omitted, presumably by inadvertence, may be included within its scope. To supply omissions transcends the judicial function.

Iselin v. United States, 270 U.S. 245, 250–251 (1926).[7]

---

[7] WVUH at least asks us to guess the preferences of the enacting Congress. *Justice Stevens* apparently believes our role is to guess the desires of the *present* Congress, or of Congresses yet to be. "Only time will tell," he says, "whether the Court, with its literal reading of § 1988, has correctly interpreted the will of Congress," *post*, at 14. The implication is that today's holding will be proved wrong if Congress amends the law to conform with his dissent. We think not. The "will of Congress" we look to is not a will evolving from Session to Session, but a will expressed and fixed in a particular enactment. Otherwise, we would speak not of "interpreting" the law but of "intuiting" or "predicting" it. Our role is to say what the law, as hitherto enacted, *is;* not to forecast what the law, as amended, *will be*.

For the foregoing reasons, we conclude that § 1988 conveys no authority to shift expert fees. When experts appear at trial, they are of course eligible for the fee provided by §§ 1920 and 1821—which was allowed in the present case by the Court of Appeals. * * *

JUSTICE MARSHALL, dissenting.

As Justice Stevens demonstrates, the Court uses the implements of literalism to wound, rather than to minister to, congressional intent in this case. That is a dangerous usurpation of congressional power when any statute is involved. It is troubling for special reasons, however, when the statute at issue is clearly designed to give access to the federal courts to persons and groups attempting to vindicate vital civil rights. * * *

Note Justice Marshall's implicit invocation of the Remedial Canon here.

JUSTICE STEVENS, with whom JUSTICE MARSHALL and JUSTICE BLACKMUN join, dissenting.

Since the enactment of the Statute of Wills in 1540, careful draftsmen have authorized executors to pay the just debts of the decedent, including the fees and expenses of the attorney for the estate. Although the omission of such an express authorization in a will might indicate that the testator had thought it unnecessary, or that he had overlooked the point, the omission would surely not indicate a deliberate decision by the testator to forbid any compensation to his attorney.

In the early 1970s, Congress began to focus on the importance of public interest litigation, and since that time, it has enacted numerous fee-shifting statutes. In many of these statutes, which the majority cites at length, see *ante*, at 4–8, Congress has expressly authorized the recovery of expert witness fees as part of the costs of litigation. The question in this case is whether, notwithstanding the omission of such an express authorization in 42 U.S.C. § 1988, Congress intended to authorize such recovery when it provided for "a reasonable attorney's fee as part of the costs." In my view, just as the omission of express authorization in a will does not preclude compensation to an estate's attorney, the omission of express authorization for expert witness fees in a feeshifting provision should not preclude the award of expert witness fees. We should look at the way in which the Court has interpreted the text of *this statute* in the past, as well as *this statute's* legislative history, to resolve the question before us, rather than looking at the text of the many other statutes that the majority cites in which Congress expressly recognized the need for compensating expert witnesses.

I

Under either the broad view of "costs" typically assumed in the fee-shifting context or the broad view of "a reasonable attorney's fee" articulated by this Court, expert witness fees are a proper component of an award under § 1988. Because we are not interpreting these words for the first time, they should be evaluated in the context that this and other courts have already created.

The term "costs" has a different and broader meaning in fee-shifting statutes than it has in the cost statutes that apply to ordinary litigation. The cost bill in this case illustrates the point. Leaving aside the question of expert witness fees, the prevailing party sought reimbursement for $45,867 in disbursements, which plainly would not have been recoverable costs under 28 U.S.C. 1920. These expenses, including such items as travel and long-distance telephone calls, were allowed by the District Court, and were not even questioned by respondent. They were expenses that a retained lawyer would ordinarily bill to his or her client. They were accordingly considered proper "costs" in a case of this kind.

The broad construction typically given to "costs" in the feeshifting context is highlighted by the *Chief Justice*'s contrasting view in *Missouri v. Jenkins*, 491 U.S. 274 (1989), in which he argued that paralegal and law clerk fees could not even be awarded as "costs" under 28 U.S.C. § 1920. One of the issues in *Jenkins* was the *rate* at which the services of law clerks and paralegals should be compensated. The State contended that actual cost, rather than market value, should govern. It did not, however, even question the propriety of reimbursing the prevailing party for the work of these nonlawyers. Only the *Chief Justice*—in a lone dissent the reasoning of which is now endorsed by the Court—advanced a purely literal interpretation of the statute. He wrote:

> I also disagree with the State's suggestion that law clerk and paralegal expenses incurred by a prevailing party, if not recoverable at market rates as 'attorney's fees' under § 1988, are nonetheless recoverable at actual cost under that statute. The language of § 1988 expands the traditional definition of 'costs' to include 'a reasonable attorney's fee,' but it cannot fairly be read to authorize the recovery of all other out-of-pocket expenses actually incurred by the prevailing party in the course of litigation. Absent specific

statutory authorization for the recovery of such expenses, the prevailing party remains subject to the limitations on cost recovery imposed by Federal Rule of Civil Procedure 54(d) and 28 U.S.C. § 1920 which govern the taxation of costs in federal litigation where a cost-shifting statute is not applicable. Section 1920 gives the district court discretion to tax certain types of costs against the losing party in any federal litigation. The statute specifically enumerates six categories of expenses which may be taxed as costs: fees of the court clerk and marshal; fees of the court reporter; printing fees and witness fees; copying fees; certain docket fees; and fees of court-appointed experts and interpreters. We have held that this list is exclusive. *Crawford Fitting Co. v. J. T. Gibbons, Inc.*, 482 U.S. 437 (1987). Since none of these categories can possibly be construed to include the fees of law clerks and paralegals, I would also hold that reimbursement for these expenses may not be separately awarded at actual cost.

Id., at 297–298.

Although the *Chief Justice* argued that charges for the work of paralegals and law clerks were not part of the narrowly defined "costs" that were reimbursable under § 1920, nor were they part of an "attorney's fee" reimbursable under 1988, the Court did not reach the *Chief Justice's* point about costs because it held in *Jenkins* that such expenses were part of a "reasonable attorney's fee" authorized by § 1988, and thus, could be reimbursed at market rate. In the Court's view, a "reasonable attorney's fee" referred to "a reasonable fee for the work product of an attorney." *Id.*, at 285. We explained:

> [T]he fee must take into account the work not only of attorneys, but also of secretaries, messengers, librarians, janitors, and others whose labor contributes to the work product for which an attorney bills her client; and it must also take account of other expenses and profit. The parties have suggested no reason why the work of paralegals should not be similarly compensated, nor can we think of any. We thus take as our starting point the self-evident proposition that the 'reasonable attorney's fee' provided for by statute should compensate the work of paralegals, as well as that of attorneys.

Ibid.

In *Jenkins*, the Court acknowledged that the use of paralegals instead of attorneys reduced the cost of litigation, and " 'by reducing the spiraling cost of civil rights litigation, further[ed] the policies underlying civil rights statutes.' " *Id.*, at 288. If attorneys were forced to do the work that paralegals could just as easily perform under the supervision of an attorney, such as locating and interviewing witnesses or compiling statistical and financial data, then "it would not be surprising to see a greater amount of such work performed by attorneys themselves, thus increasing the overall cost of litigation." *Id.*, at 288, n. 10.

This reasoning applies equally to other forms of specialized litigation support that a trial lawyer needs and that the client customarily pays for, either directly or indirectly. Although reliance on paralegals is a more recent development than the use of traditional expert witnesses, both paralegals and expert witnesses perform important tasks that save lawyers' time and enhance the quality of their work product. In this case, it is undisputed that the District Court correctly found that the expert witnesses were "essential" and "necessary" to the successful prosecution of the plaintiff's case, and that their data and analysis played a pivotal role in the attorney's trial preparation. Had the attorneys attempted to perform the tasks that the experts performed, it obviously would have taken them far longer than the experts and the entire case would have been far more costly to the parties. As Judge Posner observed in a comparable case:

> The time so spent by the expert is a substitute for lawyer time, just as paralegal time is, for if prohibited (or deterred by the cost) from hiring an expert the lawyer would attempt to educate himself about the expert's area of expertise. To forbid the shifting of the expert's fee would encourage underspecialization and inefficient trial preparation, just as to forbid shifting the cost of paralegals would encourage lawyers to do paralegals' work. There is thus no basis for distinguishing *Jenkins* from the present case so far as time spent by these experts in educating the plaintiffs' lawyer is concerned. . . .

FYI Judge Posner is a revered judge on the U.S. Court of Appeals for the Seventh Circuit who is typically associated with the "Chicago School" of Law and Economics. Note how in this passage Judge Posner employs economic analysis in his effort to resolve statutory ambiguity.

Friedrich v. Chicago, 888 F. 2d 511, 514 (CA7 1989).

In *Jenkins*, we interpreted the award of "a reasonable *attorney's* fee" to cover charges for paralegals and law clerks, even though a paralegal or law clerk is not an attorney. Similarly, the federal courts routinely allow an attorney's travel expenses or long-distance telephone calls to be awarded, even though they are not literally part of an "*attorney's fee*," or part of "costs" as defined by 28 U.S.C. § 1920. To allow reimbursement of these other categories of expenses, and yet not to include expert witness fees, is both arbitrary and contrary to the broad remedial purpose that inspired the fee-shifting provision of § 1988.

II

The Senate Report on the Civil Rights Attorneys' Fees Awards Act explained that the purpose of the proposed amendment to 42 U.S.C. § 1988 was "to remedy anomalous gaps in our civil rights laws created by the United States Supreme Court's recent decision in *Alyeska Pipeline Service Co. v. Wilderness Society*, 421 U.S. 240 (1975), and to achieve consistency in our civil rights laws." S. Rep. No. 94–1011, p. 1 (1976). The Senate Committee on the Judiciary wanted to level the playing field so that private citizens, who might have little or no money, could still serve as "private attorneys general" and afford to bring actions, even against state or local bodies, to enforce the civil rights laws. The Committee acknowledged that "[i]f private citizens are to be able to assert their civil rights, and if those who violate the Nation's fundamental laws are not to proceed with impunity, then citizens must have the opportunity to recover *what it costs them* to vindicate these rights in court." *Id.*, at 2 (emphasis added). According to the Committee, the bill would create "no startling new remedy," but would simply provide "the technical requirements" requested by the Supreme Court in *Alyeska*, so that courts could "continue the practice of awarding attorneys' fees which had been going on for years prior to the Court's May decision." *Id.*, at 6.

To underscore its intention to return the courts to their pre-*Alyeska* practice of shifting fees in civil rights cases, the Senate Committee's Report cited with approval not only several cases in which fees had been shifted, but also all of the cases contained in Legal Fees, Hearings before the Subcommittee on Representation of Citizen Interests of the Senate Committee on the Judiciary, 93rd Cong., 1st Sess., pt. 3, pp. 888–1024, 1060–1062 (1973) (hereinafter Senate Hearings). See S. Rep. No. 94–1011, p. 4, n. 3 (1976). The cases collected in the 1973 Senate Hearings included many in which courts had permitted the shifting of costs, including expert witness fees. At the time when the Committee referred to these cases, though several were later reversed, it used them to make the point that prior to *Alyeska*, courts awarded attorney's fees and costs, including expert witness fees, in civil rights cases, and that they did so in order to encourage private citizens to bring such suits. It was to this pre-*Alyeska* regime, in which courts could award expert witness fees along with attorney's fees, that the Senate Committee intended to return through the passage of the fee-shifting amendment to § 1988.

The House Report expressed concerns similar to those raised by the Senate Report. It noted that "[t]he effective enforcement of Federal civil rights statutes depends largely on the efforts of private citizens" and that the House bill was "designed to give such persons effective access to the judicial process. . . ." H. R. Rep. No. 94–1558, p. 1 (1976). The House Committee on the Judiciary concluded that "civil rights litigants were suffering very severe hardships because of the *Alyeska* decision," and that the case had had a "devastating impact" and had created a "compelling need" for a feeshifting provision in the civil rights context. *Id.*, at 2–3. * * *

This Court's determination today that petitioner must assume the cost of $104,133.00 in expert witness fees is at war with the congressional purpose of making the prevailing party whole. As we said in *Hensley v. Eckerhart*, 461 U.S. 424, 435 (1983), petitioner's recovery should be "fully compensatory," or, as we expressed in *Jenkins*, petitioner's recovery should be "comparable to what 'is traditional with attorneys compensated by a fee-paying client.' S. Rep. No. 94–1011, p. 6 (1976)." 491 U. S., at 286.

III

In recent years the Court has vacillated between a purely literal approach to the task of statutory interpretation and an approach that seeks guidance from historical context, legislative history, and prior cases identifying the purpose that motivated the legislation. Thus, for example, in *Christiansburg Garment Co. v. EEOC*, 434 U.S. 412 (1978), we rejected a "mechanical construction," *id.*, at 418, of the feeshifting provision in § 706(k) of Title VII of the Civil Rights Act of 1964 that the prevailing defendant had urged upon us. * * * That holding rested entirely on our evaluation of the relevant congressional policy and found no support within the four corners of the statutory text. Nevertheless, the holding was unanimous and, to the best of my knowledge, evoked no adverse criticism or response in Congress.

On those occasions, however, when the Court has put on its thick grammarian's spectacles and ignored the available evidence of congressional purpose and the teaching of prior cases construing a statute, the congressional response has been dramatically different. It is no coincidence that the Court's literal reading of Title VII, which led to the conclusion that disparate treatment of pregnant and nonpregnant persons was not discrimination on the basis of sex, see *General Electric Co. v. Gilbert*, 429 U.S. 125 (1976), was repudiated by the 95th Congress; [Justice Stevens went on to catalog a number of other examples of congressional rejections of literal interpretations].

In the domain of statutory interpretation, Congress is the master. It obviously has the power to correct our mistakes, but we do the country a disservice when we needlessly ignore persuasive evidence of Congress' actual purpose and require it "to take the

> Do you agree that the Court has ignored congressional purpose here?

time to revisit the matter". . . and to restate its purpose in more precise English whenever its work product suffers from an omission or inadvertent error. As Judge Learned Hand explained, statutes are likely to be imprecise.

> All [legislators] have done is to write down certain words which they mean to apply generally to situations of that kind. To apply these literally may either pervert what was plainly their general meaning, or leave undisposed of what there is every reason to suppose they meant to provide for. Thus it is not enough for the judge just to use a dictionary. If he should do no more, he might come out with a result which every sensible man would recognize to be quite the opposite of what was really intended; which would contradict or leave unfulfilled its plain purpose.

L. Hand, *How Far Is a Judge Free in Rendering a Decision?*, in THE SPIRIT OF LIBERTY 103, 106 (I. Dilliard ed. 1952).

The Court concludes its opinion with the suggestion that disagreement with its textual analysis could only be based on the dissenter's preference for a "better" statute, *ante*, at 17. It overlooks the possibility that a different view may be more faithful to Congress' command. The fact that Congress has consistently provided for the inclusion of expert witness fees in fee-shifting statutes when it considered the matter is a weak reed on which to rest the conclusion that the omission of such a provision represents a deliberate decision to forbid such awards. Only time will tell whether the Court, with its literal reading of § 1988, has correctly interpreted the will of Congress with respect to the issue it has resolved today.

NOTES & QUESTIONS

1. How many intrinsic interpretive tools can you find in the *Casey* decisions? How many other (non-intrinsic) types of interpretive tools or arguments can you find?

2. Justice Stevens' dissent included this final footnote:

   Seventy years ago, Justice Cardozo warned of the dangers of literal reading, whether of precedents or statutes:

   > [Some judges'] notion of their duty is to match the colors of the case at hand against the colors of many sample cases spread out upon their desk. The sample nearest in shade supplies the applicable rule. But, of course, no system of living law can be evolved by such a process, and no judge of a high court, worthy of his office, views the function of his place so narrowly. If that were all there was to our calling, there would be little of intellectual interest about it. The man who had the best card index of the cases would also be the wisest judge. It is when the colors do not match, when the references in the index fail, when there is no decisive precedent, that the serious business of the judge begins.

   B. Cardozo, The Nature of the Judicial Process 20–21 (1921).

One way to view *Casey* is as the paradigmatic example of the so-called "Whole Code rule" discussed in Chapter 20. The majority interprets the relevant civil-rights fee-shifting provision (42 U.S.C. § 1988) by drawing on fee-shifting provisions in statutes far afield (e.g., Toxic Substances Control Act, Consumer Product Safety Act, Public Utility Regulatory Policies Act). Arguably, what the majority has done is to treat fee-shifting provisions throughout the U.S. Code as the background linguistic *context* for understanding the words in § 1988. In other words, the majority interprets the statutes so that there is textual coherence among numerous fee-shifting provisions across the United States Code. The dissent, in contrast, wants to focus on *"this statute"* (42 U.S.C. § 1988), rather than the rest of the U.S. Code. In the next chapter, we turn to what are known as statutes *"in pari materia,"* a Latin phrase meaning statutes "on the same subject matter." The core of *in pari materia* is that statutes that are related to each other *should* cohere. Thus, another way to think about the dispute in *Casey* is to ask yourself whether the various statutes should cohere: Ordinarily, is there any reason to think a civil rights statute should cohere with, say, the Endangered Species Act? They are clearly not "on the same subject matter," are they? On the other hand, notice that the majority views the interpretive problem through the lens of fee-shifting *provisions*. If we frame the subject as "fee-shifting," then aren't all the statutes on which the majority relies in Part III of its opinion "on the same subject matter" as § 1988? For further discussion of this question, see Anuj C. Desai, *The Dilemma of Interstatutory Interpretation*, 77 Wash. & Lee L. Rev. 177, 232–244 (2020).

Test Your Understanding

To assess your understanding of the material in this chapter, click here to take a quiz.

Part VI—Extrinsic Tools and Techniques of Statutory Interpretation

In Part V, we studied a number of textual and substantive "canons of construction." These canons are often called "intrinsic" tools of interpretation, even though they require going beyond the text itself (dictionaries, for example, are external to the statute), because they offer interpretive assistance using generally applicable guidance applied to the statutory text alone. In this Part, we look at what are often referred to as "extrinsic" tools of interpretation. These extrinsic tools are also sometimes treated as "canons," collectively referred to as the "reference canons." However, the label "canons" is more commonly used to identify the tools of interpretation discussed in Part V. Today, extrinsic tools are almost always deployed in combination with at least some of the textual or substantive canons, not in place of them (as in the *Casey* decision you read as a transition case at the end of the last chapter).

The next several chapters consider the major categories of extrinsic tools of interpretation. These include: (1) the relationship between the specific text at issue and any relevant **common law** principles; (2) the relationship between the specific text at issue and **other statutes or regulations**: and (3) interpretive guidance that may be available through the study and analysis of the **legislative and statutory history** of the text at issue. The term "legislative history" is a term of art. It generally refers to the documentary record produced by the lawmaking authorities themselves during the legislative process. A given measure's legislative history may include a variety of types of evidence of the measure's meaning, from official reports of legislative committees to remarks of individual legislators to presidential or gubernatorial signing statements to testimony at legislative hearings. This part of the book reviews each of these types of legislative history materials, with a focus on the importance of assessing their reliability in individual cases. Although the notion of consulting "extrinsic" tools (or aids) of interpretation is a long-standing one (dating at least to the early decades of the twentieth century), it is worth noting that in an earlier era, courts generally viewed recourse to legislative history as neither helpful nor appropriate in resolving textual ambiguity. For a brief summary of these earlier judicial attitudes towards legislative history, see SCALIA & GARNER, READING LAW, at 369–90.

24

The Context of Enactment

Key Concepts

- Context of enactment
- Remedy common law defects
- Adopt common law definitions
- Follow common law principles
- Borrowed statutes
- Statutes *in pari materia*
- Societal circumstances of enactment

Chapter Summary

The next four chapters focus on a variety of what are sometimes called "extrinsic" interpretive tools. One category of extrinsic tools frequently used to resolve statutory ambiguity focuses on the broader *legal and social* context of the statute at issue. Contextual factors can include the common law existing at the time of the enactment, other statutes already in place, and the societal circumstances in which the measure arose. This contrasts with Chapter 20 above, which focused on the linguistic context of the statutory text. As we noted later in Part V, you can think of some of the substantive canons of construction (such as the Constitutional Avoidance Canon) as tools for taking account of the broader legal context in which legislatures draft all statutes.

The existing common law at the time of adoption is an aid respected by interpreters across the spectrum, including New Textualists. Legislators are assumed to know the contours of the common law at the time of enacting a statutory measure, and this assumption factors into statutory interpretation, whether or not it is true. Other statutes can also play a role in interpretation, as when a legislature copies language from a statute already in its own code, or "borrows" a measure in use in another jurisdiction. Courts often presume that a legislature copying or borrowing language also intends to incorporate the interpretive jurisprudence already developed around that language. Finally, the societal circumstances at

> the time of enactment can play a role in interpretation, as interpreters can use these circumstances to make assumptions about how the enacting legislature intended a law to function.

This chapter explores several principal ways that an interpreter might seek to contextualize a piece of statutory text. The term "context" is notoriously slippery in statutory interpretation. Etymologically, the prefix "con" means "together" or "with." So, you can think of "context" as literally "together with the text." That is why the term can be used in different ways: it can mean "the *words* that immediately precede and follow any particular passage of text and that clarify its meaning," or it can mean "the *circumstances* that form the setting for" the statutory text. You can think of the former as the *linguistic context* and the latter, for interpretive purposes, as the *legal and social context*. As analytically distinct as these two concepts of context are, courts often fail to specify which they mean when referring to statutory "context."

As we noted in Chapter 20, courts often look to the *linguistic context* of statutory language. The way in which the presumptions of consistent usage and meaningful variation operate within the Whole Act Rule is an example of courts considering linguistic context. In fact, even *noscitur a sociis* and *ejusdem generis* can be thought of as doctrines about linguistic context, since they direct judges to interpret one term in light of the language surrounding that term. On the other hand, in this chapter, we generally use "context" to mean the legal and social context of a statute. In this latter sense, context can be found in the common law doctrinal foundation on which a legislature erects a given statutory provision; in other statutes treating similar or related issues; and in the societal circumstances present at the time of the enactment, sometimes including the legislature's previous course of dealing with a particular issue.

A. Interpretation Based on Common Law

The common law contributes to the interpretive enterprise in at least three distinguishable ways. First, it will sometimes be helpful for the interpreter to understand the related common law in order to recognize the gap that the statutory or regulatory text is intended to fill. Placing the enacted text in the context of its relationship to pre-existing law is akin to using the "mischief" rule identified as early as *Heydon's Case*. (See Chapter 15, pp. 346–347.) Second, the common law may also be helpful when lawmakers have used words with established common law meanings, to the extent that an understanding of those common law meanings may aid in construing the statutory text. (Note, however, that this deployment of the common law may run counter to the preceding type, as reference to common law definitions may reinforce existing doctrine, rather than fill gaps.) Third, applying common law principles may itself provide an aid in construing an ambiguous provision.

1.   Construing Statutes as Remedying Common Law Defects

If the statutory text seeks to remedy a defect in the existing common law, then understanding the common law background can help in understanding the purpose behind the statute, which in turn can shape the interpretive task. As an example of referring to the common law to supply an understanding of the mischief to which a statute is directed, consider the admiralty case of *Isbrandtsen Company v. Johnson*, 343 U.S. 779 (1952). At common law, maritime employers liable to their employees for unpaid wages were entitled to deduct or set-off damages for the employees' alleged derelictions of duty. But in *Isbrandtsen*, the Supreme Court concluded that because Congress had intended "to change the general maritime law so as to improve the lot of seamen," federal statutory law now preempted what would have been the employer's common-law deductions. The Court acknowledged the interpretive rule that "[s]tatutes which invade the common law . . . are to be read with a presumption favoring the retention of long-established and familiar principles" (a version of the **Derogation Canon**, which as Chapter 22 explained provides that statutes in derogation of the common law are to be narrowly construed), but observed that this rule did not govern "when a statutory purpose to the contrary is evident." The Court saw federal maritime legislation as designed to depart from the common law, "emphasiz[ing] that such legislation is largely remedial and calls for liberal interpretation in favor of the seamen." *Id.* at 782–83.

Of course, this is an example of the tension between the **Derogation Canon** and the **Remedial Canon**. Furthermore, the presumption that a statute should be construed to remedy a defect in the common law, even if only very narrowly, is just a presumption, which may not always hold true. Sometimes a legislative measure is intended merely to codify, clarify, and render more stable or permanent specific common law principles already in place, not to expand upon them or correct a shortcoming. Thus, as with so many interpretive challenges, deciding when particular interpretive tools and analyses are appropriate is itself an exercise in judgment.

2.   Reading Statutes as Adopting Common Law Definitions

Sometimes statutes will use a term with an established common law meaning. As an example, consider *Buckhannon Board & Care Home, Inc. v. West Virginia Dep't of Health and Human Resources,* 532 U.S. 598 (2001). At issue was how to construe the statutory term "prevailing party," under provisions of both the Americans with Disabilities Act and the Fair Housing Amendments Act that provided for the award of attorneys' fees to a prevailing party. The Supreme Court followed common law doctrine to conclude that to be a prevailing party, a party must have prevailed formally in the outcome of a legal proceeding; securing a legislative change that rendered the underlying legal proceeding moot was not sufficient. *See also People ex rel Dickinson v. Van de Carr,* 84 N.Y.S. 461 (1903) (construing state bribery statute in light of "what was embraced in [the term 'bribery'] at common law").

3.   Using Common Law Principles as an Aid to Resolving Ambiguity

On occasion, an interpreter may apply common law doctrine to resolve textual ambiguity. For instance, consider *Smith v. Wade,* 461 U.S. 30 (1983). At issue was whether a state prison inmate injured at the hands of other inmates could obtain both compensatory *and punitive* damages against prison officials, under 42 U.S.C. 1983, if their conduct in failing to protect him was in reckless disregard of his safety. Section 1983 provides a federal cause of action—specifically a kind of tort liability—against state actors who deprive an individual of federal rights. The Supreme Court explained that in determining how to apply section 1983, it often considered principles of common law tort liability, particularly those in place in 1871 when section 1983 was enacted. In this case, the question was whether at common law punitive damages were available in tort only on a showing of actual malicious intent, or instead could be imposed for reckless conduct alone. After a somewhat extensive consideration of the historical context, the majority opinion and one dissenting opinion reached opposite conclusions about what to make of the common law tort principles that existed in 1871.

> **?** How would you justify using the common law principles at the time of the interpretation, if they differ from those existing at the time of the statute's enactment?

Sometimes interpreters may look not to the common law in existence at the time of a measure's enactment, but to the common law at the time of the interpretation. For instance, in another section 1983 case, the Supreme Court decided that a common-law liability immunity for prosecutors that was not even recognized until a quarter century after 1871 nevertheless was available in actions brought under section 1983 in the later twentieth century. *See Imbler v. Pachtman,* 424 U.S. 409 (1976). Likewise, in an important state law example, the California Supreme

Court updated a statutory provision of its tort law so that it embraced the newer common law doctrine of comparative negligence, even though the same provision had years earlier been construed instead to codify the quite different common law tort rule of contributory negligence. *See Li v. Yellow Cab of California,* 532 P.2d 1226 (Cal. 1975).

B. Interpretation Based on Other Statutes

Much as common law understandings or principles may shed light on an interpretive problem in a statute or regulation, occasionally the purposes, policies, or principles enshrined in other statutes or regulations may provide interpretive assistance. Likewise, a definition included in one statute may prove helpful when the same term is used without definition in another similar statute. Often the key interpretive issue is whether the referenced text is sufficiently related to the text being interpreted.

1. "Borrowed" Statutes

One way in which other statutes may influence an interpretive problem is under the "borrowed" statute rule. When a legislature adopts language from another statute, the presumption is that the legislature intends the new statute to receive the same construction

In what circumstances do you think this presumption is strongest?

that the copied statute has already received. Statutory copying can occur not only when Congress or a state legislature adopts language from its own prior handiwork, but also when a legislature adopts a measure from another jurisdiction, as frequently occurs when state legislatures borrow ideas from other states or Congress.

For instance, in *Menard v. Alaska,* 578 P.2d 966 (Alaska 1978), the Alaska supreme court looked to Oregon jurisprudence to construe the meaning of the term "assault" in a provision of the Alaska criminal law that the Alaska legislature had borrowed from Oregon. The court explained that "statutes are presumed to have been adopted with the interpretations which had been placed upon them, prior to their Alaska enactment, by the highest court of the states from which they were borrowed." But state courts interpreting a provision of their own state law derived from another state's law may feel much less constrained to adopt the other state's interpretive approaches to that measure, absent a persuasive interpretation by the other state's highest court and fairly clear evidence that the adopting state's legislature knew and approved of that interpretation. *See Zerbe v. Alaska,* 583 P.2d 845 (Alaska 1978); *see also Smith v. Bayer Corp.,* 564 U.S. 299, (2011) (discussing potential interpretive variations between Federal Rule of Civil Procedure 23 and identically worded state rule).

As an example of Congress's borrowing its own handiwork, consider *Lorillard v. Pons,* 434 U.S. 575 (1978). There, the Supreme Court assumed that when Congress enacted the Age Discrimination in Employment Act (ADEA) and included in the Act enforcement provisions that tracked the enforcement provisions of the Fair Labor Standards Act (FLSA), Congress meant for the ADEA's enforcement provisions to have the same meaning and interpretation as the enforcement provisions it had borrowed from the FLSA.

2. Statutes Identified as *"In Pari Materia"*

Closely related to the borrowed statute rule is the *in pari materia* canon. This Latin phrase, which translates as "upon the same or like subject matter," encourages interpreters to interpret similar or related statutes coherently. Depending on the judge, the coherence between related statutes can either be linguistic coherence (for instance, apply presumptions of consistent usage and meaningful variation across the related statutes) or policy coherence (that is, ensure the related statutes work harmoniously in the real world). For a discussion of the distinction between linguistic and policy coherence in the *in pari materia* doctrine, see Anuj C. Desai, *The Dilemma of Interstatutory Interpretation,* 77 WASH. & LEE L. REV. 177, 182–94 (2020).

Many commentators classify *Lorillard v. Pons,* above, as an example of the use of this canon, though its enforcement provisions involved essentially the wholesale adoption of the statutory text on which it was modeled. As we noted in the final paragraph at the end of the previous chapter (pp. 578–579), *West Virginia University Hospitals v. Casey,* 499 U.S. 83 (1991), is an excellent example of the deployment of the *in pari materia* canon.

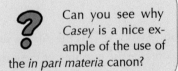
Can you see why *Casey* is a nice example of the use of the *in pari materia* canon?

Before going further, a bit of reflection is in order concerning the classification of the *in pari materia* canon. As we've noted before, while "intrinsic" and "extrinsic" labels are used by many commentators and some courts, they are far from mutually exclusive or accurately descriptive categories for understanding the tools of statutory interpretation. The *in pari materia* doctrine is a perfect example of this phenomenon. In some lexicons of statutory interpretation, *in pari materia* is considered an intrinsic canon, applicable either as an (obvious) explanation for why two parallel provisions of a *single* statute should be construed holistically under the Whole Act Rule, or as a similar (if not quite as obvious) explanation for why two analogous or comparable provisions in *different* statutes should be construed in light of each other, now as an instantiation of the Whole Code Rule. But in other lexicons, *in pari materia* is treated as an extrinsic interpretive tool for reasoning from one statute to another. These lexicons classify it as an extrinsic tool because the focus is on how a settled meaning in some other statute can help resolve an interpretive problem in an ambiguous statute. It is fair to note, however, that on this basis the Whole Code Rule, typically deemed a corollary of the Whole Act Rule, could in its entirety instead be classified as an extrinsic tool of interpretation.

3. Coherence with Other Law

Other statutes also can be used to enhance the overall coherence of the law, sometimes in fairly dramatic ways. In its more straightforward deployment, this is arguably an application of the Whole Code Rule, as for instance when the Supreme Court in *Casey* construed the scope of the phrase "reasonable attorney's fee" through reference to congressional usage of the same term in a number of other statutes. Similarly, when interpreting the 1938 Food, Drug, and Cosmetic Act in *FDA v. Brown & Williamson Tobacco Corp.*, 529 U.S. 120 (2000) (a case that will be featured in its own right in Chapter 36), the Court relied on a half-dozen other federal statutes to reject FDA's asserted authority to regulate tobacco products. The other statutes required disclosure of information about the health effects of tobacco products but did not ban them, a circumstance that the Court saw as incompatible with FDA's assertion of jurisdiction over tobacco products. And in a 1995 New York case, *Matter of Jacob*, 660 N.E.2d 397 (N.Y. 1995), which we will read in Chapter 27 as an example of a judicial response to changed legal and social conditions, the state court tried to harmonize several provisions of its family law in an effort to make the state's overall adoption scheme coherent.

C. Circumstances of Enactment

The next chapter will concentrate in earnest on interpretive guidance that can be derived from what we typically call "legislative history," or the contemporaneous records of the legislative process that produced a particular statute. As a final preliminary, however, it is worth distinguishing "legislative history" from "statutory history." Occasionally, the latter term is used quite narrowly, to describe only the way in which the enacted text itself, through amendment, may have changed over time. On the other hand, occasionally the phrase "statutory history" is also used much more broadly, to describe the entire context of a measure, including not only the range of legislative history materials generated by the enacting legislature, but also the broader circumstances surrounding a measure's enactment. This broader context—legal, social, economic—can often be relevant to an interpretive problem. In particular, both the narrower and the broader context at times can help the interpreter understand the "mischief" that the legislature sought to remedy.

For example, in construing an ambiguous provision of the Patient Protection and Affordable Care Act (ACA), the Supreme Court described in some detail the circumstances of the American health care system and health insurance marketplace, as we saw in Chapter 3. *See King v. Burwell,* 576 U.S. 988 (2015). At issue was whether federal subsidies available to individuals who purchased health insurance through an insurance exchange "established by the state" were also available to individuals who purchased insurance on a federal exchange. Central to the Court's resolution of the interpretive issue was its description and analysis of the economics of health care. The Court concluded that it was implausible that Congress had intended the terms of the subsidy provision to exclude the federal exchange and to cover only exchanges established by state governments, because that would render the ACA unworkable and could plunge "a State's individual insurance market into a death spiral."

Now consider this well-known and much earlier example:

Leo Sheep Co. v. United States
440 U.S. 668 (1979)

MR. JUSTICE REHNQUIST delivered the opinion of the Court.

This is one of those rare cases evoking episodes in this country's history that, if not forgotten, are remembered as dry facts and not as adventure. Admittedly the issue is mundane: Whether the Government has an implied easement to build a road across land that was originally granted to the Union Pacific Railroad under the Union Pacific Act of 1862—a grant that was part of a governmental scheme to subsidize the construction of the transcontinental railroad. But that issue is posed against the backdrop of a fascinating chapter in our history. As this Court noted in another case involving the Union Pacific Railroad, "courts, in construing a statute, may with propriety recur to the history of the times when it was passed; and this is frequently necessary, in order to ascertain the reason as well as the meaning of particular provisions in it." *United States v. Union Pacific R. Co.,*

91 U.S. 72, 79 (1875). In this spirit we relate the events underlying passage of the Union Pacific Act of 1862.

I

The early 19th century—from the Louisiana Purchase in 1803 to the Gadsden Purchase in 1853—saw the acquisition of the territory we now regard as the American West. During those years, however, the area remained a largely untapped resource, for the settlers on the eastern seaboard of the United States did not keep pace with the rapidly expanding western frontier. A vaguely delineated area forbiddingly referred to as the "Great American Desert" can be found on more than one map published before 1850, embracing much of the United States' territory west of the Missouri River. As late as 1860, for example, the entire population of the State of Nebraska was less than 30,000 persons, which represented one person for every five square miles of land area within the State.

With the discovery of gold at Sutter's Mill in California in 1848, the California gold rush began and with it a sharp increase in settlement of the West. Those in the East with visions of instant wealth, however, confronted the unenviable choice among an arduous 4-month overland trek, risking yellow fever on a 35-day voyage via the Isthmus of Panama, and a better than 4-month voyage around Cape Horn. They obviously yearned for another alternative, and interest focused on the transcontinental railroad.

The idea of a transcontinental railroad predated the California gold rush. From the time that Asa Whitney had proposed a relatively practical plan for its construction in 1844, it had, in the words of one of this century's leading historians of the era, "engaged the eager attention of promoters and politicians until dozens of schemes were in the air." The building of the railroad was not to be the unalloyed product of the free-enterprise system. There was indeed the inspiration of men like Thomas Durant and Leland Stanford and the perspiration of a generation of immigrants, but animating it all was the desire of the Federal Government that the West be settled. This desire was intensified by the need to provide a logistical link with California in the heat of the Civil War. That the venture was much too risky and much too expensive for private capital alone was evident in the years of fruitless exhortation; private investors would not move without tangible governmental inducement.

In the mid-19th century there was serious disagreement as to the forms that inducement could take. Mr. Justice Story, in his Commentaries on the

Constitution, described one extant school of thought which argued that "internal improvements," such as railroads, were not within the enumerated constitutional powers of Congress. Under such a theory, the direct subsidy of a transcontinental railroad was constitutionally suspect—an uneasiness aggravated by President Andrew Jackson's 1830 veto of a bill appropriating funds to construct a road from Maysville to Lexington within the state of Kentucky.

The response to this constitutional "gray" area, and source of political controversy, was the "checkerboard" land-grant scheme. The Union Pacific Act of 1862 granted public land to the Union Pacific Railroad for each mile of track that it laid. Land surrounding the railway right-of-way was divided into "checkerboard" blocks. Odd-numbered lots were granted to the Union Pacific; even-numbered lots were reserved by the Government. As a result, Union Pacific land in the area of the right-of-way was usually surrounded by public land, and vice versa. The historical explanation for this peculiar disposition is that it was apparently an attempt to disarm the "internal improvement" opponents by establishing a grant scheme with "demonstrable" benefits. As one historian notes in describing an 1827 federal land grant intended to facilitate private construction of a road between Columbus and Sandusky, Ohio:

> Though awkwardly stated, and not fully developed in the Act of 1827, this was the beginning of a practice to be followed in most future instances of granting land for the construction of specific internal improvements: donating alternate sections or one half of the land within a strip along the line of the project and reserving the other half for sale. . . . In later donations the price of the reserved sections was doubled so that it could be argued, as the Congressional Globe shows ad infinitum, that by giving half the land away and thereby making possible construction of the road, canal, or railroad, the government would recover from the reserved sections as much as it would have received from the whole.

In 1850 this technique was first explicitly employed for the subsidization of a railroad when the Illinois delegation in Congress, which included Stephen A. Douglas, secured the enactment of a bill that granted public lands to aid the construction of the Illinois Central Railroad. The Illinois Central and proposed connecting lines to the south were granted nearly three million acres along rights of way through Illinois, Mississippi, and Alabama, and by the end of 1854 the main line of the Illinois Central from Chicago to Cairo, Ill., had been put into operation. Before this line was constructed, public lands had gone begging at the Government's minimum price; within a few years after its completion, the railroad had disposed of more than one million acres and was rapidly selling more at prices far above those at which land had been originally offered by the Government.

The "internal improvements" theory was not the only obstacle to a transcontinental railroad. In 1853 Congress had appropriated moneys and authorized Secretary of War Jefferson Davis to undertake surveys of various proposed routes for a transcontinental railroad. Congress was badly split along sectional lines on the appropriate location of the route—so badly split that Stephen A. Douglas, now a Senator from Illinois, in 1854 suggested the construction of a northern, central, and southern route, each with connecting branches in the East. That proposal, however, did not break the impasse.

The necessary impetus was provided by the Civil War. * * * As is often the case, war spurs technological development, and Congress enacted the Union Pacific Act in May 1862. Perhaps not coincidentally, the Homestead Act was passed the same month.

The Union Pacific Act specified a route west from the 100th meridian, between a site in the Platte River Valley near the cities of Kearney and North Platte, Neb., to California. The original plan was for five eastern terminals located at various points on or near the Missouri River; but in fact Omaha was the only terminal built according to the plan.

The land grants made by the Union Pacific Act included all the odd-numbered lots within 10 miles on either side of the track. When the Union Pacific's original subscription drive for private investment proved a failure, the land grant was doubled by extending the checkerboard grants to 20 miles on either side of the track. Private investment was still sluggish, and construction did not begin until July 1865, three months after the cessation of Civil War hostilities. Thus began a race with the Central Pacific Railroad, which was laying track eastward from Sacramento, for the Government land grants which went with each mile of track laid. The race culminated in the driving of the golden spike at Promontory, Utah, on May 10, 1869.

II

This case is the modern legacy of these early grants. Petitioners, the Leo Sheep Co. and the Palm Livestock Co., are the Union Pacific Railroad's successors in fee to specific odd-numbered sections of land in Carbon County, Wyo. These sections lie to the east and south of the Seminoe Reservoir, an area that is used by the public for fishing and hunting. Because of the checkerboard configuration, it is physically impossible to enter the Seminoe Reservoir sector from this direction without some minimum physical intrusion upon private land. In the years immediately preceding this litigation, the Government had received complaints that private owners were denying access over their lands to the reservoir area or requiring the payment of access fees. After negotiation with these owners failed, the Government cleared a dirt road extending from a local county road to the reservoir across both public domain lands and fee lands of the Leo Sheep Co. It also erected signs inviting the public to use the road as a route to the reservoir.

Petitioners initiated this action pursuant to 28 U.S.C. 2409a to quiet title against the United States. The District Court granted petitioners' motion for summary judgment, but was reversed on appeal by the Court of Appeals for the Tenth Circuit. 570 F.2d 881. The latter court concluded that when Congress granted land to the Union Pacific Railroad, it implicitly reserved an easement to pass over the odd-numbered sections in order to reach the even-numbered sections that were held by the Government. Because this holding affects property rights in 150 million acres of land in the Western United States, we granted certiorari, and now reverse.

The Government does not claim that there is any express reservation of an easement in the Union Pacific Act that would authorize the construction of a public road on the Leo Sheep Co.'s property. Section 3 of the 1862 Act sets out a few specific reservations to the "checkerboard" grant. The grant was not to include land "sold, reserved, or otherwise disposed of by the United States," such as land to which there were homestead claims. 12 Stat. 492. Mineral lands were also excepted from the operation of the Act. Ibid. Given the existence of such explicit exceptions, this Court has in the past refused to add to this list by divining some "implicit" congressional intent. In *Missouri, K. & T. R. Co. v. Kansas Pacific R. Co.*, 97 U.S. 491, 497 (1878), for example, this Court in an opinion by Mr. Justice Field noted that the intent of Congress in making the Union Pacific grants was clear: "It was to aid in the construction of the road by a gift of lands along its route, without reservation of rights, except such as were specifically mentioned. . . ." The Court held that although a railroad right-of-way under the grant may not have been located until years after 1862, by the clear terms of the Act only claims established prior to 1862 overrode the railroad grant; conflicting claims arising after that time could not be given effect. To overcome the lack of support in the Act itself, the Government here argues that the implicit reservation of the asserted easement is established by "settled rules of property law" and by the Unlawful Inclosures of Public Lands Act of 1885.

Where a private landowner conveys to another individual a portion of his lands in a certain area and retains the rest, it is presumed at common law that the grantor has reserved an easement to pass over the granted property if such passage is necessary to reach the retained property. These rights-of-way are referred to as "easements by necessity." There are two problems with the Government's reliance on that notion in this case. First of all, whatever right of passage a private landowner might have, it is not at all clear that it would include the right to construct a road for public access to a recreational area. More importantly, the easement is not actually a matter of necessity in this case because the Government has the power of eminent domain. Jurisdictions have generally seen eminent domain and easements by necessity as alternative ways to effect the same result. For example, the State of Wyoming no longer recognizes the common-law easement by necessity in cases involving landlocked estates. It provides instead for a procedure whereby the landlocked owner can have an access route condemned on his behalf upon payment of the necessary compensation to the owner of the servient estate. For similar reasons other state courts have held that the "easement by necessity" doctrine is not available to the sovereign.

The applicability of the doctrine of easement by necessity in this case is, therefore, somewhat strained, and ultimately of little significance. The pertinent inquiry in this case is the intent of Congress when it granted land to the Union Pacific in 1862. The 1862 Act specifically listed reservations to the grant, and we do not find the tenuous relevance of the common-law doctrine of ways of necessity sufficient to overcome the inference prompted by the omission of any reference to the reserved right asserted by the Government in this case. It is possible that Congress gave the problem of access little thought; but it is at least as likely that the thought which was given focused on negotiation, reciprocity considerations, and the power of eminent domain as obvious devices for ameliorating disputes. So both as a matter of common-law doctrine and as a matter of construing congressional intent, we are unwilling to imply rights-of-way, with the substantial impact that such implication would have on property rights granted over 100 years ago, in the absence of a stronger case for their implication than the Government makes here.

The Government would have us decide this case on the basis of the familiar canon of construction that, when grants to federal lands are at issue, any doubts "are resolved for the Government, not against it." *Andrus v. Charlestone Stone Products Co.*, 436 U.S. 604, 617 (1978). But this Court long ago declined to apply this canon in its full vigor to grants under the railroad Acts. In 1885 this Court observed:

> The solution of [ownership] questions [involving the railroad grants] depends, of course, upon the construction given to the acts making the grants; and they are to receive such a construction as will carry out the intent of Congress, however difficult it might be to give full effect to the language used if the grants were by instruments of private conveyance. To ascertain that intent we must look to the condition of the country when the acts were passed, as well as to the purpose declared on their face, and read all parts of them together.

Winona & St. Peter R. Co. v. Barney, 113 U.S. 618, 625 (1885).

The Court harmonized the longstanding rule enunciated most recently in *Andrus* with the doctrine of *Winona* in *United States v. Denver & Rio Grande R. Co.*, 150 U.S. 1, 14 (1893), when it said:

> It is undoubtedly, as urged by the plaintiffs in error, the well-settled rule of this court that public grants are construed strictly against the grantees, but they are not to be so construed as to defeat the intent of the legislature, or to withhold what is given either expressly or by necessary or fair implication. . . .

> . . . When an act, operating as a general law, and manifesting clearly the intention of Congress to secure public advantages, or to subserve the public interests and welfare by means of benefits more or less valuable, offers to individuals or to corporations as

an inducement to undertake and accomplish great and expensive enterprises or works of a quasi public character in or through an immense and undeveloped public domain, such legislation stands upon a somewhat different footing from merely a private grant, and should receive at the hands of the court a more liberal construction in favor of the purposes for which it was enacted.

Thus, invocation of the canon reiterated in *Andrus* does little to advance the Government's position in this case. * * *

It is certainly true that the problem we confront today was not a matter of great concern during the time the 1862 railroad grants were made. The order of the day was the open range—barbed wire had not made its presence felt—and the type of incursions on private property necessary to reach public land was not such an interference that litigation would serve any motive other than spite. Congress obviously believed that when development came, it would occur in a parallel fashion on adjoining public and private lands and that the process of subdivision, organization of a polity, and the ordinary pressures of commercial and social intercourse would work itself into a pattern of access roads. * * * It is some testament to common sense that the present case is virtually unprecedented, and that in the 117 years since the grants were made, litigation over access questions generally has been rare.

> How does the Court's perception of the context of the enactment, described here, affect its interpretation of the statute?

Nonetheless, the present times are litigious ones and the 37th Congress did not anticipate our plight. Generations of land patents have issued without any express reservation of the right now claimed by the Government. Nor has a similar right been asserted before. When the Secretary of the Interior has discussed access rights, his discussion has been colored by the assumption that those rights had to be purchased. This Court has traditionally recognized the special need for certainty and predictability where land titles are concerned, and we are unwilling to upset settled expectations to accommodate some ill-defined power to construct public thoroughfares without compensation. The judgment of the Court of Appeals for the Tenth Circuit is * * * Reversed.

NOTES & QUESTIONS

1. The interpretive issue in this case derives not from ambiguity in a particular statutory phrase, but from a question about whether to construe the statute to contain some unstated (implicit) meaning. How does this change the interpretive task?

2. What interpretive tools can you find in use in the Court's opinion in *Leo Sheep*?

3. Is any particular consideration or circumstance most driving the Court's interpretation? If so, what and why?

4. Are any of the extrinsic canons covered in this chapter more helpful than others?

Test Your Understanding

To assess your understanding of the material in this chapter, click here to take a quiz.

25

Legislative History: Overview; Committee Reports

Key Concepts

- Legislative history
- "New Synthesis"
- Reports of standing committees
- Conference committee reports
- Individual member statements

Chapter Summary

The term "legislative history" usually refers to a variety of materials generated during the legislative process that are frequently used as extrinsic tools of statutory interpretation. Textualists generally reject the use of legislative history. Defenders argue, however, that these tools enable jurists most effectively to find and faithfully follow legislative intent. Further, many legislators increasingly expect jurists to rely on legislative materials when interpreting ambiguous statutes. Opponents counter that the legislature, as a collection of individuals, has no singular intent to be found except within the text of its enacted statutes. Even more, they argue that the large quantity of legislative utterances relating to a specific piece of enacted law may enable jurists, consciously or subconsciously, selectively to locate and rely on only those pieces of legislative history that support their preferred interpretation.

Ultimately, most interpreters at the federal level will turn to legislative history at least on occasion. Reports of legislative committees are frequently considered the most authoritative and reliable forms of legislative history. Because these reports are officially sanctioned by the legislative body, they are often trusted to express its collective intent. Within the committee report category, conference committee reports can be even more influential than reports of standing committees, because conference committees are the last step before a bill's final passage and represent the collective view of both chambers.

Using the common law as an extrinsic aid in interpretation is widely accepted under most interpretive theories, as is the use of other statutes, even if essentially as a variation on the "Whole Code Rule." In contrast, the use of what is typically called the "legislative history" of the measure in question is more contested. Most Textualists today will rarely rely on legislative history. Rather, the use of a measure's legislative history is largely the province of Purposivist and Intentionalist interpreters, precisely because these interpreters find these extrinsic tools to be potentially valuable in discerning and understanding the legislative purpose or intent behind an ambiguous provision.

A. Types of "Legislative History"

In the United States, the phrase "legislative history" has acquired a term-of-art status, referring to specific kinds of materials produced as part of a legislature's consideration of a particular measure. These materials typically include different versions of the measure that the legislature considered at various points; committee reports about the measure or different versions of the measure; proposed amendments to the measure; legislative branch and executive branch staff analyses; testimony at committee hearings; statements of individual legislators (whether offered on the floor of the legislative chamber during debate, or in letters to other legislators, or as press releases concerning the measure); executive branch messages about the measure; and, occassionally, press accounts about the legislature's consideration of the measure, particularly in some state circumstances.

The many types of legislative history materials (as that term is used in its narrow sense) are sometimes categorized by their reliability. By way of overview, the reliability of legislative history materials that the legislature itself has generated is usually categorized as follows: At the top of the hierarchy of reliability come committee reports, which are the official work product of a set of legislative actors to whom the legislature has officially delegated institutional authority to understand and recommend individual legislative proposals. Among committee reports, the reports of conference committees are generally seen as the most dependable sources of legislative history, both because they represent the views of both houses of the legislature and because the members of each body are asked to vote on them. After committee reports usually come individual statements of the sponsors of a measure, explaining its purpose or operation. A sponsor's responsibility to shepherd a measure is seen as diminishing the chances that the sponsor's statements will be disingenuous or hyperbolic. Following far behind sponsors' statements are the statements, opinions, or explanations made by other individual legislators in support of or opposition to a specific measure. Interpreters receive these materials much more skeptically (in fact refusing to consider them at all in earlier eras), as lacking much assurance that they are candid or accurate.

As for legislative history materials generated by non-legislators—such as executive branch analyses or witness testimony—interpreters may assess their reliability or persuasive power partly on where and when in the legislative process those materials became relevant. Although these materials may also merit evaluation for reliability on their own merits, it is more important to determine how much of a factor these materials were in the legislative process, for instance determining whether they were a central component of an important committee hearing, or instead were merely an exchange of views with one legislator. But in every category of legislative history, reliability is a somewhat fluid characteristic, often depending not only on the type of legislative history involved but also on case-specific indicia of whether the particular content was likely to be persuasive to, influential on, reflective of, or relied upon by a critical mass of legislators.

B.   Note About Objections to Using Legislative History

Before considering examples of how the primary categories of legislative history materials may factor in the interpretive enterprise, a reminder is in order about the primary arguments for and against the use of legislative history in interpretation. Jurists Antonin Scalia and Frank Easterbrook have been two of the most prominent critics of interpretation based on legislative history, arguing repeatedly and consistently that because legislative history is not enacted law, it is entirely irrelevant as an authoritative indicator of meaning. "To be 'a government of laws, not men' is to be governed by what the law says, not what the people who drafted the law intended." SCALIA & GARNER, *supra*, at 375; *see* ANTONIN SCALIA, A MATTER OF INTERPRETATION (1997); *In re Sinclair*, 870 F.2d 1340 (7th Cir. 1989) (Judge Easterbrook). This is the essence of the Textualists' philosophical objection to even inquiring about extrinsic indicia of "intent" as a touchstone of interpretation (though Textualists are open to using legislative history simply as an example of meaning, to the extent that, like dictionaries, legislative history may simply provide some evidence of the ways in which words are used).

In addition to the philosophical objection that legislative history itself is not law, another primary objection to using legislative history as an aid to interpretation is premised on a claim about the impact of doing so on the legislators themselves: that if interpreters rely on legislative intent, this might encourage legislators and their staff members to deliberately manipulate the legislative history by seeding it with content that might influence subsequent interpretation. This criticism often includes the refrain that a legislator who could not get a provision into the text itself (because the legislator was unable to persuade enough colleagues to agree to it) can instead simply plant the same idea somewhere in the legislative history. What is more, even staffers and lobbyists may similarly be able to influence the content of various types of legislative history much more easily than they could influence actual legislative text.

A third critique is that legislative history is far too easy for judges to manipulate: for many interpretive issues, the legislative history may provide material for a bevy of arguments on either side of the issue. This could be because of the difficulty of ascertaining one single intent for an institution composed of multiple actors, each with their own individual intentions. It could also be because that same multiplicity of legislators, in anticipation of the interpretive problem, have laced the record with arguments on either side. Thus, as Judge Harold Leventhal of the United States Court of Appeals for the District of Columbia Circuit is reported to have said, using legislative history can be like entering a cocktail party and looking over the heads of the crowd to pick out one's friends. *See* Patricia M. Wald, *Some Observations on the Use of Legislative History in the 1981 Supreme Court Term,* 68 Iowa L. Rev. 195, 214 (1983).

Yet defenders of the use of legislative history to identify statutory purpose or intent respond not only that the will of the enacting legislature is what ought to matter most to the interpretive enterprise, but also that courts have the capability to at least seek to identify that will. Although courts that undertake that search must be sensitive to the potential hazards of relying on extra-textual evidence of legislative purpose, they should not be precluded from a judicious exploration of all relevant evidence. Indeed, a balanced exploration, including a weighing of the reliability of each piece of evidence, is an activity to which the courts of our common-law tradition are well suited. This search is worth the candle, proponents argue, because in some cases legislative history may provide the best evidence of the legislature's intent. Furthermore, the legislature is always able to respond to an interpretation with which it disagrees by amending the statute.

Defenders of the use of legislative history in interpretation also argue that legislatures are constitutionally entitled to determine their internal operating procedures. If they decide to delegate much of their work to committees operating pursuant to internal rules and norms, then courts should respect that internal delegation. Thus, when committees, in compliance with these internal processes and expectations, report on their work to the full legislature, their reports are both authorized and, unless contrary evidence appears, appropriately presumed to be acceptable to the full legislature.

In addition, many legislatures increasingly seem to expect that legislative history materials will provide interpreters with additional interpretive context. Furthermore, the Constitution commands Congress to keep a "Journal of its Proceedings, and from time to time publish the same" (Article I, section 5), a requirement that some observers view as creating a justification for looking at records other than the statutory text to understand Congress's work.

Today, Textualist criticism of the use of legislative history is often credited with leading to what some commentators have called the New Synthesis, in which legislative history may have an important seat at the interpretive table but is secondary in importance to the statutory text and must be carefully scrutinized for its reliability. On its face, this is a rather unremarkable proposition, even if it represents a position perhaps at odds with some previous approaches to interpretation. Yet even this proposition may raise contested questions of interpretive approach.

One case that highlights these questions is *Exxon Mobile Corporation v. Allapattah Services, Inc.*, 545 U.S. 546 (2005), in which Justice Kennedy wrote a majority opinion discounting key evidence from a committee report as both irrelevant and unreliable, while Justice Stevens wrote a dissenting opinion arguing that the same evidence was relevant and reliable. Among other things, the majority opinion is notable for its claim that the committee report, which included language stating that "the legislative history was an attempt to correct [an] oversight" in the text of the statute itself, directly proved the Textualists' "worst fears" that legislative history would be used to circumvent the Article I lawmaking process. *Id.* at 570. Meanwhile, the dissenting opinion concluded that the very same portion of the report merely clarified that what was otherwise an ambiguous statutory provision should not be given an overly broad meaning. Justice Stevens' dissent is also noteworthy for this assertion: "I believe that we as judges are more, rather than less, constrained when we make ourselves accountable to *all* reliable evidence of legislative intent." *Id.* at 572 (Stevens, J., dissenting).

As the following discussion of each of the primary types of legislative history shows, this debate persists at both the federal and state levels (though at the state level it usually occurs regarding less developed legislative history materials), with most courts seeking to evaluate on a case-by-case basis which legislative history materials are relevant and reliable, but not until concluding that the text alone is ambiguous.

C. Examples of the Uses of Legislative Committee Reports

Legislative history materials are usually categorized based on where and when they have been generated in the legislative process. These categories, in turn, tend to have different degrees of reliability. The discussion to follow begins with two categories of committee reports because, as a general rule, they are seen as the most reliable kind of legislative history. But in any given interpretive problem, the reliability of each specific piece of legislative history must be considered on its own terms. Furthermore, as federal statutes have increasingly resulted from "unorthodox" lawmaking, these categories may have less significance. Yet they continue to form the backdrop for thinking about types of legislative history (and their significance may rebound at the federal level if at some point the country enters a post-gridlock era of more traditional congressional lawmaking).

1. Reports of Standing Committees

At the federal level, congressional committee reports are generally viewed as the most reliable sources of legislative history. They also are certainly the source most widely used by courts. In substantial part this is because of the process that produces these reports and the role that the reports play within the legislature. Committee reports historically have been the result of a collaborative, bipartisan, regularized process designed to provide the entire legislature with the benefit of the committee's experience and expertise. As previously discussed, Congress has made a deliberate decision to rely on subject-matter committees to increase the efficiency of its work. In turn, each House of Congress expects that its committees will report back to the full body with a reliable accounting of its thorough consideration of whatever measures it has been assigned. Formal written committee reports are the primary means by which committees fulfill this responsibility.

In many instances, members pay more attention to congressional committee reports than to the language of a bill itself. Although reports generally include the text of the bill, they also include other more user-friendly sections intended to assist legislators (and their staff) to digest and understand each measure. These sections include a summary of the bill, a section-by-section analysis, and the written statements of individual members who have opted to add their own concurring or dissenting views to the report of the committee majority. Reports must be distributed to the full membership at least 48 hours in advance of the floor debate, the body's formal consideration of the measure.

Throughout Justice Scalia's tenure on the Supreme Court, he consistently raised questions concerning the appropriateness of relying on legislative committee reports, in addition to objecting to the use of legislative history generally. But to some degree or another, his Supreme Court colleagues and successors have continued to deploy committee reports in support of their interpretive conclusions, and the practice is widespread throughout the federal judiciary. The practice is also widespread at the state level, although many state legislatures do not regularly produce published committee reports like the reports that congressional committees produce. That has been changing, however, as more and more state legislatures adjust their processes and practices to make more materials available. *See* WILLIAM H. MANZ, GUIDE TO STATE LEGISLATION, LEGISLATIVE HISTORY, AND ADMINISTRATIVE MATERIALS (7th ed. 2008).

At the federal level, committee reports are often a primary means by which members of Congress communicate with each other. They therefore are obviously relevant to an interpreter who seeks to discern congressional intent. But how much familiarity with the details of a committee report is it realistic to expect legislators to have? Consider the following problem.

DIY
What Is "a Reasonable Attorney's Fee"

The Civil Rights Attorney's Fees Awards Act of 1976, as set forth in 42 U.S.C. § 1988, states:

. . . In any action or proceeding to enforce a provision of sections 1981, 1982, 1983, 1985, and 1986 of [title 42 of the U.S. Code], title IX of Public Law 92–318, or title VI of the Civil Rights Act of 1964, the court, in its discretion, may allow the prevailing party, other than the United States, a reasonable attorney's fee as part of the costs.

> Yes, this is the same federal statute at issue in the *West Virginia University Hospitals v. Casey* case that we considered at the end of Part V.   **FYI**

Under this statute, think first for a moment about what should constitute a reasonable attorney's fee generally, and how a court would calculate it. After giving that a moment's thought, next consider how a court should decide what is a reasonable attorney's fee for a prevailing party who has retained a lawyer using a contingency fee agreement? In particular, can the fee amount recovered under section 1988 be greater than the fee calculated under the contingency agreement? If a congressional report concerning section 1988 addressed this issue, would you want to consider it?

The Supreme Court confronted this interpretive issue in the case that follows. As background for that case, it may help to know that the case makes repeated references to a circuit court decision in *Johnson v. Georgia Highway Express, Inc.*, 488 F.2d 714 (5th Cir. 1974), in which the Fifth Circuit identified twelve factors for determining reasonable attorney's fee awards under a related provision, section 706(k) of Title VII of the Civil Rights Act of 1964, 42 U.S.C. § 2000e–5(k). Those twelve factors were: (1) the time and labor required; (2) the novelty and difficulty of the questions; (3) the skill requisite to perform the legal service properly; (4) the preclusion of other employment by the attorney due to acceptance of the case; (5) the customary fee; (6) whether the fee is fixed or contingent; (7) time limitations imposed by the client or the circumstances; (8) the amount involved and the results obtained; (9) the experience, reputation, and ability of the attorneys; (10) the "undesirability" of the case; (11) the nature and length of the professional relationship with the client; and (12) awards in similar cases.

Blanchard v. Bergeron
489 U.S. 87 (1989)

JUSTICE WHITE delivered the opinion of the Court.

The issue before us is whether an attorney's fee allowed under 42 U.S.C. § 1988 is limited to the amount provided in a contingent-fee arrangement entered into by a plaintiff and his counsel.

I

Petitioner Arthur J. Blanchard brought suit in the United States District Court for the Western District of Louisiana alleging violations of his civil rights under 42 U.S.C. § 1983. Blanchard asserted that he was beaten by Sheriff's Deputy James Bergeron while he was in Oudrey's Odyssey Lounge. Blanchard brought his claim against the deputy, the sheriff, and the St. Martin Parish Sheriff's Department. He also joined with his civil rights claim a state-law negligence claim against the above defendants and against the owners and a manager of the lounge and the lounge itself. The case was tried and a jury awarded Blanchard compensatory damages in the amount of $5,000 and punitive damages in the amount of $5,000 on his

1983 claim. Under the provisions of 42 U.S.C. § 1988, which permit the award of attorney's fees to a prevailing party in certain federal civil rights actions, Blanchard sought attorney's fees and costs totaling more than $40,000. The District Court, after reviewing the billing and cost records furnished by counsel, awarded $7,500 in attorney's fees and $886.92 for costs and expenses.

Petitioner appealed this award to the Court of Appeals for the Fifth Circuit, seeking to increase the award. The Court of Appeals, however, reduced the award because petitioner had entered into a contingent-fee arrangement with his lawyer, under which the attorney was to receive 40% of any damages awarded should petitioner prevail in his suit. While recognizing that other Circuits had different views, the court held that it was bound by its prior decision in *Johnson v. Georgia Highway Express, Inc.*, 488 F.2d 714, 718 (1974), to rule that the contingency-fee agreement "serves as a cap on the amount of attorney's fee to be awarded." 831 F.2d 563, 564 (1987). The court further found that hours billed for the time of law clerks and paralegals were not compensable since they would be included within the contingency fee. *Ibid.* Accordingly, the court limited the fee award to 40% of the $10,000 damages award—$4,000.

Because other Courts of Appeals have concluded that a 1988 fee award should not be limited by a contingent-fee agreement between the attorney and his client, we granted certiorari to resolve the conflict, 487 U.S. 1217 (1988). We now reverse.

II

Section 1988 provides that the court, "in its discretion, may allow . . . a reasonable attorney's fee. . . ." The section does not provide a specific definition of "reasonable" fee, and the question is whether the award must be limited to the amount provided in a contingent-fee agreement. The legislative history of the Act is instructive insofar as it tells us: "In computing the fee, counsel for prevailing parties should be paid, as is traditional with attorneys compensated by a fee-paying client, 'for all time reasonably expended on a matter.' " S. Rep. No. 94–1011, p. 6 (1976) (citing *Davis v. County of Los Angeles*, 8 EPD § 9444 (CD Cal. 1974); and *Stanford Daily v. Zurcher*, 64 F. R. D. 680, 684 (ND Cal. 1974)).

In many past cases considering the award of attorney's fees under 1988, we have turned our attention to *Johnson v. Georgia Highway Express, Inc.*, a case decided before the enactment of the Civil Rights Attorney's Fee Award Act of 1976. As we stated in *Hensley v. Eckerhart*, 461 U.S. 424, 429–431 (1983), *Johnson* provides guidance to Congress' intent because both the House and Senate Reports refer to the 12 factors set forth in *Johnson* for assessing the reasonableness of an attorney's fee award. The Senate Report, in particular, refers to three District Court decisions that "correctly applied" the 12 factors laid out in *Johnson*.

[In a footnote here, the Court then quoted this portion of the Senate Report: "The appropriate standards, see *Johnson v. Georgia Highway Express*, 488 F.2d 714 (5th Cir. 1974), are correctly applied in such cases as *Stanford Daily v. Zurcher*, 64 F. R. D. 680 (N. D. Cal. 1974); *Davis v. County of Los Angeles*, 8 E. P. D. § 9444 (C. D. Cal. 1974); and *Swann v. Charlotte-Mecklenburg Board of Education*, 66 F. R. D. 483 (W. D. N.C. 1975). These cases have resulted in fees which are adequate to attract competent counsel, but which do not produce windfalls to attorneys." S. Rep. No. 94–1011, p. 6 (1976).]

In the course of its discussion of the factors to be considered by a court in awarding attorney's fees, the *Johnson* court dealt with fee arrangements:

> Whether or not [a litigant] agreed to pay a fee and in what amount is not decisive. Conceivably, a litigant might agree to pay his counsel a fixed dollar fee. This might be even more than the fee eventually allowed by the court. Or he might agree to pay his lawyer a percentage contingent fee that would be greater than the fee the court might ultimately set. Such arrangements should not determine the court's decision. The criterion for the court is not what the parties agree but what is reasonable.

488 F.2d, at 718.

Yet in the next sentence, *Johnson* says "In no event, however, should the litigant be awarded a fee greater than he is contractually bound to pay, if indeed the attorneys have contracted as to amount." 488 F.2d, at 718. This latter statement, never disowned in the Circuit, was the basis for the decision below. But we doubt that Congress embraced this aspect of *Johnson*, for it pointed to the three District Court cases in which the factors are "correctly applied." Those cases clarify that the fee arrangement is but a single factor and not determinative. In *Stanford Daily v. Zurcher*, for example, the District Court considered a contingent-fee arrangement to be a factor, but not dispositive, in the calculation of a fee award. In *Davis v. County of Los Angeles*, supra, the court permitted a fee award to counsel in a public interest firm which otherwise would have been entitled to no fee. Finally, in *Swann v. Charlotte-Mecklenburg Board of Education,* 66 F. R. D. 483 (WDNC 1975), the court stated that reasonable fees should be granted regardless of the individual plaintiff's fee obligations. *Johnson's* "list of 12" thus provides a useful catalog of the many factors to be considered in assessing the reasonableness of an award of attorney's fees; but the one factor at issue here, the attorney's private fee arrangement, standing alone, is not dispositive.

The *Johnson* contingency-fee factor is simply that, a factor. The presence of a pre-existing fee agreement may aid in determining reasonableness. " 'The fee quoted to the client or the percentage of the recovery agreed to is helpful in demonstrating the attorney's fee expectations when he accepted the case.' " *Pennsylvania v. Delaware Valley Citizens' Council for Clean Air,* 483 U.S. 711, 723 (1987) quoting *Johnson,* 488 F.2d, at 718. But as we see it, a contingent-fee contract does not impose an automatic ceiling on an award of attorney's fees, and to hold otherwise would be inconsistent with the statute and its policy and purpose.

As we understand 1988's provision for allowing a "reasonable attorney's fee," it contemplates reasonable compensation, in light of all of the circumstances, for the time and effort expended by the attorney for the prevailing plaintiff, no more and no less. Should a fee agreement provide less than a reasonable fee calculated in this manner, the defendant should nevertheless be required to pay the higher amount. The defendant is not, however, required to pay the amount called for in a contingent-fee contract if it is more than a reasonable fee calculated in the usual way. It is true that the purpose of 1988 was to make sure that competent counsel was available to civil rights plaintiffs, and it is of course arguable that if a plaintiff is able to secure an attorney on the basis of a contingent or other fee agreement, the purpose of the statute is served if the plaintiff is bound by his contract. On that basis, however, the plaintiff should recover nothing from the defendant, which would be plainly contrary to the statute. And Congress implemented its purpose by broadly requiring all defendants to pay a reasonable fee to all prevailing plaintiffs, if ordered to do so by the court. Thus it is that a plaintiff's recovery will not be reduced by what he must pay his counsel. Plaintiffs who can afford to hire their own lawyers, as well as impecunious litigants, may take advantage of this provision. And where there are lawyers or organizations that will take a plaintiff's case without compensation, that fact does not bar the award of a reasonable fee. All of this is consistent with and reflects our decisions in cases involving court-awarded attorney's fees.

Hensley v. Eckerhart, 461 U.S. 424 (1983), directed lower courts to make an initial estimate of reasonable attorney's fees by applying prevailing billing rates to the hours reasonably expended on successful claims. And we have said repeatedly that "[t]he initial estimate of a reasonable attorney's fee is properly calculated by multiplying the number of hours reasonably expended on the litigation times a reasonable hourly rate." *Blum v. Stenson*, 465 U.S. 886, 888 (1984). The courts may then adjust this lodestar calculation by other factors. We have never suggested that a different approach is to be followed in cases where the prevailing party and his (or her) attorney have executed a contingent-fee agreement. To the contrary, in *Hensley* and in subsequent cases, we have adopted the lodestar approach as the centerpiece of attorney's fee awards. The *Johnson* factors may be relevant in adjusting the lodestar amount, but no one factor is a substitute for multiplying reasonable billing rates by a reasonable estimation of the number of hours expended on the litigation. * * *

It is clear that Congress "intended that the amount of fees awarded * * * be governed by the same standards which prevail in other types of equally complex Federal litigation * * * and not be reduced because the rights involved may be nonpecuniary in nature." S. Rep. No. 94–1011, at 6. "The purpose of 1988 is to ensure 'effective access to the judicial process' for persons with civil rights grievances." *Hensley*, supra, at 429, quoting H. R. Rep. No. 94–1558, p. 1 (1976). Even when considering the award of attorney's fees under the Clean Air Act, 42 U.S.C. 7401, the Court has applied the 1988 approach, stating: "A strong presumption that the lodestar figure—the product of reasonable hours times a reasonable rate—represents a 'reasonable fee' is wholly consistent with the rationale behind the usual fee-shifting statute. . . ." *Pennsylvania v. Delaware Valley Citizens' Council for Clean Air*, 478 U.S. 546, 565 (1986).

If a contingent-fee agreement were to govern as a strict limitation on the award of attorney's fees, an undesirable emphasis might be placed on the importance of the recovery of damages in civil rights litigation. The intention of Congress was to encourage successful civil rights litigation, not to create a special incentive to prove damages and shortchange efforts to seek effective injunctive or declaratory relief. Affirming the decision below would create an artificial dis-incentive for an attorney who enters into a contingent-fee agreement, unsure of whether his client's claim sounded in state tort law or in federal civil rights, from fully exploring all possible avenues of relief. Section 1988 makes no distinction between actions for damages and suits for equitable relief. Congress has elected to encourage meritorious civil rights claims because of the benefits of such litigation for the named plaintiff and for society at large, irrespective of whether the action seeks monetary damages.

It should also be noted that we have not accepted the contention that fee awards in 1983 damages cases should be modeled upon the contingent-fee arrangements used in personal injury litigation. "[W]e reject the notion that a civil rights action for damages constitutes nothing more than a private tort suit benefiting only the individual plaintiffs whose rights were violated. Unlike most private tort litigants, a civil rights plaintiff seeks to vindicate important civil and constitutional rights that cannot be valued solely in monetary terms." *Riverside v. Rivera*, 477 U.S. 561, 574 (1986).

Respondent cautions us that refusing to limit recovery to the amount of the contingency agreement will result in a "windfall" to attorneys who accept 1983 actions. Yet the very nature of recovery under 1988 is designed to prevent any such "windfall." Fee awards are to be reasonable, reasonable as to billing rates and reasonable as to the number of hours spent in advancing the successful claims. Accordingly, fee awards, properly calculated, by definition will represent the reasonable worth of the services rendered in vindication of a plaintiff's civil rights claim. It is central to the awarding of attorney's fees under 1988 that the district court judge, in his or her good judgment, make the assessment of what is a reasonable fee under the circumstances of the case. The trial judge should not be limited by the contractual fee agreement between plaintiff and counsel.

The contingent-fee model, premised on the award to an attorney of an amount representing a percentage of the damages, is thus inappropriate for the determination of fees under 1988. The attorney's fee provided for in a contingent-fee agreement is not a ceiling upon the fees recoverable under 1988. Accordingly, we reverse and remand.

* * *

JUSTICE SCALIA, concurring in part and concurring in the judgment.

I concur in the judgment and join the opinion of the Court except that portion which rests upon detailed analysis of the Fifth Circuit's opinion in *Johnson v. Georgia Highway Express, Inc.*, 488 F.2d 714 (1974), and the District Court decisions in *Swann v. Charlotte-Mecklenburg Board of Education*, 66 F. R. D. 483 (WDNC 1975); *Stanford Daily v. Zurcher*, 64 F. R. D. 680 (ND Cal. 1974); and *Davis v. County of Los Angeles*, 8 EPD § 9444 (CD Cal. 1974). The Court carefully examines those opinions, separating holding from dictum, much as a lower court would study our opinions in order to be faithful to our guidance. The justification for this role reversal is that the Senate and House Committee Reports on the Civil Rights Attorney's Fees Awards Act of 1976 referred approvingly to *Johnson*, and the Senate Report alone referred to the three District Court opinions as having "correctly applied" *Johnson*. The Court resolves the difficulty that *Johnson* contradicts the three District Court opinions on the precise point at issue here by concluding in effect that the analysis in *Johnson* was dictum, whereas in the three District Court opinions it was a holding. Despite the fact that the House Report referred only to *Johnson*, and made no mention of the District Court cases, the Court "doubt[s] that Congress embraced this aspect of *Johnson*, for it pointed to the three District Court cases in which the factors are 'correctly applied.' "

In my view Congress did no such thing. Congress is elected to enact statutes rather than point to cases, and its Members have better uses for their time than poring over District Court opinions. That the Court should refer to the citation of three District Court cases in a document issued by a single committee of a single house as the action of Congress displays the level of unreality that our unrestrained use of legislative history has attained. I am confident that only a small proportion of the Members of Congress read either one of the Committee Reports in question, even if (as is not always the case) the Reports happened to have been published before the vote; that very few of those who did read them set off for the nearest law library to check out what was actually said in the four cases at issue (or in the more than 50 other cases cited by the House and Senate Reports); and that no Member of Congress came to the judgment that the District Court cases would trump *Johnson* on the point at issue here because the latter was dictum. As anyone familiar with modern-day drafting of congressional committee reports is well aware, the references to the cases were inserted, at best by a committee staff member on his or her own initiative, and at worst by a committee staff member at the suggestion of a lawyer-lobbyist; and the purpose of those references was not primarily to inform the Members of Congress what the bill meant (for that end *Johnson* would not merely have been cited, but its 12 factors would have been described, which they were not), but rather to influence judicial construction. What a heady feeling it must be for a young staffer, to know that his or her citation of obscure district court cases can transform them into the law of the land, thereafter dutifully to be observed by the Supreme Court itself.

I decline to participate in this process. It is neither compatible with our judicial responsibility of assuring reasoned, consistent, and effective application of the statutes of the United States, nor conducive to a genuine effectuation of congressional intent, to give legislative force to each snippet of analysis, and even every case citation, in committee reports that are increasingly unreliable evidence of what the voting Members of Congress actually had in mind. By treating *Johnson* and the District Court trilogy as fully authoritative, the Court today expands what I regard as our cases' excessive preoccupation with them—and with the 12-factor *Johnson* analysis in particular. * * * Except for the few passages to which I object, today's opinion admirably follows our more recent approach of seeking to develop an interpretation of the statute that is reasonable, consistent, and faithful to its apparent purpose, rather than to achieve obedient adherence to cases cited in the committee reports. I therefore join the balance of the opinion.

NOTES & QUESTIONS

1. Throughout his service on the Court, Justice Scalia maintained his staunch opposition to reliance on legislative history, including committee reports. Largely as a result of his influence, most observers have detected a decline in the Supreme Court's reliance on legislative history materials, and committee reports in particular. Nevertheless, many judges have continued to cite legislative history for evidence of congressional intent. In general, reports of congressional committees remain widely respected and frequently used in resolving interpretive issues at the federal level. And notwithstanding the refusal of some judges to cite legislative history in their opinions, lawyers litigating cases need to continue to cite (and to be able to make compelling arguments from) relevant legislative history.

2. What do you make of the Court's use of congressional reports here? Should it matter whether a member's staff, rather than a member directly, reads the reports?

3. We will see another example of the extensive use of congressional committee reports in Part III of the Supreme Court's decision in *Sweet Home Chapter v. Babbitt*, which we have saved for the last chapter of the book.

2. Conference Committee Reports

Reports of congressional conference committees often have an even more exalted status than reports of each chamber's standing committees, for two central reasons: (1) they are the joint product of both houses of Congress working together; and (2) they are written at the final stage of the legislative process and therefore describe the bill at the very moment when its text is no longer subject to further amendment. The purpose of a conference committee is to work out differences between the two chambers after each has passed its own version of a bill. Usually, some points of disagreement remain to be resolved as part of achieving the agreement of both Houses on precisely the same text. Although conference committees are *ad hoc* committees, rather than standing committees, their members are especially trusted. They are appointed by the leaders of both major political parties in both chambers because of their extra familiarity with the specific subject of the conference committee and their ability to represent their respective house and party effectively in resolving remaining differences as a measure nears completion. Conference committees, by definition, also are joint committees of both Houses, and therefore speak on behalf of the Congress as a whole rather than just the House or the Senate. Furthermore, once the conference committee completes its work and refers its report to both chambers, each chamber then approves the same report if the measure is to become law. The content of conference committee reports thus can be especially probative in ascertaining meaning. The most noticeable weakness in conference reports is that they address only the points of disagreement, so any aspects of a measure on which the two chambers were already in agreement prior to the conference are not likely to receive much elucidation in the conference report.

> **FYI** We first encountered Judge Easterbrook in Chapter 17 when we read his *Marshall* opinion. What else can you glean about his judicial philosophy from his *In re Sinclair* opinion here?

The following circuit court case, again authored by Seventh Circuit Judge Frank Easterbrook, involves an interesting rejection of the apparent implication of a conference committee report.

In re Sinclair
870 F.2d 1340 (7th Cir. 1989)

EASTERBROOK, CIRCUIT JUDGE.

This case presents a conflict between a statute and its legislative history. The Sinclairs, who have a family farm, filed a bankruptcy petition in April 1985 under Chapter 11 of the Bankruptcy Act of 1978. In October 1986 Congress added Chapter 12, providing benefits for farmers, and the Sinclairs asked the bankruptcy court to convert their case from Chapter 11 to Chapter 12. The bankruptcy judge declined, and the district court affirmed. Each relied on Sec. 302(c)(1) of the Bankruptcy Judges, United States Trustees, and Family Farmer Bankruptcy Act of 1986, Pub. L. 99–554, 100 Stat. 3088:

> The amendments made by subtitle B of title II shall not apply with respect to cases commenced under title 11 of the United States Code before the effective date of this Act.

The Sinclairs rely on the report of the Conference Committee, which inserted Sec. 302(c)(1) into the bill:

> It is not intended that there be routine conversion of Chapter 11 and 13 cases, pending at the time of enactment, to Chapter 12. Instead, it is expected that courts will exercise their sound discretion in each case, in allowing conversions only where it is equitable to do so.

> Chief among the factors the court should consider is whether there is a substantial likelihood of successful reorganization under Chapter 12.

> Courts should also carefully scrutinize the actions already taken in pending cases in deciding whether, in their equitable discretion, to allow conversion. For example, the court may consider whether the petition was recently filed in another chapter with no further action taken. Such a case may warrant conversion to the new chapter. On the other hand, there may be cases where a reorganization plan has already been filed or confirmed. In cases where the parties have substantially relied on current law, availability [sic] to convert to the new chapter should be limited.

H.R. Conf. Rep. 99-958, 99th Cong., 2d Sess. 48–49 (1986), U.S.Code Cong. & Admin.News 1986, pp. 5227, 5249–5250. The statute says conversion is impossible; the report says that conversion is possible and describes the circumstances under which it should occur.

Which prevails in the event of conflict, the statute or its legislative history? The statute was enacted, the report just the staff's explanation. Congress votes on the text of the bill, and the President signed that text. Committee reports help courts understand the law, but this report contradicts rather than explains the text. So the statute must prevail. Such is the holding of *In re Erickson Partnership*, 856 F.2d 1068 (8th Cir. 1988).

Yet the advice from the Supreme Court about how to deal with our situation seems scarcely more harmonious than the advice from the legislature. The reports teem with statements such as: "When we find the terms of a statute unambiguous, judicial inquiry is complete", *Rubin v. United States*, 449 U.S. 424, 430 (1981). Less frequently, yet with equal conviction, the Court writes: "When aid to the construction of the meaning of words, as used in the statute, is available, there certainly can be no 'rule of law' which forbids its use, however clear the words may appear on 'superficial examination.'" *United States v. American Trucking Associations, Inc.*, 310 U.S. 534, 543–44 (1940). Some cases boldly stake out a middle ground, saying, for example: "only the most extraordinary showing of contrary intentions from [the legislative history] would justify a limitation on the 'plain meaning' of the statutory language." *Garcia v. United States*, 469 U.S. 70, 75 (1984). This implies that once in a blue moon the legislative history trumps the statute (as opposed to affording a basis for its interpretation) but does not help locate such strange astronomical phenomena. These lines of cases have coexisted for a century, and many cases contain statements associated with two or even all three of them, not recognizing the tension.

> Does the structure of this paragraph seem familiar? Doesn't it resemble Llewelyn's "thrust and parry" number 12 that we studied in Chapter 23? Here, the Conference Report would serve as evidence of what Llewelyn referred to as Congress's "manifest purpose." Notice how Judge Easterbrook reconciles the "tension" in the next paragraph.

What's a court to do? The answer lies in distinguishing among uses of legislative history. An unadorned "plain meaning" approach to interpretation supposes that words have meanings divorced from their contexts—linguistic, structural, functional, social, historical. Language is a process of communication that works only when authors and readers share a set of rules and meanings. What "clearly" means one thing to a reader unacquainted with the circumstances of the utterance—including social conventions prevailing at the time of drafting—may mean something else to a reader with a different background. Legislation speaks across the

> Take note of the clarity of Judge Easterbrook's ensuing discussion here about the use(s) of legislative history.

decades, during which legal institutions and linguistic conventions change. To decode words one must frequently reconstruct the legal and political culture of the drafters. Legislative history may be invaluable in revealing the setting of the enactment and the assumptions its authors entertained about how their words would be understood. It may show, too, that words with a denotation "clear" to an outsider are terms of art, with an equally "clear" but different meaning to an insider. It may show too that the words leave gaps, for short phrases cannot address all human experience; understood in context, the words may leave to the executive and judicial branches the task of adding flesh to bones. These we take to be the points of cases such as *American Trucking* holding that judges may learn from the legislative history even when the text is "clear". Clarity depends on context, which legislative history may illuminate. The process is objective; the search is not for the contents of the authors' heads but for the rules of language they used.

Quite different is the claim that legislative intent is the basis of interpretation, that the text of the law is simply evidence of the real rule. In such a regimen legislative history is not a way to understand the text but is a more authentic, because more proximate, expression of legislators' will. One may say in reply that legislative history is a poor guide to legislators' intent because it is written by the staff rather than by members of Congress, because it is often losers' history ("If you can't get your proposal into the bill, at least write the legislative history to make it look as if you'd prevailed"), because it becomes a crutch ("There's no need for us to vote on the amendment if we can write a little legislative history"), because it complicates the task of execution and obedience (neither judges nor those whose conduct is supposed to be influenced by the law can know what to do without delving into legislative recesses, a costly and uncertain process). Often there is so much legislative history that a court can manipulate the meaning of a law by choosing which snippets to emphasize and by putting hypothetical questions—questions to be answered by inferences from speeches rather than by reference to the text, so that great discretion devolves on the (judicial) questioner. Sponsors of opinion polls know that a small change in the text of a question can lead to large differences in the answer. Legislative history offers willful judges an opportunity to pose questions and devise answers, with predictable divergence in results. These and related concerns have led

How might you counter this argument?

to skepticism about using legislative history to find legislative intent. E.g., *Blanchard v. Bergeron*, ___ U.S. ___, 109 S. Ct. 939, 946–47 (1989) (SCA-

LIA, J., concurring). These cautionary notes are well taken, but even if none were salient there would still be a hurdle to the sort of argument pressed in our case.

Statutes are law, not evidence of law. References to "intent" in judicial opinions do not imply that legislators' motives and beliefs, as opposed to their public acts, establish the norms to which all others must conform. "Original meaning" rather than "intent" frequently captures the interpretive task more precisely, reminding us that it is the work of the political branches (the "meaning") rather than of the courts that matters, and that their work acquires its meaning when enacted ("originally"). Revisionist history may be revelatory; revisionist judging is simply unfaithful to the enterprise. Justice Holmes made the point when denouncing a claim that judges should give weight to the intent of a document's authors:

> [A statute] does not disclose one meaning conclusively according to the laws of language. Thereupon we ask, not what this man meant, but what those words would mean in the mouth of a normal speaker of English, using them in the circumstances in which they were used. . . . But the normal speaker of English is merely a special variety, a literary form, so to speak, of our old friend the prudent man. He is external to the particular writer, and a reference to him as the criterion is simply another instance of the externality of the law. . . . We do not inquire what the legislature meant; we ask only what the statute means.

Oliver Wendell Holmes, *The Theory of Legal Interpretation*, 12 HARV. L. REV. 417, 417–19 (1899), reprinted in COLLECTED LEGAL PAPERS 204, 207 (1920). Or as Judge Friendly put things in a variation on Holmes's theme, a court must search for "what Congress meant by what it said, rather than for what it meant simpliciter." Henry J. Friendly, *Mr. Justice Frankfurter and the Reading of Statutes*, in BENCHMARKS 218–19 (1967).

An opinion poll revealing the wishes of Congress would not translate to legal rules. Desires become rules only after clearing procedural hurdles, designed to encourage deliberation and expose proposals (and arguments) to public view and recorded vote. Resort to "intent" as a device to short-circuit these has no more force than the opinion poll—less, because the legislative history is written by the staff of a single committee and not subject to a vote or veto. The Constitution establishes a complex of procedures, including presidential approval (or support by two-thirds of each house). It would demean the constitutionally prescribed method of legislating to suppose that its elaborate apparatus for deliberation on, amending, and approving a text is just a way to create some evidence about the law, while the real source of legal rules is the mental processes of legislators. We know from *INS v. Chadha*, 462 U.S. 919 (1983), that the express disapproval of one house of Congress cannot change the law, largely because it removes the President from the process; it would therefore be surprising if "intents" subject to neither vote nor veto could be sources of law.

If Congress enacts a *parens patriae* statute "intending" thereby to allow states to represent indirect purchasers of overpriced goods, that belief about the effects of the enactment does not become law. *Illinois Brick Co. v. Illinois*, 431 U.S. 720, 733–34 n. 14 (1977). If Congress were to reduce the rate of taxation on capital gains, "intending" that this stimulate economic growth and so yield more in tax revenue, the meaning of the law would be only that rates go down, not that revenue go up—a judge could not later rearrange rates to achieve the "intent" with respect to federal coffers. On the other hand, doubt about the meaning of a term found in the statute could well be resolved by harmonizing that provision with the structure of the rest of the law, understood in light of a contemporaneous explanation. In this sense legislative intent is a vital source of meaning even though it does not trump the text.

Concern about the source of law—is the statute law, or is it just evidence of the law?—lies behind statements such as: "[T]he language being plain, and not leading to absurd or wholly impracticable consequences, it is the sole evidence of the ultimate legislative intent." *Caminetti*, 242 U.S. at 490, 37 S. Ct. at 196. To treat the text as conclusive evidence of law is to treat it as law—which under the constitutional structure it is. Legislative history then may help a court discover but may not change the original meaning. *Pierce v. Underwood*, 487 U.S. 552 (1988). The "plain meaning" rule of *Caminetti* rests not on a silly belief that texts have timeless meanings divorced from their many contexts, not on the assumption that what is plain to one reader must be clear to any other (and identical to the plan of the writer), but on the constitutional allocation of powers. The political branches adopt texts through prescribed procedures; what ensues is the law. Legislative history may show the meaning of the texts—may show, indeed, that a text "plain" at first reading has a strikingly different meaning—but may not be used to show an "intent" at variance with the meaning of the text. *Caminetti* and *American Trucking* can comfortably coexist when so understood. This approach also supplies the underpinning for the belief that legislative history is "only admissible to solve doubt and not to create it", *Wisconsin R.R.*

Comm'n, 257 U.S. at 589, which punctuates the U.S. Reports. Legislative history helps us learn what Congress meant by what it said, but it is not a source of legal rules competing with those found in the U.S. Code.

Ours is now an easy case. Section 302(c)(1) of the statute has an ascertainable meaning, a meaning not absurd or inconsistent with the structure of the remaining provisions. It says that Chapter 11 cases pending on the date the law went into force may not be converted to Chapter 12. No legislative history suggests any other meaning. The committee report suggests, at best, a different intent. Perhaps a reader could infer that the committee planned to allow conversion but mistakenly voted for a different text. So two members of the committee have said since, calling Sec. 302(c)(1) an oversight.

FYI Judge Easterbrook now calls this an "easy case." But wasn't it always this easy, even before his extended discussion of interpretive doctrine, at least as his opinion has framed the issue? Unfortunately, the way the case was briefed and argued may have made it too easy: the analysis here entirely omits the existence of another provision within the statute itself (and not just the committee report) that potentially conflicts with section 302. The second Note following this case excerpt invites you to explore this further.

See 133 Cong. Rec. S2273–76 (daily ed. Feb. 19, 1987) (Sen. Grassley), E544 (daily ed. Feb. 19, 1987) (Rep. Coelho). Not only the committee's remarks on conversion but also the omission of Sec. 302(c)(1) from the section-by-section description of the bill suggest that whoever wrote the report (a staffer, not a Member of Congress) wanted Sec. 302(c)(1) deleted and may have thought that had been accomplished. Still another possibility is that the Conference Committee meant to distinguish Chapter 11 from Chapter 13: to ban conversions from Chapter 11 (covered by Sec. 302(c)(1)) but allow them from Chapter 13. On this reading the gaffe is the failure to delete the reference to Chapter 11 from the report, which could still stand as a treatment of conversions from Chapter 13.

Congress has done nothing to change Sec. 302(c)(1), implying that the statement in the committee report may have been the error. It is easy to imagine opposing forces arriving at the conference armed with their own texts and legislative histories, and in the scramble at the end of session one version slipping into the bill and the other into the report. Whichever was the blunder, we know which one was enacted. What came out of conference, what was voted for by House and Senate, what was signed by the President, says that pending Chapter 11 cases may not be converted. Accordingly, pending Chapter 11 cases may not be converted.

NOTES & QUESTIONS

1. How would you structure a dissenting opinion in the *Sinclair* case?

2. The Conference Committee Report on the Bankruptcy Act amendment at issue in the *Sinclair* case is available online at the Congressional Record link for October 2, 1986, here: https://www.congress.gov/bound-congressional-record/1986/10/02/house-section?s=1&r=10. The Report begins at page 28131 and continues through page 28148. Take a look at it, and especially page 28139, to see if you can find a potentially directly relevant section of subtitle B of the act itself (subtitle B begins on page 28136, starting with sec. 251, if that helps you track its provisions) that the *Sinclair* opinion somehow omits from its analysis? What do you see as the import of this unacknowledged statutory section? What do you make of its omission from the opinion?

3. In light of what you found in Question 2, now how would you structure a dissenting opinion in the *Sinclair* case?

D. The State Perspective

With respect to state statutes as well, interpreters may see committee reports as especially probative. However, at the state level it is much less common for legislative committees to issue written reports. Rather, legislative committees often fulfill their role as the entire body's delegate in a less recorded way (other than a committee's performance of its responsibility to "mark up" or revise the bill). For instance, state legislative committees may report orally in private conversations or caucus meetings between committee members and other legislators not on the committee. But in states whose legislatures produce written committee reports, interpreters will readily look to them for interpretive guidance. Some states' legislative processes also may generate various other types of official reports, such as analyses by legislative drafting bureaus, joint study committee reports, or executive branch budget messages.

For instance, the New Jersey Supreme Court relied upon the report of the New Jersey Senate Judiciary Committee to construe the terms of the state's Products Liability Act in *Perez v. Wyeth Laboratories, Inc.*, 734 A.2d 1245 (N.J. 1999). At issue was whether the "learned intermediary" doctrine relieved the manufacturer of the drug Norplant from tort liability for the drug's side-effects when the manufacturer had engaged in direct marketing of the drug to consumers. The state statute provided that "in the case of prescription drugs," an adequate warning of its potential dangers sufficient to avoid tort liability would be one "taking into account the characteristics of, and the ordinary knowledge common to, the prescribing physician." The committee report stated that "in the case of prescription drugs, the warning is owed to the physician."

The case is interesting in part because the statute at issue included its own interpretive direction, which provided that committee statements "shall be consulted in the interpretation and construction of this act." In the view of the dissenting justice, both the statute and the committee report supported the view that the manufacturer was relieved of liability as long as it had informed the physician—the learned intermediary—of the potential side effects. But the majority concluded from a variety of evidence, including the committee report, that the statutory specification of what constituted an adequate warning reflected the circumstances of an earlier era, when "drugs were then marketed to the physician," and did not provide a safe harbor for drug manufacturers who were now marketing directly to the consumer. One implication is that even if judges agree to consider congressional reports, they can often disagree about how to read this legislative history. Another implication is that legislative history (evidence of legislative intent at the time the legislature adopted the statute) may become less relevant when courts interpret a statute after circumstances have changed. We address interpretation in light of new or changed circumstances in Chapter 27.

Test Your Understanding

To assess your understanding of the material in this chapter, click here to take a quiz.

26

Other Sources of Legislative History

Key Concepts

- Sponsor statements
- Legislative hearings
- Floor debates
- The Dog That Didn't Bark ("canine silence") Canon
- "Dear Colleague" letters
- Outside correspondence
- Presidential vetoes and signing statements
- Post-enactment legislative action & inaction

Chapter Summary

In the hierarchy of legislative history materials, the statements made by a bill's legislative sponsors typically come next after committee reports. These statements are highly regarded by many interpreters. Sponsor statements are assumed to be reliable because sponsors are tasked with helping other legislators understand the functioning of their own bills.

Comments at legislative hearings and statements in floor debates from non-sponsors are largely viewed as far less reliable. Since any legislator can say anything about a bill, they can and often do intentionally make comments on the record to lead (or mislead) future interpreters to their own personal policy views. Indeed, this reality highlights the New Textualist critique of Legislative History. Therefore, even those interpreters who employ legislative history are often quite cautious in how to employ these statements.

Meanwhile, courts will also occasionally treat total silence from legislators as evidence of statutory meaning. The so-called dog that didn't bark, or "canine silence," canon assumes that if one possible interpretation of a new law or statutory amendment would significantly (or unexpectedly) change the existing legal landscape, that putative change should have triggered debate before the law's passage. Thus, if not one legislator said anything for or against such an interpretation, that "silence" may be treated as reliable evidence that the interpretation was not the legislature's intent.

Other forms of legislative history include "Dear Colleague" letters, outside correspondence, presidential statements, and post-enactment legislative action or inaction. These materials are relied upon far less often, in large part because it can be much harder to reliably conclude that the content of these materials actually affected the legislative process.

A. Statements of Sponsors and Drafters

Although committee reports are generally seen as the most authoritative and reliable sources of legislative history, a measure's principal drafters and sponsors are often seen as best understanding the measure's purpose or intent. Sponsors and drafters will frequently find opportunities to make on-the-record statements about the meaning of some portions of their measures, typically in fulfillment of their responsibility to shepherd a measure's consideration by the full chamber. These opportunities most often include explanations offered when introducing a measure, and colloquies (planned or spontaneous) with colleagues. As Justice Frankfurter said more than sixty years ago, "Whatever we may think about the loose use of legislative history, it has never been questioned that the reports of committees *and utterances of those in charge of legislation* constitute authoritative exposition of the meaning of legislation." *Orloff v. Willoughby,* 345 U.S. 83, 98 (1953) (Frankfurter, J., dissenting) (emphasis added). Nevertheless, interpreters must consider critical questions about the reliability of any individual statement.

For instance, in construing the employment nondiscrimination provisions of Title VII of the Civil Rights Act of 1964, the Supreme Court relied on several floor statements uttered by the primary Senate sponsors of the measure. As discussed previously in Chapter 18, at issue in *United Steelworkers of America v. Weber,* 443 U.S. 193 (1979), was whether Title VII's prohibition against racial discrimination in employment precluded a private employer from using a voluntary affirmative action program that benefitted members of racial minority groups. Senator Hubert Humphrey, the floor manager of the bill, had described the purpose of the title as "to open employment opportunities for Negroes in occupations which have been traditionally closed to them." Relying on this and similar statements by other senators holding prominent leadership roles with respect to this measure, the Court concluded that Title VII should not be construed to preclude voluntary affirmative action programs.

However, Justice Rehnquist's dissenting opinion concluded that other statements of key legislators provided support for the opposite result, including statements by Senator Humphrey that the bill "provides that race shall not be a basis for making personnel decisions" and that it "forbids discriminating against anyone on account of race." The House floor manager, Representative Emmanuel Celler, also had said on the House floor that the bill would prevent "employers from discriminating against or in favor of workers because of their race. . . ." The dissenting opinion thus saw in these sponsors' statements evidence that the purpose of the bill was to end all race-based distinctions in employment, while the majority opinion derived from other sponsors' statements that the purpose was to remedy the plight of minority workers. The majority opinion also distinguished the statements on which the dissent had relied as occurring at an earlier stage in the enactment process, before critical adjustments to the bill had occurred.

Consider also *Hamdan v. Rumsfeld*, 548 U.S. 557 (2006), in which Justice Stevens compared contradictory statements of Senator Levin, on the one hand, and Senators Graham and Kyl, on the other. All three were sponsors of the Detainee Treatment Act of 2005, the retroactivity of which was at issue in the case. But the statements of Senators Graham and Kyl were less authoritative, in Justice Stevens' view, because they were not uttered on the floor but instead were inserted into the Congressional Record after the fact (as all Members of Congress are usually allowed to do). Justice Stevens instead credited Senator Levin's actual on-the-floor statement that the act was to be retroactive.

In *Kosak v. United States*, 465 U.S. 848 (1984), a case roughly contemporaneous with *Weber*, the Supreme Court disagreed about another interpretive problem (involving the Federal Tort Claims Act), but this time over what reliance to place on an explanation of a *nonlegislator* who, in the 1930s, had had the key responsibility of drafting the language at issue. The Court majority relied on a report prepared by this drafter, a Special Assistant to the U.S. Attorney General who would later serve as a federal judge, about the proposed measure, even though the Court had no evidence that Congress had been aware of the report. Justice Stevens' dissenting opinion argued in reply that "the intent of a lobbyist—no matter how public spirited he may have been—should not be attributed to the Congress without positive evidence that elected legislators were aware of and shared the lobbyist's intent." Justice Stevens also offered this cautionary advice from a 1902 English precedent: "[T]he worst person to con-

> Contrast the statement of Justice Stevens at the end of this paragraph with the statement of Justice Frankfurter in the first paragraph of this section above! **FYI**

strue [a statute] is the person who is responsible for its drafting. He is very much disposed to confuse what he intended to do with the effect of the language which in fact has been employed." *Id.* at 863–64.

For another example of interpretation in light of the statements of non-legislative participants in the drafting process, consider the dissenting opinion in *Circuit City Stores, Inc. v. Adams*, 532 U.S. 105 (2001). The case involved the scope of the Federal Arbitration Act, specifically the universe of employees covered by the act. The majority opinion reached its result using a plain meaning approach, while the dissent would have relied on an explanation of the American Bar Association committee, which had pressed for the statute's enactment, and statements of the Secretary of Commerce about the act.

Until relatively recently, the British rule for over two hundred years had been that "Parliamentary materials" (in other words, legislative history) were not admissible in court to determine statutory meaning. But in *Pepper v. Hart*, [1992] UKHL 3, the House of Lords relied extensively on the equivalent of legislators' floor statements to resolve an interpretive problem. The opinion included an extended discussion of the arguments for and against modifying the British exclusionary rule. Central to the decision to admit these Parliamentary materials was the view that when faced with statutory ambiguity, courts should not "blind themselves to a clear indication of what Parliament intended," if they found that evidence reliable.

The Textualist critique, of course, is that legislative history is never reliable. In addition to Textualism's general criticisms that reliance on legislative history circumvents the lawmaking requirements of Article I and enables sloppy drafting, the use of sponsor statements is subject to the additonal critique that sponsors, more easily than entire committees, may deliberately include claims in their floor remarks strategically, precisely to provide arguments for a subsequent interpretive problem. When it comes to floor statements, the criticism runs, talk is cheap. Furthermore, the use of sponsor statements also is subject to the critique that not even sponsors are able to speak about a measure on behalf of the legislature as an institution; interpreters should not encourage this circumvention of the legislative process.

However, those interpreters who use legislative history will undertake an individualized look at each potentially relevant statement by a sponsor or drafter to see whether the statement bears sufficient indicia of its reliability. Underlying this inquiry is a sense of the importance to a legislative body of building and maintaining relationships of trust among its members. Colleagues may cease to trust one another if they engage in hyperbole or distortion at moments when others might expect to rely on their assertions, as in particular when sponsors are characterizing their own measures. Factors by which interpreters therefore seek to assess the reliability of individual member statements include: (1) Was the statement made under circumstances in which other legislators would have had full awareness of it? (2) Would other legislators have relied upon it? (3) Would other legislators have had an opportunity to seek additional information in light of the statement? (4) Is the statement consistent with other statements concerning the statute? Central to considering all these factors is whether the statement likely expresses an understanding that is fairly attributable to the enacting coalition.

At the state level, courts frequently rely on statements of legislative sponsors, sometimes more so than on committee reports. In part, this may reflect the fact that at the state level transcripts of floor debate and committee proceedings are more common than published committee reports. In addition, and perhaps as a result, floor debate in state legislatures can involve a more genuine and substantive exchange of views and information than in Congress, as committee chairs are called upon to explain their committee's view on a measure for the benefit of all members. State court interpreters of state legislative output are therefore often quite willing to consider the views of the key proponents of a measure.

B. Floor Debate & Remarks at Committee Hearings by Non-Sponsors

Distinguishable from statements made by sponsors are statements made by other legislators during debate over a proposed measure. Sponsors' statements, although they have their own reliability issues, may nonetheless carry with them some indicia of reliability. In contrast, statements made by legislators *opposed* to a measure are usually greatly discounted, again on the theory that talk is cheap in this context and opponents may readily overstate reasons for their opposition by mischaracterizing how a measure might operate. But occasionally statements made in debate by those in favor of a measure may have explanatory force if the views can fairly be understood as representative of those who supported the measure. Likewise, interpreters may on occasion derive interpretive assistance by referring to testimony at a committee hearing.

As an example of the influence of floor debate on an interpretive issue, consider *BankAmerica Corp. v. United States*, 462 U.S. 122 (1983). One provision of the Clayton Act (one of Congress's principal pieces of anti-trust legislation) generally prohibited interlocking corporate boards, but excepted banks from this prohibition. At issue was whether the exception allowed bank-nonbank interlocks, or excepted only bank-bank interlocks, which were regulated in a separate provision. An opponent of the bill had complained that the conference committee had produced a version of the bill that no longer prohibited bank-nonbank interlocks, although he understood the earlier versions from both the House and Senate to have done so. Two proponents of the bill, while agreeing that the conference committee version did not prohibit bank-nonbank interlocks, argued that this had also been true of the earlier versions. The Supreme Court credited this exchange to support its conclusion that the act did not bar bank-nonbank interlocks.

> **FYI** An "interlocking board" or "interlocking directorate" describes two or more companies whose boards of directors share one or more members. When the same person serves on multiple boards of directors of companies that may be in competition with each other, the person may not be able to fully and fairly serve both companies and instead may experience conflicted loyalties.

Another example of the use of floor debate is the Ninth Circuit's unpublished initial decision in *Montana Wilderness Association v. United States Forest Service*, which the court subsequently withdrew and replaced in response to a request for rehearing. (Section D of this chapter includes portions of the published replacement opinion.) In initially determining that a provision of the Alaska National Interest Lands Conservation Act that granted access to private lands within the National Forest System applied only to National Forest lands in Alaska, rather than nationwide, the circuit court's unpublished opinion noted that the act "was discussed endlessly on the Senate floor," yet the court could not find "one single suggestion [during that debate] that [the act] would affect access rights in the rest of the country." Because the statute's effect on access rights throughout the country would have been a significant change in the law, the court inferred that Congress could not have intended the law to have effect outside of Alaska.

This kind of negative inference from the absence of evidence is an example of what is sometimes called "**the dog that didn't bark**" canon (or what Justice Scalia called the "canine silence" canon), after the Arthur Conan Doyle story "Silver Blaze," in which the fact that a watchdog didn't bark suggested to Sherlock Holmes that the crime had been an inside job. Similarly, when no legislator raises an alarm about a possible construction that ought to have raised an alarm in at least some quarters, legal interpreters occasionally conclude that it is not appropriate to give the text that construction. And although the *Montana Wilderness* court did find evidence that a few members of the House of Representatives had viewed the provision as applying nationwide and had corresponded with the Department of Justice about this understanding, the court said that these "off-the-record views . . . are not attributed to Congress as a whole. . . . This is particularly

> "The dog that didn't bark" or "canine silence" canon attaches meaning to the absence of any congressional alarm or awareness, where such alarm or awareness would have been expected if the statute had been intended to produce a particular result. The silence then is construed to mean Congress did not intend to produce that particular result.

true where, as here, there is no indication that the House as a whole was aware of the correspondence." 655 F.2d 951, 956 nn. 7 & 10. You can think of this "canon" as like a clear-statement rule for interpretations that a court sees as working a significant and unexpected change to the preexisting legal landscape. See Anita S. Krishnakumar, *The Sherlock Holmes Canon*, 84 GEO. WASH. L. REV. 1 (2016). Judges also see it as an attempt to apply "common sense" about the legislative process to statutory interpretation. *See, e.g., Church of Scientology of Calif. v. IRS*, 484 U.S. 9, 17–18 (1987).

C. Other Contemporaneous Legislative History Materials

Although committee reports, sponsor statements, and other remarks in committee meetings or on the legislative floor constitute by far the most widely consulted sources of contemporaneous legislative history, several other categories of materials receive occasional attention.

"Dear Colleague" letters. These are letters or memoranda from one legislator to another, typically circulated to all other members (or all committee members) in advance of a debate or vote. For instance, prior to the Senate debate on the Alaska Lands Act at issue in the Ninth Circuit's opinion in the *Montana Wilderness* case that follows below, Senator Melcher, the author of the relevant provision, sent a letter about the Act to his 99 Senate colleagues. How much weight should a court give to a document like this? Think about this question when you read *Montana Wilderness*.

Correspondence between legislators and executive branch officials or private lobbyists. As we have seen earlier, many external influences shape the legislative process. On occasion, non-legislator participants may create records during the enactment process that shed light on legislative intent. Interpreters considering such evidence must of course exercise great care to use it only to ascertain what it was that the legislature meant, not what the executive branch or private sector lobbyists wanted.

For instance, in *Lindahl v. Office of Personnel Management,* 470 U.S. 768 (1985), the Supreme Court reviewed letters from the Director of the federal Office of Personnel Management to the chairs of the relevant House and Senate committees. The Court wrote, "Yet while Congress' understanding of the enactment is of course our touchstone, in discerning what it was that Congress understood we necessarily attach "great weight" to agency representations to Congress when the administrators participated in drafting and directly made known their views to Congress in committee hearings." *Id.* at 788 (internal quotations omitted).

Presidential/gubernatorial vetoes and signing statements. Because the head of the executive branch is a necessary part of the lawmaking process in all fifty states and the federal system, the views of this participant might in theory be every bit as relevant as the views of a sponsor or other key legislator in understanding the intent behind a measure. On the other hand, except in the case of an executive veto, the President and governors do not have any official opportunity to participate in the lawmaking process until the work of the legislative branch is complete, making it very difficult for the other actors to respond to or rebut effectively whatever the President or governor might say about a measure at that point. However, if the executive responds to a legislative measure with a veto or "disapproval," the veto includes a statement of reasons. These reasons can be especially influential in understanding the scope of the measure either if it is subsequently enacted into law in identical form notwithstanding the veto, or if an alternative measure that responds to the objections is enacted.

For instance, in *United States v. Yermian,* 468 U.S. 63 (1984), the Court noted that President Roosevelt had vetoed Congress's 1934 attempt to amend the False Statements Act, 18 U.S.C. 1001, because it did not do enough to expand the scope of the existing law. In response, Congress passed and the President signed a broader measure. The Court in *Yermian* invoked the President's veto statement to help construe the scope of the enacted measure.

On rare occasions, presidential signing statements have also factored into a court's interpretive reasoning. For instance, at issue in *United States v. Story,* 891 F.2d 988

(2d Cir. 1989), was whether the Sentencing Reform Act of 1984, as applied to criminal offenses that continued over a period of time, covered only ongoing criminal offenses begun after the act's effective date, or also covered offenses begun before but continuing after its effective date. The statute was ambiguous, but President Reagan's signing statement expressed agreement with floor statements of key sponsors of the measure that the act applied to conduct "begun prior to, but not completed until on or after" the act's effective date. The court relied on the signing statement as one of several sources of interpretive evidence, noting that while signing statements might often carry little weight, in this case the President's views were "significant . . . because the Executive Branch participated in the negotiation of the compromise legislation." *Id.* at 994.

Press accounts. In the federal system, it has long been the practice to publish in the Congressional Record a transcript of the proceedings of both houses of Congress, as well as to prepare transcripts of most committee hearings and to require committees to publish official reports on proposed legislation. As discussed in earlier chapters, these materials form the bulk of the legislative history sources relied upon in construing federal legislation. But state legislatures often lack the analogous documents. In those circumstances, press accounts are often the closest form of contemporaneous record of what occurred in a committee proceeding or floor debate. For instance, in *In re Jason W.,* 378 Md. 596, 602–04 (Md. 2003), the court relied on newspaper articles to understand the committee debate on a bill passed in 1970, an era before the state legislature routinely prepared committee reports or otherwise preserved committee records. It is worth considering when and to what extent interpreters might rely on press accounts of the legislative process to shed light on the legislative intent.

> Consider, for instance, *The Federalist Papers*, **FYI** published as newspaper essays in 1787–1788. The essays, written by three proponents of ratification of the proposed U.S. Constitution, articulated their views of the meaning of and rationale for specific provisions of the document. *The Federalist Papers* have had a substantial influence on matters of constitutional interpretation.

D. Post-Enactment Legislative Action and Inaction

On occasion, interpreters consider legislative activity that post-dates the enactment of the measure in question. To the extent that the interpreter's goal in doing so is to understand the intent of the enacting legislature, such an approach can be deeply problematic. That is because after enactment, it can be even easier than during the enactment process for an individual legislator to make purely strategic statements or to attempt to characterize the purpose of a measure without much accountability. Thus, post-enactment explanations of meaning or purpose are usually ignored or, at best, greatly discounted. Every now and then, however, some subsequent legislative activity does influence the interpretive process. Consider the following case:

Montana Wilderness Association v. U.S. Forest Service
655 F.2d 951 (9th Cir. 1981)

NORRIS, CIRCUIT JUDGE:

Environmentalists and a neighboring property owner [plaintiffs-appellants] seek to block construction by Burlington Northern of roads over parts of the Gallatin National Forest. * * * The district court held that Burlington Northern has an easement by necessity or, alternatively, an implied easement under the Northern Pacific Land Grant of 1864. The defendants argue that the Alaska National Interest Lands Act of 1980, passed subsequent to the district court's decision, also grants Burlington Northern assured access to its land. * * *

I.

Defendant-Appellee Burlington Northern, Inc. owns timberland located within the Gallatin National Forest southwest of Bozeman, Montana. This land was originally acquired by its predecessor, the Northern Pacific Railroad, under the Northern Pacific Land Grant Act of 1864, 13 Stat. 365. The Act granted odd-numbered square sections of land to the railroad, which, with the even-number sections retained by the United States, formed a checkerboard pattern.

To harvest its timber, Burlington Northern in 1979 acquired a permit from defendant-appellee United States Forest Service, allowing it to construct an access road across national forest land. The proposed roads would cross the Buck Creek and Yellow Mules drainages, which are protected by the Montana Wilderness Study Act of 1977 as potential wilderness areas. The proposed logging and road-building will arguably disqualify the areas as wilderness under the Act.

The plaintiffs, Montana Wilderness Association, The Wilderness Society, and Nine Quarter Circle Ranch, having contested the granting of the permit, filed suit after it was granted, seeking declaratory and injunctive relief. A temporary restraining order was granted. Before the scheduled preliminary injunction hearing, the Forest Service suspended the permit and submitted the legal question of Burlington Northern's right of access to the Attorney General. The case lay dormant until Attorney General Civiletti issued his opinion [in June 1980]. Of the three theories given in support of Burlington Northern's right of access, the Attorney General rejected two [that there is a right of access under the Forest Service Organic Administrative Act of 1897, 16 U.S.C. § 478, and that there is an easement by necessity,] but left open the issue whether Burlington Northern has an implied easement under the Northern Pacific Land Grant of 1864.

After the Attorney General's opinion was issued, the Forest Service reconsidered the case, and reinstated the permit on the grounds that Burlington Northern had an assured right of access under the 1864 land grant. [If Burlington Northern does not have an enforceable right of access, the protected status of the federal land may remove the Secretary of Agriculture's usual discretion to grant access over Forest Service land. In that case, Burlington Northern's remedy would be the exchange of its inholdings for other federal land of comparable value.] The parties immediately filed cross-motions for summary judgment on the assured access issue. The district court denied the plaintiffs' motion and granted the defendants' partial summary judgment motion. * * *

II.

The sole issue on appeal is whether Burlington Northern has a right of access across federal land to its inholdings of timberland. Appellees contend that the recently enacted Alaska National Interest Lands Conservation Act (Alaska Lands Act), Pub. L. No. 96–487, 94 Stat. 2371 (1980), establishes an independent basis for affirming the judgment of the district court. They argue that § 1323(a) of the Act requires that the Secretary of Agriculture provide access to Burlington Northern for its enclosed land.

Section 1323 is a part of the administrative provisions, Title XIII, of the Alaska Lands Act. Appellees argue that it is the only section of the Act which applies to the entire country; appellants argue that, like the rest of the Act, it applies only to Alaska. Section 1323 reads as follows:

Sec. 1323. (a) Notwithstanding any other provision of law, and subject to such terms and conditions as the Secretary of Agriculture may prescribe, the Secretary shall provide such access to nonfederally owned land within the boundaries of the National Forest System as the Secretary deems adequate to secure to the owner the reasonable use and enjoyment thereof: Provided, That such owner comply with rules and regulations applicable to ingress and egress to or from the National Forest System.

(b) Notwithstanding any other provision of law, and subject to such terms and conditions as the Secretary of the Interior may prescribe, the Secretary shall provide such access to nonfederally owned land surrounded by public lands managed by the Secretary under the Federal Land Policy and Management Act of 1976 (43 U.S.C. 1701–82) as the Secretary deems adequate to secure to the owner the responsible use and enjoyment thereof: Provided, That such owner comply with rules and regulations applicable to access across public lands.

This section provides for access to nonfederally-owned lands surrounded by certain kinds of federal lands. Subsection (b) deals with access to nonfederal lands "surrounded by public lands managed by the Secretary (of the Interior)." Section 102(3) of the Act defines "public lands" as certain lands "situated in Alaska." Subsection (b), therefore, is arguably limited by its terms to Alaska, though we do not find it necessary to settle that issue here. Our consideration of the scope of § 1323(a) proceeds under the assumption that § 1323(b) is limited to Alaska.

Subsection (a) deals with access to nonfederally-owned lands "within the boundaries of the National Forest System." The term "National Forest System" is [not defined].

The question before the court is whether the term "National Forest System" as used in § 1323(a) is to be interpreted as being limited to national forests in Alaska or as including the entire United States. We note at the outset that the bare language of § 1323(a) does not, when considered by itself, limit the provision of access to Alaskan land. We must look, however, to the context of the section to determine its meaning.

Elsewhere in the Act, Congress used the term "National Forest System" in a context which refers to and deals with national forests in Alaska. Title V of the Act is entitled "National Forest System." Section 501(a) states: "The following units of the National Forest System are hereby expanded. . . ." It is not unreasonable to read Section 1323(a) as referring to the "National Forest System" in the context in which it is used in Title V of the Act, rather than to all national forests in the United States.

Congress did, however, supply us with a general definition of the term in another statute. Pub. Law 93–378, 88 Stat. 480 (1974). 16 U.S.C. § 1609(a) states *inter alia* that:

> Congress declares that the National Forest System consists of units of federally owned forest, range, and related lands through- out the United States and its territories, united into a nationally significant system dedicated to the long-term benefit for present and future generations, and that it is the purpose of their section to include all such areas into one integral system. The 'National Forest System' shall include all national forest lands reserved or withdrawn from the public domain of the United States. . . .

Application of this definition to § 1323(a) would necessarily yield the conclusion that the section was intended to have nation-wide effect. This seems especially so when Congress uses the term "National Forest System" in § 1323(a) without limitation or qualification.

As the parties agreed at oral argument, however, § 1323(b) is *in pari materia* with § 1323(a). The two subsections are placed together in the same section, and use not only a parallel structure but many of the same words and phrases. The natural interpretation is that they were meant to have the same effect, one on lands controlled by the Secretary of Agriculture, the other on lands controlled by the Secretary of the Interior. Since we assume that § 1323(b), by definition of public lands in § 102(3), applies only to Alaskan land, we face a presumption that § 1323(a) was meant to apply to Alaska as well.

That interpretation is supported by a review of the entire Act which discloses no other provision having nation-wide application. We therefore conclude that the language of the Act provides tentative support for the view that § 1323(a) applies only to national forests in Alaska. Bearing in mind that "(a)bsent a clearly expressed legislative intent to the contrary, (the statutory) language must ordinarily be regarded as conclusive," *Consumer Product Safety Commission v. GTE Sylvania*, 447 U.S. 102, 108 (1980), we turn to the legislative history.

The legislative history concerning § 1323 is surprisingly sparse.[5] The report of the Senate committee which drafted the section is ambiguous.[6] At times when the Senate could have been expected to comment on its intention to make a major change in current law, it did not.[7] The only expression of intent that § 1323 apply nation-wide came from a single senator eight

---

[5]   Section 1323 was added to the Alaska Lands Bill by the Senate Committee on Energy and Natural Resources in its amendment to H.R. 39, originally passed by the House. S.Rep.No.96–413, 96th Cong. 1st Sess. (1979), reprinted in (Feb. 1981) U.S. Code Cong. & Admin. News 9130. It was incorporated in the Tsongas substitute bill which replaced by amendment the Energy Committee's proposed bill, 126 Cong. Rec. S11099, S11140 (daily ed. Aug. 18, 1980). The Tsongas substitute bill was passed by the Senate, 126 Cong. Rec. S11193 (daily ed. Aug. 19, 1980), and House, 126 Cong. Rec. H10552 (daily ed. Nov. 12, 1980), and became law on December 1, 1980, 94 Stat. 2371.

[6]   The Energy Committee report discussed it in its section-by-section analysis, S.Rep.No.96–413 at 310, (Feb. 1981) U.S. Code Cong. & Admin. News at 9314. (The Committee analysis mixes up §§ 1323 and 1324. Thus, the analysis entitled § 1324 is really concerned with § 1323 and vice versa.) Although the appellees contend that the language of the Energy Committee report makes perfectly clear the Committee's intent that § 1323 apply nationwide, we do not find their interpretation of the report's language persuasive:

> This section is designed to remove the uncertainties surrounding the status of the rights of the owners of non-Federal lands to gain access to such lands across Federal lands. It has been the Committee's understanding that such owners had the right of access to their lands subject to reasonable regulation by either, the Secretary of Agriculture in the case of national forests, or by the Secretary of the Interior in the case of public lands managed by the Bureau of Land Management under the Federal Land Policy and Management Act of 1976. However, a recent District Court decision in Utah (*Utah v. Andrus et al.*, C79-0037, October 1, 1979, D.C. Utah) has cast some doubt over the status of these rights. Furthermore, the Attorney General is currently reviewing the issue because of differing interpretations of the law by the Departments of Agriculture and the Interior.
>
> The Committee amendment is designed to resolve any lingering legal questions by making it clear that non-Federal landowners have a right of access (across) National Forests and public land, subject, of course, to reasonable rules and regulations.

S.Rep.No.96–413 at 310, (Feb. 1981) U.S. Code Cong. & Admin. News at 9314.

While the Committee's intent to guarantee access is clear, it is less than clear whether this provision was meant to guarantee access outside of Alaska. The problem raised in the first paragraph the differing interpretations of the law of access is not confined to Alaska, but the scope of the remedy as set forth in the last paragraph could be so confined. As with § 1323 itself, the report uses indiscriminately terms defined in the Act as applying only to Alaskan land ("public land") and terms not so defined ("National Forests").

The absence of any reference to Alaska is not of much import. The report's discussion of other access provisions such as § 1110 and § 1111, which all parties agree apply only to Alaska, fails to mention Alaska and is as ambiguous about whether § 1110 and § 1111 apply nationwide as is the discussion of § 1323. S.Rep. No.96–413 at 299–300, (Feb. 1981) U.S. Code Cong. & Admin. News at 9303–04.

[7]   The Alaska Lands bill was discussed endlessly on the Senate floor. There are numerous occasions when one would expect a change in current laws of access of the magnitude of the appellees' proposed interpretation of § 1323 to be discussed, mentioned or at least alluded to. Yet we have not found in the Senate debates, and appellees have not called to our attention, one single suggestion that anything in the Alaska Land Bill would affect access rights in the rest of the country. In Senator Tsongas' long, detailed comparison of his substitute bill with the Energy Committee bill, § 1323 is not mentioned. 126 Cong. Rec. S11193 (daily ed. Aug. 19, 1980). In discussion about the adequacy of the substitute bill's access provisions (which include § 1323) no mention is made of a change in the law of access for the rest of the country. 126 Cong. Rec. S11061–62 (daily ed. Aug. 18, 1980).

Neither did Senator Tsongas remark on § 1323 when it was first proposed in the Energy Committee bill, even though in his statement in the Committee report he spends several pages criticizing the bill's overbroad provisions on access. S.Rep.No.96–413 at 422-24, (Feb. 1981) U.S. Code Cong. & Ad. News at 9422–23 (additional views of Senators Metzenbaum and Tsongas). Yet the extension of § 1323(a) to the entire country would certainly have a greater impact than the other measures he discusses.

days after the Alaska Lands Act was passed by Congress.[8] In the House debates, three representatives suggested that § 1323 did apply nation-wide, but the chairman of one of the responsible committees said it did not.[9] Two chairmen of House subcommittees responsible for the bill did state in a letter to the Attorney General that they believed that § 1323 applied nation-wide, but there is no indication that the contents of this letter were generally known by members of the House, and so the letter carries little weight in our analysis.[10] All this gives only slight support at best to the * * * interpretation that § 1323 applies nation-wide.

---

[8] Senator Melcher, the author of the section, discussed it on the floor of the Senate, 126 Cong. Rec. S14770–71 (daily ed. Nov. 20, 1980). The remarks of Senator Melcher, however, were made on November 20th, eight days after Congress passed H.R. 39. His remarks clearly demonstrate that his personal understanding of the section is that it applies nationwide, but because they are the remarks of but one senator made subsequent to the passage of the bill they do not provide a reliable indication of the understanding of the Senate as a whole.

[9] On October 2, 1980, Representative Udall, chairman of the Committee on Interior and Insular Affairs which had joint responsibility for the bill, introduced an amendment one section of which was to "make clear that (the bill) applies only to Alaska." 127 Cong. Rec. 10376 (daily ed. October 2, 1980). This amendment was never adopted. Representative Udall subsequently declared in prepared remarks inserted into the Congressional Record that although the final version of the bill was "ambiguously drafted and not expressly limited to Alaskan lands, the House believes that, as with all the other provisions of the bill, the language of the section applies only to lands within the State of Alaska." 126 Cong. Rec. H10549 (daily ed. Nov. 12, 1980). Representative Weaver stated that the section granting access rights to inholders on national forest and BLM lands "apparently applies not only to Alaska but also to the entire United States." 126 Cong. Rec. H8638 (daily ed. September 9, 1980). Representative Sieberling inserted into the record a summary of proposed amendments, which refers to Section 1323 as the "nationwide access amendment." 126 Cong. Rec. H10350 (daily ed. October 2, 1980). Representative AuCoin stated that one of the flaws of the final bill is that it "grants private inholders carte blanche access across national forest and public lands nationwide." 126 Cong. Rec. H10529-30 (daily ed. Nov. 12, 1980).

[10] Appellees rely heavily upon an exchange of letters between Representatives Sieberling and Weaver, chairmen of the subcommittees responsible for the bill (Public Lands of the Committee on Interior and Insular Affairs and Forest of the Committee on Agriculture), and the Attorney General's office. In their letter, the representatives express concern over § 1323, which they state applies nationwide, and ask for a clarification of how different the § 1323 access language is from existing access provisions. It is indeed clear from their letter that they believed that § 1323 applies nation-wide.

Appellees argue, on the basis of the September 5, 1980 return letter from Assistant Attorney General Alan Parker, that the Department of Justice confirmed this interpretation of § 1323. We interpret the letter differently. As we read the letter, the Assistant Attorney General assumed without analysis that the representatives' interpretation of § 1323 was correct, and proceeded to discuss in detail the effect of such a change in the law.

The exchanged letters are entitled to little weight. In general, off-the-record views of congressmen are not attributed to Congress as a whole. This is particularly true where, as here, there is no indication that the House as a whole was aware of the correspondence. *Id*. at 191–92.

DIY
Does the Alaska Lands Act Apply Nationwide?

 The court is not yet finished with its opinion, and neither are we, BUT DO NOT TURN THE PAGE JUST YET! Instead, at this point in the court's discussion of the text and legislative history of section 1323(a), pause for a few minutes to consider whether you think the section's proper scope is (1) nationwide, or instead (2) limited to Alaska. Be sure to consider the legislative history that the court has described in some detail in the footnotes to the preceding paragraph. Then write down your view of the proper scope, along with a brief summary of why this is your view, including your sense of what interpretive tools are most persuasive. Be mindful that a right answer to this question does not exist, only an answer that is most persuasive to you! Once you have decided what you think is the proper scope of section 1323(a), continue to the next page to read the remainder of the 9th Circuit's opinion.

The appellees, however, have uncovered subsequent legislative history that, given the closeness of the issue, is decisive. Three weeks after Congress passed the Alaska Lands Act, a House-Senate Conference Committee considering the Colorado Wilderness Act interpreted § 1323 of the Alaska Lands Act as applying nation-wide:

> Section 7 of the Senate amendment contains a provision pertaining to access to non-Federally owned lands within national forest wilderness areas in Colorado. The House bill has no such provision.
>
> The conferees agreed to delete the section because similar language has already passed Congress in Section 1323 of the Alaska National Interest Lands Conservation Act.

H.R.Rep.No.1521, 96th Cong., 2d Sess., 126 Cong. Rec. H11687 (daily ed. Dec. 3, 1980) (emphasis supplied).

This action was explained to both Houses during discussion of the Conference Report. See 126 Cong. Rec. S15571 (daily ed. Dec. 4, 1980) (remarks of Sen. Hart); *Id.* at S15573 (remarks of Sen. Armstrong); *Id.* at H11705 (daily ed. Dec. 3, 1980) (remarks of Rep. Johnson). Both houses then passed the Colorado Wilderness bill as it was reported by the Conference Committee.

Although a subsequent conference report is not entitled to the great weight given subsequent legislation, *Consumer Product Safety Commission v. GTE Sylvania*, 447 U.S. 102, 118 n.13 (1980), it is still entitled to significant weight, *Seatrain Shipbuilding Corp. v. Shell Oil Co.*, 444 U.S. 572 (1980), particularly where it is clear that the conferees had carefully considered the issue. *See Consumer Product Safety Commission, supra*, at 120; *Skidmore v. Swift & Co.*, 323 U.S. 134, 140 (1944). The conferees, including Representatives Udall and Sieberling and Senator Melcher, had an intimate knowledge of the Alaska Lands Act. Moreover, the Conference Committee's interpretation of § 1323 was the basis for their decision to leave out an access provision passed by one house. In these circumstances, the Conference Committee's interpretation is very persuasive. We conclude that it tips the balance decidedly in favor of the broader interpretation of § 1323. We therefore hold that Burlington Northern has an assured right of access to its land pursuant to the nation-wide grant of access in § 1323. * * *

NOTES & QUESTIONS

1. Note that the Ninth Circuit initially issued a different, unpublished opinion, based on everything except the Colorado Wilderness Act, that reached the opposite result. It then vacated that initial decision, after the appellees brought the Colorado act to its attention, and issued the opinion excerpted above. This revised opinion reads very much like the initial opinion until it reaches its discussion of the Colorado act.

2. The circuit court calls this a "close" issue. Is it? (Consider your answer from the exercise on the previous page.) If so, is the legislative history of the Colorado Wilderness Act a legitimate basis for the court to reverse the tentative position it appeared to have reached before it considered the impact of the Colorado act? If not, why does the court do this? Is it possible that Section 1323(a) of the Alaska Lands Act, when passed, really didn't apply nationwide, but that the members of the Colorado Wilderness Act's Conference Committee in effect "amended" the Alaska Lands Act—without changing its language?

3. Consider the final paragraph of the court's opinion: What is the difference between the "great weight" to which the court says subsequent history is not entitled, and the "significant weight" to which the court says it is entitled here? How much weight do *you* think it should receive?

4. What parts of the legislative history of the Alaska Lands Act are most probative of the proper scope of section 1323(a), and why? Did you notice the implied use of the "canine silence canon"?

5. How does the circuit court's use of legislative history affect your thoughts about the use of legislative history more generally? You should by now recognize that Textualists would find virtually every word of the court's opinion starting with "The legislative history . . ." objectionable. But isn't the court doing its best here to determine what Congress meant when it adopted section 1323(a)? Isn't the legislative history relevant here, at least if the court's goal is to defer to Congress on this important policy question potentially affecting the entire country? Or is there yet some sense in which the court is selectively using or manipulating the legislative history to favor a result it sought to make on other grounds?

6. How might a Textualist resolve this difficult interpretive problem? By simply ending the analysis before the discussion of the legislative his-

tory, at the point where the court "conclude[s] that the language of the Act provides tentative support for the view that § 1323(a) applies only to national forests in Alaska"? If so, does that mean a Textualist would necessarily have dissented? Or can you imagine how a Textualist could write a concurrence? If a Textualist could write both a dissent and a concurrence in this case, what factors, if not the legislative history, would a Textualist use to resolve the interpretive dispute? What are the advantages to using those factors rather than the legislative history in a case like this?

A Word About Legislative Acquiescence. Another occasional use of subsequent legislative activity is to determine whether the legislature, as a dynamic institution, has ratified or implicitly now concurs in a prior interpretation of an ambiguity. This use of subsequent legislative activity (or inactivity) may be less problematic, although reliance on this factor is also deeply contested by Textualist interpreters who view their role as solely to understand the text *as enacted*. The Supreme Court itself also has cautioned against the practice, observing that subsequent congressional activity "is a hazardous basis for inferring the intent of an earlier Congress." *Pension Benefit Guaranty Corporation v. LTV Corporation,* 496 U.S. 633, 650 (1990) (internal quotations omitted). Nevertheless, over the years a number of prominent Supreme Court decisions have relied on the notion that Congress has acquiesced in previous judicial or agency interpretations of a provision.

A quintessential example of interpretation in light of subsequent congressional action is *Flood v. Kuhn,* 407 U.S. 258 (1972), which you will see in full flower in Chapter 27. In *Flood,* the Supreme Court reconsidered its own previous decisions in 1922 and 1953 exempting Major League Baseball from federal antitrust laws. Although for reasons you will read in Chapter 27 the time would have been ripe for the Court to overrule its prior decisions, the Court relied on the fact that Congress had been well aware of the Court's earlier decisions exempting baseball from the antitrust laws, and yet had done nothing to reverse this exemption, to conclude that Congress approved of the exemption, or at least did not disapprove of it. The Court refused to overrule its earlier cases "when Congress, by its positive inaction, has allowed those decisions to stand for so long and . . . has clearly evinced a desire not to disapprove of them legislatively." *Id.* at 283.

In a similar vein, a few years after the Court in *Weber* had construed Title VII to permit a private employer's voluntary affirmative action program on behalf of racial minorities, the Court relied on what it saw as Congress's apparent acceptance of this construction of the statute to also uphold a public employer's affirmative action program on behalf of women employees. *See Johnson v. Transportation Agency,*

Santa Clara County, 480 U.S. 616 (1987). The Court's underlying reasoning in *Weber* had depended quite substantially on two considerations not present in *Johnson*, namely the Court's understanding that the overwhelming purpose behind Title VII was to promote employment opportunities for racial minorities, and the Court's view that it should construe Title VII to not interfere with the prerogatives of private employers any more than necessary. Although neither of these factors was present in the facts of *Johnson* (because it was not about racial discrimination, and because it involved a public employer), the Court chose to follow rather than distinguish *Weber* because "Congress has not amended the statute to reject our construction, nor have any such amendments even been proposed, and we therefore may assume that our [*Weber*] interpretation was correct." *Id.* at 629 n.7. In dissent, Justice Scalia thought it "patently false" to use the current Congress' view as evidence of what the law meant when enacted.

As another example, consider the Supreme Court's use of subsequent congressional activity to construe the Food, Drug, and Cosmetic Act (FDCA) in *FDA v. Brown & Williamson Tobacco Corp.,* excerpted below in Chapter 36. Although the dissenting opinion and the FDA argued that the FDCA's plain language gave the FDA jurisdiction to regulate tobacco products, the majority opinion rejected this construction of the act partly on the basis that a number of congressional proposals enacted or considered after the enactment of the FDCA seemed to assume that the FDCA had not given the FDA jurisdiction over tobacco products.

E. The Charitable Exemption Problem

What do you think about the concept of "legislative acquiescence"? In what circumstances should a court consider it? After reflecting on this question, consider the following problem involving apparent congressional acquiescence in a prior *agency* construction of a statute.

DIY
The Charitable Exemption Problem from the Early 1980s

Section 501(c)(3) of the Internal Revenue Code lists the following kinds of organizations as exempt from federal income taxation under § 501(a) unless denied tax exemptions under other specified sections of the Code:

Corporations, and any community chest, fund, or foundation, *organized and operated exclusively for religious, charitable,* scientific, testing for public safety, literary, *or educational purposes,* or to foster national or international amateur sports competition (but only if no part of its activities involve the provision of athletic facilities or equipment), or for the prevention of cruelty to children or animals, no part of the net earnings of which inures to the benefit of any private shareholder or individual, no substantial part of the activities of which is carrying on propaganda, or otherwise attempting, to influence legislation . . . and which does not participate in, or intervene in (including the publishing or distributing of statements), any political campaign on behalf of any candidate for public office.

(Emphasis added.) ***What limitations if any do you think this provision imposes on the types of religious or educational organizations entitled to federal tax exemption? If you were an attorney for the IRS, how would you counsel it to decide whether to treat an organization as exempt under section 501(c)(3)?***

The IRS reversed its own view on this issue in 1970, giving rise to the following court challenge. Pay extra attention to part II-D of the the majority opinion, Justice Powell's concurrence, and the second half of Justice Rehnquist's dissent, which responds to the arguments the majority makes in part II-D.

Bob Jones University v. United States
461 U.S. 574 (1983)

CHIEF JUSTICE BURGER **delivered the opinion of the Court.**

* * * Until 1970, the Internal Revenue Service granted tax-exempt status to private schools, without regard to their racial admissions policies, under § 501(c)(3) of the Internal Revenue Code and granted charitable deductions for contributions to such schools under § 170 of the Code.

On January 12, 1970, a three-judge District Court for the District of Columbia issued a preliminary injunction prohibiting the IRS from according tax-exempt status to private schools in Mississippi that discriminated as to admissions on the basis of race. *Green v. Kennedy,* 309 F.Supp. 1127, *appeal dism'd sub nom. Cannon v. Green,* 398 U.S. 956 (1970). Thereafter, in July, 1970, the IRS concluded that it could "no longer legally justify allowing tax-exempt status [under § 501(c)(3)] to private schools which practice racial discrimination." IRS News Release, July 7, 1970. At the same time, the IRS announced that it could not "treat gifts to such schools as charitable deductions for income tax purposes [under § 170]." *Ibid.* By letter dated November 30, 1970, the IRS formally notified private schools, including those involved in this litigation, of this change in policy, "applicable to all private schools in the United States at all levels of education."

* * * The revised policy on discrimination was formalized in Revenue Ruling 71–447, 1971–2 Cum.Bull. 230:

> Both the courts and the Internal Revenue Service have long rec-
> ognized that the statutory requirement of being "organized and
> operated exclusively for religious, charitable, . . . or educational
> purposes" was intended to express the basic common law concept
> [of "charity"]. All charitable trusts, educational or otherwise, are
> subject to the requirement that the purpose of the trust may not
> be illegal or contrary to public policy.

Based on the "national policy to discourage racial discrimination in education," the IRS ruled that

> a [private] school not having a racially nondiscriminatory policy
> as to students is not 'charitable' within the common law concepts
> reflected in sections 170 and 501(c)(3) of the Code.

Id. at 231.

The application of the IRS construction of these provisions to * * * private schools with racially discriminatory admissions policies, is now before us.

* * * Bob Jones University is not affiliated with any religious denomina-
tion, but is dedicated to the teaching and propagation of its fundamentalist Christian religious beliefs. It is both a religious and educational institution. Its teachers are required to be devout Christians, and all courses at the University are taught according to the Bible. Entering students are screened as to their religious beliefs, and their public and private conduct is strictly regulated by standards promulgated by University authorities.

The sponsors of the University genuinely believe that the Bible forbids interracial dating and marriage. To effectuate these views, Negroes were completely excluded until 1971. From 1971 to May, 1975, the University accepted no applications from unmarried Negroes, but did accept applications from Negroes married within their race. * * * Since May 29, 1975, the University has permitted unmarried Negroes to enroll; but a disciplinary rule prohibits interracial dating and marriage [and provides for expulsion of students who violate the rule, and the University continues to deny admission to applicants known to advocate interracial marriage or dating.]

[Until 1970, the IRS extended tax-exempt status to Bob Jones University under § 501(c)(3). On January 19, 1976, the IRS officially revoked the University's tax-exempt status, effective as of December 1, 1970, the day after the University was formally notified of the change in IRS policy. The United States District Court for the District of South Carolina held that revocation of the University's tax-exempt status exceeded the delegated powers of the IRS, was improper under the IRS rulings and procedures, and violated the University's rights under the Religion Clauses of the First Amendment. The Court of Appeals for the Fourth Circuit reversed.]

II-A

In Revenue Ruling 71–447, the IRS formalized the policy, first announced in 1970, that § 170 and § 501(c)(3) embrace the common law "charity" concept. Under that view, to qualify for a tax exemption pursuant to § 501(c)(3), an institution must show, first, that it falls within one of the eight categories expressly set forth in that section, and second, that its activity is not contrary to settled public policy. * * *

It is a well-established canon of statutory construction that a court should go beyond the literal language of a statute if reliance on that language would defeat the plain purpose of the statute:

> The general words used in the clause . . . , taken by themselves, and literally construed, without regard to the object in view, would seem to sanction the claim of the plaintiff. But this mode of expounding a statute has never been adopted by any enlightened tribunal—because it is evident that, in many cases, it would defeat the object which the Legislature intended to accomplish. And it is well-settled that, in interpreting a statute, the court will not look merely to a particular clause in which general words may be used, *but will take in connection with it the whole statute . . . and the objects and policy of the law. . . .*

Brown v. Duchesne, 19 How. 183, 194 (1857) (emphasis added).

Section 501(c)(3) therefore must be analyzed and construed within the framework of the Internal Revenue Code and against the background of the congressional purposes. Such an examination reveals unmistakable evidence that, underlying all relevant parts of the Code, is the intent that entitlement to tax exemption depends on meeting certain common law standards of charity—namely, that an institution seeking tax-exempt status must serve a public purpose and not be contrary to established public policy.

This "charitable" concept appears explicitly in § 170 of the Code. That section contains a list of organizations virtually identical to that contained in § 501(c)(3). It is apparent that Congress intended that list to have the same meaning in both sections. In § 170, Congress used the list of organizations in defining the term "charitable contributions." On its face, therefore, § 170 reveals that Congress' intention was to provide tax benefits to organizations serving charitable purposes.[11] The form of § 170 simply makes plain what common sense and history tell us: in enacting both § 170 and § 501(c)(3), Congress sought to provide tax benefits to charitable organizations, to encourage the development of private institutions that serve a useful public purpose or supplement or take the place of public institutions of the same kind.

Tax exemptions for certain institutions thought beneficial to the social order of the country as a whole, or to a particular community, are deeply rooted in our history, as in that of England. The origins of such exemptions lie in the special privileges that have long been extended to charitable trusts.

[Here the Court discussed its view of the historical development of the common law of charitable trusts and the preferential treatment of charities.]

What little floor debate occurred on the charitable exemption provision of the 1894 [revenue] Act and similar sections of later statutes leaves no doubt that Congress deemed the specified organizations entitled to tax benefits because they served desirable public purposes. * * *

---

[11] The dissent suggests that the Court "quite adeptly avoids the statute it is construing" and "seeks refuge . . . by turning to § 170." This assertion dissolves when one sees that § 501(c)(3) and § 170 are construed together, as they must be. The dissent acknowledges that the two sections are "mirror" provisions; surely there can be no doubt that the Court properly looks to § 170 to determine the meaning of § 501(c)(3). It is also suggested that § 170 is "at best of little usefulness in finding the meaning of § 501(c)(3)," since "§ 170(c) simply tracks the requirements set forth in § 501(c)(3)." That reading loses sight of the fact that § 170(c) defines the term "charitable contribution." The plain language of § 170 reveals that Congress' objective was to employ tax exemptions and deductions to promote certain *charitable* purposes. While the eight categories of institutions specified in the statute are indeed presumptively charitable in nature, the IRS properly considered principles of charitable trust law in determining whether the institutions in question may truly be considered "charitable" for purposes of entitlement to the tax benefits conferred by § 170 and § 501(c)(3).

In enacting the Revenue Act of 1938, ch. 289, 52 Stat. 447, Congress expressly reconfirmed this view with respect to the charitable deduction provision:

> The exemption from taxation of money or property devoted to charitable and other purposes is based upon the theory that the Government is compensated for the loss of revenue by its relief from financial burdens which would otherwise have to be met by appropriations from other public funds, and by the benefits resulting from the promotion of the general welfare.

H.R. Rep. No. 1860, 75th Cong., 3d Sess., 19 (1938).

A corollary to the public benefit principle is the requirement, long recognized in the law of trusts, that the purpose of a charitable trust may not be illegal or violate established public policy. In 1861, this Court stated that a public charitable use must be "consistent with local laws and public policy," *Perin v. Carey*, 24 How. at 501. Modern commentators and courts have echoed that view. *See, e.g.*, Restatement (Second) of Trusts § 377, Comment *c* (1959); 4 Scott § 377, and cases cited therein; Bogert § 378, at 191–192.

When the Government grants exemptions or allows deductions all taxpayers are affected; the very fact of the exemption or deduction for the donor means that other taxpayers can be said to be indirect and vicarious "donors." Charitable exemptions are justified on the basis that the exempt entity confers a public benefit—a benefit which the society or the community may not itself choose or be able to provide, or which supplements and advances the work of public institutions already supported by tax revenues. History buttresses logic to make clear that, to warrant exemption under § 501(c)(3), an institution must fall within a category specified in that section and must demonstrably serve and be in harmony with the public interest. The institution's purpose must not be so at odds with the common community conscience as to undermine any public benefit that might otherwise be conferred.

II-B

We are bound to approach these questions with full awareness that determinations of public benefit and public policy are sensitive matters with serious implications for the institutions affected; a declaration that a given institution is not "charitable" should be made only where there can be no doubt that the activity involved is contrary to a fundamental public policy. But there can no longer be any doubt that racial discrimination in education violates deeply and widely accepted views of elementary justice. Prior to 1954, public education in many places still was conducted under the pall of this Court's decision in *Plessy v. Ferguson,* 163 U.S. 537 (1896); racial segregation in primary and secondary education prevailed in many parts of the country. *See, e.g.,* Segregation and the Fourteenth Amendment in the States (B. Reams & P. Wilson eds.1975). This Court's decision in *Brown v. Board of Education,* 347 U.S. 483 (1954), signaled an end to that era. Over the past quarter of a century, every pronouncement of this Court and myriad Acts of Congress and Executive Orders attest a firm national policy to prohibit racial segregation and discrimination in public education.

An unbroken line of cases following *Brown* establishes beyond doubt this Court's view that racial discrimination in education violates a most fundamental national public policy, as well as rights of individuals. [Here the Court described the development of judicial, executive, and legislative branch prohibitions on racial discrimination in education.]

Few social or political issues in our history have been more vigorously debated and more extensively ventilated than the issue of racial discrimination, particularly in education. Given the stress and anguish of the history of efforts to escape from the shackles of the "separate but equal" doctrine of *Plessy v. Ferguson,* 163 U.S. 537 (1896), it cannot be said that educational institutions that, for whatever reasons, practice racial discrimination, are institutions exercising "beneficial and stabilizing influences in community life," *Walz v. Tax Comm'n,* 397 U.S. 664, 673 (1970), or should be encouraged by having all taxpayers share in their support by way of special tax status.

There can thus be no question that the interpretation of § 170 and § 501(c)(3) announced by the IRS in 1970 was correct. That it may be seen as belated does not undermine its soundness. It would be wholly incompatible with the concepts underlying tax exemption to grant the benefit of tax-exempt status to racially discriminatory educational entities. * * * Whatever may be the rationale for such private schools' policies, and however sincere the rationale may be, racial discrimination in education is contrary to public policy. Racially discriminatory educational institutions cannot be viewed as conferring a public benefit within the "charitable" concept discussed earlier, or within the congressional intent underlying § 170 and § 501(c)(3).

II-C

Petitioners contend that, regardless of whether the IRS properly concluded that racially discriminatory private schools violate public policy, only Congress can alter the scope of § 170 and § 501(c)(3). Petitioners accordingly argue that the IRS overstepped its lawful bounds in issuing its 1970 and 1971 rulings.

Yet ever since the inception of the Tax Code, Congress has seen fit to vest in those administering the tax laws very broad authority to interpret those laws. In an area as complex as the tax system, the agency Congress vests with administrative responsibility must be able to exercise its authority to meet changing conditions and new problems. Indeed, as early as 1918, Congress expressly authorized the Commissioner "to make all needful rules and regulations for the enforcement" of the tax laws. Revenue Act of 1918, ch. 18, § 1309, 40 Stat. 1143. * * *

Congress, the source of IRS authority, can modify IRS rulings it considers improper; and courts exercise review over IRS actions. In the first instance, however, the responsibility for construing the Code falls to the IRS. Since Congress cannot be expected to anticipate every conceivable problem that can arise or to carry out day-to-day oversight, it relies on the administrators and on the courts to implement the legislative will. Administrators, like judges, are under oath to do so. * * *

Guided, of course, by the Code, the IRS has the responsibility, in the first instance, to determine whether a particular entity is "charitable" for purposes of § 170 and § 501(c)(3). This in turn may necessitate later determinations of whether given activities so violate public policy that the entities involved cannot be deemed to provide a public benefit worthy of "charitable" status. We emphasize, however, that these sensitive determinations should be made only where there is no doubt that the organization's activities violate fundamental public policy.

> Parts VII & VIII below will consider **FYI** in more detail the implications of congressional delegations of interpretive authority to executive agencies.

On the record before us, there can be no doubt as to the national policy. In 1970, when the IRS first issued the ruling challenged here, the position of all three branches of the Federal Government was unmistakably clear. The correctness of the Commissioner's conclusion that a racially discriminatory private school "is not 'charitable' within the common law concepts reflected in . . . the Code," Rev.Rul. 71–447, 1971–2 Cum.Bull., at 231, is wholly consistent with what Congress, the Executive, and the courts had repeatedly declared before 1970. Indeed, it would be anomalous for the Executive, Legislative, and Judicial Branches to reach conclusions that add up to a firm public policy on racial discrimination, and at the same time have the IRS blissfully ignore what all three branches of the Federal Government had declared. * * * We therefore hold that the IRS did not exceed its authority when it announced its interpretation of § 170 and § 501(c)(3) in 1970 and 1971.

II-D

The actions of Congress since 1970 leave no doubt that the IRS reached the correct conclusion in exercising its authority. It is, of course, not unknown for independent agencies or the Executive Branch to misconstrue the intent of a statute; Congress can and often does correct such misconceptions, if the courts have not done so. Yet, for a dozen years, Congress has been made aware—acutely aware—of the IRS rulings of 1970 and 1971. As we noted earlier, few issues have been the subject of more vigorous and widespread debate and discussion in and out of Congress than those related to racial segregation in education. Sincere adherents advocating contrary views have ventilated the subject for well over three decades. Failure of Congress to modify the IRS rulings of 1970 and 1971, of which Congress was, by its own studies and by public discourse, constantly reminded, and Congress' awareness of the denial of tax-exempt status for racially discriminatory schools when enacting other and related legislation make out an unusually strong case of legislative acquiescence in and ratification by implication of the 1970 and 1971 rulings.

Ordinarily, and quite appropriately, courts are slow to attribute significance to the failure of Congress to act on particular legislation. *See, e.g., Aaron v. SEC*, 446 U.S. 680, 694, n. 11 (1980). We have observed that "unsuccessful attempts at legislation are not the best of guides to legislative intent," *Red Lion Broadcasting Co. v. FCC*, 395 U.S. 367, 382, n. 11 (1969). Here, however, we do not have an ordinary claim of legislative acquiescence. Only one month after the IRS announced its position in 1970, Congress held its first hearings on this precise issue. Equal Educational Opportunity: Hearings before the Senate Select Committee on Equal Educational Opportunity, 91st Cong., 2d Sess., 1991 (1970). Exhaustive hearings have been held on the issue at various times since then. These include hearings in February 1982, after we granted review in this case. Administration's Change in Federal Policy Regarding the Tax Status of Racially Discriminatory Private Schools: Hearing before the House Committee on Ways and Means, 97th Cong., 2d Sess. (1982).

Nonaction by Congress is not often a useful guide, but the nonaction here is significant. During the past 12 years, there have been no fewer than 13 bills introduced to overturn the IRS interpretation of § 501(c)(3). Not one of these bills has emerged from any committee, although Congress has enacted numerous other amendments to § 501 during this same period, including an amendment to § 501(c)(3) itself. Tax Reform Act of 1976, Pub. L. 94–455, § 1313(a), 90 Stat. 1730. It is hardly conceivable that Congress—and in this setting, any Member of Congress—was not abundantly aware of what was going on. In view of its prolonged and acute awareness of so important an issue, Congress' failure to act on the bills proposed on this subject provides added support for concluding that Congress acquiesced in the IRS rulings of 1970 and 1971. * * *

> Do you agree that the congressional nonaction in this case should affect the Court's interpretation of the statute?

The evidence of congressional approval of the policy embodied in Revenue Ruling 71–447 goes well beyond the failure of Congress to act on legislative proposals. Congress affirmatively manifested its acquiescence in the IRS policy when it enacted the present § 501(i) of the Code, Act of Oct. 20, 1976, Pub. L. 94–568, 90 Stat. 2697. That provision denies tax-exempt status to social clubs whose charters or policy statements provide for "discrimination against any person on the basis of race, color, or religion." Both the House and Senate Committee Reports on that bill articulated the national policy against granting tax exemptions to racially discriminatory private clubs. S. Rep. No. 94–1318, p. 8 (1976); H.R. Rep. No. 94–1353, p. 8 (1976).

Even more significant is the fact that both Reports focus on this Court's affirmance of *Green v. Connally,* 330 F.Supp. 1150 (DC 1971), as having established that "discrimination on account of race is inconsistent with an *educational institution's* tax-exempt status." S. Rep. No. 94–1318, *supra,* at 7–8, and n. 5; H.R. Rep. No. 94–1353, *supra* at 7–8, and n. 5 (emphasis added). These references in congressional Committee Reports on an enactment denying tax exemptions to racially discriminatory private social clubs cannot be read other than as indicating approval of the standards applied to racially discriminatory private schools by the IRS subsequent to 1970, and specifically of Revenue Ruling 71–447.

[In Part III the Court then rejected a separate claim that the IRS nondiscrimination policy violated religious schools' First Amendment rights to free exercise of religion.]

JUSTICE POWELL, concurring in part and concurring in the judgment.

* * *

[T]here is force in JUSTICE REHNQUIST's argument that §§ 170(c) and 501(c)(3) should be construed as setting forth the only criteria Congress has established for qualification as a tax-exempt organization. Indeed, were we writing prior to the history detailed in the Court's opinion, this could well be the construction I would adopt. But there has been a decade of acceptance that is persuasive in the circumstances of this case, and I conclude that there are now sufficient reasons for accepting the IRS's construction of the Code as proscribing tax exemptions for schools that discriminate on the basis of race as a matter of policy.

I cannot say that this construction of the Code, adopted by the IRS in 1970 and upheld by the Court of Appeals below, is without logical support. The statutory terms are not self-defining, and it is plausible that in some instances an organization seeking a tax exemption might act in a manner so clearly contrary to the purposes of our laws that it could not be deemed to serve the enumerated statutory purposes. And, as the Court notes, if any national policy is sufficiently fundamental to constitute such an overriding limitation on the availability of tax-exempt status under § 501(c)(3), it is the policy against racial discrimination in education. Finally, and of critical importance for me, the subsequent actions of Congress present "an unusually strong case of legislative acquiescence in and ratification by implication of the [IRS'] 1970 and 1971 rulings" with respect to racially discriminatory schools. In particular, Congress' enactment of § 501(i) in 1976 is strong evidence of agreement with these particular IRS rulings.[2]

---

[2] The District Court for the District of Columbia in *Green v. Connally*, 330 F.Supp. 1150 (three-judge court), *aff'd sub nom. Coit v. Green*, 404 U.S. 997 (1971) (*per curiam*), held that racially discriminatory private schools were not entitled to tax-exempt status. The same District Court, however, later ruled that racially segregated social clubs could receive tax exemptions under § 501(c)(7) of the Code. *See McGlotten v. Connally*, 338 F. Supp. 448 (1972) (three-judge court). Faced with these two important three-judge court rulings, Congress expressly overturned the relevant portion of *McGlotten* by enacting § 501(i), thus conforming the policy with respect to social clubs to the prevailing policy with respect to private schools. This affirmative step is a persuasive indication that Congress has not just silently acquiesced in the result of *Green*. Cf. *Merrill Lynch, Pierce, Fenner & Smith v. Curran*, 456 U.S. 353, 402 (1982) (POWELL, J., dissenting) (rejecting theory "that congressional intent can be inferred from silence, and that legislative inaction should achieve the force of law").

* * *

Justice Rehnquist, dissenting.

The Court points out that there is a strong national policy in this country against racial discrimination. To the extent that the Court states that Congress, in furtherance of this policy, could deny tax-exempt status to educational institutions that promote racial discrimination, I readily agree. But, unlike the Court, I am convinced that Congress simply has failed to take this action and, as this Court has said over and over again, regardless of our view on the propriety of Congress' failure to legislate, we are not constitutionally empowered to act for it.

> Can you anticipate what the dissenting opinion will say? You might think about how you would craft a dissent before you read Justice Rehnquist's.

In approaching this statutory construction question, the Court quite adeptly avoids the statute it is construing. This I am sure is no accident, for there is nothing in the language of § 501(c)(3) that supports the result obtained by the Court. * * * With undeniable clarity, Congress has explicitly defined the requirements for § 501(c)(3) status. An entity must be (1) a corporation, or community chest, fund, or foundation, (2) organized for one of the eight enumerated purposes, (3) operated on a nonprofit basis, and (4) free from involvement in lobbying activities and political campaigns. Nowhere is there to be found some additional, undefined public policy requirement.

The Court first seeks refuge from the obvious reading of § 501(c)(3) by turning to § 170 of the Internal Revenue Code, which provides a tax deduction for contributions made to § 501(c)(3) organizations. In setting forth the general rule, § 170 states:

> There shall be allowed as a deduction any charitable contribution (as defined in subsection (c)) payment of which is made within the taxable year. A charitable contribution shall be allowable as a deduction only if verified under regulations prescribed by the Secretary.

26 U.S.C. § 170(a)(1). The Court seizes the words "charitable contribution" and with little discussion concludes that "[o]n its face, therefore, § 170 reveals that Congress' intention was to provide tax benefits to organizations

serving charitable purposes," intimating that this implies some unspecified common law charitable trust requirement.

The Court would have been well advised to look to subsection (c) where, as § 170(a)(1) indicates, Congress has defined a "charitable contribution":

> For purposes of this section, the term "charitable contribution" means a contribution or gift to or for the use of . . . [a] corporation, trust, or community chest, fund, or foundation . . . organized and operated exclusively for religious, charitable, scientific, literary, or educational purposes, or to foster national or international amateur sports competition (but only if no part of its activities involve the provision of athletic facilities or equipment), or for the prevention of cruelty to children or animals; . . . no part of the net earnings of which inures to the benefit of any private shareholder or individual; and . . . which is not disqualified for tax exemption under section 501(c) (3) by reason of attempting to influence legislation, and which does not participate in, or intervene in (including the publishing or distributing of statements), any political campaign on behalf of any candidate for public office.

26 U.S.C. § 170(c). Plainly, § 170(c) simply tracks the requirements set forth in § 501(c)(3). Since § 170 is no more than a mirror of § 501(c)(3) and, as the Court points out, § 170 followed § 501(c)(3) by more than two decades, it is, at best, of little usefulness in finding the meaning of § 501(c)(3).

Making a more fruitful inquiry, the Court next turns to the legislative history of § 501(c)(3) and finds that Congress intended in that statute to offer a tax benefit to organizations that Congress believed were providing a public benefit. I certainly agree. But then the Court leaps to the conclusion that this history is proof Congress intended that an organization seeking § 501(c)(3) status "must fall within a category specified in that section and must demonstrably serve and be in harmony with the public interest." To the contrary, I think that the legislative history of § 501(c)(3) unmistakably makes clear that Congress has decided what organizations are serving a public purpose and providing a public benefit within the meaning of § 501(c)(3), and has clearly set forth in § 501(c)(3) the characteristics of such organizations. In fact, there are few examples which better illustrate Congress' effort to define and redefine the requirements of a legislative Act.

[JUSTICE REHNQUIST then discussed the evolution of the charitable exemption.]

One way to read the opinion handed down by the Court today leads to the conclusion that this long and arduous refining process of § 501(c)(3) was certainly a waste of time, for when enacting the original 1894 statute, Congress intended to adopt a common law term of art, and intended that this term of art carry with it all of the common law baggage which defines it. Such a view, however, leads also to the unsupportable idea that Congress has spent almost a century adding illustrations simply to clarify an already defined common law term.

Another way to read the Court's opinion leads to the conclusion that, even though Congress has set forth some of the requirements of a § 501(c)(3) organization, it intended that the IRS additionally require that organizations meet a higher standard of public interest, not stated by Congress, but to be determined and defined by the IRS and the courts. This view I find equally unsupportable. Almost a century of statutory history proves that Congress itself intended to decide what § 501(c)(3) requires. Congress has expressed its decision in the plainest of terms in § 501(c)(3) by providing that tax-exempt status is to be given to any corporation, or community chest, fund, or foundation that is organized for one of the eight enumerated purposes, operated on a nonprofit basis, and uninvolved in lobbying activities or political campaigns. The IRS certainly is empowered to adopt regulations for the enforcement of these specified requirements, and the courts have authority to resolve challenges to the IRS's exercise of this power, but Congress has left it to neither the IRS nor the courts to select or add to the requirements of § 501(c)(3) * * *

Perhaps recognizing the lack of support in the statute itself, or in its history, for the 1970 IRS change in interpretation, the Court finds that "[t]he actions of Congress since 1970 leave no doubt that the IRS reached the correct conclusion in exercising its authority," concluding that there is "an unusually strong case of legislative acquiescence in and ratification by implication of the 1970 and 1971 rulings." The Court relies first on several bills introduced to overturn the IRS interpretation of § 501(c)(3). But we have said before, and it is equally applicable here, that this type of congressional inaction is of virtually no weight in determining legislative intent. See *United States v. Wise*, 370 U.S. 405, 411 (1962); *Waterman S.S. Corp. v. United States*, 381 U.S. 252, 269 (1965). These bills and related hearings indicate little more than that a vigorous debate has existed in Congress concerning the new IRS position.

The Court next asserts that "Congress affirmatively manifested its acquiescence in the IRS policy when it enacted the present § 501(i) of the Code," a provision that "denies tax-exempt status to social clubs whose charters or policy statements provide for" racial discrimination. Quite to the contrary, it seems to me that, in § 501(i), Congress showed that, when it wants to add a requirement prohibiting racial discrimination to one of the tax-benefit provisions, it is fully aware of how to do it.

[Justice Rehnquist then discussed some legislative history concerning section 501(i), and focused on some amendments intended to limit certain enforcement procedures proposed by the IRS in 1978 and 1979 for determining whether a school operated in a racially nondiscriminatory fashion. The majority had discussed this amendment in a footnote to its opinion.] The Court points out that, in proposing his amendment, Congressman Ashbrook stated: " 'My amendment very clearly indicates on its face that all the regulations in existence as of August 22, 1978, would not be touched.' " The Court fails to note that Congressman Ashbrook also said:

> The IRS has no authority to create public policy. . . . So long as the Congress has not acted to set forth a national policy respecting denial of tax exemptions to private schools, it is improper for the IRS or any other branch of the Federal Government to seek denial of tax-exempt status. . . . There exists but a single responsibility which is proper for the Internal Revenue Service: To serve as tax collector.

125 Cong. Rec. 18444 (1979). In the same debate, Congressman Grassley asserted:

> Nobody argues that racial discrimination should receive preferred tax status in the United States. However, the IRS should not be making these decisions on the agency's own discretion. Congress should make these decisions.

Id. at 18448. The same debates are filled with other similar statements. While on the whole these debates do not show conclusively that Congress believed the IRS had exceeded its authority with the 1970 change in position, they likewise are far less than a showing of acquiescence in and ratification of the new position.

This Court continuously has been hesitant to find ratification through inaction. See *United States v. Wise*, supra. This is especially true where such a finding would result in a construction of the statute which not only is at odds with the language of the section in question and the pattern of the statute taken as a whole, but also is extremely far reaching in terms of the virtually untrammeled and unreviewable power it would vest in a regulatory agency.

SEC v. Sloan, 436 U.S. 103, 121 (1978). Few cases would call for more caution in finding ratification by acquiescence than the present ones. The new IRS interpretation is not only far less than a longstanding administrative policy, it is at odds with a position maintained by the IRS, and unquestioned by Congress, for several decades prior to 1970. The interpretation is unsupported by the statutory language, it is unsupported by legislative history, the interpretation has led to considerable controversy in and out of Congress, and the interpretation gives to the IRS a broad power which, until now, Congress had kept for itself. Where in addition to these circumstances Congress has shown time and time again that it is ready to enact positive legislation to change the Tax Code when it desires, this Court has no business finding that Congress has adopted the new IRS position by failing to enact legislation to reverse it.

I have no disagreement with the Court's finding that there is a strong national policy in this country opposed to racial discrimination. I agree with the Court that Congress has the power to further this policy by denying § 501(c)(3) status to organizations that practice racial discrimination. But as of yet, Congress has failed to do so. Whatever the reasons for the failure, this Court should not legislate for Congress. * * * I would reverse the Court of Appeals.

NOTES & QUESTIONS

1. How important to the result in *Bob Jones University* is Part II-D of the Court's opinion?

2. The majority opinion and Justice Rehnquist's dissent draw different conclusions from the fact that Congress legislated on a similar issue for a different type of organization ("social clubs"). Which opinion do you think makes the better argument? As you see from Justice Powell's concurrence, Part II-D of the Court's opinion, including its discussion of Congress's adoption of section 501(i) for social clubs, was an extremely important factor for him. Looking at footnote 2 of Justice Powell's opinion, what does he view the import of that legislation to be?

3. What do you make of the Court's (and the dissent's) interpretive arguments *not* involving Part II-D? In large part, they are wrestling with how to respond to changed societal conditions. In section B of the next chapter we return briefly to *Bob Jones University* in connection with this issue.

4. Do you think the Court's *result* would have been different if the Court had been deciding this case in 1975, rather than in 1983? If you think the result would still have been the same, how would the opinion have been different?

5. "Subsequent" legislative action (or inaction) involves observing how a legislature behaves after it has passed a statute, or more particularly how a legislature behaves after a court or agency has interpreted its statute.

6. *Montana Wilderness* involved subsequent legislative action, while *Bob Jones University* involved subsequent legislative inaction (or acquiescence). Keeping in mind that the subsequent legislative action we are discussing is not an amendment to the relevant statutory language but is instead simply evidence that members of Congress accepted a particular interpretation, is there a meaningful difference between subsequent action and subsequent inaction?

7. How many different types (or categories) of subsequent legislative activity or inactivity can you imagine?

Test Your Understanding

To assess your understanding of the material in this chapter, click here to take a quiz.

27

Changed Context by the Time of Interpretation

Key Concepts

- The interpretive moment
- Changed legal context
- Changed factual context
- Enacting legislature vs. current legislature
- Judicial updating vs. legislative updating of statutes
- Statutory *stare decisis* (reprise)

Chapter Summary

We began this Part with a chapter exploring how an understanding of the context of a statute's enactment can offer interpretive guidance. But many years can pass between when a statute is enacted and when it is interpreted. During that time, both the factual conditions and the broader legal context that existed at the time of enactment may well have changed, requiring the interpreter to apply the statute to unforeseen circumstances. How should a court in such a case meet the moment? To what extent or in what ways should it consider changes in conditions since the time of enactment? This chapter considers several examples of courts confronting the issue of how to interpret a statute in light of intervening changes in context.

The previous chapter concluded with a consideration of whether and if so, when, a legislature's action or inaction *after* it has enacted a particular statute might affect the interpretation of that statute. In this chapter we take up an additional post-enactment interpretive consideration, how the broader context of the era in which an interpretation occurs can affect that interpretation. Of course, the interpretive enterprise can be implicitly influenced by a host of factors specific to that interpretive moment, including the interpretive philosophies of those doing the interpretation, the evolving relationships among the branches of government, and the "context of the times," something that may not be acknowledged or recognized even as it influences the decision-making process. But this chapter will focus specifically on acknowledged legal and factual developments that have arisen after the time of enactment.

As described in Chapter 14, one category of post-enactment interpretive difficulties arises because a statute written years earlier is being applied in circumstances or to conditions that may have been unforeseeable or unforeseen by the enacting legislature. The *Bostock* decision we read in Chapter 17, in which the question was whether the protections of the 1964 Civil Rights Act against employment discrimination "because of . . . sex" also protect against employment discrimination on the basis of sexual orientation, might be seen as an example of that difficulty. In this chapter we consider several other examples that invite reflection on what the role of interpreting courts should be in the face of circumstances present at the time of interpretation but that were likely not anticipated by the enacting legislature.

Sometimes what has changed between the moment of enactment and the moment of interpretation is the broader legal landscape into which the interpretive choice will need to fit. Other times what has changed are the facts "on the ground," including the kinds of societal problems that litigants are bringing to the legal system and the broader challenges and values of the day. And sometimes both legal and factual conditions have changed, in ways that complicate the task of determining how to construe a piece of statutory text. We will look at each of these categories in turn.

A. Changed Legal Context

The sheer volume of statutes on the books is enormous, not to mention common law and constitutional law (and, as we will see later in this book, agency regulations). It is virtually impossible for anyone to "know" all the law. Meanwhile, legislatures are constantly passing new laws. Often, a legislature consciously changes the law with awareness that it is doing so. But at other times, a legislature may adopt a law that touches on or potentially intersects or overlaps with some other law without any awareness of the potential overlap. Sometimes, that overlap may not even become apparent until later on. In such circumstances, courts must decide how to make disparate laws cohere. The Whole Code Rule and the *in pari materia* doctrine discussed in Chapters 20 and 24 are examples of the ways in which courts attempt to make laws cohere.

Of course, even at the time of enactment, full coherence with the entire body of existing law is a wholly unrealistic ideal. It is simply impossible for the legislature to know *all* the preexisting law—and all the ways a pending bill might implicate some preexisting law—before deciding whether to pass that bill. But when the surrounding law that had been part of the context at the time of enactment itself later changes, should an interpreting court take that into consideration at the time of interpretation, and if so, how? These questions can be especially tricky if it is unclear how relevant or important the surrounding legal context at the time of enactment was to the enacting legislature. Consider the following problem.

DIY
The Juror Selection Problem from the Early 20th Century

In many states, it has been common to select jurors from the pool of eligible voters. The Nineteenth Amendment, ratified in 1920, extended to women the right to vote. In the years shortly after ratification of the Nineteenth Amendment, several states confronted the issue of whether that Amendment's extension of the voting franchise to women had altered the way jurors were to be selected. The problem arose in a number of states that had not previously extended the right to vote to women, and that had juror selection statutes explicitly providing in some form that jurors were to be chosen from the list of the state's "qualified electors," or voters.

How should these juror selection statutes, enacted at a time when the term "qualified electors" in these states unquestionably described a category that excluded women, be interpreted in light of the constitutional amendment requiring that women be included among those qualified to vote? The constitutional amendment of course said nothing about its application to jury service, nor about any other aspect of gender equality beyond the right to vote.

Before reading further, take two minutes to think and write down your thoughts about what a court in 1925 required to interpret the term "qualified electors" (or its equivalent) in a juror selection statute should do. Keep in mind possible Textualist and Purposivist arguments.

In actuality, courts diverged on this issue. In *Commonwealth v. Maxwell*, 114 A. 825 (Pa. 1921), the Pennsylvania Supreme Court held that the Nineteenth Amendment's extension of the franchise to women years after the state's adoption of its juror selection statute required that women also now be part of the potential jury pool. By contrast, high courts in Illinois and Massachusetts reached the opposite result, accepting the counterargument that the legislatures responsible for enacting these jury selection statutes, in providing that jurors were to be drawn from the ranks of qualified electors, had intended to limit the class of jurors to men. Therefore, although the Nineteenth Amendment put women into the class of qualified voters, the juror statutes of these states would continue to exclude women from juries. *See People ex rel. Fyfe v. Barnett*, 150 N.E. 290 (Ill. 1925); *Commonwealth v. Welosky*, 177 N.E. 656 (Mass. 1931). In these cases, the judicial decisions were implicitly saying that it was up to the legislatures to update their juror selection statutes.

Here is an excerpt of the Massachusetts high court's decision in *Welosky*:

Commonwealth v. Welosky
177 N.E. 656 (Mass. 1931)

RUGG, C.J.

* * *

[The question] is whether the statutes of this Commonwealth require that the names of women otherwise qualified be placed upon jury lists so that they may be drawn for service as jurors.

It is plain that women could not rightly serve as jurors, save in the rare instances where a jury of matrons was called, under the Constitution and laws of this Commonwealth prior to the adoption of the Nineteenth Amendment to the Constitution of the United States. The terms of the statute, in the light of the Constitution, express decisions, universal understanding, and unbroken practice, forbid any other view. The trial by jury of the common law and that contemplated by both the Constitution of this commonwealth and that of the United States were by a jury of twelve composed exclusively of men. *Commonwealth v. Dorsey, 103 Mass. 412, 418; Capital Traction Co. v. Hof, 174 U. S. 1, 13, 19 S. Ct. 580, 43 L. Ed. 873.*

The statute to be interpreted is G. L. c. 234, § 1. Its relevant language is: 'A person qualified to vote for representatives to the general court shall be liable to serve as a juror,' with exceptions not here material.

The words of a statute are the main source for the ascertainment of a legislative purpose. They are to be construed according to their natural import in common and approved usage. The imperfections of language to express intent often render necessary further inquiry. Statutes are to be interpreted, not alone according to their simple, literal or strict verbal meaning, but in connection with their development, their progression through the legislative body, the history of the times, prior legislation, contemporary customs and conditions and the system of positive law of which they are part, and in the light of the constitution and of the common law, to the end that they be held to cover the subjects presumably within the vision of the Legislature and, on the one hand, be not unduly constricted so as to exclude matters fairly within their scope, and, on the other hand, be not

What kind of interpretive approach is the court taking in this paragraph?

stretched by enlargement of signification to comprehend matters not within the principle and purview on which they were founded when originally framed and their words chosen. General expressions may be restrained by relevant circumstances showing a legislative intent that they be narrowed and used in a particular sense.

Is the court now taking a different interpretive approach here?

It is clear beyond peradventure that the words of G. L. c. 234, § 1, when originally enacted could not by any possibility have included or been intended by the general court to include women among those liable to jury duty. The Constitution forbade the words, 'A person qualified to vote for representatives to the general court,' to comprehend women. Women have been qualified

In Massachusetts, the legislature is **FYI** known as the "General Court of Massachusetts." So, this reference to the "general court" is a reference to the state legislature.

to vote in this commonwealth only since the adoption of the Nineteenth Amendment to the Constitution of the United States. It is not argued in behalf of the defendant that the terms of the statutes preceding G. L. c. 234, § 1, that is to say of R. L. c. 176, § 1, and its predecessors in substantially the same words since a time before the adoption of the Constitution, could possibly have imposed jury duty upon women. The argument on this point is * * * that the phrase of the statute is general and therefore was intended automatically to include women if their constitutional inhibitions were ever removed. * * *

Statutes framed in general terms commonly look to the future and may include conditions as they arise from time to time not even known at the time of enactment, provided they are fairly within the sweep and the meaning of the words and falling within their obvious scope and purpose. But statutes do not govern situations not within the reason of their enactment and giving rise to radically diverse circumstances presumably not within the dominating purpose of those who framed and enacted them.

As matter of strict and abstract verbal interpretation, apart from context, circumstances, and contemporary and antecedent history, the language of G. L. c. 234, § 1, is broad enough to comprise women. The word "person" when used in an unrestricted sense includes a woman. It has been said that "The word 'person,' in its natural and usual signification, includes women as well as men." The word "person," like many other words, has no fixed and rigid signification, but has different meanings dependent upon contemporary conditions, the connection in which it is used, and the result intended to be accomplished. It has been said to be "an ambiguous word" and may refer to those of either or both sexes. * * * It has also been held not to include a woman. * * *

This brief review of authorities demonstrates that "person" by itself is an equivocal word. Its meaning in a statute requires interpretation. The statute here under examination (G. L. c. 234, § 1) is a re-enactment of a long line of statutes of the commonwealth running back to a time shortly after the adoption of the Constitution as well as through all intermediate revisions dealing with qualifications for jury service. Laws of the colony and of the province are in effect the same. In the earlier and later statutes, the same essential and almost the identical words have been employed. The word 'person' occurs in them all. The selection of jurors has constantly been required to be from those qualified to vote. Qualifications for voting have been continuously established by the Constitution. By the words of that instrument and its amendments (apart from the effect of the Nineteenth Amendment of the federal Constitution) the right to vote was confined to male inhabitants, male persons, and finally to male citizens, until the word 'male' was stricken out in 1924 by Amendment 68. See part 2, c. 1, § 2, art. 2; part 2, c. 1, § 3, art. 4; articles 3 and 32 of the Amendments. Manifestly, therefore, the intent of the Legislature must have been, in using the word 'person' in statutes concerning jurors and jury lists, to confine its meaning to men. That was the only intent constitutionally permissible. There is every presumption that the legislative department of government always intends to act strictly within the bounds of the Constitution.

Possession of property of specified value and payment of taxes as qualifications for voters were required in earlier days and from time to time, but these were gradually eliminated by Amendments to the Constitution until the last of such limitations disappeared with the approval of Amendment 32 in 1891. When the suffrage has been thus widened among male citizens, there has followed, without further legislation and without change in the phrase of the statute, a like extension of citizens liable to service as jurors. These concurring enlargements of those liable to jury service were simply an extension to larger numbers of the same classification of persons. Since the word 'person' in the statutes respecting jurors meant men, when there was an extension of the right to vote to other men previously disqualified, the jury statutes by specific definition included them. No amendment to the statute can be conceived which could have made that meaning more clear. This is the force and effect of *Neal v. Delaware, 103 U. S. 370, at page 389, 26 L. Ed. 567.*

Changes in suffrage and in liability for jury service in the past differ in kind from the change here urged.

* * * The change in the legal status of women wrought by the Nineteenth Amendment was radical, drastic and unprecedented. While it is to be given full effect in its field, it is not to be extended by implication. It is unthinkable that those who first framed and selected the words for the [juror qualification statute] had any design that it should ever include women within its scope. It is equally inconceivable that those who from time to time had re-enacted that statute had any such design. When they used the word 'person' in connection with those qualified to vote for members of the more numerous branch of the general court, to describe those liable to jury service, no one contemplated the possibility of women becoming so qualified. The same is true in general of those who from time to time re-enacted the statute in substantially the same words. No intention to include

> What interpretive approach does this assertion suggest? Do you agree it is "unthinkable" that those who wrote the juror qualification statute would have countenanced including women on juries?

women can be deduced from the omission of the word 'male.' That word was imbedded in the Constitution of the commonwealth as a limitation upon those citizens who might become voters and thereby members of a class from which jurors might be drawn. It would have been superfluous also to insert that word in the statute. * * *

The conclusion is irresistible that, according to sound principles of statutory construction, it cannot rightly be held that the scope of R. L. c. 176, § 1, the statute in force on August 26, 1920, now G. L. c. 234, § 1, was extended by the ratification of the Nineteenth Amendment so as to render women liable to jury duty. To reach that result would be directly contrary to every purpose and intent of the general court in enacting that law.

NOTES & QUESTIONS

1. Did the Massachusetts court get it right? Why or why not? If you believe *Welosky* was wrongly decided, would it matter if the statute had said, "A *man* qualified to vote for representatives to the general court. . ." rather than "A *person* qualified to vote for representatives to the general court. . ."? For cases addressing variations of this question, see *Idaho v. Kelly*, 229 P. 659 (Idaho 1924); *South Carolina v. Mittle*, 113 S.E. 335 (S.C. 1922). For a state where the basic statutes about jury service used the term "persons," but a more specific provision involving certain grand juries referred to "men," see *Browning v. Ohio*, 165 N.E. 566, 567 (Ohio 1929).

2. Why does the Massachusetts court view other changes in suffrage (particularly the elimination of property ownership requirements) differently from the expansion of voting to women?

3. One fundamental question that all cases involving changed circumstances raise is *who* should update a statute in light of social, technological, or legal change. Implicit in the *Welosky* court's rejection of the claim that the statute required women on juries was the view that the legislature, rather than a court, should decide the question. Of course, in *Commonwealth v. Maxwell* mentioned above, it was the 1921 Pennsylvania court that did the updating. In your view, who should decide the question, a court or the legislature?

4. Does it matter that the Massachusetts juror statute had numerous exceptions for those whose jobs made jury duty difficult (e.g., firemen, lighthouse keepers, surgeons), jobs that were exclusively done by men at the time? In a portion of the decision not excerpted above, the *Welosky* court thought the absence of any female-specific exceptions was another reason not to read the statute to encompass women. Does it matter that when the Massachusetts legislature eventually extended jury duty to women in 1949, it created female-specific exceptions (e.g., women attendant nurses, mothers of children under sixteen)?

B. Changed Factual Context

The *Bob Jones University* case at the end of the last chapter focused on the extent to which Congress, for more than a decade, had been aware of *and arguably acquiesced in* the IRS's 1970 determination not to grant a charitable exemption to a university that was engaging in racial discrimination. But in addition to this post-enactment "legislative inaction" dimension for which we principally read the *Bob Jones University* case, the underlying question of how to construe the charitable exemption provisions in the Internal Revenue Code, in light of the country's evolving efforts to reduce racial discrimination, offers one kind of example of how factual changes in the broader society, including changing social views and changing national policy, can affect the interpretation of a specific piece of statutory text. Recall that in the *Bob Jones University* case, the majority treated the statute as incorporating a *common-law* concept, thereby giving the *courts* the authority to update the meaning of the statute. Should courts be able to update statutes that do not incorporate the common law into statutory text? Is this what happened in the 2020 *Bostock* case when the U.S. Supreme Court held that firing an employee because the employee was gay was an adverse employment action "because of. . .sex" within the meaning of Title VII of the 1964 Civil Rights Act?

C. Hybrid Cases, Involving Changes in Both Fact and Surrounding Law

Quite often, interpreting courts confront a post-enactment, moment-of-interpretation context in which both key facts and social conditions, as well as the relevant legal landscape, have changed. We present below three fascinating examples, beginning with one you have already considered.

1.   Affirmative Action in Employment Revisited

The story of the Supreme Court's acceptance of an employer's voluntary affirmative action plan in the *Weber* case in 1979, introduced in Chapter 18 as an example of a purpose-based interpretation of Title VII, might alternatively be understood as an example of what could be called a "dynamic" reading of the statute, in light of at least two significant changes that had occurred between the statute's enactment in 1964 and the Court's decision in 1979. First, as a matter of social conditions, the problem of race-based discrimination in employment had turned out to be almost intractable, proving much harder to eradicate than the enacting Congress had probably anticipated (or hoped). Second, as a matter of law, by the time of *Weber* the Court had construed Title VII to prohibit discrimination against either Black *or white* employees (as well as employees of any other race), *see McDonald v. Santa Fe Trail Transportation Co.*, 427 U.S. 273 (1976), making it very difficult for an employer to rectify the continuing effects of past discrimination against Black individuals without leaving the employer vulnerable to a Title VII lawsuit by white individuals.

In light of these new realities, the *Weber* Court arguably adopted a construction of Title VII less true to either the original intent or the original purpose of the enacting Congress and more in line with the Court's sense of the place of the statute in American society by 1979. Justice Blackmun's concurring opinion in the case, more than the majority opinion we read earlier, is a particularly good example of this type of dynamic reasoning. As you read Justice Blackmun's concurrence below, watch for how his opinion recognizes, either explicitly or implicitly, the unforeseen difficulties that confronted the statute.

United Steelworkers of America v. Weber
443 U.S. 193 (1979)

* * *

MR. JUSTICE BLACKMUN, **concurring**.

While I share some of the misgivings expressed in MR. JUSTICE REHNQUIST's dissent concerning the extent to which the legislative history of Title VII clearly supports the result the Court reaches today [authors' note: described above on p. 423], I believe that additional considerations, practical and equitable, only partially perceived, if perceived at all, by the 88th Congress, support the conclusion reached by the Court today, and I therefore join its opinion as well as its judgment.

I

In his dissent from the decision of the United States Court of Appeals for the Fifth Circuit, Judge Wisdom pointed out that this litigation arises from a practical problem in the administration of Title VII. The broad prohibition against discrimination places the employer and the union on what he accurately described as a "high tightrope without a net beneath them." If Title VII is read literally, on the one hand they face liability for past discrimination against blacks, and on the other they face liability to whites for any voluntary preferences adopted to mitigate the effects of prior discrimination against blacks.

In this litigation, Kaiser denies prior discrimination but concedes that its past hiring practices may be subject to question. Although the labor force in the Gramercy area was approximately 39% black, Kaiser's work force was less than 15% black, and its craftwork force was less than 2% black. Kaiser had made some effort to recruit black painters, carpenters, insulators, and other craftsmen, but it continued to insist that those hired have five years' prior industrial experience, a requirement that arguably was not sufficiently job related to justify under Title VII any discriminatory impact it may have had. The parties dispute the extent to which black craftsmen were available in the local labor market. They agree, however, that after critical reviews from the Office of Federal Contract Compliance, Kaiser and the Steelworkers established the training program in question here and modeled it along the lines of a Title VII consent decree later entered for the steel industry. Yet when they did this, respondent Weber sued, alleging that Title VII prohibited the program because it discriminated against him as a white person and it was not supported by a prior judicial finding of discrimination against blacks.

Respondent Weber's reading of Title VII, endorsed by the Court of Appeals, places voluntary compliance with Title VII in profound jeopardy. The only way for the employer and the union to keep their footing on the "tightrope" it creates would be to eschew all forms of voluntary affirmative action. Even a whisper of emphasis on minority recruiting would be forbidden. Because Congress intended to encourage private efforts to come into compliance with Title VII, Judge Wisdom concluded that employers and unions who had committed "arguable violations" of Title VII should be free to make reasonable responses without fear of liability to whites. Preferential hiring along the lines of the Kaiser program is a reasonable response for the employer, whether or not a court, on these facts, could order the same step as a remedy. The company is able to avoid identifying victims of past discrimination, and so avoids claims for backpay that would inevitably follow a response limited to such victims. If past victims should be benefited by the program, however, the company mitigates its liability to those persons. Also, to the extent that Title VII liability is predicated on the "disparate effect" of an employer's past hiring practices, the program makes it less likely that such an effect could be demonstrated. And the Court has recently held that work-force statistics resulting from private affirmative action were probative of benign intent in a "disparate treatment" case.

The "arguable violation" theory has a number of advantages. It responds to a practical problem in the administration of Title VII not anticipated by Congress. It draws predictability from the outline of present law and closely effectuates the purpose of the Act. Both Kaiser and the United States urge its adoption here. Because I agree that it is the soundest way to approach this case, my preference would be to resolve this litigation by applying it and holding that Kaiser's craft training program meets the requirement that voluntary affirmative action be a reasonable response to an "arguable violation" of Title VII.

 How do you like the "arguable violation" theory?

II

The Court, however, declines to consider the narrow "arguable violation" approach and adheres instead to an interpretation of Title VII that permits affirmative action by an employer whenever the job category in question is "traditionally segregated." Ante, at 209, and n. 9. The sources cited suggest that the Court considers a job category to be "traditionally segregated" when there has been a societal history of purposeful exclusion of blacks from the job category, resulting in a persistent disparity between the proportion of blacks in the labor force and the proportion of blacks among those who hold jobs within the category.

"Traditionally segregated job categories," where they exist, sweep far more broadly than the class of "arguable violations" of Title VII. The Court's expansive approach is somewhat disturbing for me because, as Mr. Justice Rehnquist points out, the Congress that passed Title VII probably thought it was adopting a principle of nondiscrimination that would apply to blacks and whites alike. While setting aside that principle can be justified where necessary to advance statutory policy by encouraging reasonable responses as a form of voluntary compliance that mitigates "arguable violations," discarding the principle of nondiscrimination where no countervailing statutory policy exists appears to be at odds with the bargain struck when Title VII was enacted.

A closer look at the problem, however, reveals that in each of the principal ways in which the Court's "traditionally segregated job categories" approach expands on the "arguable violations" theory, still other considerations point in favor of the broad standard adopted by the Court, and make it possible for me to conclude that the Court's reading of the statute is an acceptable one.

A. The first point at which the Court departs from the "arguable violations" approach is that it measures an individual employer's capacity for affirmative action solely in terms of a statistical disparity. The individual employer need not have engaged in discriminatory practices in the past. While, under Title VII, a mere disparity may provide the basis for a prima facie case against an employer, it would not conclusively prove a violation of the Act. As a practical matter, however, this difference may not be that great. While the "arguable violation" standard is conceptually satisfying in practice the emphasis would be on "arguable" rather than on "violation." The great difficulty in the District Court was that no one had any incentive to prove that Kaiser had violated the Act. Neither Kaiser nor the Steelworkers wanted to establish a past violation, nor did Weber. The blacks harmed had never sued and so had no established representative. The Equal Employment Opportunity Commission declined to intervene, and cannot be expected to intervene in every case of this nature. To make the "arguable violation" standard work, it would have to be set low enough to permit the employer to prove it without obligating himself to pay a damages award. The inevitable tendency would be to avoid hairsplitting litigation by simply concluding that a mere disparity between the racial composition of the employer's work force and the composition of the qualified local labor force would be an "arguable violation," even though actual liability could not be established on that basis alone.

B. The Court also departs from the "arguable violation" approach by permitting an employer to redress discrimination that lies wholly outside the bounds of Title VII. For example, Title VII provides no remedy for pre-Act discrimination; yet the purposeful discrimination that creates a "traditionally segregated job category" may have entirely predated the Act. More subtly, in assessing a prima facie case of Title VII liability, the composition of the employer's work force is compared to the composition of the pool of workers who meet valid job qualifications. When a "job category" is traditionally segregated, however, that pool will reflect the effects of segregation, and the Court's approach goes further and permits a comparison with the composition of the labor force as a whole, in which minorities are more heavily represented.

Strong considerations of equity support an interpretation of Title VII that would permit private affirmative action to reach where Title VII itself does not. The bargain struck in 1964 with the passage of Title VII guaranteed equal opportunity for white and black alike, but where Title VII provides no remedy for blacks, it should not be construed to foreclose private affirmative action from supplying relief. It seems unfair for respondent Weber to argue, as he does, that the asserted scarcity of black craftsmen in Louisiana, the product of historic discrimination, makes Kaiser's training program illegal because it ostensibly absolves Kaiser of all Title VII liability. Brief for Respondents 60. Absent compelling evidence of legislative intent, I would not interpret Title VII itself as a means of "locking in" the effects of segregation for which Title VII provides no remedy. Such a construction, as the Court points out, ante, at 204, would be "ironic," given the broad remedial purposes of Title VII.

MR. JUSTICE REHNQUIST's dissent, while it focuses more on what Title VII does not require than on what Title VII forbids, cites several passages that appear to express an intent to "lock in" minorities. In mining the legislative history anew, however, the dissent, in my view, fails to take proper account of our prior cases that have given that history a much more limited reading than that adopted by the dissent. For example, in *Griggs v. Duke Power Co.*, 401 U.S. 424, 434–436, and n. 11 (1971), the Court refused to give controlling weight to the memorandum of Senators Clark and Case which the dissent now finds so persuasive. See post, at 239–241. And in quoting a statement from that memorandum that an employer would not be "permitted. . .to prefer Negroes for future vacancies," post, at 240, the dissent does not point out that the Court's opinion in *Teamsters v. United States*, 431 U.S., at 349–351, implies that language is limited to the protection of established seniority systems. Here, seniority is not in issue because the craft training program is new and does not involve an abrogation of pre-existing seniority rights. In short, the passages marshaled by the dissent are not so compelling as to merit the whip hand over the obvious equity of permitting employers to ameliorate the effects of past discrimination for which Title VII provides no direct relief.

III

I also think it significant that, while the Court's opinion does not foreclose other forms of affirmative action, the Kaiser program it approves is a moderate one. The opinion notes that the program does not afford an absolute preference for blacks, and that it ends when the racial composition of Kaiser's craftwork force matches the racial composition of the local population. It thus operates as a temporary tool for remedying past discrimination without attempting to "maintain" a previously achieved balance. See *University of California Regents v. Bakke*, 438 U.S. 265, 342 n. 17 (1978) (opinion of Brennan, White, Marshall, and Blackmun, JJ.). Because the duration of the program is finite, it perhaps will end even before the "stage of maturity when action along this line is no longer necessary." *Id.*, at 403 (opinion of Blackmun, J.). And if the Court has misperceived the political will, it has the assurance that because the question is statutory Congress may set a different course if it so chooses.

NOTES & QUESTIONS

1. What is different about Justice Blackmun's interpretive approach in *Weber* compared to the Court's majority opinion, which you read in Chapter 18?

2. What is different about the resulting doctrine Justice Blackmun would have adopted to resolve the case, compared to the majority opinion?

3. At the end of his opinion, Justice Blackmun, like the majority, refers to the affirmative action program "as a *temporary* toll for remedying past discrimination" and its duration as "finite," because it will end "when the racial composition of Kaiser's craftwork force matches the racial composition of the local population." What if the racial composition of Kaiser's craftwork force never reaches the racial composition of the local population?

4. For "the book" on the idea of "dynamic" statutory interpretation in light of changed circumstances, see William N. Eskridge Jr., Dynamic Statutory Interpretation (1994); *see also* T. Alexander Aleinikoff, *Updating Statutory Interpretation*, 87 Mich. L. Rev. 20 (1988).

2. Evolving Family Configurations and Evolving Family Law

Family law is almost exclusively a matter of state rather than federal law, and it is overwhelmingly statutory rather than judge-made. The following 1995 family law case from New York State's highest court involves a dramatic example of how both societal and legal changes (which of course can often happen in tandem) combined to produce what might fairly be called a judicial re-interpretation of a statute, in order to promote a sense of overall coherence in the law. As you read it, be on the lookout for the specific interpretive issue that the court confronts: What provision of the state code is it in, and what is the textual language at issue?

Matter of Jacob
660 N.E.2d 397 (N.Y. 1995)

CHIEF JUDGE KAYE.

Under the New York adoption statute, a single person can adopt a child (Domestic Relations Law § 110). Equally clear is the right of a single homosexual to adopt. * * * These appeals call upon us to decide if the unmarried partner of a child's biological mother, whether heterosexual or homosexual, who is raising the child together with the biological parent, can become the child's second parent by means of adoption.

Because the two adoptions sought—one by an unmarried heterosexual couple, the other by the lesbian partner of the child's mother—are fully consistent with the adoption statute, we answer this question in the affirmative. To rule otherwise would mean that the thousands of New York children actually being raised in homes headed by two unmarried persons could have only one legal parent, not the two who want them.

The Adoptions Sought

In *Matter of Jacob*, Roseanne M. A. and Jacob's biological father (from whom she is divorced) separated prior to the child's birth and Roseanne M. A. was awarded sole custody. Jacob was a year old when Stephen T. K. began living with him and his mother in early 1991. * * * Though acknowledging that "the granting of an adoption in this matter may be beneficial to Jacob," Family Court dismissed the petition for lack of standing on the ground that Domestic Relations Law § 110 does not authorize adoptions by an unmarried couple. The Appellate Division affirmed, two Justices dissenting (210 AD2d 876), and an appeal to this Court was taken as of right.

In *Matter of Dana*, appellants are G. M. and her lesbian partner, P. I., who have lived together in what is described as a long and close relationship for the past 19 years. * * * In 1989, the two women decided that P. I. would have a child they would raise together. P. I. was artificially inseminated by an anonymous donor, and on June 6, 1990, she gave birth to Dana. G. M. and P. I. have shared parenting responsibilities since Dana's birth and have arranged their separate work schedules around her needs. * * * In the court-ordered report recommending that G. M. be permitted to adopt (*see*, Domestic Relations Law § 116), the disinterested investigator described Dana as an attractive, sturdy and articulate little girl with a "rich family life," which includes frequent visits with G. M.'s three grown children from a previous marriage "who all love Dana and accept her as their baby sister." Noting that G. M. "only has the best interest of Dana in mind," the report concluded that she "provides her with a family structure in which to grow and flourish."

As in *Matter of Jacob*, Family Court, while conceding the favorable results of the home study and "in no way disparaging the ability of [G. M.] to be a good, nurturing and loving parent," denied the petition for lack of standing. In addition, the court held that the adoption was further prohibited by Domestic Relations Law § 117 which it interpreted to require the automatic termination of P. I.'s relationship with Dana upon an adoption by G. M. Despite its conclusion that G. M. had standing to adopt, the Appellate Division nevertheless affirmed on the ground that Domestic Relations Law § 117 prohibits the adoption (209 AD2d 8). We granted leave to appeal.

Limiting our analysis, as did the courts below, to the preserved statutory interpretation issues, we conclude that appellants have standing to adopt under Domestic Relations Law § 110 and are not foreclosed from doing so by Domestic Relations Law § 117. There being no statutory preclusion, we now reverse the order of the Appellate Division in each case and remit the matter to Family Court for a factual evaluation and determination as to whether these adoptions would be in the best interest of the children.

The Context of our Statutory Analysis

Two basic themes of overarching significance set the context of our statutory analysis.

First and foremost, since adoption in this State is "solely the creature of. . .statute" (*Matter of Eaton*, 305 N.Y. 162, 165), the adoption statute must be strictly construed. What is to be construed strictly and applied rigorously in this sensitive area of the law, however, is legislative purpose as well as legislative language. Thus, the adoption statute must be applied in harmony with the humanitarian principle that adoption is a means of securing the best possible home for a child.

 How did the court identify this as the statute's purpose?

* * * [I]n strictly construing the adoption statute, our primary loyalty must be to the statute's legislative purpose – the child's best interest. "The adoptive family arises out of the State's concern for the best interest of the child" (*People ex rel. Sibley v. Sheppard*, 54 N.Y.2d 320, 327). This profound concern for the child's welfare is reflected in the statutory language itself: when "satisfied that the best interests of the. . .child will be promoted thereby," a court *"shall* make an order approving the adoption" (Domestic Relations Law § 114 [emphasis added]).

This policy would certainly be advanced in situations like those presented here by allowing the two adults who actually function as a child's parents to become the child's legal parents. The advantages which would result from such an adoption include Social Security and life insurance benefits in the event of a parent's death or disability, the right to sue for the wrongful death of a parent, the right to inherit under rules of intestacy and eligibility for coverage under both parents' health insurance policies. In addition, granting a second parent adoption further ensures that two adults are legally entitled to make medical decisions for the child in case of emergency and are under a legal obligation for the child's economic support (*see*, Domestic Relations Law § 32).

Even more important, however, is the emotional security of knowing that in the event of the biological parent's death or disability, the other parent will have presumptive custody, and the children's relationship with their parents, siblings and other relatives will continue should the coparents separate. Indeed, viewed from the children's perspective, permitting the adoptions allows the children to achieve a measure of permanency with both parent figures. * * *

A second, related point of overriding significance is that the various sections comprising New York's adoption statute today represent a complex and not entirely reconcilable patch-work. Amended innumerable times since its passage in 1873, the adoption statute was last consolidated nearly 60 years ago, in 1938. Thus, after decades of piecemeal amendment upon amendment, the statute today contains language from the 1870's alongside language from the 1990's.

Though courts surely must, and do, strive to give effect to every word of a statute, our analysis must recognize the difficulty—perhaps unique difficulty – of such an endeavor here. With its long, tortuous history, New York's adoption statute today is a far cry from a "methodical[ ] and meticulous[ ]" expression of legislative judgment (dissenting opn, at 683). That the questions posed by these appeals are not readily answerable by reference to the words of a particular section of the law, but instead require the traditional and often close and difficult task of statutory interpretation is evident even in the length of today's opinions—whichever result is reached.

Against this backdrop, we turn to the particular provisions at issue.

Domestic Relations Law § 110

Despite ambiguity in other sections, one thing is clear: section 110 allows appellants to become adoptive parents. Domestic Relations Law § 110, entitled "Who May Adopt," provides that an "adult unmarried person or an adult husband and his adult wife together may adopt another person" (Domestic Relations Law § 110). Under this language, both appellant G. M. in *Matter of Dana* and appellant Stephen T. K. in *Matter of Jacob*, as adult unmarried persons, have standing to adopt and appellants are correct that the Court's analysis of section 110 could appropriately end here.

Endowing the word "together" as used in section 110 with the overpowering significance of enforcing a policy in favor of marriage (as the dissent does) would require us to rewrite the statute. The statute uses the word "together" only to describe married persons and thus does not preclude an unmarried person in a relationship with another unmarried person from adopting. Rather, by insisting on the joint consent of the married persons, the statutory term "together" simply insures that one spouse cannot adopt a child without the other spouse's knowledge or over the other's objection. Since each of the biological mothers here is not only aware of these proceedings, but has expressly consented to the adoptions, section 110 poses no statutory impediment.

The conclusion that appellants have standing to adopt is also supported by the history of section 110. The pattern of amendments since the end of World War II evidences a successive expansion of the categories of persons entitled to adopt regardless of [marital status or sexual orientation]. * * *

These amendments reflect some of the fundamental changes that have taken place in the makeup of the family. Today, for example, at least 1.2 of the 3.5 million American households which consist of an unmarried adult couple have children under 15 years old, more than a six-fold increase from 1970. Yet further recognition of this transformation is evidenced by the fact that unlike the States of New Hampshire and Florida (NH Rev Stat Annot § 170–B:4; Fla Stat Ann § 63.042[3]), New York does not prohibit adoption by homosexuals. Indeed, as noted earlier, an administrative regulation is in place in this State forbidding the denial of an agency adoption based solely on the petitioner's sexual orientation (18 NYCRR 421.16[h][2]).

A reading of section 110 granting appellants, as unmarried second parents, standing to adopt is therefore consistent with the words of the statute as well as the spirit behind the modern-day amendments: encouraging the adoption of as many children as possible regardless of the sexual orientation or marital status of the individuals seeking to adopt them.

Domestic Relations Law § 117

Appellants having standing to adopt pursuant to Domestic Relations Law § 110, the other statutory obstacle relied upon by the lower courts in denying the petitions is the provision that "[a]fter the making of an order of adoption the natural parents of the adoptive child shall be relieved of all parental duties toward and of all responsibilities for and shall have no rights over such adoptive child or to his property by descent or succession" (Domestic Relations Law § 117[1][a]). Literal application of this language would effectively prevent these adoptions since it would require the termination of the biological mothers' rights upon adoption thereby placing appellants in the "Catch-22" of having to choose one of two coparents as the child's only legal parent.

As outlined below, however, neither the language nor policy underlying section 117 dictates that result.

The Language of Section 117. Both the title of section 117 ("Effect of adoption") and its opening phrase ("After the making of an order of adoption") suggest that the section has nothing to do with the standing of an individual to adopt, an issue treated exclusively in section 110. Rather, section 117 addresses the legal effect of an adoption on the parties and their property.

Also plain on the face of section 117 is that it speaks principally of estate law. Words such as "succession," "inheritance," "decedent," "instrument" and "will" permeate the statute. Read contextually, it is clear that the Legislature's chief concern in section 117 was the resolution of property disputes upon the death of an adoptive parent or child. As we observed in *People ex rel. Sibley v. Sheppard*, where we declined to read section 117's termination language "overbroadly. . .[to] interfere with the court's ability to protect the best interest of the child" and thereby prohibit visits with the child's biological grandparents, the "bulk of the statute refers to intestacy and succession" (54 NY2d, at 325). Thus, from the very beginning of what is now section 117, both the scholarly commentary about the section and its dozen or so amendments have centered on issues of property rights and inheritance. * * *

Recent Statutory Amendments. Moving beyond the language and history of section 117 itself, our reading of the statute is further supported by recent amendments to other sections of the adoption law which provide elaborate procedural mechanisms for regulating the relationships between the child, the child's (soon-to-be former) biological parents and the persons who will become the child's parents upon adoption.

In the context of agency adoptions, Social Services Law § 383–c, enacted in 1990 (L 1990, chs 479, 480), provides that biological parents willing to give their child up for adoption must execute a written instrument, known as a "surrender," stating "in conspicuous bold print on the first page" that "the parent is giving up all rights to have custody, visit with, write to or learn about the child, forever" (Social Services Law § 383–c [5][b][ii]). * * *

The procedural safeguards contained in Social Services Law § 383–c. . .further indicate that section 117 does not invariably mandate termination in all circumstances. Under the language of section 117 alone, a biological mother's rights could theoretically be severed unilaterally, without notice as to the consequences or other procedural protections. Though arguably adequate in 1938 when the statute was enacted, such a summary procedure would be unlikely to pass muster today (*see, e.g., Santosky v. Kramer*, 455 U.S. 745, 768–770; *Matter of Sarah K.*, 66 N.Y.2d 223, 237).

The above-described amendments * * * suggest that the Legislature in recent years has devised statutory vehicles other than section 117 to carefully regulate and restrict parental rights during the adoption process, again militating against a rigid application of subdivision (1)(a).

The Ambiguity Should Be Resolved in the Children's Favor. Finally, even though the language of section 117 still has the effect of terminating a biological parent's rights in the majority of adoptions between strangers – where there is a need to prevent unwanted intrusion by the child's former biological relatives to promote the stability of the new adoptive family – the cases before us are entirely different. As we recognized in *Matter of Seaman* (78 N.Y.2d 451, 461), "complete severance of the natural relationship [is] not necessary when the adopted person remain[s] within the natural family unit as a result of an intrafamily adoption."

One example of an adoption where the Legislature has explicitly acknowledged that termination is unwarranted is when the child, with the consent of the biological parent, is adopted by a "stepparent" (Domestic Relations Law § 117[1][d]). A second, implicit exception occurs in the adoptions by teenage fathers authorized by the 1951 amendment to section 110 *(see,* at 661, *supra).* Since minor fathers adopting their own biological children are not "stepparents" under the language of Domestic Relations Law § 117(1)(d), they would be prohibited from adopting were section 117's termination language to be mandatory in all cases. The seemingly automatic cut-off language of section 117 could not have been intended to bar these adoptions, however, since they are precisely what the Legislature sought to encourage in the first place.

Yet a third class of adoptions where complete termination of parental rights appears to be contrary to legislative intent are those adoptions contemplated by Social Services Law § 383–c, a completely new statute enacted five years ago. Specifically, New York law now allows the parties to an agency adoption to "agree to different terms" as to the nature of the biological parents' postadoptive relationship with the child. The statute thus expressly permits parties to agree that the biological parent will retain specified rights * * * *after* the adoption, thereby authorizing "open adoptions" for the first time in this State.

A year prior to the enactment of Social Services Law § 383–c, this Court declined to sanction the concept of "open adoption" because of our belief that it was inconsistent with what we perceived to be section 117's requirement that termination of parental rights was mandatory in all cases (*Matter of Gregory B.,* 74 N.Y.2d 77, 91 [citations omitted]). Significantly, when enacting Social Services Law § 383–c the very next year, the Legislature saw no need to amend Domestic Relations Law § 117. Again, if section 117 automatically terminated parental rights in all circumstances, it would have the practical effect of overriding the conditional surrender/"open adoption" provisions of Social Services Law § 383–c. By passing Social Services Law § 383–c as it did, the Legislature thus necessarily rejected the reading of section 117 articulated in *Matter of Gregory B.*

Given the above, it is plain that an interpretation of section 117 that would limit the number of beneficial intrafamily adoptions cannot be reconciled with the legislative intent to authorize open adoptions and adoptions by minors. The coexistence of the statute's seemingly automatic termination language along with these more recent enactments creates a statutory puzzle not susceptible of ready resolution.

One conclusion that can be drawn, however, is that section 117 does not invariably require termination in the situation where the biological parent, having consented to the adoption, has agreed to retain parental rights and to raise the child together with the second parent. Despite their varying factual circumstances, each of the adoptions described above. . .share such an agreement as a common denominator. Because the facts of the cases before us are directly analogous to these three situations, the half-century-old termination language of section 117 should not be read to preclude the adoptions here. Phrased slightly differently, "the desire for consistency in the law should not of itself sever the bonds between the child and the natural relatives" (*People ex rel. Sibley v. Sheppard*, 54 N.Y.2d 320, 326, *supra*).

"Where the language of a statute is susceptible of two constructions, the courts will adopt that which avoids injustice, hardship, constitutional doubts or other objectionable results" (*Kauffman & Sons Saddlery Co. v. Miller*, 298 N.Y. 38, 44 [Fuld, J.]; *see also*, McKinney's Cons Laws of NY, Book 1, Statutes § 150). Given that section 117 is open to two differing interpretations as to whether it automatically terminates parental rights in all cases, a construction of the section that would deny children like Jacob and Dana the opportunity of having their two de facto parents become their legal parents, based solely on their biological mother's sexual orientation or marital status, would not only be unjust under the circumstances, but also might raise constitutional concerns in light of the adoption statute's historically consistent purpose – the best interests of the child. * * *

These concerns are particularly weighty in *Matter of Dana*. Even if the Court were to rule against him on this appeal, the male petitioner in *Matter of Jacob* could still adopt by marrying Jacob's mother. Dana, however, would be irrevocably deprived of the benefits and entitlements of having as her legal parents the two individuals who have already assumed that role in her life, simply as a consequence of her mother's sexual orientation.

> New York began authorizing same-sex marriages in 2011, sixteen years after this case.
>
> **FYI**

Any proffered justification for rejecting these petitions based on a governmental policy disapproving of homosexuality or encouraging marriage would not apply. As noted above, New York has not adopted a policy disfavoring adoption by either single persons or homosexuals. In fact, the most recent legislative document relating to the subject urges courts to construe section 117 in precisely the manner we have as it cautions against discrimination against "nonmarital children" and "unwed parents." An interpretation of the statute that avoids such discrimination or hardship is all the more appropriate here where a contrary ruling could jeopardize the legal status of the many New York children whose adoptions by second parents have already taken place. * * *

Conclusion

To be sure, the Legislature that last codified section 117 in 1938 may never have envisioned families that "include[ ] two adult lifetime partners whose relationship is. . .characterized by an emotional and financial commitment and interdependence" (*Braschi v. Stahl Assocs. Co.*, 74 N.Y.2d 201, 211). Nonetheless, it is clear that section 117, designed as a shield to protect new adoptive families, was never intended as a sword to prohibit otherwise beneficial intrafamily adoptions by second parents. * * *

BELLACOSA, J. (dissenting).

* * * These appeals share a statutory construction issue under New York's adoption laws. While the results reached by the majority are intended to have a benevolent effect on the individuals involved in these two cases, the means to those ends transform the legislative adoption charter governing countless other individuals. Additionally, the dispositional methodology transcends institutional limitations on this Court's proper exercise of its authority, fixed by internal discipline and by the external distribution of powers among the branches of government.

The majority minimizes the at-will relationships of the appellants couples who would be combined biological-adoptive parents in each case, but the significant statutory and legally central relevancy is inescapable. Unlike married and single parent households, each couple here cohabits only day-to-day, no matter the depth or length of their voluntary arrangements. Their relationships lack legal permanency and the State has not endowed them with the benefits and enforceable protections that flow from relationships recognized under color of law. Nowhere do statutes, or any case law previously, recognize de facto, functional or second parent adoptions in joint circumstances as presented here.

Specifically, in the respective cases, the availability of adoption is implicated because of the operation-of-law consequences under Domestic Relations Law § 117 based on: (1) the relationship of the biological parent and the putative adoptive child if a *male and female unmarried cohabiting couple*, one of whom is the biological mother of the child, *jointly petitions* to adopt the five-year-old child; and (2) the relationship of the biological parent and her child if the *lesbian partner* of the biological mother *petitions alone* to adopt the five-year-old child. Neither case presents an issue of ineligibility because of sexual orientation or of discrimination against adoption on that basis, despite the majority's evocations in that regard.

* * * Although adoption has been practiced since ancient times, the authorization for this unique relationship derives solely from legislation. * * * A transcendent societal goal in the field of domestic relations is to stabilize family relationships, particularly parent-child bonds. That State interest promotes permanency planning and provides protection for an adopted child's legally secure familial placement. Therefore, statutory authorizations should not be substantively transformed under the guise of interpretation, and all facets of the adoption statutes should be harmonized.

> Is Judge Bellacosa also identifying a purpose of the adoption statute here? How did Judge Bellacosa identify this goal? How does it square with the purpose that Chief Judge Kaye identified above?

Notably, too, for contextual understanding of these cases, New York State has long refused to recognize common-law marriages. It also does not recognize or authorize gay or lesbian marriages, though efforts to secure such legislation have been pursued. * * *

II.

A key societal concern in adoption proceedings is, we all agree, the best interests of children. The judicial power to grant an adoption cannot be exercised, however, by simply intoning the phrase "the best interests of the adoptive child" as part of the analysis to determine qualification for adoption. That approach bypasses crucial, threshold steps and begs inescapably interwoven questions that must be considered and answered at the outset of the purely statutory construction issue in these cases. Before a court can arrive at the ultimate conclusion that an adoption is in the best interests of a child therefore, it is first obliged to discern whether the particular application is legislatively authorized. Reversing the analysis erects the building before the foundation. * * *

III.

A principal factor in these cases must also ultimately include consideration of the inexorable operation-of-law consequences that flow from section 117, a distinctive feature of New York's adoption laws. Specifically, courts are statutorily mandated to apply Domestic Relations Law § 110 together with the interconnected features of Domestic Relations Law § 117.

Domestic Relations Law § 117 provides: "After the making of an order of adoption the natural parents of the adoptive child *shall be relieved of all parental duties toward and of all responsibilities for and* shall have no rights over such adoptive child *or* to his [or her] property by descent or succession" (emphasis added). The plain and overarching language and punctuation of section 117 cannot be judicially blinked, repealed or rendered obsolete by interpretation.

Section 117 says that it severs all facets of a biological parent's conjunctively listed relationships upon adoption of the child. This Court has recognized that "[t]he purpose of the section [former section 114, now section 117] was to define the relation, after adoption, of the child to its natural parents and to its adopting parents, together in their reciprocal rights, duties and privileges." * * *

In implementation of its prerogative to define family relationships that are accorded legal status, the Legislature even prescribed a stepparent departure from the otherwise automatic section 117 consequence. It thus sought to obviate the inevitable result that an order of adoption might actually effectuate the symbolic Solomonic threat by severing the rights of a consenting biological parent in such specifically excepted circumstances where a biological parent is married to an adopting stepparent. One would have thought promulgation of such an exception unnecessary, yet the Legislature chose certainty of statutory expression for every eventuality as to the severance or nonseverance operation-of-law consequences of section 117.

Appellants in both cases nevertheless propose the theory that section 117 is meant to apply only to inheritance succession of property rights after adoption and should have no effect on the wider expanse and array of rights and responsibilities of a biological parent with an adoptive child. The language of section 117 reveals, however, that the biological parents' duties, responsibilities and rights with respect to the adoptive child are separate and distinct from, and more comprehensive than, a single, narrow category of inheritance rights. * * *

IV.

* * * In sum, the common issue here involves a subject on which the Legislature has expressed itself. * * * [T]he Legislature has delineated its will and judgment methodically and meticulously to reflect its enactments. Ambiguity cannot directly or indirectly create or substitute for the lack of statutory authorization to adopt. * * * [I]f the Legislature had intended to alter the definitions and interplay of its plenary, detailed adoption blueprint to cover the circumstances as presented here, it has had ample and repeated opportunities, means and words to effectuate such purpose plainly and definitively as a matter of notice, guidance, stability and reliability. It has done so before (*see, e.g.*, L 1984, ch 218 [permitting adoption by adults not yet divorced]; L 1951, ch 211 [permitting adoption by a minor]).

Because the Legislature did not do so here, neither should this Court. . . . Cobbling law together out of interpretative ambiguity that transforms fundamental, societally recognized relationships and substantive principles is neither sound statutory construction nor justifiable lawmaking. * * *

NOTES & QUESTIONS

1. One key analytical move the majority makes at the beginning of its opinion (indeed, before discussing the specific statutory provisions) is to note that the "various sections comprising New York's adoption statute today represent a complex and not entirely reconcilable patch-work." This description of "a complex and not entirely reconcilable patch-work" applies equally in many areas of law. As you see here, this is why courts necessarily exercise some discretion in reconciling the "not entirely reconcilable patch-work" of law. You can probably also see why a decision about how much and which "context" to consider—and thus how much coherence courts should seek—is crucial in resolving difficult questions of statutory interpretation.

2. What do you see as the greatest strength in Chief Judge Kaye's opinion? What is its greatest weakness? Is she usurping the state legislature's role, or facilitating it?

3. What interpretive philosophy undergirds Chief Judge Kaye's majority opinion? What about Judge Bellicosa's dissenting opinion? Go back and re-read the final paragraphs in each opinion. Does this tell you anything about the different views each judge has about the relationship between courts and the legislature?

4. What interpretive tools did you see the two opinions using, or using well?

3. Statutory *Stare Decisis* Revisited

The problem of whether to let contextual factors at the time of interpretation affect the interpretation itself has special resonance with respect to the concept of statutory *stare decisis*, which we introduced in Chapter 16. Our focus there was on the question of institutional choice between courts and legislatures in changing (and arguably even correcting) a previous judicial construction of a statute when that interpretation later seems questionable. When the principle of statutory *stare decisis* is invoked, as in *Allen v. Milligan* discussed earlier, it almost always is being used by the courts to say to the legislature, "This is *your* call. If you no longer like what we once did, you are the institution to change it, not us, *even if we no longer like what we did*." In this section, we invite you to focus not so much on the institutional-choice issue *per se*, but instead on how often it is that some change in circumstance after an earlier judicial decision can give rise to that institutional-choice question and the question of whether that earlier decision deserves to have continuing force.

Consider a famous example—*Flood v. Kuhn (The Baseball Antitrust Case).*

DIY
The Evolution of Major League Baseball

Today Major League Baseball is big business, and you might think that it therefore would be subject to federal antitrust laws (known also as "competition law," which is a set of complicated laws that seek to protect trade and commerce from restraints, monopolies, price-fixing, and price discrimination). You would be wrong, as you will see in the 1972 case of *Flood v.*

Congress has passed various antitrust laws to promote more robust economic competition by regulating or limiting the ways in which powerful or dominant companies might otherwise control the economic marketplace through their size and strength.

FYI

Kuhn, which famously confronts the issue of statutory *stare decisis*. Read the case excerpts that follow not for the purpose of learning the underlying antitrust doctrine, but as (1) an example of how changed legal and factual conditions can undermine an earlier decision interpreting a statute, and (2) a lens for seeing both how the Court understands its role as legal interpreter, as well as how it assesses the congressional role as lawmaker. As you read, be thinking about how much impact the changed factual and legal context should have, as well as whether and in what circumstances "statutory *stare decisis*" should be stronger than *stare decisis* in other contexts, such as the common law and constitutional law.

Flood v. Kuhn
407 U.S. 258 (1972)

MR. JUSTICE BLACKMUN delivered the opinion of the Court.

For the third time in 50 years the Court is asked specifically to rule that professional baseball's reserve system is within the reach of the federal antitrust laws. [The reserve system confines a player to the club that has him under contract, and gives the club the unilateral power to reassign that contract to another club.] * * *

I

The Game

It is a century and a quarter since the New York Nine defeated the Knickerbockers 23 to 1 on Hoboken's Elysian Fields June 19, 1846, with Alexander Jay Cartwright as the instigator and the umpire. The teams were amateur, but the contest marked a significant date in baseball's beginnings. That early game led ultimately to the development of professional baseball and its tightly organized structure. [Justice Blackmun then continued a multi-paragraph tribute to 125 years of baseball history, its cultural impact, and its best-known icons.]

How might the Court's view of baseball's history, largely omitted here, have affected the Court's resolution of the issue? Chief Justice Burger, concurring, opted not to join just this part of the opinion of the Court.

II

The Petitioner

The petitioner, Curtis Charles Flood, born in 1938, began his major league career in 1956 when he signed a contract with the Cincinnati Reds for a salary of $4,000 for the season. He had no attorney or agent to advise him on that occasion. He was traded to the St. Louis Cardinals before the 1958 season. Flood rose to fame as a center fielder with the Cardinals during the years 1958–1969. In those 12 seasons he compiled a batting average of .293. His best offensive season was 1967 when he achieved .335. He was .301 or better in six of the 12 St. Louis years. He participated in the 1964, 1967, and 1968 World Series. He played errorless ball in the field in 1966, and once enjoyed 223 consecutive errorless games. Flood has received seven Golden Glove Awards. He was co-captain of his team from 1965–1969. He ranks among the 10 major league outfielders possessing the highest lifetime fielding averages.

* * *

But at the age of 31, in October 1969, Flood was traded to the Philadelphia Phillies of the National League in a multi-player transaction. He was not consulted about the trade. He was informed by telephone and received formal notice only after the deal had been consummated. In December he complained to the Commissioner of Baseball and asked that he be made a free agent and be placed at liberty to strike his own bargain with any other major league team. His request was denied.

Flood then instituted this antitrust suit in January 1970 in federal court for the Southern District of New York. The defendants * * * were the Commissioner of Baseball, the presidents of the two major leagues, and the 24 major league clubs. In general, the complaint charged violations of the federal antitrust laws and civil rights statutes, violation of state statutes and the common law, and the imposition of a form of peonage and involuntary servitude contrary to the Thirteenth Amendment and [federal statutes]. Petitioner sought declaratory and injunctive relief and treble damages.

Flood declined to play for Philadelphia in 1970, despite a $100,000 salary offer, and he sat out the year. After the season was concluded, Philadelphia sold its rights to Flood to the Washington Senators. Washington and the petitioner were able to come to terms for 1971 at a salary of $110,000. Flood started the season but, apparently because he was dissatisfied with his performance, he left the Washington club on April 27, early in the campaign. He has not played baseball since then.

III

The Present Litigation

[The trial court concluded that two earlier Supreme Court cases, *Federal Baseball Club v. National League*, 259 U.S. 200 (1922), and *Toolson v. New York Yankees, Inc.*, 346 U.S. 356 (1953), were controlling precedent that precluded applying the antitrust laws to Major League Baseball.] On appeal, the Second Circuit felt "compelled to affirm."

We granted certiorari in order to look once again at this troublesome and unusual situation. * * *

IV

The Legal Background

A. *Federal Baseball Club v. National League* [(1922)] * * * was a suit for treble damages instituted by a member of the Federal League (Baltimore) against the National and American Leagues and others. The plaintiff obtained a verdict in the trial court, but the Court of Appeals reversed. The main brief filed by the plaintiff with this Court discloses that it was strenuously argued, among other things, that the business in which the defendants were engaged was interstate commerce; that the interstate relationship among the several clubs, located as they were in different States, was predominant; that organized baseball represented an investment of colossal wealth; that it was an engagement in moneymaking; that gate receipts were divided by agreement between the home club and the visiting club; and that the business of baseball was to be distinguished from the mere playing of the game as a sport for physical exercise and diversion. * * *

Mr. Justice Holmes, in speaking succinctly for a unanimous Court, said:

> The business is giving exhibitions of base ball, which are purely state affairs. . . . But the fact that in order to give the exhibitions the Leagues must induce free persons to cross state lines and must arrange and pay for their doing so is not enough to change the character of the business. . . . [T]he transport is a mere incident, not the essential thing. That to which it is incident, the exhibition, although made for money would not be called trade or

commerce in the commonly accepted use of those words. As it is put by the defendant, personal effort, not related to production, is not a subject of commerce. That which in its consummation is not commerce does not become commerce among the States because the transportation that we have mentioned takes place. To repeat the illustrations given by the Court below, a firm of lawyers sending out a member to argue a case, or the Chautauqua lecture bureau sending out lecturers, does not engage in such commerce because the lawyer or lecturer goes to another State.

If we are right the plaintiff's business is to be described in the same way and the restrictions by contract that prevented the plaintiff from getting players to break their bargains and the other conduct charged against the defendants were not an interference with commerce among the States.

259 U.S., at 208–209. The Court thus chose not to be persuaded by opposing examples proffered by the plaintiff. * * *

B. * * * In the years that followed, baseball continued to be subject to intermittent antitrust attack. The courts, however, rejected these challenges on the authority of *Federal Baseball*. In some cases stress was laid, although unsuccessfully, on new factors such as the development of radio and television with their substantial additional revenues to baseball. For the most part, however, the Holmes opinion was generally and necessarily accepted as controlling authority. And in the 1952 Report of the Subcommittee on Study of Monopoly Power of the House Committee on the Judiciary, H.R.Rep.No.2002, 82d Cong., 2d Sess., 229, it was said, in conclusion:

On the other hand the overwhelming preponderance of the evidence established baseball's need for some sort of reserve clause. Baseball's history shows that chaotic conditions prevailed when there was no reserve clause. Experience points to no feasible substitute to protect the integrity of the game or to guarantee a comparatively even competitive struggle. The evidence adduced at the hearings would clearly not justify the enactment of legislation flatly condemning the reserve clause.

C. The Court granted certiorari [in the *Toolson* case and two other cases], and, by a short per curiam (WARREN, C.J., and BLACK, FRANKFURTER, DOUGLAS, JACKSON, CLARK, and MINTON, JJ.), affirmed the judgments of the respective courts of appeals in those three cases. *Toolson v. New York*

Yankees, Inc., 346 U.S. 356 (1953). *Federal Baseball* was cited as holding "that the business of providing public baseball games for profit between clubs of professional baseball players was not within the scope of the federal antitrust laws," 346 U.S., at 357, and:

> Congress has had the ruling under consideration but has not seen fit to bring such business under these laws by legislation having prospective effect. The business has thus been left for thirty years to develop, on the understanding that it was not subject to existing antitrust legislation. The present cases ask us to overrule the prior decision and, with retrospective effect, hold the legislation applicable. We think that if there are evils in this field which now warrant application to it of the antitrust laws it should be by legislation. Without re-examination of the underlying issues, the judgments below are affirmed on the authority *of Federal Baseball Club of Baltimore v. National League of Professional Baseball Clubs,* supra, so far as that decision determines that Congress had no intention of including the business of baseball within the scope of the federal antitrust laws.

Ibid.

This quotation reveals four reasons for the Court's affirmance of *Toolson* and its companion cases: (a) Congressional awareness for three decades of the Court's ruling in *Federal Baseball,* coupled with congressional inaction; (b) The fact that baseball was left alone to develop for that period upon the understanding that the reserve system was not subject to existing federal antitrust laws; (c) A reluctance to overrule *Federal Baseball* with consequent retroactive effect; (d) A professed desire that any needed remedy be provided by legislation rather than by court decree. The emphasis in *Toolson* was on the determination, attributed even to *Federal Baseball,* that Congress had no intention to include baseball within the reach of the federal antitrust laws. Two Justices (Burton and Reed, JJ.) dissented, stressing the factual aspects, revenue sources, and the absence of an express exemption of organized baseball from the Sherman Act. 346 U.S., at 357. The 1952 congressional study was mentioned. *Id.*, at 358, 359, 361.

It is of interest to note that in *Toolson* the petitioner had argued flatly that *Federal Baseball* "is wrong and must be overruled," Brief for Petitioner, No. 18, O.T.1953, p. 19, and that Thomas Reed Powell, a constitutional scholar of no small stature, urged, as counsel for an amicus, that "baseball is a unique enterprise," Brief for Boston American League Base-Ball Co. as

692 • Learning Legislation and Regulation •

Amicus Curiae 2, and that "unbridled competition as applied to baseball would not be in the public interest." *Id.*, at 14.

D. *United States v. Shubert*, 348 U.S. 222 (1955), was a civil antitrust action against defendants engaged in the production of legitimate theatrical attractions throughout the United States and in operating theaters for the presentation of such attractions. The District Court had dismissed the complaint on the authority of *Federal Baseball* and *Toolson*, 120 F.Supp. 15 (S.D.N.Y.1953). This Court reversed. Mr. Chief Justice Warren noted the Court's broad conception of "trade or commerce" in the antitrust statutes and the types of enterprises already held to be within the reach of that phrase. He stated that *Federal Baseball* and *Toolson* afforded no basis for a conclusion that businesses built around the performance of local exhibitions are exempt from the antitrust laws. 348 U.S., at 227. He then went on to elucidate the holding in *Toolson* by meticulously spelling out the factors mentioned above. * * *

E. *United States v. International Boxing Club*, 348 U.S. 236 (1955), was a companion to *Shubert* and was decided the same day. This was a civil antitrust action against defendants engaged in the business of promoting professional championship boxing contests. Here again the District Court had dismissed the complaint in reliance upon *Federal Baseball* and *Toolson*. The Chief Justice observed that "if it were not for *Federal Baseball* and *Toolson*, we think that it would be too clear for dispute that the Government's allegations bring the defendants within the scope of the Act." 348 U.S., at 240–241. He pointed out that the defendants relied on the two baseball cases but also would have been content with a more restrictive interpretation of them than the *Shubert* defendants, for the boxing defendants argued that the cases immunized only businesses that involve exhibitions of an athletic nature. The Court accepted neither argument. It again noted, 348 U.S., at 242, that "*Toolson* neither overruled *Federal Baseball* nor necessarily reaffirmed all that was said in *Federal Baseball*." * * *

The Court noted the presence then in Congress of various bills forbidding the application of the antitrust laws to "organized professional sports enterprises"; the holding of extensive hearings on some of these; subcommittee opposition; a postponement recommendation as to baseball; and the fact that "Congress thus left intact the then-existing coverage of the antitrust laws." 348 U.S., at 243–244.

Mr. Justice Frankfurter, joined by Mr. Justice Minton, dissented. "It would baffle the subtlest ingenuity," he said, "to find a single differentiating factor between other sporting exhibitions. . . .and baseball insofar as the conduct of the sport is relevant to the criteria or considerations by which the Sherman Law becomes applicable to a 'trade or commerce.'" 348 U.S., at 248. He went on:

> The Court decided as it did In the *Toolson* case as an application of the doctrine of *stare decisis*. That doctrine is not, to be sure, an imprisonment of reason. But neither is it a whimsy. It can hardly be that this Court gave a preferred position to baseball because it is the great American sport. . . . If *stare decisis* be one aspect of law, as it is, to disregard it in identical situations is mere caprice.
>
> Congress, on the other hand, may yield to sentiment and be capricious, subject only to due process. . . .
>
> Between them, this case and *Shubert* illustrate that nice but rational distinctions are inevitable in adjudication. I agree with the Court's opinion in *Shubert* for precisely the reason that constrains me to dissent in this case.

348 U.S., at 249–250. * * *

F. The parade marched on. *Radovich v. National Football League*, 352 U.S. 445 [(1957)], was a civil Clayton Act case testing the application of the antitrust laws to professional football. The District Court dismissed. The Ninth Circuit affirmed in part on the basis of *Federal Baseball* and *Toolson*. The court did not hesitate to "confess that the strength of the pull" of the baseball cases and of *International Boxing* "is about equal," but then observed that "(f)ootball is a team sport" and boxing an individual one. 9 Cir., 231 F.2d 620, 622.

This Court reversed with an opinion by Mr. Justice Clark. He said that the Court made its ruling in *Toolson* "because it was concluded that more harm would be done in overruling *Federal Baseball* than in upholding a ruling which at best was of dubious validity." 352 U.S., at 450. He noted that Congress had not acted. He then said:

> All this, combined with the flood of litigation that would follow its repudiation, the harassment that would ensue, and the retroactive effect of such a decision, led the Court to the practical result that it should sustain the unequivocal line of authority reaching over many years.

[S]ince *Toolson* and *Federal Baseball* are still cited as controlling authority in antitrust actions involving other fields of business, we now specifically limit the rule there established to the facts there involved, i.e., the business of organized professional baseball. As long as the Congress continues to acquiesce we should adhere to—but not extend—the interpretation of the Act made in those cases. . . .

If this ruling is unrealistic, inconsistent, or illogical, it is sufficient to answer, aside from the distinctions between the businesses, that were we considering the question of baseball for the first time upon a clean slate we would have no doubts. But *Federal Baseball* held the business of baseball outside the scope of the Act. No other business claiming the coverage of those cases has such an adjudication. We therefore, conclude that the orderly way to eliminate error or discrimination, if any there be, is by legislation and not by court decision. Congressional processes are more accommodative, affording the whole industry hearings and an opportunity to assist in the formulation of new legislation. The resulting product is therefore more likely to protect the industry and the public alike. The whole scope of congressional action would be known long in advance and effective dates for the legislation could be set in the future without the injustices of retroactivity and surprise which might follow court action. 352 U.S., at 450–452 (footnote omitted).

Mr. Justice Frankfurter, [Mr. Justice Harlan, and Mr. Justice Brennan] dissented. * * *

G. Finally, in *Haywood v. National Basketball Assn.*, 401 U.S. 1204 (1971), Mr. Justice Douglas, in his capacity as Circuit Justice, reinstated a District Court's injunction pendente lite in favor of a professional basketball player and said, "Basketball. . .does not enjoy exemption from the antitrust laws." 401 U.S., at 1205.

H. This series of decisions understandably spawned extensive commentary * * *; nearly all of it looked to Congress for any remedy that might be deemed essential.

I. Legislative proposals have been numerous and persistent. Since *Toolson* more than 50 bills have been introduced in Congress relative to the applicability or nonapplicability of the antitrust laws to baseball. A few of these passed one house or the other. Those that did would have expanded, not restricted, the reserve system's exemption to other professional league sports. * * *

V

In view of all this, it seems appropriate now to say that:

1. Professional baseball is a business and it is engaged in interstate commerce.

2. With its reserve system enjoying exemption from the federal antitrust laws, baseball is, in a very distinct sense, an exception and an anomaly. *Federal Baseball* and *Toolson* have become an aberration confined to baseball.

3. Even though others might regard this as "unrealistic, inconsistent, or illogical," see *Radovich*, 352 U.S., at 452, the aberration is an established one, and one that has been recognized not only in *Federal Baseball* and *Toolson*, but in *Shubert, International Boxing*, and *Radovich*, as well, a total of five consecutive cases in this Court. It is an aberration that has been with us now for half a century, one heretofore deemed fully entitled to the benefit of *stare decisis*, and one that has survived the Court's expanding concept of interstate commerce. It rests on a recognition and an acceptance of baseball's unique characteristics and needs.

4. Other professional sports operating interstate—football, boxing, basketball, and, presumably, hockey and golf—are not so exempt.

5. The advent of radio and television, with their consequent increased coverage and additional revenues, has not occasioned an overruling of *Federal Baseball* and *Toolson*.

6. The Court has emphasized that since 1922 baseball, with full and continuing congressional awareness, has been allowed to develop and to expand unhindered by federal legislative action. Remedial legislation has been introduced repeatedly in Congress but none has ever been enacted. The Court, accordingly, has concluded that Congress as yet has had no intention to subject baseball's reserve system to the reach of the antitrust statutes. This, obviously, has been deemed to be something other than mere congressional silence and passivity. * * *

7. The Court has expressed concern about the confusion and the retroactivity problems that inevitably would result with a judicial overturning of *Federal Baseball*. It has voiced a preference that if any change is to be made, it come by legislative action that, by its nature, is only prospective in operation.

8. The Court noted in *Radovich*, 352 U.S., at 452, that the slate with respect to baseball is not clean. Indeed, it has not been clean for half a century.

This emphasis and this concern are still with us. We continue to be loath, 50 years after *Federal Baseball* and almost two decades after *Toolson*, to overturn those cases judicially when Congress, by its positive inaction, has allowed those decisions to stand for so long and, far beyond mere inference and implication, has clearly evinced a desire not to disapprove them legislatively.

Accordingly, we adhere once again to *Federal Baseball* and *Toolson* and to their application to professional baseball. We adhere also to *International Boxing* and *Radovich* and to their respective applications to professional boxing and professional football. If there is any inconsistency or illogic in all this, it is an inconsistency and illogic of long standing that is to be remedied by the Congress and not by this Court. If we were to act otherwise, we would be withdrawing from the conclusion as to congressional intent made in *Toolson* and from the concerns as to retrospectivity therein expressed. Under these circumstances, there is merit in consistency even though some might claim that beneath that consistency is a layer of inconsistency.

* * *

Judgment affirmed.

Mr. Chief Justice Burger, concurring.

I concur in all but Part I of the Court's opinion but, like Mr. Justice Douglas, I have grave reservations as to the correctness of *Toolson*. * * * The error, if such it be, is one on which the affairs of a great many people have rested for a long time. Courts are not the forum in which this tangled web ought to be unsnarled. I agree with Mr. Justice Douglas that congressional inaction is not a solid base, but the least undesirable course now is to let the matter rest with Congress; it is time the Congress acted to solve this problem.

> **?** Do you agree that the Court should leave it to Congress to correct interpretive errors or to remedy disparate statutory impacts? Or has the Court given away too much power here?

DIY
When Should a Court Change Its Earlier Interpretation of a Statute?

 Excerpts from two dissenting opinions follow. But before you read them, take two minutes to outline in your notes what you think would make the most persuasive dissenting opinion. Then continue reading.

MR. JUSTICE DOUGLAS, **with whom** MR. JUSTICE BRENNAN **concurs, dissenting.**

This Court's decision in *Federal Baseball Club* * * * is a derelict in the stream of the law that we, its creator, should remove. Only a romantic view of a rather dismal business account over the last 50 years would keep that derelict in midstream.

In 1922 the Court had a narrow, parochial view of commerce. With the demise of the old landmarks of that era, * * * the whole concept of commerce has changed.

Under the modern [Commerce Clause] decisions * * *, the power of Congress was recognized as broad enough to reach all phases of the vast operations of our national industrial system. An industry so dependent on radio and television as is baseball and gleaning vast interstate revenues (see H.R.Rep. No. 2002, 82d Cong., 2d Sess., 4, 5 (1952)) would be hard put today to say with the Court in the *Federal Baseball Club* case that baseball was only a local exhibition, not trade or commerce.

Baseball is today big business that is packaged with beer, with broadcasting, and with other industries. The beneficiaries of the Federal Baseball Club decision are not the Babe Ruths, Ty Cobbs, and Lou Gehrigs.

The owners, whose records many say reveal a proclivity for predatory practices, do not come to us with equities. The equities are with the victims of the reserve clause. I use the word 'victims' in the Sherman Act sense, since a contract which forbids anyone to practice his calling is commonly called an unreasonable restraint of trade. * * *

If congressional inaction is our guide, we should rely upon the fact that Congress has refused to enact bills broadly exempting professional sports from antitrust regulation. H.R.Rep. No. 2002, 82nd Cong., 2d Sess. (1952). The only statutory exemption granted by Congress to professional sports concerns broadcasting rights. 15 U.S.C. secs. 1291–1295. I would not ascribe a broader exemption through inaction than Congress has seen fit to grant explicitly.

There can be no doubt "that were we considering the question of baseball for the first time upon a clean slate" we would hold it to be subject to federal antitrust regulation. * * * The unbroken silence of Congress should not prevent us from correcting our own mistakes.

MR. JUSTICE MARSHALL, with whom MR. JUSTICE BRENNAN joins, dissenting.

* * *

This is a difficult case because we are torn between the principle of *stare decisis* and the knowledge that the decisions in [*Federal Baseball Club* and *Toolson*] are totally at odds with more recent and better reasoned cases.

[In *Toolson*,] the Court said:

> The business has. . .been left for thirty years to develop, on the understanding that it was not subject to existing antitrust legislation. The present cases ask us to overrule the prior decision and, with retrospective effect, hold the legislation applicable. We think that if there are evils in this field which now warrant application to it of the antitrust laws it should be by legislation.

Much more time has passed since *Toolson* and Congress has not acted. We must now decide whether to adhere to the reasoning of *Toolson*—i.e., to refuse to re-examine the underlying basis of *Federal Baseball Club*—or to proceed with a re-examination and let the chips fall where they may.

In his answer to petitioner's complaint, the Commissioner of Baseball "admits that under present concepts of interstate commerce defendants are engaged therein." App. 40. There can be no doubt that the admission is warranted by today's reality. Since baseball is interstate commerce, if we re-examine baseball's antitrust exemption, the Court's decision in [*Shubert*, *International Boxing*, and *Radovich*] require that we bring baseball within the coverage of the antitrust laws. * * *

The importance of the antitrust laws to every citizen must not be minimized. They are as important to baseball players as they are to football players, lawyers, doctors, or members of any other class of workers. Baseball players cannot be denied the benefits of competition merely because club owners view other economic interests as being more important, unless Congress says so.

Has Congress acquiesced in our decisions in *Federal Baseball Club* and *Toolson*? I think not. Had the Court been consistent and treated all sports in the same way baseball was treated, Congress might have become concerned enough to take action. But, the Court was inconsistent, and baseball was isolated and distinguished from all other sports. In *Toolson* the Court refused to act because Congress had been silent. But the Court may have read too much into this legislative inaction.

Americans love baseball as they love all sports. Perhaps we become so enamored of athletics that we assume that they are foremost in the minds of legislators as well as fans. We must not forget, however, that there are only some 600 major league baseball players. Whatever muscle they might have been able to muster by combining forces with other athletes has been greatly impaired by the manner in which this Court has isolated them. It is this Court that has made them impotent, and this Court should correct its error.

We do not lightly overrule our prior constructions of federal statutes, but when our errors deny substantial federal rights, like the right to compete freely and effectively to the best of one's ability as guaranteed by the antitrust laws, we must admit our error and correct it. We have done so before and we should do so again here. * * *

To the extent that there is concern over any reliance interests that club owners may assert, they can be satisfied by making our decision prospective only. Baseball should be covered by the antitrust laws beginning with this case and henceforth, unless Congress decides otherwise.

Accordingly, I would overrule *Federal Baseball Club* and *Toolson* and reverse the decision of the Court of Appeals. * * *

NOTES & QUESTIONS

1. In your view, was *Flood v. Kuhn* rightly decided? What about *Toolson* in 1953? *Federal Baseball Club* in 1922? For a comprehensive discussion of the historical background and meaning of the *Flood v. Kuhn* case, see Brad Snyder, A Well-Paid Slave: Curt Flood's Fight for Free Agency in Professional Sports (2006).

2. What relevant factual circumstances can you identify that had changed in the fifty years between 1922 and 1972? What legal principles had changed in that period?

3. What is the proper role of the Supreme Court in construing statutes such as the antitrust laws? Note that the Sherman Act dates back to 1890, more than eight decades before *Flood v. Kuhn* and even three decades before *Federal Baseball*. Does that matter? Does it matter that the relevant language—"trade or commerce among the several States"—is vague and thus indeterminate, and that this indeterminacy is to a certain extent by design? In particular, might Congress have intended this indeterminacy to permit judicial updating?

4. Think about the variety of congressional activities described in the *Flood v. Kuhn* opinions related to Major League Baseball's exemption from the antitrust laws. In terms of resolving the case before the Court in *Flood*, what are the proper implications of these congressional activities? Should they matter at all? After all, isn't the Court supposed be interpreting the statute Congress *did* pass (back in 1890), not all the bills Congress *didn't* pass (during the 1950s and 1960s)?

5. Should the baseball industry's reliance on both *Federal Baseball* and then *Toolson* for a half-century matter? As Chief Justice Burger notes, "[t]he error. . .is one on which the affairs of a great many people have rested for a long time."

6. In 1998, more than a quarter century later (and the year after Curt Flood died), Congress passed the Curt Flood Act, which extended to Major League Baseball players the same antitrust protections already available by law to all other professional athletes and performers. But by then negotiations and arbitration between the baseball players' association and the team owners had long eliminated the reserve clause, replacing it with "free agency."

Curt Flood was not just your average professional ballplayer. He was a three-time All-Star, seven-time Gold Glove winner, and the co-captain and an integral part of the St. Louis Cardinals' World Series teams during the 1960s. He was also active in the civil rights movement. As a point of comparison to Flood's $100,000 annual salary in 1970, in 2023 Shohei Ohtani signed a ten-year contract with the Los Angeles Dodgers reported to worth an average annual salary of $70,000,000. Free agency has significantly changed the players' negotiating power!

Test Your Understanding

To assess your understanding of the material in this chapter, click here to take a quiz.

Part VII—Government Regulation and the Administrative State

Parts V and VI explored the tools of interpretation that courts use when construing or interpreting the meaning of legal texts, particularly the statutory texts enacted through the legislative process. Today, however, an even larger body of legal texts is promulgated by administrative agencies, using their delegated regulatory authority. These legal texts also can generate an additional level of interpretive difficulties, complicated by questions about the relationship between the legislative branch and the various administrative agencies of the executive branch.

This Part and Part VIII set out some of the key features of the federal administrative state (with occasional comparisons to some analogous dimensions of the administrative apparatus at the state level). The term "administrative state" usually refers to the group of all federal administrative agencies together as a single unit. Although the term is sometimes used pejoratively, our use of it in this book is purely descriptive and meant as shorthand for referring to all federal administrative agencies. The term was popularized by a 1948 book of that title by Dwight Waldo, THE ADMINISTRATIVE STATE: A STUDY OF THE POLITICAL THEORY OF AMERICAN PUBLIC ADMINISTRATION.

This Part has three chapters. It begins with Chapter 28, a chapter describing what agencies are and what they do. The next two chapters describe, respectively, the legislative and executive branch constraints on agencies. Chapter 29 addresses the delegation of lawmaking authority from Congress to particular executive branch agencies or independent agencies and discusses other ways in which legislatures act to constrain agencies. Chapter 30 describes the constraints that the President imposes on federal agencies, including what has become one of the most fundamental aspects of how federal agencies operate in twenty-first century America: centralized regulatory review by the White House. In Part VIII, the final part of the book, we then turn to a third set of constraints on agencies, judicial review and the ways in which the courts shape agency behavior.

Part VII—Government Regulation and the Administrative State

28

Introduction to Agencies in the American Legal System

Key Concepts

- Administrative agencies
- Promulgate
- Agency rulemaking
- Legislative rules vs. interpretive rules
- Agency adjudication
- Agency procedures
- The Administrative Procedure Act
- Formal vs. informal rulemaking
- Notice and Comment
- Agency accountability vs. agency independence

Chapter Summary

Administrative agencies engage in a variety of different activities that lawyers need to understand. Rather than just "executing" (i.e., enforcing or implementing) the law, administrative agencies also engage in both rulemaking and adjudicatory functions. The processes by which agencies undertake these tasks and the constraints under which agencies operate are critically important, in significant part because the connection between agencies and representative government is not as direct or apparent as in the case of legislatures or the elected chief executive (i.e., President or governors). Agencies are instead constrained by legislatures, the chief executive, and the courts, typically by being required to follow prescribed procedures to make them more accountable, including providing opportunities for public input.

We now turn in earnest to the role of agencies in administering the law. Although agencies have played an active role in American governance since the late eighteenth century, the twentieth century saw a dramatic increase in the extent to which government agencies not only implement but also shape and influence government policy. More particularly, in addition to performing an array of what are conventionally viewed as "executive" functions (e.g., enforcement of law), these administrative agencies also engage in significant activities that are more naturally characterized as "legislative" or "judicial" functions. Indeed, today these agencies are responsible for vast amounts of both rule creation and conflict adjudication, and they have become by far the dominant forum for interactions between citizens and their government. For that reason, many lawyers represent clients before agencies, and large swathes of law practice involve direct engagement with agencies. A basic understanding of their organization, role, and function is therefore essential.

> **FYI** Immediately after the Founding, the First Congress and President Washington established Departments of War, Treasury, and Foreign Affairs. These agencies wielded significant government power. As one scholar has put it, "[f]rom the beginning some administrators were clothed with broad statutory authority, made general rules, adjudicated cases, were located outside of departments, and were tightly bound to congressional oversight and direction." Jerry L. Mashaw, *Recovering American Administrative Law: Federalist Foundations, 1787–1801*, 115 YALE L.J. 1256, 1256 (2006).

At bottom, administrative agencies are a reflection that Congress, the President, and the federal courts (as well as the analogous institutional actors in the three branches of state governments) need assistance. To meet the challenges of governing an increasingly complex society, Congress has relied upon agencies to develop and enforce regulations having a much finer grain than the broadly focused statutes that Congress is well-suited to enact. The New Deal Era saw a marked increase in the responsibilities of federal agencies, though their growth has continued throughout much of the twentieth and early twenty-first centuries. Meanwhile, Congress also has tasked these same experts to resolve or adjudicate numerous controversies related to their areas of expertise, subject to court review.

Although most government agencies are typically thought of as part of the executive branch of government (or as part of an extra-constitutional "fourth branch" of government if they are "independent" agencies), they nonetheless are usually creations of the legislative branch. Even in the states, most of whose constitutions establish multiple elected executive branch positions in addition to the Governor, such as State Treasurer or State Attorney General, it remains for the state legislature to specify the contours of the various departments that these officials will direct. Legislatures, in short, decide what responsibilities to assign to administrative agencies, as well as what authority to give them to fulfill those responsibilities (subject of course to approval by the President or Governor). Executive branch departments and agencies also depend upon the legislative branch for appropriations to fund—and direct—their operations.

In Chapter 11, you read about the legislative process, or how legislatures function. In courses on Civil Procedure (and implicitly, in many of your other courses too), you have learned about the judicial process, or how courts function. This chapter will give you a deeper understanding of administrative processes, or how administrative agencies function. It describes the basics of agencies, the various roles that

As may be obvious, the words "procedure" (as in "Civil **FYI** Procedure") and "process" come from the same etymological root, from the Latin *procedere* ("pro"—'forward' + "cedere"—"to go")

As you read about agency processes, think about the pros and cons of having unelected individuals making decisions on behalf of the public, often with significant public impact.

agencies play (i.e., what, as a practical matter, agencies actually do), and a brief discussion of some of the constraints on how agencies do what they do. In subsequent chapters, we will address these constraints in more detail. These include constraints imposed by Congress, by the President, and by the courts, principally in the power of judicial review of agency action.

DIY
The Power and Impact of Government Agencies

Throughout the remaining portions of the book, be thinking about these two very different questions:

1. Have agencies been given too much power, or does the legislature retain too much control over how agencies function?

2. What examples can you identify of agency regulations that directly impact your life?

A. Who Works in Agencies

What is an administrative agency? Like a legislature and like a court, it is an institution where decisions—often, contested decisions—about law get made. Naturally then, it is a place where lawyers play a key role, both advocating on behalf of their clients and internally, as key personnel working within the agencies themselves.

> **FYI** The federal government consists of a few thousand political appointees, including approximately 1200 who need Senate confirmation.

Agencies are not, however, just lawyers. Rather, a variety of people, with a wide range of backgrounds, work for agencies. Broadly, the people who work for agencies fit into two buckets: political appointees and career civil servants. Political appointees are at the top of the organizational hierarchy of an administrative agency. These individuals are ultimately responsible for what an agency does. Indeed, as we will see, many statutes mention these individual positions by name, directly authorizing or mandating that specific political appointees within agencies do (or not do) certain things. The details of who gets these jobs, and how, are not crucial, but the key point is that they are called "political" appointees for a reason: they are chosen by a politically elected person, usually the President. As you might imagine, political appointees in the current American political landscape are generally either Democrats or Republicans. So, in practical effect, when you vote for a presidential candidate, you are choosing a cadre, a whole team, of either mostly Democrats or mostly Republicans to staff the upper echelons of federal administrative agencies.

At the most senior level of the government are individuals who report directly to the President, many of whom make up the President's Cabinet. One or two levels down are other political appointees, many of whom are formally appointed by the President but are typically chosen by an agency head or some other higher-ranked appointee. Many of these individuals must be confirmed by the United States Senate before they can take office, but they serve at the pleasure of the President (meaning the President can fire them for any reason the President wants, including political

> **!** As we will discuss in more detail in Chapter 30, the President's power to fire political appointees is one of the fundamental distinctions between an "executive agency" and an "independent agency." The President does not have the power to fire political appointees of independent agencies.

disagreement). An important corollary of this is that these individuals are usually replaced soon after a new President takes office.

The second, and much larger, group of agency employees consists of career civil servants. These individuals are hired through a merit selection process and have strong job protection (that is, they cannot be fired easily, and certainly not for political reasons). But their job is largely to follow the policy direction of the political appointees, their superiors in the agency hierarchy.

> As a point of comparison with the **FYI** few thousand political appointees, there are approximately two million civilian (i.e., non-military) civil servants in the federal government.

Importantly, many of the people who work for agencies—including the political appointees, but especially the civil servants—have subject-matter expertise relevant to the agency's specialty. As just a brief list of examples, there are toxicologists at the EPA; automotive engineers at the Department of Transportation; historians at the National Archives; statisticians at the Department of Labor; pharmacologists at the FDA; physicians at the Department of Health & Human Services; entomologists at the Department of Agriculture; nuclear physicists at the Department of Energy; intelligence analysts at the CIA; aerospace engineers at the Federal Aviation Administration; foreign service officers with fluency in an endless array of languages (say, Xhosa or Ukrainian or Tagalog) at the State Department; and macro-economists at the Federal Reserve. Of course, like all organizations, agencies also have a host of other employees: human resource professionals, financial analysts; communications specialists; and a variety of other administrators. For reasons that will become obvious, agencies also have employees—many of whom are lawyers, or at least have legal training—who specialize in relations with either the courts or legislatures.

The fact that federal agencies consist of both political appointees answerable to the President and civil servants with expertise whose job protection is intended to insulate them from political pressure raises a key tension that we will see throughout this and the next Part of this Book: agency accountability versus agency independence. Many of the issues agencies address are highly technical and require experts to develop policies without political interference. Take, for example, the regulation of nuclear power plants. As a society, we probably want experts who are independent of—indeed, insulated from—politics deciding how to ensure that nuclear power plants are safe. On the other hand, such policies have a huge impact on the public, and in a democracy, we also want agencies to be politically accountable. Many of the difficult questions in this and the next Part of this book revolve around this tension between democratic accountability and independent expertise.

As a lawyer, why will all this matter to you? As we have touched on in earlier chapters, and as we will see in more detail later, many decisions about "law" are not *just* about law in some abstract sense. Many of those decisions—whether made by legislatures, courts, or agencies—have "policy" implications with wide-ranging impact in the real world, beyond the "law." Importantly, because of the policy implications, almost all those decisions depend on facts about the world. Consider, for example, some of the court cases you've studied in your torts, contracts, or criminal law courses. In those cases, the judicial decision-making process, before coming to a legal decision, needs to determine the facts: What happened? Who did what to whom? When? As you have probably already gathered from a Civil Procedure course (and will also see in an Evidence class), the court system has a complex set of rules designed to make those factual determinations.

Ultimately, though, within that set of rules, people—often juries, sometimes judges—make those determinations. Our judicial system generally trusts juries, for example, to make credibility determinations when witnesses tell conflicting stories on the stand. But for some kinds of factual determinations, it is more difficult for lay jurors to know how to make the determination. Consider a criminal case with DNA evidence. How can the ordinary juror know whether a particular defendant's DNA was at a crime scene? In such circumstances, the judicial system brings in experts who understand the science of DNA to explain enough about (and at times, to argue about) DNA so that the jurors can better make the determination of whether the DNA found at the crime scene was the defendant's. Many determinations of this sort require knowledge beyond the ordinary person's knowledge base, and the legal system helps by incorporating expertise into the judicial process.

> **FYI** Earlier, we noted the relative size of the categories of political appointees (a few thousand) and civil servants (a couple of million) within the executive branch. As a point of comparison, there are approximately 10,000–15,000 people who work for Congress.

As we saw in Part II, the legislature is made up of people too: legislators, legislators' staff, staff who work for Committees, and even some staff who work for the institution as a whole (i.e., the House or the Senate). As with the courts, legislators too have ways of learning about the difficult factual questions that affect the decisions they must make regarding the measures they are considering, all of which also occurs within the structure of the rules that make up the legislative process we discussed in Part III. Sometimes, legislators hear from constituents; but sometimes, just like the DNA-in-court example from the previous paragraph, they learn from experts. This can happen at legislative hearings or in communications with lobbyists (many of whom are experts on matters germane to their clients). Sometimes, through their own committee experience or the staff with whom they work, the legislators acquire some "in-house" expertise about the legal decisions they face. In short, then, those in the legislature have a variety of ways to learn. And, as with the courts, the reason legislatures need to have knowledge about things other than (and, in addition to) law is that the law they make depends on and intersects with complex factual (often scientific) questions about the world, questions that cannot be answered or understood without some kind of expertise outside of law.

Agencies also make decisions involving and about law. Because this is a book about law and you are preparing to become a lawyer, much of what you will learn about agencies in this book is what sometimes gets called "administrative law," the law that empowers, but also constrains and regulates, administrative agencies. Like many of the issues of statutory interpretation we addressed in Parts IV through VI, this "law" is what we can call "trans-substantive law," because it applies broadly to many different subject-matter areas of law. So, like statutory interpretation, what you learn in this Part and Part VIII will be generally applicable across a wide variety of areas of law.

> Areas of law like "family law" or **FYI** "employment law" or "environmental law" are examples of what we mean by "substantive" law. "Trans-substantive law" is "meta-law," the law that applies across the board, irrespective of the underlying substantive law. The rules of civil procedure are another example of "trans-substantive law," since those rules apply to all kinds of civil cases. Similarly, the law that regulates the legislative process (e.g., Article I, Section 7 of the Constitution, requiring bicameralism and presentment, or Senate Rule XXII, requiring 60 votes to invoke cloture) is another example of "trans-substantive law."

As we will see, as a formal matter, it is usually a political appointee who is ultimately responsible for any decision an agency makes that has legally binding effect. In other words, since political appointees are subject to Presidential control, virtually every agency decision can, as a formal legal matter, be tied to a democratically elected individual. In contrast to decisions made by the legislature, however, the relevant individual in the case of agencies is the President (or, in the states, the governor). As is probably obvious at this point, though, the formal connection between the President and an agency decision is more attenuated than the formal connection between members of Congress and a statute, since the democratically elected Members of Congress are directly connected to statutes: even if they had little (if any) role in drafting a statute, they must vote on it.

Having already begun to learn about how legislatures and courts make their decisions, you will now turn to how agencies make theirs. As you learn about agencies, keep in mind the *type* of "legal" decisions they are making and how those decisions compare with the decisions made by legislatures and courts. Agency decisions touch virtually every aspect of modern American governance and virtually every area of law. Agencies also do much more than legislatures and courts. To give a sense of comparison, in a recent year Congress enacted about 175 statutes, while federal agencies issued more than 3,300 "rules," a form of generalized lawmaking with binding effect similar to a federal statute. And, as we will see, the "legal" decisions that agencies must make often require deep scientific knowledge, complex economic trade-offs, and an understanding of the political landscape. In short, the kind of facts that agencies deal with make their decisions about "law" different at times from the kinds of decisions about law that legislatures make and that courts make.

As you learn about agencies, you should also keep in mind the question of who is participating in shaping agency decisions. In many other law courses, you have by now learned that court decisions are largely shaped by the briefs and arguments made by the parties before the court. Indeed, unless a party raises an argument or cites a case, it is considered unfair to the other party for the court itself to consider that argument, and of course the concerns of those who are not in the case will generally not be known either. Similarly, as we saw in Part II, legislation comes from those who bring their concerns to the legislature. You'll recall our discussion in Part II about the role of campaign financing and lobbyists, and the concerns that the legislative process may favor certain interests because of who can most easily become a legislator and who can influence those legislators. Similarly, as you read through this Part, think about who influences agencies. Agencies do have expertise, but they also depend on the participants in the administrative process. So, for example, as you might imagine, those individuals or entities regulated by an agency are likely to want to actively engage with the agency when it is making decisions that might affect them. This is why many commentators fear what is known as "agency capture," the notion that a regulated industry uses its political sophistication and influence to shape—and, in the theory's strongest form, to control—an agency's decisions and actions. We discuss this in more detail in Chapter 33.

Finally, as we will see, legislatures, the chief executive, and courts all shape agencies. Indeed, the law that empowers, constrains, and regulates agencies—what, as we noted, is often described as "administrative law"—is generally written by legislatures and interpreted by courts. Meanwhile, the chief executive often plays a direct or indirect role in agency decision-making as those decisions are being made. Agencies are thus interacting with and acting in the shadow of legislatures, the chief executive, and courts all the time. This Part, Part VII, is broadly about the relationships between agencies and legislatures and between agencies and the chief executive. Later, Part VIII addresses the relationship between agencies and courts.

B. What Agencies Do: Rulemaking, Adjudication, Enforcement

Agencies have a range of powers. The way in which agencies use their powers can vary from agency to agency, and the law uses different terms to describe those different exercises of power. Accordingly, a brief overview of some nomenclature is in order.

At the most basic level, agency authority can be divided into three categories: (1) **rulemaking** (a quasi-legislative) power, (2) **adjudicatory** (a quasi-judicial) power, and (3) what is essentially executive or **enforcement** power. Agency rulemaking and adjudication are the focus of this book both because they involve agencies in activities traditionally (if simplistically) understood to belong to other branches of government, and because these activities routinely call upon agencies to interpret and apply statutory language. Furthermore, distinguishing between rulemaking and adjudicatory powers can be crucial yet difficult.

At the federal level, government agencies can conduct both their rulemaking processes and their adjudication processes in several different ways. The most fundamental distinction between these available processes is the distinction between a **formal** process and an **informal** process, a distinction that arises from the Administrative Procedure Act ("APA") discussed below. Because of their origin in the processes spelled out in the APA, these are "terms of art," with very specific meanings that do not match their colloquial, ordinary meanings. In particular, the process by which agencies engage in "informal" rulemaking is anything but informal in the ordinary sense of that word. Furthermore, agencies today in fact engage in very little "formal" rulemaking or adjudication. We touch on why this is so below.

1.   Rulemaking

Agency rulemaking power is the power to establish **rules** or **regulations** (terms used here synonymously) of legal force pursuant to a statutory provision. Often, the statutory provision will either explicitly or implicitly authorize, or even at times mandate, the agency to make such rules, but will generally do so only in broad terms, with the idea that the agency will create more specific regulatory provisions to operationalize the statutory provision. These agency rules have binding legal effect on all parties subject to the rule. For instance, when the Clean Water Act authorizes the Environmental Protection Agency to develop water quality standards, the standards the agency "promulgates" (adopts as regulatory law) have the same binding authority as if they were enacted in the original legislation.

Although rulemaking power is undoubtedly "lawmaking" power, some observers—and judges—have insisted on distinguishing rulemaking power from "legislative" power, primarily for purposes of protecting the Constitution's explicit grant to Congress of "[a]ll [federal] legislative Powers." A set of judicial decisions involving the scope of what is exclusively Congress's legislative authority has given rise to what is known as the nondelegation doctrine, a complex subject that we discuss more in the next chapter. For now, the important thing to know is that, under the current version of the nondelegation doctrine, only Congress may exercise "legislative" power, and may not "delegate" its "legislative" power to agencies. It is crucial to reiterate, however, that from the perspective of a regulated party, agencies' rulemaking power amounts to the power to regulate behavior. In other words, for your future clients, an agency rule has the same binding legal effect as a statute, and is every bit what you likely think of as "law."

Adding to the confusion, many courts and commentators frequently refer to binding agency regulations as "**legislative rules**." This label generally covers an agency's prototypical substantive regulations, as distinguished from an agency's "**interpretative rules**" or its "**general policy statements**." Legislative rules are promulgated by an agency pursuant to authority to exercise lawmaking power, while interpretative rules clarify pre-existing legal obligations—to advise the public of the agency's construction of the statutes and rules that it administers—and general policy statements provide notice of how an agency understands its authority or intends to conduct its operations. Legislative rules establish new legal obligations and carry the force and effect of law, while interpretative rules and policy statements do not. Distinguishing between legislative rules on the one hand and interpretive rules and policy statements on the other is not always easy. *See, e.g.*, *General Motors Corporation v. Ruckelshaus*, 742 F.2d 1561, 1565 (D.C. Cir. 1984) (en banc) (quoting *Noel v. Chapman*, 508 F.2d 1023, 1030 (2d Cir. 1975)) (describing the distinction as "enshrouded in considerable smog"); *American Hospital Association v. Bowen*,

834 F.2d 1037, 1046 (D.C. Cir. 1987) (calling the line between interpretive and legislative rules "fuzzy"); *Community Nutrition Institute v. Young,* 818 F.2d 943, 946 (D.C. Cir. 1987) (quoting authorities describing the distinction between legislative rules and policy statements as "tenuous," "blurred" and "baffling"). Courts have, however, developed legal tests to make that determination. *See, e.g., American Mining Congress v. Mine Safety & Health Administration,* 995 F.2d 1106 (D.C. Cir. 1993); *Professionals & Patients for Customized Care v. Shalala,* 56 F.3d 592 (5th Cir. 1995).

> **FYI** The reason this distinction between legislative rules and interpretive rules matters is that an agency may not promulgate legislative rules without jumping through a host of procedural hoops (which we discuss below in Section B.1)., whereas "interpretive rules" and "general statements of policy" are not subject to the same procedural requirements. *See* 5 U.S.C. sec. 553(b)(A), 553(d)(2).

Moreover, numerous significant government activities now result from the issuance of interpretive rules, general policy statements, and other expressions of agency and executive branch positions, including presidential orders. For instance, the Obama Administration authorized the "Deferred Action for Childhood Arrivals" (DACA) immigration policy in 2012 through a policy "memorandum" instructing immigration officials to use their discretionary authority to defer removing certain undocumented individuals who arrived in the U.S. as children. The Obama Administration also repeatedly used agency policy statements or guidance memoranda to delay the effective date of portions of the 2010 Affordable Care Act (also known as "Obamacare"). As discussed in subsection B.1 below, these non-legislative rules generally are not subject to the same procedural requirements, including an opportunity for public comment, that apply to legislative rules. *See* 5 U.S.C. §§ 553(b)(A), 553(d)(2); *Hudson v. Federal Aviation Administration,* 192 F.3d 1031 (D.C. Cir. 1999).

> **FYI** In the federal system, an "adjudication" is effectively defined as any final decision an agency makes that isn't a "rule." *See* 5 U.S.C. sec. 551(7) (defining "adjudication" as an "agency process for the formulation of an order"); *id.* sec. 551(6) (defining "order" as "the whole or a part of a final disposition . . . of an agency in a matter other than rule making . . .")

2. Adjudication

Meanwhile, agencies use adjudicatory power to resolve specific issues, typically concluding the adjudicatory process by issuing an agency "order." Although these orders, like rules, also have binding legal effect, by their terms they generally apply only to the parties to the particular adjudication, not more widely. Nevertheless, the involved parties can sometimes represent a broad swath of interests, and adjudicative orders, like court decisions, may set a precedent that can govern similar controversies. Agency adjudicatory "orders" are also thus "law" in a colloquial sense, much as you might say an appellate court decision is "law." Because orders can have broad legally binding effect beyond the directly involved parties, agencies often use adjudications to establish general policies.

FYI As you might imagine, with this reference to "*Chenery II*", there is in fact a *Chenery I*. We discuss the important principle established by *Chenery I*—that courts can review agency action only on the basis of the reasons the agency gives for its action—in Part VIII, when we discuss judicial review of agency action.

For instance, in the foundational case of *Securities and Exchange Commission v. Chenery Corporation*, 332 U.S. 194, 207 (1947) (*Chenery II*), the Supreme Court approved what it acknowledged was an "administrative order wherein a new principle is announced," over the objection that any such new principle should be treated as a rule that the agency could apply only prospectively. Although the Court suggested that when agencies are "filling in the interstices" of the statutes they are enforcing, they should use their rulemaking rather than their ad-

judicatory authority "as much as possible," the Court also said that agencies must have the flexibility to resolve unanticipated problems that arise in adjudicatory proceedings. The Supreme Court reaffirmed the same principle three decades later, holding in *National Labor Relations Board v. Bell Aerospace Company*, 416 U.S. 267 (1974), that the NLRB could use an adjudicatory proceeding rather than a rulemaking proceeding to determine that certain classes of workers were not "managerial employees" under the National Labor Relations Act.

3. Enforcement

Finally, agencies enforce statutes and regulations within their jurisdiction. The term "enforcement" may first bring to mind *criminal* enforcement—indeed, the term "law enforcement" is often used to refer to institutions like

Virtually any decision a governmental agency makes about a particularized matter can be viewed as an "adjudication." These can range from the most minor decisions to fundamental decisions affecting the entire country. For example, a city's License and Permit Department's decision to grant or deny a pet license is an "adjudication." But so too is a decision by the United States Secretary of Energy to store spent nuclear fuel and other high-level radioactive waste within Yucca Mountain, Nevada. Although both of those decisions are "adjudications," the legal processes for making each decision are different.

the police department and the FBI, the means by which most American jurisdictions investigate violations of their criminal law. There is little doubt that criminal enforcement is certainly one important facet of the broader idea of enforcement of the law. Thought of through this lens, then, a police department—whether local, state, or federal, whether one with broad powers or one related to specific types of crimes—is in fact an "agency" in the broadest sense of that word. Just as one example, the federal government's principal investigative arm—the most prominent federal "police," so to speak—is the Federal Bureau of Investigation, and it is an agency.

Criminal prosecutors are also part of an agency, whether a district attorney's office, a department of justice, or some other prosecutor's office at the federal, state, or local level. At the federal level, the United States Department of Justice (DOJ), headed by the Attorney General, prosecutes federal crimes, usually through its Criminal Division and what are known as United States Attorney offices throughout the country. Most states have a similar office, also usually headed by a lawyer whose title is "Attorney General."

> Some federal crimes are prosecuted by other DOJ divisions. For example, the Environmental Crimes Section in DOJ's Environment and Natural Resources Division is in charge of prosecuting many pollution and wildlife crimes, such as the criminal prohibitions in the Safe Drinking Water Act or Endangered Species Act.

Much enforcement of law, however, is not criminal enforcement, but instead civil enforcement. DOJ is also involved in civil enforcement, as are state Attorneys General. But much civil enforcement is done by other agencies. For example, in the federal government, the Occupational Safety and Health Administration (OSHA), part of the Department of Labor, enforces workplace health and safety laws and regulations. The Food and Drug Administration (FDA), part of the Department of Health and Human Services (HHS), enforces violations of the Food, Drug, and Cosmetic Act. The Environmental Protection Agency (EPA) enforces many laws related to, for example, air and water pollution, hazardous chemicals, and greenhouse gases.

The relationship between agency enforcement and DOJ criminal and civil enforcement, including the different types of remedies available, is an extraordinarily complex topic, well beyond the scope of this book. But agency enforcement often takes place *within the agency itself*—the Administrator of the Wage and Hour Division of the Department of Labor, for example, prosecutes violations of minimum wage laws before an Administrative Law Judge (ALJ) who works in the Department of Labor itself—while enforcement by DOJ occurs in federal court. Most federal agencies do not have the authority to bring either civil or criminal actions in court, what is known as "independent litigating authority," and instead must be represented by the DOJ, even in enforcing statutes in their subject-matter area. *See* 5 U.S.C. § 3106. A few agencies, mostly independent agencies, do have independent litigating authority. Examples include the Department of State (*not* an independent agency), *see* 22 U.S.C. § 2698, and the Board of the Federal Reserve, *see* 12 U.S.C. § 248(p). So, in those agencies, their lawyers can bring cases to court. But even in the context of enforcement by DOJ, officials in other agencies—including, not surprisingly, lawyers—often work closely with DOJ officials.

C. How Administrative Agencies Do What They Do: Procedural Constraints on Agencies

The dramatic rise in the number of federal administrative agencies in the first half of the twentieth century and the accompanying increase in the substantive responsibilities that Congress delegated to these agencies understandably led to calls to constrain and regularize the way in which federal agencies used their various powers. During the New Deal era in particular, a trenchant criticism was that agencies acted with no uniform procedure, and often without much public input. The most significant response was the Administrative Procedure Act, enacted in 1946 after a decade of consideration. Today, most states have adopted their own analogous measures to regulate state agency processes. Meanwhile, the Due Process Clause of the U.S. Constitution, applicable to both federal and state agency action, imposes an additional constraint on how agencies operate, particularly in the context of agency adjudication. Of course, Congress and state legislatures may also impose additional constraints on how individual agencies operate through statutory provisions in other statutes authorizing particular agency action.

1. The Administrative Procedure Act

The Administrative Procedure Act (APA), 5 U.S.C. §§ 551 *et seq.*, is often characterized as the "constitution" of federal administrative law because of the foundational way in which it defines the functioning and the limits of the authority of federal agencies. In the main, it specifies in significant detail certain processes (such as public comment opportunities and notification requirements) that all federal agencies must follow when promulgating various types of rules or adjudicating certain kinds of disputes. It also requires that federal agencies take a number of affirmative steps to keep the public informed of their work and it establishes processes for judicial review of agency action.

The APA broadly defines the term "agency," the entities to which the Act's provisions apply, as "each authority of the Government of the United States, whether or not it is within or subject to review by another agency." However, the APA expressly excludes Congress and the federal courts from its coverage, as well as the governments of U.S. territories and possessions. *See* 5 U.S.C. § 551(1). Additionally, the Supreme Court has held that the President is not an APA agency. *See Franklin v. Massachusetts*, 505 U.S. 788, 800–01 (1992); *Dalton v. Specter*, 511 U.S. 462, 470 (1994).

Like many things in law, even this **FYI** APA phrasing does not resolve all debate about what constitutes an "agency." There is no definition of what constitutes an "authority" of the Government of the United States, and there is no legally binding list of all federal agencies. The Administrative Conference of the United States (abbreviated "ACUS" and itself an independent federal agency!) has a <u>Sourcebook of U.S. Executive Agencies</u> that contains what may be the most comprehensive list of executive agencies.

Note that this definition makes certain formal sub-units within agencies themselves agencies. So, for example, OSHA is within the Department of Labor, but OSHA itself is an "agency" within the APA definition. Similarly, the Civil Rights Division of the Department of Justice is also an "agency" within the APA definition.

The APA divides agency actions into two broad categories: rulemaking proceedings, which produce agency rules; and adjudications, which produce agency orders. These categories reflect the potential for agencies to engage in both quasi-legislative action and quasi-judicial action. In turn, both rulemaking proceedings and adjudications can be either formal, involving more elaborate processes, or informal, giving the agency greater flexibility. Although the APA does not itself label its various processes as "formal" or "informal," its provisions specify how each type of agency action must occur.

For instance, Section 4 of the APA (often referred to as "Section 553" because it is codified at 5 U.S.C. § 553) sets forth the rulemaking requirements for one category of informal rulemaking, a category that today is generally called "notice and comment rulemaking." This most-widely used rulemaking process requires an agency to provide public notice of a pro-

The idea behind "notice and comment" rulemaking is that the public should have both a warning (or "notice") that an agency is contemplating adopting a new or revised rule, and an opportunity to provide the agency with input or feedback on the proposal (to "comment") before the agency acts.

posed rule by publishing the substance of the proposed rule (in the form of the proposed text of the rule) in the Federal Register. The notice also must describe the agency's source of legal authority to promulgate the rule and the means by which interested parties may express their views about the proposal. Typically, parties share those views by submitting written comments to the agency, although agencies on rare occasions may also conduct field hearings or allow oral presentations. Section 553 further requires that the agency incorporate into any resulting rule "a concise general statement of [its] basis and purpose." The "general statement of [a rule's] basis and purpose" describes the agency's reasons for adopting the rule. These days, though, these statements are anything but concise. As we discuss below, courts have effectively required agencies to provide a great deal of detail about their rules.

> **FYI** The federal government has a website, regulations.gov, that serves as a central repository for the public to submit comments on many proposed federal rules.

Meanwhile, section 553 also references the fact that sometimes an agency is required to conduct a full-blown, trial-like proceeding, in which rules are "to be made on the record after opportunity for an agency hearing." This is formal rulemaking, and two separate APA provisions—5 U.S.C. §§ 556 and 557—provide detailed requirements for how agencies are to conduct these proceedings. A third section—5 U.S.C. § 3105—provides for the appointment of administrative law judges (ALJs) to preside at these formal proceedings. ALJs are a type of non-Article III federal judicial officer whose appointment the APA vests in each agency. In practice, though, formal rulemakings are exceedingly rare, in substantial part because the Supreme Court has significantly limited the circumstances in which agencies must adhere to the formal hearing requirements of §§ 556 and 557. Most important, in *United States v. Florida East Coast Railway Co.*, 410 U.S. 224, 241 (1973), the Court concluded that agencies need not follow the

> **FYI** Prior to the *Florida East Coast Railway* decision, most federal courts of appeals had held that "hearing" meant an oral evidentiary hearing. Hearings under sections 556 and 557 had often been extensive affairs, involving many lawyers and much evidence from numerous witnesses, sometimes occurring over periods of months or even years. This would in turn mean lawyers billing clients for many hours of work! Because many statutes lack the magic words "on the record after opportunity for an agency hearing," *Florida East Coast Railway* had the immediate effect of sending lawyers scrambling for more work. *See* KRISTIN HICKMAN & RICHARD PIERCE, FEDERAL ADMINISTRATIVE LAW: CASES AND MATERIALS 560 (3d ed. 2020).

formal rulemaking process unless Congress has specifically required that the rule-making proceeding occur "on the record after opportunity for an agency hearing." *Florida East Coast Railway* can be thought of as almost a "magic words" holding, since the Court held that a statute that merely required that a rule be made "after hearing" could be satisfied through the informal § 553 notice-and-comment process, or what is often called a "paper hearing."

Section 553 also contemplates other types of even more informal decision-making processes akin to rulemaking. In particular, it provides that agencies may promulgate "interpretative rules" and "general statements of policy" without complying with even the notice-and-comment requirements of § 553. *See Perez v. Mortgage Bankers Ass'n*, 575 U.S. 92 (2015). However, these statements of agency position still must comply with the requirement that all agency rules of general applicability be published in the Federal Register. *See* 5 U.S.C. § 552(a)(1)(D).

Turning from the processes of agency rulemaking to the processes of agency adjudication, here too the relevant APA provisions implicitly create a distinction between formal adjudications and informal adjudications. Section 5 of the APA, 5 U.S.C. § 554, explains that agency adjudications of issues that are "required by statute to be determined on the record after opportunity for an agency hearing," like formal rulemaking issues, must follow the detailed hearing procedures of §§ 556 and 557, unless all parties to the adjudication are able to reach agreement "by consent." But the Court's 1973 decision in *Florida East Coast Railway* (which as described above concluded in the rulemaking context that a requirement of an agency "hearing" did not necessarily require the formal trial-type proceeding of §§ 556 and 557) also gave federal agencies the green light to develop and employ informal adjudicatory processes whenever a governing statute called only for adjudication "after hearing," rather than specifically calling for a hearing "on the record." The Court's subsequent decisions in *Vermont Yankee Nuclear Power Corp. v. Natural Resources Defense Council*, 435 U.S. 519 (1978) (involving rulemaking), and *Pension Benefit*

The Supreme Court itself has never held that its *Florida East Coast Railway* decision applies to adjudications. In the immediate aftermath of *Florida East Coast Railway*, the Courts of Appeals were split on the question. However, since 1984, when the Supreme Court decided the *Chevron* case (which we will address in Part VIII), every Court of Appeals to address the issue has allowed agencies to avoid formal adjudication unless the statute authorizing the agency adjudication explicitly required adjudication "on the record after opportunity for an agency hearing." *See, e.g., Dominion Energy Brayton Point, LLC v. Johnson*, 443 F.3d 12 (1st Cir. 2006).

Guaranty Corp. v. LTV Corp., 496 U.S. 633 (1990) (involving adjudication), made clear that federal agencies have great discretion to choose how to conduct both rulemaking proceedings and adjudications, subject only to constitutional limits, the narrow construction of §§ 553 and 554, and any specific constraints Congress may have imposed through some other statute, potentially including the agency's organic statute.

> **FYI** An agency's "organic statute" is the statute that creates the agency, or brings the agency to life by giving the agency its powers and duties. It is one example of a kind of "enabling statute," which is any statute that authorizes or confers some kind of power on an agency.

Today, many agency adjudications, like almost all agency rulemakings, are informal. Section 6 of the APA, 5 U.S.C. § 555, spells out certain procedural rights applicable even to informal adjudications, including the right to be represented by counsel, as well as rights to subpoena relevant witnesses, to obtain copies of records, and to receive notice and an explanation of resulting agency action. Formal adjudications are usually conducted by Administrative Law Judges (ALJs), who function like hearing officers, assisting the agency in developing a factual record and making an initial or recommended decision. But the agency itself, which has final responsibility for the matter, is not required to follow or adopt the ALJ's decision.

One fundamental question that the APA leaves open is when an agency should proceed by rulemaking rather than by adjudication. As noted above, in 1947 the Supreme Court held that an agency was free to announce even a generally applicable rule through an adjudicatory proceeding and need not promulgate such a rule through the rulemaking process. *See Chenery II*, 332 U.S. 194. The Court said that "the choice made between proceeding by general rule or by individual, ad hoc litigation is one that lies primarily in the informed discretion of the agency." *Id.* at 203. Although *Chenery II* did not involve the APA, the Court reiterated this principle in an APA case a quarter century later, though it noted that the agency's discretion was not unlimited: "there may be situations where [agency] reliance on adjudication would amount to an abuse of discretion." *National Labor Relations Board v. Bell Aerospace*, 416 U.S. at 294.

Finally, and critically, the APA specifies in great detail the manner in which federal courts are empowered to review agency action. We turn to this in earnest in Part VIII, but provide a brief comment here. Section 10 of the APA, 5 U.S.C. §§ 701–706, governs the way in which "[a] person suffering legal wrong because of agency action . . . is entitled to judicial review thereof." 5 U.S.C. § 702. In addition to establishing a presumption that agency actions are generally reviewable, *see*

Citizens to Preserve Overton Park v. Volpe, 401 U.S. 402 (1971); *Abbott Laboratories v. Gardner*, 387 U.S. 136 (1967), these provisions specify the form and venue of appellate review, as well as the scope of review. Of particular import is the standard of § 706(2)(A), which provides that a reviewing court shall hold unlawful agency action that is "arbitrary, capricious, an abuse of discretion, or otherwise not in accordance with law."

2.   State Analogs of the APA

At about the same time that Congress was developing the Administrative Procedure Act, the National Conference of Commissioners of Uniform State Laws (NCCUSL, sometimes pronounced "Necusal," but also often called the Uniform Law Commission), with the encouragement of the American Bar Association, was developing its own Model State Administrative Procedure Act (MSAPA). Most state administrative procedure statutes trace their pedigrees to this 1946 model act, and its subsequent revisions, more than to the federal APA. However, the model state act was substantively quite like the federal APA, and indeed was developed almost in tandem with the APA. By 1981, when NCCUSL released a second revision of the MSAPA, more than half the states had adopted some version of either the original 1946 MSAPA or its 1961 revision. Other states that did not adopt some version of the full model state act at least adopted portions of the model act. In 2010, NCCUSL produced a third revision of the MSAPA. *See* www.uniformlaws.org.

Do you think that every state should adopt some version of the MSAPA?

3.   Due Process Constraints

In addition to statutory constraints on agency activities (exemplified most prominently by the Administrative Procedure Act), the Due Process Clause of the U.S. Constitution provides another procedural limit on the functioning of federal and state government agencies. Decades before enactment of the APA, the Supreme Court established that in the circumstances of a government agency's individualized determination of a party's legal rights or obligations, the party must have notice of the impending agency action and an opportunity to be heard by the agency. *See Londoner v. Denver*, 210 U.S. 373 (1908). But less than a decade later, the Court clarified that this principle did not apply in the circumstances of a generalized rulemaking, where it would be "impracticable that everyone should have a direct voice in [the rule's] adoption." *Bi-Metallic Investment Co. v. State Board of Education*, 239 U.S. 441, 445 (1915). Moreover, the Due Process Clause only protects government deprivations of "life, liberty or property," *see* U.S. Const.

This distinction between individualized and generalized decisionmaking is known as the *Londoner-BiMetallic* distinction after the names of these two cases. The distinction is, in essence, the distinction between adjudication and rulemaking.

amends. V, XIV. There is a complex jurisprudence about what constitutes "liberty" or "property" for purposes of the Due Process Clause, but the important thing to note is that not every agency action, not even every agency adjudication, triggers the Due Process Clause. *See, e.g., Board of Regents v. Roth*, 408 U.S. 564 (1972).

4.   Other Statutory Provisions

While the Due Process Clause of the U.S. Constitution and the Administrative Procedure Act are trans-substantive and apply broadly to administrative processes throughout the federal government, Congress sometimes writes administrative procedure directly into substantive statutes. So, for example, the Clean Air Act contains a provision that lays out rulemaking procedures for the EPA to follow when promulgating or revising many of the regulations the Act requires. *See* 42 U.S.C. § 7607(d). Although the procedures have similarities to the informal rulemaking procedures in the Administrative Procedure Act, the statute explicitly states that the procedures replace those found in the APA. *See id.* at 7607(d)(1) ("The provisions of section 553 through 557 and section 706 of Title 5 shall not, except as expressly provided in this subsection, apply to actions to which this subsection applies."). As one example of the kind of detailed procedure Congress can impose on an agency, the Clean Air Act requires that the notice of proposed rulemaking *also* include a "statement of basis and purpose." [Recall from Section C.1 above that the APA requires that an agency's *final rule* include a "statement of basis and purpose," but does not require such a statement in the notice of proposed rulemaking.]

Test Your Understanding

To assess your understanding of the material in this chapter, click here to take a quiz.

29

Legislative Control of Government Agencies

Key Concepts

- Agency creation
- Congressional delegation
- Nondelegation doctrine
- Intelligible principle
- Legislative veto
- Fiscal control of agencies
- Legislative oversight of agencies

Chapter Summary

Today, American democracy depends on a wide array of administrative agencies to implement government policies. These agencies function pursuant to whatever authority has been granted to them by the legislative branch, under a variety of mechanisms of legislative oversight and control. Although nominally the legislative branch is not allowed to hand over its legislative power to executive branch agencies, in practice the legislature is granted wide latitude in enlisting agency assistance in developing the details of many statutory programs.

At least at the federal level, however, the Supreme Court has limited Congress's ability to micromanage federal agencies. For instance, although the President's appointment of nominees to many leadership positions in the executive branch requires Senate approval, the Senate is not allowed to exercise control over the President's removal of leaders who have lost the President's confidence. Similarly, Congress is not able to exercise a "legislative veto" over specific agency action, other than by enacting a new law.

A. Federal Agencies Are Creatures of Statute

At the federal level, Article II of the U.S. Constitution vests "[t]he executive Power" in the President of the United States. As specified in Article II, this power includes the power to oversee "each of the executive Departments," to appoint "Officers of the United States, whose Appointments . . . shall be established by law," and to "Commission all the Officers of the United States." Yet Congress in the first instance must establish these executive departments, none of which are established by the Constitution. Congress also must specify those Officers within each department whose appointments are to be made by the President (whether unilaterally or with the advice and consent of the Senate), as well as those other executive branch positions that may be filled not by the President but by "the Heads of Departments."

In 1789, three of the First Congress's early legislative acts were the creation of the first federal departments: the Department of Foreign Affairs (later that same year renamed the Department of State), the Department of War (what we today call the Department of Defense), and the Department of Treasury. Through enabling statutes, Congress gave each of these departments a specific charge and provided that each was to be led by a Secretary, who was to be appointed by the President with the advice and consent of the Senate. The First Congress also established the position of Attorney General of the United States but did so without creating a department for that official to lead.

As the country grew in size and complexity or confronted new challenges, Congress from time to time created other executive branch departments or reorganized existing federal departments. For instance, in 1870, Congress established the Department of Justice and placed the Attorney General at its head. In 1979, Congress divided the Department of Health, Education, and Welfare into a reconfigured Department of Health and Human Services and a freestanding Department of Education. After the terrorist attacks of September 11, 2001, Congress created a new Department of Homeland Security, consolidating under one head an array of functions that previously had been scattered across many other departments and agencies.

Today, as seen below, the federal government contains fifteen executive branch departments.

Executive Branch

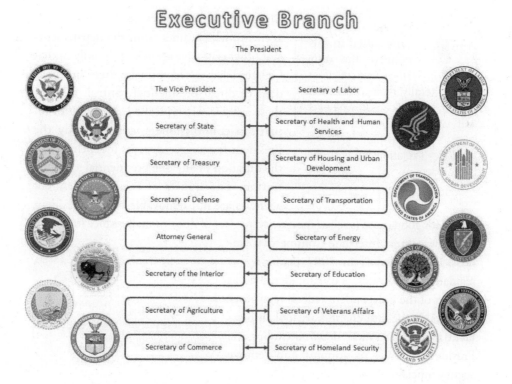

Each of these fifteen departments is created by Congress and each is led by a Secretary who is appointed by the President, with the advice and consent of the Senate, pursuant to Article II, Section 2 of the Constitution. Each of these department heads reports directly to the President and also serves as a member of the President's Cabinet. In furtherance of the President's constitutional responsibility to "take Care that the Laws be faithfully executed," U.S. CONST. art. II, sec. 3, the President retains significant control over these departments, mainly through the authority to remove at will any of the department heads.

"Cabinet" is the term frequently **FYI** used to describe the team of appointed government officials who, in addition to leading a subsidiary department of the executive branch, also function as a group of policy advisors to the chief executive.

In addition to these fifteen departments, scores of other agencies—such as the Central Intelligence Agency, the Environmental Protection Agency, and the National Science Foundation—now also are part of the federal bureaucracy.

> **!** When used in this context, the term "independent" does not literally mean "independent," as in "can do whatever it wants." Here, "independent" refers primarily to the agency's relationship with the President.

Many of these agencies are "independent" agencies, which differ from the departments and other executive agencies primarily in that Congress has opted to make them independent of direct presidential control. Instead, these agencies are typically led by a set of bipartisan commissioners, appointed by the President for staggered terms independent of the duration of any one presidential administration. The leaders of these independent agencies are not removable by the President except for good cause (such as incapacity, neglect of duty, or malfeasance in office). The now-defunct Interstate Commerce Commission, established in 1887 primarily to regulate railroad rates, is usually identified as the first of the independent federal regulatory agencies. In the next chapter, we look at presidential control in more detail, including the President's power to appoint and remove agency officials.

> **?** What sort of regulatory issues are better suited to independent agencies than to executive branch agencies?

B. State Agencies Also Are Largely Creatures of Statute

State administrative agencies also are largely creatures of state statutes, although the landscape surrounding state agencies and departments often differs somewhat from that of the federal system. Perhaps most significantly, many state constitutions expressly create several executive branch officers, in addition to the Governor, each of them separately elected. For instance, forty-three states elect their state Attorney General, while thirty-eight states elect the state Treasurer and the Secretary of State. Many other examples of independently elected state officials exist, including Insurance, Banking, or Public Utility Commissioners, heads of the Department or Board of Education, and Chief Election Officials. These elected state officers do not report to the state governor and may take policy positions at odds with other elected state officials. Nevertheless, they too are highly dependent on their respective state legislature to set the terms of their authority and to fund their activities.

C. Delegation of Authority to Administrative Agencies

Just as important as the leadership structure of an administrative agency is the legislature's choice of what authority and duties to assign to the agency. An entire judicial doctrine—the nondelegation doctrine—has developed around the question of what legislatures may empower agencies to do without violating the Constitution's separation of powers (which establishes Congress as the legislative branch of government). Primarily, this involves the question of how much lawmaking authority the legislative branch can share with the executive branch.

> The nondelegation doctrine purports to limit Congress's ability to delegate its lawmaking authority to other actors, although in practice Congress has wide latitude to rely on agencies to make legal rules.

FYI Because the nondelegation doctrine is a constitutional doctrine, when it applies, the doctrine invalidates a statutory provision that delegates authority to an administrative agency. As we will see in Part VIII, a parallel doctrine can apply when courts interpret the scope of statutes that delegate to agencies. That doctrine, arguably also rooted in separation-of-powers principles but of very recent vintage, is known as the "Major Questions Doctrine," and it provides that Congress must speak clearly in a statute if it wishes to assign to an agency decisions of vast economic and political importance. The doctrine can result in invalidating an agency action as being outside the power of the statute's delegation to an agency, but without invalidating the statute itself.

Legislatures may find it advantageous to leave to an agency the development of more detailed regulations in a specific area of law, whether it be tax law, environmental law, energy law, election law, or any other area. One reason legislators like members of Congress might do this is that, in a complex world legislators understand their cognitive and capacity limits. Arguably, government agencies have both the expertise and the capacity to develop detailed legal requirements much more carefully, appropriately, and efficiently than could Congress or a state legislature. This might be characterized as a "public interest" motivation on legislators' part. On the other hand, efficiency is not necessarily a virtue for the lawmaking process, and many inefficiencies or hurdles in the legislative process are often defended as helping produce better laws in the long run. Moreover, some argue that because agency personnel are not elected, the regulations an agency promulgates are less representative of the public's will—and thus less "democratic"—than are statutes passed by a legislature. Indeed, some argue that this is precisely why legislators delegate to agencies:

! Recall again the processes for electing legislators we studied in Chapters 4 through 9, the nature of lobbying in Chapter 10, and the process for enacting statutes in Chapter 11. To the extent that the process of passing legislation is "democratic," you now understand that democracy is mediated through the institutional structure of the legislature, as shaped by an array of rules determining who can become a legislator and what constrains them in office. In this Part of the book, we are looking at the institutional structure of administrative agencies, the processes they use to promulgate regulations, who the agency decisionmakers are, and what constrains them.

to avoid accountability and responsibility for the difficult decisions that regulation often entails, so they can continue to get re-elected. This idea is obviously premised on a more cynical notion of legislative behavior than the "public interest" motivation. This theory, which has been the focus of much work in political science and economics over the past half-century or so, is often called the "public choice" theory of legislative behavior. In any given congressional delegation of power, it is likely that both public-spirited and self-interested motivations are at play, and so, by themselves, these theories are rarely determinative as to when delegation is appropriate. But the core idea underlying the nondelegation doctrine is that some delegations may be simply too open-ended or unconstrained, and thus must be invalidated. In large measure, then, the nondelegation doctrine addresses the constitutional boundary between permissible and impermissible delegations of lawmaking authority from the legislature to agencies.

Although delegations of regulatory power have occurred since the First Congress, the Supreme Court has repeatedly noted that "Congress cannot delegate legislative power" to the executive branch. *E.g., Marshall Field & Co. v. Clark*, 143 U.S. 649, 692 (1892). The question, then, is what should count as a delegation of "legislative" power. The canonical answer to this question, and the most frequently invoked statement of the nondelegation doctrine, is found in *J. W. Hampton, Jr. & Co. v. United States*, 276 U.S. 394, 409 (1928): "If Congress shall lay down by legislative act an intelligible principle to which the person or body authorized to [take regulatory activity] is directed to conform, such legislative action is not a forbidden delegation of legislative power."

"Public Choice" theory seeks to use **FYI** tools of economic analysis to explain political decisionmaking in terms of the interactions of a host of self-interested actors.

But what is an "intelligible principle"? In the federal system, a litany of cases suggests that almost anything can be an "intelligible principle" and that the nondelegation doctrine therefore appears to have little direct bite (although as we will explore later, when a statute leaves the extent of delegated authority ambiguous, the application of either a "nondelegation canon" of interpretation, or the newer "Major Questions Doctrine," often may limit the scope of the delegation). In only two cases, both involving the same statute and both in 1935 during the height of the Supreme Court's rejection of New Deal legislation, has the Court held that Congress unconstitutionally delegated legislative power to the executive branch: In *Panama Refining Co. v. Ryan*, 293 U.S. 388 (1935), and again in *A.L.A. Schechter Poultry Corp. v. United States*, 295 U.S. 495 (1935), the Court struck down provisions of the 1933 National Industrial Recovery Act (NIRA) as unconstitutional legislative delegations. At issue in *Schechter Poultry* was a provision authorizing the President to impose "codes of fair competition" on certain trades or industries. In reviewing a challenge to a resulting poultry code, the Court found this authority "virtually unfettered," notwithstanding NIRA's "statement of the general aims of rehabilitation, correction, and expansion described in section one." *Id.* at 541–42.

> The National Industrial Recovery Act **FYI** was one of several laws enacted in the midst of the Great Depression by the Seventy-Third Congress and supported by President Franklin Roosevelt. Congress passed the NIRA in June 1933, a mere three months after Roosevelt took office.

Yet beyond those two cases, the Supreme Court has so far always found an adequate "intelligible principle" in every nondelegation issue that it has addressed. As the Court explained in 1989, "our jurisprudence has been driven by a practical understanding that in our increasingly complex society . . . Congress simply cannot do its job absent an ability to delegate power." *Mistretta v. United States*, 488 U.S. 361, 372 (1989). Indeed, early in the twenty-first century, in *Whitman v. American Trucking Associations, Inc.*, 531 U.S. 457, 474–75 (2001), the Court seemed to suggest that it would be unlikely ever to "second-guess Congress regarding the permissible degree of policy judgment that can be left to those executing or applying the law."

However, it is possible that things could change. At least five of the Court's current Justices have indicated a willingness to reconsider this highly-deferential-to-Congress approach to the nondelegation doctrine. One key moment that signals the potential shift was a dissenting opinion in 2019 in a case called *Gundy v. United States*, 139 S. Ct. 2116, 2131 (Gorsuch, J., dissenting, joined by Chief Justice Roberts and Justice Thomas); *see also id.* at 2130–31 (Alito, J., concurring) (indicating willingness "to reconsider the approach we have taken for the past 84 years"); *Paul v. United States*, 140 S. Ct. 342 (2019) (Statement of Justice Kavanaugh respecting the denial of certiorari) (noting that "Justice Gorsuch's scholarly analysis of the Constitution's nondelegation doctrine in his *Gundy* dissent may warrant further consideration in future cases").

What follows are fuller excerpts of the 2001 *Whitman* case and each of the opinions in the 2019 *Gundy* case:

Whitman v. American Trucking Associations, Inc.
531 U.S. 457 (2001)

Justice Scalia delivered the opinion of the Court.

These cases present the following questions: (1) Whether § 109(b)(1) of the Clean Air Act (CAA) delegates legislative power to the Administrator of the Environmental Protection Agency (EPA). * * *

I

? Why do you think a statute like the Clean Air Act requires that an agency like the EPA revisit its air quality standards for air pollutants every five years? Might this help us understand at least one reason why Congress wants to delegate the power to promulgate air quality standards to the EPA?

Section 109(a) of the CAA * * * requires the Administrator of the EPA to promulgate NAAQS [national ambient air quality standards] for each air pollutant for which "air quality criteria" have been issued under § 108. Once a NAAQS has been promulgated, the Administrator must review the standard (and the criteria on which it is based) "at five-year intervals" and make "such revisions . . . as may be appropriate." CAA § 109(d)(1), 42 U.S.C. § 7409(d)(1). These cases arose when, on July 18, 1997, the Administrator revised the NAAQS for particulate matter (PM) and ozone. American Trucking Associations, Inc., and its co-respondents in No. 99–1257—which include, in addition to other private companies, the States of Michigan, Ohio, and West Virginia— challenged the new standards in the Court of Appeals for the District of Columbia Circuit.

The District of Columbia Circuit accepted some of the challenges and rejected others. It agreed with the No. 99–1257 respondents (hereinafter respondents) that § 109(b)(1) delegated legislative power to the Administrator in contravention of the United States Constitution, Art. I, § 1, because it found that the EPA had interpreted the statute to provide no "intelligible principle" to guide the agency's exercise of authority. The court thought, however, that the EPA could perhaps avoid the unconstitutional delegation by adopting a restrictive construction of § 109(b)(1), so instead of declaring the section unconstitutional the court remanded the NAAQS to the agency. (On this delegation point, Judge Tatel dissented, finding the statute constitutional as written.) * * *

The Administrator and the EPA petitioned this Court for review. * * *

III

Section 109(b)(1) of the CAA instructs the EPA to set "ambient air quality standards the attainment and maintenance of which in the judgment of the Administrator, based on [the] criteria [documents of § 108] and allowing an adequate margin of safety, are requisite to protect the public health." 42 U.S.C. § 7409(b)(1). The Court of Appeals held that this section as interpreted by the Administrator did not provide an "intelligible principle" to guide the EPA's exercise of authority in setting NAAQS. "[The] EPA," it said, "lack[ed] any determinate criteria for drawing lines. It has failed to state intelligibly how much is too much." 175 F.3d, at 1034. The court hence found that the EPA's interpretation (but not the statute itself) violated the nondelegation doctrine. *Id.*, at 1038. We disagree.

In a delegation challenge, the constitutional question is whether the statute has delegated legislative power to the agency. Article I, § 1, of the Constitution vests "[a]ll legislative Powers herein granted . . . in a Congress of the United States." This text permits no delegation of those powers, and so we repeatedly have said that when Congress confers decisionmaking authority upon agencies *Congress* must "lay down by legislative act an intelligible principle to which the person or body authorized to [act] is directed to conform." *J. W. Hampton, Jr., & Co. v. United States,* 276 U.S. 394, 409 (1928). We have never suggested that an agency can cure an unlawful delegation of legislative power by adopting in its discretion a limiting construction of the statute. * * * The idea that an agency can cure an

> Notice how the Court characterizes what an agency does here—as "decisionmaking authority," as opposed to "legislative power." What exactly are the American Trucking Association and the other respondents (including several states) challenging here? The EPA Administrator has established (and revised) air quality standards for particulate matter and ozone that are binding regulations. Isn't the EPA's action here "legislative" in an intuitive sense of what that word means? After you have read the concurrence below, think about this question again.

Why is this a question for the courts? What is the Court "interpreting" here? Notice how much power this places in the courts.

unconstitutionally standardless delegation of power by declining to exercise some of that power seems to us internally contradictory. The very choice of which portion of the power to exercise—that is to say, the prescription of the standard that Congress had omitted—would *itself* be an exercise of the forbidden legislative authority. Whether the statute delegates legislative power is a question for the courts, and an agency's voluntary self-denial has no bearing upon the answer.

We agree with the Solicitor General that the text of § 109(b)(1) of the CAA at a minimum requires that "[f]or a discrete set of pollutants and based on published air quality criteria that reflect the latest scientific knowledge, [the] EPA must establish uniform national standards at a level that is requisite to protect public health from the adverse effects of the pollutant in the ambient air." Requisite, in turn, "mean[s] sufficient, but not more than necessary." These limits on the EPA's discretion are strikingly similar to the ones we approved in *Touby v. United States,* 500 U.S. 160 (1991), which permitted the Attorney General to designate a drug as a controlled substance for purposes of criminal drug enforcement if doing so was " 'necessary to avoid an imminent hazard to the public safety.' " *Id.,* at 163. They also resemble the Occupational Safety and Health Act provision requiring the agency to " 'set the standard which most adequately assures, to the extent feasible, on the basis of the best available evidence, that no employee will suffer any impairment of health' "—which the Court upheld in *Industrial Union Dept., AFL-CIO v. American Petroleum Institute,* 448 U.S. 607, 646 (1980), and which even then-Justice Rehnquist, who alone in that case thought the statute violated the nondelegation doctrine, see *id.,* at 671 (opinion concurring in judgment), would have upheld if, like the statute here, it did not permit economic costs to be considered. See *American Textile Mfrs. Institute, Inc. v. Donovan,* 452 U.S. 490, 545 (1981) (REHNQUIST, J., dissenting).

The scope of discretion § 109(b)(1) allows is in fact well within the outer limits of our nondelegation precedents.

* * *

In short, we have "almost never felt qualified to second-guess Congress regarding the permissible degree of policy judgment that can be left to those executing or applying the law." *Mistretta v. United States,* 488 U.S. 361, 416 (1989) (SCALIA, J., dissenting); see *id.,* at 373 (majority opinion).

> Recall that two paragraphs earlier the Court was emphatic that the question of "[w]hether the statute delegates legislative power is a question for the courts." How can the Court square that statement with the idea that the courts are not "qualified to second-guess Congress regarding the permissible degree of policy judgement that can be left to those executing or applying the law"?

* * *

"[A] certain degree of discretion, and thus of lawmaking, inheres in most executive or judicial action." *Mistretta v. United States, supra,* at 417 (SCALIA, J., dissenting) (emphasis deleted); see 488 U.S., at 378–379 (majority opinion). Section 109(b)(1) of the CAA, which to repeat we interpret as requiring the EPA to set air quality standards at the level that is "requisite"—that is, not lower or higher than is necessary—to protect the public health with an adequate margin of safety, fits comfortably within the scope of discretion permitted by our precedent.

We therefore reverse the judgment of the Court of Appeals remanding for reinterpretation that would avoid a supposed delegation of legislative power. * * *

JUSTICE STEVENS, with whom JUSTICE SOUTER joins, concurring in part and concurring in the judgment.

* * *

The Court has two choices. We could choose to articulate our ultimate disposition of this issue by frankly acknowledging that the power delegated to the EPA is "legislative" but nevertheless conclude that the delegation is constitutional because adequately limited by the terms of the authorizing statute. Alternatively, we could pretend, as the Court does, that the authority delegated to the EPA is somehow not "legislative power." Despite the fact that there is language in our opinions that supports the Court's articulation of our holding, I am persuaded that it would be both wiser and more faithful to what we have actually done in delegation cases to admit that agency rulemaking authority is "legislative power."

The proper characterization of governmental power should generally depend on the nature of the power, not on the identity of the person exercising it. See BLACK'S LAW DICTIONARY 899 (6th ed. 1990) (defining "legislation" as, *inter alia*, "[f]ormulation of rule[s] for the future"); 1 K. DAVIS & R. PIERCE, ADMINISTRATIVE LAW TREATISE § 2.3, p. 37 (3d ed. 1994) ("If legislative power means the power to make rules of conduct that bind everyone based on resolution of major policy issues, scores of agencies exercise legislative power routinely by promulgating what are candidly called 'legislative rules' "). If the NAAQS that the EPA promulgated had been prescribed by Congress, everyone would agree that those rules would be the product of an exercise of "legislative power." The same characterization is appropriate when an agency exercises rulemaking authority pursuant to a permissible delegation from Congress.

My view is not only more faithful to normal English usage, but is also fully consistent with the text of the Constitution. In Article I, the Framers vested "All legislative Powers" in the Congress, Art. I., § 1, just as in Article II they vested the "executive Power" in the President, Art. II, § 1. Those provisions do not purport to limit the authority of either recipient of power to delegate authority to others. See *Bowsher v. Synar,* 478 U.S. 714, 752 (1986) (Stevens, J., concurring in judgment) ("Despite the statement in Article I of the Constitution that 'All legislative powers herein granted shall be vested in a Congress of the United States,' it is far from novel to acknowledge that independent agencies do indeed exercise legislative powers"); *INS v. Chadha,* 462 U.S. 919, 985–986 (1983) (WHITE, J., dissenting) ("[L]egislative power can be exercised by independent agencies and Executive departments. . ."); 1 DAVIS & PIERCE § 2.6, p. 66 ("The Court was probably mistaken from the outset in interpreting Article I's grant of power to Congress as an implicit limit on Congress' authority to delegate legislative power"). Surely the authority granted to members of the Cabinet and federal law enforcement agents is properly characterized as "Executive" even though not exercised by the President. Cf. *Morrison v. Olson,* 487 U.S. 654, 705–706 (1988) (SCALIA, J., dissenting) (arguing that the independent counsel exercised "executive power" unconstrained by the President).

It seems clear that an executive agency's exercise of rulemaking authority pursuant to a valid delegation from Congress is "legislative." As long as the delegation provides a sufficiently intelligible principle, there is nothing inherently unconstitutional about it. Accordingly, * * * I would hold that when Congress enacted § 109, it effected a constitutional delegation of legislative power to the EPA.

NOTES & QUESTIONS

1. What is the difference between the opinion of the Court, written by Justice Scalia, and Justice Stevens' concurring opinion? Is it just a different linguistic characterization of what Congress has delegated (*i.e.,* whether to call it "legislative")? Or is there some practical difference between the two?

2. Near the end of its opinion, the Court says (quoting from Justice Scalia's dissent in the earlier *Mistretta* case): " '[A] certain degree of discretion, and thus of lawmaking, inheres in most executive or judicial action.' " What are the implications of this claim for the notion of the separation of powers? Notice that the Court is explicitly acknowledging that a "certain degree . . . of *lawmaking* . . . inheres in most executive or judicial action" (emphasis added). What then makes something "legislative" within the meaning of Article I of the Constitution, as opposed to "lawmaking" in the sense the Court is using the term here?

Gundy v. United States
588 U.S. ___, 139 S.Ct. 2116 (2019)

JUSTICE KAGAN announced the judgment of the Court and delivered an opinion, in which JUSTICE GINSBURG, JUSTICE BREYER, and JUSTICE SOTOMAYOR join.

The nondelegation doctrine bars Congress from transferring its legislative power to another branch of Government. This case requires us to decide whether 34 U.S.C. § 20913(d), enacted as part of the Sex Offender Registration and Notification Act (SORNA), violates that doctrine. We hold it does not. Under § 20913(d), the Attorney General must apply SORNA's registration requirements as soon as feasible to offenders convicted before the statute's enactment. That delegation easily passes constitutional muster.

I

Congress has sought, for the past quarter century, to combat sex crimes and crimes against children through sex-offender registration schemes. In 2006, to address [the failings of previous statutes], Congress enacted SORNA. See 120 Stat. 590, 34 U.S.C. § 20901 *et seq.*

SORNA makes "more uniform and effective" the prior "patchwork" of sex-offender registration systems. *Reynolds v. United States*, 565 U.S. 432, 435 (2012). The Act's express "purpose" is "to protect the public from sex offenders and offenders against children" by "establish[ing] a comprehensive national system for [their] registration." § 20901. To that end, SORNA covers more sex offenders and imposes more onerous registration requirements than most States had before. The Act also backs up those requirements with new criminal penalties. Any person required to register under SORNA who knowingly fails to do so (and who travels in interstate commerce) may be imprisoned for up to ten years. See 18 U.S.C. § 2250(a).

The basic registration scheme works as follows. A "sex offender" is defined as "an individual who was convicted of" specified criminal offenses: all offenses "involving a sexual act or sexual contact" and additional offenses "against a minor." Such an individual must register—provide his name, address, and certain other information—in every State where he resides, works, or studies. And he must keep the registration current and periodically report in person to a law enforcement office for a period of between fifteen years and life (depending on the severity of his crime and his history of recidivism). See §§ 20915, 20918.

Section 20913—the disputed provision here—elaborates the "[i]nitial registration" requirements for sex offenders. §§ 20913(b), (d). Subsection (b) sets out the general rule: An offender must register "before completing a sentence of imprisonment with respect to the offense giving rise to the registration requirement" (or, if the offender is not sentenced to prison, "not later than [three] business days after being sentenced"). Two provisions down, subsection (d) addresses (in its title's words) the "[i]nitial registration of sex offenders unable to comply with subsection (b)." The provision states:

"The Attorney General shall have the authority to specify the applicability of the requirements of this subchapter to sex offenders convicted before the enactment of this chapter . . . and to prescribe rules for the registration of any such sex offenders and for other categories of sex offenders who are unable to comply with subsection (b)."

Subsection (d), in other words, focuses on individuals convicted of a sex offense before SORNA's enactment—a group we will call pre-Act offenders. Many of these individuals were unregistered at the time of SORNA's enactment, either because pre-existing law did not cover them or because they had successfully evaded that law (so were "lost" to the system). And of those potential new registrants, many or most could not comply with subsection (b)'s registration rule because they had already completed their prison sentences. For the entire group of pre-Act offenders, once again, the Attorney General "shall have the authority" to "specify the applicability" of SORNA's registration requirements and "to prescribe rules for [their] registration."

Under that delegated authority, the Attorney General issued an interim rule in February 2007, specifying that SORNA's registration requirements apply in full to "sex offenders convicted of the offense for which registration is required prior to the enactment of that Act." The final rule, issued in December 2010, reiterated that SORNA applies to all pre-Act offenders. That rule has remained the same to this day.

Petitioner Herman Gundy is a pre-Act offender. The year before SORNA's enactment, he pleaded guilty under Maryland law for sexually assaulting a minor. After his release from prison in 2012, Gundy came to live in New York. But he never registered there as a sex offender. A few years later, he was convicted for failing to register, in violation of § 2250. He argued below (among other things) that Congress unconstitutionally delegated legislative power when it authorized the Attorney General to "specify the applicability" of SORNA's registration requirements to pre-Act offenders. § 20913(d). The District Court and Court of Appeals for the Second Circuit rejected that claim, as had every other court (including eleven Courts of Appeals) to consider the issue. We nonetheless granted certiorari. Today, we join the consensus and affirm.

II

Article I of the Constitution provides that "[a]ll legislative Powers herein granted shall be vested in a Congress of the United States." § 1. Accompanying that assignment of power to Congress is a bar on its further delegation. Congress, this Court explained early on, may not transfer to another branch "powers which are strictly and exclusively legislative." But the Constitution does not "deny[ ] to the Congress the necessary resources of flexibility and practicality [that enable it] to perform its function[s]." Congress may "obtain[ ] the assistance of its coordinate Branches"—and in particular, may confer substantial discretion on executive agencies to implement and enforce the laws. "[I]n our increasingly complex society, replete with ever changing and more technical problems," this Court has understood that "Congress simply cannot do its job absent an ability to delegate power under broad general directives." So we have held, time and again, that a statutory delegation is constitutional as long as Congress "lay[s] down by legislative act an intelligible principle to which the person or body authorized to [exercise the delegated authority] is directed to conform."

Given that standard, a nondelegation inquiry always begins (and often almost ends) with statutory interpretation. The constitutional question is whether Congress has supplied an intelligible principle to guide the delegee's use of discretion. So the answer requires construing the challenged statute to figure out what task it delegates and what instructions it provides. Only after a court has determined a challenged statute's meaning can it decide whether the law sufficiently guides executive discretion to accord with Article I. And indeed, once a court interprets the statute, it may find that the constitutional question all but answers itself.

That is the case here, because § 20913(d) does not give the Attorney General anything like the "unguided" and "unchecked" authority that Gundy says. * * * The text, considered alongside its context, purpose, and history, makes clear that the Attorney General's discretion extends only to considering and addressing feasibility issues. Given that statutory meaning, Gundy's constitutional claim must fail. Section 20913(d)'s delegation falls well within permissible bounds.

A

This is not the first time this Court has had to interpret § 20913(d). In *Reynolds*, the Court considered whether SORNA's registration requirements applied of their own force to pre-Act offenders or instead applied only once the Attorney General said they did. We read the statute as adopting the latter approach. But even as we did so, we made clear how far SORNA limited the Attorney General's authority. And in that way, we effectively resolved the case now before us.

Everything in *Reynolds* started from the premise that Congress meant for SORNA's registration requirements to apply to pre-Act offenders. The majority recounted SORNA's "basic statutory purpose," found in its text, as follows: "the 'establish[ment of] a comprehensive national system for the registration of [sex] offenders' that *includes* offenders who committed their offenses before the Act became law." * * *

But if that was so, why had Congress (as the majority held) conditioned the pre-Act offenders' duty to register on a prior "ruling from the Attorney

General"? The majority had a simple answer: *"[I]nstantaneous* registration" of pre-Act offenders "might not prove feasible," or "[a]t least Congress might well have so thought." Here, the majority explained that SORNA's requirements diverged from prior state law. Some pre-Act offenders (as defined by SORNA) had never needed to register before; others had once had to register, but had fulfilled their old obligations. And still others (the "lost" or "missing" offenders) should have registered, but had escaped the system. As a result, SORNA created a "practical problem[ ]": It would require "newly registering or reregistering a large number of pre-Act offenders." * * *

On that understanding, the Attorney General's role under § 20913(d) was important but limited: It was to apply SORNA to pre-Act offenders as soon as he thought it feasible to do so. That statutory delegation, the Court explained, would "involve[ ] implementation delay." But no more than that. Congress had made clear in SORNA's text that the new registration requirements would apply to pre-Act offenders. So (the Court continued) "there was no need" for Congress to worry about the "unrealistic possibility" that "the Attorney General would refuse to apply" those requirements on some excessively broad view of his authority under § 20913(d). Reasonably read, SORNA enabled the Attorney General only to address (as appropriate) the "practical problems" involving pre-Act offenders before requiring them to register. The delegation was a stopgap, and nothing more.

* * *

B

* * *

And no Attorney General has used (or, apparently, thought to use) § 20913(d) in any more expansive way. To the contrary. Within a year of SORNA's enactment (217 days, to be precise), the Attorney General determined that SORNA would apply immediately to pre-Act offenders. That rule has remained in force ever since (save for a technical change to one of the rule's illustrative examples). And at oral argument here, the Solicitor General's office—rarely in a hurry to agree to limits on the Government's authority—acknowledged that § 20913(d) does not allow the Attorney General to excuse a pre-Act offender from registering, except for reasons of "feasibility." We thus end up, on close inspection of the statutory scheme, exactly where *Reynolds* left us. The Attorney General's authority goes to transition-period implementation issues, and no further.

C

Now that we have determined what § 20913(d) means, we can consider whether it violates the Constitution. The question becomes: Did Congress make an impermissible delegation when it instructed the Attorney General to apply SORNA's registration requirements to pre-Act offenders as soon as feasible? Under this Court's long-established law, that question is easy. Its answer is no.

As noted earlier, this Court has held that a delegation is constitutional so long as Congress has set out an "intelligible principle" to guide the delegee's exercise of authority. Or in a related formulation, the Court has stated that a delegation is permissible if Congress has made clear to the delegee "the general policy" he must pursue and the "boundaries of [his] authority." Those standards, the Court has made clear, are not demanding. "[W]e have 'almost never felt qualified to second-guess Congress regarding the permissible degree of policy judgment that can be left to those executing or applying the law.'" Only twice in this country's history (and that in a single year) have we found a delegation excessive—in each case because "Congress had failed to articulate *any* policy or standard" to confine discretion. By contrast, we have over and over upheld even very broad delegations. Here is a sample: We have approved delegations to various agencies to regulate in the "public interest." We more recently affirmed a delegation to an agency to issue whatever air quality standards are "requisite to protect the public health." *Whitman*, 531 U.S. at 472. And so forth.

In that context, the delegation in SORNA easily passes muster (as all eleven circuit courts to have considered the question found). The statute conveyed Congress's policy that the Attorney General require pre-Act offenders to register as soon as feasible. Under the law, the feasibility issues he could address were administrative—and, more specifically, transitional—in nature. * * * That statutory authority, as compared to the delegations we have upheld in the past, is distinctly small-bore. It falls well within constitutional bounds.

Indeed, if SORNA's delegation is unconstitutional, then most of Government is unconstitutional—dependent as Congress is on the need to give discretion to executive officials to implement its programs. * * *

It is wisdom and humility alike that this Court has always upheld such "necessities of government." *Mistretta*, 488 U.S. at 416 (SCALIA, J., dissenting) (internal quotation marks omitted); see *ibid.* ("Since Congress is no less endowed with common sense than we are, and better equipped to inform itself of the 'necessities' of government; and since the factors bearing upon those necessities are both multifarious and (in the nonpartisan sense) highly political . . . it is small wonder that we have almost never felt qualified to second-guess Congress regarding the permissible degree of policy judgment that can be left to those executing or applying the law"). We therefore affirm the judgment of the Court of Appeals.

It is so ordered.

JUSTICE ALITO, concurring in the judgment.

The Constitution confers on Congress certain "legislative [p]owers," Art. I, § 1, and does not permit Congress to delegate them to another branch of the Government. Nevertheless, since 1935, the Court has uniformly rejected nondelegation arguments and has upheld provisions that authorized agencies to adopt important rules pursuant to extraordinarily capacious standards.

If a majority of this Court were willing to reconsider the approach we have taken for the past 84 years, I would support that effort. But because a majority is not willing to do that, it would be freakish to single out the provision at issue here for special treatment.

Because I cannot say that the statute lacks a discernable standard that is adequate under the approach this Court has taken for many years, I vote to affirm.

JUSTICE GORSUCH, with whom THE CHIEF JUSTICE and JUSTICE THOMAS join, dissenting.

The Constitution promises that only the people's elected representatives may adopt new federal laws restricting liberty. Yet the statute before us scrambles that design. It purports to endow the nation's chief prosecutor with the power to write his own criminal code governing the lives of a half-million citizens. Yes, those affected are some of the least popular among us. But if a single executive branch official can write laws restricting the liberty of this group of persons, what does that mean for the next?

Today, a plurality of an eight-member Court endorses this extraconstitutional arrangement but resolves nothing. Working from an understanding of the Constitution at war with its text and history, the plurality reimagines the terms of the statute before us and insists there is nothing wrong with Congress handing off so much power to the Attorney General. But JUSTICE ALITO supplies the fifth vote for today's judgment and he does not join either the plurality's constitutional or statutory analysis, indicating instead that he remains willing, in a future case with a full Court, to revisit these matters. Respectfully, I would not wait.

I

For individuals convicted of sex offenses *after* Congress adopted the Sex Offender Registration and Notification Act (SORNA) in 2006, the statute offers detailed instructions. * * * On and on the statute goes for more than 20 pages of the U.S. Code.

But what about those convicted of sex offenses *before* the Act's adoption? At the time of SORNA's enactment, the nation's population of sex offenders exceeded 500,000, and Congress concluded that something had to be done about these "pre-Act" offenders too. But it seems Congress couldn't agree what that should be. The treatment of pre-Act offenders proved a "controversial issue with major policy significance and practical ramifications for states." Among other things, applying SORNA immediately to this group threatened to impose unpopular and costly burdens on States and localities by forcing them to adopt or overhaul their own sex offender registration schemes. So Congress simply passed the problem to the Attorney General. For all half-million pre-Act offenders, the law says only this, in 34 U.S.C. § 20913(d):

"The Attorney General shall have the authority to specify the applicability of the requirements of this subchapter to sex offenders convicted before the enactment of this chapter . . . and to prescribe rules for the registration of any such sex offender."

Yes, that's it. The breadth of the authority Congress granted to the Attorney General in these few words can only be described as vast. As the Department of Justice itself has acknowledged, SORNA "does not require the Attorney General" to impose registration requirements on pre-Act offenders "within a certain time frame or by a date certain; it does not require him to act at all." If the Attorney General does choose to act, he can require all pre-Act offenders to register, or he can "require some but not all to register." For those he requires to register, the Attorney General may impose "some but not all of [SORNA's] registration requirements," as he pleases. And he is free to change his mind on any of these matters "at any given time or over the course of different [political] administrations." Congress thus gave the Attorney General free rein to write the rules for virtually the entire existing sex offender population in this country—a situation that promised to persist for years or decades until pre-Act offenders passed away or fulfilled the terms of their registration obligations and post-Act offenders came to predominate.

Unsurprisingly, different Attorneys General have exercised their discretion in different ways. For six months after SORNA's enactment, Attorney General Gonzales left past offenders alone. Then the pendulum swung the other direction when the Department of Justice issued an interim rule requiring pre-Act offenders to follow all the same rules as post-Act offenders. A year later, Attorney General Mukasey issued more new guidelines, this time directing the States to register some but not all past offenders. Three years after that, Attorney General Holder required the States to register only those pre-Act offenders convicted of a new felony after SORNA's enactment. Various Attorneys General have also taken different positions on whether pre-Act offenders might be entitled to credit for time spent in the community before SORNA was enacted.

These unbounded policy choices have profound consequences for the people they affect. Take our case. Before SORNA's enactment, Herman Gundy pleaded guilty in 2005 to a sexual offense. After his release from prison five years later, he was arrested again, this time for failing to register as a sex offender according to the rules the Attorney General had then prescribed for pre-Act offenders. As a result, Mr. Gundy faced an additional 10-year prison term—10 years more than if the Attorney General had, in his discretion, chosen to write the rules differently.

II

A

Our founding document begins by declaring that "We the People . . . ordain and establish this Constitution." At the time, that was a radical claim, an assertion that sovereignty belongs not to a person or institution or class but to the whole of the people. From that premise, the Constitution proceeded to vest the authority to exercise different aspects of the people's sovereign power in distinct entities. In Article I, the Constitution entrusted all of the federal government's legislative power to Congress. In Article II, it assigned the executive power to the President. And in Article III, it gave independent judges the task of applying the laws to cases and controversies.

To the framers, each of these vested powers had a distinct content. When it came to the legislative power, the framers understood it to mean the power to adopt generally applicable rules of conduct governing future actions by private persons—the power to "prescrib[e] the rules by which the duties and rights of every citizen are to be regulated," or the power to "prescribe general rules for the government of society."

The framers understood, too, that it would frustrate "the system of government ordained by the Constitution" if Congress could merely announce vague aspirations and then assign others the responsibility of adopting legislation to realize its goals. Through the Constitution, after all, the people had vested the power to prescribe rules limiting their liberties in Congress alone. No one, not even Congress, had the right to alter that arrangement. As Chief Justice Marshall explained, Congress may not "delegate . . . powers which are strictly and exclusively legislative." Or as John Locke, one of the thinkers who most influenced the framers' understanding of the separation of powers, described it:

"The legislative cannot transfer the power of making laws to any other hands; for it being but a delegated power from the people, they who have it cannot pass it over to others. The people alone can appoint the form of the commonwealth, which is by constituting the legislative, and appointing in whose hands that shall be. And when the people have said we will submit to rules, and be governed by laws made by such men, and in such forms, nobody else can say other men shall make laws for them; nor can the people be bound by any laws but such as are enacted by those whom they have chosen and authorised to make laws for them."

Why did the framers insist on this particular arrangement? They believed the new federal government's most dangerous power was the power to enact laws restricting the people's liberty. An "excess of law-making" was, in their words, one of "the diseases to which our governments are most liable." To address that tendency, the framers went to great lengths to make lawmaking difficult. In Article I, by far the longest part of the Constitution, the framers insisted that any proposed law must win the approval of two Houses of Congress—elected at different times, by different constituencies, and for different terms in office—and either secure the President's approval or obtain enough support to override his veto. Some occasionally complain about Article I's detailed and arduous processes for new legislation, but to the framers these were bulwarks of liberty.

Nor was the point only to limit the government's capacity to restrict the people's freedoms. Article I's detailed processes for new laws were also designed to promote deliberation. "The oftener the measure is brought under examination," Hamilton explained, "the greater the diversity in the situations of those who are to examine it," and "the less must be the danger of those errors which flow from want of due deliberation, or of those missteps which proceed from the contagion of some common passion or interest."

* * *

If Congress could pass off its legislative power to the executive branch, the "[v]esting [c]lauses, and indeed the entire structure of the Constitution," would "make no sense." Without the involvement of representatives from across the country or the demands of bicameralism and presentment, legislation would risk becoming nothing more than the will of the current President. And if laws could be simply declared by a single person, they would not be few in number, the product of widespread social consensus, likely to protect minority interests, or apt to provide stability and fair notice. Accountability would suffer too. Legislators might seek to take credit for addressing a pressing social problem by sending it to the executive for resolution, while at the same time blaming the executive for the problems that attend whatever measures he chooses to pursue. In turn, the executive might point to Congress as the source of the problem. These opportunities for finger-pointing might prove temptingly advantageous for the politicians involved, but they would also threaten to " 'disguise . . . responsibility for . . . the decisions.' "

* * *

B

Accepting, then, that we have an obligation to decide whether Congress has unconstitutionally divested itself of its legislative responsibilities, the question follows: What's the test? * * *

First, we know that as long as Congress makes the policy decisions when regulating private conduct, it may authorize another branch to "fill up the details." [Justice Gorsuch then proceeded to discuss several cases.]

* * * Through all these cases, small or large, runs the theme that Congress must set forth standards "sufficiently definite and precise to enable Congress, the courts, and the public to ascertain" whether Congress's guidance has been followed.

Second, once Congress prescribes the rule governing private conduct, it may make the application of that rule depend on executive fact-finding.

Third, Congress may assign the executive and judicial branches certain non-legislative responsibilities. * * *

III

A

Returning to SORNA with this understanding of our charge in hand, problems quickly emerge. Start with this one: It's hard to see how SORNA leaves the Attorney General with only details to fill up. Of course, what qualifies as a detail can sometimes be difficult to discern and, as we've seen, this Court has upheld statutes that allow federal agencies to resolve even highly consequential details so long as Congress prescribes the rule governing private conduct. But it's hard to see how the statute before us could be described as leaving the Attorney General with only details to dispatch. As the government itself admitted in *Reynolds*, SORNA leaves the Attorney General free to impose on 500,000 pre-Act offenders all of the statute's requirements, some of them, or none of them. The Attorney General may choose which pre-Act offenders to subject to the Act. And he is free to change his mind at any point or over the course of different political administrations. In the end, there isn't a single policy decision concerning pre-Act offenders on which Congress even tried to speak, and not a single other case where we have upheld executive authority over matters like these on the ground they constitute mere "details." This much appears to have been deliberate, too. Because members of Congress could not reach consensus on the treatment of pre-Act offenders, it seems this was one of those situations where they found it expedient to hand off the job to the executive and direct there the blame for any later problems that might emerge.

Nor can SORNA be described as an example of conditional legislation subject to executive fact-finding. * * * Instead, it gave the Attorney General unfettered discretion to decide which requirements to impose on which pre-Act offenders. The Attorney General's own edicts acknowledge the considerable policy-making powers he enjoys, describing his rules governing pre-Act offenders as " 'of fundamental importance to the initial operation of SORNA, and to its practical scope . . . since [they] determin[e] the applicability of SORNA's requirements to virtually the entire existing sex offender population.' " These edicts tout, too, the Attorney General's "discretion to apply SORNA's requirements to sex offenders with pre-SORNA convictions if he determines (as he has) that the public benefits of doing so outweigh any adverse effects." Far from deciding the factual predicates to a rule set forth by statute, the Attorney General himself acknowledges that the law entitles him to make his own policy decisions.

Finally, SORNA does not involve an area of overlapping authority with the executive. Congress may assign the President broad authority regarding the conduct of foreign affairs or other matters where he enjoys his own inherent Article II powers. But SORNA stands far afield from any of that. It gives the Attorney General the authority to "prescrib[e] the rules by which the duties and rights" of citizens are determined, a quintessentially legislative power.

* * *

It would be easy enough to let this case go. After all, sex offenders are one of the most disfavored groups in our society. But the rule that prevents Congress from giving the executive *carte blanche* to write laws for sex offenders is the same rule that protects everyone else. Nor is it hard to imagine how the power at issue in this case—the power of a prosecutor to require a group to register with the government on pain of weighty criminal penalties—could be abused in other settings. To allow the nation's chief law enforcement officer to write the criminal laws he is charged with enforcing—to " 'unit[e]' " the " 'legislative and executive powers . . . in the same person' "—would be to mark the end of any meaningful enforcement of our separation of powers and invite the tyranny of the majority that follows when lawmaking and law enforcement responsibilities are united in the same hands.

Nor would enforcing the Constitution's demands spell doom for what some call the "administrative state." The separation of powers does not prohibit any particular policy outcome, let alone dictate any conclusion about the proper size and scope of government. Instead, it is a procedural guarantee that requires Congress to assemble a social consensus before choosing our nation's course on policy questions like those implicated by SORNA. What is more, Congress is hardly bereft of options to accomplish all it might wish to achieve. It may always authorize executive branch officials to fill in even a large number of details, to find facts that trigger the generally applicable rule of conduct specified in a statute, or to exercise non-legislative powers. Congress can also commission agencies or other experts to study and recommend legislative language. Respecting the separation of powers forecloses no substantive outcomes. It only requires us to respect along the way one of the most vital of the procedural protections of individual liberty found in our Constitution.

B

What do the government and the plurality have to say about the constitutional concerns SORNA poses? Most everyone, the plurality included, concedes that if SORNA allows the Attorney General as much authority as we have outlined, it would present "a nondelegation question." So the only remaining available tactic is to try to make this big case "small-bore" by recasting the statute in a way that might satisfy any plausible separation-of-powers test. So, yes, just a few years ago in *Reynolds* the government represented to this Court that SORNA granted the Attorney General nearly boundless discretion with respect to pre-Act offenders. But *now*, faced with a constitutional challenge, the government speaks out of the other side of its mouth and invites us to reimagine SORNA as compelling the Attorney General to register pre-Act offenders "to the maximum extent feasible." And, as thus reinvented, the government insists, the statute supplies a clear statement of legislative policy, with only details for the Attorney General to clean up.

But even this new dream of a statute wouldn't be free from doubt. A statute directing an agency to regulate private conduct to the extent "feasible" can have many possible meanings: It might refer to "technological" feasibility, "economic" feasibility, "administrative" feasibility, or even "political" feasibility. Such an "evasive standard" could threaten the separation of powers if it effectively allowed the agency to make the "important policy choices" that belong to Congress while frustrating "meaningful judicial review." And that seems exactly the case here, where the Attorney General is left free to make all the important policy decisions and it is difficult to see what standard a court might later use to judge whether he exceeded the bounds of the authority given to him.

* * *

In a future case with a full panel, I remain hopeful that the Court may yet recognize that, while Congress can enlist considerable assistance from the executive branch in filling up details and finding facts, it may never hand off to the nation's chief prosecutor the power to write his own criminal code. That "is delegation running riot."

NOTES & QUESTIONS

1. Can you define what an "intelligible principle" is? That is, what kind of statutory language has sufficient detail to withstand a nondelegation doctrine challenge to a statutory grant of lawmaking authority to an agency?

2. In addition to delegating authority to agencies to capitalize on their expertise, what other reason(s) can you think of for a legislature to task an agency with the role of specifying some (or many) of the details of a statutory scheme?

3. How important is it to have a robust nondelegation doctrine? On the one hand, isn't Justice Scalia correct, as he put it in his dissent in *Mistretta* (which the *Whitman* majority and *Gundy* plurality both quote), that a court isn't really "qualified to second-guess [a legislature] on the permissible degree of policy judgment that can be left to those executing or applying the law"? Aren't legislatures, as Justice Scalia put it, "no less endowed with common sense than [courts] are, and better equipped to inform [themselves] of the 'necessities' of government"? On the other hand, isn't Justice Gorsuch right that delegation of important policy decisions to agencies allows legislatures to avoid accountability for those decisions? Isn't that an abdication of their responsibility? Shouldn't legislatures actually do the legislating? Isn't that why we elect them? In particular, if policymaking requires difficult trade-offs, shouldn't the elected representatives be required to decide how to balance those trade-offs? Or, would it sometimes be better to have an agency, with expertise but only indirect electoral accountability through the President, make those decisions?

4. In contrast to the relative impotence of the *federal* nondelegation doctrine under current law, the nondelegation doctrine is stronger at the state level, at least in many states. By one account, some twenty states permit legislative delegations only if the legislature has provided specific and definite standards to guide the delegated authority, a formulation that courts in these states enforce with some strictness. *See* Jim Rossi, *Institutional Design and the Lingering Legacy of Antifederalist Separation of Powers Ideals in the States*, 52 VAND. L. REV. 1167, 1193–97 (1999); *see also* Jason Iuliano & Keith E. Whittington, *The Nondelegation Doctrine: Alive and Well*, 93 NOTRE DAME L. REV. 619, 626 (2017) (arguing that the nondelegation doctrine, in both state courts and lower federal

courts, "not only survived the New Deal revolution, but has thrived in the eighty years since"). Another two-dozen states enforce a less strict but still meaningful version of the nondelegation doctrine, while only a handful of states appear willing to tolerate almost any delegation, as has been the federal pattern. *See id.* at 1191–93, 1197–1200; *see also* Gary J. Greco, *Survey, Standards or Safeguards: A Survey of the Delegation Doctrine in the States*, 8 ADMIN. L. J. AM. U. 567, 580–99 (1994). *But see* Joseph Postell & Randolph J. May, *The Myth of the State Nondelegation Doctrines*, 74 ADMIN. L. REV. 263, 267 (2022) (arguing "that only ten states have relatively robust nondelegation doctrines in this typical conventional context, and even those states rarely invalidate laws"). Since *Gundy*, there has been a flurry of scholarly interest in the operation of the nondelegation doctrine in the states. *See id.*; Jason Iuliano & Keith E. Whittington, *supra*; Benjamin Silver, *Nondelegation in the States*, 75 VAND. L. REV. 1211 (2022); Daniel E. Walters, *Decoding Nondelegation After Gundy: What the Experience in State Courts Tells Us About What to Expect When We're Expecting*, 71 EMORY L.J. 417 (2022).

D. Legislative Veto of Agency Action

After Congress has delegated authority to an agency, how can it control what the agency does? As a theoretical matter, the most direct approach would be for Congress to pass new legislation. After all, if agencies' power derives from a delegation of power from Congress—in other words, if Congress is the principal and agencies are its agents—then Congress can control that power with the very tool it used to give agencies power. Legislation can grant an agency new powers, take powers away from an agency, or amend an agency's power. As with all legislation, when we use the term "Congress" here, we really are referring to the full lawmaking process, usually with the President's assent or with Congress overriding the President's veto.

For many years, Congress sought to retain some measure of control over agency uses of delegated lawmaking authority through the use of a "legislative veto," a procedure in which some subset of Congress, either one House of Congress, both Houses of Congress, or even a congressional committee, acting by majority vote, could override a proposed agency action. The Supreme Court invalidated this veto mechanism in *INS v. Chadha*, 462 U.S. 919 (1983). The Court reasoned that the exercise of a legislative veto by one chamber of Congress amounted to lawmaking in contravention of the requirement in Article I of the U.S. Constitution that both Houses and the President must agree for a measure to become law.

In place of the invalidated legislative veto mechanism, some congressional delegations of authority now contain a "report and wait" requirement. Under these
requirements, an agency must report to Congress about its proposed use of delegated authority, and then wait a specified amount of time before implementing
its proposal. In theory, this delay provides Congress the opportunity to use the
lawmaking process to seek to enact a new measure to override the agency proposal.

Meanwhile, other federal laws continue to call for agencies to obtain congressional
committee approval before undertaking certain actions. Although under *Chadha*
these requirements are not legally enforceable, most agencies adhere to them because of their desire to maintain good working relationships with Congress. For
more on these dynamics, see Louis Fisher, *The Legislative Veto: Invalidated, It Sur-
vives*, 56 L. & CONTEMP. PROBS. 273 (1993); *see also* Stephen Breyer, *The Legislative Veto After* Chadha, 72 GEO. L.J. 785 (1984).

In 1996, Congress enacted what might be viewed as a "*Chadha*-compliant" version
of the legislative veto. The statute, called the Congressional Review Act (CRA),
creates what is in effect a comprehensive "report and wait" requirement. *See* Subtitle E ("Congressional Review") of the Small Business Regulatory Enforcement
Fairness Act of 1996, Title II of the Contract with America Advancement Act of
1996, Pub. L. No. 104–121, 101 Stat. 847, 868-74, codified at 5 U.S.C. §§ 801–
808. Under the CRA, Congress can veto a "major rule" by passing, within 60
legislative days of being notified of an agency's announcement of the rule, a joint
resolution of disapproval that must also be presented to the President for approval
or potential veto. [This is the import of *Chadha*: legislative vetoes of agency action
are invalid unless they satisfy the bicameralism and presentment requirements of
Article I, Section 7 of the Constitution.] Such a resolution would invalidate the
rule and prevent the agency from passing any other rule that is "substantially the
same." 5 U.S.C. § 801(b)(2). The CRA provides expedited Congressional procedures for these "joint resolution[s] of disapproval," most importantly excluding
them from the Senate filibuster process. *Id.* at § 802. However, because the President usually supports the rules that the Administration's agencies promulgate, the
President will usually veto any such joint resolution. For this reason, the CRA is
rarely used. In its first twenty years, Congress used the CRA only once, in 2001.
Then, in 2017, during the first few months of the 115th Congress, with Republican majorities in both Houses of Congress and a Republican President (President
Trump), Congress used the CRA to overturn 14 rules that agencies had promulgated during the previous Democratic (Obama) Administration. Congress used
the CRA to overturn two more rules in 2018. In 2021, the partisan tables turned,
with Democratic majorities in both Houses of Congress and a Democratic President (President Biden), and Congress used the CRA to overturn three more rules.

Many states also have experimented with variations on a legislative veto mechanism. The *Chadha* decision, predicated as it was on the U.S. Constitution's Article I lawmaking requirements for Congress, did not directly affect the validity of these state legislative vetoes. Nevertheless, most states that have addressed the issue have chosen to adopt the *Chadha* reasoning, invalidating legislative vetoes of agency action if they do not comply with their particular state constitution's lawmaking requirements. But in a departure from the *Chadha* rule, at least three states (Idaho, Iowa, and New Jersey), either through court decision or explicit constitutional permission, allow a bicameral legislative veto, without gubernatorial presentment or approval. Other states with some version of a legislative veto mechanism have yet to address the question of whether it violates their state constitution.

FYI During the COVID-19 pandemic, several state legislatures considered creating new mechanisms to allow the legislature to override state agency health directives.

E. Fiscal Control of Agencies

Congress and state legislatures also retain substantial control over the activities of government agencies through the "power of the purse." This fiscal control exists both through current limits on the purposes for which an agency is permitted to spend government funds, and by explicit or implied threats to withhold future agency funding after the fact, if the legislature perceives the agency as having engaged in activities of which the legislature disapproves.

As noted in Chapter 12, at the federal level Congress must both authorize agencies to spend federal funds in pursuit of specified activities, and then separately appropriate actual dollars for the agencies to spend in doing so. At either stage, Congress in various ways may constrain the way in which an agency operates. For instance, when appropriating funds for an agency such as the Centers for Disease Control and Prevention, Congress may provide that "None of the funds made available for injury prevention and control at the Centers for Disease Control and Prevention may be used to advocate or promote gun control." *See* Omnibus Consolidated Appropriations Act, 1997, Pub. L. No. 104–208, 110 Stat. 3009, 3009–244 (1996).

Because the federal appropriations process occurs annually, Congress has the opportunity to revisit the scope of each federal agency's permitted activities every year. In turn, each year every agency must submit to Congress a budget request, specifying the intended uses of the agency's desired level of funding. Congress has unfettered authority to decide how much funding to appropriate, as well as with how fine a grain to specify the permitted uses of the funding, from a lump sum appropriation to a program-by-program funding allocation. Congress also may choose to attach "riders" to appropriations measures, which are specific statutory provisions that may impose additional substantive obligations or limits on an agency.

F. Control of Agencies Through Other Forms of Legislative Oversight

The appropriations process is an example—but only one example—of legislative "oversight" of agency activity. Congress and state legislatures also have other means of overseeing or supervising how government agencies behave. At any point, legislative committees may schedule hearings concerning a particular agency's operations, requiring key agency personnel to appear and answer questions, often under oath. Sometimes these oversight hearings occur in response to a particular controversy, but they may also occur as a matter of routine monitoring or audits. As part of the oversight process, legislators also may request (or demand through subpoena) agency documents, although agencies frequently seek to protect some of their internal information from disclosure on the basis of a legal privilege, such as "executive privilege" or "deliberative process privilege." Further, individual legislators may occasionally share concerns or ideas with agency leaders, always under the shadow of more formal oversight hearings, if warranted.

Legislative oversight has something of a mixed history, at least at the federal level. A number of high-profile congressional investigations have been incredibly important to ferreting out governmental misconduct, such as the Watergate hearings or the Iran-Contra hearings. At times, however, oversight investigations may be nothing more than raw attempts to gain partisan advantage. The House Un-American Activities Committee hearings and the Senate McCarthy hearings of the 1950s, ostensibly intended to rid the government of Communists, were undoubtedly a low point of legislative oversight. In both of these series of hearings, Congress abused its oversight authority to embarrass and humiliate government employees and private citizens. By contrast, most agency oversight today is much more routine, seeking to understand the details of how an agency is pursuing its legislative charge.

NOTES & QUESTIONS

1. Do you think a legislative veto ought to be part of the mechanisms of legislative control over agencies? Why or why not?

2. How important is the power of the purse to legislative control over agencies? How do you think it compares to other tools of legislative control?

Test Your Understanding

 To assess your understanding of the material in this chapter, click here to take a quiz.

30

Presidential Control of Government Agencies

Key Concepts

- Executive agencies
- Independent agencies
- Presidential appointment powers
- Presidential removal power
- Executive Order 12866
- Regulatory planning
- Regulatory review
- Interagency coordination
- Benefit-cost analysis (or cost-benefit analysis)
- Budgets and appropriations

Chapter Summary

Although legislatures create agencies, set the parameters of their power through legislation, and have significant oversight authority over them, agencies are part of the "executive branch," and Presidents have authority over them too. In the federal system, agencies are generally divided into two categories: independent agencies and executive agencies. The former are more insulated from the President than the latter. For both types of agencies, the President has the initial power to appoint agency heads and other political appointees (subject in most cases to Senate approval). Under current doctrine, however, the President has the power to remove political appointees only from executive agencies, not independent agencies. These appointment and removal powers are a form of presidential control over agency actions. Presidents have also created a process of regulatory "planning" and "review" of agency rulemaking that also serves as an important tool of presidential control. Presidents also control agencies' budget requests, a power that has a significant impact on agencies' ability to act.

A. Overview

In the previous chapter, we described the ways in which Congress can shape what federal agencies do. Specifically, federal agencies may only do what Congress either requires or at least permits them to do through legislation. Once Congress has passed legislation, moreover, Congress may continue to shape what agencies do through the variety of means we described in the previous chapter.

But, what about the President? How can the President shape what agencies do? As with Congress, the President will generally want agencies to further the President's policy agenda. Moreover, the U.S. Constitution arguably gives the President a responsibility—a constitutional obligation—to oversee agency action. Article II, Section 3, Clause 3 of the Constitution provides that the President "shall take Care that the laws be faithfully executed." *See generally* Gillian E. Metzger, *The Constitutional Duty to Supervise*, 124 YALE L.J. 1836 (2015).

How can the President assert control over agencies? After all, the President is just one person, while the federal government is vast, with a sweeping array of responsibility. As we will see, the President has many ways to control agencies. Some are formal, while others are more informal and a matter of practice or norms. Understanding the relationship between the President and agencies will help you understand not only how the world of "administrative law" really works, but also where opportunities for legal advocacy lie, so you can understand where lawyers play a role in shaping agencies' actions.

The normative questions that shape presidential control over agencies touch on some of the fundamental themes that we have raised elsewhere in this book. On the one hand, because the President is democratically elected, presidential control over agencies has the potential to increase the democratic accountability of agency action. In a democracy, one fundamental premise is control over the levers of government by the people. Within the executive branch, the President is the only elected official, the only one directly answerable to the voters. This accountability usually presumes a level of transparency: the public needs to know what agencies are doing. We will soon see whether, and if so how, administrative processes promote that transparency. So at least theoretically, if voters don't like what administrative agencies do, they can hold the President responsible. The President should generally thus seek to ensure that agencies' actions serve voters' interests.

Moreover, as we will see in some detail in Section B below, the President can coordinate the actions of the sprawling bureaucracy. This can help agencies avoid either duplicating, or acting in ways that conflict with, the work of other agencies. This in turn can increase the efficiency of government action.

On the other hand, recall that one of the key benefits of agencies is their expertise—and the fact that their expertise is in some ways insulated from meddling by non-experts. Agency independence from political constraints is to some degree vital for agencies to be able to do their work. Sometimes, a President's policy desires might conflict with the scientific or other expertise that an agency brings to bear on a problem. In such circumstances, presidential control could undermine expertise, a principal virtue that agencies bring to government policy. Moreover, sometimes a President's policy agenda might conflict with the congressional policy embedded in the statutes that Congress wrote, statutes that direct agencies to act in certain ways. While conflicts of this sort are inevitable in some sense, at the extreme, presidential control over agencies could undermine the value and authority of agency action.

This potential tension between public accountability and bureaucratic expertise pervades dilemmas raised in the administrative state, and it speaks to a fundamental question that runs throughout this book: who should make the decisions about how best to regulate behavior in a complex world? In this chapter, when thinking about how much control the President should have over administrative agencies, we are often asking how much, and what types of, public accountability society wants to impose on the expertise of administrative agencies.

B. The President's Power to Appoint and Remove Political Appointees

As we explained in Chapter 28, officials at the top of an agency's bureaucracy are political appointees. The fact that they are political appointees itself underlies one important aspect of the idea of presidential "control," i.e., the ability of the President to shape agency behavior. In this section, we address two fundamental aspects of political appointees and their relationship with the President: (1) the process by which they are appointed; and (2) the circumstances in which the President may remove them.

1. Appointments

One fundamental question that speaks to the President's (and Congress's) power to shape agency behavior is how the officials within agencies are chosen. The Constitution's Appointments Clause specifies the process of appointment for "officers" of the United States and distinguishes between principal officers and "inferior officers." The Constitution gives the President the "Power . . . to nominate, and by and with the Advice and Consent of the Senate, [to] appoint . . . all . . . Officers of the United States." U.S. CONST. Art. II, sec. 2, cl. 2. However, for "inferior Officers," the Constitution also permits Congress to diverge from the "Presidential nomination, Senate confirmation" process: "Congress may by Law vest the Appointment of such inferior Officers, as they think proper, in the President alone, in the Courts of Law, or in the Heads of Departments." *Id.*

In several cases, the Court has addressed both the distinction between "officers" and "mere employees," and the distinction between "principal officers" and "inferior officers." To qualify as an "officer," whose appointment is subject to the Appointments Clause of the Constitution, "an individual must occupy a 'continuing' position established by law" and must "exercis[e] significant authority pursuant to the laws of the United States." *Lucia v. S.E.C.*, 585 U.S. 237, 244 (2018) (concluding that Administrative Law Judges who "have all the authority needed to ensure fair and orderly adversarial hearings—indeed, nearly all the tools of federal trial judges"—are "officers" within the meaning of the Constitution's Appointments Clause); *see also Buckley v. Valeo*, 424 U.S. 1 (1976) (concluding that Commissioners of the Federal Election Commission with discretionary enforcement power, including "primary responsibility for conducting civil litigation in the courts of the United States" and "rulemaking, advisory opinions, and determinations of eligibility for funds and even for federal elective office itself," are "officers" and thus cannot be appointed by Congress).

> **FYI** As we noted above, approximately 1200 positions in the federal government require Senate confirmation. Importantly, though, that is because statutes, rather than the Constitution, require such confirmation. Many of those positions are inferior officers for whom Senate confirmation is not constitutionally required. When Congress requires that an official be Senate confirmed, rather than having an official simply be appointed by the President or a lower-ranked official, it is another way that Congress can play a role in how agencies act.

The distinction between a principal officer, whose appointment constitutionally requires Senate confirmation, and an "inferior officer," for whom Congress may create a different appointment process (i.e., "in the President alone, in the Courts of Law, or in the Heads of Departments") is also one the Court has addressed. Although it raises some questions on the margins, there is no question that cabinet Secretaries are principal officers who must be nominated by the President and undergo the Senate confirmation process. The most recent case law makes the distinction depend on two factors. To be an "inferior officer" requires both that an individual have a "superior" in a formal sense, and that the individual's work be "directed and supervised at some level" by someone who is a principal officer. *Edmond v. United States*, 520 U.S. 651, 663 (1997) (civilian members of the Coast

Guard Court of Criminal Appeals were "inferior officers" because (1) they were administratively overseen by the Judge Advocate General, who in turn was subordinate to the Secretary of Transportation, and (2) their decisions could be reviewed by another executive branch entity, the Court of Appeals for the Armed Forces); *see also United States v. Arthrex*, 141 S. Ct. 1970 (2021) (under the Appointments Clause, Administrative Patent Judges appointed solely by the Secretary of Commerce may not have "the final word within the Executive Branch on the validity of a challenged patent"). *But cf. Morrison v. Olson*, 487 U.S. 654, 671–73 (1988) (even though "independent counsel" was not directed or supervised by a principal officer, "independent counsel" was an "inferior officer" who could be appointed by "the Courts of Law" because she was removable by the Attorney General, had no policy making power, had a limited jurisdiction, and had a limited tenure).

2. Presidential Removal and the Notion of the "Independent" Agency

A second fundamental question that also affects the ability of the President or Congress to shape agency behavior is how officers may be removed from office. Agency heads and other top officials in agencies wield a great deal of power, often power that statutes explicitly give to the agency official, not the President. Although the Constitution does not have a "Removal Clause" comparable in specificity to the Appointments Clause, the Supreme Court has held that both the Vesting Clause of Article II, Section 1, Clause 1 of the Constitution ("The executive Power shall be vested in a President of the United States of America") and the Take Care Clause of Article II, Section 3 ("[H]e shall take Care that the Laws be faithfully executed") speak to this question. Two competing concerns have shaped the Court's jurisprudence in this area: accountability and independence. On the one hand, Officers are not elected, and the President's ability to remove an official is thus an important power requisite to making these unelected Officers

FYI As an example of the power of top agency officials, the Clean Air Act explicitly gives the Administrator of the EPA the power to prescribe regulations under that Act. *See* 42 U.S.C. 7601. The power is the Administrator's, not the President's.

FYI The Constitution's only reference to removing officers is the Impeachment Clause, Article II, Section 4, which provides that "[t]he President, Vice President and all civil Officers of the United States, shall be removed from Office on Impeachment for, and Conviction of, Treason, Bribery, or other high Crimes and Misdemeanors." Although this is the only reference to the removal of civil officers, the Court has never even considered, let alone concluded, that this Clause implies that impeachment is the only means to remove Officers.

somehow accountable to the people. On the other hand, Congress will want at times to protect Officers from Presidential control, so as to give them independence from political pressure. Independence can ensure impartiality, elevate technical expertise, promote continuity across Presidential administrations, and prevent short-term electoral interests from distorting long-term policy. One classic example is the Federal Reserve Board (the "Fed"), which regulates monetary policy and is designed to be insulated from the electoral cycle: for example, no President wants the Federal Reserve to raise interest rates before an election, but the Fed's Governors are insulated from Presidential removal, so that if necessary, they can raise interest rates when it is appropriate for the long-term health of the economy.

FYI The author of the 1926 *Myers* opinion was Chief Justice William Howard Taft. Taft had previously been President of the United States—which no doubt influenced his view of Presidential power! Taft is the only person in American history to have held both offices. In between his time as President (1909–1913) and his time as Chief Justice (1921–1930), he was a law professor at Yale Law School and, among other things, wrote a treatise on presidential power.

In its first major foray into grappling with this tension, the Supreme Court ruled decisively in favor of accountability. In *Myers v. United States*, 272 U.S. 52 (1926), a divided Court concluded that an inherent component of the President's constitutional responsibility to execute the laws was a unilateral power to remove those executive branch officials—a local postmaster in this case—who no longer had the President's trust or support. Although the congressional statute creating the positions of postmasters had conditioned both their appointment and their removal on the advice and consent of the Senate, the Court held that conditioning the President's removal power on Senate consent was unconstitutional. As the Court explained, the President's ability to execute the laws depended on the assistance of subordinates who would act under presidential direction; it therefore was "essential" that the President have the "power of removing those for whom he cannot continue to be responsible." *Id.* at 117.

However, less than a decade later, the Supreme Court in *Humphrey's Executor v. United States*, 295 U.S. 602 (1935), unanimously limited the scope of its *Myers* decision by distinguishing *independent* federal agencies from government departments under presidential control. Although the President's removal power remained "exclusive and illimitable" with respect to officials in the prototypical "units in the executive department," the Court explained that Congress was free to create agencies not subject to presidential direction or control, including agencies—in this case, the Federal Trade Commission (FTC)—whose commissioners were not removable at will by the President. The Court characterized the FTC as "an administrative body created by Congress" to perform duties of a "legislative" and "judicial" character, not just executive duties. These broader functions that the FTC performed allowed the Court to distinguish *Myers* by concluding that the FTC "cannot in any proper sense be characterized as an arm or an eye of the executive." *Id.* at 627–28.

Although the holding of *Humphrey's Executor* pertained only to whether the President had removal power over the commissioner of an independent agency, the decision also had the effect of granting Congress wide latitude to decide how to structure government agencies. The Court made clear that Congress had the power, as it deemed fit, to create administrative bodies "free from executive control," in furtherance of whatever legitimate policy or purpose Congress intended the agency to pursue.

Today, however, independent agencies like the FTC are not generally classified as agencies of the legislative or judicial branches. Rather, it is common to speak of these independent agencies as still part of the executive branch, despite the fact that (1) Congress often gives these agencies (as well as the prototypical executive branch departments) quasi-legislative or quasi-judicial responsibilities, and (2) the agencies are largely insulated from presidential control because of the job security that Congress has given the agencies' leaders. Alternatively, the independent federal agencies are sometimes referred to as the "fourth branch" of government, reflecting the reality that these agencies do not fit cleanly into the typical tripartite separation of powers. Meanwhile, both the legislative branch and the judicial branch also each now have a handful of their own "agencies" (such as the Congressional Budget Office and the Government Accountability Office in the legislative branch, and the Judicial Conference of the United States and the U.S. Sentencing Commission in the judicial branch) that per-

As noted previously, many agencies in the modern American system of government, whether denominated "independent" or "executive," perform what we would conventionally view as legislative, executive, and judicial functions related to the agency's area of expertise. That is, some individuals who work within those agencies help to promulgate regulations that have a legislative form and character; other individuals implement federal law through enforcement actions; and yet other agency officials adjudicate disputes that arise out of federal law.

form important functions to assist their respective branches. These legislative and judicial branch agencies are not usually included in the category of independent agencies.

Many independent agencies do extraordinarily important work regulating vast swathes of the modern economy. A few examples of independent agencies within the federal government include the National Labor Relations Board, the Securities and Exchange Commission, the Federal Election Commission, the Federal Communications Commission, and the Federal Reserve Board. But in the eyes of many scholars of federal bureaucracy, agency "independence" is not an all-or-nothing characteristic. Rather, the degree of agency "independence" may be a function of several congressionally specified factors, including not only the protection of agency heads against removal at will, but also such other criteria as requirements of bipartisan leadership, terms of office of the agency leaders, the nature of the agency's adjudicative responsibilities, and how the agency is funded. *See generally, e.g.*, Kirti Datla and Richard L. Revesz, *Deconstructing Independent Agencies (and Executive Agencies)*, 98 CORNELL L. REV. 769 (2013).

> **FYI** Notwithstanding the theoretical idea that there is a range of "independence" among agencies such that agencies do not fit neatly into two distinct categories of "independent agencies" versus "executive agencies," federal law does explicitly designate some agencies as "independent agencies" for many purposes, including regulatory review, which we discuss below. *See* 44 U.S.C. sec. 3502(5); Executive Order 12866, sec. 3(b).

Thus, consistent with *Humphrey's Executor*, Congress has substantial control over how it structures administrative agencies, including over the factors that determine a given agency's degree of independence. Congressional flexibility is not unlimited, however.

In *Bowsher v. Synar*, 478 U.S. 714, 726 (1986), the Supreme Court held that "Congress cannot reserve for itself the power of removal of an officer charged with the execution of laws." At issue was the Comptroller General's role in executing the Balanced Budget and Emergency Deficit Control Act of 1985 by preparing program-by-program budget reductions sufficient to achieve specified spending targets, which the Act mandated the President to follow. The Comptroller General was the head of what was then called the General Accounting Office (now the Government Accountability Office), a legislative branch agency. The Court explained: "To permit the execution of laws to be vested in an officer answerable only to Congress would, in practical terms, reserve in Congress control over the execution of laws." This would be an untenable "usurpation of Executive Branch functions." In response to the Court's decision, Congress once again was able to restructure the statutory scheme with relative ease (by moving the responsibility to oversee the budget reduction targets from the Comptroller General, within the legislative branch, to the White House Office of Management and Budget, within the executive branch) to preserve the Balanced Budget Act's underlying substantive ends.

Most recently, in *Seila Law LLC v. Consumer Financial Protection Bureau*, 591 U.S. ___, 140 S. Ct. 2183 (2020), the Court has swung decidedly back towards the theme of strong presidential power in *Myers*, significantly limiting *Humphrey's Executor*. In *Seila Law*, the Court held that Congress could not impose any restrictions on the President's ability to remove the director of the Consumer Financial Protection Bureau, an "independent" agency led by a single director and vested with significant executive power. The Court reframed the past precedents on removal to mean that there were only two exceptions to the President's power to remove Officers: "one for multimember expert agencies that do not wield substantial executive power, and one for inferior officers with limited duties and no policymaking or administrative authority." 591 U.S. at ___, 140 S. Ct. at 2199–2200; *see also Free Enterprise Fund v. Public Company Accounting Oversight Board*, 561 U.S. 477 (2010) (holding unconstitutional a "dual-layer for-cause" limitation on removing members of the Public Company Accounting Oversight Board, whereby they could be removed only for cause and only by the Securities and Exchange Commission, whose Commissioners themselves could only be removed by the President for cause).

As we noted above, part of the original **FYI** rationale for *Humphrey's Executor* was that the FTC performed duties of a legislative and judicial character. Today, the FTC has far more "executive," i.e., enforcement, powers than it did during the 1930s when the Court decided *Humphrey's Executor*. Some scholars are now arguing that, even under *Humphrey's Executor*, the current FTC Commissioners should not enjoy for-cause removal protection. This issue is currently in the courts. *See Federal Trade Commission v. Walmart, Inc.*, Brief for Amicus Curiae Professor Jennifer L. Mascott in Support of Defendant's Motion to Dismiss.

C. Agency Control by the Office of Management and Budget (OMB)

1. The Office of Management and Budget in the Executive Office of the President

Recall again that the federal government has about 2 *million* civilian employees, making it about 1000 times larger than the EOP. Just as one point of comparison, the Social Security Administration has more than 1500 Administrative Law *Judges* just to adjudicate claims involving retirement, survivors, disability insurance and supplemental security income benefits. In short, in the grand scheme of the federal government, the EOP is tiny. As a historical matter, though, the EOP is a large "presidential staff." President McKinley, the last President of the 19th century, had a staff of about a dozen aides! *See* Dickinson at 138.

Central to presidential control over agency action is an entity known as the Executive Office of the President (EOP). President Franklin Roosevelt formally established the EOP in 1939 as an umbrella organization that contains a number of what one scholar refers to as "staff agencies." *See* Mathew J. Dickinson, *The Executive Office of the President: The Paradox of Politicization, in* THE EXECUTIVE BRANCH 135 (Joel D. Aberbach and Mark A. Peterson, eds., 2005). The components of EOP are far smaller than most agencies. Indeed, the entire staff of the Executive Office of the President is about 2000 employees. Compared with other agencies, a far higher percentage of EOP staff is political appointees. Moreover, EOP staff all work in close physical proximity to the President, either in the White House itself or in one of the two government "executive office buildings," one right next to the White House and the other across the street.

The EOP has a number of components, most of which have a subject-matter specialty, although often one that crosses the boundaries of multiple executive agencies. For example, the Biden Administration's EOP includes the Gender Policy Council, the Climate Policy Office, the Office of the Intellectual Property Enforcement Coordinator, the Council on Environmental Quality, the Office of National Drug Control Policy, the National Security Council, and the Council of Economic Advisers.

The largest component of the Executive Office of the President, though, is known as the Office of Management and Budget, or OMB. The Office of Management and Budget has around 600–700 employees, and it helps implement the President's goals across the executive branch. Though OMB has one of the most boring names one could imagine, it has its hands in much of importance that happens in the executive branch. As noted earlier, modern Presidents cannot possibly be personally involved in overseeing the vast array of agency actions. OMB has now become one of the central means through which Presidents further their policy agenda. Some scholars refer to it as "the most powerful agency in Washington." *See* CHARLES H. KOCH, JR. & RICHARD MURPHY, 3 ADMINISTRATIVE LAW AND PRACTICE § 7.32 (3d ed.).

OMB serves a number of vital roles, but four are key to your understanding of OMB's ability to help an administration implement the President's policies. First, OMB coordinates the executive branch's relationship with Congress and legislation and clears all communications between the executive branch and Congress. Enrolled bills all pass through OMB, which works with (and advises) the President

> **FYI** An "enrolled bill" is one that has passed both houses of Congress, and is ready to be presented to the President for approval or veto.

on whether to sign or veto the bill. OMB also clears and coordinates the executive branch's position on legislative proposals (i.e., pending or prospective bills). This is crucial, because, as we noted in Chapter 11, executive agencies are often deeply involved in the statutory drafting process. Moreover, when an administration official from an executive agency (such as a member of the Cabinet) testifies before a congressional committee, whether about pending legislation or anything else, the testimony gets cleared and coordinated through OMB.

> **FYI** Historically, Executive Orders have served as one of the President's most important tools for unilaterally furthering his policy objectives. To give an example, President Roosevelt's Executive Order 9066 directed the Secretary of War to "prescribe certain parts of the country as 'military areas.'" Relying on the authority of Executive Order 9066, the U.S. military ordered the interning of all Americans of Japanese descent during the Second World War.

Second, OMB clears all Executive Orders. An Executive Order is a directive from the President to someone else (or many people) in the executive branch. Executive Orders can be thought of as "internal memos" within the government, though they are issued publicly and published in the Federal Register. Importantly, despite being internal government memos, because the recipients of the memos are themselves powerful government actors who have the power to enforce law, promulgate regulations, and adjudicate cases, an Executive Order can have significant ripple effects throughout not only the government but also the rest of the country. Executive Orders do not, however, create any causes of action against the government. Moreover, in the hierarchy of law, they are constrained by (and thus, may not conflict with) the Constitution and statutes. Finally, because Executive Orders are framed as orders to officials with their official titles, Executive Orders remain in effect unless and until revoked (or they expire of their own terms). In that sense, their legal effect is similar to statutes. Just as statutes generally do not have "sunset clauses" and so remain in effect when Congress changes hands, so too do Executive Orders when a new President comes into office. Of course, Executive Orders are easier to revoke (or even just amend) than statutes are to repeal, because the President can act unilaterally, while Congress, as we saw in Chapter 11, has many more hurdles to overcome. But many Executive Orders remain in effect over the course of Presidents from both parties.

> **FYI** As just one of many recent examples, President Trump issued Executive Order E.O. 13864, *Improving Free Inquiry, Transparency, and Accountability at Colleges and Universities* in 2019. Though it raised significant political controversy at the time, President Biden did not revoke it.

Third, OMB coordinates and reviews all significant federal regulations from executive agencies. As described in earlier chapters and as we will discuss further in Part VIII, agencies promulgate regulations pursuant to Congressional authority. But, through OMB, the President plays a significant role in shaping those regulations. Since the early 1980s, pursuant to a series of Executive Orders, all agencies must (1) publish an annual "regulatory plan" that describes "the most important significant regulatory actions that the agency reasonably expects to issue" in the year to come; and (2) for executive agencies (but not independent agencies), clear those regulatory actions through an agency in OMB known as the Office of Information and Regulatory Affairs (OIRA).

> If you're saying it out loud, insiders pronounce OIRA "oh-EYE-rah."

Finally, OMB works with agencies to develop a single coordinated budget request to Congress. Although shaped by agency requests, the budget sets the *President's* priorities. Ultimately, as we saw in Chapter 12, Congress sets the budget and appropriates funds for the government to spend. But, as a practical matter, the President's budget helps set the agenda for the entire federal government. Importantly, while the budget might seem like a niche area of little interest to most lawyers, it is crucial. An agency cannot do anything—even things that Congress has elsewhere in the law mandated the agency to do—without money in the budget to act. Importantly, in the twenty-first century, most agencies do not have enough resources to do all the things they have statutory authority to do. So, the budget—and in the first instance, the President's budget request—effectively determines what agencies can and cannot do. *See generally* Eloise Pasachoff, *The President's Budget as a Source of Agency Policy Control*, 125 YALE L.J. 2182 (2016). As a lawyer, if you can prevent the President, through OMB, from requesting funds to do something your client wants an agency not to do, that can be sufficient to prevent the agency from acting.

2. Regulatory Review Under Executive Order 12866

As we described in the previous subsection, the Office of Information and Regulatory Affairs (OIRA) reviews all significant regulations that agencies promulgate. Next you will read an excerpt from an Executive Order first issued by President Clinton, which sets forth the process of OIRA review of significant regulations. As you read it, first notice its structure. Like statutes, Executive Orders look quite different from judicial opinions. Many lawyers spend far more of their time reading documents that look like this than ones that look like judicial opinions. So, knowing how to read this kind of a document carefully is itself a skill that you will need as a lawyer. Second, focus on the process described in Section 6 of the Order. As you do, one question you should ask yourself is whether there is place for advocacy, where a lawyer whose client has a stake in the outcome of an agency's proposed regulation might be able to intervene. You'll recall our discussion of rulemaking and the notice-and-comment rulemaking process in Chapter 28. This regulatory review by OIRA has created another step in that process. When in that process is OIRA review? And, as a procedural matter, what actually happens when OIRA reviews an agency regulation? Third, and finally, think about the substance of this review process. What exactly is OIRA reviewing? Who is doing the review? Who do you think works at OIRA doing this review? Is this a "legal" review? Is there place in the process for a "legal" review? Even if so, is a legal review the primary goal of the OIRA review process? If not, then, what does all this have to do with *law*?

Executive Order 12866 of September 30, 1993, as amended by Executive Order 13258 of February 26, 2002, and Executive Order 14094 of April 6, 2023: Regulatory Planning and Review

The American people deserve a regulatory system that works for them, not against them: a regulatory system that protects and improves their health, safety, environment, and well-being and improves the performance of the economy without imposing unacceptable or unreasonable costs on society; regulatory policies that recognize that the private sector and private markets are the best engine for economic growth; regulatory approaches that respect the role of State, local, and tribal governments; and regulations that are effective, consistent, sensible, and understandable. We do not have such a regulatory system today.

 Why do we "not have such a regulatory system today"? What do you think this assertion reflects?

With this Executive order, the Federal Government begins a program to reform and make more efficient the regulatory process. The objectives of this Executive order are to enhance planning and coordination with respect to both new and existing regulations; to reaffirm the primacy of Federal agencies in the regulatory decision-making process; to restore the integrity and legitimacy of regulatory review and oversight; and to make the process more accessible and open to the public. In pursuing these objectives, the regulatory process shall be conducted so as to meet applicable statutory requirements and with due regard to the discretion that has been entrusted to the Federal agencies.

Accordingly, by the authority vested in me as President by the Constitution and the laws of the United States of America, it is hereby ordered as follows:

Section 1. Statement of Regulatory Philosophy and Principles.

(a) The Regulatory Philosophy. Federal agencies should promulgate only such regulations as are required by law, are necessary to interpret the law, or are made necessary by compelling public need, such as material failures of private markets to protect or improve the health and safety of the public, the environment, or the well-being of the American people. In deciding whether and how to regulate, agencies should assess all costs and benefits of available regulatory alternatives, including the alternative of not regulating. Costs and benefits shall be understood to include both quantifiable measures (to the fullest extent that these can be usefully estimated) and qualitative measures of costs and benefits that are difficult to quantify, but nevertheless essential to consider. Further, in choosing among alternative regulatory approaches, agencies should select those approaches that maximize net benefits (including potential economic, environmental, public health and safety, and other advantages; distributive impacts; and equity), unless a statute requires another regulatory approach.

(b) The Principles of Regulation. To ensure that the agencies' regulatory programs are consistent with the philosophy set forth above, agencies should adhere to the following principles, to the extent permitted by law and where applicable:

(1) Each agency shall identify the problem that it intends to address (including, where applicable, the failures of private markets or public institutions that warrant new agency action) as well as assess the significance of that problem.

(2) Each agency shall examine whether existing regulations (or other law) have created, or contributed to, the problem that a new regulation is intended to correct and whether those regulations (or other law) should be modified to achieve the intended goal of regulation more effectively.

(3) Each agency shall identify and assess available alternatives to direct regulation, including providing economic incentives to encourage the desired behavior, such as user fees or marketable permits, or providing information upon which choices can be made by the public.

(4) In setting regulatory priorities, each agency shall consider, to the extent reasonable, the degree and nature of the risks posed by various substances or activities within its jurisdiction.

(5) When an agency determines that a regulation is the best available method of achieving the regulatory objective, it shall design its regulations in the most cost-effective manner to achieve the regulatory objective. In doing so, each agency shall consider incentives for innovation, consistency, predictability, the costs of enforcement and compliance (to the government, regulated entities, and the public), flexibility, distributive impacts, and equity.

(6) Each agency shall assess both the costs and the benefits of the intended regulation and, recognizing that some costs and benefits are difficult to quantify, propose or adopt a regulation only upon a reasoned determination that the benefits of the intended regulation justify its costs.

"Justify" is a crucial word here. What do you think it means?

(7) Each agency shall base its decisions on the best reasonably obtainable scientific, technical, economic, and other information concerning the need for, and consequences of, the intended regulation.

(8) Each agency shall identify and assess alternative forms of regulation and shall, to the extent feasible, specify performance objectives, rather than specifying the behavior or manner of compliance that regulated entities must adopt.

(9) Wherever feasible, agencies shall seek views of appropriate State, local, and tribal officials before imposing regulatory requirements that might significantly or uniquely affect those governmental entities. Each agency shall assess the effects of Federal regulations on State, local, and tribal governments, including specifically the availability of resources to carry out those mandates, and seek to minimize those burdens that uniquely or significantly affect such governmental entities, consistent with achieving regulatory objectives. In addition, as appropriate, agencies shall seek to harmonize Federal regulatory actions with related State, local, and tribal regulatory and other governmental functions.

(10) Each agency shall avoid regulations that are inconsistent, incompatible, or duplicative with its other regulations or those of other Federal agencies.

(11) Each agency shall tailor its regulations to impose the least burden on society, including individuals, businesses of differing sizes, and other entities (including small communities and governmental entities), consistent with obtaining the regulatory objectives, taking into account, among other things, and to the extent practicable, the costs of cumulative regulations.

(12) Each agency shall draft its regulations to be simple and easy to understand, with the goal of minimizing the potential for uncertainty and litigation arising from such uncertainty.

Sec. 2. Organization. An efficient regulatory planning and review process is vital to ensure that the Federal Government's regulatory system best serves the American people.

(a) The Agencies. Because Federal agencies are the repositories of significant substantive expertise and experience, they are responsible for developing regulations and assuring that the regulations are consistent with applicable law, the President's priorities, and the principles set forth in this Executive order.

(b) The Office of Management and Budget. Coordinated review of agency rulemaking is necessary to ensure that regulations are consistent with applicable law, the President's priorities, and the principles set forth in this Executive order, and that decisions made by one agency do not conflict with the policies or actions taken or planned by another agency. The Office of Management and Budget (OMB) shall carry out that review function. Within OMB, the Office of Information and Regulatory Affairs (OIRA) is the repository of expertise concerning regulatory issues, including methodologies and procedures that affect more than one agency, this Executive order, and the President's regulatory policies. To the extent permitted by law, OMB shall provide guidance to agencies and assist the President and regulatory policy advisors to the President in regulatory planning and shall be the entity that reviews individual regulations, as provided by this Executive order.

(c) Assistant. In fulfilling his responsibilities under this Executive order, the President shall be assisted by the regulatory policy advisors within the Executive Office of the President and by such agency officials and personnel as the President may, from time to time, consult.

Sec. 3. Definitions. For purposes of this Executive order:

* * *

(b) "Agency," unless otherwise indicated, means any authority of the United States that is an "agency" under 44 U.S.C. 3502(1), other than those considered to be independent regulatory agencies, as defined in 44 U.S.C. 3502(10).

(c) "Director" means the Director of OMB.

(d) "Regulation" or "rule" means an agency statement of general applicability and future effect, which the agency intends to have the force and effect of law, that is designed to implement, interpret, or prescribe law or policy or to describe the procedure or practice requirements of an agency. It does not, however, include:

(1) Regulations or rules issued in accordance with the formal rulemaking provisions of 5 U.S.C. 556, 557;

(2) Regulations or rules that pertain to a military or foreign affairs function of the United States, other than procurement regulations and regulations involving the import or export of non-defense articles and services;

(3) Regulations or rules that are limited to agency organization, management, or personnel matters; or

(4) Any other category of regulations exempted by the Administrator of OIRA.

(e) "Regulatory action" means any substantive action by an agency (normally published in the FEDERAL REGISTER) that promulgates or is expected to lead to the promulgation of a final rule or regulation, including notices of inquiry, advance notices of proposed rulemaking, and notices of proposed rulemaking.

(f) "Significant regulatory action" means any regulatory action that is likely to result in a rule that may:

(1) have an annual effect on the economy of $200 million or more (adjusted every year by the Administrator of OIRA for changes in gross domestic product); or adversely affect in a material way the economy, a sector of the economy, productivity, competition, jobs, the environment, public health or safety, or State, local, territorial, or tribal governments or communities;

(2) create a serious inconsistency or otherwise interfere with an action taken or planned by another agency;

(3) materially alter the budgetary impact of entitlements, grants, user fees, or loan programs or the rights and obligations of recipients thereof; or

(4) raise legal or policy issues for which centralized review would meaningfully further the President's priorities or the principles set forth in this Executive order, as specifically authorized in a timely manner by the Administrator of OIRA in each case.

Sec. 4. Planning Mechanism. * * *

Sec. 5. Existing Regulations. * * *

Sec. 6. Centralized Review of Regulations. The guidelines set forth below shall apply to all regulatory actions, for both new and existing regulations, by agencies other than those agencies specifically exempted by the Administrator of OIRA:—

(a) Agency Responsibilities. (1) Each agency shall (consistent with its own rules, regulations, or procedures) provide the public with meaningful participation in the regulatory process. In particular, before issuing a notice of proposed rulemaking, each agency should, where appropriate, seek the involvement of those who are intended to benefit from and those expected to be burdened by any regulation (including, specifically, State, local, and tribal officials). In addition, each agency should afford the public a meaningful opportunity to comment on any proposed regulation, which in most cases should include a comment period of not less than 60 days. Each agency also is directed to explore and, where appropriate, use consensual mechanisms for developing regulations, including negotiated rulemaking.—

* * *

(3) In addition to adhering to its own rules and procedures and to the requirements of the Administrative Procedure Act, the Regulatory Flexibility

Act, the Paperwork Reduction Act, and other applicable law, each agency shall develop its regulatory actions in a timely fashion and adhere to the following procedures with respect to a regulatory action:—

(A) Each agency shall provide OIRA, at such times and in the manner specified by the Administrator of OIRA, with a list of its planned regulatory actions, indicating those which the agency believes are significant regulatory actions within the meaning of this Executive order. Absent a material change in the development of the planned regulatory action, those not designated as significant will not be subject to review under this section unless, within 10 working days of receipt of the list, the Administrator of OIRA notifies the agency that OIRA has determined that a planned regulation is a significant regulatory action within the meaning of this Executive order. The Administrator of OIRA may waive review of any planned regulatory action designated by the agency as significant, in which case the agency need not further comply with subsection (a)(3)(B) or subsection (a)(3)(C) of this section.—

(B) For each matter identified as, or determined by the Administrator of OIRA to be, a significant regulatory action, the issuing agency shall provide to OIRA:—

(i) The text of the draft regulatory action, together with a reasonably detailed description of the need for the regulatory action and an explanation of how the regulatory action will meet that need; and—

(ii) An assessment of the potential costs and benefits of the regulatory action, including an explanation of the manner in which the regulatory action is consistent with a statutory mandate and, to the extent permitted by law, promotes the President's priorities and avoids undue interference with State, local, and tribal governments in the exercise of their governmental functions.—

(C) For those matters identified as, or determined by the Administrator of OIRA to be, a significant regulatory action within the scope of section 3(f)(1), the agency shall also provide to OIRA the following additional information developed as part of the agency's decision-making process (unless prohibited by law):—

(i) An assessment, including the underlying analysis, of benefits anticipated from the regulatory action (such as, but not limited to, the promotion of the efficient functioning of the economy and private markets, the enhancement of health and safety, the protection of the natural environment, and

> ❗ As you are no doubt reading carefully, you will have noticed that the set of regulatory actions to which this sub-paragraph (subparagraph (C)) applies is more limited than the set to which the previous subparagraph (subparagraph (B)) applies. What does this phrase "within the scope of section 3(f)(1)" mean? Go back and re-read section 3(f) above, in the "Definitions" section of this Executive Order. As you do, compare section 3(f)(1) with the rest of section 3(f). Once you've done that, return here and read the remainder of this subparagraph (C), and notice how much more an agency must submit to OIRA for regulatory actions within the scope of section 3(f)(1). Why do you think that is?

the elimination or reduction of discrimination or bias) together with, to the extent feasible, a quantification of those benefits;—

(ii) An assessment, including the underlying analysis, of costs anticipated from the regulatory action (such as, but not limited to, the direct cost both to the government in administering the regulation and to businesses and others in complying with the regulation, and any adverse effects on the efficient functioning of the economy, private markets (including productivity, employment, and competitiveness), health, safety, and the natural environment), together with, to the extent feasible, a quantification of those costs; and

(iii) An assessment, including the underlying analysis, of costs and benefits of potentially effective and reasonably feasible alternatives to the planned regulation, identified by the agencies or the public (including improving the current regulation and reasonably viable nonregulatory actions), and an explanation why the planned regulatory action is preferable to the identified potential alternatives.

(D) In emergency situations or when an agency is obligated by law to act more quickly than normal review procedures allow, the agency shall notify OIRA as soon as possible and, to the extent practicable, comply with subsections (a)(3)(B) and (C) of this section. For those regulatory actions that are governed by a statutory or court-imposed deadline, the agency shall, to the extent practicable, schedule rulemaking proceedings so as to permit sufficient time for OIRA to conduct its review, as set forth below in subsections (b)(2) through (4) of this section.

(E) After the regulatory action has been published in the Federal Register or otherwise issued to the public, the agency shall:

(i) Make available to the public the information set forth in subsections (a)(3)(B) and (C);

(ii) Identify for the public, in a complete, clear, and simple manner, the substantive changes between the draft submitted to OIRA for review and the action subsequently announced; and—

(iii) Identify for the public those changes in the regulatory action that were made at the suggestion or recommendation of OIRA.

(F) All information provided to the public by the agency shall be in plain, understandable language.

(b) OIRA Responsibilities. The Administrator of OIRA shall provide meaningful guidance and oversight so that each agency's regulatory actions are consistent with applicable law, the President's priorities, and the principles set forth in this Executive order and do not conflict with the policies or actions of another agency. OIRA shall, to the extent permitted by law, adhere to the following guidelines:—

> How do you think the Administrator of OIRA will know if the agency's proposed regulatory actions "do not conflict with the policies or actions of another agency"? What might the Administrator of OIRA do to find out?

(1) OIRA may review only actions identified by the agency or by OIRA as significant regulatory actions under subsection (a)(3)(A) of this section.—

(2) OIRA shall waive review or notify the agency in writing of the results of its review within the following time periods:

(A) For any notices of inquiry, advance notices of proposed rulemaking, or other preliminary regulatory actions prior to a Notice of Proposed Rulemaking, within 10 working days after the date of submission of the draft action to OIRA;

(B) For all other regulatory actions, within 90 calendar days after the date of submission of the information set forth in subsections (a)(3)(B) and (C) of this section, unless OIRA has previously reviewed this information and, since that review, there has been no material change in the facts and circumstances upon which the regulatory action is based, in which case, OIRA shall complete its review within 45 days; and

(C) The review process may be extended (1) once by no more than 30 calendar days upon the written approval of the Director and (2) at the request of the agency head.

(3) For each regulatory action that the Administrator of OIRA returns to an agency for further consideration of some or all of its provisions, the Administrator of OIRA shall provide the issuing agency a written explanation for such return, setting forth the pertinent provision of this Executive order on which OIRA is relying. If the agency head disagrees with some or all of the bases for the return, the agency head shall so inform the Administrator of OIRA in writing.

(4) Except as otherwise provided by law or required by a Court, in order to ensure greater openness, accessibility, and accountability in the regulatory review process, OIRA shall be governed by the following disclosure requirements:

(A) Only the Administrator of OIRA (or a particular designee) shall receive oral communications initiated by persons not employed by the executive branch of the Federal Government regarding the substance of a regulatory action under OIRA review;

(B) All substantive communications between OIRA personnel and persons not employed by the executive branch of the Federal Government regarding a regulatory action under review shall be governed by the following guidelines: (i) A representative from the issuing agency shall be invited to any meeting between OIRA personnel and such person(s);

(ii) OIRA shall forward to the issuing agency, within 10 working days of receipt of the communication(s), all written communications, regardless of format, between OIRA personnel and any person who is not employed by the executive branch of the Federal Government, and the dates and names of individuals involved in all substantive oral communications (including meetings to which an agency representative was invited, but did not attend, and telephone conversations between OIRA personnel and any such persons); and

(iii) OIRA shall publicly disclose relevant information about such communication(s), as set forth below in subsection (b)(4)(C) of this section.

(C) OIRA shall maintain a publicly available log that shall contain, at a minimum, the following information pertinent to regulatory actions under review:

(i) The status of all regulatory actions, including if (and if so, when and by whom) Presidential consideration was requested;

(ii) A notation of all written communications forwarded to an issuing agency under subsection (b)(4)(B)(ii) of this section; and—

(iii) The dates and names of individuals involved in all substantive oral communications, including meetings and telephone conversations, between OIRA personnel and any person not employed by the executive branch of the Federal Government, and the subject matter discussed during such communications.

(D) After the regulatory action has been published in the FEDERAL REGISTER or otherwise issued to the public, or after the agency has announced its decision not to publish or issue the regulatory action, OIRA shall make available to the public all documents exchanged between OIRA and the agency during the review by OIRA under this section.

(5) All information provided to the public by OIRA shall be in plain, understandable language.

Sec. 7. Resolution of Conflicts. * * *

Sec. 8. Publication. Except to the extent required by law, an agency shall not publish in the FEDERAL REGISTER or otherwise issue to the public any regulatory action that is subject to review under section 6 of this Executive order until (1) the Administrator of OIRA notifies the agency that OIRA has waived its review of the action or has completed its review without any requests for further consideration, or (2) the applicable time period in section 6(b)(2) expires without OIRA having notified the agency that it is returning the regulatory action for further consideration under section 6(b)(3), whichever occurs first. If the terms of the preceding sentence have not been satisfied and an agency wants to publish or otherwise issue a regulatory action, the head of that agency may request Presidential consideration through the Director, as provided under section 7 of this order. Upon receipt of this request, the Director shall notify OIRA and the Advisors. The guidelines and time period set forth in section 7 shall apply to the publication of regulatory actions for which Presidential consideration has been sought.—

Sec. 9. Agency Authority. Nothing in this order shall be construed as displacing the agencies' authority or responsibilities, as authorized by law.—

Sec. 10. Judicial Review. Nothing in this Executive order shall affect any otherwise available judicial review of agency action. This Executive order is intended only to improve the internal management of the Federal Government and does not create any right or benefit, substantive or procedural, enforceable at law or equity by a party against the United States, its agencies or instrumentalities, its officers or employees, or any other person.—

Sec. 11. Revocations. * * *

NOTES & QUESTIONS

1. When an agency promulgates a rule, that rule has binding effect on affected parties, just like a statute. Notice what Section 6 of Executive Order 12866 does: it creates more procedural hurdles for an agency to go through if the rule is a "significant regulatory action." Go back and take a look at the definition of "significant regulatory action" in Section 3(f). It covers a lot. Now that you have a sense of what kind of "regulatory action[s]" are covered, what exactly does OIRA do with them? What are they reviewing? What is OIRA supposed to be looking for? Does EO 12866 tell you? Re-read the introductory language to EO 12866, and the "Regulatory Philosophy" described in Section 1. Does that help?

2. As you saw in the previous question, Section 6(a)(3)(C) makes the agency do even more if the agency's proposed action amounts to a "significant regulatory action" under the definition in Section 3(f)(1). What is Section 3(f)(1), and what more does the agency need to do under Section 6(a)(3)(C)? Why do you think agencies are required to do that? This is what economists and policy analysts refer to as "cost-benefit analysis" (or "benefit-cost analysis"). EO 12866 requires agencies to do a comprehensive cost-benefit analysis for any proposed action that has "an annual effect on the economy of $200 million or more (adjusted every 3 years by the Administrator of OIRA for changes in gross domestic product); or adversely affect[s] in a material way the economy, a sector of the economy, productivity, competition, jobs, the environment, public health or safety, or State, local, territorial, or tribal governments or communities." OIRA then has to review not only the proposed regulation, but also the cost-benefit analysis supporting the regulation. Does this give you a sense of who works at OIRA? The Administrator of OIRA is a political appointee. What kind of background should the Administrator of OIRA have? Might it surprise you to know that many OIRA Administrators have been law professors?

3. When the agency or OIRA does a cost-benefit analysis, what happens if the costs exceed the benefits? What happens if the costs exceed the benefits, but the statute requires the agency to regulate nonetheless? Take a look at Section 9. Does that answer it?

4. Notice Section 6(c)(4), the aspects of the EO 12866 process that create transparency. At any moment, anyone can see what OIRA is reviewing. You can find it all at https://www.reginfo.gov/public/. Can you see opportunities for advocacy for clients in this process? Check out https://www.reginfo.gov/public/do/eo/neweomeeting. Anyone who wants can go to this webpage and request a meeting with OIRA. Yes, we mean anyone! Do you think this part of the process mitigates or exacerbates potential problems of agency capture by regulated entities?

5. As you saw in Section 6(b), part of the OIRA Administrator's job is to ensure that an agency's proposed action "not conflict with the policies or actions of another agency." How will the Administrator of OIRA know if the agency's proposed regulatory actions "conflict with the policies or actions of another agency"? In fact, this is actually pretty straightforward: OIRA just asks the other agencies! No one expects the Administrator of OIRA to know everything. You can think of it a little like hub and spokes. OIRA sits in the middle and coordinates a government-wide review of an agency action. OIRA performs its own review, but just as importantly, it also permits other interested agencies to review as well. OIRA then serves as a mediator between and among agencies that may not necessarily have the same views about policy and do not always see things the same way.

Test Your Understanding

To assess your understanding of the material in this chapter, click here to take a quiz.

Part VIII—Judicial Review of Agency Action

This final Part of the book introduces the complex landscape surrounding the judicial role in overseeing how government agencies have used their delegated authority, including how agencies have resolved ambiguities in the legal texts that they administer. This Part is thus a culmination of all that has come before, weaving together the various approaches to the interpretive problem with the dynamic relationships between agencies, courts, and legislatures. It begins, however, with an overview of the way in which the judicial branch enforces the procedural requirements of the Administrative Procedure Act. It then turns to the essential question of how much deference the judiciary should give to agencies with respect to how agencies construe the statutes they are charged with administering. The *Chevron* Doctrine, named for a 1984 Supreme Court decision, has been central to this jurisprudence, although judicial developments before and after the *Chevron* decision continue to loom large, including the emergence of the Court's "major questions doctrine" in 2022 and new cases in the pipeline.

Part VIII—Judicial Review of Agency Action

31

Introduction to Judicial Review of Agency Actions

Key Concepts

- Judicial review of agency action
- Institutional choice
- *Chenery I* principle
- Final agency action
- Standards of review
- Fact/Law distinction
- Judicial review of agency factfinding
- Substantial evidence

Chapter Summary

The Administrative Procedure Act explicitly provides for judicial review of agency action. This review raises difficult questions about the relationship between courts and agencies, particularly about where primary responsibility for legal and policy decisionmaking should lie in our system of government. Courts review final agency actions based on the agency's own articulation of its decision. In doing so, courts have power to review an agency's factual findings, an agency's processes (including its reasoning process), and an agency's legal conclusions. Courts review agency actions through the lens of different standards of review. In this chapter, we address judicial review of agency factfinding, in which courts ask whether the agency's decision is supported by "substantial evidence." In the next chapter, we address judicial review of agency processes. Finally, in the remaining chapters of this Part VIII, we address judicial review of agency interpretation of their legal authority.

A. Overview

Implicit in the notion that the activities of government administrative agencies are constrained by law, including the U.S. Constitution and statutes such as the APA (and state analogs), is the promise of judicial review of agency action for conformance with these safeguards and constraints. As previously noted, the APA itself provides for judicial review of administrative activities in specific circumstances. In addition, both the organic statutes that establish agencies and other statutes granting agencies authority to act often include their own provisions for judicial review, which may supersede the generic APA judicial review provisions if the congressional intent to do so is clear. *See Dickinson v. Zurko*, 527 U.S. 150 (1999). Meanwhile, general federal question jurisdiction and mandamus actions also may provide opportunities for federal courts to review agency action, as may agency enforcement proceedings brought against parties who have failed to adhere to an agency directive.

FYI "Federal question jurisdiction" refers to the power that federal courts have to hear civil cases in which a plaintiff alleges a violation of federal law. See 28 U.S.C. § 1331. You will learn more about this in an advanced civil procedure course or a course on federal courts. Meanwhile, "mandamus" is a special writ that courts may issue to force a party to comply with an obligatory legal duty of a public nature. Mandamus is extremely rare and usually granted only when there is no other way the party seeking the writ can obtain adequate relief. In the federal system, it is only available in appellate courts.

Judicial review of agency action raises difficult questions about the relationship between courts and agencies, including when and to what degree courts should defer to agency expertise (which after all is a primary rationale for delegating substantial discretionary authority to agencies in the first place). Accordingly, courts have developed several distinct doctrines of judicial review for a variety of agency rulemaking and adjudication contexts. The paragraphs below sketch the outlines of several of the most significant of these doctrines. Other topics concerning judicial review of agency action that are beyond the scope of this book include the "exhaustion" requirement, which requires aggrieved parties to exhaust all avenues for relief within the administrative process before turning to courts for relief; related requirements that an agency action must be "final" before it is reviewable in court; the APA provision that judicial review is not available for agency actions "committed to agency discretion by law"; the presumption that an agency's refusal to act is not reviewable; and the question of who has standing to seek judicial review of agency action. For more detail about these topics, see Ernest Gellhorn, Ronald M. Levin & Jeffrey Lubbers, Administrative Law & Process In A Nutshell (6th ed. 2016).

One framework (though by no means the only one) for understanding and thinking about judicial review of agency action is through the lens of "institutional choice." By "institutional choice," we mean thinking comparatively about how different institutions—specifically agencies and courts—perform. This entails in turn thinking about the relative strengths and weaknesses of agencies and courts as decision-making bodies. We have already touched on some of the strengths of agencies, but some of the key ones are said to be 1) policy making expertise; 2) capacity to do a lot; 3) capacity to involve a variety of relevant interests in the decision-making process; and 4) some measure of political accountability. In contrast, courts are said to have the advantage of fostering "rule-of-law" values such as 1) independence, or what might be thought of as a *lack* of political accountability; 2) disinterestedness when the government's interests are at stake; 3) concern for individual rights and due process; and 4) expertise at legal analysis.

> Recall that agencies often enforce laws—indeed, the police department is itself an executive agency. Broader separation-of-powers principles suggest that a society may not want the enforcement arm of government to decide the extent of its own power, including (as we will see in the later chapters of this Part) the power to have the final word on the meaning of laws granting the agency power.

One of the fundamental premises of judicial review of agency action is that it is *review* of agency action. At the core, this means that the court is not addressing the problem the agency addressed from scratch. Instead, thought of through the lens of the etymological origins of the word "review," it is "viewing" the agency's action "again." Many questions related to judicial review revolve around how much it matters that the court is engaged in review. For example, in a case just before the enactment of the APA, *Securities and Exchange Commission v. Chenery Corporation*, 318 U.S. 80 (1943) (*Chenery I*), the U.S. Supreme Court established a fundamental premise of judicial review of agency action, which has continued validity today: a court may not sustain an agency action on any basis that the agency itself did not explicitly articulate at the time of its decision. As the Court put it, "the Commission's order must be measured by what the Commission did, not by what it might have done. . . . The Commission's action cannot be upheld merely because findings might have been made and considerations disclosed which would justify its order. . . . There must be such a responsible finding." *Id.* at 93–94. A fortiori, the agency must set forth its rationale with clarity: "the process of review requires that the grounds upon which the administrative agency acted be clearly disclosed and adequately sustained. " *Id.* at 94. As your high school math teacher might have put it, the Court was effectively telling agencies, "Show your work!" The rationale for this holding dovetails both with the reason Congress delegates to agencies and the reason we have judicial review. If Congress committed certain decisions to an agency because of its expertise, then the agency should demonstrate that it actually exercised that expertise. Just as importantly, "courts cannot exercise their duty of review unless they are advised of the considerations underlying the action under review." *Id.* at 94.

As you think about judicial review of agency action, including how much there should be and what form it should take, it may be helpful to think about another form of judicial review with which you are already familiar from other law courses: appellate review of trial court decisions. While judicial review of agency action is not the same as appellate review of trial court decisions, it is similar. First, in both situations, the reviewing court is engaged in the act of "reviewing." Second, generally speaking, only *final* **judgments** in a trial court may be appealed. *See, e.g.,* 28 U.S.C. § 1291 (giving federal appellate courts jurisdiction over appeals from all "final decisions" of the federal district courts). Of course, there are exceptions to this rule, in the form of what are called interlocutory appeals. So too with judicial review of agency action: While there are exceptions, the general principle is that only **"*final* agency action"** is reviewable. *See* 5 U.S.C. § 704.

Third, you also may be familiar from other courses with the **"standard of review"** or the standard that appellate courts use when reviewing trial court decisions (including jury decisions). The standard of review is usually seen through the **fact/law paradigm**. The fact/law distinction, which is fundamental to virtually every area of law, is more easily stated in the abstract than applied in practice, at least at the margins. But it is one that structures the way in which appellate courts review trial courts. As you likely have already learned, the longstanding rule is that a trial court's conclusions of law are subject to **de novo** review, while its findings of fact are subject to a more deferential review, in many jurisdictions known as **"clearly erroneous"** review or by some other similar moniker. The central rationale for this fact/law distinction is the belief that, in general, trial courts are better positioned to find facts and appellate courts are better suited to determine the meaning of law.

> **FYI** The term "de novo" simply means "afresh" or "from the beginning." The essence of *de novo* review is, at least theoretically, that the trial court's conclusion on a legal question is irrelevant to the appellate court's conclusion.

A separate standard of review derives from the fact that, at times, a trial judge will make decisions that the law either explicitly or implicitly vests in the trial judge's "discretion." These are often procedural or evidentiary decisions. (Think, for example, of a decision to exclude certain evidence because it is more prejudicial than probative. *See, e.g.,* Federal Rule of Evidence 404.) In most jurisdictions, appellate courts review such decisions through an **"abuse of discretion"** standard. These standards of review necessarily shape the relationship between trial and appellate courts. In particular, they allocate decision-making authority between appellate and trial courts. As you might imagine, then, trial courts generally determine "facts" and appellate courts generally determine "law."

> Standards of review also are another example of what we have previously referred to as trans-substantive law, law that applies across a variety of different areas of law.

> In the federal system, appellate courts have exclusive jurisdiction to review much agency action. There are, however, many exceptions. The jurisdictional questions related to review of agency action are complex and dependent on specific statutory authority. As a default matter, it is probably best to think about an appellate court as the court exercising judicial review of agency decisions, since even when trial courts have jurisdiction, it is the agency that has the power to determine facts and the courts' review power usually precludes the court from finding new facts. In other words, whatever court is reviewing the agency action, it is doing so in an appellate capacity, so to speak, and does so solely on the basis of the record that was before the agency (just as an appellate court reviews a trial court's decision based on the record before the trial court).

Although the relationship between agencies and appellate courts is by no means the same as the relationship between trial and appellate courts, the standards of review that courts use in reviewing agency decisions do bear some similarities to those that appellate courts use in reviewing trial court decisions. In particular, the fact/law distinction remains paramount. Moreover, there is an important aspect of judicial review of agency action that corresponds directly to the "abuse of discretion" category, although as we will see, the nature of that review differs somewhat from its appellate-review-of-trial-court-decisions counterpart.

In this chapter, you will read a short case excerpt from a longstanding precedent involving judicial review of agency fact-finding. In the following chapter, we turn to judicial review of agency procedures and processes, the counterpart to appellate "abuse of discretion" review of trial court decisions. As we will see, the nature of that review—known as "arbitrary and capricious" review—is a crucial aspect of judicial control of agency action, far more fundamental than "abuse of discretion" review of trial courts. Finally, in Chapters 33–38, we address judicial review of agency legal determinations, i.e., agency *interpretations of law.*

FYI

As we will also see in the next chapter, this reference to "procedures and processes" is somewhat fraught, as much of "arbitrary and capricious" review intertwines with the substance of agency decisions.

As we will see, that review is not the same as appellate court review of trial court legal interpretations, and the question of how much deference, if any, courts should give to agency interpretations of law is one of the most hotly disputed (and unsettled) issues in modern American law.

As you read through the materials in this Part, you will encounter numerous legal doctrines about the standard of judicial review in various contexts. The doctrines will be relatively straightforward to articulate, but they will at times be very difficult to apply. As you read these materials, then, think about why the doctrines are framed the way that they are, and what the doctrines' *purposes* are. These standards of review shape the relationship between courts and agencies, but, as we indicated in Chapter 29, they do so in the context of legislative delegation of authority to agencies. Thus, although most of the reading in the remainder of this book is from judicial opinions, these materials will also allow you to explore the respective roles of legislatures, agencies, and courts in legal and policy decision-making in modern American society. Understanding the way that judges think about these respective roles will be crucial for you as a lawyer, no matter the area in which you practice: In the modern American legal system, most areas of law involve a complex interplay among legislation, regulation, and judicial decision-making.

B. Judicial Review of Agency Fact-Finding

In agency adjudications in particular, agencies are engaged in the type of fact-finding reminiscent of exactly what trial courts do and in a very similar manner. Although adjudications in agencies are generally nowhere nearly as formalized as in federal court, agencies often must find facts in the context of their decision-making, often from conflicting evidence.

FYI

The kind of facts in these sort of cases (the "who did what, where, when, how, why, with what motive or intent") are often referred to as "adjudicative facts." Especially in rulemaking, agencies also often determine "legislative facts," a term that refers to facts that "do not usually concern the immediate parties but are the general facts which help the tribunal decide questions of law and policy and discretion." See KENNETH CULP DAVIS, ADMINISTRATIVE LAW TREATISE (1958), quoted in KRISTIN E. HICKMAN & RICHARD J. PIERCE, JR., ADMINISTRATIVE LAW TREATISE (6th ed. 2019).

Huge swathes of agency adjudications largely involve fact-finding. For example, the Social Security Administration adjudicates hundreds of thousands of cases per year about benefits. The U.S. Citizenship and Immigration Service similarly adjudicates millions of cases each year, involving immigrant visa petitions, applications to adjust residency status, asylum applications, and others.

1. Formal Adjudication and Rulemaking

The Administrative Procedure Act provides that, in formal adjudication and formal rulemaking, reviewing courts shall set aside agency action that is "unsupported by substantial evidence." 5 U.S.C. § 706(2)(E). The next case is the leading case articulating the meaning of that term. As you read the decision, think to yourself how the "substantial evidence" standard compares with the "clearly erroneous" standard ordinarily used in appellate court review of trial-court factual findings.

Universal Camera Corp. v. National Labor Relations Board
340 U.S. 474 (1951)

Mr. Justice Frankfurter delivered the opinion of the Court.

The essential issue raised by this case * * * is the effect of the Administrative Procedure Act and the legislation colloquially known as the Taft-Hartley Act on the duty of Courts of Appeals when called upon to review orders of the National Labor Relations Board.

The Court of Appeals for the Second Circuit granted enforcement of an order directing, in the main, that petitioner reinstate with back pay an employee found to have been discharged because he gave testimony under the Wagner Act, and cease and desist from discriminating against any employee who files charges or gives testimony under that Act. The court below, Judge Swan dissenting, decreed full enforcement of the order. Because the views of that court regarding the effect of the new legislation on the relation between the Board and the courts of appeals in the enforcement of the Board's orders conflicted with those of the Court of Appeals for the Sixth Circuit we brought both cases here. The clash of opinion obviously required settlement by this Court.

I.

FYI As with virtually every question related to agencies and courts, remember that the standard of review depends on the agency's statutory authority. So, while the APA generally applies, Congress sometimes specifically sets a standard of review. *See, e.g.,* 7 U.S.C. sec. 2023(a)(15) (*de novo* trial in federal district court).

The Wagner Act provided: 'The findings of the Board as to the facts, if supported by evidence, shall be conclusive.' This Court read 'evidence' to mean 'substantial evidence,' *Washington, V. & M. Coach Co. v. Labor Board*, 301 U.S. 142 (1937), and we said that '(s)ubstantial evidence is more than a mere scintilla. It means such relevant evidence as a reasonable mind might accept as adequate to support a conclusion.' *Consolidated Edison Co. v. National Labor Relations Board*, 305 U.S. 197, 229 (1939). * * *

The very smoothness of the 'substantial evidence' formula as the standard for reviewing the evidentiary validity of the Board's findings established its currency. But the inevitably variant applications of the standard to conflicting evidence soon brought contrariety of views and in due course bred criticism. Even though the whole record may have been canvassed in order to determine whether the evidentiary foundation of a determination by the Board was 'substantial,' the phrasing of this Court's process of review readily lent itself to the notion that it was enough that the evidence supporting the Board's result was 'substantial' when considered by itself. * * *

Criticism of so contracted a reviewing power reinforced dissatisfaction felt in various quarters with the Board's administration of the Wagner Act in the years preceding the war. The scheme of the Act was attacked as an inherently unfair fusion of the functions of prosecutor and judge. Accusations of partisan bias were not wanting. The 'irrespon-

! Remember that agencies (in this case, the NLRB) often both prosecute laws and also decide individual cases under those same laws.

sible admission and weighing of hearsay, opinion, and emotional speculation in place of factual evidence' was said to be a 'serious menace.' No doubt some, perhaps even much, of the criticism was baseless and some surely was reckless. What is here relevant, however, is the climate of opinion thereby generated and its effect on Congress. Protests against 'shocking injustices' and intimations of judicial 'abdication' with which some courts granted enforcement of the Board's order stimulated pressures for legislative relief from alleged administrative excesses.

* * *

It is fair to say that in all this Congress expressed a mood. And it expressed its mood not merely by oratory but by legislation. As legislation that mood must be respected, even though it can only serve as a standard for judgment and not as a body of rigid rules assuring sameness of applications. Enforcement of such broad standards implies subtlety of mind and solidity of judgment. But it is not for us to question that Congress may assume such qualities in the federal judiciary.

* * *

Whether or not it was ever permissible for courts to determine the substantiality of evidence supporting a Labor Board decision merely on the basis of evidence which in and of itself justified it, without taking into account contradictory evidence or evidence from which conflicting inferences could be drawn, the new legislation definitively precludes such a theory of review and bars its practice. **The substantiality of evidence must take into account whatever in the record fairly detracts from its weight. This is clearly the significance of the requirement in both statutes that courts consider the whole record.** * * * (emphasis added)

To be sure, the requirement for canvassing 'the whole record' in order to ascertain substantiality does not furnish a calculus of value by which a reviewing court can assess the evidence. Nor was it intended to negative the function of the Labor Board as one of those agencies presumably equipped or informed by experience to deal with a specialized field of knowledge, whose findings within that field carry the authority of an expertness which courts do not possess and therefore must respect. Nor does it mean that even as to matters not requiring expertise a court may displace the Board's choice between two fairly conflicting views, even though the court would justifiably have made a different choice had the matter been before it *de novo*. Congress has merely made it clear that a reviewing court is not barred from

> This is the Court's key holding. Even though the phrase "substantial evidence" might, on its face, imply that the reviewing court need only look at the evidence that supports the agency's conclusion (*i.e.*, might ask simply whether there is enough evidence to support the agency's conclusion), the Court is clear that this is not what "substantial evidence" means in the context of the APA.

setting aside a Board decision when it cannot conscientiously find that the evidence supporting that decision is substantial, when viewed in the light that the record in its entirety furnishes, including the body of evidence opposed to the Board's view.

* * *

We conclude, therefore, that the Administrative Procedure Act and the Taft-Hartley Act direct that courts must now assume more responsibility for the reasonableness and fairness of Labor Board decisions than some courts have shown in the past. Reviewing courts must be influenced by a feeling that they are not to abdicate the conventional judicial function. Congress has imposed on them responsibility for assuring that the Board keeps within reasonable grounds. That responsibility is not less real because it is limited to enforcing the requirement that evidence appear substantial when viewed, on the record as a whole, by courts invested with the authority and enjoying the prestige of the Courts of Appeals. * * *

2. "Informal" Agency Adjudication and Rulemaking

The *Universal Camera* decision above arose from a formal adjudication. However, as we indicated in Part VII, formal rulemaking has largely disappeared from the administrative state, in the wake of the Supreme Court's 1973 decision in *Florida East Coast Railway*. So, courts are often reviewing agency factfinding in the context of informal rulemaking or informal adjudication. Under the APA, courts review informal agency decisions under what is known as the "arbitrary and capricious" standard. *See* 5 U.S.C. § 706(1)(A) (instructing courts to "hold unlawful and set aside agency action, findings, and conclusions found to be . . . (A) arbitrary, capricious, an abuse of discretion, or otherwise not in accordance with law"). We will encounter this "arbitrary and capricious" standard again in a different context in the next chapter, but for now, the most important thing to know about this standard in the context of agency fact-finding is this: the law is not clear. The Supreme Court has on occasion intimated that the standard is *more deferential* than the "substantial evidence" standard. *See, e.g., Abbott Labs. v. Gardner*, 387 U.S. 136, 143 (1967) (noting that the "substantial evidence" standard provides "a considerably more generous [that is, more searching] judicial review than the 'arbitrary and capricious' test"). At the same time, many lower courts have effectively treated the standards as equivalent. *See, e.g., ADAPSO v. Board of Governors of the Federal Reserve*, 745 F.2d 677, 683–85 (D.C. Cir. 1984).

Test Your Understanding

To assess your understanding of the material in this chapter, click here to take a quiz.

32

Judicial Review of Agency Procedures and Policymaking

Key Concepts

- Judicial review of agency action
- "Arbitrary and capricious" standard
- "Hard look" review
- "Reasoned decision-making"
- The *State Farm* Case
- Rescission of agency action
- The *UC Regents* Case

Chapter Summary

The previous chapter provided an overview of judicial review of agency fact-finding and the "supported by substantial evidence" standard. This chapter turns to the topic of judicial review of agency procedures. Of central importance here is the "arbitrary and capricious" standard, one of the Administrative Procedure Act's several bases on which federal courts may set aside an agency action. This standard is also notoriously squishy, as several prominent cases show, but it has come to mean that an agency must at least be able to show that it has engaged in "reasoned decision-making." Of course, this too is not a straightforward standard to apply, especially as applied to an agency's complex rulemaking processes.

A. Overview

The last chapter introduced you to one of the most important phrases in the American legal system, "arbitrary and capricious." Like the term "reasonable" in the field of Tort law, the phrase "arbitrary and capricious" is a legal term of art that bears some resemblance to its use in ordinary language but has taken on something more in its legal context. And, despite endless jurisprudence about the term, "arbitrary and capricious," just like "reasonable," is nearly impossible to pin down precisely.

> ❗ *Chenery I* is the principle that a reviewing court may uphold an agency action only based on the reasons that the agency itself explicitly articulated at the time of its decision.

The concept of "arbitrary and capricious" is a fundamental standard that courts use when reviewing agency action: if an agency acts in a manner that is "arbitrary and capricious," a reviewing court must invalidate the agency's action. Like the *Chenery I* principle discussed in the previous chapter, this idea also predates the APA, *see, e.g., Pacific States Box & Basket Co., v. White*, 296 U.S. 176, 180–82 (1935) (assessing Due Process Clause challenge to agency action by inquiring as to whether action was "arbitrary or capricious"), but it was explicitly written into the APA.

Section 706(2) of the APA requires a reviewing court to "hold unlawful and set aside" an agency action if the court determines that it falls into any one of six categories. These categories include "agency action, findings, and conclusions" that are:

(A)   arbitrary, capricious, an abuse of discretion, or otherwise not in accordance with law;

(B)   contrary to constitutional [law];

(C)   in excess of statutory [authority], or short of statutory right;

(D)   without observance of procedure required by law;

(E)   unsupported by substantial evidence in a case . . . reviewed on the record of an agency hearing . . . ; or

(F)   unwarranted by the facts to the extent that the facts are subject to trial de novo by the reviewing court.

Paragraph (E) is applicable only to the narrow category of formal on-the-record agency proceedings conducted under 5 U.S.C. §§ 556 and 557 (or analogous proceedings), and paragraph (F) is also a very limited exception involving a few circumstances that call for the reviewing court to conduct a trial de novo. Meanwhile, paragraphs (B), (C), and (D) are limited to situations in which an agency has acted contrary to law. So, on their face at least, they seem to be squarely within the purview of reviewing courts.

> **Recall** from the Chapter 28 discussion of *Florida East Coast Railway* that agencies today rarely use the formal procedures of sections 556 and 557.

> **?** What does the phrase "arbitrary or capricious" mean to you? How would you attempt to explain or define it? (Notice that, despite the fact that judicial review under section 706(2)(A) is often colloquially referred to as "arbitrary *and* capricious" review, the text of the APA requires only that the agency action be either arbitrary *or* capricious.)

But paragraph (A)—in particular, the first three terms, "arbitrary," "capricious," and "an abuse of discretion"—provides potentially wide latitude for reviewing courts to second-guess agency action. It has not been easy for federal courts to determine just what this so-called "arbitrary and capricious review" (and, depending on the circumstances, sometimes also called "abuse of discretion review") should entail. In particular, although the Administrative *Procedure* Act primarily concerns agency *procedures*, "arbitrary and capricious" review can bleed over into the *substance* of an agency's decision. As several cases summarized or excerpted below will show, the line between a court reviewing an agency's compliance with procedural requirements and a court reviewing aspects of the substance of the agency's underlying decision is fuzzier than one might think.

> **FYI** Careful readers will have noticed that the final clause of paragraph (A)—"otherwise not in accordance with law"—fits linguistically more naturally with paragraphs (B), (C), and (D). Although the first two terms in particular, "arbitrary and capricious," are usually thought of as single unit, one commentator has articulated the distinction among the first three terms of paragraph (A) as follows: "Capriciousness seems to be a lesser included element of arbitrariness. It is action made arbitrary because it is based solely on whim. Abuse of discretion often refers, not to review of true discretion, but to weak review of judgments and hence often refers to review identical to that of arbitrariness." Charles H. Koch, Jr. and Richard Murphy, Administrative Law and Practice sec. 9.25 at n.3 (3d ed. Feb. 2022 update).

B. *Vermont Yankee v. Natural Resources Defense Council*

During the late 1960s and 1970s, the federal courts of appeals, including in particular the D.C. Circuit, used judicial review, usually under the guise of "arbitrary and capricious" review, to engage in what came to be called "hard look review": reviewing the agency decision to ensure that the agency took a "hard look" at the issues before it, and engaged in "reasoned decision-making" to come to its conclusion. *See, e.g., National Tire Dealers & Retreaders Ass'n, Inc. v. Brinegar*, 491 F.2d 31 (D.C. Cir. 1974). Over time, the phrase "hard look review" also came to mean that courts would themselves take a "hard look" at the underlying substance of the agency's decision. Then, in 1978, in *Vermont Yankee Nuclear Power Corp. v. Natural Resources Defense Council, Inc.*, 435 U.S. 519 (1978), the Supreme Court seemed to indicate that courts should take a more hands-off attitude towards judicial review of agency action. In *Vermont Yankee*, the Court reviewed the process by which the Atomic Energy Commission had developed a rule concerning the reprocessing of spent nuclear fuel. The D.C. Circuit had overturned the rule as arbitrary and capricious on the basis that the rulemaking process was inadequate "to ventilate the issues" surrounding questions of nuclear safety. The Supreme Court reversed, concluding that as long as the agency had complied with the APA's statutorily prescribed rulemaking processes, it was beyond the reviewing court's authority to impose its own view of the desired procedures. In other words, the APA establishes the *procedures* (the minimum *and* maximum procedures) an agency must follow, and courts are not to impose more.

C. *Motor Vehicle Manufacturers Association v. State Farm*

Vermont Yankee was initially perceived as signaling that the Supreme Court might be prepared to grant agencies quite a bit of deference under "arbitrary and capricious" review. But only five years later, the Court in the following case conducted a somewhat more searching review of agency rulemaking proceedings before invalidating the resulting rule under the "arbitrary and capricious" standard. The case, *Motor Vehicle Manufacturers Association v. State Farm Mutual Automobile Insurance Company*, is now viewed as a paradigmatic example of a court ensuring that an agency engaged in "reasoned decision-making" under the "arbitrary and capricious" standard.

Motor Vehicle Manufacturers Association v. State Farm Mutual Automobile Insurance Co.
463 U.S. 29 (1983)

Justice White delivered the opinion of the Court.

The development of the automobile gave Americans unprecedented freedom to travel, but exacted a high price for enhanced mobility. Since 1929, motor vehicles have been the leading cause of accidental deaths and injuries in the United States. In 1982, 46,300 Americans died in motor vehicle accidents and hundreds of thousands more were maimed and injured. While a consensus exists that the current loss of life on our highways is unacceptably high, improving safety does not admit to easy solution. In 1966, Congress decided that at least part of the answer lies in improving the design and safety features of the vehicle itself. But much of the technology for building safer cars was undeveloped or untested. Before changes in automobile design could be mandated, the effectiveness of these changes had to be studied, their costs examined, and public acceptance considered. This task called for considerable expertise and Congress responded by enacting the National Traffic and Motor Vehicle Safety Act of 1966 (Act), 80 Stat. 718, as amended, 15 U.S.C. 1381 et seq. (1976 ed. and Supp. V). The Act, created for the purpose of "reduc[ing] traffic accidents and deaths and injuries to persons resulting from traffic accidents," 15 U.S.C. 1381, directs the Secretary of Transportation or his delegate to issue motor vehicle safety standards that "shall be practicable, shall meet the need for motor vehicle safety, and shall be stated in objective terms." 15 U.S.C. 1392(a) (1976 ed., Supp. V). In issuing these standards, the Secretary is directed to consider "relevant available motor vehicle safety data," whether the proposed standard "is reasonable, practicable and appropriate" for the particular type of motor vehicle, and the "extent to which such standards will contribute to carrying out the purposes" of the Act. 15 U.S.C. 1392(f)(1), (3), (4).

The Act also authorizes judicial review under the provisions of the Administrative Procedure Act (APA) of all "orders establishing, amending, or revoking a Federal motor vehicle safety standard," 15 U.S.C. 1392(b). Under this authority, we review today whether NHTSA acted arbitrarily and capriciously in revoking the requirement in Motor Vehicle Safety Standard 208 that new motor vehicles produced after September 1982 be equipped with passive restraints to protect the safety of the occupants of the vehicle in the event of a collision. Briefly summarized, we hold that the agency failed to present an adequate basis and explanation for rescinding the passive restraint requirement and that the agency must either consider the matter further or adhere to or amend Standard 208 along lines which its analysis supports.

I

The regulation whose rescission is at issue bears a complex and convoluted history. Over the course of approximately 60 rulemaking notices, the requirement has been imposed, amended, rescinded, reimposed, and now rescinded again.

As originally issued by the Department of Transportation in 1967, Standard 208 simply required the installation of seatbelts in all automobiles. It soon became apparent that the level of seatbelt use was too low to reduce traffic injuries to an acceptable level. The Department therefore began consideration of "passive occupant restraint systems"—devices that do not depend for their effectiveness upon any action taken by the occupant except that necessary to operate the vehicle. Two types of automatic crash protection emerged: automatic seatbelts and airbags. The automatic seatbelt is a traditional safety belt, which when fastened to the interior of the door remains attached without impeding entry or exit from the vehicle, and deploys automatically without any action on the part of the passenger. The airbag is an inflatable device concealed in the dashboard and steering column. It automatically inflates when a sensor indicates that deceleration forces from an accident have exceeded a preset minimum, then rapidly deflates to dissipate those forces. The lifesaving potential of these devices was immediately recognized, and in 1977, after substantial on-the-road experience with both devices, it was estimated by NHTSA that passive restraints could prevent approximately 12,000 deaths and over 100,000 serious injuries annually.

In 1969, the Department formally proposed a standard requiring the installation of passive restraints, thereby commencing a lengthy series of proceedings. In 1970, the agency revised Standard 208 to include passive protection requirements, and in 1972, the agency amended the Standard to require full passive protection for all front seat occupants of vehicles manufactured after August 15, 1975. In the interim, vehicles built between August 1973 and August 1975 were to carry either passive restraints or lap and shoulder belts coupled with an "ignition interlock" that would prevent starting the vehicle if the belts were not connected. On review, the agency's decision to require passive restraints was found to be supported by "substantial evidence" and upheld.

In preparing for the upcoming model year, most car makers chose the "ignition interlock" option, a decision which was highly unpopular, and led Congress to amend the Act to prohibit a motor vehicle safety standard from requiring or permitting compliance by means of an ignition interlock or a continuous buzzer designed to indicate that safety belts were not in use. The 1974 Amendments also provided that any safety standard that could be satisfied by a system other than seatbelts would have to be submitted to Congress where it could be vetoed by concurrent resolution of both Houses. 15 U.S.C. 1410b(b)(2).

> This provision in the statute is an example of a legislative veto. Recall from Chapter 29 that the Court held legislative vetoes unconstitutional in *I.N.S. v. Chadha*, 462 U.S. 919 (1983). Interestingly enough, the Court decided *Chadha* one day before this case.

The effective date for mandatory passive restraint systems was extended for a year until August 31, 1976. But in June 1976, Secretary of Transportation William T. Coleman, Jr., initiated a new rulemaking on the issue. After hearing testimony and reviewing written comments, Coleman extended the optional alternatives indefinitely and suspended the passive restraint requirement. Although he found passive restraints technologically and economically feasible, the Secretary based his decision on the expectation that there would be widespread public resistance to the new systems. He instead proposed a demonstration project involving up to 500,000 cars installed with passive restraints, in order to smooth the way for public acceptance of mandatory passive restraints at a later date.

Coleman's successor as Secretary of Transportation disagreed. Within months of assuming office, Secretary Brock Adams decided that the demonstration project was unnecessary. He issued a new mandatory passive restraint regulation, known as Modified Standard 208. The Modified Standard mandated the phasing in of passive restraints beginning with large cars in model year 1982 and extending to all cars by model year 1984. The two principal systems that would satisfy the Standard were airbags and passive belts; the choice of which system to install was left to the manufacturers. In *Pacific Legal Foundation v. Department of Transportation*, 193 U.S. App. D.C. 184, 593 F.2d 1338, *cert. denied*, 444 U.S. 830 (1979), the Court of Appeals upheld Modified Standard 208 as a rational, nonarbitrary regulation consistent with the agency's mandate under the Act. The Standard also survived scrutiny by Congress, which did not exercise its authority under the legislative veto provision of the 1974 Amendments.

Over the next several years, the automobile industry geared up to comply with Modified Standard 208. * * * In February 1981, however, Secretary of Transportation Andrew Lewis reopened the rulemaking due to changed economic circumstances and, in particular, the difficulties of the automobile industry. Two months later, the agency ordered a one-year delay in the application of the Standard to large cars, extending the deadline to September 1982, and at the same time, proposed the possible rescission of the entire Standard. After receiving written comments and holding public hearings, NHTSA issued a final rule (Notice 25) that rescinded the passive restraint requirement contained in Modified Standard 208.

II

In a statement explaining the rescission, NHTSA maintained that it was no longer able to find, as it had in 1977, that the automatic restraint requirement would produce significant safety benefits. This judgment reflected not a change of opinion on the effectiveness of the technology, but a change in plans by the automobile industry. In 1977, the agency had assumed that airbags would be installed in 60% of all new cars and automatic seatbelts in 40%. By 1981 it became apparent that automobile manufacturers planned to install the automatic seatbelts in approximately 99% of the new cars. For this reason, the lifesaving potential of airbags would not be realized. Moreover, it now appeared that the overwhelming majority of passive belts planned to be installed by manufacturers could be detached easily and left that way permanently. Passive belts, once detached, then required "the same type of affirmative action that is the stumbling block to obtaining high usage levels of manual belts." For this reason, the agency concluded that there was no longer a basis for reliably predicting that the Standard would lead to any significant increased usage of restraints at all.

In view of the possibly minimal safety benefits, the automatic restraint requirement no longer was reasonable or practicable in the agency's view. The requirement would require approximately $1 billion to implement and the agency did not believe it would be reasonable to impose such substantial costs on manufacturers and consumers without more adequate assurance that sufficient safety benefits would accrue. In addition, NHTSA concluded that automatic restraints might have an adverse effect on the public's attitude toward safety. Given the high expense and limited benefits of detachable belts, NHTSA feared that many consumers would regard the Standard as an instance of ineffective regulation, adversely affecting the public's view of safety regulation and, in particular, "poisoning . . . popular sentiment toward efforts to improve occupant restraint systems in the future."

State Farm Mutual Automobile Insurance Co. and the National Association of Independent Insurers filed petitions for review of NHTSA's rescission of the passive restraint Standard. The United States Court of Appeals for the District of Columbia Circuit held that the agency's rescission of the passive restraint requirement was arbitrary and capricious. * * *

> Why are insurers challenging NHTSA's action in this case? What is the insurers' interest in opposing the agency's decision to rescind the passive-restraint requirement?

DIY
Reviewing Agency Decisionmaking Processes

Before continuing, pause here for a moment, and ask yourself:

"What might be wrong with the agency's decision-making process?"

Take two minutes to think about this and to write down your thoughts.

III

* * * The scope of review under the "arbitrary and capricious" standard is narrow and a court is not to substitute its judgment for that of the agency. Nevertheless, the agency must examine the relevant data and articulate a satisfactory explanation for its action including a "rational connection between the facts found and the choice made." *Burlington Truck Lines, Inc. v. United States*, 371 U.S. 156, 168 (1962). In reviewing that explanation, we must "consider whether the decision was based on a consideration of the relevant factors and whether there has been a clear error of judgment."

> **!** Here, the Court identifies four ways in which an agency rule might "normally" be arbitrary and capricious.

Normally, an agency rule would be arbitrary and capricious if the agency has relied on factors which Congress has not intended it to consider, entirely failed to consider an important aspect of the problem, offered an explanation for its decision that runs counter to the evidence before the agency, or is so implausible that it could not be ascribed to a difference in view or the product of agency expertise. The reviewing court should not attempt itself to make up for such deficiencies; we may not supply a reasoned basis for the agency's action that the agency itself has not given. *SEC v. Chenery Corp.*, 332 U.S. 194, 196 (1947). We will, however, "uphold a decision of less than ideal clarity if the agency's path may reasonably be discerned." *Bowman Transportation, Inc. v. Arkansas-Best Freight System, Inc.*, supra, at 286. * * *

V

The ultimate question before us is whether NHTSA's rescission of the passive restraint requirement of Standard 208 was arbitrary and capricious. * * *

A.

The first and most obvious reason for finding the rescission arbitrary and capricious is that NHTSA apparently gave no consideration whatever to modifying the Standard to require that airbag technology be utilized. Standard 208 sought to achieve automatic crash protection by requiring automobile manufacturers to install either of two passive restraint devices: airbags or automatic seatbelts. There was no suggestion in the long rule-making process that led to Standard 208 that if only one of these options were feasible, no passive restraint standard should be promulgated. Indeed, the agency's original proposed Standard contemplated the installation of inflatable restraints in all cars. Automatic belts were added as a means of complying with the Standard because they were believed to be as effective as airbags in achieving the goal of occupant crash protection. At that time, the passive belt approved by the agency could not be detached. Only later, at a manufacturer's behest, did the agency approve of the detachability feature—and only after assurances that the feature would not compromise the safety benefits of the restraint. Although it was then foreseen that 60% of the new cars would contain airbags and 40% would have automatic seatbelts, the ratio between the two was not significant as long as the passive belt would also assure greater passenger safety.

The agency has now determined that the detachable automatic belts will not attain anticipated safety benefits because so many individuals will detach the mechanism. Even if this conclusion were acceptable in its entirety, standing alone it would not justify any more than an amendment of Standard 208 to disallow compliance by means of the one technology which will not provide effective passenger protection. It does not cast doubt on the need for a passive restraint standard or upon the efficacy of airbag technology. In its most recent rulemaking, the agency again acknowledged the lifesaving potential of the airbag. * * *

Given the effectiveness ascribed to airbag technology by the agency, the mandate of the Act to achieve traffic safety would suggest that the logical response to the faults of detachable seatbelts would be to require the installation of airbags. At the very least this alternative way of achieving the objectives of the Act should have been addressed and adequate reasons given for its abandonment. But the agency not only did not require compliance through airbags, it also did not even consider the possibility in its 1981 rulemaking. Not one sentence of its rulemaking statement discusses the airbags-only option. Because, as the Court of Appeals stated, "NHTSA's . . . analysis of airbags was nonexistent," what we said in *Burlington Truck Lines, Inc. v. United States*, 371 U.S., at 167, is apropos here:

> There are no findings and no analysis here to justify the choice made, no indication of the basis on which the [agency] exercised its expert discretion. We are not prepared to and the Administrative Procedure Act will not permit us to accept such . . . prac-

> Notice the Court's reference to agency expertise. How is agency expertise connected to the Court's rationale for invalidating NHTSA's rescission of the passive-restraint requirement?

tice. . . . Expert discretion is the lifeblood of the administrative process, but 'unless we make the requirements for administrative action strict and demanding, expertise, the strength of modern government, can become a monster which rules with no practical limits on its discretion.' *New York v. United States*, 342 U.S. 882, 884 (dissenting opinion) (footnote omitted).

We have frequently reiterated that an agency must cogently explain why it has exercised its discretion in a given manner, and we reaffirm this principle again today.

The automobile industry has opted for the passive belt over the airbag, but surely it is not enough that the regulated industry has eschewed a given safety device. For nearly a decade, the automobile industry waged the regulatory equivalent of war against the airbag and lost—the inflatable restraint was proved sufficiently effective. Now the automobile industry has decided to employ

> How does this argument about the industry's response to the regulation relate to the "capture theory" of agency behavior?

a seatbelt system which will not meet the safety objectives of Standard 208. This hardly constitutes cause to revoke the Standard itself. Indeed, the Act was necessary because the industry was not sufficiently responsive to safety concerns. The Act intended that safety standards not depend on current technology and could be "technology-forcing" in the sense of inducing the development of superior safety design. If, under the statute, the agency should not defer to the industry's failure to develop safer cars, which it surely should not do, a fortiori it may not revoke a safety standard which can be satisfied by current technology simply because the industry has opted for an ineffective seatbelt design.

Although the agency did not address the mandatory airbag option and the Court of Appeals noted that "airbags seem to have none of the problems that NHTSA identified in passive seatbelts," petitioners recite a number of difficulties that they believe would be posed by a mandatory airbag standard. These range from questions concerning the installation of airbags in small cars to that of adverse public reaction. But these are not the agency's reasons for rejecting a mandatory airbag standard. Not having discussed the possibility, the agency submitted no reasons at all. The short—and sufficient—answer to petitioners' submission is that the courts may not accept appellate counsel's post hoc rationalizations for agency action. It is well established that an agency's action must be upheld, if at all, on the basis articulated by the agency itself.

Petitioners also invoke our decision in *Vermont Yankee Nuclear Power Corp. v. Natural Resources Defense Council, Inc.*, 435 U.S. 519 (1978), as though it were a talisman under which any agency decision is by definition unimpeachable. Specifically, it is submitted that to require an agency to consider an airbags-only alternative is, in essence, to dictate to the agency the procedures it is to follow. Petitioners both misread *Vermont Yankee* and misconstrue the nature of the remand that is in order. In *Vermont Yankee*, we held that a court may not impose additional procedural requirements upon an agency. We do not require today any specific procedures which NHTSA must

The Court makes clear that it is unwilling to entertain arguments that were not discussed by the agency in its rulemaking process. So, the determination of whether an agency action was arbitrary and capricious is based on the articulation the agency gave for its decision at the time it made that decision. This idea, as you may recall, derives from the so-called *Chenery I* doctrine.

Why do you think the Court is insisting on this? What is the point of a doctrine that insists that the agency, rather than its lawyers during litigation, determine the reasons for an agency's decisions? As you try to answer this question, think about the role the Court sees itself playing in the process of administrative decisionmaking.

follow. Nor do we broadly require an agency to consider all policy alternatives in reaching decision. It is true that rulemaking "cannot be found wanting simply because the agency failed to include every alternative device and thought conceivable by the mind of man . . . regardless of how uncommon or unknown that alternative may have been. . . ." *Id.*, at 551. But the airbag is more than a policy alternative to the passive restraint Standard; it is a technological alternative within the ambit of the existing Standard. We hold only that given the judgment made in 1977 that airbags are an effective and cost-beneficial life-saving technology, the mandatory passive restraint rule may not be abandoned without any consideration whatsoever of an airbags-only requirement.

B.

* * * Although the issue is closer, we also find that the agency was too quick to dismiss the safety benefits of automatic seatbelts. NHTSA's critical finding was that, in light of the industry's plans to install readily detachable passive belts, it could not reliably predict "even a 5 percentage point increase as the minimum level of expected usage increase." The Court of Appeals rejected this finding because there is "not one iota" of evidence that Modified Standard 208 will fail to increase nationwide seatbelt use by at least 13 percentage points, the level of increased usage necessary for the Standard to justify its cost. Given the lack of probative evidence, the court held that "only a well justified refusal to seek more evidence could render rescission non-arbitrary."

Petitioners object to this conclusion. In their view, "substantial uncertainty" that a regulation will accomplish its intended purpose is sufficient reason, without more, to rescind a regulation. We agree with petitioners that just as an agency reasonably may decline to issue a safety standard if it is uncertain about its efficacy, an agency may also revoke a standard on the basis of serious uncertainties if supported by the record and reasonably explained. Rescission of the passive restraint requirement would not be arbitrary and capricious simply because there was no evidence in direct support of the agency's conclusion. It is not infrequent that the available data do not settle a regulatory issue, and the agency must then exercise its judgment in moving from the facts and probabilities on the record to a policy conclusion. Recognizing that policymaking in a complex society must account for uncertainty, however, does not imply that it is sufficient for an agency to merely recite the terms "substantial uncertainty" as a justification for its actions. As previously noted, the agency must explain the evidence which is available, and must offer a "rational connection between the facts found and the choice made." Generally, one aspect of that explanation would be a justification for rescinding the regulation before engaging in a search for further evidence.

In these cases, the agency's explanation for rescission of the passive restraint requirement is not sufficient to enable us to conclude that the rescission was the product of reasoned decisionmaking. To reach this conclusion, we do not upset the agency's view of the facts, but we do appreciate the limitations of this record in supporting the agency's decision. * * *

The agency also failed to offer any explanation why a continuous passive belt would engender the same adverse public reaction as the ignition interlock, and, as the Court of Appeals concluded, "every indication in the record points the other way." We see no basis for equating the two devices: the continuous belt, unlike the ignition interlock, does not interfere with the operation of the vehicle. More importantly, it is the agency's responsibility, not this Court's, to explain its decision.

VI

"An agency's view of what is in the public interest may change, either with or without a change in circumstances. But an agency changing its course must supply a reasoned analysis . . . ." *Greater Boston Television Corp. v. FCC*, 143 U.S. App. D.C. 383, 394, 444 F.2d 841, 852 (1970) (footnote omitted), cert. denied, 403 U.S. 923 (1971). We do not accept all of the reasoning of the Court of Appeals but we do conclude that the agency has failed to supply the requisite "reasoned analysis" in this case. Accordingly, we vacate the judgment of the Court of Appeals and remand the cases to that court with directions to remand the matter to the NHTSA for further consideration consistent with this opinion.

JUSTICE REHNQUIST, with whom THE CHIEF JUSTICE, JUSTICE POWELL, and JUSTICE O'CONNOR join, concurring in part and dissenting in part.

I join parts I, II, III, IV, and V–A of the Court's opinion. In particular, I agree that, since the airbag and continuous spool automatic seatbelt were explicitly approved in the standard the agency was rescinding, the agency should explain why it declined to leave those requirements intact. In this case, the agency gave no explanation at all. Of course, if the agency can provide a rational explanation, it may adhere to its decision to rescind the entire standard.

I do not believe, however, that NHTSA's view of detachable automatic seatbelts was arbitrary and capricious. The agency adequately explained its decision to rescind the standard insofar as it was satisfied by detachable belts.

* * * The agency chose not to rely on a study showing a substantial increase in seatbelt usage in cars equipped with automatic seatbelts *and* an ignition interlock to prevent the car from being operated when the belts were not in place *and* which were voluntarily purchased with this equipment by consumers. It is reasonable for the agency to decide that this study does not support any conclusion concerning the effect of automatic seatbelts that are installed in all cars whether the consumer wants them or not and are not linked to an ignition interlock system.

* * * It seems to me that the agency's explanation, while by no means a model, is adequate. The agency acknowledged that there would probably be some increase in belt usage, but concluded that the increase would be small and not worth the cost of mandatory detachable automatic belts. The agency's obligation is to articulate a "rational connection between the facts found and the choice made." I believe it has met this standard.

* * *

The agency's changed view of the standard seems to be related to the election of a new President of a different political party. It is readily apparent that the responsible members of one administration may consider public resistance and uncertainties to be more important than do their counterparts in a previous administration. A change in administration brought about by the people casting their votes is a perfectly reasonable basis for an executive agency's reappraisal of the costs and benefits of its programs and regulations. As long as the agency remains within the bounds established by Congress, it is entitled to assess administrative records and evaluate priorities in light of the philosophy of the administration.

NOTES & QUESTIONS

1. Part I of the Court's opinion discusses the "complex and convoluted history" of Standard 208. Why do you think the regulation went through so many iterations over so many years? Look carefully at when each of the changes took place and note who was President at the time. Does that help explain what happened? If so, does that support the view that NHTSA was politically accountable? Is there a tension here between the agency's expertise and the agency's political accountability? Relatedly, is the political accountability in this case a good thing? Or not? What might the majority say? What about Justice Rehnquist's partial dissent?

2. Why did the court find that the agency's conduct in this case was "arbitrary and capricious"? What exactly did the agency do wrong? Did the agency fail to follow some procedure that the Court thought it should follow? Or was the Court questioning the underlying substance of the agency's decision to rescind the passive-restraint requirement? Most

scholars view *State Farm* as a re-affirmation of "hard look" judicial review, a variation of what the D.C. Circuit was often doing in the 1970s.

3.   Notice that the Court requires the agency to supply a "reasoned analysis," to provide a "rational connection between the facts found and the choice made," and to engage in "reasoned decision-making." How are these ideas about "reason[ ]" and "rational[ity]" connected to the idea of "arbitrary and capricious" behavior? One scholar has argued that an agency that based a decision on astrological charts would be acting "arbitrarily." Even if there were facts to support the agency's decision and even if the agency followed all the APA-mandated procedures (in, for example, 5 U.S.C. § 553), an agency that consulted astrological charts to make its decision would, in this view, be subject to reversal by a court for being "arbitrary and capricious." *See* Gary Lawson, *Outcome, Procedures, and Process: Agency Duties of Explanation for Legal Conclusions,* 48 RUTGERS L. REV. 313, 318–19 (1996).

4.   Relatedly, does the *State Farm* case seem like a case about the agency's "procedures" in any way? One way to think of the word "procedure" or "process" is, as we often see in law, as a contrast to "substance." But, in *State Farm,* the Court pretty clearly engaged, at some level, with the substance of NHTSA's decision, didn't it? Another way to think of "procedure" is as the agency's *decision-making* or *reasoning* process (i.e., the reasoning the agency used to come to its conclusion), as opposed to the tangible *procedures* it used (e.g., whether it properly published a notice of its proposed rule or gave the public enough time to provide comments)? *See, e.g., FCC v. Fox Television Stns., Inc.,* 556 U.S. 502, 548 (2009) (BREYER, J., dissenting) (noting that "it is not so much a particular set of substantive commands but rather it is a *process,* a process of learning through reasoned argument, that is the antithesis of the 'arbitrary' ").

D. *State Farm* Applied: *DHS v. Regents of the University of California*

Now consider a more recent case, in which once again the Supreme Court is invalidating agency action because it found the agency action to have been "arbitrary and capricious." As you will see, the Court concludes that the Secretary of Homeland Security, in seeking to rescind, in 2017, the immigration program started in 2012 known as DACA, made precisely the same mistake as NHTSA did in the *State Farm* case. But the factual scenario in this case is quite different from *State Farm*. Moreover, in contrast to *State Farm*, the agency action here is not even a regulation.

Department of Homeland Security v. Regents of the University of California
140 S. Ct. 1891 (2020)

CHIEF JUSTICE ROBERTS **delivered the opinion of the Court, except as to Part IV.**

In the summer of 2012, the Department of Homeland Security (DHS) announced an immigration program known as Deferred Action for Childhood Arrivals, or DACA. That program allows certain unauthorized aliens who entered the United States as children to apply for a two-year forbearance of removal. Those granted such relief are also eligible for work authorization and various federal benefits. Some 700,000 aliens have availed themselves of this opportunity.

Five years later, the Attorney General advised DHS to rescind DACA, based on his conclusion that it was unlawful. The Department's Acting Secretary issued a memorandum terminating the program on that basis. The termination was challenged by affected individuals and third parties who alleged, among other things, that the Acting Secretary had violated the Administrative Procedure Act (APA) by failing to adequately address important factors bearing on her decision. For the reasons that follow, we conclude that the Acting Secretary did violate the APA, and that the rescission must be vacated.

I

A

In June 2012, the Secretary of Homeland Security issued a memorandum announcing an immigration relief program for "certain young people who were brought to this country as children." Known as DACA, the program applies to childhood arrivals who were under age 31 in 2012; have continuously resided here since 2007; are current students, have completed high school, or are honorably discharged veterans; have not been convicted of any serious crimes; and do not threaten national security or public safety. DHS concluded that individuals who meet these criteria warrant favorable treatment under the immigration laws because they "lacked the intent to violate the law," are "productive" contributors to our society, and "know only this country as home."

[T]he DACA Memorandum instructs Immigration and Customs Enforcement to "exercise prosecutorial discretion[ ] on an individual basis . . . by deferring action for a period of two years, subject to renewal." In addition, it directs U.S. Citizenship and Immigration Services (USCIS) to "accept applications to determine whether these individuals qualify for work authorization during this period of deferred action," as permitted under regulations long predating DACA's creation. Pursuant to other regulations, deferred action recipients are considered "lawfully present" for purposes of, and therefore eligible to receive, Social Security and Medicare benefits.

In November 2014, two years after DACA was promulgated, DHS issued a memorandum announcing that it would expand DACA eligibility by removing the age cap, shifting the date-of-entry requirement from 2007 to 2010, and extending the deferred action and work authorization period to three years. In the same memorandum, DHS created a new, related program known as Deferred Action for Parents of Americans and Lawful Permanent Residents, or DAPA. That program would have authorized deferred action for up to 4.3 million parents whose children were U. S. citizens or lawful permanent residents. These parents were to enjoy the same forbearance, work eligibility, and other benefits as DACA recipients.

Before the DAPA Memorandum was implemented, 26 States, led by Texas, filed suit in the Southern District of Texas. The States contended that DAPA and the DACA expansion violated the APA's notice and comment requirement, the Immigration and Nationality Act (INA), and the Executive's duty under the Take Care Clause of the Constitution. The District Court found that the States were likely to succeed on the merits of at least one of their claims and entered a nationwide preliminary injunction barring implementation of both DAPA and the DACA expansion.

A divided panel of the Court of Appeals for the Fifth Circuit affirmed the preliminary injunction. This Court affirmed the Fifth Circuit's judgment by an equally divided vote, which meant that no opinion was issued. For the next year, litigation over DAPA and the DACA expansion continued in the Southern District of Texas, while implementation of those policies remained enjoined.

Then, in June 2017, following a change in Presidential administrations, DHS rescinded the DAPA Memorandum. In explaining that decision, DHS cited the preliminary injunction and ongoing litigation in Texas, the fact that DAPA had never taken effect, and the new administration's immigration enforcement priorities.

Three months later, in September 2017, Attorney General Jefferson B. Sessions III sent a letter to Acting Secretary of Homeland Security Elaine C. Duke, "advis[ing]" that DHS "should rescind" DACA as well. Citing the Fifth Circuit's opinion and this Court's equally divided affirmance, the Attorney General concluded that DACA shared the "same legal defects that the courts recognized as to DAPA" and was "likely" to meet a similar fate. "In light of the costs and burdens" that a rescission would "impose[ ] on DHS," the Attorney General urged DHS to "consider an orderly and efficient wind-down process."

The next day, Duke acted on the Attorney General's advice. In her decision memorandum Duke summarized the history of the DACA and DAPA programs, the Fifth Circuit opinion [invalidating DAPA] and ensuing affirmance, and the contents of the Attorney General's letter. "Taking into consideration the Supreme Court's and the Fifth Circuit's rulings" and the "letter from the Attorney General," she concluded that the "DACA program should be terminated."

Duke then detailed how the program would be wound down: No new applications would be accepted, but DHS would entertain applications for two-year renewals from DACA recipients whose benefits were set to expire within six months. For all other DACA recipients, previously issued grants of deferred action and work authorization would not be revoked but would expire on their own terms, with no prospect for renewal.

B

Within days of Acting Secretary Duke's rescission announcement, multiple groups of plaintiffs ranging from individual DACA recipients and States to the Regents of the University of California and the National Association for the Advancement of Colored People challenged her decision in [three] U.S. District Courts. * * * The relevant claim [is] that the rescission was arbitrary and capricious in violation of the APA. * * *

All three District Courts ruled for the plaintiffs, albeit at different stages of the proceedings. [T]he D.C. District Court * * * granted partial summary judgment to the plaintiffs on their APA claim, holding that Acting Secretary Duke's "conclusory statements were insufficient to explain the change in [the agency's] view of DACA's lawfulness." The District Court stayed its order for 90 days to permit DHS to "reissue a memorandum rescinding DACA, this time providing a fuller explanation for the determination that the program lacks statutory and constitutional authority."

Two months later, Duke's successor, Secretary Kirstjen M. Nielsen, responded via memorandum. She explained that, "[h]aving considered the Duke memorandum," she "decline[d] to disturb" the rescission. Secretary Nielsen went on to articulate her "understanding" of Duke's memorandum, identifying three reasons why, in Nielsen's estimation, "the decision to rescind the DACA policy was, and remains, sound." First, she reiterated that, "as the Attorney General concluded, the DACA policy was contrary to law." Second, she added that, regardless, the agency had "serious doubts about [DACA's] legality" and, for law enforcement reasons, wanted to avoid "legally questionable" policies. Third, she identified multiple policy reasons for rescinding DACA, including (1) the belief that any class-based immigration relief should come from Congress, not through executive non-enforcement; (2) DHS's preference for exercising prosecutorial discretion on "a truly individualized, case-by-case basis"; and (3) the importance of "project[ing] a message" that immigration laws would be enforced against all classes and categories of aliens. In her final paragraph, Secretary Nielsen acknowledged the "asserted reliance interests" in DACA's continuation but concluded that they did not "outweigh the questionable legality of the DACA policy and the other reasons" for the rescission discussed in her memorandum.

The Government asked the D.C. District Court to revise its prior order in light of the reasons provided by Secretary Nielsen, but the court declined. In the court's view, the new memorandum, which "fail[ed] to elaborate meaningfully" on the agency's illegality rationale, still did not provide an adequate explanation for the September 2017 rescission.[After the Ninth Circuit affirmed a nationwide injunction, and while appeals were pending in the Second and D.C. Circuits,] we granted the petitions and consolidated the cases for argument.

II

The dispute before the Court is not whether DHS may rescind DACA. All parties agree that it may. The dispute is instead primarily about the procedure the agency followed in doing so.

* * *

III

A

Deciding whether agency action was adequately explained requires, first, knowing where to look for the agency's explanation. The natural starting point here is the explanation provided by Acting Secretary Duke when she announced the rescission in September 2017. But the Government urges us to go on and consider the June 2018 memorandum submitted by Secretary Nielsen as well. That memo was prepared after the D.C. District Court vacated the Duke rescission and gave DHS an opportunity to "reissue a memorandum rescinding DACA, this time providing a fuller explanation for the determination that the program lacks statutory and constitutional authority." According to the Government, the Nielsen Memorandum is properly before us because it was invited by the District Court and reflects the views of the Secretary of Homeland Security—the official responsible for immigration policy. Respondents disagree, arguing that the Nielsen Memorandum, issued nine months after the rescission, impermissibly asserts prudential and policy reasons not relied upon by Duke.

It is a "foundational principle of administrative law" that judicial review of agency action is limited to "the grounds that the agency invoked when it took the action." If those grounds are inadequate, a court may remand for the agency to do one of two things: First, the agency can offer "a fuller explanation of the agency's reasoning *at the time of the agency action.*" This route has important limitations. When an agency's initial explanation "indicate[s] the determinative reason for the final action taken," the agency may elaborate later on that reason (or reasons) but may not provide new ones. Alternatively, the agency can "deal with the problem afresh" by taking *new* agency action. An agency taking this route is not limited to its prior reasons but must comply with the procedural requirements for new agency action.

The District Court's remand thus presented DHS with a choice: rest on the Duke Memorandum while elaborating on its prior reasoning, or issue a new rescission bolstered by new reasons absent from the Duke Memorandum. Secretary Nielsen took the first path. Rather than making a new decision, she "decline[d] to disturb the Duke memorandum's rescission" and instead "provide[d] further explanation" for that action. Indeed, the Government's subsequent request for reconsideration described the Nielsen Memorandum as "additional explanation for [Duke's] decision" and asked the District

Court to "leave in place [Duke's] September 5, 2017 decision to rescind the DACA policy." Contrary to the position of the Government before this Court, and of JUSTICE KAVANAUGH in dissent, the Nielsen Memorandum was by its own terms not a new rule implementing a new policy.

Because Secretary Nielsen chose to elaborate on the reasons for the initial rescission rather than take new administrative action, she was limited to the agency's original reasons, and her explanation "must be viewed critically" to ensure that the rescission is not upheld on the basis of impermissible "*post hoc* rationalization." But despite purporting to explain the Duke Memorandum, Secretary Nielsen's reasoning bears little relationship to that of her predecessor. Acting Secretary Duke rested the rescission on the conclusion that DACA is unlawful. Period. By contrast, Secretary Nielsen's new memorandum offered three "separate and independently sufficient reasons" for the rescission, only the first of which is the conclusion that DACA is illegal.

Her second reason is that DACA is, at minimum, legally *questionable* and should be terminated to maintain public confidence in the rule of law and avoid burdensome litigation. No such justification can be found in the Duke Memorandum. Legal uncertainty is, of course, related to illegality. But the two justifications are meaningfully distinct, especially in this context. While an agency might, for one reason or another, choose to do nothing in the face of uncertainty, illegality presumably requires remedial action of some sort.

The policy reasons that Secretary Nielsen cites as a third basis for the rescission are also nowhere to be found in the Duke Memorandum. That document makes no mention of a preference for legislative fixes, the superiority of case-by-case decisionmaking, the importance of sending a message of robust enforcement, or any other policy consideration. * * *

JUSTICE KAVANAUGH asserts that this "foundational principle of administrative law," actually limits only what lawyers may argue, not what agencies may do. While it is true that the Court has often rejected justifications belatedly advanced by advocates, we refer to this as a prohibition on *post hoc* rationalizations, not advocate rationalizations, because the problem is the timing, not the speaker. The functional reasons for requiring contemporaneous explanations apply with equal force regardless whether *post hoc* justifications are raised in court by those appearing on behalf of the agency or by agency officials themselves. * * *

The basic rule here is clear: An agency must defend its actions based on the reasons it gave when it acted. This is not the case for cutting corners to allow DHS to rely upon reasons absent from its original decision.

B

We turn, finally, to whether DHS's decision to rescind DACA was arbitrary and capricious. As noted earlier, Acting Secretary Duke's justification for the rescission was succinct: "Taking into consideration" the Fifth Circuit's conclusion that DAPA was unlawful because it conferred benefits in violation of the INA, and the Attorney General's conclusion that DACA was unlawful for the same reason, she concluded—without elaboration—that the "DACA program should be terminated."

Respondents maintain that this explanation is deficient for three reasons. Their first and second arguments work in tandem, claiming that the Duke Memorandum does not adequately explain the conclusion that DACA is unlawful, and that this conclusion is, in any event, wrong. While those arguments carried the day in the lower courts, in our view they overlook an important constraint on Acting Secretary Duke's decisionmaking authority—she was *bound* by the Attorney General's legal determination.

The same statutory provision that establishes the Secretary of Homeland Security's authority to administer and enforce immigration laws limits that authority, specifying that, with respect to "all questions of law," the determinations of the Attorney General "shall be controlling." 8 U.S.C. § 1103(a)(1). Respondents are aware of this constraint. Indeed they emphasized the point in the reviewability sections of their briefs. But in their merits arguments, respondents never addressed whether or how this unique statutory provision might affect our review. They did not discuss whether Duke was required to explain a legal conclusion that was not hers to make. Nor did they discuss whether the current suits challenging Duke's rescission decision, which everyone agrees was within her legal authority under the INA, are proper vehicles for attacking the Attorney General's legal conclusion.

Because of these gaps in respondents' briefing, we do not evaluate the claims challenging the explanation and correctness of the illegality conclusion. Instead we focus our attention on respondents' third argument—that Acting Secretary Duke "failed to consider . . . important aspect[s] of the problem" before her. *Motor Vehicle Mfrs. Assn. of United States, Inc. v. State Farm Mut. Automobile Ins. Co.*, 463 U.S. 29, 43, (1983).

Whether DACA is illegal is, of course, a legal determination, and therefore a question for the Attorney General. But deciding how best to address a finding of illegality moving forward can involve important policy choices, especially when the finding concerns a program with the breadth of DACA. Those policy choices are for DHS.

Acting Secretary Duke plainly exercised such discretionary authority in winding down the program. Among other things, she specified that those DACA recipients whose benefits were set to expire within six months were eligible for two-year renewals.

But Duke did not appear to appreciate the full scope of her discretion, which picked up where the Attorney General's legal reasoning left off. The Attorney General concluded that "the DACA policy has the same legal . . . defects that the courts recognized as to DAPA." So, to understand those defects, we look to the Fifth Circuit, the highest court to offer a reasoned opinion on the legality of DAPA. That court described the "core" issue before it as the "Secretary's decision" to grant "eligibility for benefits"—including work authorization, Social Security, and Medicare—to unauthorized aliens on "a class-wide basis." The Fifth Circuit's focus on these benefits was central to every stage of its analysis. And the Court ultimately held that DAPA was "manifestly contrary to the INA" precisely because it "would make 4.3 million otherwise removable aliens" eligible for work authorization and public benefits.

But there is more to DAPA (and DACA) than such benefits. The defining feature of deferred action is the decision to defer removal (and to notify the affected alien of that decision). And the Fifth Circuit was careful to distinguish that forbearance component from eligibility for benefits. As it explained, the "challenged portion of DAPA's deferred-action program" was the decision to make DAPA recipients eligible for benefits. The other "[p]art of DAPA," the court noted, "involve[d] the Secretary's decision—at least temporarily—not to enforce the immigration laws as to a class of what he deem[ed] to be low-priority illegal aliens." Borrowing from this Court's prior description of deferred action, the Fifth Circuit observed that "the states do not challenge the Secretary's decision to 'decline to institute proceedings, terminate proceedings, or decline to execute a final order of deportation.' " And the Fifth Circuit underscored that nothing in its decision or the pre-liminary injunction "requires the Secretary to remove any alien or to alter" the Secretary's class-based "enforcement priorities." In other words, the Secretary's forbearance authority was unimpaired.

Acting Secretary Duke recognized that the Fifth Circuit's holding addressed the benefits associated with DAPA. In her memorandum she explained that the Fifth Circuit concluded that DAPA "conflicted with the discretion authorized by Congress" because the INA " 'flatly does not permit the reclassification of millions of illegal aliens as lawfully present and thereby make them newly eligible for a host of federal and state benefits, including work authorization.' " Duke did not characterize the opinion as one about forbearance.

In short, the Attorney General neither addressed the forbearance policy at the heart of DACA nor compelled DHS to abandon that policy. Thus, removing benefits eligibility while continuing forbearance remained squarely within the discretion of Acting Secretary Duke, who was responsible for "[e]stablishing national immigration enforcement policies and priorities." 116 Stat. 2178, 6 U.S.C. § 202(5). But Duke's memo offers no reason for terminating forbearance. She instead treated the Attorney General's conclusion regarding the illegality of benefits as sufficient to rescind both benefits and forbearance, without explanation.

That reasoning repeated the error we identified in one of our leading modern administrative law cases [*State Farm*]. * * *

While the factual setting is different here, the error is the same. Even if it is illegal for DHS to extend work authorization and other benefits to DACA recipients, that conclusion supported only "disallow[ing]" benefits. It did "not cast doubt" on the legality of forbearance or upon DHS's original reasons for extending forbearance to childhood arrivals. Thus, given DHS's earlier judgment that forbearance is "especially justified" for "productive young people" who were brought here as children and "know only this country as home," the DACA Memorandum could not be rescinded in full "without any consideration whatsoever" of a forbearance-only policy.

* * * According to the Government, "It was not arbitrary and capricious for DHS to view deferred action and its collateral benefits as importantly linked." Perhaps. But that response misses the point. The fact that there may be a valid reason not to separate deferred action from benefits does not establish that DHS considered that option or that such consideration was unnecessary.

* * * Duke also failed to address whether there was "legitimate reliance" on the DACA Memorandum. When an agency changes course, as DHS did here, it must "be cognizant that longstanding policies may have 'engendered

serious reliance interests that must be taken into account.' " It would be arbitrary and capricious to ignore such matters." Yet that is what the Duke Memorandum did.

For its part, the Government does not contend that Duke considered potential reliance interests; it counters that she did not need to. In the Government's view, shared by the lead dissent, DACA recipients have no "legally cognizable reliance interests" because the DACA Memorandum stated that the program "conferred no substantive rights" and provided benefits only in two-year increments. But neither the Government nor the lead dissent cites any legal authority establishing that such features automatically preclude reliance interests, and we are not aware of any. These disclaimers are surely pertinent in considering the strength of any reliance interests, but that consideration must be undertaken by the agency in the first instance, subject to normal APA review. There was no such consideration in the Duke Memorandum.

* * * DHS could respond that reliance on forbearance and benefits was unjustified in light of the express limitations in the DACA Memorandum. Or it might conclude that reliance interests in benefits that it views as unlaw-ful are entitled to no or diminished weight. And, even if DHS ultimately concludes that the reliance interests rank as serious, they are but one factor to consider. DHS may determine, in the particular context before it, that other interests and policy concerns outweigh any reliance interests. Making that difficult decision was the agency's job, but the agency failed to do it. * * *

Had Duke considered reliance interests, she might, for example, have con-sidered a broader renewal period based on the need for DACA recipients to reorder their affairs. Alternatively, Duke might have considered more accommodating termination dates for recipients caught in the middle of a time-bounded commitment, to allow them to, say, graduate from their course of study, complete their military service, or finish a medical treat-ment regimen. Or she might have instructed immigration officials to give salient weight to any reliance interests engendered by DACA when exercising individualized enforcement discretion.

To be clear, DHS was not required to do any of this or to "consider all policy alternatives in reaching [its] decision." *State Farm*, 463 U.S. at 51. Agencies are not compelled to explore "every alternative device and thought conceivable by the mind of man." But, because DHS was "not writing on a blank slate," *post*, at 1929, n. 14 (opinion of THOMAS, J.), it *was* required to assess whether there were reliance interests, determine whether they were significant, and weigh any such interests against competing policy concerns.

* * *

We do not decide whether DACA or its rescission are sound policies. "The wisdom" of those decisions "is none of our concern." *Chenery II*, 332 U.S. at 207. We address only whether the agency complied with the procedural requirement that it provide a reasoned explanation for its action. Here the agency failed to consider the conspicuous issues of whether to retain forbearance and what if anything to do about the hardship to DACA recipients. That dual failure raises doubts about whether the agency appreciated the scope of its discretion or exercised that discretion in a reasonable manner. The appropriate recourse is therefore to remand to DHS so that it may consider the problem anew.

It is so ordered.

JUSTICE THOMAS, with whom JUSTICE ALITO and JUSTICE GORSCH join, concurring in the judgment in part and dissenting in part. * * *

* * *

II

" '[A]n agency literally has no power to act . . . unless and until Congress confers power upon it.' " *Arlington v. FCC*, 569 U.S. 290, 317 (2013) (ROBERTS, C.J., dissenting) (quoting *Louisiana Pub. Serv. Comm'n v. FCC*, 476 U.S. 355, 374 (1986)). When an agency exercises power beyond the bounds of its authority, it acts unlawfully. The 2012 memorandum creating DACA provides a poignant illustration of *ultra vires* agency action.

> **!** *Ultra vires* is a Latin term meaning "beyond one's power or authority."

DACA alters how the immigration laws apply to a certain class of aliens. * * * DACA in effect created a new exception to the statutory provisions governing removability and, in the process, conferred lawful presence on an entire class of aliens.

To lawfully implement such changes, DHS needed a grant of authority from Congress to either reclassify removable DACA recipients as lawfully present, or to exempt the entire class of aliens covered by DACA from statutory removal procedures. No party disputes that the immigration statutes lack an express delegation to accomplish either result. And, an examination of the highly reticulated immigration regime makes clear that DHS has no implicit discretion to create new classes of lawful presence or to grant relief from removal out of whole cloth. Accordingly, DACA is substantively unlawful.

This conclusion should begin and end our review. The decision to rescind an unlawful agency action is *per se* lawful. No additional policy justifications or considerations are necessary. And, the majority's contrary holding—that an agency is not only permitted, but required, to continue an ultra vires action—has no basis in law. * * *

* * *

IV

Even if I were to accept the majority's premise that DACA's rescission required additional policy justifications, the majority's reasons for setting aside the agency's decision still fail.

A

[The majority] cites no authority for the proposition that arbitrary and capricious review *requires* an agency to dissect an unlawful program piece by piece, scrutinizing each separate element to determine whether it would independently violate the law, rather than just to rescind the entire program.

The then-Attorney General reviewed the thorough decisions of the District Court and the Fifth Circuit. Those courts exhaustively examined the INA's text and structure, the relevant provisions of other federal immigration statutes, the historical practice of deferred action, and the general grants of statutory authority to set immigration policy. Both decisions concluded that DAPA and expanded DACA violated the carefully crafted federal immigration scheme, that such violations could not be justified through reference to past exercises of deferred action, and that the general grants of statutory authority did not give DHS the power to enact such a sweeping nonenforcement program. Based on the reasoning of those decisions, then-Attorney General Sessions concluded that DACA was likewise implemented without statutory authority. He directed DHS to restore the rule of law. DHS followed the then-Attorney General's legal analysis and rescinded the program. This legal conclusion more than suffices to supply the "reasoned analysis" necessary to rescind an unlawful program. *State Farm*, 463 U.S. at 42.

The majority has no answer except to suggest that this approach is inconsistent with *State Farm*. But in doing so, the majority ignores the fact that, unlike the typical "prior policy" contemplated by the Court in *State Farm*, DACA is unlawful. Neither *State Farm* nor any other decision cited by the majority addresses what an agency must do when it has inherited an unlawful program. It is perhaps for this reason that, rather than responding with authority of its own, the majority simply opts to excise the "unlawful policy" aspect from its discussion.

B

Second, the majority claims that DHS erred by failing to take into account the reliance interests of DACA recipients. But reliance interests are irrelevant when assessing whether to rescind an action that the agency lacked statutory authority to take. No amount of reliance could ever justify continuing a program that allows DHS to wield power that neither Congress nor the Constitution gave it.

Even if reliance interests were sometimes relevant when rescinding an ultra vires action, the rescission still would not be arbitrary and capricious here. Rather, as the majority does not dispute, the rescission is consistent with how deferred action has always worked. As a general matter, deferred action creates no rights—it exists at the Government's discretion and can be revoked at any time. . . . The Government has made clear time and again that, because "deferred action is not an immigration status, no alien has the right to deferred action. Thus, contrary to the majority's unsupported assertion, this longstanding administrative treatment of deferred action provides strong evidence and authority for the proposition that an agency need not consider reliance interests in this context.

* * *

President Trump's Acting Secretary of Homeland Security inherited a program created by President Obama's Secretary that was implemented without statutory authority and without following the APA's required procedures. Then-Attorney General Sessions correctly concluded that this *ultra vires* program should be rescinded. These cases could—and should—have ended with a determination that his legal conclusion was correct.

Instead, the majority today concludes that DHS was required to do far more. Without grounding its position in either the APA or precedent, the majority declares that DHS was required to overlook DACA's obvious legal deficiencies and provide additional policy reasons and justifications before restoring the rule of law. This holding is incorrect, and it will hamstring all future agency attempts to undo actions that exceed statutory authority. I would therefore reverse the judgments below and remand with instructions to dissolve the nationwide injunctions.

Justice Kavanaugh, concurring in the judgment in part and dissenting in part.

[R]egardless of whether the Court is correct about the Duke Memorandum, the Nielsen Memorandum more fully explained the Department's legal reasons for rescinding DACA, and clarified that even if DACA were lawful, the Department would still rescind DACA for a variety of policy reasons. The Nielsen Memorandum also expressly addressed the reliance interests of DACA recipients. The question under the APA's deferential arbitrary-and-capricious standard is not whether we agree with the Department's decision to rescind DACA. The question is whether the Nielsen Memorandum reasonably explained the decision to rescind DACA. Under ordinary application of the arbitrary-and-capricious standard, the Nielsen Memorandum—with its alternative and independent rationales and its discussion of reliance—would pass muster as an explanation for the Executive Branch's action.

The Nielsen Memorandum was issued nine months after the Duke Memorandum. Under the Administrative Procedure Act, the Nielsen Memorandum is itself a "rule" setting forth "an agency statement of general . . . applicability and future effect designed to implement . . . policy." 5 U.S.C. § 551(4). Because it is a rule, the Nielsen Memorandum constitutes "agency action." § 551(13). As the Secretary of Homeland Security, Secretary Nielsen had the authority to decide whether to stick with Secretary Duke's decision to rescind DACA, or to make a different decision. Like Secretary Duke, Secretary Nielsen chose to rescind DACA, and she provided additional explanation. Her memorandum was akin to common forms of agency action that follow earlier agency action on the same subject—for example, a supplemental or new agency statement of policy, or an agency order with respect to a motion for rehearing or reconsideration. Courts often consider an agency's additional explanations of policy or additional explanations made, for example, on agency rehearing or reconsideration, or on remand from a court, even if the agency's bottom-line decision itself does not change.

Yet the Court today jettisons the Nielsen Memorandum by classifying it as a *post hoc* justification for rescinding DACA. Under our precedents, however, the *post hoc* justification doctrine merely requires that courts assess agency action based on the official explanations of the agency decisionmakers, and not based on after-the-fact explanations advanced *by agency lawyers during litigation* (or by judges). As the D.C. Circuit has explained, the *post hoc* justification doctrine "is not a time barrier which freezes an agency's exercise of its judgment after an initial decision has been made and bars it from further articulation of its reasoning. It is a rule directed at reviewing courts which forbids judges to uphold agency action on the basis of rationales offered by anyone other than the proper decisionmakers." *Alpharma, Inc. v. Leavitt*, 460 F.3d 1, 6 (2006) (GARLAND, J.) (internal quotation marks omitted). * * *

Because the Court excludes the Nielsen Memorandum, the Court sends the case back to the Department of Homeland Security for further explanation. Although I disagree with the Court's decision to remand, the only practical consequence of the Court's decision to remand appears to be some delay. The Court's decision seems to allow the Department on remand to relabel and reiterate the substance of the Nielsen Memorandum, perhaps with some elaboration as suggested in the Court's opinion.

[A]s to the narrow APA question presented here, I appreciate the Court's careful analysis, but I ultimately disagree with its treatment of the Nielsen Memorandum. I therefore respectfully dissent from the Court's judgment on plaintiffs' APA claim. * * *

NOTES & QUESTIONS

1. Notice that the majority in *UC Regents* refers to the "procedural requirement" to "provide a reasoned explanation for its action." Does that seem like a "procedural" requirement or a "substantive" requirement? Either way, as you now see, this requirement that an agency not act in an "arbitrary and capricious" manner, that it "provide a reasoned explanation for its action," is a fundamental constraint on all agency action.

2. At the beginning of its analysis, the Court makes clear that "[a]ll parties agree" that "DHS may rescind DACA." Notice first how different that is from the *State Farm* case, where the disagreement was at core about whether the agency could in fact rescind the passive-restraint requirement in Standard 208. Even more than *State Farm*, then, is the dispute here in *UC Regents* really just about "procedure," i.e., "how" DHS may

rescind DACA? In Justice Kavanaugh's opinion, he notes that, "the only practical consequence of the Court's decision to remand appears to be some delay. The Court's decision seems to allow the Department on remand to relabel and reiterate the substance of the Nielsen Memorandum, perhaps with some elaboration as suggested in the Court's opinion." Is the upshot of administrative law doctrine of this sort simply to impose delay on agencies doing what they have authority to do? Is that all that is at stake here, just a question of how long it takes for an agency to act? Do you know what happened to DACA after the Supreme Court issued its opinion? Hint: The Court issued its opinion in June 2020, a little more than four months before a presidential election.

3. The Court states explicitly that "[t]he wisdom of [the agency's] decisions is none of our concern." Do you think the wisdom of the agency's decision (which, as the Court noted, involved more than 700,000 DACA recipients) really played no role in its decision?

4. The principal dissent by Justice Thomas argues that the original DACA program was illegal from the start and the original 2012 memorandum establishing DACA was thus *ultra vires*. Because of that, the dissent argues, the agency should not have needed to go through *any* process to rescind it. What does the majority say about that? Does the majority state that the agency *did* have power to issue the original 2012 DACA memorandum? If not, is the majority saying that the requirement of a "reasoned explanation" applies even to rescind an illegal action?

5. Justice Kavanaugh's dissent argues that the Nielsen Memorandum was itself part of the *agency's* rationale for its action. In contrast, the majority refuses to consider the Nielsen Memorandum. They are debating about the "no *post hoc* rationales" principle. This, you may recall, derives from *Chenery I*. Based on the rationale for *Chenery I*, who do you think has the better of the argument as to whether the agency should get to rely on the Nielsen Memorandum, the majority or Justice Kavanaugh?

6. *UC Regents*, *State Farm*, and *Vermont Yankee* are but three of many Supreme Court decisions addressing "arbitrary and capricious" review under paragraph (A) of APA section 706(2). Of course, what is at issue in these paragraph (A) cases is an agency's use (or abuse) of its discretionary authority. Meanwhile, paragraphs (B) and (C) of section 706(2) suggest that reviewing courts might engage in *de novo* review of an agency's determination of questions of law. That is certainly what appellate courts usually do when reviewing trial court conclusions on legal questions. In

the context of court review of agency interpretations, however, agencies often have some discretion in how they construe the statutes that govern them, which may entitle agencies to some judicial deference even on questions of law. We turn to these questions in earnest next.

Test Your Understanding

To assess your understanding of the material in this chapter, click here to take a quiz.

33

Agency Interpretation of Statutes and Regulations

Key Concepts

- Agencies as interpreters of legal text
- Agency expertise as a distinctive interpretive factor
- Agency political accountability as a distinctive interpretive factor
- Canons of agency interpretation
- ALJs (Administrative Law Judges)
- Agency reinterpretation of statutory provisions
- Judicial reviewability of agency statutory interpretation
- Presumption of reviewability

Chapter Summary

In the course of performing both rulemaking and adjudicatory functions, administrative agencies are routinely called upon to interpret the meaning of legal text. Whether in the form of clarifying ambiguity or of filling gaps, agency interpretations are a fundamental feature of the American legal system. Agencies bring to these interpretive tasks at least two capacities or "virtues" that courts generally lack when engaged in statutory interpretation. One is that agencies frequently have special expertise concerning the subject matter under interpretation, and as a result may even have been intimately involved in the process of drafting the statutory provisions at issue. Another is that agencies are legitimately influenced by political considerations, which may affect their interpretive decisions.

On the other hand, agencies also have the potential to bring certain drawbacks or "vices" to the interpretive task relative to courts. First, they may be too close to the industries they regulate, leading to what scholars refer to as "agency capture," meaning the agency is "captured" by the parties the agency is supposed to regulate. Second, they have a self-interest in regulating: as bureaucracies with a specific mission, they have incentives to aggrandize their own power; so, their own interpretations may be biased towards giving themselves unwarranted power.

Some observers of agency interpretation have even argued that a distinctive set of interpretive canons are appropriate to guide agency interpretation, although it is not clear that agencies themselves in fact recognize how distinctive their interpretive processes might be. These features distinguishing agencies from courts help explain why agencies not only may perform their interpretive tasks quite distinctively in the first instance, but also may often justify an agency's reinterpretation or changed interpretation. All of these considerations are important background to the following chapter's consideration of how courts should review agency interpretation, although it is important to note that not all agency interpretations are always subject to judicial review.

Many different types of actors—from citizens to lawyers to judges to executive branch officials—must confront the task of legal interpretation. Nevertheless, as Parts V and VI reflect, the primary focus of interpretive theory is on how judges construe legal text, given the judiciary's role to declare what the law is. However, every bit as much (actually much more) official interpretation of statutory text occurs at the hands of agency officials, in fulfillment of their rulemaking and adjudicatory responsibilities summarized in Chapter 28. These responsibilities give rise to a host of agency regulations and orders. Meanwhile, agencies also must frequently interpret their own regulations and orders—a responsibility that is not always easy, given that agencies can be vast, complicated bureaucracies.

Although some of these agency interpretations will eventually come before courts for review under the standards discussed in the remaining chapters, many agency interpretations will not, either because they are not challenged in court, or because by law they may be insulated from judicial review. In those cases, the agency's construction would effectively be the final interpretive word. It therefore is important to understand something about the distinctive way in which agencies in their own right may interpret legal text. This understanding then will also be a helpful prerequisite to considering how the judicial branch reviews these agency interpretations.

To that end, this chapter discusses several characteristics of agencies that shape their implementation of their legal authority and their interpretation of statutory and regulatory text. These agency characteristics include their delegated lawmaking authority, their frequently close working relationships with the legislature during the process of drafting agency legislation, their expertise, and their relative political accountability. This chapter also briefly considers several potential weaknesses of executive agencies, before turning to the question of how all these characteristics influence agency rulemaking, agency adjudication, and the principle of *stare decisis* with respect to administrative precedents. It concludes by summarizing key doctrine that affects which agency actions will or will not be subject to judicial review.

A. Agency Delegation Reprise: Legislative Reliance on Agency Interpretation and Implementation

All lobbyists worth their salt know that even after a bill becomes a law, many opportunities remain to influence its implementation. This is primarily because the complexity of American law today frequently requires the promulgation of additional regulations to clarify and enforce the statute, or relies on the administrative adjudication of a range of associated issues. Responsibility for promulgating these regulations and conducting these adjudications generally rests with the executive branch departments and independent agencies whose existence, organization, and function were briefly described in Chapter 28.

Congress and state legislatures now routinely delegate to these organs of the administrative state the explicit authority to make rules and adjudicate controversies. In turn, these agencies, by law, conduct many of their most important proceedings in public meetings, formal on-the-record hearings, or notice-and-comment rulemaking procedures. The primary point of these processes is to help the agency collect additional information relevant to its execution of its responsibilities. Meanwhile, the public nature of these processes makes it easy for citizens and other interested parties to renew their efforts to affect the ultimate policy outcome, while also making the agencies more accountable for how they exercise the authority delegated to them.

As Chapter 29 explored, the nondelegation doctrine imposes some limits on a legislature's ability to give agencies unbridled discretion to make law. Nevertheless, agencies regularly construe and refine the statutes they are implementing in ways that create new legal rights and duties. Indeed, in the typical case of a delegation of authority, this is exactly what an agency is expected to do, as long as the agency's resulting rules and orders are consistent with its delegated powers. Congress and state legislatures often will enact measures that they know are vague or incompletely specified, with the expectation that the administrative agency will further clarify the text's meaning when it promulgates regulations or adjudicates controversies.

Furthermore, agencies have the authority and responsibility to do more than just resolve ambiguities in the statutes they are charged to administer. Even in the course of implementing unambiguous statutory language, they also have the power to make subsidiary policy decisions, provided once again that their action is

> ! Agencies routinely expand the body of written law in the course of implementing those statutes that they are charged to administer.

consistent with the overall policy established by the legislature. Additionally, from time to time agencies may need to construe, clarify, or otherwise refine their own previously issued regulations.

In all these contexts, agencies must necessarily interpret legal text. Although agencies will frequently invoke many of the same interpretive strategies and tools as courts, their interpretive role typically has some distinctive features as compared to the judiciary's interpretive role discussed in Parts V and VI. In particular, the most trenchant caution about the potential hazards of judicial interpretation—that in the guise of interpretation, courts may usurp the legislative function—is often less potent with respect to agency interpretation. Agencies regularly function in a

> ? For what reasons might agencies decide to change or refine their interpretations of the statutes they are implementing?

quasi-legislative fashion, and in fact are expected to function in this way, within established limits and safeguards. Provided that the agency complies with these limits and safeguards, it may be no complaint that an agency has engaged in policy making, nor can it fairly be said that in doing so it has usurped the legislative role; rather, the agency has done exactly what the legislature tasked the agency to do when the legislature gave it lawmaking power. Furthermore, the agency is most likely to be in harmony with the legislative delegation if the agency is able to predicate its action upon a reasonable understanding of what it is that the legislature (or its key leaders) intended. In this sense, agencies arguably are functioning as both the legislature's faithful agents and its cooperative partners, within the sphere of their delegated authority.

> ! Agencies frequently are active participants in the legislative process.

Moreover, the interpreting agencies often will have been active partners, even if behind-the-scenes, in the statutory drafting process. As a result, it not only may be appropriate (or even necessary) for agencies to identify and understand the legislature's underlying purpose, it also may be easier for them to do so than for courts. Thus, with respect to agency interpretations rendered in furtherance of an agency's delegated authority to implement a statute, the debate between Textualists and Purposivists may have less salience.

Furthermore, agencies exercising their delegated authority may be influenced—sometimes heavily—by several important factors: their own subject-matter expertise, their adaptable political accountability (relative to courts); the influences and parties with which they interact; and their own self-interest. These factors, which deserve brief additional discussion in their own right, make agencies very different kinds of interpreters than courts.

B. Some Important Agency Characteristics

In today's complex administrative state, several agency characteristics shape agencies, as a matter of comparative institutional competency, compared with both courts and legislatures: their expertise, their political accountability (relative to courts); the influences and parties with which they interact; and their own self-interest. Depending on the circumstances, these characteristics can be seen as either virtues or vices.

1. Agency Expertise

In substantial part, agencies are justified in serving as a cooperative partner of the legislature because agencies possess far greater expertise, an expertise that the legislature often specifically seeks to tap. While legislatures prototypically consist of a cadre of generalists who legislate across the complete range of public policy issues, agencies are highly specialized in particular subject matters. Their normal functioning depends upon having a leadership team and a support staff who possess deep knowledge of and experience with their specific subjects.

> For what issues, and in what circumstances, would agency expertise be most valuable?

Across the government bureaucracy, this expertise takes a variety of forms. It can include scientific training, engineering background, foreign policy experience, economic knowledge, military training, public budgeting and finance experience, and any number of other areas in which formal training or practical experience (or both) can be especially valuable. Indeed, one benefit of agency decision-making is that within a single agency, multiple kinds of expertise often can be brought to bear at one time on the same problem. Agencies in turn organize themselves around this expertise, seeking to ensure that they can contribute to whatever policy issues they confront.

The legislature may deliberately employ this expertise in at least three very different ways. One is by charging a particular agency to fill in the gaps of an enacted statute, on the premise that the agency is better suited than the legislature to specify the detailed rules that will best accomplish the legislative aim. A second is to allow the agency to adjudicate the application of the statute and its regulations to specific controversies, on the premise that the agency is better suited than the judicial branch to understand how the rules apply to the relevant facts within the agency's purview, especially in a complex or technical field.

A third way is for the legislature to rely on the agency's expertise during the drafting process itself, inviting agency personnel to the table to participate in the development of the statutory text. Indeed, agencies are often the primary behind-the-scenes drafters or architects of legislative measures; in many other cases, agencies may provide an invaluable source of technical assistance. *See* CHRISTOPHER J. WALKER, FEDERAL AGENCIES IN THE LEGISLATIVE PROCESS: TECHNICAL ASSISTANCE IN STATUTORY DRAFTING (2015). With this level of involvement in the legislative process, agencies frequently have an insider's perspective on the legislature's underlying purpose behind its enactment (including whether it is even fair to ascribe a specific purpose to a given legislative action). This perspective has obvious potential relevance to an agency resolving subsequent interpretive issues in both the rulemaking and adjudicatory contexts, provided the agency has a meaningful way to preserve its institutional memory of what transpired in the drafting process.

> **FYI** This concern for the role of expertise in democracy is by no means new. The renowned journalist and political commentator Walter Lippmann pointed a century ago to the inability of most ordinary people to glean or have enough accurate information about to govern themselves. *See* WALTER LIPPMANN, PUBLIC OPINION (1922).

Some argue, however, that expertise is not always a virtue. Experts can sometimes view themselves as immune from criticism by those with less expertise. The very quality that makes them experts—their specialized knowledge—can also prevent them from seeing the broader contours of some problems. Moreover, to the extent that an agency's expertise is driving its decision-making, a tension exists between "rule by experts" and "rule by the people." In this sense, experts are inherently "elitist" in the literal sense of that word, since the very point of experts is to put decisions in the hands of those who have experiences and knowledge that others do not. As we have seen, the structure of agencies, with political appointees (and ultimately, the elected President) at the top, along with the basic principle that agencies are confined by legislative delegations, aim to mitigate this potential problem by connecting the agencies' decisions to the democratic polity. But, as suggested by the discussion of the non-delegation doctrine in Chapter 29, agencies are often acting within broad delegations of authority and, within those broad contours, can sometimes exercise significant authority. In practice, then, agencies make many of the most important policy decisions in American society.

2. Agency Political Accountability

A completely different reason that agency interpretation of statutes can be quite unlike judicial interpretation is that many agencies are to some degree politically accountable (though theoretically less so than legislatures), in a way that federal courts are not. Executive agencies led by a cabinet secretary appointed by the President or Governor serve at the plea-

> **!** The word "elitist" often has a pejorative tint to it, but as with the phrase "administrative state," we mean it here in a neutral sense. We recognize, though, that the lens through which one sees the word "elitist" very much shapes one's views about the appropriateness of experts playing such an outsized role in legal and policy decisionmaking in a democracy.

sure of that executive branch leader, and therefore must be politically responsive. To whatever degree these agencies have discretionary authority to fill in policy gaps when implementing and interpreting legislative statutes, they are likely to be mindful of public opinion and of the political impact of their choices. Typically, this is even more true of those state executive agencies that are led by an official who is independently elected in a statewide popular election, rather than by an official appointed by the Governor.

> **?** Is it a good thing for agencies to be politically responsive? When and why?

Courts, in contrast, are expected to make their decisions free from political considerations. In theory this is true even of the many state court judges across the country who must stand for election. Although these judges may be politically accountable for their judicial philosophy and temperament, the ideal of judicial impartiality usually suggests that they are not supposed to be politically accountable for any specific judicial decision, including ones in which they construe and apply a piece of statutory text. Agency officials, however, may very well expect to be indirectly politically accountable for each specific interpretive decision, and therefore to be responsive to the executive branch leaders to whom they report.

The extent to which agency officials are politically accountable for matters of textual interpretation may vary across agencies. For instance, political accountability may matter more for agencies with a single head, such as a cabinet secretary, than for multi-member boards or commissions. And political accountability is generally much more important for agencies within the executive branch than it is for agencies with a high degree of independence from the executive branch. The extent to which an agency is influenced by its sense of political accountability for a given issue may also be affected by the extent to which the issue involves technical, scientific, or other kinds of expertise the agency possesses that might trump any other bases for decision.

Of course, agencies are politically accountable only indirectly, in contrast with legislators, who are at least theoretically accountable directly. But this mediated accountability may often allow agencies to be nimble in adapting to changing attitudes. Although some administrative processes are cumbersome, they ultimately conclude with the action of a single decisionmaker (or, in the case of multi-member commissions, a small number of decisionmakers), rather than, as in the case of a federal statute, a majority of two large houses of Congress and a President. Moreover, other administrative processes (such as issuing agency policy statements or interpretative rules) are generally less cumbersome than the legislative process and can be streamlined or relatively informal. The result is that assigning responsibility to an agency may often permit more timely or efficient responses to new or changed circumstances or concerns.

Moreover, the fact that agencies are more insulated from politics than are legislatures allows them greater leeway to rely on their expertise. Indeed, as we noted above, the idea of political accountability—a notion of public responsiveness, and that agencies might at least in some cases seek to respect public preferences—is potentially in tension with the idea of being guided by expertise—a notion that agencies should make decisions based on facts and expert opinion, not public opinion. Yet expertise and political accountability are both frequently identified as important features of the administrative state (and also, as we will discuss later, as reasons for courts sometimes to defer to an agency's interpretation, even if the court might otherwise have reached a different result). In what circumstances political accountability should carry the day, and in what circumstances expert judgment should hold sway, may itself be an important aspect of an agency's discretionary power, except to the extent that a legislative directive may specify the proper basis for a particular agency decision.

Political accountability through the President may, however, undermine political accountability to Congress, the delegator of authority to the agency in the first place. Presidents may not share the same views about policy as Congress, undermining the principles of legislative delegation that established the agency's authority. In contrast, courts are independent of the President's political control and thus may be better suited to determine neutrally what the legislature would have wanted, as opposed to what the current chief executive wants; in other words, to serve more faithfully as "faithful agents" of the enacting Congress's will. If Congress, not the President, should be the prime mover of policy, then agency political accountability may undermine that goal.

3. Agency Capture

When legislatures, agencies, or courts make decisions, their decisions are shaped by the voices and views they hear. One key question, then, is who has access to those decisionmakers. For many lawyers, the ability to have access to and the ability to influence legal decisionmakers is part of their stock-in-trade. Some scholars have long argued that government decision-making institutions such as legislatures or agencies (or even courts) are likely to become "captured" by the industries they are supposed to be regulating. *See, e.g.*, George J. Stigler, *The Theory of Economic Regulation*, 2 Bell J. Econ. & Mgmt. Sci 3 (1971). Regulatory capture theory is premised on the idea that a regulated industry often constitutes the most concentrated interest in legal and policy decisions. So, just as one example, automakers have the greatest interest in the regulation of motor vehicles; likewise, pharmaceutical companies have the greatest interest in drug regulation, and so forth. Because of this concentrated interest, those industries will play an outsized role in the decisions that an agency makes.

In Part II, we studied how legislatures are formed and, in turn, how legislatures pass statutes. The discussion of interest group politics in Chapter 4 touched on different categories of legislative activity. Parts II and III also explored how legislative decision-making depends on the process by which legislators get elected. We considered the impact that, for example, campaign finance laws and voting rules have on our lawmaking institutions, and on the statutes they produce. We also saw that legislators are constrained—by time, by complex legislative rules, by the need to raise money, by the need to spend time getting re-elected—in what they do (and can do). One criticism of legislatures is that they can thus be "captured" by interest groups, those interests that help the legislators themselves get elected and re-elected.

Courts too are not completely free from this problem, although judges are generally immune from what are viewed as the crassest aspects of politics. For example, federal judges do not need to worry about re-election or re-appointment, and even those state judges who are elected generally have longer terms than legislators. Indeed, this insulation from the direct impact of political accountability is why courts are often viewed as the institution best positioned to protect individual rights. Judges can theoretically act "without fear or favor" or as "umpires," "calling balls and strikes."

FYI With respect to the judicial role discussed in the prior paragraph, Justice Ketanji Brown Jackson used the phrase "without fear or favor" to describe how she would act as a judge during her confirmation hearing to become an Associate Justice of the Supreme Court of the United States. (The New York Times has long used the phrase to describe its reporting.) Meanwhile, Chief Justice John Roberts used the analogy of judges to baseball umpires during his confirmation hearing to become Chief Justice of the United States.

But it is the administrative agencies that, in the view of many scholars and activists, are most susceptible to being captured, by the very entities they regulate. Why might agencies fare worse on this front than other lawmaking institutions? In part because agencies are specialized, the industries that a given agency regulates have an outsized interest in that agency's decisions. Industries are also repeat players with agencies. Banks must engage with the Federal Reserve and the Federal Deposit Insurance Corporation on a regular basis. So too must nuclear-power plant owners engage repeatedly with the Nuclear Regulatory Commission. The list could go on. Moreover, the very expertise that the agency and its employees have is often precisely the expertise that the industry itself has. Consider the market for automotive engineers who understand the environmental impacts of motor vehicles: the EPA and Department of Transportation hire experts of that sort, but so too do General Motors, Toyota, Tesla, and Rivian. Given the far higher salaries in private industry, there has long been concern about the "revolving door" between government and industry: given the more lucrative opportunities in industry, government officials may have an incentive to be friendly with an industry where they might hope to work some day.

During the 1960s and 1970s, public-interest groups and citizen advocacy organizations argued that federal agencies had become far too cozy with industry. *See generally* Paul Sabin, Public Citizens: The Attack on Big Government and the Remaking of American Liberalism (2021). This may have been part of what led courts, particularly the D.C. Circuit, to take a more active role in reviewing agency actions, as we discussed in Chapter 32. *See* Thomas W. Merrill, *Capture Theory and the Courts: 1967–1983*, 72 Chi.-Kent L. Rev. 1039 (1997). You will recall, for example, the Supreme Court's criticism of NHTSA for acceding to the auto manufacturers' decision to choose automatic seatbelts over airbags in its 1983 *State Farm* decision. The potential problem is by no means limited to the auto industry and NHTSA. Is the FDA captured by the pharmaceutical industry? Is the FCC captured by the telecommunications companies? Is the U.S. Department of Agriculture captured by "big agrobusinesses"? Is the Department of Education captured by universities? These are the kind of questions scholars trying to understand agency action try to answer. Of course, agency capture may simply be an extension of agency engagement, and so may not always be a bad thing. For example, the auto industry almost certainly has unique information of relevance for NHTSA when it seeks to regulate motor vehicle safety. Pharmaceutical companies similarly bring unique expertise on questions related to drug development and safety that the FDA needs before it regulates. Whether agencies exhibit the undesirable qualities of a "captured" entity, and if so, whether they do so to any extent greater than legislatures or even courts, is a fundamental question in thinking about how agencies work. As you read through the remaining materials, think about the role of agency capture in agency decision-making and what implications agency capture might have for judicial review of agency action.

4. Agency Self-Interest

One other factor that scholars and theorists have explored is the broad category of agency bias. Bias could be thought of as we just described it, through the lens of "capture," or the idea that the agency is biased in favor of the industry it regulates. But a broader sense of bias also deserves attention, which involves agency power and self-interest. The theory here is that agencies are bureaucracies with their own self-interest, a self-interest that does not necessarily line up with either the legal authority that Congress has given them or the public interest in an abstract sense. In this way of thinking, one agency motivation is to seek to increase their power as much as they can. They are "biased," in other words, in favor of themselves. This can involve, most pointedly, trying to maximize their budget, and this budget-maximization goal might be seen as a proxy for everything an agency might self-interestedly want. *See* William A. Niskanen, *Nonmarket Decision Making: The Peculiar Economics of Bureaucracy*, 58 AM. ECON. REV. 293–305 (1968).

In the specific context of agency interpretation of statutes, though, this self-interest can involve maximizing the agency's regulatory authority. One way to think about this problem might be through an example. Imagine that a parent leaves a child home alone for a few hours and says, "You may have a few cookies while I'm gone." While the parent is away, who exactly should interpret the phrase "a few" in this grant of permission? The child? Some neutral third party with no stake in the outcome? Thinking about the self-interestedness of an agency as the delegee of power may be helpful for understanding the broader question of who should wield interpretive authority. As you read through the remaining materials, think about the role that agency self-interest might have for understanding judicial review of agency action.

C.   Impact of Agency Characteristics on Agency Action

Administrative agencies' characteristics can be important in both the rulemaking and adjudicatory contexts, as well as in various other ways in which agencies offer guidance about the statutes they are charged with administering.

1.   Agency Rulemaking

Federal agencies may engage in three distinct types of rulemaking processes under the Administrative Procedure Act: formal on-the-record rulemaking after a live hearing (quite rare today); informal notice-and-comment rulemaking, typically based on a paper record; and the development of interpretative rules, policy statements, and the like. Rulemaking proceedings can take months and even years. During this time, the agency has plenty of opportunity both to assess public opinion and to deepen its own expertise. Rulemaking is a quasi-legislative activity, by which an agency promulgates legal text beyond the text of a statute. These rulemaking processes enhance the democratic legitimacy of the resulting agency regulations because they permit the involvement of anyone who wants to participate in the process.

As part of the rulemaking process, agencies not only determine how to operationalize a legislative directive, but they also fill in gaps and interpret ambiguities in legislative enactments. However, in doing so they must function within many more constraints than the legislature. These constraints encompass not only constitutional limits on government activities, including Due Process requirements, but also whatever limits the legislature has imposed through the agency's enabling statutes or other measures (often including requirements of conducting cost-benefit analysis), the limits of any applicable executive branch orders and directives, and the procedural requirements of the Administrative Procedure Act (or state law analogs).

At the federal level, the importance to agency interpretation of advancing the legislative purpose is implicit in the APA requirement that agencies incorporate within the text of their rules a "concise general statement of their basis and purpose." Agencies always tie these statements back to their enabling legislation, articulating a purpose for the rule that traces its pedigree to the congressional purpose and authorization of agency action. But subject to the constraints just identified, agencies otherwise have wide latitude to determine for themselves what rules to promulgate, based on their expert evaluation of the evidence in the record, their own evaluation of the public interest, and the legislative purpose to which they must remain faithful under their statutory mandate, consistent with the nondelegation doctrine. Their role as a cooperative partner of the legislature thus subsumes the element of also being its faithful agent, even while having substantial freedom within those limits.

As a normative matter, some recent scholarship has argued that within those limits, agencies are the superior governmental institution to exercise primary responsibility for the interpretation of statutes, largely because of their substantive expertise and democratic legitimacy. *See, e.g.,* William N. Eskridge Jr., *Expanding* Chevron's *Domain: A Comparative Institutional Analysis of the Relative Competence of Courts and Agencies to Interpret Statutes,* 2013 Wisc. L. Rev. 411; Kevin M. Stack, *Purposivism in the Executive Branch: How Agencies Interpret Statutes,* 109 Nw. U. L. Rev. 871 (2015). But the beginnings of these arguments about the comparative advantages of agency statutory interpretation trace back at least a quarter century. *See* Peter L. Strauss, *When the Judge Is Not the Primary Official with Responsibility to Read: Agency Interpretation and the Problem of Legislative History,* 66 Chi.-Kent L. Rev. 321 (1990).

Recognition of the institutional competence and other advantages that agencies have in construing statutes also has produced an argument for a separate set of interpretive canons to guide agency interpretations. These include, for instance, "interpret to give energy and breadth to all legislative programs within your jurisdiction," "follow presidential directives," "use legislative history as a primary interpretive guide," and "engage in activist lawmaking." *See* Jerry L. Mashaw, *Norms, Practices, and the Paradox of Deference: A Preliminary Inquiry into Agency Statutory Interpretation,* 57 Admin. L. Rev. 501, 521–23 (2005). To be sure, the advisability of some (or all) of these distinct interpretive tools for agencies is controversial. Indeed, an agency that uses these tools might serve as the very poster-child for the self-interest that some have argued characterizes agencies. Each of these tools has an element of self-aggrandizement to them. But, even if there are reasons for agencies to approach the interpretive task in a more robust manner, these interpretive suggestions for agencies might be seen as inappropriate for courts.

Of course, these arguments over how agencies might approach the interpretive enterprise quite differently from how courts do so are not necessarily reflective of what agencies actually do. As a descriptive matter, empirical research is only just beginning to explore which interpretive tools and approaches agencies in fact rely upon the most when construing statutes. At the federal level, early work suggests that agencies do rely heavily on legislative history materials, as well as on a few textual canons (primarily the Whole Act Rule, the ordinary meaning canon, and the *noscitur a sociis* canon, described in Chapter 20). Agencies also engage in statutory interpretation mindful of the way in which courts may review their work and the circumstances in which courts will most defer to the agency interpretation. *See* Christopher J. Walker, *Inside Agency Statutory Interpretation*, 67 STAN. L. REV. 999 (2015).

2.   Agency Adjudication

Problems of statutory meaning also regularly arise in the context of agency adjudications. At the federal level, agency adjudicatory processes, both formal and informal, differ dramatically from agency rulemaking processes. Yet agencies have few constraints for deciding which interpretive issues are most appropriate for resolution through the promulgation of an administrative regulation, and which through the issuance of an adjudicatory order. As a result, agencies often rely on adjudicatory processes to establish new policies that arise through the agencies' clarification of ambiguities in statutes. And the Supreme Court has explicitly held that agencies may choose rulemaking or adjudication when deciding to establish new policies. *See SEC v. Chenery Corp.* (*Chenery II*), 332 U.S. 194 (1947).

Legislatures task agencies with adjudicatory responsibilities in part because of the sheer number of cases that arise under the authority of the statutes and regulations that agencies administer, which would swamp the regular courts. But in many cases, agencies also are tasked with adjudicative responsibilities because agency adjudications may more efficiently produce reasonable outcomes, again because of agencies' institutional competencies. In formal agency adjudications, neutral Administrative Law Judges (ALJs), who usually have some degree of independence from the involved agency, are responsible for the vast majority of initial decisions or recommendations. However, the agency itself typically is then free to review the ALJ's determination de novo. In so doing, the agency may once again rely upon its own expertise, or be influenced by broader concerns about consistency or democratic legitimacy. Meanwhile, in informal agency adjudications, agencies have even greater leeway to rely on these institutional competencies, often subject only to the requirements of Due Process.

As we will consider later, when courts are called upon to review how an agency has construed a particular piece of statutory text, it usually makes little difference whether the agency interpretation has occurred as part of an adjudication or as part of a rulemaking proceeding. Both are avenues through which agencies adopt official positions regarding what the text means and how the agency will administer and enforce it.

D. Agencies' Subsequent Revisions of Interpretations of Statutes They Administer, or of Their Own Regulations

An additional feature of agency interpretation is the flexibility that agencies have to revise how they have interpreted the statutes that they are charged with administering. As we explored previously, the principle of *stare decisis* typically has extra strength with respect to judicial interpretations of statutory provisions, because courts are even more reluctant to overturn a statutory precedent than they ordinarily might be to overturn a common law decision or doctrine. By contrast, agencies have great freedom to overturn their previous constructions of statutory meaning.

Of course, it goes almost without saying that Congress must have the ability to revise its own handiwork; indeed, updating the law is a core legislative function. Agencies may also be able to make important contributions in this regard (within the accepted limits of the nondelegation doctrine), whether in response to changing public and political views, or in response to new information developed or evaluated by the agency experts. Agencies therefore not only are allowed to revise their own regulations (consistent with APA rulemaking requirements), but also in many circumstances may be expected to do so when a regulation interpreting a statute has become outmoded.

E. Presumption of Reviewability

When considering how courts review agency interpretations of statutes and regulations, a threshold question lurks: Which agency interpretations are judicially reviewable, and which are not?

At the federal level, when Congress delegates rulemaking or adjudicatory authority to an agency, Congress is free to specify whether or not the agency's use of that authority is subject to judicial review. Congress occasionally does so by including in a statute a preclusion of judicial review of specified agency actions, as for instance in a Department of Veterans' Affairs statute which provides that "the decisions of [the agency] on any question of law or fact under any law administered by the Veterans Administration providing benefits for veterans and their dependents or survivors shall be final and conclusive and no other official or any court of the United States shall have power or jurisdiction to review any such decision." 38 U.S.C. 211(a); *see Johnson v. Robison*, 415 U.S. 361 (1974). Additionally, under the Administrative Procedure Act, certain agency actions may be unreviewable if they are "committed to agency discretion by law." 5 U.S.C. 701(a)(2); *see Webster v. Doe*, 486 U.S. 592 (1988).

Often, however, a statute may be silent or ambiguous about whether a particular agency action is reviewable. For these circumstances, the Supreme Court has construed the Administrative Procedure Act to create a presumption that agency actions will be reviewable, absent strong evidence that Congress intended otherwise. *See Citizens to Preserve Overton Park v. Volpe*, 401 U.S. 402 (1971); *Abbott Laboratories v. Gardner*, 387 U.S. 136 (1967). Although at one time this standard required "clear and convincing evidence" that Congress wanted to insulate an agency action from judicial review, the Court relaxed this standard somewhat in *Block v. Community Nutrition Board*, 467 U.S. 340 (1984). *Block* listed five ways of establishing congressional intent to preclude judicial review: (1) clear statutory text; (2) specific legislative history; (3) a judicial interpretation to which Congress has acquiesced; (4) the collective impact of legislative history and judicial construction; and (5) inferences drawn from the statute as a whole.

When any of those factors persuade a court that an agency's authority to act is unreviewable, the agency becomes the final interpreter, even of legal meaning. Yet when what is at stake is the legal meaning of the words of a legislative enactment, courts are unlikely to find that any of the five *Block* factors overcome the presumption of reviewability. Instead, judicial review will likely be available, with the key question becoming just how much deference the reviewing court should grant to the agency's interpretation of a statute that it is charged with administering. The chapters that follow will begin to explore how courts conduct review in such cases. First, however, we provide an example of an agency's statutory interpretation.

F.   An Example of Agency Interpretation: What Does "Appropriate" Mean?

The following excerpt comes from what is known as the "preamble" to an agency rule. The preamble to a rule is, as the word suggests, what comes before the rule. The rule itself is "law," just like a statute, and, in the federal system, is codified in what is called the Code of Federal Regulations or CFR. The CFR is to regulations what the United States Code is to statutes, the place where you can find the actual regulatory text, organized by subject matter category. In contrast, the preamble is explanatory, the *why*. In that sense, it is more similar to a judicial opinion or the legislative history of a statute. Recall again that under informal notice-and-comment rulemaking, agencies must provide "a concise general statement of [the] basis and purpose" of any rule they promulgate. 5 U.S.C. § 553(c). The "preamble" to a rule provides that "general statement."

The original document from which the following excerpt comes, though, is anything but concise. In the Federal Register (which prints in three columns and small font!), the original document is 211 pages. That's about 230,000 words, far longer than almost any judicial opinion. So, although the excerpt below might seem long, we have cut it dramatically to focus on the agency's discussion of statutory interpretation. As you read it, ask yourself what else might be in that document? What else might be in it that has nothing to do with statutory interpretation? Might there be other portions of the document that are relevant for the statutory interpretation? Do you think it needs to be that long? If so, why? And, does the length affect your views about the respective roles of agencies and courts in interpreting statutes?

As a point of comparison, the Supreme Court's combined opinion (*i.e.*, majority, concurrences, and dissent) in the 2022 decision overturning *Roe v. Wade*, *Dobbs v. Jackson Women's Health Organization*, which was one of the longest Supreme Court opinions in memory, was "only" about 73,000 words. As another point of comparison, *The Great Gatsby* is 47,000 words, and even *Moby Dick* comes in at a mere 206,000 words.

This rule involves the EPA's regulation of the emissions of mercury and certain other so-called "hazardous air pollutants" (HAP) from coal- and oil-fired electric utility steam generating units (EGUs) under Clean Air Act section 112 (42 U.S.C. § 7412). As you will see, the statute requires the Administrator of the EPA to regulate EGUs, but only if the Administrator finds it "appropriate and necessary" to do so. The relevant statute, section 112 of the Clean Air Act, is complex, and the EPA must interpret a lot of statutory text. But, as you read the excerpt, you should focus on the EPA's interpretation of the word "appropriate." How important is it in the statute? Is the other language in section 112 (what in Parts V and VI we called the "context" surrounding the word "appropriate") helpful for interpreting "appropriate"?

For those less steeped in the specialized nomenclature, laypeople would usually refer to an EGU as a "power plant."

National Emission Standards for Hazardous Air Pollutants From Coal- and Oil-Fired Electric Utility Steam Generating Units and Standards of Performance for Fossil-Fuel-Fired Electric Utility, Industrial-Commercial-Institutional, and Small Industrial-Commercial-Institutional Steam Generating Units

77 Federal Register 9304–01 (Thursday, February 16, 2012)

> ❗ Notice the title of this document. In contrast to a judicial opinion, there are no "parties" listed in the title. It is simply a description (though a dense one!) of the agency action. In this sense, it resembles the title of a statute.

AGENCY: Environmental Protection Agency (EPA).

ACTION: Final rule.

SUMMARY: On May 3, 2011, under authority of Clean Air Act (CAA) sections 111 and 112, the EPA proposed both national emission standards for hazardous air pollutants (NESHAP) from coal- and oil-fired electric utility steam generating units (EGUs) and standards of performance for fossil-fuel-fired electric utility, industrial-commercial-institutional, and small industrial-commercial-institutional steam generating units. After consideration of public comments, the EPA is finalizing these rules in this action.

* * *

Pursuant to CAA section 112, the EPA is establishing NESHAP that will require coal- and oil-fired EGUs to meet hazardous air pollutant (HAP) standards reflecting the application of the maximum achievable control technology. This rule protects air quality and promotes public health by reducing emissions of the HAP listed in CAA section 112(b)(1).

* * *

II. Background Information on the NESHAP

On May 3, 2011, the EPA proposed this rule to address emissions of toxic air pollutants from coal and oil-fired electric generating units as required by the CAA. The proposal explained at length the statutory history and requirements leading to this rule, the factual and legal basis for the rule and its specific provisions, and the costs and benefits to the public health and environment from the proposed requirements.

The EPA received over 900,000 comments from members of the public on the proposed rule, substantially more than for any other prior regulatory proposal. The comments express concerns about the presence of Hg [Hg is the chemical symbol for mercury] in the environment and the effect it has on human health, concerns about the costs of the rule, how challenging it may be for some sources to comply and questions about the impact it may have on this country's electricity supply and economy. Many comments provided additional information and data that have enriched the factual record and enabled EPA to finalize a rule that fulfills the mandate of the CAA while providing flexibility and compliance options to affected sources—options that make the rule less costly and compliance more readily manageable.

This rule establishes uniform emissions-control standards that sources can meet with proven and available technologies and operational processes in a timeframe that is achievable. They will put this industry, now the single largest source of Hg emissions in the United States (U.S.) with emissions of 29 tons per year, on a path to reducing those emissions by approximately 90 percent. Emissions of other toxic metals, such as arsenic (As) and nickel (Ni), dioxins and furans, acid gases (including hydrochloric acid (HCl) and SO_2) will also decrease dramatically with the installation of pollution controls. And the flexibilities established in this rule along

Does the number of comments surprise you? Does this tell you something about the notice-and-comment rulemaking process? As the EPA notes, this is "substantially more than for any other prior regulatory proposal," but still . . . isn't that a lot? Who do you think these 900,000 commenters are? What are the implications of this volume of comments for the process itself? Imagine if the Supreme Court received 900,000 briefs in one of its cases!

Relatedly, what does this volume of comments tell you, if anything, about the potential for direct democratic engagement in the agency rulemaking process and how that might compare with the legislative process Congress uses for adopting statutes?

with other available tools provide a clear pathway to compliance without jeopardizing the country's energy supply.

This preamble explains EPA's appropriate and necessary finding, the elements of the final rule, key changes the EPA is making in response to comments submitted on the proposed rule, and our responses to many of the comments we received. A full response to comments is provided in the response to comments document available in the docket for this rulemaking.

A. What is the statutory authority for this final rule?

! As you read through this section of the EPA's preamble, notice how complex the statute is. What is the nature of the complexity? What might that suggest about the respective roles that the agency (here, the EPA) and courts play or ought to play in the interpretive task?

Congress established a specific structure for determining whether to regulate EGUs under CAA section 112. Specifically, Congress enacted CAA section 112(n)(1).

Section 112(n)(1)(A) of the CAA requires the EPA to conduct a study to evaluate the remaining public health hazards that are reasonably anticipated to occur as a result of EGUs' HAP emissions after imposition of CAA requirements. The EPA must report the results of that study to Congress and regulate EGUs "if the Administrator finds such regulation is appropriate and necessary," after considering the results of that study. Thus, CAA section 112(n)(1)(A) governs how the Administrator decides whether to list EGUs for regulation under CAA section 112. See New Jersey v. EPA, 517 F.3d 574 at 582 (D.C. Cir. 2008) ("Section 112(n)(1) governs how the Administrator decides whether to list EGUs; it says nothing about delisting EGUs.").

As directed, the EPA conducted the study to evaluate the remaining public health hazards and reported the results to Congress (Utility Study Report to Congress (Utility Study)). We discuss this study below in conjunction with other studies that CAA section 112(n)(1) requires concerning EGUs.

Once the EPA lists a source category pursuant to CAA section 112(c), the EPA must then establish technology-based emission standards under CAA section 112(d). For major sources, the EPA must establish emission standards that "require the maximum degree of reduction in emissions of the hazardous air pollutants subject to this section" that the EPA determines are achievable taking into account certain statutory factors. See CAA section 112(d)(2).

These standards are referred to as "maximum achievable control technology" or "MACT" standards. The MACT standards for existing sources must be at least as stringent as the average emission limitation achieved by the best performing 12 percent of existing sources in the category (for which the Administrator has emissions information) or the best performing 5 sources for source categories with less than 30 sources. See CAA section 112(d)(3)(A) and (B), respectively. This level of minimum stringency is referred to as the "MACT floor," and the EPA cannot consider cost in setting the floor. For new sources, MACT standards must be at least as stringent as the control level achieved in practice by the best controlled similar source. See CAA section 112(d)(3).

The EPA also must consider more stringent "beyond-the-floor" control options. When considering beyond-the-floor options, the EPA must consider the maximum degree of reduction in HAP emissions and take into account costs, energy, and non-air quality health and environmental impacts when doing so. See Cement Kiln Recycling Coal. v. EPA, 255 F.3d 855, 857–58 (D.C. Cir. 2001).

Alternatively, the EPA may set a health-based standard for HAP that have an established health threshold, and the standard must provide "an ample margin of safety." See CAA section 112(d)(4). As these standards could be less stringent than MACT standards, the Agency must have detailed information on HAP emissions from the subject sources and sources located near the subject sources before exercising its discretion to set such standards.

For area sources, the EPA may issue standards or requirements that provide for the use of generally available control technologies or management practices (GACT standards) in lieu of promulgating MACT or health-based standards. See CAA section 112(d)(5).

As noted above, CAA section 112(n) requires completion of various reports concerning EGUs. For the first report, the Utility Study, Congress required the EPA to evaluate the hazards to public health reasonably anticipated to occur as the result of HAP emissions from EGUs after imposition of the requirements of the CAA. See CAA section 112(n)(1)(A). The EPA was required to report results from this study to Congress by November 15, 1993. Id. Congress also directed the EPA to conduct "a study of mercury emissions from [EGUs], municipal waste combustion units, and other sources, including area sources" (Mercury Study). See CAA section 112(n)(1)(B). The EPA was required to report the results from this study to Congress by November 15, 1994. Id. In conducting this Mercury Study, Congress directed the EPA to "consider the rate and mass of such emissions, the health and environmental effects of such emissions, technologies which are available to control such emissions, and the costs of such technologies." Id. Congress directed the National Institute of Environmental Health Sciences (NIEHS) to conduct the last required evaluation, "a study to determine the threshold level of mercury exposure below which adverse human health effects are not expected to occur" (NIEHS Study). See CAA section 112(n)(1)(C). The NIEHS was required to submit the results to Congress by November 15, 1993. Id. In conducting this study, NIEHS was to determine "a threshold for mercury concentrations in the tissue of fish which may be consumed (including consumption by sensitive populations) without adverse effects to public health." Id.

In addition, Congress, in conference report language associated with the EPA's fiscal year 1999 appropriations, directed the EPA to fund the National Academy of Sciences (NAS) to perform an independent evaluation of the available data related to the health impacts of methylmercury (MeHg) (NAS Study or MeHg Study). H.R. Conf. Rep. No 105–769, at 281–282 (1998). Specifically, Congress required NAS to advise the EPA as to the appropriate reference dose (RfD) for MeHg. 65 FR 79826. The RfD is the amount of a chemical which, when ingested daily over a lifetime, is anticipated to be without adverse health effects to humans, including sensitive subpopulations. In the same conference report, Congress indicated that the EPA should not make the appropriate and necessary regulatory determination for Hg emissions until the EPA had reviewed the results of the NAS Study. See H.R. Conf. Rep. No 105–769, at 281–282 (1998).

As directed by Congress through different vehicles, the NAS Study and the NIEHS Study evaluated the same issues. The NIEHS completed the NIEHS Study in 1995, and the NAS completed the NAS Study in 2000. Because NAS completed its study 5 years after the NIEHS Study, and considered additional information not earlier available to NIEHS, for purposes of this document we discuss the content of the NAS Study as opposed to the NIEHS Study.

The EPA conducted the studies required by CAA section 112(n)(1) concerning utility HAP emissions, the Utility Study and the Mercury Study, and completed both by 1998. Prior to issuance of the Mercury Study, the EPA engaged in two extensive external peer reviews of the document.

On December 20, 2000, the EPA issued a finding pursuant to CAA section 112(n)(1)(A) that it was appropriate and necessary to regulate coal- and oil-fired EGUs under CAA section 112 and added such units to the list of source categories subject to regulation under CAA section 112(d). In making that finding, the EPA considered the Utility Study, the Mercury Study, the NAS Study, and certain additional information, including information about Hg emissions from coal-fired EGUs that the EPA obtained pursuant to an information collection request (ICR) under the authority of CAA section 114. 65 FR 79826–27.

B. What is the litigation history of this final rule?

Shortly after issuance of the December 2000 finding, an industry group challenged that finding in the Court of Appeals for the D.C. Circuit (D.C. Circuit). Utility Air Regulatory Group (UARG) v. EPA, 2001 WL 936363, No. 01–1074 (D.C. Cir. July 26, 2001). The D.C. Circuit dismissed the lawsuit holding that it did not have jurisdiction because CAA section 112(e)(4) provides, in pertinent part, that "no action of the Administrator * * * listing a source category or subcategory under subsection (c) of this section shall be a final agency action subject to judicial review, except that any such action may be reviewed under section 7607 of (the CAA) when the Administrator issues emission standards for such pollutant or category." Id. (emphasis added).

> You can think of this section as the equivalent of the "procedural posture" portion of a judicial opinion. Notice how long it is!

Pursuant to a settlement agreement, the deadline for issuing emission standards was March 15, 2005. However, instead of issuing emission standards pursuant to CAA section 112(d), on March 29, 2005, the EPA issued the Section 112(n) Revision Rule (2005 Action). That action delisted EGUs after finding that it was neither appropriate nor necessary to regulate such units under CAA section 112. In addition, on May 18, 2005, the EPA issued the Clean Air Mercury Rule (CAMR). 70 FR 28606. That rule established standards of performance for emissions of Hg from new and existing coal-fired EGUs pursuant to CAA section 111.

Environmental groups, states, and tribes challenged the 2005 Action and CAMR. Among other things, the environmental and state petitioners argued that the EPA could not remove EGUs from the CAA section 112(c) source category list without following the requirements of CAA section 112(c)(9).

On February 8, 2008, the D.C. Circuit vacated both the 2005 Action and CAMR. The D.C. Circuit held that the EPA failed to comply with the requirements of CAA section 112(c)(9) for delisting source categories. Specifically, the D.C. Circuit held that CAA section 112(c)(9) applies to the removal of "any source category" from the CAA section 112(c) list, including EGUs. The D.C. Circuit found that, by enacting CAA section 112(c)(9), Congress limited the EPA's discretion to reverse itself and remove source categories from the CAA section 112(c) list. The D.C. Circuit found that the EPA's contrary position would "nullify § 112(c)(9) altogether." New Jersey v. EPA, 517 F.3d 574, 583 (D.C. Cir. 2008). The D.C. Circuit did not reach the merits of petitioners' arguments on CAMR, but vacated CAMR for existing sources because coal-fired EGUs were already listed sources under CAA section 112. The D.C. Circuit reasoned that even under the EPA's own interpretation of the CAA, regulation of existing sources' Hg emissions under CAA section 111 was prohibited if those sources were a listed source category under CAA section 112. Id. The D.C. Circuit vacated and remanded CAMR for new sources because it concluded that the assumptions the EPA made when issuing CAMR for new sources were no longer accurate (i.e., that there would be no CAA section 112 regulation of EGUs and that the CAA section 111 standards would be accompanied by standards for existing sources). Id. at 583–84. Thus, CAMR and the 2005 Action became null and void.

On December 18, 2008, several environmental and public health organizations filed a complaint in the U.S. District Court for the District of Columbia. They alleged that the Agency had failed to perform a nondiscretionary duty under CAA section 304(a)(2), by failing to promulgate final CAA section 112(d) standards for HAP from coal- and oil-fired EGUs by the statutorily-mandated deadline, December 20, 2002, 2 years after such sources were listed under CAA section 112(c). The EPA settled that litigation. The consent decree resolving the case requires the EPA to sign a notice of proposed rulemaking setting forth the EPA's proposed CAA section 112(d) emission standards for coal- and oil-fired EGUs by March 16, 2011, and a notice of final rulemaking by December 16, 2011.

* * *

III. Appropriate and Necessary Finding

A. Overview

In December 2000, the EPA issued a finding pursuant to CAA section 112(n)(1)(A) that it was appropriate and necessary to regulate coal- and oil-fired EGUs under CAA section 112 and added such units to the list of source categories subject to regulation under section 112(d). The EPA found that it was appropriate to regulate HAP emissions from coal- and oil-fired EGUs because, among other reasons, Hg is a hazard to public health, and U.S. EGUs are the largest domestic source of Hg emissions. The EPA also found it appropriate to regulate HAP emissions from EGUs because it had identified certain control options that would effectively reduce HAP emissions from U.S. EGUs. The EPA found that it was necessary to regulate HAP emissions from U.S. EGUs under section 112 because the implementation of other requirements under the CAA will not adequately address the serious public health and environmental hazards arising from HAP emissions from U.S. EGUs and that CAA section 112 is intended to address HAP emissions. See 76 FR 24984-20985 (for further discussion of 2000 finding).

> As you read this section, think about what factors the EPA is considering when asking whether it is "appropriate" to regulate EGUs.

Because several years had passed since the 2000 finding, the EPA performed additional technical analyses for the proposed rule, even though those analyses were not required. These analyses included a national-scale Hg risk assessment focused on populations with high levels of self-caught fish consumption, and a set of 16 case studies of inhalation cancer risks for non-Hg HAP. The analyses confirm that it remains appropriate and necessary to regulate U.S. EGUs under section 112.

In the preamble to the proposed rule, the EPA reported the results of those additional technical analyses. Those analyses confirmed the 2000 finding that it is appropriate to regulate U.S. EGUs under section 112 by demonstrating that (1) Hg continues to pose a hazard to public health because up to 28 percent of watersheds were estimated to have Hg deposition attributable to U.S. EGUs that contributes to potential exposures above the reference dose for methylmercury (MeHg RfD), a level above which there is increased risk of neurological effects in children, (2) non-Hg HAP emissions pose a hazard to public health because case studies at 16 facilities demonstrated that lifetime cancer risks at 4 of the facilities exceed 1 in 1 million, and (3) U.S. EGUs remain the largest domestic source of Hg emissions and several HAP (e.g., HF, Se, HCl), and are among the largest contributors for other HAP (e.g., As, Cr, Ni, HCN). Thus, in the preamble to the proposed rule, the EPA found that Hg and non-Hg HAP emissions from U.S. EGUs pose hazards to public health, which confirmed the 2000 finding and demonstrated that it remains appropriate to regulate U.S. EGUs under section 112.

In the preamble to the proposed rule, the EPA also found that it is appropriate to regulate U.S. EGUs because (1) Hg emissions pose a hazard to the environment and wildlife, adversely impacting species of fish-eating birds and mammals, (2) acid gas HAP pose a hazard to the environment because they contribute to aquatic acidification, and (3) effective controls are available to reduce Hg and non-Hg HAP emissions from U.S. EGUs.

* * *

Based on our consideration of the peer reviews, public comments, and our updated analyses, we confirm the findings that Hg and non-Hg HAP emissions from U.S. EGUs pose hazards to public health and that it remains appropriate to regulate U.S. EGUs under CAA section 112. We also conclude that it remains appropriate to regulate U.S. EGUs under CAA section 112 because of the magnitude of Hg and non-Hg emissions, environmental effects of Hg and certain non-Hg emissions, and the availability of controls to reduce HAP emissions from EGUs.

* * *

F. Public Comments and Responses to the Appropriate and Necessary Finding

1. Legal Aspects of Appropriate and Necessary Finding

* * *

b. Interpretation of "Appropriate" and "Necessary"

* * *

Comment: Several commenters assert that in the 1990 amendments to the Clean Air Act, Congress directed the EPA to base its determination regarding regulation of fossil-fuel-fired generating units on consideration of any adverse public health effects identified in the study mandated by the first sentence of section 112(n)(1)(A) and that Congress did not dictate in section

112(n)(1)(A) that the EPA must regulate electric utility steam generating units under section 112.

According to the commenters the sponsor of the House bill that became section 112(n)(1)(A) provides an explanation that contradicts the EPA's approach to regulating EGUs:

> Pursuant to section 112(n), the Administrator may regulate fossil fuel fired electric utility steam generating units only if the studies described in section 112(n) clearly establish that emissions of any pollutant, or aggregate of pollutants, from such units cause a significant risk of serious adverse effects on the public health. Thus, * * * he may regulate only those units that he determines—after taking into account compliance with all provisions of the act and any other Federal, State, or local regulation and voluntary emission reductions—have been demonstrated to cause a significant threat of serious adverse effects on the public health.

136 Cong. Rec. H12,934 (daily ed. Oct. 26, 1990) (statement of Rep. Michael Oxley).

The commenters stated that the EPA position is premised on the assumption that "regulation under section 112" necessarily means "regulation under 112(d)" and falsely premised on the assumption that source categories listed by operation of section 112(n)(1)(A) cannot be regulated differently. The commenters conclude that the language of section 112(n)(1)(a) reflects Congress' intent that "regulation of HAP from EGUs was not intended to operate under section 112(d) but was instead intended to be tailored to the findings of the utility study mandated by section 112(n)(1)(A)."

Response: The commenters maintain that the Agency's interpretation of CAA section 112(n)(1) is flawed in many respects. The primary support for one commenter's arguments against EPA's interpretation, including in the comment above, is legislative history in the form of statements from one Congressman, Representative Oxley. The Supreme Court has repeatedly stated that the statements of one legislator alone should not be given much weight. * * * As these cases show, the Supreme Court does not give weight to the statements of an individual legislator, except when the statements are supported by other legislative history and the clear intent of the statute. The commenters cited no case law that would support reliance on such limited legislative history.

The commenter has not cited any other legislative history to support Representative Oxley's statement, and the lack of additional support makes the statement of little utility or import under the case law. In fact, there does not appear to be anything in the House, Senate, or Committee Reports that supports Oxley's statement. The lack of support for Oxley's statement in the Committee Report is particularly telling since, as the commenter notes, the House and Senate bills required different approaches to regulating EGUs under section 112, with the Senate bill requiring EGUs be regulated prior to the Utility Study. In fact, legislative statements from Senator Durenberger, a supporter of the Senate version, demonstrate that others would almost certainly not have agreed with Oxley's interpretation. For example, Senator Durenberger stated, "It seems to me inequitable to impose a regulatory regime on every industry in America and then exempt one category, especially a category like power plants which are a significant part of the air toxics problem."

Senator Durenberger discussed the negotiations with the Administration and the industry push to avoid regulation, including industry arguments for not regulating Hg from U.S. EGUs:

> The utility industry continued to adamantly oppose [regulation under section 112]. First, they argued that mercury isn't much of an environmental problem. But as the evidence mounted over the summer and it became clear that mercury is a substantial threat to the health of our lakes, rivers and estuaries and that power plants are among the principal culprits, they changed their tactic. Now they are arguing that mercury is a global problem so severe that just cleaning up U.S. power plants won't make enough of a difference to be worth it. They've gone from 'we're not a problem' to 'you can't regulate us until you address the whole global problem.' Recasting an issue that way is not new around here. So, it is not a surprise. But it does suggest the direction in which this debate will be heading in the next few years.

Senator Durenberger also explained why the House version was adopted:

> Given that a resolution of the difficult issues in the conference were necessary to conclude work on this bill, the Senate proposed to recede to the House provision which was taken from the original administration bill. It provides for a 3-year study of utility emissions followed by regulation to the extent that the Administrator finds them necessary.

Senator Durenberger's statements indicate that it is unlikely that he would agree with Oxley's interpretation of CAA section 112(n)(1), a provision that provides the Agency with considerable discretion, and nothing indicates that others in the Senate (or for that matter anyone else in the House) would agree with that interpretation. Given the Supreme Court's views on the use of such limited legislative history, the EPA reasonably declined to consider (or even discuss) the legislative history in the preamble to the proposed rule and we believe it would be improper to ascribe Representative Oxley's statements to the entire Congress.

Moreover, Representative Oxley's statement directly conflicts with the statutory text. Representative Oxley stated that "[the Administrator may regulate only those units that he determines—after taking into account compliance with all provisions of the act and any other Federal, State, or local regulation and voluntary emission reductions—have been demonstrated to cause a significant threat of serious adverse effects on the public health." However, the Utility Study required under CAA section 112(n)(1)(A) directs the Agency to consider the hazards to public health reasonably anticipated to occur after "imposition of the requirements of [the Clean Air Act]." EPA was not required to consider state or local regulations or voluntary emission reduction programs in the Utility Study, and that study is the only condition precedent to making the appropriate and necessary finding.

The legislative history the commenters rely on is not controlling. The Agency believes that it has reasonably interpreted section 112(n)(1)(A), for all the reasons described herein and in the proposal. The commenters also cite Representative Oxley's statements as support for alternative interpretations of CAA section 112(n)(1). We believe that any arguments that rely on such limited legislative history are without merit.

* * *

Comment: A number of commenters agreed with the Agency's interpretation of section 112(n)(1) and the terms appropriate and necessary. The commenters also agreed that the EPA's interpretation of that provision was reasonable and consistent with the statute.

Response: We agree with the commenters and appreciate their support.

* * *

e. Considering Costs in Finding

Comment: Several commenters assert that the EPA must consider costs in assessing whether regulation of EGUs is appropriate under CAA section 112(n)(1)(A). Commenters posit that the EPA's position that "the term 'appropriate' * * * does not allow for the consideration of costs in assessing whether hazards * * * are reasonably anticipated to occur based on EGU emissions" does not withstand scrutiny. According to the commenters, the treatment of "costs" under section 112(c) does not support the Agency's position, and the process by which sources may be "delisted" under section 112(c)(9), including no consideration of costs, sheds no light on the circumstances under which it may be "appropriate" to regulate EGUs under section 112(n)(1)(A).

Commenters characterize as "unintelligible" the EPA's position that it is "reasonable to conclude that costs may not be considered in determining whether to regulate EGUs" when "hazards to public health and the environmental are at issue." Two commenters stated that a natural reading of the term "appropriate" would include the consideration of costs. According to the commenters, something may be found to be "appropriate" where it is "specially suitable," "fit," or "proper." See Webster's Third New International Dictionary at 106 (1993). The term "appropriate" carries with it the connotation of something that is "suitable or proper in the circumstances." See New Oxford American Dictionary (2d Ed. 2005). Considering the costs associated with undertaking a particular action is inextricably linked with any determination as to whether that action is "specially suitable" or "proper in the circumstances." One commenter notes that in 2005, the EPA used the dictionary definition of "appropriate," as being "especially suitable or compatible" and that it would be difficult to fathom how a regulatory program could be either "suitable" or "compatible" for a given public health objective without consideration of cost.

One commenter asserts that on the face of CAA section 112(n)(1)(A), it is clear that the EPA is expected to consider costs. According to the commenter, that Congress intended that the EPA investigate and consider "alternative control strategies" for emissions as part of the section 112 (n)(1) Utility Study when making the "appropriate and necessary" determination refutes the notion that the Agency can, and indeed must, disregard the cost of regulation in making that determination, because the cost of a given emission "control strategy" is a central factor in any evaluation of "alternative" controls.

Further, according to commenters, it is well-settled that CAA regulatory provisions should be read with a presumption in favor of considering costs (citing Michigan v. EPA, 213 F.3d 663, 678 (D.C. Cir. 2000)), and the legislative history of section 112(n)(1)(A) confirms that Congress intended EPA to consider costs (citing Oxley Statement at 1417).

Commenters also assert that the EPA falsely represents that it "did not consider costs when making the "appropriate" determination in the EPA's December 2000 notice (76 FR at 24,989/2).

Response: The commenters first take issue with EPA's explanation of why the Agency determined that costs should not be considered in making the appropriate determination. What commenters do not identify is an express statutory requirement that the Agency consider costs in making the appropriate determination. Congress treated the regulation of HAP emissions differently in the 1990 CAA amendments because the Agency was not acting quickly enough to address these air pollutants with the potential to adversely affect human health and the environment. See New Jersey, 517 F.3d at 578. Specifically, following the 1990 CAA amendments, the CAA required the Agency to list source categories and nothing in the statute required us to consider costs in those listing decision[s], and we have not done so when listing other source categories. Thus, it is reasonable to make the listing decision, including the appropriate determination, without considering costs.

The commenters next argue that the Agency is compelled by the statute to consider costs based on a dictionary definition of "appropriate" and the CAA section 112(n)(1)(A) direction to consider alternative control strategies for regulating HAP emissions in the Utility Study.

Concerning the definition of "appropriate", commenters stated:

> Not only is it "reasonable" for EPA to consider costs in determin-
> ing whether it is "appropriate" to regulate EGU HAP emissions, a
> natural reading of the term indicates that excluding the consideration
> of costs would be entirely unreasonable. Something may be found
> to be "appropriate" where it is "specially suitable," "fit," or "proper."
> See Webster's Third New International Dictionary at 106 (1993).
> The term "appropriate" carries with it the connotation of something

that is "suitable or proper in the circumstances." See New Oxford American Dictionary (2d Ed. 2005) at 76. Considering the costs associated with undertaking a particular action is inextricably linked with any determination as to whether that action is "specially suitable" or "proper in the circumstances."

The EPA believes the definition[s] of "appropriate" that the commenters provide wholly support its interpretation and nothing about the definition compels a consideration of costs. It is appropriate to regulate EGUs under CAA section 112 because EPA has determined that HAP emissions from EGUs pose hazards to public health and the environment, and section 112 is "specially suitable" for regulating HAP emissions, and Congress specifically designated CAA section 112 as the "proper" authority for regulating HAP emissions from stationary sources, including EGUs. Section 112 of the CAA is "suitable [and] proper in the circumstances" because EPA has identified a hazard to public health and the environment from HAP emissions from EGUs and Congress directed the Agency to regulate HAP emissions from EGUs under that provision if we make such a finding. Cost does not have to be read into the definition of "appropriate" as commenter suggests. In addition, as stated elsewhere in response to comments, the Agency does not consider costs in any listing or delisting determinations, and the EPA maintains that it is reasonable to assess whether to list EGUs (i.e. the appropriate and necessary finding) without considering costs.

The commenters' argument that costs must be considered based on the CAA section 112(n)(1)(A) requirement to "develop and describe alternative control strategies" in the Utility Study is equally flawed. The argument is flawed because Congress did not direct the Agency to consider in the Utility Study the costs of the controls when evaluating the alternative control strategies. In addition, the EPA did not consider the costs of the alternative controls in the Utility Study, as implied by the commenter. Thus, even viewing section 112(n)(1)(A) in isolation, there is nothing in that section that compels EPA to consider costs. For the reasons described herein, we do not believe that it is appropriate to consider costs in determining whether to regulate EGUs under section 112.

* * *

G. EPA Affirms the Finding That It Is Appropriate and Necessary to Regulate EGUs To Address Public Health and Environmental Hazards Associated With Emissions of Hg and Non-Hg HAP From EGUs

In response to peer reviews of both the Hg and non-Hg HAP risk analyses, and taking into account public comments, the EPA conducted revised analyses of the risks associated with emissions of Hg and non-Hg HAP from U.S. EGUs. These revised analyses demonstrated that the risk results reported in the preamble to the proposed rule are robust to revisions in response to the peer reviews and public comments.

Specifically, the revised Hg Risk TSD shows that up to 29 percent of modeled watersheds have populations potentially at-risk from exposure to Hg from U.S. EGUs. This 29 percent of watersheds with populations potentially at-risk includes up to 10 percent

A "TSD" is a "Technical Support Document."

of modeled watersheds where deposition from U.S. EGUs alone leads to potential exposures that exceed the MeHg RfD, and up to 24 percent of modeled watersheds where total potential exposures to MeHg exceed the RfD and U.S. EGUs contribute at least 5 percent to Hg deposition. Each of these results independently supports our conclusion that U.S. EGUs pose hazards to public health.

In the preamble to the proposed rule and in the 2000 finding, the EPA explained at length the serious nature of the health effects associated with Hg exposures, and the persistent nature of Hg in the environment. Congress specifically recognized the significant impacts of persistent bioaccumulative pollutants, like Hg, when it enacted section 112(c)(6), which requires the EPA to subject source categories listed pursuant to that section to MACT standards. Congress also required certain studies be conducted under CAA section 112(n) regarding the health effects of Hg. The EPA interprets CAA section 112(n)(1), with regard to Hg, as intended to protect the public, including sensitive populations, against exposures to Hg from EGUs that would exceed the level determined by the EPA to be without appreciable risk, e.g., exposures that are above the RfD for methylmercury (MeHg), or would contribute additional risk in areas where Hg exposures exceed the RfD due to contributions from all sources of Hg. Our recent technical analyses show that 98 percent of the watersheds for which we had fish tissue data have total Hg deposition such that potential exposures exceed the MeHg RfD, above which there is an increased risk of adverse effects on human health. In these watersheds, any reductions in exposures to Hg will reduce risk, and thus the incremental contribution to Hg exposure from any individual source or group of sources, such as EGUs, may reasonably be anticipated to cause additional risk.

* * *

Given these findings, and considering that (1) the revised risk analysis showed the percent of modeled watersheds with populations potentially at-risk increased from 28 to 29 percent, and (2) the revised analysis includes 36 percent more watersheds, which significantly expands the coverage in several states, we conclude that the finding that emissions of Hg from U.S. EGUs pose a hazard to public health is confirmed by the national-scale revised Hg Risk TSD. As a result, we conclude that it remains appropriate to regulate Hg emissions from U.S. EGUs because those Hg emissions pose a hazard to public health.

* * *

In summary, we confirm the findings that Hg and non-Hg HAP emissions from U.S. EGUs each pose hazards to public health and that it remains appropriate to regulate U.S. EGUs under CAA section 112 for those reasons. We also conclude that it remains appropriate to regulate EGUs under CAA section 112 because of the magnitude of Hg and non-Hg emissions and the environmental effects of Hg and some non-Hg emissions, each of which standing alone, supports the appropriate finding. The availability of controls to reduce HAP emissions from EGUs only further supports the appropriate finding.

* * *

NOTES & QUESTIONS

1. What are the key reasons the EPA found it "appropriate" to regulate coal- and oil-fired EGUs? Given what you know about agencies in general (and the fact that the EPA is the *Environmental Protection* Agency"), do these seem like the kind of things on which an agency should

base its decision to regulate? Were there aspects of the EPA's interpretation that it might be more appropriate (if you'll pardon the pun!) for a court to do?

2. How does the approach to interpretation the EPA took compare with the approach taken in the judicial opinions interpreting statutes that you read in Parts V and VI of this book? When the EPA "interprets" a statute as it did here, is it engaged in essentially the same activity as when the courts do it?

3. As you saw, the EPA disagreed with many commenters. Thus, as you might imagine, many commenters were unhappy with the EPA's decision to conclude that it was "appropriate and necessary" to regulate HAPs from EGUs? (Have you figured out all the acronyms yet?) Who in particular do you think was most unhappy? As you will see in Chapter 36, the EPA's finding in this 2012 action was by no means the final word on the question of whether it is "appropriate and necessary" to regulate HAPs from EGUs because the unhappy parties turned to their lawyers and sought judicial review.

4. Is the agency's expertise on display in this excerpt? If so, what kind of expertise? Is it scientific expertise? Economic? Legal? Political? Some combination of all four types?

5. What role is the agency's political accountability playing here? Is the agency's political accountability affecting its interpretation of "appropriate"? Look again at the section of the preamble describing the litigation history (Section II.B). Consider when things happened at the EPA and who the President was at each moment. Does that tell us something about political accountability? If so, is that a good thing?

6. Relatedly, in what sense is the agency's political accountability connected to the original Congress that adopted the relevant language in the Clean Air Act Amendments of 1990? The EPA made determinations about whether it is "appropriate" to regulate coal- and oil-fired EGUs in 2000, 2005, and (in the document you read) in 2012. As you will see in Chapter 36, this saga may still not be over as this book goes to press. The EPA *again* made determinations about whether it is "appropriate" to regulate coal- and oil-fired EGUs in 2016, 2020, and 2023. How does the political accountability of the Presidents at each of these six points compare with an agency being accountable to the 1990

Congress? When interpreting a statute more than two decades (now, three decades) later, should the agency still be accountable to the 1990 Congress? Or does it make more sense for it to be accountable to the current President? Does it matter that the word that Congress used in 1990 is "appropriate," an open-ended term?

7. Does anything in this document seem like the product of agency "capture"? Remember, there were over 900,000 commenters on this rule? Who are all those commenters? In literal terms, they are of course "interests" in the sense that we used the term in the section above on agency capture. They all have an "interest" in the regulation of hazardous air pollutants from power plants. Does the fact that it is possible for there to be so many interests affect your thinking about how "capture" might work in the real world?

Test Your Understanding

 To assess your understanding of the material in this chapter, click here to take a quiz.

34

Introduction to Judicial Review of Agency Interpretation of Statutes

---

Key Concepts

- Judicial deference to agency interpretation
- Determining when Congress has delegated interpretive authority
- *Skidmore* deference
- "Power to persuade, if lacking power to control"

Chapter Summary

One of the most important questions in the field of statutory interpretation is when and how much a reviewing court should defer to the interpretation that an agency has given to a piece of legal text that it is charged with administering. The question remains live today, but especially at the federal level it has a rich history as well. Importantly, the legal doctrine on this question is in flux. Thus, to understand the competing concerns requires some understanding of the jurisprudential history. The Supreme Court's 1984 decision in *Chevron v. Natural Resources Defense Council* remains an important decision in the field, but as we will see in Chapter 37, by the early 2020s the Supreme Court had overlaid the so-called "*Chevron* doctrine" with what it called the "Major Questions Doctrine." But to understand how *Chevron* works in practice, as well as how the Major Questions Doctrine is layered on top of it, first requires some familiarity with what preceded *Chevron*. In particular, this chapter summarizes two labor and employment law cases from the 1940s: *NLRB v. Hearst Publications, and Skidmore v. Swift & Company*. *Skidmore* gave rise to a set of factors that purported to guide federal courts in deciding how much weight to afford an agency interpretation, but in the forty years between *Skidmore* and *Chevron* the deference doctrine had become confused.

Notwithstanding—or perhaps because of—the unique agency characteristics discussed in the previous chapter, federal courts in particular have wrestled for many years with the question of how much deference to give to agency interpretations of statutes that the agency is charged with administering. The next chapter will discuss a centrally important Administrative Law decision, *Chevron, U.S.A., Inc. v. Natural Resources Defense Council, Inc.*, 467 U.S. 837 (1984), which has framed this question for most of the past four decades. *Chevron* is a case about judicial review of agency interpretations of statutory text. To situate *Chevron* properly, however, it is helpful to know a little about the principal doctrines of judicial review of agency construction that preceded *Chevron*.

A. The *Skidmore* Framework

Two Supreme Court cases from forty years before *Chevron* figure most prominently in setting the stage for the *Chevron* decision. Both cases involved questions of labor and employment law, one under the National Labor Relations Act, and the other under the Fair Labor Standards Act. In turn, the National Labor Relations Board, and the Wage and Hour Division of the U.S. Department of Labor, each played a role in the Court's resolution of the interpretive problems. As you read about these cases, think particularly about the agencies' roles and the Court's view of these roles.

1. Who Is an Employee? (the "Newsboy" Issue)

A long-standing problem in the field of labor law is whether a person performing labor or service for another is an employee, or instead is an independent contractor. On that distinction hang a host of legal implications. In particular, the National Labor Relations Act of 1935 (NLRA, also sometimes called "The Wagner Act") guaranteed private-sector "employees" the right to organize into trade unions. The Act included this explanation of the term "employee":

> The term "employee" shall include any employee, and shall not be limited to the employees of a particular employer, unless the Act explicitly states otherwise, and shall include any individual whose work has ceased as a consequence of, or in connection with, any current labor dispute or because of any unfair labor practice, and who has not obtained any other regular and substantially equivalent employment, but shall not include any individual employed as an agricultural laborer, or in the domestic service of any family or person at his home, or any individual employed by his parent or spouse. 29 U.S.C. 152(3).

But long before 1935, a host of common-law factors and tests had developed for categorizing workers as either employees or contractors, frequently focused on the extent to which the entity paying the worker controlled the work. One frequent (though not necessarily determinative) touchstone was whether or not liability for a worker's tort extended to the entity paying the worker.

DIY
Who Is an "Employee"?

 At the time of the NLRA's enactment, newspaper publishers in Los Angeles, as in many big cities, relied on a cadre of "newsboys" (mostly men, not "boys") to sell papers. Newsboys generally purchased newspapers on credit from the publishers and then resold them on the street at a price the publishers set. Their compensation was the difference between the newspapers' purchase price and their sale price. The newsboys desired to unionize and engage in collective bargaining under the NLRA. Imagine you are counsel to the National Labor Relations Board, advising the Board whether the newsboys are "employees" entitled to the benefits of the NLRA. What would you want to know? How would you recommend that the Board respond to the newsboys' request?

The publishers argued that the newsboys were not covered by the NLRA because they were independent contractors, not employees. The publishers had a strong argument if the term "employee" in the NLRA were construed using established common-law principles. But the newsboys argued that the NLRA was deliberately broader in its scope. The decision below presents the resolution of this issue. Before reading it, predict which way you think the case will come out, and why.

NLRB v. Hearst Publications
322 U.S. 111 (1944)

Mr. Justice Rutledge delivered the opinion of the Court.

These cases arise from the refusal of respondents, publishers of four Los Angeles daily newspapers, to bargain collectively with a union representing newsboys who distribute their papers on the streets of that city. Respondents' contention that they were not required to bargain because the newsboys are not their 'employees' within the meaning of that term in the National Labor Relations Act, 49 Stat. 450, 29 U.S.C. 152, presents the important question which we granted certiorari to resolve. The proceedings before the National Labor Relations Board were begun with the filing of four petitions for investigation and certification by Los Angeles Newsboys Local Industrial Union No. 75. * * *

[The findings of the Board disclose that the] papers are distributed to the ultimate consumer through a variety of channels, including independent dealers and newsstands often attached to drug, grocery or confectionery stores, carriers who make home deliveries, and newsboys who sell on the streets of the city and its suburbs. Only the last of these are involved in this case.

The newsboys work under varying terms and conditions. They may be 'bootjackers,' selling to the general public at places other than established corners, or they may sell at fixed 'spots.' They may sell only casually or part-time, or full-time; and they may be employed regularly and continuously or only temporarily. The [bargaining] units which the Board determined to be appropriate are composed of those who sell full-time at established spots. Those vendors, misnamed boys, are generally mature men, dependent upon the proceeds of their sales for their sustenance, and frequently supporters of families. Working thus as news vendors on a regular basis often for a number of years, they form a stable group with relatively little turnover, in contrast to schoolboys and others who sell as bootjackers, temporary and casual distributors.

Over-all circulation and distribution of the papers are under the general supervision of circulation managers. But for purposes of street distribution each paper has divided metropolitan Los Angeles into geographic districts. Each district is under the direct and close supervision of a district manager. His function in the mechanics of distribution is to supply the newsboys in his district with papers which he obtains from the publisher and to turn over to the publisher the receipts which he collects from their sales, either directly or with the assistance of 'checkmen' or 'main spot' boys. * * *

The newsboys' compensation consists in the difference between the prices at which they sell the papers and the prices they pay for them. The former are fixed by the publishers and the latter are fixed either by the publishers or, in the case of [one of the papers], by the district manager. In practice the newsboys receive their papers on credit. They pay for those sold either sometime during or after the close of their selling day, returning for credit all unsold papers. Lost or otherwise unreturned papers, however, must be paid for as though sold. Not only is the 'profit' per paper thus effectively fixed by the publisher, but substantial control of the newsboys' total 'take home' can be effected through the ability to designate their sales areas and the power to determine the number of papers allocated to each. While as a practical matter this power is not exercised fully, the newsboys' 'right' to decide how many papers they will take is also not absolute. In practice, the Board found, they cannot determine the size of their established order without the cooperation of the district manager. And often the number of papers they must take is determined unilaterally by the district managers.

In addition to effectively fixing the compensation, respondents in a variety of ways prescribe, if not the minutiae of daily activities, at least the broad terms and conditions of work. * * * [D]istrict managers' instructions in what the publishers apparently regard as helpful sales technique are expected to be followed. Such varied items as the manner of displaying the paper, of emphasizing current features and headlines, and of placing advertising placards, or the advantages of soliciting customers at specific stores or in the traffic lanes are among the subjects of this instruction. Moreover, newsboys are furnished with sales equipment, such as racks, boxes and change aprons, and advertising placards by the publishers. In this pattern of employment the Board found that the newsboys are an integral part of the publishers' distribution system and circulation organization. And the record discloses that the newsboys and checkmen feel they are employees of the papers and respondents' supervisory employees, if not respondents themselves, regard them as such.

In addition to questioning the sufficiency of the evidence to sustain these findings, respondents point to a number of other attributes characterizing their relationship with the newsboys and urge that on the entire record the latter cannot be considered their employees. They base this conclusion on the argument that by common-law standards the extent of their control and direction of the newsboys' working activities creates no more than an 'independent contractor' relationship and that common-law standards determine the 'employee' relationship under the Act. They further urge that the Board's selection of a collective bargaining unit is neither appropriate nor supported by substantial evidence.

I.

The principal question is whether the newsboys are 'employees.' Because Congress did not explicitly define the term, respondents say its meaning must be determined by reference to common-law standards. In their view 'common-law standards' are those the courts have applied in distinguishing between 'employees' and 'independent contractors' when working out various problems unrelated to the Wagner Act's purposes and provisions.

The argument assumes that there is some simple, uniform and easily applicable test which the courts have used, in dealing with such problems, to determine whether persons doing work for others fall in one class or the other. Unfortunately this is not true. Only by a long and tortuous history was the simple formulation worked out which has been stated most frequently as 'the test' for deciding whether one who hires another is responsible in tort for his wrongdoing. But this formula has been by no means exclusively controlling in the solution of other problems. And its simplicity has been illusory because it is more largely simplicity of formulation than of application. Few problems in the law have given greater variety of application and conflict in results than the cases arising in the borderland between what is clearly an employer-employee relationship and what is clearly one of independent entrepreneurial dealing. This is true within the limited field of determining vicarious liability in tort. It becomes more so when the field is expanded to include all of the possible applications of the distinction.

It is hardly necessary to stress particular instances of these variations or to emphasize that they have arisen principally, first, in the struggle of the courts to work out common-law liabilities where the legislature has given no guides for judgment, more recently also under statutes which have posed the same problem for solution in the light of the enactment's particular terms and purposes. It is enough to point out that, with reference to an identical problem, results may be contrary over a very considerable region of doubt in applying the distinction, depending upon the state or jurisdiction where the determination is made; and that within a single jurisdiction a person who, for instance, is held to be an 'independent contractor' for the purpose of imposing vicarious liability in tort may be an 'employee' for the purposes of particular legislation, such as unemployment compensation. In short, the assumed simplicity and uniformity, resulting from application of 'common-law standards,' does not exist.

Mere reference to these possible variations as characterizing the application of the Wagner Act in the treatment of persons identically situated in the facts surrounding their employment and in the influences tending to disrupt it, would be enough to require pause before accepting a thesis which would introduce them into its administration. This would be true, even if the statute itself had indicated less clearly than it does the intent they should not apply.

Two possible consequences could follow. One would be to refer the decision of who are employees to local state law. The alternative would be to make it turn on a sort of pervading general essence distilled from state law. Congress obviously did not intend the former result. It would introduce variations into the statute's operation as wide as the differences the forty-eight states and other local jurisdictions make in applying the distinction for wholly different purposes. Persons who might be 'employees' in one state would be 'independent contractors' in another. They would be within or without the statute's protection depending not on whether their situation falls factually within the ambit Congress had in mind, but upon the accidents of the location of their work and the attitude of the particular local jurisdiction in casting doubtful cases one way or the other. Persons working across state lines might fall in one class or the other, possibly both, depending on whether the Board and the courts would be required to give effect to the law of one state or of the adjoining one, or to that of each in relation to the portion of the work done within its borders.

Both the terms and the purposes of the statute, as well as the legislative history, show that Congress had in mind no such patchwork plan for securing freedom of employees' organization and of collective bargaining. The Wagner Act is federal legislation, administered by a national agency, intended to solve a national problem on a national scale. It is an Act, therefore, in reference to which it is not only proper, but necessary for us to assume, 'in the absence of a plain indication to the contrary, that Congress . . . is not making the application of the federal act dependent on state law.' Nothing in the statute's background, history, terms or purposes indicates its scope is to be limited by such varying local conceptions, either statutory or judicial, or that it is to be administered in accordance with whatever different standards the respective states may see fit to adopt for the disposition of unrelated, local problems. Consequently, so far as the meaning of 'employee' in this statute is concerned, 'the federal law must prevail no matter what name is given to the interest or right by state law.'

II.

Whether, given the intended national uniformity, the term 'employee' includes such workers as these newsboys must be answered primarily from the history, terms and purposes of the legislation. The word 'is not treated by Congress as a word of art having a definite meaning. . . .' Rather 'it takes color from its surroundings. . .(in) the statute where it appears,' *United States v. American Trucking Associations, Inc.*, 310 U.S. 534, 545, and derives meaning from the context of that statute, which 'must be read in the light of the mischief to be corrected and the end to be attained.' *South Chicago Coal & Dock Co. v. Bassett*, 309 U.S. 251, 259.

Congress, on the one hand, was not thinking solely of the immediate technical relation of employer and employee. It had in mind at least some other persons than those standing in the proximate legal relation of employee to the particular employer involved in the labor dispute. It cannot be taken, however, that the purpose was to include all other persons who may perform service for another or was to ignore entirely legal classifications made for other purposes. Congress had in mind a wider field than the narrow technical legal relation of 'master and servant,' as the common law had worked this out in all its variations, and at the same time a narrower one than the entire area of rendering service to others. The question comes down therefore to how much was included of the intermediate region between what is clearly and unequivocally 'employment,' by any appropriate test, and what is as clearly entrepreneurial enterprise and not employment.

It will not do, for deciding this question as one of uniform national application, to import wholesale the traditional common-law conceptions or some distilled essence of their local variations as exclusively controlling limitations upon the scope of the statute's effectiveness. To do this would be merely to select some of the local, hairline variations for nation-wide application and thus to reject others for coverage under the Act. That result hardly would be consistent with the statute's broad terms and purposes.

Congress was not seeking to solve the nationally harassing problems with which the statute deals by solutions only partially effective. It rather sought to find a broad solution, one that would bring industrial peace by substituting, so far as its power could reach, the rights of workers to self-organization and collective bargaining for the industrial strife which prevails where these rights are not effectively established. Yet only partial solutions would be provided if large segments of workers about whose technical legal position such local differences exist should be wholly excluded from coverage by reason of such differences. Yet that result could not be avoided, if choice must be made among them and controlled by them in deciding who are 'employees' within the Act's meaning. Enmeshed in such distinctions, the administration of the statute soon might become encumbered by the same sort of technical legal refinement as has characterized the long evolution of the employee-independent contractor dichotomy in the courts for other purposes. The consequences would be ultimately to defeat, in part at least, the achievement of the statute's objectives. Congress no more intended to import this mass of technicality as a controlling 'standard' for uniform national application than to refer decision of the question outright to the local law.

The Act, as its first section states, was designed to avert the 'substantial obstructions to the free flow of commerce' which result from 'strikes and other forms of industrial strife or unrest' by eliminating the causes of that unrest. It is premised on explicit findings that strikes and industrial strife themselves result in large measure from the refusal of employers to bargain collectively and the inability of individual workers to bargain successfully for improvements in their 'wages, hours, or other working conditions' with employers who are 'organized in the corporate or other forms of ownership association.' Hence the avowed and interrelated purposes of the Act are to encourage collective bargaining and to remedy the individual worker's inequality of bargaining power by 'protecting the exercise . . . of full freedom of association, self-organization, and designation of representatives of their own choosing, for the purpose of negotiating the terms and conditions of their employment or other mutual aid or protection.' 49 Stat. 449, 450.

The mischief at which the Act is aimed and the remedies it offers are not confined exclusively to 'employees' within the traditional legal distinctions separating them from 'independent contractors.' Myriad forms of service relationship, with infinite and subtle variations in the terms of employment, blanket the nation's economy. Some are within this Act, others beyond its coverage. Large numbers will fall clearly on one side or on the other, by whatever test may be applied. But intermediate there will be many, the incidents of whose employment partake in part of the one group, in part of the other, in varying proportions of weight. And consequently the legal pendulum, for purposes of applying the statute, may swing one way or the other, depending upon the weight of this balance and its relation to the special purpose at hand.

Unless the common-law tests are to be imported and made exclusively controlling, without regard to the statute's purposes, it cannot be irrelevant that the particular workers in these cases are subject, as a matter of economic fact, to the evils the statute was designed to eradicate and that the remedies it affords are appropriate for preventing them or curing their harmful effects in the special situation. Interruption of commerce through strikes and unrest may stem as well from labor disputes between some who, for other purposes, are technically 'independent contractors' and their employers as from disputes between persons who, for those purposes, are 'employees' and their employers. * * *

? Why does the Court believe that the task has been assigned primarily to the NLRB? Notice that the Court uses the passive voice, avoiding explicitly saying who (if anyone!) assigned the task to the agency. Is the Court making a claim that Congress in fact assigned the task to the agency? If so, does it cite to any evidence in the statute or legislative history suggesting Congress gave the agency interpretive authority? Or, does the rest of this paragraph suggest that the Court itself is implicitly comparing the relative institutional competence of courts and the agency and concluding that the agency is the more appropriate decisionmaker?

It is not necessary in this case to make a completely definitive limitation around the term 'employee.' That task has been assigned primarily to the agency created by Congress to administer the Act. Determination of 'where all the conditions of the relation require protection' involves inquiries for the Board charged with this duty. Everyday experience in the administration of the statute gives it familiarity with the circumstances and backgrounds of employment relationships in various industries, with the abilities and needs of the workers for self-organization and collective action, and with the adaptability of collective bargaining for the peaceful settlement of their disputes with their employers. The experience thus acquired must be brought frequently to bear on the question who is an employee under the Act. Resolving that question, like determining whether unfair labor practices have been committed, 'belongs to the usual administrative routine' of the Board.

In making that body's determinations as to the facts in these matters conclusive, if supported by evidence, Congress entrusted to it primarily the decision whether the evidence establishes the material facts. Hence in reviewing the Board's ultimate conclusions, it is not the court's function to substitute its own inferences of fact for the Board's, when the latter have support in the record. Undoubtedly questions of statutory interpretation, especially when arising in the first instance in judicial proceedings, are for the courts to resolve, giving appropriate weight to the judgment of those whose special duty is to administer the questioned statute. But where the question is one of specific application of a broad statutory term in a proceeding in which the agency administering the statute must determine it initially, the reviewing court's function is limited. * * * [T]he Board's determination that specified persons are 'employees' under this Act is to be accepted if it has 'warrant in the record' and a reasonable basis in law.

In this case the Board found that the designated newsboys work continuously and regularly, rely upon their earnings for the support of themselves and their families, and have their total wages influenced in large measure by the publishers who dictate their buying and selling prices, fix their markets and control their supply of papers. Their hours of work and their efforts on the job are supervised and to some extent prescribed by the publishers or their agents. Much of their sales equipment and advertising materials is furnished by the publishers with the intention that it be used for the publisher's benefit. Stating that 'the primary consideration in the determination of the applicability of the statutory definition is whether effectuation of the declared policy and purposes of the Act comprehend securing to the individual the rights guaranteed and protection afforded by the Act,' the Board concluded that the newsboys are employees. The record sustains the Board's findings and there is ample basis in the law for its conclusion.

III.

The Board's selection of the collective bargaining units also must be upheld. * * *

The judgments are reversed and the causes are remanded for further proceedings not inconsistent with this opinion. * * *

MR. JUSTICE ROBERTS [dissenting].

I think the judgment of the Circuit Court of Appeals should be affirmed. The opinion of that court * * * seems to me adequately to state the controlling facts and correctly to deal with the question of law presented for decision. I should not add anything were it not for certain arguments presented here and apparently accepted by the court.

I think it plain that newsboys are not 'employees' of the respondents within the meaning and intent of the National Labor Relations Act. When Congress * * * said: 'The term 'employee' shall include any employee, . . .'

it stated as clearly as language could do it that the provisions of the Act were to extend to those who, as a result of decades of tradition which had become part of the common understanding of our people, bear the named relationship. Clearly also Congress did not delegate to the National Labor Relations Board the function of defining the relationship of employment so as to promote what the Board understood to be the underlying purpose of the statute. The question who is an employee, so as to make the statute applicable to him, is a question of the meaning of the Act and, therefore, is a judicial and not an administrative question.

> **?** In contrast to the majority, notice that Justice Roberts is using the active voice to make the opposite point from the majority. In what sense does the majority think Justice Roberts is wrong here?

I do not think that the court below suggested that the federal courts sitting in the various states must determine whether a given person is an employee by application of either the local statutes or local state decisions. Quite the contrary. As a result of common law development, many prescriptions of federal statutes take on meaning which is uniformly ascribed to them by the federal courts, irrespective of local variance. *Funk v. United States*, 290 U.S. 371. This court has repeatedly resorted to just such considerations in defining the very term 'employee' as used in other federal statutes, as the opinion of the court below shows. There is a general and prevailing rule throughout the Union as to the indicia of employment and the criteria of one's status as employee. Unquestionably it was to this common, general, and prevailing understanding that Congress referred in the statute and, according to that understanding, the facts stated in the opinion below,

> **!** Justice Roberts' approach to the question of whether to defer to an agency's interpretation will recur in many of the judicial opinions you will read in the remainder of this book. Focus again on how he states the point: if a question is "a question of the meaning of the Act," it "is a judicial and not an administrative question." If something is a legal question, Justice Roberts seems to be saying, the courts (and not the administrative agencies) must decide it.

and in that of this court, in my judgment, demonstrate that the newsboys were not employees of the newspapers. * * *

NOTES & QUESTIONS

1. How did the majority opinion and the dissenting opinion comport to your response to the DIY exercise preceding the case excerpts?

2. Why did the Court decide to defer to the Board in this case?

3. In Chapter 31, we addressed judicial review of agency fact-finding. Although *Hearst Publications* can be thought of as a case about judicial review of agency legal interpretation, notice how important some of the facts are to the ultimate legal conclusion. For example, the Court relied on the Board's findings that "the newsboys are an integral part of the publishers' distribution system and circulation organization" and that "the newsboys and checkmen feel they are employees of the papers and respondents' supervisory employees, if not respondents themselves, regard them as such."

4. Of course, we are now addressing judicial review of an agency's legal interpretation. What exactly is the interpretive question in this case? Is the question "Does the common-law meaning of the word 'employee' apply to the Wagner Act?"? Or, is the question, "Does the Wagner Act's definition of 'employee' apply to the newsboys?"? Didn't the Court ultimately answer both of those questions? Is the former question a pure question of law? How about the latter? Or, is the latter an application of law to fact? If the question were being asked in a trial court, do you think it would be a question for the jury? Or for the judge? Does that help you think about who should answer it here?

2. What Is "Overtime"? *Skidmore v. Swift & Co.*

A few months after *Hearst Publications*, the Supreme Court in *Skidmore v. Swift & Company* considered whether the Fair Labor Standards Act (FLSA) gave company employees serving at a company fire house a claim for overtime compensation for their hours on-call when not attending to alarms. In this instance, the case came to the Court not from an agency decision but from a suit initiated in federal district court. As in *Hearst Publications*, this case again presented a "mixed" question of the application of law to fact. The record before the Court included informal rulings, an interpretive bulletin, and an *amicus curiae* brief of the Wage and Hour Division of the Department of Labor. In denying the employees' request for overtime compensation, the district court had disregarded these agency views as inconsistent with its understanding of the FLSA. As you read the opinion below, think about what explains the Court's different approach to the "deference" question here compared to in *Hearst Publications*.

Skidmore v. Swift & Co.
323 U.S. 134 (1944)

MR. JUSTICE JACKSON delivered the opinion of the Court.

Seven employees of the Swift and Company packing plant at Fort Worth, Texas, brought an action under the Fair Labor Standards Act, 29 U.S.C.A. § 201 et seq., to recover overtime, liquidated damages, and attorneys' fees, totaling approximately $77,000. The District Court rendered judgment denying this claim wholly, and the Circuit Court of Appeals for the Fifth Circuit affirmed. 136 F.2d 112.

It is not denied that the daytime employment of these persons was working time within the Act. Two were engaged in general fire hall duties and maintenance of fire-fighting equipment of the Swift plant. The others operated elevators or acted as relief men in fire duties. They worked from 7:00 a.m. to 3:30 p.m., with a half-hour lunch period, five days a week. They were paid weekly salaries.

Under their oral agreement of employment, however, petitioners undertook to stay in the fire hall on the Company premises, or within hailing distance, three and a half to four nights a week. This involved no task except to answer alarms, either because of fire or because the sprinkler was set off for some other reason. No fires occurred during the period in issue, the alarms were rare, and the time required for their answer rarely exceeded an hour. For each alarm answered the employees were paid in addition to their fixed compensation an agreed amount, fifty cents at first, and later sixty-four cents. The Company provided a brick fire hall equipped with steam heat and air-conditioned rooms. It provided sleeping quarters, a pool table, a domino table, and a radio. The men used their time in sleep or amusement as they saw fit, except that they were required to stay in or close by the fire hall and be ready to respond to alarms. It is stipulated that 'they agreed to remain in the fire hall and stay in it or within hailing distance, subject to call, in event of fire or other casualty, but were not required to perform any specific tasks during these periods of time, except in answering alarms.' The trial court found the evidentiary facts as stipulated; it made no findings of fact as such as to whether under the arrangement of the parties and the circumstances of this case, which in some respects differ from those of the

Armour case (*Armour & Co. v. Wantock*, 323 U.S. 126), the fire hall duty or any part thereof constituted working time. It said, however, as a 'conclusion of law' that 'the time plaintiffs spent in the fire hall subject to call to answer fire alarms does not constitute hours worked, for which overtime compensation is due them under the Fair Labor Standards Act, as interpreted by the Administrator and the Courts,' and in its opinion (53 F.Supp. 1020, 1021) observed, 'of course we know pursuing such pleasurable occupations or performing such personal chores does not constitute work.' The Circuit Court of Appeals affirmed.

* * *

Congress did not utilize the services of an administrative agency to find facts and to determine in the first instance whether particular cases fall within or without the Act. Instead, it put this responsibility on the courts. But it did create the office of Administrator, impose upon him a variety of duties, endow him with powers to inform himself of conditions in industries and employments subject to the Act, and put on him the duties of bringing injunction actions to restrain violations. Pursuit of his duties has accumulated a considerable experience in the problems of ascertaining working time in employments involving periods of inactivity and a knowledge of the customs prevailing in reference to their solution. From these he is obliged to reach conclusions as to conduct without the law, so that he should seek injunctions to stop it, and that within the law, so that he has no call to interfere. He has set forth his views of the application of the Act under different circumstances in an interpretative bulletin and in informal rulings. They provide a practical guide to employers and employees as to how the office representing the public interest in its enforcement will seek to apply it. Wage and Hour Division, Interpretative Bulletin No. 13.

The Administrator thinks the problems presented by inactive duty require a flexible solution, rather than the all-in or all-out rules respectively urged by the parties in this case, and his Bulletin endeavors to suggest standards and examples to guide in particular situations. In some occupations, it says, periods of inactivity are not properly counted as working time even though the employee is subject to call. Examples are an operator of a small telephone exchange where the switchboard is in her home and she ordinarily gets several hours of uninterrupted sleep each night; or a pumper of a stripper well or watchman of a lumber camp during the off season, who may be on duty twenty-four hours a day but ordinarily 'has a normal night's sleep, has ample time in which to eat his meals, and has a certain amount of time for relaxation and entirely private pursuits.' Exclusion of all such hours the Administrator thinks may be justified. In general, the answer depends 'upon the degree to which the employee is free to engage in personal activities during periods of idleness when he is subject to call and the number of consecutive hours that the employee is subject to call without being required to perform active work.' 'Hours worked are not limited to the time spent in active labor but include time given by the employee to the employer. . . .'

The facts of this case do not fall within any of the specific examples given, but the conclusion of the Administrator, as expressed in the brief amicus curiae, is that the general tests which he has suggested point to the exclusion of sleeping and eating time of these employees from the work-week and the inclusion of all other on-call time: although the employees were required to remain on the premises during the entire time, the evidence shows that they were very rarely interrupted in their normal sleeping and eating time, and these are pursuits of a purely private nature which would presumably occupy the employees' time whether they were on duty or not and which apparently could be pursued adequately and comfortably in the required circumstances; the rest of the time is different because there is nothing in the record to suggest that, even though pleasurably spent, it was spent in the ways the men would have chosen had they been free to do so.

There is no statutory provision as to what, if any, deference courts should pay to the Administrator's conclusions. And, while we have given them notice, we have had no occasion to try to prescribe their influence. The rulings of this Administrator are not reached as a result of hearing adversary proceedings in which he finds facts from evidence and reaches conclusions of law from findings of fact. They are not, of course, conclusive, even in the cases with which they directly deal, much less in those to which they apply only by analogy. They do not constitute an interpretation of the Act or a standard for judging factual situations which binds a district court's processes, as an authoritative pronouncement of a higher court might do. But the Administrator's policies are made in pursuance of official duty, based upon more specialized experience and broader investigations and information than is likely to come to a judge in a particular case. They do determine the policy which will guide applications for enforcement by injunction on behalf of the Government. Good administration of the Act and good judicial administration alike require that the standards of public enforcement and those for determining private rights shall be at variance only where justified by very good reasons. The fact that the Administrator's policies and standards are not reached by trial in adversary form does not mean that they are not entitled to respect. This Court has long given considerable and in some cases decisive weight to Treasury Decisions and to interpretative regulations of the Treasury and of other bodies that were not of adversary origin.

We consider that the rulings, interpretations and opinions of the Administrator under this Act, while not controlling upon the courts by reason of their authority, do constitute a body of experience and informed judgment to which courts and litigants may properly resort for guidance. The weight of such a judgment in a particular case will depend upon the thoroughness evident in its consideration, the validity of its reasoning, its consistency with earlier and later pronouncements, and all those factors which give it power to persuade, if lacking power to control.

> Take note of the final sentence of this paragraph, which becomes known as the *Skidmore* test."

The courts in the *Armour* case weighed the evidence in the particular case in the light of the Administrator's rulings and reached a result consistent therewith. The evidence in this case in some respects, such as the understanding as to separate compensation for answering alarms, is different. Each case must stand on its own facts. But in this case, although the District Court referred to the Administrator's Bulletin, its evaluation and inquiry were apparently restricted by its notion that waiting time may not be work, an understanding of the law which we hold to be erroneous. Accordingly, the judgment is reversed and the cause remanded for further proceedings consistent herewith.

Reversed.

NOTES & QUESTIONS

1. What do you make of the *Skidmore* framework? Is it too much deference to the agency, too little, or just the right amount?

2. Does the *Skidmore* framework invite abuse from willful judges who will only adopt the agency's reasoning when it comports with their preconceived outcome? (Note the court's language: ". . . courts and litigants *may* properly resort for guidance.") Put another way, is it actually any deference at all? What does it mean when the Court refers to the "power to persuade, if lacking power to control"? Does that simply mean that a court is to defer if it is persuaded the agency is correct and not to defer if the court is not so persuaded? If so, does that amount to any deference at all?

B. From *Skidmore* to *Chevron*

After *Skidmore*, federal courts in the pre-*Chevron* era eventually came to rely on something of a sliding scale, in which the extent to which a reviewing court would defer to an agency's interpretation of a statute it was charged with administering would depend upon the cumulative impact of a range of factors. These factors included not only those outlined in *Skidmore*, but also such other factors as precisely how much rulemaking or adjudicatory power Congress had given the agency; whether the agency's position was contemporaneous with the statute's enactment; how technical and complex the interpretive issue was; whether Congress had acquiesced in an agency's previous construction of a statute; and the extent to which following the agency interpretation would promote uniformity in the law. Furthermore, a multi-factor approach also came to characterize the courts' approach to the questions of whether it was reasonable to assume that Congress had intended to give an agency formal lawmaking powers, or that Congress likely would have expected the courts to defer to the agency. Finally, settled pre-*Chevron* doctrine was that reviewing courts would show no deference to an agency interpretation of a statute if the statute's meaning was "plain" to the reviewing court using traditional interpretive tools. Overall, though, by the time of *Chevron*, the standards for judicial review of agency interpretations were seen by many as somewhat confused.

Test Your Understanding

 To assess your understanding of the material in this chapter, click here to take a quiz.

35

The *Chevron* Doctrine

Key Concepts

- *Chevron v. Natural Resources Defense Council*
- The EPA "bubble" concept
- Has Congress directly spoken to the interpretive question?
  - Is the agency's interpretation reasonable?
- *Chevron* Step One
- *Chevron* Step Two
- Highly deferential review

Chapter Summary

The Supreme Court's 1984 decision in *Chevron v. Natural Resources Defense Council* has dominated the field of judicial review of agency statutory interpretation for much of the last four decades. In *Chevron* the Court said that the federal judiciary should defer to an agency's reasonable construction of a statute, even if the court itself would not have adopted that specific construction, unless the court concluded that Congress had directly spoken to the question of the proper interpretation. The decision quickly gave rise to a two-step process, in which reviewing courts first address the question of whether Congress has already supplied the answer to the interpretive problem. If not, at the second step the reviewing court then determines whether the agency's answer to the interpretive problem is a reasonable one. However, just how to conduct each of these steps remains contested.

In the face of what many saw, in the four decades after *Skidmore*, as somewhat confused standards of judicial review of agency interpretations, in 1984 the Court took up what at the time was perceived as just one more case in the pantheon of routine questions of agency interpretation. At issue was another air pollution regulation. The 1977 amendments to the federal Clean Air Act imposed obligations on those states that had failed to meet the air pollution emissions standards that had been imposed under an earlier iteration of the Clean Air Act, standards known as "national ambient air quality standards" (NAAQS). The law required these so-called "nonattainment" states to establish a permit program aimed at limiting emissions from "major stationary sources" of air pollution. The permit requirement applied both to newly constructed sources and to those modifications of existing sources that would increase the emissions of air pollutants; the new permit requirement did not otherwise apply to retrofitting of existing sources of air pollution.

The problem was that the act did not define the term "source" in the phrase "stationary source." Did the term mean each device or apparatus that emitted a pollutant, or did the term mean each industrial plant, even if that plant might have multiple devices emitting pollutants within it? If each smokestack within an industrial plant were deemed a "source," then every new smokestack, whether it simply replaced an existing apparatus or was part of an addition of new equipment to the facility, would have to obtain a permit under the 1977 Amendments. But if the entire plant was viewed as one "source," then a new smokestack or apparatus could be added without having to obtain a permit if some other emitter of pollution within the plant was eliminated (or its emissions reduced) so as to offset the new smokestack's emissions. Similarly, an existing smokestack could be replaced if the replacement did not increase total emissions from the entire facility. In effect, the plant-wide definition of "source" imagined a bubble over the facility, with one final smokestack, or "source" of pollution, coming off the top. In other words, as long as the net emissions from the whole bubble did not increase, the owner of the plant could make changes inside the bubble without obtaining a permit.

The Clean Air Act charged the Environmental Protection Agency (EPA) with administering the Act. Throughout the 1970s, in a series of rulemaking proceedings, the EPA had resisted industry calls to adopt a "bubble" definition of "stationary source" for all purposes of the Act, although the EPA had used the bubble concept for other purposes of the Act (unrelated to the 1977 Amendments). But in 1981, under the deregulatory policies of the Reagan Administration, the EPA reconsidered its approach and issued a regulation adopting the plant-wide bubble definition for all purposes. The Natural Resources Defense Council and others then challenged this regulation as inconsistent with the language and purpose of the 1977 Amendments.

As you read the Supreme Court's opinion below, think about (1) the way(s) in which it signals a departure from the *Skidmore* style of judicial review of agency interpretation, (2) the ways in which the facts of the case and the ways in which the agency's exercise of expertise differ from cases like *Hearst Publications* and

Skidmore, and (3) what the opinion says about the underlying justifications for granting deference to an agency.

Chevron U.S.A., Inc. v. Natural Resources Defense Council, Inc.

467 U.S. 837 (1984)

JUSTICE STEVENS delivered the opinion of the Court.

In the Clean Air Act Amendments of 1977, Pub. L. 95–95, 91 Stat. 685, Congress enacted certain requirements applicable to States that had not achieved the national air quality standards established by the Environmental Protection Agency (EPA) pursuant to earlier legislation. The amended Clean Air Act required these "nonattainment" States to establish a permit program regulating "new or modified major stationary sources" of air pollution. Generally, a permit may not be issued for a new or modified major stationary source unless several stringent conditions are met. The EPA regulation promulgated to implement this permit requirement allows a State to adopt a plantwide definition of the term "stationary source." Under this definition, an existing plant that contains several pollution-emitting devices may install or modify one piece of equipment without meeting the permit conditions if the alteration will not increase the total emissions from the plant. The question presented by these cases is whether EPA's decision to allow States to treat all of the pollution-emitting devices within the same industrial grouping as though they were encased within a single "bubble" is based on a reasonable construction of the statutory term "stationary source."

I

The EPA regulations containing the plantwide definition of the term stationary source were promulgated on October 14, 1981. * * * The Court of Appeals set aside the regulations. *Natural Resources Defense Council, Inc. v. Gorsuch,* 222 U.S. App. D.C. 268, 685 F.2d 718 (1982).

The court observed that the relevant part of the amended Clean Air Act "does not explicitly define what Congress envisioned as a 'stationary source, to which the permit program . . . should apply," and further

> **FYI**
> Anne Gorsuch, the mother of Supreme Court Justice Neil Gorsuch, was the administrator of the EPA in the Reagan Administration responsible for the regulation at issue in *Chevron*.

stated that the precise issue was not "squarely addressed in the legislative history." *Id.* at 273. In light of its conclusion that the legislative history bearing on the question was "at best contradictory," it reasoned that "the purposes of the nonattainment program should guide our decision here." *Id.* at 276, n. 39. Based on two of its precedents concerning the applicability of the bubble concept to certain Clean Air Act programs, the court stated that the bubble concept was "mandatory" in programs designed merely to maintain existing air quality, but held that it was "inappropriate" in programs enacted to improve air quality. *Id.* at 276. Since the purpose of the permit program—its *"raison d'etre,"* in the court's view—was to improve air quality, the court held that the bubble concept was inapplicable in these cases under its prior precedents. *Ibid.* It therefore set aside the regulations embodying the bubble concept as contrary to law. We granted certiorari to review that judgment, 461 U.S. 956 (1983), and we now reverse.

The basic legal error of the Court of Appeals was to adopt a static judicial definition of the term "stationary source" when it had decided that Congress itself had not commanded that definition. * * *

II

> ! Note the Court's identification of these two *"Chevron"* questions.

When a court reviews an agency's construction of the statute which it administers, it is confronted with two questions. First, always, is the question whether Congress has directly spoken to the precise question at issue. If the intent of Congress is clear, that is the end of the matter; for the court, as well as the agency, must give effect to the unambiguously expressed intent of Congress.[9] If, however, the court determines Congress has not directly addressed the precise question at issue, the court does not simply impose its own construction on the statute, as would be necessary in the absence of an administrative interpretation. Rather, if the statute is silent or ambiguous with respect to the specific issue, the question for the court is whether the agency's answer is based on a permissible construction of the statute.[11]

---

[9] [this and other footnotes included in this opinion excerpt are the Court's footnotes:] The judiciary is the final authority on issues of statutory construction and must reject administrative constructions which are contrary to clear congressional intent. If a court, employing traditional tools of statutory construction, ascertains that Congress had an intention on the precise question at issue, that intention is the law and must be given effect.

[11] The court need not conclude that the agency construction was the only one it permissibly could have adopted to uphold the construction, or even the reading the court would have reached if the question initially had arisen in a judicial proceeding. * * *

The power of an administrative agency to administer a congressionally created * * * program necessarily requires the formulation of policy and the making of rules to fill any gap left, implicitly or explicitly, by Congress.

Morton v. Ruiz, 415 U.S. 199, 231 (1974). If Congress has explicitly left a gap for the agency to fill, there is an express delegation of authority to the agency to elucidate a specific provision of the statute by regulation. Such legislative regulations are given controlling weight unless they are arbitrary, capricious, or manifestly contrary to the statute. Sometimes the legislative delegation to an agency on a particular question is implicit, rather than explicit. In such a case, a court may not substitute its own construction of a statutory provision for a reasonable interpretation made by the administrator of an agency.

> Note the APA standard of review here.

We have long recognized that considerable weight should be accorded to an executive department's construction of a statutory scheme it is entrusted to administer, and the principle of deference to administrative interpretations

> has been consistently followed by this Court whenever decision as to the meaning or reach of a statute has involved reconciling conflicting policies, and a full understanding of the force of the statutory policy in the given situation has depended upon more than ordinary knowledge respecting the matters subjected to agency regulations.
>
> . . . If this choice represents a reasonable accommodation of conflicting policies that were committed to the agency's care by the statute, we should not disturb it unless it appears from the statute or its legislative history that the accommodation is not one that Congress would have sanctioned.

United States v. Shimer, 367 U.S. 374, 382, 383 (1961).

In light of these well-settled principles, it is clear that the Court of Appeals misconceived the nature of its role in reviewing the regulations at issue. Once it determined, after its own examination of the legislation, that Congress did not actually have an intent regarding the applicability of the bubble concept to the permit program, the question before it was not whether, in its view, the concept is "inappropriate" in the general context of a program designed to improve air quality, but whether the Administrator's view that it is appropriate in the context of this particular program is a reasonable one. Based on the examination of the legislation and its history which follows, we agree with the Court of Appeals that Congress did not have a specific intention on the applicability of the bubble concept in these cases, and conclude that the EPA's use of that concept here is a reasonable policy choice for the agency to make.

III

In the 1950's and the 1960's, Congress enacted a series of statutes designed to encourage and to assist the States in curtailing air pollution. *See generally Train v. Natural Resources Defense Council, Inc.*, 421 U.S. 60, 63–64 (1975). The Clean Air Amendments of 1970, Pub. L. 91–604, 84 Stat. 1676, "sharply increased federal authority and responsibility in the continuing effort to combat air pollution," 421 U.S. at 64, but continued to assign "primary responsibility for assuring air quality" to the several States, 84 Stat. 1678. Section 109 of the 1970 Amendments directed the EPA to promulgate National Ambient Air Quality Standards (NAAQS's) and § 110 directed the States to develop plans (SIP's) to implement the standards within specified deadlines. In addition, § 111 provided that major new sources of pollution would be required to conform to technology-based performance standards; the EPA was directed to publish a list of categories of sources of pollution and to establish new source performance standards (NSPS) for each. Section 111(e) prohibited the operation of any new source in violation of a performance standard.

Section 111(a) defined the terms that are to be used in setting and enforcing standards of performance for new stationary sources. It provided:

> For purposes of this section:
>
> * * *
>
> (3) The term "stationary source" means any building, structure, facility, or installation which emits or may emit any air pollutant.

84 Stat. 1683. In the 1970 Amendments, that definition was not only applicable to the NSPS program required by § 111, but also was made applicable to a requirement of § 110 that each state implementation plan contain a procedure for reviewing the location of any proposed new source and pre-

venting its construction if it would preclude the attainment or maintenance of national air quality standards.

In due course, the EPA promulgated NAAQS's, approved SIP's, and adopted detailed regulations governing NSPS's for various categories of equipment. In one of its programs, the EPA used a plantwide definition of the term "stationary source." In 1974, it issued NSPS's for the nonferrous smelting industry that provided that the standards would not apply to the modification of major smelting units if their increased emissions were offset by reductions in other portions of the same plant.

Nonattainment

The 1970 legislation provided for the attainment of primary NAAQS's by 1975. In many areas of the country, particularly the most industrialized States, the statutory goals were not attained. In 1976, the 94th Congress was confronted with this fundamental problem, as well as many others respecting pollution control. As always in this area, the legislative struggle was basically between interests seeking strict schemes to reduce pollution rapidly to eliminate its social costs and interests advancing the economic concern that strict schemes would retard industrial development with attendant social costs. The 94th Congress, confronting these competing interests, was unable to agree on what response was in the public interest: legislative proposals to deal with nonattainment failed to command the necessary consensus.

In light of this situation, the EPA published an Emissions Offset Interpretative Ruling in December, 1976, *see* 41 Fed. Reg. 55524, to "fill the gap," as respondents put it, until Congress acted. The Ruling stated that it was intended to address "the issue of whether and to what extent national air quality standards established under the Clean Air Act may restrict or prohibit growth of major new or expanded stationary air pollution sources." *Id.* at 55524–55525. In general, the Ruling provided that "a major new source may locate in an area with air quality worse than a national standard only if stringent conditions can be met." *Id.* at 55525. The Ruling gave primary emphasis to the rapid attainment of the statute's environmental goals. Consistent with that emphasis, the construction of every new source in nonattainment areas had to meet the "lowest achievable emission rate" under the current state of the art for that type of facility. *See ibid.* The 1976 Ruling did not, however, explicitly adopt or reject the "bubble concept."

IV

The Clean Air Act Amendments of 1977 are a lengthy, detailed, technical, complex, and comprehensive response to a major social issue. A small portion of the statute—91 Stat. 745–751 (Part D of Title I of the amended Act, 42 U.S.C. §§ 7501–7508)—expressly deals with nonattainment areas. The focal point of this controversy is one phrase in that portion of the Amendments.

* * *

Most significantly for our purposes, the statute provided that each plan shall

> (6) require permits for the construction and operation of new or modified major stationary sources in accordance with section 173. . . .

Id. at 747. Before issuing a permit, § 173 requires (1) the state agency to determine that there will be sufficient emissions reductions in the region to offset the emissions from the new source and also to allow for reasonable further progress toward attainment, or that the increased emissions will not exceed an allowance for growth established pursuant to § 172(b)(5); (2) the applicant to certify that his other sources in the State are in compliance with the SIP, (3) the agency to determine that the applicable SIP is otherwise being implemented, and (4) the proposed source to comply with the lowest achievable emission rate (LAER).

The 1977 Amendments contain no specific reference to the "bubble concept." Nor do they contain a specific definition of the term "stationary source," though they did not disturb the definition of "stationary source" contained in § 111(a)(3), applicable by the terms of the Act to the NSPS program. Section 302(j), however, defines the term "major stationary source" as follows:

> (j) Except as otherwise expressly provided, the terms "major stationary source" and "major emitting facility" mean any stationary facility or source of air pollutants which directly emits, or has the potential to emit, one hundred tons per year or more of any air pollutant (including any major emitting facility or source of fugitive emissions of any such pollutant, as determined by rule by the Administrator).

91 Stat. 770.

V

The legislative history of the portion of the 1977 Amendments dealing with nonattainment areas does not contain any specific comment on the "bubble concept" or the question whether a plantwide definition of a stationary source is permissible under the permit program. It does, however, plainly disclose that in the permit program Congress sought to accommodate the conflict between the economic interest in permitting capital improvements to continue and the environmental interest in improving air quality.

* * *

VI

* * *

In 1981, a new administration took office and initiated a "Government-wide reexamination of regulatory burdens and complexities." 46 Fed. Reg. 16281. In the context of that review, the EPA reevaluated the various arguments that had been advanced in connection with the proper definition of the term "source" and concluded that the term should be given the same definition in both nonattainment areas and PSD areas.

In explaining its conclusion, the EPA first noted that the definitional issue was not squarely addressed in either the statute or its legislative history, and therefore that the issue involved an agency "judgment as how to best carry out the Act." *Ibid.* It then set forth several reasons for concluding that the plantwide definition was more appropriate. It pointed out that the dual definition "can act as a disincentive to new investment and modernization by discouraging modifications to existing facilities" and "can actu-

> **FYI** Compare how the Court views the agency's explanation of this decision, prompted (as the Court notes) by a "new administration," with how the Court viewed the agency's failure to explain its decision in the *State Farm* case in Chapter 32, also prompted by a change of administration.

ally retard progress in air pollution control by discouraging replacement of older, dirtier processes or pieces of equipment with new, cleaner ones." *Ibid.* Moreover, the new definition "would simplify EPA's rules by using the same definition of "source" for PSD, nonattainment new source review, and the construction moratorium. This reduces confusion and inconsistency." *Ibid.*

Finally, the agency explained that additional requirements that remained in place would accomplish the fundamental purposes of achieving attainment with NAAQS's as expeditiously as possible. These conclusions were expressed in a proposed rulemaking in August, 1981, that was formally promulgated in October. *See id.* at 50766.

VII

In this Court, respondents * * * contend that the text of the Act requires the EPA to use a dual definition—if either a component of a plant, or the plant as a whole, emits over 100 tons of pollutant, it is a major stationary source. They thus contend that the EPA rules adopted in 1980, insofar as they apply to the maintenance of the quality of clean air, as well as the 1981 rules which apply to nonattainment areas, violate the statute.

Statutory Language

The definition of the term "stationary source" in § 111(a)(3) refers to "any building, structure, facility, or installation" which emits air pollution. *See supra* at 846. This definition is applicable only to the NSPS program by the express terms of the statute; the text of the statute does not make this definition applicable to the permit program. Petitioners therefore maintain that there is no statutory language even relevant to ascertaining the meaning of stationary source in the permit program aside from § 302(j), which defines the term "major stationary source." *See supra* at 851. We disagree with petitioners on this point.

The definition in § 302(j) tells us what the word "major" means—a source must emit at least 100 tons of pollution to qualify—but it sheds virtually no light on the meaning of the term "stationary source." It does equate a source with a facility—a "major emitting facility" and a "major stationary source" are synonymous under § 302(j). The ordinary meaning of the term "facility" is some collection of integrated elements which has been designed and constructed to achieve some purpose. Moreover, it is certainly no affront to common English usage to take a reference to a major facility or a major source to connote an entire plant, as opposed to its constituent parts. Basically, however, the language of § 302(j) simply does not compel any given interpretation of the term "source."

Respondents recognize that, and hence point to § 111(a)(3). Although the definition in that section is not literally applicable to the permit program, it sheds as much light on the meaning of the word "source" as anything in the statute. As respondents point out, use of the words "building, structure, facility, or installation," as the definition of source, could be read to impose the permit conditions on an individual building that is a part of a plant. A "word may have a character of its own not to be submerged by its association." *Russell Motor Car Co. v. United States,* 261 U.S. 514, 519 (1923). On the other hand, the meaning of a word must be ascertained in the context of achieving particular objectives, and the words associated with it may indicate that the true meaning of the series is to convey a common idea. The language may reasonably be interpreted to impose the requirement on any discrete, but integrated, operation which pollutes. This gives meaning to all of the terms—a single building, not part of a larger operation, would be covered if it emits more than 100 tons of pollution, as would any facility, structure, or installation. Indeed, the language itself implies a "bubble concept" of sorts: each enumerated item would seem to be treated as if it were encased in a bubble. While respondents insist that each of these terms must be given a discrete meaning, they also argue that § 111(a)(3) defines "source" as that term is used in § 302(j). The latter section, however, equates a source with a facility, whereas the former defines "source" as a facility, among other items.

We are not persuaded that parsing of general terms in the text of the statute will reveal an actual intent of Congress. We know full well that this language is not dispositive; the terms are overlapping, and the language is not precisely directed to the question of the applicability of a given term in the context of a larger operation. To the extent any congressional "intent" can be discerned from this language, it would appear that the listing of overlapping, illustrative terms was intended to enlarge, rather than to confine, the scope of the agency's power to regulate particular sources in order to effectuate the policies of the Act.

Legislative History

In addition, respondents argue that the legislative history and policies of the Act foreclose the plantwide definition, and that the EPA's interpretation is not entitled to deference, because it represents a sharp break with prior interpretations of the Act.

Based on our examination of the legislative history, we agree with the Court of Appeals that it is unilluminating. The general remarks pointed to by respondents "were obviously not made with this narrow issue in mind, and they cannot be said to demonstrate a Congressional desire. . . ." *Jewell Ridge Coal Corp. v. Mine Workers,* 325 U.S. 161, 168–169 (1945). * * * We find that the legislative history as a whole is silent on the precise issue before us. It is, however, consistent with the view that the EPA should have broad discretion in implementing the policies of the 1977 Amendments.

More importantly, that history plainly identifies the policy concerns that motivated the enactment; the plantwide definition is fully consistent with one of those concerns—the allowance of reasonable economic growth—and, whether or not we believe it most effectively implements the other, we must recognize that the EPA has advanced a reasonable explanation for its conclusion that the regulations serve the environmental objectives as well. Indeed, its reasoning is supported by the public record developed in the rulemaking process, as well as by certain private studies.

Our review of the EPA's varying interpretations of the word "source"—both before and after the 1977 Amendments—convinces us that the agency primarily responsible for administering this important legislation has consistently interpreted it flexibly—not in a sterile textual vacuum, but in the context of implementing policy decisions in a technical and complex arena. The fact that the agency has from time to time changed its interpretation of the term "source" does not, as respondents argue, lead us to conclude that no deference should be accorded the agency's interpretation of the statute. An initial agency interpretation is not instantly carved in stone. On the contrary, the agency, to engage in informed rulemaking, must consider varying interpretations and the wisdom of its policy on a continuing basis. Moreover, the fact that the agency has adopted different definitions in different contexts adds force to the argument that the definition itself is flexible, particularly since Congress has never indicated any disapproval of a flexible reading of the statute.

Significantly, it was not the agency in 1980, but rather the Court of Appeals that read the statute inflexibly to command a plantwide definition for programs designed to maintain clean air and to forbid such a definition for programs designed to improve air quality. The distinction the court drew may well be a sensible one, but our labored review of the problem has surely disclosed that it is not a distinction that Congress ever articulated itself, or one that the EPA found in the statute before the courts began to review the legislative work product. We conclude that it was the Court of Appeals, rather than Congress or any of the decisionmakers who are authorized by Congress to administer this legislation, that was primarily responsible for the 1980 position taken by the agency.

Policy

The arguments over policy that are advanced in the parties' briefs create the impression that respondents are now waging in a judicial forum a specific policy battle which they ultimately lost in the agency and in the 32 jurisdictions opting for the "bubble concept," but one which was never waged in the Congress. Such policy arguments are more properly addressed to legislators or administrators, not to judges.

In these cases, the Administrator's interpretation represents a reasonable accommodation of manifestly competing interests, and is entitled to deference: the regulatory scheme is technical and complex, the agency considered the matter in a detailed and reasoned fashion, and the decision involves reconciling conflicting policies. Congress intended to accommodate both interests, but did not do so itself on the level of specificity presented by these cases. Perhaps that body consciously desired the Administrator to strike the balance at this level, thinking that those with great expertise and charged with responsibility for administering the provision would be in a better position to do so; perhaps it simply did not consider the question at this level; and perhaps Congress was unable to forge a coalition on either side of the question, and those on each side decided to take their chances with the scheme devised by the agency. For judicial purposes, it matters not which of these things occurred.

> Note the three distinct reasons the Court offers for why Congress might not have provided perfect clarity in the statutory text.

Judges are not experts in the field, and are not part of either political branch of the Government. Courts must, in some cases, reconcile competing political interests, but not on the basis of the judges' personal policy preferences. In contrast, an agency to which Congress has delegated policymaking responsibilities may, within the limits of that delegation, properly rely upon the incumbent administration's views of wise policy to inform its judgments. While agencies are not directly accountable to the people, the Chief Executive is, and it is entirely appropriate for this political branch of the Government to make such policy choices—resolving the competing interests which Congress itself either inadvertently did not resolve, or intentionally left to be resolved by the agency charged with the administration of the statute in light of everyday realities.

When a challenge to an agency construction of a statutory provision, fairly conceptualized, really centers on the wisdom of the agency's policy, rather than whether it is a reasonable choice within a gap left open by Congress, the challenge must fail. In such a case, federal judges—who have no constituency—have a duty to respect legitimate policy choices made by those who do. The responsibilities for assessing the wisdom of such policy choices and resolving the struggle between competing views of the public interest are not judicial ones: "Our Constitution vests such responsibilities in the political branches." *TVA v. Hill,* 437 U.S. 153, 195 (1978).

We hold that the EPA's definition of the term "source" is a permissible construction of the statute which seeks to accommodate progress in reducing air pollution with economic growth. "The Regulations which the Administrator has adopted provide what the agency could allowably view as . . . [an] effective reconciliation of these twofold ends. . . ." *United States v. Shimer,* 367 U.S. at 383.

The judgment of the Court of Appeals is reversed.

NOTES & QUESTIONS

1. Notice the way the Court frames the issue in the last sentence in the opening paragraph: "The question presented by these cases is whether EPA's decision to allow States to treat all of the pollution-emitting devices within the same industrial grouping as though they were encased within a single 'bubble' is based on a reasonable construction of the statutory term 'stationary source.' " The focus is through the lens of the EPA's interpretation, and the Court asks whether the EPA's construction is "reasonable," *not* whether the EPA's construction is correct. If no agency were involved, how might a court frame the interpretive question differently? Wouldn't a court ask about the meaning of, or the best reading of, the statutory term "stationary source"?

2. Can you articulate what changed from the 1944 *Skidmore* framework to the 1984 *Chevron* approach to judicial review of an agency interpretation of a statute?

3. Why do you think the *Chevron* decision became such a big deal?

4. Go back through the *Chevron* decision and see which interpretive tools you can find in use. Look particularly at Part VII of the Court's opinion. How similar is what you see there to the statutory-interpretation cases you read in Parts V and VI of this book?

5. In the section on policy at the very end of the *Chevron* opinion, the Court lists three reasons why Congress might not have provided clarity on the meaning of "source." The Court then states, "For judicial purposes, it matters not which of these things occurred." Look again at those reasons. Should it matter which of these three occurred? If "Congress was unable to forge a coalition on either side of the question, and those on each side decided to take their chances with the scheme devised by the agency," should that mean the agency gets to decide? Isn't this exactly the kind of abdication of congressional responsibility that those who oppose government by bureaucrats fear? Or is this okay because, as the Court points out in the next paragraph, the EPA Administrator is ultimately responsible to the electorate through her boss, the President? Is it thus, as the Court put it, "entirely appropriate for this political branch of the Government to make . . . policy choices" that "Congress itself . . . did not resolve"? In Chapter 37 we turn to the "Major Questions Doctrine," and now some forty years after *Chevron* we will see a very different approach and attitude to "policy choices" that Congress "did not resolve."

Test Your Understanding

To assess your understanding of the material in this chapter, click here to take a quiz.

36

The Complexities of the *Chevron* Framework

Key Concepts

- *Chevron* Step One
- *Chevron* Step Two
- Highly deferential review

Chapter Summary

The *Chevron* decision quickly gave rise to a two-step process, in which reviewing courts first address the question of whether Congress has already supplied the answer to the interpretive problem. If not, at the second step the reviewing court then determines whether the agency's answer to the interpretive problem is a reasonable one. However, just how to conduct each of these steps remains contested. In the following chapter, we will see that there can even be a threshold question of whether and when to apply the *Chevron* framework.

As previously noted, the *Chevron* opinion has become the most cited Supreme Court administrative law decision. Although in part this reflects the vast number of administrative interpretations that are the subjects of judicial review, at least two other factors help explain the *Chevron* opinion's continuing influence. One is its discussion of the comparative institutional advantages that agencies have over courts in certain aspects of statutory interpretation. The other is its articulation of a clear, seemingly simple two-step framework for evaluating agency interpretations.

At what has become known as **Step One**, the court must determine, using what a footnote in the opinion called "traditional tools" of statutory interpretation, if the statute is ambiguous or silent with respect to the interpretive question raised by the agency's challenged construction. The Court phrased this question as **"whether Congress has directly spoken to the precise question at issue."** If Congress has directly spoken, the reviewing court does not reach the second step; instead, "that is the end of the matter, for the court, as well as the agency, must give effect to the unambiguously expressed intent of Congress."

If, however, the court concludes that Congress has been silent or ambiguous on the interpretive question, the court moves to the next step. At **Step Two**, the court must determine **"whether the agency's answer is based on a permissible construction of the statute."** The *Chevron* opinion alternatively phrased this inquiry as "whether [the agency's view] is a reasonable one." If it is a reasonable or permissible construction, then under the *Chevron* doctrine a reviewing court is to uphold the agency's interpretation.

Well beyond the immediate decision, *Chevron* has spawned a cottage industry of analysis and reflection by academics, jurists, and practitioners, all striving to contribute to the jurisprudence of statutory interpretation and agency discretion. Several distinct questions have arisen concerning both Step One and Step Two. Often, the beginning of finding answers to these questions is to consider the way in which the Court itself applied these two steps to the EPA's "bubble" regulation in the *Chevron* opinion. Meanwhile, questions about the threshold determination of whether a particular instance of agency statutory construction is even suited to the *Chevron* doctrine have given rise to the idea of a *Chevron* "Step Zero," which we address in the next chapter.

A. Questions About *Chevron* Step One

An initial question is whether analytically the *Chevron* doctrine in fact should involve only one step. That is, should the Step One question of "whether Congress has directly spoken to the precise question at issue" be understood as really just a specific inquiry relevant to answering the Step Two question of "whether the agency's view is reasonable"? If Congress has directly spoken to the issue, then under Step Two alone, any agency interpretation that departs from what Congress has said would be unreasonable, and not permissible. On this analysis, the sole *Chevron* question that a reviewing court needs to ask is the Step Two question of whether the agency's construction is a reasonable or permissible one. *See Entergy Corp. v. Riverkeeper*, 556 U.S. 208, 218 n.4 (2009).

> ❗ Later in this chapter, we will read a "Step Two" case, *Michigan v. EPA*, that makes clear that this wrinkle may well be endemic to the *Chevron* doctrine. *See* Section B.2, Note 2.

Nevertheless, most courts invoking the *Chevron* doctrine continue to apply it in two distinct steps, first exploring as an independent inquiry whether Congress has clearly spoken to the interpretive question at issue or instead has left the issue for the agency to decide (within the limits of reasonableness). In large part the persistence of this first step of analysis may reflect the lingering influence of *Hearst Publications* and the desire to distinguish the judicial role of declaring what the law is (Step One) from the agency role of interpreting and applying that law to specific circumstances within its delegated authority, subject to judicially enforceable APA constraints (Step Two). It also may simply reflect how difficult it frequently can be for courts to resolve the Step One inquiry of whether or not Congress has directly spoken to the issue.

Indeed, how to determine at Step One the pure law question of whether Congress has directly spoken has engendered its own controversies, even though (or perhaps because) this question looks very much like the same one that courts have long addressed when interpreting statutes generally: Has the legislature made the statute's textual meaning clear? The familiar battle over Textualist versus Purposivist interpretation thus also continues to rage in the *Chevron* Step One context.

To some, the Step One requirement of determining whether Congress has directly spoken to the precise question at issue suggested a search for *textual* clarity. On this inquiry, Step One might be concerned only with whether Congress has "directly spoken" through the statute's text. Unsurprisingly, Justice Scalia adhered to this view. *See, e.g., I.N.S. v. Cardoza-Fonseca*, 480 U.S. 421 (1987). But this approach to Step One was certainly not compelled by the *Chevron* decision, which itself had relied on the legislative history of the 1977 Clean Air Act Amendments to resolve its Step One issue. Nevertheless, other courts have occasionally thought of Step One as best resolved without resort to legislative history. *See, e.g., Bankers Life & Casualty Co. v. United States*, 142 F.3d 973, 983 (7th Cir. 1998) ("While this circuit has examined legislative history during the first step of *Chevron* . . . , we now seem to lean toward reserving consideration of legislative history and other appropriate factors until the second *Chevron* step."). This was never a widespread approach to Step One, however, and most courts have continued to use extrinsic aids such as legislative history as part of the "traditional tools" of interpretation that the *Chevron* decision approved for determining whether Congress had directly spoken to the issue.

One familiar interpretive tool that has additional impact in the *Chevron* context is the canon of constitutional avoidance. The constitutional concern embodied in the relatively limited federal nondelegation doctrine may in fact find life in at least some instances of Step One ambiguity, encouraging courts to construe the scope of delegated agency authority more narrowly to avoid raising a concern about an excessive delegation. Additionally, a number of other interpretive presumptions that are sometimes applied to reduce Step One ambiguity have been classified as a set of "nondelegation canons." These presumptions, many of which derive from the substantive canons of interpretation discussed in Parts V and VI above, function to rein in the amount of authority that an agency might otherwise enjoy. *See, e.g.,* Cass R. Sunstein, *Nondelegation Canons*, 67 U. Chi. L. Rev. 315 (2000). Meanwhile, the recent advent of the full-fledged Major Questions Doctrine may be the most direct "nondelegation canon." As we will see in Chapter 37, the Supreme Court has recently held that agencies do not have authority to act in the context of "major questions" unless Congress has explicitly given the agency authority to act. Some judges and scholars view this as a "nondelegation canon." Under this view, the reason the Court adopts narrow interpretations of congressional delegations in cases involving "major questions" is to avoid answering the question of whether a congressional delegation is unconstitutional.

As suggested by the deployment of the nondelegation canon and various substantive presumptions, another complication at Step One is that if courts can use all the traditional interpretive tools, in theory they might always be able to find a clear meaning, even for what may at first have appeared to be an ambiguous provision when considering the text alone. Indeed, on at least some interpretive theories, that is the purpose behind these tools—to allow the interpreter to identify the "correct" meaning with confidence. In that event, traditional statutory interpretation at Step One might lead to reaching Step Two only rarely. Even Textualists, relying on a more limited set of tools, might be prone to find a clear textual meaning. Justice Scalia once suggested something to this effect, observing that when Textualists like himself are reviewing agency interpretations, they are less likely to find ambiguity in the statutory text, and therefore are less likely to proceed to Step Two. *See* Antonin Scalia, *Judicial Deference to Administration Interpretations of Law*, 1989 Duke L. J. 511; *see also INS v. Cardoza-Fonseca*, 480 U.S. 421 (1987); *EEOC v. Aramco*, 499 U.S. 244 (1991); *Christensen v. Harris Cty.*, 529 U.S. 576 (2000).

Furthermore, the Textualist versus Purposivist debate at Step One potentially involves an additional element not present in the analogous debate over matters of pure judicial interpretation of statutes. Some commentators have observed that an agency's position on the meaning of a statutory provision might itself be a relevant indicator of legislative intent, perhaps even a good indicator, for the reasons that the *Chevron* opinion offered to justify deferring to the agency at Step Two. That is, the agency's experience with the subject, often including the agency's participation in the legislative drafting process, may make it uniquely familiar with the statutory scheme, while at the same time the agency's political accountability also may help the agency better understand the underlying legislative intent. Of course, most Textualists reject this additional extrinsic source of interpretive guidance in resolving the Step One inquiry.

1.   *The Long-Distance Rate Filing Case*

The case that follows is an important example of the tension between interpretive approaches at Step One. As you read it, think about how you would determine the meaning of the single statutory word at issue, "modify." This case is also an early example of what is in effect the major questions doctrine without an explicit invocation of that phrase. So, as you read the majority's and the dissent's interpretations of the word "modify," be sure to identify the policy implications of the different interpretations and why the majority might be skeptical of the agency's interpretation.

MCI Telecommunications Corp. v. AT&T

512 U.S. 218 (1994)

JUSTICE SCALIA delivered the opinion of the Court.

Section 203(a) of Title 47 of the United States Code requires communications common carriers to file tariffs with the Federal Communications Commission, and § 203(b) authorizes the Commission to "modify" any requirement of § 203. These cases present the question whether the Commission's decision to make tariff filing optional for all nondominant long distance carriers is a valid exercise of its modification authority.

I

* * * An understanding of the cases requires a brief review of the Commission's efforts to regulate and then deregulate the telecommunications industry. When Congress created the Commission in 1934, AT&T, through its vertically integrated Bell system, held a virtual monopoly over the Nation's telephone service. The Communications Act of 1934, 48 Stat. 1064, as amended, authorized the Commission to regulate the rates charged for communication services to ensure that they were reasonable and non-discriminatory. The requirements of § 203 that common carriers file their rates with the Commission and charge only the filed rate were the centerpiece of the Act's regulatory scheme.

In the 1970's, technological advances reduced the entry costs for competitors of AT&T in the market for long distance telephone service. The Commission, recognizing the feasibility of greater competition, passed regulations to facilitate competitive entry. By 1979, competition in the provision of long distance service was well established, and some urged that the continuation of extensive tariff filing requirements served only to impose unnecessary costs on new entrants and to facilitate collusive pricing. [The Commission held hearings on the matter and] issued a series of rules that have produced this litigation.

[The Court explained that in its first order, the Commission distinguished between dominant carriers (those with market power) and nondominant carriers (which in the long distance market amounted to everyone other than AT&T), and relaxed some of the filing procedures for nondominant carriers. In its second order, the Commission entirely eliminated the filing requirement for some providers of common carrier services. In its fourth and fifth orders, the Commission extended this optional tariff filing policy, referred to as "permissive detariffing," to specialized common carriers, including MCI Telecommunications Corp., and to virtually all remaining categories of nondominant carriers.]

[AT&T filed a complaint with the Commission, alleging that MCI's collection of tariffs without having a rate on-file was a violation of § 203. After a convoluted history, the complaint was dismissed on the basis that MCI was in compliance with the Commission's fourth order. The agency decision did not address AT&T's assertion that the Commission's fourth order was *ultra vires*, instead announcing a separate rulemaking proceeding to address that question. In that rulemaking proceeding, the Commission determined that the permissive detariffing policy was within its authority under the Communications Act. The D.C. Circuit reversed this order, and both MCI and the United States (together with the FCC) petitioned for certiorari.]

II

Section 203 of the Communications Act contains both the filed rate provisions of the Act and the Commission's disputed modification authority. It provides in relevant part:

(a) Filing; public display.

Every common carrier, except connecting carriers, shall, within such reasonable time as the Commission shall designate, file with the Commission and print and keep open for public inspection schedules showing all charges . . . , whether such charges are joint or separate, and showing the classifications, practices, and regulations affecting such charges. . . .

(b) Changes in schedule; discretion of Commission to modify requirements.

(1) No change shall be made in the charges, classifications, regulations, or practices which have been so filed and published except after one hundred and twenty days' notice to the Commission and to the public, which shall be published in such form and contain such information as the Commission may by regulations prescribe.

(2) The Commission may, in its discretion and for good cause shown, modify any requirement made by or under the authority of this section either in particular instances or by general order applicable to special circumstances or conditions except that the Commission may not require the notice period specified in paragraph (1) to be more than one hundred and twenty days.

(c) Overcharges and rebates.

No carrier, unless otherwise provided by or under authority of this chapter, shall engage or participate in such communication unless schedules have been filed and published in accordance with the provisions of this chapter and with the regulations made thereunder; and no carrier shall (1) charge, demand, collect, or receive a greater or less or different compensation for such communication . . . than the charges specified in the schedule then in effect, or (2) refund or remit by any means or device any portion of the charges so specified, or (3) extend to any person any privileges or facilities in such communication, or employ or enforce any classifications, regulations, or practices affecting such charges, except as specified in such schedule.

47 U.S.C. 203 (1988 ed. and Supp. IV).

The dispute between the parties turns on the meaning of the phrase "modify any requirement" in § 203(b)(2). Petitioners argue that it gives the Commission authority to make even basic and fundamental changes in the scheme created by that section. We disagree. The word "modify"—like a number of other English words employing the root "mod-" (deriving from the Latin word for "measure"), such as "moderate," "modulate," "modest," and "modicum,"—has a connotation of increment or limitation. Virtually every dictionary we are aware of says that "to modify" means to change moderately or in minor fashion. See, e.g., RANDOM HOUSE DICTIONARY OF THE ENGLISH LANGUAGE 1236 (2d ed. 1987) ("to change somewhat the form or qualities of; alter partially; amend"); WEBSTER'S THIRD NEW INTERNATIONAL DICTIONARY 1452 (1976) ("to make minor changes in the form or structure of: alter without transforming"); 9 OXFORD ENGLISH DICTIONARY 952 (2d ed. 1989) ("to make partial changes in; to change (an object) in respect of some of its qualities; to alter or vary without radical transformation"); BLACK'S LAW DICTIONARY 1004 (6th ed. 1990) ("to alter; to change in incidental or subordinate features; enlarge; extend; amend; limit; reduce").

In support of their position, petitioners cite dictionary definitions contained in or derived from a single source, WEBSTER'S THIRD NEW INTERNATIONAL DICTIONARY 1452 (1976) ("Webster's Third"), which includes among the meanings of "modify," "to make a basic or important change in." Petitioners contend that this establishes sufficient ambiguity to entitle the Commission to deference in its acceptance of the broader meaning, which in turn requires approval of its permissive detariffing policy. *See Chevron U.S.A. Inc. v. Natural Resources Defense Council, Inc.*, 467 U.S. 837, 843 (1984). In short, they contend that the courts must defer to the agency's choice among available dictionary definitions. * * *

Most cases of verbal ambiguity in statutes involve * * * a selection between accepted alternative meanings shown as such by many dictionaries. One can envision (though a court case does not immediately come to mind) having to choose between accepted alternative meanings, one of which is so newly accepted that it has only been recorded by a single lexicographer. (Some dictionary must have been the very first to record the widespread use of "projection," for example, to mean "forecast.") But what petitioners demand that we accept as creating an ambiguity here is a rarity even rarer than that: a meaning set forth in a single dictionary (and, as we say, its progeny) which not only supplements the meaning contained in all other dictionaries, but contradicts one of the meanings contained in virtually all other dictionaries. Indeed, contradicts one of the alternative meanings contained in the out-of-step dictionary itself—for as we have observed, Webster's Third itself defines "modify" to connote both (specifically) major change and (specifically) minor change. It is hard to see how that can be. When the word "modify" has come to mean both "to change in some respects" and "to change fundamentally" it will in fact mean neither of those things. It will simply mean "to change," and some adverb will have to be called into service to indicate the great or small degree of the change.

If that is what the peculiar Webster's Third definition means to suggest has happened—and what petitioners suggest by appealing to Webster's Third— we simply disagree. "Modify," in our view, connotes moderate change. It might be good English to say that the French Revolution "modified" the status of the French nobility but only because there is a figure of speech called understatement and a literary device known as sarcasm. And it might be unsurprising to discover a 1972 White House press release saying that "the Administration is modifying its position with regard to prosecution of the war in Vietnam"—but only because press agents tend to impart what is nowadays called "spin." Such intentional distortions, or simply careless or ignorant misuse, must have formed the basis for the usage that Webster's Third, and Webster's Third alone, reported. It is perhaps gilding the lily to add this: In 1934, when the Communications Act became law—the most relevant time for determining a statutory term's meaning, see *Perrin v. United States*, 444 U.S. 37, 42–45 (1979)—Webster's Third was not yet even contemplated. To our knowledge all English dictionaries provided the narrow definition of "modify," including those published by G. & C. Merriam Company. See WEBSTER'S NEW INTERNATIONAL DICTIONARY 1577 (2d ed. 1934); WEBSTER'S COLLEGIATE DICTIONARY 628 (4th ed. 1934). We have not the slightest doubt that is the meaning the statute intended.

Beyond the word itself, a further indication that the § 203 authority to "modify" does not contemplate fundamental changes is the sole exception to that authority which the section provides. One of the requirements of § 203 is that changes to filed tariffs can be made only after 120 days' notice to the Commission and the public. § 203(b)(1). The only exception to the Commission's § 203(b)(2) modification authority is as follows: "except that the Commission may not require the notice period specified in paragraph (1) to be more than one hundred and twenty days." Is it conceivable that the statute is indifferent to the Commission's power to eliminate the tariff-filing requirement entirely for all except one firm in the long-distance sector, and yet strains out the gnat of extending the waiting period for tariff revision beyond 120 days? We think not. The exception is not as ridiculous as a

Lilliputian in London only because it is to be found in Lilliput: in the small-scale world of "modifications," it is a big deal.

Since an agency's interpretation of a statute is not entitled to deference when it goes beyond the meaning that the statute can bear, see, e.g., *Pittston Coal Group v. Sebben*, 488 U.S. 105, 113 (1988); *Chevron*, 467 U.S., at 842–843, the Commission's permissive detariffing policy can be justified only if it makes a less than radical or fundamental change in the Act's tariff-filing requirement.

* * *

Bearing in mind, then, the enormous importance to the statutory scheme of the tariff-filing provision, we turn to whether what has occurred here can be considered a mere "modification." The Commission stresses that its detariffing policy applies only to nondominant carriers, so that the rates charged to over half of all consumers in the long-distance market are on file with the Commission. It is not clear to us that the proportion of customers affected, rather than the proportion of carriers affected, is the proper measure of the extent of the exemption (of course all carriers in the long-distance market are exempted, except AT&T). But even assuming it is, we think an elimination of the crucial provision of the statute for 40% of a major sector of the industry is much too extensive to be considered a "modification." What we have here, in reality, is a fundamental revision of the statute, changing it from a scheme of rate regulation in long-distance common-carrier communications to a scheme of rate regulation only where effective competition does not exist. That may be a good idea, but it was not the idea Congress enacted into law in 1934.

* * *

Finally, petitioners earnestly urge that their interpretation of § 203(b) furthers the Communications Act's broad purpose of promoting efficient telephone service. They claim that although the filing requirement prevented price discrimination and unfair practices while AT&T maintained a monopoly over long-distance service, it frustrates those same goals now that there is greater competition in that market. Specifically, they contend that filing costs raise artificial barriers to entry and that the publication of rates facilitates parallel pricing and stifles price competition. We have considerable sympathy with these arguments (though we doubt it makes sense, if one is concerned about the use of filed tariffs to communicate pricing information, to require filing by the dominant carrier, the firm most likely to be a price leader). * * * But our estimations, and the Commission's estimations, of desirable policy cannot alter the meaning of the Federal Communications Act of 1934. For better or worse, the Act establishes a rate-regulation, filed-tariff system for common-carrier communications, and the Commission's desire "to 'increase competition' cannot provide it authority to alter the well-established statutory filed rate requirements," *Maislin*, 497 U.S., at 135. As we observed in the context of a dispute over the filed-rate doctrine more than 80 years ago, "such considerations address themselves to Congress, not to the courts," *Armour Packing*, 209 U.S., at 82.

We do not mean to suggest that the tariff-filing requirement is so inviolate that the Commission's existing modification authority does not reach it at all. Certainly the Commission can modify the form, contents, and location of required filings, and can defer filing or perhaps even waive it altogether in limited circumstances. But what we have here goes well beyond that. It is effectively the introduction of a whole new regime of regulation (or of free-market competition), which may well be a better regime but is not the one that Congress established.

The judgment of the Court of Appeals is Affirmed.

DIY
The Long-Distance Telephone Problem: Interpreting the 1934 Communications Act 60 Years Later

 Before reading the dissenting opinion in the *MCI* case (which follows immediately below), spend three minutes outlining the arguments that you think would make the strongest dissenting opinion. Then go on and read the dissent.

JUSTICE STEVENS, with whom JUSTICE BLACKMUN and JUSTICE SOUTER join, dissenting.

The communications industry has an unusually dynamic character. In 1934, Congress authorized the Federal Communications Commission (FCC) to regulate "a field of enterprise the dominant characteristic of which was the rapid pace of its unfolding." *National Broadcasting Co. v. United States*, 319 U.S. 190, 219 (1943). The Communications Act (the Act) gives the FCC unusually broad discretion to meet new and unanticipated problems in order to fulfill its sweeping mandate "to make available, as far as possible, to all the people of the United States, a rapid, efficient, Nationwide and world-wide wire and radio communication service with adequate facilities at reasonable charges." 47 U.S.C. 151. This Court's consistent interpretation of the Act has afforded the Commission ample leeway to interpret and apply its statutory powers and responsibilities. The Court today abandons that approach in favor of a rigid literalism that deprives the FCC of the flexibility Congress meant it to have in order to implement the core policies of the Act in rapidly changing conditions.

I

At the time the Communications Act was passed, the telephone industry was dominated by the American Telephone & Telegraph Company and its affiliates. Title II of the Act, which establishes the framework for FCC regulation of common carriers by wire, was clearly a response to that dominance. As the Senate Report explained, "under existing provisions of the Interstate Commerce Act the regulation of the telephone monopoly has been practically nil. This vast monopoly which so immediately serves the needs of the people in their daily and social life must be effectively regulated." S. Rep. No. 781, 73d Cong., 2d Sess., 2 (1934).

The wire communications provisions of the Act address problems distinctly associated with monopoly. * * *

Section 203, modeled upon the filed rate provisions of the Interstate Commerce Act, see 49 U.S.C. 10761–10762; S. Rep. No. 781, supra, at 4, requires that common carriers other than connecting carriers "file with the Commission and print and keep open for public inspection schedules showing all charges for itself and its connecting carriers." 47 U.S.C. 203(a). A telephone carrier must allow a 120-day period of lead time before a tariff goes into effect, and, "unless otherwise provided by or under authority of this Act," may not provide communication services except according to a filed schedule,

§§ 203(c), (d). The tariff-filing section of the Communications Act, however, contains a provision that states:

> (b) Changes in schedule; discretion of Commission to modify requirements.
>
> . . .
>
> (2) The Commission may, in its discretion and for good cause shown, modify any requirement made by or under the authority of this section either in particular instances or by general order applicable to special circumstances or conditions except that the Commission may not require the notice period specified in paragraph (1) to be more than one hundred and twenty days.

47 U.S.C. 203(b)(2) (1988 ed., Supp. IV).

Congress doubtless viewed the filed rate provisions as an important mechanism to guard against abusive practices by wire communications monopolies. But it is quite wrong to suggest that the mere process of filing rate schedules—rather than the substantive duty of reasonably priced and nondiscriminatory service—is "the heart of the common-carrier section of the federal Communications Act."

* * *

III

Although the majority observes that further relaxation of tariff-filing requirements might more effectively enhance competition, it does not take issue with the Commission's conclusions that mandatory filing of tariff schedules serves no useful purpose and is actually counterproductive in the case of carriers who lack market power. * * * Thus, the sole question for us is whether the FCC's policy, however sensible, is nonetheless inconsistent with the Act.

In my view, each of the Commission's detariffing orders was squarely within its power to "modify any requirement" of § 203. Subsection 203(b)(2) plainly confers at least some discretion to modify the general rule that carriers file tariffs, for it speaks of "any requirement." Subsection 203(c) of the Act, ignored by the Court, squarely supports the FCC's position; it prohibits carriers from providing service without a tariff "unless otherwise provided by or under authority of this Act." Subsection 203(b)(2) is plainly one provision that "otherwise provides" and thereby authorizes service without a filed schedule. The FCC's authority to modify § 203's requirements in "particular instances" or by "general order applicable to special circumstances or conditions" emphasizes the expansive character of the Commission's authority: modifications may be narrow or broad, depending upon the Commission's appraisal of current conditions. From the vantage of a Congress seeking to regulate an almost completely monopolized industry, the advent of competition is surely a "special circumstance or condition" that might legitimately call for different regulatory treatment.

The only statutory exception to the Commission's modification authority provides that it may not extend the 120-day notice period set out in § 203(b)(1). See § 203(b)(2). The Act thus imposes a specific limit on the Commission's authority to stiffen that regulatory imposition on carriers, but does not confine the Commission's authority to relax it. It was no stretch for the FCC to draw from this single, unidirectional statutory limitation on its modification authority the inference that its authority is otherwise unlimited.

> **?** How strong is the *expressio unius* argument that can be made from this one exception?

According to the Court, the term "modify," as explicated in all but the most unreliable dictionaries, rules out the Commission's claimed authority to relieve nondominant carriers of the basic obligation to file tariffs. Dictionaries can be useful aids in statutory interpretation, but they are no substitute for close analysis of what words mean as used in a particular statutory context. Cf. *Cabell v. Markham*, 148 F.2d 737, 739 (CA2 1945) (Hand, J.). Even if the sole possible meaning of "modify" were to make "minor" changes, further elaboration is needed to show why the detariffing policy should fail. The Commission came to its present policy through a series of rulings that gradually relaxed the filing requirements for nondominant carriers. Whether the current policy should count as a cataclysmic or merely an incremental departure from the § 203(a) baseline depends on whether one focuses on particular carriers' obligations to file (in which case the Commission's policy arguably works a major shift) or on the statutory policies behind the tariff-filing requirement (which remain satisfied because market constraints on nondominant carriers obviate the need for rate-filing). When § 203 is viewed as part of a statute whose aim is to constrain monopoly power, the Commission's decision to exempt nondominant carriers is a rational and "measured" adjustment to novel circumstances—one that remains faithful to the core purpose of the tariff-filing section. See BLACK's LAW DICTION-ARY 1198 (3d ed. 1933) (defining "modification" as "A change; an alteration which introduces new elements into the details, or cancels some of them, but leaves the general purpose and effect of the subject-matter intact").

The Court seizes upon a particular sense of the word "modify" at the expense of another, long-established meaning that fully supports the Commission's position. That word is first defined in WEBSTER's COLLEGIATE DICTIONARY 628 (4th ed. 1934) as meaning "to limit or reduce in extent or degree." The Commission's permissive detariffing policy fits comfortably within this common understanding of the term. The FCC has in effect adopted a general rule stating that "if you are dominant you must file, but if you are nondominant you need not." The Commission's partial detariffing policy—which excuses nondominant carriers from filing on condition that they remain nondominant—is simply a relaxation of a costly regulatory requirement that recent developments had rendered pointless and counterproductive in a certain class of cases.

A modification pursuant to § 203(b)(1), like any other order issued under the Act, must of course be consistent with the purposes of the statute. . . .

The filed tariff provisions of the Communications Act are not ends in themselves, but are merely one of several procedural means for the Commission to ensure that carriers do not charge unreasonable or discriminatory rates. See 84 F.C.C.2d, at 483. The Commission has reasonably concluded that this particular means of enforcing the statute's substantive mandates will prove counterproductive in the case of nondominant long distance carriers. Even if the 1934 Congress did not define the scope of the Commission's modification authority with perfect scholarly precision, this is surely a paradigm case for judicial deference to the agency's interpretation, particularly in a statutory regime so obviously meant to maximize administrative flexibility. Whatever the best reading of § 203(b)(2), the Commission's reading cannot in my view be termed unreasonable. It is informed (as ours is not) by a practical understanding of the role (or lack thereof) that filed tariffs play in the modern regulatory climate and in the telecommunications industry. Since 1979, the FCC has sought to adapt measures originally designed to control monopoly power to new market conditions. It has carefully and consistently explained that mandatory tariff-filing rules frustrate the core statutory interest in rate reasonableness. The Commission's use of the "discretion" expressly conferred by § 203(b)(2) reflects "a reasonable accommodation of manifestly competing interests and is entitled to deference: the regulatory scheme is technical and complex, the agency considered the matter in a detailed and reasoned fashion, and the decision involves reconciling conflicting policies." *Chevron U.S.A. Inc. v. Natural Resources Defense Council, Inc.*, 467 U.S. 837, 865 (1984) (footnotes omitted). The FCC has permissibly interpreted its § 203(b)(2) authority in service of the goals Congress set forth in the Communications Act. We should sustain its eminently sound, experience-tested, and uncommonly well explained judgment.

> **?** This is the dissent's invocation of *Chevron*. What part of the *Chevron* two-step test is the dissent referring to here?

I respectfully dissent.

NOTES & QUESTIONS

1. In the *MCI* case, what, if anything, did the agency do wrong?

2. What is the primary difference between the majority opinion and the dissenting opinion?

3. Why do you think Congress wrote a statute that allowed the FCC to "modify" the filed rate requirement? How might the majority answer that question, and how might the dissent?

4. *MCI v. AT&T* is obviously a case about changed circumstances in the telecommunications industry. Here, the changes are both technological and economic, rendering the market for long-distance telephone service dramatically different from the one Congress faced in 1934. You will recall that Chapter 27 addressed the question of changed circumstances in statutory interpretation by courts. In Chapter 27, though, you had not yet learned about agencies. Now that you have, which institution is best suited to decide that the filed rate requirement no longer made sense: Congress, the Courts, or the FCC? Why?

5. When determining whether Congress has made the meaning of the statutory text clear under *Chevron* Step One, could a reviewing court properly take the agency's own views and analysis into account?

6. Might other extrinsic sources of interpretation be helpful at Step One, not to clarify an apparently ambiguous provision, but to reveal that a provision which appears to have a clear meaning actually may not be so clear?

2. *The Tobacco Case*

Now consider the following problem, and then the Supreme Court's resolution of it under *Chevron* Step One.

DIY
The Tobacco Problem: Interpreting the 1938 Food, Drug, and Cosmetic Act 60 Years Later

 The 1938 Food, Drug, and Cosmetic Act (FDCA) gives the Food and Drug Administration (FDA) authority to regulate drugs, which the Act defines as "articles (other than food) intended to affect the structure or any function of the body." 21 U.S.C. § 321. In 1996 (more than half a century after Congress adopted the statute), the FDA used this statutory authority to promulgate new regulations governing nicotine and tobacco products. Looking at the language of the FDCA, can you see any argument that "Congress has directly spoken to the precise question at issue" under *Chevron* Step One? Before reading the case that follows, take a few minutes to write some thoughts about (1) any argument that "Congress has directly spoken to the precise question at issue," whether in favor of or against the FDA's exercise of its FDCA authority to regulate nicotine and tobacco products; and (2) what additional research you would want to conduct in search of support for your argument.

FDA v. Brown & Williamson Tobacco Corp.
529 U.S. 120 (2000)

JUSTICE O'CONNOR delivered the opinion of the Court.

This case involves one of the most troubling public health problems facing our Nation today: the thousands of premature deaths that occur each year because of tobacco use. In 1996, the Food and Drug Administration (FDA), after having expressly disavowed any such authority since its inception, asserted jurisdiction to regulate tobacco products. The FDA concluded that nicotine is a "drug" within the meaning of the Food, Drug, and Cosmetic Act (FDCA or Act), as amended, 21 U.S.C. § 301 *et seq.*, and that cigarettes and smokeless tobacco are "combination products" that deliver nicotine to the body. Pursuant to this authority, it promulgated regulations intended to reduce tobacco consumption among children and adolescents. The agency believed that, because most tobacco consumers begin their use before reaching the age of 18, curbing tobacco use by minors could substantially reduce the prevalence of addiction in future generations and thus the incidence of tobacco-related death and disease.

Regardless of how serious the problem an administrative agency seeks to address, however, it may not exercise its authority "in a manner that is inconsistent with the administrative structure that Congress enacted into law." And although agencies are generally entitled to deference in the interpretation of statutes that they administer, a reviewing "court, as well as the agency, must give effect to the unambiguously expressed intent of Congress." *Chevron U.S.A. Inc.* v. *Natural Resources Defense Council, Inc.,* 467 U.S. 837, 842–843 (1984). In this case, we believe that Congress has clearly precluded the FDA from asserting jurisdiction to regulate tobacco products. Such authority is inconsistent with the intent that Congress has expressed in the FDCA's overall regulatory scheme and in the tobacco-specific legislation that it has enacted subsequent to the FDCA. In light of this clear intent, the FDA's assertion of jurisdiction is impermissible.

I

The FDCA grants the FDA * * * the authority to regulate, among other items, "drugs" and "devices." The Act defines "drug" to include "articles (other than food) intended to affect the structure or any function of the body." 21 U.S.C. § 321(g)(1)(C). It defines "device," in part, as "an instrument, apparatus, implement, machine, contrivance, * * * or other similar or related article, including any component, part, or accessory, which is * * * intended to affect the structure or any function of the body." § 321(h). The Act also grants the FDA the authority to regulate so-called "combination products," which "constitute a combination of a drug, device, or biologic product." § 353(g)(1). * * *

On August 11, 1995, the FDA published a proposed rule concerning the sale of cigarettes and smokeless tobacco to children and adolescents. The rule, which included several restrictions on the sale, distribution, and advertisement of tobacco products, was designed to reduce the availability and attractiveness of tobacco products to young people. A public comment period followed, during which the FDA received over 700,000 submissions, more than "at any other time in its history on any other subject."

On August 28, 1996, the FDA issued a final rule entitled "Regulations Restricting the Sale and Distribution of Cigarettes and Smokeless Tobacco to Protect Children and Adolescents." The FDA determined that nicotine is a "drug" and that cigarettes and smokeless tobacco are "drug delivery devices," and therefore it had jurisdiction under the FDCA to regulate tobacco products as customarily marketed—that is, without manufacturer claims of therapeutic benefit. First, the FDA found that tobacco products " 'affect the structure or any function of the body' " because nicotine "has significant pharmacological effects." Specifically, nicotine "exerts psychoactive, or mood-altering, effects on the brain" that cause and sustain addiction, have both tranquilizing and stimulating effects, and control weight. Second, the FDA determined that these effects were "intended" under the FDCA because they "are so widely known and foreseeable that [they] may be deemed to have been intended by the manufacturers"; consumers use tobacco products "predominantly or nearly exclusively" to obtain these effects; and the statements, research, and actions of manufacturers revealed that they "have 'designed' cigarettes to provide pharmacologically active doses of nicotine to consumers." Finally, the agency concluded that cigarettes and smokeless tobacco are "combination products" because, in addition to containing nicotine, they include device components that deliver a controlled amount of nicotine to the body.

Having resolved the jurisdictional question, the FDA next explained the policy justifications for its regulations, detailing the deleterious health effects associated with tobacco use. It found that tobacco consumption was "the single leading cause of preventable death in the United States." According to the FDA, "[m]ore than 400,000 people die each year from tobacco-related illnesses, such as cancer, respiratory illnesses, and heart disease." The agency also determined that the only way to reduce the amount of tobacco-related illness and mortality was to reduce the level of addiction, a goal that could be accomplished only by preventing children and adolescents from starting to use tobacco. * * *

Based on these findings, the FDA promulgated regulations concerning tobacco products' promotion, labeling, and accessibility to children and adolescents. The access regulations prohibit the sale of cigarettes or smoke-less tobacco to persons younger than 18; require retailers to verify through photo identification the age of all purchasers younger than 27; prohibit the sale of cigarettes in quantities smaller than 20; prohibit the distribution of free samples; and prohibit sales through self-service displays and vending machines except in adult-only locations. [The Court here also summarized the advertising and labelling regulations.]

Respondents, a group of tobacco manufacturers, retailers, and advertisers, filed suit in United States District Court for the Middle District of North Carolina challenging the regulations. They moved for summary judgment on the grounds that the FDA lacked jurisdiction to regulate tobacco products as customarily marketed, the regulations exceeded the FDA's authority under 21 U.S.C. § 360j(e), and the advertising restrictions violated the First Amendment. The District Court granted respondents' motion in part and denied it in part. The court held that the FDCA authorizes the FDA to regulate tobacco products as customarily marketed and that the FDA's access and labeling regulations are permissible, but it also found that the agency's advertising and promotion restrictions exceed its authority under § 360j(e). * * *

The Court of Appeals for the Fourth Circuit reversed, holding that Congress has not granted the FDA jurisdiction to regulate tobacco products. * * * Having resolved the jurisdictional question against the agency, the Court of Appeals did not address whether the regulations exceed the FDA's authority under 21 U.S.C. § 360j(e) or violate the First Amendment.

We granted the Government's petition for certiorari. * * *

II

The FDA's assertion of jurisdiction to regulate tobacco products is founded on its conclusions that nicotine is a "drug" and that cigarettes and smokeless tobacco are "drug delivery devices." Again, the FDA found that tobacco products are "intended" to deliver the pharmacological effects of satisfying addiction, stimulation and tranquilization, and weight control because those effects are foreseeable to any reasonable manufacturer, consumers use tobacco products to obtain those effects, and tobacco manufacturers have designed their products to produce those effects. * * *

A threshold issue is the appropriate framework for analyzing the FDA's assertion of authority to regulate tobacco products. Because this case involves an administrative agency's construction of a statute that it administers, our analysis is governed by *Chevron U.S.A. Inc. v. Natural Resources Defense Council, Inc.*, 467 U.S. 837 (1984). Under *Chevron*, a reviewing court must first ask "whether Congress has directly spoken to the precise question at issue." If Congress has done so, the inquiry is at an end; the court "must give effect to the unambiguously expressed intent of Congress." But if Congress has not specifically addressed the question, a reviewing court must respect the agency's construction of the statute so long as it is permissible. Such deference is justified because "[t]he responsibilities for assessing the wisdom of such policy choices and resolving the struggle between competing views of the public interest are not judicial ones," and because of the agency's greater familiarity with the ever-changing facts and circumstances surrounding the subjects regulated.

In determining whether Congress has specifically addressed the question at issue, a reviewing court should not confine itself to examining a particular statutory provision in isolation. The meaning—or ambiguity—of certain words or phrases may only become evident when placed in context. It is a "fundamental canon of statutory construction that the words of a statute must be read in their context and with a view to their place in the overall statutory scheme." A court must therefore interpret the statute "as a symmetrical and coherent regulatory scheme," and "fit, if possible, all parts into an harmonious whole." Similarly, the meaning of one statute may be affected by other Acts, particularly where Congress has spoken subsequently and more specifically to the topic at hand. In addition, we must be guided to a degree by common sense as to the manner in which Congress is likely to delegate a policy decision of such economic and political magnitude to an administrative agency. Cf. *MCI Telecommunications Corp.* v. *American Telephone & Telegraph Co.*, 512 U.S. 218, 231 (1994).

With these principles in mind, we find that Congress has directly spoken to the issue here and precluded the FDA's jurisdiction to regulate tobacco products.

A

Viewing the FDCA as a whole, it is evident that one of the Act's core objectives is to ensure that any product regulated by the FDA is "safe" and "effective" for its intended use. See 21 U.S.C. § 393(b)(2) (1994 ed., Supp. III) (defining the FDA's mission). * * * This essential purpose pervades the FDCA. * * *

In its rulemaking proceeding, the FDA quite exhaustively documented that "tobacco products are unsafe," "dangerous," and "cause great pain and suffering from illness." It found that the consumption of tobacco products "presents extraordinary health risks," and that "tobacco use is the single leading cause of preventable death in the United States." * * *

These findings logically imply that, if tobacco products were "devices" under the FDCA, the FDA would be required to remove them from the market. [Here the Court summarized its view that an unsafe device would need to be banned.] [W]ere tobacco products within the FDA's jurisdiction, the Act would deem them misbranded devices that could not be introduced into interstate commerce. Contrary to the dissent's contention, the Act admits no remedial discretion once it is evident that the device is misbranded. * * *

Congress, however, has foreclosed the removal of tobacco products from the market. A provision of the United States Code currently in force states that "[t]he marketing of tobacco constitutes one of the greatest basic industries of the United States with ramifying activities which directly affect interstate and foreign commerce at every point, and stable conditions therein are necessary to the general welfare." 7 U.S.C. § 1311(a). More importantly, Congress has directly addressed the problem of tobacco and health through legislation on six occasions since 1965. See Federal Cigarette Labeling and Advertising Act (FCLAA), Pub. L. 89–92, 79 Stat. 282; Public Health Cigarette Smoking Act of 1969, Pub. L. 91–222, 84 Stat. 87; Alcohol and Drug Abuse Amendments of 1983, Pub. L. 98–24, 97 Stat. 175; Comprehensive Smoking Education Act, Pub. L. 98–474, 98 Stat. 2200; Comprehensive Smokeless Tobacco Health Education Act of 1986, Pub. L. 99–252, 100 Stat. 30; Alcohol, Drug Abuse, and Mental Health Administration Reorganization Act, Pub. L. 102–321, § 202, 106 Stat. 394. When Congress enacted these statutes, the adverse health consequences of tobacco use were well known, as were nicotine's pharmacological effects. * * * Nonetheless, Congress stopped well short of ordering a ban. Instead, it has generally regulated the labeling and advertisement of tobacco products, expressly providing that it is the policy of Congress that "commerce and the national economy may be. . .protected to the maximum extent consistent with" consumers "be[ing] adequately informed about any adverse health effects." 15 U.S.C. § 1331. Congress' decisions to regulate labeling and advertising and to adopt the express policy of protecting "commerce and the national economy. . .to the maximum extent" reveal its intent that tobacco products remain on the market. Indeed, the collective premise of these statutes is that cigarettes and smokeless tobacco will continue to be sold in the United States. A ban of tobacco products by the FDA would therefore plainly contradict congressional policy. * * *

Considering the FDCA as a whole, it is clear that Congress intended to exclude tobacco products from the FDA's jurisdiction. * * *

B

In determining whether Congress has spoken directly to the FDA's authority to regulate tobacco, we must also consider in greater detail the tobacco-specific legislation that Congress has enacted over the past 35 years. At the time a statute is enacted, it may have a range of plausible meanings. Over time, however, subsequent acts can shape or focus those meanings. The "classic judicial task of reconciling many laws enacted over time, and getting them to 'make sense' in combination, necessarily assumes that the implications of a statute may be altered by the implications of a later statute." This is particularly so where the scope of the earlier statute is broad but the subsequent statutes more specifically address the topic at hand. * * *

Congress has enacted six separate pieces of legislation since 1965 address-ing the problem of tobacco use and human health. Those statutes, among other things, require that health warnings appear on all packaging and in all print and outdoor advertisements; prohibit the advertisement of tobacco products through "any medium of electronic communication" subject to regulation by the Federal Communications Commission (FCC); require the Secretary of Health and Human Services (HHS) to report every three years to Congress on research findings concerning "the addictive property of tobacco"; and make States' receipt of certain federal block grants contingent on their making it unlawful "for any manufacturer, retailer, or distributor of tobacco products to sell or distribute any such product to any individual under the age of 18."

In adopting each statute, Congress has acted against the backdrop of the FDA's consistent and repeated statements that it lacked authority under the FDCA to regulate tobacco absent claims of therapeutic benefit by the manufacturer. In fact, on several occasions over this period, and after the health consequences of tobacco use and nicotine's pharmacological effects had become well known, Congress considered and rejected bills that would have granted the FDA such jurisdiction. Under these circumstances, it is evident that Congress' tobacco-specific statutes have effectively ratified the FDA's long-held position that it lacks jurisdiction under the FDCA to regulate tobacco products. Congress has created a distinct regulatory scheme to address the problem of tobacco and health, and that scheme, as presently constructed, precludes any role for the FDA. * * *

[B]efore enacting the FCLAA in 1965, Congress considered and rejected several proposals to give the FDA the authority to regulate tobacco. * * *

Congress ultimately decided in 1965 to subject tobacco products to the less extensive regulatory scheme of the FCLAA, which created a "comprehensive Federal program to deal with cigarette labeling and advertising with respect to any relationship between smoking and health." Pub. L. 89–92, § 2, 79 Stat. 282. The FCLAA rejected any regulation of advertising, but it required the warning, "Caution: Cigarette Smoking May Be Hazardous to Your Health," to appear on all cigarette packages. *Id.*, § 4, 79 Stat. 283. In the Act's "Declaration of Policy," Congress stated that its objective was to balance the goals of ensuring that "the public may be adequately informed that cigarette smoking may be hazardous to health" and protecting "commerce and the national economy. . .to the maximum extent." *Id.*, § 2, 79 Stat. 282 (codified at 15 U.S.C. § 1331).

Not only did Congress reject the proposals to grant the FDA jurisdiction, but it explicitly preempted any other regulation of cigarette labeling: "No statement relating to smoking and health, other than the statement required by . . . this Act, shall be required on any cigarette package." *Id.*, § 5(a), 79 Stat. 283. The regulation of product labeling, however, is an integral aspect of the FDCA, both as it existed in 1965 and today. The labeling requirements currently imposed by the FDCA, which are essentially identical to those in force in 1965, require the FDA to regulate the labeling of drugs and devices to protect the safety of consumers. See 21 U.S.C. § 352; 21 U.S.C. § 352 (1964 ed. and Supp. IV). * * *

Further, the FCLAA evidences Congress' intent to preclude *any* administrative agency from exercising significant policymaking authority on the subject of smoking and health. In addition to prohibiting any additional requirements for cigarette labeling, the FCLAA provided that "[n]o statement relating to smoking and health shall be required in the advertising of any cigarettes the packages of which are labeled in conformity with the provisions of this Act." Pub. L. 89–92, § 5(b), 79 Stat. 283. Thus, in reaction to the FTC's attempt to regulate cigarette labeling and advertising, Congress enacted a statute reserving exclusive control over both subjects to itself.

Subsequent tobacco-specific legislation followed a similar pattern. [The Court then discussed changes to the FCLAA and the Consumer Product Safety Commission.]

Meanwhile, the FDA continued to maintain that it lacked jurisdiction under the FDCA to regulate tobacco products as customarily marketed. In 1972, FDA Commissioner Edwards testified before Congress that "cigarettes recommended for smoking pleasure are beyond the Federal Food, Drug, and Cosmetic Act." 1972 Hearings 239, 242. He further stated that the FDA believed that the Public Health Cigarette Smoking Act "demonstrates that the regulation of cigarettes is to be the domain of Congress," and that "labeling or banning cigarettes is a step that can be take[n] only by the Congress. Any such move by FDA would be inconsistent with the clear congressional intent."

* * * In 1983, Congress again considered legislation on the subject of smoking and health. HHS Assistant Secretary Brandt testified that, in addition to being "a major cause of cancer," smoking is a "major cause of heart disease" and other serious illnesses, and can result in "unfavorable pregnancy outcomes." He also stated that it was "well-established that cigarette smoking is a drug dependence, and that smoking is addictive for many people." Nonetheless, Assistant Secretary Brandt maintained that "the issue of regulation of tobacco . . . is something that Congress has reserved to itself, and we do not within the Department have the authority to regulate nor are we seeking such authority." He also testified before the Senate, stating that, despite the evidence of tobacco's health effects and addictiveness, the Department's view was that "Congress has assumed the responsibility of regulating. . .cigarettes."

Against this backdrop, Congress enacted three additional tobacco-specific statutes over the next four years that incrementally expanded its regulatory scheme for tobacco products. In 1983, Congress adopted the Alcohol and Drug Abuse Amendments, Pub. L. 98–24, 97 Stat. 175 (codified at 42 U.S.C. § 290aa *et seq.*), which require the Secretary of HHS to report to Congress every three years on the "addictive property of tobacco" and to include recommendations for action that the Secretary may deem appropriate. A year later, Congress enacted the Comprehensive Smoking Education

Act, Pub. L. 98–474, 98 Stat. 2200, which amended the FCLAA by again modifying the prescribed warning. Notably, during debate on the Senate floor, Senator Hawkins argued that the Act was necessary in part because "[u]nder the Food, Drug and Cosmetic Act, the Congress exempted tobacco products." 130 Cong. Rec. 26953 (1984). And in 1986, Congress enacted the Comprehensive Smokeless Tobacco Health Education Act of 1986 (CSTHEA), Pub. L. 99–252, 100 Stat. 30 (codified at 15 U.S.C. § 4401 *et seq.*), which essentially extended the regulatory provisions of the FCLAA to smokeless tobacco products. Like the FCLAA, the CSTHEA provided that "[n]o statement relating to the use of smokeless tobacco products and health, other than the statements required by [the Act], shall be required by any Federal agency to appear on any package . . . of a smokeless tobacco product." § 7(a), 100 Stat. 34 (codified at 15 U.S.C. § 4406(a)). Thus, as with cigarettes, Congress reserved for itself an aspect of smokeless tobacco regulation that is particularly important to the FDCA's regulatory scheme. * * *

Taken together, these actions by Congress over the past 35 years preclude an interpretation of the FDCA that grants the FDA jurisdiction to regulate tobacco products. We do not rely on Congress' failure to act—its consideration and rejection of bills that would have given the FDA this authority—in reaching this conclusion. Indeed, this is not a case of simple inaction by Congress that purportedly represents its acquiescence in an agency's position. To the contrary, Congress has enacted several statutes addressing the particular subject of tobacco and health, creating a distinct regulatory scheme for cigarettes and smokeless tobacco. In doing so, Congress has been aware of tobacco's health hazards and its pharmacological effects. It has also enacted this legislation against the background of the FDA repeatedly and consistently asserting that it lacks jurisdiction under the FDCA to regulate tobacco products as customarily marketed. Further, Congress has persistently acted to preclude a meaningful role for *any* administrative agency in making policy on the subject of tobacco and health. Moreover, the substance of Congress' regulatory scheme is, in an important respect, incompatible with FDA jurisdiction. Although the supervision of product labeling to protect consumer health is a substantial component of the FDA's regulation of drugs and devices, the FCLAA and the CSTHEA explicitly prohibit any federal agency from imposing any health-related labeling requirements on cigarettes or smokeless tobacco products.

Under these circumstances, it is clear that Congress' tobacco-specific legislation has effectively ratified the FDA's previous position that it lacks jurisdiction to regulate tobacco. As in *Bob Jones Univ. v. United States,* 461 U.S.

574 (1983), "[i]t is hardly conceivable that Congress—and in this setting, any Member of Congress—was not abundantly aware of what was going on." Congress has affirmatively acted to address the issue of tobacco and health, relying on the representations of the FDA that it had no authority to regulate tobacco. It has created a distinct scheme to regulate the sale of tobacco products, focused on labeling and advertising, and premised on the belief that the FDA lacks such jurisdiction under the FDCA. As a result, Congress' tobacco-specific statutes preclude the FDA from regulating tobacco products as customarily marketed.

C

Finally, our inquiry into whether Congress has directly spoken to the precise question at issue is shaped, at least in some measure, by the nature of the question presented. Deference under *Chevron* to an agency's construction of a statute that it administers is premised on the theory that a statute's ambiguity constitutes an implicit delegation from Congress to the agency to fill in the statutory gaps. In extraordinary cases, however, there may be reason to hesitate before concluding that Congress has intended such an implicit delegation. Cf. Breyer, Judicial Review of Questions of Law and Policy, 38 Admin. L.Rev. 363, 370 (1986) ("A court may also ask whether the legal question is an important one. Congress is more likely to have focused upon, and answered, major questions, while leaving interstitial matters to answer themselves in the course of the statute's daily administration").

This is hardly an ordinary case. Contrary to its representations to Congress since 1914, the FDA has now asserted jurisdiction to regulate an industry constituting a significant portion of the American economy. In fact, the FDA contends that, were it to determine that tobacco products provide no "reasonable assurance of safety," it would have the authority to ban cigarettes and smokeless tobacco entirely. Owing to its unique place in American history and society, tobacco has its own unique political history. Congress, for better or for worse, has created a distinct regulatory scheme for tobacco products, squarely rejected proposals to give the FDA jurisdiction over tobacco, and repeatedly acted to preclude any agency from exercising significant policymaking authority in the area. Given this history and the breadth of the authority that the FDA has asserted, we are obliged to defer not to the agency's expansive construction of the statute, but to Congress' consistent judgment to deny the FDA this power.

Our decision in *MCI Telecommunications Corp. v. American Telephone & Telegraph Co.*, 512 U.S. 218 (1994), is instructive. That case involved the proper construction of the term "modify" in § 203(b) of the Communications Act of 1934. The FCC contended that, because the Act gave it the discretion to "modify any requirement" imposed under the statute, it therefore possessed the authority to render voluntary the otherwise mandatory requirement that long distance carriers file their rates. We rejected the FCC's construction, finding "not the slightest doubt" that Congress had directly spoken to the question. In reasoning even more apt here, we concluded that "[i]t is highly unlikely that Congress would leave the determination of whether an industry will be entirely, or even substantially, rate-regulated to agency discretion—and even more unlikely that it would achieve that through such a subtle device as permission to 'modify' rate-filing requirements."

As in *MCI*, we are confident that Congress could not have intended to delegate a decision of such economic and political significance to an agency in so cryptic a fashion. To find that the FDA has the authority to regulate tobacco products, one must not only adopt an extremely strained understanding of "safety" as it is used throughout the Act—a concept central to the FDCA's regulatory scheme—but also ignore the plain implication of Congress' subsequent tobacco-specific legislation. It is therefore clear, based on the FDCA's overall regulatory scheme and the subsequent tobacco legislation, that Congress has directly spoken to the question at issue and precluded the FDA from regulating tobacco products. * * *

JUSTICE BREYER, with whom JUSTICE STEVENS, JUSTICE SOUTER, and JUSTICE GINSBURG join, dissenting.

The Food and Drug Administration (FDA) has the authority to regulate "articles (other than food) intended to affect the structure or any function of the body. . . ." Federal Food, Drug and Cosmetic Act (FDCA), 21 U.S.C. § 321(g)(1)(C). Unlike the majority, I believe that tobacco products fit within this statutory language.

In its own interpretation, the majority nowhere denies the following two salient points. First, tobacco products (including cigarettes) fall within the scope of this statutory definition, read literally. Cigarettes achieve their mood-stabilizing effects through the interaction of the chemical nicotine and the cells of the central nervous system. Both cigarette manufacturers and smokers alike know of, and desire, that chemically induced result. Hence, cigarettes are "intended to affect" the body's "structure" and "function," in the literal sense of these words.

Second, the statute's basic purpose—the protection of public health—supports the inclusion of cigarettes within its scope. Unregulated tobacco use causes "[m]ore than 400,000 people [to] die each year from tobacco-related illnesses, such as cancer, respiratory illnesses, and heart disease." 61 Fed. Reg. 44398 (1996). Indeed, tobacco products kill more people in this country every year "than. . .AIDS, car accidents, alcohol, homicides, illegal drugs, suicides, and fires, *combined*." *Ibid*. (emphasis added).

Despite the FDCA's literal language and general purpose (both of which support the FDA's finding that cigarettes come within its statutory authority), the majority nonetheless reads the statute as *excluding* tobacco products for two basic reasons:

(1) the FDCA does not "fit" the case of tobacco because the statute requires the FDA to prohibit dangerous drugs or devices (like cigarettes) outright, and the agency concedes that simply banning the sale of cigarettes is not a proper remedy; and

(2) Congress has enacted other statutes, which, when viewed in light of the FDA's long history of denying tobacco-related jurisdiction and considered together with Congress' failure explicitly to grant the agency tobacco-specific authority, demonstrate that Congress did not intend for the FDA to exercise jurisdiction over tobacco.

In my view, neither of these propositions is valid. Rather, the FDCA does not significantly limit the FDA's remedial alternatives. And the later statutes do not tell the FDA it cannot exercise jurisdiction, but simply leave FDA jurisdictional law where Congress found it. [C]f. Food and Drug Administration Modernization Act of 1997, 111 Stat. 2380 (codified at note following 21 U.S.C. § 321 (1994 ed., Supp. III)) (statute "shall" *not* "be construed to affect the question of whether" the FDA "has any authority to regulate any tobacco product").

The bulk of the opinion that follows will explain the basis for these latter conclusions. In short, I believe that the most important indicia of statutory meaning—language and purpose—along with the FDCA's legislative history (described briefly in Part I) are sufficient to establish that the FDA has authority to regulate tobacco. The statute-specific arguments against jurisdiction that the tobacco companies and the majority rely upon (discussed in Part II) are based on erroneous assumptions and, thus, do not defeat the jurisdiction-supporting thrust of the FDCA's language and purpose. The inferences that the majority draws from later legislative history are not persuasive, since (as I point out in Part III) one can just as easily infer from the later laws that Congress did not intend to affect the FDA's tobacco-related authority at all. And the fact that the FDA changed its mind about the scope of its own jurisdiction is legally insignificant because (as Part IV establishes) the agency's reasons for changing course are fully justified. Finally, as I explain in Part V, the degree of accountability that likely will attach to the FDA's action in this case should alleviate any concern that Congress, rather than an administrative agency, ought to make this important regulatory decision. * * *

III

In the majority's view, laws enacted since 1965 require us to deny jurisdiction, whatever the FDCA might mean in their absence. But why? Do those laws contain language barring FDA jurisdiction? The majority must concede that they do not. Do they contain provisions that are inconsistent with the FDA's exercise of jurisdiction? With one exception, the majority points to no such provision. Do they somehow repeal the principles of law * * * that otherwise would lead to the conclusion that the FDA has jurisdiction in this area? The companies themselves deny making any such claim. Perhaps the later laws "shape" and "focus" what the 1938 Congress meant a generation earlier. But this Court has warned against using the views of a later Congress to construe a statute enacted many years before. And, while the majority suggests that the subsequent history "control[s] our construction" of the FDCA, this Court expressly has held that such subsequent views are not "controlling."

Regardless, the later statutes do not support the majority's conclusion. That is because, whatever individual Members of Congress after 1964 may have assumed about the FDA's jurisdiction, the laws they enacted did not embody any such "no jurisdiction" assumption. And one cannot automatically *infer* an antijurisdiction intent, as the majority does, for the later statutes are both (and similarly) consistent with quite a different congressional desire, namely, the intent to proceed without interfering with whatever authority the FDA otherwise may have possessed. As I demonstrate below, the subsequent legislative history is critically ambivalent, for it can be read either as (a) "ratif[ying]" a no-jurisdiction assumption, *or* as (b) leaving the jurisdictional question just where Congress found it. And the fact that both inferences are "equally tenable," prevents the majority from drawing from the later statutes the firm, antijurisdiction implication that it needs. * * *

IV

I now turn to the final historical fact that the majority views as a factor in its interpretation of the subsequent legislative history: the FDA's former denials of its tobacco-related authority.

Until the early 1990's, the FDA expressly maintained that the 1938 statute did not give it the power that it now seeks to assert. It then changed its mind. The majority agrees with me that the FDA's change of positions does not make a significant legal difference. Nevertheless, it labels those denials "important context" for drawing an inference about Congress' intent. In my view, the FDA's change of policy, like the subsequent statutes themselves, does nothing to advance the majority's position.

When it denied jurisdiction to regulate cigarettes, the FDA consistently stated *why* that was so. * * *

What changed? For one thing, the FDA obtained evidence sufficient to prove the necessary "intent" despite the absence of specific "claims." This evidence, which first became available in the early 1990's, permitted the agency to demonstrate that the tobacco companies *knew* nicotine achieved appetite-suppressing, mood-stabilizing, and habituating effects through chemical (not psychological) means, even at a time when the companies were publicly denying such knowledge.

Moreover, scientific evidence of adverse health effects mounted, until, in the late 1980's, a consensus on the seriousness of the matter became firm. * * *

Finally, administration policy changed. Earlier administrations may have hesitated to assert jurisdiction for the reasons prior Commissioners expressed. Commissioners of the current administration simply took a different regulatory attitude.

Nothing in the law prevents the FDA from changing its policy for such reasons. By the mid-1990's, the evidence needed to prove objective intent—even without an express claim—had been found. The emerging scientific consensus about tobacco's adverse, chemically induced, health effects may have convinced the agency that it should spend its resources on this important regulatory effort. As for the change of administrations, I agree with then-Justice Rehnquist's statement in a different case, where he wrote:

> The agency's changed view. . .seems to be related to the election of a new President of a different political party. It is readily apparent that the responsible members of one administration may consider public resistance and uncertainties to be more important than do their counterparts in a previous administration. A change in administration brought about by the people casting their votes is a perfectly reasonable basis for an executive agency's reappraisal of the costs and benefits of its programs and regulations. As long as

> the agency remains within the bounds established by Congress, it
> is entitled to assess administrative records and evaluate priorities
> in light of the philosophy of the administration.
>
> *Motor Vehicle Mfrs. Assn. of United States, Inc. v. State Farm Mut. Automobile*
> *Ins. Co.,* 463 U.S. 29, 59 (1983) (Rehnquist, J., concurring in part and
> dissenting in part). * * *
>
> The upshot is that the Court today holds that a regulatory statute aimed
> at unsafe drugs and devices does not authorize regulation of a drug (nico-
> tine) and a device (a cigarette) that the Court itself finds unsafe. Far more
> than most, this particular drug and device risks the life-threatening harms
> that administrative regulation seeks to rectify. The majority's conclusion is
> counter-intuitive. And, for the reasons set forth, I believe that the law does
> not require it.

NOTES & QUESTIONS

1. What do you think best explains the Court's departure from what seems
    to be the "plain meaning" of the Food, Drug, and Cosmetic Act? Recall
    the mention of this case in the Chapter 24 discussion of "coherence
    with other law." Is the Court simply trying to reconcile the 1938 FDCA
    with the six post-1965 tobacco-specific statutes? If that seems right to
    you, does it matter that none of those statutes purports to affect the
    FDA's jurisdiction? As Justice Breyer pointed out in his dissent (in a
    passage not excerpted above), "the [six] later laws say next to nothing
    about the FDA's tobacco-related authority. Previous FDA disclaimers of
    jurisdiction may have helped to form the legislative atmosphere out of
    which Congress' own tobacco-specific statutes emerged. But a legisla-
    tive atmosphere is not a law, unless it is embodied in a statutory word
    or phrase." Or is the Court rejecting the best reading of the statutory
    text based on an intuition that Congress could not have possibly in-
    tended the FDCA's open-ended language to apply to an industry with
    "its unique place in American history and society [and] its own unique
    political history," one that "constitut[ed] a significant portion of the
    American economy"?

2. Recall the *Bostock* case in Chapter 17, which in 2020 construed Title
    VII's prohibition on discrimination in employment "because of. . .sex"

to prohibit an employer from firing an employee because the employee was gay. If the majority's "ordinary public meaning" analysis in *Bostock* had been applied to *Brown & Williamson*, would it have produced a different result concerning the scope of the Food, Drug, and Cosmetic Act?

3. As you can see, both *MCI v. AT&T* and *Brown & Williamson* involved seemingly open-ended statutory language from an old statute: In *MCI v. AT&T*, the word "modify" in the 1934 Communications Act, and in *Brown & Williamson*, the definitions of "drug" and "device" in the 1938 Food, Drug, and Cosmetic Act. Notice too that both *MCI v. AT&T* and *Brown & Williamson* are cases about statutory interpretation of this open-ended language in light of changed circumstances. In *MCI v. AT&T*, the key change between the statute's passage and the agency's interpretation more than a half-century later was the fact that the long-distance telephone market was no longer a monopoly, an assumption that Congress clearly made in 1934 when it required the dominant long-distance telephone company (AT&T) to file its rates with the FCC. The FCC's decision to exempt non-dominant carriers from the rate-filing requirement was thus meant to respond to this important change in the market. But, what about the FDA in *Brown & Williamson*? What did the FDA think had changed between 1938, when Congress passed the statute, and 1996, when the FDA promulgated its rule regulating tobacco products?

4. In contrast to *MCI v. AT&T*, *Brown & Williamson* involved the Court reviewing multiple statutes, not just the FDCA, the statute that the Court was ostensibly interpreting. The *Brown & Williamson* Court thus broadened the Step One inquiry. The Step One question is thus whether *Congress* spoke directly to the issue, *not* whether *the statute* spoke directly to the issue. Look again at the discussions of Textualism and Intentionalism in Part IV. Which of those theories does the *Brown & Williamson* emphasis on Congress (as opposed to the *statute*) seem based on?

5. Both *MCI* and *Brown & Williamson* were doctrinally viewed as *Chevron* Step One cases at the time they were decided, but many observers now view them as proto-"Major Questions Doctrine" cases. Don't worry if you don't yet see why. We will turn to this issue in more detail in Chapter 37.

6. Before we get there, though, we turn to Step Two of the *Chevron* test. Remember that a court will theoretically only get to Step Two if the

court determines that Congress has not spoken directly to the issue. When courts, commentators, and others talk about "*Chevron* deference," they are talking about Step Two, not Step One. As we hope you've seen from *MCI v. AT&T* and *Brown & Williamson*, Step One is not deferential at all.

B. Questions About *Chevron* Step Two

Recall that Step Two of the *Chevron* doctrine tells a court to defer to the agency's interpretation if that interpretation is "permissible" or "reasonable." Step Two functions like a presumption that Congress has intended to delegate lawmaking authority (including *interpretive* authority) to an agency whenever Congress has not spoken specifically or clearly enough. The basis for this presumption is that the agency's resolution is preferable to the judiciary's, for any of several reasons, alone or in combination. In addition to notions of the agency's political accountability and expertise, other arguments for deferring to an agency sometimes include the agency's greater efficiency at developing national uniformity and consistency on an issue, and the agency's ability to adapt dynamically to changed circumstances.

FYI Occasionally, Congress will explicitly give the agency interpretive authority. In such circumstances, the courts will defer to the agency interpretation without needing to go through the *Chevron* two steps. The leading case for this proposition is *Batterton v. Francis*, 432 U.S. 416 (1977).

Notably, though, the *Chevron* rationale did not explicitly require that the agency either rely upon its potentially superior expertise in resolving a given interpretive problem, or demonstrate any political accountability with respect to the interpretation in question. Nor did *Chevron* itself even require that the agency show that Congress had intended the agency to resolve the interpretive issue. Indeed, the notion that statutory ambiguity means that Congress has authorized the agency to resolve the interpretive issue is the critical presumption of *Chevron* Step Two. Thus, when *Chevron* Step Two is employed, the resulting judicial deference is independent of whether the agency in fact has capitalized on the agency's institutional competencies in resolving the particular interpretive problem.

Once courts reach Step Two, the result in practice has been a highly deferential judicial willingness to accept with little questioning any reasonable agency construction of the statutory terms at issue.

At Step Two, courts are generally highly deferential. Think about why this might be.

Although the *Chevron* doctrine does not require the reviewing court to ascertain at Step Two whether the agency relied upon its greater expertise or its greater political accountability, commentators have raised questions about whether some relatively crude proxy for these inquiries might be appropriate. These questions include, in particular: (1) whether *Chevron* deference is less appropriate for independent agencies, because they are less politically accountable; and (2) whether *Chevron* deference is less appropriate with respect to an interpretive issue for which expertise is less relevant than for an issue for which expertise is crucial. Although the U.S. Supreme Court has never explicitly refined the *Chevron* doctrine to incorporate factors like these, commentators have wondered whether they may sometimes be at play *sub silentio* in cases in which the Court has reviewed agency interpretations without mentioning *Chevron*. Thus, one Step Two question is whether *Chevron* deference is, or should be, more appropriate for those agencies with greater expertise or more political accountability.

A related Step Two question is whether, for the reviewing court to sustain the agency's interpretation as reasonable, the agency needs to have conducted an adequate process when deciding how to construe the statute. For instance, in *Gonzales v. Oregon*, 546 U.S. 243 (2006), the Court rejected one of the agency's several proffered interpretive justifications because it did not follow statutorily prescribed procedures. Here, judicial review of agency statutory interpretation also could implicate review under the Administrative Procedure Act, thus raising the question of whether there is any difference between a court reviewing the "reasonableness" of an agency *interpretation* at *Chevron* Step Two and a court reviewing the arbitrariness of an agency *action* under section 706 of the APA. *See, e.g,* Ronald M. Levin, *The Anatomy of* Chevron: *Step Two Reconsidered*, 72 Chi.-Kent L. Rev. 1253 (1997) (arguing that the two standards should be identical and describing caselaw supporting that view). In a 2016 decision, the Supreme Court announced that it would not extend *Chevron* deference to an agency rule that resulted from a "defective" procedure, including failing to give adequate reasons for a rule under the *State Farm* decision. *See Encino Motorcars, LLC v. Navarro*, 579 U.S. 211 (2016).

Many commentators have wrestled more generally with questions of how to reconcile or integrate "arbitrary and capricious" review with *Chevron* Step Two deference. Arguably, arbitrary and capricious review is more about process—especially **the facts** that this process is expected to bring to the agency's attention to support its decision—while *Chevron* Step Two is more about the reasonableness of the resulting interpretation of **the law**. Some observers have noted, somewhat critically, that with respect to arbitrary and capricious review, the *State Farm* decision seems to say that courts need not be reflexively deferential to an agency's policy decisions, but instead should give them a "hard look." In contrast, with respect to an agency's interpretation of the legal meaning of ambiguous statutory language, *Chevron* tells courts to defer to any reasonable construction that the agency chooses. Arguably, these standards reverse what might be a more natural set of deference principles, in which agency expertise and accountability would justify deferring to almost any reasonable policy choices, while it would remain the judiciary's role to establish the legal meaning of a statutory provision. The primary explanation for this counterintuitive approach, once again, is the presumption that Congress intended to delegate interpretive authority to the agency.

The high degree of deference that a *Chevron* analysis affords agencies means that courts have only rarely invalidated an agency interpretation as unreasonable at Step Two. One study of federal circuit court cases found that agencies prevail more than 90% of the time at Step Two; in the U.S. Supreme Court agency losses at Step Two have been even more unusual. But consider the following significant case.

Michigan v. Environmental Protection Agency
576 U.S. 743 (2015)

JUSTICE SCALIA delivered the opinion of the Court.

* * * The Clean Air Act Amendments of 1990 subjected power plants to various regulatory requirements [expected to reduce] power plants' emissions of hazardous air pollutants, although the extent of the reduction was unclear. Congress directed [the EPA] to "perform a study of the hazards to public health reasonably anticipated to occur as a result of emissions by [power plants] of [hazardous air pollutants]. . . ." § 7412(n)(1)(A). If the Agency "finds . . . regulation is appropriate and necessary [after considering the study]," it "shall regulate [power plants] under [§ 7412]." * * *

For each category [of pollutants], the Agency must promulgate certain minimum emission regulations, known as floor standards. * * * In some circumstances, the Agency may also impose more stringent emission regulations, known as beyond-the-floor standards. The statute expressly requires the Agency to consider cost (alongside other specified factors) when imposing beyond-the-floor standards. § 7412(d)(2).

EPA completed the study required by § 7412(n)(1)(A) in 1998 and concluded that regulation of coal- and oil-fired power plants was "appropriate and necessary" in 2000. In 2012, it reaffirmed the appropriate-and-necessary finding, divided power plants into subcategories, and promulgated floor standards. The Agency found regulation "appropriate" because (1) power plants' emissions of mercury and other hazardous air pollutants posed risks to human health and the environment and (2) controls were available to reduce these emissions. It found regulation "necessary" because the imposition of the Act's other requirements did not eliminate these risks. EPA concluded that "costs should not be considered" when deciding whether power plants should be regulated. * * *

Petitioners (who include 23 States) sought review of EPA's rule in the Court of Appeals for the D.C. Circuit. As relevant here, they challenged the Agency's refusal to consider cost when deciding whether to regulate power plants. The Court of Appeals upheld the Agency's decision. * * *

II

* * * EPA's decision to regulate power plants under § 7412 allowed the Agency to reduce power plants' emissions of hazardous air pollutants and thus to improve public health and the environment. But the decision also ultimately cost power plants, according to the Agency's own estimate, nearly $10 billion a year. EPA refused to consider whether the costs of its decision outweighed the benefits. The Agency gave cost no thought *at all*, because it considered cost irrelevant to its initial decision to regulate.

EPA's disregard of cost rested on its interpretation of § 7412(n)(1)(A), which, to repeat, directs the Agency to regulate power plants if it "finds such regulation is appropriate and necessary." The Agency accepts that it *could* have interpreted this provision to mean that cost is relevant to the decision to add power plants to the program. But it chose to read the statute to mean that cost makes no difference to the initial decision to regulate.

We review this interpretation under the standard set out in *Chevron U.S.A. Inc. v. Natural Resources Defense Council, Inc.*, 467 U.S. 837 (1984). *Chevron* directs courts to accept an agency's reasonable resolution of an ambiguity in a statute that the agency administers. *Id.*, at 842–843. Even under this deferential standard, however, "agencies must operate within the bounds of reasonable interpretation." EPA strayed far beyond those bounds when it read § 7412(n)(1) to mean that it could ignore cost when deciding whether to regulate power plants.

> Is it a fair characterization of the agency's position to say the agency thought it could ignore costs when deciding whether to regulate? Compare the dissenting opinion's discussion of the same question.

A

* * * Congress instructed EPA to add power plants to the [hazardous air pollutants] program if (but only if) the Agency finds regulation "appropriate and necessary." § 7412(n)(1)(A). One does not need to open up a dictionary in order to realize the capaciousness of this phrase. In particular, "appropriate" is "the classic broad and all-encompassing term that naturally and traditionally includes consideration of all the relevant factors." 748 F. 3d, at 1266 (opinion of KAVANAUGH, J.). Although this term leaves agencies with flexibility, an agency may not "entirely fai[l] to consider an important aspect of the problem" when deciding whether regulation is appropriate. *State Farm.*

Read naturally in the present context, the phrase "appropriate and necessary" requires at least some attention to cost. One would not say that it is even rational, never mind "appropriate," to impose billions of dollars in economic costs in return for a few dollars in health or environmental benefits. In addition, "cost" includes more than the expense of complying with regulations; any disadvantage could be termed a cost. EPA's interpretation precludes the Agency from considering *any* type of cost—including, for instance, harms that regulation might do to human health or the environment. * * *

There are undoubtedly settings in which the phrase "appropriate and necessary" does not encompass cost. But this is not one of them. Section 7412(n)(1)(A) directs EPA to determine whether "*regulation* is appropriate and necessary." (Emphasis added.) Agencies have long treated cost as a centrally relevant factor when deciding whether to regulate. Consideration of cost reflects the understanding that reasonable regulation ordinarily requires paying attention to the advantages *and* the disadvantages of agency decisions. It also reflects the reality that "too much wasteful expenditure devoted to one problem may well mean considerably fewer resources available to deal effectively with other (perhaps more serious) problems." *Entergy Corp. v. Riverkeeper, Inc.*, 556 U.S. 208, 233 (2009) (BREYER, J., concurring in part and dissenting in part). Against the backdrop of this established administrative practice, it is unreasonable to read an instruction to an administrative agency to determine whether "regulation is appropriate and necessary" as an invitation to ignore cost.

Statutory context reinforces the relevance of cost. * * * In subparagraph (A), the part of the law that has occupied our attention so far, Congress required EPA to study the hazards to public health posed by power plants and to determine whether regulation is appropriate and necessary. But in subparagraphs (B) and (C), Congress called for two additional studies.

One of them, a study into mercury emissions from power plants and other sources, must consider "the health and environmental effects of such emissions, technologies which are available to control such emissions, *and the costs of such technologies.*" This directive to EPA to study cost is a further indication of the relevance of cost to the decision to regulate. * * * EPA has not explained why § 7412(n)(1)(B)'s reference to "environmental effects . . . and . . . costs" provides "direct evidence that Congress was concerned with environmental effects," but not "direct evidence" that it was concerned with cost. *Chevron* allows agencies to choose among competing reasonable interpretations of a statute; it does not license interpretive gerrymanders under which an agency keeps parts of statutory context it likes while throwing away parts it does not.

B

EPA identifies a handful of reasons to interpret § 7412(n)(1)(A) to mean that cost is irrelevant to the initial decision to regulate. We find those reasons unpersuasive.

EPA points out that other parts of the Clean Air Act expressly mention cost, while § 7412(n)(1)(A) does not. But this observation shows only that § 7412(n)(1)(A)'s broad reference to appropriateness encompasses *multiple* relevant factors (which include but are not limited to cost); other provisions' specific references to cost encompass just cost. It is unreasonable to infer that, by expressly making cost relevant to other decisions, the Act implicitly makes cost irrelevant to the appropriateness of regulating power plants. * * * Other parts of the Clean Air Act also expressly mention environmental effects, while § 7412(n)(1)(A) does not. Yet that did not stop EPA from deeming environmental effects relevant to the appropriateness of regulating power plants.

Along similar lines, EPA seeks support in this Court's decision in *Whitman v. American Trucking Assns., Inc.*, 531 U.S. 457 (2001). There, the Court addressed a provision of the Clean Air Act requiring EPA to set ambient air quality standards at levels "requisite to protect the public health" with an "adequate margin of safety." 42 U.S.C. § 7409(b). Read naturally, that discrete criterion does not encompass cost; it encompasses health and safety. The Court refused to read that provision as carrying with it an implicit authorization to consider cost, in part because authority to consider cost had "elsewhere, and so often, been expressly granted." 531 U.S., at 467. *American Trucking* thus establishes the modest principle that where the Clean Air Act expressly directs EPA to regulate on the basis of a factor that on its face does not include cost, the Act normally should not be read as implicitly allowing the Agency to consider cost anyway. That principle has no application here. "Appropriate and necessary" is a far more comprehensive criterion than "requisite to protect the public health"; read fairly and in context, as we have explained, the term plainly subsumes consideration of cost.

Turning to the mechanics of the hazardous-air-pollutants program, EPA argues that it need not consider cost when first deciding *whether* to regulate power plants because it can consider cost later when deciding *how much* to regulate them. The question before us, however, is the meaning of the "appropriate and necessary" standard that governs the initial decision to regulate. And as we have discussed, context establishes that this expansive standard encompasses cost. Cost may become relevant again at a later stage of the regulatory process, but that possibility does not establish its irrelevance at *this* stage. In addition, once the Agency decides to regulate power plants, it must promulgate certain minimum or floor standards no matter the cost (here, nearly $10 billion a year); the Agency may consider cost only when imposing regulations *beyond* these minimum standards. By EPA's logic, someone could decide whether it is "appropriate" to buy a Ferrari without thinking about cost, because he plans to think about cost later when deciding whether to upgrade the sound system. * * *

C

The dissent does not embrace EPA's far-reaching claim that Congress made costs altogether irrelevant to the decision to regulate power plants. Instead, it maintains that EPA need not "explicitly analyze costs" before deeming regulation appropriate, because other features of the regulatory program will on their own ensure the cost-effectiveness of regulation. *Post,* at 2 (opinion of Kagan, J.). This line of reasoning contradicts the foundational principle of administrative law that a court may uphold agency action only on the grounds that the agency invoked when it took the action. *SEC v. Chenery Corp.,* 318 U.S. 80, 87 (1943). When it deemed regulation of power plants appropriate, EPA said that cost was *irrelevant* to that determination—not that cost-benefit analysis would be deferred until later. Much *less* did it say (what the dissent now concludes) that the consideration of cost at subsequent stages will ensure that the costs are not disproportionate to the benefits. What it said is that cost is irrelevant to the decision to regulate.

That is enough to decide these cases. But for what it is worth, the dissent vastly overstates the influence of cost at later stages of the regulatory process. * * *

D

Our reasoning so far establishes that it was unreasonable for EPA to read § 7412(n)(1)(A) to mean that cost is irrelevant to the initial decision to regulate power plants. The Agency must consider cost—including, most importantly, cost of compliance—before deciding whether regulation is appropriate and necessary. We need not and do not hold that the law unambiguously required the Agency, when making this preliminary estimate, to conduct a formal cost-benefit analysis in which each advantage and disadvantage is assigned a monetary value. It will be up to the Agency to decide (as always, within the limits of reasonable interpretation) how to account for cost. * * *

JUSTICE KAGAN, **with whom** JUSTICE GINSBURG, JUSTICE BREYER, **and** JUSTICE SOTOMAYOR **join, dissenting.**

The Environmental Protection Agency placed emissions limits on coal and oil power plants following a lengthy regulatory process during which the Agency carefully considered costs. At the outset, EPA determined that regulating plants' emissions of hazardous air pollutants is "appropriate and necessary" given the harm they cause, and explained that it would take costs into account in developing suitable emissions standards. Next, EPA divided power plants into groups based on technological and other characteristics bearing significantly on their cost structures. It required plants in each group to match the emissions levels already achieved by the best-performing members of the same group—benchmarks necessarily reflecting those plants' own cost analyses. EPA then adopted a host of measures designed to make compliance with its proposed emissions limits less costly for plants that needed to catch up with their cleaner peers. And with only one narrow exception, EPA decided not to impose any more stringent standards (beyond what some plants had already achieved on their own) because it found that doing so would not be cost-effective. After all that, EPA conducted a formal cost-benefit study which found that the quantifiable benefits of its regulation would exceed the costs up to nine times over—by as much as $80 billion each year. Those benefits include as many as 11,000 fewer premature deaths annually, along with a far greater number of avoided illnesses.

Despite that exhaustive consideration of costs, the Court strikes down EPA's rule on the ground that the Agency "unreasonably . . . deemed cost irrelevant." On the majority's theory, the rule is invalid because EPA did not explicitly analyze costs at the very first stage of the regulatory process, when making its "appropriate and necessary" finding. And that is so even though EPA later took costs into account again and again. * * *

That is a peculiarly blinkered way for a court to assess the lawfulness of an agency's rulemaking. I agree with the majority—let there be no doubt about this—that EPA's power plant regulation would be unreasonable if "[t]he Agency gave cost no thought *at all*." But that is just not what happened here. Over more than a decade, EPA took costs into account at multiple stages and through multiple means as it set emissions limits for power plants. And when making its initial "appropriate and necessary" finding, EPA knew it would do exactly that—knew it would thoroughly consider the cost-effectiveness of emissions standards later on. That context matters. The Agency acted well within its authority in declining to consider costs at the opening bell of the regulatory process given that it would do so in every round thereafter—and given that the emissions limits finally issued would depend crucially on those accountings. Indeed, EPA could not have measured costs at the process's initial stage with any accuracy. And the regulatory path EPA chose parallels the one it has trod in setting emissions limits, at Congress's explicit direction, for every other source of hazardous air pollutants over two decades. The majority's decision that EPA cannot take the same approach here—its micromanagement of EPA's rulemaking, based on little more than the word "appropriate"—runs counter to Congress's allocation of authority between the Agency and the courts. Because EPA reasonably found that it was "appropriate" to decline to analyze costs at a single stage of a regulatory proceeding otherwise imbued with cost concerns, I respectfully dissent.

[I-B] * * * Said otherwise, the question is not whether EPA can reasonably find it "appropriate" to regulate without thinking about costs, full stop. It cannot, and it did not. Rather, the question is whether EPA can reasonably find it "appropriate" to trigger the regulatory process based on harms (and technological feasibility) alone, given that costs will come into play, in multiple ways and at multiple stages, before any emission limit goes into effect.

In considering that question, the very nature of the word "appropriate" matters. "[T]he word 'appropriate,' " this Court has recognized, "is inherently context-dependent": Giving it content requires paying attention to the surrounding circumstances. * * * [That means considering the place of the "appropriate and necessary" finding in the broader regulatory scheme—as a triggering mechanism that gets a complex rulemaking going. The interpretive task is thus at odds with the majority's insistence on staring fixedly "at *this* stage." The task instead demands taking account of the entire regulatory process in thinking about what is "appropriate" in its first phase. The statutory language, in other words, is a directive to remove one's blinders and view things whole—to consider what it is fitting to do at the threshold stage given what will happen at every other.

And that instruction is primarily given to EPA, not to courts: Judges may interfere only if the Agency's way of ordering its regulatory process is unreasonable—*i.e.*, something Congress would never have allowed. The question here, as in our seminal case directing courts to defer to agency interpretations of their own statutes, arises "not in a sterile textual vacuum, but in the context of implementing policy decisions in a technical and complex arena." *Chevron*. EPA's experience and expertise in that arena—and courts' lack of those attributes—demand that judicial review proceed with caution and care. The majority actually phrases this principle well, though honors it only in the breach: Within wide bounds, it is "up to the Agency to decide . . . how to account for cost." That judges might have made different regulatory choices—might have considered costs in different ways at different times—will not suffice to overturn EPA's action where Congress, as here, chose not to speak directly to those matters, but to leave them to the Agency to decide.

All of that means our decision here properly rests on something the majority thinks irrelevant: an understanding of the full regulatory process relating to power plants and of EPA's reasons for considering costs only after making its initial "appropriate and necessary" finding. I therefore turn to those issues, to demonstrate the simple point that . . . EPA, in regulating power plants' emissions of hazardous air pollutants, accounted for costs in a reasonable way. * * *

III

The central flaw of the majority opinion is that it ignores everything but one thing EPA did. It forgets that EPA's "appropriate and necessary" finding was only a first step which got the rest of the regulatory process rolling. It narrows its field of vision to that finding in isolation, with barely a glance at all the ways in which EPA later took costs into account. In sum, the majority disregards how consideration of costs infused the regulatory process. * * *

The same fault inheres in the majority's secondary argument that EPA engaged in an "interpretive gerrymander[ ]" by considering environmental effects but not costs in making its "appropriate and necessary" finding. The majority notes—quite rightly—that Congress called for EPA to examine both subjects in a study of mercury emissions from all sources (separate from the study relating to power plants' emissions alone). And the majority states—again, rightly—that Congress's demand for that study "provides direct evidence that Congress was concerned with [both] environmental effects [and] cost." But nothing follows from that fact, because EPA too was concerned with both. True enough, EPA assessed the two at different times: environmental harms (along with health harms) at the threshold, costs afterward. But that was for the very reasons earlier described: because EPA wanted to treat power plants like other sources and because it thought harms, but not costs, could be accurately measured at that early stage. Congress's simple request for a study of mercury emissions in no way conflicts with that choice of when and how to consider both harms and costs. Once more, the majority perceives a conflict only because it takes so partial a view of the regulatory process.

And the identical blind spot causes the majority's sports-car metaphor to run off the road. The majority likens EPA to a hypothetical driver who decides that "it is 'appropriate' to buy a Ferrari without thinking about cost, because he plans to think about cost later when deciding whether to upgrade the sound system." The comparison is witty but wholly inapt. To begin with, emissions limits are not a luxury good: They are a safety measure, designed to curtail the significant health and environmental harms caused by power plants spewing hazardous pollutants. And more: EPA knows from past experience and expertise alike that it will have the opportunity to purchase that good in a cost-effective way. A better analogy might be to a car owner who decides without first checking prices that it is "appropriate and necessary" to replace her worn-out brake-pads, aware from prior experience that she has ample time to comparison-shop and bring that purchase within her budget. Faced with a serious hazard and an available remedy, EPA moved forward like that sensible car owner, with a promise that it would, and well-grounded confidence that it could, take costs into account down the line.

That about does it for the majority's opinion, save for its final appeal to *Chenery*—and *Chenery* cannot save its holding. Of course a court may not uphold agency action on grounds different from those the agency gave. See *Chenery*, 318 U.S., at 87. But equally, a court may not strike down agency action without considering the reasons the agency gave. *Id.*, at 95. And that is what the majority does. Indeed, it is difficult to know what agency document the majority is reading. It denies that "EPA said . . . that cost-benefit analysis would be deferred until later." But EPA said exactly that: The "costs of controls," the Agency promised, "will be examined" as "a part of developing a regulation." 65 Fed. Reg. 79830. Tellingly, these words appear nowhere in the majority's opinion. But what are they other than a statement that cost concerns, contra the majority, are *not* "irrelevant"—that they are simply going to come in later? * * *

IV

Costs matter in regulation. But when Congress does not say how to take costs into account, agencies have broad discretion to make that judgment. Far more than courts, agencies have the expertise and experience necessary to design regulatory processes suited to "a technical and complex arena." *Chevron.* * * * Congress has entrusted such matters to them, not to us. * * *

NOTES & QUESTIONS

1. The majority framed the issue in *Michigan v. EPA* as whether the word "appropriate" in section 112(n)(1)(A) of the Clean Air Act requires the EPA to consider costs. Did this interpretive question look familiar? We hope so. In Chapter 33, you read an excerpt from the preamble of the very rule challenged in this case, an excerpt that set forth the EPA's interpretation of the word "appropriate," including its conclusion that "appropriate" did *not* require it to consider costs. Re-read the portion of the EPA's preamble that addressed the question of costs. Did it seem convincing? Or is the Court majority's interpretation better?

2. Can you see why *Michigan v. EPA* is a "Step Two" case? The Court says, "*Chevron* directs courts to accept an agency's reasonable resolution of an ambiguity in a statute that the agency administers." By assuming there is "ambiguity" in the statute, that statement is a formulation of the Step Two inquiry. It turns out though that it is not obvious that this needed to be a Step Two case. Remember again that, if it's a Step Two case, that means the Court had to have concluded, under Step One, that Congress did not speak directly to the relevant interpretive question, right? So, what exactly is the interpretive question that the Court thinks Congress did not resolve? Is it simply that the word "appropriate" is open-ended ("broad and all-encompassing") and has a range of possible meanings? On the other hand, if one frames the interpretive question as, "Does the word 'appropriate' require a consideration of costs?", then at least according to the majority, didn't Congress conclude that the word "appropriate" does require the EPA to consider costs? If the question is "Does the word 'appropriate' require a consideration of

costs?", wouldn't that make this a Step One case? This little wrinkle in *Chevron*'s two steps is why some scholars have concluded that "*Chevron, properly understood, has only one step.*" Matthew C. Stephenson & Adrian Vermeule, Chevron *Has Only One Step*, 95 VA. L. REV. 597, 597 (2009). The "one step" is simply, "Is the agency's interpretation within the 'zone' of permissible interpretations?" If it is, the court accepts the agency's interpretation; if not, it doesn't. You may recall that we raised this issue right at the beginning of the section discussing Step One.

3. The dissent also sees this as a Step Two case. What is the key difference between the majority and the dissent in their treatment of *Chevron*? Re-read the paragraph in the dissent that begins, "And that instruction is primarily given to EPA, not to courts: . . ." Did you notice that the dissent quotes *Chevron* in that paragraph? Why does the dissent view that quotation as important here?

4. At the end of Part II-A, Justice Scalia's majority opinion says that "*Chevron* allows agencies to choose among competing reasonable interpretations of a statute; it does not license interpretive gerrymanders under which an agency keeps parts of statutory context it likes while throwing away parts it does not." Having read the relevant portion of the agency's own interpretation of the statute in Chapter 33, do you think this is a fair criticism of the agency's action here? Why or why not?

5. As we noted in Chapter 33, the ultimate issue raised in this 2015 case, whether it is appropriate for the EPA to regulate hazardous air pollutants from power plants under section 112(n) of the Clean Air Act, remains up for revision as this book went to press in 2024. Following the Court's decision in *Michigan v. EPA*, the EPA returned to the drawing board on remand and, in 2016, after this time taking costs into account, again concluded that it was "appropriate" to regulate power plants. In 2020, the EPA reconsidered that finding and concluded that it was *not* "appropriate" for it to regulate hazardous air pollutants from power plants. Then in 2023, the EPA reconsidered again and concluded that it *was* "appropriate." Thinking about who was President on each of those dates, does this sort of yo-yo of policy simply reflect the need for agencies to be politi-

FYI Section 112(n) is only one part of the Clean Air Act. Under another section, the EPA has long regulated emissions (including from power plants) of what environmental law specialists refer to as six "criteria" pollutants: particulate matter, ground-level ozone, carbon monoxide, sulfur dioxide, nitrogen dioxide, and lead.

cally accountable? But it has now been more than three decades since Congress passed the 1990 Clean Air Act Amendments mandating that the EPA regulate power plants if, but only if, the EPA determined that such regulation was "appropriate and necessary," and we still don't have a conclusive answer.

6. Look at the full language of section 112(n)(1)(A). It only has four sentences, and the last sentence requires the EPA Administrator to regulate hazardous air pollutants from power plants "if the Administrator finds such regulation is appropriate and necessary after considering the results of the study required by this subparagraph." Why do you think Congress wrote it that way? Is Congress passing the buck on a question that it, the more directly democratically accountable branch of government, should make? Or is Congress delegating a technical question to an agency with more expertise and capacity? If you represented an environmental non-profit advocacy organization, would you view the question as one that should be decided by Congress or the EPA? What if you represented a coal-fired power plant?

Despite the Court's invalidation in *Michigan v. EPA* of the EPA's conclusion that its regulatory choice was "appropriate," *Chevron* Step Two has traditionally been highly deferential. Remember that one fundamental point of *Chevron* is to permit the agency to use its expertise and relative political accountability to resolve ambiguity within the space Congress implicitly gave it. This zone of ambiguity raises another Step Two question: how important or relevant should traditional tools of statutory interpretation be to the agency's interpretive process? This zone of ambiguity allows the agency to act without regard to what Congress itself would have done within that zone, or even would have intended the agency to do. In other words, most of the tools of determining congressional intent discussed above in Parts V and VI are theoretically meaningless if the presumption is that Congress simply had no intent, except to let the agency use its own institutional competencies to establish the statutory meaning. In fact, however, as you saw when you read EPA's preamble to its rule regulating hazardous air pollutants from power plants in Chapter 33, agencies routinely employ many of the same interpretive tools that courts do.

On this reading, the *Chevron* doctrine's deference effectively treats agency resolution of textual ambiguities at Step Two less as a matter of interpretation and more as a matter of policy choice. *See, e.g.,* Peter L. Strauss, *"Deference" is Too Confusing—Let's Call Them "Chevron Space" and "Skidmore Weight,"* 112 COLUM. L. REV. 1143 (2012). This way of thinking would be consistent with the approach we described earlier in this chapter, in which *Chevron* Step Two "deference" is simply another way for a court to do what the Supreme Court did in the *State Farm* case we read in Chapter 32: review the agency's action to ensure that it is not "arbitrary and capricious" under section 706(2)(A) of the APA. This perspective on an agency's exercise of implicitly delegated interpretive authority potentially avoids the critique variously leveled at both Textualists and Purposivists that their interpretive approaches mask the ability to engage in ends-oriented interpretation. It does so by acknowledging without embarrassment or shame that ends-oriented declaration of textual meaning is exactly what agencies can do within the space protected under *Chevron* (but once again, only within the gap or space left by the legislature).

Still, questions linger within the academy and the judiciary about whether Step Two deference to agency interpretation of statutes either allows the legislative branch to shirk its institutional role of passing clear laws or usurps the judicial branch's role to declare what the law is, on the one hand; or instead appropriately involves the executive branch in declaring what the law is, as a "counter-*Marbury* for the administrative state." Cass R. Sunstein, *Beyond Marbury: The Executive's Power to Say What the Law Is,* 115 YALE L.J. 2580, 2589 (2006). These questions also relate to how readily an agency should be able to construe a piece of statutory text dynamically over time, or to supersede a previous judicial construction of the same statute with the agency's own subsequent interpretation.

Test Your Understanding

To assess your understanding of the material in this chapter, click here to take a quiz.

37

Chevron Step Zero, the "Major Questions Doctrine," and the Future of Agency Deference

Key Concepts

- *Chevron* "Step Zero"
- "Force of law" power
- Congressional delegation to agencies (redux)
- The Major Questions Doctrine
- "Vast economic and political significance"
- Clear statement rules
- "Clear congressional authorization"
- The fading *Chevron* Doctrine
- *Loper Bright Enterprises v. Raimondo/Relentless v. Department of Commerce*

Chapter Summary

Forty years after *Chevron*, questions of the appropriate level of deference for courts to afford agency interpretations of statutes continue to bedevil the federal judiciary. A *Chevron* "Step Zero" inquiry of whether the *Chevron* deference regime even applies to a particular agency interpretive choice has turned out to be but one off-ramp from *Chevron* deference, as on occasion courts have entirely avoided using the *Chevron* framework based on some other interpretive philosophy or consideration. But a more important development has been the Supreme Court's addition of a "major questions" exception: In certain extraordinary cases, if the interpretive question that the agency's decision confronts is of "vast economic and political significance," the Court will not defer to the agency's resolution unless the agency can point to "clear congressional authorization" for the authority that the agency claims. Otherwise, the Court will conclude that the agency does not have the power to do what it seeks to do. Meanwhile, *Chevron* itself is teetering, as the

> Court has not upheld an agency regulation based on *Chevron* since 2016, and it has a pair of consolidated cases before it that ask whether to overrule *Chevron*.

A. Supreme Court Creation of a *Chevron* "Step Zero": *United States v. Mead*

For much of the first fifteen years after the *Chevron* decision, lower federal courts functioned as though *Chevron* was the principal framework for reviewing agency interpretations of statutes. The U.S. Supreme Court was not nearly so enamored with its own *Chevron* opinion, however, citing it far less often. Yet it did little to clarify when or whether *Chevron* was ordinarily the appropriate framework for review.

That situation changed with the Court's 2001 decision in *United States v. Mead*, 533 U.S. 218 (2001). *Mead* has given rise to the notion that the *Chevron* doctrine necessitates a "Step Zero," a threshold inquiry about whether *Chevron* is even the proper frame for reviewing a given agency interpretation of a statute. That is, it has turned out that the Supreme Court deploys a range of deference regimes other than the *Chevron* two-step approach, and therefore determining when the *Chevron* deference regime applies is a key threshold question. As we will see in Part B of this chapter, another example of a doctrine that can be thought of as a threshold inquiry is the "Major Questions Doctrine."

As you will read in the excerpt below, *Mead* established that a necessary condition for *Chevron* deference is that Congress have delegated to the agency the power to act with the "force of law" and that the agency have exercised that "force of law" power. But as you read, see if you can figure out just what "force of law" power is.

United States v. Mead

533 U.S. 218 (2001)

Justice Souter delivered the opinion of the Court.

The question is whether a tariff classification ruling by the United States Customs Service deserves judicial deference. * * * [A] tariff classification has no claim to judicial deference under *Chevron*, there being no indication that Congress intended such a ruling to carry the force of law, but we hold that under *Skidmore v. Swift & Co.*, 323 U.S. 134 (1944), the ruling is eligible to claim respect according to its persuasiveness.

I

A

Imports are taxed under the Harmonized Tariff Schedule of the United States (HTSUS), 19 U.S.C. § 1202. Title 19 U.S.C. § 1500(b) provides that Customs "shall, under rules and regulations prescribed by the Secretary [of the Treasury] . . . fix the final classification and rate of duty applicable to . . . merchandise" under the HTSUS. * * * The Secretary provides for tariff rulings before the entry of goods by regulations authorizing "ruling letters" setting tariff classifications for particular imports. 19 CFR § 177.8 (2000). * * *

Any of the 46 port-of-entry Customs offices may issue ruling letters, and so may the Customs Headquarters Office, in providing "[a]dvice or guidance as to the interpretation or proper application of the Customs and related laws with respect to a specific Customs transaction [which] may be requested by Customs Service field offices . . . at any time, whether the transaction is prospective, current, or completed," 19 CFR § 177.11(a) (2000). Most ruling letters contain little or no reasoning, but simply describe goods and state the appropriate category and tariff. A few letters, like the Headquarters ruling at issue here, set out a rationale in some detail.

B

Respondent, the Mead Corporation, imports "day planners," three-ring binders with pages having room for notes of daily schedules and phone numbers and addresses, together with a calendar and suchlike. The tariff schedule on point falls under the HTSUS heading for "[r]egisters, account books, notebooks, order books, receipt books, letter pads, memorandum pads, diaries and similar articles," HTSUS subheading 4820.10, which comprises two subcategories. Items in the first, "[d]iaries, notebooks and address books, bound; memorandum pads, letter pads and similar articles," were subject to a tariff of 4.0% at the time in controversy. Objects in the second, covering "[o]ther" items, were free of duty.

> What exactly is the interpretive question that Customs answered, and how did it answer it? Put another way, what legal conclusion is the agency asking the court to defer to? See if you can state the legal conclusion in a sentence.

Between 1989 and 1993, Customs repeatedly treated day planners under the "other" HTSUS subheading. In January 1993, however, Customs changed its position, and issued a Headquarters ruling letter classifying Mead's day planners as "Diaries . . . , bound" subject to tariff under [the first subcategory.] Customs rejected Mead's [protest of the] ruling letter, and Mead filed suit in the Court of International Trade (CIT). The CIT granted the Government's motion for summary judgment, adopting Customs's reasoning without saying anything about deference.

Mead then went to the United States Court of Appeals for the Federal Circuit. While the case was pending there this Court decided *United States v. Haggar Apparel Co.*, 526 U.S. 380 (1999), holding that Customs regulations receive the deference described in *Chevron U.S.A. Inc. v. Natural Resources Defense Council, Inc.*, 467 U.S. 837 (1984). The appeals court requested briefing on the impact of *Haggar*, and the Government argued that classification rulings, like Customs regulations, deserve *Chevron* deference.

The Federal Circuit, however, reversed the CIT and held that Customs classification rulings should not get *Chevron* deference, owing to differences from the regulations at issue in *Haggar*. Rulings are not preceded by notice and comment as under the Administrative Procedure Act (APA), 5 U.S.C. § 553, they "do not carry the force of law and are not, like regulations, intended to clarify the rights and obligations of importers beyond the specific case under review."

* * * We hold that administrative implementation of a particular statutory provision qualifies for *Chevron* deference when it appears that Congress delegated authority to the agency generally to make rules carrying the force of law, and that the agency interpretation claiming deference was promulgated in the exercise of that authority. Delegation of such authority may be shown in a variety of ways, as by an agency's power to engage in adjudication or notice-and-comment rulemaking, or by some other indication of a comparable congressional intent. The Customs ruling at issue here fails to qualify, although the possibility that it deserves some deference under *Skidmore* leads us to vacate and remand.

II

A

When Congress has "explicitly left a gap for an agency to fill, there is an express delegation of authority to the agency to elucidate a specific provision of the statute by regulation," *Chevron*, 467 U.S., at 843–844, and any ensuing regulation is binding in the courts unless procedurally defective, arbitrary or capricious in substance, or manifestly contrary to the statute. See *id.*, at 844; APA, 5 U.S.C. § 706(2)(A), (D). But whether or not they enjoy any express delegation of authority on a particular question, agencies charged with applying a statute necessarily make all sorts of interpretive choices, and while not all of those choices bind judges to follow them, they certainly may influence courts facing questions the agencies have already answered. "[T]he well-reasoned views of the agencies implementing a statute 'constitute a body of experience and informed judgment to which courts and litigants may properly resort for guidance,' " *Bragdon v. Abbott,* 524 U.S. 624, 642 (1998) (quoting *Skidmore,* 323 U.S., at 139–140), and "[w]e have long recognized that considerable weight should be accorded to an executive department's construction of a statutory scheme it is entrusted to administer. . . ." *Chevron.* * * *

The fair measure of deference to an agency administering its own statute has been understood to vary with circumstances, and courts have looked to the degree of the agency's care, its consistency, formality, and relative expertness, and to the persuasiveness of the agency's position, see *Skidmore, supra,* at 139–140. The approach has produced a spectrum of judicial responses, from great respect at one end, to near indifference at the other. Justice Jackson summed things up in *Skidmore v. Swift & Co.*:

> The weight [accorded to an administrative] judgment in a particular case will depend upon the thoroughness evident in its consideration, the validity of its reasoning, its consistency with earlier and later pronouncements, and all those factors which give it power to persuade, if lacking power to control.

Since 1984, we have identified a category of interpretive choices distinguished by an additional reason for judicial deference. This Court in *Chevron* recognized that Congress not only engages in express delegation of specific interpretive authority, but that "[s]ometimes the legislative delegation to an agency on a particular question is implicit." 467 U.S., at 844. Congress, that is, may not have expressly delegated authority or responsibility to implement a particular provision or fill a particular gap. Yet it can still be apparent from the agency's generally conferred authority and other statutory circumstances that Congress would expect the agency to be able to speak with the force of law when it addresses ambiguity in the

> What tools are appropriate for determining when Congress has made an implicit delegation?

statute or fills a space in the enacted law, even one about which "Congress did not actually have an intent" as to a particular result. *Id.,* at 845. When circumstances implying such an expectation exist, a reviewing court has no business rejecting an agency's exercise of its generally conferred authority to resolve a particular statutory ambiguity simply because the agency's chosen resolution seems unwise, see *id.,* at 845–846, but is obliged to accept the agency's position if Congress has not previously spoken to the point at issue and the agency's interpretation is reasonable, see *id.,* at 842–845; cf. 5 U.S.C. § 706(2) (a reviewing court shall set aside agency action, findings, and conclusions found to be "arbitrary, capricious, an abuse of discretion, or otherwise not in accordance with law").

We have recognized a very good indicator of delegation meriting *Chevron* treatment in express congressional authorizations to engage in the process of rulemaking or adjudication that produces regulations or rulings for which deference is claimed. * * * It is fair to assume generally that Congress contemplates administrative action with the effect of law when it provides for a relatively formal administrative procedure tending to foster the fairness and deliberation that should underlie a pronouncement of such force. Thus, the overwhelming number of our cases applying *Chevron* deference have reviewed the fruits of notice-and-comment rulemaking or formal adjudication. That said, and as significant as notice-and-comment is in pointing to *Chevron* authority, the want of that procedure here does not decide the case, for we have sometimes found reasons for *Chevron* deference even when no such administrative formality was required and none was afforded. The fact that the tariff classification here was not a product of such formal process does not alone, therefore, bar the application of *Chevron*.

There are, nonetheless, ample reasons to deny *Chevron* deference here. The authorization for classification rulings, and Customs's practice in making them, present a case far removed not only from notice-and-comment process, but from any other circumstances reasonably suggesting that Congress ever thought of classification rulings as deserving the deference claimed for them here.

B

No matter which angle we choose for viewing the Customs ruling letter in this case, it fails to qualify under *Chevron*. On the face of the statute, to begin with, the terms of the congressional delegation give no indication that Congress meant to delegate authority to Customs to issue classification rulings with the force of law. We are not, of course, here making any global statement about Customs's authority, for it is true that the general rulemaking power conferred on Customs authorizes some regulation with the force of law, or "legal norms," as we put it in *Haggar*. It is true as well that Congress had classification rulings in mind when it explicitly authorized, in a parenthetical, the issuance of "regulations establishing procedures for the issuance of binding rulings prior to the entry of the merchandise concerned." 19 U.S.C. § 1502(a). The reference to binding classifications does not, however, bespeak the legislative type of activity that would naturally bind more than the parties to the ruling, once the goods classified are admitted into this country. And though the statute's direction to disseminate "information" necessary to "secure" uniformity seems to assume that a ruling may be precedent in later transactions, precedential value alone does not add up to *Chevron* entitlement; interpretive rules may sometimes function as precedents and they enjoy no *Chevron* status as a class. In any event, any precedential claim of a classification ruling is counterbalanced by the provision for independent review of Customs classifications by the CIT; the scheme for CIT review includes a provision that treats classification rulings on par with the Secretary's rulings on "valuation, rate of duty, marking, restricted merchandise, entry requirements, drawbacks, vessel repairs, or similar matters." It is hard to imagine a congressional understanding more at odds with the *Chevron* regime.

It is difficult, in fact, to see in the agency practice itself any indication that Customs ever set out with a lawmaking pretense in mind when it undertook to make classifications like these. Customs does not generally engage in notice-and-comment practice when issuing them, and their treatment by the agency makes it clear that a letter's binding character as a ruling stops short of third parties; Customs has regarded a classification as conclusive only as between itself and the importer to whom it was issued, and even then only until Customs has given advance notice of intended change. Other importers are in fact warned against assuming any right of detrimental reliance.

Indeed, to claim that classifications have legal force is to ignore the reality that 46 different Customs offices issue 10,000 to 15,000 of them each year. Any suggestion that rulings intended to have the force of law are being churned out at a rate of 10,000 a year at an agency's 46 scattered offices is simply self-refuting. Although the circumstances are less startling here, with a Headquarters letter in issue, none of the relevant statutes recognizes this category of rulings as separate or different from others; there is thus no indication that a more potent delegation might have been understood as going to Headquarters even when Headquarters provides developed reasoning, as it did in this instance.

* * * In sum, classification rulings are best treated like "interpretations contained in policy statements, agency manuals, and enforcement guidelines." They are beyond the *Chevron* pale.

C

To agree with the Court of Appeals that Customs ruling letters do not fall within *Chevron* is not, however, to place them outside the pale of any deference whatever. *Chevron* did nothing to eliminate *Skidmore*'s holding that an agency's interpretation may merit some deference whatever its form, given the "specialized experience and broader investigations and information" available to the agency, and given the value of uniformity in its administrative and judicial understandings of what a national law requires.

There is room at least to raise a *Skidmore* claim here, where the regulatory scheme is highly detailed, and Customs can bring the benefit of specialized experience to bear on the subtle questions in this case: whether the daily planner with room for brief daily entries falls under "diaries," when diaries are grouped with "notebooks and address books, bound; memorandum pads, letter pads and similar articles." * * * A classification ruling in this situation may therefore at least seek a respect proportional to its "power to persuade," *Skidmore, supra,* at 140. Such a ruling may surely claim the merit of its writer's thoroughness, logic and expertness, its fit with prior interpretations, and any other sources of weight.

D

> Notice here that the Court is referring to the agency's "implementation" of the statute, rather than its "interpretation" of the statute. Of course, the tariff ruling being challenged in this case is an interpretation, since it resolves a question about the application of law to fact. But, the Court here is recognizing that the Customs Service interprets the statute as part of its "implement[ation]" of (indeed, enforcement of) the statute.

Underlying the position we take here, like the position expressed by Justice Scalia in dissent, is a choice about the best way to deal with an inescapable feature of the body of congressional legislation authorizing administrative action. That feature is the great variety of ways in which the laws invest the Government's administrative arms with discretion, and with procedures for exercising it, in giving meaning to Acts of Congress. Implementation of a statute may occur in formal adjudication or the choice to defend against judicial challenge; it may occur in a central board or office or in dozens of enforcement agencies dotted across the country; its institutional lawmaking may be confined to the resolution of minute detail or extend to legislative rulemaking on matters intentionally left by Congress to be worked out at the agency level.

Although we all accept the position that the Judiciary should defer to at least some of this multifarious administrative action, we have to decide how to take account of the great range of its variety. If the primary objective is to simplify the judicial process of giving or withholding deference, then the diversity of statutes authorizing discretionary administrative action must be declared irrelevant or minimized. If, on the other hand, it is simply implausible that Congress intended such a broad range of statutory authority to produce only two varieties of administrative action, demanding either *Chevron* deference or none at all, then the breadth of the spectrum of possible agency action must be taken into account. Justice Scalia's first priority over the years has been to limit and simplify. The Court's choice has been to tailor deference to variety. This acceptance of the range of statutory variation has led the Court to recognize more than one variety of judicial deference, just as the Court has recognized a variety of indicators that Congress would expect *Chevron* deference.

* * * Since the *Skidmore* assessment called for here ought to be made in the first instance by the Court of Appeals for the Federal Circuit or the Court of International Trade, we go no further than to vacate the judgment and remand the case for further proceedings consistent with this opinion.

JUSTICE SCALIA, dissenting:

Today's opinion makes an avulsive change in judicial review of federal administrative action. Whereas previously a reasonable agency application of an ambiguous statutory provision had to be sustained so long as it represented the agency's authoritative interpretation, henceforth such an application can be set aside unless "it appears that Congress delegated authority to the agency generally to make rules carrying the force of law," as by giving an agency "power to engage in adjudication or notice-and-comment rulemaking, or . . . some other [procedure] indicati[ng] comparable congressional intent," and "the agency interpretation claiming deference was promulgated in the exercise of that authority." What was previously a general presumption of authority in agencies to resolve ambiguity in the statutes they have been authorized to enforce has been changed to a presumption of no such authority, which must be overcome by affirmative legislative intent to the contrary. And whereas previously, when agency authority to resolve ambiguity did not exist the court was free to give the statute what it considered the best interpretation, henceforth the court must supposedly give the agency view some indeterminate amount of so-called *Skidmore* deference. We will be sorting out the consequences of the *Mead* doctrine, which has today replaced the *Chevron* doctrine, for years to come. I would adhere to our established jurisprudence, defer to the reasonable interpretation the Customs Service has given to the statute it is charged with enforcing, and [reverse the Court of Appeals].

I

* * * While the Court disclaims any hard-and-fast rule for determining the existence of discretion-conferring intent, it asserts that "a very good indicator [is] express congressional authorizations to engage in the process of rulemaking or adjudication that produces regulations or rulings for which deference is claimed." * * * [This] doctrine is neither sound in principle nor sustainable in practice.

A

As to principle: The doctrine of *Chevron*—that all *authoritative* agency interpretations of statutes they are charged with administering deserve deference—was rooted in a legal presumption of congressional intent, important to the division of powers between the Second and Third Branches. When, *Chevron* said, Congress leaves an ambiguity in a statute that is to be administered by an executive agency, it is presumed that Congress meant to give the agency discretion, within the limits of reasonable interpretation, as to how the ambiguity is to be resolved. By committing enforcement of the statute to an agency rather than the courts, Congress committed its initial and primary interpretation to that branch as well.

> **!** This is the dissent's characterization of *Chevron*. Is it not accurate? Isn't that what *Chevron* said? How does the majority disagree with this characterization of *Chevron*?

There is some question whether *Chevron* was faithful to the text of the Administrative Procedure Act (APA), which it did not even bother to cite. But it was in accord with the origins of federal-court judicial review. Judicial control of federal executive officers was principally exercised through the prerogative writ of mandamus. See L. JAFFE, JUDICIAL CONTROL OF ADMINISTRATIVE ACTION 166, 176–177 (1965). That writ generally would not issue unless the executive officer was acting plainly beyond the scope of his authority. . . . Statutory ambiguities, in other words, were left to reasonable resolution by the Executive.

The basis in principle for today's new doctrine can be described as follows: The background rule is that ambiguity in legislative instructions to agencies is to be resolved not by the agencies but by the judges. Specific congressional intent to depart from this rule must be found—and while there is no single touchstone for such intent it can generally be found when Congress has authorized the agency to act through (what the Court says is) relatively formal procedures such as informal rulemaking and formal (and informal?) adjudication, and when the agency in fact employs such procedures. The Court's background rule is contradicted by the origins of judicial review of administrative action. But in addition, the Court's principal criterion of congressional intent to supplant its background rule seems to me quite implausible. There is no necessary connection between the formality of procedure and the power of the entity administering the procedure to resolve authoritatively questions of law. The most formal of the procedures the Court refers to—formal adjudication—is modeled after the process used in trial courts, which of course are not generally accorded deference on questions of law. The purpose of such a procedure is to produce a closed record for determination and review of the facts—which implies nothing about the power of the agency subjected to the procedure to resolve authoritatively questions of law. * * *

B

As for the practical effects of the new rule:

(1) The principal effect will be protracted confusion. As noted above, the one test for *Chevron* deference that the Court enunciates is wonderfully imprecise: whether "Congress delegated authority to the agency generally to make rules carrying the force of law, . . . as by . . . adjudication[,] notice-and-comment rulemaking, or . . . some other [procedure] indicati[ng] comparable

> Does the Court have a response to this? What difference does it make that the agency exercised its "delegated authority. . .generally to make rules carrying the force of law"?

congressional intent." * * * It is hard to know what the lower courts are to make of today's guidance.

 The GPO is the Government Printing Office.

(2) Another practical effect of today's opinion will be an artificially induced increase in informal rulemaking. Buy stock in the GPO. Since informal rulemaking and formal adjudication are the only more-or-less safe harbors from the storm that the Court has unleashed; and since formal adjudication is not an option but must be mandated by statute or constitutional command; informal rulemaking—which the Court was once careful to make voluntary unless required by statute, *see Bell Aerospace, supra,* and *Chenery, supra*—will now become a virtual necessity. As I have described, the Court's safe harbor requires not merely that the agency have been given rulemaking authority, but also that the agency have *employed* rulemaking as the means of resolving the statutory ambiguity. (It is hard to understand why that should be so. Surely the mere *conferral* of rulemaking authority demonstrates—if one accepts the Court's logic—a congressional intent to allow the agency to resolve ambiguities. And given that intent, what difference does it make that the agency chooses instead to use another perfectly permissible means for that purpose?) * * *

(3) Worst of all, the majority's approach will lead to the ossification of large portions of our statutory law. Where *Chevron* applies, statutory ambiguities remain ambiguities subject to the agency's ongoing clarification. They create a space, so to speak, for the exercise of continuing agency discretion. As *Chevron* itself held, the Environmental Protection Agency can interpret "stationary source" to mean a single smokestack, can later replace that interpretation with the "bubble concept" embracing an entire plant, and if that proves undesirable can return again to the original interpretation. 467 U.S., at 853–859, 865–866. For the indeterminately large number of statutes taken out of *Chevron* by today's decision, however, ambiguity (and hence flexibility) will cease with the first judicial resolution. *Skidmore* deference gives the agency's current position some vague and uncertain amount of respect, but it does not, like *Chevron, leave* the matter within the control of the Executive Branch for the future. Once the court has spoken, it becomes *unlawful* for the agency to take a contradictory position; the statute now *says* what the court has prescribed. It will be bad enough when this ossification occurs as a result of judicial determination (under today's new principles) that there is no affirmative indication of congressional

intent to "delegate"; but it will be positively bizarre when it occurs simply because of an agency's failure to act by rulemaking * * * before the issue is presented to the courts. * * *

(4) And finally, the majority's approach compounds the confusion it creates by breathing new life into the anachronism of *Skidmore*, which sets forth a sliding scale of deference owed an agency's interpretation of a statute that is dependent "upon the thoroughness evident in [the agency's] consideration, the validity of its reasoning, its consistency with earlier and later pronouncements, and all those factors which give it power to persuade, if lacking power to control"; in this way, the appropriate measure of deference will be accorded the "body of experience and informed judgment" that such interpretations often embody. Justice Jackson's eloquence notwithstanding, the rule of *Skidmore* deference is an empty truism and a trifling statement of the obvious: A judge should take into account the well-considered views of expert observers.

It was possible to live with the indeterminacy of *Skidmore* deference in earlier times. But in an era when federal statutory law administered by federal agencies is pervasive, and when the ambiguities (intended or unintended) that those statutes contain are innumerable, totality-of-the-circumstances *Skidmore* deference is a recipe for uncertainty, unpredictability, and endless litigation. To condemn a vast body of agency action to that regime (all except rulemaking, formal (and informal?) adjudication, and whatever else might now and then be included within today's intentionally vague formulation of affirmative congressional intent to "delegate") is irresponsible. * * *

[In parts II, III, and IV of his dissent, Justice Scalia responded to the majority's claim that it was merely clarifying existing doctrine rather than changing it, argued that *Chevron* was the appropriate doctrinal approach here, and explained why under *Chevron* these Customs' tariffs were entitled to deference.]

NOTES & QUESTIONS

1. What does *Mead* say about the circumstances in which the *Chevron* deference framework applies? Re-read the last paragraph in Section I.B, the one that begins "We hold. . . ." Notice that the first sentence of that paragraph describes two requirements, one about Congress and the other about the agency. What are those two requirements? Hint: agency *procedures* are relevant. Why might an agency's procedures be relevant in determining whether a court should give it *Chevron* deference? On the other hand, what does the dissent say about the relevance of procedures to the question of whether an agency's legal interpretation should be entitled to deference? One thing is clear: if an agency engages in notice-and-comment rulemaking pursuant to Congressional authorization to do so, then the agency is acting with the "force of law" within the meaning of *Mead*. Much else, though, is unclear.

2. Under the facts of *Mead*, what were the factors that led the Court to conclude that *Chevron* deference was not warranted? Look at Section II.B and see if you can identify three features of the tariff rulings that the Court says indicate that Congress did **not** intend tariff rulings to have the "force of law." Does that help you think about what "force of law" might mean? Near the beginning of Section II.B, the Court distinguishes the tariff ruling in *Mead* from the Customs regulations that the Court had previously held in *United States v. Haggar Apparel* **were** entitled to *Chevron* deference. In doing so, the Court says, "The reference to binding classifications does not . . . bespeak the legislative type of activity that would naturally bind more than the parties to the ruling, once the goods classified are admitted into this country." What does the Court mean there? Why is the Court referring to "legislative type of activity"? Is "legislative type of activity" what the Court means when it uses the phrase "the force of law"? If so, is the Court referring to the distinction between rulemaking (quasi-legislative) and adjudication (quasi-judicial), what we referred to in Chapter 28 as the *Londoner-Bimetallic* distinction? If not, are there aspects of the *Londoner-Bimetallic* distinction that speak to what constitutes Congressional authorization to an agency to act with the "force of law"?

3. What does *Mead* say about the relationship between *Skidmore* deference and *Chevron* deference?

4. If you were helping to craft the *Mead* decision, how might you further specify criteria for determining when Congress has given an agency the power to act with the "force of law" and when an agency has acted with the "force of law"?

5. By establishing a "*Chevron* Step Zero," *Mead* made clear that *Chevron* was not the only deference regime for courts to use when dealing with an agency interpretation of statutory language: *Skidmore* deference would sometimes be the approach that courts should take. The year after *Mead*, though, the Court seemed to muddy the *Mead* test even further. In *Barnhart v. Walton*, the Court cited *Mead*, but rather than apply what seemed to be the *Mead* test (see Note 1 above), the Court relied on a set of factors similar to the *Skidmore* factors to determine whether *Chevron* deference was appropriate. See *Barnhart v. Walton*, 535 U.S. 212, 222 (2002) ("In this case, the interstitial nature of the legal question, the related expertise of the Agency, the importance of the question to administration of the statute, the complexity of that administration, and the careful consideration the Agency has given the question over a long period of time all indicate that *Chevron* provides the appropriate legal lens through which to view the legality of the Agency interpretation here at issue.").

> Compare this with the language in *Skidmore*: "The weight [given to an agency's] judgment in a particular case will depend upon the thoroughness evident in its consideration, the validity of its reasoning, its consistency with earlier and later pronouncements, and all those factors which give it power to persuade, if lacking power to control."

B. The Rise of the "Major Questions Doctrine"

The Supreme Court has recently developed another threshold question that courts are to ask prior to *Chevron*'s two-step framework. That threshold question is known as the "Major Questions Doctrine." The core of the Major Questions Doctrine is as follows: If the action the agency is taking raises a "major question" and if Congress has not explicitly and specifically given the agency authority to do what the agency has done, the agency does *not* have the authority to do it. In contrast to the *Mead* doctrine, which affects whether the reviewing court uses *Chevron* deference or *Skidmore* deference, the Major Questions Doctrine results in courts giving no deference at all to an agency's interpretation. The Major Questions Doctrine is different from *Mead* in another way too. Recall that under *Mead*, one question the court asks whether the statute has given the agency authority to act with the "force of law"—in other words, the court is asking whether Congress gave the agency *enough* power to warrant *Chevron* deference. If not, as in *Mead*, the court applies *Skidmore* rather than *Chevron* deference. In contrast, the Major Questions Doctrine involves what is in some ways a countervailing consideration: has the agency acted in such a way that it seems to be exercising *too much* power? As we will see, the Supreme Court has not made clear exactly how to determine what constitutes a "major" question, but the doctrine depends on an intuition that sits in significant tension with one of the rationales of *Chevron*. Recall that one of the rationales underlying *Chevron* is the idea of *implicit* Congressional delegation: where statutory language does not speak directly to an issue, the court will presume that Congress intended the *agency*—not the court—to have authority to interpret. *Chevron* gave three reasons why Congress may not have spoken directly to an issue: "Perhaps [Congress] consciously desired the [agency] to strike the balance at this level, thinking that those with great expertise and charged with responsibility for administering the provision would be in a better position to do so; perhaps it simply did not consider the question at this level; and perhaps Congress was unable to forge a coalition on either side of the question, and those on each side decided to take their chances with the scheme devised by the agency." The *Chevron* Court then made clear that "[f]or judicial purposes, it matters not which of these things occurred." In other words, under *Chevron*, if Congress has not spoken directly to an issue, that statutory ambiguity is to be treated as an implicit delegation to the agency to interpret—and hence, a delegation to the agency to implement the statute based on its interpretation.

In contrast, the Major Questions Doctrine makes a very different presumption. If the agency's interpretation and the real-world effects of that interpretation implicate a major question (one of "vast economic and political significance"), the court will presume that Congress did not delegate authority to the agency to act as it has—and hence to interpret the statute in the way that it did. In other words, when a "major question" is raised, statutory ambiguity is to be treated as an implicit *lack* of delegation to the agency. You can thus think of the Major Questions Doctrine, like *Mead*'s Step Zero, as a threshold question to *Chevron*, but a very different kind of threshold question. Rather than, as in *Mead*, asking about agency procedures, a court must make an assessment about the substance addressed in the agency's action, namely whether the issue the agency is addressing is "major."

Even though the Major Questions Doctrine amounts to a threshold question that can completely preclude a court from applying *Chevron* at all, the recent development of the doctrine can be found in cases that apply *Chevron*, including several cases you have already read, such as Step One cases *MCI v. AT&T* and *Brown & Williamson*, as well as *King v. Burwell*, a case that rejects applying *Chevron* altogether.

Reconsider *MCI v. AT&T*. Applying *Chevron* Step One, the Court interpreted "modify" in the 1934 Federal Communications Act and held that the FCC did not have the authority to waive the rate-filing requirement for nondominant long-distance carriers. The Court determined that the FCC had worked "a fundamental revision of the statute, changing it from a scheme of rate regulation in long-distance common-carrier communications to a scheme of rate regulation only where effective competition does not exist." 512 U.S. 218, 231–32 (1994). While noting that "[t]hat may be a good idea," the Court concluded that "the Commission's desire to increase competition cannot provide it authority to alter the well-established statutory filed rate requirements." *Id.* at 232, 234. Instead, "such considerations address themselves to Congress. . . ." *Id.* at 234. In other words, because the FCC's interpretation implicated such a major question—how to reconcile a statute written for a world with a long-distance telephone monopoly to one with competition in the long-distance market—the Court concluded that Congress did not give the FCC authority to interpret as it did.

Similarly, in *Brown & Williamson*, the Court majority found at Step One of a *Chevron* analysis that, in light of a broad contextualized reading of the Food, Drug and Cosmetic Act (one that involved looking to many other statutes), "Congress has directly spoken to the issue here and precluded the FDA's jurisdiction to regulate tobacco products." 529 U.S. 120, 133 (2000). Yet the text of the statute on which the FDA was relying—the FDCA—was itself by no means clear on this point, and instead the majority concluded that the FDA's jurisdiction did not extend to tobacco in part because "Congress could not have intended to delegate a decision of such economic and political significance to an agency in so cryptic a fashion." *Id.* at 160.

Finally, in *King v. Burwell*, the Court did something a little different from what it did in *MCI v. AT&T* and in *Brown & Williamson*, something more directly akin to what we now refer to as the Major Questions Doctrine. Rather than analyze the interpretive question through the lens of *Chevron* Step One ("did Congress directly speak to the issue?"), the Court held that the two-step *Chevron* framework was inapplicable. The Court explained that the question of whether the Affordable Care Act's tax credits were available for insurance purchased on the federal exchanges was a centrally important question of "deep economic and political significance" that, "had Congress wished to assign" the question to an agency, "it surely would have done so expressly." 576 U.S. 473, 486 (2015).

We now turn to *West Virginia v. Environmental Protection Agency*, the 2022 case that explicitly announced the Major Questions Doctrine. The case involves another complex environmental regulation. As in *Michigan v. EPA* and *Chevron* itself, *West Virginia v. EPA* involves the authority of the EPA to regulate under the Clean Air Act. Indeed, as in *Michigan v. EPA*, the challenge here is to an EPA regulation of power plants. While *Michigan v. EPA* involved the regulation of what are known as "hazardous air pollutants" (such as mercury) from those power plants, *West Virginia v. EPA* involves the regulation of carbon dioxide, a greenhouse gas.

As you read the majority opinion, see if you can identify exactly what it is that makes the majority treat this as a "major questions" case. What exactly is the "major question"? Is it a question? Or is it an issue? Or is it just that the resulting regulation itself is "major"? Or is it that the agency's approach to regulating is "major"?

West Virginia v. Environmental Protection Agency
597 U.S. 697 (2022)

CHIEF JUSTICE ROBERTS delivered the opinion of the Court.

FYI This is an example of what is known as "cooperative federalism," a legal structure that involves overlapping functions of the national and state governments. Under this provision of the Clean Air Act, the federal EPA establishes the "standard of performance" but the states, through their own environmental administrative agencies, then promulgate their own regulations to implement the federal "standard of performance."

The Clean Air Act authorizes the Environmental Protection Agency to regulate power plants by setting a "standard of performance" for their emission of certain pollutants into the air. 84 Stat. 1683, 42 U.S.C. § 7411(a)(1). That standard may be different for new and existing plants, but in each case it must reflect the "best system of emission reduction" that the Agency has determined to be "adequately demonstrated" for the particular category. §§ 7411(a)(1), (b)(1), (d). For existing plants, the States then implement that requirement by issuing rules restricting emissions from sources within their borders.

Since passage of the Act 50 years ago, EPA has exercised this authority by setting performance standards based on measures that would reduce pollution by causing plants to operate more cleanly. In 2015, however, EPA issued a new rule [the Clean Power Plan] concluding that the "best system of emission reduction" for existing coal-fired power plants included a requirement that such facilities reduce their own production of electricity, or subsidize increased generation by natural gas, wind, or solar sources.

The question before us is whether this broader conception of EPA's authority is within the power granted to it by the Clean Air Act. * * *

I

A

The Clean Air Act establishes three main regulatory programs to control air pollution from stationary sources such as power plants. Clean Air Amendments of 1970, 84 Stat. 1676, 42 U.S.C. § 7401 *et seq.* One program is the New Source Performance Standards program of Section 111, at issue here. The other two are the National Ambient Air Quality Standards (NAAQS) program, set out in Sections 108 through 110 of the Act, 42 U.S.C. §§ 7408–7410, and the Hazardous Air Pollutants (HAP) program, set out in Section 112, § 7412. To understand the place and function of Section 111 in the statutory scheme, some background on the other two programs is in order. * * *

> **FYI**
>
> The NAAQS program was the Clean Air Act program at issue in *Chevron* itself. The "HAP" or "Hazardous Air Pollutants" program under Section 112 of the Clean Air Act is the basis for the regulation at issue in *Michigan v. EPA*.

* * * [Section 111] directs EPA to list "categories of stationary sources" that it determines "cause[ ], or contribute[ ] significantly to, air pollution which may reasonably be anticipated to endanger public health or welfare." § 7411(b)(1)(A). Under Section 111(b), the Agency must then promulgate for each category "Federal standards of performance for new sources," § 7411(b)(1)(B). A "standard of performance" is one that

> reflects the degree of emission limitation achievable through the application of the best system of emission reduction which (taking into account the cost of achieving such reduction and any nonair quality health and environmental impact and energy requirements) the [EPA] Administrator determines has been adequately demonstrated.

§ 7411(a)(1).

Thus, the statute directs EPA to (1) "determine[ ]," taking into account various factors, the "best system of emission reduction which . . . has been adequately demonstrated," (2) ascertain the "degree of emission limitation achievable through the application" of that system, and (3) impose an emissions limit on new stationary sources that "reflects" that amount. Generally speaking, a source may achieve that emissions cap any way it chooses; the key is that its pollution be no more than the amount "achievable through the application of the best system of emission reduction . . . adequately demonstrated," or the BSER. § 7411(a)(1); see § 7411(b)(5). EPA undertakes this analysis on a pollutant-by-pollutant basis, establishing different standards of performance with respect to different pollutants emitted from the same source category.

Although the thrust of Section 111 focuses on emissions limits for *new* and *modified* sources—as its title indicates—the statute also authorizes regulation of certain pollutants from *existing* sources. * * *

B

* * *

The BSER that the Agency selected for existing coal-fired power plants . . . was quite different from the BSER it had chosen for new sources. The BSER for existing plants included three types of measures, which the Agency called "building blocks." The first building block was "heat rate improvements" at coal-fired plants—essentially practices such plants could undertake to burn coal more efficiently. But such improvements, EPA stated, would "lead to only small emission reductions," because coal-fired power plants were already operating near optimum efficiency. On the Agency's view, "much larger emission reductions [were] needed from [coal-fired plants] to address climate change."

So, the Agency included two additional building blocks in its BSER, both of which involve what it called "generation shifting from higher-emitting to lower-emitting" producers of electricity. Building block two was a shift in electricity production from existing coal-fired power plants to natural-gas-fired plants. Because natural gas plants produce "typically less than half as much" carbon dioxide per unit of electricity created as coal-fired plants, the Agency explained, "this generation shift [would] reduce[ ] CO2 emissions." Building block three worked the same way, except that the shift was from both coal- and gas-fired plants to "new low- or zero-carbon generating capacity," mainly wind and solar. "Most of the CO2 controls" in the rule came from the application of building blocks two and three.

The Agency identified three ways in which a regulated plant operator could implement a shift in generation to cleaner sources. First, an operator could simply reduce the regulated plant's own production of electricity. Second, it could build a new natural gas plant, wind farm, or solar installation, or invest in someone else's existing facility and then increase generation there. Finally, operators could purchase emission allowances or credits as part of a cap-and-trade regime. Under such a scheme, sources that achieve a reduction in their emissions can sell a credit representing the value of that reduction to others, who are able to count it toward their own applicable emissions caps.

* * * The Agency settled on what it regarded as a "reasonable" amount of shift, which it based on modeling of how much more electricity both natural gas and renewable sources could supply without causing undue cost increases or reducing the overall power supply. Based on these changes, EPA projected that by 2030, it would be feasible to have coal provide 27% of national electricity generation, down from 38% in 2014.

From these significant projected reductions in generation, EPA developed a series of complex equations to "determine the emission performance rates" that States would be required to implement. The calculations resulted in numerical emissions ceilings so strict that no existing coal plant would have been able to achieve them without engaging in one of the three means of shifting generation described above.

> If at first you don't understand the description of what the EPA has done, don't worry. It's very complex. Just read it again (and, if necessary, again). What exactly is the EPA regulation doing here and how does the Court view it as different in kind from the "heat rate improvements" it calls the "first building block"?

* * *

III

A

In devising emissions limits for power plants, EPA first "determines" the "best system of emission reduction" that—taking into account cost, health, and other factors—it finds "has been adequately demonstrated." 42 U.S.C. § 7411(a)(1). The Agency then quantifies "the degree of emission limitation achievable" if that best system were applied to the covered source. *Ibid.*; see also 80 Fed. Reg. 64719. The BSER, therefore, "is the central determination that the EPA must make in formulating [its emission] guidelines" under Section 111. The issue here is whether restructuring the Nation's overall mix of electricity generation, to transition from 38% coal to 27% coal by 2030, can be the "best system of emission reduction" within the meaning of Section 111.

> ❓ Notice that the Court begins here with a fundamental principle of statutory interpretation, one that we first encountered back in Part V, in Chapter 20. As you read through the rest of the opinion, think about the relationship between this principle (statutes should be read "in context") and the Major Questions Doctrine. Is this doctrine just a way for courts to think about "context" in a much broader way, such that it includes the "economic and political" aspects of a statute? To be sure, in doctrinal terms, it is framed differently. The question you should think about, though, is whether the Major Questions Doctrine is just another way to say that courts should think broadly about the statute.

"It is a fundamental canon of statutory construction that the words of a statute must be read in their context and with a view to their place in the overall statutory scheme." *Davis v. Michigan Dept. of Treasury*, 489 U.S. 803, 809 (1989). Where the statute at issue is one that confers authority upon an administrative agency, that inquiry must be "shaped, at least in some measure, by the nature of the question presented"— whether Congress in fact meant to confer the power the agency has asserted. * * * In the ordinary case, that context has no great effect on the appropriate analysis. Nonetheless, our precedent teaches that there are "extraordinary cases" that call for a different approach—cases in which the "history and the breadth of the authority that [the agency] has asserted," and the "economic and political significance" of that assertion, provide a "reason to hesitate before concluding that Congress" meant to confer such authority.

* * * Extraordinary grants of regulatory authority are rarely accomplished through "modest words," "vague terms," or "subtle device[s]." *Whitman*, 531 U.S., at 468. Nor does Congress typically use oblique or elliptical language to empower an agency to make a "radical or fundamental change" to a statutory scheme. *MCI Telecommunications Corp. v. American Telephone & Telegraph Co.*, 512 U.S. 218, 229 (1994). * * * We presume that "Congress intends to make major policy decisions itself, not leave those decisions to

agencies." *United States Telecom Assn. v. FCC*, 855 F.3d 381, 419 (CADC 2017) (Kavanaugh, J., dissenting from denial of rehearing en banc).

Thus, in certain extraordinary cases, both separation of powers principles and a practical understanding of legislative intent make us "reluctant to read into ambiguous statutory text" the delegation claimed to be lurking there. *Utility Air*, 573 U.S., at 324. To convince us otherwise, something more than a merely plausible textual basis for the agency action is necessary. The agency instead must point to "clear congressional authorization" for the power it claims. *Ibid.*

The dissent criticizes us for "announc[ing] the arrival" of this major questions doctrine, and argues that each of the decisions just cited simply followed our "ordinary method" of "normal statutory interpretation[.]" But in * * * *Brown & Williamson*, the Court could not have been clearer: "In extraordinary cases . . . there may be reason to hesitate" before accepting a reading of a statute that would, under more "ordinary" circumstances, be upheld. 529 U.S. at 159. * * *

As for the major questions doctrine "label[ ]," it took hold because it refers to an identifiable body of law that has developed over a series of significant cases all addressing a particular and recurring problem: agencies asserting highly consequential power beyond what Congress could reasonably be understood to have granted. Scholars and jurists have recognized the common threads between those decisions. So have we. * * *

B

Under our precedents, this is a major questions case. In arguing that Section 111(d) empowers it to substantially restructure the American energy market, EPA "claim[ed] to discover in a long- extant statute an unheralded power" representing a "transformative expansion in [its] regulatory authority." *Utility Air*, 573 U.S., at 324. It located that newfound power in the vague language of an "ancillary provision[ ]" of the Act, *Whitman*, 531 U.S., at 468, one that was designed to function as a gap filler and had rarely been used in the preceding decades. And the Agency's discovery allowed it to adopt a regulatory program that Congress had conspicuously and repeatedly declined to enact itself. * * *

Prior to 2015, EPA had always set emissions limits under Section 111 based on the application of measures that would reduce pollution by causing the regulated source to operate more cleanly. It had never devised a cap by looking to a "system" that would reduce pollution simply by "shifting" polluting activity "from dirtier to cleaner sources." 80 Fed. Reg. 64726. * * *

This consistent understanding of "system[s] of emission reduction" tracked the seemingly universal view, as stated by EPA in its inaugural Section 111(d) rulemaking, that "Congress intended a technology-based approach" to regulation in that Section. 40 Fed. Reg. 53343 (1975). * * * A technology-based standard is one that focuses on improving the emissions performance of individual sources. * * *

But, the Agency explained, in order to "control[ ] CO_2 from affected [plants] at levels . . . necessary to mitigate the dangers presented by climate change," it could not base the emissions limit on "measures that improve efficiency at the power plants." * * * Instead, to attain the necessary "critical CO_2 reductions," EPA adopted [the Clean Power Plan regulations] forcing a shift throughout the power grid from one type of energy source to another. * * *

> **?** Does *MCI v. AT&T's* "fundamental change" to the filed rate requirement seem similar to the change the EPA has effected with its generation-shifting here? What assumption is the Court making, both here and in *MCI v. AT&T*, about what Congress did in these statutes? Relatedly, note that by the time the Court hears these two cases, the original statutory language in both cases dates back more than half a century.

This view of EPA's authority was not only unprecedented; it also effected a "fundamental revision of the statute, changing it from [one sort of] scheme of . . . regulation" into an entirely different kind. *MCI*, 512 U.S. at 231. Under the Agency's prior view of Section 111, its role was limited to ensuring the efficient pollution performance of each individual regulated source. Under that paradigm, if a source was already operating at that level, there was nothing more for EPA to do. Under its newly "discover[ed]" authority, however, EPA can demand much greater reductions in emissions based on a very different kind of policy judgment: that it would be "best" if coal made up a much smaller share of national electricity generation. And on this view of EPA's authority, it could go further, perhaps forcing coal plants to "shift" away virtually all of their generation—*i.e.*, to cease making power altogether.

* * *

We also find it "highly unlikely that Congress would leave" to "agency discretion" the decision of how much coal-based generation there should be over the coming decades. *MCI*, 512 U.S. at 231; see also *Brown & Williamson*, 529 U.S. at 160 ("We are confident that Congress could not have intended to delegate a decision of such economic and political significance to an agency in so cryptic a fashion."). The basic and consequential tradeoffs involved in such a choice are ones that Congress would likely have intended for itself. See W. ESKRIDGE, INTERPRETING LAW: A PRIMER ON HOW TO READ STATUTES AND THE CONSTITUTION 288 (2016) ("Even if Congress has delegated an agency general rulemaking or adjudicatory power, judges presume that Congress does not delegate its authority to settle or amend major social and economic policy decisions."). Congress certainly has not conferred a like authority upon EPA anywhere else in the Clean Air Act. The last place one would expect to find it is in the previously little-used backwater of Section 111(d).

The dissent contends that there is nothing surprising about EPA dictating the optimal mix of energy sources nationwide, since that sort of mandate will reduce air pollution from power plants, which is EPA's bread and butter. But that does not follow. Forbidding evictions may slow the spread of disease, but the CDC's ordering such a measure certainly "raise[s] an eyebrow." We would not expect the Department of Homeland Security to make trade or foreign policy even though doing so could decrease illegal immigration. And no one would consider generation shifting a "tool" in OSHA's "toolbox," even though reducing generation at coal plants would reduce workplace illness and injury from coal dust.

* * * Finally, we cannot ignore that the regulatory writ EPA newly uncovered conveniently enabled it to enact a program that, long after the dangers posed by greenhouse gas emissions "had become well known, Congress considered and rejected" multiple times. * * * It has also declined to enact similar measures, such as a carbon tax. * * * "The importance of the issue," along with the fact that the same basic scheme EPA adopted "has been the subject of an earnest and profound debate across the country, makes the oblique form of the claimed delegation all the more suspect. . . ."

C

Given these circumstances, our precedent counsels skepticism toward EPA's claim that Section 111 empowers it to devise carbon emissions caps based on a generation shifting approach. To overcome that skepticism, the Government must—under the major questions doctrine—point to "clear congressional authorization" to regulate in that manner.

All the Government can offer, however, is the Agency's authority to establish emissions caps at a level reflecting "the application of the best system of emission reduction adequately demonstrated." 42 U.S.C. § 7411(a)(1). As a matter of "definitional possibilities," generation shifting can be described as a "system" * * * capable of reducing emissions. But of course almost anything could constitute such a "system"; shorn of all context, the word is an empty vessel. Such a vague statutory grant is not close to the sort of clear authorization required by our precedents.

> **?** Notice again the Court's reference to "context." What kind of "context" is the Court referring to? Does it seem like the semantic or linguistic context of the word "system"? Or, is the Court using the term "context" more broadly here? Would this be an "intrinsic tool" of statutory interpretation of the kind you learned in Chapter 20 or more like an "extrinsic tool"?

* * *

[T]he only interpretive question before us, and the only one we answer, is * * * whether the "best system of emission reduction" identified by EPA in the Clean Power Plan was within the authority granted to the Agency in Section 111(d) of the Clean Air Act. For the reasons given, the answer is no.

* * *

Capping carbon dioxide emissions at a level that will force a nationwide transition away from the use of coal to generate electricity may be a sensible "solution to the crisis of the day." *New York v. United States*, 505 U.S. 144, 187 (1992). But it is not plausible that Congress gave EPA the authority to adopt on its own such a regulatory scheme in Section 111(d). A decision of such magnitude and consequence rests with Congress itself, or an agency acting pursuant to a clear delegation from that representative body. The judgment of the Court of Appeals for the District of Columbia Circuit is reversed, and the cases are remanded for further proceedings consistent with this opinion.

JUSTICE GORSUCH with whom JUSTICE ALITO joins, concurring.

To resolve today's case the Court invokes the major questions doctrine. Like many parallel clear-statement rules in our law, this one operates to protect foundational constitutional guarantees. I join the Court's opinion and write to offer some additional observations about the doctrine on which it rests.

I

One of the Judiciary's most solemn duties is to ensure that acts of Congress are applied in accordance with the Constitution in the cases that come before us. To help fulfill that duty, courts have developed certain "clear-statement" rules. These rules assume that, absent a clear statement otherwise, Congress means for its laws to operate in congruence with the Constitution rather than test its bounds. In this way, these clear-statement rules help courts "act as faithful agents of the Constitution." A. Barrett, *Substantive Canons and Faithful Agency*, 90 B.U. L. REV. 109, 169 (2010) (Barrett).

> Justice Gorsuch is drawing here on a variation of the "Constitutional Avoidance" canon. This is a doctrine of statutory interpretation that we discussed in Chapter 21, Section B.

> **FYI** Yes, Justice Gorsuch is citing to a law review article written by Justice Amy Coney Barrett when she was a law professor at Notre Dame Law School. Justice Gorsuch sprinkles a lot of cites to this article throughout his concurring opinion.

* * * The major questions doctrine works in much the same way to protect the Constitution's separation of powers. In Article I, "the People" vested "[a]ll" federal "legislative powers . . . in Congress." Preamble; Art. I, § 1. As Chief Justice Marshall put it, this means that "important subjects . . . must be entirely regulated by the legislature itself," even if Congress may leave the Executive "to act under such general provisions to fill up the details." *Wayman v. Southard*, 10 Wheat. 1, 42–43 (1825). Doubtless, what qualifies as an important subject and what constitutes a detail may be debated. See, *e.g., Gundy v. United States*, 139 S.Ct. 2116, 2122–2124 (2019) (plurality opinion); id., at 2135–2137 (GORSUCH, J., dissenting). But * * * the Constitution's rule vesting federal legislative power in Congress is "vital to the integrity and maintenance of the system of government ordained by the Constitution." *Marshall Field & Co. v. Clark*, 143 U.S. 649, 692 (1892).

> **!** Notice that Justice Gorsuch is making the argument that only Congress is politically accountable and that agencies are comparable to "a ruling class of largely unaccountable 'ministers.' "

It is vital because the framers believed that a republic—a thing of the people—would be more likely to enact just laws than a regime administered by a ruling class of largely unaccountable "ministers." THE FEDERALIST No. 11, p. 85 (C. Rossiter ed. 1961) (A. Hamilton). From time to time, some have questioned that assessment. But by vesting the lawmaking power in the people's elected representatives, the Constitution sought to ensure "not only that all power [w]ould be derived from the people," but also "that those [e]ntrusted with it should be kept in dependence on the people." *Id.*, No. 37, at 227 (J. Madison). * * *

Permitting Congress to divest its legislative power to the Executive Branch would "dash [this] whole scheme." *Department of Transportation v. Association of American Railroads*, 575 U.S. 43, 61 (2015) (ALITO, J., concurring). Legislation would risk becoming nothing more than the will of the current President, or, worse yet, the will of unelected officials barely responsive to him. See S. BREYER, MAKING OUR DEMOCRACY WORK: A JUDGE'S VIEW 110 (2010) ("[T]he president may not have the time or willingness to review [agency] decisions"). In a world like that, agencies could churn out new laws more or less at whim. Intrusions on liberty would not be difficult and rare, but easy and profuse. See THE FEDERALIST No. 47, at 303 (J. Madison); *id.*, No. 62, at 378 (J. Madison). Stability would be lost, with vast numbers of laws changing with every new presidential administration. Rather than embody a wide social consensus and input from minority voices, laws would more often bear the support only of the party currently in power. Powerful special interests, which are sometimes "uniquely" able to influence the agendas of administrative agencies, would flourish while others would be left to ever-shifting winds. T. Merrill, *Capture Theory and the Courts: 1967–1983*, 72 CHI.-KENT L. REV. 1039, 1043 (1997). * * *

> **?** Given what you now know about the legislative process for promulgating statutes and the administrative process for regulations, does this seem right to you? Are statutes adopted by the legislature more likely to "embody a wide social consensus and input from minority voices" than agency regulations?

B

* * * Article I's Vesting Clause has its own [clear-statement rule]: the major questions doctrine. See *Gundy*, 139 S. Ct. at 2141–2142 (GORSUCH, J., dissenting). * * *

The Court has applied the major questions doctrine for the same reason it has applied other similar clear-statement rules—to ensure that the government does "not inadvertently cross constitutional lines." Barrett 175. And the constitutional lines at stake here are surely no less important than those this Court has long held sufficient to justify parallel clear-statement rules. At stake is not just a question of retroactive liability or sovereign immunity, but basic questions about self-government, equality, fair notice, federalism, and the separation of powers. The major questions doctrine seeks to protect against "unintentional, oblique, or otherwise unlikely" intrusions on these interests. *NFIB v. OSHA*, 595 U.S., at ___ (GORSUCH, J., concurring). The doctrine does so by ensuring that, when agencies seek to resolve major questions, they at least act with clear congressional authorization and do not "exploit some gap, ambiguity, or doubtful expression in Congress's statutes to assume responsibilities far beyond" those the people's representatives actually conferred on them. *Ibid.* * * *

> This is Justice Gorsuch's articulation of his rationale for the Major Questions Doctrine. According to Justice Gorsuch, how does the Major Questions Doctrine help to protect against intrusions on the interests of "self-government, equality, fair notice, federalism, and the separation of powers"?

II

A

Turning from the doctrine's function to its application, * * * our cases supply a good deal of guidance about when an agency action involves a major question for which clear congressional authority is required.

First, this Court has indicated that the doctrine applies when an agency claims the power to resolve a matter of great "political significance" or end an "earnest and profound debate across the country." * * *

Second, this Court has said that an agency must point to clear congressional authorization when it seeks to regulate " 'a significant portion of the American economy". * * *

Third, this Court has said that the major questions doctrine may apply when an agency seeks to "intrud[e] into an area that is the particular domain of state law." * * *

? What do you think the EPA's response to this characterization of generation-shifting as "forc[ing] coal and gas-fired power plants 'to cease [operating] altogether'" would be?

While this list of triggers may not be exclusive, each of the signs the Court has found significant in the past is present here, making this a relatively easy case for the doctrine's application. The EPA claims the power to force coal and gas-fired power plants "to cease [operating] altogether." Whether these plants should be allowed to operate is a question on which people today may disagree, but it is a question everyone can agree is vitally important. * * *

JUSTICE KAGAN, with whom JUSTICE BREYER and JUSTICE SOTOMAYOR join, dissenting.

Today, the Court strips the Environmental Protection Agency (EPA) of the power Congress gave it to respond to "the most pressing environmental challenge of our time." *Massachusetts v. EPA*, 549 U.S. 497, 505 (2007).

* * *

Congress charged EPA with addressing [the] potentially catastrophic harms [caused by greenhouse gases], including through regulation of fossil-fuel-fired power plants. Section 111 of the Clean Air Act directs EPA

! Notice how the dissent characterizes this: it is the Court that is "strip[ping] the. . .EPA. . .of the power Congress gave it." But what would the majority say to this? Wouldn't the majority say that Congress didn't give the EPA the power the dissent says it gave? So, wouldn't the majority just say the Court is instead simply enforcing Congress's will in ensuring that the agency doesn't go beyond the power Congress gave it?

to regulate stationary sources of any substance that "causes, or contributes significantly to, air pollution" and that "may reasonably be anticipated to endanger public health or welfare." 42 U.S.C. § 7411(b)(1)(A). Carbon dioxide and other greenhouse gases fit that description. * * *

The limits the majority now puts on EPA's authority fly in the face of the statute Congress wrote. The majority says it is simply "not plausible" that Congress enabled EPA to regulate power plants' emissions through genera tion shifting. But that is just what Congress did when it broadly authorized EPA in Section 111 to select the "best system of emission reduction" for power plants. The "best system" full stop—no ifs, ands, or buts of any kind relevant here. The parties do not dispute that generation shifting is indeed the "best system"—the most effective and efficient way to reduce power plants' carbon dioxide emissions. And no other provision in the Clean Air Act suggests that Congress meant to foreclose EPA from selecting that system; to the contrary, the Plan's regulatory approach fits hand-in-glove with the rest of the statute. The majority's decision rests on one claim alone: that generation shifting is just too new and too big a deal for Congress to have authorized it in Section 111's general terms. But that is wrong. A key reason Congress makes broad delegations like Section 111 is so an agency can respond, appropriately and commensurately, to new and big problems. Congress knows what it doesn't and can't know when it drafts a statute; and Congress therefore gives an expert agency the power to address issues—even significant ones—as and when they arise. That is what Congress did in enacting Section 111. The majority today overrides that legislative choice. In so doing, it deprives EPA of the power needed—and the power granted—to curb the emission of greenhouse gases.

> Does the "key reason" Justice Kagan says Congress delegates here sound familiar? It is indeed one of the rationales for legislative delegation of rulemaking authority discussed in Part VII, in Chapter 29. Notice the implication of Justice Kagan's point here, that many agency actions are those that the enacting Congress could not have anticipated at the time of enactment. In other words, broad language in a statute—words like "best system of emission reduction"— are an implicit indication that Congress was delegating to the agency the power to confront unanticipated questions in the future. This idea of an implicit delegation is of course one of the underlying premises of the *Chevron* doctrine.

I

The Clean Air Act was major legislation, designed to deal with a major public policy issue. * * * [T]he statutory language * * * does not impose *any* constraints—technological or otherwise—on EPA's authority to regulate stationary sources. * * *

"Congress," this Court has said, "knows to speak in plain terms when it wishes to circumscribe, and in capacious terms when it wishes to enlarge, agency discretion." *Arlington v. FCC*, 569 U.S. 290, 296 (2013). In Section

111, Congress spoke in capacious terms. It knew that "without regulatory flexibility, changing circumstances and scientific developments would soon render the Clean Air Act obsolete." *Massachusetts*, 549 U.S., at 532. So the provision enables EPA to base emissions limits for existing stationary sources on the "best system." That system may be technological in nature; it may be whatever else the majority has in mind; or, most important here, it may be generation shifting. The statute does not care. And when Congress uses "expansive language" to authorize agency action, courts generally may not "impos[e] limits on [the] agency's discretion." *Little Sisters of the Poor Saints Peter and Paul Home v. Pennsylvania*, 591 U.S., (2020). That constraint on judicial authority—that insistence on judicial modesty—should resolve this case.

II

The majority thinks not, contending that in "certain extraordinary cases"—of which this is one—courts should start off with "skepticism" that a broad delegation authorizes agency action. The majority labels that view the "major questions doctrine" * * * and claims to find support for it in our caselaw. But the relevant decisions do normal statutory interpretation: In them, the Court simply insisted that the text of a broad delegation, like any other statute, should be read in context, and with a modicum of common sense. Using that ordinary method, the decisions struck down agency actions (even though they plausibly fit within a delegation's terms) for two principal reasons. First, an agency was operating far outside its traditional lane, so that it had no viable claim of expertise or experience. And second, the action, if allowed, would have conflicted with, or even wreaked havoc on, Congress's broader design. In short, the assertion of delegated power was a misfit for both the agency and the statutory scheme. But that is not true here. The Clean Power Plan falls within EPA's wheelhouse, and it fits perfectly * * * with all the Clean Air Act's provisions. That the Plan addresses major issues of public policy does not upend the analysis. Congress wanted EPA to do just that. * * *

The majority claims it is just following precedent, but that is not so. The Court has never even used the term "major questions doctrine" before. And in the relevant cases, the Court has done statutory construction of a familiar sort. It has looked to the text of a delegation. It has addressed how an agency's view of that text works—or fails to do so—in the context of a broader statutory scheme. And it has asked, in a common-sensical (or call it purposive) vein, about what Congress would have made of the agency's view—otherwise said, whether Congress would naturally have delegated authority over some important question to the agency, given its expertise and experience. In short, in assessing the scope of a delegation, the Court has considered—without multiple steps, triggers, or special presumptions—the fit between the power claimed, the agency claiming it, and the broader statutory design.

* * *

This is not the Attorney General regulating medical care [as in *Gonzales v. Oregon*], or even the [Centers for Disease Control and Prevention (CDC)] regulating landlord-tenant relations [as in *Alabama Assn. of Realtors v. Department of Health and Human Servs.*]. It is the EPA (that's the Environmental Protection Agency, in case the majority forgot) acting to address the greatest environmental challenge of our time. * * *

> Does this seem right to you? Think back to the several cases you read leading up to *West Virginia v. EPA: MCI v. AT&T* (1994), *Brown & Williamson v. FDA* (2000), and *King v. Burwell* (2015). It is certainly true that the Court never used the phrase "major questions doctrine." But, when treating the agency's interpretations, did the Court in each of those cases merely engage in "statutory construction of a familiar sort"?

[G]eneration shifting has a well-established pedigree as a tool for reducing pollution; even putting aside other federal regulation, both state regulators and power plants themselves have long used it to attain environmental goals. The technique is, so to speak, a tool in the pollution-control toolbox. And that toolbox is the one EPA uses. So that Agency, more than any other, has the desired "comparative expertise." The majority cannot contest that point frontally: It knows that cap and trade and similar mechanisms are an ordinary part of modern environmental regulation. Instead, the majority protests that Congress would not have wanted EPA to "dictat[e]," through generation shifting, the "mix of energy sources nationwide." But that statement reflects a misunderstanding of how the electricity market works. *Every* regulation of power plants—even the most conventional, facility-specific controls— "dictat[es]" the national energy mix to one or another degree. That result follows because regulations affect costs, and the electrical grid works by taking up energy from low-cost providers before high-cost ones. Consider an example: Suppose EPA requires coal-fired plants to use carbon-capture technology. That action increases those plants' costs, and automatically (by virtue of the way the grid operates) reduces their share of the electricity market. So EPA is always controlling the mix of energy sources. In that

> ❓ What do you think about this argument? The core idea is that regulation of any kind always has an impact on the broader market. So, no matter what the EPA does, it will necessarily result in "generation shifting," a change in the aggregate market share of the different sources of electricity. Justice Kagan is saying that, in effect, even heat-rate improvements—which the majority says are okay—lead to generation shifting. What would the majority say to this? Would the majority say that it is the means rather than the ends of the regulation that makes this a "major questions" case? Or, is the majority mainly concerned just with the ends?

sense (though the term has taken on a more specialized meaning), everything EPA does is "generation shifting." The majority's idea that EPA has no warrant to direct such a shift just indicates that courts sometimes do not really get regulation.

Why, then, be "skeptic[al]" of EPA's exercise of authority? When there is no misfit, of the kind apparent in our precedents, between the regulation, the agency, and the statutory design? Although the majority offers a flurry of complaints, they come down in the end to this: The Clean Power Plan is a big new thing, issued under a minor statutory provision. * * * I have already addressed the back half of that argument: In fact, there is nothing insignificant about Section 111(d), which was intended to ensure that EPA would limit existing stationary sources' emissions of otherwise unregulated pollutants (however few or many there were). And the front half of the argument doesn't work either. The Clean Power Plan was not so big. It was not so new. And to the extent it was either, that should not matter. * * *

And contra the majority, it is [the enacting] Congress's choice which counts, not any later one's. The majority says it "cannot ignore" that Congress in recent years has "considered and rejected" cap-and-trade schemes. But under normal principles of statutory construction, the majority *should* ignore that fact (just as I should ignore that Congress failed to enact bills barring EPA from implementing the Clean Power Plan). As we have explained time and again, failed legislation "offers a particularly dangerous basis on which to rest an interpretation of an existing law a different and earlier Congress" adopted. *Bostock v. Clayton County*, 140 S.Ct. 1731, 1747 (2020) (internal quotation marks omitted).

> **FYI** Notice that Justice Kagan is quoting from the *Bostock* case we read in Chapter 17. (This is the case in which the Court interpreted Title VII to prohibit employment discrimination based on sexual orientation.) Why do you think Justice Kagan is quoting from it here? Do you remember who wrote the majority opinion in that case?

III

Some years ago, I remarked that "[w]e're all textualists now." Harvard Law School, *The Antonin Scalia Lecture Series: A Dialogue with Justice Elena Kagan on the Reading of Statutes* (Nov. 25, 2015). It seems I was wrong. The current Court is textualist only when being so suits it. When that method would frustrate broader goals, special canons like the "major questions doctrine" magically appear as get-out-of-text-free cards. Today, one of those broader goals makes itself clear: Prevent agencies from doing important work, even though that is what Congress directed. * * *

It is not surprising that Congress has always delegated, and continues to do so—including on important policy issues. As this Court has recognized, it is often "unreasonable and impracticable" for Congress to do anything else. In all times, but ever more in "our increasingly complex society," the Legislature "simply cannot do its job absent an ability to delegate power under broad general directives." *Mistretta v. United States*, 488 U.S. 361, 372 (1989). Consider just two reasons why.

First, Members of Congress often don't know enough—and know they don't know enough—to regulate sensibly on an issue. Of course, Members can and do provide overall direction. But then they rely, as all of us rely in our daily lives, on people with greater expertise and experience. Those people are found in agencies. Congress looks to them to make specific judgments about how to achieve its more general objectives. And it does so especially, though by no means exclusively, when an issue has a scientific or technical dimension. Why *wouldn't* Congress instruct EPA to select "the best system of emission reduction," rather than try to choose that system itself? Congress knows that systems of emission reduction lie not in its own but in EPA's "unique expertise."

Second and relatedly, Members of Congress often can't know enough—and again, know they can't—to keep regulatory schemes working across time. Congress usually can't predict the future—can't anticipate changing circumstances and the way they will affect varied regulatory techniques. Nor can Congress (realistically) keep track of and respond to fast-flowing developments as they occur. Once again, that is most obviously true when it comes to scientific and technical matters. The "best system of emission reduction" is not today what it was yesterday, and will surely be something different tomorrow. So for this reason too, a rational Congress delegates. It enables an agency to adapt old regulatory approaches to new times, to ensure that a statutory program remains effective.

Over time, the administrative delegations Congress has made have helped to build a modern Nation. Congress wanted fewer workers killed in industrial accidents. It wanted to prevent plane crashes, and reduce the deadliness of car wrecks. It wanted to ensure that consumer products didn't catch fire. It wanted to stop the routine adulteration of food and improve the safety and efficacy of medications. And it wanted cleaner air and water. If an American could go back in time, she might be astonished by how much progress has occurred in all those areas. It didn't happen through legislation alone. It happened because Congress gave broad-ranging powers to administrative agencies, and those agencies then filled in—rule by rule by rule—Congress's policy outlines.

This Court has historically known enough not to get in the way. * * *

In short, when it comes to delegations, there are good reasons for Congress (within extremely broad limits) to get to call the shots. Congress knows about how government works in ways courts don't. More specifically, Congress knows what mix of legislative and administrative action conduces to good policy. Courts should be modest.

Today, the Court is not. * * * And nothing in the rest of the Clean Air Act, or any other statute, suggests that Congress did not mean for the delegation it wrote to go as far as the text says. In rewriting that text, the Court substitutes its own ideas about delegations for Congress's. And that means the Court substitutes its own ideas about policymaking for Congress's. The Court will not allow the Clean Air Act to work as Congress instructed.

> ❗ Notice Justice Kagan's reference to "policymaking." Remember that one of the rationales for *Chevron* was to give agencies policymaking leeway. Remember too, though, that the limits of that policymaking were supposed to be within the zone of ambiguity in the statutory language.

The subject matter of the regulation here makes the Court's intervention all the more troubling. Whatever else this Court may know about, it does not have a clue about how to address climate change. And let's say the obvious: The stakes here are high. Yet the Court today prevents congressionally authorized agency action to curb power plants' carbon dioxide emissions. The Court appoints itself—instead of Congress or the expert agency—the decision-maker on climate policy. I cannot think of many things more frightening. Respectfully, I dissent.

NOTES & QUESTIONS

1. Here is the full language for the definition of "standard of performance" that includes the reference to the "best system of emission reduction":

    > The term "standard of performance" means a standard for emissions of air pollutants which reflects the degree of emission limitation achievable through the application of the best system of emission reduction which (taking into account the cost of achieving such reduction and any non-air quality health and environmental impact and energy requirements) the Administrator determines has been adequately demonstrated.

    42 U.S.C. § 7411(a)(1). What do you think? Does the reference to the "best system of emission reduction" here include the possibility of generation shifting? If not, couldn't the whole case have been decided against the EPA under *Chevron* Step One without even getting into the Major Questions Doctrine?

2. Of course, the question above is the *dissent's* framing of the case ("Does the text of that provision, when read in context and with a common-sense awareness of how Congress delegates, authorize the agency action here?"). From the perspective of the majority, the question in Note 1 isn't the right question. Since the generation-shifting approach involves the EPA engaging in something "major," making a decision of "vast economic and political significance," the question instead is whether there is "*clear* congressional authorization" (emphasis added). If not, then even if a plausible, or even a better, reading of the phrase "best system of emission reduction" would include generation shifting, that would still be insufficient for the EPA to require such generation shifting.

3. The key inquiry in whether the Major Questions Doctrine applies is whether the agency is making a decision of "vast economic and political significance." Notice that, though the Court refers to the doctrine as a Major *Questions* Doctrine, it could more appropriately be thought of as a Major *Actions* Doctrine, or perhaps a Major *Answers* Doctrine, given that the trigger for the doctrine is the economic or political significance of the agency's *action*. *See* Lisa Heinzerling, *The Major Answers Doctrine*, 16 NYU J. L. & Lib. 506 (2023). Does this seem like the kind of question a court should be asking? Does this even seem like a question of *law* at all? How do judges know whether a decision is of

"vast economic and political significance"? Will it just be a question of the judges' intuition, a "we know it when we see it" inquiry? Part II.A of Justice Gorsuch's concurrence lays out his attempt to establish the contours of the inquiry. What do you think of judges' ability to make the determinations he lays out?

4. Part I of Justice Gorsuch's concurrence discusses what he views as the constitutional underpinnings of the Major Questions Doctrine: the nondelegation doctrine. Recall Justice Gorsuch's dissent in the nondelegation case of *Gundy v. United States* in Chapter 29: in that case, he sought to curb Congress's power to delegate altogether. Here, he views the Major Questions Doctrine as the way to use statutory interpretation to enforce the nondelegation principle. So, Justice Gorsuch's view of the Major Questions Doctrine is as a doctrine of "constitutional avoidance": apply the doctrine to hold that the statute does not authorize the agency's action, so as to avoid having to answer the constitutional question of whether Congress even *could* authorize the agency's action. You will recall from Chapter 21 that the "constitutional avoidance" doctrine is what is known as a "substantive canon." If his characterization is correct, is Justice Gorsuch saying that it might violate the nondelegation doctrine for Congress to authorize the EPA to use generation shifting as a means to reduce greenhouse gases? Relatedly, does this seem like the other contexts in which the courts engage in constitutional avoidance in statutory interpretation? Consider the *Catholic Bishop* case in Chapter 21, Section B: Does that case seem like this one?

5. Notice that the Major Questions Doctrine applies only to delegations to *agencies*. So, for example, the majority states, "Extraordinary grants of *regulatory* authority are rarely accomplished through 'modest words,' 'vague terms,' or 'subtle device[s]' " (emphasis added). Yet, when legislatures draft statutes with broad language or "vague terms" outside of the agency context, who ordinarily has the power to interpret that language? The courts! *Broad or vague language in a statute*—at least in our system of government where courts have the power to interpret that language—*amounts to a delegation of power to courts*. Yet, the Major Questions Doctrine doesn't apply unless there is a delegation to an *administrative agency*, and so doesn't apply to the implicit delegation to *courts* that results from broad or vague language in statutes. Consider the following sentence from Justice Gorsuch's concurrence, citing the majority: "[T]he [major questions] doctrine addresses 'a particular and

recurring problem: agencies asserting highly consequential power beyond what Congress could reasonably be understood to have granted.'" Don't *courts* assert highly consequential power of this sort all the time? As suggested by the cases on statutory interpretation that we read in Parts IV, V, and VI, this is what the interpretive power often involves. One example might be the *Bostock* case in Chapter 17, written by none other than Justice Gorsuch. Recall that in that 2020 case, the Court interpreted the prohibition of employment discrimination "because of . . . sex" in Title VII of the Civil Rights Act of 1964 to include discrimination based on sexual orientation. Whether or not you agree with the Court's decision, couldn't one characterize the decision in *Bostock* as "asserting highly consequential power beyond what Congress could reasonably be understood to have granted"? Would you view *Bostock* as addressing a "major question"?

6. How, if at all, does the dissent respond to the core of the Court's holding, that Congress could not have intended to delegate so great a power to the EPA with language like the "best system of emission reduction"? What does the dissent mean when it says that Congress should "get to call the shots"? Doesn't the majority think that *it* is letting Congress "call the shots"? Which opinion is more faithfully giving Congress the power to "call the shots"? Relatedly, what does the dissent mean when it says, "Courts should be modest."? As you think about these questions, think about the differences in the big-picture framing between the majority and dissenting opinions. One thing both opinions share is a claim to be furthering what Congress would want—in other words, to be acting as Congress's faithful agent. Yet the majority is constraining the agency, while the dissent is empowering the agency. But notice what each side believes the other side is doing: The majority essentially argues that the dissent is acquiescing in an inappropriate exercise of *executive* (i.e., agency) power, while the dissent claims that the majority is engaged in an inappropriate exercise of *judicial* power. Both the majority and the dissent are thinking about what we have called "institutional choice." The majority believes the Court needs to step in to constrain an agency attempting to aggrandize its own power, and the dissent believes the Court is aggrandizing *its* power. What is your view of who has the better of this fight?

C. *Chevron*'s Uncertain Future

Before concluding this chapter, we confess substantial uncertainty about how much longer the highly deferential aspect of *Chevron* Step Two will remain part of the doctrine of judicial review of agency statutory interpretation. As described above, *Chevron* is not the only doctrine relevant for judicial review of agency actions: refinements like the Major Questions Doctrine or the requirement that the agency have exercised "Force of Law Power" mean that reviewing courts may depart from the *Chevron* framework and its deferential Step Two. Indeed, the Supreme Court has not upheld an agency regulation based on *Chevron* Step Two deference since 2016, although the United States Courts of Appeals continue to do so.

In 2024, the Supreme Court is hearing two consolidated cases, *Loper Bright Enterprises v. Raimondo* and *Relentless v. Department of Commerce,* that present the question of whether to overrule *Chevron* entirely. Thus, there is some possibility that *Chevron*'s two-step doctrinal formulation for judicial review of agency interpretation may be gone by the time you read this. And given the Court's recent direction, it seems likely that, whatever the Court does with the *Loper Bright* and *Relentless* cases, courts will be less deferential to agency interpretations than they have been. But exactly how much so, and in what ways, remains very much unknown. Importantly, though, remember that, even under current doctrine, courts need not—and do not—give unquestioning deference to agencies' interpretations. Although the *Chevron* two-step doctrine seems straightforward and is often thought to be highly deferential, Step One has always allowed courts to give the agencies no deference at all. So, courts have always been able to reject agency interpretations when they desired. As we hope you gathered from the previous chapter, figuring out when courts would use Step One rather than Step Two has never been straightforward, as cases like *MCI v. AT&T* and *FDA v. Brown & Williamson* show. Still, when coupled with Justice Gorsuch's dissenting opinion in *Gundy* and the serious interest that several current members of the Supreme Court have shown in reinvigorating the federal nondelegation doctrine, the relationships between Congress, federal agencies, and the courts are particularly in flux today.

Nonetheless, we do feel confident that, whatever the doctrinal changes, the kinds of considerations you have seen expressed by Justices in the cases you have read throughout this Part—both majority and dissenting opinions—will continue to matter, as will the characteristics of agencies we raised in Chapter 33, Section B. As just a few examples of those considerations, you can expect that, no matter what the doctrine, courts will consider how explicit the congressional delegation to the agency is; the possibility that that delegation is so broad as to raise nondelegation concerns (that is, the sense that *Congress,* not the agency, should make the policy decision that the agency has made); the complexity of the statutory scheme and the role of agency expertise relative to courts; an agency's political accountability relative to courts, and also relative to Congress; how long the agency's interpretation has been in place and how embedded that interpretation is, if at all, in other agency implementing actions; the potential for agency capture by one set of interests; the potential that agency self-interestedness will lead to an aggrandizement of its own power; and the clarity of the legal text being interpreted. Different judges will of course weigh these concerns in different ways, but each of these concerns depends on courts' implicit understanding about the relationships among the branches of government, especially including judges' views about their own role in the larger system of lawmaking. In short, whatever the future holds for the doctrine of judicial review of agency interpretation, the courts are likely to continue to care about the broad question of institutional choice in legal decision-making and the role that different legal institutions (courts versus Congress versus agencies) play. Whether or not the Court overturns *Chevron* and, if so, whatever new doctrine replaces it, you will still need to understand the big-picture questions, subtle and difficult as they are, about the role of the judiciary in shaping agencies' regulations and congressional delegations.

D. Analogous State Doctrines

The preceding portions of Part VIII have focused exclusively on the federal doctrines of judicial review of agency interpretations of statutes. As previously noted, the number of cases and secondary discussions of this topic is extensive. However, much less has been written about judicial review of agency statutory interpretation in the various state systems. A couple of helpful analyses or summaries of state practice include Aaron Saiger, Chevron *and Deference in State Administrative Law*, 83 FORD. L. REV. 555 (2014); and William R. Anderson, *Chevron in the States: An Assessment and A Proposal*, 58 ADMIN. L. REV. 1017 (2006).

Briefly, the *Chevron* doctrine is not widely followed in state courts. Instead, most state courts have maintained that it is for courts to decide *de novo* what a statute means, even though in the course of doing so most state courts will consider an agency's construction. This approach is more like the federal pre-*Chevron* doctrine, in which courts evaluate in something like a *Skidmore* fashion whether the agency has offered persuasive reasons for courts to follow its interpretation. These agency justifications may provide the reviewing court with more than just good arguments, instead having greater weight or influence akin to that of expert witness testimony, or even functioning like non-binding persuasive authority from other jurisdictions. Still, in states employing this kind of *Skidmore* approach, the courts remain the final arbiter of statutory meanings.

However, a dozen or more states have now developed something like a *Chevron* doctrine, usually with far fewer of the complexities about when the doctrine applies than the federal counterpart. That is, the courts in these states more often simply make a threshold Step One determination of whether the state legislature has plainly spoken on the interpretive issue, and if not then uphold the agency's interpretation at Step Two if it is a reasonable use of the authority that the state legislature has delegated to the agency. Meanwhile, some commentators have observed a slow movement in the direction of *Chevron* in other state courts and in state administrative law jurisprudence generally.

Of course, given the flux in the federal jurisprudence of judicial deference to agency statutory interpretation, it is even harder to predict where state law on the subject is headed. Perhaps in the field of statutory interpretation, as in other fields, states can serve as laboratories of democracy, refining the complex relationships between the three branches of American government. In any event, it seems safe to assume that as long as federal and state government agencies continue to play the substantial and significant roles that they have increasingly come to play over the past century, issues of the appropriate extent of judicial deference to agency statutory interpretation will remain of central importance to American law.

Test Your Understanding

To assess your understanding of the material in this chapter, click here to take a quiz.

38

A Review and Synthesis Case: *Babbitt v. Sweet Home Chapter*

We conclude our exploration of the ways in which statutory interpreters—particularly courts and agencies—resolve textual ambiguities with a famous Endangered Species Act issue, addressed in the 1995 Supreme Court case *Babbitt v. Sweet Home Chapter of Communities for a Greater Oregon*. (With the significant caveat that the extent to which the Court in 1995 showed deference to the agency interpretation now seems somewhat quaint, in light of the dramatic shift in judicial review of agency activity apparently now underway at the Court.)

DIY
Deploying Interpretive Tools: The *Sweet Home* Case as Course Summary

As you read the edited versions of the three opinions from the *Sweet Home* case that follow, consider the following questions:

1. In the statute at issue, has Congress's effort to exhaustively define the term "take" led to the kind of problem Francis Lieber warned about (Chapter 14, pp. 334–335) when he said that providing additional specifications of meaning might not prevent ambiguity, because "the various specifications would have required new ones. Where would be the end?"?

2. How many interpretive tools can you identify? (You might make a list as you read.)

3. What differences, explicit or implicit, do you see in the three opinions' interpretive philosophies?

---

4.   Does any particular tool, or philosophy, seem to drive the conclusion of any one opinion?

5.   Is anything missing from any of the opinions? Do they fully respond to each other?

6.   What sense do you get of the Justices' views of the agency and its role? Of the judicial role?

7.   What do you think of the structure of the opinions? How would you approach things differently?

Be sure to revisit these questions after you finish reading the opinion excerpts.

Babbitt v. Sweet Home Chapter of Communities for a Greater Oregon
515 U.S. 687 (1995)

JUSTICE STEVENS delivered the opinion of the Court.

The Endangered Species Act of 1973 (ESA or Act), 87 Stat. 884, 16 U.S.C. § 1531, contains a variety of protections designed to save from extinction species that the Secretary of the Interior designates as endangered or threatened. Section 9 of the Act makes it unlawful for any person to "take" any endangered or threatened species. The Secretary has promulgated a regulation that defines the statute's prohibition on takings to include "significant habitat modification or degradation where it actually kills or injures wildlife." This case presents the question whether the Secretary exceeded his authority under the Act by promulgating that regulation.

I

Section 9(a)(1) of the Endangered Species Act [16 U.S.C. § 1538(a)(1)] provides the following protection for endangered species:

Except as provided in sections 1535(g)(2) and 1539 of this title, with respect to any endangered species of fish or wildlife listed pursuant to section 1533 of this title it is unlawful for any person subject to the jurisdiction of the United States to—

. . .

> (B) take any such species within the United States or the territorial sea of the United States[.]

Section 3(19) of the Act [16 U.S.C. § 1532(19)] defines the statutory term "take":

> The term "take" means to harass, harm, pursue, hunt, shoot, wound, kill, trap, capture, or collect, or to attempt to engage in any such conduct.

The Act does not further define the terms it uses to define "take." The Interior Department regulations that implement the statute, however, define the statutory term "harm":

> *Harm* in the definition of "take" in the Act means an act which actually kills or injures wildlife. Such act may include significant habitat modification or degradation where it actually kills or injures wildlife by significantly impairing essential behavioral patterns, including breeding, feeding, or sheltering.

50 CFR § 17.3 (1994). This regulation has been in place since 1975.

A limitation on the § 9 "take" prohibition appears in § 10(a)(1)(B) of the Act, which Congress added by amendment in 1982. That section authorizes the Secretary to grant a permit for any taking otherwise prohibited by § 9(a)(1)(B) "if such taking is incidental to, and not the purpose of, the carrying out of an otherwise lawful activity." 16 U.S.C. § 1539(a)(1)(B).

In addition to the prohibition on takings, the Act provides several other protections for endangered species. Section 4, 16 U.S.C. § 1533, commands the Secretary to identify species of fish or wildlife that are in danger of extinction and to publish from time to time lists of all species he determines to be endangered or threatened. Section 5, 16 U.S.C. § 1534, authorizes the Secretary, in cooperation with the States, see 16 U.S.C. § 1535, to acquire land to aid in preserving such species. Section 7 requires federal agencies to ensure that none of their activities, including the granting of licenses and permits, will jeopardize the continued existence of endangered species "or result in the destruction or adverse modification of habitat of such species which is determined by the Secretary . . . to be critical." 16 U.S.C. § 1536(a)(2).

Respondents in this action are small landowners, logging companies, and families dependent on the forest products industries in the Pacific Northwest and in the Southeast, and organizations that represent their interests. They brought this declaratory judgment action against petitioners, the Secretary of the Interior and the Director of the Fish and Wildlife Service, in the United States District Court for the District of Columbia to challenge the statutory validity of the Secretary's regulation defining "harm," particularly the inclusion of habitat modification and degradation in the definition. Respondents challenged the regulation on its face. Their complaint alleged that application of the "harm" regulation to the red cockaded woodpecker, an endangered species, and the northern spotted owl, a threatened species, had injured them economically. * * *

II

* * * The text of the Act provides three reasons for concluding that the Secretary's interpretation is reasonable. First, an ordinary understanding of the word "harm" supports it. The dictionary definition of the verb form of "harm" is "to cause hurt or damage to: injure." Webster's Third New International Dictionary 1034 (1966). In the context of the ESA, that definition naturally encompasses habitat modification that results in actual injury or death to members of an endangered or threatened species.

Respondents argue that the Secretary should have limited the purview of "harm" to direct applications of force against protected species, but the dictionary definition does not include the word "directly" or suggest in any way that only direct or willful action that leads to injury constitutes "harm."[10] Moreover, unless the statutory term "harm" encompasses indirect as well as direct injuries, the word has no meaning that does not duplicate the meaning of other words that § 3 uses to define "take." A reluctance to treat statutory terms as surplusage supports the reasonableness of the Secretary's interpretation. * * * [11]

---

[10] Respondents and the dissent emphasize what they portray as the "established meaning" of "take" in the sense of a "wildlife take," a meaning respondents argue extends only to "the effort to exercise dominion over some creature, and the concrete effect of [sic] that creature." This limitation ill serves the statutory text, which forbids not taking "some creature" but "tak[ing] any [endangered] *species*"—a formidable task for even the most rapacious feudal lord. More importantly, Congress explicitly defined the operative term "take" in the ESA, no matter how much the dissent wishes otherwise, thereby obviating the need for us to probe its meaning as we must probe the meaning of the undefined subsidiary term "harm." Finally, Congress' definition of "take" includes several words—most obviously "harass," "pursue," and "wound," in addition to "harm" itself—that fit respondents' and the dissent's definition of "take" no better than does "significant habitat modification or degradation."

[11] In contrast, if the statutory term "harm" encompasses such indirect means of killing and injuring wildlife as habitat modification, the other terms listed in § 3—"harass," "pursue," "hunt," "shoot," "wound," "kill,"

Second, the broad purpose of the ESA supports the Secretary's decision to extend protection against activities that cause the precise harms Congress enacted the statute to avoid. In *TVA v. Hill*, 437 U.S. 153 (1978), we described the Act as "the most comprehensive legislation for the preservation of endangered species ever enacted by any nation." Whereas predecessor statutes enacted in 1966 and 1969 had not contained any sweeping prohibition against the taking of endangered species except on federal lands, the 1973 Act applied to all land in the United States and to the Nation's territorial seas. As stated in § 2 of the Act, among its central purposes is "to provide a means whereby the ecosystems upon which endangered species and threatened species depend may be conserved. . . ." 16 U.S.C. § 1531(b).

In *Hill*, we construed § 7 as precluding the completion of the Tellico Dam because of its predicted impact on the survival of the snail darter. Both our holding and the language in our opinion stressed the importance of the statutory policy. "The plain intent of Congress in enacting this statute," we recognized, "was to halt and reverse the trend toward species extinction, whatever the cost. This is reflected not only in the stated policies of the Act, but in literally every section of the statute." *Id.*, at 184. Although the § 9 "take" prohibition was not at issue in *Hill*, we took note of that prohibition, placing particular emphasis on the Secretary's inclusion of habitat modification in his definition of "harm." In light of that provision for habitat protection, we could "not understand how TVA intends to operate Tellico Dam without 'harming' the snail darter." Congress' intent to provide comprehensive protection for endangered and threatened species supports the permissibility of the Secretary's "harm" regulation. * * *

Third, the fact that Congress in 1982 authorized the Secretary to issue permits for takings that § 9(a)(1)(B) would otherwise prohibit, "if such taking is incidental to, and not the purpose of, the carrying out of an otherwise lawful activity," 16 U.S.C. § 1539(a)(1)(B), strongly suggests that Congress understood § 9(a)(1)(B) to prohibit indirect as well as deliberate takings. * * * The permit process requires the applicant to prepare a "conservation plan" that specifies how he intends to "minimize and mitigate" the "impact" of his activity on endangered and threatened species, 16 U.S.C. § 1539(a)(2)(A),

---

"trap," "capture," and "collect"—generally retain independent meanings. Most of those terms refer to deliberate actions more frequently than does "harm," and they therefore do not duplicate the sense of indirect causation that "harm" adds to the statute. In addition, most of the other words in the definition describe either actions from which habitat modification does not usually result (*e.g.*, "pursue," "harass") or effects to which activities that modify habitat do not usually lead (*e.g.*, "trap," "collect"). To the extent the Secretary's definition of "harm" may have applications that overlap with other words in the definition, that overlap reflects the broad purpose of the Act.

making clear that Congress had in mind foreseeable rather than merely accidental effects on listed species. No one could seriously request an "incidental" take permit to avert § 9 liability for direct, deliberate action against a member of an endangered or threatened species, but respondents would read "harm" so narrowly that the permit procedure would have little more than that absurd purpose. "When Congress acts to amend a statute, we presume it intends its amendment to have real and substantial effect." *Stone v. INS*, 514 U.S. 386, 397 (1995). Congress' addition of the § 10 permit provision supports the Secretary's conclusion that activities not intended to harm an endangered species, such as habitat modification, may constitute unlawful takings under the ESA unless the Secretary permits them.

The Court of Appeals made three errors in asserting that "harm" must refer to a direct application of force because the words around it do. First, the court's premise was flawed. Several of the words that accompany "harm" in the § 3 definition of "take," especially "harass," "pursue," "wound," and "kill," refer to actions or effects that do not require direct applications of force. Second, to the extent the court read a requirement of intent or purpose into the words used to define "take," it ignored § 9's express provision that a "knowing" action is enough to violate the Act. Third, the court employed *noscitur a sociis* to give "harm" essentially the same function as other words in the definition, thereby denying it independent meaning. The canon, to the contrary, counsels that a word "gathers meaning from the words around it." The statutory context of "harm" suggests that Congress meant that term to serve a particular function in the ESA, consistent with but distinct from the functions of the other verbs used to define "take." The Secretary's interpretation of "harm" to include indirectly injuring endangered animals through habitat modification permissibly interprets "harm" to have "a character of its own not to be submerged by its association." *Russell Motor Car Co. v. United States*, 261 U.S. 514, 519 (1923).

Nor does the Act's inclusion of the § 5 land acquisition authority and the § 7 directive to federal agencies to avoid destruction or adverse modification of critical habitat alter our conclusion. Respondents' argument that the Government lacks any incentive to purchase land under § 5 when it can simply prohibit takings under § 9 ignores the practical considerations that attend enforcement of the ESA. Purchasing habitat lands may well cost the Government less in many circumstances than pursuing civil or criminal penalties. In addition, the § 5 procedure allows for protection of habitat before the seller's activity has harmed any endangered animal, whereas the Government cannot enforce the § 9 prohibition until an animal has actually been killed or injured. The Secretary may also find the § 5 authority useful for preventing modification of land that is not yet but may in the future become habitat for an endangered or threatened species. The § 7 directive applies only to the Federal Government, whereas the § 9 prohibition applies to "any person." Section 7 imposes a broad, affirmative duty to avoid adverse habitat modifications that § 9 does not replicate, and § 7 does not limit its admonition to habitat modification that "actually kills or injures wildlife." Conversely, § 7 contains limitations that § 9 does not, applying only to actions "likely to jeopardize the continued existence of any endangered species or threatened species," 16 U.S.C. § 1536(a)(2), and to modifications of habitat that has been designated "critical" pursuant to § 4, 16 U.S.C. § 1533(b)(2). Any overlap that § 5 or § 7 may have with § 9 in particular cases is unexceptional, and simply reflects the broad purpose of the Act set out in § 2 and acknowledged in *TVA v. Hill.*

We need not decide whether the statutory definition of "take" compels the Secretary's interpretation of "harm," because our conclusions that Congress did not unambiguously manifest its intent to adopt respondents' view and that the Secretary's interpretation is reasonable suffice to decide this case. *See generally Chevron U.S.A. Inc. v. Natural Resources Defense Council, Inc.,* 467 U.S. 837 (1984). The latitude the ESA gives the Secretary in enforcing the statute, together with the degree of regulatory expertise necessary to its enforcement, establishes that we owe some degree of deference to the Secretary's reasonable interpretation.

III

Our conclusion that the Secretary's definition of "harm" rests on a permissible construction of the ESA gains further support from the legislative history of the statute. The Committee Reports accompanying the bills that became the ESA do not specifically discuss the meaning of "harm," but they make clear that Congress intended "take" to apply broadly to cover indirect as well as purposeful actions. The Senate Report stressed that " '[t]ake' is defined . . . in the broadest possible manner to include every conceivable way in which a person can 'take' or attempt to 'take' any fish or wildlife." S. Rep. No. 93–307, p. 7 (1973). The House Report stated that "the broadest possible terms" were used to define restrictions on takings. H. R. Rep. No. 93–412, p. 15 (1973). The House Report underscored the breadth of the "take" definition by noting that it included "harassment, *whether intentional or not.*" *Id.*, at 11 (emphasis added). The Report explained that the definition "would allow, for example, the Secretary to regulate or prohibit the activities of birdwatchers where the effect of those activities might disturb the birds and make it difficult for them to hatch or raise their young." *Ibid.* These comments, ignored in the dissent's welcome but selective foray into legislative history, support the Secretary's interpretation that the term "take" in § 9 reached far more than the deliberate actions of hunters and trappers.

Two endangered species bills, S. 1592 and S. 1983, were introduced in the Senate and referred to the Commerce Committee. Neither bill included the word "harm" in its definition of "take," although the definitions otherwise closely resembled the one that appeared in the bill as ultimately enacted. See Hearings on S. 1592 and S. 1983 before the Subcommittee on Environment of the Senate Committee on Commerce, 93d Cong., 1st Sess., pp. 7, 27 (1973) (hereinafter Hearings). Senator Tunney, the floor manager of the bill in the Senate, subsequently introduced a floor amendment that added "harm" to the definition, noting that this and accompanying amendments would "help to achieve the purposes of the bill." 119 Cong. Rec. 25683 (July 24, 1973). Respondents argue that the lack of debate about the amendment that added "harm" counsels in favor of a narrow interpretation. We disagree. An obviously broad word that the Senate went out of its way to add to an important statutory definition is precisely the sort of provision that deserves a respectful reading.

The definition of "take" that originally appeared in S. 1983 differed from the definition as ultimately enacted in one other significant respect: It included "the destruction, modification, or curtailment of [the] habitat or range" of fish and wildlife. Hearings, at 27. Respondents make much of the fact that the Commerce Committee removed this phrase from the "take" definition before S. 1983 went to the floor. See 119 Cong. Rec. 25663 (1973). We do not find that fact especially significant. The legislative materials contain no indication why the habitat protection provision was deleted. That provision differed greatly from the regulation at issue today. Most notably, the habitat protection in S. 1983 would have applied far more broadly than the regulation does because it made adverse habitat modification a categorical violation of the "take" prohibition, unbounded by the regulation's limitation to habitat modifications that actually kill or injure wildlife. The S. 1983 language also failed to qualify "modification" with the regulation's limiting adjective "significant." We do not believe the Senate's unelaborated disavowal of the provision in S. 1983 undermines the reasonableness of the more moderate habitat protection in the Secretary's "harm" regulation.

The history of the 1982 amendment that gave the Secretary authority to grant permits for "incidental" takings provides further support for his reading of the Act. The House Report expressly states that "[b]y use of the word 'incidental' the Committee intends to cover situations in which it is known that a taking will occur if the other activity is engaged in but such taking is incidental to, and not the purpose of, the activity." H. R. Rep. No. 97–567, p. 31 (1982). This reference to the foreseeability of incidental takings undermines respondents' argument that the 1982 amendment covered only accidental killings of endangered and threatened animals that might occur in the course of hunting or trapping other animals. Indeed, Congress had habitat modification directly in mind: both the Senate Report and the House Conference Report identified as the model for the permit process a cooperative state federal response to a case in California where a development project threatened incidental harm to a species of endangered butterfly by modification of its habitat. See S. Rep. No. 97–418, p. 10 (1982); H. R. Conf. Rep. No. 97–835, pp. 30–32 (1982). Thus, Congress in 1982 focused squarely on the aspect of the "harm" regulation at issue in this litigation. Congress' implementation of a permit program is consistent with the Secretary's interpretation of the term "harm."

IV

When it enacted the ESA, Congress delegated broad administrative and interpretive power to the Secretary. The task of defining and listing endangered and threatened species requires an expertise and attention to detail that exceeds the normal province of Congress. Fashioning appropriate standards for issuing permits under § 10 for takings that would otherwise violate § 9 necessarily requires the exercise of broad discretion. The proper interpretation of a term such as "harm" involves a complex policy choice. When Congress has entrusted the Secretary with broad discretion, we are especially reluctant to substitute our views of wise policy for his. See *Chevron*, 467 U.S., at 865–866. In this case, that reluctance accords with our conclusion, based on the text, structure, and legislative history of the ESA, that the Secretary reasonably construed the intent of Congress when he defined "harm" to include "significant habitat modification or degradation that actually kills or injures wildlife."

* * *

The judgment of the Court of Appeals is reversed.

JUSTICE O'CONNOR, concurring.

My agreement with the Court is founded on two understandings. First, the challenged regulation is limited to significant habitat modification that causes actual, as opposed to hypothetical or speculative, death or injury to identifiable protected animals. Second, even setting aside difficult questions of scienter, the regulation's application is limited by ordinary principles of proximate causation, which introduce notions of foreseeability. * * *

With this understanding, I join the Court's opinion.

JUSTICE SCALIA, with whom THE CHIEF JUSTICE and JUSTICE THOMAS join, dissenting.

I think it unmistakably clear that the legislation at issue here (1) forbade the hunting and killing of endangered animals, and (2) provided federal lands and federal funds *for the acquisition of private lands,* to preserve the habitat of endangered animals. The Court's holding that the hunting and killing prohibition incidentally preserves habitat on private lands imposes unfairness to the point of financial ruin-not just upon the rich, but upon the simplest farmer who finds his land conscripted to national zoological use. I respectfully dissent.

I

* * * In my view petitioners must lose—the regulation must fall—even under the test of *Chevron U.S.A. Inc. v. Natural Resources Defense Council, Inc.,* 467 U.S. 837, 843 (1984), so I shall assume that the Court is correct to apply *Chevron.* * * *

If "take" were not elsewhere defined in the Act, none could dispute what it means, for the term is as old as the law itself. To "take," when applied to wild animals, means to reduce those animals, by killing or capturing, to human control. *See, e.g.,* 11 Oxford English Dictionary (1933) ("Take . . . To catch, capture (a wild beast, bird, fish, etc.)"); Webster's New International Dictionary of the English Language (2d ed. 1949) (take defined as "to catch or capture by trapping, snaring, etc., or as prey"); *Geer v. Connecticut,* 161 U.S. 519, 523 (1896) ("[A]ll the animals which can be taken upon the earth, in the sea, or in the air, that is to say, wild animals, belong to those who take them") (quoting the Digest of Justinian); 2 W. Blackstone, Commentaries 411 (1766) ("Every man . . . has an equal right of pursuing and taking to his own use all such creatures as are *ferae naturae*"). This is just the sense in which "take" is used elsewhere in federal legislation and treaty. *See, e.g.,* Migratory Bird Treaty Act, 16 U.S.C. § 703 (1988 ed., Supp. V) (no person may "pursue, hunt, take, capture, kill, [or] attempt to take, capture, or kill" any migratory bird); Agreement on the Conservation of Polar Bears, Nov. 15, 1973, Art. I, 27 U. S. T. 3918, 3921, T. I. A. S. No. 8409 (defining "taking" as "hunting, killing and capturing"). And that meaning fits neatly with the rest of § 1538(a)(1), which makes it unlawful not only to take protected species, but also to import or export them (§ 1538(a)(1)(A)); to possess, sell, deliver, carry, transport, or ship any taken species (§ 1538(a)(1)(D)); and to transport, sell, or offer to sell them in interstate or foreign commerce (§§ 1538(a)(1)(E), (F). The taking prohibition, in other words, is only part of the regulatory plan of § 1538(a)(1), which covers all the stages of the process by which protected wildlife is reduced to man's dominion and made the object of profit. It is obvious that "take" in this sense—a term of art deeply embedded in the statutory and common law concerning wildlife—describes a class of acts (not omissions) done directly and intentionally (not indirectly and by accident) to particular animals (not populations of animals).

The Act's definition of "take" does expand the word slightly (and not unusually), so as to make clear that it includes not just a completed taking, but the process of taking, and all of the acts that are customarily identified with or accompany that process ("to harass, harm, pursue, hunt, shoot, wound, kill, trap, capture, or collect"); and so as to include attempts. § 1532(19).

The tempting fallacy—which the Court commits with abandon—is to assume that *once defined*, "take" loses any significance, and it is only the definition that matters. The Court treats the statute as though Congress had directly enacted the § 1532(19) definition as a self-executing prohibition, and had not enacted § 1538(a)(1)(B) at all. But § 1538(a)(1)(B) *is* there, and if the terms contained in the definitional section are susceptible of two readings, one of which comports with the standard meaning of "take" as used in application to wildlife, and one of which does not, an agency regulation that adopts

> What do you make of the claim at the end of this paragraph that the agency's interpretation is "necessarily" unreasonable? Is this a claim that the interpretation is logically unsound? And if so, therefore that Justice Scalia's colleagues in the majority are illogical? Or do those in the majority instead just have a different but not necessarily illogical approach to understanding language and meaning?

the latter reading is necessarily unreasonable, for it reads the defined term "take"—the only operative term—out of the statute altogether.

That is what has occurred here. The verb "harm" has a *range* of meaning: "to cause injury" at its broadest, "to do hurt or damage" in a narrower and more direct sense. *See, e.g.,* 1 N. WEBSTER, AN AMERICAN DICTIONARY OF THE ENGLISH LANGUAGE (1828) ("Harm, *v.t.* To hurt; to injure; to damage; *to impair soundness of body, either animal* or vegetable") (emphasis added); AMERICAN COLLEGE DICTIONARY 551 (1970) ("harm . . . *n.* injury; damage; hurt: *to do him bodily harm*"). In fact the more directed sense of "harm" is a somewhat more common and preferred usage; "*harm* has in it a little of the idea of specially focused hurt or injury, as if a personal injury has been anticipated and intended." J. OPDYCKE, MARK MY WORDS: A GUIDE TO MODERN USAGE AND EXPRESSION 330 (1949). See also AMERICAN HERITAGE DICTIONARY OF THE ENGLISH LANGUAGE (1981) ("*Injure* has the widest range. . . . *Harm* and *hurt* refer principally to what causes physical or mental distress to living things"). To define "harm" as an act or omission that, however remotely, "actually kills or injures" a population of wildlife through habitat modification, is to choose a meaning that makes nonsense of the word that "harm" defines—requiring us to accept that a farmer who tills his field and causes erosion that makes silt run into a nearby river which depletes oxygen and thereby "impairs [the] breeding" of protected fish, has "taken" or "attempted to take" the fish. It should take the strongest evidence to make us believe that Congress has defined a term in a manner repugnant to its ordinary and traditional sense.

Here the evidence shows the opposite. "Harm" is merely one of 10 prohibitory words in § 1532(19), and the other 9 fit the ordinary meaning of "take" perfectly. To "harass, pursue, hunt, shoot, wound, kill, trap, capture, or collect" are all affirmative acts (the provision itself describes them as "conduct," see § 1532(19)) which are directed immediately and intentionally against a particular animal—not acts or omissions that indirectly and accidentally cause injury to a population of animals. The Court points out that several of the words ("harass," "pursue," "wound," and "kill") "refer to actions or effects that do not require direct *applications of force*." That is true enough, but force is not the point. Even "taking" activities in the narrowest sense, activities traditionally engaged in by hunters and trappers, do not all consist of direct applications of force; pursuit and harassment are part of the business of "taking" the prey even before it has been touched. What the nine other words in § 1532(19) have in common—and share with the narrower meaning of "harm" described above, but not with the Secretary's ruthless dilation of the word—is the sense of affirmative conduct intentionally directed against a particular animal or animals.

I am not the first to notice this fact, or to draw the conclusion that it compels. In 1981 the Solicitor of the Fish and Wildlife Service delivered a legal opinion [Memorandum of April 17, 1981, reprinted in 46 Fed. Reg. 29490, 29491 (emphasis in original)] on § 1532(19) that is in complete agreement with my reading:

> The Act's definition of 'take' contains a list of actions that illustrate the intended scope of the term. . . . With the possible exception of 'harm,' these terms all represent forms of conduct that are directed against and likely to injure or kill *individual* wildlife. Under the principle of statutory construction, *ejusdem generis*, . . . the term 'harm' should be interpreted to include only those actions that are directed against, and likely to injure or kill, individual wildlife.

I would call it *noscitur a sociis*, but the principle is much the same: the fact that "several items in a list share an attribute counsels in favor of interpreting the other items as possessing that attribute as well." The Court contends that the canon cannot be applied to deprive a word of all its "independent meaning." That proposition is questionable to begin with, especially as applied to long lawyers' listings such as this. If it were true, we ought to give the word "trap" in the definition its rare meaning of "to clothe" (whence "trappings")—since otherwise it adds nothing to the word "capture." In any event, the Court's contention that "harm" in the narrow sense adds nothing to the other words underestimates the ingenuity of our own species in a way that Congress did not. To feed an animal poison, to spray it with mace, to chop down the very tree in which it is nesting, or even to destroy its entire habitat in order to take it (as by draining a pond to get at a turtle), might neither wound nor kill, but would directly and intentionally harm.

* * * So far I have discussed only the immediate statutory text bearing on the regulation. But the definition of "take" in § 1532(19) applies "[f]or the purposes of this chapter," that is, it governs the meaning of the word *as used everywhere in the Act.* Thus, the Secretary's interpretation of "harm" is wrong if it does not fit with the use of "take" throughout the Act. And it does not. In § 1540(e)(4)(B), for example, Congress provided for the forfeiture of "[a]ll guns, traps, nets, and other equipment . . . used to aid the taking, possessing, selling, [etc.]" of protected animals. This listing plainly relates

to "taking" in the ordinary sense. If environmental modification were part (and necessarily a major part) of taking, as the Secretary maintains, one would have expected the list to include "plows, bulldozers, and back hoes." As another example, § 1539(e)(1) exempts "the taking of any endangered species" by Alaskan Indians and Eskimos "if such taking is primarily for subsistence purposes"; and provides that "[n]on edible byproducts of species taken pursuant to this section may be sold . . . when made into authentic native articles of handicrafts and clothing." Surely these provisions apply to taking only in the ordinary sense, and are meaningless as applied to species injured by environmental modification. The Act is full of like examples. *See, e.g.*, § 1538(a)(1)(D) (prohibiting possession, sale, and transport of "species taken in violation" of the Act). "[I]f the Act is to be interpreted as a symmetrical and coherent regulatory scheme, one in which the operative words have a consistent meaning throughout," *Gustafson v. Alloyd Co.*, 513 U.S. 561, 569 (1995), the regulation must fall.

The broader structure of the Act confirms the unreasonableness of the regulation. Section 1536 [16 U.S.C. § 1536(a)(2) (emphasis added)] provides:

> Each Federal agency shall . . . insure that any action authorized, funded, or carried out by such agency . . . is not likely to jeopardize the continued existence of any endangered species or threatened species or *result in the destruction or adverse modification of habitat* of such species which is determined by the Secretary . . . to be critical.

The Act defines "critical habitat" as habitat that is "essential to the conservation of the species," §§ 1532(5)(A)(i), (A)(ii), with "conservation" in turn defined as the use of methods necessary to bring listed species "to the point at which the measures provided pursuant to this chapter are no longer necessary." § 1532(3).

These provisions have a double significance. Even if §§ 1536(a)(2) and 1538(a) (1)(B) were totally independent prohibitions—the former applying only to federal agencies and their licensees, the latter only to private parties—Congress's explicit prohibition of habitat modification in the one section would bar the inference of an implicit prohibition of habitat modification in the other section. "[W]here Congress includes particular language in one section of a statute but omits it in another . . . , it is generally presumed that Congress acts intentionally and purposely in the disparate inclusion or exclusion." *Keene Corp. v. United States*, 508 U.S. 200, 208 (1993) (internal quotation marks omitted). And that presumption against implicit prohibition would be even stronger where the one section which uses the language carefully defines and limits its application. That is to say, it would be passing strange for Congress carefully to define "critical habitat" as used in § 1536(a)(2), but leave it to the Secretary to evaluate, willy nilly, impermissible "habitat modification" (under the guise of "harm") in § 1538(a)(1)(B).

In fact, however, §§ 1536(a)(2) and 1538(a)(1)(B) do *not* operate in separate realms; federal agencies are subject to *both*, because the "person[s]" forbidden to take protected species under § 1538 include agencies and departments of the Federal Government. See § 1532(13). This means that the "harm" regulation also contradicts another principle of interpretation: that statutes should be read so far as possible to give independent effect to all their provisions. By defining "harm" in the definition of "take" in § 1538(a)(1)(B) to include significant habitat modification that injures populations of wildlife, the regulation makes the habitat modification restriction in § 1536(a)(2) almost wholly superfluous. As "critical habitat" is habitat "essential to the conservation of the species," adverse modification of "critical" habitat by a federal agency would also constitute habitat modification that injures a population of wildlife. * * *

II

The Court makes four other arguments. First, "the broad purpose of the [Act] supports the Secretary's decision to extend protection against activities that cause the precise harms Congress enacted the statute to avoid." I thought we had renounced the vice of "simplistically . . . assum[ing] that *whatever* furthers the statute's primary objective must be the law." *Rodriguez v. United States*, 480 U.S. 522, 526 (1987) *(per curiam)* (emphasis in original). Deduction from the "broad purpose" of a statute begs the question if it is used to decide by what *means* (and hence to what *length*) Congress pursued that purpose; to get the right answer to that question there is no substitute for the hard job (or in this case, the quite simple one) of reading the whole text. "The Act must do everything necessary to achieve its broad purpose" is the slogan of the enthusiast, not the analytical tool of the arbiter.

Second, the Court maintains that the legislative history of the 1973 Act supports the Secretary's definition. Even if legislative history were a legitimate and reliable tool of interpretation (which I shall assume in order to rebut the Court's claim); and even if it could appropriately be resorted to when the enacted text is as clear as this; here it shows quite the opposite of what the

Court says. I shall not pause to discuss the Court's reliance on such statements in the Committee Reports as " '[t]ake' is defined . . . in the broadest possible manner to include every conceivable way in which a person can 'take' or attempt to 'take' any fish or wildlife.' " S. Rep. No. 93–307, p. 7 (1973). This sort of empty flourish—to the effect that "this statute means what it means all the way"—counts for little even when enacted into the law itself.

Much of the Court's discussion of legislative history is devoted to two items: first, the Senate floor manager's introduction of an amendment that added the word "harm" to the definition of "take," with the observation that (along with other amendments) it would "help to achieve the purposes of the bill"; second, the relevant Committee's removal from the definition of a provision stating that "take" includes " the destruction, modification or curtailment of [the] habitat or range " of fish and wildlife. The Court inflates the first and belittles the second, even though the second is on its face far more pertinent. But this elaborate inference from various pre-enactment actions and inactions is quite unnecessary, since we have *direct* evidence of what those who brought the legislation to the floor thought it meant—evidence as solid as any ever to be found in legislative history, but which the Court banishes to a footnote.

Both the Senate and House floor managers of the bill explained it in terms which leave no doubt that the problem of habitat destruction on private lands was to be solved principally by the land acquisition program of § 1534, while § 1538 solved a different problem altogether—the problem of takings. Senator Tunney stated [119 Cong. Rec. 25669 (1973) (emphasis added)]:

> *Through [the] land acquisition provisions, we will be able to conserve habitats necessary to protect fish and wildlife from further destruction.*

> Although most endangered species are threatened primarily by the destruction of their natural habitats, a significant portion of these animals are subject to *predation by man for commercial, sport, consumption, or other purposes.* The provisions of [the bill] would prohibit the commerce in or the importation, exportation, or taking of endangered species. . . .

The House floor manager, Representative Sullivan, put the same thought in this way [*id.,* at 30162 (emphasis added)]:

> [T]he principal threat to animals stems from destruction of their habitat. . . . [*The bill] will meet this problem by providing*

funds for acquisition of critical habitat. . . . It will also enable the Department of Agriculture to cooperate with willing landowners who desire to assist in the protection of endangered species *but who are understandably unwilling to do so at excessive cost to themselves.* Another hazard to endangered species arises from those who would *capture or kill them for pleasure or profit.* There is no way that Congress can make it less pleasurable for a person to take an animal, but we can certainly make it less profitable for them to do so.

Habitat modification and takings, in other words, were viewed as different problems, addressed by different provisions of the Act. The Court really has no explanation for these statements. All it can say is that "[n]either statement even suggested that [the habitat acquisition funding provision in § 1534] would be the Act's exclusive remedy for habitat modification by private landowners or that habitat modification by private landowners stood outside the ambit of [§ 1538]." That is to say, the statements are not as bad as they might have been. Little in life is. They are, however, quite bad enough to destroy the Court's legislative history case, since they display the clear understanding (1) that habitat modification is separate from "taking," and (2) that habitat destruction on private lands is to be remedied by public acquisition, and *not* by making particular unlucky landowners incur "excessive cost to themselves." The Court points out triumphantly that they do not display the understanding (3) that the land acquisition program is "the [Act's] only response to habitat modification." *Ibid.* Of course not, since that is not so (all *public* lands are subject to habitat modification restrictions); but (1) and (2) are quite enough to exclude the Court's interpretation. They identify the land acquisition program as the Act's only response to habitat modification *by private landowners*, and thus do not in the least "contradic[t]," *ibid.*, the fact that § 1536 prohibits habitat modification *by federal agencies.*

Third, the Court seeks support from a provision which was added to the Act in 1982, the year after the Secretary promulgated the current regulation. The provision states:

> [T]he Secretary may permit, under such terms and conditions as he shall prescribe—
>
> . . . any taking otherwise prohibited by section 1538(a)(1)(B) . . . if such taking is incidental to, and not the purpose of, the carrying out of an otherwise lawful activity.

16 U.S.C. § 1539(a)(1)(B). This provision does not, of course, implicate our doctrine that reenactment of a statutory provision ratifies an extant judicial or administrative interpretation, for neither the taking prohibition in § 1538(a)(1)(B) nor the definition in § 1532(19) was reenacted. The Court claims, however, that the provision "strongly suggests that Congress understood [§ 1538(a)(1)(B)] to prohibit indirect as well as deliberate takings." That would be a valid inference if habitat modification were the only substantial "otherwise lawful activity" that might incidentally and nonpurposefully cause a prohibited "taking." Of course it is not. This provision applies to the many otherwise lawful takings that incidentally take a protected species—as when fishing for unprotected salmon also takes an endangered species of salmon. Congress has referred to such "incidental takings" in other statutes as well—for example, a statute referring to "the incidental taking of . . . sea turtles in the course of . . . harvesting [shrimp]" and to the "rate of incidental taking of sea turtles by United States vessels in the course of such harvesting," 103 Stat. 1038 § 609(b)(2), note following 16 U.S.C. § 1537 (1988 ed., Supp. V); and a statute referring to "the incidental taking of marine mammals in the course of commercial fishing operations," 108 Stat. 546, § 118(a). The Court shows that it misunderstands the question when it says that "[n]o one could seriously request an 'incidental' take permit to avert . . . liability for direct, deliberate action *against a member of an endangered or threatened species*" (emphasis added). That is not an *incidental* take at all.

This is enough to show, in my view, that the 1982 permit provision does not support the regulation. I must acknowledge that the Senate Committee Report on this provision, and the House Conference Committee Report, clearly contemplate that it will enable the Secretary to permit environmental modification. See S. Rep. No. 97–418, p. 10 (1982); H. R. Conf. Rep. No. 97–835, pp. 30–32 (1982). But the *text* of the amendment cannot possibly bear that asserted meaning, when placed within the context of an Act that must be interpreted (as we have seen) not to prohibit private environmental modification. The neutral language of the amendment cannot possibly alter that interpretation, nor can its legislative history be summoned forth to contradict, rather than clarify, what is in its totality an unambiguous statutory text. There is little fear, of course, that giving no effect to the relevant portions of the Committee Reports will frustrate the real life expectations of a majority of the Members of Congress. If they read and relied on such tedious detail on such an obscure point (it was not, after all, presented as a revision of the statute's prohibitory scope, but as a discretionary waiver provision) the Republic would be in grave peril. * * *

III

* * * The Endangered Species Act is a carefully considered piece of legislation that forbids all persons to hunt or harm endangered animals, but places upon the public at large, rather than upon fortuitously accountable individual landowners, the cost of preserving the habitat of endangered species. There is neither textual support for, nor even evidence of congressional consideration of, the radically different disposition contained in the regulation that the Court sustains. For these reasons, I respectfully dissent.

After you have finished reading the *Sweet Home* opinion excerpts, remember to revisit the questions that preceded the opinion (pp. 991–992).

Test Your Understanding

 To assess your understanding of the material in this chapter, click here to take a quiz.

INDEX

References are to Pages

For an index of court decisions, see the Table of Cases.
For an index of secondary authorities, see the Table of Works Cited.